SPAIN

J. Malburet/ MICHELIN

Editorial Director	Cynthia Clayton Ochterbeck

THE GREEN GUIDE SPAIN

Editor	Gwen Cannon
Principal Writer	Paul Glassman
Production Coordinator	Natasha G. George
Cartography	Alain Baldet, Michèle Cana, Peter Wrenn
Photo Editor	Lydia Strong
Proofreader	Jonathan P. Gilbert
Layout & Design	Heinrich Grieb and Nicole D. Jordan
Cover Design	Laurent Muller and Frank Ladd

Contact Us:

The Green Guide
Michelin Maps and Guides
One Parkway South
Greenville, SC 29615
USA
www.michelintravel.com
michelin.guides@us.michelin.com

Michelin Maps and Guides
Hannay House
39 Clarendon Road
Watford, Herts WD17 1JA
UK
☏(01923) 205 240
www.ViaMichelin.com
travelpubsales@uk.michelin.com

Special Sales:

For information regarding bulk sales, customized editions and premium sales, please contact our Customer Service Departments:

USA	1-800-432-6277
UK	(01923) 205 240
Canada	1-800-361-8236

One Team ...
A Commitment to Quality

There's just one reason our team is dedicated to producing quality travel publications—you, our reader.

Throughout our guides we offer **practical information**, **touring tips** and **suggestions** for finding the best places for a break.

Michelin driving tours help you hit the highlights and quickly absorb the best of the region. Our descriptive **walking tours** make you your own guide, armed with directions, maps and expert information.

We scout out the attractions, classify them with **star ratings**, and describe in detail what you will find when you visit them.

Michelin maps featured throughout the guide offer vibrant, detailed and easy-to-follow outlines of everything from close-up museum plans to international maps.

Places to stay and eat are always a big part of travel, so we research **hotels and restaurants** that we think convey the essence of the destination, and arrange them by geographic area and price. We walk you through the best shopping districts and point you towards the host of entertainment and recreation possibilities available.

We **test, retest, check and recheck** to make sure that our guidebooks are truly just that: a personalized guide to help you make the most of your visit. And if you still want a speaking guide, we list local tour guides who will lead you on all the boat, bus, guided, historical, culinary, and other tours you shouldn't miss.

In short, we remove the guesswork involved with travel. After all, we want you to enjoy traveling with Michelin as much as we do.

The Michelin Green Guide Team

PLANNING YOUR TRIP

INTRODUCTION TO SPAIN

E. Baret/MICHELIN

SYMBOLS

- Tourist Information
- Hours of Operation
- Periods of Closure
- A Bit of Advice
- Details to Consider
- Entry Fees
- Especially for Children
- Tours
- Wheelchair Accessible

CONTENTS

DISCOVERING SPAIN

HOW TO USE THIS GUIDE

Orientation

To help you grasp the "lay of the land" quickly and easily, so you'll feel confident and comfortable finding your way around the region, we offer the following tools in this guide:

- Detailed table of contents for an overview of what you'll find in the guide, and how the guide is organized.
- Map of the country on the cover flap, with the Principal Sights highlighted for easy reference.
- Detailed maps for major cities and villages, including driving tour maps and larger-scale maps for walking tours.
- Map of Regional Driving Tours, each one numbered and color coded.
- Principal Sights organized alphabetically for quick reference.

Practicalities

At the front of the guide, you'll see a section called "Planning Your Trip" that contains information about planning your trip, the best time to go, different ways of getting to the region and getting around, and basic facts and tips for making the most of your visit. You'll find driving and themed tours, and suggestions for outdoor fun. There's also a calendar of popular annual events. Information on shopping, sightseeing, kids' activities and sports and recreational opportunities is included as well.

WHERE TO STAY

We've made a selection of hotels and arranged them within the cities by price category to fit all budgets (*see the Legend on the cover flap for an explanation of the price categories*). For the most part, we've selected accommodations based on their unique regional quality, their Spanish feel, as it were. So, unless the individual hotel embodies local ambience, it's rare that we include chain properties, which typically have their own imprint. If you want a more comprehensive selection of accommodations, see the red-cover **Michelin Guide España & Portugal**.

WHERE TO EAT

We thought you'd like to know the popular eating spots in the country. So we selected restaurants that capture the Spanish experience—those that have a unique regional flavor and local atmosphere. We're not rating the quality of the food per se. As we did with the hotels, we selected restaurants for many towns and villages, categorized by price to appeal to all wallets (*see the Legend on the cover flap for an explanation of the price categories*). If you want a more comprehensive selection of dining recommendations, see the red-cover **Michelin Guide España & Portugal**.

Attractions

Principal Sights are arranged alphabetically. Within each Principal Sight, attractions for each town, village, or geographical area are divided into local Sights or Walking Tours, nearby Excursions to sights outside the town, or detailed Driving Tours—suggested itineraries for seeing several attractions around a major town. Contact information, admission charges and hours of operation are given for the majority of attractions. Unless otherwise noted, admission prices shown are for a single adult only. Discounts for children, seniors, students, teachers, etc. may be available; be sure to ask. If no admission charge is shown, entrance to the attraction is free.

If you're pressed for time, we recommend you visit the three- and two-star sights first: the stars are your guide.

STAR RATINGS

Michelin has used stars as a rating tool for more than 100 years:

★★★	Highly recommended
★★	Recommended
★	Interesting

SYMBOLS IN THE TEXT

Besides the stars, other symbols in the text indicate sights that are closed to the public ⊶; on-site eating facilities ✗; also see ◉; breakfast included in the nightly rate ☕; on-site parking P; spa facilities Spa; camping facilities △; swimming pool ♒; and beaches ⛱.

See the box appearing on the Contents page and the Legend on the cover flap for other symbols used in the text.

See the Maps explanation below for symbols appearing on the maps.

Throughout the guide you will find peach-coloured text boxes or sidebars containing anecdotal or background information. Green-coloured boxes contain information to help you save time or money

Maps

All maps in this guide are oriented north, unless otherwise indicated by a directional arrow. See the map Legend at the back of the guide for an explanation of other map symbols. A complete list of the maps found in the guide appears at the back of this book.

Addresses, phone numbers, opening hours and prices published in this guide are accurate at press time. We welcome corrections and suggestions that may assist us in preparing the next edition. Please send your comments to:

Michelin Maps and Guides
Hannay House
39 Clarendon Road
Watford, Herts WD17 1JA
UK
travelpubsales@uk.michelin.com
www.michelin.co.uk

Michelin Maps and Guides
Editorial Department
P.O. Box 19001
Greenville, SC 29602-9001
USA
michelin.guides@us.michelin.com
www.michelintravel.com

Ceramic tiles, Casa de Pilatos, Sevilla
H. Le Gac/ MICHELIN

PLANNING YOUR TRIP

MICHELIN DRIVING TOURS

Refer to the Driving Tours Map on the inside back cover and to Michelin maps nos. 571, 572, 574, 577 and 578 in order to make the most of the following driving tours.

1 GALICIA

Round trip of 1 031km/644mi from A Coruña/La Coruña – This tour provides an insight into a region with magnificent towns and cities, verdant landscapes, an indented coastline and villages full of character and charm, known in ancient times as *finis terra*, or "end of the world." Galicia is also renowned for its delicious seafood. After visiting A Coruña/La Coruña, with its old quarter and attractive seafront promenade *(avenida de la Marina)*, head south to **Santiago de Compostela**, one of Spain's finest cities, to marvel at the spectacular plaza del Obradoiro, dominated by the impressive cathedral – the final destination for hundreds of thousands of pilgrims every year. The tour continues along the **Rías Bajas** to the mouth of the Miño, forming a natural border with Portugal. Along this magnificent stretch of coastline, with its genuine fishing villages and summer resorts popular with Spanish holidaymakers, the sea has created a series of beautiful inlets. Having followed the Miño as far as the historic town of **Tui/Tuy**, continue by motorway to **Orense/Ourense**. After visiting the town, the itinerary continues along the spectacular gorges cut by the Sil, before following the same road into the province of León, and the town of Ponferrada, the gateway to the magical landscapes of **Las Médulas**. Heading back into Galicia, make your way to **Lugo**, which has managed to preserve its exceptional Roman walls. Continue north to the coast, driving along the **Rías Altas** before returning to A Coruña/La Coruña.

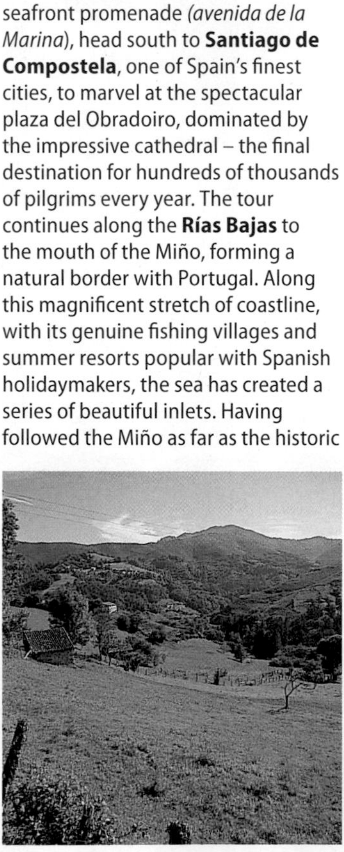

J. Malburet/ MICHELIN

Picos de Europa

2 AROUND THE MONTES DE CANTABRIA

Round trip of 764km/477mi from Santander – The Cantabrian mountains form a natural boundary between Castilla y León and the autonomous communities of Cantabria and Asturias. To the north, the highest summits of the Picos de Europa rise up close to the stunning coast, while in the lands of Castilla to the south you won't want to miss some of the towns and villages along the Way of St James, or two outstanding jewels of Gothic art, the cathedrals of León and Burgos. Leaving behind the seigniorial town of **Santander**, with its superb location on a magnificent bay, head west to the charming medieval town of **Santillana del Mar**, making sure you visit the replica of the **Cuevas de Altamira**, a masterpiece of prehistoric cave art. Continue along the same road to the picturesque pueblo of **Comillas**, before reaching the seaside resort of **San Vicente de la Barquera**. From here, the tour heads into the mountains, passing through the northern section of the **Parque Nacional de los Picos de Europa**, before returning to the coastal city of **Gijón**, renowned for its extensive beach, and then south to nearby **Oviedo**, with its well-maintained historical centre containing some outstanding examples of Asturian architecture. Continue inland to visit the historic city of **León**, and then east across the Meseta towards Burgos along the Way of St James, visiting Villalcázar de Sirga, Carrión de los Condes and **Frómista** en route, the latter famous for the Iglesia de San Martín, a masterpiece of Romanesque architecture. Having spent time exploring **Burgos** and its magnificent religious heritage, the tour continues towards **Aguilar de Campoo**, overlooked by its castle, and from here to Reinosa, at the foot of the Montes Cantábricos, an ideal departure point for an excursion to the **Pico de Tres Mares**; alternatively, make your way back to Santander, stopping at **Puente Viesgo** to admire the wall paintings in the Cueva del Castillo.

3 THE BASQUE COUNTRY, RIOJA AND NAVARRA

Round trip of 696km/435mi from Bilbao – This tour combines stunning coastline dotted with picturesque villages, the delightful inland landscapes of northern Spain and the Way of St James, as well as charming towns and cities renowned for their wonderful gastronomy.
The tour starts with an obligatory visit to the **Guggenheim Museum** in Bilbao before following the indented **Costa Vasca** eastwards through quaint fishing villages to **Donostia-San Sebastián**, with its majestic setting on one of Spain's most breathtaking bays. From here, continue the short distance to **Hondarribia**, a pleasant resort and fishing port with an attractive old quarter, close to the French border. The magnificent Valle del Bidasoa provides the backdrop as you head inland to **Pamplona/Iruña**, a medieval town built around its imposing cathedral and famous for the annual running of the bulls. The route then heads deeper into Navarra, past monasteries and important staging-posts on the **Way of St James** (Leyre, La Oliva, Sangüesa/Zangoza and Puente la Reina) and historic towns such as Sos del Rey Católico and Olite), before reaching **Estella/Lizarra**, one of the most important stops along the famous pilgrimage route. After visiting the nearby Monasterio de Irache, the pilgrims' path continues west to **Logroño**, the capital of La Rioja, known for its cathedral and old streets, and then through the extensive vineyards for which this region is justifiably renowned; the most famous halts on this section of the path are undoubtedly **Nájera** and **Santo Domingo de la Calzada**. Between the two, nestled in a delightful valley, is the village of San Millán de la Cogolla, the cradle of the written Castilian language. Before returning to the Basque country via the capital of the province of Álava, **Vitoria-Gasteiz**, with its atmospheric old quarter and several museums of interest, take time to visit Haro and the Museo del Vino de La Rioja. Return to Bilbao via the motorway, which winds its way through an impressive mountain landscape.

4 CATALUNYA

Round trip of 1 020km/637mi from Barcelona – This driving tour through Catalunya is characterised by high Pyrenean peaks, rugged coasts with charming coves, long sandy beaches, picturesque villages, exquisite Romanesque churches, impressive monasteries, and towns and cities overflowing with history.
Once you've spent time in the region's capital, **Barcelona**, a city with a fascinating mix of modernity and history, begin your tour along the **Costa Brava**, a beautiful stretch of coastline dotted with authentic fishing villages and summer resorts. After visiting the old Roman colony of **Empùries/Ampurias**, the Golfo de Roses, the picture-postcard small town of **Cadaqués** and the **Monasterio de Sant Pere de Rodes**, head inland to **Figueres**, home of the museum dedicated to Salvador Dalí, and **Girona/Gerona**, a city that still retains the vestiges of its Roman, Jewish, Moorish and Christian past.

From here, the tour climbs up into the **Pyrenees**, a land of spectacular mountain roads, beautiful valleys and charming villages with small Romanesque churches of singular purity and simplicity. The itinerary abandons the mountains via the Valle de la Noguera Ribagorzana to reach **Lleida/Lérida**, watched over by the remains of its former Moorish fortress and by the city's cathedral (Seo). The journey back to the Mediterranean provides an opportunity to visit **Poblet**, the most famous Cistercian monastery in Spain, as well as the walled town of **Montblanc**, before arriving in **Tarragona**, capital of Tarraconensis under the Romans. Have a fun day out at the **Port Aventura** theme park before heading back to Barcelona. The final leg of the tour runs along the coast past the attractive resort town of **Sitges** on the **Costa Dorada**.

5 CASTILLA Y LEÓN

Round trip of 756km/472mi from Salamanca – Historic towns and lofty castles dominate this tour through the lands of old Castile. If your trip coincides with Holy Week, head for Zamora or Valladolid to witness their solemn Semana Santa processions. After spending time exploring **Salamanca**, a lively university city teeming with sumptuous monuments, head north to **Zamora** to admire the scallop tiling on the cupola of the cathedral. The road east towards Valladolid passes through **Toro**, where the dome of the town's collegiate church is similar in style to the cupola of Zamora's cathedral, and **Tordesillas**, where the famous treaty dividing the lands of the New World between Spain and Portugal was signed. In **Valladolid**, renowned for fine examples of Isabelline art, it is well worth visiting the Museo Nacional de Escultura, Spain's national sculpture museum. Continue your journey through an extensive landscape of cereal crops, passing through Medina de Rioseco en route to **Palencia**, with its magnificent cathedral. Heading east into the province of Burgos, the itinerary takes in charming small towns and villages such as **Lerma** and **Covarrubias**. One of the highlights of this tour is the **Monasterio de Santo Domingo de Silos**, the cloisters of which are a masterpiece of Romanesque art. From here, the itinerary heads south, skirting along the banks of the Duero, to visit a series of **castles** built to defend the lands conquered by Christians from the Moors, such as the ruined fortress at Peñaranda de Duero; the impressive castle at **Peñafiel**; **Cuéllar**; and the more unusual **Castillo de Coca**, in Mudejar style. The tour continues to **Segovia**, famous for its aqueduct and fairytale castle, and on to **Ávila**, a city of convents and churches, encircled by its famous walls. Before completing your circuit, it is well worth making a last stop in the small town of Alba de Tormes.

6 ZARAGOZA, SORIA, GUADALAJARA AND TERUEL

Round trip of 869km/543mi from Zaragoza – This tour travels across several inland provinces, passing through impressive mountain landscapes, villages crowned by old castles and towns full of character and charm. The journey begins with a foray into Navarra to visit **Tudela**, with its interesting examples of Mudéjar architecture and its fine cathedral. Returning to the province of Zaragoza, head for **Tarazona**, famous for its old quarter and cathedral, and the **Monasterio de Veruela**, which is well worth a visit. From Tarazona, continue to **Soria**, a quiet provincial capital embellished with impressive churches, on the banks of the Duero. The itinerary then continues southwest, passing through **Calatañazor**, a picturesque village overlooked by a medieval castle, to **Burgo de Osma**, yet another charming town, renowned for its magnificent cathedral. Head across country to **Berlanga de Duero**, the site of another castle built to defend the Duero, and **San Baudelio**

de Berlanga, with its unusual and remote 11C Mozarabic chapel. Once past **Atienza**, crowned by the ruins of its castle, continue to historic **Sigüenza**, whose highlights include the fortified cathedral with its impressive array of sculptures, and the castle (now a parador). Join up with the fast highway heading east towards Zaragoza, passing through attractive scenery along the banks of the Jalón, crossing the river briefly to visit the magnificent **Monasterio de Santa María de Huerta**, built in sober Cistercian style with a number of Renaissance additions. As the road passes Ateca, head directly south past the La Tranquera Reservoir to the **Monasterio de Piedra**, to enjoy a stroll through its delightful park. The tour continues via Molina de Aragón, with yet another castle, before entering the Sierra de **Albarracín** en route to the charming medieval village of the same name. The next stop on the itinerary is **Teruel**, a town enjoying a superb location, and adorned with a number of interesting examples of Mudéjar architecture. To complete the tour, head north to **Daroca**, with its 4km/2.5mi of walls, before joining the motorway for the final leg to Zaragoza.

7 AROUND MADRID

Round trip of 689km/431mi from Madrid – The area around the Spanish capital is home to several towns of major interest, a number of royal palaces and the scenic, mountainous landscapes of the Sierras de Gredos and Sierra de Guadarrama.
One of the closest towns to Madrid is **Alcalá de Henares**, the birthplace of Miguel de Cervantes, where the major attraction is the former university, the Colegio de San Ildefonso. From here, the route passes through **Chinchón**, with one of the country's prettiest main squares, and on to **Aranjuez**, nestled in a verdant setting on the banks of the Tagus. After visiting the royal palace and pavilions and strolling through the delightful gardens here, continue your journey southwest to the historic city of

B. Juge/ MICHELIN

La Granja

Toledo, magnificently perched in a loop of the Tagus, with the sumptuous vestiges of its rich past. Continue your journey west to **Talavera de la Reina**, famous for its ceramics, and then north along a mountain road through the **Sierra de Gredos** en route to Ávila, visiting along the way the Cueva del Águila, a cave 4km/2.5mi from the main road via an unsurfaced track. Ávila, a city of churches and convents, and the cradle of St Teresa, has preserved intact its magnificent 11C walls. From Ávila, the tour heads east to the **Monasterio de El Escorial**, an immense monastery built by order of Philip II. On the way to Segovia, you may wish to branch off to the **Valle de los Caídos**, or Valley of the Fallen, impressively situated amid the stunning landscapes of the Sierra de Guadarrama. In **Segovia**, admire the incredible Roman aqueduct, the city's Romanesque churches and the exotic Alcázar. Close to the city, at the foot of the Sierra de Guadarrama, are the palace and magnificent gardens of **La Granja de San Ildefonso**, built by Philip IV – the grandson of Louis XIV – in nostalgia for the Versailles of his childhood. Return to the mountains, and after crossing the **Navacerrada Pass**, head northeast through a valley to the **Monasterio de El Paular**. A twisting road farther north traverses the Navafría Pass, before descending into **Pedraza de la Sierra**, a seigniorial town full of charm. Before returning by motorway to Madrid via the Somosierra

Pass, the small town of **Sepúlveda** is worth a visit to admire its impressive site overlooking a deep gorge of the River Duratón.

8 EXTREMADURA AND THE PEÑA DE FRANCIA

Round trip of 780km/487mi from Plasencia – This tour through the region of Extremadura has a strong historic focus because of its links with the Romans, the great conquistadors and Emperor Charles V. The tour ends with the Peña de Francia, in the province of Salamanca.

After visiting the cathedral and old quarter of **Plasencia**, the tour starts in the verdant **Valle de La Vera**, the setting for the **Monasterio de Yuste**, to which Charles V withdrew following his abdication, and the 15C castle in **Jarandilla de la Vera** (now a parador). Leaving the valley along a country road that crosses the Valdecañas Reservoir, you come to the village of **Guadalupe**, huddled around its magnificent monastery. Following a visit to this shrine, continue westwards to the monumental town of **Trujillo**, the birthplace of several of the famous conquistadors, and the site of one of Spain's most impressive and original main squares. From Trujillo, the tour then heads southwest by fast highway to **Mérida** to admire the city's Roman remains (theatre, amphitheatre etc) and the Museo Nacional de Arte Romano, which bears witness to Mérida's importance during this period. The next stops on the itinerary are **Cáceres**, a monumental town with a stunning and superbly preserved old town where time seems to have stopped in the 16C and 17C, and **Alcántara**, whose main sights of interest are a monastery – the seat of the military order of the same name – and an exceptional Roman bridge spanning the Tagus. Head northeast to **Coria** to visit its cathedral, and then into the province of Salamanca, to **Ciudad Rodrigo**, a pleasant small town with several buildings of interest hidden behind its walls. The tour ends with a visit to the **Peña de Francia**, a crag rising to 1 723m/5 682ft, and the Sierra de Béjar, with its typical mountain villages.

9 THE LANDS OF LA MANCHA

Round trip of 849km/531mi from Cuenca – For many, La Mancha conjures up a scene of seemingly endless fields of cereal crops and vines, interspersed with the occasional village or town and the evocative silhouette of a windmill or castle. Yet it is also an area of impressive mountains and landscapes that have little in common with this image.

Cuenca, with its spectacular position between the ravines of the Júcar and Huécar rivers, is the starting-point for this tour, which begins with a drive through the **sierra** of the same name, famous for sights such as the Ciudad Encantada (with its unusual stone formations), the source of the River Cuervo, and the Beteta Ravine. Returning to Cuenca, the itinerary then heads out along the flat landscapes to the southwest to **Belmonte**, with its castle and interesting collegiate church, and **Campo de Criptana**, a typical La Mancha village, whose houses are framed by the silhouette of its windmills. After passing through **Alcázar de San Juan**, the largest town in the area, continue on to **Consuegra**, where the castle and line of windmills on a hill overlooking the town offers one of the region's most enduring sights. From here, head south for a visit to the **Parque Nacional de las Tablas de Daimiel,** a wetland area at the confluence of the River Guadiana and River Cigüela. The next stop on the itinerary is in **Almagro**, a historic town that has preserved its delightful old quarter, including a magnificent main square and the Corral de Comedias, a 16C theatre. A short distance to the southeast stands **Valdepeñas**, the capital of La Mancha's wine industry. Continuing east, the tour passes through **Villanueva de los Infantes**, containing several fine examples of Renaissance and Baroque architecture, and the village of **Alcaraz**, with its outstanding main square lined by elegant buildings, protected by the mountain range in which the River Mundo has its source. The next stop is the city of **Albacete**, home to a provincial museum with an interesting archaeology section. From here, head north to **Alarcón**, impressively situated on a hill almost completely encircled by the River Júcar and crowned by an imposing medieval castle (now a parador), before returning to Cuenca.

10 THE LEVANTE REGION

Round trip of 715km/447mi from Valencia – This tour running along the coast and inland through the provinces of Valencia, Alicante and Murcia is characterised by long sandy beaches and charming villages and towns with a fascinating artistic and architectural heritage.

Having spent time exploring **Valencia**, start the tour along the Mediterranean, visiting **El Saler**, with its extensive sandy beaches, and the nearby **Parque Natural de la Albufera**, a large freshwater lake and important rice-growing area. The itinerary then passes through a series of large resorts such as **Cullera**, **Gandía**, home to the former palace of the Dukes of Borja, and Denia, watched over by its castle. **Xàbia/Jávea**, with its picturesque old quarter, is just a few miles north of the Cabo de la Nao headland, offering spectacular views of the coast, and **Calp/Calpe**, located close to the impressive **Penyal d'Ifac** rock. **Altea**, the next resort to the south, is one of the area's most attractive coastal towns with its steep and narrow streets. Continue along the coast to **Benidorm**, where the backdrop to the beach is a mass of high-rise hotels and apartment buildings, and from here to the **Terra Mítica** theme park. The tour then heads inland through the mountains to visit **Guadalest**, in a spectacular location on a rocky ridge, **Alcoi/Alcoy**, nestled in a fertile river valley, and to the south, **Xixona**, famous for its nougat, and reached via the Carrasqueta Pass. Returning to the coast, the next major city on the itinerary is **Alicante**, a pleasant and relaxed provincial capital overlooked by an imposing fortress, the Castillo de Santa Bárbara. The itinerary continues southwards, skirting the resorts of Guardamar del Segura and Torrevieja, before arriving at **Mar Menor**, a shallow lagoon separated from the sea by a long sand bar, at the southern tip of which stands the resort of **La Manga del Mar Menor**. After a visit to **Cartagena**, on the curve of a deep bay, leave the coast for the town of **Murcia**, whose main sights are its fine cathedral and the Museo Salzillo, a museum dedicated to the 18C sculptor Francisco Salzillo. Continue northeast to **Orihuela**, a tranquil town with numerous churches of interest, and then to **Elx/Elche**, famous for its palm grove. From here the itinerary heads farther inland by dual carriageway to **Villena**, protected by its imposing castle. The final stop on this driving tour is **Xàtiva/Játiva**, the town of a thousand fountains. Situated on a fertile plain, the town has preserved a number of buildings of architectural interest.

11 CÓRDOBA, SEVILLA, CÁDIZ AND MÁLAGA

Round trip of 890km/556mi from Córdoba – This tour takes in some of the finest cities of inland Andalucía, the delightful whitewashed towns and villages (*pueblos blancos*) in the

B. Kaufmann/ MICHELIN

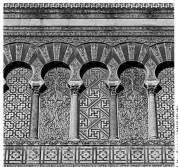

Blind arches, La Mezquita, Córdoba

provinces of Cádiz and Málaga, and the famous Costa del Sol resorts. **Córdoba**, one of the three emblems of Andalucía, along with Sevilla and Granada, is one of Spain's most beautiful cities with monuments such as the Mezquita, typical whitewashed streets and a history influenced by the Christian, Muslim and Jewish faiths. From here, head west to **Écija**, the so-called "frying pan" of Andalucía, a town of churches, convents, palaces and numerous bell towers. Farther west stands the breathtaking city of **Sevilla**, a name that conjures up passion and colour, where several days are needed to explore it to the full. The itinerary then heads towards the Atlantic, pausing in the elegant town of **Jerez de la Frontera**, famous for its sherry, equestrian history, and delightful architecture, before arriving in **Cádiz**, reached via an impressive causeway. This charming provincial capital and port is one of Spain's best-kept secrets, with its 18C architecture, historic squares, impressive monuments and super beaches. **Chiclana de la Frontera**, to the south, is the closest town to the Playa de la Barrosa, a magnificent, and seemingly endless sandy beach. From here, the tour heads inland to **Medina Sidonia**, a quaint town with a medieval quarter perched on a hill with expansive views of the surrounding area. The whitewashed town of **Arcos de la Frontera**, the next stop, has an even more outstanding location, straddling a ridge above a gorge of the River Guadalete. Arcos is one of the region's famous **Pueblos Blancos**, which include **Ronda**, renowned for its dramatic location, stunning architecture and tradition of bullfighting. From Ronda, the itinerary winds its way through stunning mountain scenery down to the coast, dominated by the impressive **Rock of Gibraltar**. The coast road east to Málaga passes through some of the Costa del Sol's most famous resorts (Estepona, **Marbella**, Fuengirola, Benalmádena etc), with their luxury developments, hotels and apartments. From **Málaga**, follow the fast highway inland to **Antequera**, the ideal base from which to explore local nature, and from here to **Estepa**, crowned by the remains of a fortress. The hilltop town of **Osuna**, the last stage on the journey, has preserved an interesting architectural heritage with numerous palaces and noble mansions amid its old whitewashed centre. From Osuna, return directly to Córdoba.

1 2 GRANADA, ALMERÍA AND JAÉN

Round trip of 835km/522mi from Granada – This tour through the eastern half of Andalucía is characterised by historic towns and cities with an outstanding artistic heritage, magnificent deserted beaches, breathtaking mountain scenery and a landscape carpeted with olive trees as far as the eye can see.

For many, a visit to the Alhambra, overlooking **Granada**, is the highlight of a trip to Spain. It marks the starting-point for this driving tour, which begins with a journey across the spectacular **Alpujarras** mountain range, passing through verdant valleys and picturesque whitewashed small towns and villages to reach **Almería**, a provincial capital overlooked by a Moorish fortress perched on a hill above the city. The itinerary continues through the **Parque Natural de Cabo de Gata** and along the Almerian coast, an area of luminous skies, sand dunes, wild beaches and impressive desert landscapes that conjure up images of nearby Africa; **Mojácar**, perched on a hill, is the most attractive town in this area. From here, follow the fast highway north, cutting inland to the area known as Los Vélez, in the foothills of the Sierra de María, and the town of **Vélez Blanco**, overlooked by its unusual Renaissance castle. Once you have crossed the Sierra de María, a cross-country route leads to **Pontones**, in the province of Jaén, at the heart of the **Parque Natural de las Sierras de Cazorla, Segura y las Villas**. The tour through the park as far as **Cazorla** passes through impressive mountain landscapes cut by deep ravines, rivers and streams. Following a restorative sojourn at the heart of nature, the tour continues to **Úbeda** and **Baeza**, two monumental towns renowned for their magnificent Renaissance architecture. The last leg of the tour traverses extensive olive groves before reaching **Jaén**, spread out at the foot of the Cerro de Santa Catalina, a hill crowned by the city's imposing Arab fortress. Apart from the castle, the other major sights of interest in Jaén are its sumptuous cathedral and the Arab baths in the Palacio de Villardompardo.

Local Driving Tours

Listed below are the sights within the *Discovering Spain* section of the guide, where you can find local driving tours not listed on the Driving Tours Map.

- Pico de Tres Mares
- Cuevas de Canalobre and Jijona
- Sierra de Béjar and Sierra de Candelario
- East from Almería
- Desfiladero de los Gaitanes
- The Ribagorza
- Monte Hacho
- Sierra de Andía and Sierra de Urbasa
- The Alpujarras
- Los Mallos de Riglos
- Sierra de Loarre
- Serrablo
- Monasterio de San Juan de la Peña
- Valle de Hecho
- Roncal and Ansó Valleys
- Cistercian Monasteries of Catalunya
- Río Sil
- Valle del Bidasoa
- Upper Valley of the Ter
- La Cerdanya
- Vall del Segre
- Vall del Noguera Pallaresa
- La Vall d'Arán
- Vall del Noguera Ribagorçana
- Rías Bajas
- East of Vitoria-Gasteiz: Medieval Paintings
- Mallorca's Rocky Coast
- Mallorca's East Coast and Caves
- Tenerife, Canaries
- Lanzarote, Canaries
- La Palma, Canaries
- La Dehesa, El Hierro, Canaries

WHEN AND WHERE TO GO

When to Go

SEASONS

As a guideline, the best two seasons to visit Spain are spring and autumn, when temperatures across the country are generally pleasant.

Spring is the best time to explore Extremadura, Castilla-La Mancha and Andalucía, which in summer are the hottest regions in Spain. Late spring is also a good time to visit the Mediterranean and Balearic Islands, as the sea temperature starts to warm up.

In **summer**, the country's north coast comes into its own, offering a pleasant climate for sightseeing and relaxing on the beach without the oppressive heat of other parts of the country. This time of year is also ideal for discovering the magnificent mountain landscapes of the Pyrenees, Picos de Europa, and the Sierra de Gredos, Sierra de Guadarrama and Sierra Nevada ranges.

Autumn is a generally pleasant season across most of Spain.

In **winter**, skiing enthusiasts can head for the Pyrenees or the Sierra Nevada, while those preferring to escape the cold wet winter in northern Europe can travel south to the Canary Islands for some winter sunshine.

For up-to-date information on **weather** in Spain, log onto the Spanish Meteorological Office website at www.inm.es.

WHAT TO PACK

Since Spain has so many days of sunshine and its temperatures are generally warmer than many other European countries, pack as few clothes as possible. Unless you choose

Temperature chart

Maximum temperatures in black.
Minimum temperatures in red.

Month	Jan	Feb	Mar	Apr	May	Jun	Jul	Aug	Sep	Oct	Nov	Dec
	13	14	16	18	21	25	28	28	25	21	16	13
Barcelona	6	7	9	11	14	18	21	21	19	15	11	7
	9	11	15	18	21	27	31	30	26	19	13	9
Madrid	1	2	5	7	10	14	17	17	14	9	5	2
	12	12	15	15	17	20	22	22	21	18	15	12
Santander	7	6	8	9	11	14	16	16	15	12	9	7
	15	17	20	23	26	32	36	36	32	26	20	16
Sevilla	6	6	9	11	13	17	20	20	18	14	10	7
	15	16	8	20	23	26	29	29	27	23	19	16
Valencia	5	6	8	10	13	16	19	20	17	13	9	6

to visit in winter, light-weight clothing is usually an ideal choice. It's a good idea to pack a sturdy pair of walking shoes, or even hiking boots. An umbrella, rainwear, a light-weight jacket and suntan lotion are good to have with you. Try to pack everything in one suitcase and a carry-on bag. Take an extra tote bag for bringing new purchases back home.

Ideas for Your Visit

SPAIN'S COASTLINES

MEDITERRANEAN COAST

Spain has thousands of miles of beautiful coastline, with the Mediterranean continuing to attract millions of Spanish and foreign visitors every year to its delightful waters and magnificent beaches.

The rugged and indented **Costa Brava**, or Wild Coast, with its charming coves and lively resorts, extends from north of Barcelona as far as the French border.

The **Levante** coast, characterised by long sandy beaches and built-up resorts such as Benidorm, Cullera and Gandía, continues to be as popular as ever. This area is also favoured by Spanish families, and is occupied by a large number of second homes.

The **Costa del Sol**, in particular the famous stretch between Málaga and Estepona, is a succession of luxury developments and golf courses. Marbella is considered the leading resort here, reinforced by its reputation as the playground of the international jet-set.

The remainder of the Andalucían coast is generally quieter, attracting mainly Spanish visitors.

The **Balearic Islands** are one of the country's most popular tourist destinations. Of the three main islands, Mallorca and Ibiza attract large numbers of Spanish and foreign (particularly German) visitors, who come here to enjoy their magnificent landscapes and beaches and lively nightlife. Menorca tends to be quieter, finding popularity with those in search of a more relaxing holiday.

F. Vidal/ MICHELIN

ATLANTIC COAST

Spain's North Atlantic coast stretches from the Basque Country in the east to Galicia in the west. In general, its resorts are popular with Spanish visitors attracted by the temperate climate, delightful beaches, excellent fish and seafood, impressive landscapes and fascinating towns and cities, including renowned resorts such as Donostia-San Sebastián and Santander. With the exception of a few places, the coast of Northern Spain has escaped the frenetic development of the Mediterranean, and as such has managed to preserve its natural beauty.
Although less popular with foreign visitors, the **Costa de la Luz** (Coast of Light), stretching between the southernmost tip of Spain and the Portuguese border, has some of the country's finest beaches, dotted with charming family resorts and historic cities such as Cádiz, the oldest in Spain.

CANARY ISLANDS

The Canary Islands come into their own in winter, when thousands of visitors flock here to escape the cold of Northern Europe. High season in the Canaries runs from 1 November to 30 April. The main tourist centres on the archipelago can be found in the south of Gran Canaria (Maspalomas, Playa del Inglés and Playa de San Agustín) and on Tenerife (Playa de las Américas to the south, and Puerto de la Cruz to the north).

NATIONAL PARKS

Spain is a country that acts as a bridge between Europe and Africa, and as such has a wealth of different landscapes including salt marshes, conifer forests, high mountains, desert areas and Mediterranean woodland.
The country's national parks protect those areas of major ecological interest to ensure their continuing survival. The main aim of these parks is to preserve their unique flora and fauna and to control public access. In total, Spain has 12 national parks – seven on the mainland and five spread across the islands. For many animal and plant species, Spain's mountain parks provide the most southerly habitat in Europe.

MOUNTAIN PARKS

The country's first national park was the Parque de Montaña de Covadonga, created in 1918. In 1995, this protected area was significantly extended (from 16 925ha/41 822 acres to 64 600ha/159 626 acres) and became known as the **Parque Nacional de los Picos de Europa**. This magnificent park is charac-terised by breathtaking landscapes with glacial lakes and extensive forests of beech (between 800m/2 624ft and 1 500m/ 4 920ft) as well as chestnut and oak, where water, in the shape of rivers, streams, lagoons and lakes, is an ecological factor of great impor-tance. In terms of fauna, the main spe-cies found here are chamois, mountain cats, polecats, foxes, otters, squirrels, imperial eagles and partridges, with the occasional sighting of the brown bear. The main types of fish found in the park's rivers are trout and salmon.
The **Parque Nacional de Ordesa y Monte Perdido**, at the heart of the Pyrenees in the province of Huesca, covers an area of 15 608ha/ 38 567 acres, and was also established in 1918. The park is spread across four valleys, in which the landscape is dominated by bubbling mountain rivers and streams, waterfalls, impressive precipices and forests of mountain pine, beech and fir, inhabitated by polecats, wild boar, foxes, pine martens, otters etc.
The present-day appearance of the **Parc Nacional de Aigüestortes i Estany de Sant Maurici**, covering 9 851ha/24 342 acres in the province of Lleida, in the Catalan Pyrenees, was created by the ice that invaded this area during the Quater-nary Era. The park's varied landscape includes lakes, forests of mountain pine, fir and Alpine meadows, popu-lated by a variety of fauna, including wild boar, ermine, pine martens, dor-mice, imperial eagles and partridge.
The **Sierra Nevada** (90 000ha/ 222 390 acres) is a mountain park with

several summits over 3 000m/9 840ft, including Mul-hacén, the highest peak on mainland Spain at 3 482m/11 421ft. This range is also renowned for the variety of its flora and fauna, which is the result of the unique climatic and topographical features that exist here.

PARQUE NACIONAL DE CABAÑEROS

Spread across a flatland area between two rocky formations in the Montes de Toledo, this protected national park covering some 40 000ha/98 840 acres is characterised by a Mediterranean-style wooded landscape abundant with deer, wild boar and birds of prey, in particular black and griffon vultures.

WETLAND PARKS

The Tablas de Daimiel and the Parque de Doñana are of vital ecological importance due to the protection they offer flora and fauna in danger of extinction, and their role as a breeding, migration and wintering area for numerous species of birds.

The **Tablas de Daimiel** (Ciudad Real) is the smallest of Spain's national parks, with an area of just 1 928ha/4 764 acres. The flooding of the Cigüela and Guadiana rivers has resulted in the formation of areas of shallow bodies of water ideal for the creation of typical marshland vegetation that has been colonised by various species of birds, some of which migrate here for the winter or to nest (grey herons, lesser egrets, red-crested pochard etc).

The extraordinary wealth of species in the **Parque Nacional de Doñana** (50 720ha/125 329 acres) is the result of its three distinct habitats: the coastal dunes, the salt marshes, and the former hunting grounds or cotos. Its strategic location on the southern tip of Europe, almost within sight of the coast of Africa, has resulted in its development as an important wetland for migratory birds. Various birds and ani-mals in danger of extinction can still be found here, such as the lynx, ichneumon and imperial eagle.

PARKS ON THE SPANISH ISLANDS

The **Cabrera archipelago,** in the Balearics, is Spain's only maritime and terrestrial national park, stretching across an area of some 10 000ha/24 700 acres. The remaining four parks not on the Spanish mainland are found in the Canary Islands: the Parque Nacional del **Teide**, on Tenerife; the **Caldera de Taburiente**, on the island of La Palma; **Timanfaya**, on Lanzarote; and **Garajonay**, on the island of La Gomera.

OVER THE BORDER

If you're staying close to Spain's national borders, you may wish to consider a day trip into southwest France or Portugal to visit a number of sights of interest within easy distance. The Green Guide collection covers these areas (Atlantic Coast; Languedoc Roussillon Tarn Gorges; and Portugal), in addition to the *Michelin Guide France*, the *Michelin Guide España Portugal*, and a comprehensive range of maps and plans to enhance your touring itineraries.

PLACES OF INTEREST CLOSE TO THE SPANISH BORDER

FRANCE

Across the border from the province of **Guipúzcoa**, the Basque country of France boasts some of the country's most beautiful and most famous resorts such as St Jean de Luz, Biarritz and Bayonne.

Less than 30km/18mi from **Roncesvalles** (Navarra) is the town of St-Jean-Pied-de-Port, a famous staging-post on the Way of St James.

From various places in the **Pirineos Aragoneses**, such as Somport and the Portalet Pass, it is possible to drive into the Parc National des Pyrénées, a protected area within the French Pyrenees. From the **Pirineos Catalanes**, it is also easy to cross the border to admire the impressive landscapes on the French side of the range. From **Cerbère** (Girona), the coast road winds its way north to the delightful village of Collioure, where the poet Antonio Machado died, and then inland to Perpignan, the capital of French Catalunya.

PORTUGAL

Opposite the Galician town of **Tui/Tuy** (Pontevedra), and linked by a bridge designed by Gustave Eiffel over the River Miño, stands Valença do Minho, where you can ascend Monte do Faro to enjoy a magnificent view.
To the south of **Puebla de Sanabria**, in the province of Zamora, it is also well worth visiting the historic Portuguese city of Braganza, while from **Ciudad Rodrigo** (Salamanca) you may wish to explore the fortified town of Almeida.
From **Cáceres**, the N 521 runs directly west into Portugal and the attractive mountain landscapes of the Serra de São Mamede, including the fortified town of Marvão and Castelo de Vide.
The walled town of Elvas is located just across the border from **Badajoz**, with Estremoz and its attractive old quarter some 50km/31mi farther west.
Ayamonte (Huelva), the closest town to Portugal in southern Spain, is the perfect starting-point from which to explore the summer playground of the Algarve, with its beautiful beaches, lively resorts and quaint fishing villages.

B. Kaufmann/MICHELIN

Bayonne

KNOW BEFORE YOU GO

Useful Websites

www.spain.info
The official site of the Spanish Tourist Board, providing comprehensive information on all aspects of the country, including transport, accommodation, sport and leisure activities.

www.tourspain.co.uk
The Spanish Tourist Board's site for UK visitors.

www.okspain.org
The Spanish Tourist Board's site for US visitors.

www.tourspain.toronto.on.ca
The Spanish Tourist Board's site for Canadian visitors.

www.fco.gov.uk
The British Government's Foreign and Commonwealth Office website provides up-to-date information on travel around the globe.

www.state.gov
American visitors may check the US State Department website for travel advice around the globe.

www.fac-aec.gc.ca
Website of Foreign Affairs Canada with relevant travel updates.

www.tourspain.es
The business-to-business site of the Spanish Tourist Board is useful for travel professionals.

Tourist Offices

London

2nd floor, 79 New Cavendish Street
Lonond W1W 6XB
☎ (020) 7486 8077;
24-hour brochure line: 084 59 400 180 (charged at national rate);
londres@tourspain.es

New York
666 Fifth Avenue,
New York, NY 10103
☎212-265-8822;
nuevayork@tourspain.es

Chicago
Water Tower Place, Suite 915 East,
845 North Michigan Avenue,
Chicago, IL 60611 ☎312-642-1992;
chicago@tourspain.es

Los Angeles
8383 Wilshire Blvd, Suite 960,
Beverly Hills, CA 90211
☎323-658-7195/7192
losangeles@tourspain.es

Miami
1395 Brickell Avenue,
Miami, FL 33131 ☎305-358-1992;
miami@tourspain.es

Toronto
2 Bloor St West, 34th Floor,
Toronto, Ontario M4W 3E2
☎416-961-3131;
toronto@tourspain.es

International Visitors

EMBASSIES AND CONSULATES

US Embassy
Serrano 75, 28006 Madrid
☎91 587 22 40 (emergencies,
☎91 587 22 40); www.embusa.es

US Consulates
Paseo Reina Elisenda de Montcada 23, 08034 **Barcelona**, ☎93 280 2227.
In addition there are consular agencies in **Málaga** (☎952 47 48 91), **Sevilla** (☎654 22 87 51), **Valencia** (☎963 51 69 73), **Las Palmas** (☎928 22 25 52), **La Coruña** (☎981 21 32 33) and **Palma de Mallorca** (☎971 40 37 07).

Australian Embassy
Plaza del Descubridor Diego de Ordás 3, 2º, 28003 Madrid,
☎913 53 66 00;
www.embaustralia.es.

Australian Consulates
Barcelona (honourary, ☎93 490 90 13);
Sevilla (honourary, ☎95 422 09 71).

British Embassy
Calle Fernando el Santo 16, 28010 Madrid, ☎91 700 82 00;
www.ukinspain.com

British Consulate-General
Paseo de Recoletos 7/9, 28004 Madrid, ☎91 524 97 00.

British Consular Offices
Alicante (☎965 21 61 90);
Barcelona (☎93 366 62 00);
Bilbao (☎94 415 76 00);
Granada (☎ 669 89 50 53);
Ibiza (☎971 30 18 18);
Las Palmas, Canary Islands (☎928 26 25 08);
Málaga (☎952 35 23 00);
Palma de Mallorca, Mallorca (☎971 71 24 45);
Santa Cruz de Tenerife, Canary Islands (☎922 28 68 63)

Canadian Embassy
Calle Núñez de Balboa 35, 28001 Madrid, ☎91 423 32 50;
www.canada-es.org

Canadian Consulate
Barcelona (☎93 204 27 00);
Málaga (☎952 22 33 46).

Embassy of Ireland
Ireland House, Paseo de la Castellana 46, 4ª, 28046 Madrid,
☎91 436 40 93;
embajadairlanda@terra.es

Honorary Irish Consulates
Alicante (☎965 10 74 85)
Barcelona (☎93 491 50 21);
Bilbao (☎944 23 04 14);
Las Palmas, Canary Islands (☎928 29 77 28);
Málaga (☎952 47 51 08);

Palma de Mallorca, Mallorca (☎971 72 25 04);
(☎954 21 63 61); and
Santa Cruz de Tenerife, Canary Islands (☎922 24 56 71).

DOCUMENTS

Visitors must be in possession of a valid **passport**. Holders of British, Irish and US passports do not need a visa for a visit of less than 90 days. Visitors from some Commonwealth countries or those planning to stay longer than 90 days should enquire about visa requirements at their local Spanish consulate. US citizens should view *Tips for Traveling Abroad* online (travel.state.gov/travel/tips/brochures/brochures_1225.html) for general information on visa requirements, customs regulations, medical care etc.

CUSTOMS REGULATIONS

UK residents may bring home goods on which taxes have been paid (Canary Islands excluded). Contact HM Customs and Excise, ☎(0845) 010 9000; www.hmce.gov.uk. US citizens can obtain a pamphlet, **Know Before You Go**, from the US Customs Service, ☎202-354-1000; www.customs.gov

HEALTH

British citizens should apply for the European Health Insurance Card (www.ehic.org.uk or at a post office) to obtain free or low-cost treatment in the EU. All visitors should consider insurance for uncovered medical expenses, lost luggage, theft, , etc.
Pets (cats and dogs) – A general health certificate and proof of rabies vaccination should be obtained from your local vet before departure.

Accessibility

Information on facilities for the disabled within Spain is available from Polibea, Ronda de la Avutarda 3, 28043 Madrid, ☎91 759 53 72; www.polibea.com/turismo.

GETTING THERE

By Plane

A number of Spanish and international airlines operate direct scheduled services to airports across Spain. These include:

- **Iberia Airlines**: ☎902 400 500; www.iberia.com. Reservations in the U.K. ☎ 0870 609 0500; in the US and Canada: ☎800-772-4642 (toll-free)
- **British Airways**: ☎0870 850 9850; www.ba.com. Reservations within the US and Canada: ☎1-800-AIRWAYS.

A number of low-cost airlines also offer inexpensive flights to several Spanish cities from the UK. Some airlines only allow bookings to be made via the Internet, while others offer small discounts for Internet bookings:

- **Bmibaby**: www.bmibaby.com
- **EasyJet**: ☎0871 244 2366 (charged per minute); 807 260026 (Spain); www.easyJet.com
- **Ryanair**: ☎0871 246 0000 (UK) 0818 30 30 30 (Ireland); www.ryanair.com

Hundreds of weekly charter flights also operate from the UK to Spanish cities, particularly along the Mediterranean coast and in the Balearic and Canary islands.

By Ship

Brittany Ferries and P&O Ferries both operate services to northern Spain from the UK.

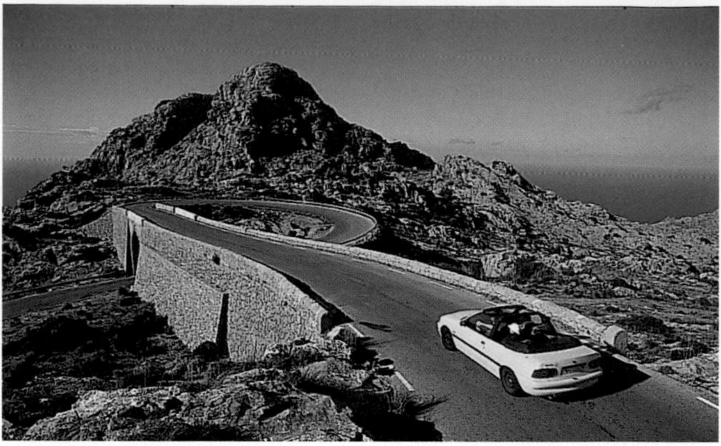
B. Pérousse/MICHELIN

Brittany Ferries run a ferry service between Plymouth and Santander from mid-March to mid-November; journey time: approx. 24hr. For reservations, contact:

Brittany Ferries: ☎0870 907 6103 (UK); ☎942 36 06 11 (Santander); www.brittany-ferries.com

P&O Portsmouth offers a twice-weekly crossing from Portsmouth to Bilbao from March to December; journey time: approx. 30hr. For reservations, contact:

P&O Portsmouth: ☎08705 980 333; ☎902 02 04 61 (Spain); www.poferries.com

By Train

Eurostar (☎08705 186 186; www.eurostar.com) operates high-speed passenger trains to Paris, from where overnight train-hotel services operate to Madrid and Barcelona, with onward connections to destinations across the country. Services from Paris, as well as train tickets within Spain, can be booked through the Spanish State Railway Network's (RENFE) UK agent, the Spanish Rail Service, ☎(020)7725 7063; www.spanish-rail.co.uk. Alternatively, log onto the official **RENFE** website at www.renfe.es.

By Coach/Bus

Regular long-distance bus services operate from London to all major towns and cities in Spain. For information, contact: Eurolines UK, ☎08705 808080; www.eurolines.co.uk

GETTING AROUND

By Plane

Spain has over 40 airports, including 12 on the islands. Information on these is available from AENA (Aeropuertos Españoles y Navegación Aérea) at www.aena.es, ☎902 40 47 04.
The largest airports in the country are as follows:

Madrid-Barajas ☎902 35 35 70.
Barcelona ☎902 40 47 04.
Bilbao ☎94 486 96 64.
Sevilla ☎95 444 90 00.
Málaga ☎95 204 88 04.
Valencia ☎96 159 85 00.
Palma ☎971 78 92 08.

MAJOR AIRLINE COMPANIES:

Iberia and **Aviaco**: Inforiberia, ☎902 400 500 (information and bookings); www.iberia.com

Air Europa: ☎902 401 501; www.aireuropa.com

Spanair: ☎902 13 14 15; www.spanair.com

By Ship

Several ferry companies operate services between the Spanish mainland and the Balearics, Canaries and North Africa.

Trasmediterránea – Daily services to the Balearics (from Valencia and Barcelona), a weekly service from Cádiz to the Canary Islands, and daily crossings to Ceuta and Melilla from Almería, Málaga and Algeciras. Information and reservations: ☎902 45 46 45 and www.trasmediterranea.es

Regional offices: Madrid: Avenida Europa 10, Parque Empresarial La Moraleja, 28108 Madrid, ☎91 423 85 00; Barcelona: Estació Marítima, Muelle San Beltrán, 08039 Barcelona, ☎93 295 91 34/35; Cádiz: Estación Marítima, Muelle Alfonso XIII, 11006 Cádiz, ☎956 22 20 38.

Baleària – Baleària operates services to and from the Balearics and from island to island. For information, call ☎902 160 180 or log onto www.balearia.com. Regional offices: Madrid: calle O'Donnell 38, ☎91 409 14 42; Denia (Alicante), Estación Marítima, Puerto de Denia, ☎96 642 86 00.

By Train

RENFE ☎902 24 02 02 (24hr information and reservation, except 11.45pm-12.15am; Sat and Sun 11.45pm-2.30am); www.renfe.es.

AVE (Alta Velocidad Española) high-speed trains run from Madrid (Atocha Station) to Córdoba in 1h 50min and Sevilla in 2h 35min; to Zaragoza in 1h 40min; to Lleida/Lérida in 2h 30min and Huesca in 2h 25min; and to Toledo in just 30min.

"Green" railway stations – Dozens of stations are so designated (*estaciones verdes*) due to their location near nature reserves, or because of their suitability for hikers, mountain bikers or for nature lovers wishing to discover the beauty of rural Spain. Information about attractions near designated stations is available on line at www.renfe.es/empresa/mundo/medio_ambiente/.

TOURIST TRAINS

El Expreso Al Andalus – A seven-day trip across Andalucía in carriages built in the 1920s and 1930s. The tour includes excursions, meals and accommodation and operates from April to June and September to November. Departures from Madrid and Sevilla. For current state of operations call ☎91 570 96 92 (from 9am-1pm); or check http://www.spanish-rail.co.uk/trains/alandalus.html.

El Transcantábrico – This narrow-gauge train skirts the coastline of Cantabria from San Sebastián (Donostia) to Santiago de Compostela. The trip lasts a week and combines rail and bus travel. The service operates from April to October. ☎91 571 66 92 (9am-1.30pm and 4-7.30pm). www.transcantabrico.feve.es

El Tren de la Fresa – The Strawberry Train operates vintage cars between Madrid and Aranjuez, from April to July from Atocha station. ☎902 24 02 02 (Spanish Railways).

By Coach/Bus

The Spanish bus network is a comfortable, modern and relatively inexpensive way of travelling across the country. Numerous companies offer local and long-distance services. Information on routes, timetables and prices can be obtained from local bus stations.
Two of the companies with the largest networks are:

Alsa – Extensive routes across the country, particularly in the northwest, center, and along the Mediterranean. For information, call ☎902 42 22 42 or log onto www.alsa.es.

Auto Res – Numerous services in the Valencia region, Castilla y León, Extremadura, etc. For information, call ☎902 02 00 52 or log onto www.auto-res.net.

By Car

ROAD NETWORK

Spain has over 340 000km/212 500mi of roads, including 7 000km/4 375mi of divided highways and expressways.
Speed limits in Spain are as follows:

- 120kph/75mph on expressways and divided highways;
- 100kph/62mph on the open road (with a hard shoulder of at least 1.5m/5ft);
- 90kph/56mph on the open road (without a hard shoulder);
- 50kph/31mph in built-up areas.

DOCUMENTS

In general, motorists need only have a current driving licence from their country of origin and valid papers (vehicle documentation and valid insurance) to drive in Spain, although in certain situations an International Driving Permit may be required. If in doubt, visitors should check with the AA or RAC in the United Kingdom or with the American Automobile Association in the US.

DRIVING REGULATIONS

The minimum driving age is 18. Traffic drives on the right. It is compulsory for passengers in both front and rear seats to wear **seat belts**. Motorcyclists (on all sizes of machine) must wear safety helmets. It is now a legal requirement for motorists to carry two red warning triangles, in addition to a spare tyre and a set of replacement bulbs.

Motorists should note that it is illegal to use a **mobile phone** when driving, unless the vehicle is fitted with a hands-free unit. Heavy on-the-spot fines are frequent for those caught using hand-held phones.

INSURANCE

Those motorists entering Spain in their own vehicles should ensure that their insurance policy includes overseas cover. Visitors are advised to check with their respective insurance company prior to travel. Motorists are also advised to take out adequate accident and **breakdown** cover for their period of travel overseas. Various motoring organisations (AA, RAC etc) will be able to provide further details on options available. Bail bonds are no longer necessary, although travellers may wish to take this precaution (consult your insurance company). Members of the American Automobile Association should obtain the free brochure, *Offices to Serve You Abroad*, which gives details of affiliated organisations in Spain.

If the driver of the vehicle is not accompanied by the owner, he or she must have written permission from the owner to drive in Spain.

ROAD INFORMATION

The **National Traffic Agency** (Dirección General de Tráfico) is able to provide information in English on road conditions, driving itineraries, regulations etc. For further information, call ☎900 12 35 05 (toll-free) or log onto the agency's website at www.dgt.es.

TOLLS

Tolls are payable on some sections of the Spanish highway network. On Michelin maps, these sections are indicated by kilometre markers in red; toll-free sections are marked in blue.

MAPS AND PLANS

Michelin's España/Portugal spiral **road atlas** and general **road maps** will assist you in the planning of your journey. These are listed in the **Maps and plans** section at the back of the guide.

MOTORING ORGANISATIONS

RACE (Royal Automobile Club of Spain) ☎902 40 45 45 and 902 30 05 05 (roadside assistance); www.race.es

CAR HIRE

Vehicles in Spain can be hired through the offices of all major international car hire companies around the world. Alternatively, cars can be hired at major airports, train stations, large hotels and in all major towns and cities around the country:

Avis ☎902 13 55 31; www.avis.com

Europcar ☎902 10 50 30 or 913 43 45 12. www.europcar.com

Hertz ☎902 22 00 24. www.hertz.com

Visitors should bear in mind that although the legal driving age in Spain is 18, most companies will only rent out vehicles to drivers over the age of 21.

WHERE TO STAY AND EAT

Hotel and Restaurant recommendations are located in the Address Books throughout the *Discovering Spain* section of this guide. For coin ranges and for a description of the symbols used in the Address Books, see the Legend on the cover flap.

Hotel and Restaurant listings fall within the description of each region in order to enhance your stay and enable you to make the most of your holiday. These have been recommended for their location, comfort, excellent value for money and in some cases for their charm. We have also made a conscious effort to cover all budgets, although some regions (for example, the Costa Brava, Costa del Sol and the Balearic Islands) are more expensive than others, and prices in Madrid and Barcelona can be as high as in other major cities in Europe.

As a general rule, restaurants serve lunch from 1:30pm-3:30pm and dinner from 9pm-11pm.

Finding a Hotel

This section lists a selection of hotels, *hostales* and *pensiones* based on the price of a double room in high season and generally excluding breakfast and VAT, unless otherwise indicated. The difference in rates between high and low season can be significant, particularly on the coast and islands, so it is always advisable to receive

J. Malburet/MICHELIN

Parador, Pontevedra

confirmation of prices in writing at the time of booking.

PARADORS

Almost all of the state-run network of luxury hotels are in restored historic monuments (castles, palaces, monasteries etc) in magnificent locations. For more information, contact Paradores de Turismo, calle Requena 3, 28013 Madrid ☎91 561 66 66; www.parador.es The official UK representative is Keytel International, 402 Edgware Road, London W2 1ED ☎(020) 7616 0300; Fax (020) 7616 0317; paradors@keytel.co.uk. In the US, contact PTB Hotels, ☎1-800-467-0772, info@paradors.com; in Canada, ADSUM Tourism Services, ☎416-728-5356, paradores-ca@adsum.ws. Special weekend **offers** are often available, in addition to a five-night "go as you please" accommodation **card**.

RURAL ACCOMMODATION

The number of visitors to Spain who wish to stay in rural accommodation is steadily increasing. Most autonomous communities publish a practical guide listing details of every type of accommodation available, including rooms in private houses, hostels for groups, entire houses for rent, and farm campsites. Contact local tourist offices listed within the Principal Sights for further details, or www.ecoturismorural.com.

CAMPSITES

The Secretaría General de Turismo publishes an annual campsite guide. Further details on camping and caravanning are supplied by the Federación Española de Campings, calle San Bernardo 97-99, Edificio Colomina, 3° planta, 28015 Madrid, ☎91 448 12 34, www.fedcamping.com. Book in advance for popular resorts during summer.

YOUTH HOSTELS

Spain's 160 youth hostels are open to travellers with an **international card**, available from international youth hostelling offices and youth hostels themselves. For further information, contact the **Spanish Youth Hostel Network** (Red Española de Albergues Juveniles), Castello 24, 28001 Madrid, ☎915 227 007. Information and online bookings are available at www.reaj.com.

SPECIAL OFFERS

Many chains and hotels catering to business travellers often offer reduced rates at weekends. It is also possible to purchase vouchers for one or several nights at advantageous prices. For further information on these special offers, contact the following:

NH Hoteles ☎902 115 116 (24 hours); www.nh-hoteles.es Weekend rates with activities from 160 € double, Sleep and Go rates for under-30s for 29 € per person.

Bancotel ☎91 509 61 22, 00800 1001 1002 from Europe; www.bancotel.com/ing/index.htm Booklets of five vouchers on sale exclusively at travel agencies and on its website. Three-, four- and five-star hotels. Good discounts on standard rates.

Halcón Viajes ☎807 227 222 (information and reservations); www.halcon-viajes.es Individual vouchers (for a one-night stay for one or two people) with a discount on the official rate.

Hoteles Meliá ☎902 14 44 40; www.solmelia.com Discounts via the

MAS loyalty card and special weekend offers.

DON'T FORGET THE MICHELIN GUIDE

The red-cover **Michelin Guide España & Portugal** is revised annually and is an indispensable complement to this guide with additional information on hotels and restaurants including category, price, degree of comfort and setting.

Where to Eat

The restaurants listed in the Address Books in this guide have been chosen for their surroundings, ambience, typical dishes or unusual character. Coin symbols (see Legend on cover flap) correspond to average cost of a meal and are given as a guideline only.

TAPAS

Given the country's reputation for tapas, we have also included a list of tapas bars where visitors can enjoy an aperitif or meal throughout the day and late into the evening. Prices of tapas are often not listed, although as a general rule the cost of a reasonably priced tapas lunch or supper should not exceed 14 €.

TAKING A BREAK, SHOPPING AND NIGHTLIFE

These headings, which appear periodically in Address Books throughout the guide, include a variety of addresses from cafés and bars to shops and theatres, as well as nightclubs and concert venues. Some may be quiet cafés during the day, transforming themselves into lively bars at night.

WHAT TO SEE AND DO

Outdoor Fun

As a result of its climate and varied landscapes, Spain is able to offer a whole range of activities for nature-lovers and outdoor sports enthusiasts.

WINTER SPORTS

There are 31 ski resorts in Spain including 17 in the Pyrenees, six in the Cordillera Cantábrica, four in the Cordillera Central, three in the Cordillera Ibérica and one in the Sierra Nevada (near Granada). Information on these is available from the Federación Española de Deportes de Invierno, Avenida de los Madroños 36, 28043 Madrid, ☎91 376 99 30, www.rfedi.es, or from ATUDEM (Asociación Turística de Estaciones de Esquí y Montaña), calle Padre Damián 43 1°, office 11, 28036 Madrid, ☎91 359 15 17 (snow conditions: ☎91 350 20 20), www.atudem.org. Maps and brochures showing the major resorts, including their altitude and facilities (ski-lifts, downhill and cross-country runs), are available from tourist offices.

GOLF

There are approximately 180 golf courses across the country, a number that is steadily growing, particularly in coastal areas. For further information, contact the Federación Española de

B. Kaufmann/ MICHELIN

Playing golf in Jávea

Golf, calle Provisional Arroyo del Fresno Dos, 5°, 28035 Madrid, ☎91 555 26 82, www.golfspainfederacion.com.
A map of golf courses is also available from tourist offices.
Golf courses and their telephone numbers are also listed in the current edition of the **Michelin Guide España Portugal** under the nearest town or city.

HUNTING

Spain boasts the largest hunting area of any European country, populated by large game including wild boar, deer and moufflon, and smaller prey such as partridge, pheasant, rabbits, hare and duck. The hunting season generally runs from September to February, although this varies from species to species.
Hunting and fishing permits can be obtained from local autonomous community authorities. For further details, as well as information on the official hunting calendar, contact the Federación Española de Caza, calle Francos Rodríguez 70, 2°, 28039 Madrid, ☎91 311 14 11, www.fedecaza.com.

FISHING

Spain's 76 000km/47 500mi of river courses provide a wealth of options for freshwater fishing enthusiasts, although seasons can vary from one region to another. Fishing permits are issued by the Environment Agency (Agencia de Medio Ambiente) in the relevant autonomous community.
For further information on sea and freshwater fishing, contact the Spanish Sea and Freshwater Fishing Federation (Federación Española de Pesca en Agua Dulce y Marítima), calle Navas de Tolosa 3, 1°, 28013 Madrid, ☎91 532 83 53, www.fepyc.es.

B. Kaufmann/ MICHELIN

SAILING

The waters of the Mediterranean and Atlantic are one of Spain's major attractions. As a result, hundreds of sailing clubs and pleasure marinas have been established along the coastlines. For further information, apply to the Royal Sailing Federation (Real Federación de Vela), calle Luis de Salazar 12, 28002 Madrid, ☎91 519 50 08; www.rfev.es.

SCUBA-DIVING

The Spanish coast, in particular the waters of the Mediterranean, is becoming increasingly popular with scuba-divers, with the development of diving sites such as the Cabo de Gata, the Islas Medes, on the Costa Brava, and resorts in the Balearic and Canary islands. For further information, contact the Spanish Scuba-Diving Federation (Federación Española de Actividades Subacuáticas), calle Santaló 15, 3° 1ª, 0821 Barcelona; ☎93 200 67 69; www.fedas.es.

HIKING AND MOUNTAINEERING

Hiking is becoming increasingly popular across Spain. For information on hiking routes and paths, as well as mountaineering, contact the Spanish Mountaineering Federation (Federación Española de Montañismo), calle Floridablanca 84, 08015 Barcelona, ☎93 426 42 67, www.fedme.es.

HORSE RIDING

A wide choice of options is available to horse-riding enthusiasts, ranging from short excursions to treks lasting several days. Every autonomous community has a large number of companies and organisations offering equestrian activities. For further information, contact the Spanish Horse Riding Federation (Federación Hípica Española), calle Monte Esquinza 28 - 3º, 28010 Madrid, ☎91 436 42 00; www.rfhe.com.

OTHER SPORTS

Information on clubs offering paragliding, hang-gliding, microlight flying, rafting etc is available from local tourist offices.

Spas

The hectic pace of modern life has resulted in an increasing number of people visiting the country's spa resorts for a few days in which to relax, recharge their batteries and help ease certain illnesses and ailments through treatments that are based on the medicinal qualities of the resorts' mineral-rich waters.
Generally speaking, spa complexes are found in areas of outstanding beauty where visitors and patients are also able to enjoy the surrounding nature and leisure facilities available. In Spain, there are a number of spa resorts dotted around the country, inheriting a tradition that has been passed down from the Greeks, Romans and Moors. For information on the treatments and facilities available at individual spas, contact the National Spa Resort Association (Asociación Nacional de Estaciones Termales), calle Rodríguez San Pedro 56, 3º, 28015 Madrid, ☎902 11 76 22, www.balnearios.org.

Activities for Children

In this guide, sights of particular interest to children are indicated with a KIDS symbol (Kids). Some attractions may offer discounted fees for children. In recent years, the number of leisure attractions popular with families has increased dramatically with the opening of several major theme and water parks. The following are just a few examples of places that will guarantee a fun day out for children and their parents alike.
The country's best-known **theme parks** are Port Aventura (near Tarragona), Terra Mítica (Benidorm), Isla Mágica (Sevilla) and Warner Bros. Park on the outskirts of Madrid. The country's capital is also home to one of Spain's best amusement parks.
Wildlife parks, such as the Parque de la Naturaleza de Cabárceno (near Santander), zoos (Madrid) and aquariums (Barcelona, Madrid, Donostia-San Sebastián, and O Grove, in Galicia), continue to be popular with youngsters of all ages, as do the bird and animal parks in the Canary Islands, including the Parque Ecológico Las Águilas del Teide, Loro Parque and Cactus and Animal Park (all on Tenerife); Palmitos Park, on Gran Canaria; and Tropical Park, on Lanzarote.
The Spanish coastline, particularly the Mediterranean, boasts numerous **water parks**, which are invariably full throughout the summer.
Interactive science museums, such as those in Valencia, Granada and La Coruña, offer an interesting and educational alternative to the leisure options above, as does a visit to the **Parque Minero** in Minas de Riotinto (Huelva), where visitors are transported by miners' train to discover this fascinating site.
Lastly, for those families on holiday close to Almería, a visit to **Oasys**, a desert park where many of the early Spaghetti Westerns were filmed, is an absolute must for young and old alike.

Calendar of Events

Spain's major festivals are mentioned in the list below. In order to confirm exact dates and times, which may vary slightly, contact the relevant local tourist office, which will be able to provide an up-to-date calendar of events. During the summer months, practically every small town and village in the country hosts a fiesta in honour of its own patron saint.

WEEK BEFORE ASH WEDNESDAY

Carnival festivities
Cádiz, Santa Cruz de Tenerife

1ST SUNDAY IN MARCH

International Vintage Car Rally
Sitges (Barcelona)

3RD SUNDAY IN LENT

Feast of the Magdalen; bullfights, processions
Castellón de la Plana

12-19 MARCH

Las Fallas Festival
Valencia

HOLY WEEK

Processions
Cartagena, Cuenca, Málaga, Murcia, Sevilla, Valladolid, Zamora

FIRST WEEK AFTER EASTER

Spring Festival
Murcia

APRIL

April Fair
Sevilla

22-24 OR 24-26 APRIL

St George's Festival: "Moors and Christians"
Alcoi/Alcoy

LAST SUNDAY IN APRIL

Romería (pilgrimage) to the Virgen de la Cabeza
Andújar (Jaén)

APRIL OR MAY

Horse Fair
Jérez de la Frontera

1ST FORTNIGHT IN MAY

Las Cruces Festival
Córdoba

15 MAY

San Isidro Festival
Madrid

WHITSUN

Pilgrimage to the Nuestra Señora del Rocío shrine
El Rocío (Huelva)
La Caballada Festival
Atienza (Guadalajara)

2ND SUNDAY AFTER WHITSUN: CORPUS CHRISTI CELEBRATION

Streets carpeted with flowers; competitions; processions
Puenteareas
Sitges (Barcelona)
Toledo

24 JUNE

"Hogueras" St John Festival
Alicante
Midsummer's Day Festival
Ciutadella (Menorca)

4-6 JULY

"A Rapa das Bestas" Festival
A Estrada (Pontevedra)

6-14 JULY

"Los Sanfermines" Festival with bull-running
Pamplona/Iruña

1ST OR 2ND SATURDAY IN AUGUST

Kayak races on the River Sella
Arriondas – Ribadesella (Asturias)

11-15 AUGUST

Elche Mystery Play
Elche (Alicante)

7-17 SEPTEMBER

Fair (Feria)
Albacete

19 SEPTEMBER

America Day in Asturias
Oviedo

21 SEPTEMBER

St Matthew's Festival
Oviedo

20-26 SEPTEMBER

La Rioja Wine Harvest Festival
Logroño

24 SEPTEMBER

Festival of Our Lady of Mercy (Virgen de la Merced)
Barcelona

8 OCTOBER

Procession of the Virgin
Guadalupe (Cáceres)

WEEK OF 12 OCTOBER

Pilar Festival
Zaragoza

FESTIVALS

Holy Week
Sacred Music Festival
Cuenca

June and July
International Music and Dance Festival ☎958 276 200
Granada

July
Internacional Classical Theatre Festival
www.festivaldealmagro.com
☎926 261 449
Almagro (Ciudad Real)

3rd week of July
Jazz Festival
www.jazzvitoria.com,
☎945 141 919
Vitoria

Last week of July
Jazz Festival www.jazzaldia.com,
☎943 48 19 00
Donostia-San Sebastián

July – August
Classical Theatre Festival
www.festivaldemerida.es
☎924 004 930
Mérida (Cáceres)
Castell de Perelada Festival
Perelada (Girona)

Last two weeks of September
San Sebastián International Film Festival www.sansebastian-festival.com/ ☎943 481 212
Donostia-San Sebastián

First two weeks of October
Catalunya International Film Festival www.cinemasitges.com/ ☎938 949 990
Sitges (Barcelona)

Last week of October
Seminci (International Film Week) www.seminci.com
☎983 42 64 60
Valladolid

End of November
Ibero-American Film Festival
www.festicinehuelva.com
Huelva

Shopping

Spain has a rich tradition of arts and crafts reflecting the character of each region as well as the influence of the civilisations – Iberian, Roman, Visigothic, and Muslim – that have marked the country's history. Traditional wares such as pottery, ceramics, basketwork and woven goods are produced countrywide.

POTTERY AND CERAMICS

The difference between pottery and ceramics is that pottery has been baked just once. In Castilla, pottery is mainly made by women who use a primitive technique. Among their specialities are kitchen utensils, jars and water pitchers. The basic items of crockery used in farmhouses – dishes, soup tureens and bowls made of glazed earthenware (*barro cocido*) – appear in villages and on stalls in every market. Many of the techniques (metal lustre, *cuerda seca*, decorative motifs, and colour) used in ceramics have been influenced by Islamic traditions. There are two large pottery centres in the Toledo region. The first, **Talavera de la Reina** is famous for its blue, green, yellow, orange and black ceramics, while the second, **El Puente del Arzobispo**, mainly uses shades of green. Pottery from **La Bisbal d'Empordà** in Catalunya has a yellow background with green decorative motifs. The Mudéjar tradition is evident in Aragón and the Levante region where blue and white pottery is made in **Muel**, green and purple ceramics in **Teruel** and lustreware in **Manises** (Valencia). Most of the figurines used as decoration for cribs at Christmas are produced in **Murcia**. Spain's richest pottery region is Andalucía, with workshops in **Granada** (glazed ceramics with thick green and blue strokes), **Guadix** (red crockery), **Triana** in Sevilla, (polychrome animal figures, glazed and decorated), **Úbeda, Andújar** (jars with cobalt blue patterns) and in **Vera** (white pottery with undulating shapes). In Galicia, porcelain and earthenware goods with contemporary shapes and designs are factory-made at the **Sargadelos** centre in the province of La Coruña, but there is also a craft industry at **Niñodaguia** in Orense (where the yellow glaze only partially covers the pottery) and at **Bruño** (where yellow motifs set off a dark brown background). Mention should be made of the famous *xiurels*, whistles decorated in red and green from the Balearic Islands.

LACE, WOVEN AND EMBROIDERED GOODS

The textile industry prospered under the Muslims and several workshops still thrive today. Brightly coloured blankets and carpets are woven in the Alpujarras region, la Rioja, the area around Cádiz (Grazalema) and at Níjar near Almería (where *tela de trapo* carpets are made from strips of cloth). Blankets from Zamora, Palencia and Salamanca are well known. The village of **El Paso**, on the island of La Gomera, in the Canary Islands, is the only place in Spain that still produces silk fabrics. In some villages in the province of Ciudad Real (particularly in **Almagro**) female lacemakers may still be seen at work in their doorways with bobbins and needles. Lacework from **Camariñas** in Galicia is also widely known. The most popular craft, however, is embroidery, often done in the family. The most typical, geometrically patterned embroideries come from the Toledo region (**Lagartera** and **Oropesa**). Embroidery has been raised to the level of a veritable art in two thoroughly Spanish domains: firstly, in the ornaments used for *pasos* during Holy Week and secondly in bullfighters' costumes.

METALWORK

Iron forging, a very old practice in Spain, has produced outstanding works of art such as the wrought-iron grilles and screens that adorn many churches. Blacksmiths continue to make the grilles for doors and

windows so popular in architecture in the south of Spain (La Mancha, Extremadura and Andalucía). **Guadalupe**, in Extremadura, is an important centre for copper production (boilers, braziers etc). Damascene weapons (steel inlaid with gold, silver and copper) are still produced, in **Eibar** (País Vasco) and in **Toledo** particularly, according to pure Islamic tradition. The best switch-blades and knives in Spain are produced in **Albacete**, Las Palmas de Gran Canaria and Taramundi (Asturias).
Gold- and silver-smithing were developed in antiquity and throughout the Visigothic period and have retained some traditional methods. One example is filigree ornamentation (soldered, intertwined gold and silver threads) crafted in **Córdoba** and **Toledo**. Salamanca, Cáceres and Ciudad Rodrigo specialise in gold jewellery. **Santiago de Compostela** is the world's leading centre for black amber ornaments.

LEATHERWORK

Leather-making has always been an important trade, especially in Andalucía, and has become industrialised in some areas. The town of Ubrique (Cádiz) is the leading producer of leatherwork in Spain, followed by the Alicante area and the Balearic Islands. The production of famous **Córdoba** leather, including embossed polychrome leatherwork, continues to the same high standards. Workshops specialising in the manufacture of harnesses and horse-riding and hunting accessories are predominantly found in Andalucía (Jerez de la Frontera, Alcalá de los Gazules, Villamartín, Almodóvar del Río and Zalamea la Real) .
Typically Spanish gourds and wineskin containers are made in the provinces of Bilbao, Pamplona/Iruña and Burgos and in other wine-growing areas. The wineskins produced in Valverde del Camino (Huelva) are known throughout Spain.

BASKETWORK

Basket-making remains one of the most representative of Spanish crafts. Although carried out countrywide, it is particularly rich on the Mediterranean coast and in the Balearic Islands.
The type of product and the material used vary from region to region. Baskets, hats and mats are made of reeds, willow, esparto grass, strips of olive-wood and birch and chestnut bark, while furniture may be rush or wickerwork. Willow is used in Andalucía and in the Levante, hazel and chestnut in Galicia and in Asturias, and straw and esparto grass on the island of Ibiza.

Sightseeing

Opening times and entrance fees for monuments, museums, churches etc are included in the "Discovering Spain" section of this guide. This information is given as a guideline only, as times and prices are liable to change without prior warning.
Prices shown are for individual visitors and do not take into account discounts for groups, who may also benefit from private visits. As many monuments require frequent maintenance and restoration, it is advisable to phone ahead to avoid disappointment.
Information for churches is only given if the interior contains a sight of particular interest with specific opening times or if an entrance fee is payable. In general, religious buildings should not be visited during services, although some only open for Mass, in which case visitors should show appropriate respect.

Books

Biography

Franco. Paul Preston (1995). A definitive life of the man who shaped Spain for decades, and whose Spain was unshaped on his demise.

Reference

Barcelona. Robert Hughes (1999). An enthusiastic and scholarly celebration of the coming-out of Catalunya's distinct culture after Franco.

History

Moorish Spain. Richard Fletcher (1993). An illumination through literature and history of the culture that was expelled from Spain but never expurgated.

Homage to Catalonia. George Orwell (1938; 2003). An inside look at the Spanish Civil War from the Republican side, and at conditions that led to the conflict.

Fiction

Don Quixote de La Mancha. Miguel de Cervantes (1605; 2003). The classic novel of Castille and of Spanish character.

Serpent's Tail. Manuel Vásquez Montalbán (1999). A leading contemporary writer probes murder and a changing society where many are spiritually imprisoned in a totalitarian past.

The Shadow of the Wind. Carlos Ruiz Zafón (2001; 2004). A contemporary allegory of post-Civil War Barcelona infused with Latin American magical realism.

Travel

Death in the Afternoon. Ernest Hemingway (1932; 2000). A terse take on tauromarchy, tradition, and the Spanish soul.

Iberia. James A Michener (1968; 1991). Vintage Michener in a ramble through vintage Spain in the throes of entering modern Europe.

Driving Over Lemons. Chris Stewart (1999). An account of living unconventionally in rural Granada.

South from Granada. Gerald Brenan (1992). A literary and folkloric account of a region in the last century.

Spain. Jan Morris (1986, 2003). The Morris take on Spain: history, enounters, and pleasures.

The Way of St James: a Walker's Guide. Alison Raju (1998, 2003). A modern guide to one of the first tourist routes.

Art

Picasso. Timothy HIlton (1976). An attempt to define the Spanish master's place in world art.

Films

Women on the Edge of a Nervous Breakdown (1976). Post-Franco Spanish cinema's (and Almodóvar's) coming out before the world, presenting a country freeing itself from social shackles.

Bad Education (La Mala Educación, 2004). Almodóvar's metaphor of his own life and of Spain: flourishing and passionate, despite a dark period.

The Sea Inside (Mar Adentro, 2004). An Oscar-winner about a dignified struggle with disability, ending in assisted suicide.

Belle Epoque (1992). A look at forbidden sexuality against the background of the Spanish Civil War.

Starting Over (1982). Spain's first Oscar winner depicts the return of a Civil War exile to his native Asturias.

Thesis (1996). Mystery, horror and secret lives unroll and unravel a beautiful university student.

The Others (2001). Alejandro Amenábar directs Nicole Kidman to great advantage in a Gothic thriller set in wartime England.

Lovers or the Arctic Circle (1998). A boy and girl are linked from childhood by fate, coincidence and attraction, across time and geography.

Take My Eyes (2003). A woman faces pressures to return to an abusive husband.

The Secret Life of Words (2005). A deaf nurse and a blinded oil worker discover each other and themselves.

Secrets of the Heart (1997). A boy is sent away to stay with relatives and uncovers family secrets.

Land Without Bread (1933). Buñuel's classic documents the hard lives of peasants in Las Hurdes.

Un Chien Andalou (1929). A pioneer short surrealist work by Salvador Dali and Luis Bunuel abandons plot and provokes reaction by the power of its images.

The Lucky Star (1997). A triangle of afflicted persons who love, hate and complete each other.

Alone (1998). Mother and daughter are opposites, but circumstances lead them to come to terms.

USEFUL WORDS AND PHRASES

Common words

yes, no .... **sí, no**
good morning .... **buenos días**
good afternoon .... **buenas tardes**
goodbye......... **hasta luego, adiós**
please .... **por favor**
how are you?............... **¿qué tal?**
thank you (very much)................
.... **(muchas) gracias**
excuse me .... **perdone**
I don't understand ...... **no entiendo**
sir, Mr; you .... **señor; usted**
madam, Mrs .... **señora**
miss .... **señorita**

Time

when? .... **¿cuándo?**
what time?.............. **¿a qué hora?**
today .... **hoy**
yesterday .... **ayer**
tomorrow morning...................
.... **mañana por la mañana**
tomorrow afternoon ....
.... **mañana por la tarde**

Shopping

how much?.......... **¿cuánto (vale)?**
(too) expensive.... **(demasiado) caro**
a lot, little.............. **mucho, poco**
more, less............... **más, menos**
big, small .... **grande, pequeño**
credit card .... **tarjeta de crédito**
Correspondence
post box .... **buzón**
post office .... **çorreos**
telephone .... **teléfono**
letter .... **carta**
post card .... **(tarjeta) postal**
poste restante...... **lista (de çorreos)**
stamp .... **sello**
telephone call........... **conferencia**
tobacco shop ...... **estanco, tabacos**

On the road, In town

coche .... car
gasolina .... petrol, gasoline
a la derecha............. on the right
a la izquierda .... on the left
obras...................... road works
peligro, peligroso danger, dangerous
cuidado........... beware, take care
dar la vuelta a...... to go round, tour
después de............ after, beyond
girar .... to go round, to circle

Numbers

0 .... cero
1 .... uno / una
2 .... dos
3 .... tres
4 .... cuatro
5 .... cinco
6 .... seis
7 .... siete
8 .... ocho
9 .... nueve
10 .... diez
11 .... once
12 .... doce
13 .... trece
14 .... catorce
15 .... quince
16 .... dieciséis
17 .... diecisiete
18 .... dieciocho

19 .... diecinueve
20 .... veinte
21 .... veintiuno
22 .... veintidós
23 .... veintitrés
24 .... veinticuatro
25 .... veinticinco
26 .... veintiséis
27 .... veintisiete
28 .... veintiocho
29 .... veintinueve
30 .... treinta
40 .... cuarenta
50 .... cincuenta
60 .... sesenta
70 .... setenta
80 .... ochenta
90 .... noventa
100 .... cien
1,000 .... mil

Food and Wine

For further hotel and restaurant vocabulary, consult the current edition of the **Michelin Guide España & Portugal.**

aceite, aceitunas .... oil, olives
sin gas .... sparkling/still water
ajo .... garlic
alcachofa .... artichoke
alergia: tengo alergia a... .... I'm allergic to...
alubias .... beans
anchoas .... anchovies
arroz .... rice
atún .... tuna
ave .... poultry
azúcar .... sugar
bacalao .... cod
berenjena .... aubergine/eggplant
café con leche ... coffee with hot milk
café solo .... black coffee
calamares .... squid
cangrejo .... crab
carne .... meat
cebolla .... onion
cerdo .... pork
cerveza .... beer
chorizos .... spicy sausages
cordero (lechal) ...... mutton (lamb)
crema (de leche) .... cream
ensalada .... green salad
entremeses .... hors-d'œuvre
fiambres .... cold cooked meats
gambas .... prawns
garbanzos .... chick peas
guisantes .... garden peas
helado .... ice cream
hígado .... liver
huevo; ....
huevos al plato ...... egg; fried eggs
jamón .... ham
judías verdes .... French beans
langostino .... (king) prawns
leche .... milk
legumbres .... vegetables
limón .... lemon
mantequilla .... butter
manzana .... apple
mariscos .... seafood, shellfish
naranja .... orange
nata .... cream
nuez (nueces) .... nut(s)
pan .... bread
patatas .... potatoes
pescados .... fish
pimienta (negra) ..... (black) pepper
pimiento (rojo/verde) .... (red/green) pepper
plátano .... banana
pollo .... chicken
postre .... dessert
potaje .... soup
queso .... cheese
sal .... salt
salchichas .... sausages
sandía .... water-melon
setas/hongos .... mushrooms
ternera .... veal
tortilla .... omelette
trucha .... trout
vaca/buey .... beef
vegetariano/a .... vegetarian
vino blanco/rosado/tinto .... white/rosé/red wine
zanahoria .... carrot
zumo de frutas .... fruit juice

Places and Things to See

See also architectural terms in the Introduction.

Words in italics are in Catalan.

where is? .... **¿dónde está?**
may one visit? ..... **¿se puede visitar?**
key .... **llave**
light .... **luz**
sacristan .... **sacristán**
guide .... **guía**

porter, caretaker ... **guarda, conserje**
open, closed .... **abierto, cerrado**
no entry, not allowed...... **prohibido**
entrance, exit ....**entrada, salida**
apply to.................. **dirigirse a**
wait ....**esperar**
beautiful............**bello, hermoso**
storey, stairs, steps .... **piso, escalera**
alcazaba ....Muslim fortress
alcázar...............Muslim palace
alrededores.......environs, outskirts
alto .... pass, high pass
ayuntamiento, *ajuntament*.......... ....town hall
audiencia...........audience, court
balneario .... spa
barranco...............gully, ravine
barrio, *barri* .... quarter
bodega ....wine cellar/store
cabo, *cap*............cape, headland
calle, *carrer*.................. street
calle mayor ....main street
camino.................. road, track
campanario.................. belfry
capilla .... chapel
capitel .... capital
carretera................main road
cartuja........ Carthusian monastery
casa........................house
casa consistorial..........town hall
castillo...................... castle
castro................. Celtic village
ciudad, *ciutat*............. town, city
claustro....................cloisters
colegio, colegiata................. ....college, collegiate church
collado, *coll* .... pass, high pass
convento........ monastery, convent
cruz.................. cross, Calvary
cuadro ....picture
cueva, gruta, cava ...... cave, grotto
desfiladero ....defile, cleft
embalse..............reservoir, dam
ermita ....hermitage, chapel
estación...................station
excavaciones .... excavations
finca ....property, domain
fuente .... fountain
gargantas...................gorges
gruta................cavern, grotto
hoz .... defile, narrow pass, gorge
huerto, huerta .... vegetable/market garden
iglesia......................church
imagen ....religious statue/sculpture
isla......................island, isle
lago, *estany*.....................lake
mezquita ....mosque
monasterio, *monestir*..... monastery
monte.............mount, mountain
mirador....... belvedere, viewpoint, ... lookout point
museo, *museu* .... museum
nacimiento .... source, birthplace
palacio (real), *palau* ....(royal) palace
pantano............... artificial lake
paseo, *passeig* .... avenue, esplanade, ... promenade
paso .... sculptured figures: ....the Passion
pazo .... manor-house (Galicia)
plaza, *plaça* .... square
plaza mayor............main square
plaza de toros..............bullring
portada...........portal, west door
pórtico................portal, porch
presa......................... dam
pueblo, *poble*....village, market town
puente, *pont* .... bridge
puerta .... door, gate, entrance
puerto .... pass, harbour, port
ría.......................... estuary
río.....................river, stream
romano; románico................. ....Roman; Romanesque
santuario .... church
siglo .... century
talla..................carved wood
tapices.................... tapestries
techo....................... ceiling
tesoro.............treasury, treasure
torre .... tower, belfry
torre del homenaje ....keep
torrente.... mountain stream, torrent
valle, *vall*...................... valley
vega .... fertile plain
vidriera ....window: plain ....or stained glass
vista .... view, panorama

BASIC INFORMATION

Business Hours

Shops are generally open 10am-2pm and 5-8:30pm, although an increasing number of larger stores and shopping centres do not close for lunch. The majority of shops close on Sundays, and a few still close on Saturday afternoon.

Discounts

Consult the website of the **Instituto de la Juventud**, www.injuve.mtas.es (Calle Marqués de Riscal 16, 28010 Madrid, ☎91 363 77 00) for links to youth-oriented travel services.
The **Oficina Nacional de Turismo e Intercambio de Jóvenes y Estudiantes (TIVE)**, centrally located at Gran Via 10, Madrid, ☎91 720 13 24/25/26, tive.juventude@madrid.org, arranges hostel reservations, discounted transportation and language study, and sells certain student cards. There are offices in other major cities.
The **EURO<26 Card**, issued by student organisations in 27 countries, entitles young people between the ages of 14 and 25 to a whole series of discounts on travel, cultural events, accommodation etc. In Spain, some 50 000 outlets participate in the scheme. For information, see www.eyca.org. In Spain, ☎91 363 76 85, carnetjoven@mtas.es or at TIVE offices (see above).
The **Student Card**, available to those aged 12 and over, also provides numerous discounts on a variety of services.
Senior citizens aged 65 and over qualify for significant discounts on transport, entrance fees to monuments, and events and shows. Many museums offer half-price entry, with free entrance to many national monuments.

Electricity

220 volts AC (some older establishments may still have 110 V). Plugs are two-pin.

Emergencies

☎112 conects with all emergency services in Spain.

Police ☎091(national), 092 (local) or 112
Medical emergencies ☎061 or 112
Fire ☎080, 085 or 112
Civil Guard ☎062
Mossos d'Esquadra (Catalan police) ☎088

Emergency services: ☎112
Medical emergencies: ☎061
Directory enquiries: ☎1003
International directory enquiries: ☎025

Public Holidays

Because autonomous communities and individual towns and cities have their own local festivals and feast days, it is difficult to draw up a definitive list of public holidays.
The following list represents those public holidays that are taken throughout the country:
1 January (New Year's Day), 6 January (Epiphany), Good Friday, 1 May (Labour Day), 15 August (Assumption of Our Lady), 12 October (Virgin of the Pillar: Day of the Hispanidad), 1 November (All Saints), 6 December (Spanish Constitution Day), 8 December (Immaculate Conception) and 25 December (Christmas Day).

Mail/Post

Post offices are open 8.30am-2.30pm, Monday-Friday, and 9.30am-1pm on Saturdays.
Stamps (*sellos*) can also be purchased at tobacconists (*estancos*). **The** red-cover **Michelin Guide España & Portugal** gives the postcode for every town and city covered.

Money

The unit of currency in Spain is the **euro**, written as €. Coins come in the following denominations: 1, 2, 5, 10, 20 and 50 cents and 1 and 2 euro with notes in 5, 10, 20, 50, 100, 200 and 500 values (*see the illustrations opposite*). There are no restrictions on the amount of currency (euro or other) that foreigners may bring with them into Spain.

Changing Money

Travellers' cheques and foreign cash can be exchanged at banks and exchange offices (*cambios*). International credit cards are accepted in most shops, hotels and restaurants. Visitors can also obtain cash from bank machines using credit and debit cards; a pin number will be required.

Banks

Banks are generally open 8.30am-2pm, Monday to Saturday. The same opening times apply in summer, except on Saturdays, when banks are closed.

Credit Cards

In the event of a **lost or stolen credit card**, contact the relevant issuer as soon as possible:

CC **Mastercard**: ☎ 900 97 1231
CC **Visa** ☎900 99 1124
CC **American Express** ☎ 902 37 56 37
CC **Diners Club** ☎902 40 11 12

Telephones

Public telephones accept coins as well as phone cards (*tarjetas telefónicas*).
For **international calls** from Spain, dial 00, then dial the country code (44 for the United Kingdom, 353 for Ireland, 1 for the United States and Canada), followed by the area code (minus the first 0 of the STD code when dialling the UK), and the number.
For number information, dial 11818 or 11823 for Spain; 025 or 11825 for other countries.
For calls within Spain, dial the full 9-digit number of the person you are calling.
When calling Spain from abroad, dial the international access code, followed by 34 for Spain, then the full 9-digit number.

Time

Spain is 1hr ahead of GMT. The Spanish keep very different hours from either the British or North Americans.
As a general rule, restaurants serve lunch from 1:30pm to 3:30pm and dinner from 9pm to 11pm.

Price and Tips

Restaurants and other establishments in Spain usually include both taxes and service in prices. It is customary to leave an additional cash tip of from 5 to 10 percent of a restaurant cheque or taxi fare. Tip porters 1 € per bag for assistance, and chambermaids 1 € per day. Guides may be tipped 3 to 5 € per day at your discretion.

CONVERSION TABLES

Weights and Measures

1 kilogram (kg)	**2.2 pounds (lb)**	**2.2 pounds**	*To convert kilograms to pounds, multiply by 2.2*
6.35 kilograms	14 pounds	1 stone (st)	
0.45 kilograms	16 ounces (oz)	16 ounces	
1 metric ton (tn)	**1.1 tons**	**1.1 tons**	
1 litre (l)	**2.11 pints (pt)**	**1.76 pints**	*To convert litres to gallons, multiply by 0.26 (US) or 0.22 (UK)*
3.79 litres	1 gallon (gal)	0.83 gallon	
4.55 litres	1.20 gallon	1 gallon	
1 hectare (ha)	**2.47 acres**	**2.47 acres**	*To convert hectares to acres, multiply by 2.4*
1 sq. kilometre (km²)	**0.38 sq. miles (sq.mi.)**	**0.38 sq. miles**	
1 centimetre (cm)	**0.39 inches (in)**	**0.39 inches**	*To convert metres to feet, multiply by 3.28; for kilometres to miles, multiply by 0.6*
1 metre (m)	3.28 feet (ft) or 39.37 inches or 1.09 yards (yd)		
1 kilometre (km)	**0.62 miles (mi)**	**0.62 miles**	

Clothing

Women			
Shoes	35	4	2½
	36	5	3½
	37	6	4½
	38	7	5½
	39	8	6½
	40	9	7½
	41	10	8½
Dresses & suits	36	6	8
	38	8	10
	40	10	12
	42	12	14
	44	14	16
	46	16	18
Blouses & sweaters	36	06	30
	38	08	32
	40	10	34
	42	12	36
	44	14	38
	46	16	40

Men			
Shoes	40	7½	7
	41	8½	8
	42	9½	9
	43	10½	10
	44	11½	11
	45	12½	12
	46	13½	13
Suits	46	36	36
	48	38	38
	50	40	40
	52	42	42
	54	44	44
	56	46	48
Shirts	37	14½	14½
	38	15	15
	39	15½	15½
	40	15¾	15¾
	41	16	16
	42	16½	16½

Sizes often vary depending on the designer. These equivalents are given for guidance only.

Speed

KPH	10	30	50	70	80	90	100	110	120	130
MPH	6	19	31	43	50	56	62	68	75	81

Temperature

Celsius (°C)	0°	5°	10°	15°	20°	25°	30°	40°	60°	80°	100°
Fahrenheit (°F)	32°	41°	50°	59°	68°	77°	86°	104°	140°	176°	212°

To convert Celsius into Fahrenheit, multiply °C by 9, divide by 5, and add 32.
To convert Fahrenheit into Celsius, subtract 32 from °F, multiply by 5, and divide by 9.

NB: Conversion factors on this page are approximate.

UNESCO World Heritage Sites

In 1972, the United Nations Educational, Scientific and Cultural Organization (UNESCO) adopted a Convention for the preservation of cultural and natural sites. Over 600 sites "of outstanding universal value" are now on the World Heritage List. Each year, representatives from 21 countries, assisted by technical organizations evaluate proposals for new sites. A site must be nominated by the country in which it is located.

The protected cultural heritage may be monuments (buildings, sculptures, archaeological structures etc) with unique historical, artistic or scientific features; groups of buildings (such as religious communities, ancient cities); or sites (human settlements, examples of exceptional landscapes, cultural landscapes) which are the combined works of man and nature of exceptional beauty. Natural sites may be a testimony to the stages of the earth's geological history or to the development of human cultures and creative genius or represent significant ongoing ecological processes, contain superlative natural phenomena or provide a habitat for threatened species. Signatories of the Convention pledge to cooperate to preserve and protect these sites around the world as a common heritage to be shared by all humanity.

UNESCO World Heritage sites included in this guide:	
Alcalá de Henares: University and historic quarter	**Lugo**: Roman walls
Altamira: Cave	**Mérida**: Archaeological site
Atapuerca (Burgos): Prehistoric remains	**Oviedo**: Monuments in the city and the kingdom of Asturias
Ávila: Old town and extra-muros churches	**Poblet**: Monastery
Barcelona: Parque Güell, Palacio Güell, Casa Milà, Palau de la Música Catalana and Hospital de Sant Pau	**Salamanca**: Old town
Burgos: Cathedral	**San Millán de la Cogolla**: Monasterio de Yuso and Monasterio de Suso
Cáceres: Old town	**Santiago de Compostela**: Old town
Córdoba: Historic centre	**Santiago de Compostela**:Way of St James
Cuenca: Historic fortified town	**Segovia**: Old town and aqueduct
Doñana: National Park	**Sevilla**: Cathedral, Alcázar and Archivo de Indias
Elche: El Palmeral palm grove	**Tarragona**: Roman town (Tarraco)
El Escorial: Monastery	**Tenerife**: San Cristóbal de la Laguna
La Gomera: Garajonay National Park	**Teruel**: Mudéjar architecture
Granada: Alhambra, Generalife and Albaicín	**Toledo**: Historic city
Guadalupe: Monasterio Real de Santa María	**Valencia**: La Lonja de la Seda
Ibiza: Biodiversity and culture	**Vall de Boí (Lleida)**: Romanesque churches

Equestrian statue of Philip III, Plaza Mayor, Madrid
E. Baret/MICHELIN

INTRODUCTION TO SPAIN

NATURE

Because of its geographical location, Spain acts as a bridge between two continents – Europe and Africa. The country has myriad natural attractions, ranging from long sandy beaches, sheltered coves and steep cliffs to breathtaking mountain landscapes characterised by high peaks and enclosed valleys. By contrast, the centre of Spain, known as the Meseta, is marked by seemingly endless expanses of flat terrain.

Regions and Landscape

Relief – The average altitude in Spain is 650m/2,100ft above sea level and one sixth of the terrain rises to more than 1,000m/3,300ft. The highest peak on the Spanish mainland is Mulhacén (3,482m/11,424ft) in the Sierra Nevada. The dominant feature of the peninsula is the immense plateau at its centre. This is the **Meseta**, a Hercynian platform between 600m/2,000ft and 1,000m/3,300ft high, which tilts slightly westwards. The Meseta is surrounded by long mountain ranges which form barriers between the central plateau and the coastal regions. All these ranges, the **Cordillera Cantábrica** in the northwest (an extension of the Pyrenees), the **Cordillera Ibérica** in the northeast and the **Sierra Morena** in the south, were caused by Alpine folding. Other mountains rising here and there from the Meseta are folds of the original, ancient massif. They include the **Sierras de Somosierra, Guadarrama** and **Gredos**, the **Peña de Francia** and the **Montes de Toledo**. The highest massifs in Spain, the **Pyrenees** (Pirineos) in the north and the **Sierras Béticas**, including the **Sierra Nevada**, in the south, are on the country's periphery, as are Spain's greatest depressions, those of the Ebro and Guadalquivir rivers.

Climate – Although most of Spain enjoys 300 days of sunshine a year, the great diversity of its landscapes is partly due to the country's variety of climates: the Meseta has a **continental** climate with extremes of temperature ranging from scorching hot in summer to freezing cold in winter. On the north coast, where mist often develops into drizzle, the climate is **mild and very humid**. The east and south coasts have a **Mediterranean** climate verging on a desert climate in the Almería region.

J. Malburet/MICHELIN

Mallorca

ATLANTIC SPAIN

País Vasco, Cantabria, Principado de Asturias: a maritime Switzerland – The mountain chain that borders the northern edge of the Meseta emerged in the Tertiary Era and now runs through each of the coastal provinces. The **Montes Vascos**, secondary limestone ranges, continue westwards from the Pyrenean foothills and rise to 1,500m/4,900ft. The **Cordillera Cantábrica** farther west forms an imposing barrier which has given the province of Cantabria the name of La Montaña. The range rises above 2,500m/8,200ft in the **Picos de Europa**, less than 50km/31mi from the sea.

The **País Vasco** (Basque Country) is a markedly undulating region with small villages and isolated farms nestling in the valleys. Local architecture is very distinctive: half-timbered houses with broad whitewashed fronts. The land sandwiched between the mountains and the sea in **Cantabria** and the principality of **Asturias** is very hilly. Roads wind along valley floors hemmed in by lush meadows, cider apple orchards and fields of maize. Dairy produce is a major source of livelihood, especially in Cantabria. Maize, originally imported from America, has since become an important crop, judging by the large number of hórreos or squat drying sheds, so typical of Asturian villages.

The coast is indented by deep inlets or rías and lined by low cliffs in many places. There are beautiful beaches, particularly in Cantabria.

Galicia – This remote region fronting the Atlantic on its northern and western borders is reminiscent of Ireland, Wales or Brittany. Galicia is an ancient eroded granite massif that was displaced and rejuvenated as a result of Alpine folding. Although peaks rise to 2,000m/6,600ft (that of Peña Trevinca is 2,124m/6,968ft high) the average altitude is less than 500m/1,600ft. Yet the overall impression of Galicia is that of a hilly and mountainous region.

The coast, cut by deep **rías**, is more densely populated than the interior. It is Spain's chief fishing region where most of the catch is canned. The interior is primarily an agricultural region where mixed farming is the norm: maize, potatoes, grapes and rye. The Orense province produces beef for export.

The climate is strongly influenced by the sea: temperatures are mild and vary little (the annual average is 13°C/55°F), and rainfall is abundant.

THE PYRENEES AND THE EBRO REGION

The autonomous communities of Aragón, Navarra and La Rioja are characterised by their varied landscapes and colour.

The Pyrenees (Pirineos) – **Alta (Upper) Aragón** (Huesca) embraces the Pirineos Centrales, a region of mountain valleys and piedmont vales, spring waterfalls (Parque Nacional de Ordesa) and villages of rough-stone houses with slate roofs. The main source of livelihood is farming around Huesca and stock-raising in the valleys. There are some industries in Zaragoza.

In **Navarra** the Pyrenees are watered by Atlantic rain. They rise regularly from the 900m/2,953ft of Mont La Rhune to the 2,504m/8,215ft of the Pic d'Anie (both peaks just over the French border). East of Orreaga/Roncesvalles, the terrain becomes more mountainous and the harshness of the climate becomes visible in the ruggedness of the forest cover and the steeply sloped slate roofs and stone fronts of the houses. Resemblance to the Basque provinces is apparent west of Roncesvalles where small parcels of land are used alternately as pasture or to grow maize and the houses have tiled roofs with half-timbered whitewashed fronts. To the south, beyond the limestone range of the Andía, Urbasa, Navascués and Leyre sierras, the land drops away to the Ebro basin.

Ebro depression – This clay basin was formerly a gulf that has since been filled with sediment. The terraces on either side of the river are deeply ravined, providing a sharp contrast with the lower valley, which has been transformed by irrigation into fertile market gardens, or *huertas*.

Cereals predominate in the Cuenca region, also known as the Pamplona basin, in **Navarra**. The western **ribera**, a continuation of the famous **Rioja**, is a wine-growing area, while the well-irrigated eastern part of the province around Tudela has become a prosperous horticultural region growing and canning asparagus, artichokes and peppers. Tall brick houses are typical of the architecture in this area.

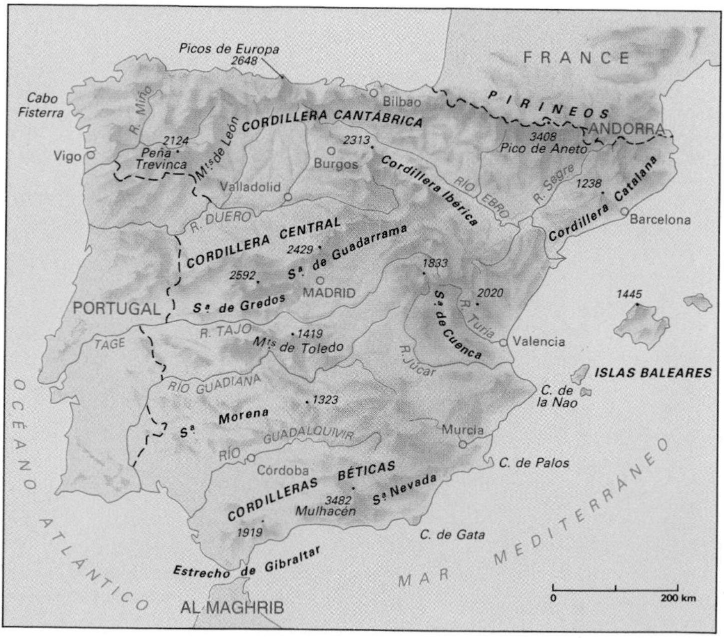

Picos de Europa

Cordillera Ibérica – The clay hills bordering the Ebro basin in **Bajo Aragón** (Lower Aragón) around Daroca and Alcañiz are planted with vineyards and olive groves. Brick villages and ochre-coloured houses merge in with the tawny shade of the deeply scored hillsides. The plateaux surrounding Teruel form part of the massive spread of the **Montes Universales**, one of Spain's great watersheds where the Cabriel, Turia, Júcar and Tajo (Tagus) rivers rise. The climate here is continental, as the mountains prevent maritime weather systems from exerting their influence this far inland.

THE MESETA

This tableland accounts for 40% of the surface area of the Iberian Peninsula, and occupies the autonomous communities of Castilla y León, Castilla-La Mancha, Madrid and Extremadura. Its horizons appear infinite, broken only here and there by a rock-brown village clustered at the foot of a castle, or by the indistinct outline of **páramos** (bare limestone heights).

The northern Meseta – The autonomous community of Castilla y León (Old Castile) in the north consists almost entirely of the Duero basin. This area is about 1,000m/3,300ft above sea level and is ringed by the Montes de León in the northwest, the Cordillera Cantábrica in the north, the Cordillera Ibérica in the east and the Cordillera Central in the southeast. As the Tertiary sediment on the Meseta resists erosion in different ways, there are different landscape features such as wide terraced valleys dotted with rock pinnacles, narrow defiles and gently rolling hills.

Cereal growing predominates everywhere: wheat on the better land, oats and rye elsewhere. Only the southwest peneplains near Salamanca are used for stock-raising: sheep on small properties and fighting bulls on larger ones of often over 500ha/1,200 acres.

The southern Meseta – This section covers the whole of Madrid-Castilla-La Mancha (New Castile) and Extremadura. It is a vast tableland slightly tilted towards the west, watered by two large rivers – the Tajo (Tagus), which cuts a deep gorge through the limestone Alcarria region, and the sluggish Guadiana. The terrain is flatter than in Castilla y León and rises to an average altitude of less than 700m/2,300ft compared to between 800m/2,600ft and 1,000m/3,300ft in the north. The aridity of the region is particularly apparent in summer and the name **La Mancha** comes from the Arab manxa meaning dry land. Despite this there is considerable cultivation and a sweeping look across the Meseta would take in wind-ruffled cereal fields, stretches of saffron turned purple in the flowering season, and straight lines of olives and vines. The region is Spain's leading area for the production of table wines, and is also famous for its *manchego* cheese.

The bare, eroded and virtually uninhabited **Montes de Toledo** separate the Tajo basin from that of the Guadiana, while the other massifs in the region ring the borders. The **Cordillera Central** runs along the northern edge (Sierras de Gredos and Guadarrama), the **Sierra Morena** is in the south, and the **Serranía de Cuenca**, a limestone plateau pitted with swallow-holes (*torcas*) and cut by gorges (*hoces*), lies to the northeast. The **Alcarria** farther north is a region of remote villages where the Tajo and its tributaries flow through deeply eroded gullies. Its upper mountain slopes grow aromatic plants such as thyme, rosemary, lavender and marjoram from which a well-known honey is produced.

The rural character of the region persists; small towns look more like large villages with the arcaded *plaza mayor* (the main square) still acting as the nerve-centre.

Extremadura in the southwest is a schist and granite Hercynian platform that levels off at about 400m/1,300ft. The immense plateaux of the region are used for sheep grazing but lie deserted in summer when the animals are moved to higher pastures. Cork provides supplementary income as does traditional pig farming. The population is concentrated along the rivers that supply irrigation for a variety of crops including tobacco, cotton and wheat as well as market-garden produce. The Badajoz Plan that controls the flow of the Guadiana by means of a series of dams has made it possible to reafforest a large area and to develop high-yield crops such as maize, sunflowers, market-garden produce and above all animal fodder.

MEDITERRANEAN REGIONS

These comprise Catalunya, the Comunidad Valenciana, Murcia and the Balearic Islands.

Catalunya – Catalunya is a triangle of varied landscapes between the French border, Aragón and the Mediterranean. In the north, the eastern stretch of the Pyrenees, between Andorra and the Cabo de Creus headland, is a green wooded area with peaks over 3,000m/9,800ft high. The limestone foothills of the Pyrenees are similar in appearance to the sierras of Aragón.

The **Costa Brava** between France and Barcelona is a rocky area with many bays and inlets. It has a Mediterranean climate as does the **Costa Dorada** (Gold Coast) farther south with its vast sandy beaches. The hinterland, separated from the coast by the Catalan *sierras*, is a drier region with harsh winters.

The southern part of the triangle is composed of green hills sloping down to an intensively cultivated plain around the lower Ebro and its delta. Although fertile (cereals, vines, olives and market-garden produce), Catalunya is primarily an industrial region with its main activities centred around Barcelona.

Levante – The whole of the Levante, including Valencia and Murcia, comprises a narrow alluvial plain between the Mediterranean coast and the massifs of the interior (the Cordillera Ibérica in the north and the Sierras Béticas in the south).

The coast, called **Costa del Azahar** (Orange Blossom Coast) near Valencia and the **Costa Blanca** (White Coast) around Alicante and Murcia, consists of dunes and offshore sand bars that form pools and lagoons.

The climate is Mediterranean but drier than average in this area. Little rain falls except during the autumn months when the rivers flood. Thanks to an ingenious system of irrigation (*acequias*) developed since Antiquity, the natural vegetation, of olives, almond and carob trees and vines, has gradually been replaced, and the countryside transformed into **huertas** (irrigated areas), lush citrus orchards and market gardens, with orange trees between Castellón and Denia and lemons near Murcia. The prosperous *huertas* are among the most densely populated areas in Spain. There are palm groves around Elche and Orihuela in the south and rice is grown in swampy areas.

The region's economy is based on the mining of mineral deposits, port activities, and the booming tourist industry.

Olive groves near Jaén

The arid **interior** is devoted to the growing of cereal crops and the breeding of livestock. Here, the climate is cooler than on the coast, which has more abundant rainfall.

Balearic Islands (Islas Baleares) – The Balearic archipelago consists of three large islands (Mallorca, Menorca and Ibiza), two smaller ones (Formentera and Cabrera), and numerous tiny islets.

The limestone hills, none of which exceed 1,500m/4,900ft, differ in origin. Ibiza and Mallorca are an extension of the Cordillera Bética in Andalucía while Menorca belongs to the submerged massif from which Corsica, Sardinia and the Catalan cordilleras rise.

The lush vegetation produced by the autumn rains is one of the sunny islands' greatest attractions. Pines shade the indented shores, junipers and evergreen oaks cover the upper hillsides, while almonds, figs and olives cloak the plains.

The three larger islands differ considerably in character although they share the same contrast between the tranquillity of the hills inland and the bustling tourism along the coast. Their beaches are washed by a wonderfully calm, clear sea.

ANDALUCÍA

This magnificent region is known for its varied landscapes, whitewashed villages and towns, flowers and patios, and the charming character of its people. In geographical terms, it can be divided into three distinct areas:

Sierra Morena – This mountain chain separates the Meseta from Andalucía. It is rich in minerals and thickly covered by a scrub of oaks, lentisks (mastic trees) and arbutus (strawberry trees). Jaén province's extraordinary landscape consists of row upon row of olive trees as far as the eye can see.

Guadalquivir depression – This Quaternary basin, a former gulf, opening broadly onto the Atlantic, is one of the richest agricultural areas in Spain. Cereals, cotton, olives and citrus fruit are grown on the plains, and rice and vines (around Jerez) on the coast, where fighting bulls are also bred. The centre of the region is Sevilla, Spain's fourth largest city. The whole area is a vast tract of cultivated land divided into large properties known as **fincas**.

Cordilleras Béticas – The **Sierra Nevada**, which includes mainland Spain's highest peak, Mulhacén (3,482m/11,424ft), is continued westwards by the Serranía de Ronda and Sierra de Ubrique. The range's snow-capped heights dominate a series of basins like the wide *vega* (plain) of Granada.

Despite its semi-desert climate, the province of Almería, at the eastern end of the Costa del Sol (Sun Coast), produces citrus and early fruit and vegetables which are grown on irrigated land.

CANARY ISLANDS

It would appear that these volcanic islands were created following the compression of the Atlantic plate at the time of the formation of the Saharan Atlas mountains. **Mount Teide**, on the island of Tenerife, is the highest peak in Spain, rising to a height of 3,718m/12,195ft.

As a result of the archipelago's delightful scenery and superb climate, characterised by pleasant temperatures all year round due to the influence of the trade winds and the cooler Canarian current, it has developed into one of Europe's major tourist destinations.

HISTORY

Modern Spain represents the culmination of centuries of crossbreeding, political union, exclusion and division. The country's history is a complex one, enlivened by myths and legends, and punctuated by significant historical and cultural landmarks, which have combined to create a unique people.

Time Line

FROM ANTIQUITY TO THE VISIGOTHIC KINGDOM

BC

11C-5C – Phoenician and Greek trading posts founded on the eastern and southern coasts of Spain, inhabited by **Iberians** and **Tartessians** respectively. In the 9C BC, the central-European Celts settle in west Spain and on the Meseta, intermingling with the Iberians (forming **Celtiberians**).

3C-2C – The **Carthaginians** take over the southeast after conquering the Greeks and Tartessians. The capture of Sagunto by Hannibal leads to the Second Punic War (218-201 BC). Rome expels the Carthaginians and begins the conquest of peninsular Spain (with resistance at **Numancia**).

1C BC-1C AD – Cantabria and Asturias are finally pacified in AD 19. Spain is now known as Iberia or Hispania.

AD

1C – Christianity reaches the Iberian Peninsula and begins to spread.

5C-6C – Early Suevi (Swabian) and Vandal invasions are followed by those of the **Visigoths** (411) who establish a powerful monarchy with Toledo as capital. The peninsula unites under King Leovigild (584-85).

MUSLIM SPAIN AND THE RECONQUEST

8C – Moors invade and annihilate the Visigothic kingdom after the **Battle of Guadalete** in 711. Pelayo's victory at **Covadonga** in 722 heralds a 700-year-long Christian War of Reconquest. The first Muslim invaders are subjects of the Umayyad Caliphate in Damascus. **Abd ar-Rahman I** breaks with Damascus by founding an independent emirate at Córdoba in 756.

9C – Settlement of uninhabited land by Christians.

10C – Golden age of the emirate of Córdoba, which is raised to the status of a caliphate (929-1021) by **Abd ar-Rahman III**. A period of great prosperity ensues during which the expansion of Christian kingdoms is checked. Fortresses are built in the north along the Duero river.

11C – Christian Spain now includes the kingdoms of León, Castilla, Navarra and Aragón, and the county of Barcelona. On the death of al-Mansur in 1002, the Caliphate of Córdoba disintegrates into about 20 ***taifa*** (faction) kingdoms (1031). Alfonso VI of Castilla conquers Toledo (1085), and the area around the Tajo river is resettled by Christians. The taifa kings call upon the **Almoravids** (Saharan Muslims) for assistance and in a short time the tribe overruns a large part of Spain. Pilgrims begin to tread the Way of St James of Compostela. **El Cid** conquers Valencia (1094).

12C – Dissension stemming from a second age of taifa kingdoms assists the Reconquest, especially in the Ebro Valley (Zaragoza is taken in 1118, Tortosa in 1148 and Lleida in 1149), but after Yacoub al-Mansur's victory in Alarcos (1195), the **Almohads** (who routed the Almoravids) recover Extremadura and check Christian expansion towards the Guadiana and Guadalquivir rivers. Sevilla, with Córdoba under its control, enjoys great prosperity. Great military orders are founded (Calatrava, Alcántara, and Santiago).
Unification of the kingdoms of Aragón and Catalunya (1150).

13C – The *taifa* kingdoms enter their third age. The decline of the Muslims begins with the **Battle of Las Navas de Tolosa** (1212). Muslim influence is reduced to the Nasrid kingdom of Granada (modern provinces of Málaga, Granada and Almería) which holds out until its capture in

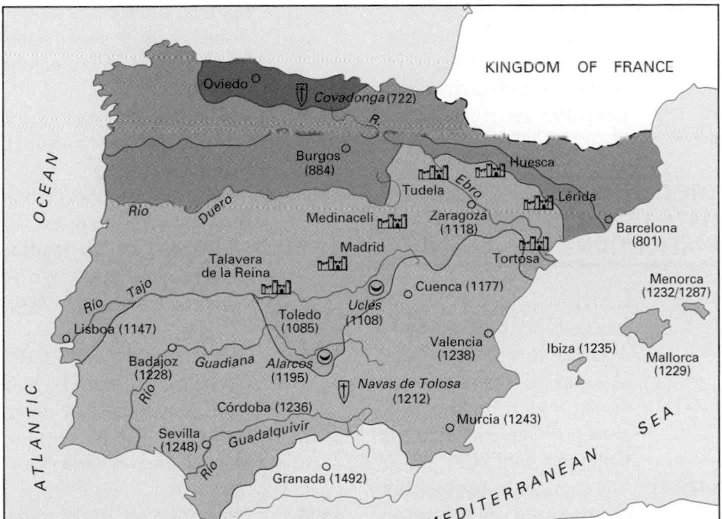

THE CHRISTIAN RECONQUEST OF THE IBERIAN PENINSULA

Kingdom of Asturias C 750

Recovered territory: C 850; C 1040; C 1150; C 1270; Between 1270 and 1492

Christian victories; Muslim victories; Muslim strongholds

1492

If there were only one important date to remember in Spanish history, it would be 1492. That year, after 781 years of Muslim occupation, the Reconquest ended with the fall of Granada on 2 January. This was also the year that the Jews were expelled, the Spaniard Rodrigo Borja (Borgia) became Pope Alexander VI and on 12 October, Christopher Columbus discovered America.

Christopher Columbus (Cristóbal Colón) (1451?-1506) and the discovery of America – Born in Genoa, the son of a weaver, Columbus began his seafaring career at an early age. He travelled to Lisbon in 1476 where he developed a passion for mapmaking on discovering Ptolemy's Geography and the Frenchman Pierre d'Ailly's Imago Mundi. Convinced that the Indies could be reached by sailing west, he submitted a navigation plan to João II of Portugal and to the kings of France and England. He ultimately managed to gain the support of the Duke of Medinaceli and that of the Prior of the Monasterio de La Rábida, Juan Pérez, who was Isabel the Catholic's confessor. The Catholic Monarchs agreed to finance his expedition and, if he succeeded, to bestow upon him the hereditary title of Admiral of the Ocean and the viceroyship of any lands discovered.

On 3 August 1492, heading a fleet of three caravels (the Santa María, under his command, and the Pinta and the Niña captained by the Pinzón brothers), he put out from Palos de la Frontera. On 12 October, after a difficult crossing, San Salvador (Bahamas) came into sight and a short time later Hispaniola (Haiti) and Cuba were discovered. On his return to Spain on 15 March 1493, Christopher Columbus was given a triumphant welcome and the means with which to organise new expeditions. This marked the beginning of the great Spanish discoveries of the New World.

1492. Unification of Castilla and León under Ferdinand III (1230).

The crown of Aragón under James I, the Conqueror (1213-76), gains control over considerable territory in the Mediterranean.

THE CATHOLIC MONARCHS (1474-1516) AND THE UNIFICATION OF SPAIN

1474 – Isabel, wife of Ferdinand, succeeds her brother Henry IV to the throne of Castilla. She has to contend with opposition from the supporters of her niece Juana la Beltraneja until 1479.

1478-79 – The court of the **Inquisition** is instituted by a special Papal Bull and **Torquemada** is later appointed Inquisitor-General.

The court, a political and religious institution directed against Jews, Moors and later Protestants, survives until the 19C.

Ferdinand becomes King of Aragón in 1479 and Christian Spain is united under one crown.

1492 – Fall of Granada marks the end of the Reconquest. Expulsion of Jews.

12 October 1492 – Christopher Columbus discovers America.

1494 – The **Treaty of Tordesillas** divides the New World between Spain and Portugal.

1496 – Juana, daughter of the Catholic Monarchs, marries Philip "the Handsome" (Felipe el Hermoso), son of Emperor Maximilian of Austria (Maximiliano I).

1504 – Death of Isabel. The kingdom is inherited by her daughter, "Mad" Joan (Juana la Loca) but Ferdinand governs as regent until Juana's son Charles (b 1500), future Emperor Charles V, comes of age.

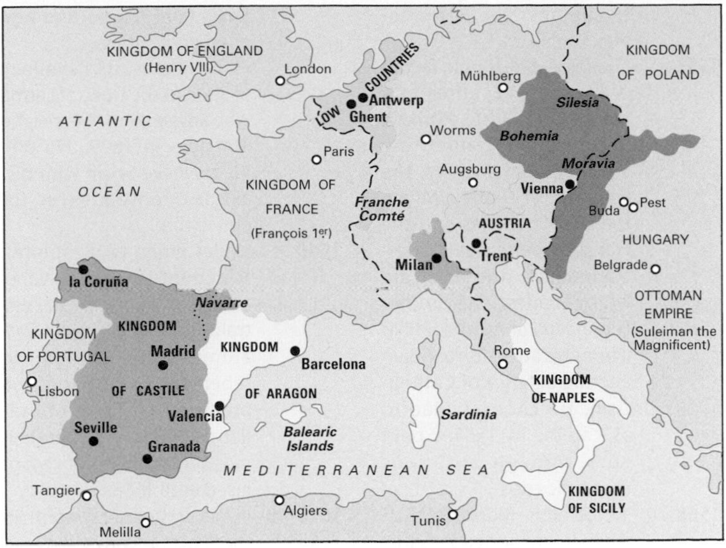

THE EMPIRE OF CHARLES V

Burgundian inheritance | Austrian inheritance | Other possessions
Spanish inheritance | Charles V's conquests | The Holy Roman Empire

1512 – The Duke of Alba conquers Navarra, thus bringing political unity to Spain.

THE HABSBURGS (1516-1700) AND THE CONQUEST OF AMERICA

1516 – **The apogee: Charles I** (1516-56) and **Philip II** (1556-98). On the death of Ferdinand, his grandson becomes Charles I (Carlos I) of Spain. Through his mother, Charles inherits Spain, as well as Naples, Sicily, Sardinia and American territories. Cardinal Cisneros governs until the new king arrives for the first time in Spain in 1517.

1519 – On the death of Maximilian of Austria, Charles I is elected Holy Roman Emperor under the name of **Charles V** (Carlos V). He inherits Germany, Austria, the Franche-Comté and the Low Countries.

1520-22 – The Spanish, incensed by Charles V's largely Flemish court advisers and the increasing number of taxes, rise up in arms. The emperor quells **Comuneros** and **Germanías** revolts.

1521-56 – Charles V wages five wars against France in order to secure complete control of Europe. In the first four he conquers Francis I (imprisoned at Pavia in 1525) and in the fifth he routs the new French king, Henri II, and captures Milan.
The conquistadores move across America. **Núñez de Balboa** discovers the Pacific; **Cortés** seizes Mexico in 1521; **Pizarro** and **Diego de Almagro** subdue Peru in 1533; **Francisco Coronado** explores the Colorado river in 1535; **Hernando de Soto** takes possession of Florida in 1539; and **Pedro de Valdivia** founds Chile in 1541.

1555 – Charles V signs the Peace of Augsburg with the Protestants in Germany after failing to suppress the Reformation.

1556 – Charles V abdicates in favour of his son and retires to a monastery in Yuste. **Philip II** becomes king, inheriting Spain and its colonies, the kingdom of Naples, Milan, the Low Countries and the Franche-Comté, but not Germany and Austria which are left by Charles to his brother Ferdinand I of Austria. Philip II turns his attention to Spain and the defence of Catholicism. He chooses Madrid as capital in 1561. Spain goes through a serious economic crisis.

1568-70 – Revolt of the Moriscos (Muslims who converted to Christianity) in Granada.

1571 – The Turks are defeated in the **Battle of Lepanto** by a fleet of ships sent by the Pope, the Venetians and the Spanish, under the command of **Don Juan of Austria**, the king's natural brother. The victory seals Spain's mastery of the Mediterranean.

1580 – The King of Portugal dies without an heir. Philip II asserts his rights, invades Portugal and is proclaimed king in 1581.

1588 – Philip II sends the **Invincible Armada** against Protestant England, which supports the Low Countries. The destruction of the fleet marks the end of Spain as a sea power.

1598 – Philip II dies, leaving a vast kingdom which, in spite of huge wealth from the Americas, is crippled by debt after 70 years of almost incessant war and monumental building projects like El Escorial.

1598-1621 – **The decline** – The last Habsburgs, **Philip III** (Felipe III, 1598-1621), **Philip IV** (Felipe IV, 1621-65) and **Charles II** (Carlos II, 1665-1700), lack the mettle of their forebears. Paradoxically, Spain enjoys a **golden age** of art and culture.

Philip III entrusts the affairs of State to the Duke of Lerma who advises him to expel the Moriscos in 1609. 275 000 Moors leave Spain with disastrous consequences for agriculture.

1640 – Under Philip IV (Felipe IV), the Count-Duke of Olivares adopts a policy of decentralisation which spurs Catalunya and Portugal to rebellion. The Portuguese proclaim the Duke of Braganza King John IV, but their independence is not recognised until 1668.

1618-48 – Spain wastes her strength in the **Thirty Years War.** In spite of victories like that of Breda (1624), the defeat in the Netherlands at Rocroi (1643) signals the end of Spain as a European power.

The **Treaty of Westphalia** gives the Netherlands independence.

1659 – The **Treaty of the Pyrenees** ends war with France. Philip IV arranges the marriage of his daughter María Teresa to Louis XIV of France.

1667-97 – Spain loses strongholds in Flanders to France during the **War of Devolution** (1667-68). The Dutch Wars (1672-78) end with the **Treaty of Nijmegen.** The **Treaty of Ryswick** (1697) concludes the war waged by the Confederation of Augsburg (Spain is a member) against France (1688-97).

THE BOURBONS, NAPOLEON AND THE WAR OF INDEPENDENCE (1808-14)

1700 – Charles II dies without issue. He wills the crown to Philip, Duke of Anjou, grandson of his sister María Teresa and Louis XIV. Emperor Leopold, who had renounced his rights to the Spanish throne in favour of his son, the Archduke Charles, is displeased, but the appointment of the Bourbons to the Spanish throne stabilises the balance of power in Europe.

1702-14 – **War of the Spanish Succession** – England, the Netherlands, Denmark and Germany support the Archduke of Austria against France and Philip of Anjou. Catalunya, Valencia and Aragón also side with the Archduke and war spreads throughout Spain (1705). By the **Treaty of Utrecht**, Spain forfeits Gibraltar and Menorca (taken by the English) and many of her Italian possessions. **Philip V** (Felipe V) is proclaimed King of Spain (1714-45).

1759-88 – The reign of **Charles III** (Carlos III), an enlightened despot, is the most brilliant of those of the Bourbons. He is assisted by competent ministers (Floridablanca and Aranda) who draw up important economic reforms. Expulsion of the Jesuits in 1767.

1788 – **Charles IV** (Carlos IV) succeeds to the throne. A weak-willed king, he allows the country to be governed by his wife María Luisa and her favourite, Godoy.

1793 – On the death of Louis XVI, Spain declares war on France (then in the throes of the Revolution).

1796-1805 – Spain signs an alliance with the French Directorate against England (Treaty of San Ildefonso, 1796).
Napoleon enters Spain with his troops on the pretext that he is going to attack Portugal. The renewed offensive against England in 1804 ends disastrously with the **Battle of Trafalgar** the following year.

1805-08 – Napoleon takes advantage of the disagreement between Charles IV and his son Ferdinand to engineer Charles IV's abdication and appoint his own brother, Joseph, King of Spain. The Aranjuez Revolt takes place in March 1808.

2 May 1808 – The Madrid uprising against French troops marks the beginning of the **War of Independence** (The Peninsular War) which lasts until Napoleon is exiled by Wellington in 1814. During the war there are battles at Bailén (1808), Madrid, Zaragoza and Girona.

1812 – The French are routed by Wellington in the Arapiles Valley; King Joseph flees from Madrid. Valencia is taken by the French general, Suchet. Spanish patriots convene the Cortes (parliament) and draw up the liberal **Constitution of Cádiz.**

1813-14 – Anglo-Spanish forces expel Napoleon after successive victories.
Ferdinand VII (Fernando VII) returns to Spain, repeals the Constitution of Cádiz and so reigns as an absolute monarch until 1820. Meanwhile, the South American colonies struggle for independence.

THE DISTURBANCES OF THE 19C

1820-23 – The liberals oppose the king's absolute rule but their uprisings are all severely quelled. The 1812 constitution is reinstated after a liberal revolt led by **General Riego** in Cádiz in 1820, but only for three years.
In 1823 Ferdinand VII appeals to Europe for assistance and 100 000 Frenchmen are sent in the name of St Louis to re-establish absolute rule (which lasts until 1833).

1833-39 – On the death of Ferdinand VII, his brother Don Carlos disputes the right to the throne of his niece Isabel II, daughter of the late king and Queen María Cristina. The traditionalist Carlists fight Isabel's liberal supporters who, after six years, win the **First Carlist War** (Convention of Vergara). In 1835, the government minister **Mendizábal** has a series of decrees passed which do away with religious orders and confiscate their property (*desamortización*).

1840 – A revolutionary junta forces the regent María Cristina into exile. She is replaced by General Espartero.

1843-68 – Queen Isabel II comes of age. The **Narváez** uprising forces Espartero to flee. A new constitution is drawn up in 1845. The Second Carlist War (1847-49) ends in victory for Isabel II but her reign is troubled by a succession of uprisings on behalf of progressives and moderates.
The 1868 revolt led by General Prim puts an end to her reign. Isabel leaves for France and General Serrano is appointed leader of the provisional government.

1869 – The Cortes passes a progressive constitution which however envisages the establishment of a monarchy. Amadeo of Savoy is elected king.

1873 – The Third Carlist War (1872-76). The king abdicates on finding himself unable to keep the peace. The National Assembly proclaims the **First Spanish Republic**.

1874 – General Martínez Campos leads a revolt. The head of the government, Cánovas de Castillo, proclaims Isabel's son **Alfonso XII**, King of Spain. The Bourbon Restoration opens a long period of peace.

1885 – Death of Alfonso XII (at 28). His widow María Cristina (who is expecting a baby) becomes regent.

1898 – Cuba and the Philippines rise up with disastrous losses for Spain.
The United States, which supports the rebel colonies, occupies Puerto Rico and the Philippines, marking the end of the Spanish Empire.

1902 – **Alfonso XIII** (born after the death of his father Alfonso XII) succeeds to the throne at 16.

THE FALL OF THE MONARCHY AND THE SECOND REPUBLIC (1931-36)

1914-18 – Spain remains neutral throughout the First World War. A general strike in 1917 is severely put down.

1921 – Insurrection in Morocco; General Sanjurjo occupies the North (1927).

1923 – General **Miguel Primo de Rivera** establishes a dictatorship with the king's approval. Order is restored, the country grows wealthier but opposition increases among the working classes.

1930 – In the face of hostility from the masses, Primo de Rivera is forced into exile and General Berenguer is appointed dictator.

1931 – April elections bring victory to the Republicans in Catalunya, the País Vasco, La Rioja and the Aragonese province of Huesca. The king leaves Spain and the Second Republic is proclaimed.

June 1931 – A constituent Cortes is elected with a socialist republican majority; a Constitution is promulgated in December. Don Niceto Alcalá Zamora is elected President of the Republic. Agrarian reforms, such as compulsory purchase of large properties, meet strong right-wing opposition.

1933 – The **Falange Party**, which opposes regional separation, is founded by **José Antonio Primo de Rivera**, son of the dictator. The army plots against the régime.

Oct 1934 – Catalunya proclaims its autonomy. Miners in Asturias spark off a revolt against the right-wing government and are brutally repressed.

Feb 1936 – The Popular Front wins the elections, precipitating a revolutionary situation. Anarchy hits the streets and the right promptly retaliates.

THE CIVIL WAR (1936-39)

17 July 1936 – The Melilla uprising triggers the Civil War. The army takes control and puts an end to the Second Republic. Nationalist troops based in Morocco and led by General Franco cross the Straits of Gibraltar and make their way to Toledo which is taken at the end of September. Franco is proclaimed Generalísimo of the armed forces and Head of State in Burgos. Nationalists lead an unsuccessful attack against Madrid.

While Madrid, Catalunya and Valencia remain faithful to the Republicans, the conservative agricultural regions – Andalucía, Castilla and Galicia – are rapidly controlled by the Nationalists. These latter outnumber the Republicans tenfold and the Republicans themselves are torn by dissension between anarchists and communists within their own ranks. They do, however, receive assistance from International Brigades.

1937 – Industrial towns in the north are taken by Nationalist supporters in the summer (Gernika is bombed by German planes). The Republican Government is moved to Barcelona in November. In the battle of Teruel in December, the Republicans try to breach the Nationalist front in Aragón and thereby relieve surrounded Catalunya. Teruel is taken by the Republicans and recaptured by the Nationalists soon after.

1938 – The Nationalist army reaches the Mediterranean, dividing Republican territory into two parts. The **Battle of the Ebro** lasts from July to November: the Republican army flees eastwards and Franco launches an offensive against Catalunya which is occupied by the Nationalists in February 1939.

1 April 1939 – The war ends with the capture of Madrid.

THE FRANCO ERA

1939-49 – Spain is declared a monarchy with Franco as regent and Head of State and remains neutral in the Second World War. Period of diplomatic isolation.

1952 – Spain joins UNESCO.

1955 – Spain becomes a member of the United Nations.

1969 – Prince Juan Carlos is named as Franco's successor.

20 Dec 1973 – Prime Minister Carrero Blanco is assassinated.

20 Nov 1975 – Death of Franco. **Juan Carlos I** becomes King of Spain.

DEMOCRACY

15 June 1977 – General elections – **Adolfo Suárez** is elected Prime Minister. A new constitution is passed by referendum in 1978. Statutes of autonomy are approved for Catalunya, the País Vasco (Euskadi) and Galicia.

1981-82 – Suárez resigns. There is an attempted military coup on 23 February 1981. The general elections on 28 October 1982 are won by the Socialist Party and **Felipe González** becomes Prime Minister.

1 Jan 1986 – Spain joins the **European Economic Community**.

11 March 1986 – Spain's continued membership in NATO is voted by referendum.

11 June 1986 – General elections – Felipe González, leader of the Socialist Party (PSOE), is re-elected Prime Minister.

Oct 1989 – General elections again won by the Socialists under Felipe González.

1992 – Barcelona hosts the 1992 Summer Olympics, and Sevilla hosts Expo 1992.

3 March 1996 – General election is won by the Popular Party; **José María Aznar** becomes Prime Minister.

2000 – José María Aznar is re-elected Prime Minister.

11 March 2004 – A **terrorist attack** by Islamic fundamentalists in Madrid leaves 192 dead and 1,500 injured, convulsing the country.

14 March 2004 – The Socialist Party carries the general elections. **José Luis Rodríguez Zapatero** becomes Prime Minister.

22 May 2004 – The Prince of Asturias, heir to the Spanish crown, marries to Letizia Ortiz Rocasolano, a journalist and divorcee.

31 October 2005 – Princess Leonor is born in Madrid to the crown prince and princess.

30 December 2006 – Basque separatists of the ETA explode a car bomb at Madrid airport, breaking a truce.

15 February 2007 – Trial of alleged 2004 Madrid train bombers begins

ART AND CULTURE

ABC of Architecture

Ground plan

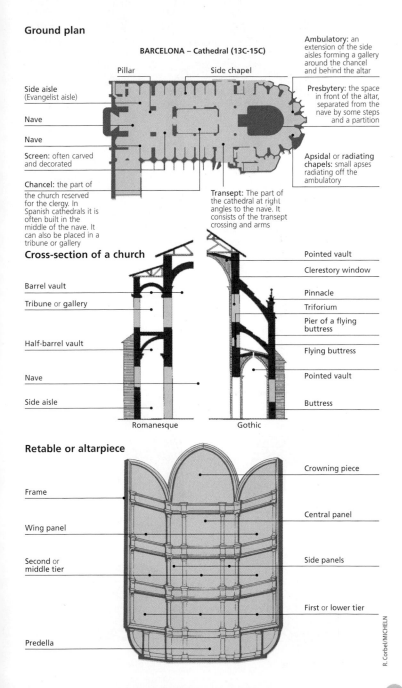

BARCELONA – Cathedral (13C-15C)

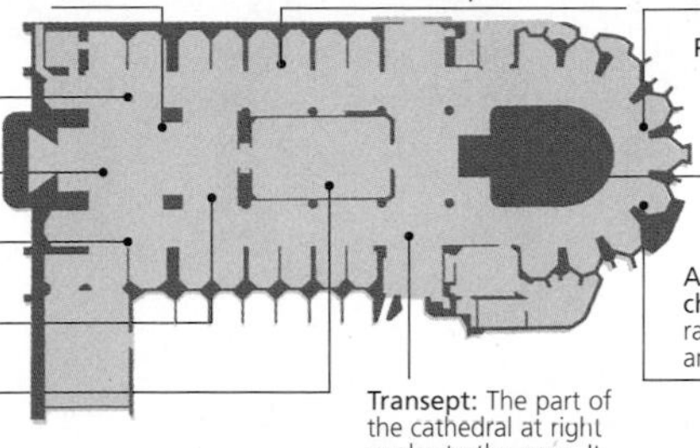

Cross-section of a church

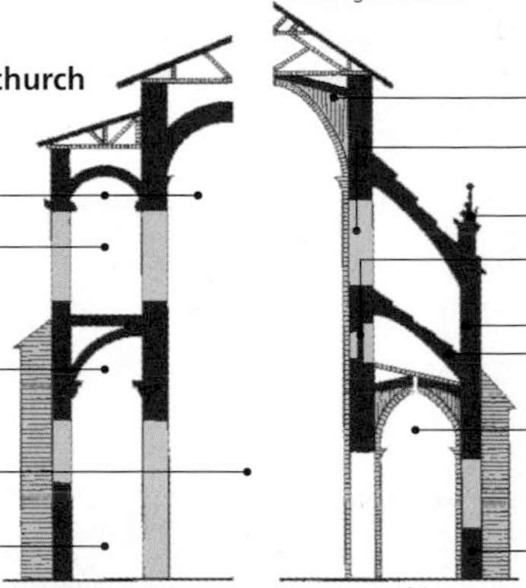

Retable or altarpiece

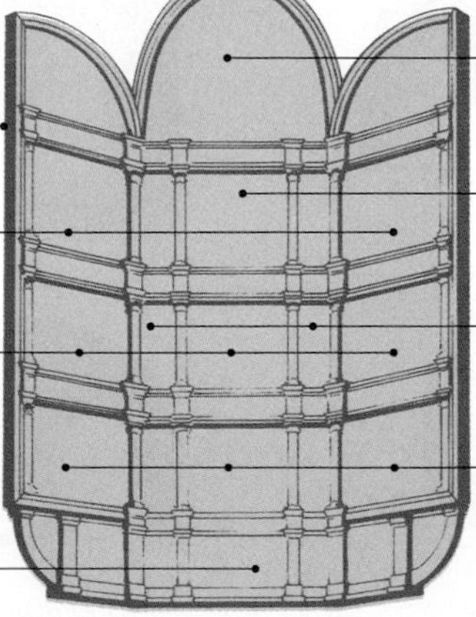

R. Corbel/MICHELN

Arcos

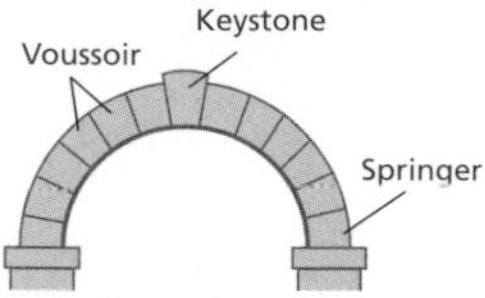

Semicircular

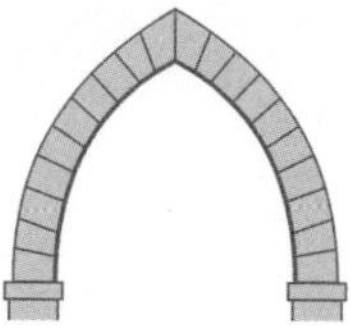
Pointed

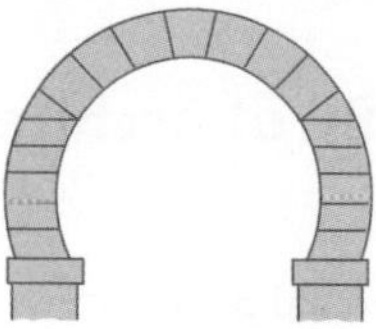
Horseshoe (Moorish)

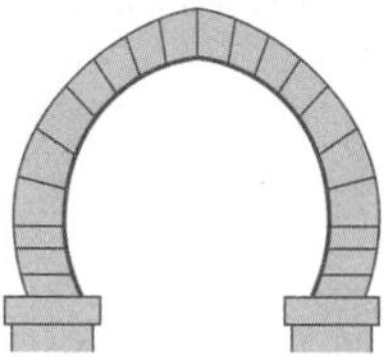
Pointed horseshoe

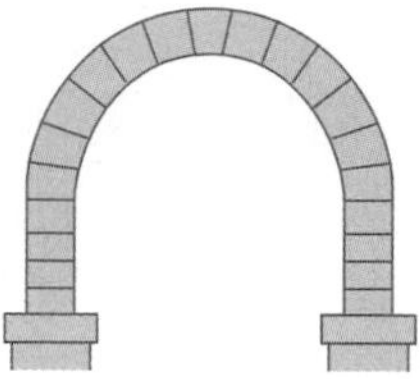
Raised

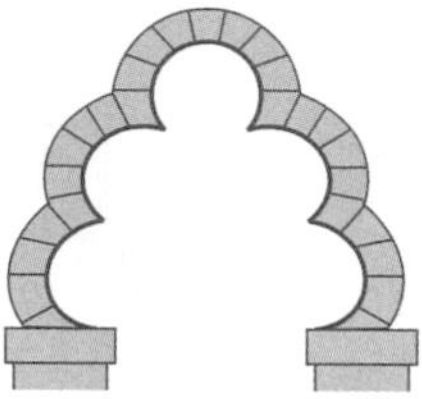
Multifoil

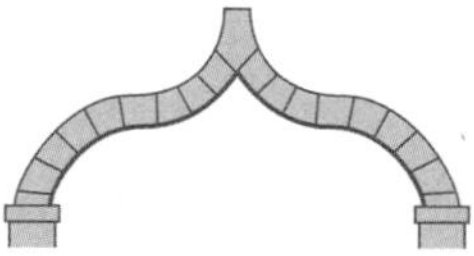
Ogee

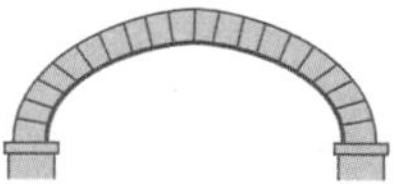
Basket-handle

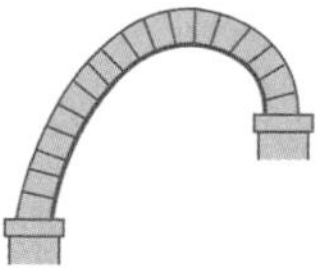
Rampant

Vaults

Barrel

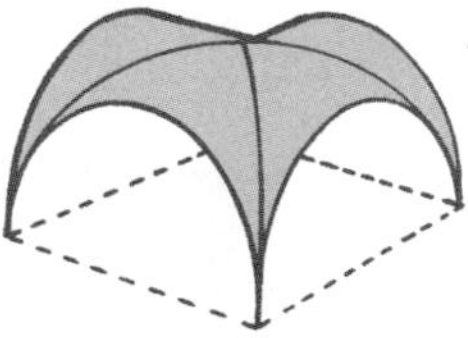
Arris

Pointed

Fan

Cylindrical

Oven

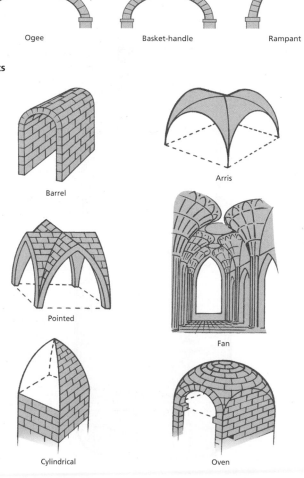

R. Corbel/MICHELN

Hispano-Moorish art

CÓRDOBA – Mezquita: Puerta de Alhakem II (10C)

Eight centuries of Moorish rule in Spain had a fundamental influence on Spanish art.

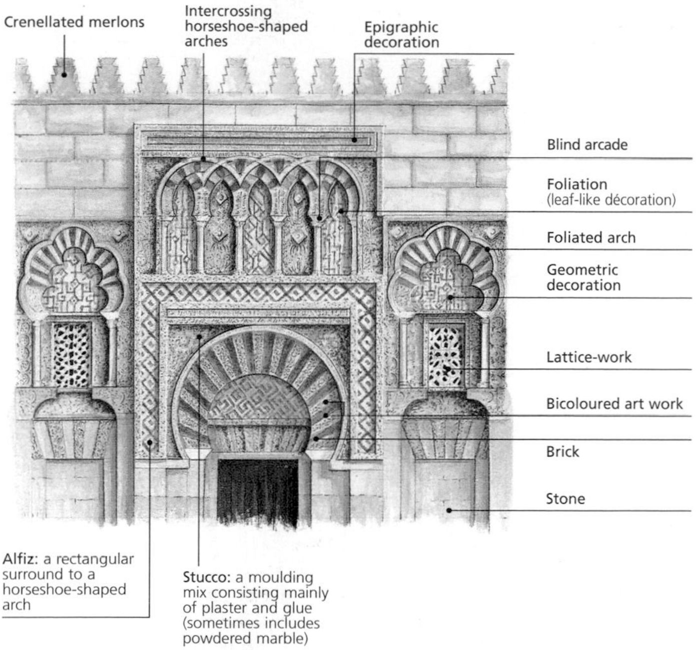

GRANADA – La Alhambra (14C)

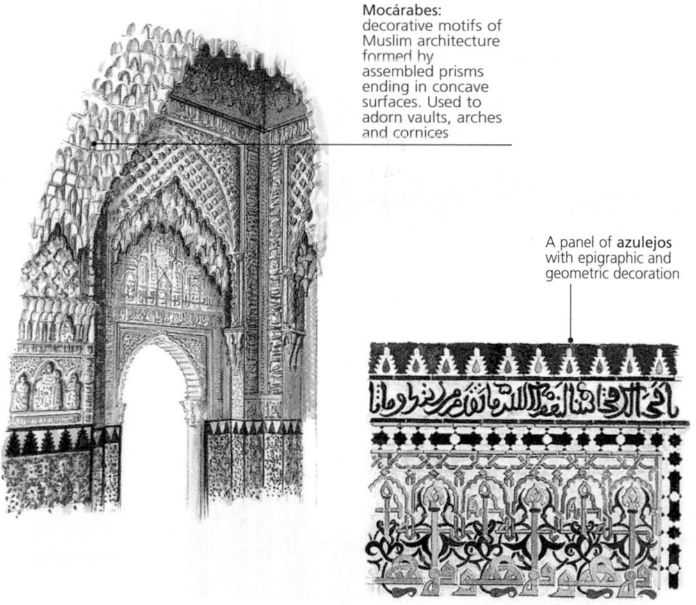

Mocárabes: decorative motifs of Muslim architecture formed by assembled prisms ending in concave surfaces. Used to adorn vaults, arches and cornices
A panel of azulejos with epigraphic and geometric decoration

R. Corbel/MICHELN

Romanesque

SANTIAGO DE COMPOSTELA – Cathedral: Interior (11C-13C)

Santiago cathedral is a typical example of a Spanish pilgrimage church and shows clear French influence.

Corinthian capital

R. Corbel/MICHELN

Gothic

LEÓN – Cathedral: side façade (13C-14C)

In Gothic architecture, light was considered the essence of beauty and the symbol of truth. León cathedral is the brightest and most delicate of all the major Spanish cathedrals and is viewed as the best example of this concept. The beauty and magnificence of its stained glass attracts the admiration of its many thousands of visitors every year. French influence is clearly evident in its ground plan (Reims) and sculptures (Chartres).

Tympanum

R. Corbel/MICHELN

Plateresque

SALAMANCA – University: façade (16C)

Although the exuberant decoration used to cover the entire façade is somewhat Gothic in style, the motifs used are Classical.

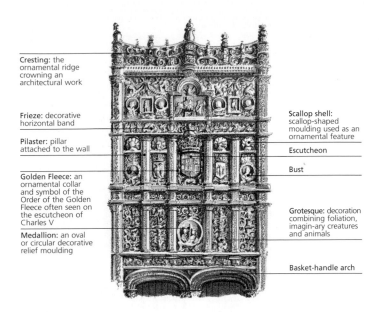

Renaissance

TOLEDO - Hospital Tavera: patio (16C)

The sense of proportion, visible on both the ground and first floors surrounding the double patio of this hospital, is a typical feature of pure Renaissance style.

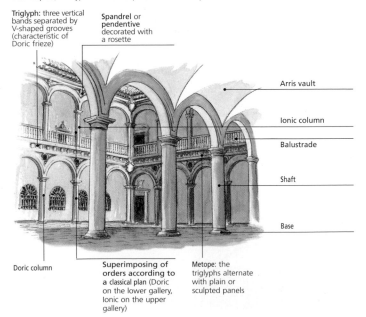

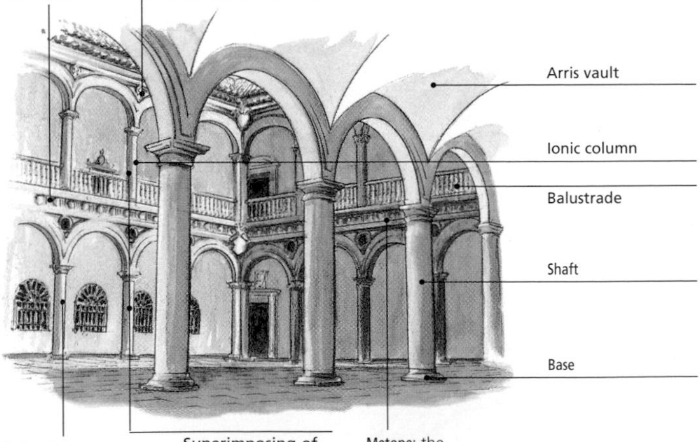

R. Corbel/MICHELN

Baroque

MADRID – Museo Municipal (Antiguo Hospicio): portal (18C)

The Baroque retable or altarpiece, which reached new architectural heights in Spain, was occasionally created on the façade of a building, rather than inside it.

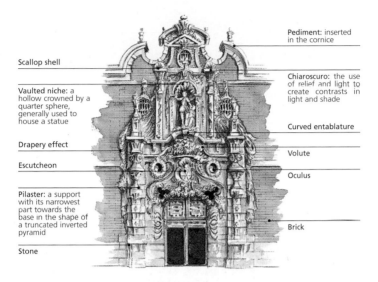

Neo-Classical

MADRID - Observatório Astronómico (18C)

This small building designed by Juan de Villanueva is a model of simplicity and purity which shows clear Palladian influence in its proportions and design.

R. Corbel/MICHELN

Modernist

BARCELONA –Casa Batlló (Antoni Gaudí: 1905-07)

Modernism is a colourful, decorative and sensual style which recreates organic forms in a world dominated by curves and reverse curves.

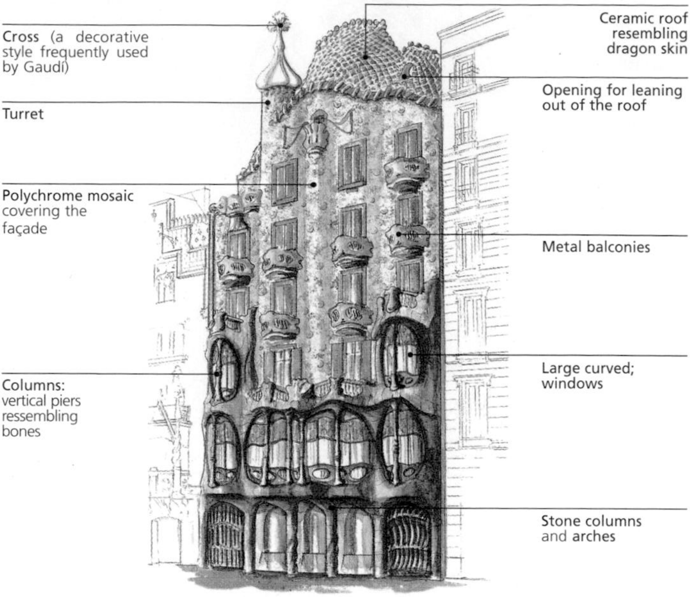

Mediterranean Rationalist

BARCELONA – Fundació Joan Miró (JL Sert: 1972-75)

The building consists of a series of interrelated architectural features and open spaces in which natural light plays a fundamental role.

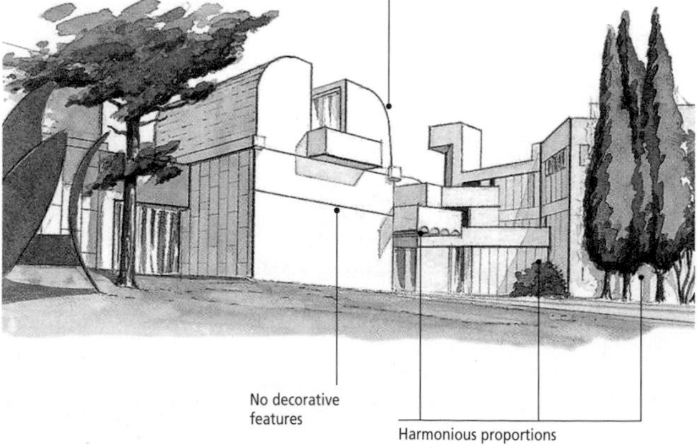

R. Corbel/MICHELN

Glossary of Architecture

Some of the terms below are illustrated on the previous pages. Words in italics are Spanish.

Ajimez: paired window or opening separated by a central column.

Alfarje: wooden ceiling, usually decorated, consisting of a board resting on cross beams (a feature of the Mudéjar style).

Alfiz: rectangular surround to a horseshoe-shaped arch in Muslim architecture.

Alicatado: section of wall or other surface covered with sheets of ceramic tiles (azulejos) cut to form geometric patterns. Frequently used to decorate dados (a Mudéjar feature).

Aljibe: Arab word for cistern.

Altarpiece: also retable. Decorative screen above and behind the altar.

Apse: far end of a church housing the high altar; can be semicircular, polygonal or horseshoe-shaped.

Apsidal or radiating chapel: small chapel opening from the apse.

Arch: *See illustrations p 64.*

Archivolt: ornamental moulding on the outer edge of an arch.

Artesonado: marquetry ceiling in which raised fillets outline honeycomb-like cells in the shape of stars. This decoration, which first appeared under the Almohads, was popular throughout the country, including Christian Spain, in the 15C and 16C.

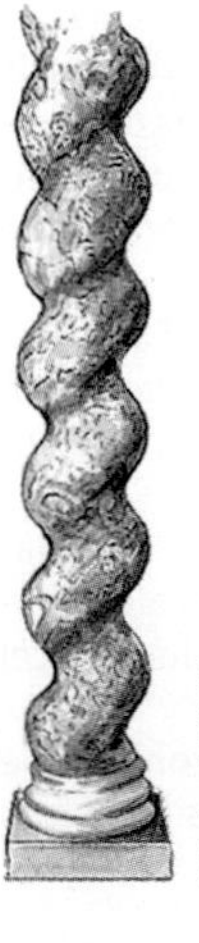

H.Choimet/MICHELIN

Ataurique: decorative plant motif on plaster or brick which was developed as a feature of the Caliphate style and was subsequently adopted by the Mudéjar.

Azulejos: glazed, patterned, ceramic tiles.

Barrel vaulting: vault with a semicircular cross-section.

Caliphate: the architectural style developed in Córdoba under the Caliphate (8C-11C) of which the finest example is the mosque in that city.

Churrigueresque: in the style of the Churrigueras, an 18C family of architects. Richly ornate Baroque decoration.

Estípite: pilaster in the shape of a truncated inverted pyramid.

Gargoyle: projecting roof gutter normally carved in the shape of a grotesque animal.

Groined vaulting: vault showing lines of intersection of two vaults or arches (usually pointed).

Grotesque: typical Renaissance decoration combining vegetation, imaginary beings and animals.

Kiblah: sacred wall of a mosque from which the mihrab is hollowed, facing towards Mecca.

Lacerías: geometric decoration formed by intersecting straight lines making star-shaped and polygonal figures. Characteristic of Moorish architecture.

Lombard bands: decorative pilaster strips typical of Romanesque architecture in Lombardy.

Lonja: commodity exchange building.

Mihrab: richly decorated prayer-niche in the sacred wall (kiblah) in a mosque.

Minaret: tower of the mosque (mezquita), from which the muezzin calls the faithful to prayer.

Minbar: pulpit in a mosque.

Mocárabes: decorative motifs of Muslim architecture formed by assembled prisms ending in concave surfaces. They resemble stalactites or pendants and adorn vaults and cornices.

Mozarabic: the work of Christians living under Arab rule after the Moorish invasion of 711. On being persecuted in the 9C, they sought refuge in Christian areas bringing with them Moorish artistic traditions.

Mudéjar: the work of Muslims living in Christian territory following the Reconquest (13C-14C).

Mullion: slender column or pillar dividing an opening in a door or window.

Naveta: megalithic monument found in the Balearic Islands, which has a

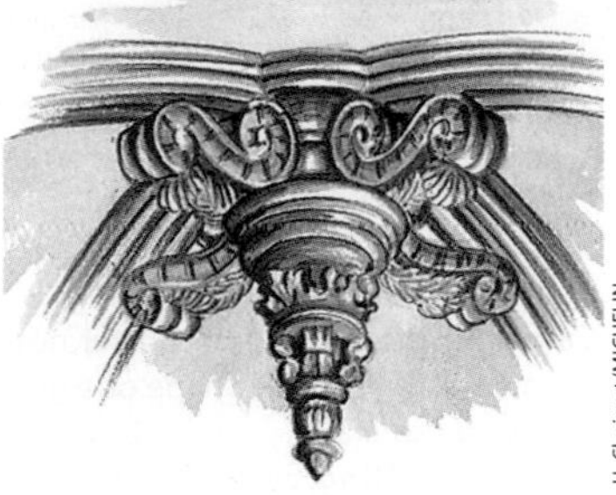

H. Choimet/MICHELIN

pyramidal shape with a rectangular base, giving the appearance of an upturned boat.

Plateresque: term derived from *platero* (ie silversmith); used to describe the early style of the Renaissance characterised by finely carved decoration.

Predella: the lower part of an altarpiece.

Sebka: type of brick decoration developed under the Almohads consisting of an apparently endless series of small arches forming a network of diamond shapes.

Seo or *seu*: cathedral.

Soportales: porticoes of wood or stone pillars supporting the first floor of houses. They form an open gallery around the plaza mayor of towns and villages.

Star vault: vault with a square or polygonal plan formed by several intersecting arches.

Stucco: type of moulding mix consisting mainly of plaster, used for coating surfaces. It plays a fundamental role in wall decoration in Hispano-Muslim architecture.

H. Choimet/MICHELIN

Talayot: megalithic monument found in the Balearic Islands, which takes the form of a truncated cone of stones.

Taula (*mesa* in the Mallorcan language): megalithic monument found in the Balearic Islands, which consists of a monolithic horizontal stone block placed on top of a similar vertical stone block.

Triforium: arcade above the side aisles which opens onto the central nave of a church.

Tympanum: inner surface of a pediment. This often ornamented space is bounded by the archivolt and the lintel of the doors of churches.

Venera: scallop-shaped moulding frequently used as an ornamental feature. It is the symbol of pilgrimages to Santiago de Compostela.

Yesería: plasterwork used in sculptured decoration.

Following are Spanish terms and their translations used in the guide. Words like coro *are in the original Spanish; there is no equivalent in English.*

Cabecera: the east or apsidal end of a church.

Camarín: a small chapel on the first floor behind the altarpiece or retable. It is plushly decorated and very often contains a lavishly costumed statue of the Virgin Mary.

Capilla Mayor: the area of the high altar containing the **retablo mayor** or monumental altarpiece which often rises to the roof.

Coro: a chancel in Spanish canonical churches often built in the middle of the nave. It contains the **stalls** (*sillería*) used by members of religious orders. When placed in a tribune or gallery it is known as the coro alto.

Crucero: transept. The part of a church at right angles to the nave which gives the church the shape of a cross.

Girola (also *deambulatorio*): ambulatory. An extension to the aisles forming a gallery around the chancel and behind the altar.

Presbiterio: the space in front of the altar. (The presbytery is known as the casa del cura.)

Púlpito: pulpit.
Sagrario: chapel containing the Holy Sacrament. May sometimes be a separate church.
Sillería: the stalls.
Trasaltar: back wall of the capilla mayor in front of which there are frequently sculptures or tombs.
Trascoro: the wall, often carved and decorated, which encloses the coro.

Architecture and the Visual Arts

Over the centuries, Spain has amassed countless artistic and architectural treasures across the length and breadth of the country, ranging from diminutive Romanesque chapels, lofty Gothic cathedrals and exuberant Baroque churches to awe-inspiring Hispano-Moorish monuments, imposing castles, magnificent paintings and outstanding sculptures.

FROM PREHISTORY TO THE MOORISH CONQUEST

Prehistoric art

Prehistoric inhabitants of the Iberian Peninsula have left some outstanding examples of their art. The oldest are the Upper Palaeolithic (40000-10000 BC) cave paintings in Cantabria (Altamira and Puente Viesgo), Asturias (El Pindal, Ribadesella and San Román) and the Levante region (Cogull and Alpera). Megalithic monuments like the famous Antequera dolmens were erected during the Neolithic Era (7500-2500 BC), or New Stone Age, while in the Balearic Islands strange stone monuments known as **talayots** and *navetas* were built by a Bronze Age people (2500-1000 BC).

First millennium BC

Iberian civilisations produced gold and silverware (treasure of Carambolo in the Museo Arqueológico in Sevilla), and fine sculpture. Some of their work, such as the Córdoba lions, the Guisando bulls and, in the Museo Arqueológico in Madrid, the *Dama de Baza* and the *Dama de Elche*, is of a remarkably high standard. Meanwhile, Phoenician, Carthaginian and in turn Greek colonisers introduced their native art: Phoenician sarcophagi in Cádiz, Punic art in Ibiza and Greek art in Empúries.

Roman Spain (1C BC-5C AD)

Besides roads, bridges, aqueducts, towns and monuments, Roman legacies include the Mérida theatre, the ancient towns of Italica and Empúries, and the Segovia aqueduct and Tarragona triumphal arch.

The Visigoths (6C-8C)

Christian Visigoths built small stone churches (Quintanilla de las Viñas, San Pedro de la Nave) adorned with friezes carved in geometric patterns with plant motifs. The apsidal plan was square and the arches were often horseshoe-shaped. The Visigoths were outstanding gold and silversmiths who made sumptuous jewellery in the Byzantine and Germanic traditions. Gold votive crowns (Guarrazar treasure in Toledo), fibulae and belt buckles adorned with precious stones or cloisonné enamel were presented to churches or placed in the tombs of the great.

HISPANO-MOORISH ARCHITECTURE (8C-15C)

The three major periods of Hispano-Moorish architecture correspond to the

H. Stierlin

Dama de Elche

The Alhambra, Granada

reigns of successive Arab dynasties over the Muslim-held territories in the peninsula.

Caliphate or Córdoba architecture (8C-11C)

This period is characterised by three types of building: **mosques**, built to a simple plan consisting of a minaret, a courtyard with a pool for ritual ablutions and finally a square prayer room with a *mihrab* (prayer-niche marking the direction of Mecca); **alcázares** (palaces), built around attractive patios and surrounded by gardens and fountains; and **alcazabas** (castle fortresses), built on high ground and surrounded by several walls crowned with pointed merlons – one of the best examples of these can be found in Málaga. The most famous monuments from this period are in Córdoba (the Mezquita and the Medina Azahara palace) and in Toledo (Cristo de la Luz) where, besides the ubiquitous horseshoe arch which virtually became the hallmark of Moorish architecture, other characteristics developed including ornamental brickwork in relief, cupolas supported on ribs, turned modillions, arches with alternating white stone and red-brick voussoirs, multifoil arches and doors surmounted with blind arcades. These features subsequently became popular in Mudéjar and Romanesque churches.

The Umayyads brought a taste for profuse decoration from Syria. As the Koran forbids the representation of human or animal forms, Muslim decoration is based on calligraphy (Cufic inscriptions running along walls), geometric patterns (polygons and stars made of ornamental brickwork and marble) and lastly plant motifs (flowerets and interlacing palm leaves).

The Decorative Arts

Extremely rich and varied decorative artifacts from the Almohad period include geometric wood strapwork, brocades, weapons, ceramics with metal lustre decoration and small ivory chests.

Almohad or Sevilla architecture (12C-13C)

The religious puritanism of the Almohad dynasty, of which Sevilla was the capital, was expressed in architecture by a refined, though sometimes rather austere, simplicity. One of the characteristics of the style consisted of brickwork highlighted by wide bands of decoration in relief, without excessive ornamentation (the Giralda tower in Sevilla is a good example.) The style was later used in the Mudéjar architecture of Aragón. Other features that emerged at this time include *artesonado* ceilings and *azulejos*. Arches of alternate brick and stonework disappeared, the horseshoe arch became pointed and the multifoil arch was bordered by a curvilinear festoon (ornament like a garland) as in the Aljafería in Zaragoza. Calligraphic decoration included cursive (flowing) as well as Cufic script to which floral motifs were added to fill the spaces between vertical lines.

Nasrid or Granada architecture (14C-15C)

This period of high sophistication, of which the **Alhambra** in Granada is the masterpiece, produced less innovation in actual architectural design than in the decoration, whether stucco or ceramic, that covered the walls.

Surrounds to doors and windows became focal points for every room's design and the spaces between them were filled by perfectly proportioned panels. Arch outlines were simplified – the stilted round arch became widespread – while detailed lacework ornamentation was used as a border.

Mudéjar architecture

This is the name given to work carried out by Muslims while under the Christian yoke, yet executed in the Arab tradition. It was fashionable from the 11C to the 15C in different regions depending on the area recovered by the Reconquest, although some features, like *artesonado* ceilings, continued as decorative themes for centuries.

Court Mudéjar, developed by Muslim artists (in buildings ordered by Peter the Cruel in Tordesillas and Sevilla, and in synagogues in Toledo), was an extension of the Almohad or contemporary Nasrid style. Popular Mudéjar, on the other hand, was produced by local Muslim workshops and reflects marked regional taste: walls were decorated with blind arcades in Castilla (Arévalo, Sahagún and Toledo) and belfries were faced with *azulejos* and geometric strapwork in Aragón.

PRE-ROMANESQUE AND ROMANESQUE ART AND ARCHITECTURE (8C-13C)

Asturian architecture

A highly sophisticated style of court architecture, characterised by sweeps of ascending lines, developed in the small kingdom of Asturias between the 8C and the 10C. Asturian churches (Naranco, Santa Cristina de Lena) followed the precepts of the Latin basilica in their rectangular plan with a narthex, a nave and two aisles separated by semicircular arches, a vast transept and an east end divided into three. Decoration inside consisted of frescoes, and borrowings from the East including motifs carved on capitals (strapwork, rosettes and monsters) and ornamental openwork around windows. Gold and silversmiths in the 9C and 10C produced rich treasures, many of which may be seen in the Cámara Santa in Oviedo Cathedral.

Mozarabic architecture

This term is given to work carried out by Christians living under Arab rule after the Moorish invasion of 711. Churches built in this style, especially in Castilla (San Miguel de Escalada, San Millán de la Cogolla), brought back Visigothic traditions (horseshoe arches) enriched by Moorish features such as ribbed cupolas and turned modillions.

Illuminated manuscripts provide the earliest known examples of Spanish medieval painting (10C). They were executed in the 10C and 11C by Mozarabic monks and have Moorish features such as horseshoe arches and Arab costumes. They portray St John's Commentary on the Apocalypse written in the 8C by the monk **Beatus de Liébana**, after whom the manuscripts were named.

Catalunya, home of the earliest Romanesque style in Spain

Catalunya had intimate links with Italy and France and consequently developed an architectural style strongly influenced by Lombardy from the 11C to the 13C. This evolved in the Pyrenean valleys, isolated from the more travelled pilgrim and trade routes. Sober little churches were built often accompanied by a separate bell tower decorated with Lombard bands. Interior walls in the 11C and 12C were only embellished with frescoes which, in spite of their borrowings from Byzantine mosaics (heavy black outlines, rigid postures, and themes like Christ in Glory portrayed within a mandorla), proved by their realistic and expressive details to be typically Spanish. Altar fronts of painted wood, executed in bright colours, followed the same themes and layout.

European Romanesque art along the pilgrim routes

Northwest Spain opened its gates to foreign influence during the reign of Sancho the Great of Navarra early in the 11C. Cistercian abbeys were founded and French merchants allowed to settle rate-free in towns (Estella, Sangüesa and Pamplona). Meanwhile, the surge of pilgrims to Compostela and the fever to build along the routes brought about the construction of a great many religious buildings in which French influence was clearly marked (characteristics from Poitou in Soria and Sangüesa, and from Toulouse in Aragón and Santiago de Compostela). The acknowledged masterpiece of this style is the cathedral of Santiago de Compostela.

In Aragón, Romanesque art was particularly evident in sculpture. The artists who carved capitals in the manner of their leader, the Maestro de San Juan de la Peña, had a seemingly clumsy style because their emphasis was more on symbolism than realistic portrayal. Disproportionate faces with bulging eyes were the means by which the sculptor illustrated the soul, while gestures such as outstretched hands conveyed religious meaning.

In the early 12C, reform of the **Cistercian Order** with emphasis on austerity brought an important change to architecture. The transitional style which heralded the Gothic (intersecting ribbed vaulting, squared apses) was introduced and the profusion of Romanesque decoration disappeared. Examples of this style may be seen in the monasteries of Poblet, Santes Creus, La Oliva and Santa María de Huerta.

THE GOTHIC PERIOD (FROM THE 13C)

The early stages

French Gothic architecture made little headway into Spain except in Navarra where a French dynasty had been in power since 1234. The first truly Gothic buildings (Roncesvalles church, Cuenca and Sigüenza cathedrals) appeared in the 13C. Bishops in some of the main towns in Castilla (León, Burgos, Toledo) sent abroad for cathedral plans, artists and masons. An original style of church, with no transept, a single nave (aisles, if there were any, would be as high as the nave), and pointed stone arches or a wooden roof resting on diaphragm arches, developed in **Valencia**, **Catalunya** and the **Balearic Islands**. The unadorned walls enclosed a large, homogeneous space in which there

Turespaña

Catedral Nueva, Salamanca

Gothic Decoration, Sevilla Cathedral (detail)

was little carved decoration, and purity of line supplied a dignified elegance. Civil architecture followed the same pattern and had the same geometrical sense of space, used with rare skill particularly in the *lonjas* or commodity exchanges of Barcelona, Palma, Valencia and Zaragoza.

The Gothic style develops

During the 14C and 15C in Castilla, the influence of artists from the north such as **Johan of Cologne** and **Hanequin of Brussels**, brought about the flowering of a style approaching Flamboyant Gothic. As it adapted to Spain, the style developed simultaneously in two different ways: in one, decoration proliferated to produce the Isabelline style; in the other, structures were simplified into a national church and cathedral style which remained in favour until the mid 16C (Segovia and Salamanca).

The last of the Gothic cathedrals

Following the example of Sevilla, the dimensions of Gothic cathedrals became ever more vast. Aisles almost as large as the nave increased the volume of the building, while pillars, though massive, retained the impression of thrusting upward lines. A new plan emerged in which the old crescendo of radiating chapels, ambulatory, chancel and transept was superseded by a plain rectangle. Gothic decoration accumulated around doors, on pinnacles and in elaborate star vaulting; a style echoed in some Andalucían cathedrals.

Painting

Artists in the Gothic era worked on polyptyches and altarpieces which sometimes reached a height of more than 15m/50ft. The Primitives, who customarily painted on gold backgrounds, were influenced by the Italians (soft contours), the French and the Flemish (rich fabrics with broken folds and painstaking detail). Nonetheless, as they strove for expressive naturalism and lively anecdotal detail, their work came across as distinctively Spanish.
There was intense artistic activity in the states attached to the Crown of Aragón, especially in Catalunya. The Vic, Barcelona and Valencia museums contain works by **Ferrer Bassá** (1285-1348) who was influenced by the Sienese **Duccio**, paintings by his successor **Ramón Destorrents** (1346-91), and by the **Serra** brothers, Destorrents' pupils. Among other artists were **Luis Borrassá** (c 1360-1425) who had a very Spanish sense of the picturesque, **Bernat Martorell** (d 1452) who gave special importance to landscape, **Jaime Huguet** (1415-92) who stands out for his extreme sensitivity and is considered to be the undisputed leader of the Catalan School, and finally **Luis Dalmau** and **Bartolomé Bermejo**,

both influenced by Van Eyck (who accompanied a mission sent to Spain by the Duke of Burgundy).

In Castilla, French influence predominated in the 14C and Italian in the 15C until about 1450 when Flemish artists like **Rogier van der Weyden** arrived. By the end of the 15C, **Fernando Gallego** had become the main figure in the Hispano-Flemish movement in which **Juan of Flanders** was noted for his appealingly delicate touch.

Sculpture

Gothic sculpture, like architecture, became more refined. Relief was more accentuated than in Romanesque carving, postures more natural and details more meticulous. Decoration grew increasingly abundant as the 15C progressed and faces became individualised to the point where recumbent funerary statues clearly resembled the deceased. Statues were surmounted by an openwork canopy, while door surrounds, cornices and capitals were decorated with friezes of intricate plant motifs. After being enriched by French influence in the 13C and 14C and Flemish in the 15C, sculpture ultimately developed a purely Spanish style, the Isabelline.

Portals showed a French influence. Tombs were at first sarcophagi decorated with coats of arms, sometimes surmounted by a recumbent statue in a conventional posture with a peaceful expression and hands joined. Later, more attention was paid to the costume of the deceased; with an increasingly honed technique marble craftsmen were able to render the richness of brocades and the supple quality of leather. In the 15C, sculptors produced lifelike figures in natural positions, kneeling for instance, or even in nonchalant attitudes like that of the remarkable Doncel in Sigüenza Cathedral. Altarpieces comprised a predella or plinth, surmounted by several levels of panels and finally by a carved openwork canopy. Choir stalls were adorned with biblical and historical scenes or carved to resemble delicate stone tracery.

The Isabelline style

At the end of the 15C, the prestige surrounding the royal couple and the grandees in the reign of Isabel the Catholic (1474-1504) provided a favourable context for the emergence of a new style in which exuberant decoration covered entire façades of civil and religious buildings. Ornamentation took the form of supple free arcs, lace-like carving, heraldic motifs and every fantasy that imagination could devise (*see VALLADOLID*). The diversity of inspiration was largely due to foreign artists: **Simon of Cologne** (son of Johan) – San Pablo in Valladolid, Capilla del Condestable in Burgos; **Juan Guas** (son of the Frenchman, Pierre) – San Juan de los Reyes in Toledo; and **Enrique Egas** (nephew of Hanequin of Brussels) – Capilla Real in Granada.

THE RENAISSANCE (16C)

In the 16C, at the dawn of its golden age, Spain was swept by a deep sense of its own national character and so created a style in which Italian influence became acceptable only when hispanicised.

Architecture

Plateresque was the name given to the early Renaissance style because of its finely chiselled, lavish decoration reminiscent of silverwork (platero: silversmith). Although close to the Isabelline style in its profusion of carved forms extending over entire façades, the rounded arches and ornamental themes (grotesques, foliage, pilasters, medallions and cornices) were Italian. The Plateresque style was brought to a climax in Salamanca in the façade of the Universidad and that of the Convento de San Esteban. Among architects of the time were **Rodrigo Gil de Hontañón** who worked at Salamanca (Palacios de Monterrey and Fonseca) and at Alcalá de Henares (university façade), and **Diego de Siloé**, the main architect in Burgos (Escalera de la Coronería). Together with **Alonso de Covarrubias** (d 1570) who worked mainly in Toledo (Alcázar and Capilla de los Reyes Nuevos in the cathedral),

Diego de Siloé marked the transition from the Plateresque style to the Classical Renaissance. **Andrés de Vandelvira** (1509-76) was the leading architect of the Andalucían Renaissance (Jaén cathedral). His work introduces the austerity which was to characterise the last quarter of the century.

The Renaissance style drew upon Italian models and adopted features from Antiquity such as rounded arches, columns, entablatures and pediments. Decoration became of secondary importance after architectonic perfection. **Pedro Machuca** (d 1550) who studied under Michelangelo, designed the palace of Charles V in Granada, the most classical example of the Italian tradition. Another important figure, **Bartolomé Bustamante** (1500-70), built the Hospital de Tavera in Toledo.

The greatest figure of Spanish Classicism was **Juan de Herrera** (1530-97) who gave his name to an architectural style characterised by grandeur and austerity. He was the favourite architect of Philip II. The king saw in him the sobriety that suited the Counter-Reformation and in 1567 entrusted him with the task of continuing work on El Escorial, his greatest achievement.

Sculpture

Sculpture in Spain reached its climax during the Renaissance. In the 16C, a great many choir stalls, mausoleums and altarpieces (also known as retables or reredos) were still being made of alabaster and wood. These latter were then painted by the estofado technique in which gold leaf is first applied, then the object is coloured and finally delicately scored to produce gold highlights. Carved altarpiece panels were framed by Corinthian architraves and pilasters. The sculptures of **Damián Forment** (c 1480-1540), who worked mainly in Aragón, belong to the transition period between Gothic and Renaissance styles. The Burgundian **Felipe Vigarny** (d 1543) and the architect **Diego de Siloé**, who was apprenticed in Naples, both worked on Burgos Cathedral. **Bartolomé Ordóñez** (d 1520) studied in Naples and carved the trascoro (choir screen) in Barcelona Cathedral and the mausoleums of Juana the Mad, Philip the Handsome (Capilla Real in Granada) and Cardinal Cisneros (Alcalá de Henares).

The home of the Renaissance School moved from Burgos to Valladolid in the mid-16C by which time the Spanish style had absorbed foreign influences and Spain's two great Renaissance sculptors had emerged. The first, **Alonso Berruguete** (1488-1561), who studied in Italy under Michelangelo, had a style which drew closely on the Florentine Renaissance and reflected a strong personality. He sought strength of expression rather than formal beauty and his tormented fiery human forms are as powerful as those of his master (statue of San Sebastián in the Museo de Valladolid). The second, **Juan de Juni** (d 1577), a Frenchman who settled in Valladolid, was also influenced by Michelangelo and founded the Catalan School of sculpture. His statues, recognisable by their beauty and the fullness of their forms, anticipated the Baroque style through the dramatic postures they adopted to express sorrow. Many of his works, such as the famous Virgen de los Siete Cuchillos (Virgin of the Seven Knives) in the Iglesia de las Angustias in Valladolid and the Entombments in the Museo de Valladolid and Segovia Cathedral, were subsequently copied.

Most of the finely worked wrought-iron grilles closing off chapels and coros (chancels) were carved in the 15C and 16C. Members of the Arfe family, Enrique, Antonio and Juan, stand out in the field of gold- and silversmithing. They made the monstrances of Toledo, Santiago de Compostela and Sevilla cathedrals respectively.

Painting

Under Italian Renaissance influence, Spanish painting in the 16C showed a mastery of perspective, a taste for clarity of composition and glorification of the human body. These features found their way into Spanish painting mainly through the Valencian School where **Fernando Yáñez de la Almedina** and **Fernando de Llanos** introduced the style of Leonardo da Vinci, while

Vicente Macip added that of Raphael and his son **Juan de Juanes** produced Mannerist works. In Sevilla, **Alejo Fernández** painted the famous *Virgin of the Navigators* in the Alcázar. In Castilla, the great master of the late 15C was **Pedro Berruguete** (c 1450-1504) whose markedly personal style drew upon all the artistic influences in the country. His successor, **Juan de Borgoña**, specialised particularly in landscape, architecture and decorative motifs. Another artist, **Pedro de Campaña** from Brussels, used chiaroscuro to dramatic effect while **Luis de Morales** (c 1520-86), a Mannerist, gave his work a human dimension through the portrayal of feelings. Ordinary people with religious sentiments responded favourably to the spiritual emotion expressed in his paintings. At the end of the 16C, Philip II sent for a great many Italian or Italian-trained artists to paint pictures for El Escorial. During his reign he introduced portrait painting under the Dutchman **Antonio Moro** (1519-76), his disciple **Alonso Sánchez Coello** (1531-88) and **Pantoja de la Cruz** (1553-1608). **El Greco**, on the other hand, was scorned by the court and settled in Toledo.

BAROQUE (17C-18C)

Spanish art reached its apogee in the mid-17C. Baroque met with outstanding success in its role as an essentially religious art in the service of the Counter-Reformation and was particularly evident in Andalucía, then enriched by trade with America.

Architecture

Architects in the early 17C were still under the influence of 16C Classicism and the Herreran style to which they added decorative details. Public buildings proliferated and many continued to be built throughout the Baroque period.

Public buildings of the time in Madrid include the plaza Mayor by **Juan Gómez de Mora**, built shortly before the Ayuntamiento (town hall), and the most significant building of all, the present Ministerio de Asuntos Exteriores (Ministry of Foreign Affairs) by **Juan Bautista Crescenzi**, the architect of the Panteón de los Reyes at El Escorial. Church architecture of the period showed greater freedom from Classicism. A style of Jesuit church, with a cruciform plan and a large transept that served to light up altarpieces, began to emerge. Madrid has several examples including the Iglesia de San Isidro by the Jesuits **Pedro Sánchez** and **Francisco Bautista**, and the Real Convento de la Encarnación by **Juan Gómez de Mora**. In the middle of the century, architects adopted a less rigid style, changing plans and façades, breaking up entablatures and making pediments more elaborate. A good example of this Italian Baroque style is the Iglesia Pontificia de San Miguel (18C) in Madrid. A new feature, the **camarín**, was introduced: at first simply a passage behind the high altar leading to the retable niche containing a statue venerated by the faithful, it developed into a highly ornate chapel. Decoration of this kind may be seen in Zaragoza's Basílica de Nuestra Señora del Pilar designed by **Francisco Herrera the Younger** (1622-85). The Clerecía in Salamanca is a magnificent Baroque creation with a patio that anticipates the audacity and superabundant decoration characteristic of the Churrigueresque style.

The Churrigueresque style

In this style, named after the Churriguera family of architects (late 17C), architecture became no more than a support for dense concentrations of ornament covering entire façades. The style is typified by the use of *salomónicas*, or barley sugar columns entwined with vines, and *estípites*, or pilasters arranged in an inverse pyramid. Early examples of this extravagance, the altarpiece of the Convento de San Esteban in Salamanca and the palace in Nuevo Baztán near Madrid, were by **José de Churriguera** (1665-1725) who was the instigator of the style but did not make any architectural changes. His brothers **Joaquín** (1674-1724) and especially **Alberto** (1676-1750) who designed the plaza Mayor in Salamanca, took greater liberties in their work.

Pedro de Ribera (1683-1742), a Castilian architect who worked mainly in Madrid, surpassed the Churriguera brothers in decorative delirium. The other great Castilian, **Narciso Tomé**, is remembered for the façade of the Universidad de Valladolid (1715) and particularly for the *Transparente* in Toledo Cathedral (1720-32).

Regional variations

The popularity of the Baroque spread countrywide, differing from province to province. In **Galicia**, where the hardness of the granite precluded delicate carving, Baroque took the form of softer lines and decorative mouldings. The best example of the style and the masterpiece of its designer, **Fernando de Casas y Novoa**, is the Obradoiro façade of Santiago de Compostela Cathedral (1750).

In **Andalucía**, Baroque attained its utmost splendour, especially in decoration. Undulating surfaces characterised the façades of palaces (Écija), cathedrals (Guadix) and the doorways of countless churches and mansions (Jerez) in the 18C. As well as sculptor and painter, **Alonso Cano** was the instigator of Andalucían Baroque and designed the façade of Granada Cathedral. The major exponent of the style was, however, **Vicente Acero**, who worked on the façade of Guadix Cathedral (1714-20), designed Cádiz Cathedral and built the tobacco factory in Sevilla. Mention should also be made of **Leonardo de Figueroa** (1650-1730) for the Palacio de San Telmo in Sevilla and **Francisco Hurtado** (1669-1725) and **Luis de Arévalo** for La Cartuja in Granada; Hurtado worked on the monastery's tabernacle and Arévalo on the sacristy, the most exuberant Baroque works in Andalucía.

In the **Levante**, Baroque artists used polychrome tiles to decorate church cupolas and spires like that of Santa Catalina in Valencia. In the same town, the Palacio del Marqués de Dos Aguas by **Luis Domingo** and **Ignacio Vergara** is reminiscent of façades by Ribera, although its design is more like French Rococo. The cathedral in Murcia has an impressive façade by **Jaime Bort**.

The Golden Age of Spanish painting

This was characterised by the rejection of the previous century's Mannerism and the adoption of naturalism. The starting point was Caravaggio's tenebrism, powerful contrasts of light and shade, and his stern realism. Painters took up portraiture and still life *(bodegón)*, while allegories on the theme of *vanitas* (still-life paintings showing the ephemerality of life) reflected a philosophical purpose by juxtaposing everyday objects with symbols of decay to illustrate the transience of wealth and the things of this world and the inevitability of death. Among 17C artists were two from the Valencian School – **Francisco Ribalta** (1565-1628), who introduced tenebrism into Spain, and **José de Ribera** (1591-1652), known for his forceful realism.

Some of the greatest Baroque artists worked in Andalucía. One was **Francisco Zurbarán** (1598-1664), master of the Sevilla School; light in his paintings springs from within the subjects themselves. Other artists included **Murillo** (1618-82), who painted intimate, mystical scenes, and **Valdés Leal** whose powerful realism clearly challenged earthly vanities. **Alonso Cano** (1601-67), architect, painter and sculptor, settled in Granada and painted delicate figures of the Virgin.

The Castilian painters of the century, **Vicente Carducho** (1575-1638) and the portraitists **Carreño de Miranda** (1614-85) and **Claudio Coello** (1642-93), all excellent artists, nonetheless pale beside **Velázquez**. His aerial perspective and outstanding sense of depth are beyond compare.

Sculpture

Spanish Baroque sculpture was naturalistic and intensely emotive. The most commonly used medium was wood, and while altarpieces continued to be carved, pasos or statues specially made for Semana Santa processions proved a great novelty.

The two major schools of Baroque sculpture were in Castilla and Andalucía. **Gregorio Hernández**, Juni's successor, worked in Valladolid, the Castilian centre. His style was a lot more natural than that of his master, and his Christ Recumbent for the Convento de Capuchinos in El Pardo was widely copied. Sevilla and Granada were the main centres for the Andalucían School. **Juan Martínez Montañés** (1568-1649) settled in Sevilla and worked exclusively in wood, carving a great many *pasos* and various altarpieces. Alonso Cano, Granada's illustrious artist, became famous for the grace and femininity of his Immaculate Conceptions while his best-known disciple, **Pedro de Mena**, produced sculptures of great dramatic tension which contrasted with his master's understated style. The statue of Mary Magdalene (Museo Nacional de Escultura Policromada, Valladolid), St Francis (Toledo Cathedral) and the Dolorosa (Monasterio de las Descalzas Reales, Madrid) are telling examples of his work.

The 18C saw the rise to prominence of the great Murcian, Francisco Salzillo, whose dramatic sculptures were inspired by Italian Baroque.

Churrigueresque excess in sculpture took the form of immense altarpieces which reached the roof. These huge constructions took on such grand proportions that they began to be designed by architects. Their statues seemed smothered by decoration, lost in an overabundance of gilding and stucco.

BOURBON ART

Austrian imperialism was succeeded by enlightened Bourbon despotism which resulted in artistic as well as political change in the 18C. Henceforth the rules of art were to be governed by official bodies like the Academia de Bellas Artes de San Fernando.

Architecture

During the first half of the century architecture still bore the stamp of Spanish Baroque, itself influenced at the time by French Rococo. The king and queen had palaces built in a moderate Baroque style (El Pardo, Riofrío, La Granja and Aranjuez) and began work on Madrid's Palacio Real modelled on Versailles. These buildings sought to ally French Classical harmony with Italian grace, and to this end most of the work was entrusted to Italian architects who generally respected the traditional quadrangular plan of *alcázares*, so typically Spanish. The vast gardens were given a French design.

Excavations of Pompeii and Herculaneum contributed to the emergence of a new, neo-Classical style which flourished between the second half of the 18C and 19C. It repudiated Baroque excess and aspired to Hellenistic beauty through the use of Classical orders, pediments, porticoes and cupolas. The kings of Spain, Charles III in particular, set about embellishing the capital by building fountains (Cibeles, Neptune), gates (Alcalá and Toledo), and planting botanic gardens.

The first Spanish neo-Classical architect, **Ventura Rodríguez** (1717-85), who was actually apprenticed in Italian Baroque, quickly developed an academic neo-Classical style. His works include the façade of Pamplona Cathedral, the paseo del Prado in Madrid and the Basílica de Nuestra Señora del Pilar in Zaragoza. **Sabatini** (1722-97), whose style developed along similar lines, designed the Puerta de Alcalá and the building that now houses the Ministerio de Hacienda (Ministry of Finance) in Madrid. The leading architect was without doubt **Juan de Villanueva** (1739-1811), schooled in Classical principles during a stay in Rome. He designed the façade of the Ayuntamiento in Madrid, the Casita del Príncipe at El Escorial and most importantly, the Museo del Prado. Two notable town planners emerged during the 19C: **Ildefonso Cerdà** in Barcelona and **Arturo Soria** (1844-1920) in Madrid.

Painting

Bourbon monarchs took pains to attract the greatest painters to court and grant them official positions. In 1752 Ferdinand VI founded the Academia de Bellas Artes de San Fernando where it was intended that students should learn official painting techniques and study the Italian masters. Leading artists of the time were **Anton Raffael Mengs** (1728-79) from Bohemia and the Italian **Gian Battista Tiepolo** (1696-1770), both of whom decorated the Palacio Real. There was also **Francisco Bayeu** (1734-95) from Aragón, who painted a great many tapestry cartoons, as did his brother-in-law **Francisco Goya** (1746-1828). Goya's work, much of which may be seen in the Prado, Madrid, was to dominate the entire century.

Painters working in the post-Goya period did not follow in the master's footsteps as academic neo-Classical influences and Romanticism took over; Goya's legacy was not taken up until the end of the 19C. The following stand out among artists of the academic Romantic trend: **Federico de Madrazo**, representative of official taste in royal portraits and historical scenes, **Vicente Esquivel**, portrait-painter, and lastly **Leonardo Alenza**, and **Eugenio Lucas**, the spokesmen for **Costumbrismo** which had attained full status as a genre. (This was a style of painting illustrating scenes of everyday life which gradually developed from the simply anecdotal to a higher calling, the evocation of the Spanish soul.) Historical themes became very popular in the 19C with works by José Casado de Alisal, Eduardo Rosales and Mariano Fortuny. Impressionist features began to appear in naturalist paintings by **Martí Alsina** and in post-Romantic landscapes by **Carlos de Haes**. The style secured a definitive hold in the works of **Narciso Oller, Ignacio Pinazo**, the best Valencian Impressionist, **Darío Regoyos** and lastly, **Joaquín Sorolla**, who specialised in light-filled folk scenes and regional subjects. The Basque artist **Ignacio Zuloaga** (1870-1945) expressed his love for Spain in brightly coloured scenes of everyday life at a time when Impressionism was conquering Europe.

The decorative arts

Factories were built under the Bourbons to produce decorative material for their royal palaces. In 1760, Charles III founded the Buen Retiro works, where ceramics for the famous Salones de Porcelana in the royal palaces of Aranjuez and Madrid were made. The factory was destroyed during the Napoleonic invasion.

In 1720, Philip V opened the Real Fábrica de Tapices de Santa Bárbara (in Madrid), the equivalent of the French Gobelins factory in Paris. Some of the tapestries were of Don Quixote while others depicted scenes of everyday life based on preparatory cartoons by Bayeu and Goya.

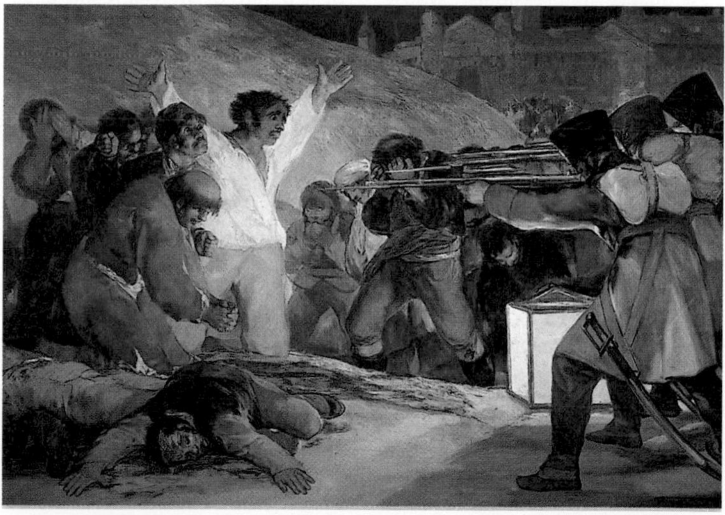

The Third of May, Goya

Llibre-mur, Tàpies

20C ART

From Modernism to Surrealism

The barren period that Spanish art in general experienced at the end of the 19C was interrupted in Catalunya by a vast cultural movement known as **Modernism**. This was particularly strong in architecture, with outstanding work by **Antoni Gaudí, Lluís Domènech i Montaner** and **Josep María Jujol**.

In the field of sculpture, **Pau Gargallo** broke new ground through the simplicity of his shapes, the attention he gave to volume and the use of new materials like iron.

Painting was varied and prolific. The following stand out among the many artists of the time: **Ramón Casas**, the best Spanish Impressionist, whose works are suffused with an atmosphere of grey melancholy, **Santiago Rusiñol, Isidro Nonell**, instigator of Spanish Expressionism, and **Pablo Ruiz Picasso** (1881-1973), the dominant figure whose innovations were to mark the entire history of 20C painting.

Picasso's attention was first devoted to academic naturalism *(Science and Charity)*. He subsequently became a Modernist and social Expressionist. Later, once he had moved to Paris (1904), his style developed through the successive blue and rose periods to Cubism *(Les Demoiselles d'Avignon)*, Surrealism and Expressionism *(Guernica)*, which in turn led to a totally personal and subjective lyrical style *(La Joie de Vivre)*.

In the 1920s a movement began to emerge that was influenced by Cubism and more particularly, by Surrealism. Its sculptors were **Angel Ferrant, Victorio Macho, Alberto Sánchez** and lastly **Julio González**, who strove towards abstract Expressionism through the use of iron and simple shapes. Painters of the movement included **Daniel Vázquez Díaz**, Juan Gris, Joan Miró and Salvador Dalí. **Juan Gris** (1887-1927), the most faithful analytical Cubist, worked in Paris. The works of Joan Miró (1893-1983), champion of Surrealism, are characterised by child-like spontaneity and an original attitude to everyday objects. Miró used very bright colours and magic symbols in all his paintings. **Salvador Dalí** (1904-89), a quasi-Surrealist, dreamed up his own creative method which he called the paranoic critical. Some of his best paintings were a result of his interest in the subconscious and his vision of a dream world. All his works attest to an excellent drawing technique and many show an attention to detail worthy of the best miniaturists.

Post-war art

Spanish art was crucially affected by the Civil War in two ways: firstly, the fact that several artists went into exile meant that the country suffered cultural loss, and secondly, official taste in architecture developed a penchant for the monumental. This is clearly apparent in a number of colossal edifices. Many government buildings, all in Madrid, were designed in the manner of El Escorial, including the Ministerio del Aire, the Museo de América, the Arco del Triunfo and the Consejo de

Investigaciones Científicas. The most striking example is the monument of the Valle de los Caídos (Valley of the Fallen) outside Madrid. However, among exponents of the nationalist style, there were several innovative architects like **Miguel Fisac**.

In 1950 the first signs of a new style, based on rational and functional criteria, began to emerge. Examples abound in Barcelona – the Vanguardia building by **Oriol Bohigas** and **José María Martorell**, the residential block by **Ricardo Bofill** in carrer de Nicaragua – and in Madrid – the Colegio Monfort by **A Fernandez Alba**, the Maravillas secondary school *(gimnasio)* by **Alejandro de la Sota** and the Torres Blancas (White Towers) by **F Javier Sáenz de Oíza**.

Post-war sculpture and painting are basically academic but there are some notable artists such as **José Gutiérrez Solana**, whose paintings are full of anguish, and the landscape painters **Benjamín Palencia**, who glorifies the country and light of Castilla, and **Rafael Zabaleta**, who is more interested in painting the region's country folk.

Avant-garde painters also began to emerge after the war. The first post-war Surrealists are members of a group called **Dau al Set** including **Modest Cuixart**, **Antoni Tàpies** and **Juan José Tharrats**. Tàpies is a veritable pioneer, one of the major abstract artists.

New artistic trends

In the 1950s two abstract groups, with different qualities but with the common aim of artistic innovation, were formed: the **El Paso** group in Madrid with **Antonio Saura, Manuel Millares, Rafael Canogar, Luis Feito, Manuel Viola and Martín Chirino,** all representatives of what was known as action painting; and the **El Equipo 57** group in Cuenca with **Duart, Ibarrola, Serrano** and **Duarte**, who were more interested in drawing. The movement's sculptors included **Jorge Oteiza, Andréu Alfaro** and lastly **Eduardo Chillida**, who worked in iron and wood and stripped his sculptures of any figurative suggestion.

Spanish Gardens

The gardens of Spain are a further example of the country's rich culture, and bear witness to an enviable ability to adapt to a varied climate. Although Spanish landscape gardening has inherited many of its traditions from within Europe, particularly from the Greco-Roman era, the long period of Moorish occupation added a completely new dimension to the country's landscape.

THE GENERALIFE (14C), GRANADA

The Moors were truly gifted gardeners. The Generalife is *the* Moorish garden par excellence, despite the alterations it has undergone over the centuries. As a result of its extraordinary position it is a magnificent balcony, but above all it has been able to preserve an intimate, sensual character which was such a feature of Muslim gardens.

A Moorish garden is always an evocation of paradise; it is a feast for the senses and a harmonious whole which avoids grandiloquence. Nothing has been left to chance: the colour of the plants and flowers, their scent, and the omnipresence of water combine to create a serene ambience full of intimate charm.

A. de la Rosa

The Generalife has been laid out on several levels to ensure that the trees in one garden do not interfere with the views from another. In fact, the Generalife is a series of landscaped areas and enclosures each with its own individuality yet part of an overall design. The garden's architectural features and vegetation, reflected in the water channels, blend together to create a perfect whole.

H. Le Gac/MICHELIN

LA GRANJA (18C), LA GRANJA DE SAN ILDEFONSO, SEGOVIA

Once he came to the Spanish throne, Philip V, the grandson of Louis XIV, chose a beautiful spot in the Segovian countryside at the foot of the Sierra de Guadarrama to create these magnificent Baroque gardens. They bring to mind those of Versailles, where the monarch spent his childhood. Philip V was to make La Granja his personal retreat.

Although the Versailles influence is clearly evident, the differences are also obvious. Because of its position, hemmed in by the mountains, the grandiose perspectives of Versailles are not to be found at La Granja. The rigidity of the French garden is also lost here as there is no clear central axis; instead, La Granja consists of a succession of parts each with a certain independence, thus adopting hints of Moorish design. Although the gardeners brought with them a variety of species from France, they were able to adapt perfectly to the features of the local landscape and to preserve the somewhat wild appearance which gives it an undoubted charm. Magnificent fountains and sculptures scattered in small squares and along avenues add a theatrical touch.

FOTOSEARCH

PAZO DE OCA (18C-19C), LA ESTRADA, LA CORUÑA

A pazo is a Baroque-style manor typically found in Galicia. These large rustic residences are built on plots of land which generally comprise a recreational garden, a kitchen garden and cultivated farmland.

The Pazo de Oca garden, the oldest in Galicia, is a magnificent example of a garden in the wet part of Spain. What comes as a complete surprise is its perfect integration into its surroundings, where the damp climate has enabled vegetation to grow on rocks, creating an intimate relationship between its architectural and vegetal features. Water plays a vital role, appearing in basins or fountains or trickling through the garden. The most attractive part, with its two ponds, is hidden behind a parterre. A delightful bridge, with benches enabling visitors to enjoy this enchanting spot, separates the two sections, overcoming the difference in height between them. The lower pond contains the pazo's most representative and famous feature: the stone boat, with its two petrified sailors, planted with hydrangeas.

The combination of both climate and vegetation gives the site an unquestionably romantic air.

JARDÍN BOTÁNICO DE MARIMURTRA (20C), BLANES, GIRONA

Carlos Faust, the German impresario who settled on the Costa Brava, created this botanical garden in 1921 for research purposes to enable scientists to carry out studies on flora, and to catalogue and preserve plants threatened with extinction. It is situated in a delightful spot between the sea and the mountains and offers visitors magnificent views of the coast.

Marimurtra is a fine example of a contemporary Mediterranean garden, although a number of exotic species from every continent have also adapted perfectly here. It contains an interesting cactus garden, an impressive aquatic garden, as well as a collection of medicinal, toxic and aromatic plants. The scientific aims of the garden have not interfered in any way with the aesthetic direction it has taken. The only architectural feature with a purely decorative function is the small temple built at the end of the steps running down to the sea.

At present, only a third of Marimurtra is open to the public.

Literature

Errant knights, Don Juan characters, mystics and highwaymen occupy a hallowed place in Spanish letters. Spanish literature reached its peak during the Golden Age of the 16C and 17C, and has enjoyed a renewed period of acclaim

TURESPAÑA

since the beginning of the 20C, through the works of a new generation of writers from within Spain and across the Spanish-speaking world.

Roman Spain produced great Latin authors such as **Seneca the Elder** or the Rhetorician, his son **Seneca the Younger** or the Philosopher, Quintilian the Rhetorician, and the epic poet **Lucan**. In the 8C, the monk Beatus wrote the Commentary on the Apocalypse which gave rise to a series of outstanding illuminated manuscripts known as Beatus. Arab writers won

H. Stierlin/Monasterio de El Escorial

Beatus – El Escorial

renown during the same period. Works written in Castilian began to emerge only in the Middle Ages.

THE MIDDLE AGES

The first milestone of Spanish literature appeared in the 12C in the form of *El Cantar del Mío Cid*, an anonymous Castilian poem inspired by the adventures of **El Cid**. In the 13C, the monk **Gonzalo de Berceo**, drawing on religious themes, won renown through his works of *Mester de Clerecía*, the learned poetry of clerics and scholars. **Alfonso X, the Wise**, an erudite king who wrote poetry in Galician, decreed that in his kingdom, Latin should be replaced as the official language by Castilian, an act subsequently followed throughout Spain except in Catalunya where Catalan remained the written language. In the 14C, **Don Juan Manuel** introduced the use of narrative prose in his moral tales while Juan Ruiz, **Archpriest of Hita**, wrote a brilliant satirical verse work titled *El Libro de Buen Amor*, which later influenced the picaresque novel.

THE RENAISSANCE

In the 15C, lyric poetry flourished under Italian influence with poets such as **Jorge Manrique** and the **Marquis of Santillana**. **Romanceros**, collections of ballads in an epic or popular vein, perpetuated the medieval style until the 16C when *Amadís de Gaula* (1508) set the model for a great many romances or tales of chivalry. In 1499, *La Celestina*, a novel of passion in dialogue form by **Fernando de Rojas**, anticipated modern drama in a subtle, well-observed tragicomic intrigue.

THE GOLDEN AGE (SIGLO DE ORO)

Spain enjoyed its greatest literary flowering under the Habsburgs (1516-1700), with great lyric poets such as **Garcilaso de la Vega**, disciple of Italian verse forms, **Fray Luis de León** and above all **Luis de Góngora** (1561-1627) whose obscure, precious style won fame under the name of Gongorism. Pastoral novels became popular with works by Cervantes and Lope de Vega. The **picaresque** novel, however, was the genre favoured by Spanish writers at the time. The first to appear in 1554 was *Lazarillo de Tormes*, an anonymous autobiographical work in which the hero, an astute rogue (*pícaro* in Castilian), casts a mischievous and impartial eye on society and its woes. There followed Mateo Alemán's *Guzmán de Alfarache* with its brisk style and colourful vocabulary, and *La Vida del Buscón*, an example of the varied talents of **Francisco de Quevedo** (1580-1645), essayist, poet and satirist. The genius of the Golden Age, however, was **Cervantes** (1547-1616), with his masterpiece, the universal **Don Quixote** (1605). **Lope de Rueda** paved the way for *comedia*, which emerged at the end of the 16C. Dramatists proliferated, among them the master **Lope de Vega** (1562-1635), who perfected and enriched the art form. This "phoenix of the mind" wrote more than 1 000 plays on the most diverse subjects. His successor, **Calderón de la Barca** (1600-81), wrote historical and philosophical plays *(La vida es sueño or Life's a Dream* and *El alcalde de Zalamea* or *The Mayor of Zalamea)* in which he brilliantly reflects the mood of Spain in the 17C. **Tirso de Molina** (1583-1648) left his interpretation of Don Juan for posterity while **Guillén de Castro** wrote *Las Mocedades del Cid* (*Youthful Adventures of the Cid*). Mention should also be made of works on the conquest of America by **Cortés** and **Bartolomé de las Casas** among others. Finally, the moralist **Fray Luis de Granada** and the mystics **Santa Teresa de Ávila** (1515-82) and **San Juan de la Cruz** (St John of the Cross) (1542-91) wrote theological works.

18C AND 19C

The critical mode found expression in the works of essayists such as **Benito Jerónimo Feijóo** and **Jovellanos**, while elegance dominated the plays of **Moratín**. The great romantic poet of the 19C was **Bécquer** (1836-70) from Sevilla, while **Larra** was a social satirist,

Menéndez Pelayo a literary critic and **Ángel Ganivet** a political and moral analyst. Realism was introduced to the Spanish novel by **Alarcón** (*The Three-Cornered Hat*) and **Pereda** (*Peñas arriba*) who concentrated on regional themes. By the end of the 19C, the best realist was **Pérez Galdós** whose prolific, lively work (*National Episodes*) is stamped with a great sense of human sympathy.

20C

A group of intellectuals known as the Generation of '98, saddened by Spain's loss of colonies like Cuba, pondered over the future and character of their country and, more generally, the problems of human destiny. The atmosphere was reflected in the work of essayists such as **Miguel de Unamuno** (1864-1936) who wrote *El sentimiento trágico de la vida (The Tragic Sense of Life)*, and **Azorín**, as well as the philologist **Menéndez Pidal**, the novelist **Pío Baroja** and the aesthete **Valle Inclán**, who created an elegant poetic prose style. Among their contemporaries were **Jacinto Benavente** (winner of the 1922 Nobel Prize for literature), who developed a new dramatic style, and the novelist **Vicente Blasco Ibáñez**. Henceforth Spain opened up to literary contributions from abroad. Some great poets began to emerge, including **Juan Ramón Jiménez** (Nobel Prize 1956), who expressed his feelings through simple unadorned prose poems *(Platero y yo)*, **Antonio Machado** (1875-1939) the bard of Castilla, and **Rafael Alberti**. **Federico García Lorca** (1898-1936) equally great as both poet and dramatist *(Bodas de sangre)*, was Andalucían through and through. His work was, perhaps, the most fascinating reflection of a Spain whose mystery **Ortega y Gasset** (1883-1925), essayist and philosopher, spent his life trying to fathom.

POST-WAR WRITING

Several years after the Civil War, writing rose from its ashes with works by essayists (Américo Castro), playwrights (Alfonso Sastre) and above all, novelists such as **Miguel Delibes, Camilo José Cela** *(La familia de Pascual Duarte)* who won the Nobel Prize for Literature in 1989, **Juan Goytisolo, Ramón Sender** and Antonio Ferres, all preoccupied with social issues.
Among contemporary authors, mention should be made of novelists Juan Benet, Juan Marsé, **Manuel Vázquez Montalbán**, Terenci Moix, Javier Marías and **Eduardo Mendoza**, and playwrights Antonio Gala, Fernando Arrabal and Francisco Nieva.
The Spanish-speaking countries of Latin America are making enormous contributions to literature in Spanish with works by Jorge Luis Borges, Gabriel García Márquez, Pablo Neruda and Miguel Ángel Asturias.

Cinema and Music

Over the centuries, Spain has produced countless musicians and thespians of world renown. In more recent times, the genius of film directors such as **Luis Buñuel**, **Juan Antonio Bardem** and **Pedro Almodóvar**, composers such as **Manuel de Falla**, and classical guitarists such as **Antonio Segovia**, has thrilled audiences the world over.

CINEMA

Spanish cinema dates back to a short film in 1897 which shows people leaving the Basílica de Nuestra Señora del Pilar in Zaragoza after Mass. Studios for silent movies were later set up in Barcelona.
In the 1920s, several Surrealists tried their hand at the new art form. Among them were **Dalí** and above all **Buñuel**, the master of Spanish cinema, who made *Un chien Andalou (Un perro andaluz, An Andalusian Dog)* in 1928 and *L'Age d'Or* (*La edad de oro, The Golden Age)* in 1930. When talking films appeared in the 1930s, Spain was in the throes of a political and economic crisis and so her studios lacked the means to procure the necessary equipment.
At the end of the 1930s, when films like *Sister Angelica (Sor Angélica)* by Gargallo tended to address religious themes,

Juan Piqueras launched a magazine called Nuestro Cinema which was strongly influenced by Russian ideas, and gave star billing to films such as *Las Hurdes – Land without Bread (Las Hurdes – Tierra sin pan*, 1932) by Buñuel, depicting poverty in a remote part of Spain.
During the Civil War and the ensuing Franco era, films were heavily censored and the cinema became one of the major vehicles for the ideology of the time, with historical and religious themes glorifying death and the spirit of sacrifice. One such success was *Marcelino, Bread and Wine (Marcelino, pan y vino*, 1955) by Ladislao Vajda. Change came with works by Juan Antonio Bardem like *Death of a Cyclist (Muerte de un ciclista*, 1955) and with Berlanga's *Welcome Mr Marshall (Bienvenido, Mr Marshall*, 1953) and *The Executioner (El verdugo*, 1964).
The 1960s enjoyed a period of renewal with directors like **Carlos Saura**, whose first film, *The Scoundrels (Los golfos)*, came out in 1959. More than ever before, the 1970s saw a new wave in Spanish cinema with outstanding directors and films. These were mainly concerned with the problems of childhood and youth marked by the Franco régime. Saura's *Ana and the Wolves (Ana y los lobos*, 1973) shows a young girl arriving as an outsider in a family in which three 50-year-old brothers personify the all-powerful hold of the army and religion during the Franco era. Mention should also be made of Saura's *Cría cuervos* (1975); *The Spirit of the Beehive (El espíritu de la colmena*, 1973) and *The South (El sur*, 1983) by **Víctor Erice**, *The Beehive (La colmena*, 1982) by **Mario Camus**, and films by **Manuel Gutiérrez Aragón** such as *Demons in the Garden (Demonios en el jardín*, 1982) and *The Other Half of Heaven (La Otra mitad del cielo*, 1986) which illustrate the economic changes between Spain under Franco and Spain as a democracy. **Pedro Almodóvar** breaks with this serious, nostalgic type of cinema so critical of the Franco era. His films are of a completely different, modern Spain is shown in a comic light, but not without an edgy criticism, as in *Qué he hecho yo para merecer esto* (*What have I done to deserve this?*, 1984), *Women on the Edge of a Nervous Breakdown (Mujeres al borde de un ataque de nervios*, 1987) and *Volver* (2006).

© The Bettmann Archive/CORBIS

Louis Buñuel

Four Spanish films have won an Oscar for Best Foreign Film: *To Begin Again (Volver a empezar*, 1982), directed by **JL Garci, F Trueba's** *Belle Epoque* (1993), *All about my mother (Todo sobre mi madre*, 1999), by **Pedro Almodóvar**, and *Mar adentro* (*The Sea Inside*, 2004) by **Alejandro Amenabar**. There has been a resurgence in Spanish cinema in recent years with young directors such as **Amenabar** (*Tesis*, 1996; *Los otros*, 2001), **Julio Medem** *(Los amantes del Círculo Polar*, 1998), Icíar Bollaín (*Te doy mis ojos*, 2003) and Isabel Coixet (*La vida secreta de las palabras*, 2005). This development has resulted in huge box office triumphs, such as *The Dog in the Manger (El perro del hortelano*, 1996) by the late **Pilar Miró,** and *Secrets of the Heart (Secretos del corazón*, 1997) by **Montxo Armendáriz**. Other successful films of recent years include *The Lucky Star (La buena estrella*, 1997) by **Ricardo Franco**, *Barrio* (1998) by F**ernando León de Aranoa**, *El abuelo* (1998) by JL Garci, *The Girl of your Dreams (La niña de tus ojos*, 1998) by **F Trueba**, and *Solas* (1998) by **Benito Zambrano**.

MUSIC

Alongside its folk music, Spain has developed an extraordinarily rich musical repertory since the Middle Ages, marked by a large number of influences including Visigothic, Arabic, Mozarabic and French. Polyphonic chants were studied in the 11C and the oldest known piece for three voices, the *Codex calixtinus*, was composed at Santiago de Compostela c 1140. During the Reconquest, the church encouraged great musical creativity in the form of liturgical chants, plays *(autos)* like the *Elche Mystery* which is still performed today, and poetry like the 13C **Cantigas de Santa María** by Alfonso the Wise.

At the end of the 15C, the dramatist **Juan de la Encina** composed secular songs, thus proving that he was also an excellent musician. Music, like the other arts, however, reached its climax in the second half of the 16C, under the protection of the early Habsburgs. **Victoria** (1548-1611) was one of the most famous composers of polyphonic devotional pieces, while among his contemporaries, **Francisco de Salinas** and **Fernando de las Infantas** were learned musicologists and **Cristóbal de Morales** and **Francisco Guerrero** were accomplished religious composers. As for instruments, the organ became the invariable accompaniment to sacred music, while a favourite for profane airs was the *vihuela*, a sort of guitar with six double strings which was soon replaced by the lute and eventually by the five-string Spanish guitar. In 1629, Lope de Vega wrote the text for the first Spanish opera. **Pedro Calderón de la Barca** is credited with creating the **zarzuela** (1648), a musical play with spoken passages, songs and dances, which, since the 19C, has based its plot and music on popular themes. The major composer of religious and secular music in the 18C was Padre **Antonio Soler**, a great harpsichord player.

In the 19C, the Catalan **Felipe Pedrell** brought Spanish music onto a higher plane. He opened the way for a new generation of musicians and was the first to combine traditional tunes with classical genres. At the beginning of the century, while works by French composers (Ravel's *Bolero*, Bizet's *Carmen*, Lalo's *Symphonie Espagnole* and Chabrier's *España*) bore a pronounced Hispanic stamp, Spanish composers turned to national folklore and traditional themes: **Isaac Albéniz** (1860-1909) wrote *Iberia*, **Enrique Granados** (1867-1916) became famous for his *Goyescas* and **Joaquín Turina** (1888-1949) for his *Sevilla Symphony*. This popular vein culminated in works by **Manuel de Falla** (1876-1946) including Nights in the Gardens of Spain, *El amor brujo* and *The Three-Cornered Hat*.

Among the best-known classical guitar players of our day, **Andrés Segovia** (1894-1987), **Joaquín Rodrigo** (1901-99), famous for his *Concierto de Aranjuez*, and **Narciso Yepes** (b 1927), have shown that this most Spanish of instruments can interpret a wide variety of music. Another Spaniard, **Pablo Casals** (1876-1973), was possibly the greatest cellist of all time. Spain holds a leading position in the world of opera with singers such as Victoria de los Ángeles (1923-2005), Montserrat Caballé, Plácido Domingo, Alfredo Kraus (1927-99), José Carreras and Teresa Berganza.

THE COUNTRY TODAY

Spain is living testimony that countries *can* change profoundly and permanently: from a closed society where views were rarely expressed in public to one where people speak their minds; from economically backward to a dynamic economy that attracts immigrants; from a centralised government to a land that thrives on regional diversity; from a repressive state to one whose prosecutors relentlessly pursue human rights abuses worldwide. And yet all this transformation has come about while maintaining essential values and the Spanish way of life. Elsewhere, the penetration of worldwide brands and fashion and slang will make the visitor feel at times as if he has never left home. But when you are in Spain, it is clear that you are nowhere else.

Government and Administration

The Spanish Constitution, which was approved by referendum on 6 December 1978, defines the political status of the Spanish State as a constitutional monarchy in which sovereignty rests with the Spanish people. This political system can be broken down as follows: a **Head of State**, in the shape of the King, the **Cortes Generales** (Parliament), and a **Government**. The **Cortes** are elected by universal suffrage every four years. They are divided into two chambers: the **Congreso de los Diputados** and the **Senado**. The Government (*Gobierno*) performs executive functions and comprises a head of government (*Presidente del Gobierno* or prime minister), vice-presidents and ministers. Judicial power is an independent authority administered by judges and magistrates. The Supreme Court acts as the highest tribunal in the land.

The **Iberian Peninsula**, which is separated from the rest of Europe by the Pyrenees, is made up of continental Spain and Portugal. Spain covers an area of 504,750km2/194,960sq mi, including the Canary Islands and Balearic Islands, and is the fourth largest European country after Russia, the Ukraine and France. It has over 4,000km/2,500mi of coastline lapped by the waters of the Mediterranean and Atlantic. The country's population currently stands at just under 40,000,000.

Spain can be broken down into the following administrative divisions:

Autonomous communities: Spain is divided into 17 *comunidades autónomas*, in addition to two autonomous enclaves (Ceuta and Melilla). These communities may comprise a single province or several provinces. The leading political figure in these is the *Presidente de la Comunidad*, who is elected by universal suffrage every four years. The transfer of decision-making to autonomous bodies has yet to be fully achieved; however, the system of autonomy developed in Spain is one of the most advanced in Europe.

Provinces: The need for greater administrative efficiency led the governments under Isabel II (19C) to establish an initial division of the country into provinces. At present, Spain has 50 provinces.

Municipalities: This is the smallest territorial division, comprising a town council (*ayuntamiento*) headed by a mayor (*alcalde*).

Given the new adminstrative system now operating within Spain, communities and municipalities are better able to administer their territory.

A Way of Life

Whenever foreigners conjure up an image of Spain, their thoughts inevitably turn to a leisurely lifestyle, plentiful sunshine, noisy and lively towns and cities, and an extroverted, friendly peo-

J. Malburet/MICHELIN

Plaza Mayor, Madrid

ple whose daily timetable is impossible to comprehend!

Yet, irrespective of the crazy rhythms imposed by the demands of modern life, the Spanish always attempt to extract the very maximum from life; the maxim that most applies to them is that of having to work to live rather than living for work.

Despite the differences that exist between the north and south, the coast and inland areas, and towns and cities, it can be said that a common bond exists among all Spaniards in the manner in which they approach life.

LIFE IN THE STREET

There's no doubt that the excellent climate enjoyed by most parts of the country is one of the main reasons for the Spaniards' "passion" for living outdoors; there are of course others, of lesser or equal importance. Spain is a country of informal get-togethers and social gatherings, in bars, cafés, restaurants, at work, and of chance meetings of a couple of friends – any excuse is good enough to indulge in a friendly chat or animated discussion. This affection for going out as a group, meeting friends for dinner, or enjoying an aperitif or drink, is to the Spanish a sign of identity, irrespective of their age or social standing. Nor is it uncommon for Spaniards to have a relaxed drink with friends or colleagues before heading home after a long day's work.

DAILY SCHEDULE

The daily schedule of the Spanish is completely different from that of the rest of Europe and as such is the major characteristic that distinguishes the country from its European neighbours. Spaniards don't usually have lunch before 2pm or 2.30pm, or dinner before 9.30pm, a custom that results in long mornings and afternoons and provides ample time for them to indulge in their passion for a leisurely stroll, shopping or meeting up for a snack with friends and work acquaintances.

TAPAS AND APERITIF TIME

This gastronomic pastime is one of the most deeply rooted traditions in Spain, with youngsters, couples and entire families heading for bars to *tapear*, either standing at the counter or, if time allows, sitting down on a café terrace. An aperitif can be a frugal affair, although by ordering a number of tapas you can quite easily create an alternative to lunch or dinner.

These traditional appetisers come in many guises, ranging from the small tapa itself to larger portions known as a *media ración* or *ración*. Choose a *media ración* of *manchego* cheese or Jabugo cured ham, a *ración* of chorizo sausage, or a selection of vegetarian, fish, seafood or meat dishes – washed down perhaps with a glass of draught beer (*una caña*) or a glass of fino sherry

B. Pérousse/MICHELIN

Las Ramblas, Barcelona

(*una copa de fino*). Every region has its own specialities and its own way of presenting tapas, yet whether you're in the Basque country, Andalucía or in the middle of the Meseta, tapas are appreciated the length and breadth of the country.

BARS

There are literally tens of thousands of bars in Spain, including in the smallest and most remote hamlets and villages. They act as a focal point for locals, who congregate here with friends or family in the evening and at weekends. During the afternoon and early evening in smaller towns and villages you're bound to come across locals playing cards or indulging in a game of dominoes over a coffee or something stronger. The mornings are busy in bars as well, with regulars stopping by for a pastry and coffee for breakfast.

TERRACES

With the onset of fine weather, terraces spring up across Spain – outside restaurants, cafés, bars and ice-cream parlours, on pavements and patios and in gardens and narrow alleyways. During the warmer months, it is pleasant at any time of day to take the weight off your feet for a short while and watch the world go by in front of your table.
In summer, many of the most crowded bars and clubs, particularly those by the sea, provide outdoor terraces for their customers.

BEACH BARS

These typical features of resorts along the Spanish coast come in various guises, ranging from the cheap and cheerful to the expensive and luxurious. These *chiringuitos*, as they are known, have grown in popularity, particularly given that customers can enjoy a drink or have a meal wearing only their swim suits. In the more popular tourist areas they have become a meeting-point for locals and visitors alike, with some also open for dinner.

NIGHTLIFE

The lively character of Spanish towns and cities and summer resorts is often a cause of great surprise to visitors. Nowadays, the choice of venues is often overwhelming, with something to suit every budget and taste: quiet cafés for a drink and a chat with friends; lively bars packed to the rafters, with dance floors and music played at full volume; clubs offering a variety of shows; and nightclubs ranging from holes-in-the-wall to mega-venues where the pace doesn't stop until late the next morning. On Thursday and Friday nights and on weekends, as well as in summer and during holidays, the action is almost constant, with nightclubbers migrating from one club or bar to the next – don't be surprised if you get stuck in a traffic jam at three or four in the morning! An example of this is on the paseo de la Castellana, in Madrid, with its numerous outdoor bars open until the wee hours.

THE SIESTA

Although the demands of modern life prevent most people from perpetuating this healthy custom, most Spaniards long to have an afternoon nap and will make sure that they take a restorative siesta on weekends and when they're on holiday. Although less common nowadays, those Spaniards whose work schedule allows them three hours off from 2 to 5pm will try to make it home for lunch and a short sleep.

THE FAMILY

In line with other Latin countries, the family remains the bedrock of Spanish life, and is a determining factor in the behaviour and many of the habits of Spanish society at large. Without a solid family base, it would be hard to understand how a country with a high rate of unemployment and one in which children continue to live with their parents until their late-20s and even early-30s could prosper without too many problems. It should also be added that numerous Spanish celebrations and fiestas are based upon these close family ties.

THE WORK ETHIC

Those foreigners who have chosen to live in Spain soon realise that the old image of Spain as a country where very little work is done – a view perpetuated by the country's way of life and daily schedule, and the Spaniards' well-documented liking for enjoying themselves to the full – is far removed from modern reality.

Nowadays, the work ethic in Spain is similar to that in any other European country. Visitors may wonder how this is possible, given the unusual lifestyle. The answer is simple: the Spanish sleep less. Working hours are little different from those in the rest of Europe, but from an early age the Spanish are brought up used to sleeping less during the week and trying to catch up on lost sleep on the weekend.

Traditions and Folklore

Spain has kept alive its old traditions, as can be witnessed by the huge number of fiestas fervently celebrated around the country throughout the year. These unique and varied outpourings of religious sentiment and joy are a clear demonstration of Spain's rich cultural heritage and diversity.

A LAND OF FIESTAS AND TRADITIONS

Numerous fiestas are celebrated across Spain. Unbridled joy, pomp and ceremony, and a sense of theatre are just some of the characteristics associated with these traditional aspects of Spanish life.

A detailed list of major festivals in Spain can be found in the Planning Your Trip section of this guide.

Major festivals

To a greater or lesser degree, every Spanish town and city celebrates one main festival every year, normally in honour of its patron saint. These celebrations, many of which take place over the summer months, attract the entire local population, as well as inhabitants from outlying villages and rural areas. Typical events will include religious celebrations and processions, bullfights and bull-running, while many will attend just to indulge in animated discussions with friends until the early hours, or to enjoy rides on the fairground attractions that are traditional features of these events.

The most important festivals in Spain include:

Los Sanfermines de Pamplona, in honour of San Fermín (7 July), which starts with the setting-off of a huge firework rocket or *"chupinazo"*. For an entire week the city is the backdrop for a non-stop celebration that enjoys its most spectacular moments during the morning running of the bulls *(encierros)* and at the early-evening bullfights.

Las Fallas de Valencia, held in March in honour of San José, are renowned for

J. Malburet/MICHELIN

firework displays, culminating in the *"Nit del foc"* (Night of Fire), when the impressive *"ninots"* (pasteboard figures) dotted around the city are set alight.

Andalucían fiestas

Sevilla's April Fair is the most famous of these festivals, with a reputation that has stretched far beyond the borders of Spain. Andalucían fiestas are renowned for their exciting atmosphere, colourful costumes and spontaneous dance, with mountains of tapas consumed, accompanied by a glass or two of chilled dry sherry *(fino)* or *manzanilla*. The streets of the fairground area are a mass of colour as Andalucían women parade up and down on foot or on horseback dressed in the breathtaking flamenco dresses for which the region is famous.

Romerías

Romerías (pilgrimages) are an important aspect of religious life in Spain. Although each of these colourful events has its own specific characteristics, the basic principle is the same: a pilgrimage on foot, and occasionally on horseback, to a hermitage or shrine to venerate a statue. Usually, this religious peregrination will also include a procession, music, dancing and a festive meal in the countryside.

The pilgrimage to El Rocío (Huelva) is the most extravagant and popular romería in the whole of Spain, attracting around one million pilgrims every year.

Semana Santa

Holy Week processions are another vivid expression of the Spanish character. Numerous villages, towns and cities around the country participate in these outpourings of religious fervour, which see thousands of people taking to the streets to accompany the passion of Christ and the pain of his mother. Semana Santa tends to be a more sober affair in Castilla, and more festive in Andalucía, although across Spain the beauty of the statues (often works of art in their own right), the solemnity of the processions, some of which take place against a magnificent backdrop, and the fervour of those involved, create an atmosphere that will impress believers and non-believers alike.

Although Holy Week in Sevilla is undoubtedly the most famous, the processions in Valladolid, Málaga, Zamora and Cuenca are also worthy of particular note.

Carnival

Carnival celebrations in Spain are generally extravagant affairs where the imagination is stretched to its limits and joy is unbounded. They often involve many months of hard work during which performances are rehearsed and costumes made.

In the Canaries, particularly on Tenerife, Carnival is an important aspect of island tradition, involving a procession of floats and the election of the Carnival queen – events that bring the island to a standstill. The Carnival in Cádiz, which is known for its groups of musicians and folk dancers, is the liveliest on mainland Spain.

Christmas

The Christmas period in Spain is traditionally a time for family celebration. At home, where the Christmas tree and crib are essential decorative features, families congregate for dinner either on Christmas Eve or on Christmas Day, depending on the custom of their region. An equally traditional aspect of Christmas is the procession of the Kings: as a prelude to the most eagerly awaited night of the year, the Three Wise Men and their pages ride through the streets of towns and cities on the night of 5 January, handing out sweets to excited children lining their path.

Bullfighting festivals

It is impossible to broach the subject of fiestas without mentioning bullfighting – a subject that raises passions and criticism in equal measure. Bullfighting festivals are, indeed, just as much a part of Spanish culture as Holy Week processions; it is also true that the bullfighting world is indelibly linked with the major festivals around the country, and it is rare to find a town in which bullfighting is not present in some shape or form.

Very few cultural events are as regimented as a bullfight; consequently, a basic understanding of the various moves and stages of the contest is required to make any attempt to appreciate the spectacle. The bullfighting season runs from the spring to the autumn, and the most important festivals are those in Sevilla, held during the April Fair, and the San Isidro festival in Madrid.

FOLKLORE

Andalucía

Flamenco, derived from gypsy and Arab sources, is a befitting expression of the Andalucían soul. It is based on the *cante jondo*, or deep song, which describes the performer's profound emotions in ancient poetic phrases. The rhythm is given by hand-claps, heel-clicks and castanets. The **sevillana**, from Sevilla, is a more popular type of dance and song. Sevilla and Málaga are the best places to see **tablaos** or performances of Andalucían music. Flamenco and the sevillana owe much of their grace to the Andalucían costume of brilliantly coloured flounced dresses for women and close-fitting short jacketed suits, wide flat hats and heeled boots for men.

Aragón

No general rejoicing here goes without a **jota**, a bounding, leaping dance in which couples hop and whirl to the tunes of a *rondalla* (group of stringed instruments), stopping only for the occasional brief singing of a *copla* by a soloist.

Catalunya and the Comunidad Valenciana

The **sardana** dance is still very popular in Catalunya where it is performed in a circle in main squares on Sundays. The **Castells**, who form daring human pyramids, may be seen in festivals at El Vendrell and Valls.

In the Levante, the rich local costume notable for its colour and intricate embroidery is worn during lively, colourful festivals. Valencia's **Fallas** in March are a veritable institution which Alicante's **Fogueres** try to rival. Lastly, the *Moros y Cristianos* festivals – those of Alcoy are the best known – give a colourful replay of the confrontations between Moors and Christians during the Reconquest.

Galicia, Asturias and Cantabria

Romerías in Asturias and Galicia are always accompanied by the shrill tones of the **gaita**, a type of bagpipe, and sometimes by drums and castanets. The gaita is played during events in honour of cowherds, shepherds, sailors and others who work in the country's oldest occupations. The most typical festivals are those held in summer for *vaqueiros*, or cowherds, in Aristébano and others for shepherds near the Lago de Enol. Common dances in Galicia include the *muñeira* or dance of the miller's wife, the sword dance performed only by men, and the *redondela*. Bowls *(bolos)* is a very popular game.

País Vasco and Navarra

The Basque Country and Navarra have preserved many of their unusual traditions. Men dressed in white with red sashes and the famous red berets dance in a ring accompanied by **zortzikos** (songs), a **txistu** (flute) and a *tamboril*. The most solemn dance, the *aurresku*, is a chain dance performed by men after Mass on Sundays. The **espata-dantza**, or sword dance, recalls warrior times while others, like the spinners' dance or another in which brooms are used, represent daily tasks. The Basques love contests, such as tug-of-war, trunk cutting, stone lifting and pole throwing. But by far the most popular sport is *pelota*, played in different ways: with a

TURESPAÑA

The Castells forming a human pyramid in Valls

chistera, or wickerwork scoop, or with the very similar **cesta punta** in an enclosed three-walled court *(jai alai)*, or with a wooden bat or *pala* or, finally, simply with the hand, **a mano**. There is a famous pelota university at Markina in Vizcaya.

Castilla

Few regions in Spain are as mystical or have such sober customs as Castilla. Traditional dances include the **seguidilla** and the **paloteo**, also known as the **danza de palos**, which is accompanied by flute, tambourine, and sometimes by a bass drum or the most typical of Castilian instruments, the local reed-pipe, or **dulzaina**. Peasant costumes around Salamanca are richly embroidered with precious stones, silk thread and sequins.

Balearic Islands

Mallorca's traditional dances include the *copeo*, the *jota*, the *mateixes* and the *bolero*. Dances and festivals are accompanied by a *xeremía* (local bagpipes) and a tambourine. In Menorca, a festival dating back to medieval times and calling for about 100 horsemen in elegant costumes, is held at Ciutadella on Midsummer's Day. Popular dances in Ibiza have a poetical accompaniment to guide the performers' movements.

Canary Islands

The folklore of the Canaries shows influences from the Spanish mainland, Portugal and South America (the latter as a consequence of the strong links created by emigration); these in turn have become intertwined with local traditions. The **isa**, the **malagueña**, the *folía* and the *tajaraste* are the four best-known types of dance from the islands. The *timple* is a type of small guitar which is typical of the archipelago.

Food and Drink

Spanish food is distinctively Mediterranean: it is cooked with an olive oil base, seasoned with aromatic herbs and spiced with hot peppers. It nevertheless varies enormously from region to region. Among dishes served throughout the country are garlic soup, cocido (a type of stew accompanied by beans or chick-peas), omelettes with potatoes, like the famous tortilla, typical pork meats like chorizo (a kind of spicy sausage), savoury rice dishes and delicious lean serrano hams. Fish and seafood are also used in a great many dishes.

No description of Spanish food should be complete without mentioning the ubiquitous tapas – the hors d'œuvres which appear on the counters of most bars and cafés just before lunch and dinner. This often vast array of colourful appetisers comes in two different forms: *tapas* (small saucer-size amounts) or *raciones*, more substantial portions. A selection of two or three tapas or one or two raciones makes for a very pleasant lunch accompanied by a glass (*caña*) of draught beer.

The country is also renowned for its magnificent wines, which include famous appellations such as Rioja and Penedès, and the sherries of the Jerez region.

GALICIA

Galicia's cuisine owes its delicacy to the quality of its **seafood**: octopus, hake, gilthead, scallops (*vieiras*), mussels (*mejillones*), goose-barnacles (*percebes*), prawns (*gambas*), king prawns (*langostinos*) and mantis shrimps (*cigalas*). There is also el **caldo gallego**, a local soup, **lacón con grelos** (hand of pork with turnip tops) and another common traditional recipe, **pulpo gallego** (Galician-style octopus), often served as a tapa or ración. All these dishes may be accompanied by local wines such as red or white Ribeiro or white Albariño. The region's desserts include *tarta de Santiago*, an almond-flavoured tart, and *filloas*, a type of sweet fritter.

ASTURIAS AND CANTABRIA

In Asturias, fish and seafood are also important but the main speciality is a casserole dish called **fabada** made with white beans, pork, bacon and spicy sausages. As far as cakes and pastries are concerned, mention should be made of **sobaos**, delicious biscuits which originated in Cantabria and are cooked in oil. Cider is often drunk at meals.

PAÍS VASCO

Cooking in the Basque Country has been raised to the level of a fine art and requires laborious preparation. Meat is mostly served roasted, grilled or cooked in a sauce, while fish such as cod or hake is often accompanied by a green parsley sauce *(salsa verde)* or by peppers. *Chipirones en su tinta* is a dish of baby squid in their own ink. *Marmitako*, a typical fishing village dish, is composed of tuna fish, potatoes and hot red peppers, and is often served with a good *txacolí*, a tart white wine.

NAVARRA AND LA RIOJA

Navarra and La Rioja are the regions for game, excellent market-garden produce and the best Spanish wines, especially reds. The food is varied and refined, with partridge, quail and woodpigeon competing with trout for pride of place in local dishes. Navarra has noteworthy rosés and fruity white wines. Delicious Roncal cheese is made in the valleys from ewes' milk.

ARAGÓN

Aragón is the land of **chilindrón**, a stew made with meat or poultry and peppers, and of **ternasco** (roast kid or lamb). These dishes may be washed down with heavy red Cariñena wines.

TURESPAÑA

CATALUNYA

Catalunya has a typically Mediterranean cuisine. Look out in particular for *pan con tomate* (bread rubbed with a cut tomato and occasionally garlic and sprinkled with olive oil), red peppers cooked in oil, and wonderful fish dishes with a variety of sauces such as *all i oli* (crushed garlic and olive oil) and *samfaina* (tomatoes, peppers and aubergines).
Among pork meats are **butifarra** sausages, various kinds of slicing sausage and the *fuet* sausage from Vic. Dried fruit is used in a great many dishes or may be served at the end of a meal. The most widespread dessert is **crema catalana**, a kind of crème brûlée. Catalunya is also home to *cava*, a sparkling wine. Excellent light wines are made in the Empordà region, fruity whites in Penedès and reds in Priorato.

CASTILLA AND EXTREMADURA

Castilian specialities from local produce include roast lamb **(cordero asado)**, suckling-pig (**cochinillo tostón** or **tostado**) and the ubiquitous **cocido**, all of which may be accompanied by a light fresh Valdepeñas red.

GAZPACHO

On a gastronomic level, Andalucía is renowned mainly for its fried fish dishes, and also its gazpacho, a cold soup which is particularly refreshing and tasty during the hot summer months.

Ingredients: Tomatoes, peppers (red or green), cucumber, garlic, olive oil vinegar, seasoning, breadcrumbs and water.

Method would be to add the diced peppers and tomatoes and the breadcrumbs and pound by hand until well mixed – but these days, most people liquidise everything with the help of a food processor! Slowly pour the oil onto the mixture stirring all the time. Leave to soak for a while, then add some cold water and strain the mixture through a sieve. Add a little vinegar and seasoning. Serve well chilled, with croutons, diced cucumber, red peppers and raw onion sprinkled on top.

PAELLA VALENCIANA

Paella is best prepared in a wide, shallow pan known as a *paellera*. It is essentially a dish for a festive occasion with family or friends, and can take a variety of forms. The following recipe is for a mixed meat and seafood paella:

Ingredients (serves 4):
small cup of olive oil
2 cloves of garlic (crushed)
1 green pepper (finely sliced)
half a cup of tomato purée
100g chicken (diced into medium-sized pieces)
100g pork (diced into medium-sized pieces)
250g arborio rice
1 tsp/half a dozen strands of saffron
salt and pepper
500ml fish stock
500ml chicken stock
100g clams
100g mussels
100g prawns
50g squid (cut into thin slices)
50g sweet red peppers (cut into thin slices)

Method: Heat the olive oil in a large frying pan or paella dish. Add the garlic and green peppers and fry for 2min. Add the chicken, pork and squid and cook, stirring, for a further 5min. Add the rice, saffron and tomato purée, followed immediately by the fish and chicken stock and salt and pepper. Cook for 10min, stirring occasionally. Once the rice is almost cooked, add the mussels, clams, prawns, sweet red peppers and green peas. Cook for a further 3-5min or until shellfish are cooked through. Garnish with slices of lemon.

Que aproveche! Enjoy!

Rueda wines from the province of southern Valladolid are fresh fruity whites, while those from Ribera del Duero are generally acidic reds.
Castilla is also known for its cheeses, with a ewe's milk speciality from Burgos and many varieties of *manchego*, Spain's best-known cheese. Among local sweets are the famous marzipans *(mazapán)* from Toledo.
Extremadura enjoys an excellent reputation for its hams, such as those from Guijuelo (Salamanca) and Montánchez (Cáceres).

LEVANTE

The Levante is the kingdom of rice dishes, including the famous **paella** which is cooked with a saffron rice base and chicken, pork, squid, mussels, shrimps and king prawns. As for sweets, **turrón** (made of almonds and honey or castor sugar, rather like nougat) is a Levantine speciality.

BALEARIC ISLANDS

Soups are specialities in the Balearics; Mallorca's *mallorquina* has bread, leeks and garlic, while other soups are made with fish. **Tumbet** is a well-known casserole of potatoes, onions, tomatoes, courgettes and peppers. **Sobrasada**, a spicy sausage, flavours many local dishes. **Cocas**, pastries with sweet or savoury fillings, and **ensaimadas**, light spiral rolls, make delicious desserts.

ANDALUCÍA

The region's best-known dish is **gazpacho**, a cold cucumber and tomato soup made with oil and vinegar and flavoured with garlic. Andalucíans love their food fried, especially fish and seafood. Pigs are reared in the Sierra Nevada and Sierra de Aracena for the exquisite *serrano* ham. Among local desserts, *tocino de cielo* is as sweet as an Oriental pastry.
The region is especially well known for its dessert wines: the famous **Jerez** or sherries *(see JEREZ DE LA FRONTERA)*, **Montilla-Moriles** and **Málaga.**

The Mezquita, Córdoba
B. Kaufmann/MICHELIN

DISCOVERING SPAIN

AGUILAR DE CAMPOO

POPULATION: 7,594.

MICHELIN MAP 575 D 17 – CASTILLA Y LEÓN (PALENCIA)

The Castillo de Aguilar stands on a desolate outcrop typical of this part of the Meseta. Below the castle stretches the old town, displaying its medieval heritage in gateways, walls and mansions adorned with coats of arms.

- **Information:** *Plaza de España 30, ☎979 12 36 41.*
- **Orient Yourself:** Aguilar is in northern Spain, inland from the coast and west of the Basque region.
- **Don't Miss:** A drive to the Pico de Tres Mares.
- **Organizing Your Time:** Take an hour or so before seeing the sourroundings.
- **Also See:** BURGOS, PALENCIA, The WAY OF ST JAMES, SANTANDER and COSTA DE CANTABRIA

Worth a Visit

Colegiata de San Miguel

Guided tour (1hr) mid-Jun–mid-Oct 10.30am–1.30pm and 3–6pm. Rest of the year noon–1.30pm and 5–8pm. 1.50 €. ☎979 12 22 31.

This Gothic church with Romanesque elements is at an end of the long **Plaza de España.** Two fine 16C tombs bear statues of the Marquessses of Aguilar at prayer. In the north apsidiole is the realistically sculpted tomb of archpriest García González.

Monasterio de Santa María la Real

On the edge of town towards Cervera de Pisuerga. Open Mon-Fri 4-7pm; weekends and public hols 10.30am-2pm and 4.30-7.30pm; summer daily 10.30am-2pm and 4-8pm. 1.80€ (museum). ☎616 99 46 51.

This fine, thoroughly restored transitional (12C-13C) monastery houses a Romanesque interpretation centre.

Tours

To the Pico de Tres Mares Via Reinosa *66km/41mi N*

Cross a vast plain and ascend the south face of the Cordillera Cantábrica.

Follow the A 67.

Cervatosa

The **antigua colegiata**★, a Romanesque former collegiate church, bears imaginative carved **decoration**★. The portal tympanum bears a meticulous openwork design. There is a frieze of lions while varied figures decorate the modillions. Inside are harmonious blind arcades. The carving on the capitals and consoles supporting the arch ribs is dense and sophisticated with lions, eagles, plant motifs and strapwork. The late 14C nave was raised with intersecting rib vaulting. *Ask for the key next door (Don Julio). ☎942 75 50 49.*

Continue, then turn off to the right.

Retortillo

Only an oven-vaulted apse and arch with two finely carved capitals illustrating warriors remain of a small Romanesque **church**. Adjacent are the ruins of a villa of the Roman city of **Julióbriga**.

Return to the A 67.

Reinosa

The nearby Embalse del Ebro (a reservoir) and the Alto Campoo ski resort make this a growing tourist centre.

From Reinosa, take the CA 183 to the Pico de Tres Mares (27km/17mi).

Pico de Tres Mares★★★

On the way, paths from Fontibre lead to a greenish pool, the **source of the Ebro**

(Fuente del Ebro), Spain's largest river, at an altitude of 881m/2 890ft.

To the Pico de Tres Mares by chairlift. Rivers flow from the peak (2 175m/7 136ft) to three seas (*mares* in Spanish), hence its name. The Híjar joins the Ebro to reach the Mediterranean; the Pisuerga flows into the Duero to the Atlantic. The Nansa flows north into the Cantabrian sea. At the crest is a splendid **panorama**★★★: to the north, of the Nansa and the Embalse de la Cohilla (Cohilla Dam) below Monte Cueto (1 517m/4 977ft), and circling right, the Embalse del Ebro, the Sierra de Peña Labra, the Embalse de Cervera de Pisuerga and the Montes de León; due west, the Picos de Europa including 2 618m/8 589ft Peña Vieja, and Peña Sagra (2 042m/6 699ft). In the foreground is the eroded mass of the Peña Labra (2 006m/6 581ft).

PARC NACIONAL D'AIGÜESTORTES I ESTANY DE SANT MAURICI★★

MICHELIN MAP 574 E 32-33 –
LOCAL MAP SEE PIRINEOS CATALANES – CATALUNYA (LLEIDA)

This national park in the Catalan Pyrenees abounds in falls and rushing streams. Twisting waterways—aigües tortes—wind between mossy meadows and wooded slopes. Glaciers created the harsh beauty of U-shaped valleys, high mountain lakes, and snow-covered peaks. Vegetation includes firs and Scots pines. Birch and beech trees provide a stunning splash of colour in autumn.

- **Information:** *Centro del Parque de Boí: Calle de los Graieres 2, ☎973 69 61 89; Centro del Parque de Espot: Prat del Guarda 4, ☎973 62 40 36.*
- **Orient Yourself:** The park is just west of Andorra and south of France.
- **Don't Miss:** A forest walk up to grand panoramas.
- **Organizing Your Time:** Allow a day for the park, with hikes.
- **Also See:** PIRINEOS CATALANES and PIRINEOS ARAGONESES

Worth a Visit

The park's 14 119ha/34 888 acres, between altitudes of 1 500m/4 900ft and 3 000m/900ft, are mainly granite and slate.

Both entries (Espot, to the east, and Boí, to the west) have parking areas.

Take an organised excursion by four-wheel drive (private vehicles are prohibited). Paths are well-signposted, and there are four mountain refuges.

Head first for the Casa del Parque Nacional L'Estudi in Boí or the Casa del Parque Nacional in Espot. Both open Jun-Sep 9am-1pm and 3.30-6.45pm; Oct-May 9am-2pm and 3.30-5.45pm; Sun and public hols

B. Brillion/MICHELIN

A landscape dominated by mountains

9am–2pm. Closed 1 and 6 Jan and 25-26 Dec. Tours 6.70€ (half-day); 13.30€ (full-day); 23.20€ (with hikes) 973 69 61 89.

Lago de Sant Maurici
Reached by a tarmac road from Espot. The lake, surrounded by forest, reflects the peaks of the Sierra dels Encantats.

Portarró d'Espot
3hr there and back on foot from the Estany de Sant Maurici. The path crosses the Sant Nicolau Valley. At Redó lake, admire the splendid **panoramas★★**.

Estany Gran
3hr there and back on foot from Sant Maurici lake. Beside the lake, mountain streams form impressive waterfalls.

Estany Negre
5hr there and back on foot from Espot; 4hr from Sant Maurici lake. Cross the stunning Peguera Valley to Estany Negre (Black Lake), hemmed in by awesome summits.

Aigüestortes
Western section. The entry road leads to Aigüestortes where a stream winds through rich pastures. Hike to Estany Llong *(3hr there and back)*.

ALACANT/ALICANTE★

POPULATION: 275 111.
MICHELIN MAP 577 Q 28 (TOWN PLAN) – MAP 123 COSTA BLANCA – 110KM/69MI FROM CARTAGENA – COMUNIDAD VALENCIANA (ALICANTE)

The Greeks called Alicante *Akra Leuka* (white citadel), the Romans *Lucentum* (city of light). It combines provincial calm with the bustle of tourism.

- **Information:** *Rambla de Méndez Núñez 23, 96 520 00 00.*
- **Orient Yourself:** Alicante is the midpoint of Spain's Mediterranean coast.
- **Don't Miss:** A stroll along the Explanada by the harbour.
- **Organizing Your Time:** Start with a view from the Castillo de Santa Bárbara.
- **Especially for Kids:** Kids love castles; the Castillo de Santa Bárbara is a must.
- **Also See:** COSTA BLANCA and MURCIA (81km/51mi SW).

Special Features

OLD TOWN
Follow the route marked on the town plan

Explanada de España★
The most pleasant promenade in the region, running past the marina, is shaded by magnificent palms. Sunday concerts are held on the bandstand.

Catedral de San Nicolás
Open 7.30am-12.30pm (noon in winter) and 5.30-7.30pm (8.30pm in winter); Sun and public hols, 8.30am-1.30pm and 5.30-8.30pm. 96 521 26 62. The 17C building on the site of a mosque – the city was only reconquered in 1296 – has a well-proportioned cupola, 45m/15ft high, over a Herreran nave. On calle Labradores, with its terraces, are the 18C Palacio Maisonnave, no. 9 (now the

Capital of the Costa Blanca
Because of its mild climate and proximity to vast beaches (El Postiguet, La Albufereta and San Juan), Alicante has developed into the tourist capital of the Costa Blanca *(see COSTA BLANCA)*, with seaside resorts such as Santa Pola, Guardamar del Segura, Torrevieja, and Campoamor springing up all along the southern part of this flat, sandy coastline.

Address Book

For coin ranges, see the Legend on the cover flap.

WHERE TO EAT

La Taberna del Gourmet
San Fernando 10 – ☎96 520 42 33. Near the seafront promenade, the Taberna del Gourmet specializes in rice dishes, ham, seafood, sandwiches and an array of tapas along the bar. Nautical decor.

La Goleta
Paseo Explanada de España 8 – ☎965 21 43 92 – .On a busy street near the marina, this restaurant has a pleasant covered terrace and marine decor inside. It offers regional sausages, fried seafood, faultless paella, and good homemade desserts.

TAPAS

Piripi
Oscar Esplá 30 – ☎96 522 79 40 – – 7.50€. Enjoy tapas *and* regional specialties, in the right combination of variety and quality.

WHERE TO STAY

Residencia La Milagrosa
Villavieja 8 – ☎96 521 69 18 – 29 rooms. A basic pensión frequented by the young and worldly. The rooms, some sharing baths, are bright and uncluttered; the terrace is huge and flower-filled. Try for a room with a view of picturesque plaza de Santa María.

Hostal Les Monges Palace
San Agustín 4 – ☎96 521 50 46 – www.lesmonges.net P *– 22 rooms.* An excellent location in the heart of old Alicante, with a standard not normally found in a pensión. Features of this charming 18C building include a marble staircase and large mirrors and windows.

TAKING A BREAK

Horchateria Azul
Calderón de la Barca – Open Mon-Sat 9am-1pm and 4pm-midnight.
A tiny shop without pretension, specialising in horchata, a drink made from barley and almonds. Friendly staff.

NIGHTLIFE

Barrio del Carmen
Alicante's old quarter is pleasant by day, and after 11pm, the whole district is transformed into one huge disco.

Puerto de Alicante
One of the liveliest areas on summer nights. On one side are locales with Latin and Spanish rhythms, on the other the shops and cafés and terraces of the Panoramis complex.

SHOPPING

Mercado Central
Av. Alfonso X El Sabio – Open 6am-1pm. This large covered market sells meat on the first floor and fish in the basement.

FIESTAS

Alicante celebrates its **fiestas del "foc"** (festival of fire) at midnight on 24 June, when giant pasteboard figures are set alight around the city, and the sky is lit up by a huge firework display.

Municipal Archives); and an 18C mansion, no. 14, now a cultural centre.

Ayuntamiento (Town Hall)

This imposing 18C palace of golden stone, with two tiers of balconies, is flanked by two towers. Visit the Rococo **capilla** (chapel) with *azulejos* from Manises, and reception rooms with blue silk hangings. *Open 9am-2pm. Closed Sun and public hols. ☎ 965 14 91 10.*

Nearby on calle Gravina is the early 18C palace of the Museo de Bellas Artes Gravina (art museum), with 16-19C works. *Open 10am-2pm and 4-8pm; May-Sep 10am-2pm and 5-9pm; Sun and public hols 10am-2pm. Closed Mon. ☎ 96 514 67 80.*

Iglesia de Santa María

Open 10.30am-1pm and 6-7.30pm. ☎96 521 60 26. The church is in a square below Santa Bárbara Castle. The 18C Baroque **façade**★ has wreathed columns, pillars and breaks in its cornices. Once a mosque, it altered in the 17C when Churrigueresque decoration was added. Note the graceful Renaissance marble fonts and a painting of John the Baptist and John the Apostle by Rodrigo de Osuna the Younger.

Museo de la Asegurada★

Closed for restoration. ☎96 514 07 68. On the same plaza, in a 17C granary, this museum exhibits 20C painting and sculpture donated by sculptor Eugenio Sempere. There are works by artists both Spanish (Miró, Picasso, Gargallo, Tàpies and Dalí) and foreign (Vasarely, Braque, Chagall and Kandinsky).

Castillo de Santa Bárbara

Ascend by lift and walk down, either all the way (good views) or to the halfway stop. Open Oct-Mar, 9am-7pm; Apr-Sep, 10am-8pm; last admission 30min before closing. 3€ by lift, no charge to drive or walk up. ☎965 26 31 31.
This fortress atop Benacantil hill dates from the 9C in Muslim times, though outbuildings were raised in the 16C.

Alacant – Alicante

Alfonso X el Sabio Av. de	AY		Gabriel Miró Pl. de	AZ	31	Mendez Núñez Rambla	AYZ	
Ayuntamiento Pl. del	BY	8	Jijona Av. de	AY	33	Montañeta Pl. de la	AZ	41
Calvo Sotelo Pl.	AZ	10	Jovellanos Av. de	BY	35	Poeta Carmelo Calvo Av.	AY	47
Castaños	AYZ	14	Juan Bautista Lafora Av. de	BY	36	Puerta del Mar Pl.	BZ	48
Constitución Av. de la	AY	21	López Torregrosa	AY	37	Rafael Altamira	BZ	50
Elche Portal de	AZ	28	Manero Mollá	AZ	39	Ramiro Pas.	BY	51
			Mayor	BYZ		San Fernando	ABZ	53
						Teatro Principal	AY	58

Ayuntamiento	BY	H	Colección de Arte del s. XX. Museo de La Asegurada	BY	M1	MUBAG (Museo de Bellas Artes Gravina)	BY	M2v
Catedral de San Nicolás	BY	A						

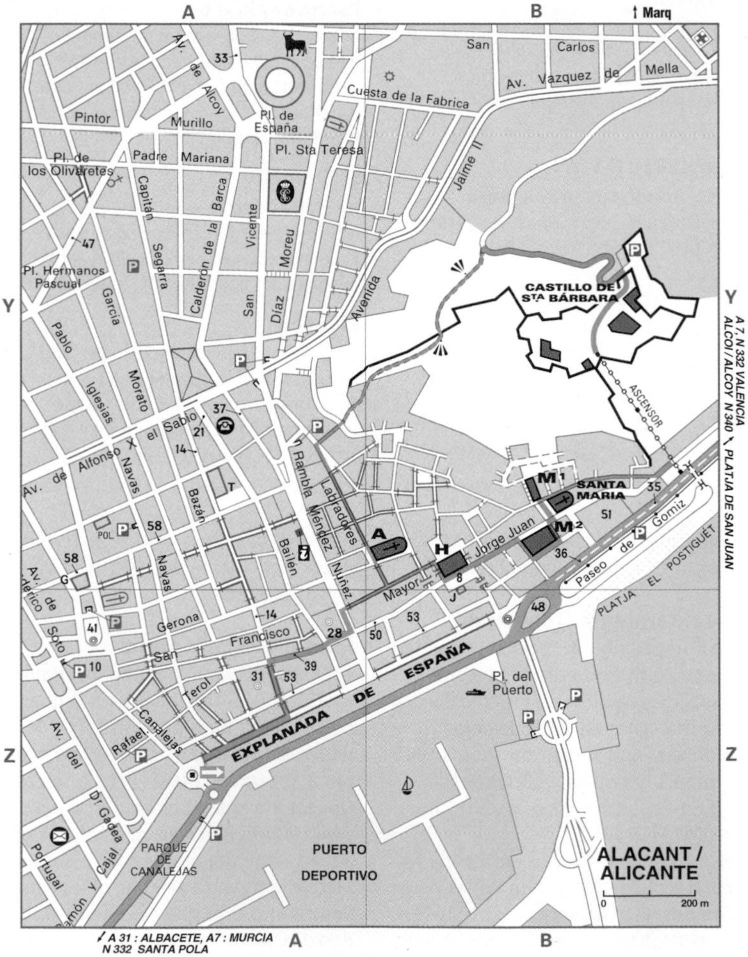

View of the city from the Castillo de Santa Bárbara

The **Fundación Capa sculpture collection** (mainly by 19 and 20C Spanish artists) is shown in the open and in three halls of the castle. *Open Tue-Sat 10am-2pm and 4-7pm; Apr-Sep 10am-2pm and 5-8pm; Sun & public hols 10am-3pm; last admission 30 min before closing. Closed Mon, 1 Jan, 24 Jun and25 Dec. 965 15 29 69.*

The Plaza de la Torreta is surrounded by the oldest buildings. A platform commands a fine **view★** of the harbour and town. The 16C section is at the halfway stop on the lift; the 17C perimeter is lower down. A footpath leads into the medieval streets and tiny squares of the working-class Santa Cruz quarter.

Worth a Visit

MARQ (Museo Arqueológico Provincial de Alicante)★★

Open 10am-7pm; Sun and public hols 10am-8pm. Closed Mon. 3€. 96 514 90 00.

MARQ opens archaeology to all, with a magnificent presentation focused on the ancients of this area.

The museum is orgnized into large halls (Prehistory, Iberian, Roman, Middle Ages, and Modern) around a space devoted to archaeology itself. Here you can get right into excavations in a cave, a church, and an underwater site.

Excursions

ELX/ELCHE★

24km/15mi SW. Pl. del Parc 3, 03202 Elx, 96 545 27 47.

Elche (Elx in Valencian) lies along the Vinalopó river. The **Dama de Elche** (4C BC), a masterpiece of Iberian art now in the Museo Arqueológico de Madrid *(see Art and Architecture)*, was discovered in **La Alcudia** *(2km/1.2mi S, see below)*. **El Misteri** is a medieval verse drama with an all-male cast. It recounts the Dormition, Assumption and Coronation of the Virgin. It is played in the Basílica de Santa María on 14 and 15 August, and is on UNESCO's Oral and Intangible Heritage of Humanity list.

El Palmeral★★ (Palm Grove) – The groves, planted by the Phoenicians and expanded by the Arabs, are the largest in Europe with more than 200 000 trees, and are a UNESCO World Heritage Site. The palms flourish with the aid of a remarkable irrigation system. Female trees produce dates, and the fronds from the male trees are used in Palm Sunday processions and handicrafts.

Huerta del Cura★★ – *Open May-Sep daily 10am-6pm. Rest of the year daily 10am-5pm. 5€. 96 545 19 36.*

This delightful garden of Mediterranean and subtropical plants lies under magnificent palm trees; one, with seven trunks, is said to be 160 years old.

Parque Municipal★ – A well-tended garden covered with palm trees.

Museo Arqueológico y de Historia de Elche (MAHE) – *Open May–Nov, noon-9pm. Rest of year 10am-1.30pm and 4-8pm; 96 545 36 03.*
The museum is in the Moorish Palacio de Altamira. The archaeological section traces Elche from its origins to the Visigoth era. Notable are sculpture and ceramics from the Iberian period and the *Venus of Illicis*, a delicately carved white marble Roman sculpture.
Basílica de Santa María – This monumental 17-18C Baroque basilica with a beautiful portal by Nicolás de Bussi is the setting for the annual mystery play. View the palm groves from the tower. Nearby are the 17-18C Almohad tower, **La Calaforra**, and the Baños árabes.
Baños árabes – *Access by a side door of the Convento de la Mercè. Open 10am-1pm and 4.30-8.30pm. Closed Mon. 96 545 14 03.*
A well-prepared exhibition details the culture of the bath in the 12C.
La Alcudia: archaeological site and museum – *2km/1.2mi S. Open 10am-5pm; summer 10am-2pm and 4-8pm. Sun and public hols 10am-2pm. Closed Mon. 96 661 15 06.*
The remains and museum reveal the story of a city from the Neolithic period to its decline in Visigoth times.

WHERE TO EAT

Datil de Oro – *Paseo de la Estación – 96 545 34 15 – www.datildeoro.com* – . Placed amid the palms of the Parque Municipal, with large conservatory dining rooms the better to enjoy the surrounding vegetation. Assorted menus include choices such as *arroz con costra* (crusted rice), the specialty.

WHERE TO STAY

Huerto del Cura – *Porta de la Morera 14 – Elche – 96 661 00 11 – www.huertodelcura.com* – – *12€.* Marvelous location right in a palm grove, opposite the famous Huerto del Cura. Bungalow-style rooms combine complete comfort with attention to all details.

TOUR INLAND *176km/110mi N.*

Take the N 340. In San Juan, then the Alcoi road and then turn right.

Cuevas de Canalobre

Guided tours (40min), 11am-5.50pm; 21 Jun-30 Sep and during Holy Week, 10.30am-7.50pm. Closed 1 Jan and 25 Dec. 4 €. 96 569 92 50.
The caves are at 700m/2 300ft up Mount Cabezón de Oro, with candelabra *(canalobre)* formations.

Return to the N 340.

Cross dry country of figs and carobs.

Xixona/Jijona

The speciality of this town is *turrón*, an almond-honey sweet. Visit a **museum** (El Lobo) and factories.
Beyond Xixona the road twists up through almond terraces to the **Puerto de la Carrasqueta**★ (1 024m/3 360ft), a pass with a view toward Alicante.

Alcoi/Alcoy

Alcoi is an industrial town in a mountain setting. At the end of April, the colourful **Moors and Christians** (Moros y Cristianos) **festivals** celebrate a Christian victory in 1276.

Take the CV 795 to Barxell, then follow the CV 794.

Bocairent

The church in this hilltop market village has an interesting **Museo Parroquial** (Parish Museum) with works by **Juan de Juanes** (1523-79) – who died here – and his school, and a 14C Last Supper by Marcial de Sax.
Guided tours (45min) by appointment. Open Sun and public hols from 12.30pm. 1.80 €. 96 235 00 62 .

Take the CV81.

Villena

Castillo la Atalaya – *Guided tours 10.30am-1pm every 30min; Sat-Sun and public hols 11am-1.30pm. 96 580 38 04 (Turismo).*
This castle of Arabic origin dominates its former feudal domain. Among its

owners have been famed men of letters: **Don Juan Manuel** in the 14C, and Prince **Henry of of Aragon** (**Marqués de Villena,** 1384-1434), poet and magic fan. Its keep survives, with circular towers in the corners, and large Homenaje (homage) tower (upper section 15C). Fine views from the walls.

Iglesia de Santiago – *Open 11am-1pm; Sun and public hols 10am-noon. ☎ 96 580 38 04.*

This Gothic-Renaissance church (14-17C) with notable bell tower stands near the town hall. Note unusual **spiral pillars★** supporting Gothic vaults, and a Renaissance-style baptismal font.

Museo Arqueológico (Archaeological Museum) – *Open Tue-Fri, 10am-2pm and 5-8pm; Sat-Sun and public hols, 11am-2pm. Closed Mon, 1 and 6 Jan, 1 May, 8 Sep and 25 Dec. ☎96 580 11 50 (ext. 769).*

The museum, in the town hall *(Palacio Municipal*, fine Renaissance façade and patio), displays solid gold from the Bronze Age (1500-1000 BC). The outstanding **Villena Treasure★★** includes jewellery and gourds decorated with sea urchin shell patterns.

▶ *Return to Alicante on the A 31.*

ALBACETE

POPULATION: 135 889.

MICHELIN MAP 576 O-P 24 – CASTILLA LA MANCHA (ALBACETE)

Albacete (from *Al Basite*, "plain" in Arabic), capital of Lower La Mancha, stands on a dry plateau that juts into the fertile east. Heritage structures stand alongside modern buildings and residential districts.

- **Information:** *Tinte 2, Edificio Posada del Rosario, ☎96 758 05 22.*
- **Orient Yourself:** The A 35 and A 30, lead to Valencia (NE) and Murcia (SE); the A 32 runs SW to Andalucía.
- **Don't Miss:** Stroll Pasaje de Lodares for a taste of old Albacete.
- **Organizing Your Time:** Spend a morning, then see caves and castles nearby.
- **Also See:** CUENCA (144km/90mi N), MURCIA (147km/92mi SE) and ALACANT/ALICANTE (168km/105mi SE).

Worth a Visit

Museo de Albacete

Open Tue-Sat 10am-2pm and 4.30-7pm. Sun and public hols, 9am-2pm. Closed Mon, 1 Jan, Maundy Thu, Good Fri and 25 Dec. 1.20 € (no charge Sat afternoon and hols). ☎96 722 83 07.

This modern building is in Abelardo Sánchez park. Its Fine Arts Museum (Museo de Bellas Artes) collects works of landscape artist Benjamín Palencia (1900-80). The Joaquín Sánchez Jiménez Archaeology Museum displays Iberian sculptures (Room 6) including the **sphinx of Haches**, the **hind of Caudete**, and the lion from Bienservida, and above all **Roman dolls with movable joints★** (Room 9).

Cathedral

Construction began in the late 16C. The façade and side doorway are additions. Three naves are separated by large Ionic columns. Mannerist paintings decorate the sacristy. The Capilla de la Virgen de los Llanos is a fine chapel dedicated to the Virgin of the Plains, the city's patron. The Renaissance altarpiece is by the Maestro de Albacete.

Pasaje de Lodares

This narrow conservatory passageway, lined by shops and homes, links calle Mayor with calle del Tinte. It is emblematic of Albacete. Decorative columns and allegorical figures proliferate.

Address Book

WHERE TO STAY & EAT

Hotel-Restaurante Juanito – *Mártires 15 – La Roda – 36km/22.5mi NW of Albacete on the A 31 – ☎96 754 80 41 – www.hoteljuanito.com – – 29 rooms – 3 € – Restaurant 20€.* Forerunner of the roadside restaurant of the same name, this re-done hotel is reasonably priced with comfortable, well-decorated rooms. The restaurant serves La Mancha specialities prepared with an innovative touch.

SHOPPING

Since Moorish times, Albacete has been famous for the manufacture of knives. Nowadays, the range of knives and penknives is vast, with a huge choice in terms of size, shape and decoration.

Excursions

Alarcón★

103km/65mi NW. Take the A 31 to Honrubia, then turn right onto the A 3.
Alarcón, named for Alaric, its Visigothic founder, rises above a loop of the Júcar river. The 13C-14C castle is now a parador. The **location**★★★ made the fortress practically impregnable. It follows a triangular plan, with a double protective enclosure. **Don Juan Manuel** (1284-1348) wrote many of his cautionary tales while living there.

Amid the whitewashed façades of Albacete, note the **Iglesia de Santa María**, a Renaissance church with an elegant Plateresque doorway and a fine sculpted 16C altarpiece. On **Plaza de Don Juan Manuel** are the Ayuntamiento (town hall), with its porticoed façade, the Iglesia de San Juan Bautista, a Herreran church, and the Casa-Palacio, adorned with attractive grilles.

Alcalá del Júcar★

60km/37mi NE along the CM 3218.
The road winds through steep **gorges**. The Júcar river encircles the magnificent **site**★ of the village, between its castle and church overlooking a fertile plain unusual for arid La Mancha. A walk through Alcalá's maze of steep alleyways reveals attractive views at every turn. Dwellings hollowed out of rock have long corridors leading to cliff-side balconies; some can be visited.

Cueva de la Vieja

70km/44mi E along the A 35, via Alpera.
Exceptionally, this easily reached cave retains clearly visible paintings. Stylised human silhouettes are shown hunting stags with bows and arrows. Note females in robes and a figure with a plumed headdress, the best-preserved painting in the entire cave.

Almansa

74km/46mi E along the A 35.
Almansa's maze of streets and lanes spreads around a limestone crag crowned by a medieval castle.

Iglesia de la Asunción – *Below the castle.* The church owes its mix of styles to a remodeling. The Renaissance portal is attributed to Vandelvira.

Palacio de los Condes de Cirat – The fine Mannerist-style doorway of this mansion, the **Casa Grande**, bears an escutcheon flanked by crude figures.

Castle – Stroll restored 15C ramparts, perched along the rock ridge, commanding a view of the plain. Keystones in the keep *(torre de homenaje)* bear the coat of arms of the Marqués de Villena.

Alcaraz

79km/49mi SW along the A 32. Alcaraz stands isolated on a red clay rise. The town grew rich manufacturing carpets and retains its Renaissance character in buildings influenced by **Andrés de Vandelvira**, born here in 1509.

Plaza Mayor – On the main square are: the 15C Pósito, once a granary; the 16C **Ayuntamiento** (town hall) with emblazoned façade; the 17C **Lonja** del Corregidor, standing against the **Torre del Tardón** (clock tower); and the 15C **Iglesia de la Trinidad**, with Flamboyant Gothic portal.

Old houses front the **calle Mayor** (main street). Note a façade with the two warriors and the Plateresque **Puerta de la Aduana** (Customs Doorway) of the Casa Consistorial. Stepped alleys head from the right-hand side of the square. The path to the cemetery passes under two arches to attractive views of brown rooftops and the countryside.

Excursion to the source of the River Mundo – *46km/29mi S of Alcaraz.* Wind along the CM 412 through a wooded valley, past Ríopar, known for its bronzework. Turn right towards Siles. After 6km/4mi turn left to the Cueva (cave) de los Chorros. A spring is the source of the Mundo, a tributary of the Segura, which drops down a wall of rock in a series of falls. The best time to visit is in the spring. *For further information contact the Albacete Tourist Office.*

LA ALBERCA★★

POPULATION: 958

MICHELIN MAP 575 K 11 – CASTILLA Y LEÓN (SALAMANCA)

La Alberca is a delightful village in the Sierra de la Peña de Francia, where stunning scenery joins heritage architecture, rooted traditions, and gastronomic treats, including sausages, honey and walnuts and chestnuts in autumn.

Information: *Plaza Mayor, ☎92 341 52 91*

Orient Yourself: La Alberca is west of Madrid in Salamanca province.

Also See: CIUDAD RODRIGO (50km/31mi NW); SALAMANCA (76km/47mi NE).

Walking About

La Alberca's haphazard streets lead to the main square (plaza Mayor), irregular and arcaded. Old architecture abounds: houses of stone on the first floor, half-timbered and balconied above. Tradition is strong, especially during the Feast of the Assumption.

Excursions

Peña de Francia★★

15km/9mi W. The Peña, a shale crag, at 1 732m/5 682ft is the peak of the Peña de Francia range. The approach affords stunning **panoramas**★★ of the Hurdes mountains, the heights of Portugal, and the Sierra de Gredos. There is a Dominican monastery with a hostelry *(open in summer only)* at the top.

Las Batuecas road★

To the S. This road climbs gradually to the Portillo Pass (1 240m/4 068ft) then plunges into a deep, green valley where lies the Batuecas Monastery. Beyond Las Mestas is the desolate, long isolated **Las Hurdes** region, setting for Buñuel's 1932 film *Land without Bread.*

TOUR OF THE SIERRA DE BÉJAR AND SIERRA DE CANDELARIO

76km/47mi to the SE – allow one day. Meander through the gorges of the Alagón and Cuerpo de Hombre rivers amid walnut and oak forests.

Head east. After 2km/1.2mi, turn to Cepeda, then Sotoserrano. Head towards Lagunilla to reach the N 630 at Puerto de Béjar.

Baños de Montemayor, a pleasant spa, and **Hervás**, with its old **judería** (Jewish quarter) are in this area.

Fiestas

On 15 August, the village performs the ancient mystery play or Loa relating the triumph of the Virgin Mary over the devil, in which participants dress up in colourful and intricately embroidered costumes.

Address Book

WHERE TO EAT

Mesón La Romana
Núñez Losada 4 – Candelario – ☎ 923 41 32 72 – open hols – reservation recommended. This delightful restaurant, situated next to the church and behind the town-hall, in a restored house in the upper village, is the ideal place to enjoy the renowned grilled meats of the region. Make sure you also try the delicious grilled fresh goat cheese or a mushroom specialty.

WHERE TO STAY

Hotel Artesa
*Mayor 57 – Candelario – ☎923 41 31 11 – www.artesa.es – 9 rooms – 4.30 € – Restaurant 12/28 €.*This simple hotel occupies an old house in the centre of the village. Rooms are modest but clean and tastefully decorated. The hotel also has a pleasant rear terrace. Other facilities include a restaurant, a shop selling local products and various arts and crafts workshops.

Return to Puerto de Béjar. One road heads towards Candelario.

Candelario★★

This picturesque village on the flank of the *sierra* retains its traditional stone homes with elegant balconies on steep streets, where water is channeled during the annual mountain snow melt.

Béjar

4km/2.5mi NW. Béjar, known for sheets and woollens, stretches along a narrow rock platform.

Leave Béjar along the SA 515.

Miranda del Castañar

34km/21mi W. Pass the 15C **castle**, cross the bullring, and penetrate the old quarter through the Puerta de San Ginés. Narrow streets are lined by houses adorned with coats of arms. Charming **Mogarraz** (10km/6mi W) and **San Martín del Castañar** (10km/6mi N) are well worth a visit.

Continue towards the Peña de Francia; take SA 202 back to La Alberca.

F. Gouverneur/MICHELIN

Plaza Mayor

ALCALÁ DE HENARES★

POPULATION: 162 780.
MICHELIN MAPS 575 AND 576 K 19 – MADRID

Alcalá has a historic centre★ of 16C-17C colleges and convents and spacious squares. Medieval calle Mayor is adorned with impressive gateways. The university and historic centre are a UNESCO World Heritage site.

- **Information:** *Plaza de los Santos Niños, ☎91 881 06 34.*
- **Orient Yourself:** Alcalá is on the edge of metropolitan Madrid.
- **Parking:** Spots are tight in the old quarter.
- **Don't Miss:** The old university
- **Organizing Your Time:** Take a half-day to see Alcalá from Madrid.

Worth a Visit

Antigua Universidad or Colegio de San Ildefonso★

Guided tours (45min), at 11, noon, 1, 5 and 6pm (and 4pm Oct-Apr); Sat-Sun and public hols, every 30 mins 11am-2pm and 5-6.30pm (7.30pm May-Sep). Closed 1 Jan and 25 Dec. 3 € (includes Capilla de San Ildefonso). ☎91 885 64 87.

The original university, on plaza de San Diego, has a beautiful **Plateresque façade**★ (1543) by Rodrigo Gil de Hontañón crowned by a balustrade. The imperial escutcheon of Charles V decorates the pediment of the central section. The majestic 17C **Patio Mayor** was designed by Juan Gómez de Mora, pupil of Herrera and architect of the Plaza Mayor and Ayuntamiento (Town Hall) in Madrid; at the centre is a well-head with a swan motif, emblem of Cardinal Cisneros. Across the 16C Renaissance Patio de los Filósofos stands the delightful **Patio Trilingüe** (1557) where Latin, Greek and Hebrew were taught. The **Paraninfoa** (1520), formerly used for examinations and degree ceremonies, now sees the solemn opening of the university year and the awarding of the Cervantes literary prize. A gallery is in the Plateresque style, with superb Mudéjar **artesonado**★★ work.

Capilla de San Ildefonso★

Next to the university. The nave and presbytery of this early-16C chapel are crowned with magnificent **Mudéjar artesonado** ceilings. The delicate **stucco** on the Epistle side of the church is late-Gothic, while the Evangelist side opposite is Plateresque. In the presby-

WHERE TO EAT

Miguel de Cervantes
Imagen 12 – ☎91 883 12 77 – www.hostalmcervantes.com – Closed Sun exc. May – .
This restaurant, behind Cervantes' birthplace in a restored town house, serves traditional cuisine in a Castillian setting. A few reasonably priced rooms are also available.

Historical Notes

Under the Romans the city was an important centre known as **Complutum** but the history of Alcalá is mainly linked to that of its university, founded by Cardinal Cisneros in 1498. It became famous for its language teaching and in 1517, Europe's first Polyglot Bible was published with parallel texts in Latin, Greek, Hebrew and Chaldean. The university was moved to Madrid in 1836.

Alcalá's famous citizens include **Catherine of Aragon,** daughter of the Catholic Monarchs and first wife of Henry VIII, the Renaissance architect **Bustamante**, who designed the Hospital de Tavera in Toledo, and **Miguel de Cervantes**, whose **birthplace** is open to the public. Open 10.15am-1.30pm and 4-6.15pm. Closed Mon. No charge. ☎ 91 889 96 54.

Cervantes

Adventure and storytelling are the words that best sum up the life of **Miguel de Cervantes Saavedra** (1547-1616). As a young man he spent four years in Italy after which he enlisted and fought at the Battle of Lepanto (1571) where he was wounded. In 1575 he was captured by the Turks, taken off to Algeria as a slave and rescued after five years by the Fathers of the Holy Trinity. In 1605 he published the first part of **Don Quixote** which was an immense and immediate success. In this tragicomic masterpiece an elderly gentleman sets out as a doughty knight errant in search of adventure, hoping to redress wrongs in the terms of the storybooks he loves; he is accompanied by his simple but astute squire, Sancho Panza. The interaction of the ideal and the real, the true and the illusory, reveals the meditations of a man of 58 deeply involved in philosophy, life and the Spain of his day. His writing continued with *Exemplary Novels* or humorous stories of adventure and intrigue, comedies, *entremeses* or one-act prose farces, novels and, in 1615, the second part of *Don Quixote*. He died a year later, on 23 April 1616 – the same day as Shakespeare.

tery is the Carrara marble **mausoleum**★★ of Cardinal Cisneros, by Domenico Fancelli and Bartolomé Ordóñez, one of the finest examples of 16C Spanish sculpture.

Catedral Magistral

Plaza de los Santos Niños. Built between 1497 and 1515, the cathedral has been remodelled several times. The central portal mixes Gothic, Plateresque and Mudéjar features. The late-Gothic interior contains attractive wrought-iron **grilles**. The cloisters (*entrance on calle Tercia*) house the **Museo de la Catedral**. *Open 9-11.30am and 6.30-8.30pm; Sun and public hols, 9am-12.45pm and 6.30-9pm. Closed Mon. 1.80 €. ☎ 91 888 09 30.*

Palacio Arzobispal

Plaza de Palacio. In the 13C, the bishops of Toledo, lords of Alcalá, erected a palace-fortress here. The Renaissance **façade**, by Alonso de Covarrubias, once fronted a courtyard. The Baroque coat of arms was added later.

On adjoining plaza de San Bernardo, the 17C church of the **Convento de San Bernardo** is crowned by an elliptical dome. The **Museo Arqueológico de la Comunidad de Madrid** (archaeological museum) is in the 17C former Convento de la Madre de Dios. *Open 11am-7pm (3pm Sun and public hols). Closed Mon. ☎ 91 879 66 66.*

ALCAÑIZ

POPULATION: 12,820.

MICHELIN MAP 574 I 29 – ARAGÓN (TERUEL)

Alcañiz, set in olive groves, is the capital of Lower Aragón. The region is famous for Holy Week ceremonies.

- **Information:** *Mayor 1, ☎ 97 883 12 13.*
- **Orient Yourself:** Alcañiz is in the northeastern province of Teruel.
- **Also See:** MORELLA (67km/42mi S), TORTOSA (102km/ 63mi E), ZARAGOZA (103km/64mi NW) and LLEIDA/LÉRIDA (116km/72mi NE).

Worth a Visit

Plaza de España★

Two memorable façades meet on the square: the tall Catalan Gothic arcade of the **Lonja**, once a market, and the Renaissance town hall *(ayuntamiento)*. Both are crowned by an Aragón gallery with overhanging eaves.

Colegiata de Santa María la Mayor

Open 10am-1pm and 4-7.30pm. ☎ 97 883 12 13.

Vertical lines and curves and a Baroque **portal**★ mark the collegiate church, rebuilt in the 18C. Massive columns with composite capitals rise to a projecting cornice.

> **Luis Buñuel (1900-83)**
>
> The film director was born in **Calanda**, 17km/10.5mi SW of Alcañiz.

Castillo

The hilltop castle was the local seat of the Order of Calatrava in the 12C. The part used as a parador largely dates from the 18C. Note the Gothic chapel, with its aisle of equilateral arches, and in the keep, 14C wall paintings.

ALMAGRO★

POPULATION: 8,962.

MICHELIN MAP 576 P 18 – CASTILLA LA MANCHA (CIUDAD REAL)

Set in the red earth of La Mancha, Almagro's stone-paved streets and façades with coats of arms recall the the Military Order of the Knights of Calatrava. The 16C Convento de San Francisco is now a parador.

- **Information:** *Plaza Mayor 1, ☎926 86 07 17; Daimiel: Plaza de España, ☎926 26 06 39.*
- **Orient Yourself:** Almagro is on the plain south of Madrid.
- **Don't Miss:** A walk though streets frozen in time.
- **Also See:** ARANJUEZ (115km/72mi N) and TOLEDO (145km/90mi N).

Walking About

This walk takes you along cobbled streets past whitewashed houses and convents and monasteries with fine stone doorways.

Plaza Mayor★★

This long square, one of the most beautiful in Castile, was the scene of bullfights and tournaments. A stone colonnade frames two sides, under two rows of windows with green surrounds.

The 17C **Corral de Comedias**★, at n°18, is the only intact original theatre in Europe. Wooden porticoes, oil lamps, stone well and scenery wall combine in a superb example of popular architecture. Summer performances are part of the International Festival of Classical Drama. *Open 11 Oct-Feb, 10am-2pm and 4-7pm (6pm Sat-Sun and public hols); Apr-Jun and Sep-10 Oct, 10am-2pm and 5-8pm (7.30pm Sat-Sun and public hols); Jul-Aug, 10am-2pm and 6-9pm (8.30pm Sat-Sun and public hols). Closed Mon, 1 Jan, 24-25 and 31 Dec. 1.50 € (Mon-Fri morning), 2.80 € (afternoons, Sat-Sun and public hols). ☎926 86 15 39.*

From near the statue of Diego de Almagro, take calle de Nuestra Señora de las Nieves (note fine doorways) to the left, to the triangular plaza Santo Domingo, surrounded by mansions. Turn left into calle de Bernardas, to face the spectacular Baroque doorway of the **Palacio de los Condes de Valparaíso.** Follow calle de Don Federico Relimpio; go left on calle de Don Diego de Almagro, dominated by the 16C **Convento de la Asunción de Calatrava** (or **de los Dominicos**) , with its fine Renaissance staircase. *Open noon-2pm and 4-6pm (5-7pm Apr-Jun and Sep; 6-8pm, Jul-Aug); Sun and public hols, noon-2pm. 1.50 €. ☎926 86 03 50.*

At the Plaza Mayor, turn right at the end onto Calle Gran Maestre and the **Museo Nacional del Teatro**, in an 18C palace,

Address Book

For coin ranges, see the Legend on the cover flap.

WHERE TO EAT

El Corregidor
Gerónimo Ceballos 2 – ☎92 686 06 48 – www.lacasadelrector.com – Closed last week of July – . This old Castilian inn, just a few metres from the Plaza Mayor, serves tasty and innovative regional cuisine. The dining room on the first floor is crowned by an attractive glass ceiling, while the bar is in the former carriage entrance. Note also the restaurant's attractive patio.

WHERE TO STAY

Hospedería Almagro
Ejido de Calatrava – ☎926 88 20 87 – 42 rooms – 2.86 €– Restaurant 14/35€. A former 16C convent now houses this hostelry which retains a certain monastic austerity with its high-ceilinged sober rooms. The large patio is shady and pleasant.

FESTIVALS

During the month of July, Almagro hosts its **International Festival of Classical Drama**, during which the Corral de Comedias and the patios and cloisters of the town are transformed into lively outdoor theatres. For further information: www.festivaldealmagro.com.

SHOPPING

Almagro is famous for its delicious aubergines in vinegar and its traditional lacework and embroidery.

showing old documents, costumes, and models of theatre sets. *Open 10am-2pm and 4-7pm; Sat 11am-2pm and 4-6pm; Jul 10am-2pm and 6-9pm; Sat 11am-2pm and 6-8pm; Sun and public hols 11am-2pm. Closed Mon and public hols. 2.40 €. ☎926 26 10 14.*

Excursions

Parque Nacional de las Tablas de Daimiel

31km/19mi N by the CM 4107 and N 420. From Daimiel, take a tarmac road to the right (7km/4.5mi). Open 9am-7pm (9pm in summer). ☎926 69 31 18.

These wetlands cover 1 928ha/4 764 acres in the heart of dry La Mancha. The "tablas" are flood plains, where marshes of the Guadiana and Cigüela rivers are a habitat for a huge variety of birds in winter and dry out in summer. Observation points allow views of mallard duck and grebe.

Soldiering Monks

In the mid-12C, the Campo de Calatrava plain was the scene of unceasing warfare between Christians and Muslims. The old Fortaleza de Calatrava, a fortress built originally by the Moors on the banks of the Guadiana, was handed over by Sancho III to Raimundo, the abbot of Fitero, around 1157. Raimundo defended the fortress from Almohad attacks and founded the **Orden Militar de Calatrava**, the first of Spain's military orders. Following the Battle of Alarcós (1195) and the capture of the castle by Al-Mansur, the knights were forced to flee to a safer haven.

Parque Natural Lagunas de Ruidera

67km/42mi NE. This park, covering 3 772ha/9 320 acres, comprises 15 lagoons linked by streams, gullies and waterfalls,

San Carlos del Valle★

46km/29mi E. The 18C **Plaza Mayor★** is charming, with a Baroque church with four lantern turrets. The house at no5, a former hospice, retains a stone doorway and typical patio.

Valdepeñas

34km/21mi SE along the CM 412. This wine centre is at the southern tip of the vast grape-growing area of La Mancha. Blue- and white-coloured houses rise above shady porticoes on plaza de España. The late-Gothic **Iglesia de la Asunción** (Church of the Assumption),

Historical Notes

The impressive architecture of this charmng town, the birthplace of the explorer Diego de Almagro (1475-1538), can be explained by its eventful history. From the 13C until the end of the 15C, Almagro was the stronghold of the Military Order of the Knights of Calatrava and the base from which they administered their possessions. Between 1750 and 1761, the town became the capital of the province as a result of the favours of the Count of Valparaíso, the then Minister of Finance under Ferdinand VI. From the 16C to the 19C, a number of religious orders established convents and monasteries here.

has a Plateresque upper gallery. The Ermita de la Veracruz (hermitage) is locally venerated. Visit the cellars of the **Cooperativa La Invencible**, the largest bodega, *Open by appointment 9am-1pm and 3-7pm. Closed Sat-Sun and public hols. ☎926 32 27 77.*

Las Virtudes

58km/36mi SE (24km/15mi S of Valdepeñas). The village claims the oldest **bullring** *(plaza de toros)* in Spain (1641), square and blocked on one side by the 14C **Santuario de Nuestra Señora de las Virtudes** (Sanctuary of Our Lady of Holy Virtue) which has a Mudéjar ceiling and Churrigueresque retable.

Castillo-Convento de Calatrava la Nueva★

32km/20mi SW. 7km/4.5mi SW of Calzada de Calatrava, go right onto a paved road (2.5km/1.5mi). The semi-ruined citadel on a magnificent **hilltop site** dominates the route to Andalucía.

The gateway leads into vaulted stables. The second perimeter, built into rock, houses religious buildings, including the impressive **church**, lit by an immense rose window, and brick swallow's nest vaulting, probably the work of Moorish prisoners. . Views from the towers encompass the ruins of the **Castillo de Salvatierra** across the road, as well as the reddish La Mancha plain.

ALMERÍA

POPULATION: 159,587.

MICHELIN MAP 578 V 22 – MAP 124 COSTA DEL SOL – ANDALUCÍA (ALMERÍA)

Almería is a swathe of white between the Mediterranean and a fortress crowned hill. Its magnificent climate – hills shelter it from winds – has made it a major tourist destination. Life in the city centres on the paseo de Almería, a tree-lined avenue. Another oasis, the parque de Nicolás Salmerón, stretches along the harbour. Houses in La Chanca, the fishermen's quarter, are built into rock.

- **Information:** *Parque Nicolás Salmerón, ☎950 27 43 55.*
- **Orient Yourself:** Almería lies on the southern coast on the Mediterranean.
- **Don't Miss:** the Alcazaba
- **Organizing Your Time:** Take a half day at least for the fortress and a stroll.
- **Especially for Kids:** Kids always love castles.
- **Also See:** *COSTA DEL SOL and GUADIX (109km/68mi NW).*

Worth a Visit

Alcazaba★

Open 9.30am-6.30pm (8.30pm Apr-Oct). Closed Mon, 1 Jan and 25 Dec. 1.50 €; no charge for citizens of the European Union. ☎950 27 16 17.

Abd ar-Rahman III ordered this fortress built in the 10C. Almotacín built a splendid palace, enlarged by the Catholic Monarchs. Its crenellated, ochre walls dominate Almería. A section of old ramparts links the fort to San Cristóbal hill, once crowned by a castle.

Attractive **gardens** are laid out in the first walled enclosure where rivulets spring from fountains. The bell in the Muro de la Vela, a wall separating the enclosures, once warned of pirates. In the third enclosure, the keep *(torre del homenaje)*, with incredibly thick walls, looks down on the Christian *alcázar*. The **view**★ from the battlements takes in the town, surrounding hills and sea.

Catedral★

Open daily for guided tours, 10am-5pm. No visits during religious services. 2 €. 950 23 48 48.

The cathedral was built in 1524, fortified against raids by Barbary pirates. It has two well-designed **portals**★ and, at the east end, a **delicately carved sunburst**★. The high altar and pulpits of inlaid marble and jasper are 18C, the choir stalls are from 1560 and the jasper *trascoro* with three alabaster statues is 18C. A chapel in the ambulatory houses a statue of the Cristo de la Escucha.

Aljibes de Jayrán

Open 9am-2pm. Closed Sat-Sun and public hols. 950 27 30 39.

On calle Tenor Iribarne are the Moorish cisterns that once supplied the city.

Iglesia de Santiago

This 16C church on one of the city's main shopping streets (calle de las Tiendas) has a fine **Renaissance doorway**★ similar to the cathedral's.

Museo Arqueológico de Almería

Carretera de Ronda 91. Open Tue 2.10-8.30pm, Wed-Sat 9-8.30pm, Sun and public hols 9am-2.30pm. Closed Mon. 950 64 98 00.

Museum exhibits cover prehistory through the Islamic era, with pieces from sites in the province, notably the El Argar and Los Millares cultures

Tours

THE EAST COAST★

Approx. 240km/150mi.

Take the airport road and turn right after 14.5km/9mi.

Parque Natural de Cabo de Gata-Níjar★★

South of the volcanic Cabo de Gata mountains, past the Acosta salt flats, this park is a haven of wild, unspoilt beaches. The lighthouse faces Mermaid Reef, popular for underwater fishing. On the other side of the mountain is the small summer resort of San José with two beautiful beaches; los **Genoveses**★ and **Monsul**★ (about 2km/1.2mi from the centre of the town).

Take the AL 12; turn at Venta del Probe.

Agua Amarga

Agua Amarga is a pleasant seaside complex with an attractive beach.

Follow the coast road to Mojácar (32km/20mi).

The road twists upward, offering views of the coast, a 17C fortified tower and a 13-14C Moorish watchtower.

Mojácar★

The village stands on a splendid **site**★ on an outcrop with **views** of the coast

Historical Notes

The city was founded by Abd ar-Rahman II in the 9C, and played an important role in the 11C when it was the capital of a taifa kingdom. It was captured by Alfonso VII in 1147; however, upon his death, 10 years later, it fell into Moorish hands once more. Almería formed part of the Nasrid kingdom of Granada until 1489, the year in which it was reconquered by the Catholic Monarchs.

In the last third of the 20C, the development of advanced agricultural techniques and the opening-up of modern infrastructures have placed this provincial capital at the forefront of Spanish agriculture.

Address Book

For coin ranges, see the Legend.

WHERE TO EAT

Asador La Gruta
5km/3mi W of the city on the Aguadulce road – ☎950 23 93 35 – www.asadorlagruta.com – Dinner only. Closed Sun, 15-28 Feb and 15-31 Oct – . The enormous caves of a former quarry are the setting of this unusual restaurant specialising in grilled meats and high-quality ingredients.

TAPAS

Casa Puga
Jovellanos 7 (old quarter) – ☎950 23 15 30 – Closed 3 weeks Sep and public hols except Holy Week – . Almería is teeming with tapas bars, of which Casa Puga is the oldest, with a choice of tapas, excellent wines and sausages, and friendly patrons.

WHERE TO STAY

Hotel Costasol
Paseo de Almería 58 – ☎950 23 40 11 - www.hotelcostasol.com – – 55 rooms – 8 €. The Costasol is housed in a 1960s-style building on Almería's busiest shopping street, although the rooms are spacious and comfortable, some with a balcony. .

Las Salinas de Cabo de Gata
Almadraba de Monteleva. Las Salinas. 4km/2.5mi SE of El Cabo de Gata – ☎ 950 37 01 03 www.lasalinascabodegata.com Closed in Oct – – 20 rooms – 6 €. The hotel's tranquil location in Parque Natural de Cabo de Gata makes this an ideal base from which to enjoy a number of excursions. All the rooms offer views of the bright-white salt pans or the beach.

(2km/1.2mi away) and a plain broken by odd rock formations. The steep, narrow village streets are clearly Moorish.

Follow the AL 12 back towards Almería, turning off at Níjar.

Níjar

This one-time Arab village carries on the craft of weaving *jarapas* (blankets), using strips of material *(trapos)*.

The road to the northeast

55km/34mi along the N 370. Sand dunes stretching from Benahadux to Tabernas were used as a desert film location. Film sets are open to the public at **Oasys**, a desert theme park. *Open 10am-9pm (7 pm Nov-Holy Week). ☎950 36 52 36.* Beyond Tabernas, the land is red and barren; pottery-making is the main occupation. **Sorbas** has an amazing **setting★**. Its houses cling to a cliff, circled below by a river loop.

TURESPAÑA

Monsul beach

PRINCIPAT D'ANDORRA★★

PRINCIPALITY OF ANDORRA

POPULATION: 62,400.
MICHELIN MAP 574 E 34-35.

The seven parishes that make up the principality of Andorra occupy high plateaux and valleys cut by charming mountain roads. In recent years Andorra has seen urbanization, hydroelectric schemes and a tourism boom. But tradition remains in the terraced slopes planted with tobacco and in religious pilgrimages (the famous Catalan *aplec*).

- **Information:** *Andorra la Vella: Doctor Vilanova, ☎00 376 82 02 14.*
- **Orient Yourself:** Andorra is tucked between Spain and France. Andorra La Vella is located 20km/12mi from La Seu d'Urgell.
- **Parking:** Forget about parking on the crowded streets of Andorra la Vella.
- **Also See:** PIRINEOS CATALANES

Worth a Visit

Andorra la Vella

Houses in the capital cluster onto a terrace overlooking the Gran Valira. Streets in the old quarter remain almost intact, as has the **Casa de les Valls**. This ancient stone building houses the Consell General de les Valls, both Parliament and courthouse to the small nation. *Guided tours (30min, must be booked one month in advance), 9.30am-1pm and 3-6.30pm; Sun and public hols 10am-2pm. Closed Sun and public hols Nov-Apr, 1 and 6 Jan, 14 Mar, 1 May, 8 Sept, 1 Nov, 21, 25 and 26 Dec. ☎ 00 376 82 91 29.*

To the east, Andorra la Vella joins the lively municipality of Les Escaldes, dominated by **Caldaea**, a thermal spa with futuristic lines featuring Turkish baths, jacuzzis, bubble beds, hot marble slabs etc.

Historical Notes

Until 1993 Andorra was a co-principality subject to an unusual political regime dating back to the days of feudalism. The neighboring rulers, the Bishop of Urgell and the President of the French Republic, enjoyed rights and exercised powers over this small territory, which was jointly governed by them. At present Andorra is a sovereign state – a full member of the United Nations.

Estany d'Engolasters (Engolasters Lake)

The Engolasters plateau is a pastured extension of Andorra la Vella used for sports and recreation. The fine Romanesque tower of the church of Sant Miquel rises above the rolling plains.

Climb over the crest among the pine trees at the end of the road and descend on foot to an impressive hydroelectric dam, surrounded by trees, which has raised the waters of the lake (alt 1 616m/5 301ft) by a total of 10m/33ft.

Santuari de Meritxell

Beyond Los Bons pass lies a lovely **site**★ of houses gathered under a ruined castle and the Capilla de Sant Romà. Nearby stands the church of Nuestra Señora de Meritxell, national sanctuary of the principality since 1976.

Canillo

The bell tower of the church set against rocks is the highest in Andorra. At its side is the white-painted ossuary, characteristic of early Iberian occupation.

Iglesia de Sant Joan de Caselles

Open Jul-Aug, 10am-1pm and 3-6pm; otherwise by prior arrangement. ☎ 00 376 85 14 34.

Below an openwork tower and rows of ornamental windows, this church is one

Practical Information

CUSTOMS AND OTHER FORMALITIES

Visitors need a valid passport and, for those driving a car, a green card and current driving licence. There are customs checkpoints on the borders.

CURRENCY

The euro is the currency of Andorra and can be easily obtained from banks and post offices. Withdrawals can also be made from cash machines using credit and debit cards.

POSTAL SERVICE

Andorra has both Spanish and French postal services, with full-time post offices in Andorra la Vella and local offices elsewhere. There are plans to create an Andorran mail service at an as yet unspecified future date.

SHOPPING

Andorra has long held a reputation as a shopper's paradise, due to its duty-free status. A wide variety of products are on offer at very reasonable prices (food, luxury items, clothes, electronic goods etc). Shops are generally open from 9am to 1pm and 4pm to 8pm, although department stores tend to open all day.

TELEPHONING

The code for Andorra is 376 followed by the correspondent's number.

WEBSITE

www.turisme.ad

of the best examples of Romanesque architecture in Andorra. Behind the wrought-iron grid of the presbytery stands a painted altarpiece by the master **Canillo** (1525), representing the life and visions of the Apostle St John. The Romanesque **Crucifixion**★ was restored in 1963: a Christ in stucco was placed atop of a fresco illustrating the Calvary.

Port d'Envalira★★

Roads may be snow-blocked but usually reopen within 24hr. Alt 2 407m/7 897ft. Envalira boasts the highest altitude of major Pyrenean passes. On the Atlantic-Mediterranean divide, it commands a lovely mountain panorama.

Pas de la Casa★

Alt 2 091m/6 861ft. Once only a frontier post, the highest village in Andorra is the main ski resort of the region.

Ordino

Leave your car on the church square, in the upper town. Ordino is a quaint village with a maze of charming alleyways. Admire the wrought-iron grilles of the church, similar to those still seen in sanctuaries near old Catalan forges. Nearby, note another fine example of wrought-iron artistry: an 18m/60ft balcony adorning the casa de Don Guillem, built for a master blacksmith.

ANTEQUERA★

POPULATION: 38,827.

MICHELIN MAP 578 U 16 – ANDALUCÍA (MÁLAGA)

In whitewashed Antequera, set in a fertile valley, the new and venerable co-exist. Cobblestone alleys, grilled windows, and the churches and fine Mudéjar brick belfry of San Sebastián are the essence of Andalucía.

- **Information:** *Plaza de San Sebastián 7, ☎95 270 25 05.*
- **Orient Yourself:** Antequera lies in southern Andalucía, inland from the Costa del Sol.
- **Don't Miss:** Ancient dolmens (burial chambers).
- **Also See:** MÁLAGA (55km/34mi S), COSTA DEL SOL and OSUNA (74km/46mi NW).

Worth a Visit

Alcazaba

Closed for restoration. ☎95 270 25 05 (Tourist Office).
This was the first fortress taken by the Christians during the reconquest of the kingdom of Granada (1410), but it was soon lost again. Today, its walls shelter a pleasant garden and its towers offer a fine **view**★ over Antequera.

Colegiata de Santa María★

Access this church, at the foot of the castle gardens, by the 16C **Arco de los Gigantes** (Arch of Giants). Built in 1514, it has one of the earliest Renaissance façades in Andalucía. The adjacent observation point looks out on 1C Roman baths.

Iglesia del Carmen

Open 10am-2pm and 4-7pm; in summer, 10am-2pm and 5-8pm (10.30pm Wed-Fri); Sun and public hols, 10am-2pm. 1.50 €. ☎95 270 25 05.
The central nave of the church boasts a Mudéjar artesonado ceiling and a magnificent Churrigueresque altarpiece.

Museo Municipal

Guided tours (40min), 10am-1.30pm and 4.30-6.30pm (8.30-10.30pm 1 July-15Sep); Sun 11am-1.30pm. Closed Mon and public hols. 3 €. ☎95 270 40 21.

> **A Bit of Advice**
>
> Given the dangerous nature of the defile and to ensure the safety of visitors, we recommend that you go no farther than the metal bridge suspended high above the El Chorro defile.

The museum in the 17C **Palacio de Nájera** exhibits archaeological pieces. The most outstanding item is the **Ephebus of Antequera**★, a 1C bronze Roman sculpture.

Dolmens★

To the left of the Antequera exit on the A 354, towards Granada. The **Menga** and **Viera dolmens**, dating from 2500 to 2200 BC, are enormous funerary chambers beneath great stone slabs. Menga, the older and larger, is oblong, divided by pillars supporting stone slabs. *Open 9am-6pm; Sun and public hols 9.30am-2.30pm. Closed Mon, 1 and 6 Jan, 9 Apr, 1 May, 16 and 20 Aug, 1 Nov, 6, 24, 25 and 31 Dec. ☎95 270 25 05.*

Continue along the A 354 and turn left onto the N 331.

The **El Romeral** dolmen (1800 BC), the most recent chamber, consists of small flat stones laid to create a trapezoidal section. *Open 9am-5.30pm; Jul-15 Sep 9am-6pm; Sun 9.30am-2.30pm. Closed Mon, 1 and 6 Jan, 9 Apr, 1 May, 25 Dec. ☎95 270 25 05.*

B. Kaufmann/MICHELIN

Menga dolmen

Excursions

Parque Natural de El Torcal★

14km/9mi SE. ▶ Take the C 3310 towards Villanueva de la Concepción; go right at the **Centro de Recepción "El Torcal"** *signpost. Reception centre closed for reconstruction. ☎952 70 25 05.*

The park, spread over 12ha/30 acres, has some of Spain's most unusual eroded karst scenery. Two sign posted paths *(1hr and 3hr)* lead to strangely shaped limestone rocks.

Tour to the Desfiladero de Los Gaitanes★★

50km/31mi SW. ▶ Take the A 343 to Álora. After the Abdajalís valley, the road zig-zags through superb mountain scenery up to **Álora**★, an attractive village of twisting alleyways overlooking the Guadalhorce River. ▶*Take the MA 444 from Álora. Leave your car at the El Chorro campsite.* Continue on foot along a tarmac track *(30min there and back) up* to a metal bridge with magnificent canyon **views**★★★.

From Antequera to Málaga★

62km/39mi S by the A 45, C 356 and C 345.

These pleasant roads, within sight of majestic hills, afford splendid **views**★★ beyond the Puerto del León (Lion Pass, 960m/3 150ft) of Málaga and the sea.

ARACENA★

POPULATION: 6,500.

MICHELIN MAP 578 S 10 – ANDALUCÍA (HUELVA)

Aracena rises in tiers up a hillside, crowned by the remains of a Templars' castle, its whitewashed houses adorned with ornate grilles.

- **Information:** *Plaza de San Pedro, ☎959 12 82 66.*
- ▶ **Orient Yourself:** Aracena is in west-central Andalucía
- **Especially for Kids:** Kids might love the Cave of Marvels
- **Also See:** SEVILLA (93km/58mi SE), ZAFRA (98km/61mi N) and HUELVA (108km/67mi SW) .

Worth a Visit

Plaza Alta, the local hub, is fronted by the Renaissance Iglesia de Nuestra Señora de la Asunción and the **Cabildo Viejo** (Centro de Información del Parque Natural Sierra de Aracena y Picos de Aroche, park information centre). Aracena lies at the centre of this nature park. *Open 10am-2pm and 4-6pm; in summer, 10am-2pm and 6-8pm. Closed Mon, 1 Jan and 25 Dec. ☎959 12 88 25.*

The **Museo al Aire Libre de Escultura Contemporánea**, an open-air exhibition of modern art around town, adds a touch of modernity.

Gruta de las Maravillas★★★ (Cave of Marvels)

Guided tours (50 min) 10am-1.30pm and 3-6pm. 7.70 €. ☎959 12 83 55 (advance booking recommended).

Rivers below the castle formed vast caves with limpid pools. Formations include draperies and pipes coloured by iron and copper oxide or brilliant white calcite crystal as in the **Salón de la Cristalería de Dios**★★ (God's Crystalware Chamber). Here also is the **Museo Geológico Minero**, a geological and mining museum.

Castle

The castle was built in the 9C over an Almohad fortress. Note the decoration on the north side of the tower next to the church, similar to that of the Giralda in Sevilla.

B. Kaufmann/MICHELIN

Corta Atalaya

Excursions

Parque Natural de la Sierra de Aracena y Picos de Aroche★★

The cool forests of this park are punctuated by slender peaks and picturesque villages such as whitewashed **Alájar**★, and **Almonaster la Real**★, concealed amid chestnut, eucalyptus, cork and holm oak, which has a rare intact **mosque**★. *Open Sat-Sun and public hols, 11am-7pm.*
Nearby **Jabugo** is justifiably famous for its delicious cured hams.

Minas de Riotinto★★

35km/22mi S. The mining tradition of this area dates back to Antiquity.

Parque Minero de Riotinto★★
Open 10.30am-3pm and 4-7pm. Fees vary by activity. Closed 1 and 6 Jan and 25 Dec. 959 59 00 25.
This mining theme park takes in the mining and railway museum, the **Museo Minero y Ferroviario**★, the spectacular open-cast mines of **Corta Atalaya**★★★ and **Cerro Colorado**★★, and a **tourist train** along a 19C line built by the Río Tinto Company.

Address Book

For coin ranges, see the Legend on the cover flap.

WHERE TO EAT

José Vicente
Avenida Andalucía 53 – 959 12 84 55 – Closed Tue and 20 Jun-15 Jul – . One of the best restaurants in the province where, according to its owner, only fresh produce is served. The menu in this tastefully decorated restaurant includes local cep mushrooms and a range of cured ham and pork dishes.

WHERE TO STAY

Hotel Los Castaños
Avenida de Huelva 5 – 959 12 63 00 – www.loscastanoshotel.com – – 33 rooms – 7€ – Restaurant 12€. This modern, three-storey Andalucían-style building is in the centre of town. Accommodation is functional, comfortable and well-maintained. Some rooms face a large inner patio. The hotel also has a fine restaurant.

SPECIALITIES

No trip to Aracena would be complete without trying the exquisite **pata negra cured ham** in one of the town's *mesones*.

ARANJUEZ★★

POPULATION: 35,872.

MICHELIN MAPS 575 AND 576 L 19 – MADRID

Aranjuez, on the banks of the Tagus *(Tajo)*, is an oasis in the Castilian plain, renowned for its greenery, particularly around the royal palace. The shaded walks sung by composers (Joaquín Rodrigo's *Concierto de Aranjuez*) and painted by artists are popular with Madrileños at weekends.

- **Information:** *Plaza de San Antonio 9, ☎91 891 04 27.*
- **Orient Yourself:** Aranjuez is off the A 4 highway linking Madrid with Andalucía, 47km/29mi from both the capital and Toledo.
- **Don't Miss:** The Palace and Prince's Garden.
- **Also See:** MADRID, TOLEDO and ALCALÁ DE HENARES (85km/53mi NE).

A Bit of History

The Aranjuez Revolt *(El motín de Aranjuez)* – In March 1808, Charles IV, his queen and the prime minister, Godoy, were at Aranjuez. They were preparing to flee (on 18 March) first to Andalucía, then to America, in the face of popular opposition to the passage transit privileges granted to Napoleon's armies.

On the night of 17 March, Godoy's mansion was attacked by followers of the heir apparent, Prince Ferdinand; Charles IV then abdicated in favour of his son; but Napoleon soon forced both royals to abdicate in his own favour (5 May). These intrigues and the presence of a French garrison in Madrid stirred the revolt of May 1808, the beginning of the War of Independence.

Special Features

ROYAL PALACE AND GARDENS★★

The Catholic Monarchs enjoyed the original 14C palace, enlarged by Emperor Charles V. The present palace is mainly the result of an initiative by Philip II who called on the future architects of the Escorial to erect a new palace amid gardens.

In the 18C, the town became a principal royal residence and was considerably embellished. It was, however, ravaged by fire in 1727 and again in 1748, after which the present façade was built. Ferdinand VI built the town to a grid plan; Charles III added two palace wings and Charles IV erected the delightful Labourer's Cottage.

Palacio Real★

Guided tours, 10am-5.15pm (10am-6.15pm Apr-Sep). Closed Mon, 1 and 6 Jan, 1 and 30 May, 24, 25 and 31 Dec and during official ceremonies. 4.50€ (6 € with tour of private chambers); no charge Wed for E. U. citizens. ☎91 891 07 40.

This Classical-style royal palace of brick and stone was built in the 16C and restored in the 18C. In spite of many modifications it retains considerable unity of style. The entry and façades of the wings are marked by archways and domed pavilions mark the angles. The apartments have been left as they were at the end of the 19C.

The **Salón del Trono** (Throne Room), with crimson velvet hangings and Rococo furnishings, has a ceiling painted with an allegory of monarchy – ironically it was in this room that Charles IV abdicated in 1808.

The **Salón de Porcelana**★★ (Porcelain Room) is the palace's most notable room, covered in white garlanded porcelain tiles, illustrating in relief scenes of Chinese life, exotica and children's games, all made in the Buen Retiro factory in Madrid in 1763.

In the king's apartments a music room precedes the Smoking or Arabian Room – a reproduction of the Hall of the Two Sisters in the Alhambra. A fine Mengs *Crucifixion* hangs in the bedroom, and the walls of another room are decorated with **203 small pictures** on rice paper with Oriental-style motifs. A museum of palace life in the days of Alfonso XIII includes a gymnasium, and items such as a tricycle.

Parterre and Jardín de la Isla★ (Parterre and Island Garden)

Open 8am-6.30pm (8.30pm Apr-Sep). Closed 1 and 6 Jan, 1 and 30 May, 5 Sep, 24, 25 and 31 Dec. 91 542 00 59.

The **Parterre** is a formal garden laid out before the east front by the Frenchman Boutelou in 1746. The fountain of Hercules brings a mythological touch to the balanced display.

The **Jardín de la Isla** was laid out on an island in the Tajo river in the 16C. Cross the canal to reach the park and its fountains hidden among chestnut, ash and poplar trees and boxwood hedges.

Jardín del Príncipe★★ (The Prince's Garden)

Entrance in calle de la Reina. Open 8am-6.30pm (8.30 Apr-Sep). Closed 1 and 6 Jan, 1 and 30 May, 5 Sep and 24-25 and 31 Dec. 91 891 13 44.

This vast garden beside the Tajo (150ha/371 acres) has four monumental gateways by Juan de Villanueva. In 1763, Boutelou landscaped the park for the future Charles IV according to the romantic vision then in fashion. A farm, greenhouses with tropical plants and stables for exotic animals were added.

Casa del Labrador★★ (The Labourer's Cottage) – *Guided tours by prior arrangement, 10am-5.15pm (6.15pm in summer). Closed Mon. 5 €; no charge Wed for citizens of the European Union. 91 891 13 44.*

The so-called cottage at the eastern end of the Jardín del Príncipe, named after the humble cottages originally on the site, was built on the whim of Charles IV in neo-Classical style with sumptuous decoration. The iron railing is topped by 20 Carrara marble busts of figures from Antiquity.

The interior is a reflection of Spanish Bourbon taste.

Casa de Marinos (The Sailors' House) – *Guided tours by prior arrangement, 10am-6.15pm (5.15pm in summer). Closed Mon. 3.40 €; no charge Wed for E. U. citizens. 91 891 13 44.*

A museum beside the former landing stage exhibits **falúas reales**★★ *(royal vessels)* that ferried the royals and guests to the Labourer's Cottage. One, a gift to Philip V from a Venetian count, is remarkable for its ornate decoration in gilded, finely carved wood.

J. Balanya/MICHELIN

One of the numerous fountains adorning the gardens (detail)

Excursions

Chinchón★

21km/13mi NE along the M 305.

Chinchón is famous for its aniseed spirit and, more importantly, the Countess of Chinchón, wife of a 17C viceroy of Peru, to whom the West owes quinine, extracted from the bark of a Peruvian tree (named chinchona in the countess' honour).

Plaza Mayor★★ – The picturesque arcaded square, dominated by its church, is surrounded by houses with wooden balconies. Bullfights are held in summer.

The brick former monastery beside the square now houses a parador.

ÁVILA★★

POPULATION: 49,868.
MICHELIN MAPS 575 OR 576 K 15 – MAP 121
ALREDEDORES DE MADRID – CASTILLA Y LEÓN (ÁVILA)

Ávila's numerous convents and churches shelter behind magnificent 11C walls. Under winter snow, distant chants and prayers seem to echo through the air.

- **Information:** *Plaza Catedral 4, ☎920 21 13 87.*
- **Orient Yourself:** At 1 131m/3 710ft, NW of Madrid, Ávila has a harsh and windy winter climate.
- **Don't Miss:** The city walls
- **Organizing Your Time:** Start with the walls and cathedral.
- **Also See:** Sierra de GREDOS, Monasterio de EL ESCORIAL (64km/40mi E), SEGOVIA (67km/42mi NE), SALAMANCA (98 km/61mi NW) and MADRID (107km/66mi SE).

Worth a Visit

Murallas★★ (City walls)

Europe's most striking medieval fortifications, with 90 bastions and towers and eight gateways, enclose an area 900m/2 953ft by 449m/1 476ft. Most date from the 11C; and despite 14C modifications, maintain their unity. Walk the sentry path along the top; the best **view** of the walls is from **Cuatro Postes**, on the Salamanca road.

Catedral★★

Open 9.30am-5pm (Sat 6pm); Sun and public hols noon-5pm; Apr-Oct 9.30am-6pm (Sat 7pm). Last entry 45 min before closing. Closed 1 and 6 Jan, Maundy Thu, 15 Oct and 25 Dec. 4 € ☎920 21 16 41.

The fortified **east end** of the cathedral is set into the ramparts, crowned with a double row of battlements. Granite and defensive design make it austere, despite window tracery, portal carvings and decoration along the upper tower, buttresses and pinnacles. The 14C **north doorway** with French Gothic decoration, its stone eroded, was removed in the 15C from the **west front** during a renovation by Juan Guas. Its current placement, from the 18C, is more suitable for a palace.

The surprising **interior** has a high Gothic nave, a chancel with sandstone patches of red and yellow and many **works of art**★★. The **trascoro** (1531)

R. Mattes/MICHELIN

A view of the walls at dusk

The City of St. Theresa

Santa Teresa de Jesús (1515-82), whose visions deeply affected her contemporaries, is one of the greatest mystics of the Roman Catholic Church. Living at a time when the Reformation was gaining adherents throughout Europe, and the monastic orders, grown rich in power and possessions, were relaxing their discipline, she succeeded in widely re-establishing the strict observance of the Carmelites, gaining converts and founding convents.

Her letters are famous, particularly those to her spiritual director, St John of the Cross, as are her mystical writings and her autobiography, Life, published in 1588. She was canonised in 1622 and made a Doctor of the Church in 1970.

Several buildings in Ávila preserve the memory of the saint, including the museums in the **Convento de San José (Las Madres)** and the **Convento de La Encarnación**. The crypt of the **Convento de Santa Teresa (La Santa)**, built on the site of the house where she was born, is home to the most comprehensive museum dedicated to her life. Her remains, however, are not in Ávila but in Alba de Tormes.

holds lovely Plateresque statues (left to right): the Presentation of Jesus in the Temple, the Adoration of the Magi and the Massacre of the Innocents). The **choir stalls** are from the same period. There are two delicate wrought-iron **pulpits** – Renaissance and Gothic. Construction lasted from 1135 to the 14C; windows in the apse are Romanesque. The large painted **altarpiece** (c 1500) by Pedro Berruguete and Juan de Borgoña has a gilt wood surround with Isabelline features and Italian Renaissance pilasters. Four carved panels on the the high altar show the Evangelists and the four Holy Knights. The central panel is Vasco de la Zarza's masterpiece: the alabaster **tomb**★★ of Don Alonso de Madrigal, Bishop of Ávila in the 15C, called El Tostado (Swarthy). He is shown before a beautiful Epiphany.

Museo – *Open 10am-5pm (6pm Apr-Oct; Sat 10am-6pm (7pm Apr-Oct); Sun and public hols noon-5pm (6pm Apr-Oct).*

Address Book

For coin ranges, see the Legend on the cover flap.

WHERE TO EAT

Siglo Doce
Plaza de la Catedral 6 – ☎920 252 885 – www.siglodoce.com – reservations recommended. A 12C house right beside the Cathedral, rustic, unpretentious, with charming exposed beams and peaked tile roof. Many choices, but the most popular is Ávila veal chop.

Doña Guiomar
Tomás Luis de Victoria 3 – ☎920 25 37 09 – Closed Sun – . A popular choice with locals, recently renovated with minimalist touches. Good views of the market across the street.

WHERE TO STAY

Hostería de Bracamonte
Bracamonte 6 – ☎920 25 12 80 – www.hospederiadebracamonte.com – 20 rooms – 6€ – Restaurant 20/40€. A charming hotel right in the centre of Ávila. The decoration in this old inn includes wooden beams, attractive brickwork and pictures hanging from the walls. The pleasant guest rooms are arranged around a plant-filled inner patio. The restaurant fills on weekends.

Palacio de los Velada
Plaza de la Catedral 10 – ☎920 25 51 00 – www.veladahoteles.com – – 144 rooms. 150/190€ – 12€ – Restaurant 32/44€. Enjoy all the comforts in a 16C building redolent of history in Castillian decor. The hotel focuses on its beautiful patio.

SPECIALITIES

The city is also famous for its candied egg yolks *(yemas de Santa Teresa)*, named for Ávila's patron saint. Give them a try.

Last entry 45 mins before closing. Closed 1 and 6 Jan, Maundy Thu, 15 Oct and 25 Dec. 4 €. 920 21 16 41.

Enter the museum via a 13C **sacristy**★★ with notable eight-ribbed vault, massive 16C altarpiece and sculptures of the Passion in imitation alabaster. View a head of Christ by Morales painted on a tabernacle door, a portrait by El Greco, a huge Isabelline grille, late-15C antiphonaries and a colossal 1571 monstrance (1.70m/5ft 8in) by Juan de Arfe. The Gothic **cloisters** are restored.

In plaza de la Catedral, the **Palacio de Valderrábanos**, now a hotel, has a fine 15C doorway with family crest.

Basílica de San Vicente★★

Open 10am-1.30pm (2pm in summer) and 4-6.30pm (7pm in summer). No visits during religious services. 1.40 €. 920 25 52 30.

This vast 12-14C Romanesque basilica, with ogive vaulting, is on the reputed site of the 4C martyrdom of St Vincent of Zaragoza and his sisters. The ensemble includes the 14C south gallery with slender columns, a cornice over the length of the nave, the tall west front porch and two incomplete towers.

The **west portal**★★ is outstanding for the statue columns below the richly decorated cornice and lifelike covings. Beneath the 14C **lantern**★ is the **martyrs' tomb**★★, a late 12C masterpiece under a rare 15C Gothic canopy with pagoda top. The martyrdom of St Vincent and his sisters is attributed to the unknown sculptor of the west portal. The scenes of their capture, flaying and torture are particularly powerful.

Monasterio de Santo Tomás★

Open 10am-1pm and 4-8pm. Closed 1-6 Feb, 15 Oct and 25 Dec. 3 € (cloisters and choir). 920 22 04 00.

This late 15C Dominican monastery, at times a summer residence of the Catholic Monarchs, was also the university.

The **church** façade includes the common motifs of the monastery: details are emphasised with long lines of balls, and

Ávila

			Don Geronimo	B	13	San Segundo	B	22
			Esteban Domingo	B	14	San Vicente	B	24
Alemania	B	2	Jimena Blásquez	A	15	Santa Pl. de la	A	25
Caballeros	B	6	López Núñez	B	16	Santo Tomas Pas. de	B	26
Calvo Sotelo Pl.	B	8	Marqués de Benavites	AB	18	Sonsoles Bajada de	B	27
Cardenal Pla y Deniel	B	10	Peregrino Bajada del	B	19	Los Telares	A	28
Cortal de las Campanas Pl. del	A	12	Ramón y Cajal	A	20	Tomás luis de Victoria	B	30
			Reyes Católicos	B	21	Tostado	B	31

Convento de San José (Las Madres)	B	R	Palacio de Núñez Vela (Palacio de Justicia)	A	J	Palacio de los Dávila	B	V
Convento de Santa Teresa	A	B	Palacio de Polentinos	A	N	Palacio de los Verdugos	B	P
Iglesia de San Pedro	B	A	Palacio de Valderrábanos	B	F	Torre de Guzmán	A	D

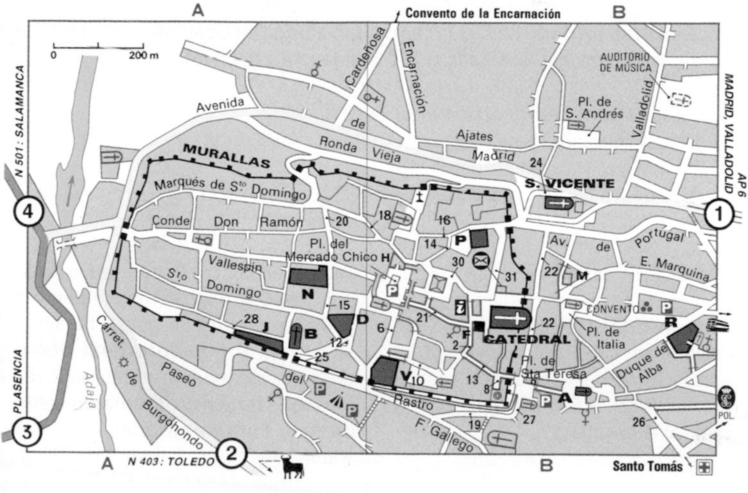

the yoke and fasces emblem of Ferdinand and Isabel. The church has a single aisle, its arches on clusters of slender columns. Two galleries were accessible only from the cloisters by the monks. The fine **mausoleum**★ (1512) is of Prince Juan, only son of the Catholic Monarchs. Its alabaster table with delicate Renaissance sculpting is by Domenico Fancelli, who created the Catholic Monarchs' mausoleum in Granada. In a north chapel is the Renaissance tomb of Juan Dávila and his wife, the prince's tutors. **Claustro (Cloisters)** – Beyond the plain 15C **Claustro de los Novicios** is the **Claustro del Silencio**★, intimate and generously carved on its upper gallery. The Claustro de los Reyes (Catholic Monarchs' Cloister) is larger and more solemn with spectacularly bare upper arching. From the Claustro del Silencio, stairs lead to beautiful 15C Gothic **choir stalls** with pierced canopies and arabesques; and from the upper gallery, to the high altar gallery where one can see Berruguete's high relief masterpiece, the **retable of St Thomas Aquinas**★★ (c 1495).

Iglesia de San Pedro

Open 10am-12.30pm and 6.30-8.30pm. No visits during religious services. ☎920 22 93 28.

This Romanesque church on vast **plaza Santa Teresa** has early Gothic pointed arches and delicate rose window.

Palacio de los Verdugos

The façade of this Gothic Renaissance palace, marked with a family crest, is flanked by two stout square towers.

Palacio de Polentinos

This palace, now a barracks, has a fine Renaissance entrance and patio.

Torre de Guzmán

Also called the Oñates Palace, it has a massive square corner tower with battlements, dating from the early 16C.

Palacio de Núñez Vela

The Renaissance palace of the Viceroy of Peru is now the Law Courts. Windows are framed by slender columns and coats of arms. The patio is lovely.

Palacio de los Dávila

Two 14C Gothic buildings with coats of arms give onto plaza Pedro Dávila and two others, belonging to the Episcopal Palace, face plaza de Rastro.

BADAJOZ

POPULATION: 130,247.

MICHELIN MAP 576 P 9 (TOWN PLAN) – EXTREMADURA (BADAJOZ)

Once an Arab fortress, Badjoz crowns a hill along the Guadiana river and the border with Portugal. Old walls, a 16C bridge and a gateway remain.

- **Information:** *Plaza de la Libertad 3, ☎924 01 36 58.*
- **Orient Yourself:** The A 5 links with Mérida (62km/39mi W), the EX 100 connects the town with Cáceres (91km/57mi NE).
- **Also See:** MÉRIDA, CÁCERES and ZAFRA (80km/50mi SE)

Background

An eventful history – Badajoz became capital in the 11C of a Moorish kingdom or *taifa*. It was besieged and pillaged in the 16C Wars of Succession between Spain and Portugal.

Today, Badajoz recalls its frontier heritage through fortress and ramparts while projecting an open character, shown by the **Puente Real** (Royal Bridge) and a modern art museum, the **Museo Extremeño e Iberoamericano de Arte Contemporáneo**. *Open 10am-1.30pm and 5-8pm; Sun, 10am-*

1.30pm. ⏲ *Closed Mon and public hols.* ☎*924 01 30 60.*

Worth a Visit

Catedral

⏲ *Open 11am-1pm and 5-7pm.* ⏲ *No visits on Sun because of religious services.* *1.80 € (museum).* ☎*924 23 90 27.*

The 13C Gothic cathedral was considerably remodelled during the Renaissance. Its fortress tower contrasts delicate Plateresque friezes and window surrounds. The impressive coro has stalls carved in 1557. The sacristy to the right of the chancel holds six fine 17C Flemish tapestries.

Museo Arqueológico Provincial

⏲ *Open 10am-3pm.* ⏲ *Closed Mon and public hols.* *1.20 €.* ☎*924 00 19 08.*

This modern museum in the 16C Palacio de la Roca in the *alcazaba* displays prehistoric and protohistoric stelae and figurines; Roman mosaics and bronze tools; Visigothic **pilasters** carved with plant and geometric motifs; medieval artefacts; and Islamic pieces.

Museo Provincial de Bellas Artes

⏲ *Open Sep-May, 10am-2pm and 4-6pm (Jun-Aug 6-8pm); Sat-Sun, 10am-2pm.* ⏲ *Closed Mon and public hols.* ☎*924 21 24 69 or 924 24 80 34.*

This fine arts museum in two elegant 19C mansions holds a collection of paintings, sculpture and sketches, particularly from the 19C and 20C.

Excursions

Olivenza

25km/15mi SW. Portuguese influence shows in this white-walled town set in olive groves. The Manueline style of architecture, named for King Manuel of Portugal (1495-1521), is late Gothic, with Renaissance, Moorish and maritime elements (knots, ropes and armillary spheres).

Iglesia de Santa María Magdalen★★ – The brothers Diego and Francisco de Arruda, architects of the Torre de Belém in Lisbon, are believed to have designed the church's nave. The sober elegance of the lierne and tierceron vaulting on cabled pillars contrasts the sumptuous altarpieces and *azulejos* in the Baroque sanctuary.

Museo Etnográfico González Santana – ⏲ *Open Oct-Apr, 11am (10am Sat) to 2pm and 4-7pm; May-Sep, 11am (10am Sat) to 2pm and 5-8pm; Sun and public hos 11am-2pm.* ⏲ *Closed Mon.* *1€.* ☎*924 49 02 22.*

The Fall From Grace of Don Manuel

Manuel Godoy Álvarez de Faria (1767-1851), the son of a modest provincial *hidalgo*, left his family at 17 for the Court where he enlisted in the Guards. Favours from Queen María Luisa assisted him in a meteoric career in politics; by the age of 25 he had been appointed Prime Minister. His rapid success earned him little sympathy from the Court, or from the common people who, outraged, accused him of being in Napoleon's pay. They insisted on his leaving the country. After the Aranjuez uprising (*see p 128*), he followed the royal family into exile at Bayonne where he drew up Charles IV's act of abdication which was to deliver Spain to Napoleon. He died, unknown, in Paris.

The War of the Oranges

At the end of the 13C, Olivenza was given in dowry to King Denis of Portugal. In 1801, it was ceded to Spain to prevent the Alentejo invasion – begun by Godoy's troops – becoming a major conflict between the two nations. The skirmish, however, left no other souvenir than the story of Godoy's futile gesture of sending oranges to Queen María Luisa from trees at the foot of the Elvas ramparts (see *The Green Guide Portugal*).

This ethnographic museum is in the 18C Panadería del Rey (King's Bakery) within a medieval castle. A keep built by João III of Portugal in 1488 offers fine views. Re-created workshops include a tailor's and a blacksmith's.

Ayuntamiento (town hall) – The **doorway**, in graceful Manueline style, is adorned with two armillary spheres, symbols of 15-16C Portuguese discoveries.

BAEZA★★

POPULATION: 17,691.

MICHELIN MAP 578 S 19 – ANDALUCÍA (JAÉN)

Noble Baeza stretches across a hill above olive groves and grain fields. Renaissance-style churches and mansions witness a bygone importance.

- **Information:** *Plaza del Pópulo, ☎953 74 04 44*
- **Orient Yourself:** With nearby, Úbeda, Baeza is in the green centre of Jaén province, near Parque Natural de Cazorla (to the E).
- **Don't Miss:** The heritage plazas.
- **Organizing Your Time:** Take half a day for the old quarter.
- **Also See:** ÚBEDA (9km/5.5mi W), Parque Natural de las SIERRAS DE CAZORLA, SEGURA Y LAS VILLAS and JAÉN (48km/30mi SW).

Walking About

MONUMENTAL CENTRE★★★

Route marked on town plan – allow half a day.

Plaza del Pópulo★

In the small, irregular square is the **Fuente de los Leones** (Lion Fountain), built with fragments from Cástulo. The Renaissance building to the left, bearing the coat of arms of Charles V, was, surprisingly, the **carnicería** (abattoir). The **Casa del Pópulo** (now the tourist office), at the end of the square, has Plateresque windows and medallions. Six doors once opened on six notaries' offices; court hearings were held upstairs. A balcony projects onto the **Puerto de Jaén**, which, along with the Villalar arch, honoured Charles V. The Jaén gate marked the emperor's visit on his way to Sevilla to marry Isabel of Portugal in 1526. The **Arco de Villalar** was erected in submission to the king after his victory, in 1521, over the Comuneros, whom the town had supported.

Plaza de Santa María

The walls of the 17C **Seminario de San Felipe Neri** bear inscriptions – traditionally done in bull's blood upon graduation. Behind the **Fuente de Santa María**, an arch adorned with atlantes, is the Gothic façade of the **Casas Consistoriales Altas**, with the coats of arms of Juana the Mad and Philip the Fair.

Catedral★ – *Open 10am-1pm and 4-6pm; Jun-Sep, 10am-1pm and 5-7pm. 2€ (museum). ☎953 74 41 57.*

The **interior★★** was remodelled by Vandelvira and his followers in the 16C. The outstanding Capilla Dorada (Gold Chapel) bears Italianate relief; St James' chapel has a fine Antique setting and St Joseph's is flanked by caryatids. The sacristy door has scrollwork and angels' heads. A monumental iron grille by Bartolomé closes the first bay in the nave; a pulpit of painted metal (1580) is in the transept. In the Capilla del Sagrario, to one end on the right, is a Baroque silver monstrance carried in procession on the feast of Corpus Christi

In the cloisters are four Mudéjar chapels with *atauriques,* inscribed in Arabic.

Palacio de Jabalquinto★

Open 9am-2pm. Closed Sat-Sun and public hols.

The palace **façade★★**, in perfect Flamboyant-Gothic style, is best seen in the

Address Book

WHERE TO EAT

Vandelvira
San Francisco 14 – ☎953 74 81 72 – www.vandelvira.es – Closed Sun evening and Mon. This elegant restaurant occupies part of the 16C Monasterio de San Francisco. Enter through impressive cloisters. The dining room is one floor up.

WHERE TO STAY

Puerta de la Luna
Melgares Raya 7 – ☎953 74 70 19 – www.hotelpuertadelaluna.com – – 40 rooms. 12€ - This 16C palace by the cathedral perfectly melds contemporary service with the tranquility of another era. Most rooms are doubles, with attention to details.

morning when the sun accentuates the decoration of windows and pinnacles. The **patio** (c 1600) is more sober, with a monumental Baroque stairway guarded by two lions.

Opposite is the Romanesque church of Santa Cruz, built immediately after the town's reconquest, with a Gothic chapel and wall paintings in the apse. *Open 11am-1pm and 4-5pm; Sun and public hols, noon-2pm.*

Antigua Universidad

Now a secondary school, the seat of the university was built between 1568 and 1593 and functioned until the 19C. Past the plain façade is an elegant Renaissance patio.

Plaza del Mercado Viejo (or Plaza de la Constitución)

This busy square is lined by bars and cafés. Fronting it are the Antigua Alhóndiga (former corn exchange), with porticoed façade (1554), and the Casas Consistoriales Bajas, built in 1703 as a gallery for officials to view celebrations held in the square.

Ayuntamiento★ (Town Hall)

The former law courts and prison has a Plateresque façade and balconies with heraldic decoration.

Ruinas de San Francisco

Construction of the convent began in 1538 under the direction of Vandelvira

Baeza

Aguayo	Y	2
Barbacana	Z	3
Cardenal Benavides Pas.	Y	5
Compañía	Z	6
Conde Romanones	Z	7
Córdoba Puerta de	Z	9
Gaspar Becerra	Y	12
General Cuadros	Y	13
José M. Cortés	Y	15
Magdalena	Y	16
Obispo Mengíbar	Z	17
Sacramento	Z	20
San Andrés	Y	21
San Felipe Neri Cuesta	Z	23
San Francisco	Y	
San Gil Cuesta de	Z	25

Antigua Carnicería	Z	A
Antigua Universidad	Z	E
Ayuntamiento	Y	H
Casas Consistoriales Atlas	Z	K
Ruinas de San Francisco (Auditorio)	Y	R
Seminario de San Felipe Neri	Z	S

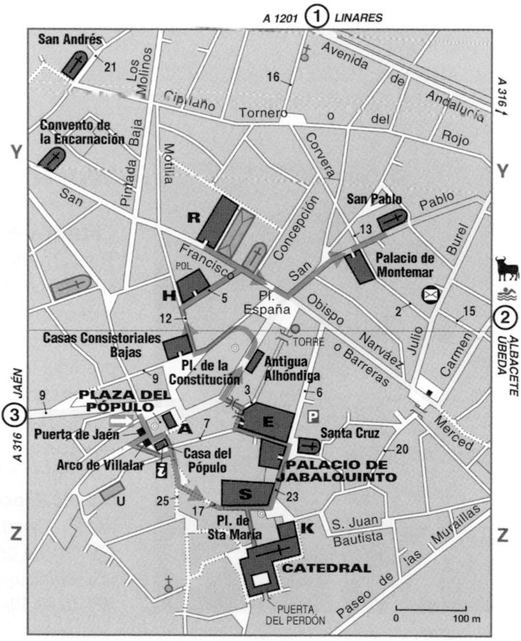

B. Kaufmann/MICHELIN

Façade of the Palacio de Jabalquinto

and lasted a century. The vast transept and apse and majestic carved stone altarpieces suggest the beautiful 16C church that once stood here. It is now an auditorium.

Palacio de Montemar (Palace of the Counts of Garcíez)

Beautiful Gothic windows and a Plateresque patio adorn this early-16C nobleman's palace. Along the street is the **Iglesia de San Pablo**, with its Renaissance façade.

Iglesia de San Andrés (note the **Gothic paintings**★ in the sacristy); the Convento de la Encarnación.

BARBASTRO

POPULATION: 15,827.

MICHELIN MAP 574 F 30 – ARAGÓN (HUESCA)

Barbastro's interesting architecture bears witness to its 16C importance. It is a base for excursions into the Central Pyrenees and capital of the Somontano wine region.

- **Information:** *Avenida de la Merced 64, ☎974 30 83 50.*
- **Orient Yourself:** Barbastro is at the end of two Pyrenean valleys, one leading to Parque de Ordesa, the other to the Maladeta range, via the Congosto de Ventamillo canyon.
- **Also See:** PIRINEOS ARAGONESES, HUESCA (52km/32mi NW) and LLEIDA/LÉRIDA (68km/42mi SE).

B. Brillion/MICHELIN

Alquézar

Worth a Visit

Catedral★

The cathedral is a standard hall-church with three elegant aisles beneath richly ornamented vaulting with gilded decoration, borne by slender columns. The predella on the high altar **retable** is an important work by Damián Forment. Several side chapels are Churrigueresque; the first on the left-hand side holds a fine early-16C retable. The **Museo Diocesano** is open to the public. *Open 9.30am-noon and 5-8pm. Closed on public hols. No visits during religious services. ☎974 31 16 82 or 974 30 83 50.*

Complejo de San Julián y Santa Lucía

The former Hospital de San Julián houses the Tourist Office, a wine shop, and a **museum** dedicated to the excellent Somontano appellation. The 16C Renaissance church of San Julián opposite houses the **Centro de Interpretación del Somontano★**, highlighting the area and its tourist sites via a short film. *Open 10am to 2pm and 4.30-8pm. Closed Sun (except in summer), Mon morning, 1 and 6 Jan, 1-8 Sep, and 25 Dec. 974 31 55 75.*

Excursions

Alquézar★

23km/14mi NW on the A 1232, following the Río Vero. Alquézar enjoys a magnificent isolated **setting★★** amid red earth, appearing to cling to a rocky promontory in a loop of the river.

Old quarter – The medieval old quarter is a maze of uneven streets lined by houses adorned with rounded stone doorways and coats of arms. The arcaded main square is enchanting.

Colegiata★ – *Guided tours, 11am-1.30pm and 4-6pm; in summer, 11am-1pm and 4.30-7.30pm. Closed Tue. 2 €. 974 31 89 40/60.* A Moorish **alcázar** on the site fell to Sancho Ramírez, King of Aragón. In the late 11C and early 12C, the walls were constructed, along with a church (rebuilt in 1530). A beautiful Romanesque Christ dates from the 12C.

Cañón del río Vero★ – Allow a day to walk up and in some places wade or swim this spectacular canyon. Or hike only to the Roman bridge at Villacantal (*2 hrs round trip*) for an overview and to see impressive ochre and grey walls.

TOUR THROUGH THE RIBAGORZA

85km/53mi– allow one day

Follows the Esera and Isábena rivers, through the historic county of Ribagorza, in the pre-Pyrenees of Aragón.

Leave Barbastro on the N 123; after 16km/10mi go right onto the A 2211.

Santuario de Torreciudad

In 1804, an 11C Romanesque statue of Our Lady of Torreciudad was placed in a small shrine and locally venerated. In 1975 a pilgrimage church was built under the auspices of Monsignor José María Escrivá de Balaguer (now canonised), founder of Opus Dei (1928). Before the brick buildings, a vast esplanade affords beautiful **views★** of the Pyrenees and the El Grado dam. The statue of Our Lady of Torreciudad is in the lower part of the altarpiece. *Open 10am-2pm and 4-7pm (7.30pm 1 May-15 Jun; 8.30pm Jul-15 Sep). 974 30 40 25.*

From Torreciudad, return to the A 2211, heading towards La Puebla de Castro, then take the N 123ª.

Graus

The village huddles around the irregular **Plaza de España**, lined by old houses decorated with frescoes, carved beams and brick galleries. The 16C **Santuario de la Virgen de la Peña★★** has a Renaissance doorway and single aisle crowned by pointed vaulting.

The A 1605 acrosses the Esera river.

Roda de Isábena★

26.5km/16.5mi from Graus. This picturesque village perches on a promontory in a beautiful mountain **setting★**. Construction of the impressive **cathedral★** began in the 11C. Most of the interior, basilical in plan with three aisles, was built in the 12C. In the central **crypt** is the **tomb of San Ramón★★**, with interesting polychrome low reliefs. A 13C fresco adorns a chapel off the cloisters. *Guided tours at 11.15am, noon, 12.45pm, 1.30pm, 4pm, 4.45pm, 5.30pm and 6.15pm; in summer at 5.15pm, 6pm and 6.45pm 1.80 €. 974 54 45 35.*

Continue 16km/10mi N on A 1605.

Monasterio de Santa María de Obarra

Only the 10-11C church, built by Lombard masters, remains of this monastery. A 12C hermitage, the Ermita de San Pablo, stands to one side.

BARCELONA★★★

POPULATION: 1 681 132

MICHELIN MAP 574 H 36 (TOWN PLAN) – MAP 122 COSTA BRAVA – MICHELIN CITY PLANS BARCELONA 40, 41 AND 2040 – CATALUNYA (BARCELONA)

Most cosmopolitan of Spanish cities, capital of Cataluña, Barcelona is open and welcoming, melding tradition and the avant-garde. It is a Mediterranean metropolis, a major port, and a centre of modern art that lives life to the full.

- **Information:** *Paseo de Gracia 107 (Palau Robert), ☎93 238 80 91; Plaza de Catalunya 17, ☎807 11 72 22; Sants Estació, ☎807 11 72 22. www.gencat.es/probert/indexfo.htm and www.barcelonaturisme.com.*
- **Orient Yourself:** Seaside Barcelona is the hub of northeastern Spain. The AP7 motorway runs from Murcia to Girona and France; the C32 heads to the resorts to the north and south to Tarragona; the C 16 veers inland to Manresa (59km/37mi NE) and the C 17 to Vic.
- **Parking:** It's impossible in the Gothic Quarter, difficult elsewhere except in car parks.
- **Don't Miss:** Sagrada Familia church, and Modernist masterpieces of architecture along Passeig de Gràcia.
- **Organizing Your Time:** Start from the Gothic Quarter, and see the Ramblas, Passeig de Gràcia and Sagrada Familia before all else.
- **Especially for Kids:** El Poble Espanyol, Parc Güell and the Aquarium.
- **Also See:** SITGES (45km/28mi SW), GIRONA/GERONA (97km/60mi NE), COSTA BRAVA (NE), VIC (66km/41mi N), TARRAGONA (109km/68mi SW) and COSTA DORADA (SW).

A Bit of History

The growth of the city – Founded by the Phocaeans, the city grew as Roman **Barcino**, within a 3C fortified wall. In the 12C, Barcelona became the capital of Catalunya and seat of the expanding kingdom of Aragón-Catalunya. Catalan Gothic architecture blossomed.

Catalunya sided with the Archduke of Austria in the War of the Spanish Succession (1701-14), and in defeat lost its autonomy. Montjuïc hill was fortified by the victors, and construction was prohibited except in the old city. Building outside the walls began again in the mid-19C. Industrialisation followed, along with two International Exhibitions, in 1888 and 1929. Modernist architecture flowered.

Barcelona present and future – Today's Barcelona is an industrial centre and busy port, seat of the Generalitat de Catalunya. It is a cultural centre and university town with an opera house, museums, theatres and concert halls. The 1992 Olympic Games brought large-scale planning projects that changed the city. The Forum of Cultures in 2004 led to the redevelopment of the Sant Adrià del Besòs waterfront.

Catalan identity – Catalan, banned under the Franco regime, is the proud language along with Castilian Spanish, used on all street names and with a flourishing literature.

A thriving centre for artists – Barcelona remains a hub for great artists. Painters Picasso, Miró, Dalí, Tàpies, sculptor Subirachs and the architects Gaudí, Josep Lluís Sert, Bofill and Bohigas all lived here.

Visit

El Ensanche and Modernist Architecture★★

See general plan

Barcelona's Eixample (*Ensanche*, or enlargment) grew in the 19C. In Ildefonso Cerdà's 1859 grid plan, streets circumscribe blocks of houses (*mançanes* in Catalan or *manzanas* in Castilian) octagonal in shape with trimmed corners. Wide avinguda Diagonal and La Meridiana cross the grid to meet on plaça de les Glòries Catalanes. In this ordered new section architects transformed El Ensanche into the centre of Modernism in Barcelona.

La Sagrada Familia★★★ (Church of the Holy Family)

Open Jan-Feb, 9am-6pm (8pm Apr-Sep). Closed 1, 6 Jan and 25 Dec. 8 €. 93 208 04 14.

The project, begun in 1882, was taken over by Gaudí in 1883. He planned a Latin Cross church with five aisles and a transept with three aisles. Three façades were each to be dominated by four spires representing the Apostles with a central spire to represent Christ and the Evangelists. The nave was to be a forest of columns. In his lifetime, only the crypt, the apsidal walls, one of the towers and the **Nativity façade**★★ were finished. The Nativity façade comprises three doorways, Faith, Hope and Charity. Work resumed in 1940. The Passion façade was completed in 1981.

The top of the east spire affords a good **view**★★ of the work on the church, and of Barcelona. Domènech i Montaner's **Hospital Sant Pau**★, with its remarkable glazed tile roofs, may be seen at the end of avinguda de Gaudí.

Passeig de Gràcia★★

Along this boulevard, with elegant wrought-iron **street lamps**★ by Pere Falqués (1900), lies some of Barcelona's finest Modernist architecture, in the **Manzana de la Discordia**★★ (Block of Discord): n°35 **Casa Lleó Morera**★ (1905) by Domènech i Montaner, n°41 **Casa Amatller**★ (1900) by Puig i Cadafalch (now the Instituto Amatller and the Centro del Modernismo, which arranges tours of Modernist Barcelona), and n°43 **Casa Batlló**★★ (1904-06) by Gaudí, with its extraordinary mosaic façade and undulating roof. *Open 9am-8pm. 16.50€. 93 216 03 06*

La Pedrera or Casa Milà★★★

Open 10am-8pm; last admission 30min before closing. Closed 1, 6 Jan, second week of Jan and 25-26 Dec. 8€. 902 40 09 73.

With its undulating lines, this magnificent Gaudí building resembles a submarine cliff. Visit the **roof and attic**★ and a **residential floor**★.The **Espai Gaudí** exhibits drawings and models by the artist. The roof, with its forest of chimneys, provides fine **views**★.

El Piso★ is a re-created apartment of an early 20C upper-class family.

Turn right from plaça de Joan Carles I into avinguda Diagonal.

Gaudí (1852-1926)

Antoni Gaudí, born in Reus, studied architecture in Barcelona. His style was influenced first by Catalan Gothic architecture with its emphasis on large areas of space (wide naves, the effect of airy spaciousness) and subsequently by the Islamic and Mudejar styles. He also studied nature, observing plants and animals which inspired his shapes, colours and textures. He gave full rein to these images – liana-like curves, the rising and breaking of waves, rugged rocks and the serrations on leaves and flowers – when designing his fabulous buildings. Part of his great originality lay in his use of parabolic arches and spirals (as can be seen in the chimneys of Casa Milà). An intensely religious man, Gaudí drew upon a great many religious symbols for his buildings, especially for the Sagrada Familia (Church of the Holy Family) on which he worked for over 40 years. He spent his last years here, hidden away in a small room in the middle of the site, until his tragic death when he was run over by a tram.

Gaudí worked a great deal for the banker **Eusebi Güell**, his patron and admirer, who asked him to design his private houses.

Gaudí's main works are the Sagrada Familia, Casa Batlló, La Pedrera, Casa Vicens, Palau Güell, Pavellons Güell and the Parc Güell.

Diagonal

Casa Quadras (1904), a Modernist building on the right, was designed by Puig i Cadafalch. Along on the left, his **Casa de les Punxes** (**Casa Terrades**★) bears the stamp of Flemish influence.

Parc Güell★★

Kids *Open Nov-Feb, 10am-6pm (7pm Mar and Oct; 8pm Apr and Sep; 9pm May-Aug). ☎93 413 24 00.*

Gaudí's imagination shines in the most famous of his commissions by Güell. In this enchanted forest are mushroom-shaped pavilions, a mosaic dragon, the **Chamber of the Columns**, whose undulating mosaic roof covers a forest of sloping columns, and the remarkable **rolling bench**★★. **Casa-Museu Gaudí**★, is the architect's house. (*Open 10am-6pm (7pm Mar-Apr and Oct; 8pm May-Sep). Closed 1 Jan, 6 Jan (afternoon) and 25 and 26 Dec (afternoon). 4 €. (9 € with Sagrada Familia) ☎93 219 38 11).*

Palau de la Música Catalana★★

In Carrer de Sant Pere Mès Alt. Guided tours (1hr), 10am-3.30pm; 10am-5pm Aug and Holy Week. Closed 1 Jan and 25 Dec. 8 €. Advance sales ☎902 44 28 82.

This concert hall (1905-1908) is Domènech i Montaner's most famous work. The **exterior**★ displays lavish mosaics. The interior, dominated by an **inverted cupola**★★ of polychrome glass, is decorated with sculpted groups and mosaic figurines. A concert in this odd venue is a memorable.

> **Touring Tip**
>
> The Multiticket de la Ruta del Modernismo offers half-price entry to nine of the main Modernist sights in Barcelona (Palau Güell, Palau de la Música, La Pedrera, Sagrada Familia etc). *For further information, contact the Casa Amatller, ☎902 07 66 21.*

Fundació Antoni Tàpies★★

Open 10am-8pm. Closed Mon, 1 and 6 Jan and 25-26 Dec. 6 €. ☎ 93 487 03 15.

Tàpies established his foundation in an ex-publishing house designed by Domènech i Montaner. The brick building is crowned by an aerial sculpture by Tàpies, *Núvol i Cadira* (cloud and chair), the emblem of the museum.

The bare interior, where everything is painted in the brown, beige, grey and ochre favoured by Tàpies, is lit by skylights (a cupola and a pyramid). Paintings and sculptures trace the development of Tàpies' work since 1948.

Walking About

BARRi GÒTIC★★ (GOTHIC QUARTER)

See plan of old city.

R. Mattès/MICHELIN

Detail on the towers of the Sagrada Familia

Practical Information

GETTING THERE

Airport – ☎02 404 704. 18km/11mi from the city centre. Can be reached by local train *(tren de cercanía)* every 15min from 6am to 10.30pm, or by the bus service from the plaça de Catalunya and plaça de Espanya, departing every 15min from 5.30am to 11pm. By taxi, the fare from the city centre will be approximately 20 €.

Taxis – The city's black and yellow taxis are an efficient, inexpensive way of getting around the city. Radio Taxi Barcelona: ☎93 303 30 33; Tele-Taxi: ☎ 93 466 56 56.

Metro – *Metro stations (Ⓜ) are shown on the maps in this guide.* For further information: ☎93 318 70 74 or visit www.tmb.net Information on access for the disabled can be obtained on ☎ 93 412 44 44.

The network is open 5am-midnight Mon-Thu; 5am-2am Fri, Sat and days preceding public holidays; 6am-midnight Sun; and 6am-11pm on weekday public holidays. A free metro guide is available. Metro **tickets and cards** can also be used on buses, the "Tramvía Blau" (a tourist tram in the Diagonal section of the city) and train services operated by Ferrocarriles de la Generalitat de Catalunya. In addition to single tickets, multi-journey cards include the T-1 (valid for 10 trips), T-DIA (unlimited travel for one day), T50-30 (50 trips in 30 days) and the T-MES (unlimited travel for one month).

Streetcars – There are four lines (T1, T2, T3 and T4).

Regional railway network – *Ferrocarriles Catalanes train stations are shown on the maps in this guide.* For further information, call ☎93 205 15 15. Free connections to the metro system may be made at these stations: Avenida Carrilet /L'Hospitalet, Espanya, Catalunya and Diagonal/Provença.

Bus Turístic – This excellent service offers visitors a variety of bus itineraries throughout the city. Daily departures from plaça de Catalunya starting at 9am.

Boat trips – The Las Golondrinas company organises trips around the port *(approx 35min)*. Departures from Portal de la Pau, opposite the Columbus monument. ☎93 442 31 06.

SIGHTSEEING

Publications – *The Guía del Ocio* is a weekly guide on sale at newspaper stands containing a list of every cultural event in the city. The city's airport and tourist offices are also able to provide visitors with a full range of booklets and leaflets produced by the Generalitat de Catalunya's Department of Industry, Commerce and Tourism.

Combined tickets and discounts – Three tickets offering discounts are available to tourists:

- **Barcelona Card** (2, 3, 4 or 5 days): unlimited transport, discounts from 20 to 50% or free entry in 30 museums, and other reductions for shows and in shops and restaurants. On sale at the city's tourist offices *(plaça de Catalunya and plaça de Sant Jaume)*. For further information: ☎ 906 30 12 82 or visit www.barcelonaturisme.com
- **Articket**: Valid six months, cost 20€, for entry to MNAC, Fundació Joan Miró, Fundació Antoni Tàpies, the CCCB, Centre de Cultura de la Caixa and the MACBA. ☎902 101 212, www.telentrada.com.
- **Multiticket de la Ruta del Modernismo**: see Special Features, "El Ensanche and Modernist Architecture".

DISTRICTS

Barri Gòtic – Following an intense restoration programme undertaken during the 1920s, the area containing the city's major historical buildings was renamed the Gothic quarter.

Ciutat Vella – The old city includes districts as diverse as Santa Anna, La Mercè, Sant Pere and El Raval. The latter, which used to be known as the Barri Xino (Chinatown), now contains Barcelona's leading cultural centres and is a fine example of urban renovation.

Eixample – Eixample (Ensanche) developed following the destruction of the city's medieval walls. The district personifies the bourgeois, elegant Barcelona of the end of the 19C, with its

R. Mattès/MICHELIN

La Boquería market

prestigious boutiques, smart avenues and some of the best examples of Modernist architecture.

Gràcia – This *barrio*, situated at the end of the Passeig de Gràcia, is one of the city's most characteristic areas. Gràcia developed from its early agricultural origins into an urban area as a result of the influx of shopkeepers, artisans and factory workers. During the 19C, Gràcia was renowned for its Republican sympathies. Today, it still hosts a number of popular fiestas.

Ribera – With its narrow alleyways and Gothic architecture, this former fishermen's quarter still retains an unquestionable charm. Its main attractions are the Calle Montcada and the Iglesia de Santa María del Mar.

Barceloneta – Barceloneta is famous for its outdoor stalls, restaurants and nautical atmosphere.

Vila Olímpica – The Olympic Village was built to accommodate sportsmen and sportswomen participating in the 1992 games. Nowadays, it is a modern district with wide avenues, landscaped areas and direct access to some of Barcelona's restored beaches.

Les Corts – This district is located at the upper end of Diagonal and includes the **Ciudad Universitaria** and the **Camp Nou**, the home of Barcelona Football Club and its football-orientated **Museo del Barça**.

Sarrià – Sarrià nestles at the foot of the Sierra de Collserola and has managed to retain its traditional, tranquil character. The neighbouring districts of **Pedralbes** and **Sant Gervasi de Cassoles**, at the foot of Tibidabo, have become a favourite hangout for the city's well-heeled inhabitants.

Sants – One of the city's main working class districts close to the railway station of the same name.

Horta-Guinardó – This barrio at the foot of Collserola was first populated by peasants and then by factory workers. It is home to the **Laberinto de Horta** (to the north), an 18C property with attractive gardens, and the **Velódromo**, a venue for sporting events and major music events.

For coin ranges, see the Legend at the back of the guide.

WHERE TO EAT

Ca l´Estevet

Valldonzella 46 (Ciutat Vella) – Universitat – 93 302 41 86 – Closed Sun and public hols – . A small, family-run restaurant with a friendly atmosphere, decorated with attractive azulejos and photographs of famous people.

Agut

Gignàs 16 (Ciutat Vella) – Jaume I – 93 315 17 09 – Closed Sun eve, Mon and in Aug – Reservations advisable. This cosy restaurant is on a lane in the old city. Agut has been serving traditional Catalan cuisine for over 80 years. The environment is subtly lit, intimate and bohemian, the walls covered with paintings.

El Tragaluz

Passatge de la Concepció 5 (Eixample) – Diagonal – 93 487 06 21 – www.grupotragaluz.com/tragaluz – Closed 1 Jan, Sat evening-Sun, and Aug. One of Barcelona's most charismatic and dynamic restaurants takes up three storeys with unique sliding greenhouse roof. It serves Mediterranean and avante garde fare.

7 Portes

Passeig d'Isabel II 14 (Ciutat Vella) – Jaume I – 93 319 30 33 – www.7portes.com – . This late-hours restaurant in the emblematic Porxos d'en Xifre building (1836) preserves period decor. The fare is traditionally Catalan.

La Provença

Provença 242 (Eixample) – Provença – 93 323 23 67 – www.laprovenza.com – . In the Eixample district, just a stone's throw from the Passeig de Gràcia, pleasant and with cheerful, tasteful, decor, serving a range of regional cuisine. Good for the price.

Agua
Passeig Marítim Barceloneta 30 (Vila Olimpica) – Barceloneta – 93 225 12 72 – www.grupotragaluz.com – Closed 24-25 Dec. A spacious restaurant with designer furniture and African sculpture. Its terrace, always crowded in summer, Is the perfect spot for a quiet dinner by the sea. Mediterranean cuisine and rice dishes prepared in a charcoal oven.

Los Caracoles
Escudellers 14 (Ciutat Vella) – Liceu – 93 302 31 85 – . Founded in 1835, this famous restaurant, one of the gastronomic emblems of Barcelona, is located on the corner of calles Escudellers and Nou de Sant Franc. The decor here consists of tiled floors, wine barrels, murals and photos. Regional and traditional cuisine.

Casa Leopoldo
Sant Rafel 24 (Ciutat Vella) – Liceu – 93 441 30 14 – www.casaleopoldo.com – Closed Mon, evenings of public hols, Holy Week, and August. This classic Barcelona restaurant is decorated with bullfighting mementoes, signed photos of famous customers and a superb bottle collection.

Casa Calvet
Casp, 48 (Eixample) – Urquinaona – 93 412 40 12 – www.casacalvet.es – Closed Sun, public hols and Holy Week and Christmas week – . The former offices of a textile company, in a magnificent Modernist building designed by Gaudí, are dominated by iron beams and wood floors. Traditional Mediterranean dishes show creative touches.

TAPAS

Irati Taverna Basca
Cardenal Casanyes 17 (Barri Gòtic) – Liceu – 93 302 30 84 – www.sagardi.com – . Near the plaza de la Boqueria, in one of the busiest districts, a typical tapas bar with a counter full of Basque skewers along with a grill room with a limited menu.

Euskal Etxea
Placeta Montcada 1-3 (Ribera) – Liceu – 93 310 21 85 – Closed Sun, Christmas week and 15-30 Aug – . By the church of Santa María del Mar, a bar and cosy dining room, the perfect setting for a glass of txacolí (a Basque white wine) and Basque pork chops and fried fish.

El Xampanyet
Montcada 22 (Ribera) – Jaume I – 93 319 70 03 – Closed Sun evening, Mon, evenings of public hols, in Aug and during Holy Week – 6 €. Famous for anchovies and sparkling wine.

WHERE TO STAY

Hotel Condal
Boquería 23 (Barrio Gótico) – Liceu – 93 318 18 82 – www.hotelcondal.es – – 52 rooms. Steps from La Rambla, this hotel is a fine base for visiting the Old City. Personnel are attentive, and the rooms are adequate.

Hostal d'Uxelles
Gran Vía de les Corts Catalanes, 688 and 667 (at the plaza de Tetuan) – Tetuan – 93 265 25 60 – www.hotelduxelles.com – 21 rooms – 7 €. Rooms in this inn, in two buildings, are a delightful combination of comfort, antiques, and attention to details. Most have a private terrace, all have Andalusian-style baths.

Hotel Hesperia Metropol
Ample 31 (Ribera) – Jaume I – 93 310 51 00 – www.hesperia-metropol.com – – 68 rooms – 10.50 €. This pleasant hotel close to the waterfront is situated in a narrow street in the old quarter, between the Post Office and the Basílica de La Mercè. An attractive feature here is the lobby in a covered patio. The guest rooms are comfortable, with the usual creature comforts.

Hotel Medicis
Castillejos 340 (Eixample) – Hospital Sant Pau – 93 450 00 53 – www.mediumhoteles.com – – 29 rooms – 7 €. This modern hotel near the Sagrada Familia, has functional but comfortable rooms, a good value for those who prefer to stay along the "Modernist Route".

Hotel Gaudí
Nou de la Rambla 12 (Ciutat Vella) – Liceu – 93 317 90 32 – www.hotelgaudi.es – – 73 rooms – 10€. Its location opposite the Palacio Güell and Modernist decor evoke the namesake artist. Try for a rooms with balcony on an upper floors for superb

views of the city and the Palacio Güell.

Hotel Granvía
Gran Vía de les Corts Catalanes 642 (Eixample) – Catalunya – 93 318 19 00 – www.nnhotels.es – – 55 rooms – 10 €. This impressive banker's residence from the late 19C was converted into a hotel in 1936. The room rates here are very reasonable given the charming setting.

Hotel Arts Barcelona
Marina 19 – Ciutadella – 93 221 10 00 – – 397 rooms – 26 €. – Restaurant 43/62 €. Barcelona's most luxurious hotel, with an emphasis on modern art and design, is in the Vila Olímpica. Every room enjoys impressive views of the city and Mediterranean.

TAKING A BREAK

Café de la Opera
Rambla dels Caputxins 74 (Ciutat Vella) – Drassanes – 93 317 75 85 – www.cafeoperabcn.com – Open 8am-2.30am (holidays 8.30am-3am). Because of its history, Modernist façade and 19C atmosphere, this café is one of the most famous in the city. Not to be missed!

El Paraigua
Passatge de l'Enseyança 2 (Horta)-

J. Malburet/MICHELIN

Hotel Arts and Torre Mapfre

Jaime I – 93 302 11 31 – www.elparaigua.com – Open 8am-2am; bar from 6pm (closed Sun). This unusual café, in an ex-umbrella factory, is decorated with mirrors and Modernist furnishings. Its cocktail bar is in a vaulted 1650 cellar; the music is classical.

Xiringuito Escribà
Platja del Bogatell – Ronda Litoral, 42 (Vila Olímpica-Poble Nou) – Ciutadella-Vila Olímpica – 932 21 07 29 – www.

TURESPAÑA

A street café in Barcelona

escriba.es – Open Tue-Thu 11am-5pm, Fri-Sun 9am-11pm. Open along the sea since 1906, this is a Barcelona summer institution, a good place to enjoy paella and music in a genuine setting.

Quatre Gats
Carrer Montsió 3 bis (Ciutat Vella) – Catalunya – 93 302 41 40 – www.4gats.com – Open 8am-2am. The symbol of Modernist and bohemian Barcelona. This landmark café was a meeting-place for artists such as Picasso, Casas and Utrillo. Reasonable lunchtime menu.

BARS AND CAFÉS

Jamboree
Plaça Reial 17 (Ciutat Vella) – Liceu – 933 01 75 64 – Open 10.30pm-5.30am. The meeting point in Barcelona for jazz musicians and aficionados.

La Fira
Provença 171 (Eixample) – Diagonal - 933 23 72 71 – Open Mon-Thu, 10.30pm-3am; Fri-Sat, 10.30pm-4.30am. An attractive bar decorated with robots and fairground amusements.

La Paloma
Tigre 27 (Sant Antoni) – Universitat – 933 01 68 97 – Open Thu-Sat, 6-9.30am and 11.30am-5am; Sun, 6-9.30am. One of the most packed of the city's clubs since 1903, with live music and a guest DJs from all over.

London Bar
Nou de la Rambla 34 (Ciutat Vella) – Liceu – 93 318 52 81 – www.londonbarbcn.com – Open Tue-Thu and Sun, 7.30pm-4am; Fri-Sat, 7.30pm-5am. A favourite with circus performers when it first opened in 1909. Hemingway, Miró and others also came here to enjoy its lively atmosphere.

Luz de Gas-Port Vell
Moll del Dipósit (Port Vell-delante de Palau de Mar)- Barceloneta – 93 484 23 26 – www.luzdegas.com – Open noon-3am. One of the busiest and most unusual summer drinking spots, at the port, it is partly on the pier as an open-air bar, and partly an enclosed wooden bar with a small dance floor.

Margarita Blue
Josep Anselm Clavé 6 (Ciutat Vella) – Drassanes – 934 12 54 89 – Open Mon-Thu, 11am-2pm and 7pm-2am; Fri-Sat, 7am-3pm. Unusual decoration (mirrors of all shapes and sizes, weird objects and antique lamps) helps make this one of the city's most popular bars, hosting weekly shows and concerts. The cuisine is Tex-Mex.

Marina Port Olympic
Passeig Maritim Port Olympic – Ciutadella Vila Olímpica. One of the lieveliest spots has something for every taste, from restaurants to fast food, bars like the Gran Casino, and discos, including the popular Luna Mora.

Pastís
Santa Mònica 4 (Ciutat Vella) – Drassanes – 933 18 79 80 – Open Sun-Thu 7.30pm-2.30am, Fri-Sat 7.30pm-3.30am. Enjoy a pastís in this bar with 40 years of tradition as you listen to Jacques Brel, Moustaki and Edith Piaf; or dance a tango until dawn on Tuesday or enjoy French chansons late Saturday.

Torres de Ávila
Avenida del Marquès de Comillas 25 (Sants – Montjuïc) – Espanya – 934 24 93 09 – Open Fri-Sat, 12.30pm-7am. This popular venue, refurbished by designers Mariscal and Arribas, attracts large crowds in summer.

ENTERTAINMENT

The **Palau de la Música Catalana** (*see p 148*), **Gran Teatre del Liceu** (*see p 151*) and the recently opened **Auditorio** are the biggest concert halls. Major pop and rock concerts are held in the **Palau Sant Jordi** (*see p 163*), **Velódromo de Horta, Plaza de Toros Monumental** and **Sot del Migdia**. The **Festival del Grec** (end of June to early August) is held at several venues, including the **Teatre Grec de Montjuïc**.

SHOPPING

ANTIQUES

Bulevard Antiquaris – *Passeig de Gràcia 55 (Eixample)*
An area containing over 70 shops selling a range of artwork and antiques.

Plaza de la Catedra – *(Ciutat Vella)*
A small market with stalls selling antiques is held here on public holidays.

Plaza Sant Josep Oriol – *(Ciutat Vella)*
Mirrors, furniture, and paintings are sold at this popular weekend market.

Calle de la Palla and calle Banys Nous – *(Ciutat Vella)*
These two streets are well-known for their reputable antique shops.

ART GALLERIES

Barcelona's most prestigious galleries can mainly be found in the calle Consell de Cent **(Carles Tatché, René Metras, Sala Gaudí)**, along the Rambla de Catalunya **(Joan Prats)**, on the periphery of the Born market and around the MACBA. The **Galeria Maeght** and the **Sala Montcada** are both located in the calle Montcada.

The Gothic quarter, named for the many buildings constructed between the 13C and 15C, holds traces of Roman settlement and massive 4C walls.

Plaça Nova

This is the heart of the quarter, where the Romans built an enclosure with walls 9m/30ft high. Two watchtowers that flanked the West Gate (converted to a house in the Middle Ages) remain.

Opposite the cathedral, the **Collegi d'Arquitectes** (College of Architects) is a modern surprise, its decorative band of cement engraved by Picasso.

Catedral★

Choir, roof and chapter museum open 1-4.30pm. 4 €. Separate visits at other times to roof (2 €), museum (1 €) or choir (2 €). 93 315 15 54 or 93 315 22 13.
The cathedral is on **pla de la Seu**, marked on one side by the **Casa de**

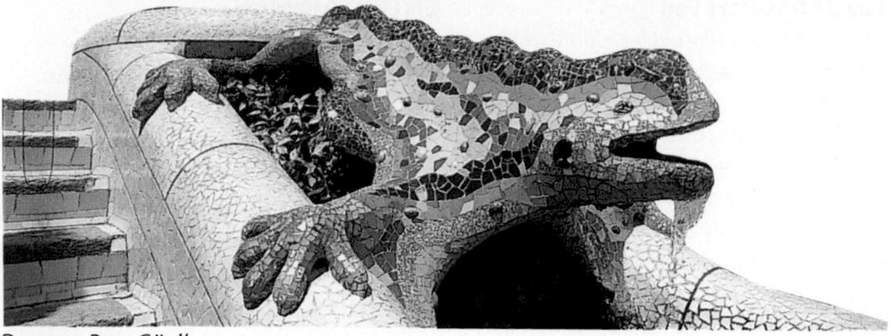
J. Malburet/MICHELIN

Dragon, Parc Güell

l'Ardiaca★ (12C-15C), and on the other by the **Casa de la Canonja** (16C) and **pia Almoina**, which house the **Museo Diocesano de Barcelona** (*Open 10am-2pm and 5-8pm; Sun, 11am-2pm. Closed Mon. 6 €. 93 315 22 13).* The cathedral was built on the site of a Romanesque church, from the late 13C to 1450. The façade and spire are 19C, based on old French designs.

The Catalan Gothic **interior**★ has an outstanding elevation with slender pillars. The nave is lit by a fine lantern-tower; the perspective is broken by the **coro**★★, with double rows of beautifully carved **stalls**. Note the humorous scenes adorning the misericords. In the early 16C, the backs were painted with the coats of arms of knights of the Order of the Golden Fleece by Juan de Borgoña, in one of the most impressive achievements of European heraldry.

The side chapels hold exquisite retables and marble tombs. The white marble **choir screen**★ was sculpted in the 16C after drawings by Bartolomé Ordóñez. Statues illustrate the martydom of St Eulàlia, patron of Barcelona. Her relics lie in the **crypt**★ in a 14C Pisan-style alabaster sarcophagus.

The Capilla del Santísimo (right of the entry) contains the 15C *Christ of Lepanto,* said to have been on the prow of the galley of Don Juan of Austria in the Battle of Lepanto (1571). In the next chapel is a Gothic retable by Bernat Martorell, also the artist of the **retable of the Transfiguration**★ in the ambulatory.

Cathedral roof visit – *by elevator from an ambulatory chapel.* Metal walkways under the imposing silhouettes of the cathedral towers and cupola allow exceptional **views**★★ of the city.

Modernist Architecture

Modernism developed between 1890 and 1920 alongside similar movements in other parts of Europe, such as Art Nouveau in both France and Great Britain and Jugendstil in Germany. Modernist architecture sprang from artistic exploration that combined new industrial materials with modern techniques, using decorative motifs like curve and counter-curve and asymmetrical shapes in stained glass, ceramics and metal. It enjoyed great success in Catalunya at a time when large fortunes were being made as a result of industrialisation. The most representative architects of the style were Antoni Gaudí, Domènech i Montaner, Puig i Cadafalch and Jujol. A parallel movement in Catalan literature known as Renaixença also flourished during this period.

Claustro★

The cloisters are an oasis, and are home to a flock of geese. In the chapter house, a museum houses a Pietà by Bermejo (1490), altarpiece panels by the 15C artist Jaime Huguet and the missal of St Eulàlia, enhanced by delicate miniatures. (*Open 10am-12.45pm and 5-6.45pm; Sun and public hols, 10am-1.15pm. 1 €. 93 315 15 54.)*

Return to pla de la Seu and head along carrer dels Comtes.

Museu Frederic Marès★

The entry (in the Palau Reial Major) is on tiny **plaça de Sant Iu**, always full of mime artists and street musicians (see description under Worth a Visit).

Palau del Lloctinent
This 16C late-Gothic palace was the residence of the viceroys of Catalunya.

Plaça del Rei★★
On this splendid square stand the Palau Reial Major (at the back), the Capilla de Santa Àgata (right) and the Palau del Lloctinent. In the right corner, the Casa Clariana-Padellàs, housing the **Museu d'Història de la Ciutat**★★ (*see Worth a Visit*), is a 15C Gothic mansion moved stone by stone when the via Laietana was built in 1931.

Palau Reial Major
Built in the 11C and 12C, the palace acquired its present appearance in the 14C. It was the seat of the counts of Barcelona and the kings of Aragón. Arches link huge buttresses in the façade; the original façade has rose windows.

Plaça Ramón Berenguer el Gran
From the plaza, Roman walls are visible, incorporated into the Palau Reial.

Carrer Paradis
At no. 10 stand four Roman **columns**★, remains of the Temple of Augustus.
Carrer Paradis leads into carrer de la Pietat, bordered on the left by the Gothic façade of the Casa dels Canonges. The cathedral cloister doorway opposite is adorned with a wooden 16C sculpture of a *Pietà*.

Ajuntament (Town Hall)
The town hall façade on plaça Sant Jaume is neo-Classical; that on carrer de la Ciutat is an outstanding 14C Gothic construction.

Palau de la Generalitat (Provincial Council)
This vast 15C-17C edifice is the seat of the Autonomous Government of Catalunya. It has a Renaissance-style façade on plaça Sant Jaume (c 1600). (*Guided tours (50min) 2nd and 4th Sun of each month, 10.30am-1.30pm, with appointment. ☎93 402 46 16.*

> **Two Modernist Masters**
>
> **Josep Puig i Cadafalch** (1867-1956) – The mixture of regional and foreign architectural tradition in his work reflects the Plateresque and Flemish styles. His main works are the Casa de les Punxes, the **Casa Macaya** (1901) and the Casa Quadras (1904).
>
> **Lluís Domènech i Montaner** (1850-1923) – He attained his highly decorative style through extensive use of mosaics, stained glass and glazed tiles. His main works include the Palau de la Música Catalana, Casa Lleó Morera, Castell dels Tres Dragons, Hospital de Sant Pau and Casa Montaner i Simó.

Carrer del Bisbe
To the left is the side wall of the Palau de la Generalitat (Provincial Council). Above a door is a fine early-15C medallion of St George by Pere Johan.
On the right side is the **Casa dels Canonges** (Canons' Residence), residence of the President of the Generalitat. A neo-Gothic covered gallery (1929), over a star-vaulted arch, links the two.

Plaça Sant Felip Neri
The Renaissance houses on this square were moved here when via Laietana was built. The **Museu del Calçat** (footwear museum) includes Columbus' shoes. (*Open 11am-2pm. Closed Mon. 2.50 €. ☎93 301 45 33.*)

▶ *Return to carrer del Bisbe along carrer Sant Sever.*

LA RAMBLA★★
The most famous promenade in Barcelona, La Rambla's five sections follow an old riverbed bordering the Gothic quarter. La Rambla separates the Eixample district from the old quarter, and is alive at all hours with locals, tourists and down and outs and vendors.
The upper section, by plaça de Catalunya, is Rambla de Canaletes, followed by Rambla dels Estudis or Rambla dels Ocells (Avenue of the Birds).

Iglesia de Betlem
This Baroque church – the interior was razed by a fire in 1936 – has retained its imposing façade, facing carrer Carme.

▶ *Follow carrer Carme.*

Antic Hospital de la Santa Creu
These Gothic, Baroque and neo-Classical buildings are a haven in this district. An ex-hospital is the Library of Catalunya. A charming planted **Gothic patio★** (Jardines de Rubio y Lluch) can be reached through a hall decorated with azulejos.

▶ *Return to La Rambla.*

Palau de la Virreina★
The elegant 1778 palace of the Vicereine of Peru, with Baroque and Rococo decorations, hosts major exhibitions. Alongside is the traditional Mercat (market) de Sant Josep (La Boqueria). Down La Rambla on the right side stands the city's opera house, the **Gran Teatre del Liceu**, rebuilt after a 1994 fire. Opposite lies **pla de la Boqueria**, a charming esplanade whose pavement was decorated by the artist Joan Miró.

▶ *Turn left onto carrer del Cardenal Casañas.*

Iglesia de Santa Maria del Pi★
This 14C Catalan Gothic church on a square is striking for its simplicity and the size of its single nave.

▶ *Return to La Rambla.*

Plaça Reial★★
This vast pedestrian square shaded by palms and lined with cafés is surrounded by neo-Classical buildings. Gaudí designed the lampposts by the fountain. A stamp and coin market is held Sunday mornings.

▶ *Turn left at carrer Nou de la Rambla.*

Palau Güell★★
Open 10am-1pm and 4-7pm; 16 Oct-30 Dec 10am-6pm. Closed Sun and public hols. 2.40€. ☎93 317 39 74.
Gaudí designed the Güell residence (1886-1890). Note the parabolic entry arches and the extravagant bars typical of the Modernist movement. The most striking interior features are the **grand hall** and the innovative use of materials and the treatment of light as a design element of each space.

▶ *Return to La Rambla.*

La Rambla meets the sea at **La Rambla de Santa Mònica**. The former **Convento de Santa Mònica** is a modern art centre that hosts exhibitions. The wax museum (**Museu de Cera**) is here. (*Open 10am-1.30pm and 4-7.30pm; Sat-Sun and public hols, 11am-2pm and 4.30-8.30pm; Jul-Sep, 10am-10pm; 7.50€; ☎93 317 26 49*).

Columbus Memorial
This 1886 monument commemorates the return of the great navigator.

Worth a Visit

BARRI GÒTIC AND LAS RAMBLAS

Museu d'Història de la Ciutat★★
Entrance on calle Veguer. Open 10am-2pm and 4-8pm; Sun and public hols 10am-3pm; Jun-Sep 10am-8pm. Closed Mon, 1 Jan, 1 May, 24 Jun, 25 Dec. 4€. ☎93 225 47 00.
The visit includes Roman remains, and outbuildings of the Palau Reial Major.

The Roman city★★★
Under the museum and plaça del Rei are Roman foundations, drainage, and reservoirs. In adjoining vaulted rooms are sculptures from the 1C-4C (busts of Agrippina, Faustina and Antoninus Pius). Two 13C Gothic frescoes were uncovered in the Sala Jaime I in 1998.

Capilla de Santa Àgata★★
This 14C palatine chapel is covered by intricate polychrome woodwork panelling. The **Altarpiece of the Constable★★** by Jaime Huguet (1465) depicts the life of Jesus and the Virgin Mary. In the centre, the *Adoration of the Three Wise Men* is a Catalan masterpiece.

A staircase leads to the **Mirador del Rei Martí**, a five-storey tower with a lovely **view**★★ of the old city.

Salón del Tinell

This lofty 14C room, 17m/56ft high, is topped with a double-sloped ceiling set on six monumental arches. It is said that the Catholic Monarchs welcomed Columbus here after his first voyage.

Museu d'Art Contemporàni de Barcelona (MACBA)★★

Open 11am-7.30pm (25 Jun-30 Sep, 11am-8pm); Sat, 10am-8pm; Sun and public hols, 10am-3pm. Closed Tue, 1 Jan, 25 Dec. 7.50 €. 93 481 33 68.

The monumental museum **building**★★, designed by American Richard Meyer, fuses the rationalist Mediterranean tradition with contemporary architecture. Two significant works can are outside: *La Ola* by Jorge Oteiza and Eduardo Chillida's mural, *Barcelona* (*see description under Worth a Visit).*

The **standing collections**★ in pristine white halls cover major artistic movements of the past 50 years. Exhibits include works influenced by Constructivism and Abstract art (Klee, Oteiza, Miró, Calder, Fontana), as well as creations by experimental artists (Kiefer, Boltanski, Solano) and names of the 1980s (Hernández, Pijuán, Barceló, Tàpies, Ràfols Casamada, Sicilia).

Centre de Cultura Contemporània de Barcelona (CCCB)

Open 11am-2pm and 4-8pm; Wed and Sat, 11am-8pm; Sun and public hols, 11am-3pm; Closed Mon, 1 Jan and 25 Dec. 4.40 € (higher with special exhibitions). 93 306 41 00.

This centre of art exhibitions, near MACBA, is in restored premises. Its **patio**★ combines original mosaics and silk-screen floral motifs with modern elements, like the side wall of glass.

Museu Frederic Marès★

Open 10am-7pm; Sun and public hols 10am-3pm. Closed Mon, 1 Jan, 1 May, 24 Jun and 25 Dec. 3 €; no charge Wed afternoon and first Sun. 93 310 58 00.

The collections, in the Palau Reial Major *(enter by plaça de Sant Lu)*, were left to the city by sculptor Frederic Marès (1893-1991).

Sculpture Section

The works on two floors and in the crypt are in chronological order from the Iberian period to the 19C. Note the **Christs and Calvaries**★ in polychrome wood (12C-14C), Romanesque and Gothic **Virgins with Child**★; a 16C **Holy Entombment**★ and **The Vocation of St Peter**★, an expressive 12C relief attributed to the master Cabestany.

Gabinete del Coleccionista

Everyday objects, mainly 19C, include items from recreational rooms, the smoking parlour and the women's boudoir (spectacles, fans, clothes etc).

CARRER DE MONTCADA★★

1hr 30min including a visit to the Museu Picasso – see plan of old city.

Museu Picasso★

Open 10am-8pm. Closed Mon, 1 Jan, Good Fri, 1 and 31 May, 24 Jun, 1 Nov and 25-26 Dec. 6 €, free first Sun of month. 93 319 63 10.

The Gothic palaces of Berenguer de Aguilar and Baron de Castellet and the Baroque Palau Meca are the setting for the museum. The works here are dedicated, in most cases, to Picasso's friend Sabartès, shown in several portraits.

Picasso's early genius is evident in portraits of his family, *First Communion* and *Science and Charity* (1896). Among examples of his early Paris work are *La Nana* and *La Espera; Los Desemparados* (1903) is from his Blue Period, *Señora Casals* from his Rose Period. His **Las Meninas series**★ consists of variations on the famous picture by Velázquez.

Picasso's skill as an engraver is seen in his outstanding etchings of bullfighting and his talent as a ceramist in vases, dishes and plates made in the 1950s.

Museu Barbier-Mueller d'Art Precolombí

Open 11am-7pm; Sat 10am-7pm; Sun and public hols 10am-3pm. Closed Mon, 1 Jan, Good Fri, 1 May, and 25-26

© Felix Carretto/SXC

La Rambla

Dec. *3 €; free first Sun of month.* *93 310 45 16.*
The 12C Palacio Nadal houses this collection of pre-Columbian art.

Iglesia de Santa María del Mar★★

Open 10am-1.30pm and 4.30-8pm; no visits during religious services. *93 319 05 16.*

This church is one of the most beautiful in the Catalan Gothic style, built in the 14C by humble sailors to compete with the cathedral of the wealthy. The result is a graceful church of outstanding simplicity. The west front is adorned only by a portal gable and the buttresses flanking the superb Flamboyant **rose window**★. The **interior**★★★ gives the impression of spaciousness due to the elevation of the nave, and side aisles divided only by slender pillars.

THE SEAFRONT★ *allow half a day*

Bus 14 follows the seafront to Vila Olímpica.

The seafront, from Montjuïc to the Besòs river, was completely redesigned for the 1992 Olympic Games, turning Barcelona once again toward the sea.

Drassanes (Shipyards)★★ and Museu Marítim★★

Open 10am-8pm. *Closed 1 and 6 Jan and 25-26 Dec.* *6 € (8.50 € with ride; 6.50 € with Columbus monument).* *93 342 99 20.*

The **ropeworks** are among the best examples of civil Gothic architecture in Catalunya. Ten sections remain from the shipyard, under a timber roof supported by sturdy stone arches. This is an ideal setting for a **Maritime Museum** with its interactive displays and priceless artefacts. Among many models is a lifesize replica of the **Royal Galley of Don Juan of Austria**★★, Christian flagship at the Battle of Lepanto (1571). The **Portulan of Gabriel de Vallseca** (1439) belonged to Amerigo Vespucci.
The area around the port includes the Moll de Bosch i Alsina (or **Moll de la Fusta**), a palm-lined promenade.

Port Vell★

The old harbour is a lively leisure area featuring bars, the **Maremàgnum** shopping and leisure centre, an **aquarium** and the **Imax** cinema.

Aquarium★

Kids *Open Oct-May, 9.30am-9pm (9.30pm Jun and Sep; 11pm Jul-Aug); last admission one hour before closing.* *15 € (10 € (children aged 4-14).* *93 221 74 74.*

One of Europe's most impressive subaquatic zoos includes a spectacular viewing tunnel, 80m/262ft long.

Basílica de la Mercè★

Open 10am-1pm and 6-8pm (8.30 Sat); Sun and public hols, 10am-2pm and 7-9pm. *93 310 51 51.*

The Ribera District

During the 13C and the 14C the Catalan fleet exercised unquestionable supremacy over the western basin of the Mediterranean. Important merchant families acquired considerable social status and the carrer de Montcada became a showcase for their high expectations and new standards of living. This street, named after the Montcada, an influential family of noble descent, is a unique ensemble of merchants' palaces and aristocratic mansions, most of which date back to the late Middle Ages. Behind the austere façades are quaint little patios with galleries and porches typical of Catalan Gothic architecture.

The following is a selection of small palaces: the 15C Palau de Berenguer de Aguilar, now the Museu Picasso, the 14C Palau del Marqués de Llió which houses the **Museu Tèxtil i d'Indumentària** (Textile and Costume Museum), the 17C Palau Dalmases at no20 with Baroque frieze decorations on the staircase, and the 16C Palau Cervelló-Giudice at no25, now the Maeght Gallery, with a fine flight of steps.

Open 10am-6pm; Sun and pub hold 1am-3pm. Closed Mon, 1 Jan, Good Friday, 1 and 31 May, 24 Jun, 1 Nov, and 6 and 25 Dec. 3.50 €. 93 310 45 16.

The entry of this 1760 church has the only curved Baroque façade in Barcelona. The façade on carrer Ample is Renaissance and was moved from elsewhere. A Gothic statue in the interior, the **Mare de Déu de la Mercè★**, is by Pere Moragues (1361).

Cross vía Laietana; continue along the passeig d'Isabel II.

La Llotja★
The building housing the Chamber of Commerce and Industry was completely rebuilt in the 18C. The **Gothic hall★★**, a lofty chamber with three naves separated by triple round arches, remains from the medieval building.

Estació de França★
This huge iron structure with glass roof is the terminal for trains to France and stages events such as the Comics Fair.

Parc de la Ciutadella★
Open 10am-nightfall. 93 413 25 00.
Built by Philip V to control rebellious Barcelona, the citadel was demolished in 1868 and replaced by gardens. It hosted the 1888 World Fair.

Castell dels Tres Dragons★★
Domènech i Montaner built this pavilion for the World Fair in neo-Gothic style, using unadorned brick and iron. It houses the **Museu de Zoologia★**, with a collection of all zoological species. *Open 10am-2.30pm (6.30pm Thu). Closed Mon, 1 Jan and 25 Dec. 3.50 € (5 € with Museu de Geologia and Botanical Garden), no charge first Sun of the month. 93 319 68 95.*

Waterfall
Gaudí collaborated on the design of this waterfall while still a student.

Parc Zoològic★
Kids *Open Jan-Feb and Nov-Dec, 10am-5pm; Mar-May and Oct, 10am-6pm; JunSep, 10am-7pm. Closed 25 Dec. 14.50 €, (8.75 € child). 93 225 67 80.*
This zoo covers much of Parc de la Ciutadella. Animals from all over the world are kept in a natural setting. A dolphin show is held in the Aquarama.

Return to pla del Palau along avenida Marquès d'Argentera and take the passeig Nacional.

La Barceloneta★
The "Iberian Naples" has quaint narrow streets, and restaurants and stalls offering seafood dishes.

Museu d'Història de Catalunya★
Open 10am-7pm (8pm Thu); Sun and public hols, 10am-2.30pm. Closed Mon, 1 and 6 Jan, 25-26 Dec. 3 €; free entry

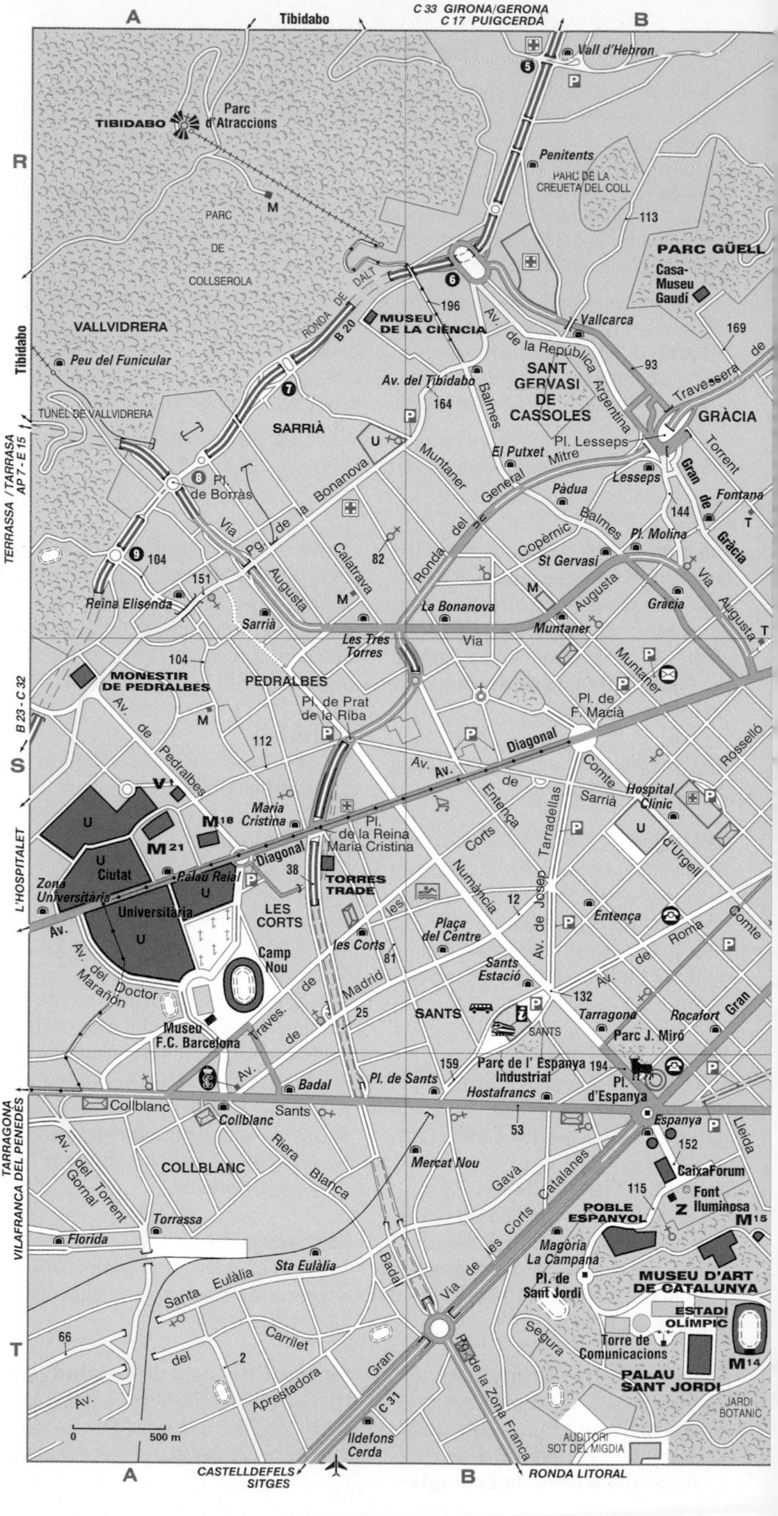
A
B
R
S
T
Tibidabo
C 33 GIRONA/GERONA
C 17 PUIGCERDÀ
TIBIDABO
Parc d'Atraccions
PARC DE COLLSEROLA
Vall d'Hebron
Penitents
PARC DE LA CREUETA DEL COLL
113
PARC GÜELL
Casa-Museu Gaudí
RONDA DE DALT
B 20
MUSEU DE LA CIÈNCIA
196
Vallcarca
169
VALLVIDRERA
Peu del Funicular
Av. de la República Argentina
SANT GERVASI DE CASSOLES
93
Travessera de
GRÀCIA
TÚNEL DE VALLVIDRERA
Av. del Tibidabo
164
Balmes
SARRIÀ
Pl. Lesseps
Torrent
Muntaner
El Putxet
Mitre
Lesseps
Gran de Gràcia
Fontana
TERRASSA / TARRASA
AP 7 - E 15
Pl. de Borràs
Pg. de la Bonanova
Pàdua
144
Via Augusta
Calatrava
Ronda del General
Copèrnic
Pl. Molina
82
St Gervasi
104
Reina Elisenda
151
Sarrià
La Bonanova
Gràcia
Muntaner
Les Tres Torres
Via
104
MONESTIR DE PEDRALBES
PEDRALBES
Pl. de Prat de la Riba
Pl. de F. Macià
B 23 - C 32
Av. de Pedralbes
112
Diagonal
Av.
Av. de Sarrià
Comte d'Urgell
Rosselló
Hospital Clínic
Entença
Tarradellas
Maria Cristina
Pl. de la Reina Maria Cristina
M 18
M 21
Corts
L'HOSPITALET
Zona Universitària
Ciutat Universitària
Palau Reial
Diagonal
38
TORRES TRADE
Numància
Av. de Josep
Av.
LES CORTS
12
Entença
Plaça del Centre
Les Corts
81
Roma
Comte
Av. del Doctor Marañón
Camp Nou
Av. de Madrid
Sants Estació
132
Av.
Museu F.C. Barcelona
Traves. de
25
SANTS
SANTS
Tarragona
Rocafort
Gran
Parc J. Miró
159
Parc de l' Espanya Industrial
194
Pl. d'Espanya
Av.
Badal
Pl. de Sants
Hostafrancs
TARRAGONA
VILAFRANCA DEL PENEDÈS
Collblanc
Collblanc
Sants
53
Espanya
Lleida
Av. del Torrent Gornal
Riera Blanca
Mercat Nou
152
COLLBLANC
CaixaForum
Gavà
115
Font Iluminosa
Via de les Corts Catalanes
POBLE ESPANYOL
M 15
Torrassa
Florida
Magòria La Campana
Sta Eulàlia
Santa Eulàlia
Pl. de Sant Jordi
MUSEU D'ART DE CATALUNYA
Badal
ESTADI OLÍMPIC
Carrilet
Segura
Torre de Comunicacions
66
del
2
Gran
Rd. de la Zona Franca
M 14
PALAU SANT JORDI
Aprestadora
C 31
JARDI BOTANIC
Av.
0
500 m
Ildefons Cerdà
AUDITORI SOT DEL MIGDIA
CASTELLDEFELS
SITGES
RONDA LITORAL

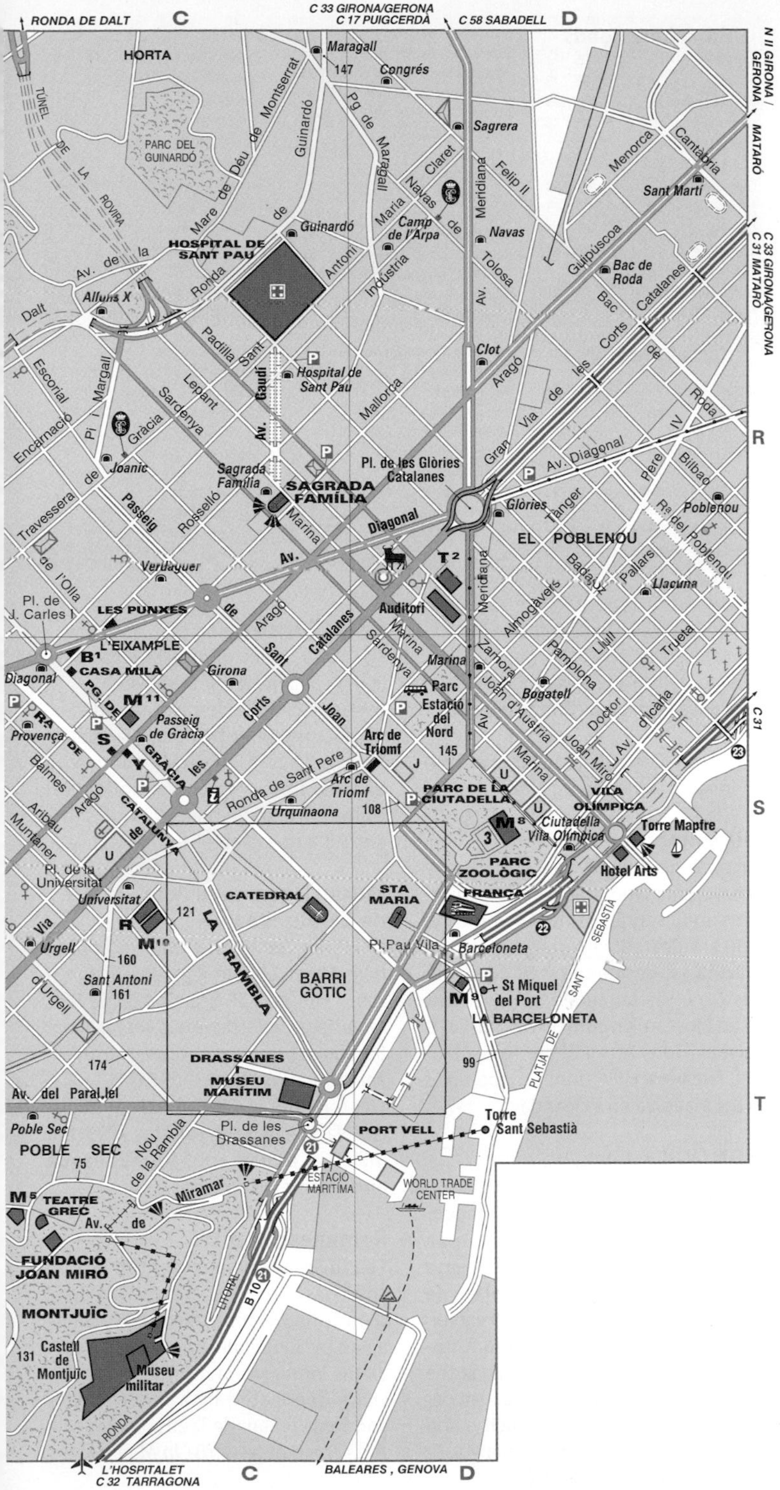
RONDA DE DALT
C 33 GIRONA/GERONA
C 17 PUIGCERDÀ
C 58 SABADELL
N II GIRONA / GERONA
MATARÓ
C 33 GIRONA/GERONA
C 31 MATARÓ
C 31
HORTA
PARC DEL GUINARDÓ
TÚNEL DE LA ROVIRA
HOSPITAL DE SANT PAU
Hospital de Sant Pau
Maragall
Congrés
Sagrera
Guinardó
Camp de l'Arpa
Navas
Sant Martí
Bac de Roda
Clot
Alfons X
Joanic
Sagrada Família
SAGRADA FAMÍLIA
Pl. de les Glòries Catalanes
Glòries
Poblenou
EL POBLENOU
Llacuna
Verdaguer
Pl. de J. Carles I
LES PUNXES
L'EIXAMPLE
CASA MILÀ
Diagonal
Girona
Passeig de Gràcia
Provença
Auditori
Marina
Bogatell
Parc Estació del Nord
Arc de Triomf
PARC DE LA CIUTADELLA
VILA OLÍMPICA
Ciutadella Vila Olímpica
Torre Mapfre
Hotel Arts
PARC ZOOLÒGIC
FRANÇA
Urquinaona
Pl. de la Universitat
Universitat
Urgell
Sant Antoni
CATEDRAL
STA MARIA
LA RAMBLA
BARRI GÒTIC
Pl. Pau Vila
Barceloneta
St Miquel del Port
LA BARCELONETA
DRASSANES MUSEU MARÍTIM
Av. del Paral.lel
Poble Sec
POBLE SEC
Pl. de les Drassanes
PORT VELL
Torre Sant Sebastià
ESTACIÓ MARÍTIMA
WORLD TRADE CENTER
TEATRE GREC
FUNDACIÓ JOAN MIRÓ
MONTJUÏC
Castell de Montjuïc
Museu militar
PLATJA DE SANT SEBASTIÀ
L'HOSPITALET
C 32 TARRAGONA
BALEARES , GENOVA

Barcelona Roads

Armes Pl.	DS	3
Berlín	BS	12
Brasil Rambla del	AS	25
Carles III Gran Via de	AS	38
Corts Catalanes Gran Via de les	BCRS	
Creu Coberta	BT	53
Exposició Pas. de	CT	75
Galileu	AS	81
Ganduxer	AR	82
Gràcia Pas. de	CS	
Guinardó Ronda del	CR	91
Hospital Militar Av. de l'	BR	93
Joan de Borbó Comte de Barcelona Pas. de	DST	99
Josep V Foix	AR	104
Lluís Companys Pas. de	DS	108
Manuel Girona Pas. de	AS	112
Mare de Déu del Coll Pas. de la	BR	113
Marquès de Comillas Av. del	BT	115
Montalegre	CS	121
Olímpic Pas.	CT	131
Països Catalans Pl. dels	BS	132
Príncep d'Astúries Av. del	BR	144
Pujades Pas. de	DS	145
Ramon Albó	CR	147
Reina Elisenda de Montcada Pas. de la	AR	151
Reina Maria Cristina Av. de la	BT	152
Sant Antoni	BT	159
Sant Antoni Ronda de	CS	160
Sant Antoni Abat	CS	161
Sant Gervasi Pas. de	BR	164
Sant Josep de la Muntanya Av. de	BR	169
Sant Pau Ronda de	CT	174
Tarragona	BT	194
Tibidabo Av. del	BR	196
Universitat Pl. de la	CS	

Barcelona Sights

Casa Quadras	CS	B^{1}
Casas : Amatlier, Batlió, Bonet, Morera, Mulleras	CS	Y
Centre de Cultura Contemporàna de Barcelona (Centre d'Estudis i de Recurses Culturals)	CS	R
Fundació Antoni Tàpies	CS	S
Galería olímpica	BT	M^{14}
Museu Egipci de Barcelona	CS	M^{11}
Museu Etnológic	BT	M^{15}
Museu d'Arqueològia de Catalunya	CT	M^{5}
Museu d'Art Contemporàni	CS	M^{10}
Museu d'Art Modern	DS	M^{8}
Museu d'Història de Catalunya	DS	M^{9}
Museu dels Carrosses	AS	M^{18}
Palau de Pedralbes	AS	M^{21}
Pavelló Güell	AS	V^{1}
Pavelló Mies van der Rohe	BT	Z
Teatre Nacional de Catalunya	DR	T^{2}

23 Apr, 18 May, 11 and 24 Sep and first Sun of month). ☎93 225 47 00.

This museum in an ex-warehouse details Catalunya from prehistory to now.

At the end of the passeig Nacional, continue into the passeig Marítim.

Vila Olímpica★

Built for the 1992 Olympics, this is one of Barcelona's most modern areas. Gardens and avenues of the Olympic Village are dotted with sculptures. The **marina**★★ designed by JR de Clascà has bars, restaurants and pavement cafés. Most striking are two 153m/502ft **towers** (Hotel Arts and the Torre Mapfre). The **view**★★★ from the top takes in the Mallorca on a clear day.

MONTJUÏC★ *1 day, including museum visits – see general plan*

The fort built on this 173m/568ft mountain during the 1640 rebellion is now a military museum. The castle commands city and harbour **views**★. The **plaça de Espanya** remains from the 1929 exhibition, along with the illuminated **fountain** (*Font Magica*) by Carles Buïgas, the **reception pavilion**★★ by Mies van der Rohe, of outstanding simplicity, and the Spanish Village (Poble Espanyol, or Pueblo Español in Castilian).

CaixaForum

Open 10am-8pm. Closed Mon (except pub holidays). ☎476 86 00.

A magnificent Modernist early 20C textile factory, built by Puig i Cadafalch, now houses a cultural center with exhibits from a splendid modern art collection of more than 800 works. The entry is a tree of steel and glass.

Museu Nacional d'Art de Catalunya★★★

Open 10am-7pm; Sun and public hols, 10am-2.30pm. Closed Mon, 1 Jan, 1 May and 25 Dec. 4.80 €; 15 € for Articket (valid three months for major Barcelona art museums); no charge first Thu of month. ☎93 622 03 75/76.

This museum of Catalan art in the Palacio Nacional built for the 1929 fair includes remarkable **Romanesque and Gothic collections**★★★.

Romanesque art

The display evokes contemporary churches. Note 12C frescoes by Sant Joan de Boí *(Room 2)*, the late 11C lateral apses by Sant Quirze de Pedret *(Room 3)*, the Santa María de Taüll ensemble (12C), dominated by a fine *Epiphany* and Sant Climent de Taüll *(Room 5)* with the remarkable *Christ in Majesty:* the apse is a Renaissance masterpiece. Note the anti-naturalism and geometry. **Altar frontals** are painted on a panel or carved. In the magnificent sculpture galleries is the polychrome *Majestad de Batlló* (13C). The museum also presents superb **capitals★** *(Room 6)*, silverware and enamels. Paintings from the chapter house of **Sigena** (1200) evidence a great stylistic shift.

Gothic art

Exhibits of 13-14C Catalan Gothic art include stone retables attributed to **Jaime Cascalls** *(Rooms 15 and 16)*; the collection of Catalan Gothic art *(Room 30)*, with works by **Guerau Gener, Juan Mates, Ramón de Mur, Juan Antigó, Bernardo Despuig** and **Jaime Cirera**; a room dedicated to **Bernardo Martorell** (*Room 32*), for whom detail and shading were paramount; the famous *Virgin of the Councillors* by **Luis Dalmau**; works by the **Master of La Seu d´Urgell** (*Room 34*) and, lastly, 14-15C funerary sculpture (*Room 50*).

Other Collections

The **Cambó Collection** includes painters of the rank of Zurbarán, Tintoretto, El Greco, Rubens, Cranach the Elder and Goya. The **Thyssen-Bornemisza Collection** selected from the Museo Thyssen comprises works from the Middle Ages to the 18C, notably paintings of the Virgin and Child. Portraits represent several schools of the 15-18C.
Resented In the **Renaissance and Baroque** section are Flemish and Italian masters along with works of Ayne Bru, Pere Nunyes and Pedro Berruguete. **19-20C** art includes paintings by Fortuny, Modernist furniture, sculpture, and posters by Gaudí, Doménech i Montaner, Casas, Rusiñol and others.

Poble Espanyol★ (Spanish Village)

Enter by avenida Marqués de Comillas. Kids *Open Mon, 9am-8pm (2am Tue-Thu, 4am Fri-Sat, midnight Sun); last entry 1hr before closing. Closed 1 Jan and 25 Dec. 7.50 €. 93 508 63 00.*
The village was built for the 1929 exhibition. Walk through a small Castilian square, a street in an Andalucían village with white houses set off by flowering geraniums, or by a Mudéjar tower from Aragón. There are restaurants, bars and shops, and craftsmen making traditional Spanish wares. The **Collection of Contemporary Art** has works of Picasso, Miró, Dalí and Spanish artists from the 1950s to the present.

Anella Olímpica★

This complex high on the mountain consists of the **Olympic Stadium★**, with its 1929 façade, and the nearby **Palau Sant Jordi★★**, a sports centre designed by Arata Isozaki. The **telecommunications tower** is the work of Santiago Calatrava.

Fundació Joan Miró★★★

Open 10am-7pm (8pm Jul-Sep, 9.30pm Thu); Sun and public hols, 10am-2.30pm; last entry 30min before closing. Closed Mon (except public hols), 1 Jan and 25-26 Dec. 7.50€. 93 443 94 70.
Joan Miró (1893-1983), a leading figure in avant-garde art, is linked to Barcelona: a mural at the airport, pavement mosaics on La Rambla, the famous logo of the savings bank La Caixa. Born in Barcelona, Miró spent 1921 and 1922 in Paris, where he painted **La Masía**, signaling his departure from figurative art. Between 1939 and 1941 he executed **Constellations**, 23 panels expressing the horror of the Second World War.
Miró's Foundation is housed in a modern building of harmonious proportions designed by Josep Lluís Sert, a close friend. The 10 000 items were largely executed during the last 20 years of his life. A small exhibition of contemporary art includes Alexander Calder's **Fountain of Mercury**.

Teatre Grec★

This 1929 open-air theatre hosts dance, concerts and stage performances organised by the **Festival del Grec**.

Museu d'Arqueologia de Catalunya★

Open 9.30am-7pm; Sun and public hols, 10am-2.30pm. Closed Mon, 1 Jan and 24-25 Dec. 2.40 €, no charge Sun and public hols. 93 424 65 77.

Barcelona

Bacardí Ptge de	MY	5
Banys Nous	MX	7
Bergara	LV	10
Bisbe	MX	15
Bòria	MV	18
Born Pas. del	NX	20
Boters	MX	23
Canaletes Rambla de	LV	27
Canonge Colom Pl. del	LY	28
Canvis Vells	NX	32
Caputxins Rambla dels	MY	35
Cardenal Casañas	LX	36
Catalunya Pl. de	LV	
Catedral Av. de la	MV	40
Ciutat	MX	43
Comercial Pl. de	NV	45
Cucurulla	LX	55
Doctor Joaquím Pou	MV	61
Estudis Rambla dels	LX	
Francesc Cambó Av. de	MV	79
Garriga i Bachs Pl. de	MX	83
Isabel II Pas. d'	NX	98
Montcada	NV	122
Montjuïc del Bisbe	MX	123
Nou de Sant Francesc	MY	126
Nova Pl.	MX	128
Paradis	MX	133
Pi Pl. del	LX	137
Pintor Fortuny	LX	140
Portal Santa Madrona	MX	142
Ramon Berenguer el Gran Pl. de	MX	148
Rei Pl. del	MX	150
Sant Felip Neri Pl. de	MX	163
Sant Josep Rambla de	LX	168
Sant Josep Oriol Pl. de	LX	171
Sant Lu Pl. de	MX	172
Sant Miquel Pl. de	MX	173
Sant Sever	MX	181
Santa Maria Pl. de	NX	189
Santa Mònica Rambla de	MY	
Seu Pl. de la	MX	192
Tapineria	MX	193
Universitat Ronda de la	LV	199

Ajuntament	MX	H
Capella Santa Agata	MX	F
Casa de l'Ardiaca	MX	A
Casa de la Canonja	MX	V
Casa dels Canonges	MX	B
Castell dels Tres Dragons (Museu de Zoologia)	NV	M[7]
Collegi d'Arquitectes	MX	L
Convento de Santa Mònica	MY	M[20]
Duana Nova	NX	G
Mirádor del Rei Martí	MX	K
Museu Barbier-Mueller d'Art Precolombi	NVX	M[12]
Museu Frederic Marès	MX	M[2]
Museu d'Història de la Ciutat	MX	M[1]
Museu de Cera	MY	M[3]
Museu de Geología	NV	M[13]
Museu del Calçat	MX	M[17]
Palau Marc	MY	S
Palau del Lloctinent	MX	E
Palau del Marquès de Llió (Museu Tèxtil i de la Indumentària)	NV	M[16]
Pia Almoina	MX	N
Saló del Tinell	MX	C

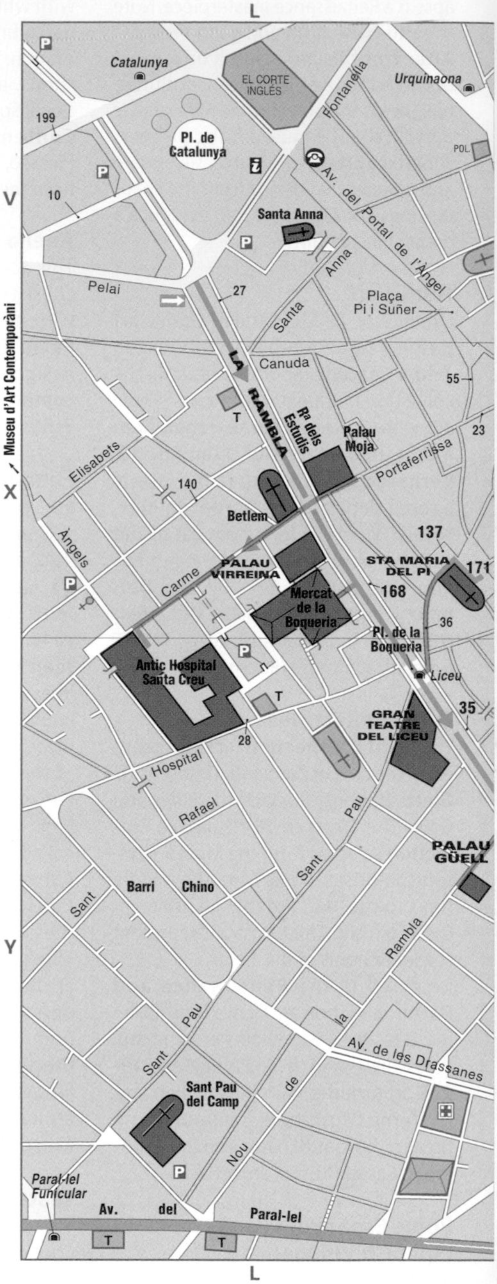

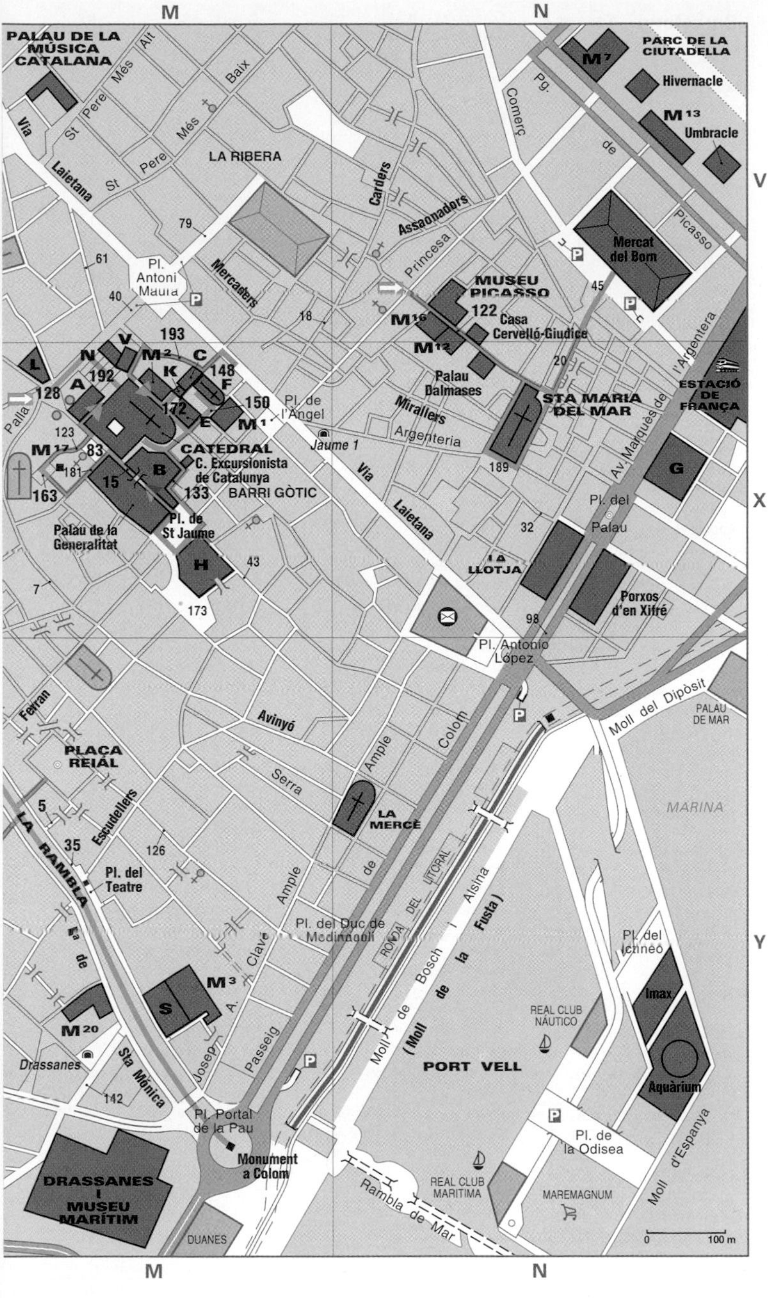
PALAU DE LA MÚSICA CATALANA
LA RIBERA
Pl. Antoni Maura
MUSEU PICASSO
Casa Cervelló-Giudice
Palau Dalmases
STA MARIA DEL MAR
PARC DE LA CIUTADELLA
Hivernacle
Umbracle
Mercat del Born
ESTACIÓ DE FRANÇA
CATEDRAL
C. Excursionista de Catalunya
BARRI GÒTIC
Palau de la Generalitat
Pl. de St Jaume
Pl. de l'Àngel
Jaume 1
LA LLOTJA
Porxos d'en Xifré
Pl. del Palau
Pl. Antonio López
Moll del Dipòsit
PALAU DE MAR
MARINA
PLAÇA REIAL
LA RAMBLA
Pl. del Teatre
LA MERCÈ
Pl. del Duc de Medinaceli
RONDA DEL LITORAL
Moll de Bosch i Alsina (Moll de la Fusta)
PORT VELL
REAL CLUB NÀUTICO
REAL CLUB MARITIMA
MAREMAGNUM
Imax
Aquàrium
Pl. de la Odisea
Moll d'Espanya
Drassanes
Pl. Portal de la Pau
Monument a Colom
DRASSANES I MUSEU MARÍTIM
DUANES
Rambla de Mar
0 100 m

Barcelona – Streets

Almogàvers	DR	
Ample	MNY	
Àngel	LX	
Àngel Pl. de l'	MX	
Antóni López Pl. d'	NY	
Antóni Maura Pl. d'	MX	
Aragó	CDRS	
Argenteria	NX	
Aribau	CS	
Armes Pl.	DS	3
Assaonadors	NV	
Augusta Via	ABR	
Avinyó	MY	
Bac de Roda	DR	
Bacardí Ptge de	MY	5
Badajoz	DR	
Badal	AT	
Balmes	BCRS	
Banys Nous	MX	7
Bergara	LV	10
Berlín	BS	12
Bilbao	DR	
Bisbe	MX	15
Bonanova Pas. de la	AR	
Boqueria Pl. de la	LXY	
Bòria	MV	18
Born Pas. del	NX	20
Borràs Pl. de	AR	
Bosch i Alsina Moll de	NY	
Boters	MX	23
Brasil Rambla del	AS	25
Calatrava	AR	
Canaletes Rambla de	LV	27
Canonge Colom Pl. del	LY	28
Cantàbria	DR	
Canuda	LX	
Canvis Vells	NX	32
Caputxins Rambla dels	MY	35
Cardenal Casañas	LX	36
Carders	NV	
Carles III Gran Via de	AS	38
Carme	LX	
Catalunya Pl. de	LV	
Catalunya Rambla de	CS	
Catedral Av. de la	MV	40
Ciutat	MX	43
Colom Pas. de	MNY	
Comerç	NV	
Comercial Pl. de	NV	45
Comte d'Urgell	BCS	
Copèrnic	BR	
Corts Travessera de les	ABS	
Corts Catalanes Gran Via de les	BCRS	
Creu Coberta	BT	53
Cucurulla	LX	55
Dalt Travessera de	BCR	
Diagonal Av.	BCRS	
Dipósit Moll del	NY	
Doctor Joaquím Pou	MV	61
Doctor Marañón Av. del	AS	
Doctor Trueta	DS	
Drassanes Av. de les	LY	
Drassanes Pl. de les	CT	
Duc de Medinaceli Pl. del	MNY	
Elisabets	LX	
Encarnació	CR	
Entença	BS	
Escorial	CR	
Escudellers	MY	
Espanya Moll d'	NY	
Espanya Pl. d'	BT	
Estudis Rambla dels	LX	
Exposició Pas. de	CT	75
Felip II	DR	
Ferrán	MY	
Fontanella	LV	
Francesc Cambó Av. de	MV	79
Francesc Macià Pl. de	BS	
Galileu	AS	81
Ganduxer	AR	82
Garriga i Bachs Pl. de	MX	83
Gaudí Av. de	CR	
Gavà	BT	
General Mitre Ronda del	BR	
Glòries Catalanes Pl. de les	DR	
Gràcia Pas. de	CS	
Gràcia Travessera de	CR	
Gran de Gràcia	BR	
Guinardó Ronda del	CR	
Guipúscoa	DR	
Hospital	LY	
Hospital Militar Av. de l'	BR	93
Icària Av. d'	DS	
Ictíneo Pl. del	NY	
Indústria	DR	
Isabel II Pas. d'	NX	98
Joan Carles I Pl. de	CRS	
Joan d'Austria	DS	
Joan de Borbó Comte de Barcelona Pas. de	DST	99
Joan Miró	DS	
Josep Anselm Clavé	MY	
Josep Tarradellas Av. de	BS	
Josep V Foix	AR	104
Laietana Via	MNVX	
Lepant	CR	
Lesseps Pl. de	BR	
Lleida	BT	
Lluís Companys Pas. de	DS	108
Llull	DS	
Madrid Av. de	AS	
Mallorca	DR	
Manuel Girona Pas. de	AS	112
Maragall Pas. de	DR	
Mare de Déu de Montserrat Av. de la	CR	
Mare de Déu del Coll Pas. de la	BR	113
Marina	CDRS	
Marquès de Comillas Av. del	BT	115
Marquès de l'Argentera Av. del	NX	
Menorca	DR	
Mercaders	MX	
Meridiana Av.	DRS	
Mirallers	NX	
Miramar Av. de	CT	
Montalegre	CS	121
Montcada	NV	122
Montjuïc del Bisbe	MX	123
Muntaner	BCRS	
Navas de Tolosa	DR	
Nou de la Rambla	CT	
Nou de Sant Francesc	MY	126
Nova Pl.	MX	128
Numància	BS	
Odisea Pl. de la	NY	
Olímpic Pas.	CT	131
Padilla	CR	
Països Catalans Pl. dels	BS	132
Palau Pl. del	NX	
Palla	MX	
Pallars	DR	
Pamplona	DS	
Paradis	MX	133
Paral.lel Av. del	CT	
Pau Vila Pl. de	DS	
Pedralbes Av. de	AS	
Pelai	LV	
Pere IV	DR	
Pi Pl. del	LX	137
Pi i Margall	CR	
Pi i SuñerPl. de	LV	
Picasso Pas. de	NV	
Pintor Fortuny	LX	140
Poblenou Rambla del	DR	
Portaferrissa	LX	
Portal de la Pau Pl. del	MY	
Portal de l'Àngel Av. del	LV	
Portal Santa Madrona	MX	142
Prat de la Riba Pl. de	AS	
Príncep d'Astúries Av. del	BR	144
Princesa	NV	
Pujades Pas. de	DS	145
Rambla La	LMXY	
Ramon Albó	CR	147
Ramon Berenguer el Gran Pl. de	MX	148
Rei Pl. del	MX	150
Reial Pl.	MY	
Reina Elisenda de Montcada Pas. de la	AR	151
Reina Maria Cristina Av. de la	BT	152
Reina Maria Cristina Pl. de la	AS	
República Argentina Av. de la	BR	
Roma Av. de	BS	
Rosselló	BCRS	
Sant Antoni	BT	159
Sant Antoni Ronda de	CS	160
Sant Antoni Abat	CS	161
Sant Antoni Maria Claret	DR	
Sant Felip Neri Pl. de	MX	163
Sant Gervasi Pas. de	BR	164
Sant Jaume Pl. de	MX	
Sant Joan Pas. de	CRS	
Sant Jordi Pl. de	BT	
Sant Josep Rambla de	LX	168
Sant Josep de la Muntanya Av. de	BR	169
Sant Josep Oriol Pl. de	LX	171
Sant Lu Pl. de	MX	172
Sant Miquel Pl. de	MX	173
Sant Pau	LY	
Sant Pau Ronda de	CT	174
Sant Pere Ronda de	CS	
Sant Pere Més Alt	MV	
Sant Pere Més Baix	MV	
Sant Rafael	LY	
Sant Sever	MX	181
Santa Anna	LV	
Santa Maria Pl. de	NX	189
Santa Mònica Rambla de	MY	
Sants	AT	
Sardenya	CDRS	
Sarrià Av. de	BS	
Segura	BT	
Serra En	MY	
Seu Pl. de la	MX	192

Tànger	DR	
Tapineria	MX	193
Tarragona	BT	194
Teatre Pl. del	MY	
Tibidabo Av. del	BR	196
Torrent de l'Olla	BCR	
Universitat Pl. de la	CS	
Universitat Ronda de la	LV	199
Zamora	DS	
Zona Franca Pas. de la	BT	

Barcelona – Sites

Ajuntament	MX	H
Antic Hospital Santa Creu	LY	
Aquàrium	NY	
Arc de Triomf	DS	
Auditori	DR	
Barri Chino	LY	
Barri Gòtic	MX	
Betlem	LX	
CaixaForum	BT	
Camp Nou	AS	
Capella Santa Agata	MX	F
Casa – Museu Gaudí	BR	
Casa Cervelló-Giudice	NV	
Casa Milà	CS	
Casa Quadras	CS	B1
Casa de l'Ardiaca	MX	A
Casa de la Canonja	MX	V
Casa de les Punxes	CR	
Casa dels Canonges	MX	B
Casas: Amatlier, Batlló, Donet, Morera, Mulleras	CS	Y
Castell de Montjuïc	CT	
Castell dels Tres Dragons (Museu de Zoologia)	NV	M7
Catedral	MX	
Centre Excursionista de Catalunya	MX	
Centre de Cultura Contemporàna de Barcelona (Centre d'Estudis i de Recurses Culturals)	CS	R
Ciutat Universitària	AS	
Collegi d'Arquitectes	MX	L
Convento de Santa Mònica	MY	M20
Drassanes i Museu Marítim	MY	
Duana Nova	NX	G
Eixample	CS	
Estació de França	DS	
Estadi olímpic	BT	
Font lluminosa	BT	
Fundació Antoni Tàpies	CS	S
Fundació Jean Miró	CT	
Galería olímpica	BT	M14
Gran Teatre del Liceu	LY	
Hivernacle	NV	
Hospital de Sant Pau	CR	
Hotel Arts Barcelona	DS	
Imax	NY	
La Barceloneta	DS	
La Llotja	NX	
La Mercè	NY	
La Ribera	MV	
Mercat de la Boqueria	LX	
Mercat del Born	NV	
Mirádor del Rei Martí	MX	K
Monestir de Pedralbes	AS	
Montjuïc	BCT	
Monument a Colom	MY	
Museu Barbier-Mueller d'Art Precolombi	NVX	M12
Museu Egipci de Barcelona	CS	M11
Museu Etnològic	BT	M15
Museu F. C. Barcelona	AS	
Museu Frederic Marès	MX	M2
Museu Picasso	NV	
Museu d'Arqueològia de Catalunya	CT	M5
Museu d'Art Contemporàni	CS	M10
Museu d'Art Modern	DS	M8
Museu d'Art de Catalunya	BT	
Museu d'Història de Catalunya	DS	M9
Museu d'Història de la Ciutat	MX	M1
Museu de Cera	MY	M3
Museu de Geología	NV	M13
Museu de la Ciència	AR	
Museu del Calçat	MX	M17
Museu dels Carrosses	AS	M18
Museu militar	CT	
Palau Dalmases	NX	
Palau Güell	LY	
Palau Marc	MY	S
Palau Moja	LX	
Palau Sant Jordi	BT	
Palau de Pedralbes	AS	M21
Palau de la Generalitat	MX	
Palau de la Música Catalana	MV	
Palau de la Virreina	LY	
Palau del Lloctinent	MX	E
Palau del Marquès de Lió (Museu Tèxtil i de la Indumentària)	NV	M16
Parc Estació del Nord	DS	
Parc Güell	BR	
Parc Joan Miró	BS	
Parc d'Atraccions	AR	
Parc de l'Espanya Industrial	BT	
Parc de la Ciutadella	DS	
Parc zoològic	DS	
Pavelló Güell	AS	V1
Pavelló Mies van der Rohe	BT	Z
Pia Almoina	MX	N
Poble Espanyol	BT	
Poble Sec	CT	
Port Vell	DT	
Porxos d'en Xifré	NX	
Sagrada Familia	CR	
Saló del Tinell	MX	C
Sant Miquel del Port	DS	
Sant Pau del Camp	LY	
Santa Anna	LV	
Santa María del Mar	NX	
Santa María del Pi	LX	
Teatre Grec	CT	
Teatre Nacional de Catalunya	DR	T2
Tibidado	AR	
Torre Mapfre	DS	
Torre Sant Sebastià	DT	
Torre de Communicacions	BT	
Torres Trade	AS	
Umbracle	NV	
Vila olímpica	DS	

Household effects, ceramics, and votive figures trace Catalunya from Palaeolithic times through to the Visigothic.

The Ciutat Universitària District

Monastir de Santa Maria de Pedralbes★★

Open 10am-2pm (5pm Jun-Sep). Closed Mon, 1 Jan, 1 May, 24 Jun and 25-26 Dec. 4€. 93 203 92 82.

Founded in the 14C by King James II of Aragón and his fourth wife, the monastery has a fine Catalan Gothic **church**★ with the tomb of the foundress. The three-storey **cloisters**★ surrounded by cells and oratories are sober and elegant. The Sant Miquel Chapel is adorned with beautiful **frescoes**★★★ by Ferrer Bassá (1346) whose works combine the attention to detail of the Siena School with the acute sense of volume and perspective of Tuscan masters.

Palau de Pedralbes (Pedralbes Palace)

Enter from avinguda Diagonal.

Open 10am-6pm; Sun and public hols, 10am-3pm. Closed Mon, 1 Jan, Good Fri, 25 Dec. 3.50€ (with Museu Tèxtil i d'Indumentària). 93 280 50 24).

This residence for King Alfonso XIII (1919-1929) was influenced by palaces of the Italian Renaissance. It houses the **Museu de les Artes Decoratives**★,

People, birds, star by Joan Miró – Fundació Joan Miró

with household items from the Middle Ages to the industrial design era; and the **Museu de Ceràmica**, showing evolutions in ceramics from the 13C.

CosmoCaixa (Museu de la Ciència); Iglesia de Sant Pau del Camp (10C, **cloisters**★); Teatre Nacional de Catalunya (Ricardo Bofill), Auditorio (Rafael Moneo); Torre Agbar (tower by Jean Nouvel).

Excursions

Monasterio de Sant Cugat del Vallès★★

20km/12mi W by BP 1417. Open 10am-1.30pm and 3-7pm (8pm Jun-Sep). Closed Mon. exc public hols, 1 Jan, 25 Dec. 3 € (museum). 93 589 63 66.

A Benedictine **monastery** was built in the Middle Ages where an earlier chapel held the relics of St Cucufas (murdered here around AD 304).

The oldest part of the **Iglesia**★ (church) is the 11C belfry. The flat, crenellated wall supported by buttresses was relieved by a rose window. There are three apses with engaged pillars, the central one with radiating vaulting (a mark of the transition to Gothic). Note the 14C **All Saints Altarpiece**★ by Pere Serra.

The **Claustro**★, among the largest Romanesque cloisters in Catalunya, is a museum. During the 11C-12C a double row of columns (144 in all) was built around a close; in the 16C an upper gallery was added above a blind arcade. Skilfully carved **Romanesque capitals**★ are Corinthian, ornamental, figurative and historiated (biblical scenes). The sculptor, Arnaud Cadell, portrayed himself at work on a northeast corner column, and inscribed his name.

Terrassa/Tarrasa

31km/19mi NW along the C 58. This industrial town retains pre-Romanesque churches.

Conjunto Monumental de Iglesias de Sant Pere★★

Open 10am-1.30pm and 4-7pm; Sun, 11am-2pm. Closed Mon and public hols. 93 783 37 02.

These fine churches, recalling the 5C bishopric of Egara, are a haven in a bustling city, showing Pyrenean influence and Roman and Visigothic features.

The **Antiguo baptisterio de Sant Miquel**★ was built in the 9C using late Roman remains. The dome rests on eight pillars; four have Roman capitals, four are Visigothic. Alabaster windows in the apse filter light onto 9C-10C pre-Romanesque wall paintings. The crypt's three apses have horseshoe arches.

The magnificent Romanesque Lombard church of **Santa Maria**★ has an octagonal cupola and a *cimborrio* (lantern); a 5C mosaic survives in front. A 13C wall fresco in the south transept, of the mar-

tyrdom of Thomas à Becket, retains bright colours. Note the 15C north transept altarpiece by Jaime Huguet, **St Abdon and St Sennen★★.**
Sant Pere is a rustic church begun in the 6C on a trapezoid plan with a Romanesque transept crossing. In the apse is a curious **stone altarpiece★**.

Masía Freixa★
This odd Modernist mansion (1907) is in Sant Jordi Park. Note parabolic arches.

Museu de la Ciencia y la Tècnica de Catalunya★
Open 10am-7pm (2.30pm Jul-Aug); Sat-Sun, 10am-2.30pm. Closed Mon, 1 and 6 Jan, and 25-26 Dec.. 2.40 €, no charge first Sun. 93 736 89 63.
The technology museum is in a Modernist 1909 steam works (Aymerich, Amat i Jover).

Sierra de Montserrat★★
49km/31mi NW along the C 58.
The grand **site★★★** of the Macizo de Montserrat (Montserrat Massif) was the setting for Wagner's Parsifal. Hard Eocene conglomerates rise above eroded formations. It is the main site of devotion to the Virgin in Catalunya.
Views★★ from the road are impressive. The Montserrat cable car runs from near Monistrol de Montserrat.

The Monastery
Benedictines arrived in the 9C. Every century saw additions to the monastery. In 1812, it was sacked by the French. The present buildings are 19C and 20C. At the end of the dark, ornate **basilica** (15C) is the shrine of the Black Madonna. *Open 7am-7.30pm (8.30pm Jul-Sep). 93 877 77 66.*

La Moreneta★★
The 12C polychrome statue of the Black Madonna, above the high altar, was discovered in a cave by shepherds.
The services are known for their Gregorian chants, particlularly Mass at 11am and Vespers at 6.45pm.
The **Escolanía**, one of the world's oldest boys' choirs, may be heard daily at 1pm (Virolai) and 7.10pm (Salve).

R. Manet/MICHELIN

Retable of Saints Abdon and Sennen, Iglesia de Santa María

Hermitages and viewpoints
Information from the Tourist Office. Access via the mountain trails, cable cars or funiculars. Sant Joan: Jan-Mar, Nov and Dec, 11am-4pm; Sat-Sun and public hols, 10am-4pm; Apr-Jun, Sep and Oct, 10am-5.40pm; Jul-Aug, 10am-7pm. 6.30 € round trip (every 20min). 93 205 15 15. Santa Cova: 10am-1pm and 2-5pm (4pm Nov-Feb). 2.50 € (every 20min).
The 13 hermitages, abandoned since the arrival of Napoleon's troops, are interesting stopping-points.
Ermita de la Trinitat, *45min on foot,* charmingly nestled in a bucolic plain, is sheltered by three mountains: El Elefante (The Elephant), La Preñada (Pregnant Woman) and La Momia (The Mummy). **Sant Jeroni★**, *1hr 30min on foot or by car,* at1 238m/4 062ft offers a **panorama**, on a clear day, from the Pyrenees to the Balearic islands. **Ermita de Santa Cecilia** has an attractive 11C **Romanesque church★** with asymmetric belfry. Its east end is circled by Lombard bands. The statue of the Virgin was found in **Santa Cova** (holy cave), *1hr walk,* which has views of the Llobregat Valley. **Sant Miquel★**, *30min from the monastery; 1hr from the upper terminal of the Sant Miquel funicular.* has a general monastery view. **Sant Joan**, *30min from upper terminal of the Sant Joan funicular,* offers a beautiful panorama; the Ermita de San Onofre may be seen clinging to the rock face.

BELMONTE★

POPULATION: 2 601.

MICHELIN MAP 576 N 21 – CASTILLA LA MANCHA (CUENCA)

The birthplace of 16C writer Fray Luis de León is classic La Mancha: whitewashed houses overlooked by an imposing church and castle. It's easy to conjure up the image of Don Quixote astride his trusty steed Rocinante.

- **Orient Yourself:** Belmonte is SE of Madrid (157km/98mi NW) in the heart of La Mancha.
- **Also See:** CUENCA (101km/63mi NE) and ALBACETE (107km/67mi SE).

Visit

The Town

Belmonte retains three old gateways; best preserved is Puerta de Chinchilla.

Antigua Colegiata★

This 15C collegiate church holds 15-17C **altarpieces**. **Choir stalls**★ from the cathedral in Cuenca starkly illustrate scenes from Genesis and the Passion.

Castillo★

Open 10am to 1.30pm and 3.30-5.30pm (Apr-30 Sep 10am-1.30pm and 4.30-7.30pm). 1 Jan, 24 Aug and 25 Dec. 2 €. ☎967 17 00 08.

This 15C fortress with six circular towers was built by the Marqués de Villena, and long abandoned. In 1870 the new owner, Eugenia de Montijo, installed an ugly brick facing in the patio. The empty rooms hold beautiful Mudéjar **artesonado**★ ceilings – the audience chamber is outstanding – and delicately carved stone window surrounds. Follow the curtain walls to the stepped merlons for views of the village and countryside.

Excursions

Villaescusa de Haro

6km/4mi NE along the N 420. The magnificent 1507 **Capilla de la Asunción**★ (Chapel of the Assumption) of the parish church has crenels, a Gothic-Renaissance altarpiece and a wrought-iron screen with three florid Gothic arches.

BILBAO★

POPULATION: 372 054.

MICHELIN MAP 573 C 21 (TOWN PLAN) – PAÍS VASCO (VIZCAYA) – LOCAL MAP SEE COSTA VASCA

Bilbao has renewed itself with a new metro system, with distinctive glazed station entrances by Sir Norman Foster; a new footbridge and airport terminal, both by Santiago Calatrava; and a riverside development by Cesar Pelli (of London's Canary Wharf tower). But Bilbao's jewel is the Guggenheim, its spectacular modern art museum designed by Frank Gehry. Bilbao was the birthplace of writer and humanist Miguel de Unamuno (1864-1936).

- **Information:** *Plaza Arenal 1, ☎94 479 57 60.*
- **Orient Yourself:** Bilbao is in northeastern Spain's Basque country.
- **Parking:** It can be difficult to find a space in this industrial city.
- **Don't Miss:** The Guggenheim is a must-see for Spain, not just Bilbao.
- **Organizing Your Time:** Spend a few hours at the Guggenheim for starters, try out the metro and stroll the riverside.
- **Also See:** COSTA VASCA, VITORIA-GASTEIZ and DONOSTIA-SAN SEBASTIÁN.

Location

The capital of Vizcaya province is an excellent base from which to explore the Basque country, with Vitoria-Gasteiz 69km/43mi to the south, Donostia-San Sebastián 102km/63mi to the east, and Santander 103km/64mi to the west.

Background

The city – Founded in the early 14C, old Bilbao is on the right bank of the Nervión, under the Santuario de Begoña (Begoña Sanctuary). It was originally named *las siete calles*, or seven streets, for its layout.

The modern *El Ensanche* business district (*ensanche* means "enlargement"), across the river, developed in the 19C. The wealthy residential quarter spreads around Doña Casilda Iturriza park and along Gran Vía de Don Diego López de Haro.

Industry – Industry developed in the middle of the 19C when iron mined nearby was shipped to England. Iron and steelworks were subsequently established.

Greater Bilbao and the ría – Since 1945 Greater Bilbao has included the towns from Bilbao itself to Getxo on the sea. Industry is concentrated along the left bank in **Baracaldo, Sestao, Portugalete** with its **transporter bridge** built in 1893, and in Somorrostro where there is an oil refinery. **Santurtzi**, a fishing port, is known for its sardines. **Algorta**, a residential town on the right bank, is a contrast to heavy industry; **Deusto** is famous for its university.

Special Features

Museo Guggenheim★★★

Open 10am-8pm. Closed Mon (except Jul-Aug). 10.50 € (12.50 € special exhibitions). 94 435 90 80

This is the European showcase for the collection founded in New York by art patron Solomon R. Guggenheim (1861-1949), the youngest of the prestigious museums managed by the Guggenheim Foundation.

With this stunning museum complex, inaugurated in 1997, acclaimed architect **Frank Gehry** created one of the great buildings of the late 20C, a counterpart to Frank Lloyd Wright's famous 1950 spiral housing the Guggenheim's Fifth Avenue Museum.

Emblem of the city

The museum rises from the banks of the Nervión like a complex ship with billowing sails. Formal geometry and symmetry are abandoned to free forms, creating harmony and lines flowing gracefully out of potential chaos. The composition, shimmering in titanium, demands to be seen from all angles and alters with

Museo Guggenheim, Bilbao

Address Book

For coin ranges, see the Legend on the cover flap.

WHERE TO EAT

⊜⊜⊜ **Goizeko Kabi** – *Particular de Estraunza 4 – ☎94 442 11 29 – Closed Sun and 31 Jul-15 Aug* – ▤. This regional gastronomic institution near the Museo de Bellas Artes is renowned for its high-quality cuisine offering a balanced combination of the traditional and innovative, with outstanding seafood dishes.

TAPAS

El Viandar de Sota – *Gran Vía de Don Diego López de Haro 45 – ☎94 415 25 00* – ▤. This complex of five different places to eat and drink is another famous landmark in the modern section of the city, also near the Museo de Bellas Artes. Take your pick from the traditional tapas bar, the sidrería, serving excellent local cider, or the vinoteca.

WHERE TO STAY

⊜ **Hotel Iturrienea** – *Santa María 14 – ☎94 416 15 00 – 21 rooms. 48 € –* ☕ *4.28 €*. This charming hotel at the heart of the old quarter is housed in a tastefully refurbished old building with a distinctive blue façade. The emphasis here is on antiques, along with works by local artists. Although the rooms are generally on the small side, the wooden floors add to the homely feel.

⊜⊜ **Hotel Sirimiri** – *Plaza de la Encarnación 3 – ☎94 433 07 59 – hsirimirieuskalnet.net* – **P** – *28 rooms* – ☕ *6 €*. Nestled in the old quarter, on the right bank of the River Bilbao, close to the Museo de Arte Sacro. The rooms here are modern, spacious and functional with large fully equipped bathrooms.

CAFÉS

Café Iruña – *Jardines de Albia-Berástegui 5*. This café, which was founded in 1903, has become something of an institution in Bilbao. It is situated in a pleasant square and contains some attractive Mudéjar-inspired ceilings and decoration. An enjoyable place for a drink, particularly at night.

Café La Granja – *Plaza Circular 3*. This famous café dates from 1926 although its style is more in keeping with the 19C with its marble tables, wooden chairs and decadent air. On evenings during the weekend the quiet, contemplative mood is replaced by a more lively atmosphere and loud music.

FIESTAS

Bilbao's main annual festival takes place during **Semana Grande** in August with bullfights, Basque pelota championships and other events.

every change of light. The south entrance, of golden limestone, opens to a soaring **central atrium** (50m/165ft high) which echoes Wright's great spiral, transformed here into a whirl of smoothly moulded shapes and natural light. Access to the galleries is by glass-fronted lifts or vertiginous suspended walkways and staircases. The largest measures 130m/450ft long and 25m/80ft wide, running the length of the riverside site, culminating in a V-shaped metal and stone tower.

Collections

Drawing on the vast Guggenheim collections (more than 6 000 paintings, sculptures and works on paper), the latest Guggenheim Museum focuses on art from the 1950s to the present. Well represented are Modern masters (Picasso, Mondrian, Kandinsky) and major movements such as Abstract Expressionism (Rothko, De Kooning, Pollock), Pop art (Oldenburg, Rosenquist, Warhol), and Conceptual and Minimalist art (Carl André, Donald Judd). Contemporary artists likely to be on view include Anselm Kiefer, Francesco Clemente and Damien Hirst. The museum's own acquisitions include a vast mural by Sol LeWitt and Richard Serra's Snake, three gigantic sheets of undulating steel. Notable Spanish works are by Antoni Tàpies, Eduardo Chillida, Francesc Torres, Cristina Iglesias

BILBAO

Street	Grid	No.
Arenal Puente	EY	2
Arriaga Pl.	EYZ	3
Arriquíbar Pl.	DYZ	4
Ayuntamiento Puente	EY	5
Bidebarrieta	EZ	7
Bilbao la Vieja	EZ	8
Correo	EZ	
Cosme Echevarrieta	DY	14
Cruz	EZ	15
Gran Vía Don Diego de López de Haro	DEY	
Jado Pl. de	DY	28
Ledesma	EY	32
Lersundi	DX	36
Marqués del Puerto	DY	38
Merced Muelle	EZ	40
Merced Puente	EZ	41
Moraza Pl. de	EX	45
Pablo Picasso	DZ	50
Pedro Eguillor Pl.	DY	52
Pedro Martínez Artola	DZ	53
Pío Baroja Pl.	EZ	55
Plaza Nueva	EZ	57
Puerto de la Paz Av.	DX	60
Ribera Puente	EZ	65
Santiago Pl.	EZ	71
Santos Juanes Pl.	EZ	73
Sombrereía	EZ	75
Viuda de Epalza	EY	80
Museo de Bellas Artes	DY	M

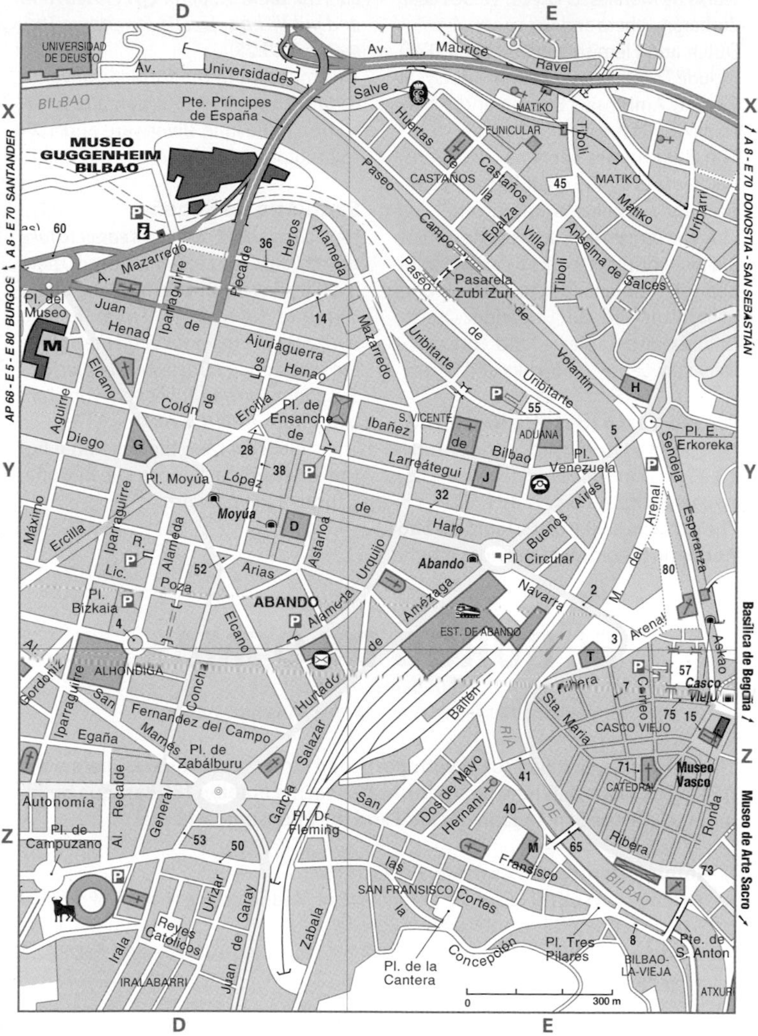

and Susana Solano. Space is reserved for **Picasso's** *Guernica*, now in Madrid's Reina Sofía museum.

Worth a Visit

Museo de Bellas Artes★

Open 10am-8pm; Sun and public hols, 10am-2pm; last admission 15 min before

closing. *Closed Mon, 1 Jan and 25 Dec.* *5 €, no charge Wed.* *94 439 60 60.*
The fine arts museum is in two buildings in Doña Casilda Iturriza park.
The **ancient art section**★★ *(old building, ground floor)* exhibits 12-17C Spanish paintings. Romanesque works include a 12C Crucifixion from the Catalan School. The 16C-17C Spanish classical section has works by Morales, El Greco, Valdés Leal, Zurbarán, Ribera and Goya.
Dutch and Flemish canvases (15C-17C) include *The Usurers* by Quentin Metsys, a *Pietà* by Ambrosius Benson and a *Holy Family* by Gossaert.
The **Basque art section** (*first floor*) holds works by the great Basque painters: Regoyos, Zuloaga, Iturrino etc.
The **contemporary art section** *(new building)* displays works by artists both Spanish – Solana, Vázquez Díaz, Gargallo, Blanchard, Luis Fernández Otieza, Chillida and Tàpies – and foreign – Delaunay, Léger, Kokoschka and Bacon.

Museo Vasco (Basque Museum)

Open 11am-5pm (4pm Sun). *Closed Mon and public hols.* *3 €, no charge Thu.* *94 415 54 23.*
The museum, in the ex-**Colegio de San Andrés** in the old town, provides insight into traditional Basque activities (linen weaving, arts and crafts, fishing). In the centre of the classicist cloisters stands the primitive, animal-like **idol of Mikeldi**.

Museo Diocesano de Arte Sacro (Diocesan Sacred Art Museum)

Open 10.30am-1.30pm and 4-7pm; Sun, 10.30am-1.30pm. *Closed Mon and public hols.* *3 €, no charge Thu.* *94 432 01 25.*
This museum in the former Convento de la Encarnación (16C), contains a collection of Basque silverware and 12C-15C sculptures of the Virgin and Child.

Santuario de Begoña

You can drive up but it's easier to take the lift from Calle Esperanza Ascao. There is a fine **view of Bilbao** from the upper terminus footbridge. *From Mallona park, take the main street on the right to the sanctuary.* *Open 8am-1.30pm and 5-8.30pm; Sun and public hols, 9am-2pm and 5-9pm.* *94 412 70 91.*
The church contains the venerated figure of Nuestra Señora de Begoña, patron of the province.

EL BURGO DE OSMA★

POPULATION: 5 054
MICHELIN MAP 575 H 20 – CASTILLA Y LEÓN (SORIA)

This attractive Castilian town with porticoed streets and squares, below the ruins of its castle, has long been a bishop's seat. Its notable 18C Baroque buildings include the San Agustín hospital and the imposing cathedral.

- **Information:** *Plaza Mayor 9,* *975 36 01 16.*
- **Orient Yourself:** El Burgo de Osma is NE of Madrid on the N 122, 56km/35mi SW of Soria and 139km/87mi SE of Burgos.
- **Also See:** SORIA, COVARRUBIAS (95km/59mi NW), BURGOS and PEDRAZA (111km/69mi SW)

Visit

Catedral★

Open 11am-1pm and 4.30-5.30pm; Jul-Nov 10am-1pm and 4-7pm. *Closed Mon.* *3 €.* *639 57 33 37.*
This Gothic sanctuary was built after a Cluniac monk, Don Pedro de Osma, vowed to replace the former cathedral. The east end, transept and chapter house were built in the 13C; the late-Gothic cloisters and chancel received Renaissance embellishments in the

16C. The sacristy, royal chapel and 72m/236ft belfry are from the 18C.

The Gothic decoration on the late-13C **south portal** includes, on the splays, statues of Moses, Gabriel, the Virgin, Judith, Solomon and Esther; on the lintel, a Dormition and on the pier, Christ showing his wounds (late 15C).

The interior is remarkable for the elevation of the nave, the delicate wrought-iron screens (16C) by Juan de Francés, the **high altar retable** by Juan de Juni, and the 16C white marble **pulpit** and **trascoro altarpiece**.

The 13C polychrome limestone **tomb of San Pedro de Osma**★ is in the west transept. In the **museum**, among the **archives** and **illuminated manuscripts**★ are a richly illustrated 1086 **Beatus** and a 12C manuscript with the signs of the Zodiac.

Excursions

Peñaranda de Duero★

47km/29mi W along the N 122 and BU 924. The small Castilian town is dominated by the ruins of its castle.

Plaza Mayor★

Around the 15C pillory in the square are half-timbered houses on stone piers.

To one side is the **Palacio de Avellaneda**★, a palace with a Renaissance façade. A patio with a two-tier gallery, a grand staircase and chambers with **artesonado ceilings**★ make this one of the finest Renaissance residences in Spain. *Guided tours (30min), 10am-2pm and 4-7.30pm (Oct-Mar, 3-6pm); last admission 1hr before closing. Closed Mon, 1 Jan and 24-25 and 31 Dec. 947 55 20 13.*

Cañón del Río Lobos

15km/10mi N on the SO 920. The landscape along this 25km/15m stretch of the Río Lobos is riddled with caves, depressions and chasms. *For further information, contact the Centro de Interpretación del Parque Natural, 975 36 35 64.*

Calatañazor

25km/15mi NE on the N 122. Along Calatañazor's steep, stone-paved streets, time has stood still. From the castle ruins, view the plain where Almanzor is said to have been defeated by the Christians.

Castillo de Gormaz

14km/9mi S on the SO 160. These 10C Moorish castle ruins, overlooking the Duero, are the largest in Europe (446m/1 463ft in length, 26 towers).

Berlanga del Duero

28km/17mi SE on the C 116 and SO 104. Berlanga, below its massive 15C castle, was a strongpoint along the Duero. In the Gothic **Colegiata**, a monumental 16C hall-church, two chapels contain Flamboyant altarpieces and the 16C recumbent alabaster statues of its founders. *To visit the church, follow the instructions on the door. 975 34 30 49.*

Some 8km/5mi southeast in **Casillas de Berlanga** is the **Iglesia de San Baudelio de Berlanga**, an unusual 11C Mozarabic chapel, its roof supported by a massive pillar. The gallery rests on a double tier of arches. All was covered with frescoes in the 12C. Hunting scenes and geometric patterns can still be made out. (*Open Oct-Mar, 10am-2pm and 3.30-6pm (Apr-Sep 10am-2pm and 4-8pm; Sun and public hols all year, 10am-2pm. Closed Mon and Tue, 1 Jan and 24-25 and 31 Dec. 0.60 €, no charge Sat-Sun. 975 22 13 97.)*

BURGOS★★

POPULATION: 169 111

MICHELIN MAP 575 E 18-19 (TOWN PLAN) – CASTILLA Y LEÓN (BURGOS)

Burgos sits on the banks of the River Arlanzón, on a windswept plateau at the heart of the Spanish Meseta. The most famous of its monuments is the magnificent cathedral, whose lofty Gothic spires dominate the city's skyline.

- **Information:** *Plaza Alonso Martínez 7, ☎947 20 31 25. www.turismoburgos.org.*
- **Orient Yourself:** Burgos is in the north of Spain, 88km/55m from Palencia, 117km/73mi from Vitoria-Gasteiz and 120km/80mi from Valladolid, at 856m/2 808ft, exposed to bitter winds in winter.
- **Don't Miss:** The cathedral and the monasteries.
- **Organizing Your Time:** Noble Burgos merits at least a day of exploration.
- **Also See:** COVARRUBIAS (39km/24mi SE), La RIOJA (Santo Domingo de la Calzada: 75km/47mi E), AGUILAR DE CAMPOO (79km/49mi NW) and PALENCIA.

Background

Historical notes – Founded by Diego Rodríguez in 884, Burgos was capital of Castilla and León from 1037 until the fall of Granada in 1492. Yet commerce and the arts flourished afterward: the town became a wool centre for the sheep farmers of the Mesta *(see SORIA)*; architects and sculptors from Northern Europe transformed monuments. Burgos became Spain's Gothic capital with outstanding works including the cathedral, the Monasterio de las Huelgas Reales (Royal Convent of Las Huelgas) and the Cartuja de Miraflores (Carthusian monastery). The end of the 16C brought the decline of the Mesta and of the town's prosperity.

Burgos was the seat of Franco's government from 1936 to 1938.

Land of El Cid (1026-99) – The exploits of Rodrigo Díaz, of Vivar *(9km/5.5mi N of Burgos)* light up the late-11C history of Castilla. The brilliant captain first supported the ambitious King of Castilla, Sancho II, then Alfonso VI who succeeded his brother in dubious circumstances. Alfonso, jealous of his exploits against the Moors, banished the hero.

Díaz entered service first with the Moorish king of Zaragoza and subsequently fought Christian and Muslim armies with equal fervour. Most famously, he captured Valencia at the head of 7 000 men, chiefly Muslims, after a nine-month siege in 1094. He was finally defeated by the Moors at Cuenca and died soon after (1099). His widow held Valencia against the Muslims until 1102 when she set fire to the city, then fled to Castilla with El Cid's body. The couple were buried in San Pedro de Cardeña *(10km/6mi SE of Burgos)*, but their ashes were moved to Burgos Cathedral in 1921.

Legend has transformed the stalwart but ruthless 11C warrior, the Campeador (Champion) of Castilla, El Cid (*Seid* in Arabic), into a knight of exceptional valour. The epic poem *El Cantar del Mío Cid* appeared in 1180 and was followed by ballads. In 1618 Guillén de Castro wrote a romanticised version of El Cid, *Las Mocedades del Cid* (Youthful Adventures of El Cid) upon which Corneille, in 1636, based his drama *Le Cid*.

Special Features

CATEDRAL★★★ *1hr 30min*

Open 9.30am-1pm and 4-7.15pm (from 10am Nov-18 Apr); Jul-Sep 9.30am-7.15pm 4€. ☎947 20 47 12.

The third-largest cathedral of Spain (after Sevilla and Toledo) illustrates the transformation of French and German Flamboyant Gothic into an exuberant Spanish style. It is a showcase of European Gothic sculpture.

Ferdinand III laid the first stone in 1221. At the beginning of the 13C, under Mau-

Address Book

For coin ranges, see the Legend on the cover flap.

WHERE TO EAT

Rincón de España – *Nuño Rasura 11 – 947 20 59 55 – Closed Mon-Tue evenings Nov-Mar –* . The best feature here is two summertime terraces with views to the cathedral nearby, though there's also a covered terrace and formal dining room. Castillian fare includes house specialties prepared in a wood-fired oven.

Ponte Vecchio – *Vitoria 111 (passage) – 947 22 56 50 – Closed Mon and first two weeks Aug –* . An italian restaurant in a magnificent locale, with murals inspired by ancient Rome. Detailed neo-Mediterranean decor, good service, and a welcoming environment where couples go to dine.

WHERE TO STAY

Hotel Jacobeo – *San Juan 24 – 947 26 01 02 – www.hoteljacobeo.com – 13 rooms – 4.50 €*. The major advantage of this small hotel, housed in a restored mansion, is undoubtedly its location in the very heart of the city's historic quarter. The rooms here are pleasant if not particularly spacious.

Hotel Landa – *3.5km/2mi S along the A 1 – 947 25 77 77 – www.landahotel.com – P – 39 rooms – 16€ – Restaurant 45/50 €*. The impressive facilities occupy part of a restored medieval castle. Especially notable are the majestic lobby, a great dining hall under stone vaults, individually styled and well-appointed rooms, and the spectacular covered pool.

rice the Englishman, then Bishop of Burgos, who had collected drawings during a journey through France (at that time very much influenced by the Gothic style), the nave, aisles and portals were built by local architects.

The 15C saw the building of the west front spires and the Capilla del Condestable (Constable's Chapel) and the decoration of other chapels. Architects and sculptors from Flanders, the Rhineland and Burgundy were brought by another Burgos prelate, Alonso de Cartagena, on his return from the Council of Basel.

These artists found new inspiration in Mudéjar arabesques and other Hispano-Moorish elements. The most outstanding, the Burgundian **Felipe Vigarny**, the Fleming **Gil de Siloé** and the Rhinelander **Johan of Cologne**, integrated rapidly and with their sons and grandsons – Diego de Siloé, Simon and Francis of Cologne – created what was essentially a Burgos school of sculpture.

The cloisters were built in the 14C, while the magnificent lantern over the transept crossing – the original of which collapsed after some particulary daring design work by Simon of Cologne – was rebuilt by Juan de Vallejo in the mid-16C.

Exterior

A walk round the cathedral reveals how the architects took ingenious advantage of the sloping ground (the upper gallery of the cloisters is level with the cathedral pavement) to introduce delightful small precincts and closes.

West front

The ornate upper area, with its frieze of Spanish kings and two openwork spires, is the masterwork of Johan of Cologne

B. Juge/MICHELIN

Spires of the cathedral

Portada de la Coronería (Coronería Doorway) (1)

The statues at the jambs have the grace of their French Flamboyant Gothic originals, though their robes show more movement. The Plateresque **Portada de la Pellejería (2)** (Skinner's Doorway) in the transept was designed by Francis of Cologne early in the 16C.

Around by the east end it becomes obvious that the Constable's Chapel, with its Isabelline decoration and lantern with pinnacles, is one of the cathedral's later additions.

Portada del Sarmental (Sarmental Doorway) (3)

The covings are filled with figures from the Celestial Court. The tympanum is a remarkable showing each Evangelist in a different position as he writes.

Interior

The design of the interior is French-inspired while the decoration bears an exuberant Spanish stamp.

Crucero, Coro and Capilla Mayor★★ (Transept crossing, choir stalls and chancel)

The splendid star-ribbed lantern of the transept crossing rises on four massive pillars to 54m/177ft above the funerary stones of El Cid and Ximena, inlaid in the crossing pavement.

The imposing unit of 103 walnut choir stalls, carved by Felipe Vigarny between 1507 and 1512, illustrates biblical stories on the upper, back rows and mythological and burlesque scenes at the front. The handsome recumbent statue of wood, plated with enamelled copper, on the tomb at the centre, from the 13C, is of Bishop Maurice.

The high altar **(4)** retable is a 16C Renaissance work in high relief against an intrinsically Classical background of niches and pediments.

Claustro

The 14C Gothic cloisters present a panorama of Burgos sculpture in stone, terracotta and polychrome wood.

The **Capilla de Santiago** (St James' Chapel) **(5)** contains the cathedral treasure of plate and liturgical objects. In the **Capilla de Santa Catalina** (St Catherine's Chapel) are manuscripts and documents, including the marriage contract of El Cid. On the 15C carved and painted consoles, Moorish kings pay homage to the king of Castilla.

The **sacristía** (sacristy) **(6)** houses the *Christ at the Column* by Diego de Siloé, a supreme example of Spanish Expressionism in post-16C Iberian sculpture.

The **sala capitular** (chapter house) **(7)** displays, besides 15C and 16C Brussels tapestries symbolising the theological and cardinal virtues, a Hispano-Flemish diptych, a *Virgin and Child* by Memling and, above, a painted wood Mudéjar *artesonado* ceiling (16C).

Capilla del Condestable★★ (Constable's Chapel)

A magnificent grille closes off the area. The Isabelline chapel founded by Hernández de Velasco, Constable of Castilla, in 1482 and designed by Simon of Cologne, is lit by a lantern surmounted by an elegant cupola with star-shaped vaulting. All the great early Renaissance sculptors of Burgos cooperated in the decoration of the walls and altarpiece. The heraldic displays in the chapel are striking. On either side of the altar, the Constable's escutcheon, held by male figures, seems suspended over the balustrades of the tribune.

Statues of the Constable and his wife lie on their tomb, carved in Carrara marble, and beside them is an immense garnet-coloured marble funerary stone for the names of their descendants. On the right side of the chapel is a Plateresque door to the sacristy (1512) **(8)** where there is a painting of *Mary Magdalene* by Pietro Ricci.

Girola★ (Ambulatory)

The *trasaltar* (at the back of the high altar), carved partly by **Felipe Vigarny**, includes an expressive representation of the Ascent to Calvary.

Escalera Dorada or Escalera de la Coronería (Golden or Coronation Staircase) (9)

The majestically proportioned staircase was designed in pure Renaissance style by Diego de Siloé in the early 16C. Twin pairs of flights are outlined by an ornate, elegant gilded banister by the French master ironsmith, Hilaire.

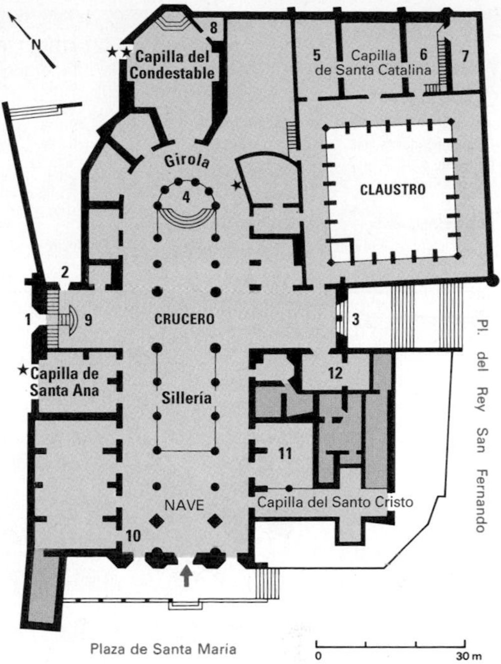

Capillas

Each of these side chapels is a museum of Gothic and Plateresque art: **Gil de Siloé** and Diego de la Cruz cooperated on the huge Gothic altarpiece in the **Capilla de Santa Ana**★ which illustrates the saint's life. In the centre is a Tree of Jesse with, at its heart, the first meeting of Anne and Joachim and at the top, the Virgin and Child.

At the beginning of the cathedral nave, near the roof, is the **Papamoscas** or **Flycatcher Clock (10)**, with a jack which opens its mouth on the striking of the hours.

In the **Capilla del Santo Cristo** (Chapel of Holy Christ) is a Crucifixion with the particularly venerated figure complete with hair and covered with buffalo hide to resemble human flesh.

The **Capilla de la Presentación** (Chapel of the Presentation) **(11)** contains the tomb of the Bishop of Lerma, carved by Felipe Vigarny and the **Capilla de la Visitación** (Chapel of the Visitation) **(12)**, the tomb of Alonso de Cartagena by Gil de Siloé.

Real Monasterio de las Huelgas★★ (Royal Convent of las Huelgas)

1.5km/1mi W of Burgos; take avenida del Monasterio de las Huelgas.

Guided tours (50min) 10am-1.15pm and 3.45-5.45pm; Sun and public hols 10.30am-2.15pm. Closed Mon, 1 and 6 Jan, 14 Apr, 1 May, 16 and 29 Jun, and 24-25 and 31 Dec. 5 €, no charge Wed for E. U. citizens. 947 20 16 30.

Las Huelgas Reales, the summer palace of the kings of Castilla, was converted in 1180 into a convent by Alfonso VIII and his wife Eleanor, daughter of Henry II of England. The nuns were Cistercians of high lineage, the abbess all-powerful; by the 13C the convent's influence, both spiritual and temporal, extended to more than 50 towns and it had become a place of retreat for members of the house of Castilla and even became the royal pantheon.

Rearrangement over the centuries has resulted in a heterogeneous and somewhat divided building in which, although the Cistercian style of the 12C and 13C predominates, there are Romanesque and even Mudéjar features (13C-15C) as well as Plateresque furnishings.

Iglesia

The clean lines of of this church are pure Cistercian. The interior is divided by a screen: from the transept, open to all, you can see the revolving pulpit (1560), in gilded ironwork, which enabled the preacher to be heard on either side. Royal and princely tombs, originally coloured, rich in heraldic devices

Burgos

Almirante Bonifaz	B	2	Eduardo Martínez del Campo	A	10	Nuño Rasura	A	23
Alonso Martínez Pl. de	B	3	España Pl.	B	12	Paloma La	A	24
Aparicio y Ruiz	A	5	Gen. Santocildes	B	15	Rey San Fernando Pl. del	A	27
Arlanzón Av. del	B	6	Libertad Pl. de la	B	16	Reyes Católicos Av. de los	B	26
Cid Campeador Av. del	B	8	Mayor Pl.	AB	18	Santo Domingo de Guzmán Pl. de	B	28
Conde de Guadalhorce Av.	A	9	Miranda	B	20	Vitoria	B	
			Monasterio de las Huelgas Av. del	A	21			

Arco de Santa Maria	A	B	Museo Marceliano Santa María	B	M^2	Museo de Burgos	B	M^1

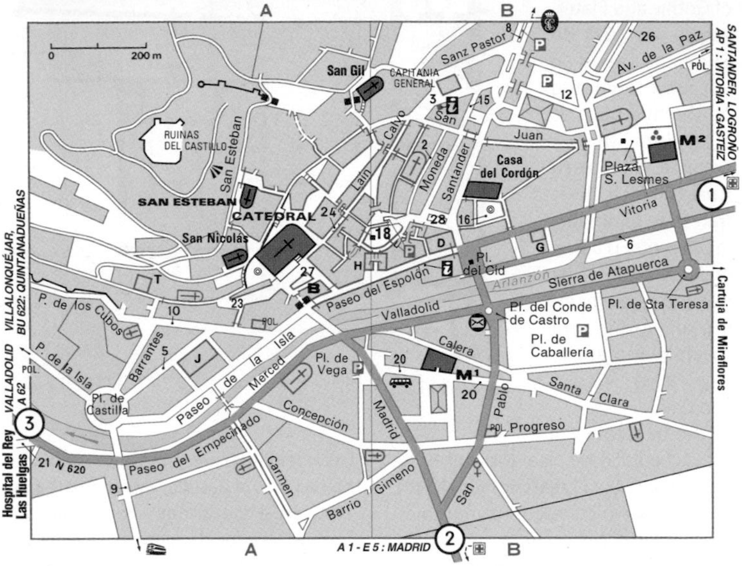

and historical legend, line the aisles, while in the middle of the nave, the nuns' *coro*, is the tomb of Alfonso VIII and Eleanor of England. The rood screen retable, delicately carved and coloured in the Renaissance style, is surmounted by a fine 13C Deposition. The altar is flanked on each side by two handsome 13C and 14C tombs.

Gothic cloisters

13C-15C. Enough fragments of Mudéjar vaulting stucco remain in these Gothic cloisters to suggest the delicacy of the strapwork inspired by Persian ivories and fabrics.

Sala Capitular

The chapter house holds the **pendón**★, a trophy from the Battle of Las Navas de Tolosa, decorated with silk *appliqué*.

Romanesque cloisters

Late 12C. In these Romanesque cloisters, slender paired columns, topped by highly stylised capitals, combine to create an effect of elegance. Several rooms in this part of Alfonso VIII's former palace were decorated by Moors. The **Capilla de Santiago** (Chapel of St James) retains an *artesonado* ceiling with original colour and stucco frieze. According to legend, the statue of the saint with articulated arms conferred knighthood on princes of royal blood.

Museo de Telas Medievales★★ (Museum of Medieval Fabrics)

The fabrics, court dress and finery displayed in the former loft provide a vivid view of royal wear in 13C Castilla. Of the clothes, (tunics, pelisses and capes) found in the tombs, the most valuable come from that of the Infante Fernando de la Cerda (who died in 1275), son of

Alfonso X, the Wise. This tomb, which excaped French desecration in 1809, contained a long tunic, *pellote* (voluminous trousers with braces) and a large mantle, all of the same material embroidered with silk and silver thread. There is also a *birrete*, a silk crown adorned with pearls and precious stones.

Cartuja de Miraflores (Miraflores Carthusian Monastery)

4km/2.5mi E. Open 10.15am-3pm and 4-6pm; Sun and public hols, 11am-3pm and 4-6pm. Closed 1 and 6 Jan and 25 Dec.

This former royal foundation, entrusted to the Carthusians in 1442, was chosen by Juan II as a pantheon for himself and his second wife, Isabel of Portugal. The church was completed in full Isabelline Gothic style in 1498.

Iglesia★

The sobriety of the façade, relieved only by the buttress finials and the founders' escutcheons, gives no indication of the elegant interior vaulting and gilded keystones.

Sculpture ensemble in the Capilla Mayor★★★ (apse)

Designed by the Fleming, Gil de Siloé at the end of the 15C, it comprises the high altarpiece, the royal mausoleum and a funerary recess.

The polychrome **altarpiece**, the work of Siloé and Diego de la Cruz, is striking. The usual rectangular compartments are replaced by circles crowded with biblical figures.

The white marble **mausoleo real** (royal mausoleum) is in the form of an eight-pointed star in which are recumbent statues of the Juan II and Queen Isabel, parents of Isabel the Catholic. Dominating the exuberant Flamboyant Gothic decoration of scrolls, canopies, pinnacles, cherubim and armorial bearings, executed with rare virtuosity, are the four Evangelists. In an ornate **recess** in the north wall is the tomb of the Infante Alfonso, whose premature death gave the throne to his sister Isabel the Catholic. The statue of the prince at prayer is technically brilliant but impersonal (compare with that of Juan de Padilla in the Museo de Burgos, *see below*). Also in the church are a 15C Hispano-Flemish triptych (to the right of the altar) and Gothic **choir stalls** carved with an infinite variety of arabesques.

Visit

Museo de Burgos★

Open 10am-2pm and 4-7pm (5-8pm in summer); Sat-Sun 10am-2pm. Closed Mon and public hols. 1.20 €, no charge Sat-Sun and public hols. 947 26 58 75.

Prehistoric and Archaeological Department

In the Casa de Miranda, a Renaissance mansion with an elegant patio, this section holds objects from the Prehistoric to Visigothic periods. Of particular interest are the rooms devoted to Iron Age sites, to the Roman settlement of Clunia and the Roman funerary steles.

Fine Arts Department

The Casa de Ángulo houses art from the region covering the period from the 9C to the 20C. There are several precious items from the Santo Domingo Monastery at Silas: an 11C **Hispano-Moorish casket★,** delicately carved in ivory in Cuenca and highlighted with enamel plaques, the 12C **Frontal** or **Urn of Santo Domingo★** in beaten and enamelled copper, and a 10C **marble diptych**. On the **tomb★** of Juan de Padilla, Gil de Siloé beautifully rendered the face and robes of the deceased.

The collection of 15C painting includes a *Christ Weeping* by Jan Mostaert.

Arco de Santa María★

Open 11am-2pm and 5-9pm. Closed Sun-Mon and public hols. 947 28 88 68.

The 14C gateway in the city walls was modified in the 16C to form a triumphal arch for Emperor Charles V and embellished with statues of the famous: below, Diego Porcelos Rodríguez is flanked by two semi-legendary judges said to have governed Castilla in the 10C; above, Count Fernán González and

El Cid (right) are with Charles V. Inside are the **Sala de Poridad**, with magnificent Mudéjar cupola, and the pharmacy of the ex-Hospital de San Juan.

Iglesia de San Nicolás

Open in summer, 10am-2pm and 4-8pm; public hols 9am-2pm and 5-6pm; in other seasons by prior arrangement. *No visits during religious services.* *1 €. 947 20 70 95.*

The **altarpiece★** of this Gothic church, carved by Simon of Cologne in 1505, is large and ornate with more than 465 figures. The upper part shows the Virgin crowned at the centre of a circle of angels; St Nicholas is surrounded by scenes from his life – note the voyage by caravel to Alexandria – and below, there is a rear view of the *Last Supper*.

Iglesia de San Esteban: Museo del Retablo

Open in summer 10.30am-2pm and 4.30-7pm; Sun 10.30am-2pm; at other times by appointment. *Closed Mon, Tu-Fri 1 Nov-31 May and 29 Jun.* *1.20 €. 947 27 37 52.*

The Retable Museum is in this delightful 14C Gothic **church★**. The interior is a magnificent setting for the 18 retables, exhibited according to their religious significance in the church's three naves. The coro alto contains a small collection of gold and silverwork.

Iglesia de San Gil

Open 10am-2pm and 4.30-7pm; by appointment in winter. *Closed Sun and public hols.* *1.20€. 947 26 11 49.*

One of the city's most beautiful churches. Hidden behind its sober façade is a late-Gothic temple. Noteworthy are the Nativity Chapel and Buena Mañana chapels, the latter containing a retable by Gil de Siloé.

Plaza Mayor

This delightful circular main square is typically lined by a portico.

Casa del Cordón

The 15C palace of the Constables of Castilla (now housing a bank, the Caja de Ahorros) displays a thick Franciscan cord motif, hence the name. It is where Columbus was received by the Catholic Monarchs on his return from his second voyage to America, and where Philip the Fair died suddenly of a chill after a game of *pelota*, reducing to despair his already disturbed wife, Juana the Mad.

Museo Marceliano Santa María

Open 10am-1.50pm and 5-9pm; Sun, 11am-1.50pm. *Closed Mon and public hols.* *0.15 €. 947 20 56 87.*

Impressionist canvases by Marceliano Santa María (1866-1952) are shown in the ruins of the former Benedictine monastery of San Juan.

Hospital del Rey

Founded by Alfonso VIII as a hospital for pilgrims, it retains its entrance, the Patio de Romeros, with its fine 16C Plateresque façade. Today, it is the seat of the University of Burgos

Castillo

This restored hilltop fortress dominates Burgos. Dating from the 9C, it was destroyed by troops of Napoleon. Views are magnificent.

Excursion

Archaeological finds in the Sierra de Atapuerca

Take the N 120 towards Logroño. In Ibeas de Juarros (13km/8mi), head to the Emiliano Aguirre hall (beside the main road). *Guided tours (2hr) of the caves and Museo Emiliano Aguirre by prior arrangement.* *4 €. 902 024 246.*

The construction of a rail line at the end of the last century led to the one of the world's most important palaeontological finds at what is now a World Heritage Site. Excavations at **La Dolina** have uncovered remains of hominids who lived around 800 000 years ago. The fossil register at the **Sima de los Huesos** (literally the Chasm of Bones), is the largest in Europe, dating from the Middle Pleistocene age between 400 000 and 200 000 years ago. Visitors can walk along the trench and visit a small archaeological museum.

CÁCERES★★★

POPULATION: 84 319.

MICHELIN MAP 576 N 10 (TOWN PLAN) – EXTREMADURA (CÁCERES)

The Almohad walls and towers of this World Heritage Site, a provincial capital, enclose a rare ensemble of intact Gothic and Renaissance noble houses.

- **Information:** *Plaza Mayor 10, ☎927 01 08 34.*
- **Orient Yourself:** Cáceres is strategically situated at the heart of Extremadura in west-central Spain.
- **Don't Miss:** The city walls and mansions redolent of the past.
- **Organizing Your Time:** Allow a half-day in Cáceres, then explore the region.
- **Also See:** *TRUJILLO (47km/29mi E), MÉRIDA (60km/37mi S), PLASENCIA (84km/52mi NE) and BADAJOZ (96km/60mi SW)*

Walking About

CÁCERES VIEJO★★★ (Old Cáceres) *1hr 30min*

Within Moorish walls lies a group of Gothic and Renaissance mansions beyond compare in Spain. The unadorned, ochre façades of the 15C and 16C reflect their owners, the Ulloas, the Ovandos and the Saavedras, who in battles against infidels and heathens won prestige, not wealth. The fortified towers of Cáceres were demolished on the command of Queen Isabel in 1477.

Follow the route on the plan.

Pass beneath the **Arco de la Estrella** (Star Arch) which was built into the wall by Manuel Churriguera in the 18C.

Plaza de Santa María★

On all sides are golden ochre façades. The front of the **Palacio Mayoralgo** (Mayoralgo Palace) has elegant paired windows while the **Palacio Episcopal** (Bishop's Palace) has a 16C bossed doorway with medallions of the Old and New Worlds on either side.

Iglesia de Santa María

Open 10am-to 1.30pm (10.45am-noon Sun and public hols) and 5-6.15pm; May-Sep, 10am-1.30pm and 6-7.15pm. 1 €. ☎92 721 53 13.

This 16C church has three Gothic aisles of almost equal height, with lierne and tierceron vaulting from which ribs descend into slender columns engaged in the main pillars. The fine carved high altar retable (16C) is difficult to see

Continue to the top of calle de las Tiendas to the **Palacio de Carvajal** (Carvajal Palace) flanked by a 15C tower. Visit chambers, patio and chapel. *Open 8am-8pm; Sat 10am-2pm and 5-8pm; Sun and public hols, 10am-2pm. Closed 1 Jan and 25 Dec. ☎92 725 55 98.*

Palacio de los Golfines de Abajo★ (Lower Golfines Palace)

This splendid late-15C Gothic-Plateresque mansion is of stone. The paired window derives from the Moorish *ajimez;* the fillet, delicately framing the windows and door, recalls the *alfiz.* A Plateresque frieze with winged griffons was added in the 16C.

Plaza San Jorge

Note the austere 18C façade of the Jesuit church of **San Francisco Javier.**

Iglesia de San Mateo

The church's high Gothic nave, begun in the 14C, abuts a 16C *coro alto* set on a vaulted arcade. Inside are a Baroque altarpiece and side chapels with tombs with decorative heraldic motifs.

Past the church the 15C **Torre de la Plata** (Silver Tower) and **Casa del Sol** (Sun House, for the Solís family crest over the arch) have unusual parapets.

Casa de las Cigüeñas

The Stork House retains the only 15C battlemented tower.

Casa de las Veletas (Weather Vane House)

This 18C mansion houses the **Museo de Cáceres**. Collections include Bronze Age steles, Celt-Iberian statues of wild boar (*verracos*) and local dress and crafts. (*Open 9am-2.30pm and 4-7.15pm; in summer, 9am-2.30pm and 5-8.15pm; Sun, 10am-2.30pm. Closed Mon and public hols. 1.20€, no charge for E.U. citizens. 92 701 08 77).*

The 11C **aljibe** (cistern) is still fed from the roof and sloping square. It is covered by five rows of horseshoe-shaped arches supported by granite capitals.

Casa del Comendador de Alcuéscar

This palace, also called the **Palacio de Torreorgaz**, with fine Gothic tower, delicate window surrounds and an unusual corner balcony, is a parador.

Down the alley is the **Palacio de los Golfines de Arriba** with plain façade and attractive patio. Further on, the **Casa de la Generala** is the law school.

Go through the ramparts opposite.

The steps to Plaza Mayor del General Mola afford an interesting view of the walls.

Extramuros

Iglesia de Santiago (St James' Church)

Open 9am-noon and 6-8pm. 92 724 49 06.

The Romanesque church is the birthplace of the Military Order of the Knights of Cáceres who in turn founded the Order of the Knights of St James. The altarpiece by Berruguete (1557) bears scenes from the Life of Christ. These surround a vigorous, finely portrayed St James the Moorslayer.

The **Palacio de Godoy** opposite has an impressive coat of arms on the corner and a fine inner patio.

Excursions

Santuario de la Virgen de la Montaña

3km/2mi E. Open 8.30am-2pm and 4-8pm (9pm in summer). Closed 22 Apr-1st Sun in May. 92 722 00 49.

In this 17C Baroque shrine is a statuette of the Virgin (*romería*, or pilgrimage, the first Sunday in May). The esplanade offers a **view**★ of the plateau.

Museo Vostell-Malpartida

10km/6mi along the N 521 to Malpartida de Cáceres; the museum is 3km/2mi beyond (follow signposts). Open

Address Book

For coin ranges, see the Legend on the cover flap.

WHERE TO EAT

El Puchero – *Plaza Mayor 9 – 92 724 54 97 – www.restauranteelpuchero.com –* . A good choice for the visitor, right in the plaza before the walled enclosure. There are two dining rooms with a local flavour where you can enjoy regional specialties at an attractive price.

El Figón de Eustaquio – *Plaza de San Juan 12 – 92 724 81 94 –* . Most traditional city, superbly located on the fringes of plaza Mayor. Traditional, local cuisine served in a rustic ambience.

WHERE TO STAY

Hotel Iberia Plaza Mayor – *Pintores 2 – 92 724 76 34 – www.iberiahotel.com – – 39 rooms.* This pleasant hotel just off the plaza Mayor is housed in a building dating from the 17C. Cosy rooms, a central location and excellent value for money. Highly recommended.

Parador de Cáceres – *Avenida Ancha 6 – 92 721 17 59 – www.parador.es – – 12.60 € – Restaurant 28.35€.* The 14C Torreorgaz Palace has been transformed into the city's delightful parador. Tasteful furnishings, comfortable rooms and well worth splashing out on.

10am-1.30pm and 4-6.30pm (summer 5-8pm; spring 5-7.30pm). ⓒ *Closed Mon and public hols.* *2 €, no charge Wed.* ☏ *92 727 64 92.*

The museum in an 18C wool-washing plant was created by Hispano-German artist Wolf Vostell. It includes works by Canogar, the Crónica team, Saura, Maciunas, Brecht, and Higgins.

Arroyo de la Luz

▶ *20km/12mi W along the N 521 and C 523. To find the Iglesia de la Asunción, head for the tower.* The 16C altarpiece has 16 **painted tablets**★ and four medallions by **Morales the Divine**, a rare assemblage of his works in one place.

Alcántara

65km/40mi NW along the N 521 and C 523. Alcántara has a Roman bridge which once brought it renown and from which it took its name (*Al Kantara* in Arabic).

Puente Romano★

2km/1.2mi NW on the road to Portugal. The magnificent bridge (106 AD), of massive unmortared granite blocks, has withstood formidable floodwaters. Note the small temple at one end and the central triumphal arch.

J. Malburet/MICHELIN

Palacio de los Golfines de Abajo

Convento de San Benito

Guided tours (30-45min), 10am (11am Sat) to 2pm and 4-5.30pm (Apr-Oct, 5-7.30pm); Sun and public hols, 11am-1.15pm. ⓒ*Closed Mon, 11 Aug-10 Oct.* ☏ *92 739 00 80.*

The old headquarters of the Military Order of Alcántara stands high above the Tajo. The 16C monastery has a Plateresque church with star vaulting, a Gothic patio and a graceful Renaissance gallery used as the backdrop for plays.

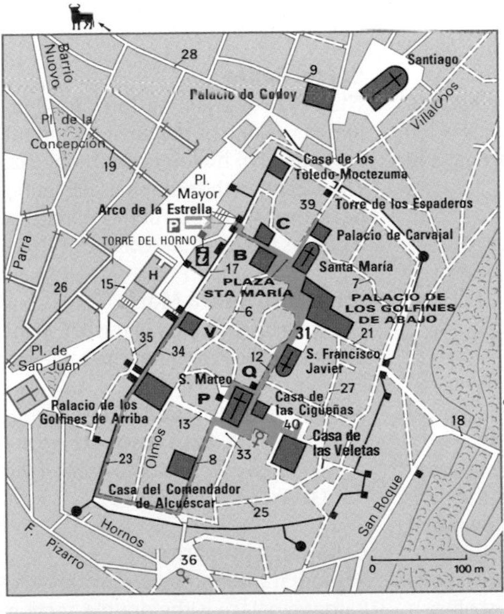

Cáceres	
Aldana Cuesta de	6
Amargura	7
Ancha	8
Camberos	9
Compañía Cuesta de la	12
Condes	13
Defensores del Alcázar	15
Estrella Adarve la	17
Fuente Concejo	18
General Ezponda	19
Marqués Cuesta del	21
Mayor Pl.	
Padre Rosalío Adarve del	23
Pereros	25
Pintores	26
Rincón de la Monja	27
San Jorge Pl.	31
San Mateo Pl. de	33
Sancti Espíritu	28
Santa Ana Adarve de	34
Santa Ana Arco de	35
Santa Clara Pl. de	36
Tiendas	39
Veletas Pl. de las	40

Casa de la Generala	V	Palacio Mayoralgo	B	Torre de los Plata	P
Casa del Sol	Q	Palacio episcopal	C		

CÁDIZ★★

POPULATION: 143 129.

MICHELIN MAP 578 W 11 – ANDALUCÍA (CÁDIZ)

Surrounded by water on three sides, Cádiz has attracted mariners for over 3 000 years. It is also one of Andalucía's most delightful provincial capitals, with charming squares, narrow alleyways and a quiet air, broken only by the exuberant Carnival, the best on the Iberian Peninsula.

- **Information:** *Avenida Ramón de Carranza, ☎95 625 86 46; Plaza de San Juan de Dios 11, ☎95 624 10 01.*
- **Orient Yourself:** This coastal city is positioned with the Atlantic to the south and west, the Bahía de Cádiz to the north and east.
- **Parking:** It's difficult in the old quarter.
- **Don't Miss:** A wander within the walls.
- **Also See:** Costa de la LUZ, JEREZ DE LA FRONTERA (35km/22mi NE) and RONDA (123km/77mi E).

Background

Oldest city in Europe – Cádiz was founded by the Phoenicians in 1100 BC. It was conquered by the Romans in 206 BC, and in turn by the Visigoths and Moors. Alfonso X reconquered the city in 1262. During the 16C, Cádiz was attacked by English corsairs, and partially destroyed by the Earl of Essex in 1596. In the 18C, Cádiz became a great port.

Constitution of Cádiz – During the French siege of 1812, patriots convened the Cortes which promulgated Spain's first liberal constitution.

Watchtowers – Between the 16C and 18C, merchants in Cádiz built over 160 towers to watch over the arrival and departure of their ships.

Walking About

Around Santa María and the Pópulo District 1

Plaza de San Juan de Dios

This 16C square is the most popular in the city. On one side stands the neo-Classical façade of the 1799 **town hall** *(ayuntamiento)*, by Torcuato Benjumeda, beside the Baroque tower of the Iglesia de San Juan de Dios. The tourist office is in an attractive neo-Classical building.

Take calle Sopranis, to the left of the Iglesia de San Juan de Dios.

Calle Sopranis

The street contains some of the best Baroque civil architecture in Cádiz, particularly the houses at nos 9, 10 and 17. At the end of the street note the 19C iron-and-brick former **tobacco factory**, and the **Convento de Santo Domingo.**

Continue along calle Plocia as far as Concepción Arenal.

Cárcel Real★

The 1792 royal jail, by Torcuato Benjumeda, is one of the most important Baroque civil buildings in Andalucía. The façade with triumphal-arch entry bears the escutcheon of the monarchy. It houses the city's law courts.

Iglesia de Santa María

The spire on the belfry of this 17C Mannerist church is adorned with azulejos.

Continue along calle Santa María, past the 18C **Casa Lasquetty** *to the left; cross calle Félix Soto towards the 13C* **Arco de los Blancos**.

Casa del Almirante

The outstanding feature of this 17C Baroque palace is the double-section Italian marble **doorway**★★, with Tuscan and Solomonic columns.

Iglesia de Santa Cruz★

Open for Mass at noon and 7pm (and usually beforehand). ☎95 628 77 04.

The old cathedral was rebuilt following the sacking by the Earl of Essex in 1596. Robust Tuscan columns define spaces. The church museum (Museo Catedralicio) is alongside in the Casa de la Contaduría (*see under Worth a Visit).*

Catedral★★

Open Tue-Sat 4.30-7pm (6.15pm Wed and Fri), Sun 11am-1pm. 4 € (includes museum). ☎95 628 61 54.

Work on the new cathedral began in 1722 and lasted over a century. The result is Baroque in character with the occasional neo-Classical feature. The **façade**★ is flanked by two lofty towers. The triple-aisle interior is surprisingly light and spacious. The crypt holds the remains of the composer **Manuel de Falla** (1876-1946).

From Plaza san Juan de Dios to the Cathedral 2

Frollow calle Nueva to plaza de San Juan de Dios. Turn left into calle Cristóbal Colón.

Casa de las Cadenas

This Baroque mansion has a Genoese marble **doorway**★ and Solomonic columns.

The Order of Alcántara

The Knights of San Juan de Pereiro changed the name of their order to Alcántara when they were entrusted with the defence of the town's fortress in 1218. Like the other great orders of chivalry in Spain – Calatrava, Santiago and Montesa – the Order of Alcántara was created to free the country from the Moors in the 12C. Each order, founded as a military unit under the command of a master, lived in a community bound by the Cistercian rule. These religious militias, always prepared for combat and capable of withstanding long sieges in their fortresses, played a major role in the Reconquest.

Continue along calles Cristóbal Colón and Cobos to plaza de la Candelaria; return to calle Nueva. Past plaza de San Agustín, take calle Rosario, to the Oratorio de la Santa Cueva (see description under Worth a Visit).

Plaza de San Francisco

This charming plaza, under the Baroque tower of the Iglesia de San Francisco, is lined by lively bars and cafés.

Plaza de Mina★★

Once the kitchen garden of the Convento de San Francisco, this verdant square is imbued with a colonial feel. Fine examples Isabelline buildings around the square include the **Museo de Cádiz** (*see under Worth a Visit).*

Head down calle de San José to the Oratorio de San Felipe Neri. The oratory stands alongside the Museo Iconográfico e Histórico de las Cortes y Sitio de Cádiz (see descriptions under Worth a Visit).

Hospital de Mujeres★

Open 10am-1.30pm. Closed Sun and public hols. 0.80 €. ☎95 622 36 47.

This Baroque building is planned around two patios linked by an extraordinary Imperial-style **stairway**★★. The Vía Crucis in the patio is created from 18C Triana azulejos.

Continue to the Torre Tavira (see description under Worth a Visit) on calle Sacramento.

Plaza de las Flores

Flower and plant stalls, cafés and shops contribute to the delightful atmosphere in one of the city's liveliest squares.

Take calle Compañía to return to plaza de la Catedral.

Worth a Visit

Museo Catedralicio★

Open 10am-1.30pm and 4.30-7pm; Sat 10.30am-1pm. 4 € (includes visit to the cathedral). ☎95 625 98 12.

Address Book

See the Legend on the cover flap.

WHERE TO EAT

El Faro – *San Félix 15 – at La Caleta beach- 902 21 10 68 – www.elfarodecadiz.com – closed evening of 24 Dec* – . This fine restaurant-tapas bar offers a cozy wood interior and a menu that emphasizes local fare.

TAPAS

Aurelio – *Zorrilla 1 – 95 622 10 31 – Closed Mon except from Jul-Sep.* This popular seafood bar is one of the places for tapas in Cádiz. Its only drawback is its small size – it soon fills up. A good central location close to Plaza de Mina.

Joselito – *San Francisco 38 – 956 25 22 51 – closed Sun.* Choose either entry, one with a covered terrace. The dining room serves fish, paella and stews.

WHERE TO STAY

Hostal Fantoni – *Flamenco 5 – 95 628 27 04 – www.hostalfantoni.net – – 12 rooms.* Why spend more when you can stay in this pleasant *hostal*? Try for a room with en-suite bathroom facing a pedestrian lane.

Hospedería Las Cortes de Cádiz – *San Francisco 9 – 956 22 04 89 – www.hotellascortes.com – – 36 rooms – Rest. 14€.* Rooms in this 19C home in the old quarter are well equipped, set around a covered patio. individually decorated, and named for a local figure. Attractive outside areas.

Hotel Francia y París – *Plaza de San Francisco 6 – 95 622 23 19 – www.hotelfrancia.com – – 57 rooms –* 5.11 €. An early-20C hotel with pleasant rooms fronting an attractive small square in the centre of the city.

BARS AND CAFÉS

El Café de Levante – *Rosario 35 – Open 4pm-3am.* A quiet café with tasteful modern decor on one of the old quarter's most typical streets. Its relaxed atmosphere attracts an eclectic crowd who come here to enjoy a quiet chat. Live music Thursday evenings.

La Cava – *Antonio López 16 – 956 21 18 66 – www.flamencolacava.com – closed Mon and in Jan – show and drink 22€ from 9.30pm (winter: Tue, Thu, Sat; summer: closed Mon).* This cosy tavern offers authentic flamenco interpreted by young artists.

FIESTAS

The **carnival** in Cádiz, the week before Ash Wednesday, is without a doubt the most famous and lively on the Iberian Peninsula.

ENTERTAINMENT

The **Gran Teatro Falla** *(plaza Falla)* organises a programme of theatre and concerts throughout the year, while the city's five **cultural centres** (El Palillero, El Bidón, La Viña, La Lechera), host a wide range of exhibitions, workshops etc, as well as flamenco concerts at the fifth venue, the **Baluarte de la Candelaria**, on alameda de Apodaca.

This medieval complex around a fine 16C **Mudéjar patio**★ holds liturgical objects and art, including the 16C **Custodia del Cogollo**★, a gold-plated monstrance attributed to Enrique Arfe, and the 18C **Custodia del Millón**.

Oratorio de la Santa Cueva★

Open 10am-1pm and 4.30-7.30pm (5-8pm in summer); Sat-Sun 10am-1pm. Closed Mon and public hols. 2 €. 95 622 22 62.

Three **canvases**★★ in this elliptical oratory were painted by Goya in 1795.

Museo de Cádiz★

Open 9am-8.30pm (Sat 8pm); Sun, 9am-2pm. Closed Mon. 1.50 €, no charge for E. U. citizens. 95 621 22 81.

The city's museum is in a small mid-19C neo-Classical palace. The collection includes vases, oil lamps and jewellery, including two 5C BC Greek **anthropoidal sarcophagi**★★ based on Egyptian models. Paintings include nine **panels**★ by Zurbarán from the Carthusian monastery in Jerez.

Torre Tavira★

Guided tours (20 min) 10am-5.30pm (8pm 15 Jun-15 Sep). 3.50 €. ☎95 621 29 10.

The first 18C watchtower houses the first **camera obscura** in Spain, a device capturing real-time images of the city.

Oratorio de San Felipe Neri

Open 10am-1.30pm. Closed Sun and public hols. 1.20 €. ☎95 621 16 12.

In this elliptical Baroque church the Cortes proclaimed the liberal Constitution of Cádiz in 1812. The **Immaculate Conception** was painted by Murillo in 1680 shortly before his death.

Museo Iconográfico e Histórico de las Cortes y Sitio de Cádiz

Open 9am-1pm and 4-7pm (15 Jun-15 Sep 5-7pm); Sat-Sun, 9am-1pm. Closed Mon and public hols. ☎95 622 17 88.

The museum's main exhibit is a **model**★ of Cádiz in the reign of Charles III.

Excursions

San Fernando

9km/5.5mi SE along the CA 33. San Fernando has been a naval base since the 18C. The main monuments are all along calle Real: the town hall (ayuntamiento), Iglesia del Carmen, and the Museo Histórico Municipal. The main civil building is the neo-Classical **Observatorio Astronómico de la Marina**, from 1753. *Visits by arrangement with the Patronato de Turismo de San Fernando, ☎956 59 93 66 or 956 94 42 26.*

The Battle of Trafalgar

On 21 October 1805, Admiral Villeneuve sailed out of Cádiz harbour with his Franco-Spanish fleet to confront the English under Nelson off the Cabo de Trafalgar headland. The ships were ill-equipped and poorly manned; after some heroic combat Villeneuve's fleet was destroyed and he was taken prisoner. Nelson had been mortally wounded during the course of the battle but England's supremacy at sea was established.

Medina Sidonia★

44km/27mi E on CA 33, A 48 and A 390.

The **Iglesia de Santa María la Mayor**★, a 15C Gothic church, holds an exquisite Plateresque **altarpiece**★ by Juan Bautista Vázquez el Viejo. *10am-2pm and 4-6pm; in summer, 9.30am-2pm and 4-9.30pm. Closed 1 Jan and 25 Dec. 2.50 €. ☎95 641 03 29.*

The Torre de Doña Blanca, a tower next to the church, provides access to the remains of the alcázar and the old quarter, with its 16C houses. The descent to

B. Kaufmann/ MICHELIN

Façade, Cádix Cathedral

Cádiz

Ancha	BY	2
Ántonio López	BCY	
Apodaca Alameda de	BY	
Argüelles Pl.	CY	
Benito Pérez Galdós	AY	
Benjumeda	BY	
Calderón de la Barca	BY	3
Calesas	CZ	
Campo del Sur	ABZ	
Candelaria Pl.	BZ	4
Cardoso	BZ	
Carlos III Paseo	ABY	
Ceballos	ABY	
Cervantes	BY	
Columela	BYZ	
Compañía	BZ	5
Concepcíon Arenal	CZ	
Constitución Pl. de la	CZ	
Cristóbal Colón	CZ	6
Diego Arias	AY	
Doctor G. Ulla Av.	AY	
Doctor Marañón	AY	7
Duque de Najera Av.	AYZ	
España Pl. de	CY	
Falla Pl.	AY	
Fernando el Católico	CY	8
Fray Félix Pl.	BZ	9
Honduras	CY	
Marqués de Comillas Alameda	BY	
Mentidero Pl. del	BY	10
Mesón Nueva	CZ	12
Mina Pl. de	BY	
Montañés	BZ	13
Moreno de Mora	AYZ	
Novena	BY	15
Nueva	CZ	16
Pelota	CZ	17
Piratas Callejón de los	BZ	18
Plocia	CZ	
Puerto Av. del	CYZ	
Ramón de Carranza Av.	CZ	19
Rep. Argentina	CY	
Rosario	BY	
Sacramento	BY	
Sagasta	ABYZ	
San Agustin Pl.	CY	20
San Antonio Pl.	BY	21
San Francisco	BCY	22
San Francisco Pl. de	BY	23
San José	ABYZ	
San Juan	BZ	
San Juan de Dios	CZ	24
San Juan de Dios Pl.	CZ	25
San Martín Pl.	CZ	26
San Roque Pl.	CZ	27
Santa Maria	CZ	28
Santo Cristo	BCZ	29
Sopranis	CZ	30
Topete Pl. de	BZ	31
Vea Murguia	BY	
Virgen de la Palma	AZ	
Viudas Pl. de las	BY	

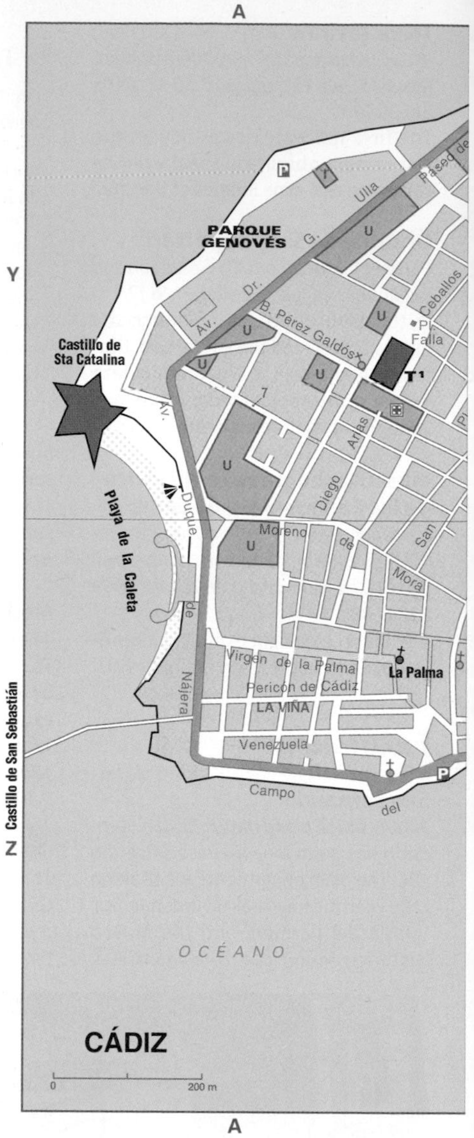

Arco de la Rosa	BZ	A^3
Arco de los Blancos	CZ	A^1
Arco del Pópulo	CZ	A^2
Ayuntamiento	CZ	H
Baluarte de la Candelaria	BY	
Casa Lasquetty	CZ	B^3
Casa de la Contaduría (Museo Catedralicio)	CZ	M^1
Casa de las Cadenas	CZ	B^2
Casa del Almirante	BZ	B^1
Castillo de San Sebastián	AZ	
Castillo de Santa Catalina	AY	
Catedral	BZ	
Convento de Santo Domingo	CZ	
Cárcel Real (Palacio de Justicia)	CZ	J
Fábrica de Tabascos (Palacio de Congresos)	CZ	K
Gran Teatro Falla	AY	T^1
Hospital de Mujeres	BZ	
Iglesia de San Antonio	BY	
Iglesia de San Francisco	BY	
Iglesia de San Lorenzo	BZ	
Iglesia de Santa Cruz	BCZ	
Iglesia de Santa María	CZ	

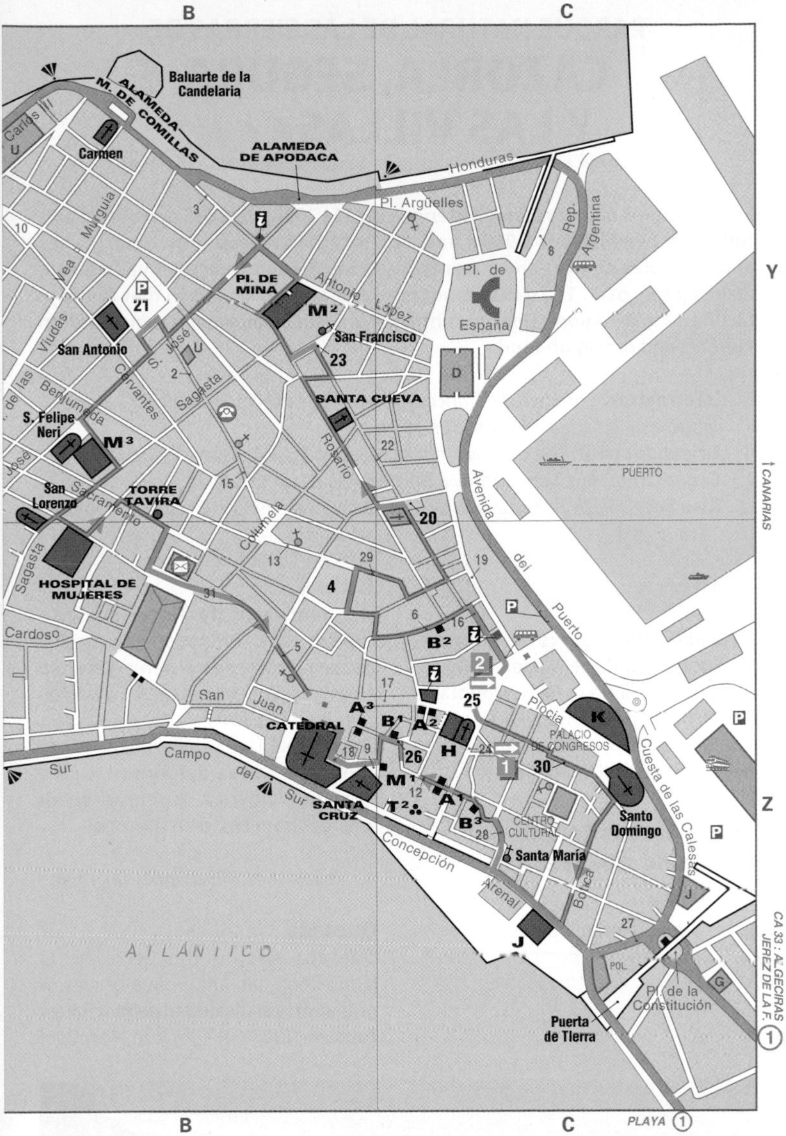

Iglesia de la Palma	AZ	
Iglesia del Carmen	BY	
Museo Iconográfico e Histórico de las Cortes y Sitio de Cádiz	BY	M3
Museo de Cádiz	BY	M2
Oratorio de San Felipe Neri	BY	
Oratorio de Santa Cueva	BY	
Parque Genovés	AY	
Playa de la Caleta	AYZ	
Teatro Romano	CZ	T
Torre Tavira	BY	

the modern town passes under the Arco de la Pastora, to reach the **Conjunto Arqueológico Romano**, a Roman complex with 30m/98ft of underground galleries from the 1C AD. *Open 10am-2pm and 4-6.30pm (8pm Apr-Jun, 5-9.30pm Jul-Oct). 3.10€. ☎95 641 24 04.*

The *cardo maximus* was the main street in Roman days. On the plaza de España lies the 18C neo-Classical **town hall**.

PARQUE NATURAL DE LAS SIERRAS DE CAZORLA, SEGURA Y LAS VILLAS★★★

MICHELIN MAP 578 S 20-21-22 R 20-21-22 Q 21-22 – ANDALUCÍA (JAÉN)

Spain's largest nature reserve extends over 214 300ha/529 535 acres at an altitude of between 600m/1 968ft and 2 017m/6 616ft. Steep cliffs, deep gorges and a complex of rivers and streams, including the source of the Guadalquivir, make up this park. The dense montane vegetation is similar to that found in Mediterranean regions. Deer, mountain goats, wild boar, golden eagles, griffon vultures and osprey abound.

- **Information:** *Carretera del Tranco, Km 48.3, Torre del Vinagre ☎95 371 30 40; Juan Domingo 2, Cazorla, ☎953 24 26 24.*
- **Orient Yourself:** The park lies in southeastern Spain, east of Úbeda.
- **Organizing Your Time:** Allow a full day at least for the park.
- **Also See:** ÚBEDA (46km/29mi NW Cazorla town) and BAEZA (55km/34mi NW)

Tours

Before setting out, visit an **information point** at Torre del Vinagre, Cazorla, Segura de la Sierra or Siles. Mountain-bikers, horse-riders and hikers can follow the extensive network of forest tracks and marked footpaths.

From Tíscar to the Embalse del Tranco de Beas

92km/67mi – allow one day.

Tíscar★

The **Santuario de Tíscar** enjoys a superb site enclosed by rocks. *Open for worship 11.30am-1pm and 4.30-6pm; Jun-Sep 11am-1pm and 5-7pm. ☎95 371 36 06.*

Below this place of pilgrimage is the impressive **Cueva del Agua**★, a cave formation where a torrent of water emerges from between the rocks.

Follow the C 323 as far as Quesada.

Quesada

Quesada sits on the Cerro de la Magdalena hill, amid olive groves. A **museum** is dedicated to painter Rafael Zabaleta (1907-60). *Open 11am-2pm*

B. Kaufmann/MICHELIN

The Castillo de la Iruela and Sierra de Cazorla

and 5-8pm (4-7pm in winter). Closed Mon-Tue. 3 € ☎95 373 30 25.
The Cañada de las Fuentes, a ravine on the outskirts, is the **source of the Guadalquivir river** *(access via a track off the A 315, to the N of Quesada)*. Wall paintings from the Palaeolithic era can be viewed in Cerro Vitar and in the Cueva del Encajero, a short distance from the town.

Take the A 315 towards Peal de Becerro; bear right on the A 319.

Cazorla★

Cazorla occupies an outstanding **site**★ below the Peña de los Halcones, dominated by its **castle**, its whitewashed houses adorned with balconies. At the centre of the plaza de Santa María stands a Renaissance fountain; the ruins of the Iglesia de Santa María, by Vandelvira, are now used as an auditorium.

Head 1.5km/1mi NE along the A 319; turn right at a signposted junction.

La Iruela

The remains of a Templar castle offer superb **views**★★ of the Guadalquivir Valley. The Iglesia (church) de Santo Domingo was designed by Vandelvira.

The road from La Iruela to the Tranco Reservoir★

The first 17km/10.5mi stretch provides **spectacular views**★★. The Parador de **El Adelantado** is 8km/5mi along a branch road up through pine forests.

Follow the A 319 along the river.

Torre del Vinagre

Open 11am-2pm and 4-6pm (7pm in spring, 9.30pm in summer). Closed 25 Dec. ☎95 371 30 40.
This information centre contains a hunting museum as well as a botanical garden with species native to the park. Several routes start here.
A game reserve, **Parque Cinegético de Collado del Almendral**, 15km/9.5mi along the A 319, has lookouts for viewing deer, mouflons and mountain goats.
Information ☎95 371 01 25.

Embalse del Tranco de Beas

Several camping areas and hotels are close to this reservoir. Water sports are available. Islands in the reservoir are Isla de Cabeza la Viña; and **Isla de Bujaraiza**, with the ruins of a Moorish castle. Both are seen from the **Mirador Rodríguez de la Fuente** viewpoint.

Santiago-Pontones to Siles

80km/50mi – allow half a day.

Santiago-Pontones

This municipality includes scattered mountain villages along with the **Cueva del Nacimiento**, a cave 9 000 years old, and the **Cuevas de Engalbo**, with their impressive wall art.

From Pontones, go NW on the A 317.

Hornos

Fortress remains rise above a steep cliff from where there are some spectacular

Address Book

For coin ranges, see the Legend on the cover flap.

WHERE TO EAT

La Sarga – *Plaza del Mercado – Cazorla –* ☎*95 372 15 07 – www.lasarga.com – Closed Tue, second half of Sep and Jan –* . This well-run restaurant in the centre of town has impressive mountain views. Good-quality regional cuisine and attentive service.

WHERE TO STAY

Molino La Fárraga – *Cazorla – at the end of calle de la Torre –* ☎*95 372 12 49 – www.molinolafarraga.com – Open 1 Mar-10 Dec – 7 rooms.* . In an 18C olive oil mill, whose machinery can still be seen under the house. Basic rooms, a garden with a small stream and a swimming pool with views of the castle and mountains.

views★ of the reservoir and the Guadalquivir Valley.

▸ *Take the A 317, then bear right to Segura de la Sierra at a junction.*

Segura de la Sierra★

This picturesque village, birthplace of the 15C poet Jorge Manrique, is at an altitude of 1 240m/4 067ft in the shelter of its Mudéjar **castle**, with its sweeping **panorama★★** of the Sierra de Segura. In the centre of the village are the **town hall** *(ayuntamiento)* with its Plateresque doorway; the **parish church**, containing a delicate, polychrome statue of the Virgin Mary carved in Gothic style from alabaster, and a recumbent Christ attributed to Gregorio Hernández; and the **Moorish baths** *(baños árabes)*.

▸ *Follow the JV 7020 to Orcera.*

Orcera

The Iglesia de Nuestra Señora de la Asunción, with its sober Renaissance portal, and the Fuente de los Chorros, a 15C fountain, can be seen in the main square. Vestiges of the former Moorish fortress are on the outskirts of Orcera.

▸ *Continue along the JV 7020 beyond Benatae, then take the JV 7021.*

Siles

The village retains sections of its old walls. Nearby is the nature reserve of Las Acebeas.

CEUTA★

POPULATION: 73 208.

MICHELIN MAP 742 FOLDS 5 AND 10 – NORTH AFRICA

Ceuta, with its European architecture, is situated on a narrow isthmus on the coast of North Africa. The closest African port to Europe, it was conquered by the Portuguese in 1415, and passed to Spain in 1580, when Philip II annexed Portugal.

- **Information:** *Alcalde José Vitori Goñalons, ☎956 51 40 92 or 956 51 00 51.*
- **Orient Yourself:** Ceuta occupies a strategic position dominating the Straits of Gibraltar.
- **Also See:** *Straits of GIBRALTAR.*

Worth a Visit

Museo Municipal

Open Oct-May, 10am-2pm and 5-8pm; Jun-Sep, 10am-2pm and 7-9pm. Closed Sun and public hols in summer. ☎95 651 73 98.

This museum houses a white marble Roman sarcophagus, Punic and Roman amphorae, a collection of coins and old weapons and ceramic ware.

Parque Marítimo del Mediterráneo

Open Oct-Apr daily 11am-8pm; May-Sep 11am-8pm, Sat-Sun and public hols 10am-8pm. Closed Thu (Oct-Apr) and 1 Jan, and 24-25 and 31 Dec. Price varies by day of week. ☎956 51 77 42.

Palm trees, exotic plants, swimming pools, lakes, waterfalls and sculptures have all been perfectly integrated by César Manrique to create this spectacular leisure park on 56ha/138 acres facing the sea. Several restaurants, a nightclub and a casino operate inside the fort which dominates the park. A cinema complex is in the Poblado Marinero.

Other places of interest are the **Iglesia de Nuestra Señora de África** (Church of Our Lady of Africa), housing the statue of the patron saint of the town, the 18C **Catedral** and the **Foso de San**

Felipe, a Portuguese fort where San Juan de Dios, the founder of the Orden de los Hospitalarios (Order of the Hospitallers of St John), worked in 1530.

Tour

Monte Hacho★

10km/6mi – about 30min. Best visited in the morning.

Calle Independencia and calle Recintor Sur, parallel to the seafront, lead to the foot of Monte Hacho which has a citadel at its summit. The corniche road encircling the peninsula offers beautiful **views** of the Western Rif coastline to the south and the Spanish coast and the Rock of Gibraltar to the north.

Before reaching the lighthouse (no entry), bear left.

Ermita de San Antonio

Leave your car in the car park. The wide flight of steps leads to a charming square fronted by the 16C Capilla de San Antonio (Chapel of St Anthony). The imposing **Fortaleza de Hacho** stands atop a hill nearby.

From here there is a magnificent **view**★★ to the left, of the town spread out on its curving isthmus around the port, and to the right, the distant peninsula coastline.

GETTING TO CEUTA

By ferry – Trasmediterránea operates services between Algeciras and Ceuta. Journey time: 40min. For information and bookings, call ☎90 245 46 45.

WHERE TO EAT

MODERATE

Parador H. La Muralla – *Plaza Virgen de África, 15 – ☎956 51 49 40 –* ▤ *– €29.* A good place to pause during your visit, an attractive dining area with lush tropical plants and exposed beams. The cooking is Andausian with Arab influences.

CIUDAD RODRIGO★

POPULATION: 14 973.

MICHELIN MAP 575 K 10 – CASTILLA Y LEÓN (SALAMANCA)

Ciudad Rodrigo appears high on a hilltop, guarded by the square tower of its 14C Alcázar (now a parador) and medieval ramparts. A Roman bridge spans the río Águeda from the Portuguese side. After the reconquest in the 12C, the town was repopulated by Count Rodrigo González for whom it is named; later it became a border stronghold and was involved in all the conflicts between Castilla and Portugal. Wellington's success against the French in 1812 won him the title of Duke of Ciudad Rodrigo and Grandee of Spain. The area is planted with ilex trees, under which pigs and fighting bulls graze.

- **Information:** *Plaza de las Amayuelas 6, ☎923 46 05 61.*
- **Orient Yourself:** Ciudad Rodrigo is west of Madrid along one of the main routes to Portugal.
- **Don't Miss:** The city walls and Roman bridge.
- **Organizing Your Time:** Take at least a morning to walk into the past in Ciudad Rodrigo.
- **Also See:** SALAMANCA (89km/55mi NE) and La ALBERCA (50km/31mi SE.

Walking About

The Old Town

▶ *Start your visit at the cathedral (plaza de las Amayuelas), where you will also find the tourist office.*

Catedral★★

Open 9.30am-1pm and 3.30-7pm. No visits during religious services. 2€ (museum). 92 348 14 24.

The cathedral was built in two stages, first from 1170 to 1230 and then in the 14C; in the 16C Rodrigo Gil de Hontañón added the central apse. The stiffness of the figures of the Disciples in a gallery in the upper part of the south transept façade contrasts with the delicate ornamentation of the surrounding blind arcades. The 13C **Portada de la Virgen**★ (Doorway of the Virgin), masked outside by a classical belfry, has a line of Apostles carved between the columns beneath the splayings and covings.

In the interior, the Isabelline choir stalls in the coro were carved by Rodrigo Alemán. The fine Renaissance **altar**★ in the north aisle is adorned with an alabaster Deposition, beautifully composed and carved in low relief, a masterpiece by Lucas Mitata.

The **cloisters**★ are made up of diverse architectural styles. In the west gallery, the oldest part, Romanesque capitals illustrate man's original sin, while grotesques on the column bases symbolise greed and vanity. Opening off the east gallery is a Plateresque door in the pure Salamanca style decorated with medallions including one (on the right) of the architect Pedro Güemes.

A number of items are also on display in the **Museo Catedralicio**. The 16C Palacio de los Miranda is on the plaza de San Salvador.

▶ *Return to the cathedral; in front is the Capilla de Cerralbo.*

Capilla de Cerralbo

The chapel, built between 1588 and 1685, is pure and austere but harmonious in the Herreran style.

▶ *The arcaded plaza del Buen Alcalde is to the right. Take the street to the left to reach plaza del Conde.*

Palacio de los Castro★ (or Palacio del Conde de Montarco)

This late-15C palace, on plaza del Conde (Count), has a long façade punctuated by delicate windows. The Plateresque doorway is surrounded by an alfiz and flanked by two twisted columns showing Portuguese influence, which are further embellished by two protective lions. Note also the simple patio.

▶ *Head to the plaza Mayor, passing the 16C Palacio de Moctezuma to the right.*

Plaza Mayor★

Two Renaissance palaces stand on the city's lively main square: the first, now the **Ayuntamiento** (town hall), has a façade with two storeys of basket arcading forming a **gallery**★ and a loggia, while the second, the **Casa de los Cueto**, has a decorative frieze separating its first and second storeys.

▶ *Continue to calle Juan Arias, lined by the Casa del Príncipe or Casa de los Águilas, a 16C building in Plateresque style.*

Murallas (Ramparts)

The walls built on Roman foundations in the 12C were converted to a full defensive system on the north and west flanks in 1710. There are several stairways up to the 2km/1mi-long sentry path.

▶ *The imposing keep of Henry of Trastámara's castle stands on the SW corner of the walls, alongside the Roman bridge spanning the Águeda river. Nowadays, the castle is the town's parador.*

CÓRDOBA★★★

POPULATION: 310 388.
MICHELIN MAP 578 S 15 – ANDALUCÍA (CÓRDOBA)

Córdoba owes its fame to the brilliance of the Roman, Moorish, Jewish and Christian civilisations that have endowed its rich and varied history. The Mezquita, the city's most precious jewel, dominates the old section whose narrow, whitewashed streets and charming small squares are embellished with wrought-iron grilles and flower-filled patios.

- **Information:** *Torrijos 10, ☏95 747 12 35; Caballerizas Reales 1, ☏90 220 17 74; Alcázar de los Reyes Cristianos, ☏95 729 95 35. otcordoba@andalucia.org*
- **Orient Yourself:** Córdoba lies along the Guadalquivir river in Andalucía, between ranchland and olive country. The A 4 highway runs to Écija (52km/32mi SW) and Sevilla (143km/89mi SW).
- **Parking:** Park outside the old city and walk Córdoba´s lanes and alleys.
- **Don't Miss:** The Mesquita
- **Organizing Your Time:** See the Mesquita, followed by the Jewish quarter.
- **Also See:** OSUNA (86km/54mi SW), PRIEGO DE CÓRDOBA (98km/61mi SE) and JAÉN (107km/67mi E).

Background

The Roman city – Córdoba was the birthplace of **Seneca the Rhetorician** (55 BC-AD 39), and his son **Seneca the Philosopher** (4 BC-AD 65). A noted early bishop was **Ossius** (257-359), counsellor to Emperor Constantine.

Of Roman Córdoba only the mausoleum in the Jardines de la Victoria, the ruins of a 1C temple, and the bridge linking the old section with the Torre de la Calahorra remain.

The Córdoba Caliphate – Emirs from Damascus established themselves in Córdoba as early as 719. In 756 **Abd ar-Rahman I**, sole survivor of the **Umayyads**, founded the dynasty which was to rule Muslim Spain for three centuries. In 929 **Abd ar-Rahman III** proclaimed himself caliph of independent Spain. In the 10C a university was founded. Christians, Jews and Muslims lived side by side and enriched each other intellectually and culturally. On the accession, in 976, of the feeble **Hisham II**, power fell into the hands of the ruthless **Al-Mansur** (the Victorious). Al-Andalus fragmented into warring kingdoms, the **reinos de taifas**. Córdoba became part of the kingdom of Sevilla in 1070. Intellectual life flourished, however. **Averroës** – physicist, astrologer, mathematician, doctor – brought the learning of Aristotle to the West. The Jew **Maimónides** (1135-1204) was famed in medicine, theology and philosophy, but fled to escape persecution.

Reconquered in 1236, Córdoba declined until the 16C and 17C, when its tooled leatherwork became fashionable.

Special Features

The Mezquita and the Judería★★★ 3hr

Mezquita-Catedral★★★ (Mosque-Cathedral)

Open Dec-Jan 10am-5.30pm (6pm Feb and Nov, 6.30pm Mar and Jul-Oct, 7.30 pm Apr-Jun); last admission 30min before closing. 8 € ☏95 747 05 12..

The Mezquita

The traditional Muslim crenellated square encloses the Patio de los Naranjos (Orange Tree Court) with a **Basin of Al-Mansur (1)** for ritual ablution, a hall for prayer and a minaret.

The first Muslims in Córdoba shared the Visigothic church of St Vincent with the Christians. Soon Abd ar-Rahman I (758-88) purchased part of the site. He razed the church and around the year 780

Address Book

For coin ranges, see the Legend on the cover flap.

WHERE TO EAT

⊖ **Taberna los Faroles** – *Velázquez Bosco 1 – ☎95 748 56 29 – 10/30 € – closed 22 Dec-8 Jan.*. This tavern is named for the lanterns that illuminate its attractive patio. Specialities here include local dishes such as salmorejo (a variant of gazpacho), aubergine with honey and *rabo de toro* (braised oxtail). A cool, pleasant atmosphere is enhanced by the *azulejos* on the walls.

⊖ **El Rincón de Carmen** – *Romero 4 – ☎ 95 729 10 55 – Closed Mon –* ▤. The patio provides an escape from the frenzied tourist activity in the Judería. Plenty of alternatives to the traditional gazpacho and an interesting wine list.

⊖ **Paseo de la Ribera** – *Plaza Cruz del Rastro 3 – ☎95 747 15 30 – www.paseoribera.com –* ▤. One of the best places for Cordoban cuisine. The dining room, between stone arches, brings to mind a Romanesque church. The terrace, on paseo de la Ribera, overlooks the Guadalquivir river. Specialties are rice dishes and oxtail.

⊖⊖ **Casa Palacio Bandolero** – *Torrijos 6 – ☎95 747 64 91 – www.restaurantebandolero.com –* ▤. The Bandolero is superbly located opposite the Mezquita and is popular with locals. Home-made tapas are served in the bar, in addition to local cuisine and a long wine list in the medieval-style dining room and on the flower-decked patio.

⊖⊖ **Almudaina** – *Jardines de los Santos Mártires 1 – ☎95 747 43 42 – www.restaurantealmudaina.com –* ▤. An attractive restaurant in a plaza, near the Alcázar. High point is the painstaking regional decor, with dining on two levels around a pleasant covered patio. The excellent food is a good introduction to Cordoban cuisine.

TAPAS

Córdoba does full justice to Andalucía's great tapas tradition with a wide range of bars offering a huge selection of local specialities such as *salmorejo* (a type of local *gazpacho*), rabo de toro (braised oxtail), *embutidos* (sausage) and sherries (finos, amontillados, olorosos).

Taberna Salinas – *Tundidores 3 – ☎ 95 748 01 35 – www.tabernasalinas.com – Closed Sun and in Aug –* ▤. Open for more than a century, this welcoming bar consists of a counter, two rooms decorated with *azulejos* and photos of celebrities, and a small patio.

Taberna San Miguel-Casa El Pisto – *Plaza San Miguel 1 – ☎95 747 01 66 – Closed Sun and in Aug –* ▤.Founded in 1886, the Taberna San Miguel, opposite the church of the same name, is popular choice for tapas. The traditional decor is enhanced by the bullfight posters and photos on the walls.

Taberna Casa Pepe de la Judería – *Romero 1 – ☎95 720 07 44 – www.casapepejuderia.com –* ▤. This bar opened in 1928 and the counter dates from this period. Several rooms around an attractive patio offer tapas, with an Andalusian restaurant upstairs.

WHERE TO STAY

⊖ **Hostal La Milagrosa** – *Rey Heredia 12 – ☎95 747 33 17 – www.lamilagrosa-hostal.com – P ▤ – 8 rooms (doubles only)*. Good central location near the Mezquita. Attractive features are the plant-filled typically Cordoban patio and well-kept, large, cool guest rooms with full bathrooms.

⊖ **Hotel González** – *Manríquez 3 – ☎ 95 747 98 19 – www.hotel-gonzalez.com – 16 rooms – Restaurant 27 €*. The rooms in this 16C palace, in the triangle of the Mezquita, the Judería and the gardens of the Alcázar, are spacious and well appointed. The Moorish-inspired patio doubles as the hotel restaurant.

⊖ **Hostal El Triunfo** – *Corregidor Luis de la Cerda 79 – ☎95 749 84 84 – www.htriunfo.com – ▤ – 55 rooms – ☕ 3.76 € – Restaurant 6/12.75 €*. Most of the rooms look onto the Mezquita, just across a narrow street. Stay on the top floor if you can to make use of the huge terrace. All rooms have a TV.

⊖ **Hostal Séneca** – *Conde y Luque 7 – ☎ 95 747 32 34 – 12 rooms – closed 2 weeks in Aug and winter.* The Seneca is a quiet *hostal* near the Mezquita with typical Andalucían decor and a flower-filled patio. Despite the rooms being fairly basic (some without a bathroom), the hotel is often full so advance booking is recommended.

Hotel Posada de Vallina – *Corregidor Luis de la Cerda 83 – 95 749 87 50 – www.hotelvallina.co – – Restaurant 8.50/24 €.* Elegance and comfort are the main features of this small hotel housed in a tastefully restored Cordoban house, whose windows open out onto the Mezquita. The pleasant restaurant on the ground floor is particularly popular.

Hotel Casa de los Azulejos – *Fernando Colón 5 – 95 747 00 00 – www.casadelosazulejos.com – – 8 rooms.* This charming hotel is a traditional Andalucian house with a colonial flavour. Outstanding features include a lovely interior garden with plants, and magnificent large rooms with period furnishings, iron headboards, original floors and colourful designer baths.

BARS AND CAFÉS

Cafetería Siena – *Plaza de las Tendillas – 95 747 46 08 – Open 8am-midnight – closed Sun..* A long-established café in Córdoba's main square, with one of the city's most popular outdoor terraces. A perfect venue for a morning coffee or an evening drink.

Málaga Café – *Málaga 3 – 95 748 63 13 – Open Mon-Thu, 4pm-2am; Fri-Sat, 4pm-4am, Sun, 4-10pm.* A quiet café with classical decor and comfortable sofas and armchairs near the plaza de las Tendillas in the centre of the city. Highly recommended for evening drinks with friends.

Sojo – *Benito Pérez Galdós 3 – 957 48 39 98 – Open 8am-4am.* Popular with the over-25s, this avant-garde bar is open from breakfast time to late at night. The Sojo also organises concerts by soloists, as well as art, photography and video exhibitions. Highly recommended, whatever the hour.

NIGHTLIFE

Chato – *Alhakem II 14 – Bellver de Cerdanya – Open 4pm-late.* A bar of modern design in the Gran Capitán area with a trendy mixed-age clientele. Pleasant for a quiet early-evening coffee or drinks in a more lively atmosphere closer to midnight.

El Puentecillo – *Poeta Emilio Prados – Open in summer, 9.30pm-5am; in winter, Thu-Sat, midnight-5am.* A small venue on the way to the El Brillante district. Warm and inviting decor inside and on the small patio. Tends to be frequented by an older, quieter crowd. Popular for drinks early in the evening.

SHOPPING

The city's traditional craftwork includes embossed leather and cordovans, in addition to gold and silver filigree. Another good buy is the local wine, **Montilla-Moriles**, produced to the south of Córdoba in the area around Montilla, Puente Genil, Lucena and Baena. The excellent wines and brandies from Montilla-Moriles are similar in style to those of Jerez.

FIESTAS

At the beginning of **May**, Córdoba celebrates the Festival of the Crosses (Cruces de Mayo), when large, flower-decked crosses adorn the city's squares and street corners. The first half of May is also the time for Córdoba's traditional patio competition, while the eagerly awaited **Feria** is held at the end of the month.

B. Kaufmann/ MICHELIN

began the construction of a splendid mosque with 11 aisles each opening onto the Patio de los Naranjos. Marble pillars and Roman and Visigothic stone were re-used. The mosque became famous for an innovation: the superimposition of two tiers of arches to add height and spaciousness. After the

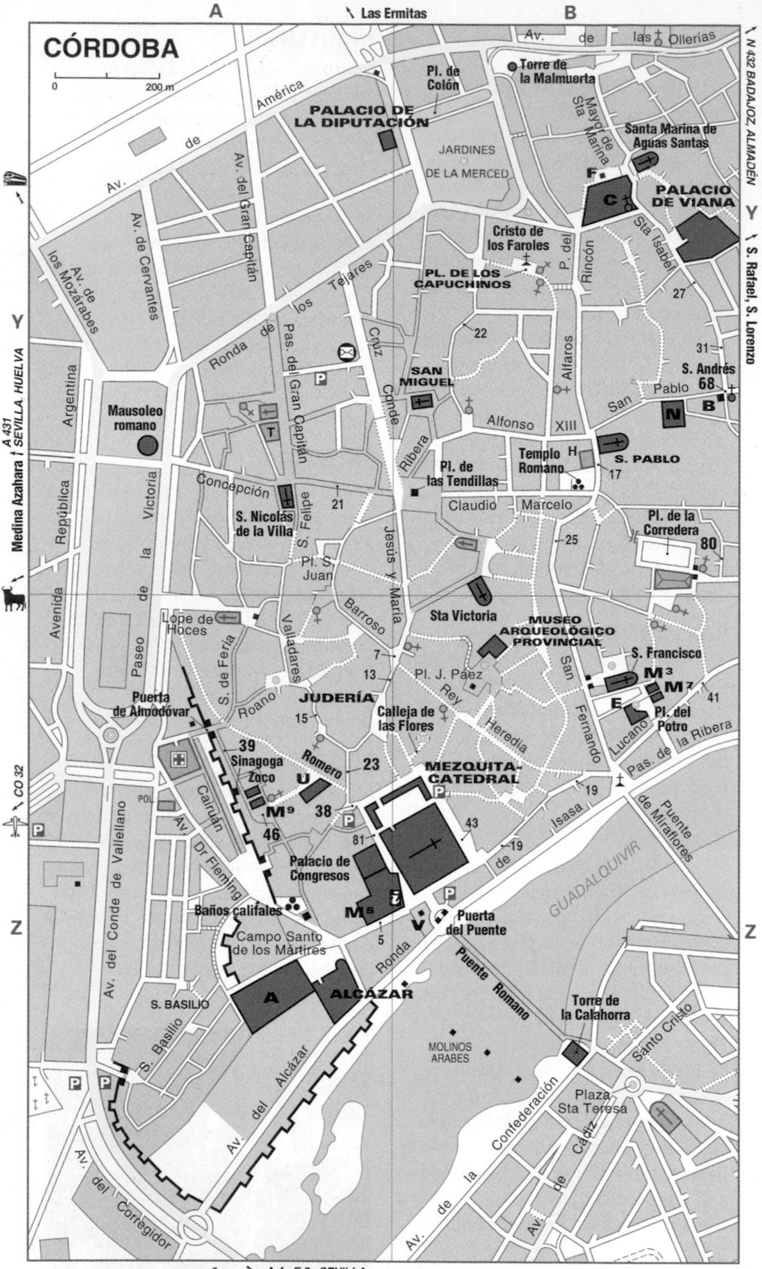

Cordoba

Amador de los Ríos	AZ	5
Ángel Saavedra	ABZ	7
Blanco Belmonte	AZ	13
Buen Pastor	AZ	15
Capitulares	BY	17
Cardenal González	BZ	19
Conde de Gondomar	AY	21
Conde de Torres	BY	22
Cruz Conde	ABY	
Deanes	AZ	23
Diario de Córdoba	BY	25
Enrique Redel	BY	27
Hermanos López Dieguez	BY	31
Judería	AZ	38
Judíos	AZ	39
Lineros	BZ	41
M. González Francés	BZ	43
Maimónides Pl. del	AZ	46
San Andrés Pl. de	BY	68
Toril Calleja del	BY	80
Torrijos	AZ	81

Caballerizas Reales	AZ	A	Monumento a Manolete	BY	F	Museo Municipal Taurino	AZ	M^9
Casa de los Luna	BY	B	Museo Diocesano de Bellas Artes	ABZ	M^5	Museo de Bellas Artes	BZ	M^3
Convento de Santa Isabel	BY	C	Museo Julio Romero de Torres	BZ	M^7	Palacio de los Villalones	BY	N
Facultad de Filosofía y Letras	AZ	U				Posada del Potro	BZ	E
						Triunfo de San Rafael	BZ	V

reconquest, Christians built chapels in the west nave, including the 17C **Capilla de la Purísima Concepción (2)**, completely covered with marble.

In 848 Abd ar-Rahman II had the mosque extended to the present-day Capilla de Villaviciosa (Villaviciosa Chapel). In 961 El Hakam II built the *mihrab*, and in 987, Al-Mansur added eight aisles (with red-brick floors).

Interior

Enter by the Puerta de las Palmas. The interior is a forest of columns (about 850) and the horseshoe-shaped arches. The wide main aisle off the doorway has a beautiful *artesonado* ceiling. It leads to the **kiblah** wall, where the faithful prayed, and the **mihrab**★★★, normally a simple niche, but here a sumptuous room preceded by a triple **maksourah (3)** (enclosure) reserved for the caliph. Its three ribbed domes rest on unusual apparently interweaving multifoil arches. Alabaster plaques and ornate stucco arabesques and palm-leaf motifs sometimes framed by Cufic script enhance the architecture.

In the 13C, Christians walled off the aisles from the court. A few columns were removed and pointed arches substituted for Moorish ones when the first **cathedral (4)** was built. Alfonso X was responsible for the chancel in the **Capilla de Villaviciosa** or **Lucernario (5)**, and built the **Capilla Real**★ **(6)** decorated in the 13C with Mudéjar stucco. Chapels were built in the western nave, including the fine marble-faced 17C **Purísima Concepción (2)**.

Catedral

In the 16C the canons cut away the centre of the mosque to erect loftier vaulting. Emperor Charles V was far from pleased: "You have destroyed something unique," he said, "to build something commonplace." The roof is a mix of 16C and 17C styles (Hispano-Flemish, Renaissance and Baroque). Additional

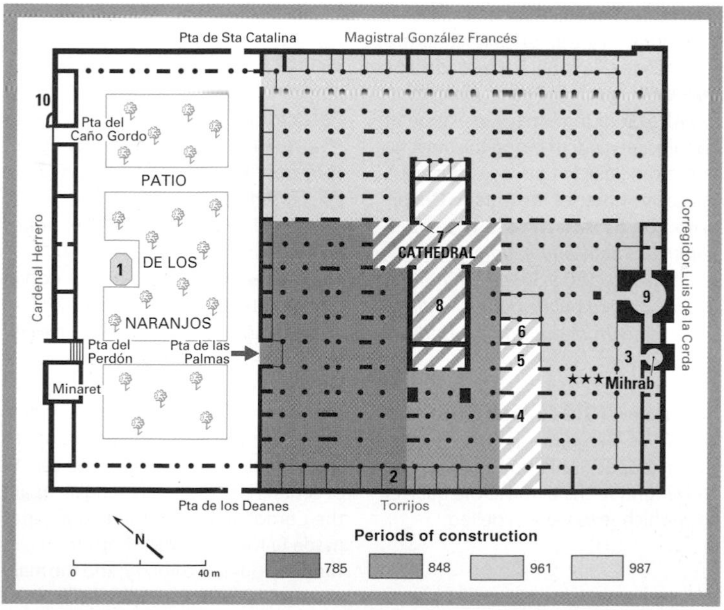

Cathedral vaults (detail)

enrichments are the Baroque **choir stalls★★ (8)** by Pedro Duque Cornejo (c 1750) and two **pulpits★★ (7)** of marble, jasper and mahogany.

Tesoro

The treasury, built by the Baroque architect Francisco Hurtado Izquierdo, in the **Capilla del Cardenal** (Cardinal's Chapel) **(9)**, includes a large 16C **monstrance★** by E Arfe and an exceptional Baroque figure of Christ in ivory.

Exterior features include the **minaret**, enveloped by a 17C Baroque tower. Giving onto the street is the 14C Mudéjar **Puerta del Perdón** (Pardon Doorway) faced with bronze. Further on is the small chapel of the **Virgen de los Faroles** (Virgin of the Lanterns) **(10)**.

The Alcázar of the Umayyads stood in magnificent gardens facing the mosque where the Palacio Episcopal (Bishop's Palace) now houses the **Museo Diocesano de Bellas Artes**. (*Open 9.30am-1.30pm and 4-6pm (9.30am-3pm Jun-Jul); Sat, 9.30am-1.30pm. Closed Sun and public hols. 1.50 € (included with Mezquita ticket). 95 747 93 75*).

Judería★★ (Old Jewish Quarter)

NW of the Mezquita. Narrow streets, flower-draped walls, cool patios, and lively nightlife characterise the quarter from which Jews were expelled.

Sinagoga

Open 10am-2pm and 3.30-5.30pm; Sun and public hols, 10am-1.30pm. Closed Mon. 0.30 €, no charge for E. U. citizens. 95 720 29 28.

Built in the early 14C, this synagogue is a small square room with a balcony for the women. The upper walls are covered in Mudéjar stucco.

Nearby is the **Zoco Municipal** (souk) where craftsmen work around a large patio, a setting for flamenco dancing in summer. In the 16C Casa de las Bulas is the **Museo Municipal Taurino** (Bullfighting Museum).

Worth a Visit

Palacio de Viana★★

Guided tours (1hr), Oct-May, 10am-1pm and 4-6pm; Jun-Sep, 9am-2pm. Closed Sat afternoon, Sun, public hols and 1-15 Jun. 6 € (3 € patios only without tour). 957 49 67 41.

This fine example of 14C-19C Cordoban civil architecture has 12 patios and an attractive garden, outstanding in a city famous for its beautiful patios.

On the ground floor are collections of porcelain, 17C-19C side-arms and tapestries. The staircase to the first floor has a beautiful Mudéjar *artesonado* ceiling of cedar. The most interesting areas are the Cordoban leather room; tapestries made in the royal workshops from cartoons by Goya; the library; and the main room with a rich *artesonado* ceiling and tapestries illustrating the Trojan War and Spanish tales.

Museo Arqueológico Provincial★★

Open 9am-8.30pm (2.30-8pm Tue); Sun, 9am-2.30pm. Closed Mon. 1.50 €, no charge for E. U. citizens. 957 35 55 31. Expansion is in under way.

The archaeological museum is in the 16C Palacio de los Páez, a palace designed by Hernán Ruiz. Displayed here are prehistoric Iberian objects, Visigothic remains and, in particular, the **Roman collection**★ (reliefs, capitals, sarcophagi and mosaics). There are also Muslim ceramics, capitals, and the outstanding 10C **stag**★ (*cervatillo*) from Medina Azahara.

Alcázar de los Reyes Católicos★

Open 10am-2pm and 4.30-6.30pm; Sun and public hols, 9.30am-2.30pm. Closed Mon. 4 €, no charge Fri. 95 742 01 51.

The 14 C complex, later expanded, retains atractive Moorish patios with ornamental basins and pools, baths, rooms with Roman **mosaics**★ and a fine 3C **sarcophagus**★. The towers afford garden and city **views**. The **gardens**★, in Arabic style, are terraced and refreshed with pools and fountains.

Iglesias Fernandinas★

The beauty of the 14 parish churches built soon after the reconquest by Ferdinand in 1236 can still be seen today, particularly in **Santa Marina de Aguas Santas**, **San Miguel** and **San Lorenzo**. Built in primitive Gothic style, they show a sober beauty in purely structural elements. Single trumpet-shaped doorways are the only lighter aspect.

Palacio de la Diputación★

The provincial Parliament building is the former Convento de la Merced, built in the 18C. The façade is graced by a

The Sephardic Jews

No history of Spain is complete without a mention of the Jews whose presence may still be felt in *juderías* (old Jewish quarters) and synagogues. The main Jewish towns in the past were Córdoba, Toledo, Sevilla, Palma de Mallorca and Girona.

©Corbis

Maimónides

The Sephardim or Sephardic Jews (Sefarad is the Hebrew word for Spain) came to the Iberian Peninsula in Antiquity at the same time as the Greeks and Phoenicians. In the 8C, during the Arab occupation, they welcomed the Muslims who regarded them as sympathetic allies. The Muslims put them in charge of negotiating with the Christian community. As merchants, bankers, craftsmen, doctors and scholars, Jews played an important economic role and influenced the domains of culture and science. Some became famous, like Maimónides of Córdoba.

The Jews were particularly prosperous under the Caliphate of Córdoba (10C-11C). However, at the end of the 11C, Jews from Andalucía moved to Toledo and Catalunya, especially Girona, as a result of intolerance and persecution under the Almohads. They were often persecuted by Christians during the Reconquest (a royal decree forced them to wear a piece of red or yellow cloth). In the end they were expelled by the Catholic Monarchs in 1492. Some chose to convert, others (known as Marranos), in spite of having publicly converted, continued practising their Jewish faith in hiding, while most emigrated to other parts of the Mediterranean, to the Netherlands, to England and to America.

Today the Sephardic Jews represent 60% of the Diaspora. Some of them have kept their language, Ladino, which is pure 15C Castilian.

B. Kaufmann/MICHELIN

Castillo de Almodóvar del Río

white marble Baroque doorway. Inside are a patio, staircase and church.

Torre de la Calahorra: Museo vivo de Al-Andalus

Open 10am-6pm; May-Sep, 10am-2pm and 4.30-8.30pm. 4 .50€. 95 729 39 29.

In the 14C Moorish fortress a museum traces the caliphate using audio and video. There is also a fine **model**★ of the mosque as it was in the 13C.

El Cristo de Los Faroles

The Calvary surrounded by lanterns (*faroles*) in **plaza de los Capuchinos**★ is known throughout Spain.

Excursions

Medina Azahara★★

Leave Córdoba on the A 431 (to the W of the plan). After 8km/5mi bear right onto a signposted road. Open 10am-6.30pm (8.30pm May-Sep); Sun 10am-2pm. Closed Mon, 1 and 6 Jan, 9 Apr, 1 May, 1 Nov, and 24-25 and 31 Dec. 1.50 €, no charge for E. U. citizens. 957 32 91 30.

A sumptuous city built by Abd ar-Rahman III from 936 was sacked by Berbers in 1013. The city rose in three tiers – mosque below, gardens and public areas, and an *alcázar* above. The jewel is the **Abd ar-Rahman III room**, with magnificent carved stone and vegetal and geometric motifs everywhere.

Castillo de Almodóvar del Río★★

25km/15mi W along the A 431. Open 11am-2.30pm and 4-7pm (8pm in summer). 5 €. 957 63 40 55.

This imposing 14C Gothic hilltop **castle**, with two enclosures and eight towers, dominates the town below and Cordoban countryside. Stroll the narrow path behind the parapet, the parade ground and the towers.

Andújar★

76km/47mi E along the A 4.

Andújar retains many 15-16C houses and churches. On the last Sunday of April, a popular *romería* (pilgrimage) is held to the Santuario de la Virgen de la Cabeza *(32km/20mi N on the J 5010)*, in the **Parque Natural de la Sierra de Andújar**★, with open pasture, grazed by fighting bulls, and dark ravines.

Iglesia de Santa María

The 15C-17C Church of St Mary holds El Greco's *Christ in the Garden of Olives*★★, in a chapel enclosed by a fine **grille**★ by Master Bartolomé. An *Assumption of the Virgin* by Pacheco is in the north apsidal chapel.

Iglesia de San Bartolomé

This church, dating from the end of the 15C, has three **Gothic portals**★.

A CORUÑA/LA CORUÑA★

POPULATION: 252 694.

MICHELIN MAP 571 B 4 (TOWN PLAN) – GALICIA (LA CORUÑA)

This pleasant Galician city is a rocky islet, linked to the mainland by a strip of sand. The Ciudad (City) at the northern end of the harbour is the charming old quarter of small squares and Romanesque churches in contrast to the wide streets of the business centre on the isthmus. The warehouses and industry of the Ensanche are a reminder that La Coruña is Spain's sixth largest port.

- **Information:** *Dársena de la Marina, ☎98 122 18 22.*
- **Orient Yourself:** La Coruña, on the north coast, links to Santiago de Compostela by the AP 9 motorway. The A 6 heads SE past Lugo (97km/60mi SE) and on to Madrid.
- **Especially for Kids:** Aquarium Finisterrae.
- **Also See:** RÍAS ALTAS and SANTIAGO DE COMPOSTELA (73km/45mi S).

Background

Invincible Armada – Philip II's **Armada** of 130 men-of-war set out for England from La Coruña in 1588, and encountered disaster, marking the end of Spanish sea power. A year later, Elizabeth sent Drake to burn La Coruña but the town was saved by **María Pita** who gave the alarm.

The 19C – During the Peninsular War, Marshal Soult of France defeated the English in the Battle of Elviña in 1809. In the late 19C, La Coruña consistently supported liberal insurgents and suffered severe reprisals.

La Coruña is the birthplace of novelist **Emilia Pardo Bazán** (1852-1921) and was the home of poet **Rosalía de Castro** (1837-85).

Walking About

Ciudad Vieja

The old town at the northern end of the harbour is characterised by narrow cobbled streets and peaceful squares.

Colegiata de Santa María del Campo

This Romanesque church has a triple barrel-vaulted nave strengthened by arches with plaster borders. Note the fine 13C-14C portal, Gothic rose window and tower. A **Museum of Sacred Art** (Arte Sacro) is on one side of the church. In the square stands a 15C Calvary.

Plazuela de Santa Bárbara

This square in the shadow of Santa Bárbara convent hosts concerts of chamber music in August (Fiestas de María Pita).

Jardín de San Carlos

General John Moore, killed in the Battle of Elviña, is buried in this park.

Castillo de San Antón: Museo Arqueológico e Histórico

This fortress dates from the period of Philip II.

Iglesia de Santiago

The church's three apses and north door are Romanesque; the west door is Gothic. Santiago Matamoros (St James the Moorslayer) is on horseback below the tympanum, while figures of St John and St Mark are carved against the piers. The stone pulpit is beautifully carved.

EL CENTRO (CENTRAL DISTRICT)

Avenida de la Marina★

The avenue, facing the harbour, is lined by tall houses with glassed balconies. Along one side is the paseo de la Dársena and on the other the **Jardines de Méndez Núñez**, gardens with a variety of flowering trees.

A Coruña/La Coruña

Alfonso VIII	2	Carmen Pl. del	20	Pósito	55
Alonso de Ojeda	5	Colegio San José	25	Puerta de Valencia	58
Andrés de Cabrera	8	Fray luis de León	30	San Nicolás Pl.	65
Angustias Bajada a las	12	Júcar Ronda del	40	San Pablo Puente de	68
Angustias Pl. de las	15	Julián Romero Ronda de	43	Trabuco	71
		Mayor Pl.	44		
		Obispo Valero	45		

Colegiata de Santa María del Campo	BY	M[1]	Museo de Bellas Artes	AY	M[2]

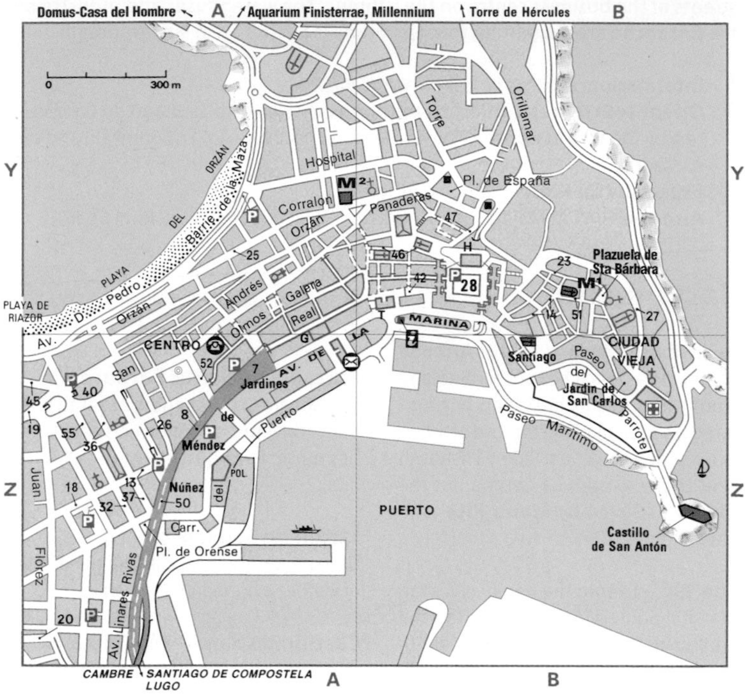

Plaza de María Pita

The vast square behind avenida de la Marina honours the 16C heroine. It has a great many terrace cafés

Worth a Visit

Castillo de San Antón: Museo Arqueológico e Histórico

Open 10am-7pm (9pm Jul-Aug); Sun and public hols, 10am-2.30pm (3pm Jul-Aug). Closed Mon, 1 Jan, Mon-Wed during Carnival, and 24-25 and 31 Dec. 2€. 98 118 98 50.

The castle's casemates, once a prison, now house an archaeological museum, which includes a room dedicated to prehistoric gold and silverware.

Museo de Bellas Artes

Open 10am-8pm; Sat, 10am-2pm and 4-8pm; Sun, 10am-2pm. Closed Mon and public hols. 2.40€, no charge Sat afternoon and Sun. 98 122 37 23.

Light and spacious exhibition rooms are dedicated to art from the 16C to the 20C, including sketches by Goya.

Domus-Casa del Hombre

Open 10am-7pm; Jul-Aug, 11am-9pm. 2€. 98 118 98 40.

This **building**★ designed by **Arata Isozaki**, is emblematic of the city. The façade facing Riazor bay is a double curve in the shape of a sail, covered with slate. The other wall uses an old quarry to create a screen of large stone blocks. The museum deals with the human species: genetics, reproduction

©iStockphoto/Rainer Walter Schmied

Glassed-in Balconies Along Avenida de la Marina

and the senses through texts and interactive displays.

Aquarium Finisterrae

Kids *Open 10am-7pm (9pm Jul-Aug); Sat-Sun and public hols, 10am-8pm (9pm Jul-Aug). 10 € (12 € including Casa de las Ciencias, Domus). 98 118 98 42.*

The aquarium highlights marine ecosystems off the Galician coast.

Torre de Hércules (Hercules Tower or Lighthouse)

Open Oct-Mar 10am-5.45pm (6.45pm Apr-Jun and Sep; 8.45pm Jul-Aug; 11.45pm Fri-Sat and holiday eves Jul-Aug). Closed 1 and 6 Jan and 25 Dec. 2 €. 981 22 37 30.

This is the oldest functioning lighthouse in the world, from the 2C AD. The original outer ramp was enclosed in 1790. From the top (104m/341ft), there is a **view** of the town and the coast.

COSTA DEL AZAHAR

MICHELIN MAP 577 K 31, L 30, M 29, N 28-29, O 28-29 – COMUNIDAD VALENCIANA (CASTELLÓN, VALENCIA)

The mountain-sheltered Orange Blossom Coast is one of Spain's major tourist centres, marked by high-rise blocks and hotels along sandy beaches and orange groves. A number of small towns and villages preserve old quarters redolent of history.

- **Information:** *Castellón de la Plana: Plaza María Agustina 5, 964 35 86 88; Gandía: Marqués de Campo, 964 287 77 88; Peñíscola: Paseo Marítimo, 964 48 02 08.*
- **Orient Yourself:** Costa del Azahar stretches along the Mediterranean coast in eastern Spain, from Valencia. The AP 7 Autopista connects the beaches.
- Kids **Especially for Kids:** Sand, surf and kids go together; apply the sunblock.
- **Also See:** COSTA DORADA (to the NE), TORTOSA (to the N), MORELLA (NW of Vinaròs) and the COSTA BLANCA (to the S).

Tours

FROM VINARÒS TO CASTELLÓN

72km/45mi

Follow either the N 340 or the AP 7 toll motorway.

The northern coast of the province of Castellón is separated from the interior by the Maestrazgo mountains, recalling knights from the Templar and Montesa orders who controlled this area during the Middle Ages. Large resorts include Peñíscola and Benicàssim.

Vinaròs

Vinaròs has the 16C **Iglesia de Nuestra Señora de la Asunción**, and a pleasant promenade close to the fishing port.

Peñíscola★★

The **old quarter**★, surrounded by walls, sits on a small rocky peninsula in the shadow of an imposing fortress, while its sandy beaches extend to either side. A small **fishing port** is still active.

Castillo★

Open 16 Oct-Palm Sunday, 9.30am-1pm and 3.15-6pm; during Holy Week and 15 Jun-15 Sep, 9am-2.30pm and 4.30-9.30pm; other times 9am-8pm. Closed 1 and 6 Jan, 9 Sep, 9 Oct and 25 Dec. 2 €. 96 448 00 21.

Built by Templars in the early 14C, the castle was subsequently modified by Pope Luna, whose coat of arms, featuring a crescent moon in allusion to his name, can be seen on a gate. Grouped around the parade ground are the vast church, with pointed vaulting and a free-standing tower containing the conclave room and the study of the learned antipope who confirmed the foundation in 1411 of the University of St Andrew's in Scotland (*see The Green Guide Scotland).*

The terrace offers a **panorama**★ of the village and coastline. The castle is the setting for events such as the Festival of Baroque and Ancient Music, in August.

The castal road passes through an arid landscape. The resort of Alcossebre, popular with Spanish families, stands between Peñíscola and Benicàssim.

Benicàssim

The other major tourist centre in the province of Castellón is separated from the interior by the **Desierto de las Palmas** (Palm Desert), which has suffered badly from fire in the past few years. Benicàssim has excellent beaches, lined by villas and apartments. The quieter town of Oropesa is located to the north.

Castellón de la Plana

Just a couple of miles separate Benicàssim from the port of Castellón, whose origins date back to the 13C. The capital of the province is situated in La Plana,

Address Book

For coin ranges, see the Legend on the cover flap.

WHERE TO EAT

El Peñón – *Santos Mártires, 22 – Peñíscola – On the way up to the castile, next to the Ermita de la Virgen – 96 448 07 16 – Closed Christmas, Jan-Feb and early Mar.* Half-hidden in one of the narrow streets of the old town, the Peñón is a friendly restaurant with attractive decor and a pleasant small terrace, where you can enjoy *dorada a la sal* (gilthead baked in salt) or an excellent grouper stew (cazuela de mero), with fish fresh from the Peñíscola market. A tradition since 1982.

El Coloso – *Plaza Marqués de la Romana – Cullera – 96 174 60 76 – Closed Tue (except May-Sep).* Classic Spanish seafood emporium, with immense windows to seaward. You'll feel as if you're on the high seas. Specialties are paella, seafood and grilled meats.

WHERE TO STAY

Hotel Simó – *Porteta 5 – Peñíscola – 96 448 06 20 – Open Mar-Sep – – 10rooms – 5.50 €.* Well-located at the seaside by the old city walls. Spectacular views more than compensate for tiny bathrooms and fluorescent lighting. Ground-floor restaurant with good wine cellar.

Albatros – *Clot de la Mota 11 (near beach) – Gandía – 96 284 56 00 – www.hotel-albatros.com – – 44 rooms – 5.50 €.* This hotel's sharp style and amenities are rare in the beach area. The coffee shop serves a limited menu in the evening.

Peñíscola

an extensive fertile area irrigated by the River Mijares. On the main square is the **Catedral de Santa María**, rebuilt after the Spanish Civil War; the octagonal bell-tower is from the late 16C. The town hall *(ayuntamiento)* is from the late 17C.

Other sights include paintings attributed to Zurbarán in the Convento de las Madres Capuchinas, and the Museo Provincial de Bellas Artes, with prehistoric objects and local canvases and ceramics.

FROM CASTELLÓN TO VALENCIA

69km/43mi

22km/14mi NW on the CV 10 and CV 160.

Vilafamés

Villafamés is an attractive town of Moorish origin with whitewashed houses and artists' workshops extending below the ruins of a castle.

Museo Popular de Arte Contemporáneo

Open 10am-1.30pm and 4-7pm (10.30am-2pm and 4-7pm Sat-Sun and public hols); Jun-Sep, 10am-1.30pm and 4-8pm. 1.80 €. 96 432 91 52.

The museum, in a 15C palace, displays works by Miró, Barjola, Serrano, Genovés, Chillida and Grupo Crónica.

Return to Castellón; continue along the A 7 for 25km/15mi to Vall d'Uxo.

Grutas de San José

In Vall d'Uxo, follow signs to the caves (grutas). Guided tours (35min), Dec-Feb, 11am-1.15pm and 3.30-5pm (5.45pm Mar and Nov; 6.30pm Apr, last two weeks of Sep and in Oct); 1 May-15 Jul, 10.30am-1.30pm and 3.30-6.30pm (8pm 15 Jul-15 Sep). Closed Mon Nov-Feb, 1 Jan and 25 Dec. 6.50 €. 96 469 67 61.

An underground river hollowed out these caves at the foot of the Parque Natural de La Sierra de Espadán. Tours by boat cover a distance of around 1.2km/0.75mi.

Continue for 20km/12mi along the CV 230, then follow the N 234.

Segorbe

The **cathedral** is chiefly important for its **museum** *(museo)* which contains a large **collection of altarpieces painted by the Valencia School**★. There are several paintings by **Juan Vicente Macip** (d 1550) who was influenced by the Italian Renaissance style. An *Ecce Homo* by his son **Juan de Juanes** bears the gentle touch favoured by Leonardo da Vinci. There are also works by Rodrigo de Osona and Jacomart and a 15C marble low relief of a Madonna by Donatello. (*Open 10.30am-1pm. Closed Mon, 1 and 6 Jan, Holy Week and 25 Dec. 2.40 €. 96 471 10 14*).

Continue along the N 234, toward the coast.

Sagunto

Historic Sagunto sits at the foot of a hill occupied by the ruins of a castle and Roman theatre. The port is 5km/3mi to the east.

A Legendary Siege

Sagunto has a place in Spain's heroic history. In 218 BC the Carthaginian general, **Hannibal**, besieged Sagunto, then a small seaport allied to Rome, for a period of 8 months. Seeing only one alternative to surrender, the local inhabitants lit a huge fire and women, children, the sick and the old then proceeded to throw themselves into the furnace while soldiers and menfolk made a suicidal sortie against the enemy. The event marked the beginning of the Second Punic War. Five years later, Scipio Africanus Major rebuilt the city which became an important Roman town.

Ruins

Open 10am-6pm (8pm in summer); Sun and public hols, 10am-2pm. Closed Mon, 1 Jan, Good Fri and 25 Dec. ☎96 266 55 81.
Access the ruins by the alleyways of the old Jewish quarter.
The 1C **theatre**, restored and still in use, with fine acoustics,was built into the hillside by the Romans. The **Acropolis** consists of the ruins and remains of ramparts, temples and houses built by Iberians, Phoenicians, Carthaginians, Romans, Visigoths and Moors. Buildings to the west date from the War of Independence, when the French general Suchet besieged the town. The **view**★ encompasses the town, countryside and sea.

Valencia (*see VALENCIA*)

FROM VALENCIA TO XÀTIVA
122km/76mi

Leave Valencia along the coast road S.

Parque Natural de La Albufera

This vast body of water (*albufera*, "small sea" in Arabic) south of Valencia is the largest freshwater lagoon in Spain, separated from the sea by an offshore bar, the Dehesa, that has been planted with rice since the 13C. Its eels appear on typical menus in restaurants in **El Palmar** *(to the S)* which also serve Valencia's famous dish, **paella**. *For further details on the park, contact the* **Centro de Interpretación del Racó de l'Olla**. (*Open Mon, Wed and Fri, 9am-2pm; Tue and Thu, 9am-2pm and 4-5.30pm (6.30pm in summer); Sat-Sun and public hols, 9am-2pm and 3-5.30pm. Closed 1 and 6 Jan and 25 Dec. ☎96 162 73 45).*
The novel *Cañas y barro*, by **Vicente Blasco Ibáñez** (1867-1928), was set in the Albufera.

Continue along the CV 500.

Cullera

This resort is at the mouth of the River Júcar; its bay is demarcated to the north by a lighthouse, the Faro de Cullera. In the town are remains of a 13C castle.

Head 27km/17mi S along the N 332.

Gandía

Gandía is at the centre of a *huerta* which produces large quantities of oranges. A resort has developed near the harbour along a 3km/1.8mi-long sandy **beach**.

The Borja Fief

Gandía became the fief of the Borja family, better known under its Italian name, Borgia, when in 1485, the Duchy of Gandía was given by Ferdinand the Catholic to Rodrigo Borgia, future Pope Alexander VI. The pope is chiefly remembered for his scandalous private life and for his children: Lucrezia, renowned for her beauty and culture, and victim of political intrigue between her father and brother; and Cesare who for political ends had his brother murdered and served as a model for Machiavelli's *The Prince*. However, the fourth duke and great-grandson of Alexander VI, who became **St Francis Borja** (1510-72), was to redeem the family name.

Palacio Ducal

Guided tours (1hr), Oct-May, 10am-2pm and 3-8pm (every hour); Jun-Sep, 10am-2pm and 4-9pm (every 30min). 5 €. ☎96 287 14 65.
The mansion in which St Francis Borja was born, now a Jesuit college, under-

went considerable modification between the 16C and 18C. Only the patio remains Gothic in appearance and typical of those along this coast.

Colegiata de Santa María , a collegiate church in nearby Plaza de la Constitució, built in the 14-15C and expanded in the 16C, is one of the finest Gothic structures in Valencia province.

Head inland along the CV 60. Before Palomar, bear right on the A 7.

Xàtiva/Játiva

Known as "the town of the thousand fountains", Xàtiva stands in a plain covered with a Mediterranean landscape of vineyards, orchards and cypress trees. The town was the birthplace of two members of the Borja family who became popes, Calixtus III (1455-58) and Alexander VI, and, in 1591, of the painter **José Ribera**.Plaza de Calixto III

The 16C **colegiata** (collegiate church) modified in the 18C, faces the former **Hospital Royal**, which has an ornate Gothic-Plateresque façade.

Museo de l'Almodí

Open 10am-2pm and 4-6pm; 15 Jun-15 Sep, 9.30am-2.30pm; Sat-Sun and public hols all year, 10am-2.30pm. Closed Mon, 1 Jan and 24-26 and 31 Dec. 2.10 €, no charge Sun. 96 227 65 97.

The Almudin, a Renaissance-style former granary with a Gothic façade, houses fine Moorish-era artifacts, along with gold and silverwork and paintings. An 11C **Moorish fountain** (*pila*) of pink marble is exceptional for its depiction of human figures, extremely rare in Islamic art.

Ermita de Sant Feliu

On the castle road. Open 10am-1pm and 3-6pm (4-7pm Apr-Oct); Sun and public hols 10am-1pm. 96 227 33 46.

Built on the flank of the hill, this chapel contains a group of 15-16C Valencian primitives. At the entrance is a white marble **stoup**★ hollowed out of a former capital.

Castillo

Open 10am-6pm (7pm in summer). Closed Mon, 1 Jan and 25 Dec. 2.10. €. 96 227 42 74.

What remains of the castle – demolished under Philip V – stands on the original town site. It commands extensive **panoramas** of the area.

COSTA BLANCA★

MICHELIN MAP 577 P 29-30, Q 29-30 –
COMUNIDAD VALENCIANA (ALACANT/ALICANTE), MURCIA

The White Coast stretches south from Valencia to Murcia. It is flat and sandy, with occasional highlands where the *sierras* drop to the sea. A hot climate, low rainfall, dazzling light, long beaches and turquoise water attract vast numbers of tourists.

- **Information:** *Altea: San Pedro 9, 96 584 41 14; Denia: Plaza del Oculista Buigues 9.*
- **Orient Yourself:** Costa Blanca towns are linked by the N 332 and the AP 7 toll motorway.
- **Don't Miss:** Beaches, sun, villages.
- **Especially for Kids:** Tierra Mítica amusement park at Benidorm.
- **Also See:** ALACANT/ALICANTE and Costa del AZAHAR.

Tours

FROM DÈNIA TO GUADALEST

115km/71mi – allow 2 days

Dènia (Denia)

The former Greek colony became Roman *Dianium*. Dènia today is a fishing harbour, toy manufacturing centre, and seaside resort. In the fortress above town is an archaeological museum.

The coast south of Dènia becomes steep and rocky with pine forests.

Cap de Sant Antoni★

Near the lighthouse on this headland, a last foothill of the Sierra del Mongó, is a good **view★** towards Xàbia and the Cabo de la Nao headland.

Xàbia (Jávea)

The old quarter is on high ground around a fortified 14C Gothic church. The modern quarter is near the harbour, beach and parador.

Cabo de la Nao★

The climb affords views over Xàbia at the foot of the Sierra del Mongó; then enter thick pinewoods where villas stand in clearings. Cabo de la Nao is an eastern extension of the Sierras Béticas (Baetic Cordillera) that continues under the sea to reappear as the island of Ibiza. There is a beautiful **view★** south from the point down the coast to the Penyal d'Ifac. Sea caves (approached by boat) and charming creeks such as **La Granadella** (south) and **Cala Blanca** (north) are excellent for diving.

Calp (Calpe)

The **Penyal d'Ifac★**, a rocky outcrop 332m/1 089ft high is the setting of Calp. A path leads to the top of the Penyal *(about 1hr walk)* with views along the coast of Calp and its salt pans, of the dark mountain chains, and northwards of the coast as far as Cabo de la Nao. The Sierra de Bernia road twists and turns before crossing the spectacular Barranco de Mascarat (Mascarat Ravine) in the hinterland to Cabo de la Nao.

Altea

Altea's white walls, rose-coloured roofs and glazed blue tile domes rise in tiers up a hillside overlooking the sea – a symphony of colour and reflected light below the Sierra de Bernia. A walk through the alleys to the church and then the view from the square over the village and beyond to the Penyal d'Ifac will reveal the attraction of so many painters towards Altea.

Benidorm

The excellent climate and two immense beaches (the Levante and the Poniente), curving away on either side of a small rock promontory, are the elements of Benidorm's incredible growth from a modest fishing village in the 1950s to a Mediterranean Manhattan with modern towers, all manner of entertainment and a lively nightlife.

From the lookout on **El Castillo** point, there are **views★** of the beaches and the Island of Plumbaria. The old quarter stands behind the point, close to the blue domed church.

J. Malburet/MICHELIN

Penyal d'Ifac

Terra Mítica

Kids 3km/2mi from Benidorm. Exit the AP 7 at exit 65 A. Open 10am-8pm (10pm mid-Jun-Aug. 33 €/day € (47 € for 2 days; 20 € evenings/nights); children 24 €/34 €/16 €. Closed Nov-Mar, Mon-Tue in May. ☎902 02 02 20.
This vast theme park is based upon the four main Mediterranean civilisations: Egypt, Greece, Rome and Iberia, covered in four areas laid out around the large central lake symbolising the "Mare Nostrum", with the fifth area, the Islands, at the centre. Terra Mítica has attractions for visitors of all ages and tastes, as well as shows and a choice of shops and restaurants.

Main attractions – In Ancient Egypt, enter a pyramid in the Mystery of Cheops, or descend the Cataracts of the Nile on an exciting white-water roller coaster ride. In Greece, emulate Theseus in the Labyrinth of the Minotaur, or experience the sensation of falling down a waterfall in the Fury of Triton. The Magnus Colossus in Rome is a spectacular wooden roller coaster. In the Flight of the Phoenix, enjoy the excitement of a free fall from 54m/177ft, or battle against currents and whirlpools in the Rapids of Argos, in the Islands section.

Take the CV 70 to Callosa d'En Sarrià then head along the CV 755 to Alcoi.

On the drive inland, you pass through small valleys cloaked in all sorts of fruit trees, including citrus and medlars. The village of **Polop** stretches up a hillside in a picturesque mountain setting. Beyond, the landscape becomes more arid but the views more extensive, the mountains more magnificent.

Guadalest★

Guadalest stands out from the terraced valleys of olive and almond trees to face the harsh limestone escarpments of the Sierra de Aitana. The **site**★ is impressive. The village, forced halfway up a ridge of rock, is a stronghold accessible

Address Book

For coin ranges, see the Legend on the cover flap.

WHERE TO EAT

⊜ **Casa Labarta** – *Conde de Altea 30 – Altea – ☎96 584 51 12 – Closed Wed.* This white building on the beachfront in Altea recalls local fishermen's houses. Traditional home cooking (rows of tapas, paella, tomato bread) served under an awning, with sea view.

⊜⊜ **Casa Modesto Vivero de Langostas** – *Cala de Finestrat – 4km/2.5mi W of Benidorm along the Playa de Poniente – ☎96 585 86 37 – Closed 15 Jan-15 Mar.* Not surprisingly, the menu at this beach restaurant revolves around fish and seafood. The views from this cove are splendid, although the high-rise towers of Benidorm are something of a blot.

TAPAS

Calle Santo Domingo – *Benidorm.* A pedestrianised street with ten or more bars. Worthy of mention are the *Aurrerá* and the *Cava Aragonesa (below).*

La Cava Aragonesa – *Plaza de la Constitución (also entry on Calle Santo Domingo) – Benidorm – ☎96 580 12 06 – www.hostallanfora.com – Open noon-3.30pm and 6.45pm-1.30am.* This typical bar makes a refreshing change from the dozens of neighbouring tower blocks, with its cured hams hanging from the ceiling and its good choice of tapas.

WHERE TO STAY

⊜ **Hostal L'Ánfora** – *Explanada Cervantes 8 – Denia – ☎96 643 01 01 – www.hostallanfora.com – – 20 rooms.* This small building with its distinctive green façade is located at the fishing port in Denia. Although small and basic, the rooms here are bright and clean. In the mornings, guests can also enjoy the sight of local fishing boats from their windows.

⊜ **Miramar** – *Plaza Almirante Bastarreche 12 (port) – Jávea – ☎96 579 01 00 – Closed 1-6 Jan – – 26 rooms.* Facing the seafront drive at one end of the beach, and an excellent choice for the price. Rooms are large and updated, well-equipped with full bathrooms.

only through an archway cut into stone. Walk round the **Castillo de San José** (now a cemetery) where ruins remain of fortifications wrecked by an earthquake in 1744. The view takes in the Guadalest reservoir with its reflections of surrounding mountain crests, the amazing site of the old village, and the sea.

COSTA BRAVA★★★

MICHELIN MAP 574 E 39, F 39, G 38-39 – CATALUNYA (GIRONA)

Spain's "Wild Coast" is the twisted, rocky shoreline where cliffs of the Catalan mountains fall away into the sea. Beautiful inlets, clear waters, picturesque harbours, and leisure and sporting activities draw tourists to these shores. Inland there are delightful medieval towns and villages.

- **Information:** *Patronat de Turisme Costa Brava Girona: Emili Grahit 13-15, no. 9, Girona, ☎972 20 84 01, www.costabrava.org; Blanes: Plaza Catalunya 2, ☎97 233 03 48, www.blanes.net; Cadaqués: Cotxe 2-A, ☎972 25 83 15.*
- **Orient Yourself:** The Costa Brava is the coastline from Blanes up to Portbou on the border with France. Lloret de Mar, Tossa de Mar and Platja d'Aro are major tourist centres; towns to the north are more low-key.
- **Especially for Kids:** Beaches are the main attractions for younger tourists.
- **Also See:** *GIRONA/GERONA, FIGUERES and BARCELONA*

Tours

THE ALBERES COASTLINE★★ 1

Portbou – Roses 65km/40mi – half a day

The foothills of the Sierra de l'Albera form huge, enclosed bays, like those of Portbou and El Port de la Selva. The clifftop **road section**★★ from Portbou to Colera offers fine views of one of the most craggy coastlines in Catalunya.

El Port de Llançà

A pleasant tourist resort sited on a bay sheltered from winds like the *tramontana* and sudden Mediterranean storms. The shallow waters are ideal for a swim.

Take the GI 612 for 8km/5mi

El Port de la Selva★

This bay is bathed in golden sunlight at dusk. Traditional white houses stand beside numerous flats and hotels. Fishing is still one of the main activities.

Monasterio de Sant Pere de Rodes★★★

7km/4mi from El Port de la Selva. Leave your car in the car park and proceed on foot for 10min. Open 10am-5.30pm (8pm Jun-Sep); last admission 20min before closing time. Closed Mon, 1 Jan and 25 Dec. 3.60 €, no charge Tue. ☎972 28 75 59.

This imposing Benedictine monastery stands in a beautiful **setting**★★ that dominates the Gulf of León and the Cabo de Creus peninsula. Begun in the 10C, it was pillaged, and abandoned in the 18C. The remarkable **church**★★★ showing pre-Romanesque influence, is an unusual example of architectural harmony. The central nave has barrel vaulting, the two lateral ones have surbased vaulting. They are separated by huge pillars, reinforced with columns on raised bases. Splendid **capitals**★ intricate tracery and acanthus leaves evoke the tradition of Córdoba and Byzantium. The left arm of the transept leads to an upper ambulatory offering a sweeping view of the central nave. The 12C **bell tower**★★ is a magnificent example of Lombardy Gothic.

The coast between El Port de la Selva and Cadaqués features many irregular creeks with crystal-clear waters, accessible only by sea. The road inland offers lovely views of the region.

Return to El Port de la Selva and turn right on the GI 613.

Cadaqués★★

Cadaqués lies south of the Cabo de Creus in a delightful **setting**★ enclosed by mountains. It was a humble fishing village until modern artists (Dalí, Picasso, García Lorca, Buñuel, André Breton, Paul Éluard etc) made it fashionable.

White houses with picturesque porticoes cluster around the **Iglesia de Santa María,** whose sober exterior contrasts with its interior: note the lovely **Baroque altarpiece**★★ in gilded wood. The town hosts an international music festival. *Open 11am-8pm. 972 25 85 00.*

Head N for 2km/1.2mi.

Portlligat★

The **Casa-Museo Salvador Dalí**★ is a cluster of fishermen's houses. Dalí's workshop, library, rooms and garden are all open to the public. *Open by appointment 10.30am-6pm (9pm 15 Jun-15 Sep). Closed Mon (except in summer, 7 Jan-14 Mar, 1 Jan and 25 Dec. 8 €. 972 25 10 15.*

Continue 4km/2.5mi N

Parque Natural Cap de Creus★★

Steep roads and paths wind between cliffs and hidden bays. Enjoy a spectacular **view**★★★ from the **lighthouse** at the highest point.

Return to Cadaqués, then head SW on the GI 614 and E on the C 260.

Roses★

Sailors of Rhodes founded a colony in a splendid natural harbour overlooking the Golfo de Roses. Its 16C Renaissance **citadel**★, a pentagon with many bastions, was commissioned by Charles V. The Benedictine monastery inside was destroyed by the French during the War of Independence. The town is both resort and fishing port.

THE EMPORDÀ PLAIN★ 2

Roses to Begur 75km/46.5mi – one day

The fertile plain lies along the coast.

Leave Roses on theC 260 towards Castelló d'Empúries.

Empuriabrava★

The luxury marina-residential development allows backyard docking.

Castelló d'Empúries★

The former capital of the principality of Empúries (11-14C) is on a promontory near the coast. The 14-15C **Iglesia de Santa Maria**★ is flanked by a typical Catalan belfry. The **portal**★★ is a unique example of Gothic art in Catalunya: the tympanum illustrates the Adoration of the Magi while the Apostles are shown on the jambs. The large central nave is lined by fine cylindrical pillars. The alabaster **retable**★ in the high altar (15C), with conical pinnacles, depicts the Passion. *(Open 1 Jun-30 Sep, 10am 1pm and 4-8pm; Sun and public hols, 11am-12.30pm and 4-8pm; rest of the year, Sat-Sun only. 972 25 80 84).*

The village retains buildings from its golden age: the **Ajuntament** (Maritime Commodities Exchange), combining Romanesque and Gothic elements, and the **Casa Gran**, of Gothic inspiration.

Leave Castelló d'Empúries toward Sant Pere Pescador. From here, continue S until you reach the GI 623.

L'Escala★

This resort has sandy beaches and a long fishing tradition (anchovies are salted). Two inlets protect its harbour. *The Empúries ruins are located to the N.*

Empúries/Ampurias★★

Open 10am-6pm (8pm Holy Week and Jun-Sep). Closed 1 Jan and 25 Dec. 2.40 €; no charge 23 Apr, 18 May and 11 Sep . 972 77 02 08.

Greco-Roman Ampurias (*Emporion* to the Greeks, meaning market) was built on a striking seaside **site**★★. It is still possible to make out the old town, or **Paliápolis**, the new town or **Neápolis**, and the Roman town.

In the mid-6C BC, the Phoenicians founded Paliápolis, on an offshore island, now joined to the mainland and occupied by the village of Sant Marti d'Empúries. A town began to develop on the shore opposite: Neápolis. As a Roman ally during the Punic Wars, it saw the arrival of an expedition led by Scipio Africanus Major in 218 BC. In 100 BC the Roman town was established to the west. The two centres coexisted until Augustus bestowed Roman citizenship upon the Greeks. The colony suffered from barbarian invasions in the 3C AD. At one time it was a bishopric, as basilica ruins show.

Neápolis

The **Templo de Asclepio** (Aesculapius – god of healing) and a sacred precinct contained altars and statues of the gods. Nearby stood a **watchtower** and drinking water cisterns. The **Templo de Zeus Serapis** (a god associated with the weather and with healing) was surrounded by a colonnade. The **Agora** was the centre of town life; three statues remain. A street from the agora to the sea was bordered on one side by the **stoa** or covered market. Behind it are the ruins of a 6C **palaeo-Christian basilica** with a rounded apse.

Museo Arqueológico de Ampurias

A section of Neápolis is displayed along with models of temples and finds from the excavations.

The Roman town

Unlike Neápolis, this is a vast, geometrically laid out town, partially excavated, with some restored walls. **House n° 1** (entrance at the back) has an atrium (inner courtyard) with six columns. Around this are residential apartments, the peristyle, or colonnaded court, and the impluvium, or rainwater catchment. The reception rooms are paved in geometric, black-and-white mosaic. .

House n° 2B has rooms paved with their original mosaic. One has been reconstituted in clay with its walls resting on stone foundations.

The **forum**, a large square lined by porticoes and, to north and south respectively, by temples and shops, was the centre of civic life. A porticoed street led through the city gate to the oval **amphitheatre** which is still visible.

▸ *Take the GI 632 to Bellcaire d'Empordà, then turn left onto the GI 640.*

Torroella del Montgrì★

Despite a Baroque front, the 14C **Iglesia de Sant Genís** is a fine example of Gothic Catalan art. The **castle** on Montaña de Montgrí (*1hr on a signposted path among the rocks*) is an extraordinary **belvedere**★★ with a view to the sea and the Gavarres mountain range.

J. Malburet/ MICHELIN

Cadaqués

▶ *Continue for 5km/3mi along the GI 641 to L'Estartit.*

Islas Medes★★
Boat trips around the islands are offered from l'Estartit. For information contact the Tourist Office. ☎972 75 19 10.
These seven islets and coral reefs are the extension of the calcareous massif of Montgrí. It is interesting to ecologists for its marine species and ecosystems. The islets are popular for diving.

▶ *Return to Torroella de Montgrí from L'Estartit, then follow the C 31.*

Pals★★
At the mouth of the Ter river, Pals has an attractive old quarter, **El Pedró**. The vestiges of fortified ramparts enclose ancient houses and winding alleyways, some with covered stairways.
Begur is located 7km/4.5mi E of Pals.

THE COAST ROAD★★ 3
Begur to Blanes
98km/61mi – one day
Plains and mountains that extend down to the sea alternate with long beaches and **coves** of astounding beauty: **Alguafreda, Aigua Blava, Tamariu**, sheltered by pine trees and dotted with luxury villas and exclusive hotels.

Begur★
The town overlooks pretty creeks from an altitude of 200m/656ft above the sea. The castle ruins (16-17C) offer a nice view of Begur.

▶ *Leave Begur and head for Llafranc.*

Far de Sant Sebastià★
2km/1.2mi from Llafranc. Built in 1857, the lighthouse stands on a tiny isthmus surrounded by steep cliffs. The nearby hermitage commands a lovely **view**★.

Calella de Palafrugell★
This fishing port is known for its **Festival de Habaneras** on the first Saturday in July. Visitors enjoy Afro-Cuban songs and dances while sipping *cremat*, flambéed coffee with rum.
A road southward leads to the **Jardin Botánic del Cap Roiga**. A terraced park carved out of the rock, overlooking the Mediterranean, presents more than 1 200 plant species laid out along shaded avenues. These gardens offer some wonderful **views**★★ of the coast. *(Open 9am-6pm (8pm Apr-Sep). 3 €. ☎972 61 45 82).*

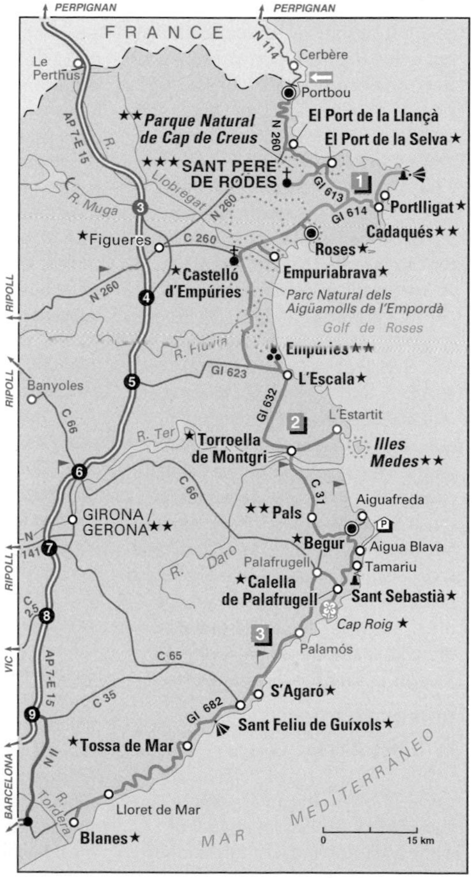

Address Book

For coin ranges, see the Legend on the cover flap.

WHERE TO EAT

⊜ **La Brasa** – *Plaça Catalunya 6 – El Port de LLançà – ☎972 38 02 02 – www.restaurantlabrasa.com– Closed Mon eves, Tue (except Jul-Aug) and 15 Dec- Feb –* ▤. The low-key atmosphere invites visitors in to enjoy grilled fish and meat. There's also a pleasant shady terrace.

⊜⊜ **Eldorado Mar** – *President Irla 15 – Sant Feliu de Guíxols – ☎972 32 62 86 – www.doradomar.com – Closed Wed Oct-May.* This restaurant in upper town specialises in seafood. Despite plain decor, large windows offer stunning sea views. Reasonable fixed menu.

⊜⊜ **La Gua-gua** – *Platja Canyelles Petites – Roses – 2.5km/1.5mi SE of Roses – ☎972 25 77 82 – Closed Oct-Holy Week. Reservation recommended.* This delightful restaurant serves traditional fish dishes (try the *suquet de peix* – a fish stew) on a beach terrace with lovely sea views. A disadvantage is the hordes of sunbathers on the beach in summer.

⊜⊜ **Can Rafa** – *Passeig 7 – Cadaqués – Exit 4 from AP 7 toward Cadaqués ☎ 972 15 94 01 – Reservation recommended.* Good local cuisine in a dining room covered with photos from the 1970s. Great bay views from the terrace.

⊜⊜ **Ca la Maria** – Unió 5 – *Mollet de Peralada – 4km/2.5mi N of Peralada – ☎ 972 56 33 82 – Closed nights, Tue and 15 Feb-15 Mar –* ▤ *– Reservation recommended.* A large restaurant in quiet Mollet, 16km/10mi inland. An unpretentious setting for real Catalan cuisine. Always busy at weekends.

⊜⊜ **Santa Marta** – *Francesc Aromir 2 – Tossa de Mar – ☎972 34 04 72 – Closed Wed (except Jun-Aug).* Located in the old town, the Santa Marta offers a range of fish and meat dishes. Despite its irregular shape, the dining room has a warm, relaxed feel. Pleasant terrace.

WHERE TO STAY

⊜ **Hotel Ubaldo** – *Unió 13 – Cadaqués – ☎972 25 81 25 – www.hotelubaldo.com – 26 rooms.* The hotel's simple façade masks a pleasant interior of white walls, curving furniture and soft lighting. Comfortable rooms overlook the alleyways of the old quarter.

⊜⊜ **Hotel Plaça** – *Plaça Mercat 22 – Sant Feliu de Guíxols – ☎972 32 51 55 – www.hotelplaza.org –* ▤ *– 19 rooms –* ☕ *6 €.* A practical choice for location and functional character. Pleasant, bright rooms – some overlook a square that's lively on market days. Outdoor jacuzzi and solarium on the top floor.

⊜⊜ **Hotel Diana** – *Plaza de España 6 – Tossa de Mar – ☎972 34 18 18 86 – www.hotelesdante.com – Open Mar-Nov – 21 rooms –* ☕. The interior of this splendid Modernist building by the sea is exquisite, with an high ceilings, cool rooms and a patio adorned with a marble fountain. The rooms are comfortable and furnished in style.

⊜⊜ **Hotel La Goleta** – *Pintor Terruella 22 – El Port de LLançà – ☎ 972 38 01 25 –* 🅿 ▤ *– 28 rooms –* ☕ *– Restaurant 18€.* Close to the port, the La Goleta offers comfort and an interesting decor of paintings and other furnishings. A friendly atmosphere and good value for money.

⊜⊜**Hotel Port Lligat** – *Avenida Salvador Dalí 1 – Port Lligat – ☎972 25 81 62 – www.port-lligat.net/hotel –* 🏊 *– 30 rooms –* ☕ *8 €.* The creature comforts in this attractive blue and white building in a cove full of fishing boats near Dalí's house are particularly popular with guests. Every room is different, and if you don't mind paying a bit extra, ask for one with a sea view.

⊜⊜ **Hotel Rosa** – *Pi i Rallo 11 – Begur – ☎972 62 30 30 15 – www.hotel-rosa.com – Open Mar-Nov –* ▤ *– 21 rooms.* ☕ *– Restaurant.* This small hotel in a restored stone house by the church is popular with a younger set for its modern decor, functional furniture and well-planned lighting. The restaurant serves traditional cuisine.

⊜⊜⊜ **Hotel Almadraba Park** – *Platja Almadraba – 4km/2.5mi SE of Roses – ☎972 25 65 50 – www.almadrabapark.com – Open 5 Apr-14 Oct –* 🅿 ▤ ♿ *– 60 rooms –* ☕ *– Restaurant 36/48 €.* A hotel offering impeccable service in a delightful natural setting amid lovely gardens. The building itself, modern in design and south facing, looks onto manicured gardens that descend to the sea in terraces. All the guest rooms enjoy wonderful views.

⊖⊖⊖ **Hotel Sant Roc** – *Plaça Atlántic 2, (Sant Roc district) – Calella de Palafrugell – ☎972 61 42 50 – www.santroc.com – – Open 17 Mar-26 Nov – P ▤ – 47 rooms – ☕ 11 € – Restaurant.* This charming building crowned by a small tower enjoys a peaceful, relaxing setting amid pine groves overlooking the Mediterranean. The rooms are spacious and elegant, while the restaurant terrace enjoys fine views of neighbouring coves. Half-board compulsory in summer.

NIGHTLIFE

Avinguda Just Marlès Vilarrodona – *Av. Just Marlès Vilarrodona – Lloret de Mar.* At nightfall, this wide throroughfare sees a mix of beautiful girls, hunky men, and flower vendors at the doors to bars. At least ten discos: *Londeners, Flamingo, Moef Gaga* and *Tropics*, one of the largest and most modern on the Costa Brava; not to forget *St Trop* (one street over), the only one that can face up to *Tropics*, with three floors, seven bars, and 200,000 watts of light.

Mojito Bar – *Codolar 2 – Tossa de Mar – Open 6pm-2am.* A small cocktail bar with a relaxed air in the pedestrianised section of the resort. The Mojito mainly concentrates on salsa, flamenco and sevillanas.

Moxo – *Empuriabrava – Open 8pm-3am.* The *Moxo* is the focal point for nightlife in this modern tourist resort, which has about 20 bars, nightclubs and restaurants. The *Saloon* specialises in country music and the *Glass* in techno.

Passarel-la – *Passeig maritim 16 – Empuriabrava – by the C-260 to Roses – ☎972 45 20 97 – www.passarel-la.com – Open 18 May-mid-Sep – Cover: 10/15€ with drink.* Dance by moonlight at this beachside disco, or inside in two spaces with different music. There's also a large pool at one of the "in" discos on the Costa Brava.

Rachdingue – *Roses road – Vilajuïga – ☎972 530 023 – Open mid-Jun–mid-Sep Fri-Sat.* This disco, started up by Dalí, is in a stone barn on a promontory, with a pool and garden bar.

ENTERTAINMENT

Water World – *Vidreres road – Lloret de Mar – ☎972 36 86 13 – www.waterworld.es – Closed Oct–mid-May*. One of the great water parks of Europe offers waves, water slides, and more.

SHOPPING

Carrer de l'Aigüeta – *La Bisbal d'Empordà.* Ceramics are a centuries-old tradition, with all sorts of objects in the shops on this street. Try El Risser.

▸ *Follow directions to Palafrugell, then take the C 31 to Palamós. Beyond, the C 253 skirts the coast; beaches alternating with rocky inlets. The C 31 is quicker though less scenic.*

S'Agarò★

An elegant resort with chalets and luxury villas surrounded by tidy gardens and pine forests. The camino de Ronda offers fine views★ of the sheer cliffs.

Sant Feliu de Guíxols★

Wheltered from the last spurs of the Sierra de les Gavarres, this is one of the most popular locations of this coast. Its seaside boulevard Passeig de la Mar is lined with pavement cafés. The **Iglesia-Monasterio de Sant Feliu**★ is part of a former Benedictine monastery. Its remains tower over the small municipality. It has retained its Romanesque façade, known as the **Porta Ferrada**★★, with horseshoe arches dating to pre-Romanesque times. The interior (14C) is Gothic in style. *Open 8-11am and at 8.30pm; Sun and public hols, during Mass. Closed Mon, 1 Jan and 25 Dec. ☎972 82 15 75.*

The lookout by the chapel of Sant Elm commands beautiful **views**★★ of the coastal road.

▸ *Follow the GI 682, enjoying spectacular views of the coast.*

Tossa de Mar★

This sandy beach curves around to Punta del Faro, the promontory on which stand the lighthouse and the 13C

View of Calella de Palafrugell

walls of the **Vila Vella**★ (old town). The **Museu Municipal**★ contains artefacts from an ancient Roman villa nearby, and an **exhibition of contemporary art** by artists who stayed in the 1930s (Chagall, Masson, Benet etc). *Open 11am-1pm and 3-5pm (6pm 1-15 Jun and 16-31 Sep; 8pm 16 Jun-16 Sep); Sat-Sun and public hols 11am-5pm. Closed Mon (except in summer), 1, 6 and 22 Jan and 25-26 Dec. 3€. 972 34 07 09.*
Between Tossa and **Lloret de Mar** (the most important and popular tourist resort of the Costa Brava), the road follows a spectacular **clifftop route**★★.

Continue along the GI 682.

Blanes★

The magnificent **Passeig Marítim**★ offers a lovely panorama of Blanes and its beach. The remains of the Castillo de Sant Joan are to the east, above the 14C Gothic Iglesia de Santa Maria. To the southeast is the **Jardin Botánic de Marimurtra**★, a botanical park with 5 000 plant species including many rare exotic varieties. At each new bend the twisting paths reveal wonderful **views**★ of Cala Forcadera and the coast. *Open 9am-6pm; Nov-Mar, 10am-5pm; Sat-Sun and public hols, 10am-2pm. Last admission one hour before closing. Closed 1 and 6 Jan and 24-26 Dec. 4 €. 972 33 08 26.*

COSTA DE CANTABRIA★

MICHELIN MAP 572 B16-20 – CANTABRIA

The Cantabrian coast is a succession of gulfs, capes, peninsulas, *rías*, splendid bays as in Santander and Santoña, traditional summer beach resorts, and delightful towns dotted with impressive mansions. This area is also rich in caves bearing traces of human habitation in the Palaeolithic Age.

- **Information:** *Comillas: Aldea 6, ☎942 72 07 68; San Vicente de la Barquera: Avenida Generalísimo 20, ☎942 71 07 97.*
- **Orient Yourself:** Explore this part of Spain's northern coast via the fast inland road or the slower, winding coastal route though charming villages with spectacular views.
- **Also See:** *COSTA VERDE (to the W), PICOS DE EUROPA (to the W) and the COSTA VASCA (to the E).*

Tours

FROM EAST TO WEST

Castro Urdiales

The village, above a vast bay, clusters round its Gothic church, ruined castle and lighthouse. The Coso Blanco festival is held the first Friday in July.

Laredo

The **old town** adjoins a long beach lined by modern buildings.

Limpias

The fishing village on the banks of the ría Asón is known for a miracle which occurred in 1919, when a deeply venerated Baroque Crucifix attributed to Juan de Mena shed tears of blood.

Santuario de Nuestra Señora de la Bien Aparecida

A road winds up to the Baroque shrine. Veneration for the patron of Cantabria province dates back to 1605. Splendid **panorama**★ of the Asón Valley.

Santoña

The fishing port facing Laredo was a French headquarters in the Peninsular War. The **Iglesia de Nuestra Señora del Puerto**, remodelled in the 18C, has, in addition to Gothic aisles, Romanesque features including carved capitals and an old font. *Open 9am-1pm*

J. Malburet/MICHELIN

Comillas

and 3-8.30pm. No visits during religious services. ☎942 66 01 55.

Bareyo

The small **Iglesia de Santa María**, overlooking the ría de Ajo, retains original Romanesque moulded arches and historiated capitals. The **font** is probably Visigothic. *Guided tours Sat-Sun 9am-1pm and 5-8pm. ☎942 62 10 41.*

Peña Cabarga

A steep road rises to the summit (568m/1 863ft) and a monument to the Conquistadores and the Seamen Adventurers of Castilla. From the top there is a splendid **panorama★★**.

Santander★ (*See SANTANDER*)

Santillana del Mar★★

(*See SANTILLANA DEL MAR*)

Museo de Altamira★★

(*See SANTILLANA DEL MAR*)

Comillas★

Comillas is a pleasant seaside resort with a delightful plaza, a beach and easy access to the extensive sands at Oyambre – 5km/3mi west. It was a royal residence at the time of Alfonso XII. Buildings in the vast park surrounding the neo-Gothic **Palacio de los Marqueses de Comillas** include Gaudí's freakish **El Capricho**, now a restaurant. The Universidad Pontíficia (Papal University) overlooks the sea.

San Vicente de la Barquera★

This resort attracts visitors to its vast **beach★**, across the inlet. The hilltop **Iglesia de Nuestra Señora de los Ángeles** (Our Lady of the Angels) has two Romanesque portals, Gothic aisles and tombs from the 15C and 16C. On the Unquera road is a fine **view★** of San Vicente.

Cueva el Soplao★

Near Rábago, 20 km/12 mi S of San Vicente de la Barquera. Open 9am-9pm; Sun and public hols 10am-2pm and 4-8pm. Reservations advised. 9€. ☎902 82 02 82.

Visit this impressive cave as a regular tourist, or in adventure mode with boots, helmet and the rest. Entry is through mining tunnels. Notable are oddly shaped stalactites and salagmites and ghost figures.

Address Book

For coin ranges, see the Legend on the cover flap.

WHERE TO EAT

Mesón Marinero – *La Correría, 23 – Castro Urdiales – ☎942 86 00 05 – www.mesonmarinero.com –* .
As it suggests, this famous name in Cantabrian gastronomy specialises in seafood of excellent quality. The choice of tapas at the bar is equally impressive.

Maruja – *Avenida Generalísimo – San Vicente de la Barquera – closed two weeks in Mar and Nov, Sun evenings and Wed – ☎942 71 00 77.* This small restaurant tastefully decorated in drawing-room style is one of the best-known along the Cantabrian coast, with dishes based on fresh local products and traditional recipes.

WHERE TO STAY

Pensión La Sota – *La Correría 1 – Castro Urdiales – ☎942 87 11 88 – 19 rooms. 2.50 €.* The La Sota stands on the main square of Castro Urdiales in the heart of the old quarter. Although lacking in space, the guest rooms are adequately furnished and have modern bathrooms.

Hotel Gerra Mayor – *Los Llaos – Gerra – 5km/3mi NE of San Vicente de la Barquera – ☎942 71 14 01 – www.hgerramayor.com – Closed 15 Dec-1 Mar – P – 19 rooms – 5 €.* This simple hotel in a onetime farmhouse, superbly located between the sea and the mountains, is perfect for those searching for peace and quiet and a pleasant base from which to explore this beautiful stretch of coastline.

COSTA DE LA LUZ★

MICHELIN MAP 578 U 7-8-9-10, V 10, W 10-11, X 11-12-13 – ANDALUCÍA (HUELVA, CÁDIZ)

The southwestern coast in the provinces of Huelva and Cádiz is edged with beaches interrupted by the mouths of major rivers – the Guadiana, Tinto and Guadalquivir. Several resorts are being developed beside the dazzling white sand and translucent skies that make this the Coast of Light.

- **Information:** *El Puerto de Santa María: Luna 22, ☎956 54 24 13; Huelva: Avenida Alemania 12, ☎959 65 02 00; Sanlúcar de Barrameda: Mayor 2, ☎948 87 14 11; Tarifa: Paseo de la Alameda, ☎956 68 09 93*
- **Orient Yourself:** The Costa de la Luz extends from Ayamonte, at the mouth of the Guadiana, to Tarifa, the most southerly town on mainland Spain.
- **Also See:** *SEVILLA (96km/60mi E of Huelva), JEREZ DE LA FRONTERA (35km/22mi NW of Cádiz), Straits of GIBRALTAR and COSTA DEL SOL.*

Tours

THE HUELVA COAST★

Ayamonte to the Parque Nacional de Doñana – 135km/84mi – allow one day

Ayamonte★

This fishing port at the mouth of the Guadiana is a lively border town of cobbled streets and whitewashed and brightly coloured houses. In the old quarter are the 16C colonial-style Iglesia de las Angustias, the Convento de San Francisco, with its elegant bell tower and magnificent *artesonado* work, and the 13C Iglesia del Salvador. Boat service is available to Vila Real de Santo António in Portugal.

Coastal resorts between Ayamonte and Huelva include **Isla Canela, Isla Cristina, La Antilla** and **Punta Umbría**. This area also includes the marshland of the **Marismas del río Piedras y Flecha de El Rompido**★, the El Portil lagoon, and the Enebrales de Punta Umbría, a landscape dominated by juniper trees.

Huelva★

In the 15C and 16C, the estuary formed by the Tinto and Odiel rivers saw the departure of numerous expeditions to the New World, notably those led by Columbus. A large monument to these explorers, the **Monumento a la Fe Descubridora** (1929), stands near the harbour at Punta del Sebo.

In Huelva, see the unusual **Barrio Reina Victoria**★, an English-style district named after Queen Victoria; the **cathedral**, with its Renaissance façade and sculpture of the Virgen de la Cinta, the town's patron saint, by Martínez Montañés; and paintings by Zurbarán in the **Iglesia de la Concepción** and **Museo Provincial.** *(Open 9am-8pm; Tue 2.30-8.30pm; Sun and public hols, 9am-2pm. Closed Mon. ☎959 25 93 00).*

Paraje Natural de las Marismas del Odiel★★

2km/1.2mi SE. Exit Huelva along Avenida Tomás Domínguez. This marshland *(marisma)* of outstanding beauty, at the mouth of the Tinto and Odiel rivers, close to an industrial chemical facility, is a World Biosphere Reserve. It provides a habitat for over 200 bird species. Visited by **canoe** or small boat *(open Fri-Sun and public hols 10am-2pm and 4-6pm; 8pm in summer; Activities require advance booking; ☎959 50 90 11 or 660 41 49 20).*

La Rábida★

In 1484, the Prior of the **Monasterio de Santa Maria**, Juan Pérez, believed Columbus' claim that the world was round and interceded to obtain the support of the Catholic Monarchs.

The **church**★ preserves old frescoes, wooden *artesonado* work and the delicate 14C alabaster statue of the **Virgen de los Milagros**★ (Virgin of Miracles),

Address Book

For coin ranges, see the Legend on the cover flap.

WHERE TO EAT

⊜⊜ **Casa Bigote** – *Bajo de Guía 10 – Sanlúcar de Barrameda – ☎956 36 26 96 – www.restaurantecasabigote.com – Closed Sun and in Nov –* ▤. This old tavern in the river district of Bajo Guía has developed into famous gastronomic landmark. Run by the same family for the past 50 years, it is decorated with old photos, fishing mementoes and antique objects. Pride of place on the extensive menu is given to the excellent local fish and prawns.

⊜⊜⊜ **Trafalgar** – *Plaza de España 31 – Vejer de la Frontera – ☎956 44 76 38 – Closed Jan-10 Feb and Mon (except Jun-Aug) –* ▤. This welcome culinary surprise, on the attractive plaza de los Pescaítos, specialises in delicious fresh fish. Tapas are also served at the entrance. Guests can dine on the terrace in summer.

WHERE TO STAY

⊜ **Hotel Convento de San Francisco** – *La Plazuela – Vejer de la Frontera – ☎956 45 10 01 – www.tugasa.com – ▤ – 25 rooms – ☕ 3.70 € – Restaurant 16/40€.* This former convent for Poor Clares dating from the 17C is situated in Vejer's old quarter. Although soberly decorated, the rooms are pleasant, with high ceilings and exposed beams. The hotel also has a good restaurant.

⊜⊜ **Hotel Toruño** – *Plaza del Acebuchal 22 – El Rocío – ☎959 44 23 23 – ▤ – 30 rooms – ☕* – Restaurant 15 €. At the edge of Parque Nacional de Doñana, this traditional great house blends perfectly into the village of El Rocío. Some rooms have lovely marsh views. Prices soar for the pilgrimage.

⊜⊜ **Posada de Palacio** – *Caballeros 11 (Barrio Alto) – Sanlúcar de Barrameda – ☎956 36 48 40 – www.posadadepalacio.com – Closed 8 Jan-1Mar – 30 rooms – ☕ 9€.* This family-run hotel is in an 18C mansion opposite the town hall (ayuntamiento) in the upper section of Sanlúcar. The rooms, laid out around an attractive patio, are simply yet tastefully decorated with antique furniture.

in front of which Columbus is said to have prayed prior to setting sail. A small room displays a **mapamundi**★, by Juan de la Cosa, which outlined the coast of America for the first time (*open 10am-1pm and 4-6.15pm; summer, 10am-1pm and 4-7pm (10am-1pm and 4.45-8pm in Aug); closed Mon.* 3 €. *☎959 35 04 11).*

Full-scale replicas of Columbus' three caravels are moored at the **Muelle de las Carabelas**★, a modern dock and museum on the Tinto Estuary (*open 1-7pm; closed Mon; 3.10 €; ☎959 53 05 97).*

Palos de la Frontera★

This picturesque town on the left bank of the Río Tinto was the birthplace of the Pinzón brothers, who sailed with Columbus. The **Casa-Museo de Martín Alonso Pinzón** and the *azulejos* dotted around the town provide a reminder of the first voyage (*closed for renovation; ☎959 35 01 99).* The 15C **Iglesia de San Jorge** is fronted by an interesting Gothic-Mudéjar doorway.

Moguer★

Expeditions left this tranquil town with its elegant houses for points unknown. The verses of **Juan Ramón Jiménez** (1881-1958), Moguer's most illustrious son and winner of the Nobel Prize for Literature in 1956, adorn *azulejo* panelling dotted around the town centre. His home is a museum, the **Casa-Museo Zenobia y Juan Ramón**★ (*guided tours (45 min) 10.15am-1.15pm and 5.15-7.15pm; Sun 10.15am-1.15pm; closed Mon and public hols; 2.50 €; ☎959 37 21 48).*

The **town hall** *(ayuntamiento)* has a fine Renaissance **façade**★. Head along the pedestrianised **calle Andalucía**★, lined by interesting buildings, includ-

Pink flamingoes in the Parco Nazionale de Doñana

ing the Archivo Histórico Municipal and Biblioteca Iberoamericana; and the 15C Convento de San Francisco, with its Mannerist cloisters, Baroque altarpiece and lofty belfry. The **tower**★ of the Iglesia de **Nuestra Señora de la Granada** recalls the Giralda in Sevilla.

Monasterio de Santa Clara★

Guided tours (40min), 11am-12.30pm and 5-7pm. Closed Sun-Mon and public hols. 2€. 959 37 01 07.

The church of this Gothic-Mudéjar monastery houses the Renaissance-style marble **tombs of the Portocarrero family**★, noteworthy **tombs**★ at the high altar, and some quite exceptional 14C **Nasrid-Mudéjar choir stalls**★★.

Return to the C 442, which follows the coast.

Parque Nacional de Doñana★★★

This park, at the crossroads of continents and of the Atlantic and the Mediterranean, acts as a rest stop for African and European migratory birds. Doñana is Spain's largest wildlife reserve with a protected area (inner and outer park) of 73 000ha/180 390 acres. The **salt marshes** are the larger part of the park and are the ideal habitat for birds which

Address Book

SIGHTSEEING

Because of the park's fragile ecology, entry to the **Doñana** is rigorously controlled. The El Acebuche visitor centre co-ordinates all park activities. Open 8am-7pm (9pm Jun-Sep). Closed 1 Jan, 24-25 and 31 Dec and during the El Rocío pilgrimage. Tours of the park (4hr) by jeep are possible if booked in advance. 16.23€. 959 43 04 32. River trips (4hr) are also available if booked in advance. 13.22€. 956 36 38 13 or contact the National Park information desk. 959 44 87 11.

Tours – Several types of excursions are possible within the park:

By Jeep – These tours should be booked in advance. Two visits per day are organised: one in the morning, one in the afternoon. Excursions are by four-wheel-drive. Itineraries vary according to the time of year.

On foot – A number of paths depart from the four information centres where details are available on the level of difficulty and duration of the walks.

On horseback – Excursions are available by horseback or horse-drawn carriage. Further information can be obtained from the visitors centres.

migrate to Europe over the winter. **Sand dunes** are grouped in formation parallel to the Atlantic and advance inland at a rate of 6m/20ft per year. The stabilised sands or **cotos** are dry, undulating areas covered with heather, rockrose, rosemary and thyme, and trees such as cork oak and pine.

The Doñana is home to lynx, wild boar, deer and a wide variety of birds, including Spanish imperial eagles, flamingoes, herons, wild ducks and coots.

El Rocío

This small village is famous as the site of the **Santuario de Nuestra Señora del Rocío** (Sanctuary of the Virgin of the Dew), to which Spain's most popular religious pilgrimage *(romería)* is made during Whitsun weekend every year.

THE CÁDIZ COAST★

From Sanlúcar de Barrameda to Tarifa
160km/100mi – allow one day

Sanlúcar de Barrameda★

The fishing port of Sanlúcar, at the mouth of the Guadalquivir, is the home town of *manzanilla*, a sherry matured like Jerez *fino* but which has a special flavour thanks to the sea air. The *bodegas* (cellars) are in the old quarter on the hill around the massive **Castillo de Santiago**. The **Iglesia de Nuestra Señora de la O** close by has a fine Mudéjar **doorway**★★ and a 16C **Mudéjar artesonado ceiling**★.

In the modern town, pass the **Palacio de Orleans y Borbón**, a 19C palace built in neo-Moorish style, and now Sanlúcar's town hall, and the **covachas**★, a mysterious series of five ogee arches decorated with Gothic tracery.

The lower town has two main churches: the **Iglesia de la Trinidad**, with its magnificent 15C Mudéjar **artesonado**★★; and the **Iglesia de Santo Domingo**, with the noble proportions of a Renaissance building. The **Centro de Visitantes Fábrica de Hielo**, a visitor centre in Bajo de Guía, near the mouth of the Guadalquivir, provides information on the Parque Nacional de Doñana across the river *(open 9am-7pm (9pm in summer); ☎956 38 16 35)*. Park excursions also depart from here.

Rota

The **old town**★ inside the ramparts is laid out around the **Castillo de la Luna** (now the town hall) and the **Iglesia de Nuestra Señora de la O**★. Rota is known for beaches such as the **Playa de la Costilla**★. A large naval base is on the outskirts of the town.

El Puerto de Santa María★

The harbour, in Cádiz Bay, played an active role in trade with the New World. Today, fishing, the export of sherry and tourism (beaches and golf courses) are important.

A palm-shaded promenade overlooking the quays along the north bank

B. Kaufmann/MICHELIN

The port of Tarifa

leads to the 12C **Castillo de San Marcos**, a castle which was the seat of the Dukes of Medinaceli. The late-15C **Iglesia Mayor Prioral** stands in the centre of the town. The **Portada del Sol**★, or Sun Gateway, in plaza de España, is a mix of Plateresque and Baroque styles. The **Fundación Rafael Alberti** nearby shows photos, letters, and manuscripts by the poet (*open 11-2.30pm; closed Mon and 24-25 and 31 Dec; 3 €. 956 85 07 11*). The **Casa-Museo de Pedro Muñoz-Seca** (1879-1936), author of *La venganza de Don Mendo*, is also here (*open 11am-2pm; closed Mon, 15 Sep-14 Jun and Sun, 15 Jun-14 Sep; 1.20€; 956 85 17 31*).

Cádiz★★ (*See CÁDIZ*)

South of Cádiz, there are good beaches at **La Barrosa**★★, Chiclana de la Frontera and **Conil de la Frontera (Playa de la Fontanilla** and **Playa de los Bateles)**.

Vejer de la Frontera★

Vejer, perched on a crag, is one of the prettiest white villages of Andalucía. The best approach is along the hillside road from the south. The **Iglesia Parroquial del Divino Salvador** has a three-aisle **interior**★ a mix of Romanesque and Gothic features.

The road on to Tarifa runs through the Baetic foothills. The **Parque Natural La Breña y Marismas de Barbate**★, with spectacular cliffs and picturesque coves, such as the **Cala de los Caños de Meca**★★, is 10km/6mi from Vejer.

Ruinas Romanas de Baelo Claudia★

Open 10am-7pm (6pm Nov-Feb, 8pm Mar-Sep). Sun and public hols 10am-2pm. Last entry 30 min before closing. Closed Mon, 1 and 6 Jan and 24-25 and 31 Dec. 1.50 €, no charge for E.U. citizens. 956 68 85 30.

The remains of the Roman city of Baelo Claudia date back to the 2C BC, when a salting factory specialising in the production of *garum* (a sauce made from the remains of fish) was established here. Vestiges of the basilica, forum and a small theatre are still visble.

Tarifa

Atlantic and Mediterranean air masses converge to make Tarifa, Spain's southmost point, a major centre for windsurfing and kitesurfing. The **Castillo de Guzmán el Bueno**, taken by the Christians in 1292, was commanded by Guzmán el Bueno who accepted the execution of his sons by the Moors rather than surrender.

COSTA DEL SOL★

MICHELIN MAP 578 V16 TO 22, W 14-15-16 – MAP 124 COSTA DEL SOL – ANDALUCÍA (MÁLAGA, GRANADA, ALMERÍA)

Sheltered by the Sierra Nevada, Spain's Sun Coast enjoys mild winters and hot summers. Millions of visitors are attracted by sandy beaches, whitewashed towns and villages and a variety of leisure activities. In summer, beaches are packed, and the nightlife continues until dawn.

- **Information:** *Estepona: Avenida San Lorenzo 1, 95 280 20 02; Marbella: Glorieta de la Fontanilla, 95 277 14 42; Nerja: Puerta del Mar 2, 95 252 15 31; Salobreña: Plaza de Goya, 958 61 03 14.*
- **Orient Yourself:** The Costa del Sol stretches along the Mediterranean from the Straits of Gibraltar to east of Almería
- **Parking:** You'll have to search in beach towns, so get there early.
- **Especially for Kids:** Take the small ones to the beach, of course.
- **Also See:** Straits of GIBRALTAR (SW), RONDA (50km/31mi N of San Pedro de Alcántara), ANTEQUERA (55km/34mi N of Málaga), GRANADA (74km/46km N of Salobreña).

Tours

The Western Coastline★★

From Estepona to Málaga

139km/86mi – allow one day

Estepona★

The **old quarter**★ retains its Andalusian charm. Its attractions are the plaza de las Flores, the ruins of the castle and the 18C Iglesia de Nuestra Señora.

Casares★, 24km/15mi inland along the A 377 and MA 539, is a whitewashed town of Moorish origin with a maze of narrow streets clinging to a rock in the Sierra de Crestenilla.

San Pedro de Alcántara

Archaeological sites close to the beach include **Las Bóvedas** (thermal baths dating from the 3C AD) and the palaeo-Christian basilica of Vega del Mar (*guided tours (1hr 45min), Tue and Thu at noon). Las Bóvedas is also open to the public;* It is advisable to reserve a day ahead. *☎95 278 13 60.*

(For a description of the road from Ronda, see RONDA).

Puerto Banús★★

This magnificent marina attract some of the world's most luxurious sailing craft. Its many restaurants, bars and boutiques are popular on summer evenings.

Marbella★★

The capital of the Costa del Sol is an international jet set destination.

Old quarter★

Whitewashed old buildings stand beside shops, bars and restaurants along a maze of streets and lanes.

The enchanting **plaza de los Naranjos**★, named for its orange trees, is lined by the 16C town hall, the 17C Casa del Corregidor, and a small 15C chapel, the Ermita de Nuestro Señor Santiago. Other sights in the old quarter are the 17C Iglesia de Santa María de la Encarnación and the **Museo del Grabado Español Contemporáneo**★ devoted to contemporary prints, in a 16C former hospital (*open 10am-1.45pm and 7-9pm; in summer, 10am-2pm and 6-9pm; closed Sun, Mon and public hols; 3 €; ☎952 76 57 41).*

Marbella also has a marina, luxury accommodations, excellent beaches, a long promenade, designer boutiques, health spas and golf courses.

Fuengirola

The Castillo de Sohail, a castle of Moorish origin, dominates this large resort. The remains of some Roman baths and villas are in the Santa Fe district.

▸ *Head N towards Mijas.*

J. Malburet/MICHELIN

Puerto Banús

Mijas★

Views★ from this picturesque whitewashed town in the *sierra* encompass much of the coast. It is well worth strolling narrow, winding streets dotted with tiny squares and charming nooks and crannies. Highlights are sections of the old Moorish wall, and the 16C Iglesia de la Inmaculada Concepción, crowned by a Mudéjar tower. Shops display Andalucían arts and crafts (pottery, basketwork and textiles). Mijas also has an unusual **miniatures museum**, known as the Carromato de Max *(open 10am-7pm (10pm in summer) 3 €; 952 48 58 20).*

Benalmádena

Benalmádena stands several kilometres inland from the resort of Benalmádena Costa. Its main sights include several 16C watchtowers and a small **archaeological museum** *(open 9.30am-1.30pm and 5-7pm; 6-8pm in summer; Sun and public hols 10am-2pm; Closed Mon, 1 and 6 Jan, Good Fri, 1 May, and 24-25 and 31 Dec; 95 244 85 93).*

Torremolinos

The promenade and the long beach are the main attractions of this onetime fishing village, now a huge resort..

Málaga★ (*See MÁLAGA*)

THE EASTERN COASTLINE★

From Málaga to Almería

204km/127mi – allow one day

This beautiful coast is punctuated by the ruins of Moorish towers – defences built after the Reconquest against attacks by Barbary pirates.

Nerja★

Nerja, a large resort, overlooks the Mediterranean from the top of a promontory. The **Balcón de Europa★** is a magnificent mirador offering views of this dramatic coastline and occasional glimpses of North Africa.

Cueva de Nerja★★

4.5km/3mi E along the Motril road. Open 10am-2pm and 4-6.30pm (10am-7.30pm Jul-Aug). 7 €. 95 252 95 20.

In this cave were found paintings, weapons, jewels and bones, indicating habitation in the Palaeolithic era. Its size and stalactites and stalagmites are both impressive. An annual festival of music and dance is held in the Sala de la Cascada (Cascade Chamber) the second and third weeks of July.

The road from Nerja to La Herradura★

The scenic road snakes along a mountainside with delightful **views★★**.

Almuñécar

Bananas, medlars, pomegranates and mangoes are grown on the small alluvial plain *(hoya)* behind this resort. The **Cueva de los Siete Palacios** houses an archaeological museum *(open 10.30am-1.30pm and 4-6pm; in summer, 10.30am-1.30pm and 6.30-9pm; Sun and public hols, 10.30am-1.30pm; closed Mon, 1 Jan and 25 Dec. 2.20 € with castle; 958 63 11 25).* The **Castillo de San Miguel** is also open to the public *(open same hours except until 9.30pm in summer).*

Salobreña★

Salobreña, prettiest town on this coast, spreads across a hill, a white blanket punctuated by purple splashes of bougainvillea. An imposing Moorish **fortress** converted into a palatial residence by Nasrid kings in the 14C stands above *(open 10.30am-2pm and 4-7pm; 5-9.30pm in summer; closed Mon in winter; 2 €; 2.55€ with museum; 958 958 61 03 14).*

RESTAURANTS – TAPAS

The pedestrianised district of **La Carihuela**, alongside the beach, is the most attractive part of Torremolinos, with dozens of bars, restaurants, hotels and shops. Two of the best restaurants are Casa Juan, which has been specialising in seafood for more than 30 years, and **El Roqueo**, with its terrace overlooking the promenade.

Address Book

For coin ranges, see the Legend on the cover flap.

WHERE TO EAT

Pepe Rico – *Almirante Ferrándiz,28 – Nerja – ☎952 52 02 47 – closed 6 Jan-2 Feb –* . On a pedestrianised street, this is a cosy eatery with fireplace, ceiling fans, and oil paintings on its walls. Specialties include duck cooked in wine and suckling pig. Rooms are available around a patio (35/60€).

El Olivar – *Virgen de la Peña 6 (El Rosario building) – Mijas – ☎952 48 61 96 – closed Sat and in Feb* . This country restaurant offers fine sierra views through its large windows and finer views from its terrace.

Pacomari – *La Gloria 4 – Nerja – ☎ 952 52 01 38 – www.pacomari.com – Closed Sun in winter, midday Sun in summer and 20 Nov-20 Dec.* With a sedate Andalucian patio and modest dining room, this is a good place to try regional specialties, such as *ajo blanco* (white gaspacho), though there are also economical prix fixe meals.

Mesón Lorente – *Junquillo 32 – Ojén – ☎952 88 11 74 – closed Thu and second half of Jan and Jul – reservation recommended.* Many Andalucians and tourists looking for a breather from the coast head for this restaurant, which is well known for its home cooking. The greenhouse looks onto the liveliest street in the town.

Casa Eladio – *Virgen de los Dolores 6 (Old Town) – Marbella – ☎ 95 277 00 83 – Closed Thu and 10 Jan-10Feb.* A longstanding family establishment where you can try traditional Spanish cooking at a fair price. Choices include delicious grilled fish and regional specialties such as *ajo blanco* (white gazpacho) and *pellejo de patata* (potato peel).

La Alcazaba – *Plaza de la Constitución – Mijas – ☎952 59 02 53 – www.rest-laalcazabademijas.com- Closed Mon and 15-30 Jan.* Perched on the Arab walls of Mijas with fine vistas and careful decoration, La Alcazaba's best feature is its timeless *mozarabe* dining room, with flowing detailing and two vernerable horseshoe arches framing an endless landscape.

Marisquería La Marea – *Plaza Cantarero – Nerja – ☎95 252 57 78 – – Reservation recommended.* A good address for fish and seafood. The scallops and clams on display at the bar are grilled fresh when you order them and served either in the bar itself or in the nautically decorated restaurant.

El Balcón de la Virgen – *Remedios 2 (Old quarter) – Marbella – ☎ 95 277 60 92 – Dinner only. Closed Sun and 20 Dec-20 Jan..* In an attractive street lined by an endless succession of restau–rant terraces. The restaurant, recognis-able by the image of the Virgin Mary on its attractive façade, is mainly popular with tourists. Andalucían cuisine.

WHERE TO STAY

Hostal San Miguel – *San Miguel 36 – Nerja – ☎952 52 72 17 – www.hostalsanmiguel.com – – 12 rooms. – 4.50 €.* This hotel is in a recently restored town house near the centre, with modest but comfortable rooms. There's a bar-coffee shop, and a special feature is the top-floor terrace with small pool and sea and mountain views.

Hostal El Pilar – *Plaza de las Flores 10 – Estepona – ☎952 80 00 18 – www.ainte.net/hostalelpilar – 20 rooms.* Time would appear to have stopped in this charming *hostal* on the main square. The interior, decorated with black and white family photos, has an impressive staircase leading up to the basic but pleasant rooms.

B. Kaufmann/ MICHELIN

La Carihuela

◎ **Hostal Marissal** – *Paseo Balcón de Europa 3 – Nerja – ☎952 52 01 99 – www.hostalmarissal.com – ▤ – 22 rooms – ☐ 3 € – Restaurant. 15/25€*. In a privileged location, at the entry to the famed Balcony of Europe, with fine views to the passage from some rooms. Coffee shop and restaurant.

◎ **La Hostería de Don José** – *Paseo del Nacimiento 1 (El Chifle) – Ojén – ☎ 952 88 11 47 – hdonjose@Jjazzviajeros.com – 6 rooms*. A charming small hotel on the top of a hill overlooking the town. At the Don José everything you need for a comfortable stay is on hand: comfort, simple yet cosy furnishings, a friendly welcome and unforgettable views of Ojén's whitewashed houses set against the backdrop of the Mediterranean.

◎ **Hotel Casablanca** – *Plaza San Cristóbal 4 – Almuñécar – ☎958 63 55 75 – www.almunecar.info/casablanca – ▤ ♿ – 35 rooms – ☐ 2.50 € – Restaurant 7.49 €*. With its cupola, raspberry-coloured façade and arches that imitate the architecture of Moroccan palaces, the Casablanca is a visual experience not to be missed! Once inside your room, the crystal chandeliers and marble decor add a decidedly Oriental touch. Make sure you book in advance.

◎◎ **Hotel La Morada Más Hermosa** – *Montenebros 16 (Old Town) – Marbella – ☎ 95 292 44 67 – www.lamoradamashermosa.com – ▤ – 8 rooms – ☐ 5.80 €*. Find this hotel on a plant-bedecked alley right in the old part of town. The charming rooms have been decorated with care by the owner in a personal country Andalucian style with colonial details. Ask for room 2 with its pleasant terrace or wood-panelled room 5.

◎◎ **Hotel La Fonda** – *Santo Domingo 7 – Benalmádena – ☎ 95 256 83 24 – ⚒ ▤ – 26 rooms – ☐*. A charming hotel in the Sierra de Castillejos, overlooking the Mediterranean. Spacious rooms, indoor pool, flower-filled patios and terraces with views of the hills and sea. Very reasonably priced given the standard.

◎◎◎ **Hotel Marbella Club** – *Boulevard Príncipe Alfonso von Hohenlohe – ☎95 282 22 11 – www.marbellaclub.com – hotelmarbellaclub.com – ℗ ▤ – 84 rooms – ☐ 28 € – Restaurant 58/69 €*. One of the best hotels along the coast, built in the middle of a superb garden planted with palm trees. The bungalow accommodation here frequently hosts the rich and famous. The Marbella Club is the perfect place to unwind and enjoy the magnificent sports facilities available (swimming pool, beach, tennis etc).

SHOPPING

Marbella is one of the best places for shopping on the Costa del Sol with all the top names in international fashion represented here. Most of these stores are concentrated in Puerto Banús, where there is an impressive nucleus of modern, designer boutiques, and in the centre of Marbella, particularly along avenida Ricardo Soriano and calle Ramón y Cajal. The best indoor shopping centre on the Costa del Sol is also found in Puerto Banús.

Markets are an important feature of life on the Costa del Sol. The one in Marbella takes place on Saturday mornings next to the Nueva Andalucía bullring (plaza de toros) near Puerto Banús.

The road from Calahonda to Castell de Ferro★

The road hugs the rocky coast, offering mountain and sea views. After Balanegra the N 340 turns inland through an immense sweep of greenhouses around El Ejido, where flowers, vegetables and tropical fruit are grown.

Almería (⚲ *See ALMERÍA*)

COSTA VASCA★★

MICHELIN MAP 574 B-C 21 TO 24
PAÍS VASCO (GUIPÚZCOA, VIZCAYA)

The Basque Coast (Costa Vasca) stretches from the Golfo de Vizcaya (Bay of Biscay) to the headland of the Cabo de Machichaco. The steep shoreline, lined by cliffs and indented by estuaries, is a line of fishing villages nestling in inlets.

- **Information:** *Bermeo: Askatasun Bidea 2, ☏94 618 65 43; Getaria: Parque Aldamar, ☏943 14 09 57; Hondarribia: Javier Ugarte 6, ☏943 64 54 58; Lekeitio: Independentzia Enparantaza ☏94 684 40, 17; Zarautz:, Nafarroa, ☏943 83 09 90.*
- **Orient Yourself:** The Basque Coast runs from the French border to Bilbao.
- **Also See:** COSTA DE CANTABRIA (to the W), VITORIA-GASTEIZ (64km/40mi S of Bilbao) and PAMPLONA (79km/49mi SE of Donostia-San Sebastián).

Tours

FROM HONDARRIBIA TO BILBAO

247km/154mi – allow 2 days

Hondarribia/Fuenterrabía★

Fuenterrabía (Hondarribia in Basque) is a resort. **La Marina** is the fishermen's quarter with characteristic wood balconies and bars and cafés. On 8 September, a parade and festival honour the Virgen de Guadalupe, who is said to have delivered the town from a two-month siege by the French in 1638.

Old town

Overlooking the River Bidasoa, the old fortified town, with steep streets, retains its 15C walls. These are punctuated by the **Puerta de Santa María**, a gateway surmounted by the town's coat of arms and twin angels venerating the Virgen de Guadalupe. Picturesque **calle Mayor** is lined with houses with wrought-iron balconies.

The **Iglesia de Santa María**, a Gothic church with massive buttresses, was remodelled in the 17C and given a Baroque tower. It was the site of a proxy wedding in 1660 between Louis XIV and the Infanta María before the real marriage in France. The **Castillo de Carlos V**, a fortress (now a parador) was constructed in the 10C by Sancho Abarca, King of Navarra, and restored by Charles V in the 16C.

Cabo Higuer★

4km/2.5mi N. ▶ Leave Fuenterrabía on the harbour road. Turn left; as the road climbs, you get a **view**★ of the beach, the town and the quayside and from the end of the headland, the French coast and the town of Hendaye.

Ermita de San Marcial

9km/5.5mi SE. ▶ Leave Fuenterrabía on the Behobia road; take the first right after the Palmera factory; bear left at the first crossroads. A narrow road leads up to the wooded hilltop (225m/738ft). The **panorama**★★ from the hermitage includes Fuenterrabía, **Irún** and **Isla de los Faisanes** (Pheasant Island) in the mouth of the River Bidasoa on the border. In the distance are Donostia-San Sebastián and Hendaye beach.

Jaizkibel Road★★

The **drive**★★ along this road *(GI 3440)* is impressive at sunset. After 5km/3mi you reach the Capilla de Nuestra Señora de Guadalupe (Chapel of our Lady of Guadalupe) where there is a lovely **view**★ of the French coast. Past pines and gorse is the Hostal de Jaizkibel at the foot of a 584m/1 916ft peak and a lookout with a superb **view**★★. The road down affords **glimpses**★ of the indented coast, the Cordillera Cantábrica range and the mountains above Donostia-San Sebastián.

Pasaia/Pasajes

17km/11mi W along the Jaizkibel road. Pasaia comprises three villages around

Address Book

For coin ranges, see the Legend on the cover flap.

WHERE TO EAT

Txiki Polit – *Plaza de la Musika – Zarautz – ☎943 83 53 57 – www.txikipolit.com* – . This simple tavern with paper tablecloths has an extensive, good-quality menu with specialities that include beef cutlets and a good choice of fish. It also has a number of reasonable guest rooms on the first floor.

Iribar – *Nagusia 34 – Getaria – ☎ 943 14 04 06 – Closed two weeks in Apr and two weeks in Oct* – . The Iribar is a traditional restaurant serving reasonably priced grilled fish in the centre of this fishing village. The dining room, on two levels, is simply but pleasantly decorated.

Asador Almiketxu – *Almike Auzoa 8 – Bermeo – 1.5km/1mi S of Bermeo – ☎94 688 09 25 – www.almiketxu.com – Closed Mon and 12 Nov-2 Dec.* This restaurant, offering a varied menu of traditional Basque cuisine, is located in a house on a hill on the outskirts of Bermeo, from where there are fine views of the town and the sea.

WHERE TO STAY

Pensión Itsasmin – *Nagusia 32 – Elantxobe – ☎94 627 61 74 – 15 rooms – 4.50 €.* This small hotel in a pedestrian street in the upper part of town has 18 pleasant rooms with parquet flooring and exposed beams. Two of the rooms have dormer windows, while four have views of the port. Parking here is the only drawback.

Hotel Emperatriz Zita – *Avenida Santa Elena – Lekeitio – ☎94 684 26 55 – www.aisiahoteles.com – P – 42 rooms – 8€ – Restaurant 12.50/23.50€.* Between 1922 and 1931, this palatial building by the sea was occupied by the Empress Zita, the last empress of the Austro-Hungarian Empire. As you would expect, the rooms are spacious, comfortable and pleasantly decorated. The hotel also has its own thalasso-therapy centre.

Hotel Obispo – *Plaza del Obispo 1 – Hondarribia – ☎943 64 54 00 – www.hotelobispo.com – ♿ – 16 rooms* – . The Obispo is a charming hotel housed in a 14C-15C palace located in the upper section of Hondarribia's old quarter. All the rooms are different, with the pleasant mix of exposed beams, stone walls, old furniture and fabrics creating a warm, cosy atmosphere.

a sheltered bay. **Pasai Antxo** is a trading port, **Pasai Donibane**★ and **Pasai San Pedro** are both deep-sea fishing ports, processing cod. To get to **Pasai Donibane**★, either park at the village entrance or take a motorboat from San Pedro. The **view** from the water is picturesque – tall houses with brightly painted wooden balconies, boats and docks, and a single street. A path runs to the lighthouse *(45min)*.

Donostia-San Sebastián★★

(See DONOSTIA-SAN SEBASTIÁN)

▸ *Take the N 1; 7km/4mi S of Donostia-San Sebastián take the N 634 toward Bilbao.*

Zarautz

Queen Isabel II made this her summer residence in the 19C. Two **palaces** stand in the old quarter: the 16C property of the Marqués de Narros, and the Luzea tower, on Plaza Mayor, with mullioned windows and a machicolated corner balcony. The tower of the church of Santa María can be seen to one side. Beyond Zarautz, the road rises to a picturesque **corniche section**★★.

Getaria

Getaria is known for its *chipirones*, or squid, and its rock – *el ratón*, or Monte de San Antón – linked by a causeway. Native son **Juan Sebastián Elcano** set out with Magellan and was the first sailor to circumnavigate the world (1522). A narrow street, lined with pic-

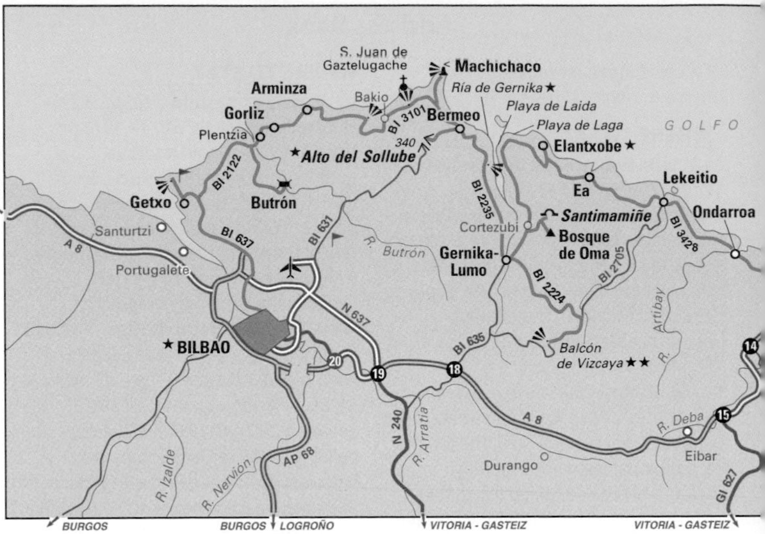

turesque houses, leads to the 13C-15C **Iglesia de San Salvador** (Church of our Saviour); its chancel rests on an arch above an alleyway. The gallery is Flamboyant Gothic.

Zumaia

Zumaia has two fine beaches: Itzurun, between cliffs, and Santiago. Near the latter is the house of painter **Ignacio Zuloaga** (1870-1945), converted into a **casa-museo** showing his works – realistic and popular themes with brilliant colours and strong lines – and his collection of paintings by El Greco, Goya, Zurbarán and Morales (*open 1 Apr-15 Sep, 4-8pm; at other times by prior arrangement; closed Mon and Tue; 5 €. 943 86 23 41).*

The 15C **Iglesia de San Pedro** (Church of St Peter) contains a 16C altarpiece by Juan de Anchieta.

Past Zumaia, go left onto the GI 631.

Santuario de San Ignacio de Loyola

Open 10am-12.30pm and 3-6.15pm; Sun 10a.m-12.30pm. 943 81 65 08.

This **sanctuary** was built by the Jesuits to plans by Italian architect Carlo Fontana around the Loyola family manor near Azpeitia at the end of the 17C. It is an important place of pilgrimage especially on St Ignatius' day (31 July).

The basement casemates of the 15C tower are vestiges of the original Loyola manor house, the **Santa Casa**. The rooms in which Ignatius was born, convalesced and converted have been transformed into profusely decorated chapels. The Baroque **basilica** is more Italian than Spanish in style, circular with a vast cupola (65m/213ft high) attributed to Churriguera.

Return to the coast

The journey by road to Deba is one of the most beautiful in the Basque country.

Icíar

The fortress-like church contains a Plateresque altarpiece in dark wood.

Deba

The **Iglesia de Santa María la Real** in this fishing port conceals, beneath the porch in its fortified front, a superb Gothic portal decorated with extremely lifelike statues. The cloister galleries have intricate tracery. There is a splendid **view★** of the coast from the **cliff road★** between Deba and Lekeitio.

Mutriku has one of the region's most delightful beaches, **Saturraran**.

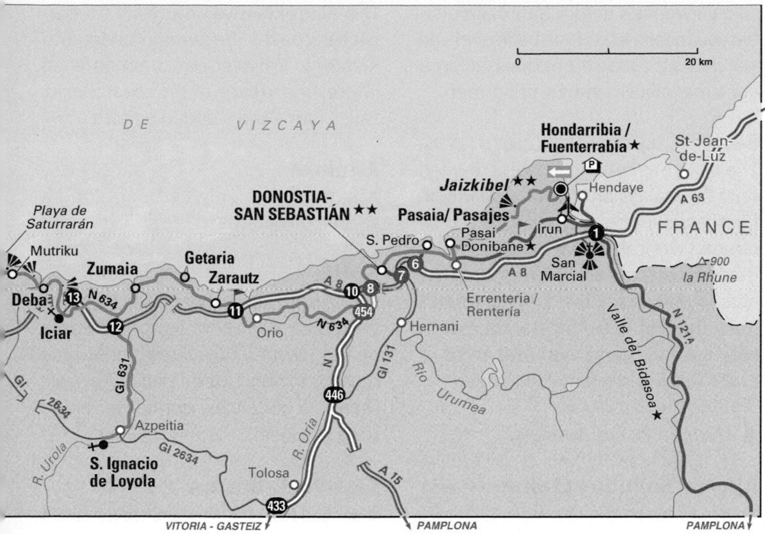

Ondarroa

The church, standing like a ship's prow, tall Basque houses with washing at the windows, and the encircling river, make an attractive **picture**★. Canning and fish salting are the main industries. Onward, on rounding a point you have a good **view**★ of Lekeitio, its beach and the island of San Nicolás, joined to the mainland at low tide.

Lekeitio

A deeply indented bay at the foot of Monte Calvario, divided by an island, is Lekeitio's fishing harbour. There are good beaches. The 15C **iglesia** guarding the harbour has three tiers of flying buttresses and a tall Baroque belfry.

Ea

This miniature harbour stands between two hills at the end of a quiet creek.

Elantxobe★

Fishermen have long used the bay as a natural harbour and built their houses overlooking the water, against steep-sided Cabo Ogoño (300m/1 000ft). Beyond rose-coloured **Playa de Laga**, a beach circling Cabo Ogoño, you can see **Gernika ría**★ (Estuary), Izaro island, the white outline of the town of Sukarrieta on the far bank, and Chacharramendi island. The resort of **Playa de Laida**, on the *ría*, is popular with Gernika residents.

▸ *Bear left at Cortézubi.*

Cuevas de Santimamiñe

Guided tours (1hr) at 10 and 11.15am and 12.30, 4.30 and 6pm. Closed Sat-Sun and public hols. ☎94 420 77 00.
Wall paintings (*closed to visitors*) and engravings from the Magdalenian Period were discovered in these caves in 1917.

Gernika

Picasso's painting, *Guernica* (*see MADRID and INTRODUCTION TO SPAIN*), immortalised a Spanish Civl War atrocity: on 26 April 1937, Nazi planes bombed the town, killing more than 2 000.
In the Middle Ages, the Gernika oak was one of the four places where newly created lords of Biscay came to swear that they would respect the local *fueros* or privileges. The remains of the 1 000-year-old tree are in the small temple behind the **Casa de Juntas**.
18km/11mi south *(via the BI 2224 and BI 3231)*, the **Balcón de Vizcaya**★★ (Balcony of Biscay) viewpoint overlooks a chequerboard of meadows and forests.

▸ *Return to Gernika.*

Two viewpoints before Mundaka enable you to take a last look back over still waters. As the road drops downhill, you get a magnificent **view★** of Bermeo.

Bermeo

The fishermen's quarter, still crowded onto the Atalaya promontory overlooking the old harbour, was protected by ramparts (traces remain), and the grim granite Torre de los Ercilla (now the Museo del Pescador, a fishermen's museum). In the Iglesia de Santa Eufemia, kings and overlords used to swear to uphold Biscay privileges.

▶ *Turn left towards Mungía.*

Alto del Sollube★ (Sollube Pass)

The road up to the low pass (340m/1 115ft) affords a good view of Bermeo.

▶ *Return to Bermeo, follow the coast road left for 3km/1.8mi then turn right.*

Faro de Machichaco

From just left of this lighthouse there is a good view west along the coastline. The road winds to a **viewpoint★** over the **San Juan de Gaztelugache** headland and its hermitage *(access via a pathway)*, the goal of a *romería* (pilgrimage) on Midsummer's Day.

There are extensive views from the **corniche road★** between Bakio and Arminza. A belvedere commands an interesting **view★** of the coast, Bakio, valley farms and wooded hinterland.

Arminza

Arminza is the only harbour along a section of wild coast.

Gorliz

Gorliz is an attractive beach resort at the mouth of the River Butrón. **Plentzia** nearby *(2km/1.2mi)* is an oyster farming centre and resort. Upon exiting Plentzia, there is a good view of the river encircling the town.

Castillo de Butrón

Closed for restoration. ☎ 94 615 11 10.

This fantasy castle is a good example of eclectic, picturesque 19C architecture. It is built on the remains of a 14C-15C construction, and provides insight into medieval castle life.

Getxo

A **paseo marítimo** (sea promenade) overlooks the coast. From the road up to Getxo's well-known golf course there is a view of the Bilbao inlet and on the far bank, Santurtzi and Portugalete.

Bilbao★ *(See BILBAO).*

J. Malburet/MICHELIN

Bermeo

COSTA VERDE★★★

MICHELIN MAPS 571 AND 572 (TOWN PLAN OF GIJÓN) B8 TO 15 – ASTURIAS

The Green Coast of Asturias is named for the colour of the sea, pine and eucalyptus trees along the shore, and wooded pastures inland. Towns and villages are nestled in picturesque coves, where fishing is the main activity. On a clear day the Picos de Europa and Cordillera Cantábrica are a stunning backdrop.

- **Information:** *Gijón: Marqués de San Esteban 1, ☎98 543 60 46; Llanes: Alfonso IX (La Torre building), ☎98 540 01 64; Luarca: Los Caleros 11, ☎98 564 00 83.*
- **Orient Yourself:** The N 634 runs the length of the northern coast of Asturias, affording sea and mountain views.
- **Especially for Kids:** The Jurassic Museum is unmissable.
- **Also See:** COSTA DE CANTABRIA (to the E), PICOS DE EUROPA (S of Ribadesella), OVIEDO (30km/19mi SW of Gijón) and RÍAS ALTAS (to the W).

Tours

Along the rocky coast, low cliffs are interrupted by sandy inlets; the estuaries are narrow and deep. West of Cudillero, the coastal plain ends in sheer cliffs overlooking small beaches.

FROM LLANES TO GIJÓN ☎

145km/90mi to the west

Llanes

The clifftop promenade affords a good view of the once fortified port, the rampart ruins and castle and the squat Iglesia de Santa María. In August, see the St Roch festival dances (the *Pericote* and the children's *Prima* dance) in brilliant local costume.

Ribadesella

The town and port of Ribadesella are on the right side of the estuary opposite a holiday resort.

Cuevas de Tito Bustillo★

Guided tours (1hr) by reservation 10am-4.15pm. Closed Mon-Tue and 9 Sep-31 Mar. 4 €. ☎98 586 11 20.
These caves are famous for their **wall of paintings**★ by Palaeolithic inhabitants (20 000 BC) of horses, stags and a doe.

La Isla

Squat drying sheds or *hórreos*, typical of Asturias, stand beside the houses in the small, attractive village.

MUJA (Museo del Jurásico de Asturias – Jurassic Museum)

Open 10.30am-2.30pm and 4-7pm (Mon 10.30am-2.30pm). Closed Tue, 1 and 6 Jan, and 24-25 and 31 Dec. 5.30€. ☎902 306 600.
Between Colunga and Lastres is this dinosaur footprint of a building dedicated to these creatures. Dinosaur prints are found in the area.

Mirador del Fito★★★

12km/8mi SE of La Isla on AS 260. This viewpoint has a spectacular panorama of the Picos de Europa and the coast.

Priesca

The capitals in the chancel in the **Iglesia de San Salvador** resemble those at Valdediós (*see below*).

Villaviciosa

Emperor Charles V arrived here at 17 to take possession of Spain. The **Iglesia de Santa María** is decorated with a Gothic rose window.
Amandi – *3km/2mi S of Villaviciosa.* The bell gable of the **Iglesia de San Juan** stands on high ground. The remodelled church retains a 13C portal with sophisticated **decoration**★. Inside the **apse**★, the frieze from the façade reappears to form a winding ribbon that follows the curves of the intercolumniation.

Valdediós★

7km/4mi S of Villaviciosa.

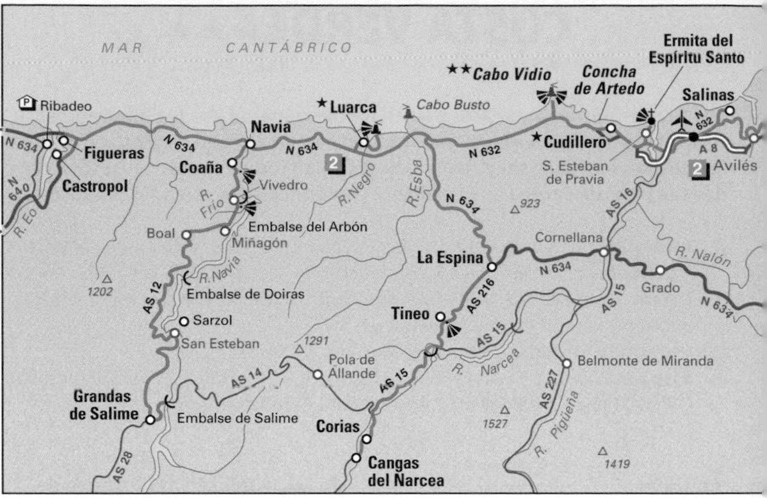

The **Iglesia de San Salvador**, consecrated in 893 and known as *El Conventín* dates from the end of the Asturian period of architecture (8C-10C). The raised nave is abutted by narrow aisles; the capitals of the triumphal arch are decorated with the Asturian cord motif. *Open 11.30am-1.30pm and 4.30-6pm; Nov-Apr, 11.30am-1.30pm. Closed Mon. 98 597 69 55.*

The **monasterio** (monastery) consists of a 13C Cistercian church and cloisters dating from the 15C, 17C and 18C (*guided tours (40min), May-Oct, 11.30am-1.30pm and 4.30-7pm; Nov-Apr, 11.30am-1.30pm and 4-6pm; Sat-Sun and public hols, 11.30am-1.30pm; closed Mon, 1 Jan, Easter and 25 Dec; 1.50 €; 98 589 23 24).*

Gijón

Gijón is a lively city with a population of over 250 000. On **Plaza del Marqués** is the late-17C **Palacio de Revillagigedo**, with an elegant façade. Nearby is the fishermen's quarter, Cimadevilla.

Vestiges of a Roman past, include the **Termas Romanas del Campo Valdés** (Roman baths) in the old quarter (*open 10am-1pm and 5-7pm (8pm Mar-Jun and Sep; 9pm Jul-Aug); Sun and public hols, 11am-2pm. and 5-7pm (8pm Jul-Aug); 2.30 € (3.60 € with Parque Arqueológico de la Campa de Torres); 985 34 51 47).*

The **Torre del Reloj** is also well worth a visit, for its history displays and splendid views (*open Jan-14 Jun 10am-2pm; Holy Week, 15-30 Jun and Sep 10am-2pm and 5-8pm (9pm Jul-Aug); Sun and public hols, 11am-2pm; 985 30 16 82).*

Practical Information

On the first Saturday in August every year, crowds of spectators flock to the area to watch the **Descenso Internacional del Sella**, a kayak race on the Sella river. The com–petition, which starts in Arriondas and ends in Ribadesella, can be followed from a train that runs parallel to the river.

From Gijón to Castropol 2

179km/119mi to the west

Cabo de Peñas★

The road runs through moorland to this cape, the northernmost point in Asturias. From the cliff near the lighthouse, there are fine **views** of the coast.

Salinas

This is a rapidly expanding resort. The rock islet of La Peñona (*footbridge*) affords a **view**★ of the beach, one of the longest on the Costa Verde.

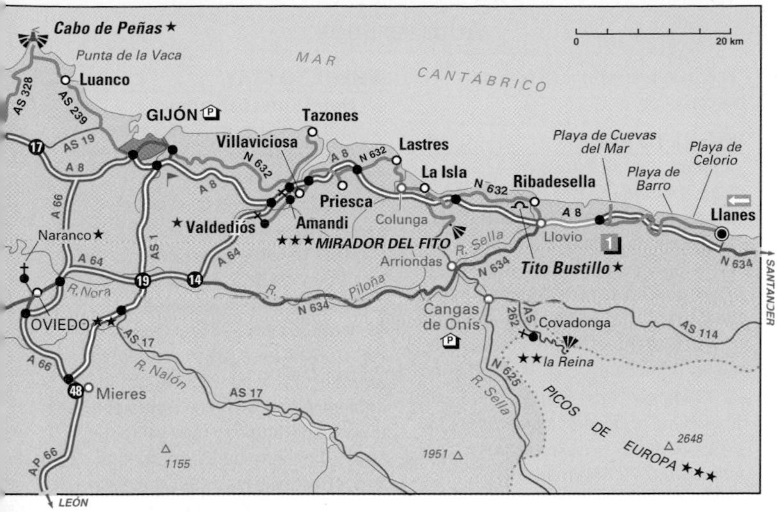

Ermita del Espíritu Santo (Hermitage of the Holy Spirit)

The hermitage commands an extensive **view**★ west along the coastal cliffs.

Cudillero★

The fishing village makes an attractive **picture**★: tall hillside houses, white cottages with brown tiled roofs leading down to the harbour full of boats.

Cabo Vidio★★

Catch the coastal **views**★★ from near the lighthouse on this headland.

Excursion to the Narcea River

91km/57mi to Cangas de Narcea along the N 634 and AS 216, branching S at the Cabo Busto.

Tineo

The town perched 673m/2 208ft up the mountainside commands an immense **panorama**★★ of the sierras.

Corias

Open 10am-12.30pm and 4-7.30pm. *98 581 01 50.*

The 11C **monastery** *(monasterio)*, rebuilt after a 19C fire, was occupied for 800 years by Benedictines. The **church** has ornate Churrigueresque altars.

Return to the coast road (N 632).

Luarca★

Luarca is in a remarkable **site**★ at the mouth of the winding río Negro, spanned by seven bridges. Its white houses have slate roofs. A lighthouse, church and cemetery stand on the headland once occupied by a fort. For an interesting **view**★, take the lighthouse road left, then circle the church to the right and return to the harbour.

Excursion inland along the Navia Valley

82km/51mi along the AS 12 (2hr 30min each way). The River Navia flows along a wild, enclosed valley below several high peaks. The road is winding.

After Coaña, turn right at a sign marked "castro".

Circular foundations and paving remain from a **Celtic village** on a mound. For a striking **panorama**★★ of the **Arbón dam**, pause at the viewpoint. Past Vivedro, there is a **panorama**★★ from a river loop in the foreground to the distant mouth of the Navia.

The **confluence**★★ of the Navia and the Frío is impressive from a giddy height. Beyond Boal, the valley is blocked by the high **Doiras dam.**

Address Book

For coin ranges, see the Legend on the cover flap.

WHERE TO EAT

Sport – *Rivero 9 – Luarca – 98 564 10 78 – Closed Wed (exc. summer and public hols) and Jan –* . This popular bar also has a dining area with a regional flavour, and a more formal area upstairs with views onto the estuary. The location near the fish market guarantees the freshness and quality of the fare.

El Álamo – *Rapalcuarto – 10km/6mi E of Figueras along the N 634 – 98 562 86 49 – www.restauranteela-lamo.com –* . This roadside restaurant is renowned for its traditional cuisine and its copious, reasonably priced lunchtime menu. Eat in the modest dining room, the larger room is for groups.

El Jornu – *Cuetu Molin – Pancar – 1.5km/1mi SW of Llanes – 98 540 16 15 – Closed in Nov.* This popular and often noisy family-run restaurant serves simple but good-quality home cooking mainly based around fish and seafood.

Casa Tista – *Toriello 47 – Toriello – 5km/3mi E of Ribadesella along the AS 263 – 98 586 09 54 –* . This long-standing family-owned restaurant is famous for its excellent fish and seafood. Although prices have gone up here in the past few years, it still represents good value for money.

WHERE TO STAY

Hotel Rural Camangu – *Camangu – 4.5km/3mi E of Camangu – 985 85 76 46 – www.camangu.com – 10 rooms – 5 €.*
This small family-run country hotel in a small village near Ribadesella is an excellent base for excursions into the local countryside. Pleasant decor, good value and a friendly welcome.

Hotel Carlos I – *Plaza Carlos I 1-4 – Villaviciosa – 98 589 01 21 – Closed Jan-Mar – 16 rooms – 4 €.* An 18C nobleman's house in the centre of the town is now home to this family-run hotel. The rooms here are spacious and attractively furnished and offer excellent value given the price. Highly recommended.

Hotel Rural Casa Manoli – *Carretera de Paredes – Almuña – 2km/1.2mi SE of Luarca along the Paredes road, then bear left – 98 547 00 40 – www.hotelluarcarural.com – 13 rooms.* This small family hotel enjoys a peaceful rural setting on the outskirts of Luarca. Pleasant small garden and inexpensive, comfortable rooms.

La Posada de Babel – *La Pereda – 4km/2.5mi S of Llanes – 98 540 25 25 – www.laposadadebabel.com – Open Mar-Oct – – 12 rooms – 7 € – Restaurant 24€.* This small hotel, with its rationalist-inspired architecture, is the perfect place for those seeking peace and quiet. The countryside around this former farm is delightful, and is enhanced by the extensive use of glass.

Grandas de Salime

The **Museo Etnográfico** (museum) in an ex-presbytery traces Asturian life through re-created rooms and artifacts (*open 11.30am-2pm and 4-6.30pm (7.30pm Jul-Sep; closed Mon; 1.50 €, no charge Tue; 985 62 72 43).*
4km/2.5mi away is the **embalse de Salime**. Viewpoints overlook the dam wall and the power station.

Return to Navia, then continue W along the N 634.

From Figueras on the ría Ribadeo you can view **Castropol**, which resembles an Austrian village, with its white-washed main square. Opposite stands Ribadeo, its Galician counterpart (*see RÍAS ALTAS*).

COVARRUBIAS★

POPULATION: 629.

MICHELIN MAP 575 F 19 – CASTILLA Y LEÓN (BURGOS)

This historic Castilian village of half-timbered houses and a Renaissance palace is partly surrounded by medieval ramparts. Covarrubias is the burial place of Fernán González, one of Castilla's great historic figures and the catalyst behind the kingdom's independence.

- **Information:** *Monseñor Vargas, ☎947 40 64 61.*
- **Orient Yourself:** Covarrubias is 40km/25mi SE of Burgos.
- **Organizing Your Time:** The Monasterio de Santo Domingo deserves a visit of several hours.
- **Also See:** BURGOS, PALENCIA (94km/59mi W) and SORIA (117km/73mi SE)

Worth a Visit

Colegiata★

Guided tours (30min), 10.30am-2pm and 4-7pm. Closed Tue. 2€. ☎947 40 63 11.

This Gothic collegiate church contains 20 medieval tombs, including those of Fernán González and the Norwegian Princess Cristina who married the Infante Philip of Castilla in 1258.

Museo-Tesoro (Museum-Treasury) – Note paintings by Pedro Berruguete and Van Eyck. A 15C Flemish **triptych**★; with central relief of the Adoration of the Magi is said to be by Gil de Siloé.

Excursions

Monasterio de Santo Domingo de Silos★★

18km/11mi SE. (35 min) 10am-1pm and 4.30-6pm; Sun-Mon and public hols, 4.30-6pm. Closed 1 Jan, 19 Mar, Maundy Thu, Good Friday, 1 May, 15 Aug, 12 Oct, 1 Nov, and 8 and 20 Dec. 3€, ☎947 39 00 49.

This site, originally Visigothic, was occupied by Benedictine monks from France in 1880. The monastery is renowned for its concerts of Gregorian chants.

Claustro★★★ – The cloisters are among the most beautiful in Spain. The lower galleries have about 60 rounded arches supported by paired columns and, in the middle of each gallery, by a group of five columns. The eight low reliefs on the corner pillars are masterpieces of Romanesque sculpture. The styles of three different sculptors can be seen.

The **capitals**, apart from those which are historiated, illustrate a fantastic bestiary which derives from the Mudéjar use of animal and plant motifs. *The most interesting have been numbered in the description of the galleries that follows.*

Southeast pillar

The Ascension is represented to the left, and Pentecost to the right.

East gallery

(1): strapwork, **(2)**: entwined plants, **(3)**: harpies defended by dogs.

Northeast pillar

This shows the Descent from the Cross and above, the earth and the moon on the point of being clouded over; on the other side is the Entombment and the

WHERE TO STAY

Hotel Tres Coronas de Silos *– Plaza Mayor 6 – Monastery of Santo Domingo de Silos – ☎947 39 00 47 – www.hoteltrescoronasdesilos.com – 16 rooms – 8€.– Restaurant 15.63 €.* A restored 18C noble mansion on the main square houses this pleasant hotel. It is decorated in typical Castilian style with exposed stone walls and plentiful wood, which combine to create a warm and inviting atmosphere.

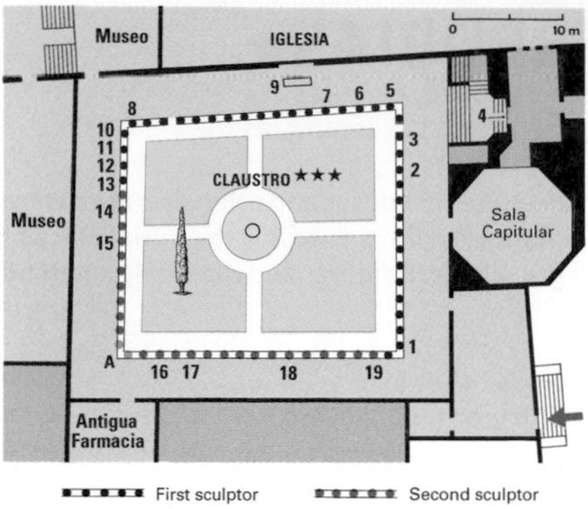

Resurrection as one composition. Opposite the pillar is the fine **Puerta de las Vírgenes** (doorway) **(4)** to the former Romanesque abbey church.

North gallery

(5): entwined plants, **(6)**: the Elders of the Apocalypse, **(7)**: harpies attacked by eagles, **(8)**: birds. The gallery also contains St Dominic's 13C tomb **(9)**: three Romanesque lions bear the saint.

Northwest pillar

This pillar shows Christ on the road to Emmaus and before St Thomas.

West gallery

(10): strapwork, **(11)**: birds with necks entwined, **(12)**: flamingoes, **(13)**: birds and lions ensnared by plant tendrils. The capitals that follow are by the second sculptor. **(14)**: the birth of Jesus, **(15)**: scenes of the Passion. Note the well-preserved 14C *artesonado* ceiling.

Southwest pillar (A)

By the third artist: an Annunciation (the Virgin Mary is crowned by two angels) and on the right a Tree of Jesse.

South gallery

(16) and **(17)**: plant tendrils ensnaring birds and stags, **(18)**: eagles clutching hares, **(19)**: grimacing monsters.

The **museo** (museum) displays an 11C chalice of St Dominic's with filigree decoration, an enamel reliquary, and a 10C-11C manuscript of the Mozarabic rite.

The **Antigua Farmacia** (old pharmacy) contains fine Talavera ceramic jars.

The present **church** (1756-1816) combines the rounded volume of Baroque with Herreran plain grandeur.

Garganta de la Yecla

21km/13mi SE and 3km/2mi SW of Santo Domingo de Silos – 20min. A footpath follows a deep narrow gorge.

Lerma

23km/14mi W along the C 110. Lerma owes its splendour and Classic town plan to the extravagance and corruption of the **Duke of Lerma**, Philip III's early 17C favourite.

The quarter built by the duke retains steep cobbled streets and houses with wood or stone porticoes. The ducal palace, with its austere façade, stands on the spacious **plaza Mayor**★. The **Colegiata** church has a 17C gilded bronze statue by Juan de Arfe of the duke's nephew, Archbishop Cristóbal de Rojas (*open 10am-2pm and 4-7pm (8pm in summer); Sun and public hols 10am-2pm (and 4-7pm in summer);*

Decorative frieze, Iglesia de Quintanilla de las Viñas

closed Mon, 1 Jan, 1 May and 25 and 31 Dec; 3 €; 947 17 70 02).

Quintanilla de las Viñas

24km/15mi N. Take the C 110, the N 234 towards Burgos, then bear right onto a signposted road. The road follows the Arlanza Valley. Below and to the right, are the ruins of the **Monasterio de San Pedro de Arlanza**.

Iglesia de Quintanilla de las Viñas★

To visit, request the key at the town hall (ayuntamiento). 947 39 20 49.

The church – reputedly 7C Visigothic – is of great archaeological interest. Only the apse and transept remain. The frieze depicts bunches of grapes, leaves and birds as well as highly stylised motifs. The foliated scrollwork is repeated inside on the keystones of the triumphal arch.

CUENCA★★

POPULATION: 46 047.

MICHELIN MAP 576 L 23 – CASTILLA-LA MANCHA (CUENCA)

Cuenca's spectacular setting★★ is a rocky platform hemmed in by the Júcar and Huécar ravines *(hoces)* in defiance of the laws of gravity. The magnificently preserved old city is on UNESCO's World Heritage List.

- **Information:** *Plaza de la Hispanidad 2, 902 10 01 31: Plaza Mayor 1, 969 23 21 19*
- **Orient Yourself:** Cuenca lies 164km/102mi east of Madrid in the Montes Universales, on the edge of the central Meseta, amid eroded limestone.
- **Parking:** Follow signs for the *casco antiguo* (old quarter). Cross the plaza Mayor and leave your car in the free car park.
- **Don't Miss:** Hanging houses and vertiginous canyon views.
- **Also See:** *TERUEL (151km/94mi NE*

Special Features

Contemporary Art

Museo de Arte Abstracto Español★★

Open 11am-2pm and 4-6pm (8pm Sat); Sun, 11am-2.30pm. Closed Mon and public hols. 3 €. 969 21 29 83.

The views from the Museum of Abstract Spanish Art are veritable works of art in themselves. The collection includes works by Chillida, Tàpies, Saura, Zóbel, Cuixart, Sempere, Rivera and Millares.

Fundación Antonio Pérez

Open 10am-8pm (11am-8pm Sat-Sun and public hols). 969 23 06 19.

This foundation, in a 17C Carmelite convent, exhibits part of the vast legacy of Antonio Pérez – work by Spanish artists such as Millares and Saura, as well as *objetos encontrados* – objects from daily life recontextualised.

Walking About

CIUDAD ANTIGUA★★ (OLD TOWN) *2hr 30min*

J. Balanya/MICHELIN

The Hanging Houses of Cuenca

From the car park, pass through the 16C Renaissance-style Arco del Bezudo, follow calle San Pedro to the San Pedro church, then turn left onto ronda Julián Romero.

Ronda Julián Romero

This delightful stepped alley runs above the Huécar gorge to the cathedral.

Convento de las Carmelitas

This ex-Carmelite convent houses the Fundación Antonio Pérez and Museo Internacional de Electrografía (*see description under Special Features*).

Catedral★

Open 10.30-1pm and 4-6pm (May-Sep 10am-2pm and 4-7pm); Sun and public hols 10am-6.30pm. 2.80€ (treasury). 969 22 00 96.

The cathedral was started in the 13C in Norman-Gothic style. One of two towers collapsed after an early-20C fire. The interior, a mix of Gothic architecture and Renaissance decoration, has superb wrought-iron chapel **grilles**★, a twin **ambulatory**, a **triforium** and an elegant Plateresque **door**★ into the chapter house with carved walnut panels by Alonso Berruguete.

Walk along the right-hand side of the cathedral and take calle Canónigos.

This street is lined by the Palacio Episcopal, housing the **Museo Diocesano**★, and the **Museo de Cuenca** (*see descriptions under Worth a Visit*).

Casas Colgadas★ (Hanging Houses)

These restored 14C houses contain the **Museo de Arte Abstracto** (*see Special Features*) and a restaurant. The best **view**★ of these gravity-defying buildings can be enjoyed from across the **Puente de San Pablo**, an iron bridge that leads to the Convento de San Pablo, the city's parador. This panorama is enchanting when illuminated.

Return to the cathedral and head along calle José T. Mena.

Address Book

For coin ranges, see the Legend on the cover flap.

WHERE TO EAT

Mesón Mangana – *Plaza Mayor 3 – 969 22 94 51 – Closed 15 Oct-15 Nov.* The perfect spot for a meal when visiting the old quarter. Good home cooking and local specialities, as well as excellent sausages, mature Manchego cheese and grilled meats. The comfortable dining room, with its decor of dark wood, is on the first floor .

Mesón Casas Colgadas – *Canónigos 3 – 969 22 35 09 – www.mesoncasascolgadas.com – Closed Mon evening and Tue –* . A well-known local landmark which is worth eating in for its location alone. As its name suggests, the restaurant is housed in one of the city's famous hanging houses (casas colgadas), with a stupendous view of the Huécar ravine. The cuisine here is a pleasant fusion of modern and traditional.

WHERE TO STAY

Posada Huécar – *Paseo del Huécar 3 – 969 21 42 01 – www.posadahuecar.com – 22 rooms.* Behind the sober, salmon-coloured façade is a pleasant hotel with simply furnished but perfectly adequate rooms, all with TV, and a delightful garden. A good location in the old part of Cuenca.

Posada de San José – *Julián Romero 4 – 969 21 13 00 – www.posadasanjose.com – 29 rooms – 8 €.* This charming inn is in a former 17C seminary. All the rooms are different, although common features include an alcove, terrace and beds with canopies. Simple, elegant and totally peaceful.

FIESTAS

Holy Week processions are considerably enhanced by the site. At dawn on Good Friday the slow ascent to Calvary is enacted along the steep alleys to the accompaniment of drums. A festival of sacred music is also held.

Cuenca	
Alfonso VIII	2
Alonso de Ojeda	5
Andrés de Cabrera	8
Angustias Bajada a las	12
Angustias Pl. de las	15
Carmen Pl. del	20
Colegio San José	25
Fray luis de León	30
Júcar Ronda del	40
Julián Romero Ronda de	43
Mayor Pl.	44
Obispo Valero	45
Pósito	55
Puerta de Valencia	58
San Nicolás Pl.	65
San Pablo Puente de	68
Trabuco	71

Convento de las Carmelitas: Fundación Antonio Pérez	M³
Museo Diocesano	M¹
Museo de Arte Abstracto Español	M
Museo de Cuenca	M²
Museo de la Ciencias de Castilla-la Mancha	M⁴

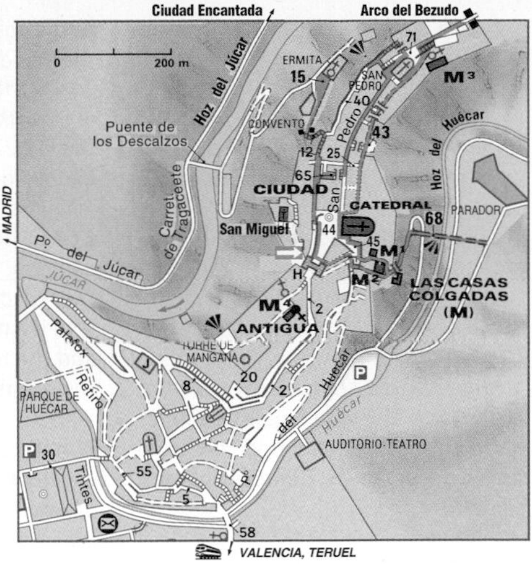

Iglesia de San Miguel

This Gothic-style former church is one of the main venues for Cuenca's Religious Music Week.

Return to the plaza Mayor. Follow calles Severo Catalina and Pilares.

Plaza de las Angustias★

An 18C Franciscan monastery and a Baroque hermitage, the Virgin in Anguish, stand in this quiet square between the town and the ravine.

Return to calle San Pedro and continue to the San Pedro church. Bear left into an alley which ends at the edge of the Júcar ravine, for a good view.

Worth a Visit

Museo Diocesano★

Open 11am-2pm and 4-7pm (Apr-Sep 5-8pm); Sun and public hols, 11am-2pm. Closed Mon. 2 €. 969 22 42 10.

This small museum holds eight **panels**★ of an altarpiece by Juan de Borgoña (c 1510), two El Grecos, a Calvary by Gérard David and exceptional gold and silver plate.

Museo de Cuenca★

Open 10am-2pm and 4-7pm; 16 Jun-15 Sep 9am-2pm and 5-7pm; Sun and public hols, 11am-2pm. Closed Mon. 1.20€, no charge Sat pm and Sun. 969 21 30 69.

This museum displays prehistoric objects, sculpture, coins and ceramics found in Roman excavations. Note the top of a **Roman altar**★ found at Ercávica illustrating ritual items.

Museo de las Ciencias de Castilla-La Mancha

Open 10am-2pm and 4-7pm (8pm May-Sep); Sun, 10am-2pm. Closed Mon, 1 Jan, Maundy Thu, Good Fri and 25 Dec. 1.20 € museum and 1.20 € planetarium. 969 24 03 20.

The science museum is on plaza de la Merced, another charming secret of Cuenca.

Excursions

Las Hoces (Ravines)

Roads parallel to the river circling Cuenca's rock spur afford amazing views of the hanging houses.The **Hoz del Júcar** is the shorter, more enclosed ravine. *Round tour of 15km/9mi.* The **Hoz del Huécar** course swings from side to side between gentler slopes given over to market gardening.

▶ *Turn left at the end of the ravine for Buenache de la Sierra and left again for the Convento de San Jerónimo.*

In a right bend, there's a **view**★ of grey rock columns and, in the distance, of Cuenca. Enter through the gateway.

Las Torcas★

▶ *Take the N 420 then bear left after 11km/6.5mi.* The road crosses a conifer wood where the *torcas*, odd and occasionally spectacular depressions, can be seen.

SERRANÍA DE CUENCA★

270km/168mi – allow 1 day

Wind and water have formed whimsical landscapes in limestone, amid pines and numerous streams.

Ventano del Diablo

25.5km/16mi from Cuenca along the CM 2105. The Devil's Window, an opening in rock, overlooks the depths of the **Garganta del Júcara** (Júcar Gorges).

Ciudad Encantada★

▶ *Follow the road signposted to the right of the CM 2105.* A circuit directs visitors through this Enchanted Forest, to the Tobogán (Toboggan Slope) and the Mar de Piedras (Sea of Stones).

To reach the **Mirador de Uña** *(2km/1mi),* ▶ *take the road from the car park.* Enjoy the **view** of the Júcar Valley dominated by towering cliffs.

Los Callejones

3km/2mi from Las Majadas. Leave your car on the esplanade. This isolated spot is a maze of eroded blocks, arches and the narrow alleyways which lend their name to the area: The Alleyways.

Nacimiento del río Cuervo★ (Source of the Cuervo)

30km/19mi N of Las Majadas towards Alto de la Vega. Leave the car after the bridge and walk up 500m. A footpath leads to **waterfalls**★ at the beginnings of the Cuervo river.

Hoz de Beteta★ (Beteta Ravine)

30km/19mi NW along the CM 2106 and CM 2201 towards Beteta. This impressive ravine was cut by the River Guadiela. From Vadillos, a road to the left leads to the spa of Solán de Cabras. The road (CM 210) continues through the **River Escabas valley**. Before reaching Priego *(3km/2mi)*, a branch to the right leads to the **Convento de San Miguel de las Victorias**, in an impressive **setting**★.

DAROCA★

POPULATION: 2 630.

MICHELIN MAP 574 I 25 – ARAGÓN (ZARAGOZA)

Daroca's battlemented walls★, originally with 100 towers and gateways, lie between two ridges. The Puerta Baja (Lower Gate) is flanked by square towers.

Information: *Plaza de España 7, ☎976 80 01 29*

▶ **Orient Yourself:** Daroca is in eastern Spain at the crossroads of the N 234 and N 330, close to Calatayud (40km/25mi N), Zaragoza (85km/53mi NE) and Teruel (96km/60mi S).

Also See: TERUEL and ZARAGOZA.

Worth a Visit

Colegiata de Santa María

Open noon-1pm and 5.30-7pm; Jun-Sep 11am-1pm and 6-8. Closed Mon. ☎976 80 07 32.

This Romanesque collegiate church, a repository for the holy cloths, was modified in the 15C and 16C. Beside the belfry is a Flamboyant Gothic portal.

The late-Gothic nave includes a Renais-cupola above the transept crossing. The **south chapels** are partly faced with 16C *azulejos*. To the right of the entrance is a 15C **altarpiece**★ in multi-coloured alabaster believed to have been carved in England. The 15C **Capilla de los Corporales**★ (Chapel of the Holy Relics) is on the site of the original Romanesque apse. The altar includes a shrine enclosing the holy altar cloths. Statues in delightful poses are carved of multicoloured alabaster. The painted Gothic **retable**★ is dedicated to St Michael.

Museo Parroquial★ (Parish Museum)

Open 11am-1pm and 5.30-7.30pm; Jun-Sep, noon-1pm and 5.30-6.30pm; Sun and public hols, 11am-1pm and 6-8pm. Closed Mon. 3 €. 976 80 07 61.

Holdings include two rare though damaged 13C panels and **altarpieces** to St Peter (14C) and St Martin (15C), and gold and silver plate mostly of local manufacture, as well as **chasubles**.

The Miracle of the Holy Alter Cloths

The miracle of the holy altar cloths took place in 1239, after the conquest of Valencia, when Christian troops in Daroca, Teruel and Calatayud were setting out to recover territory occupied by the Moors. Just as Mass was being celebrated, the Moors attacked and the priest had to hide the consecrated hosts between two altar cloths. Shortly afterwards, it was seen that the hosts had left bloodstained imprints on the linen. The three towns of Daroca, Teruel and Calatayud all claimed the precious relic. To settle the dispute the holy cloths were placed upon a mule which was then set free. It made straight for Daroca, dying, however, as it entered the Puerta Baja.

Iglesia de San Miguel

This fine church, outstanding for the purity of its Romanesque east end and its 12C portal, is restored to its original design. A short distance below is the restored Mudéjar-style belfry of the **Iglesia de Santo Domingo**.

DONOSTIA-SAN SEBASTIÁN★★

POPULATION: 176 019

MICHELIN MAPS 573 (TOWN PLAN) OR 574 C 23 – 24

SEE PLAN OF COSTA VASCA IN COSTA VASCA – PAÍS VASCO (GUIPÚZCOA)

San Sebastián (Donostia in Basque) is in a glorious setting★★★ on a scallop-shaped bay framed by two hills and the isle of Santa Clara. Two vast sand beaches follow the curve of the bay: La Concha and fashionable Ondarreta. Gardens and promenades and statuary decorate the town, along with the Peine de los Vientos, a sculpture by Eduardo Chillida.

- **Information:** *Reina Regente 8, 943 48 11 66; Fueros 1, 943 02 31 50.*
- **Orient Yourself:** Donostia-San Sebastián is on the Gulf of Vizcaya, 25km/15mi W of the French border, 102km/64mi E of Bilbao .
- **Parking:** Space is limited in the old quarter; walking is preferred.
- **Don't Miss:** A walk in the old quarter, and a fine seafood repast.
- **Organizing Your Time:** Take a day for San Sebastián and drives nearby.
- **Especially for Kids:** The Aquarium.
- **Also See:** COSTA VASCA, BILBAO and PAMPLONA/IRUÑA.

Background

The pioneer of tourism – Queen María Cristina of Habsburg chose Donostia-San Sebastián as her summer residence in the 19C, establishing it as a leading resort.

A gastronomic capital – The all-male members of 30 gourmet clubs prepare excellent meals which they consume with cider or *txacolí* wine. Specialities include hake, cod, bream and sardines and squid (*chipirones*).

Worth a Visit

Old Town

The narrow streets of the old town (rebuilt after an 1813 fire) contrast the wide avenues of modern Donostia. The area comes alive at the apéritif hour when locals and tourists (especially the

Address Book

For coin ranges, see the Legend on the cover flap.

WHERE TO EAT

⊖ **José Mari** – *Fermín Calbetón 5 – ☎ 943 42 46 45 – Closed Tue and two weeks in Oct.* For the past 10 years and more this bar-restaurant has been serving a huge variety of tapas and sandwiches. The restaurant on the first floor has an excellent menu of local dishes.

⊖⊖ **Bodegón Alejandro** – *Fermín Calbetón 4 – ☎943 42 71 58 – www.martinberasategui.com – Closed Sun evening, Mon, and Christmas week –* ▤. As befits a restaurant owned by the famous chef Martín Berasategui, the Alejandro serves excellent cuisine at surprisingly reasonable prices. Although there's just a single daily menu, the choice is quite varied. Its excellent location in the old town is an added bonus.

TAPAS

Ganbara – *San Jerónimo 21 – ☎ 943 42 25 75 – Closed Sun evening, Mon, 15-30 Jun and 15-30 Nov –* ▤. This famous tapas bar behind the plaza de la Constitución is always full of customers here to enjoy the excellent selection on offer. The cosy restaurant in the basement is also recommended.

Txepetxa – *Pescadería 5 – ☎943 42 22 27 – Closed Mon, two weeks in Jun and two weeks in Oct –* ▤. This traditional bar in the old town is worthy of its fine local reputation, particularly for its delicious anchovies, which are served in a variety of ways. The numerous prizes it has won go some way to explain its slightly high prices.

WHERE TO STAY

⊖ **Pensión Aida** – *Iztueta 9 – ☎34 943 32 78 00 – www.pensionesconencanto.com –* ☕ *3€.* You'll find surprising comfort in this pensión, Just minutes from the old town and Kursaal. Its rooms, most with balcony and a degree of enchantment, are adequately furnished. Free Internet.

⊖⊖ **Pensión Donostiarra** – *San Martín 6 1º – ☎943 42 61 67 – www.pensiondonostiarra.com – 16 rooms.* The Donostiarra, one of the city's classic addresses, has recently benefited from a facelift. Close to the new cathedral, it occupies the first floor of an early-20C building, with comfortable rooms decorated with parquet flooring, simple furniture and modern bathrooms.

⊖⊖ **Hotel Niza** – *Zubieta 56 – ☎ 943 42 66 63 – www.hotelniza.com –* 🅿 *– 41 rooms –* ☕ *9.50 €.* This elegant hotel belonging to the Chillida family opened its doors in the 1920s and has remained a Donostia-San Sebastián institution. An unbeatable location overlooking the bay and beach. Homey decoration, renovated bathrooms.

FIESTAS AND FESTIVALS

Donostia-San Sebastián's summer calendar includes the **Semana Grande** fiesta (August), an international jazz festival, Basque folklore festivals, golf and tennis tournaments, as well as horse racing and regattas.

The annual **International Film Festival** (September) is held in the new conference centre (Kursaal) designed by Rafael Moneo.

French) crowd the bars and small restaurants in the *calles* Portu, Muñoa, 31 de Agosto and Fermín Calbetón to enjoy tapas and the excellent seafood.

Plaza de la Constitución

Numbered balconies were once ringside seats for bullfights in the square.

Iglesia de Santa María

Open 9am-2pm and 5-8pm. ☎943 42 31 24.

The church has an exuberant late-18C portal and Baroque altars in a vast interior.

Museo de San Telmo

Open 10.30am-1.30pm and 4-7.30pm; April, 10.30-8pm; Sun and public hols, 10.30am-2pm. Closed Mon, 1 and 6 Jan, 1 May and 25 Dec. ☎943 48 15 80.

The museum is in a 16C monastery. The Renaissance cloisters hold Basque stone funerary crosses from the 15C-17C carved in traditional Iberian style. The upper gallery is the ethnographic section, with a reconstructed Basque interior. Paintings include a Ribera, an El Greco, and 19C artists. The chapel was decorated by **José María Sert** with scenes from the city's history.

Paseo Nuevo (Pasealekua Berria)

This promenade almost circles Monte Urgull and affords good **views** of the open sea, the bay, and fishing port.

Panoramic Views

Monte Igueldo★★★: *For access by car, follow the Concha and Ondarreta beaches and then bear left; also accessible by funicular. Open Nov-Mar, 11am-6pm (8pm Sat-Sun and public hols); Apr-Jun, 11am-8pm; Jul-Sep, 10am-10pm. Closed Wed (in winter). 1.70€ (round trip). ☎943 21 05 64.*

At the top are an amusement park, hotel and restaurant. There is also a splendid **panorama** of the sea, the harbour with Santa Clara island and Donostia-San Sebastián itself, set within a mountain cirque. The view is beautiful in the evening when the town lights up.

Monte Urgull★★: this hill, now a public park, is crowned by a fortress, the **Castillo de Santa Cruz de la Mota**. From the summit there is a good **panorama** of the monuments of the old town directly below and the Bahía de la Concha.

Aquarium San Sebastián★

Open 10am-7pm (8pm Apr-June, 9pm Jul-Aug). Closed 1 Jan and 25 Dec. 10 €. ☎943 44 00 99.

The oceanographic museum contains interesting models, but the aquarium, one of the best in Europe, is the main feature. Visitors can touch harmless species of fish. Cameras observe the under-

E. Baret/MICHELIN

La Concha Bay

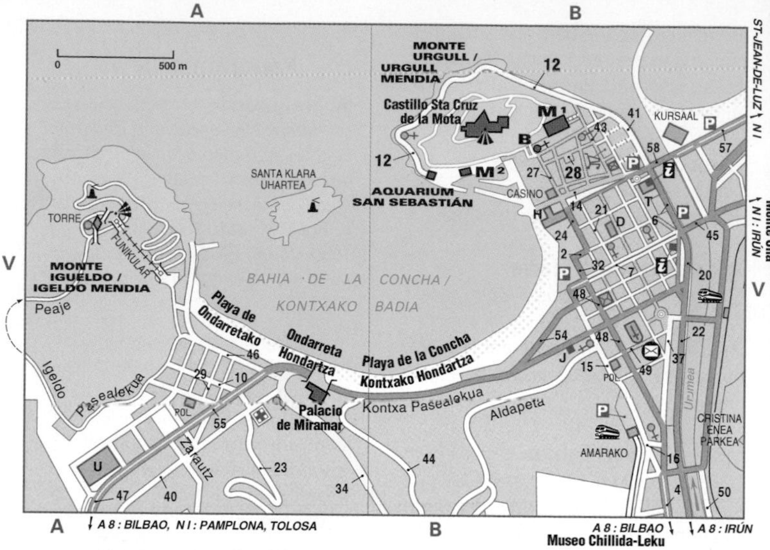

Donostia – San Sebastián

Andía	BV	2
Antso Jakitunaren Hiribidea	BV	4
Argentinako Errepublikaren Pas.	BV	6
Askatasunaren Hiribidea	BV	7
Beatriz Infantaren	AV	10
Berria Pas.	BV	12
Bulelar Zumardia	BV	14
Easo	BV	15
Ehunurteurrenaren Pl.	BV	16
Foruen Pas.	BV	20
Garibai	BV	21
Gernikako Arbolaren Pas.	BV	22
Heriz Pas.	AV	23
Hernani	BV	24
Kale Nagusia	BV	27
Konstituzio Pl.	BV	28
Kristina Infantaren	AV	29
Miramar	BV	32
Pio Baroja Pas.	AV	34
Prim	BV	37
Resurreccion Maria Azkue	AV	40
Salamanca Pas.	BV	41
San Juan	BV	43
Sanserreka Pas.	BV	44
Santa Katalina Zubia	BV	45
Satrustegi Hiribidea	AV	46
Tolosa Hiribidea	AV	47
Urbieta	BV	48
Urdaneta	BV	49
Urumea Pas.	BV	50
Zubieta	BV	54
Zumalakarregi Hiribidea	AV	55
Zurriola Pas.	BV	57
Zurriola Zubia	BV	58

Iglesia de Santa María	BV	B
Museo Naval	BV	M^2
Museo de San Telmo	BV	M^1

water life of the very smallest fish. Visitors can cross the **Oceanarium**★ in a tunnel with 360° views.

Museo Naval

Open 10am-1.30pm and 4-7.30pm; Sun, 11am-2pm. Closed Mon and public hols. 1.20 €, no charge Thu. 943 43 00 51.

This plain 18C consular building houses the naval museum, showing traditional tools and materials, models and navigational instruments, with a slant toward Basque naval history.

Excursions

View from Monte Ulía★

7km/4mi E. Follow the N 1 towards Irún and take a right before the summit.

The twisting drive up affords good **views** of the town and its setting.

Museu Chillida-Leku

6km/4mi S. Exit the N I, then take the GI 2132 from Rekalde towards Hernani and follow the signposts. Open 10.30am-3pm; July-August to 8pm (to 3pm Sun and public hols). Closed Tue (except Jul-Aug), 1 Jan and 25 Dec. 8 €. 943 33 60 06.

By creating this **museum**, Eduardo Chillida (1924-2002), native son and one of the great contemporary sculptors, realised his dream of an open site where visitors could wander among his works. The 12ha/29-acre estate is the setting for 40 large sculptures integrated into the landscape. Smaller sculptures and works on paper are shown in the 16C Zabalaga country house.

MONASTERIO DE EL ESCORIAL★★★

MICHELIN MAPS 575 OR 576 K 17 – MADRID

This symbolic building on the slopes of the Sierra de Guadarrama, commissioned by Philip II and designed by Juan de Herrera, heralded a style that combined the grandeur of a palace with the austerity of a committed monastery.

- **Information:** *Grimaldi 2, San Lorenzo de El Escorial, ☎91 890 53 13*
- **Orient Yourself:** El Escorial is 56km/40mi NW of Madrid, at 1 065m/3 494ft.
- **Don't Miss:** The sumptuous royal apartments.
- **Organizing Your Time:** El Escorial is a day trip from Madrid, often paired with El Valle de los Caídos (Valley of the Fallen).
- **Also See:** MADRID (49km/30mi SE), SEGOVIA (52km/32mi N), Sierra de GUADARRAMA (to the N) and Ávila (64km/40mi W).

Background

In memory of San Lorenzo – On 10 August 1557, St Lawrence's Day, Philip II defeated the French at St-Quentin. The king decided to dedicate a monastery to the saint, to serve as royal palace and pantheon. The stupendous project – nearly 1 200 doors and 2 600 windows; 1 500 workmen – was completed in only 21 years (1563-84) which explains the exceptional unity of style.
The general designs of Juan de Toledo were followed after his death in 1567 by **Juan de Herrera**. In reaction to the excess ornamentation of Charles V's reign, the architects produce a sober monument with clean, majestic lines.

There is a good **view**★ of the monastery and countryside from **Silla de Felipe II** (Philip II's Seat), from where the king oversaw construction (▶ *turn left after the monastery into the road marked Entrada Herrería-Golf).*

Special Features

Monastery *allow half a day*

Open 10am-5pm (6pm Apr-Sep); last admission 1hr before closing. Closed Mon, 1 and 6 Jan, 1 May, 10 Aug,14 Sep, and 8, 24-25 and 31 Dec. 8 €, no charge Wed for E. U. citizens. ☎91 890 78 18.
It is said that the monastery's gridiron plan recalls St Lawrence's martyrdom. It measures 206m x 161m (676ft x 528ft). The austerity of its grey granite empha-

Monasterio de El Escorial

TURESPAÑA

Fiestas

The feast day of San Lorenzo (St Lawrence), the patron saint of the village and monastery, is celebrated on 10 August every year.

sises the severity of the architecture. When the king commanded an increase in height, Herrera positioned windows asymmetrically to lessen monotony.

Palacios★★ (Royal Apartments)

While the Habsburgs remained on the Spanish throne, El Escorial was a place of splendour: the king resided in apartments encircling the church apse. The Bourbons preferred other palaces but when in residence, occupied suites on the north side of the church. The palace took on renewed glory in the 18C in the reigns of Charles III and IV.

A staircase built in the time of Charles IV goes up *(3rd floor)* to the **Palacio de los Borbones** (Bourbon Apartments), sumptuous with Pompeian ceilings and fine **tapestries**★, many from the Real Fábrica (Royal Tapestry Works) in Madrid based on cartoons by Spanish artists, notably Goya. Elsewhere are Flemish tapestries.

The large **Sala de las Batallas** (Battle Gallery) contains frescoes (1587): the Victory at Higueruela in the 15C against the Moors and on the north wall, the Victory at St-Quentin.

The restraint of the **habitaciones de Felipe II** (Philip II's apartments, *2nd floor*) is striking in comparison with the Bourbon rooms. Those of the Infanta Isabel Clara Eugenia comprise a suite of small rooms with dados of Talavera ceramic tiles. The king's bedroom is off the church. When he was dying of gangrene in 1598, he could contemplate the high altar from his bed. The paintings in the apartments include a *St Christopher* by Patinir and a portrait of the king in old age by Pantoja de la Cruz. Facing the gardens and the plain, the Salón del Trono (Throne Room) is hung with 16C Brussels tapestries. The Sala de los Retratos (Portrait Gallery), which follows, holds royal portraits.

Panteones★★ (Pantheons)

Access through the Patio de los Evangelistas (Evangelists' Courtyard), with frescoes by Tibaldi and his followers.

A marble and jasper staircase leads down to the **Panteón de los Reyes**★★★ (Royal Pantheon) and the remains of monarchs from the time of Charles V, with the exception of Philip V, Ferdinand VI and Amadeus of Savoy.

The octagonal chapel was begun in 1617 under Philip III and completed in 1654. Facing the door is the jasper altar; on either side stand 26 marble and bronze sarcophagi in wall niches. The kings are on the left and the queens whose sons succeeded to the throne, on the right. The ornate chandelier is the work of an Italian artist.

The 19C **Panteón de los Infantes**★ (Infantes' Pantheon) includes princes and princesses and queens whose children did not rule. The sculptures are delicately carved. Conditions are such that the room is well preserved.

Salas Capitulares★ (Chapter houses)

Two fine rooms, with ceilings painted by Italian artists with grotesques and frescoes, form a museum of 16-17C Spanish and Italian religious painting.

The first room contains canvases by El Greco and Ribera, a *St Jerome* by Titian, and *Joseph's Tunic* by Velázquez. The second room has works from the 16C Venetian School, including paintings by Tintoretto, Veronese and Titian *(Ecce Homo)*. A room at the back contains works by Bosch and his followers: the imaginative *Haywain* and the satirical *Crown of Thorns (Los Improperios)*.

Basílica★★

Herrera based his final plan on Italian drawings. He introduced the **flat vault**, in the atrium. The interior owes much to St Peter's in Rome with a Greek cross plan, a 92m/302ft high cupola above the transept crossing supported by four colossal pillars, and transept barrel vaulting. The frescoes in the nave vaulting were painted by Luca Giordano in Charles II's reign. Red marble steps lead to the sanctuary which has paintings on the vaulting of the lives of Christ and the Virgin by Cambiasso. The massive **retable**, designed by Herrera, is 30m/100ft tall and is composed of four registers of jasper, onyx and red marble columns between which stand 15 bronze sculptures by Leone and Pompeo Leoni. The tabernacle is also by Herrera. On either side of the chancel are the royal mausoleums with funerary figures at prayer by Pompeo Leoni. In the first chapel off the north aisle is the *Martyrdom of St Maurice* by Rómulo Cincinato, which Philip II preferred to that of El Greco (*see below*). In the adjoining chapel is a magnificent sculpture of Christ by Benvenuto Cellini.

Patio de los Reyes (Kings' Courtyard)

One of the three Classical gateways opens onto this courtyard, named for the statues of the kings of Judea on the west front of the church.

Biblioteca★★ (Library)

2nd floor. The shelving, designed by Herrera, is of exotic woods; the ceiling, sumptuously painted by Tibaldi, represents the liberal arts with Philosophy and Theology at each end. There are also magnificent portraits of Charles V, Philip II and Philip III by Pantoja de la Cruz, and one of Charles II by Carreño. Philip II furnished the library with over 10 000 books, many of them lost in a 1671 fire set by Napoleon's army. It is now a public library with over 40 000 books and historic manuscripts. The spines face inward for preservation purposes.

Nuevos Museos★★ (New Museums)

Paintings in the **Museo de Pintura** are on religious themes.

First room: canvases from the 16C Venetian School (Titian, Veronese and Tintoretto). Second room: two works by Van Dyck and a small painting by Rubens. Third room: works by Miguel de Coxcie, Philip II's Court Painter. Fourth room: Rogier Van der Weyden's sober and expressive *Calvary*, flanked by an *Annunciation* by Veronese and a *Nativity* by Tintoretto. Fifth room: canvases by Ribera including *St Jerome Penitent*, the *Chrysippus* and *Aesop*, with vividly portrayed faces, and Zurbarán's *St Peter of Alcántara* and the *Presentation of the Virgin*. Last room: paintings by Alonso Cano and Luca Giordano.

On the ground floor, paintings include El Greco's *Martyrdom of St Maurice and the Theban Legionary*★, commissioned by Philip II but rejected by him. Nevertheless, it is now considered one of El Greco's greater works.

Other Royal Buildings

Casita del Príncipe★ (Prince's or Lower Pavilion)

SE along the station road. Under repair. Visits by arrangement on 91 890 59 02/3. Closed Mon. 3.60 €.

Charles III commissioned Juan de Villanueva to build a lodge for the future Charles IV. Its exquisite decoration makes it a jewel of a palace in miniature. There are painted **Pompeian-style ceilings**★ by Maella and Vicente Gómez, silk hangings, canvases by Luca Giordano, chandeliers, and a beautiful mahogany and marble dining room.

Casita del Infante (Infante's or Upper Pavilion)

3km/2mi SW beyond the golf course. Open Jul-Sep 10am-6.45pm; Abr-Jun Sat-Sun and public hols 10am-1pm and 4-6.30pm. Closed Mon (Apr-Sep) and Tue-Fri (Apr-Jun). 3.40 €, no charge Wed for E.U. citizens. 91 890 59 03.

This lodge was designed by Villanueva for the Infante Gabriel, Charles IV's younger brother. The interior is furnished in period style; the first floor was used by Prince Juan Carlos before his accession to the throne.

Excursions

Valle de los Caídos★★

16km/10mi NW on the M 600 and M 527. Open 10am-5.30pm (6.30pm Apr-Sep); last admission 30min before closing. Closed Mon, 1 and 6 Jan, 1 May, 17 Jul, 10 Aug and 24-25 and 31 Dec. 5 € (8.50 € combined with El Escorial), no charge Wed for E. U. citizens. 91 890 56 11.

The Valley of the Fallen is a striking monument to the dead of the Spanish Civil War (1936-39).

Basílica★★

The basilica is hollowed out of the rock face and dominated by a monumental Cross. Its west door is a bronze work crowned by a *Pietà* by Juan de Ávalos. At the entrance to the vast interior is a fine wrought-iron screen with 40 statues of Spanish saints and soldiers. The 262m/860ft nave is lined with chapels between which are hung eight copies of 16C Brussels tapestries of the Apocalypse. Above the chapel entrances are alabaster copies of the most famous statues of the Virgin Mary in Spain. A **cupola**★, 42m/138ft in diameter, above the crossing, shows in mosaic the heroes, martyrs and saints of Spain approaching both Christ in Majesty and the Virgin Mary. On the altar stands a painted figure of Christ Crucified, the work of Beovides. At the foot of the altar are the remains of Falangist Party founder José Antonio Primo de Rivera and Francisco Franco. Ossuaries hold remains of 40 000 soldiers and civilians from both sides.

La Cruz★

The Cross is 125m/410ft high (150m /492ft including the base), the width 46m/150ft. The immense statues of the Evangelists around the plinth and the four cardinal virtues above are by Juan de Ávalos. There is a good **view** from the base *(access by funicular)*.

ESTELLA/LIZARRA★★

POPULATION: 13 569.

MICHELIN MAP 573 D 23 – NAVARRA

The brick and rough stone façades remind us that Estella (Lizarra in Basque) was the 12C capital of the kings of Navarra and the 19C base of the Carlists. It is also an important staging post on the Way of St James.

- **Information:** *San Nicolás 1, ☎948 55 40 11.*
- **Orient Yourself:** Estella lies in NE Spain near the Pyrenees on the slopes of the Sierra de Andía, along the N 111 linking Pamplona and Logroño (48km/30mi SW).
- **Organizing Your Time:** See the Palace and churches, but allow time for aimless wandering in this old town.
- **Also See:** *OLITE (44km/27mi SE), PAMPLONA (45km/28mil NE), The WAY OF ST JAMES and La RIOJA.*

Walking About

Plaza de San Martín

The once-bustling small square was originally the heart of the freemen's parish. On one side is the **former Ayuntamiento** (town hall) dating from the 16C.

Palacio de los Reyes de Navarra★ (Palace of the kings of Navarra)

This rare 12C Romanesque civil building is punctuated by arcades and twin bays with remarkable capitals.

Iglesia de San Pedro de la Rúa

Guided tours (30min), 6.30-7pm; Sat 7.30-8pm (Jun-Oct 7.30-8pm); Sun and public hols, 11am-noon. Closed 1 and 6 Jan and 25 Dec. 2.30 € (4 € with Iglesia de San Miguel). ☎948 55 00 70.

The church stands facing the royal palace on a cliff spur formerly crowned by the city castle. It retains outstanding 12C and 13C features.

The unusual **doorway**★ at the top of a steep stairway in the north wall has an equilateral scalloped arch, Caliphate influenced. Similar portals can be seen in Navarra and in the Saintonge and Poitou regions of France. Inside note

Estella La Bella

Such was the name pilgrims gave the town in the Middle Ages on their way to Santiago. As Estella was a major halt on the pilgrim road, it was endowed with several artistic buildings which date mainly from the Romanesque period. Moreover, in 1076, King Sancho Ramírez granted the town certain privileges which attracted tradesmen and innkeepers most of whom were freemen who settled on the right bank of the Ega.

Pilgrims stopped to venerate Our Lady on the Hill whose shrine, now a modern church, stands on the site on which, according to tradition, on 25 May 1085, shepherds, guided by a shower of stars, found a statue of the Virgin. Of the town's many medieval hospices, the leper hospital of St Lazarus became the most famous.

the transitional Romanesque Virgin and Child, a Gothic Christ and an unusual column of intertwined serpents in the central apse, and a Romanesque Crucified Christ in the apse on the left.

The Romanesque **cloisters** lost two galleries when the nearby castle was blown up in the 16C. The skill and invention of the masons are evident in the remaining **capitals**★★; the north gallery series illustrates scenes from the lives of Christ, St Lawrence, St Andrew and St Peter, while plant and animal themes enliven the west gallery.

Calle de la Rúa

The pilgrim road. Note the emblazoned Plateresque façade of the **Palacio de Fray Diego de Estella**, at no 7.

Iglesia del Santo Sepulcro (Church of the Holy Sepulchre)

The portal is purely Gothic. Superimposed above are the Last Supper, the three Marys at the Holy Sepulchre and Hell, and Calvary. The niches contain somewhat mannered figures of saints.

▶ *Take the Puente de la Cárcel (rebuilt in 1973) across the river.*

Iglesia de San Miguel

The church dominates a quarter that retains narrow streets and a medieval atmosphere. On the tympanum of the north **portal**★ is a figure of Christ surrounded by the Evangelists and mysterious personages. The covings are full of sculptures. The capitals illustrate the childhood of Christ. On the upper register of the walls are eight statue columns of the Apostles; on the lower register, two **high reliefs**★★, accomplished and expressive, show St Michael slaying the dragon (left) and the three Marys coming from the Sepulchre. The noble bearing, the elegant drapery and the facial expressions, make the carving a Romanesque masterpiece.

Excursions

Monasterio de Irache★

3km/2mi SW. Open 9.30am-1.30pm and 5-7pm; Jan-Mar 10am-1.30pm and 4-6pm. Closed Mon, Tue (afternoon) and in Dec. ☎948 55 44 64.

A Benedictine abbey occupied the site in the 10C. Later, this was a major pilgrimage halt and a Cistercian community before becoming a university under the Benedictines, in the 16C.

Iglesia★

This 12C-13C church's apse is purely Romanesque with rib-vaulted nave. The dome on squinches and the *coro alto* are Renaissance; the façade and most of the structures were rebuilt in the 17C.

Claustro

Brackets and capitals illustrate the lives of Christ and St Benedict.

Tour through the Sierra de Andía and Sierra de Urbasa★

94km/58mi – about 3hr.

▶ *Leave Estella on NA 120 north towards the Puerto (pass) de Lizarraga.* The road crosses *beechwoods and rises to a pass that affords extensive views.*

Monasterio de Iranzu

9km/6mi N of Estella. Signposted from NA 120. Open 10am-2pm and 4-6pm (8pm May-Sep). Closed Mon, 20 Dec-10 Jan. 2.40 €. 948 52 00 47.

The 12C Cistercian monastery, isolated in a wild **gorge**★, is now a college. It is a good example of the Cistercian transitional style from Romanesque to Gothic combining robustness and elegance.

The cloister bays, where not been given a later florid Gothic fenestration, have Romanesque blind arcades, oculi and wide relieving arches. The church, with primitive vaulting, has a flat east end decorated with three windows, symbolising the Trinity, a common Cistercian feature.

Puerto de Lizarraga road★★

Once out of the tunnel (alt 1 090m/3 576ft) pause at the **viewpoint**★ overlooking the Ergoyena Valley before the descent through woods and pastures.

Continue to Etxarri-Aranatz; take N 240 W to Olatzi; turn left to Estella.

Puerto de Urbasa road★★

The road climbs steeply between great boulders and clumps of trees. Beyond the pass (alt 927m/3 041ft) tall limestone cliffs add character to the landscape before the road enters the gorges of the sparkling river Urenderra.

FIGUERES★

POPULATION: 35 301.

MICHELIN MAP 574 F 38 – MAP 122 COSTA TBRAVA –
SEE LOCAL MAP UNDER COSTA BRAVA – CATALUNYA (GIRONA)

Figueres, capital of Alt Empordà, the birthplace of Surrealist artist Salvador Dalí (1904-89), is one of Catalunya's premier destinations. Dalí spent his last years here, building his extravagant museum.

- **Information:** *Plaça del Sol, 972 50 31 55.*
- **Orient Yourself:** Figueres is located 20km/12mi inland, at the heart of the area known as the Ampurdán, at the crossroads of routes leading to the Costa Brava and the French city of Perpignan, 58km/36mi N.
- **Don't Miss:** Everything Dalí: the Museum and Tower
- **Organizing Your Time:** Take a half-day at least, or longer if your world is Dalí's.
- **Also See:** GIRONA/GERONA (42km/26mi S), COSTA BRAVA and PIRINEOS CATALANES.

History

The end of the Spanish Civil War – The last meeting of the Rebublican Cortes was held here on 1 February 1939. Three days later, Girona fell to the Nationalists. Two days after, the Republican leaders crossed into France.

Special Features

The Dalian World

Salvador Dalí and Surrealism – Born in 1904, Dalí was to become one of most famous Surrealist aritists. His "paranoid-critical" method, based on an ironic vision of reality, resulted in his expulsion from the Surrealist ranks by its founder, André Breton. In his most famous paintings, *The Great Masturbator, The Persistence of Memory, Atomic Leda and Premonition of the Civil War,*

Address Book

For coin ranges, see the Legend on the cover flap.

WHERE TO EAT

Mas Pau – *Avinyonet de Puigventós – 5km/3mi SW of Figueres on the N 260 – ☎972 54 61 54 – www.maspau.com – Closed 6 Jan-15 Mar, Sun evenings (winter), Mon, Tue lunchtime –* . A 16C farmstead sympathetically restored and decorated in exquisite taste with numerous antiques. A lovely locale in which to discover updated Catalan cuisine. Cosy terraces by the garden, and superb rooms are also available.

WHERE TO STAY

Hotel Duràn – *Lasauca 5 – ☎972 50 12 50 – www.hotelduran.com – – 65 rooms – 8.50 € – Restaurant 17/45 €.* This recently updated hotel is in the town centre near the Dalí Museum, with large, comfortable rooms. The restaurant, specialisin in Catalan dishes, is where Dalí himself used to dine.

Hotel Mas Falgarona – *Avinyonet de Puigventós – 44.5km/3.5mi SW of Figueres on the N 260 – ☎972 54 66 28 – www.masfalgarona.com – Closed Jan – P – 11 rooms – – Restaurant 43 €.* This luxury hotel is housed in an old farmhouse. The minimalist decor, enhanced by various works of modern art, brings out the natural beauty of the stone, brick and wood. Delightful garden with pool.

Dalí expresses his personal world through bland forms loaded with sensuality and sexual connotations.

The Dalian attractions in Figueres are both located around the lively plaza de Dalí i Gala.

Teatre-Museu Dalí★★

Open 2 Jan- Jun and Oct-Dec, 10.30am-5.45pm; Jul-Sep, 9am-7.45pm (Aug also 10pm-1am); last admission 30min before closing. Closed 1 Jan and 25 Dec. 10 €. ☎972 67 75 00.

TURESPAÑA

Torre Galatea and Teatre-Museu Dalí

Dalí in the Area Around Figures

Further examples of Dalí's creativity can be seen in two museums within a short distance of Figueres: the first, the **Casa-Museo Salvador Dalí★**, is situated in the charming fishing village of **Cadaqués★★** (see COSTA BRAVA), 31km/19mi E of Figueres on the C 260 and GI 614; the second, the **Casa-Museo Castell Gala Dalía** (see GIRONA/GERONA), in Púbol, 16km/10mi E of Girona on the C 66, is housed in the castle that Dalí gave to his wife, Gala, as a gift in 1970.

The theatre-museum, a world of folly and caprice, may charm or exasperate but never fails to impress. The artist himself said: "The museum cannot be considered as such; it is a gigantic surrealist object, where everything is coherent, where nothing has eluded my design." To a restored 1850 theatre Dalí added an immense glass dome (beneath which he is buried) and patio, and decorated everything with fantasy objects: giant eggs, bread rolls, basins and gilt dummies. He gave his eccentricity full rein in the squares around the museum where figures perch on columns of tyres, as well as inside. Some of his canvases are exhibited as well as works by Pitxot and Duchamp.

Torre Galatea★

The decoration of this tower by Dalí used vivid colours and fantasy objects.

Worth a Visit

OLD TOWN

Figueres also has a pleasant historical centre with attractive squares and alleys. The Rambla is a pleasant street full of outdoor bars and restaurants,

Museu de Joguets★

Open 10am-1pm and 4-7pm; Sun and public hols 11am-1.30pm and 5-7.30pm. Closed Sun and holiday afternoons in summer; Mon Oct-May (except public hols), 1 Jan and 25 Dec. 5 €. 972 50 45 85.

The museum displays toys and stuffed animals from different countries.

Museu de l'Empordà

Open 11am-7pm (8pm Sep-Dec); Sun and public hols, 11am-2pm. Closed Mon, 1 Jan and 25-26 Dec. 3 €. 972 50 23 05.

This building houses collections devoted to the art, history and archaeology of the region. Of note is the exhibition of works by 19C and 20C painters (Nonell, Sorolla, Dalí and Tàpies).

Iglesia de Sant Pere

Open 9am-1pm and 4.30-8pm (9pm Sat); Sun 8.30am-1pm and 6-9pm. Closed Mon, 1 and 6 Jan and 25-26 Dec. 2€; no charge 18 May. 972 50 03 25.

Built in the late 13C, this church has a single nave of Gothic influence. Most of the church was rebuilt after the Spanish Civil War.

Excursions

Castillo de San Ferran★

Guided tours (2hr), 10.30am-2pm and 4-6pm; 1 Jul-16 Sep and Holy Week, 10.30am-8pm. Closed 1 Jan and 25 Dec. 3 €. 972 50 60 94.

This mid-18C fortress, with star-shaped perimeter, defended the border with France. The castle was the second largest of its kind in Europe, with a parade ground alone that covered 12 000m2/14 340sq yd. The **stables★** are worthy of particular note. The **views★** from the walls take in the Empordà plain.

GIBRALTAR★

POPULATION: 28 339.
MICHELIN MAPS 578 X 13. BRITISH CROWN COLONY

One of the last outposts of the British Empire and a self-governing Crown Colony, the towering bulk of Gibraltar is impressive and distinctive, visible for miles. For many visitors, the first contact with Gibraltar is likely to be the incredible landing strip, crossed by the main road into town.

- **Information:** *158 Main Street, ☎350 74950 (9567 749 50 from Spain); www.gibraltar.gov.gi; tourism@gibraltar.gi.*
- **Orient Yourself:** Gibraltar lies at the southwest tip of Spain only 24km/15mi from North Africa.
- **Parking:** Can be tight in town.
- **Don't Miss:** The Top of the Rock
- **Organizing Your Time:** Take a morning drive from Spain.
- **Especially for Kids:** The Den of the Barbary Apes.
- **Also See:** COSTA DE LA LUZ, COSTA DEL SOL and MÁLAGA

History

Historical notes – Archaeological discoveries on Gibraltar testify to 100 000 years of human occupation, by Carthaginians, Phoenicians and even Neanderthal Man.

The Rock of Gibraltar, considered by the Ancient Greeks to be one of the **Pillars of Hercules**, was transformed into an Islamic citadel after the Moors invaded under **Tarik-ibn-Zeyad** in AD 711. Jebel Tarik (Tarik's Mountain, hence Gibraltar) was the site of a castle, now in ruins but still known as the Moorish Castle.

Gibraltar was recaptured by Spain on 20 August 1462. During the War of Spanish Succession, Anglo-Dutch naval forces, under **Admiral Rooke**, captured the Rock in 1704. Gibraltar was ceded to Britain in the Treaty of Utrecht in 1713. The citadel guarding the Straits of Gibraltar has remained in British hands ever since. In the **Great Siege of 1779-83**, the garrison heroically resisted Spanish and French efforts to starve or bomb them into submission. The old city of Gibraltar was destroyed, but the Rock lived up to its reputation of being impregnable. Gibraltar became a British Crown Colony in 1830.

In 1967, Gibraltar's inhabitants voted resoundingly to retain their connection with Britain – by 12 138 votes to 44 – in a referendum. In 1969, Spain closed the border and maintained a blockade until 1985. It is still not unusual for Spanish customs to delay vehicles. With its people descended from a variety of races,

Geographical Features

The **Rock of Gibraltar**★ is a gigantic monolith of Jurassic limestone which forms a craggy promontory connected with mainland Spain to the north and stretching south into the Straits. It covers an area of about 6.5km2/2.5sq mi (4.5km/3mi long and 1.4km/0.9mi at its widest), rising to 423m/1 388ft at its highest point, Mount Misery. The east face of the Rock drops sheer into the sea, while the less steep west face has been partially reclaimed at the water's edge and forms the site of the town.

Neanderthal Man or Gibraltar Woman?

Eight years before the discovery in 1856 of a 60 000-year-old skeleton in the Neander Valley, east of Düsseldorf, Germany, a skull of the same age, thought to be that of a woman, was discovered on Gibraltar. However, delays in publicising the Gibraltar findings meant that Gibraltar Woman is known as Neanderthal Man.

Practical Information

Customs and other formalities – Gibraltar is a British Crown Colony. The border is open 24hr a day. Visitors must be in possession of a valid passport. Holders of UK passports and citizens of other EU countries do not need a visa. Other nationalities should check visa requirements with a British consulate, high commission, or embassy. Gibraltar is a VAT-free shopping area.
Travel and accommodation – There are daily scheduled flights from London Heathrow, Gatwick and Luton and a daily ferry service between Gibraltar and Morocco. Regular flights also operate to and from North Africa. Hotel and bed-and-breakfast accommodation is available. There are no campsites.
Money matters – The currency is Gibraltar Government notes. The euro and credit cards are widely accepted.
Language – The official language spoken on the Rock is English, but most people speak some Spanish.
Time – Gibraltar is on European time (one hour ahead of GMT).
Motoring – Driving is on the right. Drivers must have a current licence, vehicle registration documents, evidence of insurance and nationality plates.
Telephoning – The international code for Gibraltar is 350 (from Spain, dial 9567 before the five-digit local number).
Tourist information – Further tourist information is available from the Gibraltar Government Office, Arundel Great Court, 179 Strand, London WC2R 1EH; ☎(020) 7836 0777; fax (020) 7240 6612, giblondon@aol.com; Gibraltar Information Bureau 1155 15th St NW, Washington, DC 20005 ☎202-452-1108, gibinfobur@msn.com;
Website – www.gibraltar.gov.gi

religions and cultures, their identity shaped by years of resisting sieges, Gibraltar is an excellent example of a harmonious, multicultural society.
Gibraltar's economy is based on financial services and tourism. The territory is a free port and trade is based on transit and refuelling.
The naval and commercial ports, as well as the town with its mixture of English- and Spanish-style houses, pubs and shops, lie against the west face of the Rock. Numerous examples of Moorish architecture are still to be found, notably in the cathedral which has the ground plan of a mosque.

Barbary Apes

The origin of the apes, one of Gibraltar's best-known attractions, is unknown. Legend has it that British rule will last as long as the apes remain in residence on the Rock. When it looked as if they might become extinct in 1944, Churchill sent a signal ordering reinforcements. The ape colony has since flourished – there are currently just under 200 of them. They are renowned for their charm and highly inquisitive natures. The apes, in reality tailless monkeys, are the protégés of the Gibraltar Regiment.

Worth a Visit

Tour of the Rock★

Open 9.30am-6.15pm. Closed 1 Jan and 25 Dec. 8£. ☎9567 450 00
The top of the Rock can be reached on foot, by cable car and in official tour vehicles *(private cars are not allowed on the Upper Rock)*. Go down Queensway and follow the signs to Upper Rock, a **nature reserve** and home to a number of Gibraltar's most interesting historical sites. The road leads first to **St Michael's Cave**, once inhabited by Neolithic man which features some stalactites and stalagmites. From here, it is possible to walk to the top of the Rock *(1hr there and back)*, from where there are excellent **views**★★ of both sides of the rock and of the Spanish and north African coasts.

The road continues to the **Apes' Den**, home of the famous Barbary Apes.

Visitors interested in military history should not miss the **Great Siege Tunnels**, excavated in 1779 to mount guns on the north face of the Rock, creating a defence system still impressive for its ingenuity. A military heritage centre is housed in Princess Caroline's Battery. Finally there are the ancient ruins of the **Moorish Castle** (*closed for restoration*) and the northern defences dominating the hillside.

Back in town, the **Gibraltar Museum** contains extensive collections on local military and natural history. It also houses the well-preserved **Moorish Baths**. (*open 10am-2pm and 4-7pm; Sat-Sun 10am-2.30pm; 956 36 07 15*).

The **Alameda Gardens** display interesting and exotic plants, including Canary Islands dragon trees, cacti, succulents and Mediterranean vegetation. Gibraltar is home to some 600 species of flowering plant, which flourish in the subtropical climate, including a few unique to the Rock, such as its national flower, the Gibraltar Candytuft.

For those interested in seeing more examples of Gibraltar's plant and bird life, the **Mediterranean Steps**, leading from Jew's Gate (good view of the other Pillar of Hercules, Jebel Musa in Morocco) round the south of the Rock and up the east face of the Rock to the summit make a rewarding walk (*3hr walk from Jew's Gate, steep in parts; wear good boots*).

STRAITS OF GIBRALTAR★

MICHELIN MAP 578 X 13 –
ANDALUCÍA (CÁDIZ); GIBRALTAR: BRITISH CROWN COLONY

The Straits, the gateway to the Mediterranean and a mere 14km/9mi wide, have always played a strategic role in the region. The Bay of Algeciras is surrounded by Algeciras and La Línea de la Concepción, and the British outpost of Gibraltar.

- **Information:** *Algeciras: Juan de la Cierva, 956 57 26 36*
- **Orient Yourself:** The A 7 motorway links the southernmost part of Spain to the Costa del Sol.
- **Also See:** COSTA DE LA LUZ, COSTA DEL SOL and MÁLAGA

Tours

The 21km/13mi of road linking Tarifa to Algeciras provides stunning **views**★★★ of the African coast. The best viewpoint is at the Mirador del Estrecho, 8km/5mi from Tarifa.

Tarifa (*see COSTA DE LA LUZ*)

Algeciras

Population 109 000. Arabs arrived in al-Yazirat-al-jadra (Green Island, now joined to the mainland) in 711 and remained until 1344. The Bahía de Algeciras is a safe anchorage and strategic vantage point overlooking the Straits. Algeciras is Spain's busiest passenger port with crossings to Tangier and Ceuta several times a day. The main sights of interest are the the plaza Alta, the hub of the town, fronted by two churches: the 18C **Iglesia de Nuestra Señora de la Palma**, and the Baroque Iglesia de Nuestra Señora de la Aurora, and the **Museo Municipal**, displaying interesting exhibits on the **Siege of Algeciras** (1342-44, *open 10am-2pm and 5-8pm; 21 Jun-30 Sep, 10am-2pm;* closed *Sat (21 Jun-30 Sep), Sun and public hols; 956 57 06 72*).

GIRONA/GERONA★★

POPULATION: 70 409.

MICHELIN MAP 574 G 38 (TOWN PLAN) – MAP 122 COSTA BRAVA – CATALUNYA (GIRONA)

Girona, with its heritage quarter, stands on a strategic site that has made it the target of repeated sieges. Its ramparts were built and rebuilt by Iberians, Romans and Catalans. Charlemagne's troops assaulted the city, and in 1809, Girona resisted Napoleon's troops for more than seven months.

- **Information:** *Rambla de la Llibertat 1, ☎972 22 65 75; www.girona.com.*
- **Orient Yourself:** Girona connects with Barcelona (97km/60mi SW) and France via the N II and AP 7. The C 255 leads to Palafrugell (39km/24mi SW) and the C 250 to Sant Feliu de Guíxols (36km/22mi SW), both on the coast.
- **Parking:** Park along one of the wider streets and walk into the old city.
- **Don't Miss:** A walk through the old Jewish quarter is essential.
- **Organizing Your Time:** Walk around the old town, to the main sites, and also just to wander among the orange-and-ochre heritage buildings.
- **Also See:** FIGUERES, COSTA BRAVA and PIRINEOS CATALANES.

Special Features

FORÇA VELLA (OLD TOWN)

Allow 3hr

Narrow alleys lead up to the cathedral, with its monumental stairway, the **Escaleras de la Pera**. The 14C **Pia Almoina** building (*right*) is a fine example of Gothic architecture.

Catedral★

Open 10am-7pm (8pm Apr-Oct); Sun and public hols, 10am-2pm. No visits during services. Closed 1 and 6 Jan, Easter Sun and 25 Dec.. ☎972 21 58 14.

The Baroque façade is like an altarpiece with a single huge oculus. The rest of the building is Gothic: the chancel (1312) is surrounded by chapels; the single Gothic **nave**★★ is the largest in the world, and largely unadorned. A silver-gilt embossed 14C **altarpiece**★ traces the Life of Christ. The Sant Honorat chapel has the outstanding tomb, in a Gothic niche, of Bishop Bernard de Pau.

Girona and Judaism

Girona's Jewish community, which settled on both sides of **calle de la Força** in the city's old quarter, was the second largest in Catalunya after Barcelona, and became famous in the Middle Ages for its prestigious Kabbalistic School, which existed for over 600 years from the 9C until the expulsions of 1492. This past can be felt in atmospheric narrow alleyways such as calle Cúndaro and calle Sant Llorenç, the latter home to the **Centro Bonastruc ça Porta**, dedicated to the town's Jewish history.

Tesoro★★

Open 8am-2pm and 4.30-6pm (7pm Mar-Jun); 19 Mar-Jun, 8am-8pm; Sun and public hols 10am-2pm. Closed Mon. 4 €. ☎972 21 44 26.

The treasury houses one of the most beautiful copies of the **Beatus**★★, or *St John's Commentary on the Apocalypse* (8C). The 10C embossed silver **Hixem Casket** is a fine example of Caliphate art, and there is Gothic silver and plate of the 14C and 15C. The end room contains the **Tapiz de la Creación**★★★ (Tapestry of Creation), dating from about 1100, showing Christ in Majesty surrounded by the stages of creation.

The 12C-13C **cloisters**★, remain – like the 11C Torre de Carlomagno (Charlemagne Tower) – from an earlier Romanesque cathedral.

Museu d'Art de Girona★★

Open 10am-6pm (7pm Mar-Sep); Sun and public hols, 10am-2pm. Closed Mon, 1 and 6 Jan, Easter Sun and 25-26 Dec. 2 €. ☎972 20 38 34.

Address Book

For coin ranges, see the Legend on the cover flap.

WHERE TO EAT

El Celler de Can Roca – *Carretera de Taialà 40 – ☎972 22 21 57 – Closed Sun, Mon, 24 Dec-20Jan and 1-15 Jul –* . With its bold combinations, the creative cuisine here is a feast for the senses. Extensive wine list.

TAPAS

Boira – *Plaça de la Independencia 17 – ☎ 972 20 30 96 –* . This modern bar under the arcades of the square is the current in-place for Girona's young crowd. Good tapas and a great view of the colourful reflections in the river from the first floor.

WHERE TO STAY

Hotel Condal – *Joan Maragall 10 – ☎ 972 20 44 62 – 38 rooms.* Recommended for its excellent location in a busy shopping street in the city centre more than anything else. Having said this, the Condal occupies a bourgeois mansion with rooms that are simple, yet clean and bright. Note that most bathrooms have shower only.

Hotel Ultonia – *Gran Via de Jaume I 22 – ☎972 20 38 50 – – 45 rooms –* . A hotel in classic style on one of the main streets. Public areas are rather reduced, but this is balanced by large, functionally comfortable rooms.

BARS AND CAFÉS

Cu-Cut – *Plaça de la Independència 10 – ☎ 972 20 83 01.* An attractive, welcoming bar which often hosts concerts and poetry readings.

La Terra – *Ballesteries, 23 – ☎ 972 21 92 54.* A pleasant bar overlooking the Onyar River.

The museum, in the Palacio Episcopal, exhibits art from the Romanesque to the present. Holdings include a 10C portable altar from Sant Pere de Rodes of embossed silver, the 12C-13C **beam from Cruïlles★**, and apse paintings from Pyrenean churches. Among altarpieces in the Throne Room is one from **Sant Miquel de Cruïlles★★** by Luis Borrassá (15C), Catalunya's greatest Gothic artist. Note the splendid **Púbol altarpiece★,** by Bernat Martorell (1437). The panels of the **Sant Feliu altarpiece** by Juan de Borgoña mark the transition from Gothic to Renaissance style.

Colegiata de Sant Feliu★

This church outside the walls must originally have been a martyry over the tombs of St Narcissus, Bishop of Girona, and St Felix. The later Gothic church holds eight **early Christian sar-**

J. Malburet/MICHELIN

Houses overlooking the Onyar river

Girona/ Gerona

			General Fournàs	BY	16	Reina Isabel la Católica	BZ	36
			General Peralta Pas. del	BZ	17	Reina Joana Pas. de la	BY	37
Álvarez de Castro	AZ	2	Joaquim Vayreda	AY	18	Sant Cristòfol	BY	39
Argenteria	BY	3	Juli Garreta	AZ	19	Sant Daniel	BY	40
Ballesteríes	BY	4	Llibertat Rambla de la	BZ	23	Sant Domènec Pl. de	BY	42
Bellaire	BY	6	Nou	AZ		Sant Feliu Pujada de	BY	44
Berenguer Carnicer	AY	7	Nou del Teatre	BZ	27	Sant Francesc Av. de	AZ	45
Bonastruc de Porta	AY	9	Oliva i Prat	BY	26	Sant Pere Pl. de	BY	48
Carme	BZ	10	Palafrugell	BY	28	Santa Clara	ABYZ	
Ciutadans	BZ	12	Pedreres Pujada de les	BZ	29	Santa Eugénia	AZ	49
Cúndaro	BY	13	Ramon Folch Av. d'en	AY	31	Ultònia	AZ	53
Devesa Pas. de la	AY	14	Rei Ferran el Católic	BY	33			
Eduard Marquína Pl. de	AZ	15	Rei Martí Pujada del	BY	34			

Banys Àrabs	BY	S	Edifici de Les Àligues	BY	U	Museu del Cinema	AZ	M^2
Centre Bonastruc ça Porta	BY	A	Farinera Teixidor	AZ	K	Pia Almoina	BY	N
Colegiata de Sant Feliu	BY	R	Fontana d'Or	BY	E			
Convento de Sant Domènec	BY	F	Hospici	AZ	L			
			Museu d'Art	BY	M^1			

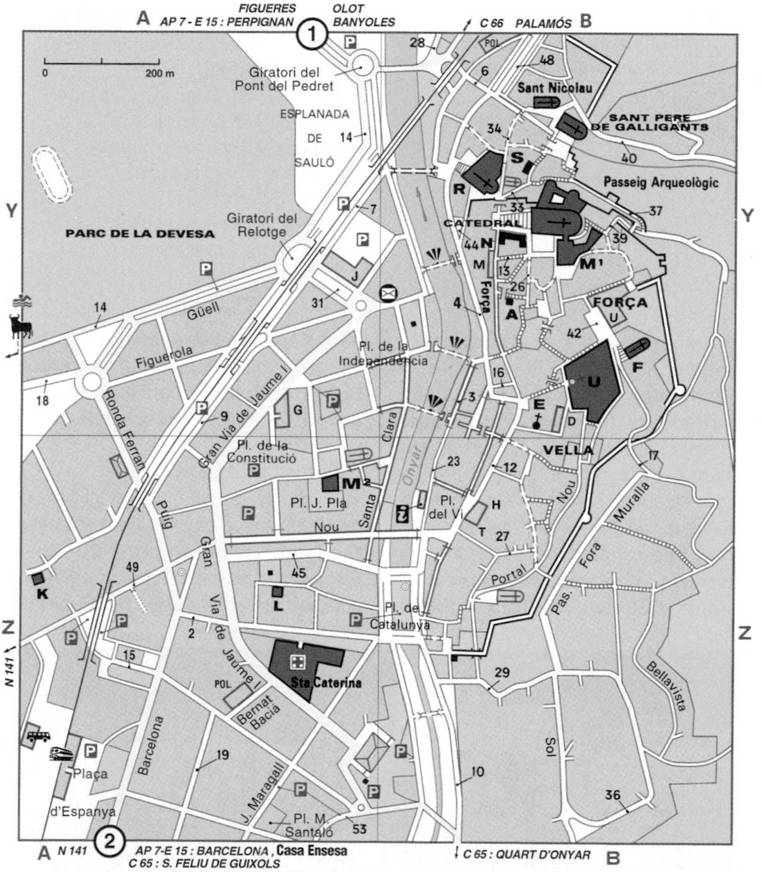

cophagi★, two with outstanding carvings, including a spirited **lion hunt**★.

Baños Árabes★ (Arab Baths)

Open 10am-2pm; Apr-Sep, 10am-7pm; Sun and public hols, 10am-2pm. Closed Mon (Oct-Mar), 1 and 6 Jan, Easter Sun and 25-26 Dec. 1.60 €. ☎972 19 07 97.

These late-12C baths were built in accordance with Muslim tradition. They consist of four rooms in a row. Steps opposite lead to the **Passeig Arqueològic (Archaeological Promenade)** from which you can view the Ter Valley.

Monasterio de Sant Pere de Galligants★

Not far from Sant Nicolau stands the fortified Romanesque church of Sant Pere, set into the town walls, housing the **Museu Arqueològic.** Shown are Medieval memorial plaques and the magnificent 4C Roman **tomb of Las Estaciones**★ (*open 10am-2pm and 4-7pm; Jun-Sep 10.30am-1.30pm and 4-7pm; Sun and public hols 10am-2pm all year; Closed Mon, 1 and 6 Jan, and 25-26 Dec; 1.80 €, no charge 23 Apr, 18 May and 11 Sep; 972 20 46 37).*

Parc de la Devesa★

This park contains the largest grove of plane trees in Catalunya.

Excursions

Casa-Museu Castell Gala Dalí★

In Púbol. 16km/10mi E along the C 66 towards La Bisbal d'Empordà. Open Nov-Dec Tue-Sat 10.30am-5pm; 15 Mar-14 June and 16 Sep-Oct Sun-Fri 10.30am-6pm; 15 Jun-15 Sep daily 10.30am-8pm. Closed Jan-14 Mar. 6€. 972 48 86 55.

In 1970, Salvador Dalí gave this 14C castle to his wife Gala. It now displays objects in a Surrealist atmosphere.

From Girona to Santa Pau

88km/55mi – allow one day. Head N from Girona along the C 66.

Banyoles

19km/12mi. Banyoles is set by a **lake**★. The **Museu Arqueològic Comarcal**★ in a Gothic building shows the Palaeolithic Jaw of Banyoles (*open 10.30am-1.30pm and 4-6.30pm (7.30pm Jul-Aug); Sun and public hols, 10.30am-2pm; closed Mon, 1 and 6 Jan and 24 and 31 Dec; 1.80 €. 972 57 23 61).*

A road 8km/5mi road around the lake passes the 13C **Iglesia de Santa Maria de Porqueres**★, its columns sculpted with odd figures (*open by arrangement, Sat 4.30-7pm and Sun 10am-1pm (daily Jul-Aug); 972 57 04 95).*

Besalù★★

A Roman **fortified bridge**★ was rebuilt in the medieval period. The **ancient city**★★ retains ramparts and many medieval buildings, including the Romanesque **Iglesia de Sant Pere**★ with unusual lion-flanked window (*guided tour by arrangement at 12.30 and 5 p.m; 2.40 €; closed 1, 6 Jan and 25-26 Dec; 972 59 12 40).*

Traditional **ritual baths** (12C) are in the Jewish quarter (*guided tour by arrangement, 10.30 a.m. noon, 1.30, 4.30pm and 6pm; Sun and public hols 1.30 and 6pm; closed 1 and 6 Jan and 25-26 Dec; 1.20 €; 972 59 12 40).*

Head 14km/9mi W along the N 260.

Castellfollit de la Roca★

The village, in **Parc Natural de la Garrotxa**★, includes a medieval centre

J. Malburet/MICHELIN

Fortified bridge, Besalù

around the church of Sant Salvador. ▶ *Continue 8km/5mi W along the N 260.*

Olot★

The 18C neo-Classical **Iglesia de Sant Esteve**★, with Baroque front, houses a fine baldaquin, Baroque retable and an unusual painting by El Greco – *Christ Bearing the Cross*★ (*open 8am-1pm; Sat 8am (Sun and public hols 10am)-1pm and 6-9pm; museum visit by appointment; ☎972 26 04 74).*

The **Museu Comarcal de la Garrotxa**★ displays a fine **collection of paintings and drawings**★★ by 19C and 20C Catalan artists (*Oopen 11am-2pm and 4-7pm; Sun and public hols, 11am-2pm. Closed Tue, 1 Jan and 25 Dec; 3 €, no charge first Sun of every month; ☎972 27 91 30).*

Note also the splendid **Modernist façade**★ of the **Casa Solà-Morales**★, a work by Domènech i Montaner.

▶ *Take the GI 524 east 9.5km/6mi.*

Santa Pau★

The Castillo de Santa Pau and the 15C-16C parish church both stand on the arcaded square of this village.

GRANADA★★★

POPULATION: 241 471

MICHELIN MAP 578 U 19 (TOWN PLAN) MAP 124

COSTA DEL SOL – ANDALUCÍA (GRANADA)

Granada enjoys a glorious setting★★★ on a fertile plain overlooked by three hills and the majestic peaks of the Sierra Nevada. Watching over the modern Christian city stands the breathtaking Alhambra, one of the most magnificent monuments ever created by man and for many, the highlight of Spain.

- **Information:** *Plaza Mariana Pineda, ☎958 24 71 28; Santa Ana 2,, ☎958 22 59 90; Centro Municipal de Recepción Turística (municipal toursim agency: hotels, tickets, tours) Virgen Blanca, 9, ☎902 405 045 www.granadatur.com.*
- **Orient Yourself:** Granada is in southern Andalucía, separated from the sea by the Sierra Nevada. The A 44 and other highways link with major cities in the region.
- **Parking:** Space is limited in the Albaicín; there is visitor parking at the Alhambra.
- **Don't Miss:** The Alhambra
- **Organizing Your Time:** Organise your stay around around your visit to the Alhambra, fitting other sights as time allows.
- **Especially for Kids:** Take the little ones to Parque de las Ciencias.
- **Also See:** *GUADIX (57km/35mi NE), JAÉN (94km/59mi N), ANTEQUERA (100km/62mi W) and COSTA DEL SOL (to the S).*

History

Historical notes – Granada gained importance in the 11C as Córdoba declined. It became capital of the Almoravids who were ousted a century later by the Almohads. In the 13C, Muslims from Córdoba, fleeing the Christians in 1236, sought refuge, enriching the city. In 1238, the new **Nasrid** ruler, Mohammed ibn Nasr, submitted to the authority of Ferdinand III, thus ensuring peace, and the kingdom flourished

The fall of Granada – In the 15C, the Catholic Monarchs turned their attention to Granada. By 2 January 1492, after a six-month siege, the city fell. Boabdil, the last Nasrid king, delivered the keys of the city and went into exile. As he looked back, his mother is said to have scolded him: "You weep like a woman for what you could not hold as a man".

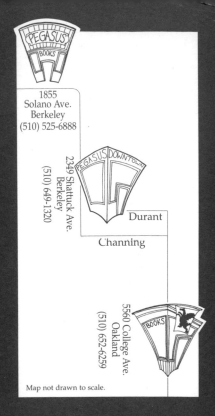

The Alhambra

Granada flourished again in the Renaissance, but its fortunes suffered during the ruthless suppression of the Las Alpujarras revolt in 1570.

Modern Granada – The old quarters east of **plaza Nueva**, havens of peace and greenery on the Alhambra and Albaicín hills, conrast with the noisy, bustling lower town and the pedestrian quarter around the cathedral between the **Gran Vía de Colón** and **calle de los Reyes Católicos**.

Special Features

The Alhambra and the Generalife★★★

Open Mar-Oct, 8.30am-8pm (and 10-11.30pm Tue-Sat: Nasrid Palace only); Nov-Feb, 8.30am-6pm (and 10-11.30pm Fri-Sat); ticket office closes 1hr before last entry. 10 €, advance purchase from any branches of the BBV bank in Spain or on www.alhambratickets.com. One ticket covers the entire Alhambra and Generalife gardens and specifies entry time to the Nasrid Palace. ☎958 22 75 25 or 902 44 12 21. Theme visits available Mon for small groups if booked on ☎902 22 44 60).

Nasrid architecture was the ultimate expression of a civilisation in decline. Nasrid princes built for the moment: beneath fabulous decoration lie ill-assorted bricks and rubble, so it is surprising how little time has diminished this masterpiece.

Decoration was the main concern. Walls and ceilings everywhere reveal an art without equal. **Stuccowork** is worked in patterns in a low relief of flat planes to catch the light; another type of decoration was made by cutting away layers of plaster to form stalactites *(mocárabes)*. This type of ornament, painted and even gilded, covered capitals, cornice mouldings, arches, pendentives and entire cupolas.

Ceramic tiles provided geometric decoration for walls: *alicatados* formed a colourful marquetry, with lines of arabesque motifs making star designs; azulejos gave colour, different hues separated by a thin raised fillet or a black line *(cuerda seca)*. **Calligraphy** employed elegant Andalucían cursive; the more decorative Cufic was reserved for religious aphorisms in scrollwork.

The Alhambra★★★

The Calat Alhambra (Red Castle) must be one of the most remarkable fortresses ever built. It commands views of the town, the Sacromonte heights, hillsides and the gardens of the Albaicín.

Enter through the Puerta de Las Granadas (Pomegranate Gateway) built by Emperor Charles V; a paved footpath then leads through to the **shrubbery**★.

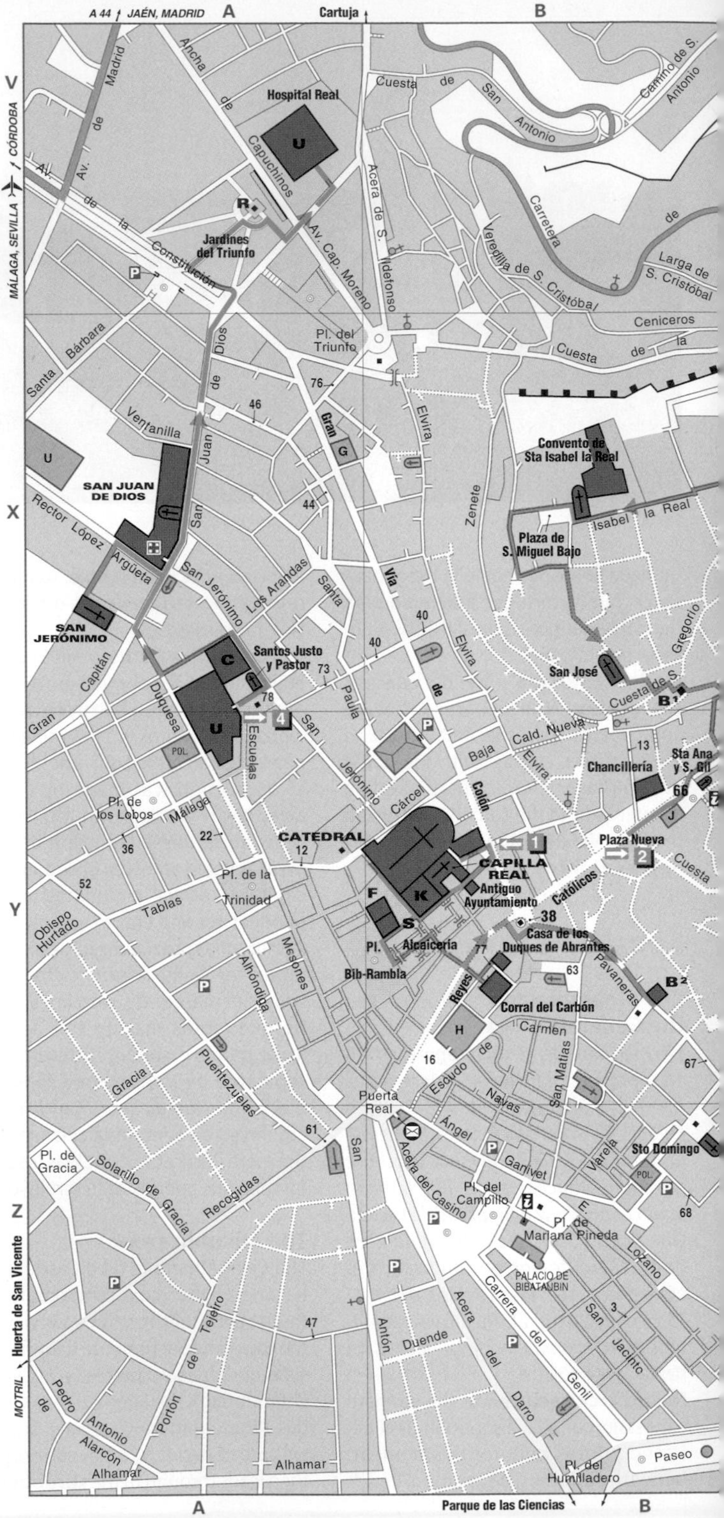
A 44 JAÉN, MADRID
Cartuja
Hospital Real
Jardines del Triunfo
SAN JUAN DE DIOS
SAN JERÓNIMO
Santos Justo y Pastor
CATEDRAL
CAPILLA REAL
Antiguo Ayuntamiento
Casa de los Duques de Abrantes
Corral del Carbón
Convento de Sta Isabel la Real
Plaza de S. Miguel Bajo
San José
Chancillería
Sta Ana y S. Gil
Plaza Nueva
Sto Domingo
PALACIO DE BIBATAUBIN
Pl. del Triunfo
Pl. de los Lobos
Pl. de la Trinidad
Pl. Bib-Rambla
Alcaicería
Puerta Real
Pl. de Gracia
Pl. del Campillo
Pl. de Mariana Pineda
Pl. del Humilladero
Paseo
MÁLAGA, SEVILLA
CÓRDOBA
MOTRIL
Huerta de San Vicente
Parque de las Ciencias

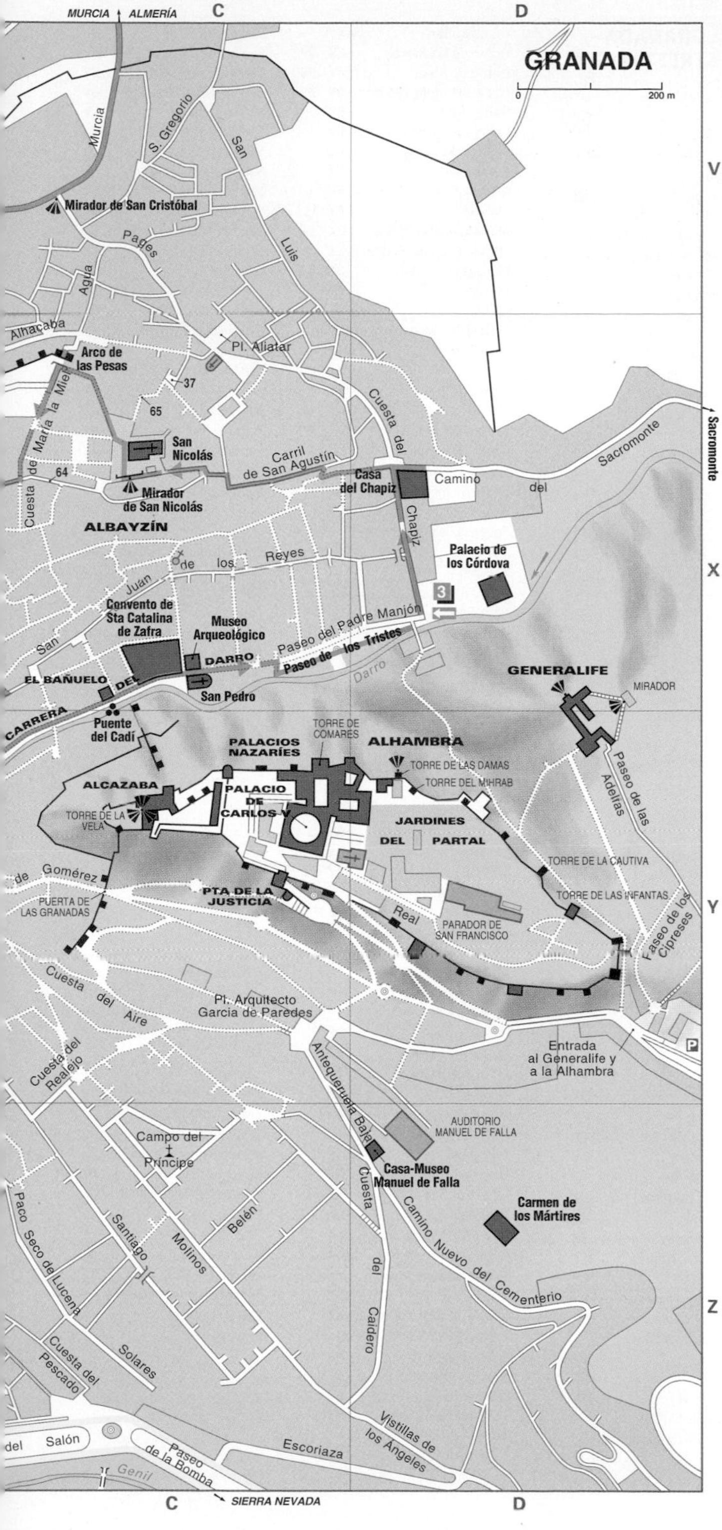
GRANADA
0
200 m
MURCIA
ALMERÍA
SIERRA NEVADA
Sacromonte
C
D
V
X
Y
Z
Murcia
S. Gregorio
San
Luis
Pages
Agua
Alhacaba
Mirador de San Cristóbal
Arco de las Pesas
Pl. Aliatar
37
65
64
Cuesta de María la Miel
San Nicolás
Mirador de San Nicolás
Carril de San Agustín
Cuesta del Chapiz
Casa del Chapiz
Camino del Sacromonte
ALBAYZÍN
de los Reyes
Juan
San
Palacio de los Córdova
Convento de Sta Catalina de Zafra
Museo Arqueológico
Paseo del Padre Manjón
Paseo de los Tristes
DARRO
Darro
EL BAÑUELO
CARRERA DEL
San Pedro
Puente del Cadí
GENERALIFE
MIRADOR
TORRE DE COMARES
PALACIOS NAZARÍES
ALHAMBRA
TORRE DE LAS DAMAS
TORRE DEL MIHRAB
ALCAZABA
PALACIO DE CARLOS V
TORRE DE LA VELA
JARDINES DEL PARTAL
Paseo de las Adelfas
TORRE DE LA CAUTIVA
TORRE DE LAS INFANTAS
Paseo de los Cipreses
de Gomérez
PUERTA DE LAS GRANADAS
PTA DE LA JUSTICIA
Real
PARADOR DE SAN FRANCISCO
Cuesta del Aire
Pl. Arquitecto Garcia de Paredes
Entrada al Generalife y a la Alhambra
Cuesta del Realejo
Antequeruela Baja
AUDITORIO MANUEL DE FALLA
Campo del Príncipe
Casa-Museo Manuel de Falla
Carmen de los Mártires
Cuesta del Caidero
Camino Nuevo del Cementerio
Paco Seco de Lucena
Santiago
Molinos
Belén
Cuesta del Pescado
Solares
Vistillas de los Angeles
Escoriaza
del Salón
Paseo de la Bomba
Genil

GRANADA – STREET INDEX

Adelfas Pas. de las	DY	
Agua	CV	
Aire Cuesta del	CY	
Alhacaba Cuesta de la	BCX	
Alhamar	AZ	
Alhóndiga	AY	
Aliatar Pl.	CX	
Ancha de Capuchinos	AV	
Ancha de la Virgen	BZ	3
Ángel Ganivet	BZ	
Antequeruela Baja	CDYZ	
Arandas Los	AX	
Belén	CZ	
Bib-Rambla Pl.	ABY	
Bomba Pas. de la	CZ	
Caldero Cuesta de	DZ	
Calderería Nueva	BY	
Campillo Pl. de	BZ	
Capitan Moreno Av.	AV	
Capuchinas	AY	12
Cárcel Alta	BY	13
Cárcel Baja	BY	
Carmen Pl. del	BZ	16
Casino Acera del	BZ	
Ceniceros	BX	
Chapiz Cuesta del	DX	
Cipreses Pas. de los	DY	
Colón Gran Via de	BXY	
Conde las Infantas	AY	22
Constitución Av. de la	AV	
Darro Acera del	BZ	
Darro Carrera del	CXY	
Duende	BZ	
Duquesa	AXY	
Elvira	BXY	
Escoriaza	CDZ	
Escudo de Carmen	BY	
Escuelas	AY	
Genil Carrera del	BZ	
Gomérez Cuesta de	BCY	
Gracia	AY	
Gracia Pl. de	AZ	
Gran Capitán	AXY	
Homo de la Charca	CX	37
Horno de Abad	AY	36
Isabel la Católica Pl. de	BY	38
Isabel la Real	BX	
Larga San Cristóbal	BV	
Lobos Pl. de los	AY	
Lozano	BZ	
Madrid Av. de	AV	
Málaga	AY	
Maria la Miel Cuesta de	CX	
Mariana Pineda Pl. de	BZ	
Marqués de Falces	BX	40
Mesones	AY	
Molinos	CZ	
Murcia Carret. de	BCV	
Navarrete	AX	44
Navas	BYZ	
Nueva Pl.	BY	
Nueva del Santísimo	AX	46
Nueva San Antón	AZ	47
Obispo Hurtado	AY	
Paco Seco de Lucena	CZ	
Padre Manjón Pas. del	CDX	
Pages	CV	
Paseo de los Tristes Pas. de los	CDX	
Pavaneras	BY	
Pedro Antonio de Alarcón	AZ	
Peña Partida	CY	
Pescado Cuesta del	CZ	
Picón Carril del	AY	52
Portón de Tejeiro	AZ	
Príncipe Campo del	CZ	
Puentezuelas	AYZ	
Real	DY	
Real Puerta	BYZ	
Realejo Cuesta del	CY	
Recogidas	AZ	
Rector López Argüeta	AX	
Reyes Católicos	BY	
Sacromonte Camino del	DX	
Salón Pas. del	BCZ	
San Agustín Carril de	CX	
San Antón	ABZ	
San Antón Pl. de	AZ	61
San Antonio Camino de	BCV	
San Antonio Cuesta de	BV	
San Cristóbal Veredilla de	BV	
San Gregorio	CV	
San Gregorio Cuesta de	BX	
San Ildefonso Acera de	BV	
San Jacinto	BZ	
San Jerónimo	AXY	
San Juan de Dios	AX	
San Juan de la Cruz Pl.	BY	63
San Juan de los Reyes	CX	
San Luis	CV	
San Matias	BY	
San Miguel Bajo Pl. de	BX	
San Nicolás Camino Nuevo de	CX	64
San Nicolás Cuesta de	CX	65
Santa Ana Pl. de	BY	66
Santa Bárbara	AX	
Santa Escolástica	BY	67
Santa Paula	AXY	
Santiago	CZ	
Santo Domingo Callejón de	BZ	68
Solares	CZ	
Solarillo de Gracia	AZ	
Tablas	AY	
Tendillas de Santa Paula	AX	73
Tinajilla	AX	76
Tovar Pl.	BY	77
Trinidad Pl. de la	AY	
Triunfo Pl. del	ABX	
Universidad Pl. de la	AX	78
Varela	BZ	
Ventanilla	AX	
Vistillas de los Ángeles	DZ	
Zenete	BX	

GRANADA – SITES INDEX

Albayzín	CX	
Alcaicería	BY	
Alcazaba	CY	
Alhambra	DY	
Arco de las Pesas	CX	
Baños árabes (El Bañuelo)	CX	
Capilla Real	BY	
Carmen de los Mártires (Jardines)	DZ	
Cartuja	BV	
Casa de Porras	BX	B[1]
Casa de los Duques de Abrantes	BY	
Casa de los Tiros	BY	B[2]
Casa del Chapiz	DX	
Casa-Museo Manuel de Falla	DZ	
Catedral	ABY	
Chancillería	BY	
Colegio de San Bartolomé y Santiago	AX	C
Convento de Santa Catalina de Zafra	CX	
Convento de Santa Isabel la Real	BX	
Corral del Carbón	BY	
Curia eclesiástica	BY	F
Generalife	DX	
Hospital Real	AV	
Hospital de San Juan de Dios	AX	
Huerta de San Vicente	AZ	
Iglesia de San José	BX	
Iglesia de San Juan de Dios	AX	
Iglesia de San Nicolás	CX	
Iglesia de San Pedro	CX	
Iglesia de Santa Ana y San Gil	BY	
Iglesia de Santo Domingo	BZ	
Iglesia de los Santo Justos y Pastor	AX	
Iglesia del Sagrario	BY	K
Jardines del Partal	DY	
Jardines del Triunfo	AV	
Jardines y Torres de la Alhambra	DY	
Madraza o Antiguo Ayuntamiento	BY	
Mirador de San Cristóbal	CV	
Mirador de San Nicolás	CX	
Monasterio de San Jerónimo	AX	
Monumento a la Immaculada Concepción	AV	R
Museo Arqueológico	CX	
Palacio Arzobispal	BY	S
Palacio de los Córdova	DX	
Palacios Nazaríes	CY	
Palácio de Carlos V	CY	
Parque de las Ciencias	BZ	
Puente del Cadí	CXY	
Puerta de la Justicia	CY	
Sacromonte	DX	
Universidad	AXY	U

Address Book

For coin ranges, see the Legend on the cover flap.

WHERE TO EAT

Chikito – *Plaza del Campillo 9 – 958 22 33 64 – www.restaurantechikito.com – Closed Wed – Reservation recommended.* A hugely popular restaurant and bar with locals and visitors alike, and renowned for serving local specialities and superb cured hams. It was here that artists and intellectuals such as García Lorca used to meet in the 1930s.

La Ermita en la Plaza de Toros – *Avenida Doctor Olóriz 25 (at the bullring) – 958 29 02 57 – www.ermitaplazadetoros.com –* . Its unusual location within the confines of the city's bullring and its tasteful decoration of exposed brickwork, wooden tables, rustic-style chairs and bullfighting memorabilia on the walls have made this a popular restaurant in which to enjoy typical Andalucían cuisine. The restaurant is on the first floor, and a tapas bar on the ground floor.

Mirador de Morayma – *Pianista García Carrillo 2 – 958 22 82 90 – www.alqueriamorayma.com/mirador – Closed Sun July-Aug and Sun evening rest of year.* This restaurant in the Albaicín district has one of the best settings of any in the city. Rustic decor, a plant-filled terrace and magnificent views of the Alhambra. Private-label wines, Flamenco show Tue evening.

TAPAS

La Trastienda – *Plaza de Cuchilleros 11 – 958 22 69 95 – Closed in Aug –* . Founded in 1836. Once through the small entrance door, head down some steps to the former grocery store, which has retained its original counter, where you can enjoy excellent chorizo and tapas, either at the bar or in the small room to the rear.

Bodegas Castañeda – *Almireceros 1 – 958 21 54 64 – Closed Sun –* . The bar and tables in this typical bodega, its decor enhanced by the myriad bottles on display, are often full with customers enjoying the delicious hot and cold tapas and regional specialties. A good central location just a few metres from plaza Nueva.

Casa Enrique – *Acera del Darro 8 – 958 25 50 08 – Closed Sun –* . This tavern dates from 1870 and has become a symbol of the city. Its small size and careful decoration make it a good meeting-point. Outstanding wine cellar, Iberian ham and local cheeses.

Pilar del Toro – *Hospital de Santa Ana 12 – 958 22 38 47 – www.hotelcasadelpilar.com.* Housed in an old 17C house, the Pilar del Toro is worth a visit for its distinctive architecture alone. The iron gate leads to the bar with a small counter to the left and a large Andalucían patio to the right, with an attractive restaurant upstairs and enchanting rooms as well.

WHERE TO STAY

Hotel Los Tilos – *Plaza Bib-Rambla 4 – 958 26 67 12 – www.hotellostilos.com – – 30 rooms – 5 €.* This no-frills hotel fronts a charming square filled with flower stalls, just a few metres from the cathedral. Although on the basic side, the rooms are comfortable, some with the bonus of a view over the plaza.

Hotel Maciá Plaza – *Plaza Nueva 4 – 958 22 75 36 – www.maciahoteles.com – – 44 rooms – 6 €.* A four-storey building with an attractive façade in a central square at the foot of the Alhambra. Standard-quality rooms with carpets and wicker furniture.

Hotel América – *Real de la Alhambra 53 – 958 22 74 71 – www.hotelamericagranada.com – Closed Mar-Nov – 17 rooms – 8 €. Restaurant 15/25€.* A small, family-run hotel superbly located within the confines of the Alhambra. A warm welcome and friendly service are the trademarks of the América, which also has a pleasant patio.

Hotel Palacio de Santa Inés – *Cuesta de Santa Inés 9 – 958 22 23 62 – www.palaciosantaines.com – – 35 rooms – 10 €.* This 16C Mudéjar-inspired building is situated in the Albaicín district, with several rooms enjoying views of Granada's number one attraction. In the charming colonnaded patio, you can still make out what's left of the building's original Renaissance frescoes.

BARS AND CAFÉS

El Tren – *Carril del Picón, 22 – Open 8am-10pm.* This unusual bar has a warm and friendly atmosphere and an extensive choice of teas, coffees and cakes. The bar has an electric train running on tracks suspended from the ceiling, hence the name. A varied clientele which changes according to the time of day.

Teterías – *Caldererría Nueva.* Calle Caldererría Nueva, between the city centre and the Albaicín, is a typical example of a street found in the Moorish quarter of any city. The small and cosy teterías are typical cafés which give a welcoming feel to this particular street. Two are worth mentioning: the quiet and pleasant Pervane, with its huge selection of teas, coffees, milk shakes and cakes; and Kasbah, decorated with cushions and rugs on the floor in true Moorish coffee shop style.

NIGHTLIFE

El Camborio – *Sacromonte 47 (in the Sacromonte district) – Open Tue-Sat, midnight-6am.* One of Granada's oldest and most established nocturnal haunts El Camborio has been open for the past 30 years. Best approached by car or taxi as it is located in one of the city's least salubrious districts. The venue itself is quite unique with four interconnected caves and with good dance music. Popular with an eclectic crowd, though predominantly frequented by students. A good place to end the night.

El Tercer Aviso – *Plaza de Toros 1-18 – ☎958 20 60 42 – www.terceraviso.com – Open 4pm-5am.* A surprising location inside the bullring, where its spacious design combines with modern, tasteful decor. The café is located on several floors, and from each floor it is possible to look down onto the floors below. Good chart music popular with the 25-45 crowd, and also quiet areas for those wanting to enjoy a chat.

La Fontana – Carrera del *Darro 19 – ☎958 22 77 59 – Open 4pm-3am.* Housed in an old residence at the foot of the Alhambra and Albaicín hills, this inviting antique-adorned café is an ideal place for a quiet drink in an atmosphere dominated by lively conversation. An excellent choice of coffees, herbal teas and cocktails.

Sala Príncipe – *Campo del Príncipe 7 – ☎958 22 80 08 – Open Tue-Sun in summer, 11pm-6am; Wed-Sun in winter.* This large venue is the place to be seen for the city's in-crowd, hosting regular concerts by leading Spanish groups. Always crowded with a mix of ages.

FIESTAS

The city's religious festivals are lively, colourful events, especially those held in Holy Week and at Corpus Christi. The city also holds an annual **music and dance festival** in June and July in the delightful surroundings of the Generalife gardens.

Palacios Nazaríes★★★ (Nasrid Palace)

The 14C Nasrid Palace was built around the Patio de los Arrayanes and Patio de los Leones. Its richness and the originality of its decoration defy description. In the **Mexuar**, used for government and judicial administration, a frieze of *azulejos* and an epigraphic border cover the walls. An oratory stands at one end. Cross the **Patio del Cuarto Dorado (1).** The south wall, protected by a remarkable carved wood cornice, exemplifies Granada art: windows are surrounded by panels covered with every variety of stucco and tile decoration. The **Cuarto Dorado** (Golden Room) has tiled panelling, fine stuccowork and a beautiful wooden ceiling. The delightful **view**★ extends over the Albaicín.

Adjoining is the beautiful oblong **Patio de los Arrayanes** (Myrtle Courtyard). A pool banked by myrtles reflects the **Torre de Comares** (Comares Tower) which contrasts with slender porticoes that give onto the **Sala de la Barca** (from *barakha*, benediction) and the **Salón de Embajadores** (Hall of Ambassadors), an audience chamber with a magnificent domed cedar ceiling.

At the heart of a second palace stands the **Patio de los Leones** (Lion Court-

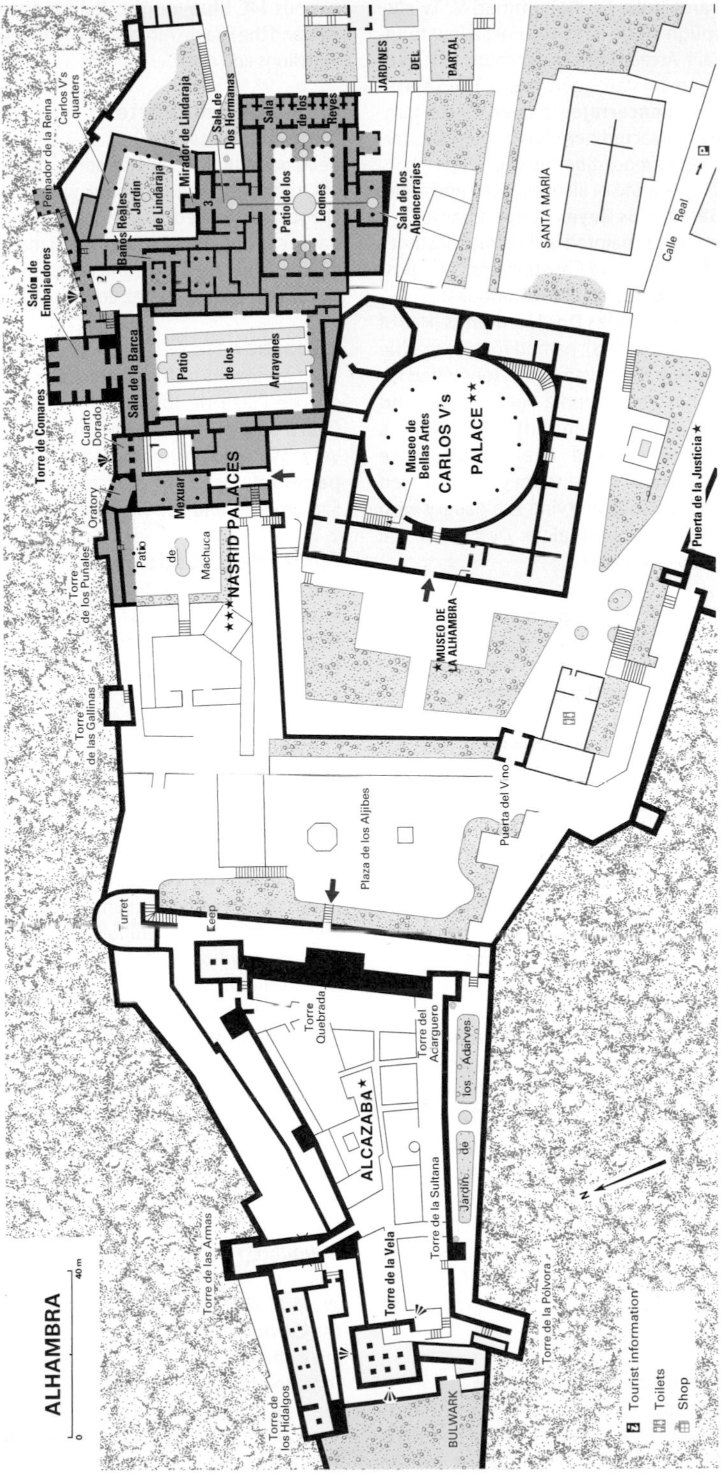
ALHAMBRA
0
40 m
Tourist information
Toilets
Shop
Torre de los Hidalgos
Torre de las Armas
BULWARK
Torre de la Vela
Torre de la Pólvora
Torre de la Sultana
ALCAZABA★
Jardín de los Adarves
Torre Quebrada
Torre del Acarguero
Turret
Keep
Plaza de los Aljibes
Puerta del Vino
Torre de las Gallinas
Torre de los Puñales
MUSEO DE LA ALHAMBRA★
Museo de Bellas Artes
CARLOS V's PALACE★★
Puerta de la Justicia★
Patio de Machuca
★★★NASRID PALACES
Oratory
Mexuar
Cuarto Dorado
Torre de Comares
Sala de la Barca
Patio de los Arrayanes
Salón de Embajadores
2
Baños Reales
3
Jardín de Lindaraja
Peinador de la Reina
Carlos V's quarters
Mirador de Lindaraja
Sala de Dos Hermanas
Patio de los Leones
Sala de los Abencerrajes
Sala de los Reyes
JARDINES DEL PARTAL
SANTA MARÍA
Calle Real
N

yard) built by Mohammed V. Twelve rough stone lions support a low fountain. Arcades of slender columns lead to the main state apartments. The **Sala de los Abencerrajes** (named for the family massacred here)has a splendid star-shaped *mocárabe* cupola.

The vaulting of alcoves at the end of the **Sala de los Reyes** (Kings' Chamber) is atypically painted to illustrate pastimes of Moorish and Christian princes – possibly done after the Reconquest.

The **Sala de las Dos Hermanas** (Hall of the Two Sisters), named for two marble slabs in the pavement, is renowned for honeycomb cupola vaulting. Beyond are the resplendent **Sala de los Ajimeces** and the **Mirador de Lindaraja**. Past a room once occupied by Washington Irving is a gallery with views of the Albaicín. *Descend to the Patio de la Reja* **(2)**.

▶ *Cross the Patio de Lindaraja to the Partal gardens.*

Gardens and perimeter towers★★

The terraced Jardines de Partal descend to the 14C porticoed **Torre de las Damas** (Lady Tower). The Torre de Mihrab (*right*) is a former oratory. The Torre de la Cautiva and Torre de las Infantas (Captive's and Infantas' towers) are sumptuously decorated inside.

▶ *Enter the Palacio de Carlos V.*

Palacio de Carlos V★★ (Emperor Charles V's Palace)

In 1526, Pedro Machuca was commissioned to design a palace to be financed by a tax on the Moors. The 1568 uprising delayed construction. It is one of the most successful Renaissance creations in Spain. Although in comparison with the Nasrid Palaces the building may at first appear lacking, its grandeur becomes apparent, in its perfect lines, its dignity, and its simple plan of a circle within a square.

Museo de la Alhambra★

This museum is devoted to Hispano-Moorish art: ceramics, wood carvings, panels and more. Outstanding are the famous 14C **blue** (or **gazelle**) **amphora**★ and the Pila de Almanzor, decorated with lions and deer.

Museo de Bellas Artes (Fine Arts Museum)

Religious sculpture and paintings of the 16C to the 18C predominate: works by Diego de Siloé, Pedro de Mena, Vicente Carducho and Alonso Cano, and a magnificent still life, *Thistle and Carrots*★★, by Brother Juan Sánchez Cotán.

Alcazaba★

The two towers of this austere fortress on the Plaza de los Aljibes (Cistern Court) date to the 13C. The Torre de la Vela (Watchtower) commands a fine **panorama**★★ of the palace, gardens, Sacromonte, and the Sierra Nevada.

Puerta de la Justicia★

The massive Justice Gateway is built into a tower in the outer walls. On the façade, a strip of delightful 16C *azulejos* bears an image of the Virgin and Child.

The Generalife★★

The **water gardens** are one of the most enjoyable parts of the 14C Generalife, the summer palace. The Patio de los Cipreses (Cypress Alley) and Patio de las Adelfas (Oleander) lead in. The nucleus is the **Patio de la Acequia** (Canal Court), a pool with fountains, a pavilion at either end, and a *mirador* in the middle. The pavilion to the rear contains the Sala Regia, with fine stuccowork. The upper gardens contain the famous **escalera del agua**, or water staircase.

CATHEDRAL QUARTER ◷*45min*

Capilla Real★★ (Chapel Royal)

◷ *Open 10.30am-1pm and 3.30-6.30pm; Apr-Oct, 10.30am-1pm and 4-7pm; Sun and public hols, 11am-1pm and 3.30-6.30pm.* ◷ *Closed 2 Jan (morning), Good Fri and 12 Oct (morning).* *3 €. ☎958 22 78 48.*

The **Catholic Monarchs** commissioned this Isabelline Gothic chapel by Enrique Egas. To enter *(by the south door)*, cross the courtyard of the old **Lonja** (Exchange), also by Egas. The south front has an elegant Renaissance façade of superimposed arcades with turned columns. Every conceivable decoration of the Isabelline style is seen inside: ribbed vaulting, coats of arms, the yoke and fasces (revived in 1934 by the Falange), monograms, and the eagle of St John. In the chancel, closed by a gilded **screen**★★★ by Master Bartolomé, are the **mausoleums**★★★ of the Catholic Monarchs on the right, and of Philip the Handsome and Juana the Mad, the parents of Charles V, on the left. The first was carved by Fancelli in Genoa in 1517, the second, magnificent in scale and workmanship, by Bartolomé Ordóñez (the sarcophagi are in the crypt). The high altar **retable**★ (1520) by Felipe Vigarny shows great movement and expression. The lower register of the predella depicts the siege of Granada and the baptism of the Moriscos.

Museo

Among objects on display are **Queen Isabel's sceptre and crown, King Ferdinand's sword,** and outstanding **paintings**★★ by Flemish (Rogier Van der Weyden), Italian (Perugino, Botticelli) and Spanish (Bartolomé Bermejo, Pedro Berruguete) artists. The central section of the ***Triptych of the Passion*** was painted by the Fleming Dirk Bouts. Two sculptures of the Catholic Monarchs at prayer are by Felipe Vigarny.

Opposite are the 18C Baroque-style former **town hall** *(ayuntamiento)*, and just below, the **Centro de Arte José Guerrero**, dedicated to modern art, especially Granada's José Guerrero (1914-1991) *(open 11am-2pm and 5-9pm; Sun 11am-2pm; closed Mon, 1 Jan, 24-25 Dec; 958 22 51 85).*

Catedral★

Enter from Gran Vía de Colón. Open 10.45am-1.30pm and 4-7pm; Sun, 4-7pm; Apr-Sep, 10.30am-1.30pm and 4-8pm; Sun, 4-8pm. 3 €. 958 22 29 59.

Construction started in 1518. Diego Siloé introduced the Renaissance style to the design of Enrique Egas. The façade (1667) is by Alonso Cano.

The **Capilla Mayor**★ is surprising. Siloé designed a rotunda circled by an ambulatory, cleverly linked to the basilica. The rotunda combines superimposed orders, the uppermost with paintings by Alonso Cano of the Life of the Virgin and beautiful 16C stained glass. Marking the rotunda entrance are figures of the Catholic Monarchs by Pedro de Mena and, in a medallion by Alonso Cano, Adam and Eve. The **organ**★ from about 1750 is by Leonardo of Ávila. The finely carved Isabelline doorway in the south transept is the original **north portal**★ of the older Capilla Real.

Alcaicería

The area, with craft and souvenir shops, was a silk market in Moorish times.

Corral del Carbón

This 14C former Moorish storehouse has an arched doorway with *alfiz* surround and panels of *sebka* decoration.

Worth a Visit

Suggested walking routes are marked on the plan.

Albaicín★★

This quarter covers a slope facing the Alhambra. It was here that the Moors lived after the Reconquest. Alleys are lined by white-walled houses. Walls enclose luxuriant gardens of *cármenes* (town houses). Go to the **Iglesia de San Nicólas** (Church of St Nicholas, *access by the Cuesta del Chapiz)* at sunset, for a **view**★★★ of the Alhambra and the Generalife. The Sierra Nevada beyond is spectacular under snow in winter.

Baños Árabes★ (El Bañuelo)

Closed for restoration. 958 02 78 00.

These 11C baths with star-pierced vaulting are the best-preserved in Spain.

Monasterio de San Jerónimo★

Open 10am-1.30pm and 3-6.30pm; Apr-Sep, 10am-1.30pm and 4-7.30pm. 3 €. 958 27 93 37.

This 16C monastery was principally designed by Diego de Siloé. Plateresque and Renaissance doorways lead to harmonious cloisters. The **church**★★, with the tomb of Gonzalo Fernández de Cór-

B. Kaufmann/MICHELIN
Sacristy, Cartuja

doba, the Gran Capitán, has a rich Renaissance apse, and superb coffers and vaulting adorned with saints, angels and animals. The **retable★★** is a jewel of the Granadine School. The paintings are from the 18C.

Iglesia de San Juan de Dios★

Guided tours (50min), 10am-1pm; open afternoons by prior arrangement. Closed Sun, public hols and in Aug. 958 22 21 44.

The Baroque Church of St John of God is noted for its richness and stylistic uniformity. Behind a massive Churrigueresque altarpiece of gilded wood is a lavish *camarín* with the funerary urn of **San Juan de Dios**, founder of the Order of Knights Hospitallers.

Cartuja★

Open 10am-1pm (noon Sun and public hols) and 3.30-6pm; Apr-Oct, 10am-1pm and 4-8pm. 3 €. 958 16 19 32 (10am-noon only).

(*To the NW; follow Gran Vía de Colón or calle San Juan de Dios.*) Go in through the cloisters. The church is exuberantly decorated with Baroque stucco. At the back of the apse is the early-18C Sancta Sanctorum, a *camarín* decorated with multi-hued marble; beneath the cupola, painted in false relief, a marble Sagrario contains the Tabernacle.

The outstanding Late Baroque **sacristy★★** (1727-64) is called the Christian Alhambra for its intricate stuccowork. The door and cedarwood furnishings, inlaid with tortoiseshell, mother-of-pearl and silver, are by a Carthusian monk, José Manuel Vásquez.

Parque de las Ciencias★

Kids *Open 10am-7pm; Sun and public hols, 10am-3pm. Closed Mon, 1 Jan, 1 May, 15-30 Sep and 24-25 Dec. 5 €, 2€ planetarium. 958 13 19 00.*

This science park comprises an interactive museum, planetarium, observatory and tropical butterfly collection.

Museo Arqueológico

Open 9am-8.30pm (Tue, 2.30-8pm; Sun, 9am-2.30pm). Closed Mon and public hols. 1.5 0€, no charge for E.U. citizens. 958 22 56 03.

The archaeological museum is in Casa Castril, a Renaissance palace with a fine **Plateresque doorway★**. It exhibits Egyptian alabaster vases found in a necropolis in Almuñecar, a bull figure from Arjona and Roman and Moorish decorative art.

Sacromonte

The hillside opposite the Generalife is the Gypsy quarter where Flamenco performances are given in troglodyte dwellings. At then end of Camino del Sacromonte is the 17-18C abbey for which the hill is named (*guided tour 11am (noon Sun)-1pm and 4-6pm; closed Mon; 3€. 958 22 14 45*).

Hospital Real

The royal hospital, now the university rectorate, was founded by the Catholic Monarchs. The plan, similar to those in Toledo and Santiago de Compostela, is of a cross within a square. Four Plateresque windows adorn the façade.

Fundación Rodríguez-Acosta★
Open 10am-2pm. Closed Mon-Tue, 1 and 6 Jan, 1 May, 1 Nov and 25 and 31 Dec. 4€ (gardens and institute), 6€ with cave, library tour). 958 22 74 97.
This foundations houses the legacies of painter José María Rodríguez-Acosta (1886-1941) and archaeologist Manuel Gómez-Moreno (1870-1970), in a fine *carmen* built between 1914 and 1928. Gómez-Moreno's personal collection includes Romanesque and Gothic pieces, and canvases by Zurbarán, Ribera, Alonso Cano and others, as well as Aztec and Chinese items.

Carmen de los Mártires
Open 10am-2pm and 4-6pm; in summer, 10am-2pm and 5-7pm; Sat-Sun and public hols, 10am-6pm. Closed in Aug. 958 22 79 53.
The romantic terraced **gardens**★ of this Carmelite monastery on the Alhambra hill are embellished with fountains and sculptures.

Excursions

Huerta de San Vicente
Federico García Lorca, poet and dramatist, was born 20km/12mi from Granada in Fuentevaqueros in 1899 (he died in 1936, shot by Franco's soldiers). His admirers will want to visit the summer home of the García Lorca family here (*guided tours (30min), 10am-1pm and 4-7pm; Apr-Jun and Sep, 10am-1pm and 5-8pm; Jul-Aug, 10am-3pm; last entry 30 min before closing; closed Mon and public hols. 3 €; 958 25 84 66).*

SIERRA NEVADA★★
The Sierra Nevada between the Costa del Sol and Granada is massive, beautiful, and often snow-capped. There is skiing at **Solynieve**★★, with over 60km/37mi of slopes, 45 runs, and 20 ski lifts. Lodging is at **Pradollano**.
Vehicular access to the **national park** is restricted; the best way to tour is on foot. The most interesting routes are the ascents to the Laguna de la Yeguas, **Mulhacén** (3 482m/11 424ft) and **Veleta** (3 394m/11 132ft). Contact **El Dornajo Visitor Centre** (*open 9am to 2pm (2.30pm in summer) and 4.30-6pm (7pm in summer); 958 34 06 25).*

Alhama de Granada★
60km/37mi SW on the A 92 and A 335.
Alhama de Granada is a village of whitewashed houses and narrow streets above a deep gorge, dominated by the **Iglesia de la Encarnación**★, a well-proportioned church built of golden stone. The stunning **view**★ from the belvedere behind the Iglesia del Carmen encompasses the canyon of the Alhama River. Baths on the outskirts date from the Roman period. A Moorish **cistern**★ survives.

Tour Through the Alpujarras★★
90km/56mi – allow one day.
This isolated region stretches across the southern slopes of the Sierra Nevada.

From Lanjarón to Valor
The High Alpujarras encompass the valley of the Guadalfeo river. Houses typically have a flat roof terrace, a *terrao*.

Lanjarón
This resort is famous for its medicinal mineral water and spa. The 16C castle affords fine valley views.

The Alpujarran Uprising
In 1499 the Arabs who did not wish to leave Spain were forced to renounce their religion and to convert to Christianity. They were known as moriscos. In 1566 Philip II forbade them their language and traditional dress, which sparked off a serious uprising, especially in Las Alpujarras where the moriscos proclaimed as king Fernando de Córdoba under the name Abén Humeya. In 1571 Philip II sent in the army under Don Juan of Austria who crushed the rebellion. However, a tense feeling of unrest remained, and in 1609 Philip III ordered the expulsion of all the Moriscos (who numbered about 275 000) from Spain.

▶ *9km/5.5mi from Lanjarón, before Órgiva, take the GR 421, a narrow mountain road.*

Pampaneira★★

Of the villages in the **Poqueira Valley**★★, Pampaneira best preserves its traditional architecture, including the 17C Iglesia de Santa Cruz.

Bubión, a centre of *morisco* resistance in 1569, is 5km/3mi further along. In **Capileira** is the **Museo Alpujarreño de Artes y Costumbres Populares**, a museum re-creating 19C Alpujarran life through its popular arts and customs *(open 11.30am-2.30pm; Sat, 4-7pm (8pm in summer); closed Mon; ☎958 76 30 51).*

▶ *Return to the GR 421.* The road enters the **Trevélez Valley**★.

Trevélez★

Trevélez, the highest municipality in Spain (1 600m/5,248ft). is famous for cured hams and dried sausages. Behind the village rises **Mulhacén**, Spain's highest peak (3,482m/11 424ft).

Beyond Trevélez, the valley opens and the verdant landscape gives way to drier terrain planted with the occasional vineyard. **Yegen** owes it fame to the Englishman Gerald Brenan, the author of *South from Granada*.

Don Fernando de Córdoba, known as **Abén Humeya**, was born and lived in Válor, the next village after Yegen. Its 16C church, like many in the region, is built in Mudéjar style.

SIERRA DE GREDOS★★

MICHELIN MAPS 575 OR 576 K 14, L 14 – CASTILLA Y LEÓN (ÁVILA)

The massif of the Sierra de Gredos includes Pico de Almanzor (2 592m/8 504ft), highest peak in the Cordillera Central. The north face of the sierra is marked by glacial cirques and lakes; the south by a steep granite wall and gullies. Fertile valleys produce apples in the north and grapes, olives and tobacco on the sheltered south slope. Wildlife is protected in the Reserva Nacional de Gredos.

- **Information:** *Plaza San Pedro, 05400 Ávila, ☎920 37 23 68.*
- **Orient Yourself:** The sierra is almost due west of Madrid (M 501 via San Martín de Valdeiglesias) and south of Ávila (N 502 to Puerto del Pico).
- **Organizing Your Time:** Take a country drive of up to a day, stopping according to your interests.
- **Especially for Kids:** Safari Madrid game park.
- **Also See:** ÁVILA, La ALBERCA and MADRID.

Special Features

San Martín de Valdeiglesias

This old market town, with 14C castle walls built by the Lord High Constable Álvaro de Luna, is a starting point for explorations.

Toros de Guisando

6km/4mi NW. The *Bulls of Guisando* are four roughly carved granite figures in an open field. Similar ancient figures, possibly Celt-Iberian, are found elsewhere in Ávila province. They are similar to the stone *porcas* (sows) seen in the Trás-os-Montes region of Portugal.

Embalse de Burguillo★ (Burguillo Reservoir)

20km/12mi NW. The man-made lake on the Alberche river is frequented by water sports enthusiasts.

Pantano de San Juan

8km/5mi E. The road down to this lake affords attractive **views**★ of the Alberche reservoir, its banks covered in pines. The area is popular with Madrid residents in summer for water sports.

Safari Madrid

27km/17mi SE at **Aldea del Fresno**.

Kids This is one of Spain's largest game parks, with animals from the world over. (*open 10.30am-6.30pm (9.30pm in summer); 10 €, 6 € children aged 3-10; ☎91 862 23 14).*

From San Martín de Valdeiglesias, take the M 501 (which becomes the C 501), towards Arenas de San Pedro.

Arenas de San Pedro

The main monument of this attractive town at the foot of the sierra is the Gothic **Iglesia de Nuestra Señora de la Asunción.**

Cuevas del Águila★ (Águila Caves)

9km/5.5mi S of Arenas de San Pedro.

Bear right immediately beyond the village of Ramacastañas and continue for 4km/2.5mi along the unsurfaced road.

A single vast chamber is open to the public. Among the many concretions are lovely frozen streams of calcite, ochre crystals coloured by iron oxide and massive pillars still in process of formation (*open 10.30am-1pm and 3-6pm (7pm in summer); 4 €. ☎920 37 71 07).*

Puerto del Pico road★

29km/18mi NE of Arenas de San Pedro.

The road through the sierra crosses **Mombeltrán** (15C castle with well-preserved exterior), then winds upward, parallel to a Roman road, used for years as a stock route. From the pass (1 352m/4 436ft) there is a good **view**★ of the mountains and, in the foreground (south), of the Tiétar Valley and, beyond, the Tajo. Beyond the pass is an austere boulder-strewn landscape.

The **Parador de Gredos**, first in Spain (1928), stands in a magnificent **setting**★★ with far-reaching views.

Laguna Grande★

12km/7.5mi S of Hoyos del Espino. Park at the end of the road. A well-marked path leads up to Laguna Grande (*2hr*), a glacial basin fed by mountain torrents. Halfway along is an unforgettable **panorama**★ of the Gredos cirque.

GUADALAJARA

POPULATION: 67 847

MICHELIN MAP 576 K 20 – MAP 121 ALREDEDORES DE MADRID – CASTILLA-LA MANCHA (GUADALAJARA)

Guadalajara ("river of stones" in Arabic) in the 14C became the fief of the Mendozas, an illustrious family in Spanish history. It includes the poet Íñigo López de Mendoza, first Marquis of Santillana (1398-1458); his son, Cardinal Pedro González de Mendoza (1428-95); and the second Duke of Infantado, who built the palace at the north entrance to the town in the 15C.

- **Information:** *Plaza de los Caídos 6, 949 21 16 26.*
- **Orient Yourself:** Guadalajara is NE of Madrid along the A 2 motorway.
- **Don't Miss:** The Palacio del Infantado.
- **Also See:** MADRID (55km/34mi SW), ALCALÁ DE HENARES (25km/15mi SW) and SIGÜENZA (75km/47mi NE).

Worth a Visit

Palacio del Infantado★ (Palace of the Duke of Infantado)

Open 10am-2pm and 4-7pm; Sun and public hols, 10.30am-2pm. Closed Mon, 1 and 6Jan, Good Fri, and 25 and 31 Dec. 949 21 33 01.

The late-15C palace, by Juan Guas, is a masterpiece of Isabelline civil architecture fusing Gothic and Mudéjar styles. The **façade**★ is adorned with diamond stonework and the Mendoza coat of arms. The upper gallery is a series of paired ogee windows interposed between corbelled loggias. The effect is splendid in spite of windows added in the 17C. The two-storey **patio**★ is just as remarkable with multifoil arches on turned columns and extremely delicate Mudéjar ornamentation. The once-sumptuous interior was damaged during the Spanish Civil War.

Francis I of France, captured at Pavia in 1525, was received here with pomp on his way to imprisonment in Madrid.

The palace houses the **Museo Provincial de Guadalajara** (*open 9am-9pm; Sun and public hols, 10am-2pm; closed 1 and 6 Jan, Good Fri, 1 May, and 25 and 31 Dec; 949 21 33 01*).

Excursion

Pastrana

42km/26mi SE on the N 320. This picturesque town was the seat of the **Princess of Eboli**, involved in intrigues in the time of Philip II. The **Palacio Ducal** stands on Hour Square, so named because a princess confined to the palace was allowed an hour at the window every day.

The 16C **Colegiata**, a collegiate church, contains, in the sacristy, four Gothic **tapestries**★ woven in Tournai after cartoons by Nuno Gonçalves which illustrate the capture of Arzila and Tangier by Alfonso V of Portugal in 1471. They reveal a mastery of composition, love of detail (armour and costume) and talent for portraiture (*open 11.30am-2pm and 4.30-5pm; Sun and public hols, 1-2pm and 4.30-5pm; 2.50 €; 949 37 00 27*).

GUADALUPE★★

POPULATION: 2 447

MICHELIN MAP 576 N 14 – EXTREMADURA (CÁCERES)

Guadalupe's monastery bristles with battlements and turrets above a picturesque village with brown tile roofs. The road above the old village★ commands a good view★ of the magical setting.

- **Information:** *Plaza Santa María de Guadalupe 1, ☎927 15 41 28.*
- **Orient Yourself:** Guadalupe is SW of Madrid, on the slopes of the Guadalupe range.
- **Don't Miss:** The monastery.
- **Also See:** TRUJILLO (82km/51mi W) and TALAVERA DE LA REINA (106km/66mi NE).

Special Features

MONASTERIO★★ *1hr 15min*

Guided tours (1hr), 9.30am-6.30pm. 3 €. ☎927 36 70 00.

The monastery, abandoned in 1835, was restored by Franciscans after 1908. The complex dates from the late 14C-early 15C, but the numerous additions result in a confused crowding of buildings within the fortified perimeter. The monastery contains artistic treasures.

Façade

15C. The façade, golden in colour, exuberant in its Flamboyant Gothic decoration, overlooks a picturesque square. Moorish influence can be seen in the sinuous decoration. Bronze reliefs on the 15C doors illustrate the Lives of the Virgin and Christ.

WHERE TO STAY

Hospedería del Real Monasterio – *Plaza Juan Carlos I – ☎927 36 70 00 – www.monasterio-guadalupe.com – Closed 15 Jan-15 Feb – – 47 rooms – 6.75 € – Restaurant 16.90€.* The hotel's superb setting, around the monastery's Gothic cloisters, and its comfortable, quiet rooms ensure a memorable stay. Excellent value for money plus a good restaurant. Highly recommended.

ARTS AND CRAFTS

Coppersmithing (jugs and pots) is still very much alive in Guadalupe.

Iglesia (Church)

14C. One of the first buildings, the church received 18C additions, such as gilt Baroque decoration on the vaulting

Patron of Todas Las Españas (All the Spains)

The first shrine is believed to have been built following the discovery of a miraculous Virgin by a cowherd in 1300. Alfonso XI, having invoked the Virgin of Guadalupe, as she was known, shortly before his victory over the Moors at the **Battle of Salado** (24 October 1340) had a grandiose monastery built in gratitude and entrusted it to the Hieronymites. The pilgrimage centre, richly endowed by rulers and deeply venerated by the people, exercised a great influence in the 16C and 17C when it became famous for craftsmanship – embroidery, gold and silversmithing, illumination – and more importantly, situated as it was at the heart of the kingdom of the Conquistadors, the symbol of the **Hispanidad** – that community of language and civilisation which links the Spanish of the Old and New Worlds. Christopher Columbus named a West Indian island after the shrine; the first American Indians converted to Christianity were brought to the church for baptism and Christians freed from slavery came in pilgrimage to leave their chains as votive offerings.

Solemn processions on 12 October celebrate the day of the Hispanidad.

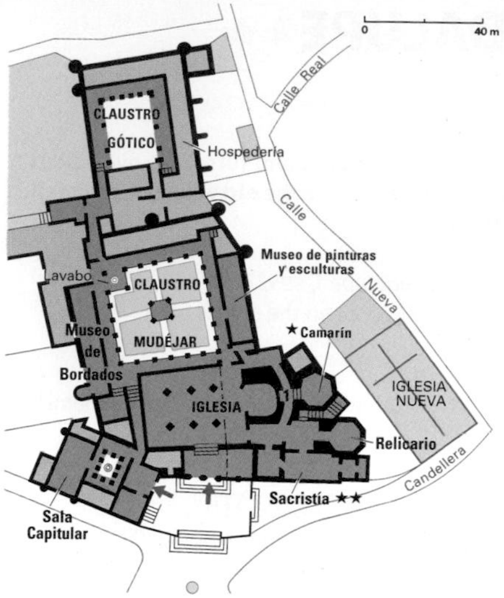

and the pierced balustrade above the nave. An intricate 16C grille by Valladolid ironsmiths closes the sanctuary, which has a large classically ordered 17C retable by Giraldo de Merlo and Jorge Manuel Theotocopuli, son of El Greco. The Virgin of Guadalupe in the altarpiece **(1)** can be seen more clearly from the *Camarín*.

Sala Capitular (Chapter house)

The chapter house contains a remarkable collection of 87 **antiphonaries and books of hours with miniatures**★ by the monks of Guadalupe.

Claustro Mudéjar

The 14C-15C cloisters are remarkable for their size and the two storeys of horseshoe arches. Note a small Mudéjar Gothic temple and, in a corner, a lavabo faced with multicoloured tiles.

Museo de Bordados (Embroidery Museum)

The museum, in the former refectory, displays a fine collection of **copes and altar-fronts**★★, embroidered by the monks between the 15C and the 19C.

Museo de Pinturas y Esculturas (Painting and Sculpture Museum)

Works include a 16C triptych of the *Adoration of the Magi* by Isembrandt, an ivory Christ attributed to Michelangelo, an *Ecce Homo* by Pedro de Mena, eight small canvases of the monks by Zurbarán, and Goya's *Prison Confession*.

Sacristía★★ (Sacristy)

17C. Canvases by Carreño de Miranda hang in the antechamber. The sacristy combines Classical architecture and ornate Baroque decoration. The unexpected harmony and rich colouring set

B. Brillion/MICHELIN

Monasterio de Guadalupe

off **paintings by Zurbarán**★★ to perfection. The 11 canvases, painted in a serene yet forceful style between 1638 and 1647, are of Hieronymite monks and scenes from the Life of St Jerome including *The Temptation*.

Relicario (Reliquary Cabinet)

This contains a collection of the Virgin of Guadalupe's mantles and the crown, worn only in solemn processions.

Camarín★

18C. A chapel-like room where the Virgin of Guadalupe rests. Riches of every description abound: jasper, gilded stucco and marble and precious wood marquetry frames for nine canvases by Luca Giordano. The Virgin sits on an enamelwork throne (1953), a small 12C figure carved in darkened oak, obscured beneath embroidered veil and mantle.

Claustro Gótico (Gothic Cloisters)

In the *hospedería* (hostelry). The cloisters were built in the 16C in Flamboyant Gothic style to serve as a dispensary for the monastery's four hospitals.

Excursions

Puerto de San Vicente (San Vicente Pass)

40km/25mi E on the C 401. The **road**★ to the pass crosses the Las Villuercas range. The climb *(8km/5mi)* beyond the Guadarranque Valley affords wonderful **views**★ of jagged green mountain ranges above the wild moorland.

SIERRA DE GUADARRAMA★

MICHELIN MAP 575 OR 576 J 17-18 – CASTILLA Y LEÓN (SEGOVIA), MADRID

The Sierra de Guadarrama is an oasis in the desert of Castilla, its snow-capped peaks visible from Ávila, Segovia and Madrid. Steep granite and gneiss slopes are covered in oaks and pines. Mountain-born streams feed the province's reservoirs. Mountain resorts, such as Navacerrada, Cercedilla, Guadarrama and El Escorial provide refuge for Castilians fleeing torrid summers on the Meseta.

- **Information:** *Puerto de Navacerrada: Caseta Punto de Información (information post), ☎91 852 33 02.*
- **Orient Yourself:** The mountain range stretches around 100km/62mi SW to NE between Ávila and Madrid.
- **Organizing Your Time:** Take a full-day drive, or longer to hike.
- **Also See:** MADRID, SEGOVIA and Monasterio de EL ESCORIAL.

Tours

FROM MANZANARES EL REAL TO SEGOVIA

106km/66mi – allow one day excluding visits to Segovia and Riofrío.

Manzanares el Real

The **castillo**★ was built by the Duke of Infantado in the 15C. This gem of civil architecture is well-proportioned, the austerity of its lines relieved by bead mouldings on the turrets and the Plateresque decoration on the south front, possibly by Juan Guas (*open 10am-5.15pm (10am-1.15pm and 4-7.15pm Jun-Sep); closed Mon and public hols; 1.80 €; ☎91 853 00 08).*

Sierra de la Pedriza★

This granite massif of the foothills, in turns rose-coloured rock and eroded screes, is popular with rock climbers, particularly near Peña del Diezmo (1 714m/5 623ft).

Address Book

For coin ranges, see the Legend on the cover flap.

WHERE TO EAT

⊖⊖ **Asador Felipe** – *Mayo 2 – Navacerrada – ☎91 853 10 41 – Open Jul-Sep and public hols rest of year.* The popular Asador Felipe is just a few metres from the Restaurante Felipe, owned by the same proprietor and in business for over 20 years. Delicious grilled meats cooked over an open fire, typically Castilian decor, and a pleasant terrace for the summer months.

WHERE TO STAY

⊖⊖ **Hotel La Posada de Alameda** – *Grande 34 – Alameda del Valle – 6km/4mi NE of El Paular along the M 604 – ☎ 91 869 13 37 – www.laposadadealameda.com – P – 22 rooms – ☕ 6 € – Restaurant 24/40 €.* This attractive rural inn started life as a dairy farm before its conversion to a modern-style hotel adorned with designer furniture. The lounge areas and bedrooms, some with dormer wndows, are simple yet cosy, with stone floors and functional bathrooms. The *posada* also has a bright, attractive restaurant.

▶ *Continue along the M 608, alongside the Santillana reservoir, to Soto del Real, then follow the M 611.*

Puerto de la Morcuera

As you reach the pass (1 796m/5 892ft), an extensive view opens toward El Vellón reservoir. A descent through moorland brings you to the wooded Lozoya depression. The río Lozoya is a well-known trout stream.

Real Monasterio de Santa María de El Paular★

2km/1.2mi from Rascafría. Castilla's earliest Carthusian monastery (1390) stands in the cool Lozoya Valley. The reconstructed complex includes a hotel in a former palace. The **church** has a Flamboyant doorway by Juan Guas. There is a magnificent 15C alabaster **altarpiece**★★ illustrating the Lives of the Virgin and Christ. The Tabernáculo (Tabernacle) is decorated in exuberant Baroque (*guided tours (45min), at noon, 1pm and 5pm; Sun and public hols at 1pm, 4pm, 5pm and 6pm; ◷ closed Thu afternoon; ☎91 869 14 25).*

Puerto de los Cotos

1 830m/6 004ft. The pass is a base for ski-lifts. From the upper terminus at Zabala, hike in summer to the Laguna de Peñalara *(15min)*, a former glacial cirque, the Picos de Dos Hermanas (Summit of the Two Sisters) *(30min)* and Peñalara (2 429m/7 967ft), the highest point in the sierra *(45min)*.

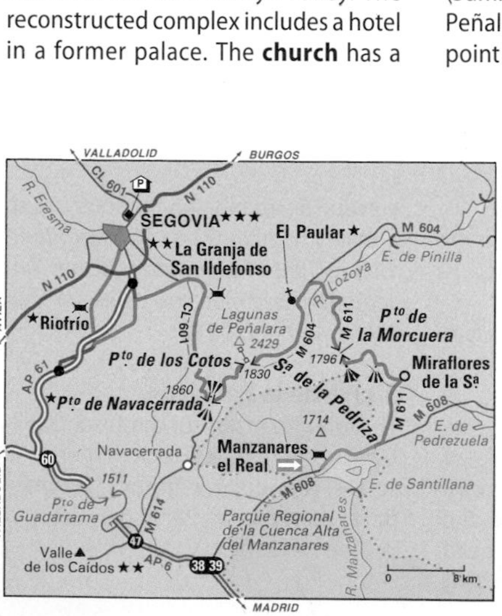

Puerto de Navacerrada★

1 860m/6 102ft. The pass, a ski resort on the borders of the two Castillas, commands a beautiful **view**★ of the Segovian plateau. A train runs to Cercedilla.

▶ *Take the CL 601 towards Valsaín and La Granja.*

Palacio de La Granja de San Ildefonso★★

◷ *Open 10am-1.30pm and 3-5pm; Sun and public hols, 10am-2pm; Easter-15 Oct, 10am-6pm.*

Gardens, Palacio de La Granja

Closed Mon, 1, 6 and 23 Jan, 1 May, 25 Aug, and 8, 24, 25 and 31 Dec. 5 €, no charge Wed for E.U.citizens. 921 47 00 19.

La Granja is a little Versailles at 1 192m/3 911ft, built in 1731 by Philip V, in pure nostalgia for the palace of his childhood. Philip V and his second wife, Isabel Farnese, are buried in the collegiate church.

The palace

Galleries and chambers, faced with marble or hung with velvet, are lit by chandeliers. A **Museo de Tapices**★★ (Tapestry Museum) contains principally 16C Flemish hangings, notably *(3rd gallery)* nine of the *Honours and Virtues* series and a 15C Gothic tapestry of *St Jerome* after a cartoon by Raphael.

Gardens★★

Open Nov-Feb, 10am-6pm (6.30pm Oct and Mar; 7pm Apr; 8pm May, first two weeks of Jun, and Sep; 9pm second two weeks of Jun, and Jul-Aug). The fountains operate at 5.30pm Wed, Sat-Sun and public hols subject to sufficient water; all the fountains operate on 30 May, 25 Jul and 25 Aug. 3.40 € (if fountains are operating). 921 47 00 19.

The ground was levelled with explosives before the French landscape gardeners (Carlier, Boutelou) and sculptors (Dumandré, Thierry) started work. The woodland vistas are more natural, however. The chestnut trees, brought from France at great expense, are magnificent. The **fountains**★★ begin at the Neptune Basin, go on to the New Cascade (Nueva Cascada), a multicoloured marble staircase in front of the palace, and end at the Fuente de la Fama (Fame Fountain), which jets up a full 40m/131ft (*see also INTRODUCTION TO SPAIN: GARDENS OF SPAIN).*

Real Fábrica de Cristales de La Granja (Royal Glass Factory)

Open 10am-6pm (7pm 15 Jun-15 Sep); Sun and public hols, 10am-3pm. Closed Mon, 1 and 6 Jan and 25 December. 3.50 €. 921 01 07 00.

Although the works date to the reign of Philip V, the present building was erected in 1770, under Charles III. It is a rare example of early industrial architecture and is now the the National Glass Centre and museum.

Riofrío★ *See SEGOVIA*

Segovia★★★ *See SEGOVIA*

GUADIX★

POPULATION: 20 322

MICHELIN MAP 578 U 20 – ANDALUCÍA (GRANADA)

Guadix, an ancient farming centre, became important under the Romans and the Visigoths a strategic road junction. It flourished under the Moors and up to the 18C, a period of artistic splendour. Guadix is known for one of the largest complexes of cave dwellings in Spain.

- **Information:** *Avenida Mariana Pineda, ☎958 66 26 65.*
- **Orient Yourself:** Guadix, at the centre of a basin in southern Spain, is 57km/35mi from Granada along the A 92, and a good base for exploring the Alpujarras (Puerto de la Ragua is just 30km/18mi to the south).
- **Also See:** Granada.

Worth a Visit

Catedral★

Open 10.30am-1pm and 4-6pm. 3€ (cathedral and museum); no charge Thu. ☎958 66 08 90.

The east end is by Diego de Siloé; the 17C Renaissance tower and Baroque **façade★** (1713) are additions. Gothic naves lead to the Renaissance apse with a large lantern above the transept.

The River of LIfe

It was the Moors who gave this old Roman camp the poetic name of Guadh-Haix, which translates as "the river of life".

Plaza de la Constitución

The 17C town hall, built during the reign of Philip III.

Barrio de Santiago★

Monuments in this typical district include the **Iglesia de Santiago**, its lovely Plateresque **doorway★** leading to a pleasant square; and mansions such as the **Palacio de Peñaflor**. The Moorish **alcazaba** *(enter via the seminary)* affords fine views to the troglodyte quarter *(closed for restoration. ☎958 66 93 00).*

Barrio de las Cuevas★ (Troglodyte Quarter)

Walk toward the Iglesia de Santiago.
Beyond the church are dwellings hol-

B. Morandi/MICHELIN

Castillo de La Calahorra

lowed out of the soft tufa hillside, with conical chimneys. These unique dwellings maintain a stable temperature. One is a **museum** (*open 10am-2pm and 4-6pm; Sat, 10am-2pm; closed Sun and public hols; 1.50 €; 958 66 93 00).*

Excursions

Purullena

6km/4mi NW. The **road**★★ winds to the **troglodyte village** of Purullena, where pottery is made. Beyond, the Granada road winds upward, to offer plateau and canyon **views**★, to the **Puerto de Mora** (Mora Pass) at 1 390m/4 560ft.

La Calahorra★

18km/11mi SE along the A 92. La Calahorra is dominated by a **castillo**★★ so austere that the graceful interior is completely unexpected. Park in the village and walk up. A heavy door opens onto a Renaissance **patio**★★, a masterpiece of refinement. The arcades and balustrade, Italian window surrounds and **staircase**★ bespeak an elegant style of life. *(Wed, 10am-1pm and 4-6pm. 958 67 70 98).*

HUESCA★

POPULATION: 50 085

MICHELIN MAP 574 F 28 – SEE LOCAL MAP UNDER JACA – ARAGÓN (HUESCA)

The tranquillity of Huesca, capital of Alto Aragón (Upper Aragón), belies its turbulent past. The old town huddles around the top of a promontory crowned by an imposing cathedral.

- **Information:** *Plaza López Allué, 974 29 21 70.*
- **Orient Yourself:** Huesca is 72km/45mi N of Zaragoza, 91km/57mi S of Jaca and 123km/77mi NW of Lleida/Lérida, along the E 7 motorway. It is a good base for excursions into the Pyrenees.)
- **Also See:** BARBASTRO (52km/32mi SE), JACA and PIRINEOS ARAGONESES.

Background

Historical notes – Huesca was the capital of a Roman state, a Moorish stronhold until its reconquest by **Pedro I of Aragón** in 1096, and capital of Aragón until 1118.

The origins of a well-known Spanish saying – "Ringing like the bell of Huesca" is a Spanish way to describe a dire event. In the 12C, King **Ramiro II**, summoned his truculent nobles to watch the casting of a bell – and promptly had them beheaded.

Worth a Visit

OLD QUARTER

Catedral★

Open 10.30am-1.30pm (Apr-May 10.30am-1.30pm and 4-6pm; Jun-Oct 10.30am-2pm and 4-7.30pm). Sun and public hols open only for religious services. 2 €. 974 23 10 99.

The 13C Gothic façade is divided unusually by a gallery and an Aragonese carved wood overhang. A gable encloses a rose window and the portal covings with weathered statues. On the tympanum are the Magi and Christ before Mary Magdalene. The alabaster **altarpiece**★★ dates from 1533. In this masterpiece by Damián Forment, three scenes of the Crucifixion appear in high relief in the middle of Flamboyant canopy and frieze decoration.

Facing the cathedral, the *Ayuntamiento* (town hall) is a tastefully decorated Renaissance town house.

Museo Arqueológico Provincial★

Open 10am-2pm and 5-8pm; Sun and public hols, 10am-2pm. Closed Mon, 1 and 6 Jan, 24-25 and 31 Dec. 974 22 05 86.

The museum is in the old university, built in 1690 around a fine octagonal patio incorporating parts of the royal palace (and notorious massacre site). The collection includes prehistoric artifacts and **Aragonese primitive paintings**★, several by the Maestro de Sigena (16C).

Iglesia de San Pedro el Viejo★

Open 10am-1.30pm and 4-7.30pm. Closed Sun. 2€. 974 22 23 87.

The 11C monastery's **cloisters**★, with their historiated capitals, are a jewel of Romanesque sculpture in Aragón. The tympanum of the cloister doorway has an unusual Adoration of the Magi with all the emphasis on movement. A Romanesque chapel holds the tombs of Kings Ramiro II and Alfonso I, the Battler.

Excursions

Monasterio de Monte Aragón

5km/3mi E along the N 240. The monastery was originally a fortress built by Sancho I Ramírez.

TOUR THROUGH LOS MALLOS DE RIGLOS – SIERRA DE LOARRE

Take the A 132 to Ayerbe. Continue 9km/5.5mi, then turn left to Agüero.

Agüero

The village is set against a spectacular background of *Mallos* (*see below*). Before Agüero, a road leads (*right*) to the Romanesque **Iglesia de Santiago**. Three aisles of the church are covered by three separate stone roofs.

Take the A 132 towards Huesca, then the HU 310 left toward Riglos.

Los Mallos de Riglos★★

The Río Gállego is banked by tall crumbling cliffs, red ochre in colour. **Los Mallos** are a formation of rose pudding-stone, eroded into sugar loaf forms. The most dramatic group (*to the right*) dominates the village of **Riglos**.

Return to Ayerbe on the A 132, then turn left to Loarre along the A 1206.

Castillo de Loarre★★

Open 11am-1pm and 3-6pm (4pm Sun and public hols); Apr-Jun and Sep-Oct, 11am-1pm and 4-7pm; Jul-Aug, 10am-2.30pm and 4.30-9pm. Closed Mon (except Jul-Aug), 1 Jan and 25 Dec. 2€. 974 38 26 27.

In the 11C, Sancho Ramírez, King of Aragón and Navarra, had this castle-fortress built at an altitude of 1 100m/3 609ft. The walls, flanked by round towers, command a vast **panorama**★★ of the Ebro basin. After the massive keep and fine covered stairway, view the 12C church. The capitals are very beautiful.

Continue SE on the A 1206.

Bolea

The main church **altarpiece** is a superb example of 15C Hispano-Flemish art.

Return to Huesca on the A 132.

JACA★

POPULATION: 14 426

MICHELIN MAP 574 E 28 – ARAGÓN (HUESCA)

Jaca stands strategically at the foot of the Pyrenees, under the Peña de Oroel. It became the capital of Aragón in the 9C.

- **Information:** *Avenida Regimiento de Galicia 2, ☎974 36 00 98.*
- **Orient Yourself:** Jaca is along the A 23, from Huesca to El Puerto de Somport, and the N 240, to Pamplona (111km/69mi NW).
- **Also See:** PIRINEOS ARAGONESES, Monasterio de LEYRE (70km/44mi W) and HUESCA (91km/57mi S).

Worth a Visit

Catedral★

Open 8am-1pm and 4-8pm. ☎ 974 35 63 78.

Spain's oldest Romanesque cathedral, from the 11C, influenced craftsmen who worked on churches along the pilgrim route to Santiago de Compostela. Note the **historiated capitals**★ of the south porch and great detail in the south doorway figures.

Gothic vaulting covers unusually wide aisles. The apse and side chapels are decorated with sculpture but the cupola on squinches over the transept crossing has retained its simplicity.

Museo Diocesano (Diocesan Museum)

Closed for restoration. ☎974 36 18 41.

The cloisters and adjoining halls contain Romanesque and Gothic **wall paintings**★ from village churches in the area, and Romanesque paintings.

Castillo de San Pedro

Open 11am-noon and 5-6pm. ☎974 36 30 18.

Built in 1595 during the reign of Philip II, the castle was one of the citadels and towers along the French border. This low fortress, surrounded by a moat, has a perfect pentagonal plan, with defensive bulwarks at each vertex.

WHERE TO STAY

Conde Aznar – *Paseo de la Constitución 3 – ☎974 36 10 50 – www.condeaznar.com – 34 rooms – – Restaurant 15 €.* A good location in an old house on the quiet paseo de la Constitución, five minutes from the cathedral. Access to the hotel, furnished with antiques, is via a small terrace; an attractive wooden staircase leads to the guest bedrooms. The hotel also has two exceptional suites and a restaurant serving some of the best cuisine in the Pyrenees.

Tours

Tour through Serrablo 1

54km/34mi – allow half a day.

▸ *Leave Jaca on the A 23 towards Sabiñánigo.*

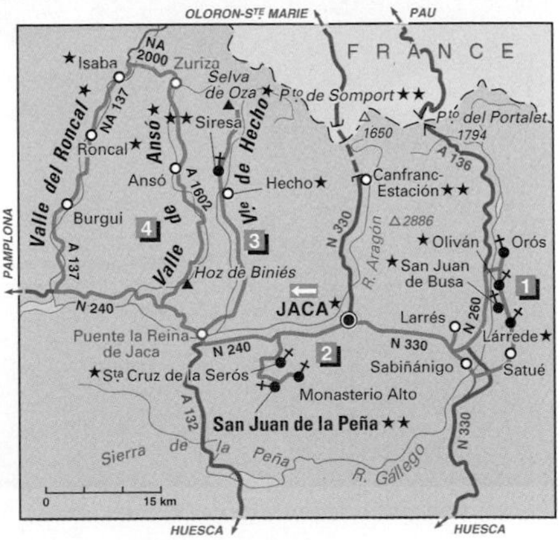

This excursion includes extraordinary 10C and 11C Mozarabic churches.

Museo de Dibujo

In Larrés, 18km/11mi E of Jaca along the A 23. Open 11am-1pm and 3-7pm (4-7pm Sun and public hols, Apr-Jun and Sep-Oct); July-Aug daily 10am-2.30pm and 4.30-8pm. 2 €. 974 48 29 81.

This museum, in the 14C Castillo de Larrés displays sketches by Martín Chirino, Salvador Dalí and others. A section covers graphic humour.

Return to the A 23. From Cartirana, take the N 260 to Puente Oliván. Follow signs to Oliván, then turn towards Orós Bajo. Follow directions below.

Mozarabic churches

The churches of the Serrablo are small and rectangular, with a semicircular apse. Walls are generally devoid of bays, while the arches are either horseshoe or semicircular; occasionally, doors are framed by an alfiz surround. The most impressive churches are in Orós Bajo, San Martín de Oliván, **San Juan de Busa**★ (with unfinished apse), **San Pedro de Lárrede**★ and Satué.

From Satué, head towards Sabiñánigo.

Museo Ángel Oresanz y Artes de Serrablo★

In Sabiñánigo, in Puente de Sabiñánigo S of the town centre. Open 10.30am-1.30pm and 3.30-6.30pm; Sun and public hols, 10.30am-1.30pm and 4-7pm. Apr-Jun and Sep, 10.30am-1.30pm and 4-7pm. Jul-Aug, 10.30am-1.30pm and 5-9pm. 2 €. 974 48 42 61.

The major ethnographic collection in the Huescan Pyrenees is in a wonderful traditional Serralbo house.

Monasterio de San Juan de la Peña★★ 2

25km/15mi – allow half a day.

Take the N 240 from Jaca. After 11km/7mi, turn off towards Santa Cruz de la Serós

Open 10am-2pm and 4-7pm; Jun-Aug, 10am-2.30pm and 3.30 (4pm in June)-8pm; 16 Oct-15 Mar, 11am-2pm and 4-5.30pm. 4.50 €. 974 35 51 19.

Santa Cruz de la Serós★

This 10C convent, endowed by nobles and princesses, was abandoned in the 16C. Only the **Romanesque church**★, surrounded by small Aragonese houses, remains. The stout belfry, crowned by an octagonal turret, abuts the lantern. The portal recalls Jaca Cathedral.

Beyond Santa Cruz de la Serós the road winds through the sierra.

Monasterio de San Juan de la Peña★★

The most spectacular feature of this monastery is its **setting**★★ in a hollow beneath overhanging rocks. The monastery was chosen as a pantheon for

B. Juge/MICHELIN

Church, Monasterio de San Juan de la Peña

the kings and nobles of Aragón and Navarra, and expanded in the 12C.

The oldest features can be seen on the lower storey, where the Lower Church dates from the early Mozarabic monastery. The **Sala de Concilios** (Council Chamber) was built by King Sancho Garcés around the year 922.

In the 11C-14C **Panteón de Nobles Aragoneses** are niches with coats of arms, sacred monograms and in many cases a cross with four roses, the emblem of Iñigo Arista, founder of the Kingdom of Navarra. The late-11C **Iglesia Alta** (Upper Church) comprises a single aisle, while the three apsidal chapels with blind arcades are hollowed out of the cliff. The **Panteón de Reyes** (Royal Pantheon) opens off the north wall.

The 12C **cloisters**★★, between precipice and cliff, are accessed by a Mozarabic door. Only two galleries and fragments of another remain. The **capitals**★★ exhibit a personal style and use of symbolism which influenced sculpture in the region for years.

Valle de Hecho★ 3

60km/37mi – allow one day.

- *Leave Jaca on the N 240. In Puente la Reina de Jaca, turn right on the A 176.*

The road follows the Aragón Subordán. The traditional houses of **Hecho**★ have stone doorways, many with coats of arms. The **Museo de Escultura al Aire Libre**, by the tourist office, shows sculpture in the open. There is also a **Museo Etnológico** (*open 1 Jul-15 Sep 10.30am-1.30pm and 5-9pm; 1.20 €*). 2km/1.2mi to the north in Siresa is the **Iglesia de San Pedro**★★, once part of a monastery. It was visited by **St Eulogus of Córdoba**, martyred in 859. The 11C **church** has a fine elevation and walls with blind arcades and buttresses. The **altarpieces**★ are principally 15C. *open 11am-1pm and 3-5pm; in summer, 11am-1pm and 5-8pm; 1.50 €).*

- *The road continues through a narrow valley towards* **Selva de Oza.**

Tour Through the Roncal and Ansó Valleys★ 4

161km/100mi – allow one day.

These two high valleys have a self-sufficient economy based on sheep rearing in common pastures. Festivals are celebrated in traditional costume.

- *Leave Jaca on the N 240, heading W. For 47km/29mi the road runs along the River Aragón through clay hills.*

- *Turn right onto the NA 137.*

The road goes up the green **Roncal Valley**★ watered by the River Esca. It crosses a narrow humpbacked bridge just before **Burgui. Roncal**★, famous for its cheese, has fine examples of noble architecture, and a museum dedicated to tenor **Julián Gayarre.** The road passes *(to the left)* the fortified tower of the Iglesia de Nuestra Señora de San Salvador de Urzainqui. **Isaba/Izaba**★ is the major valley centre.

- *A little further N, take the NA 2000 towards the Zuriza tourist complex.*

Once in the **Ansó Valley**★, this spectacular **road**★ runs along the River Veral to **Ansó**. In the church, the Museo Etnológico is dedicated to local ways (*open May-Oct, 11am-1.30pm and 4-8pm; otherwise by prior arrangement; 2 €; 974 37 01 85*).

- *Return south along the narrow, winding A 1602 through the Veral Valley.*

The river runs for 3km/2mi through the gorge known as the **Hoz de Biniés**.

WHERE TO EAT

Gaby-Casa Blasquico – *Plaza La Fuente 1 – Hecho – 974 37 50 07 – Closed 1-15 Sep.* This famous Pyrenean restaurant serves some of the best cuisine to be found anywhere in the province of Huesca, with a successful fusion of traditional and innovative ideas. The dining room is small but attractive, plus there are 6 guest and a plant-filled terrace.

JAÉN

POPULATION: 107 413

MICHELIN MAP 578 S 18 – ANDALUCÍA (JAÉN)

Jaén, dominated by its imposing fortress, is famous for the oil produced from its olive trees. The name derives from *geen* (on the caravan route). Its heritage includes Moorish remains and Renaissance buildings, many designed by Vandelvira.

- **Information:** *Maestra 13 (downstairs), ☎953 19 04 55.*
- **Orient Yourself:** Jaen is at the base of the Sierra de Jabalcuz. The A 44, heads south to Granada (94km/59mi S) past the Parque Natural de la Sierra Mágina.
- **Also See:** BAEZA (48km/30mi NE), ÚBEDA (57km/35mi NE), PRIEGO DE CÓRDOBA (67km/42mi SW) and GRANADA.

Worth a Visit

Catedral★★

Open 8.30am-1pm and 4.30-7pm (summer, 5-8pm), museum from 10am. Closed Sun afternoon in Jul-Aug. 3 €(museum). ☎953 22 46 75.

The cathedral looms over the historical quarter. It was built in the 16C and 17C by **Andrés de Vandelvira**, master of Andalucían Baroque. The façade with statues, balconies and pilasters resembles that of a palace.

The triple-nave **interior**★★ is crowned by fine ribbed vaulting and an imposing cupola above the transept. Behind the Renaissance altarpiece with its Gothic image of the **Virgen de la Antigua**★, a chapel holds the **Reliquía del Santo Rostro**★, said be a linen used by St Veronica to wipe Christ's face. The **choir stalls**★★ are carved in the Berruguete style. The sacristy, also by Vandelvira, houses the **museum** *(museo)*, which includes two canvases by Ribera, a Flemish *Virgin and Child*, large bronze candelabra by Master Bartolomé, and miniature choir books.

Baños Árabes★★

These Moorish baths are the largest in Spain (470m2/5 059sq ft). They lie beneath the 16C **Palacio de Villardompardo** and have been restored to their 11C apperance. (Open 9am-8pm; Sat-Sun, 9.30am-2.30pm; last admission 30min before closing time. Closed Mon and public hols. No charge. ☎953 24 80 00 (ext 4166).

B. Kaufmann/MICHELIN

Cathedral, Jaén

JEREZ DE LA FRONTERA★★

POPULATION: 181 602
MICHELIN MAP 578 V 11 – ANDALUCÍA (CÁDIZ)

Jerez looks out at fertile countryside. A provincial capital, it springs into life at fiesta time, sharing its tradions of wine, horsemanship, and flamenco.

- **Information:** *Alameda Cristina, Los Claustros building, ☎956 32 47 47.*
- **Orient Yourself:** Jerez is in the Andalucían countryside, just 35km/22mi from the provincial capital, Cádiz and 90km/56mi from Sevilla.
- **Don't Miss:** A *bodega* tour.
- **Organizing Your Time:** Take several hours to stroll the old quarters, with a stop at at least one *bodega* according to its hours.
- **Especially for Kids:** Take smaller visitors to the horse show for a treat.
- **Also See:** CÁDIZ, Costa de la LUZ and PUEBLOS BLANCOS.

Special Features

Bodega Domecq

Tours by arrangement. 5 € weekday mornings (7 € afternoons, Sat-Sun and public hols). ☎956 15 15 00.

The visit to the oldest Jerez bodega includes storehouses where a host of celebrities have signed their names.

Bodega González Byass

Tours at 11am, noon, 1, 5 and 6pm; Sun at 11 am, noon, 1 and 2pm. 8.50. ☎956 35 70 16/ 70 00.

The most famous storehouse is the spectacular La Concha bodega, designed by Gustave Eiffel in 1862.

Walking About

The Old Town

Plaza del Mercado

The medieval market is now a tranquil square bordered by the **Palacio de Riquelme**, with imposing Renaissance façade, the 15C **Iglesia de San Mateo**, and the **Museo Arqueológico**.

Take calle Cabezas to the **Iglesia de San Lucas**, *then calle Ánimas de Lucas, plaza de Orbaneja and calle San Juan.*

Iglesia de San Juan de los Caballeros★

This medieval church has a magnificent 14C **polygonal apse**★, topped by a ribbed cupola with jagged decoration.

Take calle Francos, then calle Canto to plaza de Ponce de León.

Note the fine **Plateresque window**★★ on one of the corners.

Go along calle Juana de Dios Lacoste, cross calle Francos. Follow calle Compañía to the Iglesia de San Marcos.

Historical Notes

Jerez was one of the first towns to be founded by the Moors on the Iberian Peninsula. A number of vestiges remain from the Moorish "Sahrish", including sections of the old walls, the fortress *(alcazaba)* and a mosque. In 1264, Jerez was conquered by the troops of Alfonso X, and developed into a settlement of strategic importance as well as a leading commercial centre. The economic resurgence experienced by the province of Cádiz in the 18C left its mark on Jerez, with the construction of fine Baroque buildings and its famous wine cellars, some of which can still be seen today.

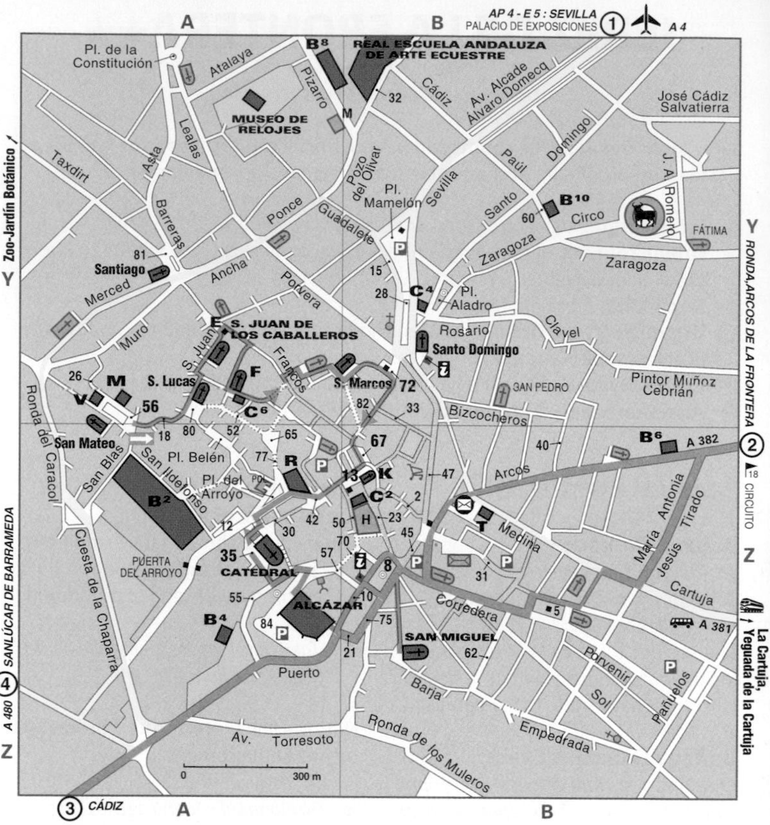

JEREZ DE LA FRONTERA

Aladro Pl.	BY	
Alcade Álvaro Domecq	BY	
Algarve	BZ	2
Ancha	AY	
Angustias Pl. de las	BZ	5
Arcos	BZ	
Arenal Pl. del	BZ	8
Armas	ABZ	10
Arroyo Calzada del	AZ	12
Arroyo Pl. del	AZ	
Asta	AY	
Asunción Pl. del	BZ	13
Atalaya	AY	
Barja	BZ	
Barreras	AY	
Beato Juan Grande	BY	15
Belén Pl.	AZ	
Bizcocheros	BY	
Cabezas	AYZ	18
Cádiz	BY	
Caracol Ronda del	AYZ	
Cartuja	BZ	
Chaparra Cuesta de la	AZ	
Circo	BY	
Clavel	BY	
Conde de Bayona	BZ	21
Consistorio	BZ	23
Constitición Pl. de la	AY	
Cordobeses	AY	26
Corredera	BZ	
Cristina Alameda	BY	28
Cruces	AZ	30
Doña Blanca	BZ	31
Duque de Abrantes Av.	BY	32
Eguilaz	BYZ	33
Empedrada	BZ	
Encarnación Pl. de la	AZ	35
Francos	AY	
Gaspar Fernández	BYZ	40
Guadalete	ABY	
José Luis Díez	AZ	42
Lancería	BZ	45
Larga	BZ	47
Lealas	AY	
Letrados	ABZ	50
Luis de Isasy	AYZ	52
Mamelón Pl.	BY	
Manuel María González	AZ	55
María Antonia Jesús Tirado	BZ	
Medina	BZ	
Mercado Pl. del	AYZ	56
Merced	AY	
Monti Pl.	BZ	57
Muleros Ronda de los	BZ	
Muro	AY	
Nuño de Cañas	BY	60
Pañuelos	BZ	
Paúl	BY	
Pedro Alonso	BZ	62
Peones Pl.	AZ	65
Pintor Muñoz Cebrián	BY	
Pizarro	AY	
Plateros Pl.	BZ	67
Ponce	AY	
Porvenir	BZ	
Porvera	ABY	
Pozo del Olivar	ABY	
Pozuelo	ABZ	70
Puerto	AZ	
Rafael Rivero Pl.	BY	72
Rosario	BY	
San Agustín	BZ	75
San Blas	AZ	
San Fernando	AZ	77
San Ildefonso	AZ	
San Juan	AY	
San Lucas Pl.	AYZ	80
Santiago Pl.	AY	81
Santo Domingo	BY	
Sevilla	BY	
Sol	BZ	
Taxdirt	AY	
Tornería	BY	82
Torresoto Av.	AZ	
Vieja Alameda	AZ	84
Zaragoza	BY	

Alcázar	AZ		Convento de Santa María de Gracia	AY	F	Museo Arqueológico de Jerez	AY	M
Bodega Domecq	AZ	B^{2}	Convento de Santo Domingo	BY		Museo de Relojes	AY	
Bodega González Byass	AZ	B^{4}	Iglesia de San Dionisio	BZ	K	Palacio de Riquelme	AY	V
Bodega Harvey	BZ	B^{6}	Iglesia de San Juan de los Caballeros	AY		Palacio del Marqués de Bertemati	AZ	R
Bodega Sandeman	ABY	B^{8}	Iglesia de San Lucas	AY		Real Escuela Andaluza de Arte Ecuestre	BY	
Bodega Williams & Humbert	BY	B^{10}	Iglesia de San Marcos	ABY		Teatro Villamarta	BZ	T
Cabildo	BZ	C^{2}	Iglesia de San Mateo	AZ		Yeguada de la Cartuja	BZ	
Casa Domecq	BY	C^{4}	Iglesia de San Miguel	BZ		Zoo-Jardín Botánico	AY	
Casa de los Ponce de León	AY	C^{6}	La Cartuja	BZ				
Catedral	AZ							
Centro Andaluz de Flamenco	AY	E						

Iglesia de San Marcos

This late-15C church has a beautiful 16C **star vault**. The apse is hidden by a 16C polygonal **altarpiece**★ showing strong Flemish influence.

From the square, calle Tonería leads to plaza de Plateros.

Plaza de Plateros

The **Torre de Atalaya**, a 15C tower, is adorned with Gothic windows.

Plaza de la Asunción★

The Renaissance façade of the **Casa del Cabildo**★★ (1575), is adorned with grotesque figures. The Gothic **Iglesia de San Dionisio** shows Mudéjar influence.

Head down calle José Luis Díez.

Plaza del Arroyo

The **Palacio del Marqués de Bertemati**★ has fine Baroque balconies.

Catedral★★

Open 11am-1pm and 6-8pm; Sat 10am-2pm and 6-8pm; Sun 11am-2pm. 956 34 84 82.

This monumental cathedral, with five aisles, combines Renaissance and Baroque features. The cupola bears bas-reliefs of the Evangelists. The annual wine harvest festival is held in front of the cathedral.

Alcázar★

Open 16 Sep-30 Apr, 10am-6pm; 1 May-15 Sep, 10am-8pm; Sun and public hols, 10am-3pm. Closed 1 and 6 Jan and 25 Dec. 3 € (5.40 € with camera oscura). 956 32 69 23.

Sherry

History would appear to show that the vine was first brought to this part of Spain by the Phoenicians, and that the Romans later exported large quantities of wine from the region during their long period of occupation. It is also known that despite the law of prohibition laid down in the Koran, the production and consumption of wine continued during the period of Moorish occupation. Following the Reconquest of 1264 by the troops of Alfonso X, and then once again at the end of the 16C, two varieties of grape were introduced here; namely Palomino and Pedro Jiménez, both of which provide sherry with a particular character.

Sherry is a blended white wine which is divided into five main types: **Fino** (15-17º), or extra dry, the lightest in body and strawlike in colour; **Amontillado** (18-24º), an older fino; **Oloroso** (18-24º), a medium, fragrant, full bodied and golden wine; **Dulce**, an oloroso with a higher concentration of sugar; and **Manzanilla**, a dry, light sherry from the coastal town of Sanlúcar de Barrameda. Their quality is the result of two principal factors: the region's special climate, and a careful maturing process which involves gradual blending and the use of solera or mother wines, with three or four American oak barrels placed one on top of the other. Each year a specific quantity of new wine is transferred to the top barrel; the same amount is then transferred from this barrel to the one immediately below it. This process continues until the very last barrel, which contains the desired wine. A visit to a **bodega**★ (a wine storehouse) is an interesting experience: **Domecq, González Byass, Sandeman** and **Williams&Humbert**.

Address Book

For coin ranges, see the Legend on the cover flap.

WHERE TO EAT

⊜⊜ **Gaitán** – *Gaitán 3 – ☎956 16 80 21 – www.restaurantegaitan.com – Closed Sun–* ▤ . This well-respected restaurant serves good-quality, innovative regional cuisine. The small whitewashed dining room is long and narrow and abundantly embellished with decorative objects.

⊜⊜ **La Taberna Flamenca** – *Angostillo de Santiago, 3 – ☎956 32 36 93 – www.latabernaflamenca.com – Closed Sun-Mon 30 Oct-30 Apr – reservation advised – 30/40€.* This restaurant in an ex-wine storehouse offers meals with a *tablao flamenco* performance (*Tue-Thu and Sat at 2.30pm and nightly at 10.30pm*).

TAPAS

Juanito – *Pescadería Vieja 8-10 – ☎ 956 33 48 38 – Closed during Jerez fair* – ▤. The Jerez classic in a pedestrian-ised street lined with outdoor terraces, has been serving its huge choice of tapas in Jerez for the past 50 years or more. The decor could not be more Andalucían, with its ceramic tiles and bullfighting-inspired pictures.

WHERE TO STAY

⊜ **Serit** – *Higueras 7 – ☎956 34 07 00 – www.hotelserit.com –* ▤ ♿ *– 35 rooms.* ☕ *6€.* A central, family-run hotel, functional and up-to-date. Best rooms, in the annex, have wood floors and wrought-iron furniture.

⊜⊜ **Hotel Doña Blanca** – *Bodegas 11 – ☎956 34 87 61 – www.hoteldonablanca.com –* ▤ *– 30 rooms –* ☕ *6.50€.* This unpretentious hotel in an attractive Andalucían-style building has the great advantage of a superb location between the market and post office in the centre of Jerez. The bedrooms here are on the spacious side with all the usual creature comforts.

NIGHTLIFE

Bereber – *Cabezas 10 – ☎956 34 42 46 – www.tablaodelbereber.com – Open 4pm-2am (hols to 6am) – dinner and show 9pm-midnight 95€ (reserve).* Bereber, in a Moorish palace, is the obligatory nighttime stopping-point. Its spaces (café, bar, patios, dance floors in wine cellars and restaurant with flamenco) are variously decorated in impeccable Arabian and Andalusian style.

ENTERTAINMENT

The **Teatro Villamarta** (*plaza Romero Martínez, ☎956 32 73 27*) offers opera, music, dance and theatre, including flamenco. The city's best-known **flamenco clubs** (*peñas flamencas*) are the Peña Tío José de Paula, at calle Merced 11 (*☎ 956 32 01 96*), and the popular Peña el Garbanzo, at calle Santa Clara 9 (*☎ 956 33 76 67*).

LEISURE

Baños Árabes Hammam Andalusí – *Salvador 6 – ☎956 34 90 66 – www.hammamandalusi.com – Baths 10am-10pm in 2hr sessions (reserve).* These re-created Moorish baths transport us to other times. The terrace and tea house look out to the cathedral.

FERIAS AND FESTIVALS

Horses are as important as sherry in Jerez and locally breeds are equally famous. In the 16C, the Carthusian monastery (Cartuja) crossed Andalucían, Neapolitan and German breeds, giving rise to the famous **Cartujana** horse. In April or May there are racing, dressage and carriage competitions at the **Feria del Caballo** (Horse Fair).

In September the **Fiesta de la Vendimia** (Wine Harvest Festival) showcases a cavalcade and a flamenco festival; the cante jondo is particularly alive and popular in Jerez, a town which is home to such famous singers as **Antonio Chacón** (1870-1929) and **Manuel Torres.**

From this 12C Almohad fortress, enjoy an excellent **view**★★ of the cathedral. Enter by the **Puerta de la Ciudad** (City Gateway). The prayer room in the **mosque**★★, located within the walls of the Alcázar, is covered by a delightful **octagonal cupola**. A **camera obscura** in the **Palacio de Villavicencio** pro-

J. Malburet/MICHELIN

Bodega González Byass

vides a unique view of Jerez via its mirrors and lenses.

Iglesia de San Miguel★★

Visits at 7pm daily. ☎626 78 54 48.
Construction began in Gothic style in the late 16C; the Baroque tower dates from two centuries later.The older San José façade is a fine example of the Hispano-Flemish style. The Renaissance **altarpiece**★ is by Martínez Montañés.

Worth a Visit

Palacio del Tiempo★★

Guided tours 10am-3pm (Mar-Oct also 6-8pm). Closed Mon except public hols, 1, 6 and10-31 Jan, 24-25 and 31 Dec. 6 € (9 € with Misterio de Jerez). ☎956 18 21 00.
This clock museum in the 19C Palacete de la Atalaya exhibits 300 18-19C timepieces in perfect working order. In the same gardens the **Misterio de Jerez** tells the story of Jerez wines (*guided tour, same hours as Palacio del Tiempo; 5€; ☎956 18 21 00).*

Fundación Real Escuela Andaluza del Arte Ecuestre★

Kids *Guided tour (30 min) including facilities and training sessions, Mon, Wed and Fri, 11am-1pm; horse show other days. Closed Sat-Sun and public hols. 8 €; show: 17 € or 23 € (23 € or 30 € during fairs). ☎956 31 80 08.*
The foundation in a 19C mansion by Charles Garnier, is dedicated to equestrian arts, including the training of horses. A **show**★★ in the main arena is not to be missed.

Museo Arqueológico de Jerez

Closed for renovation. ☎ 956 32 63 36.
The outstanding exhibit in the archaeological museum is a **Greek helmet**★.

La Cartuja★

6km/3.5mi SE.
This Carthusian monastery, founded in 1477, has a Greco-Roman portal attributed to Andrés de Ribera. The Flamboyant Gothic church has a richly decorated Baroque **façade**★★★.

La Cartuja Stud Farm★ (Yeguada de la Cartuja)

At the Finca Fuente del Suero, 6.5km/4mi from Jerez on the Medina Sidonia road. Guided tours (2hrs) Sat, 11am-1pm. Closed 15 Dec-15 Jan. 12.50 € (7.50 € child). ☎956 16 28 09.
Visitors to the stud farm get a close look at the famous Cartujana horses.

▸ Convento de Santo Domingo; Casa Domecq (18C, doorway★).

LEÓN★★

POPULATION: 147 625

MICHELIN MAP 575 E 13 (TOWN PLAN) – CASTILLA Y LEÓN (LEÓN)

León, once the capital of a kingdom, was an important pilgrim stop on the Way of St James and retains fine Romanesque and Gothic monuments.

- **Information:** *Plaza Regla 3, ☎987 23 70 82.*
- **Orient Yourself:** León is on the northern edge of the Meseta. The AP 66 motorway runs north to Oviedo (121km/75mi). Palencia (128km/80mi) and Valladolid (139km/87mi) are to the southeast.
- **Don't Miss:** The cathedral.
- **Also See:** THE WAY OF ST JAMES.

Background

The medieval town – In the 10C, the kings of Asturias moved their capital from Oviedo to León, and fortified it. By the 11C and 12C León had become virtually the centre of Christian Spain.

Ramparts and peeling stucco over old brick in the east of the city recall the early medieval period. The most evocative quarter, the Barrio Húmedo (wet quarter, for its many small bars), lies between the **Plaza Mayor** and **Plaza de Santa María del Camino**, an attractive square with wooden porticoes.

The modern city – Modern León is a sprawling industrial city. But its artistic tradition continues in Gaudí's neo-Gothic palace, **Casa de Botines** on plaza de San Marcelo.

Special Features

Catedral★★★

Open 8.30am-1.30pm and 4-7pm (8pm Jul-Sep). Closed Mon and 24 and 31 Dec. 1.70 €. ☎ 987 23 64 05.

The cathedral, built mainly between the mid-13C and late 14C, is true Gothic

Address Book

WHERE TO EAT

Rancho Chico – *Plaza San Martín 7 – ☎987 26 04 83 – Closed Wed, 15-30 Sep and 15-end Feb –* . For more than 20 years this restaurant has been earning plaudits from locals for its reasonably priced, simple, traditional fare. Its location on the pleasant and lively plaza de San Martín is an added bonus. Possible to eat on the terrace in fine weather.

Casa Pozo – *Plaza San Marcelo 15 – ☎987 22 30 39 – Closed evenings –* . This is one of the oldest restaurants in León, in business without a break since 1936. The two entries lead to separate tapas bars and assorted dining areas. A good place to sample the best of regional dishes.

WHERE TO STAY

La Posada Regia – *Regidores 11 – ☎987 21 31 73 – 20 rooms –* . A small, welcoming hotel in the old quarter of León, just a stone's throw from the cathedral. The building itself dates from the 14C and is an attractive mix of open brickwork and stone. Spacious, attractively furnished bedrooms.

Parador Hotel San Marcos – *Plaza San Marcos 7 – ☎987 23 73 00 – – 10.30 € – Restaurant 26.50 €.* Few hotels can claim to have a façade that is a masterpiece of Plateresque art! The interior continues the visual feast with its magnificent church and impressive Renaissance cloisters. Every corner of this former convent and pilgrims' hostel is a piece of art and history, in what is the most exclusive establishment in the parador chain.

in style even to the very high French-inspired nave with vast windows.

Main façade

The façade is pierced by three deeply recessed and richly carved portals. The gently smiling Santa María Blanca *(a copy: original sculpture in the apsidal chapel)* stands at the pier of the central doorway; on the lintel is a Last Judgement. The left portal tympanum illustrates scenes from the Life of Christ; the right portal includes the Dormition and the Coronation of the Virgin.

South façade

The statues decorating the jambs of the central doorway are extremely fine.

Interior

The outstanding **stained-glass windows**★★★ – 125 windows and 57 oculi with an area of 1 200m2/12 917sq ft – are unique in Spain; by their sheer number they weaken the walls. The west front rose and the three central apsidal chapels contain 13C-15C glass; the Capilla de Santiago (St James Chapel) shows Renaissance influence.
The Renaissance **trascoro**★ by Juan de Badajoz, includes four magnificent alabaster high reliefs framing Esteban Jordán's triumphal arch.
The high altar **retable**, painted by Nicolás Francés, is a good example of the 15C international style. To the left is a remarkable **Entombment**★, showing Flemish influence, attributed to the Master of Palanquinos. A silver reliquary contains the remains of San Froilán, the city patron.
Several Gothic tombs can be seen in the ambulatory and transept, in particular that of Bishop Don Rodrigo – in the Virgen del Carmen Chapel to the right of the high altar – which is surmounted by a multifoil arch.

Claustro★

The galleries are contemporary with the 13C-14C nave but the vaulting, with ornate keystones, was added at the beginning of the 16C. The galleries are interesting for the frescoes by Nicolás Francés and for the Romanesque and Gothic tombs.

Museo

Guided tours (1hr), 9.30am-1.30pm and 4-7pm; Jun-Sep, 9.30am-2pm and 4-7.30pm; Closed Sat afternoon Oct-May, Sun and public hols. 3.50 €. 987 87 57 70.
Among items in the museum are a French-inspired 15C statue of St Catherine, a Christ carved by Juan de Juni in 1576 (meant to be viewed from below), and a Mozarabic Bible.

Worth a Visit

San Isidoro★★

The **basilica**, built into the Roman ramparts, was dedicated in 1063 to Isidore, Archbishop of Sevilla, whose ashes had been brought north for burial in Christian territory. Of the 11C church only the pantheon remains. The apse and transept of the present basilica are Gothic; the balustrade and the pediment on the south front were added during the Renaissance.

Panteón Real★★★

Open 10am-1.30pm and 4-6.30pm; Sun and public hols, 10am-1.30pm; Jul-Aug, 9am-8pm; Sun and public hols, 9am-2pm. Closed 1 Jan and 25 Dec. 3 €, no charge Thu afternoon. 987 87 61 61.

© iStockphoto/Eric Naud
Catedral, León

León

Alcalde Miguel Castaño	B	2	González de Lama	B	18	Quevedo Av. de	A	40
Almirante Martín-Granizo Av. del	A	3	Guzmán el Bueno Glorieta de	A	23	Ramiro Valbuena	A	45
Ancha	B	16	Independencia Av. de	B	25	Rúa	B	
Arquitecto Ramón Cañas del Rio	B	4	Inmaculada Pl. de	A	5	Sáez de Miera Pas. de	A	47
Caño Badillo	B	8	Jorge de Montemayor	B	26	San Francisco Pas. de	B	48
Cruz Roja de León	A	9	Mariano Andrés Av. de	B	28	San Isidoro Pl. de	B	50
Espolón Pl. de	B	12	Murias de Paredes	B	30	San Marcelo Pl. de	B	52
Facultadn Av. de la	A	15	Ordoño II	A		San Marcos Pl. de	A	55
			Padre Isla Av. del	AB		San Pedro	B	38
			Palomera	B	31	Santo Domingo Pl. de	B	58
			Papalaguinda Pas. de	A	33	Santo Martino Pl. de	B	61

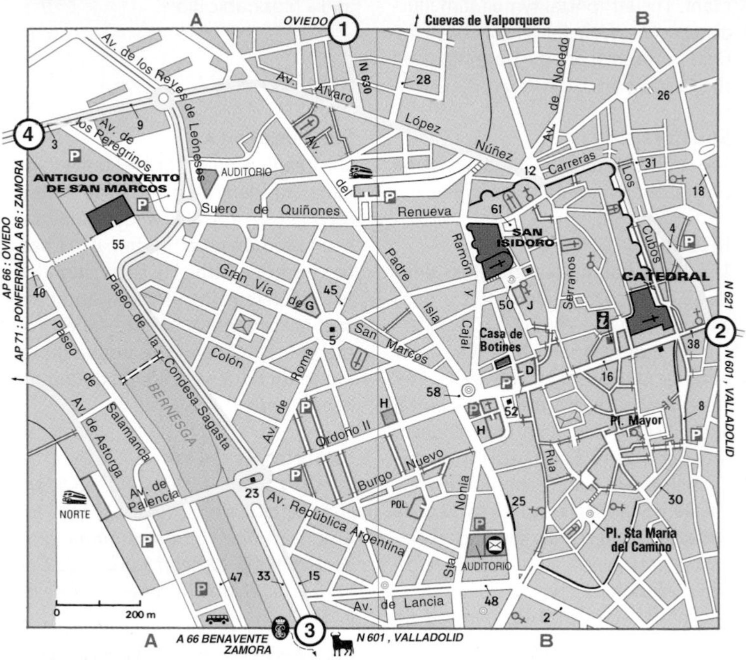

The Royal Pantheon is one of the earliest examples of Romanesque architecture in Castilla. The **capitals**★ on the short, thick columns bear traces of the Visigothic tradition yet at the same time exhibit notable advances in sculpture, showing scenes for the first time.

The 12C **frescoes**★★★ are outstanding. They illustrate not only New Testament themes but also country life.

The pantheon is the resting place of 23 kings and queens and many children.

Tesoro★★

The 11C reliquary containing the remains of San Isidoro is made of wood, faced with embossed silver and covered in a Mozarabic embroidery. The famous **Cáliz de Doña Urraca**★ (Doña Urraca chalice) comprises two Roman agate cups mounted in the 11C in a gold setting inlaid with precious stones. The plaques of the 11C **Arqueta de los Marfiles**★ (Ivory Reliquary) each represent an Apostle. The library contains over 300 incunabula and a Mozarabic Bible from 960.

Antiguo Convento de San Marcos★ (Former Monastery of St Mark)

Part of the monastery is a parador. The site has been connected with the Knights of the Order of Santiago (St James) since the 12C. Ferdinand and Isabel assumed control of the order, resulting in the present Renaissance edifice.

The 100m/328ft long **façade**★★ has a remarkable unity of style in spite of the addition of an 18C Baroque pediment.

It has two storeys of windows, niches friezes and cornices, engaged columns, pilasters and medallions in high relief illustrating Biblical and Spanish personages. The **church** front (on the extreme right), emblazoned with scallop shells, symbols of the pilgrimage to Santiago de Compostela, remains incomplete. The shell theme is repeated inside.

MUSAC (Museo de Arte Contemporáneo de Castilla y León)

Avenida de los Reyes Leoneses 24. Open 10am-3pm and 4-7pm. Closed Mon. 987 09 00 00.

This evocative building by Mansilla + Muñón, a centre for modern art, is covered in coloured crystals and focuses on living, working artists.

Museo de León★

Open 10am-2pm and 4-7pm; Jul-Sep, 10am-2pm and 5-8pm; Sun and public hols, 10am-2pm. Closed Mon, 6 Jan and 24 and 31 Dec. 1.20 €, no charge Sat-Sun, 23 Apr, 18 May, 12 Oct and 6 Dec. 987 24 18 87.

The museum displays the 10C Votive Cross of Santiago de Peñalba and an outstanding 11C ivory crucifix, the **Cristo de Carrizo**★★★. Byzantine influence is apparent in the small figure's penetrating gaze and formal pose. The **cloister** galleries, built between the 16C and 18C, serve as a lapidary museum (note the fine medallions on the keystones). The northeast corner contains a low relief of the Nativity with an interesting architectonic perspective by Juan de Juni. The **sacristy**★, a sumptuous creation by Juan de Badajoz (1549), has profusely decorated ribbed vaulting.

Excursions

San Miguel de Escalada★

28km/17mi W. Leave León via ③ on the town plan.

In the 11C, Alfonso III gave this abandoned monastery to refugee monks from Córdoba. Their church is the best-preserved Mozarabic building in Spain. The **outside gallery**★, built in 1050, has horseshoe-shaped arches resting on carved capitals at the top of smoothly polished columns. An earlier church **(iglesia**★**)** from 913 has wooden vaulting, and a balustrade of panels carved with Visigothic (birds, grapes) and Moorish (stylised foliage) motifs (*open 10.40am-2pm and 3-5.30pm; Apr-Sep, 10.15am-2pm and 4.30-8pm; Sun mornings only; closed Mon-Tue, 1 and 6 Jan, 24 Apr, 1 May, and 24-25 and 31 Dec; 987 23 70 82*).

Cuevas de Valporquero★★ (Valporquero Caves)

47km/29mi N on the LE 311. Guided tours (1hr 15min), Jun-Sep, 10am-2pm and 3.30-7pm; Oct-May, Fri-Sun and public hols only, 10am-5pm. 6.10 €. 987 57 64 08.

Neutral lighting sets off the extraordinary shapes of the concretions – there is a stalactite "star" hanging from the roof of the large chamber – and the variety of tones (35 have been counted) of red, grey and black of the mineral oxide-stained stone.

MONASTERIO DE LEYRE★

MICHELIN MAPS 573 OR 574 E 26 – NAVARRA

At the end of a winding road, a splendid panorama★★ opens up: limestone crests form majestic ramparts on whose slopes appear the ochre walls of the monastery.

- **Information:** *948 88 41 50.*
- **Orient Yourself:** The monastery is in NE Spain near the Yesa reservoir.
- **Also See:** SANGÜESA/ZANGOZA (15km/9mi SW), PAMPLONA (51km/32mi NW) and JACA (68km/42mi E).

Background

Historical notes – By the early 11C, the Abbey of San Salvador de Leyre was the spiritual centre of Navarra, and the final resting place of kings.

In the 12C, after union with Aragón, Leyre was neglected. By the 19C it had been abandoned. In 1954, however, a Benedictine community from Silos took over. They restored the 17C and 18C conventual buildings which have now been converted into a hostelry.

Special Features

Iglesia★★ (Church) *30min*

Open 10.15am-2pm and 3.30-7pm (6pm Nov-Feb). Closed 1 and 6 Jan and 25 Dec. 2.10 €. 948 88 41 50.

East end

11C. Three apses of equal height, together with the nave wall surmounted by a turret and a square tower make a delightful group. The absence of decoration, apart from several modillions, suggests the building's age.

Crypt★★

The robust 11C crypt, built to support the Romanesque church above, looks even older. The vaulting is relatively high but divided by arches with enormous voussoirs curving down onto massive plain capitals.

Interior★

In the 13C the Cistercians rebuilt the central aisle with a bold Gothic vault, while retaining earlier Romanesque bays with barrel vaulting, engaged pillars, and perfectly hewn stone. In the north bay a wooden chest contains the remains of the first kings of Navarra.

West portal★

12C. The portal is called the Porta Speciosa for its decorative richness. Carvings cover every available space. On the tympanum are archaic statues – Christ (centre), the Virgin Mary and St Peter *(on His right)* and St John *(on His left)*; the covings are alive with monsters and fantastic beasts.

Excursions

Hoz de Lumbier★

14km/9mi W. The Irati gorge between Lumbier and Liédana is barely 5km/3mi long and so narrow that it appears at either end as a crack in the cliff face. There is a good **view** of the gorge from a lookout point on the road (N 240).

Hoz de Arbayún★

31km/19mi N along the N 240 and NA 211. The river Salazar is steeply enclosed within limestone walls. From a point north of Iso there a splendid **view**★★ to the end of the canyon where the cliff walls are clad in lush vegetation.

B. Juge/MICHELIN

Crypt

LLEIDA/LÉRIDA★

POPULATION: 119 380
MICHELIN MAP 574 H 31 – CATALUNYA (LLEIDA)

Lleida, an ancient citadel, was stormed by the legions of Caesar, and occupied by the Moors from the 8C to the 12C. The Arab fortress, the Zuda, sited like an acropolis, was savaged by artillery fire in 1812 and 1936. The glacis has been converted into gardens. Lleida is an important fruit-growing centre.

- **Information:** *Plaze Ramón Berenguer IV, ☎973 24 88 40. www.catalunyaturisme.com; Major 31, ☎902 25 00 50. www.paeria.es/turisme*
- **Orient Yourself:** Lleida is linked to Barcelona by the AP 2 motorway, the Pyrenees by the C 1313 and N 240, and Huesca via the N 240.
- **Parking:** Space is limited in the old quarter.
- **Don't Miss:** A walk up to the Zuda for commanding views of city and plain.
- **Also See:** MONTBLANC (61km/38mi SE), TARRAGONA (97km/60mi SE), ZARAGOZA (150km/94mi W) and the PIRINEOS ARAGONESES.

To reach the cathedral, take the lift from plaza de Sant Joan.

Seu Vella★★★ (Old Cathedral)

Open 10am-1.30pm and 3-5.30pm; Jun-Sep, 10am-1.30pm and 4-7.30pm; last admission 20min before closing. Closed Mon, 1 Jan and 25 Dec. 2.40€, no charge Tue. ☎973 23 06 53.

The cathedral **site**★ dominates the city from inside the walls. It was built between 1203 and 1278 over a mosque; the octagonal belfry was added in the 14C. Philip V converted it into a garrison fortress in 1707.

Iglesia★★

The **capitals**★ of this transitional-style church are outstanding for their variety and detail. Those in the apses and transept illustrate the Old Testament, those in the nave and aisles, the New Testament. Moorish influences show in the exterior decoration, particularly the Puerta de Els Fillols (Godchildren's Doorway) and Puerta de la Anunciata (Annunciation Doorway). The extremely delicate carving, reminiscent of Moorish stuccowork, has come to be known as the Romanesque School of Lleida. It is seen throughout the region, in particular on the superb **portal**★★ of the Iglesia de **Agramunt** *(52km/32mi NE)*.

Claustro★★

The cloisters have an unusual position in front of the church. Their 14C galleries are remarkable for the size of the bays and the beautiful stone tracery. The Gothic style shows Moorish influence in the plant motifs on the **capitals**★. There is a fine view from the south gallery.

In the southwest corner stands the Gothic **bell tower**★★, 60m/197ft high. Along calle Major are the 13C **Palau de la Paeria**, now the town hall *(ayuntamiento)*, with its fine **façade**★; the **Hospital de Santa María**, with a **patio**★ showing Renaissance influence; and the 18C **Seu Nova** (new cathedral).

Exit through the Puerta del Lleó towards calle Sant Martí

Iglesia de Sant Martí★

Open 10am-1.30pm and 6-8pm; Sun and public hols, 10am-1.30pm. Closed Mon, 1 and 6 Jan, Good Fri, 1 May and 25-26 Dec. 1.80 €, no charge Tue. ☎ 973 28 30 75.

This 12C church was substantially remodelled three centuries after, and was later used as a barracks and a prison. **Sacred art**★ from the Museo Diocesano is on display in the nave.

Iglesia de Sant Llorenç

Open 8.30am-1pm and 5-8.30pm (7pm Sun and public hols). ☎973 26 79 94.

Address Book

WHERE TO EAT

⊜⊜ **El Celler del Roser** – *Cavallers 24 – ☎973 23 90 70 – www.cellerdelroser.com – Closed Sun evening, 25-26 Dec and 1 Jan* – ▤. In a *bodega* in the old quarter, with rustic decor. Traditional Catalan cooking includes magnificent bacalao (codfish), the house specialty.

TAPAS

Mini – *Ramón Soldevila 4 – ☎973 26 60 13 – Closed Sat evenings (summer), Sun and public hols*. Popular, a cut above the usual tapas in quality; meals are served.

WHERE TO STAY

⊜ **Hotel Goya** – *Alcalde Costa 9 – ☎ 973 26 67 88* – ⊭ – *18 rooms*. This pleasant small hotel is located in a lively district near the main shopping area and city centre. Although lacking in luxuries, the rooms are bright, clean and functional. Excellent value for money.

The late Romanesque church (13C) shows Gothic influence in its belfry and pointed arches alongside the central nave. Note the fine Gothic retables.

Hospital de Santa María

Open 10am-2pm and 5.30-8.30pm; Sat and public hols, noon-2pm and 5.30-8.30pm; Sun, 11am-2pm; Jun-Sep, 10am-2pm and 6-9pm; Sat and public hols, 11am-2pm and 7-9pm; Sun, 11am-2pm. Closed Mon, 1 Jan, Easter Mon, 1 May and 26 Dec. ☎973 27 15 00.

This former hospital, from the 15C, has a fine **patio**★, showing clear Renaissance influence. It is now used by the Institut d'Estudis Illerdencs (Institute of Lleida Studies).

Palau de la Paeria

Open 11am-2pm and 5-8pm; Sun and public hols, 11am-2pm. ☎973 70 03 94.

This 13C building in calle Major, with a lovely **façade**★, serves as the town hall, with an archaeology museum in the basement.

Palacio Episcopal (Museo Diocesano).

LUGO★

POPULATION: 87 605

MICHELIN MAP 571 C 7 (TOWN PLAN) – GALICIA (LUGO)

Lugo was capital of Roman Gallaecia, the legacy of which includes the town walls, old bridge and thermal baths. The old quarter huddles around the cathedral.

- **Information:** *Praza Maior 27, ☎982 23 13 61*
- **Orient Yourself:** Lugo is in central Galicia in NW Spain, 97km/61mi from A Coruña/La Coruña along the A 6, 96km/60mi from Orense/Ourense on the N 540, and 107km/67mi from Santiago de Compostela on the A 6 andA 54.
- **Don't Miss:** A stroll atop the walls.
- **Organizing Your Time:** See the cathedral and walls first, then explore the surrounding area.
- **Also See:** RÍAS ALTAS, The WAY OF ST JAMES and A CORUÑA/La CORUÑA.

Special Features

Old Town

Murallas★★

The Roman walls were built in the 3C, although they have been significantly modified. They are made of schist slabs levelled at a uniform 10m/33ft in a continuous 2km/1.2mi perimeter with 10 gateways. They are listed as a UNESCO World Heritage Site.

Catedral★

The Romanesque church (1129) has Gothic and Baroque additions. The Chapel of the Wide-Eyed Virgin at the east end, by Fernando Casas y Novoa (who built the Obradoiro façade of the cathedral in Santiago de Compostela) has a Baroque rotunda and stone balustrade. The north doorway has a fine Romanesque **Christ in Majesty**★. The figure is above a capital curiously suspended, carved with the Last Supper. The nave is roofed with barrel vaulting and lined with galleries, a feature common in pilgrimage churches. There are two immense wooden Renaissance altarpieces at the ends of the transept – the south one is signed by Cornelis de Holanda (1531). A door in the west wall of the south transept leads to the small but elegant **cloisters**.

City squares

The 18C **Palacio Episcopal**, facing the north door of the cathedral on **praza de Santa María**, is a typical *pazo*, one storey high with smooth stone walls, advanced square wings framing the central façade and decoration confined to the Gil Taboada coat of arms on the main doorway. **Praza del Campo**, behind the palace, is lined by old houses. Calle de la Cruz with its bars and restaurants, and **praza Maior**, dominated by the 18C **town hall,** with its gardens and esplanade, are popular meeting places. The Alejo Madarro sweet shop on rúa da Raiña first opened its doors in the middle of the 19C.

Museo Provincial

Open 10.30am-2pm and 4.30-8.30pm (8pm Sat); Sun, 11am-2pm; Jul-Aug, 11am-2pm and 5-8pm; Sat, 10am-2pm. Closed Sun and public hols (Jun-Aug) and 1 Jan, 22 May and 24-25 and 31 Dec. 982 24 21 12.

This museum of regional art, is housed in the former Monasterio de San Francisco. A room is devoted to ceramics from Sargadelos, and there are sundials and other objects from the Roman period. The former cloister of San Francisco contains an interesting collection of sundials, as well as several altars and sarcophagi. The connecting **Museo Nelson Zúmel** is dedicated to Spanish paintings from the 19C and 20C.

Lugo

Ánxel López Pérez Av.	Z	2
Bispo Aguirre	Z	3
Bolaño Rivadeneira	Y	5
CampoPr. do	Z	8
Comandante Manso Pr.	Z	12
Conde Pallarés	Z	15
Coruña Av. da	Y	21
Cruz	Z	23
Dezaoito de Xullo Av. do	Y	24
Doctor Castro	Z	27
Marior Pr.	Z	30
Montero Ríos Av.	Z	37
Paxariños	Z	39
Pío XII Pr. de	Z	43
Progreso	Y	47
Quiroga Ballesteros	Y	50
Raíña	Y	53
Ramón Ferreiro	Z	56
Rodríguez Mourelo Av.	Z	62
San Fernando	Y	65
San Marcos	Y	68
San Pedro	Z	71
Santa María Pr. de	Z	74
Santo Domingo Pr. de	YZ	77
Teatro	Y	78
Teniente Coronel Teijeiro	YZ	79
Tinería	Z	80
Vilalba	Z	83

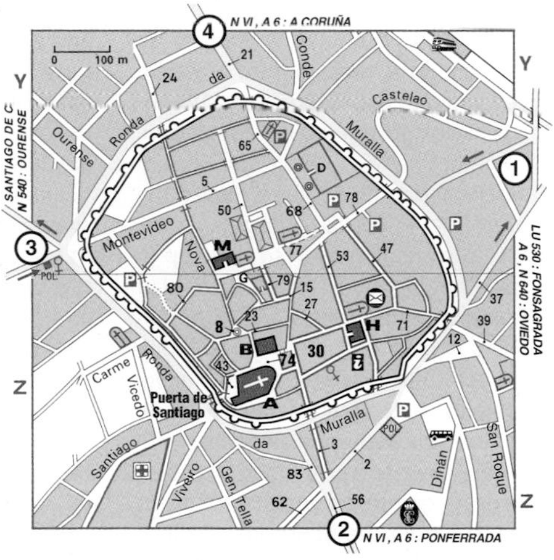

Ayuntamiento	Z	H	Museo Provincial	Y	M
Catedral	Z	A	Palacio episcopal	Z	B

MADRID★★★

POPULATION: 3 084 673

MICHELIN MAPS 575 OR 576 K 18-19 (TOWN PLAN)

Madrid is one of Europe's most cosmopolitan and lively cities, with wide avenues, attractive parks and joie de vivre. It became the capital in the 16C when Spain ruled a vast empire; its monuments were built during the 17C, 18C and 19C. An exceptional wealth of paintings has been enhanced by superb collections in the Museo Thyssen-Bornemisza and Centro de Arte Reina Sofia.

- **Information:** *Plaza Mayor 27, ☎91 588 16 36, www.esmadrid.com; Duque Medinaceli 2, ☎91 429 49 51 or 902 100 007; Barajas Airport, ☎91 305 86 56.*
- **Orient Yourself:** Europe's highest capital (646m/2 119ft), at the centre of the Iberian Peninsula, has a dry climate with hot summers and cold, sunny winters.
- **Parking:** It's best to park for the duration and use the excellent Metro.
- **Don't Miss:** The Prado, the Reina Sofía art collection, crowds in Plaza Mayor.
- **Organizing Your Time:** Start with the incomparable art museums, and be sure to nap in order to enjoy Madrid's late-hours dining and bars.
- **Especially for Kids:** Warner Bros Park, Faunia, and the Museo del Ferrocarril (railroad museum) will keep smaller visitors amused.
- **Also See:** ALCALÁ DE HENARES (32km/20mi E), Monasterio de EL ESCORIAL (49km/30mi NW), ARANJUEZ (47km/29mi S), TOLEDO (71km/44mi SW), SEGOVIA (98km/61mi NW) and Sierra de GUADARRAMA.

Background

Madrid in the past – Madrid owes its name to the 9C fortress *(alcázar)* of Majerit. In 1083 it was captured by Alfonso VI, who discovered a statue of the Virgin by a granary *(almudín)*. He converted the mosque into a church dedicated to the Virgin of the Almudena who was declared the city patron. Emperor Charles V rebuilt the Muslim *alcázar* and in 1561 Philip II moved the court from Toledo to Madrid.

The town really began to develop in Spain's Golden Age (16C). A town plan drawn up in 1656 by Pedro Texeira. King Philip IV gave his patronage to many artists including Velázquez and Murillo, as well as men of letters such as Lope de Vega, Quevedo, and Calderón.

From a town to a city – Madrid underwent its greatest transformations in the18C under the Bourbons. Philip V built a royal palace. Charles III provided Madrid with a splendour hitherto unknown in the Prado and the Puerta de Alcalá, magnificent examples of neo-Classical town planning. The nobility began building **palaces**, such as **Liria** and **Buenavista**.

The 19C began with occupation by the French and the Madrid rebellion of May 1808 and brutal reprisals. In 1857 the remaining ramparts were demolished and a vast expansion plan *(ensanche)* gave rise to the districts of Chamberí, Salamanca and Argüelles. At the end of the century, **Arturo Soria's** revolutionary *Ciudad Linea* provided for a residential quarter for 30 000 around today's avenida de Arturo Soria.

At the beginning of the 20C, architecture was French-inspired, as in the Ritz and Palace hotels; the neo-Mudéjar style was also popular and brick façades went up all over **(plaza de Toros de las Ventas)**. The **Gran Vía** linked Madrid's new districts in 1910.

Madrid today – Madrid is Spain's capital, and its business and university and administrative centre. Its industrial and technological activities are developing on the outskirts of the city. The city's most modern edifices are in the **AZCA** area, the result of one of Madrid's most revolutionary projects. Among its noteworthy buildings are the avant-garde **Banco de Bilbao-Vizcaya** and the **Torre Picasso**.

Special Features

MUSEO DEL PRADO★★★ 3hr

Open Tue-Sun 9am-7pm. Last admission 1hr before closing. Closed Mon, 1 Jan, Good Fri, 1 May and 25 Dec. 6€, no charge Sun. ☎91 330 28 00.

The Prado is the greatest gallery of Classical paintings in the world. The neo-Classical building was designed by Juan de Villanueva under Charles III for a science museum. After the Peninsular War, Ferdinand VII instead installed the Habsburg and Bourbon collections of Spanish painting, expanded over the years.

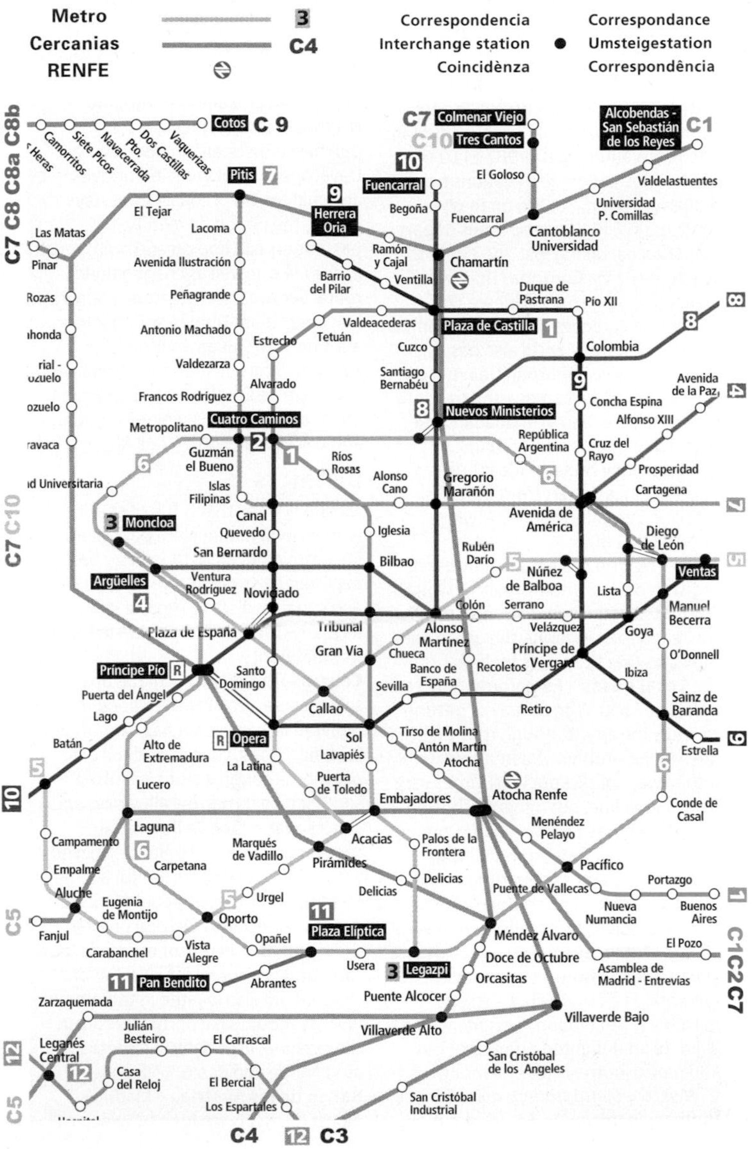

Address Book

GETTING ABOUT

Airport – Madrid-Barajas airport is located northeast of the city13km/ 8mi from downtown. Bus 200 operates to the airport from the Avenida de América interchange from 5.20am to 1.30am, with a departure every 10min between 7am and 10pm. For further information, call ☎91 431 61 92.

Metro line no8, which links up with line no4, connects the airport with the city.

Airport information ☎902 35 35 70.
Info-Iberia ☎902 400 500.

RENFE (Spanish State Railways) – The city's main railway stations are Atocha and Chamartín. For information and reservations, call ☎902 24 02 02 (24-hr information; reservations from 5.30am-11.50pm); or log on to www.renfe.es. AVE high-speed trains depart from Atocha, taking just 2hr 35min to reach Sevilla via Córdoba (1h50min); Lleida (2hr 30min) and Huesca (2hr 25min) via Zaragoza (1hr 40 min); and Toledo (30 min). Madrid also has a comprehensive suburban train network (*Cercanías*) which can be used to get to El Escorial, the Sierra de Guadarrama, Alcalá de Henares and Aranjuez.

Inter-city buses – Most buses to other cities depart from the Estación Sur, calle Méndez Álvaro. ☎ 91 468 42 00.

Taxis – Madrid has a huge number of registered taxis with distinctive white paintwork with a red diagonal stripe on the rear doors. At night, the green light indicates that the taxi is for hire.

Local buses – For information, call ☎902 507 850. A good way of getting to know the city, although traffic jams are a major problem. Passengers should also beware of pickpockets. Times vary from line to line, but generally buses operate between 6am and 11.30pm. Night buses operate from 11.30pm onwards, with most departing from plaza de Cibeles. In addition to single tickets, passengers can also purchase a 10-trip **Metro-bus** ticket *(un bono de 10 viajes)* valid on both the bus and metro network, as well as a zone-based monthly ticket *(abono mensual)* which is valid for an unlimited number of bus and metro journeys for one month.

Metro – *Metro stations are shown on the maps in this guide.* For information, call ☎ 902 444 403. The metro system is the fastest way to get around the city and consists of 11 lines. It operates from 6am to 1.30am. Passengers should beware of pickpockets.

SIGHTSEEING

The Guía del Ocio (www.guiadelocio.com/madrid) is a weekly guide containing a list of every cultural event and show in the city. It can be purchased at newspaper stands.

Bus turístico Madrid Visión – This tourist bus offers three different routes around the city (historic Madrid, modern Madrid and monumental Madrid). Tickets, which can be purchased on board, in hotels via a travel agent, or at www.madridvision.es are valid for 1 or 2 consecutive days. During the period of validity, passengers can hop on and off as much as they like as well as change their route. Services operate from 10am-7pm in winter, 10am-9pm in spring and autumn, and 9.30am-midnight in summer. Stops include the Puerta del Sol, plaza de Cibeles, paseo del Prado and Puerta de Alcalá. For information and prices, call ☎91 779 18 88.

DISTRICTS

Madrid is a city that is full of charm, with its own magnificent parks and impressive buildings. It is a city best explored by strolling through its streets and squares, discovering the delights of its many districts and getting to know its inhabitants.

Centro – This district is made up of several areas, each with their own individual character. It has a reputation for being noisy, chaotic and full of people, although visitors are often surprised by its narrow alleyways and small squares. **Sol-Callao** is the shopping area par excellence, packed with locals and visitors out for a stroll, heading for the main pedestrianised precinct (Preciados district) or for a drink or dinner in one of the many local cafés and restaurants. A number of cinemas are also located in this area. Visitors should take particular care in the evening, especially in streets such as Valverde and Barco.

Barrio de los Austrias – Madrid's oldest district is wedged between calles

Mayor, Bailén, Las Cavas and the plaza de la Cebada. Its origins are medieval and it still retains its evocatively named streets and Mudéjar towers. An excellent area for tapas, dinner or a drink. On Sundays, the famous **Rastro** flea market (*see Rastro*) is held nearby.

Lavapiés – This district is located around the square of the same name with many houses dating from the 17C. It is considered to be Madrid's most colourful district with a mix of locals, students and a large immigrant population.

Huertas – Huertas was home to the literary community in the 17C and the Movida movement in the 1980s. Nowadays, it is packed with bars and restaurants and is particularly lively at night, attracting an interesting mixture of late-night revellers.

Malasaña – This part of Madrid, which used to be known as Maravillas, is situated between Las glorietas de Bilbao y Ruiz Jiménez and around plaza del Dos de Mayo. In the mornings, this 19C *barrio* is quiet and provincial, but it is transformed at night by the legions of young people heading towards Malasaña's many bars. For those in search of a quieter night out, the district also has a number of more tranquil cafés.

Alonso Martínez – The average age and financial standing of this district's inhabitants is somewhat higher than in neighbouring Bilbao and Malasaña, as shown by the myriad upmarket bars and restaurants frequented by the city's rich and famous.

Chueca – This district covers an area around the plaza de Chueca; its approximate outer limits are the paseo de Recoletos, calle Hortaleza, Gran Vía and calle Fernando VI. At the end of the last century it was one of Madrid's most elegant districts. Today it is the city's gay area with a multitude of small and sophisticated boutiques.

Salamanca – In the 19C, Salamanca was Madrid's principal bourgeois district designed by the Marquis of Salamanca in the shape of a draughts board with wide streets at right angles. Nowadays, the district is one of the capital's most expensive areas and is home to some of Spain's leading designer boutiques (Serrano and Ortega y Gasset) and an impressive collection of stores selling luxury goods.

For coin ranges, see the Legend on the cover flap.

WHERE TO EAT

La Vaca Verónica – *Moratín, 38 – Antón Martín – 91 429 78 27 – Closed midday Sat –* . The outstanding decor re-creates a cosy, intimate space, with spider lamps, ceiling mirrors, candles and soft lighting. Posters recall Pop Art and Art Nouveau. Specialties include grilled meats and the delicious *pasta con carabineros.*

La Finca de Susana – *Arlaban 4 (Huertas) – Sevilla – 91 369 35 57 –* . Centrally located with food that's good for the price, so it's always full with a with-it young crowd that doesn't mind waiting. Food is traditional, with some *nouvelle* touches. Go early, you can't reserve.

La Bola – *Bola 5 (Centro) – Ópera – 91 547 69 30 – www.labola.es – Closed Sat evening, Sunday in Jul-Aug, Sun evenings the rest of year –* . If you're hoping to try a traditional cocido madrileño, look no further than this famous tavern which has been serving up this traditional dish in earthenware pots for over a century.

Teatriz – *Hermosilla 15 (Salamanca) – Serrano – 91 577 53 79 –* . Designed by Philippe Starck, this former theatre has been converted into an impressive-looking restaurant where you can choose between eating in the orchestra or enjoying a drink at the stage bar. The good, reasonably priced menu is based on Mediterranean dishes and Italian specialities.

Zerain – *Quevedo 3 (Huertas) – Antón Martín – 91 429 79 09 – Closed Sun, August and Holy Week –* . One of the typical menus at this Basque cider bar near plaza de Santa Ana includes

TURESPAÑA

tortilla de bacalao (cod omelette) and *chuletón* (meat cutlets). Rustic, but pleasant decor. The cider here is served directly from the barrel.

Casa Lucio – *Cava Baja 35 (La Latina) – La Latina – 91 365 32 52 – Closed Sat lunchtime and Aug –* . One of Madrid's best-known addresses frequented by politicians, actors and visitors alike. Typical Castilian decor. Famous for its *huevos estrellados* (fried eggs).

El Amparo – *Puigcerdá 8 (Salamanca) – Retiro – 91 431 64 56 – www.arturocantoblanco.com – Closed Sat lunchtime, Sun and Holy Week –* . Top-class restaurant with an original design including split-level dining rooms and roof skylights. Very pleasant atmosphere. Fine cuisine and polished service with prices to match.

TAPAS

Taberna de Dolores – *Plaza de Jesús 4 (Huertas) - Antón Martín – 91 429 22 43 -* . Tiles on the façade, a long bar and a crowd mark this as a place of character, with good draft beer, pickled anchovies, and more.

Taberna de la Daniela – *General Pardiñas 21 (Salamanca) – Goya – 91 575 23 29 –* . A bar with traditional decoration. *Azulejos* on the outside with vermouth on tap and a wide selection of canapés and *raciones* inside. Specialities here include *cocido madrileño.*

Prada a Tope – *Príncipe 11 (Huertas) – Sevilla – Closed Sun evening, Mon and in Aug – 91 429 59 21 –* . A warm locale in the spirit of El Bierzo, a traditional part of León. Outstanding rustic decor of wood and slate, with long bar, large tables, and walls covered with photos. Great variety of local products on sale.

José Luis – *Serrano, 89 (Salamanca) – Núñez de Balboa – 91 563 09 58 – www.joseluis.es –* . A Salamanca institution. In two parts, each with its distinct style, but sharing the same bar. A wide choice of superb tapas; its Spanish omelette is the most famous in the city. Tables outside in summer.

Taberna Almendro 13 – *Almendro 13 (La Latina) – La Latina – 91 365 42 52 – Closed 24-25 and 31 Dec –* . Although it has only been in business for 8 years, this new tavern with an old atmosphere is always packed. Its tapas include cheese and sausage pastries *(roscas de queso y embutido)*, fried eggs *(huevos estrellados)* and its potato-based *patatas emporradas.*

Casa Labra – *Tetuán 12 (Centro) – Sol – 91 531 00 81 – www.casalabra.es.* This old tavern dating back to the middle of the 19C is a Madrid institution. It was here that Pablo Iglesias founded the Spanish Socialist Party (PSOE) in 1879. Its house speciality is fried cod *(bacalao frito)*, which you can enjoy standing up on the street or at the marble tables inside. Also a restaurant with menu.

WHERE TO STAY

Hostal Miguel Ángel – *San Mateo 21 (Bilbao) – Tribunal – 91 447 54 00 – www.hostalmiguelangel.com – 16 rooms.* Next to the Museo Romántico. The somewhat darkened brick conceals a well-maintained hotel with a fabulous wooden staircase leading to the reception on the second floor. Friendly staff and spotless, more than adequate rooms with TV and en-suite bathroom.

Hotel Centro Sol – *Carrera de San Jerónimo 5 (Centro) – Sol – 91 522 15 82 – www.hostalcentrosol.com – – 35 rooms.* A hotel very close to the Puerta del Sol occupying the second and fourth floors of a building somewhat lacking in charm. However, its rooms, all with TVs and good bathrooms, are very reasonably priced and have been recently refurbished.

Hotel Adriano – *De la Cruz 26 (Centro) – Sol – 91 521 13 39 - www.hostaladriano.com – – 22 rooms.* A good central choice in this price range, notable for its well-equipped rooms and original decor, with personalised rooms, especially nº 114, dedicated to soprano María Callas.

Hotel Plaza Mayor – *Atocha 2 (Centro) – Sol – 91 360 06 06 – www.hostaladriano.com – – 20 rooms. –* 3.50 €. An unpretentious hotel, but with a great location right by the city's main square. Behind the modern brick façade, the rooms are small, functional but attractively decorated.

Hotel Mora – *Paseo del Prado 32 (Retiro) – Atocha – 91 420 15 69 – 60 rooms.* The Mora enjoys a superb location in an impressive building opposite the botanical gardens on paseo del Prado. Comfortable, recently

renovated rooms and reasonable rates.
⊜⊜ **Hotel Casón del Tormes** – *Río 7 (Centro) – Plaza de España – ☎91 541 97 46 – – 63 rooms – 7.50 €.* Located in a small, quiet street in the centre of the city, just behind the Senate building. Built in the middle of the 1960s, the hotel has large, comfortable rooms which have been recently renovated.
⊜⊜ **Hotel Inglés** – *Echegaray 8 (Chueca) – Sevilla – ☎91 429 65 51 – www.hotel-ingles.net – – 58 rooms – 5 €.* There's no doubting the character of this hotel built in 1853. A good central and moderately priced option in the Chueca distrct, an area renowned for its lively nightlife. Clean, comfortable rooms.
⊜⊜ **Hotel Carlos V** – *Maestro Vitoria 5 (Centro) – Sol – ☎91 531 41 00 – www.hotelcarlosv.com – – 67 rooms – .* A good central option in a pedestrianised street away from the noise of the city. Although small, the English-style rooms are pleasant and well appointed. An eclectic cafeteria on the first floor.
⊜⊜⊜ **Hotel Ritz** – *Plaza de la Lealtad 5 (Retiro) – Banco de España – ☎ 91 701 67 67 – www.ritz.es – – 137 rooms – 30 € – Restaurant €90.* A magnificent early-20C building superbly located near paseo del Prado. The hotel has all the elegance, tradition and comfort you would expect from such a famous name, plus prices to match. The terrace-garden here is an additional delight.

CAFÉS

Café de Oriente – *Plaza Oriente 2 – Ópera – ☎91 5 41 39 74 – www.grupolezama.es – Open 8.30am-2am.* This classic institution, located in the plaza de Oriente opposite the Royal Palace, is a delightful place for a drink at any time of day. Pleasant terrace.
Café del Círculo de Bellas Artes – *Marqués de Casa Riera 2 – Banco de España, Sevilla – ☎91 3 60 54 00 – Open Sun-Thu 9am-midnight, Fri-Sat 9am-3am.* The marked 19C atmosphere of this great café with its enormous columns and large windows is in sharp contrast to its young, intellectual clientele. Outdoor terrace in summer. Highly recommended.
Café Gijón – *Paseo de Recoletos 31 – Banco de España – ☎91 5 21 54 25 – www.cafegijon.com – Open 7am-2am.* This café, which has long been famous as a meeting point for writers and artists, continues the tradition to this day. Outdoor terrace in summer.
El Espejo – *Paseo de Recoletos 21 – Colón – ☎913 19 11 22 – Open 8am-1am.* An attractive, Modernist-style café close to the Café Gijón (below) with a charming wrought-iron and glass canopy.

NIGHTLIFE

Café Central – *Plaza del Ángel 10 – Antón Martin – ☎91 3 69 41 43 – www.cafecentralmadrid.com – Open 2pm-3.30am.* One of the city's main haunts for jazz-lovers since the early 1980s.
Los Gabrieles – *Echegaray 17 – Sevilla – ☎91 429 62 61 – Open Mon-Thu 12.30pm-2am, Fri-Sat 12.30pm-3.30am.* Tapas by day and a bar by night. A favourite haunt for foreign students in Madrid, attracted, no doubt, by the historical chronicles on its *azulejo*-decorated panelling.
Del Diego – *La Reina 12 – Gran Vía – ☎ 91 5 23 31 06 – Open 7pm-3.30am - Closed Sun, Holy Week and in Aug.* A pleasant bar serving some of the city's best cocktails.
Irish Rover – *Avenida de Brasil 7 – Santiago Bernabeu – ☎91 555 76 71 – Open Sun-Thu noon-2am and Fri-Sat noon-5am.* A pub within a pub. A section which looks as though it has come straight out of one of Joyce's novels and a tiny lounge are just two of the features of this Irish home-from-home. Daily performances and a small market on Sundays. Young clientele.
Libertad, 8 – *Libertad 8 – Chueca – ☎9 15 32 73 48 – Open 1am-4am.* A building over a century old is the setting for this atmospheric café, renowned for its poetry readings and storytellers, attracting young, bohemian audiences.
Joy Eslava – *Arenal 11 – Ópera, Sol – ☎913 66 37 33 – www.joy-eslava.com – Open Mon-Thu 11.30pm-5am, Fri-Sat 11.30pm-6am.* This well-known club, occupying a former 19C theatre, has been attracting a colourful crowd of club-goers and famous faces for several decades. On your way home, why not pay a visit to the famous Chocolatería de San Ginés, in the street of the same name.
Palacio de Gaviria – *Arenal 9 – Sol – ☎91 5 26 60 69 – www.palaciogaviria.com – Open Sun-*

Wed 8pm-3am, Fri-Sat 11pm-6am. A fascinating club which has been converted from one of Madrid's old palaces. Also famous for its ballroom dancing. Its Thursday-night fiesta internacional is very popular with foreigners.

ENTERTAINMENT

Madrid has over 100 cinemas, including one **Imax** cinema, 20 or so theatres, numerous concert halls and one casino. The **Auditorio Nacional** (opened in 1988) has a varied programme of classical music, the **Teatro de la Zarzuela** hosts a wide range of shows including Spanish operettas *(zarzuelas)* and ballets, while the **Teatro Real** offers a season of opera. The **Veranos de la Villa** and the **Festival de Otoño** are two events held in the summer and autumn respectively with an interesting mix of cultural performances. The **Festival Internacional de Jazz** is another event also held during November.

Berlín Cabaret – *Costanilla de San Pedro 11 – La Latina – www.einnova.com/berlincabaret – Open Sun-Thu and Sun, 11pm-5am and Fri-Sat, 11pm-6am.* One of Madrid's famous venues. Live acts (magicians, drag queens etc) and a fun atmosphere.

Café de Chinitas – *Torija 7 – Callao – 91 5 47 15 02 – www.chinitas.com – Open Mon-Sat, 10.30pm-2am.* Very popular with tourists. Dinner shows also available (70€).

Casa Patas – *Cañizares 10 – Antón Martín – 91 3 69 04 96 – Shows Mon-Thu, 10.30pm, Fri-Sat, 9pm and midnight; lunch 1-4pm, dinner 7.30pm-1am.* One of the best venues in which to enjoy a night of flamenco.

SHOPPING

Casa Mira – *Carrera San Jerónimo 30 - Sevilla - 91 429 88 95 - Open 10am-2pm and 5-9pm.* The best *turrones, mazapanes* (marzipan) and homemade sweets in Madrid. Founded in 1842, it has passed from father to son. The wares are of the highest quality, without preservatives or additives, cut and weighed at time of sale.

La Violeta – *Plaza de Canalejas 6 - Sevilla - 91 522 55 22 - Open 9.30am-2pm and 4.30-8.30pm - Closed Sun, public hols and in Aug.* This establishment has served such luminaries as King Alfonso XIII and writers Jacinto Benavente y Valle Inclán since 1915. The bonbons and caramels are popular but the *marron glacé* and glazed violets take the cake.

Capas Seseña – *Cruz 23 (Huertas) - Sevilla or Sol - 91 531 68 40 - www.sesena.com - Open 10am-1.30pm and 4.30-8pm* - A family firm that dates from 1901, where traditional and contemporary **capes** are crafted by hand from fine fabric. Photos show such clients as Hemingway, Picasso, Catherine Deneuve, Rodolfo Valentino and Marcelo Mastroianni.

Art Galleries – A number of galleries can be found in and around Atocha, close to the Centro de Arte Reina Sofía, in the Salamanca district (near the Puerta de Alcalá) and on the left side of the paseo de la Castellana, close to the calle Génova.

FIESTAS

On 15 May, the city commemorates the feast day of **San Isidro**, its patron saint, with picnics, impromptu dancing, rock concerts and above all through its famous bullfighting festival, which lasts for some six weeks. It is also traditional for *madrileños* to eat traditional pastries *(rosquillas)* on this special day.

Spanish School★★★ (15C-18C)

Bartolomé Bermejo (*Santo Domingo de Silos*) and **Yáñez de la Almedina** cultivated an international style. Masip and his son **Juan de Juanes** *(The Last Supper)* are associated with Raphael. Morales' favourite subject, a *Virgin and Child*, is also outstanding.

In those rooms devoted to the **Golden Age**, two painters stand out: **Sánchez Coello**, and his pupil **Pantoja de la Cruz**, a portraitist at the court of Philip II. **El Greco** stands apart within the Spanish School. Works here date from his early Spanish period *(Trinity)* to his maturity *(Adoration of the Shepherds)*. Other works are proof that he was a great portraitist, such as **Gentleman with his Hand on his Breast**. **Ribalta** introduced tenebrism to Spain. **José (Jusepe) de Ribera** (**Lo Spagnoletto**) is represented by the *Martyrdom of St Felipe* in which the vigorous use of chiaroscuro emphasises the horror of the scene. The portraits and still lifes of **Zurbarán** are peaceful compositions in which chiaroscuro and realism triumph. **Murillo** mainly painted the Virgin but also plain folk *(The Good Shepherd and The Boys of the Shell)*.

Velázquez (1599-1660)

The Prado possesses the greatest paintings of Velázquez. He spent time in Italy (1629-31) where he painted **The Forges of Vulcan**. He began to use richer, more subtle colours and developed his figure compositions as in his magnificent **Christ on the Cross.** On his return he painted **The Surrender of Breda** in which his originality emerges. The use of light in his pictures is crucial. He strove towards naturalism in his royal hunting portraits of **Philip IV** and **Prince Baltasar Carlos, the Hunter** (1635, a wonderful rendering of a child) and his equestrian portraits of the royal family, in particular **Prince Baltasar Carlos on Horseback** with the *sierra* in the background. In 1650 he returned to Italy where he painted landscapes, the **Gardens of the Villa Medici.** In his latter masterpiece, **The Maids of Honour (Las Meninas)** (1656), the Infanta Margarita is shown in the artist's studio in a magnificent display of light and colour. In **The Spinners** (1657), Velázquez combined myth and reality.

The Paseo del Arte

This poetic name refers to the imaginary axis linking Madrid's three greatest museums (the Prado, Thyssen-Bornemisza and the Reina Sofía), which form a close triangle in the same part of the city. The **Bono Arte**, a combined ticket on sale in each of the museums, entitles the holder to admission to all three of these magnificent art galleries. Cost: 14.40 €.

Museum Collections

El Museo del Prado está is currently completing a significant expansion. Given the large number of works in stock, some paintings are only displayed in temporary exhibitions.

Goya (1746-1828)

Goya's portraits of the royal and famous, his war scenes, his depictions of everyday life, and finally his **Majas**, all illustrate his extraordinary Realism and enthusiasm for colour. The museum contains 40 cartoons painted in oil between 1775 and 1791 for the Real

Las Meninas, by Velázquez

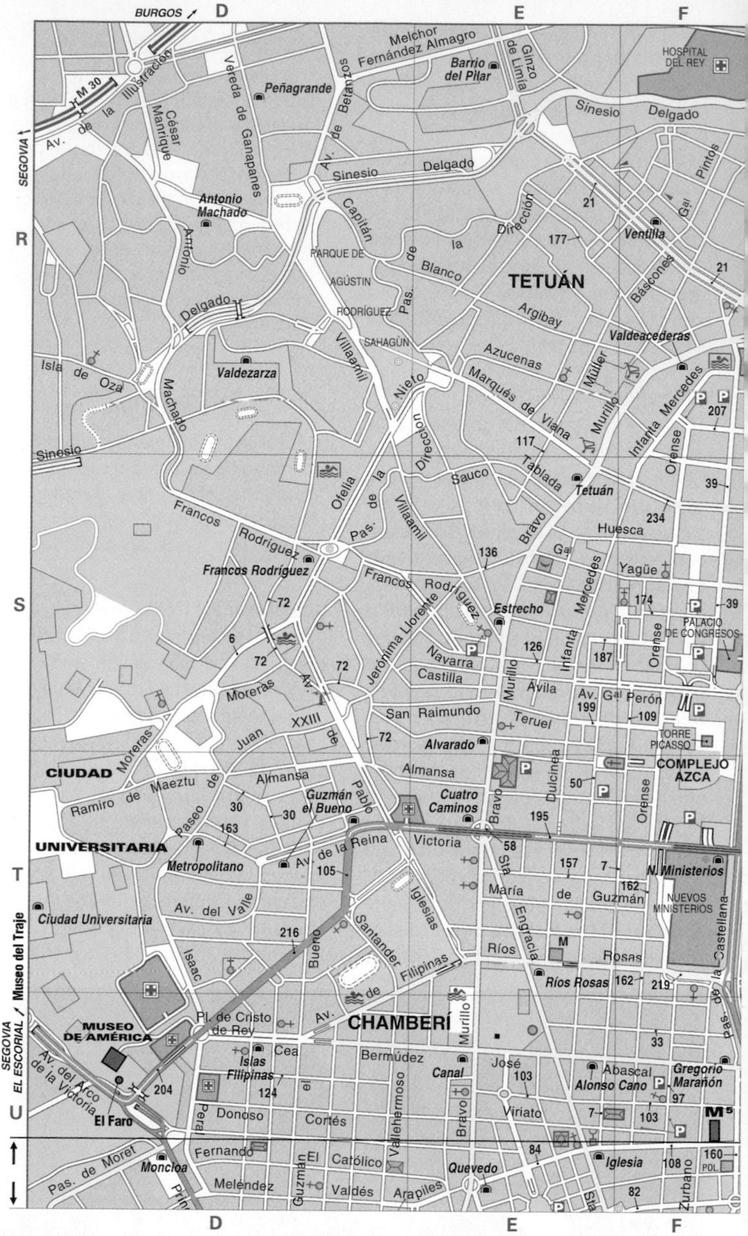

Agustín de Foxá	GR	3	Beatriz de Bobadilla	DT	30	Cuzco Pl. de	GS	61
Alcántara	JV	4	Belisana	JS	31	Daroca Av. de	JV	63
Almirante Francisco Moreno	DS	6	Bretón de los Herreros	FU	33	Diego de León	HU	67
Alonso Cano	ET	7	Caídos de la División Azul	JR	34	Doce de Octubre	JX	69
Ancora	GZ	10	Camino de los Vinateros	JY	37	Doctor Castelo	JX	70
Aniceto Marinas	DX	15	Capitán Haya	FS	39	Doctor Federico Rubio y Gali Av. del	DS	72
Ardemans	JU	17	Caracas	FV	40	Doctor Fléming	GS	73
Arroyo de la Media Legua	JY	19	Castilla Pl. de	GR	41	Don Ramón de la Cruz	HV	75
Asturias Av. de	ER	21	Claudio Coello	GV	48	Drácena	JR	76
Atocha R. de	EY	22	Comandante Zorita	ET	50	Eduardo Dato Pas. de	FU	82
Beata María Ana de Jesús Pl. de la	FZ	28	Corregidor Diego Cabeza de Vaca	JY	55	Eloy Gonzalo	EU	84
			Cuatro Caminos Glta de	ET	58	Embajadores Glta de	EY	85

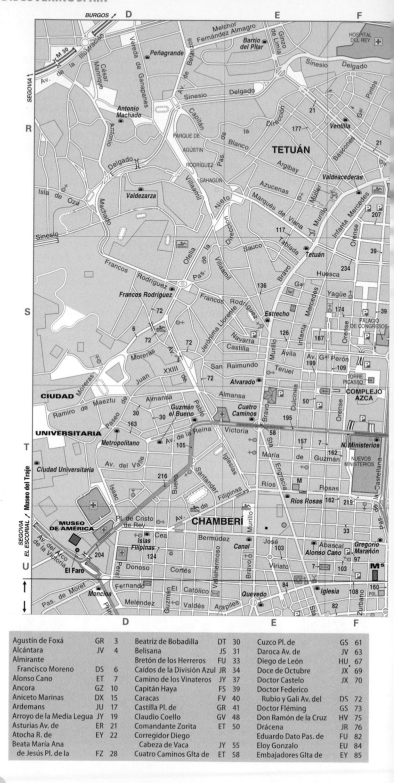

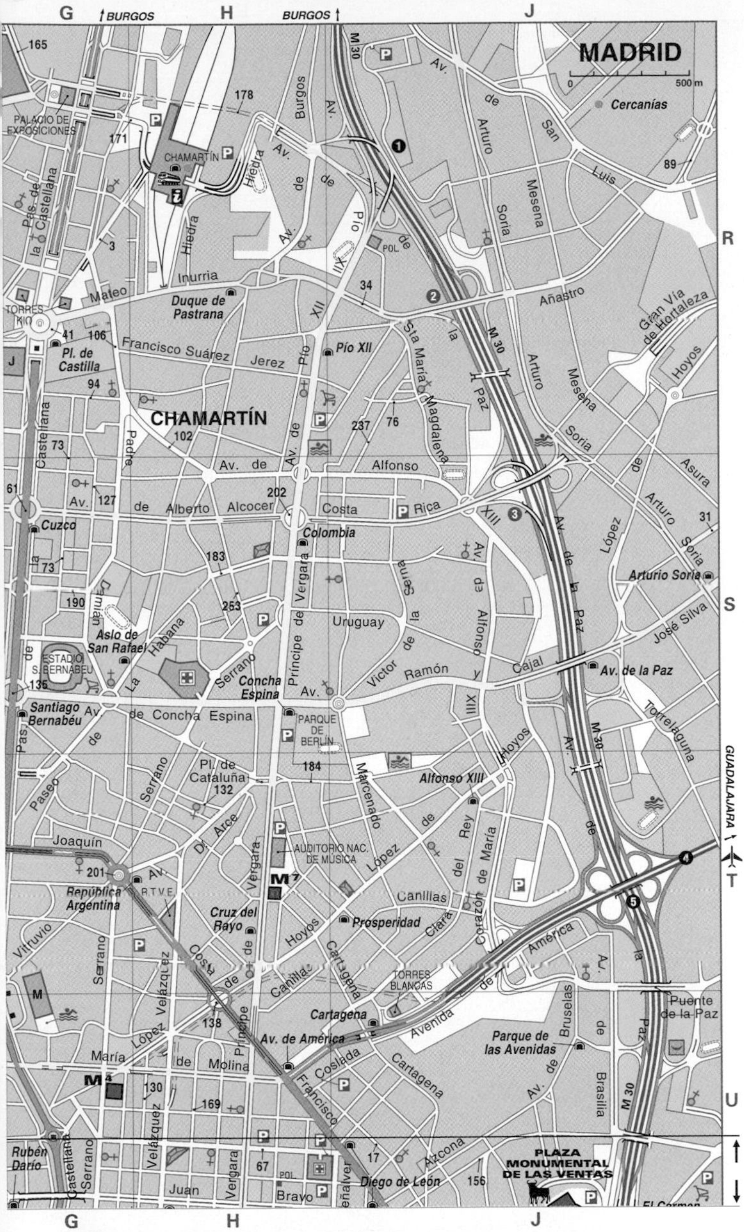

Esperanza Pas. de la	EZ	87
Estrella Polar	JY	90
Extremadura Pas. de	DY	93
Félix Boix	GR	94
Fernán González	JX	96
Fernández de la Hoz	FU	97
Florida Pas. de la	DX	100
Fray Bernardino Sahagún	HR	102
García de Paredes	EU	103
General Ibáñez de Ibero	DT	105
General López Pozas	GR	106
General Martínez Campos Pas. del	FU	108
General Moscardó	FS	109
Hierbabuena	ER	117
Jaime El Conquistador	EZ	121
Joaquín María López	DU	124
Juan de Olías	ES	126
Juan Ramón Jiménez	GS	127
Julio Camba	JV	129
Lagasca	HV	130
Leizarán	HT	132
Lima Pl. de	GS	135
Lope de Haro	ES	136
López de Hoyos Glta de	HU	138
Luis Mitjans	JZ	139
Marqués de Monistrol Pas. del	DX	147
Marqués de Salamanca Pl. del	HV	148
Marqués de Urquijo	DV	150
Marqués de Zafra Pas. del	JV	151
Marqués del Riscal	GV	153
Martínez de la Riva	JZ	155
Martínez Izquierdo	JU	156
Maudes	ET	157
Miguel Angel	FU	160
Modesto Lafuente	FT	162
Moncloa Av. de la	DT	163

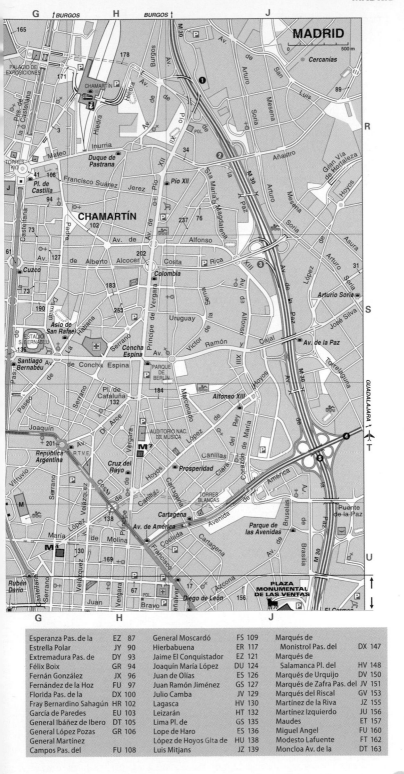

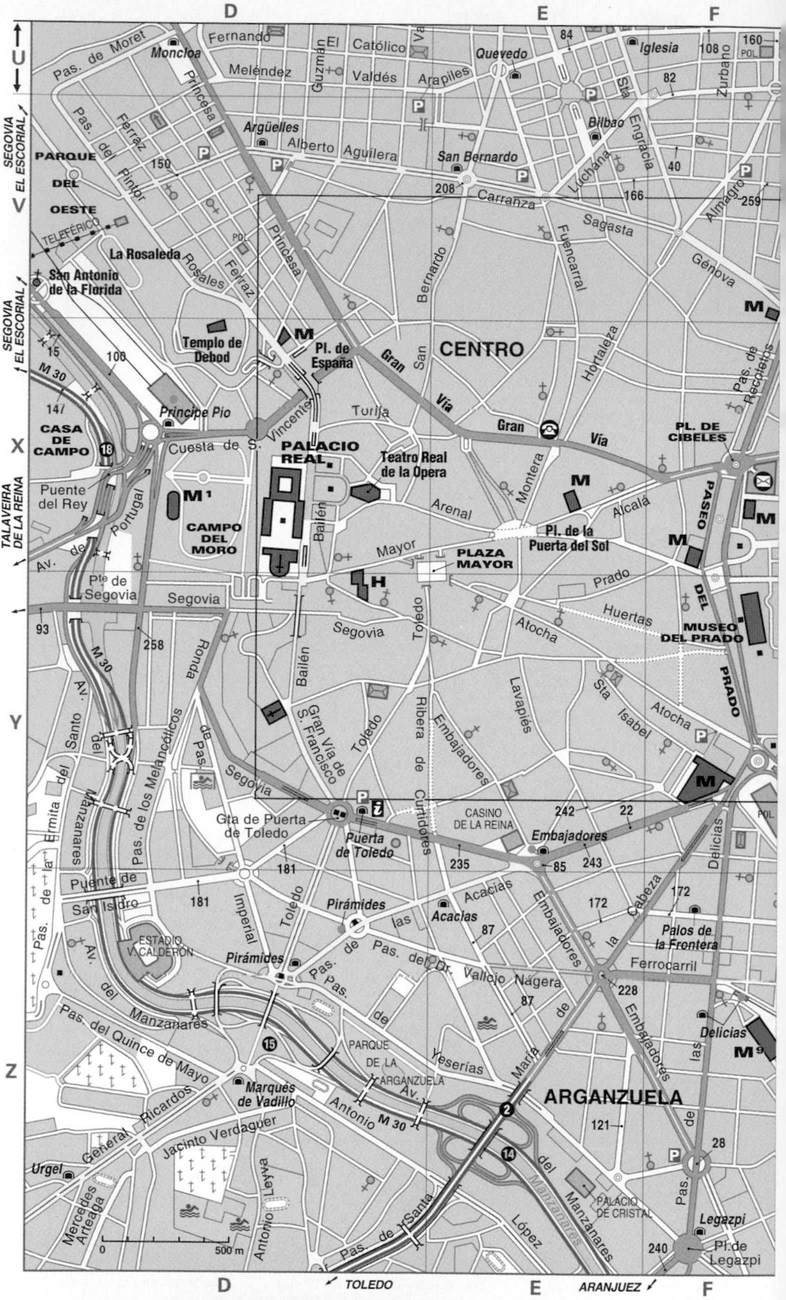

Monforte de Lemos Av. de	GR 165	Pío Baroja	JY 180	Raimundo Fernández Villaverde	ET 195
Nicasio Gallego	EV 166	Pío XII Túnel de	HR 178	Reina Cristina Pas. de la	HY 198
Núñez de Balboa	HV 169	Pontones Pas. de los	DZ 181	Reina Mercedes	ES 199
Padre Francisco Palau y Quer	GR 171	Potosí	HS 183	República Argentina Pl. de la	GT 201
Palos de la Frontera	FZ 172	Pradillo	HI 184	República Dominicana Pl. de la	HS 202
Pedro Teixeira	FS 174	Presidente Carmona Av. del	ES 187	Reyes Católicos Av. de los	DU 204
Pez Volador	JY 175	Profesor Waksman	GS 190		
Pinos Alta	ER 177	Puerto de Canfranc	JZ 193		

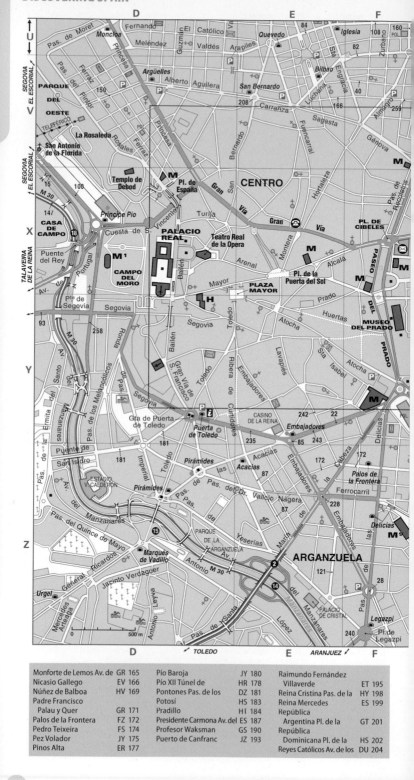

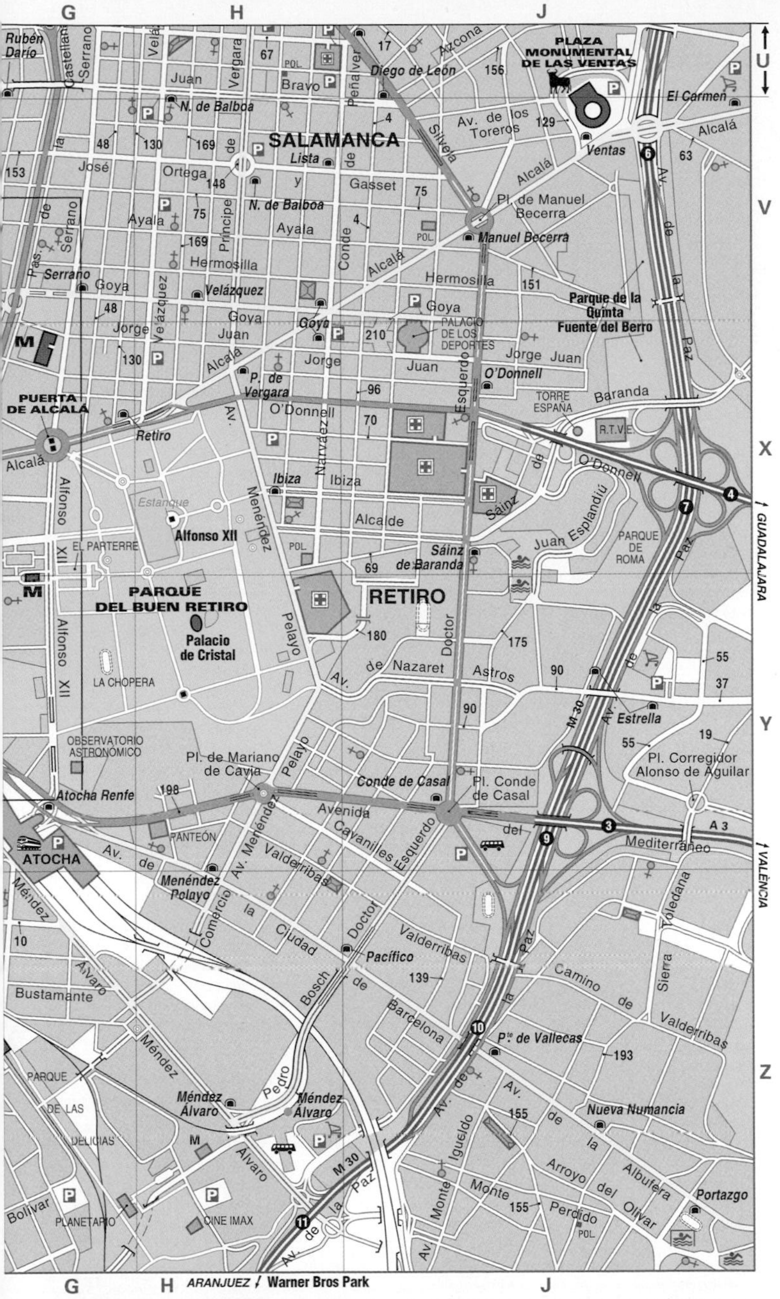

Rosario Pino	FR 207	Toledo Ronda de	EY 235
Ruiz Jiménez Glta de	EV 208	Torpedero Tucumán	JR 237
Salvador Dalí Pl. de	JX 210	Vado de Santa Catalina	FZ 240
San Francisco de Sales Pas. de	DT 216	Valencia	EY 242
San Juan de la Cruz Pl. de	FT 219	Valencia Ronda de	EY 243
Santa María de la Cabeza Glta de	EZ 228	Victor Andrés Belaunde	HS 253
Sor Angela de la Cruz	FS 234	Virgen del Puerto Pas. de la	DY 258
		Zurbarán	FV 259

Museo Lázaro Galdiano	GU	M4
Museo Nacional de Ciencia y Tecnología	FZ	M12
Museo Sorolla	FU	M5
Museo de Carruajes Reales	DX	M1
Museo de la Ciudad	HT	M7
Museo del Ferrocarril	FZ	M9

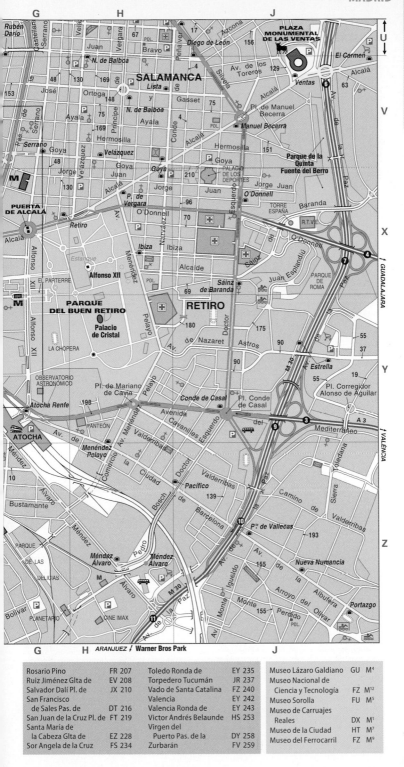

MADRID – STREET INDEX

Hortaleza LX
Hortaleza Gran Vía de JR
Huertas LY
Huesca ES
Humilladero BZ
Ibiza JX
Ilustración Av. de la DR
ImperialPas. DZ
Independencia Pl. de la NX 118
Infanta Isabel Pas. de la NZ 119
Infanta Mercedes ES
Infantas LX
Isaac Peral DT
Isabel II Pl. de KX
Isla de Oza DR
Jacinto Benavente Pl. de LY
Jacinto Verdaguer DZ
Jaime El Conquistador EZ 121
Jardines LX
Jerez HR
Jerónima Llorente DS
Jesús MY
Jesús del Valle LV 123
Jesús y María LZ
Joaquín Costa GT
Joaquín María López DU 124
Jorge Juan HX
José Abascal EU
José Ortega y Gasset HV
José Silva JS
Juan Bravo HU
Juan de Olías ES 126
Juan Esplandiú JX
Juan Ramón Jiménez GS 127
Juan XXIII Pas. de DS
Juanelo CZ
Julio Camba JV 129
Lagasca HV 130
Lavapiés LZ
Lealtad Pl. de la NY
Leganitos KX
Legazpi Pl. de FZ
Leizarán HT 132
Libreros KX 133
Lima Pl. de GS 135
Lope de Haro ES 136
López de Hoyos JT
López de Hoyos Glta de HU 138
Luchana EV
Luis Mitjans JZ 139
Luna KV
Madera LV
Madrazo MY 141
Magdalena LZ
Maldonadas BZ
Manuel Becerra Pl. de JV
Manzanares Av. del DEYZ
Marcenado JT
María de Guzmán ET
María de Molina HU
Mariano de Cavia Pl. de HY
Marqués de Cubas MY 145
Marqués de Monistrol Pas. del DX 147
Marqués de Salamanca Pl. del HV 148
Marqués de Urquijo DV 150
Marqués de Viana ER
Marqués de Zafra Pas. del JV 151
Marqués del Riscal GV 153
Marqués Viudo de Pontejos CY 154
Martínez de la Riva JZ 155
Martínez Izquierdo JU 156
Mateo Inurria HR

Maudes ET 157
Mayor KY
Mayor Pl. KY
Mediterráneo Av. del JY
Mejía Lequerica LV 159
Melancólicos Pas. de los DY
Melchor Fernández Almagro DR
Meléndez Valdés DU
Méndez Álvaro HZ
Menéndez Pelayo Av. de HX
Mercedes Arteaga DZ
Mesena JR
Mesón de Paredes LZ
Miguel Angel FU 160
Modesto Lafuente FT 162
Moncloa Av. de la DT 163
Monforte de Lemos Av. de GR 165
Montalbán NX
Monte Igueldo Av. del JZ
Monte Perdido JZ
Montera LX
Montserrat KV
Moratín MZ
Moreras DS
Moret Pas. de DU
Moreto NY
Müller ER
Murillo Pl. de NZ
Narváez HX
Navarra ES
Nazaret Av. de JY
Nicasio Gallego EV 166
Núñez de Arce LY 168
Núñez de Balboa HV 169
O'Donnell JX
Ofelia Nieto DS
Olivar LZ
Orense FS
Oriente Pl. de KX
Pablo Iglesias Av. de DT
Padre Damián GS
Padre Francisco Palau y Quer GR 171
Paja Pl. de la KZ
Palma LV
Palos de la Frontera FZ 172
La Paz Av. de JV
La Paz Puente de JU
Pedro Bosch HZ
Pedro Teixeira FS 174
Pelayo MV
Pez LV
Pez Volador JY 175
Pinos Alta ER 177
Pintor Rosales Pas. del DV
Pío Baroja JY 180
Pío XII Av. de HR
Pío XII Túnel de HR 178
Pizarro LV
Pontejos Pl. de CY
Pontones Pas. de los DZ 181
Portugal Av. de DX
Potosí HS 183
Pradillo HT 184
Prado MY
Prado Pas. del NZ
Preciados LX 186
Presidente Carmona Av. del ES 187
Prim NV
Princesa KV
Príncipe LY 188
Príncipe Anglona AZ 189
Príncipe de Vergara HS

Profesor Waksman GS 190
Provincia Pl. de la LY
Puebla LV
Puerta Cerrada Pl. de KY 191
Puerta de Moros Pl. de KZ 192
Puerta de Toledo Glta de DY
Puerta del Sol Pl. de la LY
Puerto de Canfranc JZ 193
Quince de Mayo Pas. del DZ
Raimundo Fernández Villaverde ET 195
Ramales Pl. de AY
Ramiro de Maeztu DT
Ramón y Cajal Av. de JS
Recoletos NX 196
Recoletos Pas. de NV
Redondilla AZ
Reina Cristina Pas. de la HY 198
Reina Mercedes ES 199
Reina Victoria Av. de la DET
República Argentina Pl. de la GT 201
República Dominicana Pl. de la HS 202
Requena AY
Rey Puente del DX
Reyes KV
Reyes Católicos Av. de los DU 204
Ribera de Curtidores KZ
Río KV
Ríos Rosas ET
Rollo AY
Rosario Pino FR 207
Ruda BZ
Ruiz Jiménez Glta de EV 208
Sacramento KY
Sagasta LV
Salvador Dalí Pl. de JX 210
San Bernardino KV 211
San Bernardo KV
San Buenaventura AZ
San Francisco Carrera de KZ 214
San Francisco Gran Vía de KZ
San Francisco de Sales Pas. de DT 216
San Isidro Pte de DZ
San Javier Pl. de BY 217
San Jerónimo Carrera de LY 218
San Juan de la Cruz Pl. de FT 219
San Justo KY 220
San Lorenzo LV 222
San Luis Av. de JY
San Marcos MX
San Mateo LV
San Miguel Pl. de BY
San Millán KZ 225
San Nicolás AY
San Pedro Costanilla de BZ
San Raimundo ES
San Vicente Cuesta de DX
Santa Bárbara Pl. de MV
Santa Engracia MV 226
Santa Isabel MZ
Santa María de la Cabeza Glta de EZ 228
Santa María de la Cabeza Pas. de DEZ
Santa María Magdalena JR
Santander DT
Santiago BY
Santiago Pl. de BY
Santo Domingo Cuesta de KX 230
Santo Domingo Pl. de KX 231

MADRID – SITES INDEX

Fábrica (Royal Tapestry Works), together a delightful picture of 18C Madrid life. **2 May** and the **Execution of the Rioters on 3 May 1808** were inspired by the rebellion against the French occupation *(see ARANJUEZ)*.

Flemish School★★★ (15C-17C)

The exceptional collection of Flemish painting reflects Spain's history with the Low Countries.

Among the Flemish Primitives are Robert Campen, the Mester of Flemalle (*St Barbara*). **Van der Weyden** added great richness of colour, and a sense of composition *(Descent from the Cross, Pietà)*. Drama is interpreted through melancholy by his successor, **Memling** *(Adoration of the Magi)*. There follow the weird imaginings of **Hieronymus Bosch**, El Bosco *(The Garden of Earthly Delights)* which influenced his disciple Patinir *(Crossing the Stygian Lake)*, and a **Bruegel the Elder,** *Triumph of Death*.

The most Baroque of painters, **Rubens**, breathed new life into Flemish painting *(The Three Graces)*. There is a rich collection of his work completed by that of his disciples: **Van Dyck** and **Jordaens**.

Dutch School (17C)

Two interesting works by **Rembrandt** are a *Self-portrait* and *Artemesia*.

Italian School★★ (15C-17C)

The collection is especially rich in works by Venetian painters.

The Italian Renaissance brought with it elegance and ideal beauty as in paintings by **Raphael** *(The Holy Family, Por-*

The Prado's Major Works		
SCHOOL	**ARTIST**	**PAINTING**
Spanish	Juan de Juanes	*Ecce Homo*
16C-18C	El Greco	*Gentleman with his Hand on his Breast*
		Adoration of the Shepherds
	Zurbarán	*Still Life*
		St Isabel of Portugal
	Velázquez	*The Surrender of Breda*
		The Spinners
		The Maids of Honour (Las Meninas)
		Prince Baltasar Carlos on Horseback
		Queen Mariana of Austria
		The Forges of Vulcan
		Christ on the Cross
	Murillo	*Holy Family with a Little Bird*
		Immaculate Conception of Soult
		The Good Shepherd
	Goya	*Family of Charles IV*
		Maja Naked, Maja Clothed
		Executions at Moncloa
		The Second of May
		The Witches' Coven
Flemish	Robert Campin	*St Barbara*
15C-17C	Van der Weyden	*Deposition*
	Hans Memling	*Adoration of the Magi*
	Bruegel the Elder	*Triumph of Death*
	Hieronymus Bosch	*Garden of Earthly Delights*
	Rubens	*The Three Graces*
Italian	Fra Angelico	*Annunciation*
15C-17C	Andrea Mantegna	*Dormition of the Virgin*
	Botticelli	*Story of Nastagio degli Onesti*
	Titian	*Venus with the Organist*
	Tintoretto	*Washing of the Feet*
	Veronese	*Venus and Adonis*
German and Dutch	Albrecht Dürer	*Self-portrait*
16C-17C	Rembrandt	*Artemisa*

trait of a Cardinal), Roman nobility and monumental bearing in the work of **Mantegna** *(Dormition of the Virgin)* and melancholic dreaminess in **Botticelli** *(Story of Nastagio degli Onesti)*. The spirituality of the magnificent *Annunciation* by **Fra Angelico** belongs to the Gothic tradition.

Colour and sumptuousness triumph with the Venetian school: **Titian** with his exceptional mythological scenes *(Danae and the Golden Shower, Venus with the Organist)* and his portrait of *Emperor Charles V*; **Veronese** with compositions set off by silver tones; Tintoretto's golden-fleshed figures springing from shadow *(Washing of the Feet)* and **Tiepolo's** paintings intended for Charles III's royal palace.

French School (17C-18C)

The French are represented by **Poussin** landscapes and by **Lorrain** (17C).

German School

A selection includes **Dürer's** figure and portrait paintings *(Self-portrait, Adam and Eve)* and works by Cranach.

Casón del Buen Retiro★

Entrance in calle Alfonso XII, no28. *Closed for restoration.* This annexe focuses on 19C Spanish trends. The **Gran Salón** has beautiful roof decoration by Lucas Jordán. Works from Spanish historical painting include *The Last Will and Testament of Isabel the Catholic* by Rosales, *Juana the Mad* by F Pradilla and *The Execution of Torrijos and his companions on the beaches of Málaga* by A Gisbert.

Museo thyssen-bornemisza★★★

Open 10am-7pm (11pm Jul-Aug except Sun); last admission 30min before closing. Closed Mon, 1 Jan, 1 May, 25 Dec. 6 €. 91 369 01 51.

The neo-Classical Palacio de Villahermosa houses an outstanding collection acquired by the Spanish State from **Baron Hans Heinrich Thyssen-Bornemisza.** The museum contains approximately 800 works from the late 13C to the present day, exhibited in chronological order on three floors

Second floor

The visit begins with the Italian Primitives *(Gallery 1)*: **Duccio di Buoninsegna's** *Christ and the Samaritan Woman*, with its concern for scenic realism. **Gallery 3** displays splendid examples of 15C Dutch religious painting such as **Jan van Eyck's** *The Annunciation Diptych*. Next to it is the small *Our Lady of the Dry Tree* by **Petrus Christus;** Virgin and Child symbolise the flowering of the dry tree.

The museum possesses a magnificent **portrait collection. Gallery 5** contains superb examples of the Early Renaissance and its values of identity and autonomy. These come to the fore in the *Portrait of Giovanna Tornuaboni* by the Italian painter **D Ghirlandaio.**

Raphael's *Portrait of an Adolescent* can be seen in the Villahermosa Gallery *(Gallery 6)* while **Gallery 7** (16C) reveals **Vittore Carpaccio's** *Young Knight in a Landscape* in which the protagonist's elegance stands out from a background heavy with symbolism. The *Portrait of Doge Francesco Vernier* by **Titian** should not be missed, with its sober, yet diverse tones. After admiring **Dürer's** surprising *Jesus Among the Doctors* (1506, *Gallery 8)*, move on to **Gallery 9**, with portraits from the 16C German School including **The Nymph from the Fountain**, one of several paintings by **Lucas Cranach the Elder**, and the *Portrait of a Woman* by **Hans Baldung Grien**. The 16C Dutch paintings in **Gallery 10** include **Patinir**'s *Landscape with the Rest on the Flight into Egypt*. **Gallery 11** exhibits several works by **El Greco** as well as **Titian's** *St Jerome in the Wilderness* (1575), with its characteristic use of flowing brush-strokes. One of the splendid early works of **Caravaggio** – the creator of tenebrism – *St Catherine of Alexandria*, hangs in **Gallery 12**. In the same gallery is a splendid sculpture (St Sebastian) by Baroque artist **Bernini**. Also here is the *Lamentation over the Body of Christ* (1633) by **Ribera**. The 18C Italian Painting section *(Galleries 16-18)* shows Venetian scenes by **Canaletto** and **Guardi**. Also on this floor (galleries 19-21) are 17C Dutch and Flemish works. **Van Dyck's** magnificent *Portrait of Jacques le Roy*, **De Vos'** *Antonia Canis*, and two memorable **Rubens**,

The Toilet of Venus and *Portrait of a Young Woman with a Rosary*, all hang from the walls of **Gallery 19**.

First floor

Galleries 22-26 represent 17C Dutch painting with scenes of daily life and landscapes. Note **Frans Hals'** *Family Group in a Landscape*, a fine example of a collective portrait.

Interesting portraits stand out from the 18C French and British schools, such as **Gainsborough's** *Portrait of Miss Sarah Buxton* in **Gallery 28**. 19C North American painting, virtually unknown in Europe, is in the next two rooms *(29 and 30)* with works by the Romantic landscape artists Cole, Church, Bierstadt and the Realist Homer. The European Romanticism and Realism of the 19C is expressed by **Constable's** *The Lock*, **Courbet's** *The Water Stream* and **Friedrich's** *Easter Morning*, together with the three works by **Goya** *(Gallery 31)*.

Galleries 32 and **33** are dedicated to Impressionism and Post-Impressionism: magnificent works by Monet, Manet, Renoir, Sisley, Degas, Pissarro, Gauguin, Van Gogh, Toulouse-Lautrec and Cézanne. *At the Milliner* by **Degas** is one of his major canvases. Other works which equally stand out include **Van Gogh's** *"Les Vessenots" in Auvers*, which displays the explosion of brush-strokes synonymous with some of his later works, *Mata Mua* by **Gauguin**, from his Polynesian period, and **Cézanne's** *Portrait of a Farmer*, in which his particular use of colour is used to build volumes, a forerunner of Cubism. Expressionism is represented in **Galleries 35-40**, following a small display of paintings from the Fauve movement in **Gallery 34**. The Expressionist movement, a highlight of this museum, supposes the supremacy of the artist's interior vision and colour over draughtsmanship. Two highly emblematic paintings by **Grosz**, *Metropolis* and *Street Scene*, hang in **Gallery 40**.

Ground floor

The first few galleries *(41-44)* contain exceptional Experimental avant-garde works (1907-24) from European movements: Futurism, Orphism, Suprematism, Constructivism, Cubism and Dadaism. **Room 41** displays Cubist works by **Picasso** *(Man with A Clarinet)*, **Braque** *(Woman with a Mandolin)* and **Juan Gris** *(Woman Sitting)*, while *Proun 1C* by **Lissitzky** and *New York City, New York* by **Mondrian** are in Room 43.

Gallery 45 shows post-First World War European works by **Picasso** *(Harlequin with a Mirror)* and **Joan Miró** *(Catalan Peasant with a Guitar)*, and a 1914 abstract composition by **Kandinsky** *(Picture with Three Spots)*. In the next gallery, mainly dedicated to North American painting, are *Brown and Silver I* by **Jackson Pollock** and *Green on Maroon* by **Mark Rothko**, two examples of abstract American Expressionism. The last two galleries *(47 and 48)* are given over to Surrealism, Figurative Tradition and Pop Art.

Carmen Thyssen-Bornemisza Collection

The more than 250 works on exhibit build on those in the original wing of the museum. Notable are 17C Dutch painting, Impressionism and Post-Impressionism, North American painting, and early Avant-Garde works, especially German.

Museo Nacional Centro de Arte Reina Sofía (Queen Sofia Art Center)

Open 10am-9pm; Sun, 10am-2.30pm
Closed Tue, 1 and 6 Jan, 1 May, 9 Sep, 9 Nov and 24-25 and 31 Dec. 6 € (14.40 € for Paseo del Arte ticket (Bono Arte) in combination with Museo del Prado, Museo Thyssen and MNCARS), no charge Sat from 2.30pm and all day Sun. 91 467 50 62.

The former Hospital de San Carlos was refurbished to house this outstanding museum of contemporary art. The extension is the work of Jean Nouvel.

Permanent collection★

Avant-garde movements

Second floor. The 17 rooms exhibit canvases from avant-garde movements in Spanish painting from the late 19C to the years following the Second World War. Some rooms cover the work of a single artist: Cubist works by **Juan Gris** in Room 4, Room 6 devoted to **Picasso**. His ***Guernica***★★★, commissioned for the Spanish Pavilion at the 1937 World Fair, inspired by the Fascist terror-bombing of Gernika, is renowned for its expressiveness and powerful symbolism, a stark denunciation of the atrocities of war. Room 7 shows a retrospective of **Joan Miró,** with *Snail, Woman, Flower, Star* (1934) and *Woman, Bird and Star (Tribute to Picasso)* (1970); his sculptures are in Room 16. **Dalí** is represented in Room 10, with early works *(Little Girl at the Window* – 1925), together with examples from his Surrealist period *(The Great Masturbator).*

Post-Civil War movements

Fourth floor (Rooms 18 to 45). Works reflect trends from the late 1940s to the present. Room 19 displays works by artists belonging to **Dau al Set** and **Pórtico**, which emerged in the wake of the Civil War. Rooms 20 to 23 cover the Abstract movement of the 1950s and the early 1960s, illustrated by Guerrero, Ràfols Casamada, Hernández Mompó and members of the **Equipo Crónica**. Informalism is represented in Rooms 27 to 29 with paintings associated with **El Paso** (Millares, Saura, Rivera, Canogar, Feito and Viola) and the **Cuenca Group**. Works by **Tàpies** are in Rooms 34 and 35. The collage series *Gravitaciones* by **Eduardo Chillida** in Rooms 42 and 43 is shown with his sculptures.

Works of the sixties by important U.S. artists (D. Judd, B. Nauman, B. Newman, E. Kelly) are in Room 41. Room 44 is dedicated to video.

Walking About

OLD MADRID★

2hr 30min – see town plan

Steep, narrow streets, small squares, 17C palaces and mansions, houses with wrought-iron balconies dating from the 19C and early 20C characterise Old Madrid, the very heart of the city. Try to visit early, or late in the afternoon when churches are open.

Plaza Mayor★★

The square built by Juan Gómez de Mora in 1619 is the centre of **Habsburg Madrid**. On the north side, the **Casa de la Panadería** (a former bakery) was reconstructed by Donoso in 1672. The plaza was the setting for *autos-da-fé,* mounted bullfights, and the proclamations of kings.

A stamp and coin market is held on Sunday mornings while at Christmas, stalls selli decorations. Shops around the square retain a yesteryear look.

Pass through the **Arco de Cuchilleros** into the street fronted by old houses

A

Y

Z

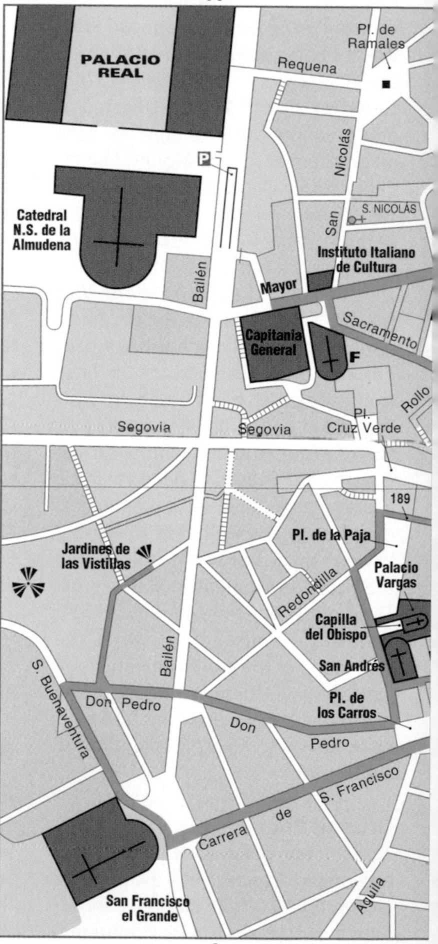

A

Paseo del Prado

With the 18C drawing to a close, Charles III wanted to develop a public area which would be worthy of Madrid's position as capital of Spain and called upon the court's best architects for his project. In an area outside of the city at the time, Hermosilla, Ventura Rodríguez, Sabatini and Villanueva designed, drained, embellished and built a curved avenue with two large fountains, Cybele and Neptune, at each end, and a third, Apollo, in the centre. To complete the project, the **Botanical Gardens, Natural History Museum** (now the Museo del Prado) and the **Observatory**, were also built. The result was a perfect combination of the functional and the ornate dedicated to science and the arts. Since the 16C, the paseo del Prado has been a favourite place for Madrileños to meet and to relax. Today, the avenue retains its dignified air, and provides locals and visitors alike with an opportunity to pass judgement on the vision and imagination of Charles III.

Cava de San Miguel	BY	45	Marqués Viudo de Pontejos	CY	154	San Javier Pl. de	BY	217
Cordón Pl. del	BY	54	Príncipe Anglonaa	AZ	189			
Cuchilleros	BY	60						

Ayuntamiento	BY	H	Iglesia Arzobispal Castrense	AY	F
Casa de Pedro Calderón de la Barca	BY	D			

B C

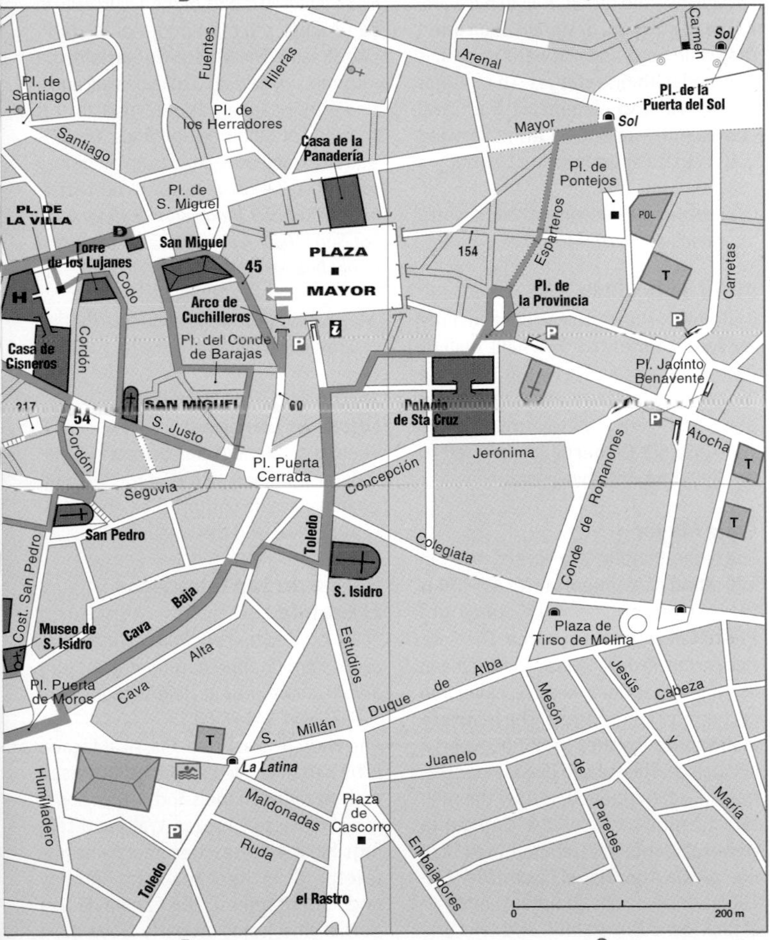

B C

Y Z

with convex façades. The **Cava de San Miguel** provides a rear view of the houses on the square. This area is crowded with small restaurants (mesones) and bars (tavernas). The **Mercado de San Miguel**, an indoor early 20C market, has an elegant iron structure.

Take calle Conde de Miranda. Cross plaza del Conde de Barajas and calle de Gómez de Mora to plaza de San Justo or Puerta Cerrada, a city gate. Continue right on calle de San Justo.

Iglesia Pontificia de San Miguel★

Open 10.30am-12.45pm and 6-8.30pm. Closed Sun and public hols. 91 548 40 11.

The basilica by Bonavia is a rare Spanish church inspired by 18C Italian Baroque. Its convex façade, designed as an interplay of inward and outward curves, is adorned with fine statues. The interior is graceful and elegant with an oval cupola, intersecting vaulting, flowing cornices and abundant stuccowork.

Follow calle Puñonrostro and calle del Codo to plaza de la Villa.

Plaza de la Villa★

Buildings around the square include the **Ayuntamiento** (town hall), built by Gómez de Mora in 1617, the **Torre de los Lujanes** (Luján Tower), a rare examplesof 15C civil architecture, and the 16C **Casa de Cisneros**, connected to the Ayuntamiento by an arch.

Calle Mayor

The name, literally Main Street, gives an indication of its importance. At n° 61 is the narrow house of 17C playright **Pedro Calderón de la Barca**. The Antigua Farmacia de la Reina Madre (Queen Mother's Pharmacy) keeps a collection of chemist's jars and pots. The **Instituto Italiano de Cultura** (n°86) occupies a 17C palace. The Palacio Uceda opposite, from the same period, is now the military headquarters of the **Capitanía General** (Captaincy General). In front of the **Iglesia Arzobispal Castrense** (17C-18C), a monument commemorates an attack on Alfonso XIII and Victoria Eugenia in 1906. In the nearby calle de San Nicolás is the Mudéjar tower of San Nicolás de los Servita.

Take calle del Sacramento to plazuela del Cordón; return to calle del Cordón; continue to calle de Segovia.

Across the street rises the 14C **Mudéjar tower** of the **Iglesia de San Pedro** (Church of St Peter), a rare example of the Mudéjar style in Madrid.

Go along calle del Príncipe Anglona.

Plaza de la Paja

This was a commercial centre in the Middle Ages. The Palacio Vargas obscures the Gothic **Capilla del Obispo**, a 16C chapel. In plaza de los Carros, the Capilla de San Isidro (chapel) is part of the 17C Iglesia de San Andrés built in honour of Madrid's patron saint. The **Museo de San Isidro**, a museum containing a miracle well and a fine Renaissance patio, is next to this complex of religious buildings. There is also an exhibit on Madrid from prehistory to the installation of the royal court in the 16C. (*Open 9.30am-8pm (2.30pm Aug); Sat-Sun, 10am-2pm. Closed Mon and public hols. 91 366 74 15).*

Cross calle de Bailén and take the first street on the right.

Jardines de las Vistillas (Vistillas Gardens)

There is a splendid **panorama**★, especially at sundown, of the Sierra de Guadarrama, Casa de Campo, the Catedral de la Almudena and the viaduct.

Iglesia de San Francisco El Grande

Guided tours (30min), 11am-12.30 and 4-7pm (5-8pm in summer); last tour 30min before closing; no tours Sun-Mon. 3 €. 91 365 38 00.

The church's vast neo-Classical façade is by Sabatini; the circular edifice itself with six radial chapels and a large dome is by Francisco Cabezas. Walls and ceilings have 19C frescoes and paintings (except 18C in the chapels of St Anthony and St Bernardino). The Capilla de San Bernardino holds an early Goya of St

Bernardino of Siena preaching before the king of Aragón (1781). Plateresque **stalls**★ from the Monasterio de El Parral outside Segovia are in the chancel. 16C **stalls**★ in the sacristy and chapter house are from the Cartuja de El Paular *(see Sierra de GUADARRAMA)*, a Carthusian monastery near Segovia.

Walk along carrera de San Francisco and Cava Alta to calle de Toledo.

Calle de Toledo

This is one of the old town's liveliest streets. The **El Rastro** flea market is held Sunday morning and on public holidays. *Beware of pickpockets.*

Iglesia de San Isidro

Open 10am-noon and 6-8pm. Closed Fri. 91 369 20 37.

Formerly the church of the Imperial College of the Company of Jesus (1622), it was the cathedral of Madrid from 1885 until 1993. It contains the relics of Madrid's patron saint, Isidro.

Puerta del Sol

On the best-known square in Madrid, a small monument displays Madrid's coat of arms, next to an equestrian statue of Charles III. The clock on the former post office (now the Madrid regional administration) chimes at New Year's.

Historical Notes

Philip IV commissioned the construction of a palace near the **monasterio de los Jerónimos** (of which only the church remains). It was subsequently destroyed during the Peninsular War and as a result only the building that formerly contained the Museo del Ejército and the Casón del Buen Retiro remain. The Duke of Olivares had the palace grounds developed into a park.

In nearby traditional shops with their colourful wood fronts customers can find fans and mantillas and delicacies.

BOURBON MADRID★★

This is the smart area with wide avenues bordered by opulent buildings, palaces and former mansions, now museums.

Plaza de Cibeles★

In the square is the 18C fountain of Cybele , goddess of fertility, emblematic of Madrid. Many an artist has been inspired to paint the perspectives opening from the square and the impressive buildings around, such as the **Banco de España** (1891), the 18C **Palacio de Buenavista** (Ministry of Defence), the late-19C **Palacio de Linares**, now the home of the Casa de América, and the **Palacio de Comunicaciones (**Post and Telegraph Office, 1919).

f. Vidal/MICHELIN

Plaza de Cibeles and Palacio de Comunicaciones at night

Paseo del Prado★

This tree-lined avenue runs from plaza de Cibeles to plaza del Emperador Carlos V., past the Ministerio de la Marina and Museo Naval (*see Worth a Visit*), the **plaza de la Lealtad** with an obelisk dedicated to the heroes of the 2 May, the neo-Classical **Bolsa** (Stock Exchange) and the emblematic **Hotel Ritz**.

Plaza de Canóvas del Castillo

This square, with its splendid Fuente de Neptuno (Neptune Fountain), is overlooked by the neo-Classical **Palacio de Villahermosa** housing the **Museo Thyssen-Bornemisza**★★★ (*see Special Features*), and the Hotel Palace.

Continuing south, along the left-hand side of the paseo del Prado are the Prado Museum and the **Real Jardín Botánico** (Royal Botanical Gardens), both the work of Juan de Villanueva (*Garden open 10am-6pm Nov-Feb (7pm Mar and Oct, 8pm Apr and Sep, 9pm May-Aug); last entry 30min before closing; to greenhouse 1hr before closing; closed 1 Jan and 25 Dec; 2 €; 91 420 04 38*).

Museo del Prado★★★

The neo-Classical building of one of the world's great art museums was built in the reign of Charles III, originally intended for the Institute of Natural Sciences. (*see Special Features*).

Plaza del Emperador Carlos V

The glass and wrought-iron façade of **Atocha railway station** dominates this square. Enter to view the tropical patio garden, and to glimpse the AVE high-speed train.

The former **Hospital de San Carlos**, opposite, houses the **Museo Nacional Centro de Arte Reina Sofía**★ (*see Special Features*).

Return toward the Jardín Botánico; walk up cuesta de Claudio Moyano with its second-hand booksellers.

Parque del Buen Retiro ★★(Retiro Park)

Open 7am-10pm (midnight in summer). 010 (municipal information).

The Retiro is close to the heart of every *madrileño*, 130ha/321 acres of greenery with dense clumps of trees, formal flower-beds and fountains, temples, colonnades and statues.

Beside the lake (Estanque) where boats may be hired, is the imposing **Monumento a Alfonso XII.** Near the graceful **Palacio de Cristal**★, in which exhibitions are held, are a pool and a grotto.

Puerta de Alcalá★ (Alcalá Arch)

The arch at the centre of plaza de la Independencia was built by Sabatini between 1769 and 1778 to celebrate the triumphant entry of Charles III into Madrid. The perspective is particularly grand at night, taking in plaza de Cibeles, calle de Alcalá and the Gran Vía.

Worth a Visit

Around the Royal Palace★★ *1 day*

Plaza de la Armería

Along the vast arcaded square (south side) is the incomplete **Catedral de la Almudena**, a cathedral begun in 1879. The neo-Baroque façade harmonises with the palace. The view toward the west extends over the Casa de Campo and the Campo del Moro gardens sloping down to the Manzanares river.

Palacio Real★★ (Royal Palace)

Visits and guided tours (40min), 9.30am-5pm (9am-6pm Apr-Sep); Sun and public hols, 9am-3pm. Closed 1 and 6 Jan, 1 and 15 May, 12 Oct, 9 Nov, 24-25 and 31 Dec and during State receptions. 8 € (9 € guided tours), no charge Wed for E.U. citizens. 91 454 88 00 or 91 542 00 03 (reservations).

The best view of the palace is from paseo de Extremadura and from the gardens of the **Campo del Moro**★. This imposing edifice built by the Bourbons following a fire at the Habsburg Alcázar, was the royal residence until 1931.

The palace is a quadrilateral made of Guadarrama granite and white stone, 140m/459ft on the sides, on a high bossaged base. The upper register, in which Ionic columns and Doric pilasters alternate, is crowned by a white limestone balustrade.

The north front gives onto the **Jardines de Sabatini**, the west the **Campo del Moro**. **Plaza de la Armería** stands to the south between the west and east wings of the palace. The east façade gives onto **plaza de Oriente**.

Palacio★ (Palace)

A monumental staircase with a ceiling painted by Giaquinto leads to the Salón de Alabarderos (Halberdier Room), with a ceiling painted by Tiepolo. This leads to the **Salón de Columnas** (Column Room) where royal celebrations and banquets are held. The **Salón del Trono**★ (Throne Room) retains decoration from the period of Charles III and is resplendent with crimson velvet hangings and a magnificent ceiling by Tiepolo (1764) symbolising *The Greatness of the Spanish Monarchy*. The consoles, mirrors and gilded bronze lions are of Italian design. The following three rooms were the king's quarters, occupied by Charles III in 1764. The Saleta Gasparini, the king's dining room, retains a ceiling painted by Mengs. The Gasparini antechamber also has a ceiling by Mengs, and Goya portraits of Charles IV and María Luisa of Parma. The **Cámara Gasparini** is covered in pure Rococo decoration.

The Salón de Carlos III was the king's bedroom. The decor is from the period of Ferdinand VII. The **Sala de Porcelana** is, along with its namesake in Aranjuez Palace, the masterpiece of the Buen Retiro Porcelain Factory. Official banquets are held in the Alfonso XII **Comedor de Gala** or Banqueting Hall (for 145 guests), adorned with 16C Brussels tapestries. The two music rooms contain instruments including several made by **Stradivarius**★. In the chapel are frescoes by Corrado Giaquinto and paintings by Mengs *(Annunciation)* and Bayeu *(St Michael the Archangel)*.

Real Farmacia (Royal Pharmacy)

Several rooms display 18C-20C jars, including a fine 18C Talavera glass jar.

Real Armería★★ (Royal Armoury)

The collection of arms and armour is outstanding. Key pieces include Charles V's suit of armour and armour belonging to Philip II and Philip III. A vaulted hall in the basement contains an excellent collection of Bourbon shotguns.

Museo de Carruajes Reales★ (Royal Carriage Museum)

Closed for restoration. ☎91 542 00 59.

A pavilion in the **Campo del Moro** winter garden houses the royal horse-drawn carriages, most from the reign of Charles IV, in the late 18C. The corona-

J. Malburet/MICHELIN

Palacio Real

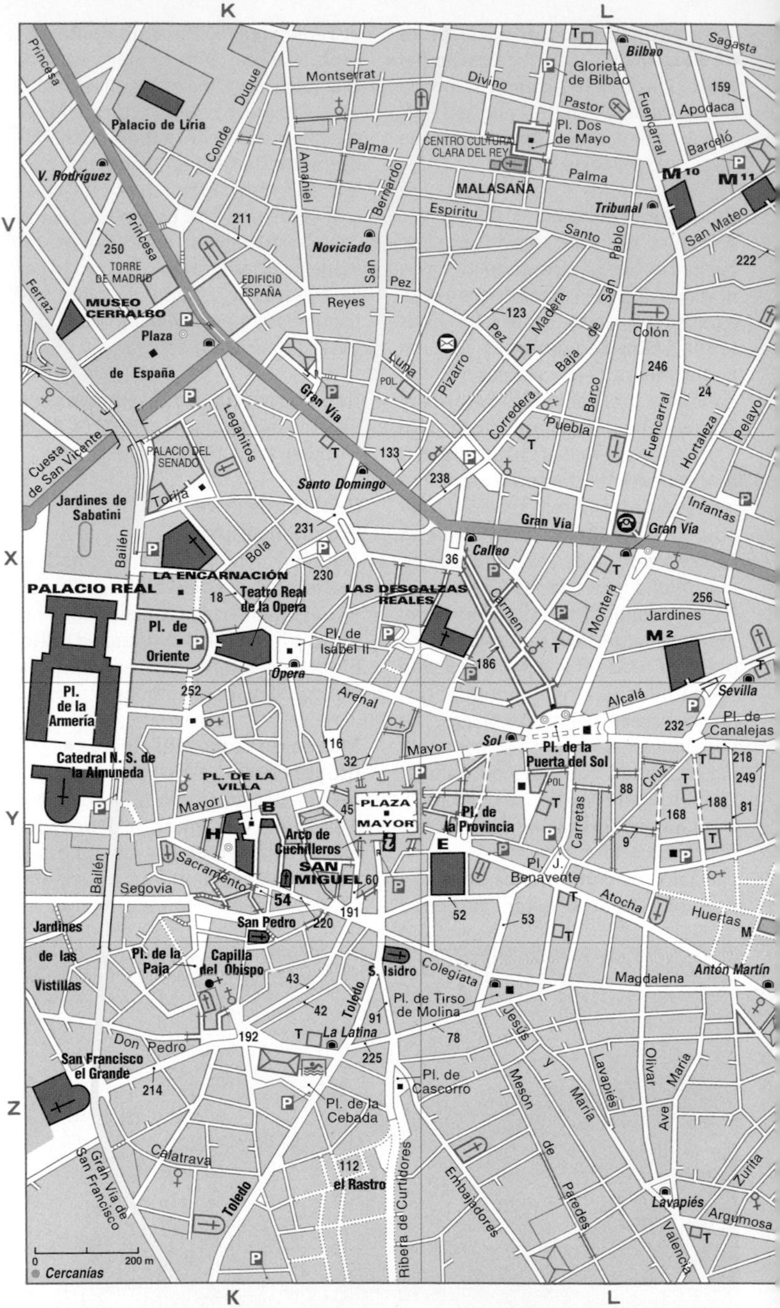

tion coach (drawn by eight horses with accompanying footmen), was built in the 19C for Ferdinand VII and still bears marks of the attempt on Alfonso XIII and his bride, Victoria Eugenia, in May 1906.

Plaza de Oriente

This attractive square between the east façade of the Palacio Real and the Teatro Real is pleasant for a stroll. The magnificent equestrian statue of Philip IV is the work of Pietro Tacca (17C).

M N

M N

V X Y Z

MADRID

Alcalá	MX	
Alvarez Gato	LY	9
Arenal	KY	
Arrieta	KX	18
Augusto Figueroa	MV	24
Ayala	NV	25
Bárbara de Braganza	NV	27
Bordadores	KY	32
Callao Pl. del	LX	36
Carmen	LX	
Cava Alta	KZ	42
Cava Baja	KZ	43
Cava de San Miguel	KY	45
Ciudad de Barcelona Av. de la	NZ	46
Colón Pl. de	NV	49
Concepción Jerónima	LY	52
Conde de Romanones	LY	53
Cordón Pl. del	KY	54
Cortes Pl. de las	MY	57
Cuchilleros	KY	60
Duque de Alba	LZ	78
Duque de Medinaceli	MY	79
Echegaray	LY	81
Espoz y Mina	LY	88
Estudios	KZ	91
Felipe IV	NY	
Fernando el Santo	NV	99
Fuencarral	LV	
General Vara del Rey Pl. del	KZ	112
Goya	NV	114
Gran Vía	LX	
Herradores Pl. de los	KY	116
Hortaleza	LX	
Independencia Pl. de la	NX	118
Infanta Isabel Pas. de la	NZ	119
Jesús del Valle	LV	123
Libreros	KX	133
Madrazo	MY	141
Marqués de Cubas	MY	145
Mayor	KY	
Mayor Pl.	KY	
Mejía Lequerica	LMV	159
Montera	LX	
Núñez de Arce	LY	168
Preciados	LX	186
Príncipe	LY	188
Puerta Cerrada Pl. de	KY	191
Puerta de Moros Pl. de	KZ	192
Puerta del Sol Pl. de la	LY	
Recoletos	NX	196
San Bernardino	KV	211
San Francisco Carrera de	KZ	214
San Jerónimo Carrera de	LMY	218
San Justo	KY	220
San Lorenzo	LV	222
San Millán	KZ	225
Santa Engracia	MV	226
Santo Domingo Cuesta de	KX	230
Santo Domingo Pl. de	KX	231
Sevilla	LY	232
Tudescos	LX	238
Valverde	LV	246
Ventura de la Vega	LY	249
Ventura Rodríguez	KV	250
Vergara	KY	252
Villa de París Pl. de la	NV	255
Virgen de los Peligros	LX	256

Ayuntamiento	KY	H
Museo Municipal	LV	M10
Museo Nacional de Artes Decorativas	NX	M8
Museo Naval	NX	M3
Museo Romántico	LV	M11
Museo Thyssen-Bornemisza	MY	M6
Palacio de Santa Cruz	LY	E
Real Academia de Bellas Artes de San Fernando	LX	M2
Torre de los Lujanes	KY	B

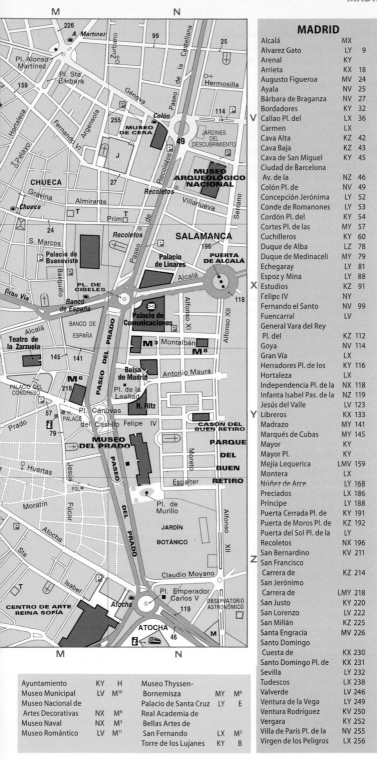

Teatro Real

This hexagonal neo-Classical building was created as an opera house in 1850 for Isabel II. It has two façades.

Monasteria de las Descalzas Reales★★

Guided tours (45min), Tue-Thu and Sat, 10.30am-12.45pm and 4-5.45pm; Fri, 10.30am-12.45pm; Sun, 11am-1.45pm. Closed Mon, 1 and 6 Jan, Wed-Sat during Holy Week, 1 and 15 May, 15 Jul, 9 Nov, and 24-25 and 31 Dec. 5 € (combined ticket with Monasterio de la Encarnación: 6 €), no charge Wed for E.U. citizens. 91 542 00 59.

Joanna of Austria, daughter of Emperor Charles V, founded the convent of Poor Clares in the palace where she was born. It served as a retreat for nobles.

The magnificent grand **staircase**★ is totally decorated with frescoes. In a former dormitory is an extraordinary collection of **tapestries**★★ depicting the Triumph of the Church, woven in Brussels in the 17C to cartoons by Rubens. The **33 small chapels** are sumptuously decorated; outstanding is that of the Virgin of Guadalupe.

Convent treasures include portraits of the royal family by Rubens, Sánchez Coello, and others.

Real Monasterio de la Encarnación★ (Royal Convent of the Incarnation)

Guided tours (45min), Tue-Thu and Sat, 10.30am-12.45pm and 4-5.45pm; Fri, 10.30am-12.45pm; Sun, 11am-1.45pm. Closed Mon, 1 and 6 Jan, Wed-Sat during Holy Week, 1 and 15 May, 27 Jul, 9 Nov, and 24-25 and 31 Dec. 3.60 € (combined with Monasterio de las Descalzas: 6 €), no charge Wed for E.U. citizens. 91 542 00 59.

The convent, on a delightful square near the former Alcázar, was founded in 1611 by Margaret of Austria. The collection of paintings from the 17C Madrid School is particularly rich and includes the interesting *Exchange of Princesses on Pheasant Island* in 1615 by Van der Meulen. There is a polychrome sculpture of *Christ at the Column* by Gregorio Hernández on the first floor.

The **Relicario**★, with ceiling painted by Vicencio Carducci, holds 1 500 relics. The church with quasi-Herreran portal was reconstructed in the 18C after the Alcázar fire.

Plaza de España

The monument to Cervantes in the middle of the city's central explanade is overwhelmed by 1950s skyscrapers. Starting from the square is the wide **Gran Vía,** lined by shops, cinemas and hotels. Calle Princesa, popular with students, leads towards the **Ciudad Universitaria**★ (University City).

MONCLOA – CASA DE CAMPO DISTRICT

Museo Cerralbo★

Open 9.30am-3pm;Sun and public hols, 10am-3pm. Closed Mon. 2.40 €, no charge Wed and Sun. 91 547 36 46.

The museum, in a late-19C mansion, displays the collection of the Marquis of Cerralbo, a patron of the Arts, including Spanish paintings, furniture, fans, clocks, armour and weaponry, porcelain, and archaeological finds.

Parque del Oeste★ (Park of the West)

This delightful garden, overlooking the Manzanares, was designed at the beginning of the 20C. In the southern part stands the small 4C BC Egyptian **Temple of Debod**, rescued from Nubia when the Aswan Dam was being built.

The **paseo del Pintor Rosales** nearby offers pavement cafés and views of Velázquez-like sunsets.

Casa de Campo★

This extensive park is popular with *madrileños.* Attractions include a lake, a swimming pool and an **amusement park**★. Kids *Consult timetables. Admission to the park: 7 €; ticket for all rides: 24.40 €, 13.90 € for children under 7. 91 463 29 00.*

A **teleférico** (cableway) connects to Parque del Oeste. (*Open noon (11am in spring and summer) to nightfall. 4.20 € round trip. 91 541 11 18 or 91 541 74 50.)*

The **zoo-aquarium**★★ here houses one of the largest assortments of animals anywhere in Europe (*Kids* *Open 10.30am-nightfall; 14.90€; 12.20€ for children under 7; 91 512 37 70).*

Museo de América★ (Museum of the Americas)

Open 9.30am-3pm; Sun and public hols, 10am-3pm. Closed Mon, 1 and 6 Jan, 1 and 15 May, 24-25 and 31 Dec. 3€, no charge Sun. 91 544 67 42.

This archaeological and ethnological museum focuses on ties between Europe and the Americas. Over 2 500 objects are accompanied by explanations, maps, models, reconstructions of dwellings etc. Outstanding items are the *Stele of Madrid* (Mayan), the powerful **Treasure of Los Quimbayas**★ (Colombian), the *Tudela Manuscript* (1553) and the prized Mayan **Tro cortesiano Manuscript**★★★, one of only four remaining.

Faro de la Moncloa (Moncloa Beacon)

Kids Open 15 Oct-30 Apr 10am-2pm and 5-7pm (8pm in May and 16 Sep-14 Oct, 9pm Jun-15 Sep); Sat-Sun and public hols, 10.30am-5.15pm. Closed Mon, 1 Jan and 25 Dec. 1 €. 91 544 81 04.

From its 76m/250ft high **observatory**★★, there is a wonderful view of Madrid and its surrounding area.

Museo del Traje (Costume Museum)

Avenida Juan Herrera 2. Open 9.30am-7pm; Sun and public hols 10am-3pm. Closed Mon. 3 €. 91 549 71 50.

This interesting museum covers clothing from before the 18C through the 20C, and ends with a re-creation of the the world of the fashion runway. The designs of couturiers Mariano Fortuny and Balenciaga are featured along with everyday wear.

SALAMANCA – RETIRO

MuseoArqueológicoNacional★★ (Archaeological Museum)

Entrance in calle Serrano. Open 9.30am-8.30pm; Sun and public hols, 9.30am-2.30pm. Closed Mon, 1 and 6 Jan, and 24 Dec. 3 €, no charge Sat (after 2.30pm) and Sun. 91 577 79 12.

Sharing a building with the **Biblioteca Nacional** (National Library), this is the best of its type in Spain.

Prehistoric, Egyptian and Greek Art★

Galleries 1-18. In the garden is a reproduction of the **Cuevas de Altamira** (*see Altamira Caves*) and their paintings of bison. Galleries are devoted to the Bronze Age and Iron Age (warlike cultures of the northeast with outstanding gold- and silver-smithing). Note the splendid bronze Costix **bulls**★ of the Megalithic culture (Talayots) of the Balearic Islands The gallery dedicated to **Ancient Egypt**, displays funerary objects. Classical Athens is also represented by magnificent **Greek vases**★.

Iberian and Roman Antiquities★★

Galleries 19-26. Exhibits in the Iberian galleries illustrate the origin of local techniques and the influence of the Phoenicians, Greeks and Carthaginians. The second gallery shows sculpture at a peak of artistic expression: the **Dama de Elche**★★★ (Lady of Elche) is an outstanding stone bust, with a sumptuous

Archivo Fotográfica/Museo Arqueológico Nacional

Votive Crown

head-dress and corsage. In the same gallery is the **Dama de Baza**★★, a realistic goddess figure of the 4C BC. Other galleries illustrate Spain's adoption of Roman techniques in sculpture, mosaics and ceramics and the incorporation of ideas from Byzantium.

Medieval Decorative Art★

Galleries 27-35. In this section are the magnificent **votive crowns of Guarrazar**★★ dating from the Visigothic period, made of embossed gold plaques, mixing Germanic and Byzantine techniques.

This section is also devoted to Muslim Spain. Gallery 31 shows the Romanesque portal from the Monasterio de San Pedro de Arlanza (12C) and treasures from San Isidoro de León, notably the magnificent 11C ivory **processional cross**★★ of Don Fernando and Doña Sancha. Rooms 32 and 33 display Romanesque and Gothic art, including engravings, grilles and capitals. Romanesque tombs and capitals, and Gothic sculpture in subsequent galleries, continue to show deep Moorish influence. Gallery 35 is a reconstruction of a Mudéjar interior, with a magnificent **artesonado**★★ ceiling.

16-19C Art

Galleries 37-38. Porcelain, furniture, jewels and arms are on display from the Kingdom of the Austrias (1516-1700). North of the Museo Arqueológico are the **Jardines del Descubrimiento** (Discovery Gardens), with monuments to the discovery of the New World. Directly below is Madrid's **Centro Cultural** (cultural centre).

Museo Lázaro Galdiano★★

Open 10am-4.30pm. Closed Tue, 1 Jan, 1 Nov, 6 and 25 Dec. 4€. 91 561 60 84.

This mansion houses **collections**★★ of editor and art lover José Lázaro Galdiano (1863-1947). On the **lower level**, are samples of outstanding paintings by the Master of Perea, Mengs, Zurbarán and Sánchez Coello. The **main floor** –which retains ceilings painted by Villamil and some lovely items of furniture – is entirely devoted to 15C-19C Spanish Art with magnificent Gothic and Renaissance panels. On the **second floor** are works of the **Flemish School** and Italian works. The **third floor** houses decorative arts (some 4 000 items): **ivories and enamel**★★★, ceramics, numismatics, arms and fabric.

Museo Nacional de Artes Decorativas

Open 9.30am-3pm; Sat-Sun, 10am-3pm. 2.40 €. 91 532 64 99.

This museum in a 19C mansion contains a splendid collection of furniture and decorative objects.

Museo Naval

Open 10am-2pm. Closed Mon, 1 and 6 Jan, 1 May, and 24-25 and 31 Dec. 91 379 52 99.

On display are ship **models**★, nautical instruments, weapons, and paintings of naval battles. The **map of Juan de la Cosa**★★ (1500) is the first to show the American continent.

CENTRO

Real Academia de Bellas Artes de San Fernando★ (San Fernando Royal Fine Arts Academy)

Open 9am-7pm; Sat-Sun and Mon, 9am-2.30pm (2pm public hols). Closed 1 and 6 Jan, 1 and 30 May, 24-25 and 31 Dec and local public hols. 3 €, no charge Wed. 91 524 08 64.

The gallery has a valuable collection of 16C-20C paintings. Spanish paintings from the Golden Age include works by Ribera, Zurbarán, Murillo, Alonso Cano *(Christ Crucified)* and Velázquez. The 18C is also present with works by artists with Bourbon connections (Van Loo, Mengs, Giaquinto, Tiepolo and Bayeu) and above all Goya, including his *Self-portrait* and studio paintings.

Museo Municipal

Open 9.30am-8pm; August, 9.30am-2.30pm. Sat-Sun, 10am-2pm. Closed Mon and public hols. 91 588 86 74.

This museum in the former city hospice, an 18C building with superb **portal**★★ retraces the history of the city.

OTHER DISTRICTS

San Antonio de la Florida★

Open 9.30am-8pm; Sat-Sun 10am-2pm. Closed Mon and public hols. 91 542 07 22.
The chapel, built in 1798 under Charles IV, and painted by Goya, contains the remains of the artist. The **frescoes**★★ on the cupola illustrate the miracle of St Anthony of Padua – but Goya used the beautiful women of 18C Madrid as models.

Museo Sorolla★

Open 9.30am-3pm (6pm Wed); Sun and public hols, 10am-3pm. Closed Mon. 1 and 6 Jan and 24-25 and 31 Dec. 2.40 €. 91 310 15 84.
The Madrid home of Joaquín Sorolla (1863-1923), the great Valencian Luminista painter, includes his studio and some of his works.

Plaza Monumental de las Ventas★ (Bullring)

The bullring (1931) is Spain's largest, with a capacity of 22 300. The **Museo Taurino** (Bullfighting Museum) honours the great fighters. (*Open 9.30am-2.30pm; Sun and public hols Mar-Sep, 10am-1pm. Closed Mon in summer, Sat all year and Sun in summer. 91 725 18 57).*

Museo de la Ciudad (City Museum)

Open 9.30am-8pm; Sat-Sun 10am-2pm. Closed Mon and public hols. 91 588 65 99.
The museum covers Madrid's history from before recorded time. It includes superb **models**★ of neighbourhoods and emblematic buildings.

Museo del Ferrocarril (Railway Museum)

Kids *Open 10am-3pm. Closed Mon, in Aug, 1 and 6 Jan, 1 May and 25 Dec. 4 €, no charge Sat. 902 22 88 22.*
The wrought-iron and glass Delicias station, built in 1880, has a collection of steam engines and a delightful restaurant car for snacks.

Faunia★

7km/4.5mi from Madrid along the A 3. Turn off to Valdebernardo.

Kids *Open Dec-Feb 10am-5.30pm (6pm Mar and Nov; 7pm Apr and Oct; 8pm May and 11-30 Sep; 9pm Jun-Aug). Closed Mon-Tue Nov-Feb. 21 €, 15 € children under 12 and seniors over 60. 91 301 62 10.* This nature-themed park re-creates the planet's ecosystems on 140 000m²/167 300sq yd, with some 4 500 small- and medium-sized animals and over 70 000 trees and plants.

Excursions

Warner Bros Park★

Kids *Check seasonal schedule. 33 €; children: 25 €. 902 02 41 00.*
This park is a great getaway, with assorted bars, restaurants and shops. Theme areas include **Hollywood Boulevard**, **Movie WB World Studios**, **Super Heroes World**, **The Old West Territory**, and **Cartoon Village**, each with rides and activities.

El Pardo

17km/10.5mi NW. The town on the outskirts of Madrid grew around one of the royal residences.

Palacio Real★

Guided tours (35min), 10.30am-5pm; Sun and public hols, 9.55am-1.40pm; Apr-Sep, 10.30am-6pm; Sun and public hols, 9.25am-1.40pm. Closed 1 and 6 Jan, 1 and 15 May, 9 Nov and 24-25 and 31 Dec and for State receptions. 5 €, no charge Wed for E.U. citizens . 91 376 15 00.
The palace was built by Philip III (1598-1621) on the site of Philip II's (1556-98) palace which had been destroyed in a fire in 1604. Franco lived here for 35 years; today, it is used by Heads of State on official visits. Decorations include more than 200 **tapestries**★; the majority are 18C from the Real Fábrica de Tápices (Royal Tapestry Factory) in Madrid based on cartoons by Goya, Bayeu, González Ruiz and Van Loo.

MÁLAGA★

POPULATION: 534 683
MICHELIN MAP 578 V 16 (TOWN PLAN) MAP 124 COSTA DEL SOL – SEE COSTA DEL SOL – 59KM/37MI E OF MARBELLA AND 124KM/77MI SW OF GRANADA – ANDALUCÍA (MÁLAGA)

Founded by Phoenicians, Málaga became a Roman colony and later, the main port of Moorish Granada. Today, it is the capital of the Costa del Sol, but it retains characteristic old houses and gardens that bespeak its importance as a 19C port. Beaches stretch eastwards from La Malagueta, at one end of the Paseo Marítimo, to El Palo *(5km/3mi E)*, **a former fishermen's quarter.**

- **Information:** *Pasaje de Chinitas 4, ☎95 221 34 45; Plaza de la Marina 11, ☎952 12 20 20. www.malagaturismo.com*
- **Orient Yourself:** Whitewashed Málaga is at the mouth of the Guadalmedina along the Mediterranean.
- **Parking:** Finding a space is difficult in the old quarter; park outside and walk.
- **Don't Miss:** The Museo Picasso and the Alcazaba.
- **Organizing Your Time:** Head first for the Picasso Museum, and allow time for strolling the castle and old quarter.
- **Also See:** *COSTA DEL SOL and ANTEQUERA (48km/30mi N).*

Worth a Visit

Museo Picasso (Picasso Museum)★★

Open 10am-8pm (9pm Fri-Sat). Closed 1 Jan and 24 and 31 Dec. 8 €, no charge last Sun of month from 3pm. ☎ 902 44 33 77.

The 16C Palacio de Buenavista houses oils, sketches, engravings, sculptures and ceramics from the collections of Christine and Bernard Ruiz-Picasso, his daughter-in-law and grandson. Among paintings are *Olga Kokholva with Mantilla* (1917), *Mother and Child* (1921-1922), *Portrait With White Cap* (1923), *Bust of Woman, Arms Crossed Behind Head* (1939), *Woman in Armchair* (1946), and *Jacqueline Seated* (1954).

Alcazaba★

Open 8.30am-7pm (9.30am-8pm in summer). Closed Mon, 1 Jan and 24-25 and 31 Dec. 1.90 € (3.15 €, joint ticket with Gibralfaro) . ☎952 22 51 06.

The ruins of a **Roman theatre** line the approach to this 11C Moorish fortress. Inside the final gateway are Moorish gardens. There is a **view**★ of the harbour and city from the ramparts. The former Nasrid palace is within.

Málaga Wine

This aperitif or dessert wine is predominantly produced from Pedro Ximénez and Moscatel grapes. The main types are Málaga Negro, Lágrima and Color. Large quantities of currants are also produced in the Málaga area, mainly for export.

Catedral★

Open 10am-6pm (7pm Sat); Sun and public hols, open for worship only. 3.50 €. ☎952 21 59 17.

Construction spanned three centuries (16C-18C); the south tower still lacks its full elevation. **Oven vaulting**★ covers the aisles. Classically ordered Corinthian columns, entablatures and cornices add a monumental appearance. **Choir stalls**★ bear figures by Pedro de Mena. There is an impressive early-15C carved and painted **Gothic retable**★ in the ambulatory.

The 18C **Palacio Episcopal** (Episcopal Palace) on the square, in Baroque style, has a lovely marble façade.

El Sagrario, an unusual 16C rectangular church in the cathedral gardens features a fine **north portal**★ in Isabelline Gothic style. The 18C interior is Baroque;

Address Book

For coin ranges, please see the Legend on the cover flap.

WHERE TO EAT

El Chinitas – *Moreno Monroy 4 – 95 221 09 72 – www.chinitas.arrakis.es – Closed evenings of 24 and 31 Dec –* . Ceramic murals, photos and pictures of popular personalities and artists make this one of the most characteristic restaurants of Málaga. The terrace on a pedestrian street is pleasant, and there are dining areas on three floors.

Restaurante-Museo La Casa del Ángel – *Madre de Dios 29 (facing Teatro Cervantes) – 95 260 87 50 – www.lacasadelangel.com – Closed Mon and 2 weeks in Jun –* . Ángel Garó captures the senses by conjuring up the best of Andalucían gastronomy in a unique artistic setting. Enjoy delicious cuisine while surrounded by original works by the likes of Picasso, Dalí, Miró, Sebastiano del Piombo and Julio Romero de Torres, master on canvas of the beauty of the Spanish woman.

TAPAS

Bar La Mesonera – *Gómez Pallete 11 – 667 52 25 32.* This small bar fills up with stars and the rich and famous before and after flamenco performances at the Teatro Cervantes opposite (and for shows right here on Wed evenings, 10€ charge). Delicious tapas and a colourful, typically Andalucían atmosphere.

WHERE TO STAY

Hotel Castilla y Guerrero – *Córdoba 7 – 95 221 86 35 – www.hotelcastillaguerrero.com – – 36 rooms.* Plain but comfortable and well-located, with everything needed for a good rest, and adequate bathrooms. Go up the stairs to check in. Good for the price.

Hotel Don Curro – *Sancha de Lara 7 – 95 222 72 00 – www.hoteldoncurro.com – – 118 rooms – 8.40€.* This slim tower is right downtown, with cosy, comfortable rooms and a game room that's always full.

Hotel Monte Victoria – *Conde de Ureña 58 – 952 65 65 25 – hotelmontevictoria.com – – Reservations advised – 8 rooms – 9€.* Quiet family hotel in a villa. Best assets are the garden terrace with impressive city views and the carefully kept rooms. Located on a narrow, climbing street where it's hard to park, though only 15 min on foot from the Casco Viejo (Old Quarter).

TAKING A BREAK

Café Central – *Plaza de la Constitución 11 – Open 8am-10pm.* One of Málaga's most typical and long-standing coffee houses, frequented by a faithful batch of regulars. Although the terrace on the square is particularly pleasant, the large tea-room stands out as the café's most impressive feature.

Casa Aranda – *Herrería del Rey – 952 22 12 84 – Open Mon-Sat 7am-1pm and 4.30-9pm; Sun and public hols 8am-12.30pm and 4.30-9pm.* This lively, atmospheric café has taken over every building on this narrow street. A great place for a chat with friends over chocolate con churros.

NIGHTLIFE

El Pimpi – *Granada 6 – 95 222 89 90 – Closed Mon morning – Open 11.30am-3am.* One of Málaga's most traditional locales, in the old city next to the Museo Picasso. Its old-time tavern decor is perfect for enjoying sweet wine and tapas. Leading luminaries have signed its casks and the walls display old bullfight posters.

Puerta Oscura – *Molina Lario 5 – 95 222 19 00 – www.malaganet.com/puertaoscura – Closed 20 Aug-1 Sep – Open 6pm-3am.* Excellent for a cup of coffee or something stronger, while you listen to chamber music. The setting is classically elegant, intimate and distinguished. During Málaga's fiesta, the decorations of religious imagery transform the space.

Liceo – *Beatas 21 – Open midnight-7am.* This disco with a lively upstairs bar, in one of Málaga's old town houses, is popular with an international crowd, particularly those in their thirties. This old mansion with its 19C feel really comes to life at the weekend.

ENTERTAINMENT

Teatro Cervantes – *Ramos Marín near plaza la Merced – ☎952 22 41 00 – www. teatrocervantes.com.* Teatro Cervantes, which first opened its doors in 1870, offers an extensive programme of theatre, concerts and dance, and hosts the Málaga Festival of Spanish Film.

FIESTAS

Málaga's major celebrations are **Holy Week** and the **Feria** (the week of August 15).

a beautiful **Mannerist altarpiece★★** is crowned by a well-preserved Calvary.

Museo-Casa Natal Picasso (Picasso's Birthplace)

Open 10am-8pm; Sun 10am-2pm. Closed 1 Jan and 25 Dec. 1€. ☎952 06 02 15.

The mid-15C building on the **plaza de la Merced** shows a number of Picasso's drawings as well as photos and ceramics; and houses the Pablo Ruiz Picasso Foundation.

Museo de Artes y Costumbres Populares (Museum of Popular Art and Costume)

Open 10am-1.30pm and 4-7pm; 15 Jun-30 Sep, 10am-1.30pm and 5-8pm; Sat, 10am-1.30pm. Closed Sun and public hols. 2€. ☎95 221 71 37.

The museum in a 17C inn displays objects once used for work on land or sea, as well as 18C and 19C costumes.

Santuario de la Virgen de la Victoria★

At the end of calle Compás de la Victoria. The sanctuary was founded by the

MÁLAGA

Aduana Pl. de la	EY	2
Arriola Pl. de la	CZ	5
Atocha Pasillo	CZ	8
Calderería	DY	13
Cánovas del Castillo Pas.	FZ	18
Cárcer	DY	27
Casapalma	DY	30
Chinitas Pasaje	DY	31
Cólon Alameda de	CZ	32
Compañía	DY	37
Constitución Pl. de la	DY	40
Cortina del Muelle	DZ	42
Especerías	DY	56
Granada	DEY	
Huerto del Conde	EY	67
Mariblanca	DY	77
Marina Pl. de la	DZ	80
Marqués de Larios	DYZ	84
Martínez	DZ	86
Molina Larios	DZ	95
Nueva	DY	
Postigo de los Abades	DY	106
Santa Isabel Pasillo de	CYZ	120
Santa Lucía	DY	123
Santa María	CY	125
Sebastián Souvirón	CDZ	130
Strachan	DYZ	133
Teatro Pl. del	DY	135
Tejón y Rodríguez	DY	138
Tetuán Puente de	CZ	140
El Sagrario	DY	F
Mercado Central	DZ	B
Museo Picasso	EY	M3
Museo de Artes y Costumbres Populares	CY	M1
Museo-Casa Natal Picasso	EY	M2
Palacio Episcopal	DY	E
Teatro romano	EY	K

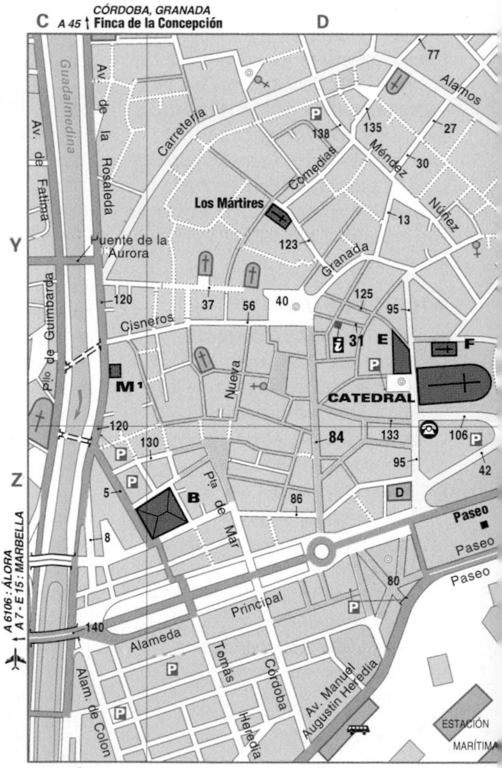

Catholic Monarchs. The church is dominated by a large 17C altarpiece at the centre of which stands the **camarín**★★, a Baroque masterpiece covered by stuccowork and presided over by a fine 15C German *Virgin and Child*.

CAC Málaga

Open 10am-8pm; summer 10am-2pm and 5-9pm. Closed Mon, 1 Jan and 25 Dec. 952 21 01 77.

The old wholesale market, a Rationalist building by Luis Gutiérrez Soto (1939), houses a modern art centre, the Centro de Arte Contemporáneo de Málaga.

Museo de Arte Sacro; Museo Interactivo de la Música.

A romantic corner of the Finca de la Concepción

Excursion

Finca de la Concepción★

7km/4mi N. Open 9.30am-5.30pm (8.30pm Apr-Sep). Closed Mon. 3.15 €. 95 225 21 48.

Visitors will enjoy strolling through this delightful jungle, planted with more than 300 tropical and subtropical species and dotted with streams, ponds, waterfalls and Roman ruins.

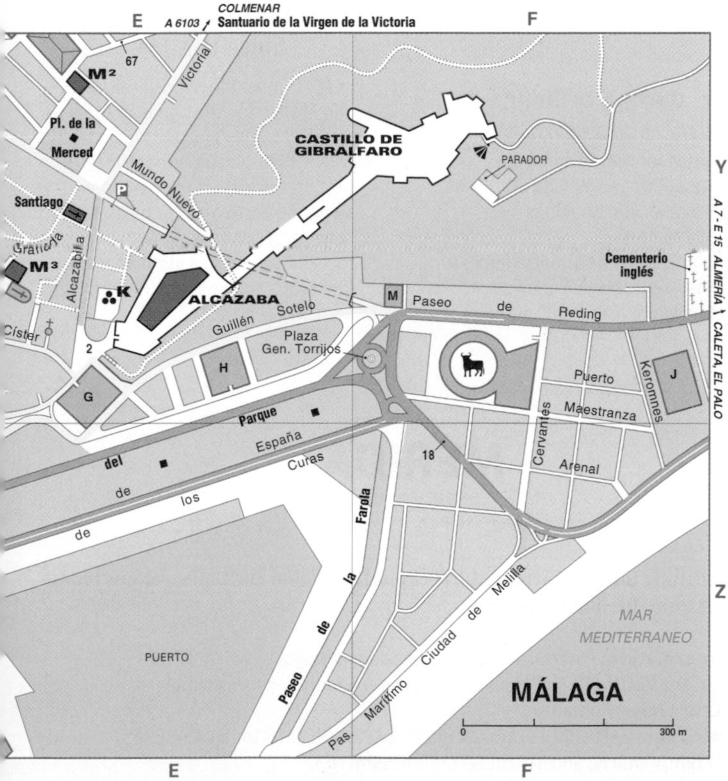

MELILLA

POPULATION: 63 670.

MICHELIN MAP 742 FOLDS 6 AND 11 – NORTH AFRICA

Melilla's wide avenues and large buildings give way to market gardens, parks and a bay full of sailing and fishing vessels.

- **Information:** *Fortuny 21, ☎95 267 54 44.*
- **Orient Yourself:** Melilla is on a peninsula jutting into the Mediterranean from the North African coast.

Worth a Visit

OLD TOWN★

- *Climb the steps the end of avenida del General Macía.*

The old town is encircled by 16C and 17C fortifications. Monuments worthy of interest include the tiny **Capilla de Santiago** *(at the end of a covered passageway)*, with its Gothic vault, and the Puerta de Santiago, a gateway bearing the escutcheon of Emperor Charles V.

Getting to Melilla

By ferry – Trasmediterránea operates services to and from Almería (7hr) and Málaga (8hr). For information and bookings, call ☎ 902 45 46 45.

By plane – Iberia has daily flights to Melilla from Málaga. For information and bookings, call ☎902 400 500.

Museo Municipal

Open 10am-1.30pm and 4-8.30pm; 1 Jul-15 Sep, 10am-1.30pm and 5-9.30pm; Sun, 10am-2pm. Closed Mon, 1 and 6 Jan, 1 May and 25 Dec. ☎95 268 13 39. In the Baluarte de la Concepción (bastion). The museum displays vases, coins and jewels from the Carthaginian, Phoenician and Roman periods, and 17C-19C weaponry. There are **panoramas**★ of the old and new towns, the port and the Cabo de Tres Forcas.

A Spanish Possession Since the 15C

In 1497, under the reign of the Catholic Monarchs, the Duke of Medinaceli's troops seized this town which then became Spanish territory. In the past, like many towns along the North African coast, Melilla fell prey to the waves of navigators and conquerors in the Mediterranean (Carthaginians, Phoenicians, Romans).

MÉRIDA★

POPULATION: 51 135

MICHELIN MAP 576 P 10 – EXTREMADURA (BADAJOZ)

This historic town in Extremadura, capital of Roman Lusitania, retains monuments from this illustrious era.

- **Information:** *Paseo José Álvarez Saénz de Buruaga, ☎924 00 97 30.*
- **Orient Yourself:** Mérida is close to the A 5 highway to Portugal
- **Don't Miss:** Roman sites.
- **Also See:** BADAJOZ (62km/39mi W), ZAFRA (66km/41mi S), CÁCERES (71km/44mil N) and TRUJILLO (88km/55mi NE).

Special Features

ROMAN MÉRIDA★★ *3hr*

In 25 BC, the Romans founded *Emerita Augusta* on the River Guadiana and at the junction of major Roman roads. They lavished upon it temples, a theatre, an amphitheatre and even a 400m/437yd circus.

Museo Nacional de Arte Romano★★ (National Museum of Roman Art)

Open 10am-2pm and 4-6pm; Mar-Nov, 10am-2pm and 4-9pm; Sun and public hols all year, 10am-2pm. Closed Mon, 1 and 6 Jan, 1 May, 3 and 8 Sep, 13 Oct, 10 and 25 Dec. 2.40 €, no charge Sat afternoon and Sun. 924 31 19 12.

An imposing brick **building**★ by Rafael Moneo Vallés, reminiscent of a Roman amphitheatre, displays Mérida's rich archaeological collections.

Sculptures include the head of Augustus *(at the end of the second bay)*. In the last bay are statues, caryatids and giant medallions (Medusa and Jupiter) which made up the frieze of Mérida's forum. Wonderful **mosaics**★ may be viewed up close.

In the basement are remains of Roman villas and tombs.

Teatro Romano★★ (Roman Theatre)

Open 9.30am-2pm and 4-6.30pm (5-7.30pm Jun-Dec). Closed 1 Jan and 24-25 and 31 Dec. 6.50 € (9 € combined ticket with church of Santa Eulalia and Alcazaba). 924 31 20 24.

The theatre. built by Agrippa in 24 BC., seated 6 000. A high stage wall was decorated in Hadrian's reign (2C AD) with colonnade and statues. Great granite blocks over the passages are skillfully secured without mortar.

Anfiteatro★ (Amphitheatre)

The 1C BC arena held 14 000 spectators. It staged chariot races and was flooded for mock sea battles. Original steps remain; a few tiers are reconstructed. A wall crowned by a cornice protected noble spectators from beasts during gladiatorial combats.

Casa Romana del Anfiteatro (Roman Villa)

Open 9.30am-1.45pm and 4-6.30pm (5-7.30pm in summer). Closed 1 Jan and 24-25 and 31 Dec. 9 € (combined ticket). 924 31 20 24.

Water channels, pavements foundations and mosaics remain.

Casa del Mitreo

Next to the bullring. The patios of this 1C villa served to distribute light and collect rainwater. Visible remains include the **Cosmological Mosaic**★.

Templo de Diana

Calle Romero Leal. Corinthian columns and fluted shafts of this temple are visible. Its stones were used In the 16C to build the palace of the Count of Corbos.

Two Roman **bridges** still span the Albarregas and Guadiana. Polychrome arches remain from two **aqueducts**.

Worth a Visit

Alcazaba

Open 9.30am-1.45pm and 4-6.30pm (5-7.30pm in summer). Closed 1 Jan and 24-25 and 31 Dec. 9 € (combined ticket). 924 31 20 24.

The Moors built this fortress in the 9C to defend the 792m/866yd **Puente Romano**★ (Roman Bridge) across the Guadiana. Inside the walls is a **cistern**.

COMBINED ENTRANCE TICKET

This ticket, on sale at all the city's major monuments, allows entry to the theatre, amphitheatre, Roman houses, Alcazaba and the Iglesia de Santa Eulalia.

CLASSICAL THEATRE FESTIVAL

During the months of July and August the Roman theatre reverts to its original function to host this prestigious festival which has been running for almost 50 years.
For information, log onto www.festivaldemerida.es.

Iglesia de Santa Eulalia★

Open 10am-1.45pm and 4-6.30pm (5-7.30pm in summer). 3.50 € (9 € with Alcazaba and Teatro). 924 31 20 24.

Excavations show that the site was occupied in turn by a palaeo-Christian necropolis, a 5C basilica and this 13C Romanesque church.

MONTBLANC★★

POPULATION: 5 612

MICHELIN MAP 574 H 33 – CATALUNYA (TARRAGONA)

Montblanc lies in an impressive setting★ amid vineyards and almond orchards. Within its ancient walls lie narrow, cobbled streets, stone buildings, and legends and deep secrets from a golden age in the 14C.

- **Information:** *Miquel Alfonso (Iglesia de Sant Francesc.), 43400 Tarragona, 977 86 17 33. www.montblancmedieval.org*
- **Orient Yourself:** Montblanc is in Catalunya at the crossroads of the N 240 (Tarragona-Lleida) and the C 240 from Reus (29km/18mi S).
- **Also See:** TARRAGONA (36km/22.5mi SE) and LLEIDA/LÉRIDA (61km/38mi NW).

Special Features

The Ramparts★★

The ramparts were commissioned by Peter IV of Aragón in the mid-14C. Two thirds of the original walls (1 500m/5 000ft) remain, along with 32 square towers and two of four gates: that of Sant Jordi (S) and Bover (NE).

Iglesia de Santa Maria★★

Open 11am-1pm and 4.30-6pm; Sun and public hols, 11am-1pm. 977 86 17 33 (tourist office).

This beautiful Gothic church overlooking the city has a single nave and radiating chapel. The unfinished façade is Baroque. The interior features a sumptuous 17C **organ**★★, a Gothic altarpiece in polychrome stone (14C) and an elegant silver monstrance.

WHERE TO STAY

Fonda dels Àngels – *Plaça Els Àngels 1 – 977 86 01 73 – Closed 1-21 Sep, Christmas and 1 Jan – – 8 rooms – 4.50 € – Restaurant 14/20 €.* This small, family-run inn at the heart of the former Jewish quarter has been converted from a Gothic-style house, of which an original ogival window has been preserved. Simple but pleasant rooms, plus a popular restaurant serving interesting local cuisine.

Museu d'Art Frederic Marès

Open 10am-2pm and 4-7pm (4.30-7.30pm in summer); Sun and public hols 10am-2pm. Closed Mon, 1 and 6 Jan, 8 Sep and 25 Dec. 2.90€. 977 86 03 49.

This museum in a late-19C former prison contains religious paintings and sculptures from the 14C to the 19C, in particular fine 14C wooden statues.

The plaza de Santa Bárbara, a little higher up, offers fine views.

Museu Comarcal de la Conca de Barberà★

Open 10am-2pm and 4-7pm (5-8pm Jun-Sep); Sun and public hols all year, 10am-2pm. Closed Mon, 1 Jan and 25-26 Dec. 2.40 €. 977 86 03 49.

A 17C house holds archaeological and ethnographical artefacts from the area as well as 18C ceramic flasks belonging to an apothecary.

Plaza Mayor

Among the arcades of shops and cafés around the main square, note the town hall *(ayuntamiento)* and the Gothic-style Casa dels Desclergue.

j. Malburet/MICHELIN

View of the town

Iglesia de Sant Miquel★

Guided tours by prior arrangement. ☎977 86 17 33 (tourism office).

Fronted by a Romanesque façade, this small 13C Gothic church has pure, sober lines. It hosted the Estates General of Catalunya several times in the 14C and15C. Next to the church stands the **Palau del Castlà**, formerly the residence of the king's representative. A 15C prison is on its ground floor.

Call Judío (Jewish Quarter)

Only the Calle dels Jueus (Street of Jews) and part of a Gothic house in plaza dels Àngels remain of the former Jewish district. Another interesting building is the 14C **Casa Alenyà**, a Gothic house of slender proportions.

OUTSIDE THE WALLS

Convento de la Serra★

Open 11am-1pm and 4-6pm. ☎977 86 17 33 (tourism office).

This ex-convent of the Order of St Clare stands on a small hill. It houses the venerated **Mare de Déu de la Serra**, an alabaster statue made in the 14C.

Hospital de Santa Magdalena★

The remarkable though small 15C **cloisters** illustrate the transition between Gothic and Renaissance. The vertical perspective on the ground floor, featuring fluted columns and pointed arches, is broken in the upper section.

Museu Molins de la Vila

1km/0.6mi toward Prenafeta.

Guided tours (1hr) by prior arrangement. 2.30 €. ☎977 86 03 49.

These are two medieval flour mills.

Tour

The Cistercians route

90km/56mi – allow one day

Along this route, visit the most important Cistercian monasteries in Catalunya, founded in the 12C after the reconquest of Catalunya by Ramón Berenguer IV.

▶ *Exit Montblanc on the N 240 to l'Espluga de Francolí. From here, follow the T 700 for 4km/2.5mi.*

Monasterio de Poblet★★★

Guided tours (45min), 10.30am-1.30pm and 4.30-6.45pm (5.30pm Nov-Feb). Closed 1 Jan and 25 Dec. 3 € (7 € with Vallbona de les Mon-

Montblanc in the Middle Ages

Until 1489, Montblanc was a thriving town with a prosperous Jewish community *(calle dels Jueus)*. Its golden age was the 14C, when its economic supremacy was reflected in the political arena with several Estates General being held in the town at the instigation of Catalan-Aragonese monarchs.

ges and Santes Creus Monasteries). ☎973 33 02 66.

The splendid **site★** of one of the largest and best preserved Cistercian monasteries is sheltered by the Prades mountains. Founded in the 12C, it enjoyed the protection of the crown of Aragón. A 2km/1mi perimeter protected the monastery and its vegetable gardens.

Capilla de Sant Jordi★★

The Late Gothic interior of this tiny 15C chapel features splendid broken barrel vaulting. An inner wall with polygonal towers enclosed annexes where visitors were received. The 15C **Porta Daurada** (Golden Door), named after the gilded bronze sheets that form its covering, was commissioned by Philip II.

Plaça Major★

On this irregular main square stand the 12C **Capilla de Santa Caterina**, shops, a hospital for pilgrims and a carpentry workshop. On the right are the ruins of the 16C Abbatial Palace and the **stone cross** erected by Abbey Guimerà, also 16C. A third wall (608m/1 995ft long, 11m/36ft high and 2m/6.5ft thick), built by Peter the Ceremonious, surrounds the monastery proper, fortified by 13 towers. On the right stands the **Baroque façade of the church**, built around 1670 and flanked, 50 years later, by heavily ornate windows. Pleasing in itself, it breaks with the overall austerity.

Porta Reial★

This is the gateway to the conventual buildings, appearing somewhat like the entrance to a fortress.

Palacio del Rei Martin★

Beyond the door, to the right, a narrow staircase rises to this 14C Gothic palace. Its splendid rooms are wonderfully light thanks to pointed bay windows.

Locutorio

Originally a dormitory for converts, this room became a wine press. The 14C vaulting rests directly on the walls.

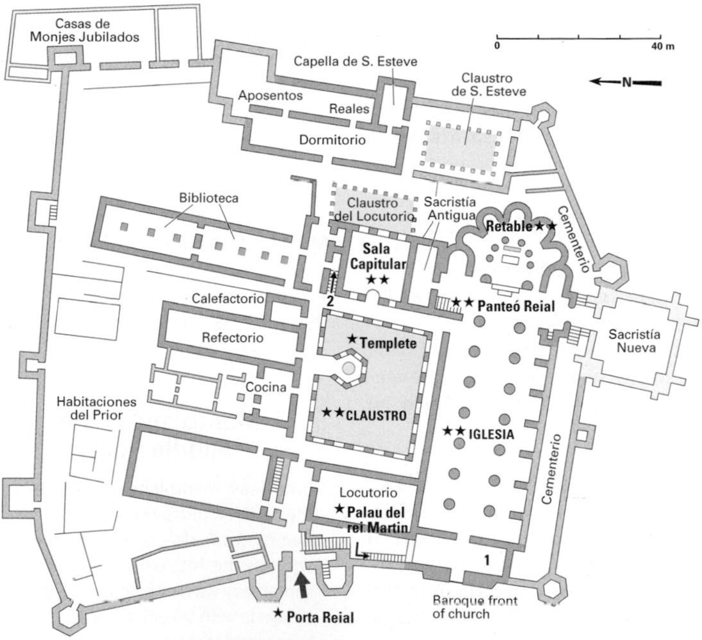

SANTA MARIA DE POBLET: THIRD PERIMETER WALL

Periods of contruction: 12C-13C, 14C, 16C, 17C-18C

Cellar
This magnificent Gothic cellar *(celler)* below the monks' sleeping quarters is used as a concert hall.

Claustro★★
The size of these cloisters (40 x 35m/131 x 115ft) and their sober lines indicate the monastery's importance. The south gallery (c 1200) and huge lavabo or **templete**★ with its marble fountain and 30 taps are in pure Romanesque style; the other galleries, built a century later, have floral motif tracery; beautiful scrollwork adorns the **capitals**★.
The **kitchen** *(cocina)* and the huge **monk's refectory** *(refectorio de los monjes)*, both built around 1200 and still in use, open onto the cloisters. The **library** *(biblioteca)* – the former scriptorium – is crowned by ogival vaulting on 13C columns. The 13C **chapter house**★★ *(sala capitular)*, through a Romanesque doorway, has four slender octagonal columns and palm-shaped vaulting.

Iglesia★★
The light, spacious church is typically Cistercian. It has pure lines, broken barrel vaulting, and unadorned capitals. The windows and wide arches dividing the nave join in a large eave. The church incorporated numerous altars for its growing community; the apse was ringed by an ambulatory and radiating chapels, a feature more commonly found in Benedictine churches.
The **royal pantheon**★★ *(panteó reial)*, the church's most original feature, has immense shallow arches spanning the transepts, surmounted by the royal tombs. These were constructed of alabaster in about 1350.
The **retable**★★ *(retablo)* at the **high altar** *(altar mayor)* is a monumental marble Renaissance altarpiece carved by Damián Forment in 1527. Figures in four superimposed registers can be seen glorifying Christ and the Virgin.
In the narthex, an opening to the outside world added in 1275, is the Renaissance **altar of the Holy Sepulchre (1)**.
A wide flight of stairs leads from the north transept to the monks' dormitory.

Dormitorio
Massive central arches support the ridge roof above the vast, 87m/285ft long gallery.

> *Leave Poblet on the T 232 towards Maldà. From here, take the road to Vallbona.*

Monasterio de Vallbona de les Monges★★
Guided tours (45min), 10.30am-1.30pm and 4.30-6.45pm (5.30pm Nov-Feb). Closed Mon, 1 Jan and 25 Dec. 3 € (7 € with Poblet and Santes Creus Monasteries). 973 33 02 66.
The Cistercian **Monasterio de Santa Maria** completes the Cistercian Trinity. The convent was founded in 1157 by the hermit Ramón de Vallbona and became a Cistercian community for women.

Iglesia★★
Built chiefly in the 13C and the 14C, this church is a fine example of transitional Gothic. The interior is simple and surprisingly light thanks to two octagonal lantern towers: one (13C) lies above the transept crossing while the other (14C) overlooks the centre of the nave. The church contains the beautiful tombs of Queen Violante of Hungary, wife of James I the Conqueror of Aragón, and her daughter, as well as a huge polychrome Virgin from the 15C.

Cloisters★
The east and west galleries are Romanesque (12C-13C). The 14C Gothic north wing features attractive capitals with plant motifs. In the south gallery (15C) note the 12C statue of Nuestra Señora del Claustro (Our Lady of the Cloisters).

> *Head toward Rocallaura then towards Montblanc along the C 240 to link up with the AP 2. Turn off onto the TP 2002 at exit 11.*

Monasterio de Santes Creus★★★
46km/29mi SE of Vallbona. Tour: 2hr. Open 15 Mar-16 Sep, 10am-1pm and 3-6.30pm (5.30pm 16 Jan-15 Mar; 5pm 16 Sep-15 Jan). Closed Mon exc public

© Ajuntament de Montblanc

The Great Cloisters

hols, 1 Jan and 25-26 Dec. 3.60 €, no charge Tue. 977 63 83 29.

The monastery was founded in the 12C by monks from Toulouse. Santes Creus hosts a festival of classical and sacred music as well as an international competition for Gregorian chant.

The monastery plan is similar to that of Poblet, with three perimeter walls. A Baroque gateway leads to the courtyard where the monastic buildings, enhanced with fine *sgraffiti*, now serve as shops and private residences. To the right is the abbatial palace, with its attractive patio, now the town hall; at the end stands the 12C-13C church, plain but for a large Gothic window and battlements added later.

The visit starts with an audio-visual presentation.

Gran Claustro★★★ (Great Cloisters)

Construction began in 1313 on the site of earlier cloisters. The ornamentation on capitals and bands illustrates Gothic motifs: plants and flowers, animals, biblical, mythological and satirical themes. The Puerta Real or Royal Gate on the south side opens onto cloisters with Gothic bays with lively carvings – note Eve shown emerging out of Adam's rib, and the fine tracery of the arches (1350-1430). In contrast, the transitional style of the **lavabo** appears almost clumsy. Carved noble tombs fill the niches.

The chapter house★★ *(sala capitular)* is an elegant hall with arches on four pillars.

Stairs next to the chapter house lead to the 12C **dormitory** *(dormitorio)*, a gallery divided by diaphragm arches supporting a timber roof, now used as a concert hall.

Iglesia★★

The church, begun in 1174, closely follows the Cistercian pattern of a flat east end and overall austerity; the square ribbed ogive vaulting, replacing the more usual broken barrel vaulting, does nothing to soften its severity. The lantern (14C), stained glass, and the superb apsidal **rose window** relieve the bareness. Ribbed vaults rest on pillars which extend back along the walls and end in unusual consoles. Gothic canopies at the transept openings shelter the **royal tombs**★★: on the north side (c 1295) that of **Pedro the Great** (III of Aragón, II of Barcelona) and on the south (14C), that of his son, **Jaime II**, the Just, and his queen, **Blanche d'Anjou**. The Plateresque decoration below the crowned recumbent figures in Cistercian habits, was added in the 16C.

Claustro Viejo (Old Cloisters)

Although they were built during the 17C, these "old cloisters" occupy the site of former cloisters dating back to the 12C. The design is simple with a small central fountain and eight cypresses in the close. Leading off are the kitchens, refectory and the **royal palace** (note a splendid 14C **patio**★).

MORELLA

POPULATION: 2 717

MICHELIN MAP 577 K 29 – COMUNIDAD VALENCIANA (CASTELLÓN)

Morella has an amazing site★: 14C ramparts, punctuated by towers, form a mile-long girdle round a 1 004m/3 294ft hill which the town ascends in tiers to castle ruins.

- **Information:** *Plaza de San Miguel, ☎964 17 30 32*
- **Orient Yourself:** Morella nestles in the Maestrazgo of Catalunya, linked to the coast by the N 232 to Peñíscola (78km/49ml) and Castellón de la Plana (98km/61mi).
- **Also See:** COSTA DEL AZAHAR and ALCAÑIZ.

Worth a Visit

A stroll around Morella's concentric streets reveals a number of mansions and religious buildings. One of the gateways, the Puerta de San Miguel, houses a small **museum** dedicated to the age of dinosaurs (*open noon-2pm and 4-6pm; Jul-Sep 11am-2pm and 4-7pm; closed Mon; 1.80€; ☎ 964 17 31 17, ext 3).*

Basílica de Santa María la Mayor★

Open noon-2pm and 4-6pm (11am-2pm and 4-7pm Jul-Sep). No visits during services. Closed 1 and 6 Jan and 25 and 31 Dec. 1.50 € (basilica-museum). ☎964 16 07 93.

The basilica is one of the most interesting Gothic churches in the Levante. It has two fine portals, the 14C Apostle Doorway, and the Virgins' Doorway with an openwork tympanum. The unusual raised Renaissance *coro* at the nave centre has a spiral staircase magnificently carved with biblical scenes and a delicate balustrade with a frieze illustrating the Last Judgement. The sanctuary was sumptuously decorated in Baroque style in the 17C and an elegant organ loft introduced in the 18C. There is a small **museum** with a beautiful Valencian *Descent from the Cross* and a 14C *Madonna* by Sassoferrato.

Castillo

On the way up there are good **views**★ of the town, the 13C-14C ruins of the Convento de San Francisco with its Gothic cloisters, the 14C-15C aqueduct and the reddish heights of the surrounding sierras.

Excursions

Santuario de la Balma

25km/15.5mi NW along the CV 14. This unusual Marian sanctuary is built into a rock wall overlooking the River Bergantes. The cave in which the Virgin appeared is enclosed by a 13C side wall

Shopping Tip

Truffles, honey, cheese and rugs are just some of the typical local products on sale in the shops lining the town's streets, in particular Virgen del Pilar, Segura Barreda, Marquesa Fuente del Sol and Blasco de Alagón.

El Maestrazgo

Morella lies at the heart of the mountain region which was the fief *(maestrazgo)* of the Knights of Montesa, a military order founded by James II of Aragón. The order, which had its seat at San Mateo *(40km/25mi SE of Morella)* as of 1317, fortified all villages in the region so as to be better defended against the Moors. Each community at the foot of its castle had a main porticoed square and narrow streets lined by balconied houses. Most occupy attractive sites in isolated, strongpoint positions and have retained considerable character.

and a 17C façade. Access is via a narrow gallery excavated into the rock.

Mirambel

30km/19mi W on the CS 840. ▶Bear left after 11km/7mi.

This small, well-preserved mountain village retains its medieval character. A number of houses bear coats of arms.

MURCIA★

POPULATION: 338 250

MICHELIN MAP 577 S 26 (TOWN PLAN) – MAP 123 COSTA BLANCA – MURCIA.

Murcia, a booming university town, lies along the Segura in a fertile market-gardening area (huerta).

- **Information:** *Plaza Cardenal Belluga, ☎968 35 87 49.*
- **Orient Yourself:** Murcia is located less than 50km/31mi from the coast.
- **Also See:** ALACANT/ALICANTE (81km/51mi NE).

History

Historical notes – The city, founded in the reign of Abd ar-Rahman II in 831 as Mursiya, was reconquered in 1266. Up to the 18C, Murcia prospered from agriculture and silk weaving.

Worth a Visit

Catedral★

Open 7am-1pm and 5-8.30pm (8pm in summer); museum, 10am-1pm and 5-8.30pm. Museum closed for renovation. Closed during the Virgen de la Fuensanta pilgrimage (dates vary). ☎ 968 21 63 44.

The original 14C cathedral is camouflaged beneath Renaissance and Baroque additions. The **façade**★, with an arrangement of columns and curves, is a brilliant example of Baroque. The impressive belfry, 95m/311ft in height, was completed by Ventura Rodríguez in the 18C.

The interior, beyond the entry cupola, is preponderantly Gothic, apart from the 16C **Capilla de los Junterones** *(fourth south chapel)* which has rich Renaissance decoration. The **Capilla de los Vélez**★ *(off the ambulatory)* is sumptuous Late Gothic with splendid star vaulting, and wall decoration with Renaissance and Mudéjar motifs.

The sacristy, approached through two successive Plateresque doors (beautiful panels on the first), is covered by an unusual radiating dome. The walls are richly panelled with Plateresque carving below and Baroque above.

Museo Salzillo★

Open 10am-2pm and 5-8pm; Sun and public hols, 11am-2pm. Closed Mon, and Sat afternoon-Sun and public hols in Jul-Aug. 3 €. ☎968 29 18 93.

The museum possesses Salzillo's masterpieces including the eight polychrome wood sculptures of **pasos** carried in the Good Friday procession during Holy Week, kept in side chapels off the nave of the Church of Jesus. The deep emotion on the faces is impressive. The museum also contains vivid terracotta pieces used to create scenes from the life of Jesus.

Excursions

Orihuela★

24km/15mi NE on the A 7. This peaceful town, with its many churches, lies along the Segura, which provides water for market gardens *(huertas)* and for the local **palm grove**. For centuries, Orihuela was a university town. The house of poet and dramatist Miguel Hernández is now a museum.

Catedral★

Guided tours (30min), 10.30am-1.30pm and 4pm (5pm in summer) to 7.30pm; Sat, 10.30am-1.30pm. 1.20 € (museum, tower and reliquary). ☎96 530 06 38.

Constructed from the 14C-16C, the cathedral has a Renaissance north doorway. The interior has three cruciform Gothic naves, ambulatory, and unusual vaulting with spiral ribs. The stalls of the choir are carved in Baroque style. There are notable Renaissance **grilles** around the choir and presbitery. The **Museo de la Catedral** houses a *Temptation of St Thomas Aquinas* by Velázquez, a *Christ* by Morales and a *Mary Magdalene* by Ribera.

The **Palacio del Obispo** on calle Ramón y Cajal behind the cathedral has a magnificent 18C patio.

Colegio de Santo Domingo

North of the City

Open 10am-2pm and 4-7pm; Jun-Sep 10am-2pm and 5-8pm; Sun and public hols 10am-2pm. Closed Mon, 1 and 6 Jan and 25 Dec. ☎96 530 27 47.

This monumental building (16C-18C), formerly the university, started out in Renaissance style and transformed into Baroque. The long college façade conceals two sober cloisters (17C and 18C). The 18C **church**★ is covered with murals and exuberant stucco mouldings.

Museo de la Muralla

Guided tour 10am-2pm and 4-7pm; Sep-Jun 10am-2pm and 5-8pm; Sun and public hols 10am-2pm. ☎96 530 46 98.

Descend below street level to the remains of the city wall, dwellings and baths from the Moorish era, and a Gothic palace and a Baroque building.

The **Iglesia de Santiago,** near the town hall, is Gothic in style, with Renaissance transept and apse. It was founded by the Catholic Monarchs whose yoke and arrow emblems, together with a statue of St James, are on the Gothic portal; the doorway on the right is Baroque. In the interior, note statues attributed to Salzillo in the side chapels (*open 10am-2pm and 4-7pm; 0.60 €; ☎96 530 27 47*).

Colegio de Santo Domingo

Santuario de la Fuensanta (La Fuensanta Shrine)

7km/4mi S. Follow the signs from Puente Viejo.

From the shrine of the Virgen de la Fuensanta, patron saint of Murcia, enjoy fine **views** of the town and the *huerta*.

Cartagena

62km/39mi SE along the N 301. In 223 BC this bay settlement was captured by the Carthaginians; it was subsequently colonised by the Romans, as *Cartago Nova*. Philip II fortified the surrounding hilltops, and Charles III built the Arsenal. The city is known for its dramatic Holy Week processions.

Near plaza del Ayuntamiento is the early **submarine** invented by native son Isaac Peral, in 1888.

From the top of the **Castillo de la Concepción**, there is a good general **view** of the harbour and the ruins of the former Romanesque cathedral of Santa María la Vieja.

Museo Nacional de Arqueología Marítima

Navidad jetty. Take the Algameca road. At Empresa Nacional Bazán, turn onto the road on the right.

Open 9.30am-3pm. Closed Mon, 1 and 6 Jan, 1 May, 24-25 and 31 Dec and local festivals. 2.40 €, no charge Sun. ☎968 12 11 66.

Address Book

WHERE TO EAT

⊜⊜ **Acuario** – *Plaza Puxmarina 3 – ☎ 968 21 99 55 – Closed Sun, Mon evening, 15-30 Aug and Holy Week –* ⊭. This established family restaurant offers regional cuisine with contemporary touches, based on local recipes and produce. Good for the price.

WHERE TO STAY

⊜ **Hispano 2** – *Radio Murcia 3 – ☎968 21 61 52 – www.hotelhispano.net – ⊭ – 35 rooms – ☕ 5€* – A local classic, known for its excellent location by the cathedral among the winding lanes and pedestrian streets. Rooms are of a basic comfort level, and public areas are limited but cosy.

SHOPPING

Pastelería Bonache – *Plaza de las Flores 8 – ☎968 21 20 83 – Closed Sat Jul-Aug – Open 9.30am-2.30pm and 5-10pm.* A tradition since 1828. Don't leave Murcia without trying a *pastel de carne* (meat pie), known throughout the province and beyond for its exquisite and unique flake pastry.

FIESTAS

Murcia's **Holy Week** processions are particularly solemn: on the morning of Good Friday, penitents in mauve robes bear eight Salzillo floats *(see below)* in procession through the town. The week after the **Spring Festival** is the occasion for general rejoicing with processions of floats and finally the Entierro de la Sardina, or Burial of the Sardine, which symbolises the end of Lent.

This museum displays underwater finds, notably Phoenician, Punic and Roman amphorae. Maps and models of vessels (galleys, biremes and triremes) illustrate seafaring in times past.

Mar Menor

At La Manga: 81km/51mi SE via the N 301 and MU 312 and 33km/21mi from Cartagena.

Mar Menor, or Little Sea, is a lagoon separated from the open Mediterranean by **La Manga**, a sand bar 500m/1 640ft wide which extends from the eastern end of the Cabo de Palos headland. Gilt-head, mullet and king prawns are fished from its shallow salt-water.

La Manga del Mar Menor is a large, elongated seaside resort with surrealistic tower blocks stretching for miles. In **Santiago de la Ribera**, where there is no natural beach, pontoons with changing cabins line the seafront. **San Javier**, nearby, is the seat of the Academia General del Aire (Air Academy).

Alcantarilla

9km/6mi W on the N 340. The **Museo de la Huerta**, on the Murcia road, is a museum dedicated to local **agriculture and irrigation**. Dispersed among the orange trees are white rustic dwellings *(barracas)* and a **noria**, a giant waterwheel devised for irrigation by the Moors(*◷ open 10am-6.30pm; Sat-Sun and public hols, 10am-1pm and 3-6pm; 4 Apr-Oct, 10am-8pm (1.30pm Aug); Sat-Sun and public hols, 10am-1.30pm and 4-6pm; ◷closed Mon, 1 and 6 Jan, Good Fri, 1 May, 1 Nov and 25 Dec; ☎968 89 25 97).*

Lorca

67km/42mi SW along the N 340-E 12.
Lorca lies in an irrigated valley at the foot of a hill crowned by as **castle**, the **Fortaleza del Sol**, where visitors may spend the day back in the Middle Ages (*Kids ◷ open 10.30am (10 am Jun-Sep) to 5pm; ◷closed Jan-Feb and 24 and 31 Dec; ⊜9 €; ☎902 40 00 47).*

The main sights are the **plaza de España,** surrounded by the Baroque façades of the **Ayuntamiento** (town hall), the **Juzgado** (Law Courts), embellished with a corner sculpture, and the **Colegiata de San Patricio**, a collegiate church built in the 16C and 18C, and the **Casa de los Guevara**. Its doorway although in poor condition, is a fine example of Baroque sculpture (1694).

MURCIA								
Alfonso X el Sabio ran Vía	DY	2	Gómez Cortina	CY	28	Platería	DY	
Cardenal Belluga Pl.	DY	5	Infante Don Juan Manuel Av.	DZ	33	Proclamación	DZ	75
Colón Alameda de	DZ		Isidoro de la Cierva	DY	40	San Francisco Plano de	CYZ	78
España Glorieta de	DZ	15	José Antonio Ponzoa	DY	44	Sociedad	DY	80
Floridablanca	DZ	18	Licenciado Cascales	DY	56	Teniente Flomesta Av.	DZ	83
Garay Pas. de	DZ	20	Marcos Redondo	CY	60	Trapería	DY	
			Martínez Tornel Pl.	DZ	65			

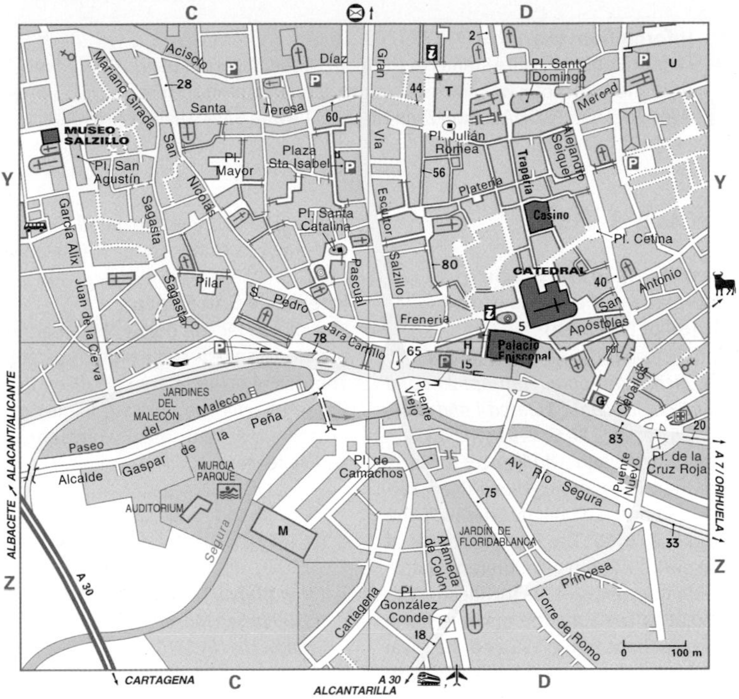

Caravaca de la Cruz

70km/44mi W along the C 415. Above Caravaca stand castle ramparts. In May, it celebrates a 1231 miracle. A Moorish king was moved to convert when a missing Cross suddenly reappeared. It was stolen in 1935.

Castillo-Iglesia de la Santa Cruz

Guided tours (45min), 11am-1pm and 4-7pm (5-8pm in Aug). Closed Mon (except Aug), 1 Jan and 1-5 May. 4 €. 968 70 56 20.

The restored ramparts of the 15C castle enclose a church which long sheltered the Holy Cross (Santa Cruz). The 1722 Herreran façade in local red marble has has an almost Latin American character. Estípites (inverted balusters) and delicately twisted pillars lend a vertical effect. From the battlements at the top of the building there is an interesting town view.

"Blancos" and "Azules"

Lorca is one of the cities of Spain where Holy Week is celebrated with full traditional panoply. Sumptuous embroideries, the pride of a local craftsmanship that is old and famous, adorn the *pasos*. Biblical and imperial Roman characters in full costume join penitents in long processions, the brilliant colours of the former contrasting with the sombre robes of the latter. Finally, there is friendly rivalry between the White and Blue Brotherhoods who compete for solemnity and magnificence.

OLITE★

POPULATION: 3 049.

MICHELIN MAP 573 E 25 – NAVARRA.

Olite, the favourite residence of the kings of Navarra in the 15C, possesses a restored fairy-tale castle the size of a city in itself. Olite's activities and setting attract numbers of summer visitors.

- **Information:** *Mayor 1, ☎948 74 17 03.*
- **Orient Yourself:** Olite stands at the heart of the Navarran plain, 4km/2.5mi from the A 15 motorway linking Zaragoza and Pamplona/Iruña.
- **Also See:** PAMPLONA(43km/27mi N), ESTELLA and SANGÜESA/ZANGOZA (44km/27.5mi NE).

Worth a Visit

Castillo de los Reyes de Navarra★★ (Fortress of the Kings of Navarra)

Entrance on plaza de Carlos III el Noble. Open 10am-6pm (7pm Apr-Jun and Sep; 8 pm Jul-Aug). Closed 1 and 6 Jan, and 25 Dec. 2.80€. ☎948 74 00 35.

The Palacio Viejo (Old Palace) is Olite's parador. The Palacio Nuevo (New Palace) was ordered built by Charles III, the Noble, in 1406. The French origins of the prince – Count of Evreux and native of Mantes – explain the fortifications, a transition between the massive stone constructions of the 13C and the royal Gothic residences of the late 15C with galleries and courtyards. During the Peninsular War, a fire almost completely destroyed the building. Behind the 15 or so towers marking the perimeter were hanging gardens, along with inner halls and chambers decorated with *azulejos*, painted stuccowork and coloured marquetry ceilings. The most impressive rooms are the Guardarropa (Wardrobe), now housing an exhibition, the Sala de la Reina (Queen's Room) and the Galería del Rey (King's Gallery).

Iglesia de Santa María la Real

Visit included in several tours. ☎948 74 12 73.

The church is the former chapel royal. An atrium of slender multifoil arches precedes the 14C **façade**★, a fine example of Navarra Gothic sculpture. The only figurative carving illustrates the lives of the Virgin and Christ. A painted 16C retable frames a Gothic statue of Our Lady.

Iglesia de San Pedro

The church façade below the tapering octagonal spire is somewhat disparate. The portal covings are set off by tori (large convex mouldings). Eagles on either side symbolise Gentleness and Violence.

Excursions

- *Head 19km/12mi NE along the NA 5300 to San Martín de Unx, then follow the NA 5310.*

Ujué★

Ujué, overlooking the Ribera region, remains, with its winding streets, much as it was in the Middle Ages.

Iglesia de Santa María

A Romanesque church was built at the end of the 11C. In the 14C, Charles II, the Bad, began a Gothic church, but the Romanesque chancel remains to this day. The central chapel contains the venerated **Santa María la Blanca**, a plated Romanesque statue honoured with a **romería** (pilgrimage) the Sunday after St Mark's Day (25 April).

Fortaleza (Fortress)

The church towers command a view which extends to Olite, the Montejurra and the Pyrenees. Of the medieval palace there remain lofty walls and a covered watch path circling the church.

B. Juge/MICHELIN

Olite Church Façade, Detail

Monasterio de La Oliva★

34km/21mi SE. Leave Olite on the N 121. ▶ After 14km/9mi, turn left onto the NA 124 to Carcastillo then follow the NA 5500. Open 9am-12pm and 3.30-4pm; Sun and public hols, 9-11.15am and 4-6pm. 1.80 €. ☎948 72 50 06.

La Oliva was one of the first Cistercian monasteries built outside. The buildings, stripped of treasure and trappings, retain a pure Cistercian beauty.

Iglesia★★

The façade of this late-12C church is mostly unadorned – a perfect setting for the interplay of lines of the portal and two rose windows. The interior is surprisingly deep with pillars and pointed arches lined with thick polygonal ribs in austere Cistercian style.

Claustro★

The bays in these late-15C cloisters appear exceptionally light. Gothic elements were grafted onto an older construction: Ogival vaults rise from Romanesque capitals at the entry to the 13C **Sala Capitular** (chapter house).

OÑATI/OÑATE

POPULATION: 10 264

MICHELIN MAP 573 C 22 – PAÍS VASCO (GUIPÚZCOA).

Oñati, with its seigniorial residences, monastery and old university, nestles amid the wild beauty of the Udana Valley. It figured prominently in the First Carlist War.

- **Information:** *Foruen Enparantza 4, ☎943 78 34 53.*
- **Orient Yourself:** Oñati stands at the foot of Monte Alona (1 321m/4 333ft), 45km/28mi NE of Vitoria-Gasteiz and 74km/46mi SW of Donostia-San Sebastián.
- **Also See:** VITORIA-GASTEIZ, DONOSTIA-SAN SEBASTIÁN and COSTA VASCA

Worth a Visit

Antigua Universidad (Old University)

Open 9am-5pm (2pm Fri). Closed Sat-Sun and public hols. ☎943 78 34 53.

The university, now administrative headquarters of Guipúzcoa province, was founded in 1542 and functioned until the early 20C. The gateway, by

Pierre Picart, is surmounted by pinnacles and crowded with statues.

Ayuntamiento (Town Hall)

This fine 18C Baroque building was designed by Martín de Carrera. At Corpus Christi, traditional dances and processions are held in the square.

Iglesia de San Miguel

Visits by prior arrangement. 1€. 943 78 34 53.

The Gothic church facing the university was modified in the Baroque period. A Renaissance chapel off the north aisle, closed by beautiful iron grilles, contains an interesting gilded wood altarpiece. The golden stone cloister exterior with gallery tracery, ogee arches, and statue niches is Isabelline Plateresque.

Excursions

Santuario de Arantzazu★

9km/5.5mi S along the GI 3591. Open 8.30am-8pm. 943 78 09 51.

The **scenic cliff road**★ follows the the River Arantzazu which flows through a narrow gorge. The **shrine** at 800m/2 625ft in a mountain **setting**★ faces the highest peak in the province, Mount Aitzgorri (1 549m/5 082ft). Dominating the church is an immense bell tower 40m/131ft high, with diamond-faceted stone symbolising the hawthorn bush (*arantzazu* in Basque) in which the Virgin appeared to a local shepherd in 1469.

PARQUE NACIONAL DE ORDESA Y MONTE PERDIDO★★★

MICHELIN MAP 574 E 29-30 –
100KM/62MI FROM HUESCA – ARAGÓN (HUESCA).

The Ordesa canyon cuts through vast, layered limestone folds. Escarpments rise nearly 1 000m/3 280ft in grey and ochre strata, streaked in spring with cascades of snowmelt. Growing up the lower slopes are pines, larches, firs – some 25m/82ft tall – and a carpet of box, hawthorn and service trees. The park's valleys lie under such impressive peaks as Monte Perdido (3 355m/11 004ft).

- **Information:** *Torla: 974 48 64 72, Aínsa: 974 50 07 67.*
- **Orient Yourself:** This national park in the central Pyrenees (with its twin on the French side) can be approached from Torla to the W or Aínsa from the SE.
- **Also See:** PIRINEOS ARAGONESES and JACA (62km/39mi S).

Walking Tours

VALLE DE ORDESA★★★

A viewpoint on the entry road offers a general panorama. A second point, near the road's end, overlooks 60m/197ft-high **cascada de Tamborrotera** ① (waterfall).

The rest of the park may only be visited on foot. The best route for inexperienced walkers or families with young children is the shaded path along the bottom of the canyon. *Allow a day from the car park to the end of the canyon and back.*

The three walks below are feasible for experienced, well-equipped hikers.

Circuito del Circo de Soaso (Soaso Cirque Route)

Start from the Cadiera hut beyond the car park; 7hr.

The walk to the valley floor is easy. The second part, via the Cola de Caballo (Horse's tail) is only recommended to those who are well equipped and in good physical condition (steep climbs).

This walk provides the best and most complete tour of the Ordesa Valley. From the Circo de Soaso path several waterfalls can be seen including the

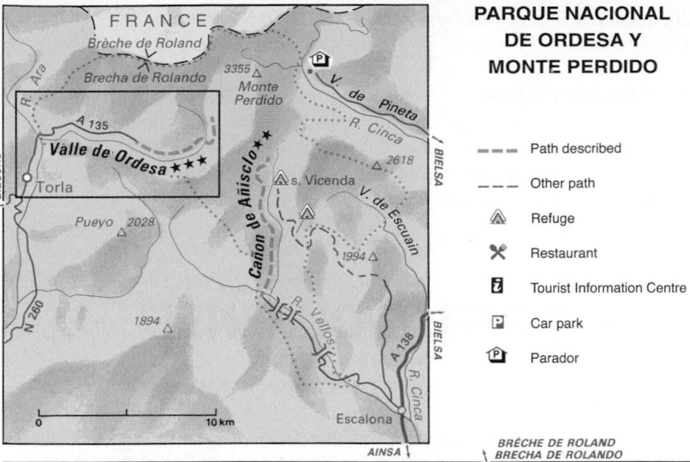

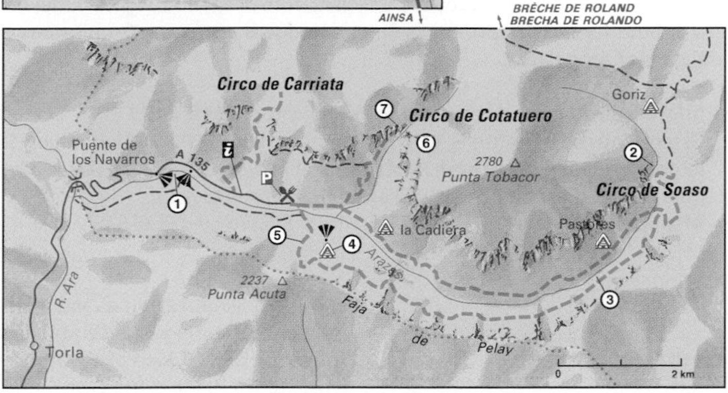

Gradas de Soaso ②, or Soaso Steps, followed by the impressive, 70m/230ft high **Cola de Caballo** ③. The path continues along the **Faja de Pelay** overlooking the canyon to a depth of 2 000m/6 550ft at the foot of the Sierra de Cutas. Continue on the **Senda de los Cazadores** (Huntsman's Path) ⑤ for a wonderful view of the canyon. The best panorama is from the **Mirador de Calcilarruego**. The path back to the hut drops almost 1 000m/3 300ft.

Circo de Cotatuero (Cotatuero Cirque)

Start from the restaurant; 4hr.

On the park's northern border are the **Cotatuero** ⑥ and the **Copos de Lana** (Tufts of Wool) *cascadas* (waterfalls) ⑦ with a drop of 250m/820ft.

Circo de Carriata

From the Centro de Información; 4hr.

The National Park

The Valle de Ordesa was declared a national park in 1918 and was expanded in 1982 to cover an area of 15 608ha/38 569 acres, including the Monte Perdido massif and the Ordesa, Añisclo, Escuain and Pineta valleys. The purpose of the park is to safeguard the region's outstanding natural beauty the massif's limestone relief of canyons, cliffs and chasms – as well as the variety and richness of its flora and fauna (Pyrenean ibex, golden eagle and izard, a goatlike antelope of the Pyrenees).

The walk is worth doing although the *clavijas* (mountaineering peg track) is not for those who suffer from vertigo. A long hike is possible to Monte Perdido via the Goriz refuge; or to the Cirque de Gavarnie in France via the Brecha de

Rolando (Roland Gap) *(ask at the Centro de Información).*

CAÑÓN DE AÑISCLO★★

Access from Escalona village on the Bielsa-Ainsa road – a 13km/8mi drive.

In the cool and lovely Añisclo Canyon, narrower than Ordesa, pine trees cling to the limestone walls.

Walk to Ripareta

Start from the San Urbez bridge. 5hr there and back.

A wide, well-defined path follows the enclosed Río Vellos down to its confluence with the Pardina.

ORENSE/OURENSE

POPULATION: 108 382

MICHELIN MAP 571 E 6, F 6 (TOWN PLAN) – GALICIA (ORENSE)

Since Antiquity, Orense (Ourense in Galician, from a legendary gold mine) has been famous for its hot springs.Its Roman bridge is a crossing for pilgrims to Santiago de Compostela.

- **Information:** *Caseta do Legoeiro-Ponte Romana, ☎988 37 20 20*
- **Orient Yourself:** Orense is 101km/63mi from Vigo (to the E) along the A 52 motorway, 100km/62mi from Pontevedra (SE) via the N 541, and 111km/69mi from Santiago de Compostela (SE) on the N 525 and the A 53.
- **Also See:** SANTIAGO DE COMPOSTELA, PONTEVEDRA and RÍAS BAJAS.

Worth a Visit

Catedral★

Open 11am-1.30pm and 4-7.30pm; Sun and public hols, 5-7pm. 1.20 € (Capilla del Santísimo Cristo); 1 € museum. ☎988 26 64 38.

The 12C-13C cathedral has been repeatedly modified. The **Portada Sur** (South Door), in the Compostelan style, lacks a tympanum, but is profusely decorated with carvings. The **Portada Norte** (North Door) has two statue columns and, beneath a great ornamental arch, a 15C Deposition framed by a Flight into Egypt and statues of the Holy Women.

The interior is noteworthy for its pure lines. At the end of the 15C, a Gothic-Renaissance transitional-style **lantern**★ was built above the transept. The ornate Gothic high altar retable is by Cornelius de Holanda. The 16C and 17C **Capilla del Santísimo Cristo** (Chapel of the Holy Sacrament), off the north transept, is decorated with exuberant sculpture in the Galician Baroque style. The triple-arched **Pórtico del Paraíso**★★ (Paradise Door) at the west end, has beautiful carvings and bright medieval colouring. The central arch shows the 24 Old Men of the Apocalypse; to the right is the Last Judgement. The pierced tympanum above, like the narthex vaulting, is 16C.

A door in the south aisle opens onto the 13C chapter house, now a **museum (Museo Catedralicio)** which includes church plate, statues, chasubles and a 12C travelling altar.

Museo Arqueológico y de Bellas Artes (Archaeological and Fine Arts Museum)

Closed for renovation. ☎988 22 38 84.

Collections in the former bishop's palace on plaza Mayor include prehistoric specimens, cultural objects (mainly statues of warriors) and an early-18C wood carving of the **Camino del Calvario**★ (Stations of the Cross).

Claustro de San Francisco★

Closed for renovation. ☎988 38 81 10.

The elegant 14C cloisters consist of horseshoe-shaped Gothic arches resting on slender, paired columns. Diamond and leaf decoration adds simple

Address Book

WHERE TO EAT

⊜⊜ **Hotel-Restaurante Zarampallo** – *Hermanos Villar 19 – ☎988 23 00 08 – www.zarampallo.com – Restaurant closed Sun evening – ▤ – 29€.* Recommended for its location in the old part of the city and first and foremost for its high-quality menu. If you're planning on staying here, the rooms are basic but comfortable.

WHERE TO STAY

⊜ **Hotel Altiana** – *Ervedelo 14 – ☎ 988 37 09 52 – 32 rooms – ☕ 3.50€.* Located near the cathedral and calle Progreso, the Altiana is a simple but friendly place to stay for those on a budget. Although far from luxurious, the bedrooms all have TVs and en-suite bathrooms and are very reasonably priced.

sophistication. Some of the **capitals** illustrate the hunt or historic figures.

Excursions

Monasterio de Santa María la Real de Oseira★

34km/21mi NW. Leave Orense on the N 525. After 23km/14mi turn right towards Cotelas. Guided tours (45min), 10am-noon and 3-5.30pm (6.30pm in spring and summer); Sun and public hols, only at noon and 3.30-6.30pm. 2 €. ☎988 28 20 04.

The grandiose 12C Cistercian monastery, called the Escorial of Galicia, was founded by Alfonso VII. It stands isolated in the Arenteiro Valley, a region that once abounded in bears (osos) as the name suggests.

The **façade** (1708) is in three sections. In a niche below the statue of Hope which crowns the doorway is the figure of a Nursing Madonna with St Bernard at her feet. Of note inside are an **escalera de honor** (grand staircase) and the **Claustro de los Medallones** (Medallion Cloisters) decorated with 40 busts of historic personages.

The **church** (12C-13C), hidden behind the Baroque façade of 1637, has retained the customary Cistercian simplicity modified only by frescoes in the transept, painted in 1694.

The **chapter house**★ dates from the late 15C and early 16C and is outstanding for its beautiful vaulting of crossed ribs descending like the fronds of a palm tree onto four spiral columns.

Verín

69km/43mi SE along the A 52. Verín is a lively, picturesque town with narrow paved streets, houses with glassed-in balconies, arcades and carved coats of arms. Its thermal springs, already famous during the Middle Ages, are reputed for their treatment of rheumatic and kidney disorders.

Castillo de Monterrei

6km/4mi W. There is a parador next to the castle, a frontier redoubt throughout the Portuguese-Spanish wars. It was more than a castle, with a monastery, hospital and a town which was abandoned in the 19C. The approach is up an avenue of lime trees which commands a full **panorama**★ of the valley below. To enter the castle pass through three walls, the outermost dating from the 17C. At the centre stand the square 15C Torre del Homenaje (Keep) and the 14C Torre de las Damas (Lady's Tower); the courtyard is lined by a three-storey arcade and is less austere. The 13C church has a **portal**★ delicately carved with a notched design and a tympanum showing Christ in Majesty between the symbols of the Evangelists.

Celanova

26km/16mi S on the N 540. The large, imposing **monastery** on plaza Mayor was founded in 936 by San Rosendo, Bishop of San Martín de Mondoñedo.

The **church** is a monumental late-17C edifice built in Baroque style. The coffered vaulting is decorated with geometrical designs, the cupola with volutes. An immense altarpiece (1697)

Touring Tip

Another way of discovering the wild beauty of this area is to take a **boat trip** along the River Sil. To get to the embarkation point, leave Orense on the C 536, turning left after 6km/4mi towards Luintra and Loureiro and following signs to San Estevo, from where the boat departs *(duration: 1hr 30min)*. For times and prices, call ☎ 988 21 51 00.

occupies the back of the apse. Note the choir stalls, Baroque in the lower part and Gothic in the upper, as well as the fine organ (*guided tours (50min) at 11am, noon, 1pm, 3pm and 4pm (and 6pm Apr-Oct); 1.20€; ☎988 43 22 01).*

The **cloisters★★**, among the most beautiful in the region, took from 1550 until the 18C to complete. The majestic staircases here are particularly worthy of note.

The **Capilla de San Miguel**, a chapel behind the church, is one of the monastery's earliest buildings (937) and one of the rare Mozarabic monuments still in good condition.

Santa Comba de Bande

52km/32.5mi S along the N 540 (26km/16mi S of Celanova). 10km/6mi beyond Bande, head along a road to the right for 400m/440yd.

The small 7C Visigothic **iglesia★** overlooks the lake. The plan is that of a Greek cross, lit by a lantern turret. The apse is square and is preceded by a horseshoe-shaped triumphal arch resting on four pillars with Corinthian capitals. Pure lines and perfect masonry enrich this unique building.

TOUR ALONG THE RÍO SIL★

65km/40mi E. ▶ *Head along the C 536; after 6km/4mi, turn left towards Luintra; continue for a further 18km/11mi. The parador (ex-monastery) is signposted.*

Parador de Santo Estevo

The ex-Benedictine monastery appears suddenly in a majestic **setting★**, spread over a great spur, against a background of granite mountains deeply cut by the Sil. Converted to a parador, it retains the church's Romanesque east end and three cloisters, built to grandiose proportions largely in the 16C.

Gargantas del Sil★ (Gorges of the Sil River)

▶ *Return downhill on the road on the left towards the Sil (not the signposted turning to the embalse de San Estevo).*

Two dams, one vaulted, the other a buttressed type, control the waters of the Sil which flow through deep gorges. The sides of the valley are dotted with vineyards and small villages.

▶ *Continue along the left bank of the river until you reach the N 120. Turn left towards Orense.*

OSUNA★★

POPULATION: 17 306

MICHELIN MAP 578 U 14 – ANDALUCÍA (SEVILLA).

This elegant town in the Sevillan countryside retains a beautiful monumental centre★ from its past as a ducal seat of the house of Osuna, one of the most powerful on the Iberian Peninsula.

- **Information:** *Plaza Mayor, ☎95 481 57 32.*
- **Orient Yourself:** Osuna rises to the south of the Guadalquivir basin, near the A 92 highway linking Granada (160km/100mi E) with Sevilla.
- **Don't Miss:** The Ducal Pantheon and heritage buildings untouched by time.
- **Also See:** ANTEQUERA (67km/42mi SE), CÓRDOBA (85km/53mi NE) and SEVILLA (92km/57mi W).

Worth a Visit

Zona Monumental★

▸ *Follow signs to Centro Ciudad (Town Centre) and Zona Monumental.*

Colegiata★

Guided tours (45min), Oct-Apr, 10am-1.30pm and 3.30-6.30pm; May-Sep, 10am-1.30pm and 4-7pm. Closed Mon, 1 and 6 (afternoon) Jan, Maundy Thu, Good Fri, and 24 (afternoon), 25 and 31 (afternoon) Dec. 2 €. 95 481 04 44.
This 16C Renaissance-style collegiate church houses five **paintings**★★ by **José (Jusepe) de Ribera "El Españoleto"** (1591-1652), including The Expiration of Christ, in the side chapel off the Nave del Evangelio. The remainder are exhibited in the sacristy.

Panteón Ducal★★ (Ducal Pantheon)

The pantheon was built in Plateresque style in 1545 for the Dukes of Osuna. It is approached by a delightful patio. The chapel (1545) stands below the Colegiata's main altar and is crowned by a blue-and-gold polychrome coffered ceiling, now blackened by candle smoke. Another crypt, built in 1901, holds the tombs of the most important dukes.
Nearby stand the 16C **former university** (Antigua Universidad) and the 17C **Monasterio de la Encarnación**★, in which the highlight is the magnificent **dado**★ of 17C Sevillian *azulejos* in the patio. The nuns here produce and sell several types of delicious biscuits and pastries (*open 10am-1.30pm and 3.30-6.30pm; in summer, 10am-1.30pm and 4-7pm; closed Sun-Mon in summer; 2 €; 95 481 11 21).*
On the descent into the town centre, note the 12C-13C Torre del Agua, a former defensive tower now a small **archaeological museum** (*open 11.30am-1.30pm and 4.30-6.30pm (5-7pm May and Sep); Jun-Aug 10am -2pm. 2 €. 95 481 12 07.*

TOWN CENTRE

Mainly around plaza del Duque and plaza España. Osuna's streets are lined by numerous Baroque **mansion houses and palaces**★★, whose massive wooden doors, darkly shining and copper-nailed, reveal fine wrought-iron grilles and cool green patios. Of particular note are the **calle San Pedro**★ (Cilla del Cabildo, Palacio de los Marqueses de la Gomera), the Antigua Audencia (former Law Courts), the Palacio de los Cepeda, the former Palacio de Puente Hermoso, several fine churches (Santo Domingo, la Compañía) and the **belfry of the Iglesia de la Merced**★, built by the same architect as the **Cilla del Cabildo**.

Excursion

Écija★

34km/21mi N along the A 351. The town lies in the Guadalquivir depression and is renowned for its lofty Baroque belfries decorated with ceramic tiles, such as the 18C **Torre de San Juan**★.

Park in plaza de España.
The **Ayuntamiento** (town hall) has two **Roman mosaic floors**★ and a *camera oscura* which offers lovely and surprising perspectives of the city (*open 10am-1.30pm; 2.50€; 95 590 29 33).*
Écija has several delightful small squares, and houses adorned with decorative columns, coats of arms and charming patios. Along the streets

B. Kaufman/MICHELIN

Cilla del Cabildo

adjoining avenida Miguel de Cervantes are several old palaces with fine **façades★**: the 18C Baroque **Palacio de Benamejí**; the concave and fresco-adorned **Palacio de Peñaflor**, its portal built on columns; and the Plateresque-style **Palacio de Valdehermoso**. Several churches are noteworthy: **Los Descalzos**, renowned for the exuberant decoration of its **interior★**; **Santa María**, crowned by an impressive tower; the Convento de los Marroquíes, with its lofty **bell tower★**, where the delicious *marroquíes* biscuits are still produced and sold by the nuns; and the **Iglesia de Santiago★**, which retains the Mudéjar windows of an earlier building and a Gothic **retable★** at the high altar illustrating the Passion and the Resurrection.

The outbuildings of the iglesia de Santa Cruz, following a restoration, house the **Museo de Arte Sacro** (sacred art museum) with 16C-19C works. (*guided tour (30 min) 10.30am-1.30pm and 6-8pm (9pm Sat-Sun and public hols); 2€; 954 83 06 13).*

OVIEDO★★

POPULATION: 204 276

MICHELIN MAPS 572 B12 (TOWN PLAN) – ASTURIAS.

The capital of Asturias has a long and eventful history. Its old quarter is sprinkled with enchanting plazas and lanes set with frozen pedestrians, who turn out to be sculptures. Strolling about this World Heritage Site is a delight.

- **Information:** *Cimadevilla 4, b902 300 202; Calle Marqués de Santa Cruz 1 (El Escorialín), b98 522 75 86.*
- **Orient Yourself:** The A 66 links Oviedo to the north coast at Gijón (29km/18mi) and to León (121km/75mi S).
- **Parking:** Avoid looking for a space in the old quarter.
- **Organizing Your Time:** Stroll the old town first.
- **Also See:** COSTA VERDE

Background

The capital of the Kingdom of Asturias (9C-10C) – Alfonso II, the Chaste (791-842), moved his court to Oviedo and rebuilt the former Muslim town. The heir to the throne of Spain is still called the Prince of Asturias.

Two Battles of Oviedo – In 1934, Oviedo was heavily damaged in fighting between insurgent miners and right-wing government forces. In 1937, Oviedo was the scene of a battle during the Spanish Civil War.

Special Features

OLD TOWN *1hr 30min*

Follow the route on the town plan..

Enter by Calle San Francisco, and proceed along the right side of the street.

Antigua Universidad (Former University)

The austere 17C stone-fronted building was restored after the civil war. Opposite the façade is *Mujer Sentada (Seated Woman)* by Manolo Hugué, one of many sculptures set in the old town.

Plaza de Porlier

View the cathedral in the next plaza. The palace of the **Count of Toreno** (*right*) dates from 1673; the **Camposagrado** (*opposite*), an 18C edifice, houses the Law Courts (note spread eaves).

Plaza de de Alfonso II el Casto (Plaza de la Catedral)

Note the coat of arms on the façade of the 17C **Palacio de Valdecarzana**. The

Address Book

For coin ranges, see the Legend on the cover flap.

WHERE TO EAT

⊜ **Las Campanas de San Bernabé** – *San Bernabé 7 – ☎98 522 49 31 – www.fade.es/lascampanas – Closed Sun and in Aug* – ▤. This restaurant is located in the middle of the main shopping area, five minutes from the cathedral. A pleasant decor of brick walls and oak beams, and good, reasonably priced regional cuisine.

⊜⊜ **El Raitán y El Chigre** – *Plaza Trascorrales 6 – ☎98 521 42 18 – www.elraitan.com – Closed Sun evening* – ▤. This rustic-style restaurant at the heart of the historic quarter serves delicious Asturian dishes. The set menus are recommended.

WHERE TO STAY

⊜ **Carreño** – *Monte Gamonal 4 – ☎98 511 86 22 – www.hotelcarreno.com* – P ♿ *– 42 rooms – ☕ 3,26€.* The best part of this hotel is its location between the rail and bus stations. Its comfortable rooms are a good value.

⊜⊜ **Hotel Casa Camila** – Fitoria de Arriba 28 – ☎ *– 98 511 48 22 www.casacamila.com – 7 rooms – ☕ – Restaurant 20 €.* This charming, well-maintained hotel on Monte Naranco is the perfect hideaway if you're looking for peace and quiet away from the city. Impressive views of Oviedo and rooms that are more than comfortable.

LOCAL SPECIALITIES

Regional gastronomic treats include *carbayones*, delicious pastries made with almonds and egg yolks, and *bollos preñaos*, filled with chorizo. The best *carbayones* can be bought at the *Camilo de Blas* pastry shop (calle Jovellanos 7) and the *Los de Peñalba* sweet shop (Calle Milicias Nacionales 4).

majestic cathedral rises at the far end of the square. The **Palacio de la Rúa** was built at the end of the 15C.

Catedral★

The main work was carried out between 1412 and 1565 in Flamboyant Gothic style. The south tower tapers into a delicate openwork spire. Three 17C Gothic portals pierce the asymmetrical façade; figures of the Transfiguration are above the central portal. On the walnut-panelled doors (also 17C) are figures of Christ and St Eulalia.

Interior – The cathedral has three aisles, the triforium surmounted by tall stained-glass windows, and an ambulatory. A splendid 16C polychrome **high altarpiece**★★ shows scenes from the Life of Christ. On either end of the transepts are 18C Baroque panels, and in the south transept, next to the main chapel, the 17C polychromed stone image of The Saviour.

The **Capilla de Alfonso II el Casto** (Alfonso II The Chaste), on the site of the original church, is the pantheon of Asturian kings. The decoration inside the gate (*end of north transept*) is Late Gothic. In the embrasures are figures of the Pilgrim St James, St Peter, St Paul and St Andrew, and on a mullion, a Virgin of Milk. Renaissance and Baroque elements intermingle.

Cámara Santa

Access by the south transept. ⌚ *Open 10am-1pm and 4-6pm (7pm Mar-15 May; 4pm 14 Sep-Oct; 8pm 16 May-13 Sep).* ⌚ *No visits Sun and public hols.* ⊜ *1.25 € (3 € complete visit). ☎98 520 31 17.*

The Cámara Santa was built by Alfonso II early in the 9C and reconstructed in the Romanesque period.

These 12 **statue columns**★★ representing the Apostles are among the most masterly sculptures of 12C Spain. The artist was obviously influenced by the Pórtico de la Gloria (Doorway of Glory) in Santiago Cathedral. Capitals illustrate the marriage of Joseph and Mary, the Holy Women at the Tomb and lion and wild boar hunts.

The **tesoro**★★ (treasury) in the apse includes outstanding ancient gold and silver plate: the **Cruz de los Ángeles** (Cross of the Angels), a gift from Alfonso II in 808, studded with precious gems,

OVIEDO

			Constitucíon Pl. de la	B	22	Riego Pl.	AB	53
			Daoiz y Velarde Pl. de	AB	23	San Antonio	B	56
Alcalde G. Conde	B	2	Jesús	AB	28	San Vicente	B	59
Alfonso II El Casto Pl. de	B	5	Juan Escalante	B	29	Santa Clara	A	60
Calvo Sotelo	A	12	Martínez Marina	A	33	Schultz	B	62
Canóniga	B	17	Palacio Valdés	A	40	Trascorrales Pl. de	B	64
Carbayón Pl. de	A	18	Pelayo	A		Uría	A	
Cimadevilla	B	20	Pérez de la Sala	A	43	Victor Chávarri	B	66
Conde de Toreno	A	21	Postigo Alto	B	48			

Ayuntamiento	B	H	Museo de Bellas Artes de Asturias	B	M^1	Palacio de Toreno	B	B
Museo Arqueológico	B	M^2	Palacio de Camposagrado	B	J	Palacio de Valdecarzana	B	A

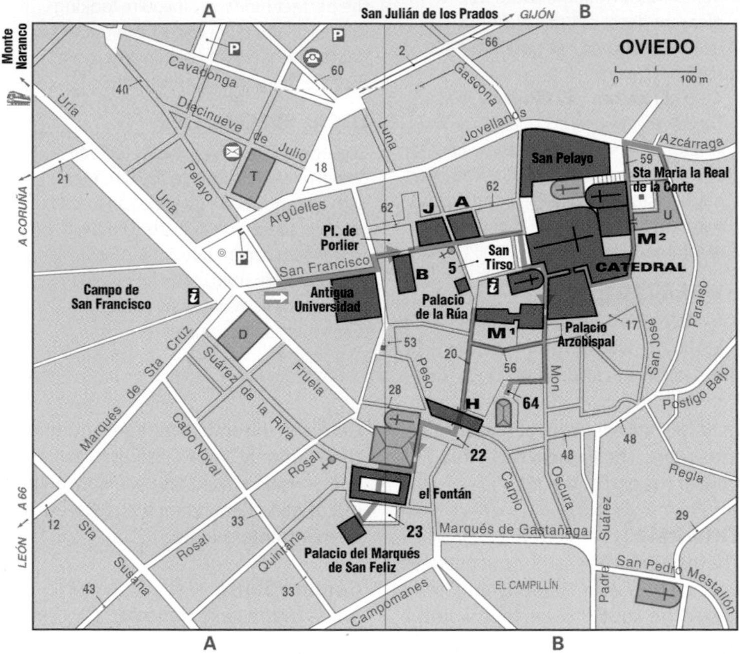

Roman cabochons and cameos; and the **Cruz de Victoria** (908), faced with chased gold, precious stones, and enamel, supposedly carried by Pelayo at Covadonga.

Claustro

The Gothic cloisters (14-15C) have intersecting pointed arches and delicate tracery in the bays. The **Capilla de Santa Leocadia** *(to the left on entering)* contains an altar, tombs from the time of Alfonso II and an unusually small stone altar. The **sala capitular** (chapter house) contains fine 15C stalls.

Return to Plaza de Alfonso II el Casto.

To the right of the cathedral (*leaving*), low reliefs and busts compose an homage to the kings of Asturias. To the left, at Calle Santa Ana, note the unexpected Moorish *alfiz* window enclosure in the remaining east wall of the 9C **Iglesia de San Tirso**.

Turn left onto Calle Tránsito de la Virgen alongside the cathedral.

Beyond the arch that connects the cathedral to the Palacio Arzobispal (archbishop's palace, *left*) is the Romanesque former cathedral. Just ahead in Plaza de la Corrada del Obispo are the rather loud façade of the **Palacio Arzobispal** (late 16C) and the imposing 18C **Puerta de la Limosna** (alms gate).

Continue along Calle San Vicente.

Museo Arqueológico (Archaeological Museum)

Closed for renovation. *985 26 91 04 or 985 26 13 58*

The museum is in the former Convento de San Vicente (16C-18C). Two galleries off the 15C Plateresque cloisters display pre-Romanesque art. Fragments and reproductions evidence the sophistication of Asturian art. Among exhibits are the Naranco altar; low reliefs showing Byzantine influence, and column bases from San Miguel de Lillo.

After the museum, go under the arch and cross the Plaza de Feijoo, past the **Iglesia de Santa María la Real de la Corte** and the palace-like façade of the 18C **Monasterio de San Pelayo**.

Turn right onto Jovellanos and look back at the city wall. Return to Calle Santa Ana.

Museo de Bellas Artes de Asturias (Fine Arts Museum)

Open 10.30am-2pm and 4.30-8.30pm; Sat, 11.30am-2pm and 5-8pm; Sun and public hols, 11.30am-2.30pm; Jul-Aug, 11am-2.30pm and 5-9pm; Sun and public hols, 11am-2.30pm. Closed Mon, 1 and 6 Jan, 1 May, 21 Sep, 12 Oct and24-25 and 31 Dec. *98 521 30 61.*

The museum is in three buildings. The core collection of Spanish painting is enriched by Italian and Flemish works. There is also a sculpture collection.

Among the works in the 18C **Palacio de Velarde** are a complete **Apostolado** by **El Greco** (ground floor); the Gothic panels of the *Santa Marina Retable* (on the stairway); the *Triptych of Don Alvaro de Carreño* by the master of the *Legend of Mary Magdalene;* a *Burial of Christ* and a magnificent *Apostle* by **Ribera***;* a *Crucifixion* by **Zurbarán**; a *San Pedro* by Murillo; the portrait of *Charles II at Ten Years* by Carreño de Miranda, and two portraits by **Goya** *(Jovellanos* and *Charles IV)* on the first floor. The second floor is devoted to Asturian and Spanish art of the 19C and early 20C.

A passageway leads to the second floor of the 17C **Casa Oviedo-Portal**. Worth seeing are a gallery dedicated to **J. Sorolla;** a *Musketeer with Sword and Cupid* by **Picasso**; and paintings by Gutiérrez-Solana, Regoyos and Nonell.

As you leave, take a look at the enchanting Plaza de Trascorrales, with its brightly coloured houses and its sculpture of *The Milkmaid.*

Take Calle Cimadevilla to reach Plaza de la Constitución.

Along **Plaza de la Constitución** are the **Ayuntamiento** (City Hall), with 17 and 18C porticoes, and the Iglesia de San Isidoro, from the same era.

Take Calle Fierro, where there is a covered market, to Calle Fontán.

Fontán is a picturesque area. Porticoed houses have an enchanting courtyard, reached by multiple archways.

Leave by the archway that faces Plaza Daoíz y Velarde.

The first sight in **Plaza Daoíz y Velarde** is the sculpture ensemble, **Las vendedoras del Fontán**, in honour of women who have sold goods in the outdoor market of these streets over the years. The beautiful tree-set plaza is the site of the noble **Palacio de Camposagrado**. Beside it is the Biblioteca de Asturias (library), with its unusual façade.

Worth a Visit

Outside The Old Quarter

Antiguo Hospital del Principado (Former Principality Hospital)

Leave Oviedo on calle Conde de Toreno (marked on the plan).

The façade of the 18C hospital, now the Hotel Reconquista, bears a fine Baroque **coat of arms**★.

Iglesia de Santullano or San Julián de los Prados★

Open May-Sep, 10am-1pm and 4-6pm; Sat, 9.30-11.30am; Oct-Apr, 9.30am-noon;, Mon, 10am-1pm. Last entry 30 min

before closing. ⌚ *Closed Sun, 25 Dec and 1 Jan.* *1.20 €.*
This outstanding early 9C work has a characteristic porch, twin aisles, wide transept and, at the east end, three chapels with barrel vaults. The walls are covered in **frescoes**★ of Roman influence. A fine transitional Romanesque **Christ in Glory**★ is in the central apse.

Santuarios del Monte Naranco★ (Mount Naranco Church and Chapel)

4km/2.5mi along Avenida de los Monumentos to the NW.
The former audience chamber (now a church) and part of the chapel remain of the 9C summer palace of Ramiro I.

Centro de Recepción e Interpretación del Prerrománico Asturiano

Just above the parking area, to the left. ⌚ *Open 10am-1pm and 3-5pm; Apr-Oct 9.30am-1.30pm y 3.30-7.30pm. Last entry 30 min before closing.* ⌚ *Closed Sun afternoon-Mon. ☎98 511 49 01.*
Panels explain Asturian art (in Spanish only); a video is narrated in English, Spanish, French and German.

Iglesia de Santa María del Naranco★★

Closed for restoration. ☎98 529 56 85.
This harmonious church is supported by grooved buttresses and lit by vast bays. The lower floor is a vaulted crypt. On the upper floor (a former reception hall), two loggias open off the great chamber. Decoration is delicate and unified. From outside, there is a fine **view** of Mount Aramo, with Oviedo in the foreground.

Iglesia de San Miguel de Lillo★

15 min on foot. *Closed for restoration. ☎98 529 56 85.*
What remains is probably only a third of the original church, which probably collapsed in the 13C.
The aisles are narrow. Several claustra-type windows remain. The delicate carving is a delight: on the door **jambs**★★ are identical scenes in relief of arena contests. An Asturian cord motif is repeated on the capitals and on vaulting in the nave and gallery.

Excursions

Iglesia de Santa Cristina de Lena★

34km/21mi S on the A 66 (junction 92). *At Pola de Lena, head for Vega del Rey then take the signposted road.* *Park before the rail viaduct and walk up the steep path (15min).* ⌚ *Open 11am-1pm and 4-6pm (4.30-6.30pm in summer).* ⌚ *Closed Mon.* *1.20 €, no charge Tue. ☎985 49 05 25.*
Santa Cristina de Lena (9C) is a well-proportioned church built of golden stone. It stands on a rocky crag, with a **panorama**★ of the Caudal Valley.
The little building has a Greek cross plan unusual in Asturias, and traditional stone vaulting, with blind arcades, and columns with pyramid-shaped capitals emphasised by a cord motif. The nave is separated from the raised choir by an iconostasis in which the superimposed arches increase the impression of balance. The low reliefs in the chancel are Visigothic sculptures (note geometric figures and plant motifs).

Teverga

43km/27mi SW on the N 634 and AS 228.
The road follows the River Trubia which, after Proaza, enters a narrow gorge. Glance back for a **view**★ of the Peñas Juntas cliff face. Beyond the Teverga fork the road penetrates the **desfiladero de Teverga**★ (Teverga Defile).
The **Colegiata de San Pedro de Teverga**, a late-12C collegiate church, is just outside La Plaza village. Built in a continuation of pre-Romanesque Asturian style, it includes a narthex, a tall narrow nave and a flat east end, originally three chapels. The narthex capitals are carved with stylised animal and plant motifs. ⌚ *Open noon-2pm and 4-6pm; Sat-Sun 11am-2pm and 4-7pm.* *2 €. ☎98 576 42 75.*

PALENCIA

POPULATION: 81 988.

MICHELIN MAP 575 F 16 – CASTILLA Y LEÓN (PALENCIA).

Palencia is a tranquil provincial capital situated in the fertile Tierra de Campos region. It was here that Alfonso VIII created the first Spanish university in 1208. Irrigation of the region has opened up an important horticultural industry.

- **Information:** *Mayor 105, ☎979 74 00 68.*
- **Orient Yourself:** Palencia is close to the A 62 heading NW to Burgos (88km/55mi) and SE to Valladolid (50km/31mi) and Salamanca (166km/104mi).
- **Don't Miss:** The Cathedral.
- **Also See:** The WAY OF ST JAMES, VALLADOLID and BURGOS.

Worth a Visit

Catedral★★

Open 8.45am-1.30pm and 4-6.30pm (4.30-7.30pm 16May-Sep); Sun 11.15am-1pm. 3 € (museum) ☎979 70 13 47.

Palencia's little-known cathedral is a 14C-16C Gothic edifice with Renaissance features. The original 7C Visigothic chapel lay forgotten during the Moorish occupation, until Sancho III de Navarra came upon it while hunting.

Interior★★

The cathedral contains an incredible concentration of art in all the styles of the early 16C: Flamboyant Gothic, Isabelline, Plateresque and Renaissance. The monumental high altar **retable** (early 16C) was carved by Felipe Vigarny, painted by Juan of Flanders and is surmounted by a Crucifix by Juan de Valmaseda. The 16C tapestries on the sides were commissioned by Bishop Fonseca. The *coro* grille, with a delicately wrought upper section, is by Gaspar Rodríguez (1563); the choir stalls are Gothic, the organ gallery, above, is dated 1716. The **Capilla del Sagrario** (Chapel of the Holy Sacrament) is exuberantly Gothic with a rich altarpiece by Valmaseda (1529). The central **triptych**★ is a masterpiece, painted in Flanders by Jan Joest de Calcar in 1505 – the donor, Bishop Fonseca, is shown at its centre.

Museo★

To the right of the west door. Guided tours (1hr) 10.30am-1.20pm and 4-6.30pm; 16 May-30 Sep, 10.30am-1.20pm and 4.30-7.20pm; Sun and public hols, 11.15am-1pm. 3€. ☎979 70 13 47.

The collection includes a *St Sebastian* by El Greco and four 15C Flemish **tapestries**★ of the Adoration, the Ascension, Original Sin and the Resurrection of Lazarus.

Excursions

Iglesia de Frómista★★

29km/18mi NE along the N 611. Open 10am-2pm and 3-6.30pm (4.30-8pm in summer). 1€. ☎979 81 01 44.

Pilgrims on the way to Santiago de Compostela used to stop here. The only vestige of the famous Benedictine **Monasterio de San Martín** is a church, built in 1066, with beautifully matched stone blocks of considerable size. This was a model for many others in the region.

Baños de Cerrato

14km/9mi SE

- *Cross the railway at Venta de Baños; turn right towards Cevico de la Torre. Bear left at the first crossroads.*

Basílica de San Juan Bautista★

Guided tours (20min), 10.30am-1.30pm and 4-7pm (5-8.30pm in summer). Closed Mon. ☎988 77 08 12 (town hall).

This, the oldest church in Spain, was built by Visigothic King Recceswinth, while he was taking the waters in Baños de Cerrato, in 661.

PAMPLONA/IRUÑA★

POPULATION: 191 197.
MICHELIN MAP 573 D 25 (TOWN PLAN) – NAVARRA.

The old quarter of Pamplona (Iruña in Basque) keeps its narrow medieval streets and arcaded squares. Streets around the plaza del Castillo are named for trades: Zapatería (shoemaker) and Tejería (tilemaker).

- **Information:** *Duque de Ahumada 3, ☎ 948 22 07 41; Eslava 1, ☎ 978 42 04 20.*
- **Orient Yourself:** Modern Pamplona extends south from the riverside old town. Roads lead to Roncesvalles in the Pyrenees and to Hendaye, both in France.
- **Parking:** Don't even try to park in the old city.
- **Also See:** DONOSTIA-SAN SEBASTIÁN (94km/59mi N), ESTELLA/LIZARRA (43km/29mi SW), SANGÜESA/ZANGOZA (46km/29mi SE) and Monasterio de LEYRE (61km/38mi SE).

Background

Historical notes – Pamplona is said to have been founded by Pompey who, gave his name to the town. The Moors briefly took over in the 8C but were repelled by Charlemagne, who demolished the walls. The townspeople in turn massacred Charlemagne's rearguard.

In the 10C Pamplona became the capital of Navarra, though it was torn for a time between proponents of Castilla and of French rule.

Worth a Visit

Catedral★★

Open 10am-1.30pm and 4-7pm; Sat 10am-1.30pm; 15 Jul-15 Sep, 10am-7pm; Sat, 10am-2pm. Closed Sun and public hols. 3.60 €. ☎948 21 08 27.

The Gothic cathedral was built in the 14C and 15C. At the end of the 18C, Ventura Rodríguez rebuilt the west front.

Interior★

The nave has wide arches and windows and great bare walls, typical of Navarra Gothic. In front of the finely wrought grille closing the sanctuary stands the alabaster **tomb**★★, commissioned in 1416 by Charles III, the Noble. The reclining figures and **mourners** were carved by Janin Lomme. Note the late-15C Hispano-Flemish altarpiece (south ambulatory chapel).

Claustro★

The 14C-15C cloisters appear delicate, with elegant Gothic arches surmounted, in some cases, by gables. Sculptured tombs and doors add interest.

Off the east gallery is the Capilla Barbazán with beautiful 14C star vaulting. On the south side, the doorway of the Sala Preciosa is a masterwork of the period, its tympanum beautifully carved with scenes from the Life of the Virgin and two statues forming a fine Annunciation. In the southeast corner, a lavabo is turned into a shrine commemorating the Battle of Las Navas de Tolosa.

Museo Diocesano★

Open 10am-1.30pm and 4-7pm; Sat, 10am-1.30pm; 15 Jul-15 Sep, 10.30am-7pm; Sat, 10am-2.30pm. Closed Sun and public hols. 4 €. ☎948 21 08 27.

The Diocesan Museum is in the old refectory and kitchen, which date from 1330. The refectory, a lofty hall with six pointed arches, contains a rostrum decorated with an enchanting scene of a unicorn hunt. The square kitchen has a central lantern rising to 24m/79ft. Displays include a 13C *Reliquary of the Holy Sepulchre* donated by St Louis (Louis IX of France) and polychrome wood statues of the Virgin and Christ.

Follow the narrow, picturesque calle del Redín to the ramparts.

PAMPLONA IRUÑA

Street	Grid	No.	Street	Grid	No.	Street	Grid	No.
Amaya	BYZ	4	Esquiroz	AZ	25	Roncesvalles Av. de	BY	59
Ansoleaga	AY	5	Estafeta	BY	26	San Fermín	BZ	63
Bayona Av. de	AY	13	García Castañón	ABY	30	San Francisco Pl. de	AY	65
Carlos III Av. de	BYZ		Juan de Labrit	BY	33	San Ignacio Av. de	BYZ	66
Castillo de Maya	BZ	16	Leyre	BYZ	36	Sancho el Mayor	ABZ	60
Chapitela	BY	17	Mayor	AY	40	Sangüesa	BZ	69
Conde Oliveto Av. del	AZ	19	Mercaderes	BY	43	Santo Domingo	AY	70
Cortes de Navarra	BY	20	Navarrería	BY	48	Sarasate Paseo de	AY	72
Cruz Pl. de la	BZ	22	Navas de Tolosa	AY	50	Taconera Recta de	AY	73
			Paulino Caballero	BZ	51	Vínculo Pl. del	AYZ	78
			Príncipe de Viana Pl. del	BZ	54	Zapatería	AY	89
			Reina Cuesta de la	AY	56			

Ayuntamiento	AY	H	Museo de Navarra	AY	M

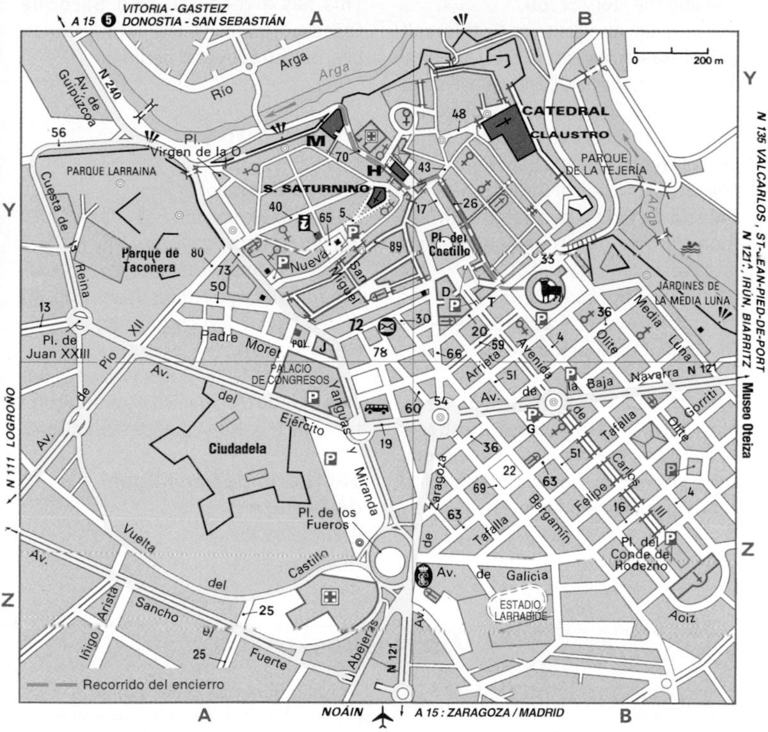

Murallas (Ramparts)

A bastion, now a garden, commands a view of the Puerta de Zumalacárregui (a gate below and to the left),and a stretch of the old walls and a bend in the rivers Arga and Monte Cristóbal.

Museo de Navarra★

Open 9.30am-2pm and 5-7pm (Thu to 9pm); Sun and public hols, 11am-2pm. Closed Mon, 1 Jan, Good Fri, 7 Jul and 25 Dec. 1 €, no charge Sun and public hols. 948 42 64 93.

This museum is on the site of the 16C Hospital de Nuestra Señora de la Misericordia. Only a Renaissance gateway and the chapel remain.

The Roman period *(basement and first floor)* is represented by funerary steles, inscriptions and **mosaic**★ pavements from 2C and 4C villas.

The main exhibit in the Hispano-Moorish section *(Room 1.8)* is an 11C ivory **casket**★ from San Salvador de Leyre sculpted in Córdoba. Romanesque **capitals**★ are from the former 12C cathedral of Pamplona, brilliantly

The "Sanfermines"

The *feria* of San Fermín is celebrated with joyous ardour from 6 to 14 July each year. Visitors pour in, doubling the town's population, to see the great evening bullfights and enjoy the carefree atmosphere (described by Hemingway in *The Sun Also Rises*). The most spectacular event, and the one most prized by "Pamploneses", however, is the **encierro** or early morning *(around 8am)* running of the bulls. The beasts selected to fight in the evening are let loose with a number of steers to rush through the streets along a set route leading to the bullring *(see route on town plan).*

carved with the Passion, the Resurrection and the Story of Job.
The museum also contains **Gothic wall paintings★** from Artaíz (13C), Artajona (14C), Pamplona (14C), and elsewhere in the province. They share an unobtrusive emphasis on faces and features reminiscent of French miniaturists.
The reconstruction of the interior of the **Palacio de Oriz** is decorated with 16C monochrome panels depicting Adam and Eve and the wars of Charles V.
On the third floor are 17C-18C paintings by Luis Paret and Francisco de Goya (portrait of the *Marqués de San Adrián*).

Iglesia de San Saturnino★

This church in a tangle of narrow streets in the old quarter mingles Romanesque brick towers, 13C Gothic **portals★** and vaulting and later additions.

Ayuntamiento (Town Hall)

This has a reconstructed **Baroque façade★** (originally late 17C) with statues, balustrades and pediments.

Excursions

Museo Oteiza

En Alzuza, 7 km/4.5mi E. ▶ Take the NA 150, then immediately turn left.
Open 10am-3pm (11am-7pm Jun-Aug); Sat-Sun and public hols 11am-7pm. Closed Mon, 1 Jan and 25 Dec. 4 €. 948 33 20 74.
Jorge Oteiza (1908-2003) was a key figures of modern Spanish abstract sculpture. The museum is beside his house.

Santuario de San Miguel de Aralar★

45km/28mi NW.

Address Book

For coin ranges, see the Legend on the cover flap.

WHERE TO EAT

Rodero – *Arrieta 3 – 948 22 80 35 – www.restauranterodero.com – Closed Sun, Mon evening and Holy Week –* . This luxury restaurant behind the bullring is one of the best in the whole province. Family-run with high-quality service and creative, innovative cuisine with prices to match.

TAPAS

Baserri – *San Nicolás 32 – 948 22 20 21 – www.restaurantebaserri.com – – 14/30 €.* The Baserri is widely recognised as being one of the best place for tapas in Pamplona, as witnessed by its numerous prizes and the huge number of locals who come here. Make sure you try the sirloin with roquefort (*solomillos al roquefort*).

WHERE TO STAY

Hotel Yoldi – *Avenida de San Ignacio 11 – 948 22 48 00 – www.hotelyoldi.com – – 50 rooms. – 9 €.* This renovated hotel is a good choice in the centre of Pamplona. Comfortable and functional rooms and a good location near the bullring. As with everywhere in the city at fiesta time, not easy to get a room here.

Follow the A 15, then shortly before Lecumberri, turn onto the NA 751.

The NA 751 crosses the Sierra de Aralar through beech woods to this sanctuary. *Open 9am-6pm (9pm Apr-Oct). 948 39 60 28.*
The sanctuary consists of a Romanesque **church**, dated 8C, which encloses a totally independent chapel. The gilt and enamel **altar front**★★ is one of the major works of European Romanesque gold- and silverwork, attributed by some to a late-12C Limoges workshop. It consists of gilded bronze plaques adorned with enamel and mounted precious stones, arranged as an altarpiece. The outstanding multicoloured honeycomb enamelwork is adorned with arabesques and plant motifs.

Epic Poems

According to legend, Roncesvalles was the site where the Basques of Navarra massacred the rearguard of Charlemagne's army in 778 as Roland was leading it back through the Pyrenees to France. The late 12C to early 13C Poem of **Bernardo del Carpio** describes Bernardo as a national hero who fought alongside his Basque, Navarra and Asturian companions in arms to avenge the Frankish invasion of Spain; the 12C **Song of Roland**, the first French epic poem, on the other hand, glorifies the heroic but ultimately despairing resistance of a handful of valiant Christian knights against hordes of Saracen fanatics.

Roncesvalles/Orreaga★

47km/29mi NE along the N 135.
This 12C mass of buildings served as an important hostelry for pilgrims to Santiago de Compostela. Its square funerary chapel is now the Capilla del Sancti Spiritus (Chapel of the Holy Spirit). A collegiate church is rich in relics.

Iglesia de la Real Colegiata

This Gothic collegiate church, inspired by those of the Paris region, was consecrated in 1219. Beneath the high altar canopy is the silver-plated statue of **Nuestra Señora de Roncesvalles**, created in France in the late 13C.

Sala Capitular (Chapter house)

The beautiful Gothic chamber contains the tombs of the founder, Sancho VII, the Strong (1154-1234), King of Navarra and his queen.

Museo★

Open 10am-2pm and 3.30-5.30pm (7pm 5 Apr-25 Oct); Jan, 10.30am-2.30pm. Closed Wed in Jan, 1 and 6 Jan, 8 Sep and 25 Dec. 2.30 €. 948 79 04 80.
The museum contains fine pieces of ancient plate: a Mudéjar casket, a Romanesque book of the Gospel, a 14C enamelled reliquary known as "Charlemagne's chessboard", a 16C Flemish triptych, an emerald, said to have been worn by Sultan Miramamolín el Verde in his turban on the day of the Battle of Las Navas de Tolosa in 1212, and a lovely *Holy Family* by Morales.

Tour Through The Valle Del Bidasoa★

100km/62mi N – allow one day.
The Bidasoa cuts through the lower foothills of the western Pyrenees, where villages of typical Basque houses lie amid lush meadows. The Bidasoa river is renowned for its salmon and trout.

Exit Pamplona along avenida de la Baja Navarra to the N 121A and over the Velate pass. Follow the NA 2540.

Elizondo, the capital of the **Valle del Baztán**, has numerous houses decorated with armorial bearings.

Return to Irutia and follow the N 121B to rejoin the N 121A, heading N towards Berrizaun.

This road heads into the ancient confederation of the **Cinco Villas**, comprising **Etxalar, Arantza, Igantzi, Lesaka** and **Bera**, where many houses bear coats of arms. The typically Basque façades have deep eaves over balconies with delicate balustrades.

PEDRAZA DE LA SIERRA★★

POPULATION: 448

MICHELIN MAPS 575 OR 576 I 18 – CASTILLA Y LEÓN (SEGOVIA).

Weekend visitors flock to Pedraza, encircled by medieval walls, to wander its enchanting streets and to eat roast lamb or suckling pig.

- **Information:** *Real 5, ☎921 50 86 66.*
- **Orient Yourself:** The village stands north of Madrid on the slopes of the Sierra de Guadarrama.
- **Also See:** SEGOVIA (35km/22mi SW) and Sierra de GUADARRAMA.

Walking About

The **Puerta de la Villa**, a fortified gateway, opens into a maze of alleys bordered by country-style houses. The first medieval building of interest is the **Cárcel de la Villa**, the former jail (*open 11.30am-2pm and 3.30-6.30pm (7.30pm autumn-winter); €2.50 €; ☎921 50 98 77 or 921 50 99 55).*

The splendid **plaza Mayor** is surrounded by ancient porticoes topped by balconies and the slender Romanesque bell tower of San Juan. A 16C **castle** houses works by artist **Ignacio Zuloaga** (*guided tours (30min) in winter, Sat-Sun and public hols, 11am-2pm and 4-6pm (other times by arrangement); in summer, Wed-Sun, 11am-2pm and 5-8pm; 4 €; ☎921 50 98 25).*

Excursion

Sepúlveda

25km/16mi N. You'll get a good view of the village's terraced **site**★ on the slopes of a deep gorge.

Park at the town hall square, overlooked by castle ruins. Walk up to the **Iglesia de San Salvador** for a fine view. The church is typical Segovia Romanesque with one of the oldest side doors in Spain, dating from 1093.

Centro de Recepción e Interpretación del Parque Natural de las Hoces del Duratón (Duratón Gorges) – *Open 10am-5pm; Jul-Sep 10am-2pm and 4-7pm; Sat and public hols Jul-Sep, 10am-6pm. ☎921 54 05 86.*

This centre provides information about hiking routes and canoe companies.

The **park** runs along the middle stretch of the river, hemmed in by spectacular 70m/230ft walls, under the simple Romanesque hermitage *(ermita)* of San Frutos.

F. Gouverneur/MICHELIN

Plaza Mayor

PICOS DE EUROPA★★★

MICHELIN MAP 572 C 14-15-16 –
CASTILLA Y LEÓN, ASTURIAS AND CANTABRIA.

The Picos de Europa, highest range in the Cordillera Cantábrica and just 30km/18mi from the sea, include deep gorges cut by gushing mountain rivers and snow-capped peaks jagged with erosion. The south face is less steep than the north, where the higher peaks are concentrated, and looks out over a harsh terrain of outstanding beauty. Parque Nacional de los Picos de Europa, covering 64 660ha/159 775 acres, protects the region's flora and fauna.

- **Information:** Cangas de Onís: Avenida de Covadonga (Plaza del Ayuntamiento), ☎98 584 80 05; Covadonga: Explanada de la Basílica, ☎98 584 60 35.
- **Orient Yourself:** The Picos de Europa rise along the northern coast, between Gijón and Santander.
- **Don't Miss:** A hike to any of several spectacular mountain viewpoints.
- **Also See:** COSTA VERDE and COSTA DE CANTABRIA.

Sights

Desfiladero De La Hermida★★ (La Hermida Defile) 1

From Panes to Potes –

27km/17mi – about 1hr

A **ravine**★★, 20km/12mi long, extends to either side of a basin containing the hamlet of La Hermida. The narrow gorge is bare and lacking in sunlight.

Iglesia de Nuestra Señora de Lebeña

Open 10am-8.30pm in summer; by arrangement in winter. ☎942 74 43 32.

The small 10C Mozarabic church stands amid poplars at the foot of tall cliffs. The belfry and porch are later additions. The church houses a venerated 15C sculpture of the Virgin Mary.

Potes

Potes is a delightful village in a pleasing **site**★ in a fertile basin set against jagged crests. From the bridge, view old stone houses and the 15C **Torre del Infantado** (tower), now the town hall.

THE CLIMB TO FUENTE DÉ★★ 2

30km/19mi on the N 621– about 3hr

Monasterio de Santo Toribio de Liébana

Approach along a signposted road on the left. Open 10am-1pm and 4-7pm. ☎942 73 05 50.

The monastery was founded in the 7C and grew to considerable importance when a fragment of the True Cross was placed in its safekeeping. A *camarín (access through the north aisle of the church)* contains the largest known piece of the True Cross in the *lignum crucis* reliquary, a silver gilt Crucifix. The transitional Romanesque church is restored to its original harmonious proportions. The monastery was the house of **Beatus**, the 8C monk famous for his **Commentary on the Apocalypse**, copied in the form of illuminated manuscripts (*see illustration under INTRODUCTION TO SPAIN: LITERATURE*).

There is a **view**★ of Potes and the central range from the lookout point at the end of the road.

Fuente Dé★★

The parador is at 1 000m/3 300ft. Nearby, the cableway **(teleférico)** rises 800m/2 625ft to the top of the sheer rock face (*only weather permitting, 10am-6pm; Jul-Sep, 9am-8pm; 12.50 €; ☎942 73 66 10*). During the **ascent** you may see wild chamois. The **Mirador del Cable**★★ commands a

splendid panorama of the upper valley of the Deva and Potes. A path leads to the Aliva refuge. Erosion of the karst limestone produces stony plateaux and huge sink-holes known as **hoyos**.

Puerto De San Glorio★ (San Glorio Pass) 3

From Potes to Oseja de Sajambre *83km/52mi – about 3hr*

The road crosses the Quiviesa Valley, then climbs through pastures. After Bores, view a changing panorama on the left.

Puerto de San Glorio★

Alt 1 609m/5 279ft. A track leads north from the pass *(1hr there and back)* to near the Peña de Llesba and the **Mirador de Llesba**, a magnificent **viewpoint**★★. To the right is the east range; to the left, the steep south face of the central massif. In the left foreground is Coriscao peak(2 234m/7 330ft).

At Portilla de la Reina, bear right onto LE 243.

Puerto de Pandetrave★★

This pass (1 562m/5 125ft) affords a **panorama** of the three ranges: in the right foreground, the Cabén de Remoña and Torre de Salinas, both in the central massif. In the distance, in a hollow, is the village of Santa Marina de Valdeón.

The road between Santa Marina de Valdeón and Posada de Valdeón is narrow but passable.

Puerto de Panderruedas★

The road climbs to pastures at 1 450m/4 757ft. Walk up the path to the left *(15min there and back)* to the **Mirador de Piedrafitas**★★ *(viewing table)* for an impressive view of the immense cirque which closes the Valdeón Valley. To the northeast is the Torre Cerredo peak (2 648m/8 688ft), highest in the range.

Puerto del Pontón★

Alt 1 280m/4 200ft. From the pass, get a fine **view**★★ of the Sajambre Valley. The descent to Oseja de Sajambre (*see below)* begins with hairpin bends in below the western range; it continues as a spectacular road cut into the mountain side (tunnels) from which you can see the formidable rock wall penetrated by the Sella river.

Desfiladero de Los Beyos★★★ (Los Beyos Defile) 4

From Oseja de Sajambre to Cangas de Onís – *38km/24mi – about 1hr*

Mirador de Oseja de Sajambre★★

There is an awe-inspiring **view**★★ of the Oseja de Sajambre basin: the sharp Niaja peak at its centre rises to 1 732m/5 682ft, and of the Los Beyos defile opens between walls of broken rock strata.

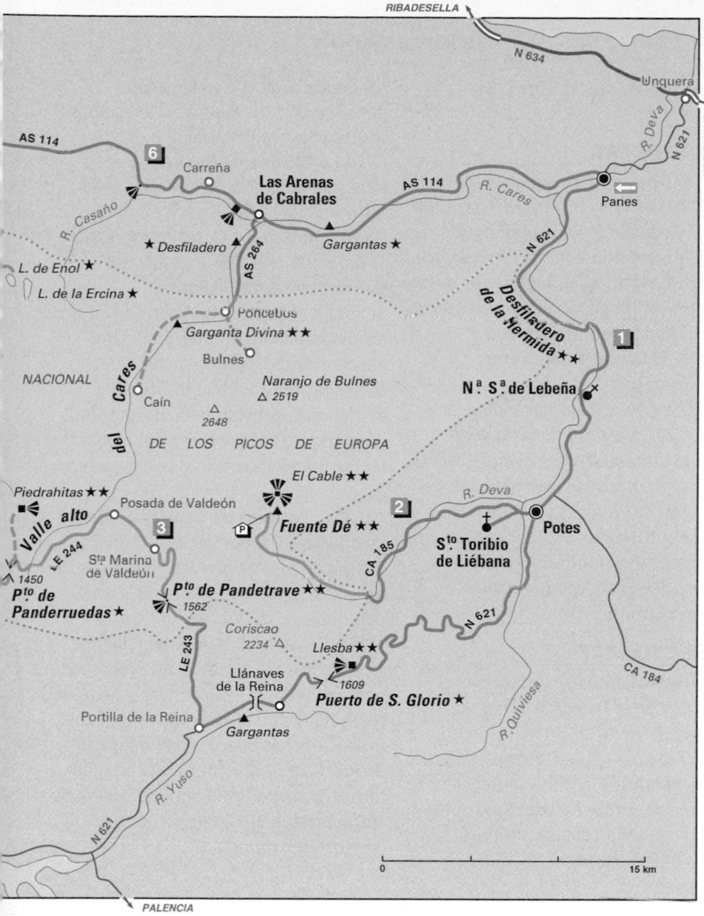

Desfiladero de Los Beyos★★★

The defile, one of the most beautiful in Europe, is 10km/6mi long, cut by the Sella in exceptionally thick limestone. An occasional tree clings to its sides.

Cangas de Onís

A humpbacked **Roman bridge** *(puente romano)* crosses the Sella to the west. The Capilla de Santa Cruz, also to the west, in Contranquil, commemmorates the victory of Covadonga. It houses the region's only dolmen.

Villanueva

The 17C Benedictine **Monasterio de San Pedro** stands at the end of the village. The monastery was built around a pre-existing Romanesque church of which there remain the apse and an elegantly decorated side portal.

The Road To Covadonga and The Lakes★★ 5

From Cangas de Onís to Covadonga *35km/22mi – about 3hr*

Cueva del Buxu

Guided tours (30min), 9am-3.30pm; restricted to 25 visitors per day; cannot be booked in advance. Closed Mon, Tue, in Nov, 1 Jan and 24-25 and 31 Dec. 3€, no charge Wed. 608 17 54 67.

The cave in the cliff face contains charcoal drawings and rock engravings from the Magdalenian period: a stag, horse and bison scarcely larger a hand.

Covadonga

This famous shrine, a landmark in Spanish history, is nestled in a magnificent

Address Book

For coin ranges, see the Legend on the cover flap.

WHERE TO EAT

El Bodegón – *San Roque – Potes – ☎942 73 02 47 – Closed Wed except Jul-Sep).* El Bodegón is a converted old stone-fronted house in the town centre. The rustic, wood-adorned interior is pleasant, although tables are somewhat close. A good, traditional menu.

El Corral del Indianu – *Avenida de Europa 14 – Arriondas – ☎98 584 10 72 – www.elcorraldelindiano.com –Closed 24 Dec-24 Jan, Sun and Wed evenings and Thu (except in Aug) –* . A pleasant surprise in the centre of Arriondas. The building's stone walls enclose a restaurant that successfully combines the modern and traditional, in terms of both decor and cuisine. A gastronomic treat.

WHERE TO STAY

Hotel Del Oso – *Cosgaya – 9km/5.5mi SE of Fuente Dé along the Potes road – ☎942 73 30 18 – Closed 1 Jan-10 Feb –* *– 51 rooms –* *5.90 €.* This hotel is at the very heart of the Picos de Europa on the banks of the River Deva, amid a spectacular high peaks. Behind the sober brick façade, rooms are large and comfortable, particularly in the annexe. The restaurant specialises in regional cuisine.

La Tahona de Besnes – *Besnes – Alles – 10km/6mi W of Panes on the AS 114 – ☎98 541 57 49 – www.latahonadebesmes.com – Closed 10 Jan-1 Mar – 13 rooms –* *5.70€ – Restaurant 12.50 €.* This former mill in Besnes, near Alles, has been transformed into an inviting country hotel. Stone and exposed wood beams are the order of the day here, with agricultural implements providing the decoration. Wood is also the predominant material on the floors and ceilings of the guest rooms.

Parador de Cangas de Onís – *Villanueva – Cangas de Onís – 3km/2mi NW of Cangas de Onís along the Arriondas road – ☎98 584 94 02 – www.parador.es –* *– 64 rooms –* *10 € – Restaurant 25.90€.* Benedictine monks chose to settle on this very spot next to the River Sella in their search for tranquillity and beauty. Nowadays, the monastery has been converted into a delightful parador offering a combination of history, nature and art. Luxurious surroundings, including elegant, comfortable rooms.

setting★★ at the bottom of a narrow valley surrounded by impressive peaks. **Don Pelayo** defeated the Moors at Covadonga (722), marking the beginning of the Spanish Reconquest.

La Santa Cueva

Open 8.30am-7pm (8pm in summer). ☎98 584 61 15.

The cave, dedicated to the Virgin of the Battlefield, holds the deeply venerated 18C wooden statue of the Virgin, patron of Asturias, **La Santina**.

Basílica

Open 9am-6.30pm (8pm in summer); no visits during religious services. ☎98 584 60 35/ 96.

Before the neo-Romanesque basilica built between 1886 and 1901 stands a statue of Pelayo. The **museo** contains gifts to the Virgin including a magnificent **crown**★ with more than 1 000 diamonds (*open 10.30am-2pm and 4-6.30pm (7.30pm in summer); closed Tue, and in Nov; 2 €; ☎98 584 60 96).*

Lago de Enol and Lago de Ercina★ (Lake Enol and Lake Ercina)

Continue to the lakes along the CO 4.

The road is steep; look back to an extensive panorama. After 8km/5mi, you reach the **Mirador de la Reina**★★ with a view of the rock pyramids which make up the Sierra de Covalierda. Beyond the pass, two rock cirques formed by *hoyos* (*see above*), are the settings of **Lago de Enol**★ and **Lago de Ercina** (lakes, alt 1 232m/4 042ft).

J. Balanya/MICHELIN

The impressive landscapes around Fuente Dé

Gargantas del Cares★★ (Cares Gorges) 6

From Covadonga to Panes

90km/56mi – allow one day

Just out of Las Estazadas village there is a splendid **panorama**★★ of the rock wall which closes off the Río Casaño Valley. From a viewpoint on the right, shortly after Carreña de Cabrales, there is a glimpse of the fang-like crest of **Naranjo de Bulnes** (2 519m/8 264ft).

Arenas de Cabrales

This is the main production centre for *cabrales*, a blue ewes' milk cheese.

- *Bear right onto AS 264 which runs through the Upper Cares Valley.*

Upper Cares Valley

The Poncebos road leads south, through a pleasant **ravine**★. After the embalse de Poncebos (reservoir) a track *(3hr there and back on foot)* leads up to the village of Bulnes. From Poncebos to Caín *(3hr 30min one way)* a path follows the Cares and plunges into the **defile**★★ to the foot of the central massif *(here you can hire a car back to Poncebos).*

- *Return to Arenas de Cabrales.*

Beyond Arenas the **gorges**★ are green with moss and the occasional tree. Humpbacked bridges and fragile footbridges span the emerald waters.

MONASTERIO DE PIEDRA★★

MICHELIN MAPS 574 OR 575 I 24 – ARAGÓN (ZARAGOZA).

Hidden in a fold of this arid plateau is an oasis fed by the River Piedra. Approach the monastery via Ateca, across a parched landscape above the Tranquera Reservoir and past the village of Nuévalos.

- **Orient Yourself:** This magnificent area is 25km/15mi S of the N II-E 90 highway from Madrid to Zaragoza (104km/65mi).
- **Also See:** Monasterio de SANTA MARÍA DE HUERTA (63km/39mi NW).

Walking About

The site was discovered by Cistercian monks, who generally chose pleasant surroundingss. Monks from the Abbey of Poblet in Tarragona established a monastery in 1194. It was rebuilt several times. The buildings have been reconstructed as a hotel.

Park and Waterfalls★★
Open 9am-5pm (8pm in summer, monastery from 10am). 11 €. ☎902 19 60 52.
Waterfalls and cascades are everywhere along the footpath through the forest *(follow red signposts to go, blue to return)*. The paths, steps and tunnels laid out last century by **Juan Federico Muntadas** have transformed an impenetrable forest into a popular park. The first fall is the **Cola de Caballo** (Horse's Tail), a cascade of 53m/174ft. You come on it again at the end of your walk if you descend steep and slippery steps into the beautiful **Cueva Iris** (Iris Grotto).
Baño de Diana (Diana's Bath) and **Lago del Espejo** (Mirror Lake), between tall cliffs, are both worth a halt.

PIRINEOS ARAGONESES★★

MICHELIN MAP 574 D 28-32, E 29-32 AND F 30-31 – ARAGÓN (HUESCA).

The central Pyrenees, in the north of Huesca province, include the highest peaks: Aneto (3 404m/11 165ft), Posets (3 371m/11 060ft) and Monte Perdido (3 355m/11 004ft). The foothills are often ravined with sparse vegetation; at the heart of the massif, accessible up the river courses, valleys lead to mountain cirques well worth exploring.

- **Information:** *Aínsa: Avenida de Pineta, ☎974 50 07 67*
- **Orient Yourself:** From Pamplona/Iruña follow the N 240 to Jaca (111km/69mi SE); from Huesca the N 330 to Jaca (91km/57mi N); from Barbastro the N 123 and the A 138 to Aínsa (52km/32.5mi N).
- **Don't Miss:** A hike in a spectacular canyon, and a surprising country repast.
- **Also See:** JACA, HUESCA and PIRINEOS CATALANES.

Location

The route described covers the Pirineos Aragoneses from east to west, divided into six sections.

Background

Structure and relief – Vast longitudinal bands are clear in this region. The **axis of Palaeozoic terrain** comprises the Maladeta, Posets, Vignemale and Balaïtous massifs, where there are remains of Quaternary glaciers. In the **Pre-Pyrenees** (Monte Perdido), deep **Mesozoic limestone** is eroded into the canyons, gorges and cirques of the upper valleys. The limestone area, which extends in broken mountain chains to the Ebro Basin, is divided at Jaca by the long depression of the River Aragón. Tertiary sediment has accumulated into hills; some are bare of vegetation, in an unusual blue marl landscape like that around the **Yesa Reservoir.**

Life in the valleys – The upper valleys of the Kingdom of Aragón developed self-contained communities. Folk traditions are still followed and native costume is worn in certain valleys. Emigration has led to the abandonment of a number of villages. Tourism is a major economic activity. Winter resorts include Candanchú, Astún, Canfranc, Panticosa, El Formigal and Benasque.

Tours

From Vielha to Benasque 1

122km/76mi – about 3hr

Vielha (*See PIRINEOS CATALANES*)
The road cuts the Maladeta massif via the Vielha tunnel to the lonely upper valley of the Noguera Ribagorçana where the attractive hamlet of **Vilaller** huddles.

Take the N 260 to Castejón de Sos, a paragliding centre, then the A 139.

Address Book

For coin ranges, see the Legend on the cover flap.

WHERE TO EAT

Casa Ruba – *Esperanza 18 – Biescas – ☎974 48 50 01 – www.hotelcasaruba.com – Closed Sun evenings (exc in summer)* – . This restaurant in a traditional house is renowned in the area. With over a century of tradition, Casa Ruba serves well-prepared, good-quality dishes, in addition to a range of tapas at the bar. 29 inexpensive rooms are also available here. Highly recommended.

Deth Gormán – *Met Día 8 – Vielha – ☎973 64 04 45 – Closed Tue and in Jun* – . A small restaurant in the village centre. The wooden front suggests the rustic, simple inteior, where regional specialties are served, such as mountain snails. .

Bodegas del Sobrarbe – *Plaza Mayor 2 – Aínsa – ☎974 50 02 37 – www.bodegasdelsobrarbe.com – Closed Jan-Feb.* This restaurant in the basement of a building on the square of this medieval town is decorated in traditional country style and serves excellent game and grilled steaks.

WHERE TO STAY

Hotel-Restaurante Casa Frauca – *Carret. de Ordesa – Sarvisé – ☎974 48 63 53 – www.casafrauca.com – Closed 8 Jan-1 Mar – 12 rooms – 4.50 € – Restaurant 16/50 €.* This hotel is well maintained with cosy rooms where wood floors and beams add to the atmosphere. The rustic-style restaurant has an extensive menu of unpretentious offerings.

Hotel Pradas – *Avenida Ordesa 7 – Broto – ☎974 48 60 04 – www.hotelpradas.com – – 24 rooms – 5 € – Restaurant 12/50 €.* The stone façade is the first thing you notice as you approach this hotel on the main road into Broto. Several rooms have their own lounge area, albeit with a more expensive price tag.

Hostal Dos Ríos – *Avenida Central 2 – Aínsa – ☎974 50 01 06 – www.hoteldosrios.com – Open Apri-Oct and 26 Dec-6 Jan – 18 rooms – 6.60 €.* This *hostal* and the hotel of the same name are the best medium-priced options in Aínsa. From its location in the lower town, the main square is easily reached on foot or by car. Guest rooms are clean and perfectly adequate.

Hotel Villa de Torla – *Plaza Aragón 1 – Torla – ☎974 48 61 56 56 – www.hotelvilladetorla.com – Closed 8 Jan-6 Mar – 38 rooms – 5 €.* The rooms in this recently renovated, attractive stone house in the centre of Torla are rustic, pleasant and comfortable. The swimming pool and terrace are welcome in summer.

H. Hospital de Benasque – *Camino Real de Francia – Benasque – 15km/9mi N of Benasque along the A 139. Follow a road to the right, signposted Los Llanos del Hospital. – ☎974 55 20 12 – www.llanosdelhospital.com – – 57 rooms – – Restaurant 20 €.* Wood and stone are the order of the day in this charming hotel established in a former pilgrims' hospital. The setting, at the foot of the Pico de Maladeta and close to the Pico de Aneto, is quite spectacular. Cosy, pleasantly decorated rooms.

Valle de Benasque★

Benasque (1 138m/3 734ft) lies in an open valley, lush and green, overshadowed by the Maladeta massif, a base for walkers, climbers (ascending the Aneto) and skiers (Cerler, 5km/3mi). Streets are lined with old mansions. **Anciles**, 1.6km/1mi away, is known for its attractive houses. 15km/9.5mi farther north, just before the road ends, a turn-off leads to the Hospital de Benasque, departure point for excursions into Parque Natural Posets-Maladeta.

From Benasque to Ainsa 2

180km/112mi – allow half a day

The road south through the Esero Valley passes through Villanova, with its two 11C-12C Lombard-Romanesque-style churches. After Castejón de Sos, it follows the **Congosto de Ventamillo**★★, a 3km/2mi defile with sheer limestone rock walls.

Ainsa★

Ainsa, one of the prettiest towns in the Pyrenees, stands on a promontory still girded by a wall, commanding the juncture of the River Cinca and River Ara. In the 11C it was the capital of the kingdom of Sobrarbe. Its arcaded **Plaza Mayor**★★ in the upper town, under the tower of a Romanesque church, is a gem of Aragonese architecture. The contemporary-style **Museo de Oficios y Artes Tradicionales**★ is a museum devoted to traditional arts and crafts (*open May-Jun, 10.30am-2pm and 4.30-8pm; Jul-15 Sep 10am-2pm and 4-9pm; closed Mon (and Tue July-Aug) and 16 Sep-Apr; 2.40€; 974 51 00 75).*

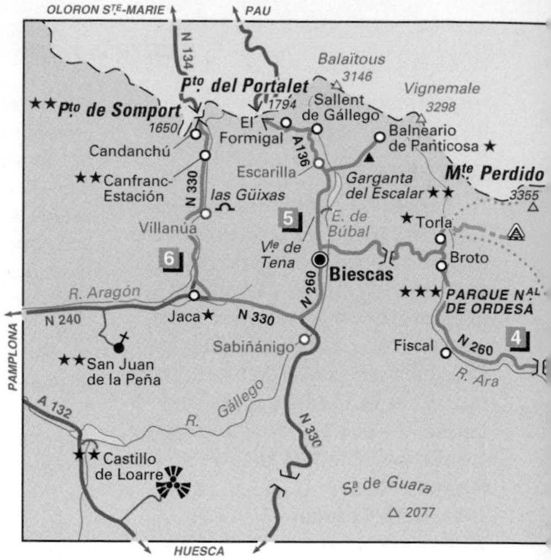

From Ainsa to Monte Perdido 3

73km/45mi – about 4hr

The A 138 follows the Cinca River northwards, through a dramatic landscape at the **Desfiladero de las Devotas**★.

Cañón de Añisclo★★ (*see Parque Nacional de ORDESA Y MONTE PERDIDO*)

Valle de Gistaín★

Exit the A 138 at Salinas de Sin. In this valley, also known as the Valle de Chistau, are some of the most picturesque villages in the Pyrenees, including **Plan**, San Juan de Plan and **Gistaín**.

Bielsa and Valle de Pineta

From the pleasant village of Bielsa, a narrow road climbs the valley of the Cinca River, traversing the impressive landscapes of the **Valle de Pineta**★★ to the Parador de Bielsa, nestled in a spectacular glacial cirque.

From Aínsa to Biescas 4

81km/51mi – about 3hr

Between **Boltaña** (16C church) and **Fiscal** (medieval tower), the river course reveals underlying strata. The church of **Broto** has an interesting Renaissance doorway. Beyond Broto, the great mass of the Mondarruego (alt 2 848m/9 341ft), closing the Ordesa Valley, backdrops the spectacular **landscape**★★ where the village of **Torla**★ lies on the western slope of the Ara Valley. The church, the Iglesia de San Salvador, houses noteworthy 18C altarpieces. The castle-abbey in Torla has an **ethnographic museum** (*for information, call 974 48 61 52 (town hall); 1 €).*

Parque Nacional de Ordesa y Monte Perdido★★★ (*See Parque Nacional de ORDESA Y MONTE PERDIDO*)

THE PORTALET ROAD 5

52km/32mi – about 2hr

The **Tena** Valley beyond Biescas widens out into the vast Búbal reservoir.

A short distance before Escarilla, bear right onto HU 610 for Panticosa.

Garganta del Escalar★★ (Escalar Gorge)

The sun rarely penetrates this gorge. The road cuts down the west slope by ramps and hairpin bends to an austere mountain cirque, the setting for the **Balneario de Panticosa**★, a spa with six sulphurous and radioactive springs, and a charming 19C air.

Return to Escarilla and continue to the Portalet Pass.

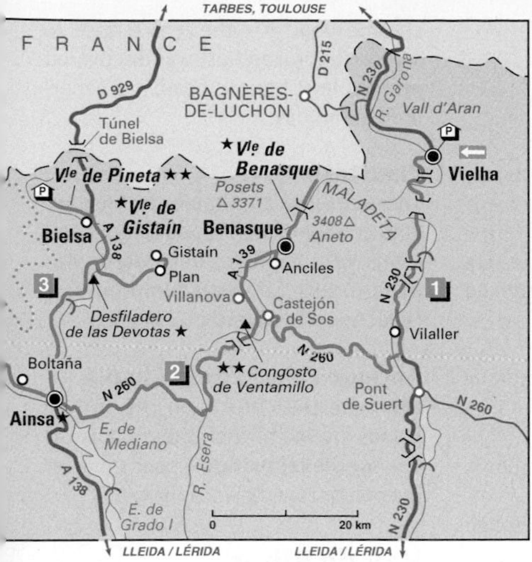

The mountain town of **Sallent de Gállego**, at 1 305m/4 281ft, hosts a summer music festival and is renowned for trout fishing and mountaineering. **El Formigal** (alt 1 480m/4 856ft), further on, is a ski resort.

Carretera del Portalet

Alt 1 794m/5 886ft. The pass lies between Portalet peak and Aneu summit to the west. The view extends to the Aneu cirque and Pic du Midi d'Ossau in France (alt 2 884m/9 462ft).

From Biescas to the Puerto De Somport 6

58km/36mi – about 2hr

Continue S on the N 260 to Sabiñánigo – from here it is possible to follow the tour through the Serrablo (see JACA: EXCURSIONS) – then take the N330 to Jaca (see JACA). From Jaca, the N 330 continues northwards.

The **Cueva de las Güixas**, a cave in Villanúa, has some 300m/330yd of galleries. (*974 37 32 17. 4 €*).

Beyond Canfranc is the abandoned early-20C **Canfranc international resort**★★, an extraordinary example of early-20C architecture.

The **Puerto de Somport**★★ (alt 1 632m/5 354ft), beside the Somport tunnel (opened in 2003), is the only pass in the Central Pyrenees which generally remains snow-free all year. **Candanchú**, best-known ski resort in Aragón, is less than 1km/0.6mi away.

Climb the mound to the right of the monument commemorating the building of the road for an extensive **panorama**★★ of the Spanish Pyrenees.

PIRINEOS CATALANES★★★

MICHELIN MAP 574 D 32, E 32-37 AND F 32-37 – CATALUNYA (GIRONA, LLEIDA).

These mountains are deeply cut by isolated valley with their own personality and traditions, especially in art developed during the Romanesque period. All offer delicious regional cuisine and opportunities for skiing, hunting, fishing, mountain climbing and adventure sports.

- **Information:** Camprodon: Plaça d'Espanya 1, 972 74 00 10; Carretera Comarcal 151, km 23,5, 972 74 09 36. www.valldecamprodon.org; Puigcerdà: Querol 1, 972 88 05 42; La Seu d'Urgell: Avinguda Valls d'Andorra 33, 973 35 15 11, www.laseu.org; Pasaje Joan Brudieu 15, 973 35 31 12; Tremp: Plaça de la Creu 1, 973 65 00 09, www.ayuntamentdetremp.com; Vielha: Sarriulera 10, 973 64 01 10; www.turisme.aran.org.
- **Orient Yourself:** The Pyrenees extend almost unbroken for 230km/143mi from the Mediterranean to the high Arán Valley (2 500m/8 202ft). The last range, the Montes Alberes, plunges into the Mediterranean from 700m/2 297ft.
- **Organizing Your Time:** Geography will oblige you to select one or two valleys to explore from the south access.
- **Also See:** PIRINEOS ARAGONESES, Principat d'ANDORRA and GIRONA/GERONA.

Tours

Upper Valley of the Ter★ 1

From the Collado de Ares to Vall de Núria

106km/66mi – allow one day

Two large valleys lie in the Ripollès area under mountains towering to 3 000m/10 000ft.

Vall De Camprodon

Molló

The 12C Romanesque church has a lovely Catalan belfry.

Take the narrow, winding road through Rocabruna to Beget.

Beget★★

This attractive mountain village with stone houses enjoys a pleasant **setting**★ deep in a peaceful valley.

The **Romanesque church**★★ (10C-12C) with Lombard arcatures and slender lantern-tower, houses the **Majestad de Beget**★, a magnificent figure of Christ carved in the 12C (*open 9am-7pm. 9-19; ask for the keys from Joan Coma, calle Bellaire; 1€; 972 74 01 36).*

Return to the C 38.

Camprodon★

Camprodon is at the confluence of the Ritort and Ter rivers, crossed by a 12C humpbacked bridge, **Pont Nou**★. The community developed around the **Monestir Sant Pere.** Only the 12C **Romanesque church**★ remains.

Monasterio de Sant Joan de les Abadesses★★

Open Nov-Feb, 10am-2pm; Mar-Apr and Oct, 10am-2pm and 4-6pm (7pm May-Sep); Jul-Aug, 10am-7pm; Sat-Sun and public hols, 10am-2pm and 4-6pm (7pm, May-Aug). 2€. 972 72 23 53.

The monastery was founded in the 9C under the rule of a Benedictine abbess, though it soon shut out women.

With its arches and columns with carved capitals the church recalls those of southwest France. A magnificent 1251 **Descent from the Cross**★★ in polychrome wood is in the central apse. In 1426 an unbroken host was discovered on the Christ figure's head; it is venerated to this day.

Claustro★

These cloisters are simple and elegant, with sweeping arches and slender columns with capitals, decorated with plant motifs. The **museum** houses a collection of embroidered fabric.

Antiguo Palacio de la Abadía

Opposite the church on the square stands the 14C former Abbatial Palace. The **medieval bridge**★ spans the Ter river on the way towards Ripoll.

Vall de Ribes

Ripoll★

Antiguo Monasterio de Santa María★

All that remains of the original monastery are the church portal and the cloisters. In 1032, Abbot Oliba consecrated an enlarged **church**★, a jewel of early Romanesque art (*Open 9am-1pm and 3-8pm; cloisters: 10am-1pm and 3-7pm. Closed Mon, except summer. 2€. 972 70 02 43)* that was damaged over the years. It was rebuilt at the end of the 19C to the original plan.

The **portada**★★★, or portal design, is composed of a series of horizontal registers illustrating the glory of God victorious over His enemies (Passage of the Red Sea). The **Claustro**★ (cloisters) abutting the church dates to the 12C; others were added in the 14C.

Head N along the N 152.

Ribes de Freser

This famous spa stands at the confluence of three rivers and is known for the healing properties of its waters. A rack railway runs to the Vall de Núria.

Vall de Núria★

The valley is surrounded by a rocky amphitheatre stretching from Puigmal to the Sierra de Torreneules. The Virgin of Núria, the patron saint of Pyrenean shepherds, is venerated in a sanctuary located in the upper part of the valley.

Address Book

WHERE TO EAT

⊜ **Can Jan** – *Sant Roc 10 – Camprodon – ☎972 13 04 07 – Closed 1-15 Nov*. The overriding features of this centrally located restaurant are the friendly welcome and service, colourful wood decor and works by local artists on display. The menu includes typical dishes from the valley based on local products.

⊜ **Grau de l'Ós** – *Jaume II de Mallorca 5 – Bellver de Cerdanya – ☎ 973 51 00 46 – Closed last two weeks May, first two weeks Nov.* This village home has been carefully restored without losing its rustic feel. Despite its traditional bent, the menu occasionally comes up with original combinations such as liver with mango, or canneloni with mushrooms.

⊜⊜ **Els Puis** – *Avinguda Dr. Morelló 13 – Esterri d'Àneu – ☎973 62 61 60 – Closed Mon and in May.* A family-run restaurant on the outskirts of the village, popular with locals and tourists alike. The menu focuses on high-quality local specialities, the wine cellar is varied and the service attentive. Seven reasonably priced rooms also available.

⊜⊜ **Casa Perú** – *Sant Antoni 6 – Bagergue – 2km/1.2mi N of Salardú – ☎ 973 64 54 37 – Closed 1-15 Jul and Wed in winter.* For many, the Casa Perú is the perfect mountain restaurant; with its excellent location in a small village of stone houses, low ceilings, rustic tableware and deliciously flavoured cuisine. Make sure you try the *olla aranesa*, a local stew, as well as the wide selection of game dishes.

WHERE TO STAY

⊜ **Hotel Casa Peyró** – *Coll – 13km/8mi S of Caldes de Boí on the L 500 – ☎973 29 70 02 – casapeiro@terra.es – Closed May and Nov – 8 rooms – ☕ 10 € – Restaurant 30/60 €.* A pretty stone-built house that is A good choice for its location between Parque Nacional d'Aiguestortes, the Caldes de Boí spa and the ski slopes of Boí-Taüll.

⊜ **Hotel Roya** – *Mayor – Espot – ☎ 973 62 40 40 – www.hotelroya.net – Closed in Nov – 34 rooms – ☕ 5 € – Restaurant 13.50/30€.* Well located between the ski slopes and hiking paths and in the middle of the resort's shops. Comfortable, bright and attractive rooms, some with views of the charming local church. Reasonably priced given the quality and location.

⊜⊜ **Hotel Cal Teixido** – *Sol de Vila 33 – Estamariu – 4km/2.5mi E of La Seu d'Urgell on the N 260, then turn left – ☎ 973 36 01 21 – www.calteixido.com – Closed 8 Jan-15 Mar – ▤ – 14 rooms – ☕ – Restaurant 18/40 €.* This large chalet decorated with brick and wood has 11 bright, comfortable rooms. With its isolated location on the side of a hill, peace and quiet is guaranteed.

⊜⊜⊜ **Maristany** – *Avinguda Maristany 20 – Camprodon – ☎972 13 00 78 – www.hotelmaristany.com – Closed 11-31 Dec – P – 10 rooms – ☕ 9 € – Restaurant 40€.* On the outskirts of town, in a quiet and well-kept area. Rooms are modern and comfortable. The cosy restaurant is in an annex.

⊜⊜⊜ **Parador de Arties** – *Carretera de Baqueira – Arties – ☎973 64 08 01 – www.parador.es – P ♿ – 54 rooms – ☕ 12 € Restaurant 27 €.* This handsome building includes parts of the architectural legacy of the Portalà family, including a 16C tower and chapel. Its exterior combines wood, stone and slate, in perfect harmony with the Pyrenees all around.

SPORT

Skiing is the most popular sport in the Pirineos Catalanes. The region has numerous resorts, some with large hotels. The best known include La Molina, in Girona province, and Baqueira-Beret, popular with the Spanish royal family, in the Val d'Aran (Lleida). For information on skiing in Catalunya, contact the **Associació Catalana d'Estacions d'Esquí i Activitats de Muntanya** (ACEM), ☎93 416 01 94 or www.acem-cat.com

La Molina ski resort: ☎972 89 20 31 or www.lamolina.com

Baqueira-Beret ski resort: ☎973 64 44 55 or www.baqueira.es.

La Cerdanya★★ 2

From Vall de Núria to La Seu d'Urgell

72km/45mi – about 2hr 30min

The fertile Cerdanya Basin, watered by the River Segre, was formed by subsidence. The northern section, La Cerdagne, was ceded to France under the Treaty of the Pyrenees in 1659.

The **Túnel del Cadí**, opened in 1984, facilitates access from Manresa.

From Ribes de Freser to Puigcerdà, the road cut into the cliff face up to the Collado de Toses commands impressive **views**★ of the Segre and its slopes.

La Molina

This is one of Catalunya's most important ski resorts. The village of Alp is popular in winter and in summer.

The N 152 joins with the E 09, which rises and offers a sweeping view of the vast Cerdanya plain.

Puigcerdà

The capital of Cerdanya, which developed on a terrace overlooking the River Segre, is one of the most popular holiday resorts of the Pyrenees, with old-fashioned shops, ancient streets and balconied buildings.

Llívia

This 12km2/5sq mi Spanish enclave in France, 6km/4mi from Puigcerdà, results from an administrative subtlety. Under the Treaty of the Pyrenees, France was to be granted the Roussillon area as well as 33 villages from Cerdanya. Since Llívia was considered to be a town, it remained part of Spain.

Llívia features Europe's oldest chemist's shop, the **Farmacia de Llívia**★(*open 10am-4.30pm Oct-Mar (6pm Apr-Jun, 7pm Jul-Sep); Sun and public hols, 10am-2pm;* closed *Mon; 1 €; 972 89 63 13).*

Return to Puigcerdà and take the N 260 towards La Seu d'Urgell.

Bellver de Cerdanya★

Poised on a rocky crag dominating the Vall del Segre, Bellver de Cerdanya has a fine main square with beautiful balconied stone houses and wooden porches.

La Seu d'Urgell/Seo de Urgel★

This city of prince-archbishops stands where the Valira, which rises in Andorra, joins the Segre River.

Catedral de Santa Maria★★

Open 10am-1pm and 4-6pm; Sun and public hols, 11am-1pm. 3 € (with museum). 973 35 01 25.

The cathedral, started in the 12C, shows strong Lombard influence. The central section of the west face, crowned by a small campanile, is typically Italian

Inside, the nave rises on cruciform pillars, surrounded in French style by engaged columns. A most effective twin-arched gallery on the east transept wall reappears outside.

Santa Maria de Ripoll Monastery

Ripoll, A Centre of Learning in the Middle Ages

Ripoll owes its celebrity to the Benedictine monastery founded in the 9C by **Wilfred the Hairy**, Count of Barcelona. The monastery was the pantheon of the counts of Barcelona, Besalù and Cerdaña until the 12C.

The library at Ripoll was one of the richest in Christendom: not only did it possess texts of the scriptures and theological commentaries but also works by non-Christian authors such as Plutarch and Virgil as well as scientific treatises. The learning of Antiquity was restored by the Arabs, who treasured and disseminated the works of the Greeks which they discovered when they captured Alexandria and, with it, its incredible library. Ripoll, previously overrun by the Moors, became, under Abbot Oliba, a link between Arab and Christian civilisations, a centre of culture, ideas and exchange to which came such men as Brother Gerbert, the future Pope **Sylvester II** (999).

The **cloisters★** are 13C; the east gallery was rebuilt in 1603 and feature granite capitals illustrating humans and animals carved by masons from the Roussillon. The Santa Maria door (southeast corner) opens into the 11C **Iglesia de Sant Miquel★**, the only remaining building of those constructed by St Ermangol.

Museo Diocesano★

The Diocesan Museum has works of art dating from the 10C to the 18C. The most precious is a beautifully illuminated 11C **Beatus★★**, one of the best-preserved copies of St John's Commentary on the Apocalypse written in the 8C by the priest, Beatus of Liébana.

Of note also are an interesting **papyrus★** belonging to Pope Sylvester II. The crypt contains the 18C funerary urn of St Ermangol (*open 10am-1pm and 4-6pm; Sat-Sun and public hols, 11am-1pm; closed 1 and 6 Jan, Easter Mon and 25 Dec; 3 €; ☎973 35 32 42).*

Vall del Segre★ 3

From La Seu d'Urgell to Tremp

73km/45mi – allow 3hr

The River Segre forms a huge basin where it flows into the Valira.

Take the N 260 towards Organyà.

Garganta de Tresponts★★

The Segre winds through dark rocks (puzolana) and pastures. Downstream, the limestone of Ares and Montsec de Tost offers a typically Pyrenean landscape dropping to a cultivated basin, where the river disappears.

Coll de Nargó

This hamlet has one of the most splendid Romanesque churches in Catalunya,

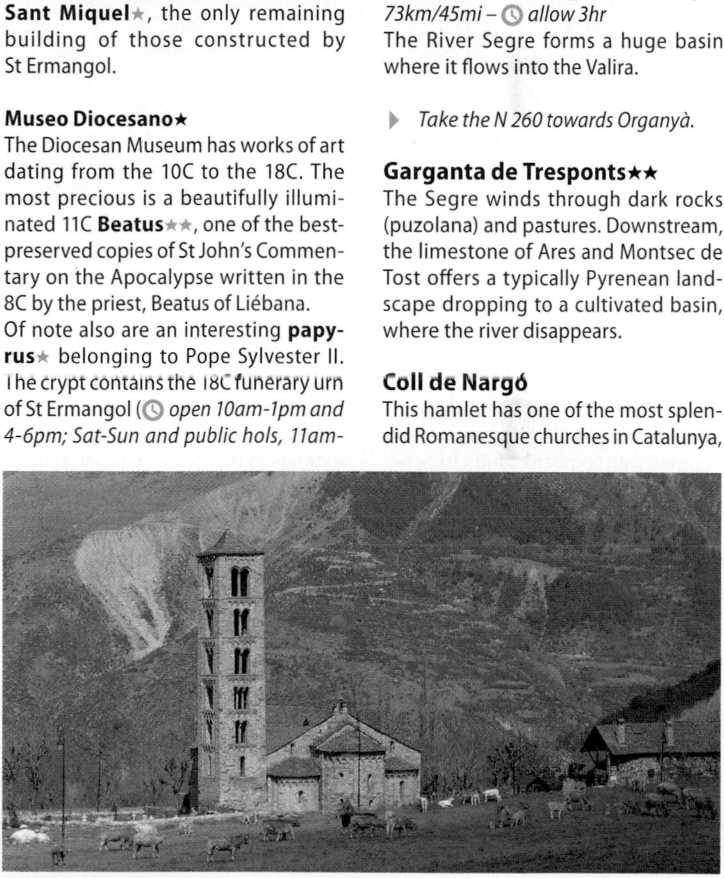

Patronat Comarcal de Turisme de L'Alta Ribagorça

Iglesia de Sant Climent

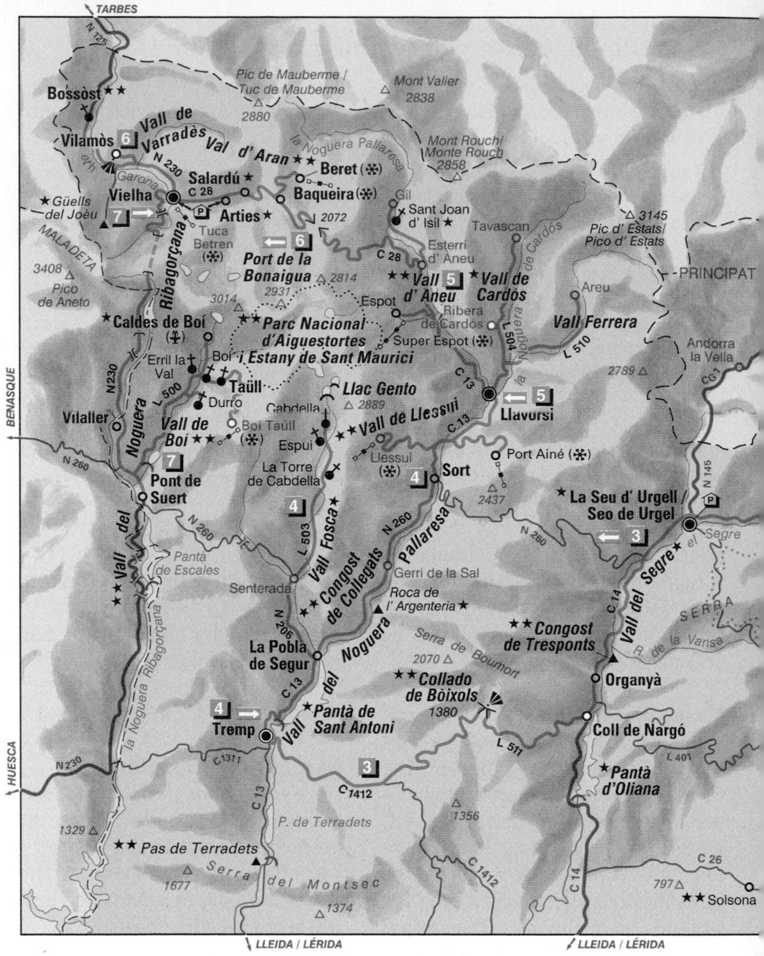

dating back to the 11C: **Sant Climent**★ has a single nave and a pretty apse adorned with Lombard bands. Its sober **bell tower**★ is pre-Romanesque.

Embalse de Oliana★

The dam is surrounded by grey rocks with lively waterfalls in spring. From the road the sight is quite spectacular.

Collado de Bòixols Road★★

Between the Coll de Nargó and Tremp, the L 511 follows canyons on slopes clad in pine and holm oak, or barren hillsides. Further on, the road proceeds up the slope, under yellow and pink crests, offering lovely **landscapes**, especially from the Collado de Bòixols.

Then the road enters a wide U-shaped valley, where terraced cultivation extends to the foot of the glacial ridge of Bòixols, to which cling the church and nearby houses. The road descends the valley until it eventually merges into the Conca de Tremp.

Vall del Noguera Pallaresa 4

From Tremp to Llavorsí

143km/89mi – allow one day

Pallars is in the uppermost region of the Catalan Pyrenees. The highest summit is Pica d'Estats (3 145m/10 318ft). To the north is **Pallars Sobirà**, at the heart of the Pyrenees; to the south, **Pallars Jussà** incorporates the vast pre-

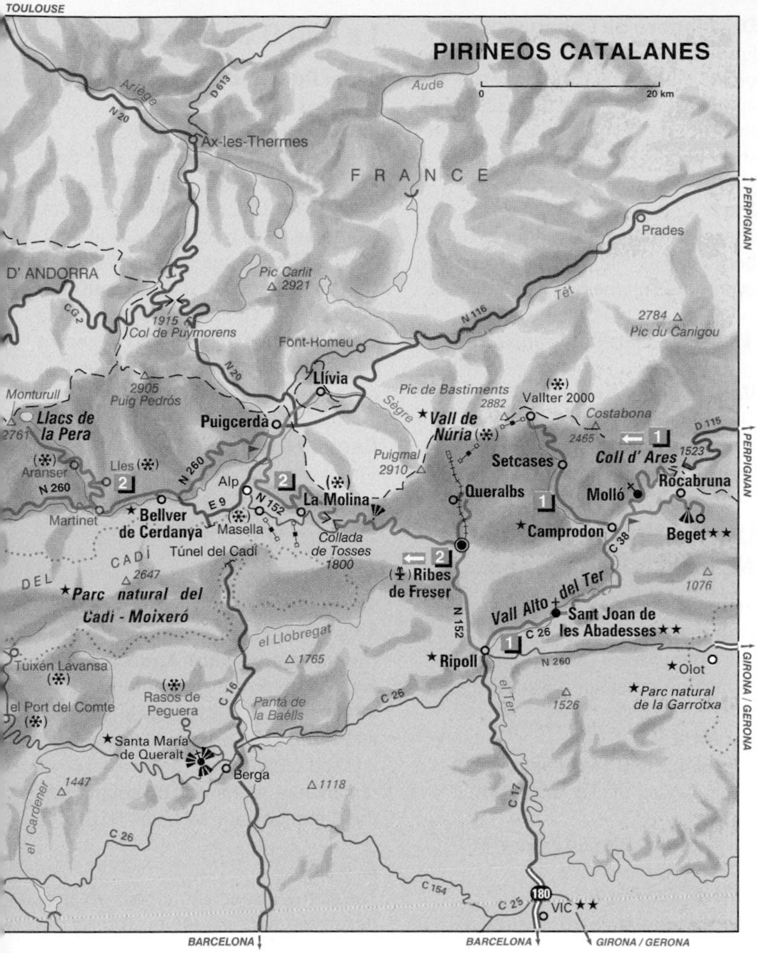

Pyrenean zone formed by Conca de Tremp. The road follows the bed of the Noguera Pallaresa, and after La Pobla de Segur, cuts across a limestone landscape of remarkable uniformity.

Tremp

In the centre of the Conca de Tremp – a huge basin with lush crops – the village retains its old quarter and three towers from its walls. The **Iglesia de Santa María**★ houses an astonishing 2m/6.5ft high Gothic statue in polychrome wood: **Santa María de Valldeflors**★ (14C). The municipality has a reservoir, the **pantano de Sant Antoni**★.

▶ *The C 13 follows the river course and spans the pantano de Sant Antoni.*

La Pobla de Segur

This popular resort is the only means of access to the Valle de Arán, Alta Ribagorça and Pallars Sobirà.

Vall Fosca★

Hemmed in by peaks, this valley is dotted with delightful hamlets, each with its Romanesque church: **Torre de Cabdella, Espui** and **Cabdella**. In the upper valley, in a large lake area; the main attraction is **lago Gento**.

▶ *Return to La Pobla de Segur and proceed upwards along the N 260.*

Desfiladero de Collegats★★
Eroded by torrents, the red, grey and ochre limestone rocks take on the appearance of spectacular cliffs. Note the **Roca de l'Argenteria**★, stalactite-shaped rocks near the Gerri de la Sal.

Sort
The resort is famous throughout Europe because of its wild waters and canoeing events held on the Noguera Pallaresa.

▶ *At Rialp, turn left towards Llessui.*

Vall de Llessui★★
The road winds way up to the north-west, through a steep granite landscape featuring a great many ravines.

Upper Valley of the Noguera Pallaresa★ 5

From Llavorsí to Puerto de la Bonaigua
▶ *105km/65mi – allow half a day*
Mountains dominate a wild landscape.

Llavorsí
The village is at the confluence of the Aneu, Cardós and Ferrera basins.

▶ *Take the L 504 and proceed N.*

Vall de Cardós★
The Noguera de Cardós is the axis of this valley.

▶ *Return to Llavorsí and take the C 13 towards Baqueira.*

Vall d'Aneu★★
Below is the valley of **Espot**, a picturesque village beside a mountain stream, gateway to the Pallars section of a **national park**★★ (*see Parc Nacional d'AIGÜESTORTES I ESTANY DE SANT MAURICI*).
Beyond Esterri d'Aneu the road crosses a breathtaking landscape, dotted with Romanesque churches such as the **Iglesia de Sant Joan d'Isil**★, glimpsed between summits, and twists up to **puerto de la Bonaigua** (2 072m/6 799ft), circled by many peaks.

La Vall D'arán★★ 6

From Puerto de la Bonaigua de Bòssost
45km/28mi – allow half a day
The **Arán Valley**, in the north-west tip of the Catalan Pyrenees, occupies the upper valley of the Garonne river. Its isolation has helped it to preserve its local traditions and language (*aranes* is a variation of the *langue d'oc* of southern France). The Vielha Tunnel ended the valley's seclusion in 1948. In recent years the region has seen the creation of several ski resorts.

Baqueira Beret
This ski resort, rising from 1 500m/4 900ft to 2 510m/8 230ft, offers excellent lodging and services.

Salardú★
Salardú is a charming village with granite and slate houses gathered around the **Iglesia de Sant Andreu**★ (12C-13C), whose interior contains some interesting 16C **Gothic paintings**★★ and a fine 12C **Christ in Majesty**★★, a stylised 65cm/25in wooden statue of remarkable anatomical precision. Note the slender octagonal belfry (15C).

Arties★
The Romanesque church has an apse decorated with scenes illustrating the Last Judgement, Heaven and Hell.

Escunhau
The **Iglesia de San Pedro**★ has a fine 12C **portal**★★ bearing an expressive Christ and unusual capitals decorated with human faces.

Betrén
The **Iglesia de San Esteve**★, built during the transition from Romanesque to Gothic, boasts archivolts on the **portal** ★★, decorated with human faces, alluding to the Last Judgement and the Resurrection.

Vielha
At an altitude of 971m/3 186ft, the capital of the Arán Valley is a holiday resort. Don't miss the 16C and 17C

homes in old town as well as the **Iglesia Parroquial de Sant Miquèu★** with its 14C octagonal tower and 13C Gothic doorway. Inside lies the **Cristo de Mijaran★**, a fragment dating from a 12C Descent from the Cross.

Bossòst

16km/10mi N of Vielha. The **Iglesia de la Purificació de Maria★★** is the area's best example of Romanesque architecture (12C). Its three naves are separated by sturdy columns. Its three apses are adorned with Lombard bands and the pretty, colourful north **doorway** features archaic relief work in its tympanum, depicting the Creator surrounded by the Sun, the Moon and symbols of the Evangelists.

Vall del Noguera Ribagorçana★★ 7

From Vielha to Caldes de Boí

54km/34mi – about 3hr

The Upper Ribagorça has summits over 3 000m/10 000ft, vast glacial cirques, pretty lake areas and steep valleys.The Vielha tunnel was constructed through the Maladeta massif in 1948.

Vilaller

Poised on an outcrop, the village is dominated by the octagonal belfry of its 18C Baroque church, Sant Climent.

El Pont de Suert

The area, dotted with attractive hamlets – **Castelló de Tor, Casòs, Malpàs** – retains its rusticity and charm.

Take the road up to Caldes de Boí.

Vall de Boí★★

Watered by the Noguera de Tor and the Sant Nicolau, this valley is renowned for its cluster of Lombard **Romanesque churches** (11C-12C), the finest in the Pyrenees. With slate roofs and irregular masonry, they stand out for their pure, sober lines and for the wall frescoes *(several reproductions remain)* now in the **Museu d'Art de Catalunya** *(see BARCELONA)*. Note the distinctive high silhouette of the belfries, separate but resting against the nave, and ornamentation of Lombard bands.

Beyond Erill la Vall turn right onto a narrow road leading to Boí.

Taüll★

This village is famous for the frescoes of its two churches. Considered to be masterpieces of Romanesque art, they are currently exhibited in Barcelona's Museu d'Art de Catalunya. The **Iglesia de Sant Climent★★**, just outside Taüll, was consecrated on 10 December 1123, only one day before Santa María *(see below)*. In the southeast corner of the sanctuary stands the slender six-storey belfry. A replica of the famous Pantocrator of Taüll can be seen in the apse (*open 10.30am-2pm and 4-7pm (8pm Jun-Sep); 1 €; 973 69 40 00).*

The village of labyrinthine streets, stone houses and wooden balconies clusters around the **Iglesia de Santa Maria★**, a Romanesque church with three naves separated by cylindrical pillars.

Return to the road to Caldes de Boí.

Parc Nacional d'Aigüestortes i Estany de Sant Maurici★★

Access by the road from Boí to Caldes de Boí *(Parc Nacional d'AIGÜESTORTES I ESTANY DE SANT MAURICI).*

Caldes de Boí★

At an altitude of 1 550m/5 084ft, Caldes de Boí is a thermal spa with 37 springs spurting out water at temperatures between 24ºC and 56ºC (75ºF to 133ºF). Nearby is **Boí-Taüll**, a ski resort.

PLASENCIA★

POPULATION: 36 826

MICHELIN MAP 576 L 11 – EXTREMADURA (CÁCERES).

In this tranquil provincial town are interesting Renaissance buildings such as the new cathedral. Between February and July migrating storks decorate rooftops and towers.

- **Information:** *Santa Clara 2, ☎927 42 38 43.*
- **Orient Yourself:** Placensia stands where the Sierra de Gredos meets the Extremadura plain.
- **Also See:** CÁCERES (85km/53mi SW), TRUJILLO (83km/52mi SE) and La ALBERCA (117km/73mi N).

Walking About

BARRIO VIEJO (OLD QUARTER)

Houses with wrought-iron balconies make up the neighbourhood.

Catedral★

The cathedral is in fact two buildings from different periods. A Romanesque-Gothic edifice was built in the 13C and 14C. At the end of the 15C, its east end was demolished for a new cathedral with a bolder design. Only the chancel and transept were completed. Enter by the north door which has rich Plateresque decoration. A door left of the *coro* opens into the **old cathedral** (parish church of Santa María). The cloisters have pointed arches and Romanesque capitals while the chapter house is covered by a fine dome. In the shortened nave is a museum of religious art.

Inside the **Catedral Nueva** (New Cathedral), the tall pillars and slender ribs illustrate the mastery of the famous architects: Juan de Java, Diego de Siloé and Alonso de Covarrubias.

The **altarpiece**★ is decorated with statues by the 17C sculptor Gregorio Fernández; the **choir stalls**★ were carved in 1520 by Rodrigo Alemán.

Start from plaza de la Catedral and leaving on your right the **Casa del Deán** (Deanery) with its unusual corner window, and the **Casa del Dr Trujillo**, now the Law Courts (Palacio de Justicia), make for the Gothic **Iglesia de San Nicolás**, a church which faces the beautiful façade of the **Casa de las Dos Torres** (House with Two Towers).

Continue to the **Palacio Mirabel**. This palace, flanked by a massive tower, contains a two-tiered patio and the Museo de Caza (Hunting Museum). A passage beneath the palace *(door on right-hand side)* leads to **calle Sancho Polo** and a quarter near the ramparts of stepped alleys, white-walled houses and washing hanging from the windows. Turn right for **plaza Mayor,** an asymmetrical square surrounded by porticoes.

Excursions

Monasterio de Yuste★

1.8km/1mi from Cuacos de Yuste. Guided tours (30min), 9.30am-12.30pm (11.50am Sun) and 3-6pm (6.30pm Apr-Oct). 2.50 €, no charge Wed morning. ☎927 17 21 30.

In 1556, a weary Emperor **Charles V** retired to this modest Hieronymite monastery in a serene setting.

The monastery, devastated during the War of Independence, is partially restored. Of Charles V's small palace one sees the dining hall, the royal bedroom adjoining the chapel, the Gothic church and, lastly, the two fine cloisters, one Gothic, the other Plateresque.

Coria

42km/26mi W. Take the N 630 S. After 7km/4.5mi turn right onto the EX 108.

This town overlooking the Alagón Valley retains Roman walls and gateways, rebuilt in the Middle Ages.

Catedral★
The Gothic cathedral, embellished with elegant Plateresque decoration in the 16C, is crowned with a Baroque tower and has a sculptured frieze. The tall, single aisle has vaulting adorned with lierne and tierceron ribs typical of the region. Note the 18C altarpiece and, in the coro, the wrought-iron grilles and the Gothic choir stalls.

PONTEVEDRA★

POPULATION: 75 148

MICHELIN MAP 571 E 4 – LOCAL MAP SEE RÍAS BAJAS

Quiet Pontevedra has a pleasant mix of fine buildings, plain arcades, cobbled streets, and attractive parks and gardens. Terrace cafés teem in summer, bars are a cosy retreat in winter.

- **Information:** *Gutiérrez Mellado 1 bajo, ☎986 85 08 14.*
- **Orient Yourself:** Pontevedra, near the northern coast, is linked by motorway with Vigo (27km/17mi S) and Santiago de Compostela (57km/35mi N).
- **Also See:** RÍAS BAJAS and SANTIAGO DE COMPOSTELA.

Special Features

Casco Antiguo★ (Old Quarter)

Allow 1hr 30min

The old quarter is tucked between calles Michelena, del Arzobispo Malvar and Cobián, and the river. Glass-covered passages and picturesque squares (**praza da Leña; do Teucro, da Pedreira**) are enchanting. There are endless places to stop for a drink and busy shopping streets such as **Sarmiento**.

Praza da Leña★

This is a delightful asymmetrical square surrounded by beautiful façades. Two 18C mansions on the square have been converted into a museum.

Museo Provincial

Open 10am-1.30pm and 4.30-8pm; Jun-Sep, 10am-2.15pm and 5-8.45pm; Sun and public hols, 11am-2pm. Closed Mon, 1 and 6 Jan and 25 Dec. 1.20 €, E.U. citizens no charge. ☎986 85 14 55.

The ground floor of the museum holds Bronze Age **Celtic treasures★** from A Golada and Caldas de Reis, and that of Foxados (2C and 1C BC), and a pre-1900 silverware collection with pieces from a number of countries. The first floor,

J. Malburet/MICHELIN

Plaza de la Leña

which is dedicated to paintings, has several 15C Aragonese Primitives.

The second mansion includes a reconstruction of a stateroom from a 19C Spanish frigate, the Numancia. On the upper floor are an interesting antique kitchen and 19C Sargadelos ceramics.

The museum encompasses the ruins of Santo Domingo and the Sarmiento building (ex-collegiate church of la Compañía de Jesús), beside the Iglesia de San Bartolomé.

Iglesia de Santa María la Mayor★

Open 10am-1pm and 6-9pm; Sat 10am 1pm; Sun 10-am-2pm and 7-9pm. No visits during services. ☎986 86 61 85.

Old alleyways and gardens surround this delightful 15C-16C Plateresque church. The **west front**★ is carved like an altarpiece, divided into separate superimposed registers on which are reliefs of the Dormition and Assumption of the Virgin and the Trinity. At the summit is the Crucifixion at the centre of an openwork coping finely carved with oarsmen and fishermen.

The **interior** mingles Gothic (notched arches), Isabelline (slender cabled columns) and Renaissance (ribbed vaulting) styles.

Touring Tip

CAFETERÍA CARABELA

This coffee house on the lively Plaça de la Ferrería, with its attractive view of both the Iglesia de San Francisco and the Capilla de la Peregrina, is a pleasant place for a drink or a bite to eat.

San Bartolomé

This 18C Baroque church has fine sculptures, some by Pedro de Mena.

San Francisco

The church's simple Gothic façade looks onto the gardens of praza da Ferrería. The interior features timber vaulting.

Capilla de la Peregrina (Pilgrim's Chapel)

Open 9am-2pm and 4-7pm. ☎986 85 13 75.

This small 18C church, with scallop-shaped floor plan and convex façade, contains a venerated statue of the patron saint of Pontevedra.

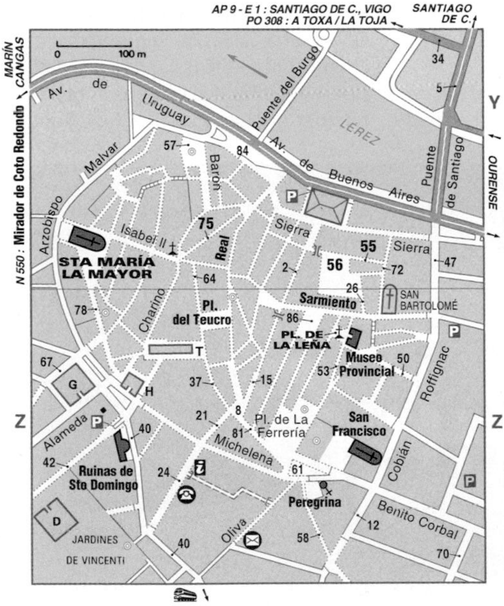

PONTEVEDRA

Benito Corbal	Z	
Buenos Aires Av. de	Y	
César Boente	Y	2
Compostela Av. de	Y	5
Curros Enríquez Pl. de	Z	8
Daniel de la Sota	Z	12
Don Gonzalo	Z	15
España Pl. de	Z	18
Fernández Villaverde	Z	21
General Gutiérrez Mellado	Z	24
Gregorio Fernández	YZ	26
Juan Manuel Pintos	Y	34
Manuel Quiroga	Z	37
Marqués de Riestra	Z	40
Michelena	Z	
Monte Rios Gran Vía de	Z	42
Oliva	Z	
Padre Amoedo Carballo	Y	47
Padre Luis María Fernández	Z	50
Pasantería	Z	53
Pedreira	Y	55
Pedreira Pl. de la	Y	56
Peirao Pl. do	Y	57
Peregrina	Z	58
Peregrina Pl.	Z	61
Princesa	YZ	64
Prudencio Landín Tobio	Z	67
Real	Y	
Sagasta	Z	70
San Bartolomé Arcos de	Y	72
San Nicolás	Y	75
Santa María Av. de	Z	78
Sarmiento	YZ	
Soportales de la Herrería	Z	81
Valentín García Escudero Pl.	Y	84
Verdura Pl. de la	Z	86

Ruinas de Santo Domingo (Santo Domingo Ruins)

Open 10.15am-1.30pm and 5-8.30pm; Oct-May, by arrangement. Closed Sat-Sun and public hols. ☎986 85 14 55.
These ruins are a perfect example of medieval romanticism. The Gothic east end is overgrown with ivy. Arranged inside, from the Museo de Pontevedra, are Roman steles, Galician coats of arms and tombs, in particular, tombs of craftsmen showing the tools they used, and tombs of noblemen.

Excursions

Mirador Coto Redondo★★

14km/9mi S on the N 550. Take the Vigo road; after 6km/4mi, turn right towards Lago Castiñeiras, climbing through pine and eucalyptus woods. The **panorama**★★ from this viewpoint extends over the Pontevedra and Vigo *rías*.

PRIEGO DE CÓRDOBA★★

POPULATION: 22 196
MICHELIN MAP 578 T 17 – ANDALUCÍA (CÓRDOBA).

This capital of Cordoban Baroque flourished with the silk industry in the 18C. Its fountains, churches and delightful old Moorish quarter, are a pleasant surprise in this isolated part of Andalucía.

- **Information:** *Real 46, ☎957 59 44 27; Río, 3, ☎957 70 06 25.*
- **Orient Yourself:** Priego is on a plain in the Subbética Cordobesa range, away from major road and rail links.
- **Also See:** JAÉN (67km/42mi NE), GRANADA (79km/49mi SE) and ANTEQUERA (85km/53m SW).

Worth a Visit

Fuentes del Rey y de la Salud★★ (Fountains of the King and of Health)

At the end of calle del Río. These fountains surprise the visitor. The older, the **Fuente de la Salud**, is a 16C Mannerist frontispiece. The lavish **Fuente del Rey** was completed at the beginning of the 19C. Its dimensions and rich design evoke Baroque palace gardens. 139 jets spout water from masks. The central display represents Neptune's chariot.

Barrio de la Villa★★

This charming quarter, dating back to Moorish times, has narrow, winding streets and flower-decked houses.

El Adarve★

This delightful viewpoint looks onto the Subbética range to the north.

Parroquia de la Asunción★ (Parish Church of the Assumption)

At the end of paseo del Abad Palomino. Visits by prior arrangement, 10.30am-1.30pm and 4-7pm; in summer, 11am 2pm and 5.30-8pm; no visits during religious services. Closed Sun afternoon and Mon. ☎606 17 16 53.
This 16C church was remodelled in Baroque style in the 18C. The presbytery is dominated by a carved and painted 16C Mannerist **altarpiece**.

El Sagrario★★

The chapel, which opens on to the Nave del Evangelio, is a masterpiece of Andalucían Baroque. An antechamber leads into an octagonal space. Light plays on the scene; intensified by white walls and ceiling, it shimmers over the extensive and lavish **yeserías**★★★ (plasterwork decoration), creating a magical atmosphere. In spite of excessive adornment, the effect is one of delicacy.

From the paseo del Abad Palomino view the remains of a Moorish **fortress**, modified in the 13C and 14C.
Priego has numerous churches: the charming Rococo-style **Iglesia de las Angustias**; the **Aurora**, with a fine portal; and **San Pedro**, adorned with interesting statues. Also noteworthy amid this Baroque splendour is the 16C **royal abattoir** (Carnicerías Reales), now an exhibition centre.

PUEBLA DE SANABRIA

POPULATION: 1 969

MICHELIN MAP 575 F 10 – CASTILLA Y LEÓN (ZAMORA).

Puebla de Sanabria is an attractive mountain village near the Portuguese border. The 15C castle of the Count of Benavente overlooks it white houses and late-12C church.

- **Information:** *Plaza Mayor, ☎980 62 00 02.*
- **Orient Yourself:** Puebla de Sanabria is along the A 52 motorway, close to the Embalse de Cernadilla (reservoir).
- **Also See:** ZAMORA (110km/69mi SE) and The WAY OF ST JAMES (to the N).

Worth a Visit

Valle de Sanabria

19km/12mi NW. Follow the lake road; turn right after 14km/9mi; after a further 6km/4mi turn left. This valley of glacial origin, now a nature reserve, was hollowed out at the foot of the Sierras de Cabrera Baja and Segundera. It is a delightful area, well-known for its hunting and fishing.

Lago de Sanabria

The largest glacial lake in Spain, at 1 028m/3 373ft, is used for water sports, and for salmon-trout fishing.

San Martín de Castañeda

There are attractive **views**★ of the rushing Tera and the mountain-encircled lake all the way to this Galician-looking village with an 11C Romanesque **church**.

RÍAS ALTAS★

MICHELIN MAP 571 A 5-7, B4-8, C 2-5, D 2 – GALICIA (LUGO, A CORUÑA/LA CORUÑA).

Although indented by *rías* – inlets of the Atlantic – the northern coast of Galicia is generally low-lying. Rocks and granite houses suggest a grim climate – yet holidaymakers arrive with the fine season for the scenery and sandy creeks. Galicia's *rías* are described below from east to west.

- **Information:** *Ferrol: Plaza Camilo José Cela, ☎981 31 11 79; Foz: Avenida de Lugo 1, ☎982 14 06 75; Viveiro: Avenida de Ramón Canosa, ☎982 56 08 79.*
- **Orient Yourself:** This series of inlets is in the far northwest corner of the Iberian Peninsula
- **Also See:** RÍAS BAJAS, A CORUÑA/La CORUÑA, COSTA VERDE and LUGO.

Special Features

Rías Altas

The Rías Altas are deep inlets backed by thick forests of pine and eucalyptus.

Ría de Ribadeo

(*See also under COSTA VERDE*). The ría de Ribadeo is the estuary of the Eo, which slackens its pace to wind gently between wide banks. There is a beauti-

Address Book

WHERE TO EAT

⊖ **O'Centolo** – *Bajada del Puerto – Fisterra – ☎981 74 04 52 – www.finisterrae.com – Closed 22 Dec-22 Jan.* This restaurant is justly popular for its excellent seafood. Choose the modern downstairs bar (with greenhouse) or upstairs dining area with fine views of the fishing port.

⊖⊖ **Hostal-Restaurante As Garzas** – *Porto Barizo 40 – Malpica de Bergantiños – 7km/4.5mi SW, towards Barizo – ☎ 981 72 17 65 – Closed Mon, Tue-Wed evenings, and Thu evening (except in summer and public holidays and eves)-* . As you would expect, the menu here is strongly influenced by the sea. The building, whitewashed and slate-roofed, has a glass-fronted dining room offering good views overlooking the sea. The rooms in the hotel are both pleasant and comfortable.

WHERE TO STAY

MODERATE

⊖⊖ **Pazo da Trave** – *Galdo – 3.5km/2mi S of Viveiro along the C 640 – ☎982 59 81 63 – P – 18 rooms – 7.21 € – Restaurant 31.25 €.* A stylish, tastefully furnished hotel in an old stone house with a garden dating back to the 15C. Inside, wood is the predominant theme, as witnessed in the flooring, exposed beams and furniture. Comfortable bedrooms and a good restaurant.

ful **view★** up the estuary from the bridge across the mouth of the river. The old port of **Ribadeo** is an important regional centre and summer resort.

Ría de Foz

Foz, at the mouth of its ría, is a small port with a fishing fleet. Its two good beaches are popular in summer.

Iglesia de San Martín de Mondoñedo

5km/3mi W. ▶ Take the Mondoñedo road, then immediately turn right. Open 11am-2pm and 4-8pm; in summer, 10am-1pm and 4-6pm by arrangement. ☎982 14 06 75 or 982 13 26 07.

Standing almost alone on a height, this archaic church was once part of a monastery and an episcopal seat until 1112. Unusually in this region, it shows no sign of Compostelan influence. The east end, with Lombard bands, is supported

TURESPAÑA

Costa de la Muerte

by massive buttresses; The transept **capitals★** are naively carved and rich in anecdotal detail: one shows a table overflowing with food while a dog licks the feet of a suffering Lazarus. The capitals, believed to date from the 10C, show Visigothic plant motifs.

Mondoñedo

23km/14mi SW along the N 634. Mondoñedo rises out of the hollow of a lush valley. Streets are lined with balconied white houses bearing coats of arms. The cathedral square is delightful with its arcades and solanas (glassed-in galleries). The immense façade of the **cathedral★** combines the Gothic grace of the three large portal arches and the rose window, all dating from the 13C, with the grandiose Baroque style of towers added in the 18C.

Late-14C frescoes decorate the interior, one above the other (below the extraordinary 1710 organ) illustrating the Massacre of the Innocents and the Life of St Peter. There are a Rococo retable at the high altar; and a polychrome wood statue of the Virgin in the south ambulatory, known as the English Virgin, as the statue was brought from St Paul's, London, in the 16C.

The classical **cloisters** were added in the 17C (*open 11am-1pm and 4-6.30pm; summer, 10am-1pm and 4-6.45pm; Sun and public hols 11am-noon and 5-7.30pm; 982 52 10 06).*

Ría de Viveiro

All **Viveiro** retains of its town walls is the Puerta de Carlos V (Charles V Gateway), emblazoned with the emperor's arms. In summer, the port is a holiday resort. On the 4th Sunday in August, visitors from all over Galicia come for the local Naseiro Romería festival.

Ría de Santa María de Ortigueira

The *ría* is deep and surrounded by green hills while **Ortigueira** port has quays bordered by well-kept gardens.

Ría de Cedeira

A small, deeply enclosed ría with beautiful beaches. The road gives good **views** of **Cedeira** (summer resort).

Ría de Ferrol

The *ría* forms a magnificent harbour entered by a channel guarded by two forts. In the 18C, **Ferrol** became (and remains) a naval base. The symmetry of the old quarter dates from the same period.

Betanzos★

Betanzos, a one-time port which has now silted up, stands on a hill at the end of a *ría*. Its old quarter retains three richly ornamented Gothic churches and old houses with glassed-in balconies.

Iglesia de Santa María del Azogue★

Open 10.30am-2pm and 4-7.30pm; no visits during religious services. 981 77 07 02.

The name of the 14C-15C church comes from *suk* (market-place in Arabic). The asymmetrical façade is given character by a projecting central bay pierced by a rose window and a portal with sculptured covings. Niches on either side contain archaic statues of the Virgin and the Archangel Gabriel. Three aisles of equal height, beneath a timber roof, create an effect of spaciousness.

Iglesia de San Francisco★

Open 9.30am-1pm and 4-7.30pm. 981 77 01 10.

This Franciscan monastery church, in the shape of a Latin Cross, with a graceful Gothic east end, was built in 1387 by the powerful Count Fernán Pérez de Andrade, Lord of Betanzos and Puentedeume. It is remarkable for the many tombs along its walls, the carved decoration on its ogives and chancel arches and the wild boar sculpted in the most unexpected places. Beneath the gallery to the left of the west door is the **monumental sepulchre★** of the founder, supported by a wild boar and a bear, his heraldic beasts. Scenes of the hunt adorn the sides of the tomb.

Iglesia de Santiago

The church, built in the 15C by the tailors' guild, stands on higher ground. Its interior resembles that of Santa María. Above the main door is a carving of St James Matamoros (Moorslayer) on horseback. The arcaded 16C **ayuntamiento** (town hall) is alongside.

Ría de La Coruña

(See A CORUÑA/La CORUÑA)

Costa de la Muerte (Coast of Death)

The coast between La Coruña and Cabo Finisterre is wild, harsh and majestic, whipped by storms, the graveyard of many a ship smashed against its rocks. Tucked in its more sheltered coves are fishing villages like **Malpica de Bergantiños**, protected by the Cabo de San Adrián (opposite the Islas Sisargas, with a bird sanctuary) or **Camariñas** famous for its bobbin-lace.

Cabo Finisterre or Fisterra★ (Cape Finisterre)

Corcubión★, near Cabo Finisterre, is an old harbour town of emblazoned houses with glassed-in balconies. The coast **road**★ to the cape looks down over the Bahía de Cabo Finisterre, a bay enclosed by three successive mountain chains. The lighthouse on the headland commands a fine **panorama**★ of the Atlantic and the bay.

RÍAS BAJAS★★

MICHELIN MAP 571 D 2-3, E 2-3, F 3-4 (TOWN PLAN OF VIGO) – GALICIA (A CORUÑA/LA CORUÑA, PONTEVEDRA).

The Rías Bajas, a coastline with deep inlets affording safe anchorages, is Galicia's most attractive region for holidaymakers, who enjoy beaches and resorts like those of A Toxa.

- **Information:** *Baiona: Paseo de Ribeira, ☎986 68 70 67; Vigo: Dánovas del Castillo 22, ☎986 43 05 77; Tui: Colón 2, ☎986 60 17 89*
- **Orient Yourself:** The Rías Bajas are four inlets: the ría de Muros y Noia; the ría de Arousa; the ría de Pontevedra; and the ría de Vigo, all along the northern coast.
- Kids **Especially for Kids:** AcquariumGalicia welcomes small marine explorers.
- **Also See:** RÍAS ALTAS, PONTEVEDRA and SANTIAGO DE COMPOSTELA.

Tours

Ría de Muros Y Noia★★ 1

From Muros to Ribeira

71km/44mi – about 1hr 15min

J. Malburet/MICHELIN

The port of Muros

Address Book

For coin ranges, see the Legend on the cover flap.

WHERE TO EAT

Tasca Típica – *Cantón 15 – Noia – ☎981 82 12 70.* This old stone building in the centre of Noia has been converted into a typical bar serving tapas and a good-value daily menu. In fine weather, customers can also eat on the terrace.

Posta do Sol – *Ribeira de Fefiñans 22 – Cambados – ☎986 54 22 85 – www.postadosol.com – Closed 15-31 Jan, 15-31 Feb and Wed (exc. Jul-Oct).* An attractive little restaurant in a one-time bar. The dining room, with fireplace, is decorated in regional style – the Camariñas lace curtains are lovely. The specialty is seafood. Also try the empanadas and house desserts.

Anduriña – *Rua do Porto 58 – A Guarda – ☎986 61 11 08 – www.restauranteandurinha.com – Closed 3-27 Nov –* . This unpretentious and well-known local restaurant has an excellent menu with creative touches, including reasonably priced fish.

Casa Ramallo – *Castro 5 – Rois – 4km/2.5mi N of Padrón on the AC 301 – ☎981 80 41 80 – Closed Mon and 24 Dec-7 Jan – – Reservation recommended.* This small, family-run hotel has an excellent reputation locally for its delicious home cooking, in particular its stews, meat dishes and seafood. Highly recommended.

La Oca – *Purificación Saavedra 8 (opposite Teis market) – Vigo – ☎986 37 12 55 – Closed Sat-Sun, Holy Week and 21 Jul-6 Aug – lunch only except Fri and holiday eves.* Don't be put off by the slightly out-of-the-way location or the neglected façade of this small family-run restaurant, as the food here is innovative and creative with notable French influences. A true pleasure for the palate!

WHERE TO STAY

Casa do Torno – *Lugar do Torno 1 – Noia – 1.1km/0.7mi S of Noia on the Boiro road. – ☎981 84 20 74 – www.crcasadotorno.com – 8 rooms – 4. 21 €.* A rural hotel in an unpretentious whitewashed village house with a garden at the rear. Cosy rooms with wood floors and antique furniture.The perfect base for a few days of relaxation.

Pazo de Hermida – *Trasmuro 21 – Lestrove – 1km/0.6mi SW of Padrón along the C 550. – ☎981 81 71 10 – Closed 21 Dec-7 Jan – – 6 rooms – 6 €.* This Galician manor house (*pazo*), built in the 17C above two former defensive towers, was for a short time home to the 19C poet Rosalía de Castro, who was undoubtedly attracted here by the tranquillity of the setting.

Hotel Convento de San Benito – *Plaza de San Benito – A Guarda – ☎ 986 61 11 66 – Closed Jan– 23 rooms – 6 €.* This former convent near the fishing port of A Guarda was founded in the 16C and originally housed an order of Benedictine nuns. A haven of peace and quiet with sober yet elegant rooms, and fine classical-style cloisters.

Hotel Pazo de Mendoza – *Elduayen 1 – Baiona – ☎986 38 50 14 – 11 rooms – 4.50 € – Restaurant 14/44 €.* A modern hotel built within the walls of an 18C house facing the sea in the centre of Baiona. The rooms are comfortable and well-furnished with attractive wood floors. The creative restaurant menu is based on local products.

The *ría* is delightfully wild, its low coastline strewn with rocks. The northern bank is wooded.

Muros is a seaside town with a harbour and local-style houses. **Noia** is notable for its square looking out to sea, upon which stands the Gothic **Iglesia de San Martín**★ with a magnificent carved portal and rose window.

Ría de Arousa 2

From Ribeira to A Toxa

115km/71mi – about 3hr

Ría de Arousa, at the mouth of the Ulla, is the largest and most indented inlet.

Ribeira

A large fishing port with vast warehouses.

Mirador de la Curota★★

10km/6mi from Puebla del Caramiñal. ▸ Take the LC 302 W towards Oleiros and after about 4km/2.5mi turn right onto a narrow road up to the viewpoint.

From a height of 498m/1 634ft there is a magnificent **panorama**★★ of the four inlets of the Rías Bajas. On a clear day the view extends from Cabo Finisterre to the River Miño.

Padrón

The legendary boat brought St James to this village. Its mooring stone *(pedrón)* can be seen beneath the altar in the **iglesia parroquial** (parish church) near the bridge. The town, renowned for its green peppers, was home to poet **Rosalía de Castro** (1837-85). Her house is a **museum** (*open 10am-1.30pm (2pm in summer) and 4-7pm (8pm in summer); Sun and public hols, 10am-1.30pm (2pm in summer); closed Mon, 1 and 6 Jan and 25 Dec; 1.40 €; ☎981 81 12 04).*

Vilagarcía de Arousa

A garden-bordered promenade overlooks the sea. The Convento de Vista Alegre, founded in 1648, on the outskirts, is an old pazo with square towers, coats of arms and pointed merlons.

Mirador de Lobeira★

4km/2.5mi S. ▸ Take a signposted forest track at Cornazo.

The view from the lookout takes in the whole *ría* and the hills inland.

Cambados★

The alleys of the old quarter are bordered by beautiful houses. At the northern entrance is the magnificent **plaza de Fefiñanes**★, lined on two sides by the emblazoned Fefiñanes *pazo*, on the third by a 17C church with lines harmonising with the *pazo*, and on the fourth by a row of arcaded houses. On the other side of the village are the romantic ruins of **Santa Mariña de Dozo**, a 12C parish church which is now a cemetery. Try the local white Albariño wine which has a light fruity flavour.

A Toxa★

A sick donkey abandoned on the island was the first creature to discover the health-giving properties of the spring

Origins

The *rías* are river valleys that have been invaded by the sea. In the case of the Galician coast, its formation is the result of tectonic movements which caused the collapse of the coastline and the advance of the sea.

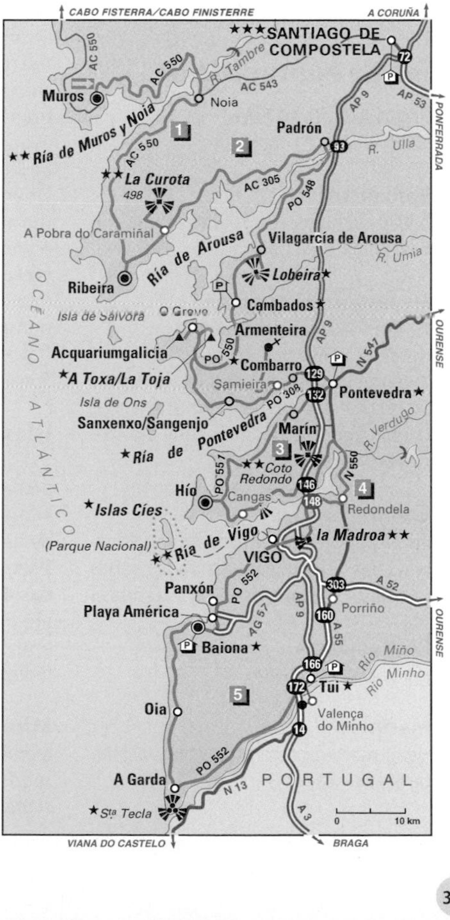

in A Toxa. The stream has run dry but the pine-covered island in a wonderful **setting**★★ remains the most elegant resort on the Galician coast, with luxury villas and an early 20C palace. A small church is covered in scallop shells.
The seaside resort and fishing harbour of **O Grove** on the other side of the causeway is renowned for its seafood.

Acquariumgalicia

Kids From O Grove head towards San Vicente and turn off at Reboredo. Open 10am-8pm (9pm Sat-Sun and public hols); 15 Oct-31 May, Fri-Sun and public hols 10am-8pm; other days by arrangement. 9 €, children 6 €. 986 73 15 15.
The only aquarium in Galicia, has over 150 species on display in 18 tanks. The complex also includes a marine farm where turbot and gilthead, are raised.
The **road**★ from A Toxa to Canelas affords views of sand dunes and rock-enclosed beaches like that of **La Lanzada.**

Ría de Pontevedra★ 3

From A Toxa to Hío

62km/39mi – about 3hr

Sanxenxo

A lively summer resort with one of the best climates in Galicia.

Monasterio de Armenteira

Visits by prior arrangement. 986 71 83 00.
In Samieira a small road leads to this Cistercian monastery, where a 12C church and 17C classical-style cloister can be visited.

Combarro★

This fishing village with winding alleyways has a good many Calvaries and is famed for its **hórreos**★ (drying sheds).

Pontevedra★

(See PONTEVEDRA)

Marín

Headquarters of the Escuela Naval Militar (naval academy).

Hío

The village at the tip of the Morrazo headland has a famous and intricately carved **Calvary**★.

Ría de Vigo★★ 4

From Hío to Baiona

70km/43mi – about 3hr
The Vigo inlet is deep and remarkably sheltered inland by hills and out to sea by islands, the Islas Cíes. By Domaio, where the steep, wooded banks draw together and the narrow channel is covered in mussel beds, it becomes really beautiful. From Cangas and Moaña you can see the white town of Vigo covering the entire hillside across the inlet.

Vigo

Vigo is Spain's principal transatlantic port and leading fishing port. Legend has it that treasure dating from the time of Philip V lies at the bottom of the inlet. Vigo's **setting**★ is outstanding: an amphitheatre on the south bank of the ría surrounded by parks and pinewoods. There are magnificent **views**★★ from El Castro hill. Berbés is the picturesque fishermen and sailors' quarter. Beside it is the unusual A Pedra market where fishwives sell oysters, served in the many bars nearby.
At Punta do Muiño, a place for splendid **views** of the *ría*, is the **Museo del Mar** (Maritime Museum), where the relationship of Vigo and the sea is explored (*open 11am-8pm (Fri-Sat to 11.30pm, Sun to 9pm); 3 €; 986 24 76 95).*

Islas Cíes★

By boat from Vigo. The beautiful archipelago of crystalline water and white sand guards the entrance to the ría de Vigo. The archipelago is a part of **Parque Nacional de las Islas Atlánticas de Galicia** (national park). There are three islands: Monteagudo, El Faro and San Martiño. The first two are linked via a beach, the playa de Rodas.

Mirador la Madroa★★

6km/4mi. Exit Vigo along the airport road. After 3.5km turn left, following signposts to the "parque zoológico" (zoo).

Getting to the Cíes Islands

From June to September, daily boat services operate from Cangas and Vigo (journey time: 30min). For information, call ☎*986 22 52 72*.

The esplanade commands a fine **view**★★ of Vigo and the *ría*.
The Alcabre, Samil and Canido beaches stretch down the coast south of Vigo.

Panxón

14km/9mi SW along the C 550. A seaside resort at the foot of Monte Ferro.

Playa América

A very popular, elegant resort in the curve of a bay.

Baiona/Bayona★

It was here, on 10 March 1493, that the caravel *Pinta* – one of the three vessels in Christopher Columbus's fleet – captained by **Martín Alonso Pinzón,** brought news of the New World.
Today, Baiona has grown into a lively summer resort with a harbour for fishing boats and pleasure craft fronted by a promenade of terrace cafés. In the old quarter houses may still be seen with coats of arms and glassed-in balconies. The **ex-colegiata** (former collegiate church) at the top of the town was built in a transitional Romanesque-Gothic style between the 12C and 14C. Chisels, axes and knives represent the various guilds that contributed to its construction (*open 11am-12.30pm and 4.30-6.30pm;* ☎*986 68 70 67).*

Monterreal

Open 10am-dusk. 0.60 €, 3 € vehicles. ☎*986 35 50 00.*
The Catholic Monarchs had a wall built around Monterreal promontory at the beginning of the 16C. The fort within has been converted into a parador, surrounded by a pleasant pinewood. A **walk round the battlements**★ *(about 30min)*, rising sheer above the rocks, affords splendid **views**★★ of the bay, Monte Ferro, the Estela islands and the coast stretching south to the cabo Silleiro headland.

The Road from Baiona to Tui★ 5 *58km/36mi*

The coast between Baiona and A Garda is flat and semi-deserted.

Oia

Houses in the fishing village cluster around the former Cistercian abbey of **Santa María la Real** with its Baroque façade. Festivals known as *curros*, during which foals are rounded up for branding, are held on certain Sundays in May and June.

A Guarda/La Guardia

This fishing village stands at the southern end of the Galician coastline. To the south, **Monte Santa Tecla**★ (341m/1 119ft) rises above the mouth of the Miño, affording fine **views**★★. (*Follow signs for Citania de Santa Trega.*) On the slopes are the extensive remains of a **Celtic city,** testimony to human habitation from the Bronze Age to the 3C AD.

From A Guarda, the PO 552 heads inland parallel to the Miño River.

Tui/Tuy★

Tui stands just across the border from Portugal in a striking **setting**★. Its old quarter, facing the Portuguese fortress of Valença, stretches down the rocky hillside. The **Parque de Santo Domingo** (Santo Domingo Park), in which stands a Gothic church of the same name, commands a good view of Tui and the Portuguese coast.
Since 1884, when a bridge was built by Gustave Eiffel across the Miño, Tui has served as a gateway to Portugal. The historic town is one of the oldest in Galicia; its emblazoned houses and narrow stepped alleys climbing towards the cathedral testify to its rich past.

LA RIOJA★

MICHELIN MAP 573 E 20-23, F 20-24 –
LA RIOJA, NAVARRA, PAÍS VASCO (ÁLAVA).

The Ebro Vally in La Rioja is carpeted with vineyards and vegetable fields under the peaks of the Sierra de Cantabria and Sierra de la Demanda. Towns and villages have a rich artistic heritage due to the proximity of the Way of St James.

- **Information:** *Logroño: Paseo del Príncipe de Vergara (Espolón), ☎941 26 06 65*; *Nájera: Constantino Garrán 8, ☎941 36 00 41; San Millán de la Cogolla: Monasterio de San Millán, ☎941 37 32 59; Santo Domingo de la Calzada: Mayor 74, ☎941 34 12 30*
- **Orient Yourself:** La Rioja (from Río Oja, a tributary of the Ebro) covers approximately 5 000km2/1 930sq mi in the provinces of La Rioja, Álava and Navarra.
- **Also See:** The WAY OF ST JAMES.

Background

Rioja Alta (Upper Rioja), to the west around Haro, is devoted to wine-growing while **Rioja Baja** (Lower Rioja), with **Logroño** and Calahorra as its main towns, is given over to the growing of early vegetables. La Rioja flourished thanks to its position on the pilgrim route to Santiago de Compostela, and later became famous for its wine.

Worth a Visit

Logroño

The capital of the Rioja region is on the banks of the Ebro. Pilgrims to Santiago de Compostela would have entered this pleasant town through the stone gateway, overlooking the cathedral.

Santa María la Redonda

Dating from 1435, the church has three naves, three polygonal apses and chapels in its side aisles. These include the Plateresque Chapel of Our Lady of Peace (Nuestra Señora de la Paz), founded in 1541 by Diego Ponce de León.

Museo de la Rioja

Closed for renovation. ☎941 29 12 59.
This regional museum is in a fine 18C Baroque palace.

Laguardia★

Hillside Laguardia is perhaps the most attractive town in Rioja Alavesa, with two imposing towers visible as you approach: San Juan to the south, and the 12C tower of the abbey to the north, once connected to the Gothic Iglesia de Santa María de los Reyes.

Iglesia de Santa María de los Reyes

Guided tours, 10am-2pm and 4-7pm (5-7 Sat); Sun and public hols, 10.45am-2pm. Closed 1 and 6 Jan, 24 and 29 Jun and 25 Dec. For information, contact the Tourist Office in Laguardia. 2 €. ☎941 60 08 45.
A superb late-14C **portal**★★ retains its 17C polychrome decoration. The tympanum is divided into three scenes relating the life of the Virgin. Note the figure of Christ holding a small child in his hands representing the soul of the Virgin.

Centro Temático del vino Villa Lucía (Villa Lucía Wine Centre)

On the way to Logroño.
Open 9am-2pm and 4.30-8pm. 5.50 €. ☎945 60 00 32.
The museum on this lovely estate traces the elaboration of wines.
The **panorama** from the **Balcón de Rioja**★★ or Rioja Balcony 12km/8mi northwest of Laguardia near the Puerto

> **TAPAS**
> The small **calle del Laurel** is without doubt one of the main attractions in Logroño with its huge choice of bars serving delicious local specialities (sweet peppers, mushrooms etc).

THE WINES OF LA RIOJA

Rioja is the only Spanish appellation with the Denominación de Origen Calificada (DOC) quality label. The wine is the result of over seven centuries of tradition and a superb position in the Ebro Valley between the Sierra de la Demanda and the Sierra de Cantabria. The wine region is traditionally divided into three sub-zones: Rioja Alavesa, Rioja Baja and Rioja Alta. Although seven grape varieties are permitted, the two most commonly used are Tempranillo and Grenache. Red wine accounts for 75% of production and is produced according to two different processes: **carbonic maceration** and **ageing**. The first produces young, fresh wines which are best consumed in the year of production, whereas the ageing process, in Bordeaux oak barrels, results in three different wines, classified according to the time spent in the barrel and the time which has elapsed between the harvest and the moment the wine leaves the cellars: **Crianza** (12 months in the barrel, one year in the bottle), **Reserva** (12 months in the barrel, two years in the bottle) and **Gran Reserva** (24 months in the barrel, three years in the bottle).

de Herrera (Herrera Pass, 1 100m/ 3 609ft), is extensive.

In Laguardia, Bodegas Ysios are the creation of Santiago Calatrava, who was inspired by the hoops of wine casks (*guided tours 11am and 1 and 4 pm; Sat-Sun by arrangement, 11am and 1pm; 945 60 06 40)*.

At El Ciego, Frank Gehry, of the Guggenheim, is responsible for the Herederos del Marqués de Riscal cellars, known as la Ciudad del Vino (City of Wine, *guided tours (1hr30min) by arrangement, Tue-Sat 10am, noon and 4pm; Sun and public hols 11am and 1pm; 6€. 945 60 60 23)*.

Haro

This centre is famous for its wines. Elegant 16C and 18C façades recall a prestigious past. In **plaza de la Paz** note the simple lines of the neo-Classical town hall (Ayuntamiento), built by Juan de Villanueva in 1769, and the Baroque tower of the **Iglesia de Santo Tomás**.

Museo del Vino de la Rioja

Open 10am-2pm and 4-8pm; Sun, 10am-2pm. Last admission 1hr before closing. Closed 1 and 6 Jan, 15 May, 25 and 29 Jun, 8 Sep and 25 and 31 Dec. 2 €, no charge Wed. 941 31 05 47.

This museum is entirely devoted to wine, from cultivation all the way through to the bottling process.

Museo de la Cultura del Vino – Dinastía Vivanco★

5km/3mi from Haro, in Briones (km 442 on the N 232). Guided tour by arrangement Oct-May 10am-6pm (8pm Fri-Sat); Jun-Sep 10am-8pm. Closed Mon and 25 Dec. 902 320 001.

This splendid museum covers the history and culture of wine and changing wine technology over 10 000 years.

Santo Domingo de la Calzada★

This staging post on the Way of St James, was founded in the 11C and owes its name to a hermit, Dominic, who built a bridge for pilgrims. Parts of the 14C ramparts can still be seen.

The **old town**★ huddles around the **plaza del Santo,** dominated by the cathedral and the ex-hospital, now a parador. The streets around the square, particularly the calle Mayor, retain 16C and 17C stone houses with fine doorways. The 18C Ayuntamiento (town hall) in nearby plaza de España, is crowned by an impressive escutcheon.

Catedral★

Open 9am1.30pm and 4-6.30pm. Closed Sun, in Jan and 12 May. 3 €. 941 34 00 33. Entrance via the 14C cloisters, housing the cathedral museum.

The church is Gothic, apart from the ambulatory and apsidal chapel which are Romanesque (second half of the 12C). The saint's tomb (13C), beneath a 1513 canopy, is in the south transept, and opposite is a sumptuous **Gothic**

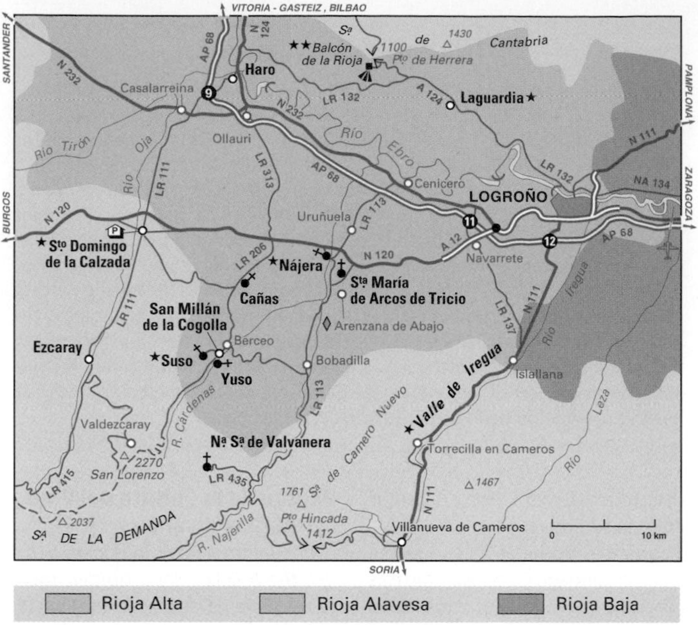

cage. This contains a live white cock and hen in memory of a miracle attributed to the saint – a cock about to be eaten sprang up and proclaimed the innocence of a convicted thief.

The **retable**★★ at the high altar (1538) is an unfinished work by Damián Forment. The cathedral also contains the **Capilla de la Magdalena**★ (Evangelist's nave) with fine Plateresque decoration and magnificent screen.

Abadía de Cañas

Open 1030am (11am Sun)-1.30pm and 4-6pm; in summer, 10am-1.30pm and 4-7pm; Sun, 11am-1.30pm and 4-7pm. Closed Sun during Eucharist (10am). 3 €. 941 37 90 83.

This monastery has been inhabited by Cistercian monks since 1170. The 16C church and chapter house are extraordinary examples of the purity and simplicity of Cistercian art.

Ezcaray

This delightful village close to Logroño is a summer resort and ski area. It has houses with stone and wood porticoes, mansions and the church of **Santa María la Mayor** as well as a former tapestry factory founded by Charles III in 1752.

Nájera

Reconquered by Sancho Garcés I in 920, Nájera was Navarra's capital until 1076.

Monasterio de Santa María la Real★

Open 10am-1pm and 4-6pm; Apr-Oct, 9.30am-1.30pm and 4-7.30pm; Sun and public hols, 10am-1pm and 4-7pm; last admission 30min before closing. Closed Mon (except in summer), 1 and 6 Jan, 17 Sep and 24-25 and 31 Dec. 2 €. 941 36 36 50.

The monastery was founded by Don García III, King of Navarra, in 1032, where he stumbled upon a statue of the Virgin. The bays in the lower galleries of the **cloisters**★ are filled with Plateresque stone tracery (1520).

Beneath the gallery of the **church**★, is the **Panteón Real**★ (Royal Pantheon) of princes of Navarra, León and Castilla of the 11C and 12C.

Basílica de Santa María de Arcos de Tricio

3km/2mi SW of Nájera. Guided tours (15-20min), in summer, 10.30am-1.30pm and 4.30-7.30pm; Sat-Sun and public hols, 10.30am-2.30pm; in winter, Sat-Sun and public hols only, 10.30am-1.30pm and 4.30-7.30pm. 636 82 05 89.

Address Book

For coin ranges, see the Legend on the cover flap.

WHERE TO EAT

Marixa – *Sancho Abarca 8 – Laguardia – ☎941 60 01 65 – www.hotelmarixa.com* – . Popular and known for traditional cooking. Good views from the dining room, plus perfectly adequate rooms available if you are planning to stay in Laguardia. *(22 rooms. 50/100€)*

WHERE TO STAY

Hotel Echaurren – *Héroes del Alcázar 2 – Ezcaray – ☎941 35 40 47 – www.echaurren.com – Closed 3 weeks in Nov – 25 rooms – 7€ – Restaurant 27/39€.* Standing opposite the church of Santa María la Mayor, this hotel is better known for its cuisine, with a choice of two menus (one traditional, the other more creative). Despite the emphasis on the food, the hotel's bedrooms are pleasantly comfortable.

Parador de Santo Domingo de la Calzada – *Plaza del Santo 3 – Santo Domingo de la Calzada – ☎941 34 03 00 – www.parador.es – – 59 rooms – 9.40€ – Restaurant 23.40€.* This state-run parador, superbly located in front of the cathedral, is housed in a former pilgrims' hospital along the Way of St James. The hotel's best feature is undoubtedly the main lounge, with its Gothic-style stone walls and arches.

This unusual church, with basilical plan, was built in the 5C above a Roman mausoleum. Thick tambours of the Roman columns support Baroque vaults.

San Millán de la Cogolla

The most attractive approach is via the turn-off from the LR 113 at Bobadilla. A World Heritage Site, San Millán de la Cogolla was already famous in the 5C when Millán or Emilian de Berceo and his followers settled as hermits. The first manuscripts in Castilian Spanish, the *Glosas Emilianenses*, were written at San Millán.

Monasterio de Suso★

Open 10am-1.30pm and 4-6.30pm (7.30pm spring-summer). Closed Mon. Housed in a Mozarabic building partly hallowed out of the rock, the monastery overlooks the Monasterio de Yuso and the Cárdenas Valley.

Monasterio de Yuso

Guided tours (50min) 10am-1pm (1.30 Tue) and 4-6pm; May-23 Sep 10.30am-1.30pm and 4-6.30pm. Closed Mon, 8-23 Jan, 9 Jun and 18 Aug. 3.50€ ☎941 37 30 49.

In the treasury are splendid **ivories**★★ from two 11C reliquaries.

Monasterio de Nuestra Señora de Valvanera

Access via the LR 113. This monastery is in a delightful, isolated wooded mountain **setting**★★. The church houses a statue of the patron saint of La Rioja, the Virgen of Valvanera, dating from the 12C. A hostel for pilgrims is also here *(☎ 941 37 70 44).*

Valle del Iregua★

50km/31mi S of Logroño on the N 111. Near Islallana, appear the **rock faces**★ of the Sierra de Cameros, overlooking the Iregua Valley from more than 500m/1 640ft. In the village of **Villanueva de Cameros**, half-timbered houses are roofed with circular tiles.

Shopping

It is well worth visiting the Hijos de Cecilio Valgañón *(Calle González Gallarza, 10, Ezcaray)*, a shop which perpetuates the local tradition of fabrics and blankets. *Open 9am-1pm and 3-7pm; Sat-Sun and public hols, 10.30am-2pm; Sat afternoon, 4.30-7.30pm. ☎941 35 40 34.*

RONDA★★

POPULATION: 35 788
MICHELIN MAP 578 V 14 – ANDALUCÍA (MÁLAGA).

Ronda stands above a deep ravine. Its isolation and legends of local highwaymen made it a place of pilgrimage for Romantic writers during the 19C. It retains cobbled streets, whitewashed houses and impressive mansions.

- **Information:** *Ronda: Plaza de España 9, ☎95 287 12 72; Paseo Blas Infante, ☎95 218 71 19; Arcos de la Frontera: Plaza del Cabildo, ☎956 70 22 64, plaza de San Sebastián 7, ☎952 70 25 05*
- **Orient Yourself:** Ronda lies in SE Spain, 60km/37mi inland and over the mountains from Marbella.
- **Also See:** Costa del SOL, MÁLAGA (96km/60mi SE) and ANTEQUERA (94km/59mi NE).

Walking About

The River Guadalevín divides Ronda into two parts, connected by the 18C Puente Nuevo, offering a **view**★ of the El Tajo ravine: to the south, the **Ciudad**, the old quarter; and, to the north, the **Mercadillo**, the old market area. The Camino de los Molinos road provides views of cliffs and the **Tajo**★.

LA CIUDAD★★

Tour: 2hr. Depart from Puente Nuevo.
The old walled town, a vestige of Moorish occupation until 1485, is a picturesque quarter of alleys and whitewashed houses with wrought-iron balconies.

Cross the bridge and follow calle Santo Domingo.

Casa del Rey Moro

This 18C building was erected in neo-Mudéjar style (*see Worth a Visit*).

Palacio del Marqués de Salvatierra

This small mansion is graced with an exceptional Renaissance **portal**★★ and a wrought-iron balcony decorated with pre-Columbian-inspired statues.

From the Arco de Felipe V, by the Puente Viejo, a stone path leads to the Baños Árabes.

Baños Árabes★

Open 10am-6pm (7pm in summer); Sat-Sun and public hols 10am-3pm. Closed Mon 1 Jan and 24 Dec. 2 €. *☎95 218 71 19 or 656 95 09 37.*
Built at the end of the 13C in the artisans' and tanners' district, the Moorish baths comprise three rooms topped with barrel vaults and illuminated by star-shaped lunettes.

Follow a stone staircase parallel to the walls, then pass through a 13C gateway, the Puerta de la Acijara.

Ronda – The Cradle of Bullfighting

Ronda is indelibly linked with the world of bullfighting. **Francisco Romero**, who was born here in 1695, laid down the rules of bullfighting, which until then had been only a display of audacity and agility. He became the father of modern bullfighting by his introduction of the cape and the **muleta**. His son Juan introduced the *cuadrillo* or supporting team and his grandson, **Pedro Romero** (1754-1839), became one of Spain's greatest bullfighters. He founded the **Ronda School**, known still for its classicism, strict observance of the rules and *estocada a recibir*.

Address Book

For coin ranges, see the Legend on the cover flap.

WHERE TO EAT

Doña Pepa – *Plaza del Socorro 10 - Ronda – ☎952 87 47 77 – www.dpepa.com – Closed evenings 24 and 31 Dec – – Reservation recommended.* Try the best of Ronda cooking, such as *rabo de toro* (bull's tail), In a house with all the charm and style of Andalucia. The set menu is reasonably priced.

Tragabuches – *José Aparicio 1 – ☎95 219 02 91 – www.tragabuches.com – Closed Sun evening, Mon and second half of January – .* This restaurant, considered by many locals to be the best in Ronda, is just a stone's throw from the parador and the bullring. Its kitchen offers guests modern cuisine in an avant-garde setting. Reservation recommended.

WHERE TO STAY

Hotel San Gabriel – *Marqués de Moctezuma 19 – ☎95 219 03 92 – www.hotelsangabriel.com – Closed 21 Dec-7 Jan and 21-31 Jul – – 16 rooms – 6.50€.* A delightful, magnificently decorated mansion dating from 1736. Some of the rooms look onto a charming patio. The hotel prides itself on its friendliness and attention to detail.

Minarete de San Sebastián★

This graceful minaret is the only one remaining from a 14C Nasrid mosque. A horseshoe arch frames the door.

Santa María la Mayor★

Open 10am-6pm). 2 €. ☎95 287 22 46.

The Collegiate Church of St Mary was built over the town's main mosque. Today, only a 13C horseshoe arch, decorated with *atauriques* and calligraphic motifs, and a minaret remain from the original building. The interior is divided into three distinct architectural styles: Gothic (aisles); Plateresque (high altar); and Baroque (choir stalls). On the exterior, note the double balcony used as a tribune by local dignitaries.

Continue along calle Manuel Montero.

Palacio de Mondragón

Two Mudéjar towers crown the Renaissance façade of the palace, now the **Museo de la Ciudad** (*see below*).

Worth a Visit

Museo de la Ciudad★★

Open 10am-7.30pm (6pm Nov-Mar); Sat-Sun and public hols, 10am-3pm. Closed 1 Jan, Good Friday and 25 Dec. 2 €. ☎952 87 84 50.

The charming **Mudéjar patio**★★ has the remains of *azulejos* and stuccowork between its arches. The collection includes an exhibition on the natural habitats of the Serranía de Ronda, and historical and ethnographic sections.

Plaza de Toros: Museo Taurino★

Open in winter, 10am-6pm (7pm spring and autumn; 8pm summer). 5 €. ☎ 95 287 15 39.

Dating from 1785 and with a capacity for 6 000, this is one of Spain's oldest and most beautiful bullrings. Enter through an elegant gateway. Traditional *Corridas Goyescas*, fights in period costumes, are held annually. The museum contains sumptuous costumes and mementoes of Ronda matadors.

Casa del Rey Moro

Open 10am-7pm (8pm spring and summer). 4 €. ☎95 218 72 00.

Inside are impressive Moorish steps, known as **La Mina,** which descend to the river. The **gardens**★ were laid out in 1912 by French landscapist **Jean-Claude Forestier,** who also designed María Luisa Park in Sevilla.

Museo del Bandolero

Open 10.15am-6.30pm (8pm summer). 2.70 €. ☎95 287 77 85.

The Serranía de Ronda range was once frequented by bandits, brigands and outlaws. This museum provides insight into these legendary figures.

Templete de la Virgen de los Dolores★ (1734)

Excursions

Iglesia Rupestre de la Virgen de la Cabeza★

2.7km/1.7mi along the A 369 towards Algeciras. Open 10.30am-2pm. Closed Sun, 1 Jan and 24 Dec. 2 €. 952 18 71 19 or 649 36 57 72.

This 9C Mozarabic monastery was excavated out of rock. The frescoes in the church were painted in the 18C. The **views★★** of Ronda are impressive.

Ruinas de Acinipo

19km/11.5mi along the A 376 towards Sevilla. Open 9am-3pm (2pm Sun and public hols). Call to confirm hours. Closed Mon, Tue, 1 Jan and 24 Dec. 952 18 71 19.

Known as Ronda la Vieja, the ruins of Acinipo retain a 1C AD theatre, with part of the stage and terraces.

Cueva de la Pileta★

20km/12mi SW. Take the A 376 towards Sevilla, then the MA 555 towards Benaoján. Bear onto the MA 561. Guided tours (1hr), 10am-1pm and 4-5pm (6pm in summer). Closed 1 Jan and 24 Dec. 6.50 €. 95 216 73 43.

The cave has over 2km/1.2mi of galleries. Red and black wall paintings predate those of Altamira, with figurative motifs from the Palaeolithic era (20 000 BC) and symbolic art and Neolithic animal drawings (goats, panthers etc, 4 000 BC).

Ronda to san pedro de alcántara by road★★

49km/30mi SE on the C 339 – about 1hr.

For 20km/12mi the road crosses a bare mountain landscape; it then climbs steeply into a **corniche★★** above the Guadalmedina valley. The route is deserted, there's not a single village.

Ronda toAlgeciras by road★

118km/73mi SW on the C 341, C 3331 and A 7 – about 3hr.

The road climbs to overlook the Genal valley, then winds around the foot of **Jimena de la Frontera** perched on a hill and crosses the **Parque Natural de los Alcornocales★,** one of the largest forests of cork oaks in Spain. After 22km/14mi, a narrow road leads (*right*) to **Castellar de la Frontera★**, a village of flower-filled alleyways huddled within the castle grounds.

Pueblos Blancos★★ (white towns of Andalucía)

To the west of Ronda, in often weirdly shaped mountains, are the remains of

R. Mattès/MICHELIN

Puente Nuevo and the ravine (El Tajo), Ronda

the *pinsapos* forest of pines dating from the beginning of the Quaternary Era. The beauty of the countryside is set off by delightful white villages *(pueblos blancos)*, often perched on rocky crags or stretched along escarpments, their whitewashed houses dominated by a ruined castle or a church.

From Ronda to Arcos de la Frontera

By the northern route; 130km/81mi – about 4hr. Take the MA 428 towards Arriate, then continue on the CA 4211.

Setenil★

In this unique village, in the gorge of the Guadalporcún river, are a number of troglodyte dwellings built into the rock. Also of interest are the **tourist office**, in an impressive building with a handsome 16C **artesonado ceiling**, the keep (torre del homenaje), and the Iglesia de la Encarnación.

Olvera

Olvera enjoys an impressive hillside **site**★★ amid olive groves, crowned by the keep of its triangular-shaped **castle** and the Iglesia de la Encarnación. Olvera is renowned for its superb olive oil *(open 10.30am-2pm and 4-6.30pm (7pm 1 Mar-1 Nov); Closed Mon; 2€ (museum and castle); 956 12 08 16, Tourist Office).*

Take the A 382 towards Algodonales; turn off to the right onto the CA 531.

Zahara de la Sierra★

The village enjoys an extraordinary hilltop **setting**★★. Zahara was a defensive enclave for the Nasrids, and later for Christians. The outlines of the 12C **castle** and the 18C Baroque **Iglesia de Santa María de Mesa** stand out.

Return to the A 382 and continue towards Villamartín.

RONDA		
Carmen Abela Pl. de	Y	5
Doctor Fleming Av.	Y	6
Duquesa de Parcent Pl. de la	Z	8
España Pl. de	Y	12
Espinel Carrera de	Y	
Gigante Pl. del	Y	14
González Campos	Z	15
Imágenes Cuesta de làs	Z	18
Juan José de Puya	Y	3
María Auxiliadora Pl.	Z	2
Marqués de Salvatierra	Z	21
Merced Pl. de la	Y	24
Padre Mariano Soubirón	Y	26
Poeta Abul-Beca Pl.	Z	27
Ruedo Gameros	Z	29
Santa Cecilia	Y	30
Santo Domingo	Y	33
Sor Ángela	Z	34
Virgen de la Paz	Y	36

Casa del Rey Moro	Y	A
Convento de Santo Domingo	Y	B
Fuente de los ocho caños	Y	E
Minarete de San Sebastián	Z	F
Museo Lara	Y	M²
Museo del Bandolero	Z	M¹
Palacio de Mondragón: Museo de la Ciudad	Z	M⁴
Palacio del Marqués de Salvatierra	Y	N
Plaza de toros : Museo taurino	Y	M⁶
Puerta de Almocabar	Z	R
Templete de la Virgen de los Dolores	Y	V

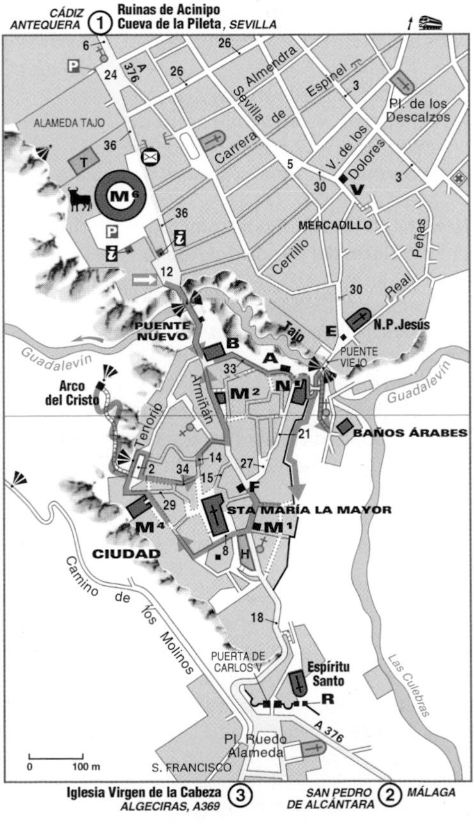

Villamartín
The **Alberite dolmen**, dating from around 4 000 BC, can be visited 4km/2.5mi to the south. A 20m/65ft gallery is formed by large stone slabs.

Bornos
The plaza del Ayuntamiento is fronted by the **Castillo-Palacio de los Ribera**★, now the tourist office. Inside are a Renaissance-style **patio** and a 16C garden. Also on the square is the **Iglesia de Santo Domingo**, a Gothic church built in the late 15C.

Espera
10km/6mi NW of Bornos on the CA 402.
This village on a small outcrop is dominated by the ruins of a Moorish castle, the **Castillo de Fatetar**.

Arcos de la Frontera★★
Arcos has a remarkable **site**★★ atop a crag enclosed by a loop in the Guadalete river. The old town huddles against formidable crenellated castle walls and those of the two churches.

Park below the village in plaza de Andalucía. Ascend the cuesta de Belén, a hill which connects modern Arcos with the medieval town.

Note the 15C Gothic-Mudéjar **façade**★ of the **Palacio del Conde del Águila.**

▶ *Continue to the right along calle Nueva to plaza del Cabildo.*

Plaza del Cabildo
Overhanging the precipice, one side of the plaza boasts a **view**★ that extends to a meander of the Guadalete. On the plaza are the town hall *(ayuntamiento)*, parador (a former palace), and the castle (closed to visitors).

Iglesia de Santa María★
Open 10am-1pm and 4-7pm; Sat, 10am-2pm. Closed Sun and public hols. 1.50€. ☎956 70 00 06.
This church was built around 1530. The **west façade**★ is Plateresque. Don't miss the 17C **altarpiece** of the Ascension of the Virgin.
A charming maze of alleys leads to the other side of the cliff, where the Capilla de la Misericordia, the Palacio del Mayorazgo (now a music conservatory) and the **Iglesia de San Pedro** can be seen.

Iglesia de San Pedro
This church dates from the early 15C and boasts a façade crowned by an impressive neo-Classical bell tower.

From Arcos de la Frontera to Ronda
By the southern route; 102km/63mi – about 3hr
Leave Arcos along the A 372 towards **El Bosque**. The Parque Natural Sierra de Grazalema visitor centre is here.

▶ *Leave El Bosque on the A 373.*

Ubrique
The **road**★ enters the heart of the Sierra de Grazalema. Beyond the **plaza del Ayuntamiento**, is the 18C parish church of **Nuestra Señora de la O**.

▶ *From Ubrique, continue 10km/6mi E along the A 374.*

Villaluenga del Rosario
This village is the highest in Cádiz province. Its irregularly shaped **bullring** *(plaza de toros)* is built on top of a rock.

▶ *Head 15km/9.5mi NE on the A 374.*

Grazalema★★
Grazalema, one of Andalucía's most charming villages, is the wettest place in the whole of Spain. It retains its Moorish layout, as well as the tower of the **Iglesia de San Juan**. The 18C **Iglesia de la Aurora** is adorned with an unusual fountain. Grazalema is famous for its white and brown woollen blankets; a traditional **hand loom** operates at the entrance to the town.

▶ *Return to Ronda on the A 372.*

SALAMANCA★★★

POPULATION: 186 322
MICHELIN MAPS 575 AND 576 J 12-13 –
CASTILLA Y LEÓN (SALAMANCA).

Salamanca reminds you of its past, through its venerable university, narrow streets, and splendid buildings of golden stone. Blessed with perhaps the most magnificent main square in Spain, Salamanca has long been a favoured destination for foreign students and visitors alike.

- **Information:** *Rúa Mayor 70 (Casa de las Conchas), ☎923 26 85 71; Plaza Mayor 14, ☎923 21 83 42.*
- **Orient Yourself:** Salamanca is in western Castilla y León region, accessible from Ávila (98km/61mi SE on the N 501), Valladolid (115km/72mi NE on the A 62) and Zamora (62km/39mi N on the N 630). It's an excellent base from which to explore the Sierra de la Peña de Francia.
- **Don't Miss:** The University and main square.
- **Also See:** CIUDAD RODRIGO (89km/55mi SW), ZAMORA (62km/39mi N) and La ALBERCA (94km/59mi S).

Background

A tumultuous past – Salamanca flourished under the Romans who built the **Puente Romano** (Roman bridge). Alfonso VI took the city from the Moors in 1085. In 1218, Alfonso IX established a centre for study, later to become an important university. In 1520, Salamanca rose against the royal authority of Emperor Charles V *(see SEGOVIA)*. In the 16C it reached its artistic and intellectual zenith.

Los Bandos – During the 15C, rivalry between noble factions *(bandos)* saw the city's streets bathed in blood. The *bandos* remained active until 1476.

The university was founded in 1218 and grew under the patronage of kings of Castilla and high dignitaries. Its great and famous members include the Infante Don Juan; St John of the Cross and his teacher, the humanist **Fray Luis de León** (1527-91); and **Miguel de Unamuno** (1864-1936), Professor of Greek, rector, and philosopher.

Art in Salamanca – In the late 15C and early 16C, two major painters were working in Salamanca: **Fernando Gallego**, one of the best Hispano-Flemish artists and **Juan of Flanders** (b 1465), whose work is outstanding for the subtle delicacy of its colours.

The 15C also saw the evolution of the original Salamanca patio arch, in which the line of the Mudéjar-curve curve is broken by counter curves and straight lines. The 16C brought Salamancan **Plateresque** art to an ebullient climax.

Special Features

MONUMENTAL CENTRE★★★

allow one day

Follow the itinerary on the town plan.

Plaza Mayor★★★

The Plaza Mayor is the life and soul of Salamanca. All the city's major streets converge on the square, where locals and visitors alike meet. It was built by Philip V between 1729 and 1755 and is among the finest in Spain, designed principally by the Churriguera brothers. Four ground-level arcades with rounded arches, decorated by a series of portrait medallions of Spanish kings and famous men such as Cervantes, El Cid, and Columbus support three storeys rising in perfect formation to an elegant balustrade. On the north and east sides are the pedimented fronts of the **Ayuntamiento** (town hall) and the Pabellón Real (Royal Pavilion).

Take calle Prior to plaza de Monterrey.

TURESPAÑA

Plaza Mayor

Casa de las Muertes (House of Death)

The early-16C Plateresque façade is attributed to Diego de Siloé.

Convento de las Úrsulas (Ursuline Convent)

Open 11am-1pm and 4-6pm. Closed last Sun of every month. 2 €. ☎923 21 98 77.

The 16C church contains the **tomb★** of Alonso de Fonseca with delicate low reliefs attributed to Diego de Siloé. The **museum**, with its artesonado and coffered ceilings, houses panels and fragments of an altarpiece by Juan de Borgoña. There are also works by Morales the Divine, an *Ecce Homo* and a *Pietà*.

Palacio de Monterrey

Built in 1539, this typical Renaissance palace has an openwork balustrade crowning a long top-floor gallery, between corner towers.

Iglesia de la Purísima Concepción (Church of the Immaculate Conception)

Open Fri-Sat noon-1pm and 5-7pm (8pm summer). Closed Sun-Thu except for worship. ☎923 21 27 38.

The **Immaculate Conception★** by Ribera hangs above the high altar.

Plaza de San Benito

On this delightful square are the **Iglesia de San Benito**, and mansions of Salamanca's old noble rival families.

Casa de las Conchas★ (House of Shells)

This late-15C house (now a library) is carved with 400 scallop shells in its golden stone wall. It has decorative Isabelline windows and beautiful wrought-iron grilles The **patio** has delicate mixtilinear arches and openwork balustrades, carved lions' heads and coats of arms.

Clerecía

Open 10.30am-12.50pm and 4-5.50pm (5-6.50pm Apr-Oct); Sat 10am-

SALAMANCA

Álvaro Gil	BY	3
Anaya Pl.	BZ	4
Ángel Pl.	BY	6
Azafranal	CY	
Bandos Pl. de los	BY	7
Bordadores	BY	9
Caldereros	BZ	10
Calderón de la Barca	BZ	12
Carmen Cuesta del	BY	13
Comuneros Av. de los	CY	16
Concilio de Trento Pl.	BZ	18
Condes de Crespo Rascón	BY	19
Constitución Pl. de la	CY	21
Corillo Pl.	BY	22
Dr. Torres Villarroel Pas. del	BY	25
Espoz y Mina	BY	28
Estación Pas. de la	CY	30
Federico Anaya Av. de	CY	31
Filiberto Villalobos Av. de	AY	33
Fray Luis de Granada	BY	34
Fuente Pl. de la	BY	36
Juan de la Fuente	BZ	37
Libertad Pl. de la	BY	39
Libreros	BZ	40
María Auxiliadora	CY	42
Marquesa de Almarza	CZ	43
Mayor Pl.	BY	
Meléndez	BY	45
Monterrey Pl. de	BY	46
Palominos	BZ	51
Patio Chico	BZ	52
Poeta Iglesias Pl.	BY	57
Pozo Amarillo	BY	58
Ramón y Cajal	AY	60
Rector Lucena	BY	15
Reina Pl. de la	CY	61
Reyes de España Av.	BZ	63
San Blas	AY	64
San Isidro Pl. de	BYZ	66
San Julián Pl.	CY	67
Sancti Spiritus Cuesta	CY	75
Santa Eulalia Pl.	CY	69
Santa Teresa Pl. de	BY	70
Santo Domingo Pl.	BZ	72
Serranos	BZ	76
Toro	BCY	
Tostado	BZ	78
Wences Moreno	BY	79
Zamora	BY	

Casa de Doña Maria la Brava	BY	Q
Casa de las Muertes	BY	S
Convento de las Dueñas	BZ	F
Convento de las Úrsulas	BY	X
Escuelas menores	ABZ	U[1]
Museo Art Nouveau y Art Déco	BZ	M[1]
Palacio de Fonseca (Diputación)	BY	D
Palacio de Monterrey	BY	R
Purísima Concepción	BY	P
Universidad	BZ	U

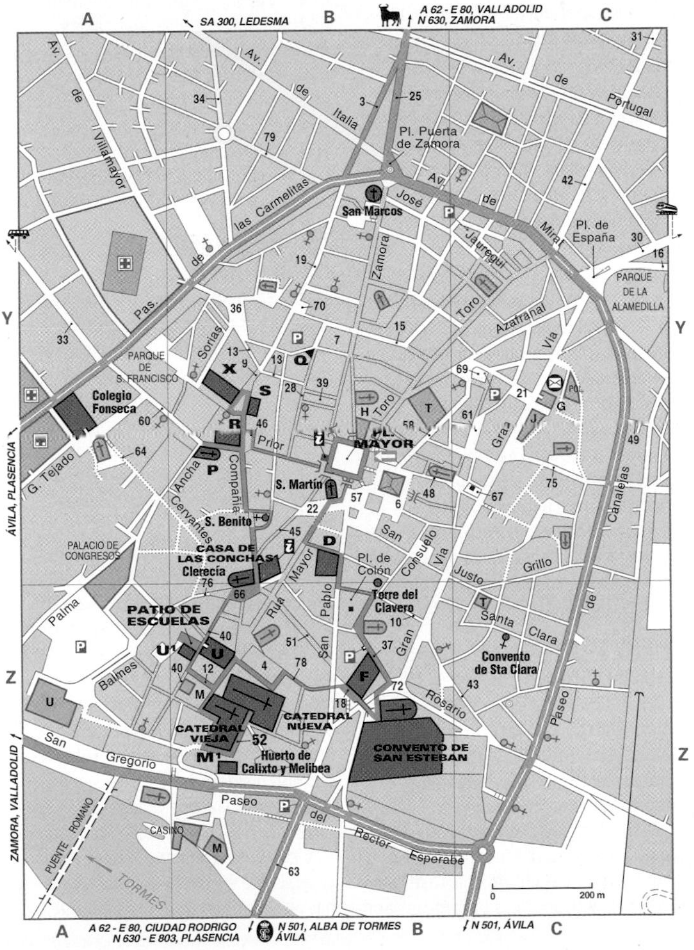

Address Book

For coin ranges, see the Legend on the cover flap.

WHERE TO EAT

La Fonda del Arcediano de Medina – *Reja 2 – 923 21 57 12 – Reservation recommended.* This restaurant has a solid local reputation as a result of its cuisine and good wine list. Meats and *bacalao* (cod) are the specialties. Pleasant decor, including subtle lighting and an interesting collage of images on the ceiling.

El Patio Chico – *Meléndez 13 – 923 26 86 16 –* . Decorated in traditional style with brick walls, exposed beams and a terracotta floor. A pleasant atmosphere with a background of the latest chart hits. The house speciality is chanfaina, the city's signature dish.

El Bardo – *Compañía 88 – 923 25 92 65 – www.restaurantesel-bardo.com.* A typical student haunt with vaulted ceilings and a lively atmosphere. A good bet for a bite to eat after visiting the nearby Casa de las Conchas. Vegetarian items available.

TAPAS

Mesón Cervantes – *Plaza Mayor 15 – 923 21 72 13 – www.mesoncervantes.com –* . A bar with typical Castilian decor and fine views of plaza Mayor serving modern, innovative cuisine. Popular with Salamanca's young crowd at night. Try the house sangría.

Momo – *San Pablo 13 – 923 28 07 98 – closed Sun in summer.* The contemporary version of a tapas bar, with minimalist decoration and allusions to the clocks in the novel *Momo*. Tapas and skewers come cold and hot, and there's a dining room in the basement.

WHERE TO STAY

Hostal Catedral – *Mayor 46 1ºB – 923 27 06 14 – – Reservation recommended – 6 rooms – 2.50€.* Because of its location (some of its windows open directly onto the cathedral), it would have been impossible to give this hostal any other name! Occupying the first floor of an attractive stone building, it is tastefully decorated with spotless bathrooms and unexpected touches such as embroidered bed linen.

Hotel Emperatriz I – *Compañía 44 – 923 21 92 00 – www.emperatrizhotel.com – – 61 rooms – 2.50€ – Restaurant 7.50/9.50€.* The name of the street refers to the Society of Jesus, as the Clerecía is located just a few metres from the hotel. The façade has a noble appearance, yet the interior is somewhat simple in style.

Hostal Plaza Mayor – *Plaza del Corrillo 20 – 923 26 20 20 – www.hostalplazamayor.es – 19 rooms.* Ideal if you want to stay in the centre of Salamanca as it is situated just behind Plaza Mayor, opposite the Romanesque church of San Martín. The hotel's interior design highlights the main features of the house, such as its attractive wooden beams.

Hotel Rector – *Rector Esperabé 10 – 923 21 84 82 – www.hotelrector.com – – 14 rooms – 10€.* A charming small hotel with spectacular views of the cathedral and elegant, well-appointed rooms.

TAKING A BREAK

Café Novelty – *Plaza Mayor 2 – 923 21 49 56 – www.cafenovelty.com.* A famous Salamanca café since 1905. Miguel de Unamuno used to meet his friends and colleagues here. The wooden chairs and marble tables conjure up images of the philosopher engaged in animated discussion, while its terrace on plaza Mayor offers a wonderful view of one of Spain's finest squares.

Café-Bar Tío Vivo – *Clavel 5 – Open from 8am.* The name originates from the tío vivo (merry-go-round) on the bar. The cine-camera, spotlights and the decoration lend an American feel.

Capitán Haddock – *Concejo 13-15 – Open 8am-1am.* The entrance is through a narrow passageway which gives no hint of the stylish decor and subdued lighting inside.

La Regenta – *Espoz y Mina 19 – 923 12 32 30 – www.cafelaregenta.com – Open 10am-noon and 2-8pm.* This typical café with a 19C atmosphere has an older feel than those above.

1.20pm and 4-6.20pm (5-7.20pm Apr-Oct); Sun and public hols 10am-1.20pm. Last admission 40 min before closing. Closed Mon; 1 and 6 Jan and 25 Dec. 2.50€. 923 27 71 22.

This Jesuit College was begun in 1617; its Baroque towers were finished by Andrés García de Quiñones in 1755.

Patio de las Escuelas★★★ (Schools' Square)

This small square, off the old Calle Libreros, is surrounded by the best examples of Salamanca Plateresque. The former university principals' residence is the **Museo Unamuno**, a museum dedicated to the philospher. *Guided tours (30min), 9.30am-1.30pm and 4-6pm (July-Sep morning only); Sat-Sun and public hols, 10am-1.30pm. Last entry 30min before closing. 3€. 923 29 44 00 (ext. 1196)*

Universidad

Open 9.30am-1.30pm and 4-6.30pm (7.30pm in summer); Sat 9.30am-1.30pm and 4-7pm; Sun and public hols, 10am-1.30pm. 4€. 923 29 44 03.

The university's sumptuous 1534 **entrance**★★★ is a brilliant composition. Above the twin doors, covered by basket arches, the carving is in ever greater relief, to compensate for increasing height. A central medallion in the first register shows the Catholic monarchs who presented the doorway; in the second are portrait heads in scallop-shell niches; in the third, flanking the pope supported by cardinals, are Venus and Hercules and the Virtues. The most famous motif is the death's head surmounted by a frog (on the right pilaster, halfway up) symbolising the posthumous punishment of lust.

The lecture halls are around the **patio**: the **Paraninfo** (Great Hall) is hung with 17C Brussels tapestries and a portrait of Charles IV from Goya's studio; the hall where Fray Luis de León lectured in theology is as it was in the 16C.

The grand staircase rises beneath star vaulting, its banister carved with foliated scrollwork and, at the third flight, a mounted bullfight.

A gallery on the first floor has its original, rich **artesonado ceiling** with stalactite ornaments and a delicate low relief frieze along the walls. A Gothic door with a fine 16C grille opens into the 18C library which contains books, incunabula and manuscripts, some of which date back to the 11C.

A Secular Tradition

The red inscriptions which appear on most of the town's monuments, in particular those of the university, are part of an old tradition that dates back to the 15C: on graduating, students would take part in a bullfight and, with the blood of the bull they had killed, write the word Victor and the date on a wall. Today the same is done with paint.

Escuelas Menores (Minor Schools)

Open 9.30am-1.30pm and 4-6.30pm (7.30pm in summer); Sat 9.30am-1.30pm and 4-7pm; Sun and public hols, 10am-1.30pm. 4€. 923 29 44 03.

Standing to the right of the hospital and crowned by the same openwork Renaissance frieze, is the entrance to the Minor (preparatory) Schools – a Plateresque portal decorated with coats of arms, roundels and scrollwork. The typical Salamanca **patio**★★ (1428) has lovely lines. To the right of the entrance is a new exhibition room with a fine Mudéjar ceiling; the University Museum opposite exhibits what remains of the ceiling painted by Fernando Gallego for the former university library. This section of the **Cielo de Salamanca**★ (Salamanca Sky) illustrates constellations and signs of the zodiac. Several works by Juan of Flanders and Juan of Burgundy stand out in the museum.

Catedral Nueva★★ (New Cathedral)

Open 9am-1pm and 4-6pm (9am-8pm in summer); Sun, 9am-2pm. 3€. 923 21 74 76.

Construction, begun in 1513, although additions continued to be made until the 18C – hence the variety of architectural styles.

The **west front★★★** is divided into four wide bays outlined by pierced stonework, carved as minutely as the keystones in the arches, the friezes and the pinnacled balustrades. The Gothic decoration of the central portal, which includes scenes such as a Crucifixion between St Peter and St Paul, overflows the covings and tympanum.

The **north doorway,** facing the **Colegio de Anaya**, bears a delicate low relief of Christ's entry into Jerusalem. The restored lower section of the last archivolt contains the surprising figure of an astronaut as well as a mythological animal eating ice-cream.

The **interior** is notable for the pattern of the vaulting, the delicacy of the cornices and the sweep of the pillars. The eight windows in the lantern are given added effect by a drum with scenes from the Life of the Virgin painted in the 18C by the Churriguera brothers, who also designed the ornate Baroque stalls in the *coro*, the *trascoro* and the north organ loft.

Catedral Vieja★★★ (Old Cathedral)

Open 10am-12.30pm and 4-5.30pm (10am-7.30pm in summer). 3.50 €. 923 21 74 76. Enter by the first bay off the south aisle in the new cathedral.

The builders of the new cathedral respected the fabric of the old which is almost totally masked outside. It was built in the 12C and is a good example of the Romanesque, the pointed arching being a legitimate, if unusual, innovation; the **cimborrio** (lantern), or Torre del Gallo, with two tiers of windows and ribbing, is outstanding. Beneath the vaulting, capitals are carved with scenes of tournaments and imaginary animals.

The **altarpiece★★** in the central apsidal chapel was painted by Nicholas of Florence in 1445 and comprises 53 compartments decorated in surprisingly fresh colours showing the architecture and dress of the times. The Virgin of the Vega is a 12C wooden statue, plated in gilded and enamelled bronze.

Recesses in the south transept contain French-influenced 13C recumbent figures and frescoes.

Claustro – Capitals from earlier Romanesque galleries destroyed during the 1755 Lisbon earthquake remain in these cloisters. The adjoining **Capilla de Talavera**, with a Mudéjar dome on carved ribs, was where the ancient Mozarabic rite was celebrated. A museum in three rooms and the Capilla de Santa Catalina contains works by Fernando Gallego and his brother Francisco and others by Juan of Flanders (St Michael altarpiece).

The **Capilla Anaya** contains the outstanding 15C alabaster **tomb★★** of Diego de Anaya, archbishop first of Salamanca and then of Sevilla. Surrounding it is a magnificent Plateresque grille. There are also a 15C **organ★** and superb 16C recumbent statues.

From the **Patio Chico** you can see the old cathedral apse and the scallop tiling on the **Torre del Gallo** (Cockerel Tower). From here, calle Arcediano leads to the delightful **Huerto de Calixto y Melibea.**

Museo de Art Nouveau y Art Déco

Open 11am-2pm and 4-7pm; Sat-Sun and public hols, 11am-8pm; 1 Apr-15 Oct, 11am-2pm and 5-9pm; Sat-Sun and public hols, 11am-9pm. Closed Mon, 1 and 6 Jan and 24-25 and 31 Dec. 3 €, no charge Thu morning. 923 12 14 25.

This modern art museum is in the Modernist Casa Lis, dating from the beginning of the 20C. Its collection includes works by R Lalique, vases by E Galle and small sculptures by Hagenauer.

Convento de San Esteban★ (St Stephen's Monastery)

Open 9am-1.30pm and 4-6pm (8pm in summer). 2 €. 923 21 50 00.

Gothic pinnacles adorn the side buttresses of this 16-17C building; the sculpture of the **façade★★** is quintessentially Plateresque. A low-relief *Martyrdom of St Stephen* is by Juan Antonio Ceroni (1610). In the 17C **cloisters★**, note the prophets' heads in **medallions** and grand staircase (1553).

The large **church** has star vaulting in the gallery and a main altarpiece by José Churriguera. Crowning it is a painting, *The Martyrdom of St Stephen*, by Claudio Coello.

Convento de las Dueñas

Open 10.30am (11am Sun)-12.45pm and 4.30-5.30pm (6.45pm in summer). 1.50 €. ☎923 21 54 42.
The Renaissance **cloisters**★★ have profusely carved capitals, extraordinarily forceful in spite of their small size.

Torre del Clavero

The octagonal keep is all that remains of a castle built in 1450. Mudéjar trelliswork decorates its turrets.

Palacio de Fonseca or Diputación (Fonseca Palace or Council)

The **patio**★ of this Renaissance palace combines Salamanca mixtilinear arches at one end with a corbelled gallery – supported by distorted atlantes – on the right and an arcade on the left.

Iglesia de San Martín; Colegio Fonseca (Gothic chapel, Renaissance **patio**★); Iglesia de San Marcos (12C); Convento de Santa Clara (Museum: 13C-16C murals, artesonado work).

J. Malburet/MICHELIN

Cloisters, Convento de las Dueñas

Excursion

Alba de Tormes

23km/14mi SE on the N 501 and C 510. Only the massive keep remains of the castle of the dukes of Alba. The remains of St Teresa of Ávila are in the Carmelite Convent. The **Iglesia de San Juan**, a church with a Romanesque-Mudéjar east end, contains an outstanding 11C **sculpture ensemble**★ in the apse, showing Christ and the Disciples in a semicircle, all noble in expression and stance.

SANGÜESA/ZANGOZA★

POPULATION: 4 447.

MICHELIN MAP 573 E 26 – NAVARRA.

Sangüesa (Zangoza in Basque) still seems to guard the bridge which in the Middle Ages brought prosperity. Its artistic heritage stems from its location on the Way of St James.

- **Information:** *Mayor 2, ☎948 87 14 11.*
- **Orient Yourself:** Sangüesa is situated 5km/3mi from the N 240, linking Jaca with Pamplona.
- **Also See:** The WAY OF ST JAMES, Monasterio de LEYRE (15km/9mi NE), OLITE (44km/27mi SW), PAMPLONA (46km/29mi NW) and JACA (81km/51mi E).

Worth a Visit

Iglesia de Santa María la Real★

Portada Sur★★ **(South Portal)** – Late 12C to 13C. The portal is amazingly crowded with sculpture. The Master of San Juan de la Peña worked on this masterpiece.
The **statue columns**, already Gothic, derive from those at Chartres and Autun. On the **tympanum**, God the Father at the centre of a group of angel

Sangüesa and the Way of St James

Fear of the Moors compelled Sangüesans to live until the 10C on the Rocaforte hillside; by the 11C, however, the citizens had moved down to defend the bridge and clear a safe passage for pilgrims. Sangüesa reached its zenith at the end of the Middle Ages when prosperous citizens began to build elegant residential mansions. These contrasted with the austere Palacio del Príncipe de Viana (Palace of the Prince of Viana), residence of the kings of Navarra, now the Ayuntamiento (town hall), with its façade (seen through the gateway) flanked by two imposing battlemented towers.

The main street, the former rúa Mayor which was once part of the pilgrim road, is lined with comfortable brick houses with the Classical carved wood eaves and windows with rich Gothic or Plateresque surrounds. In the second street on the right coming from the bridge can be seen the Baroque front of the Palacio de Vallesantoro, a palace protected by monumental overhangs carved with imaginary animals.

musicians receives the chosen at His right, but with his down-pointing left arm reproves sinners.

The **covings** swarm with motifs; the second innermost shows the humbler trades: clog-maker, lute-maker and butcher.

The older **upper arches**, marked by an Aragonese severity of style, show God surrounded by the symbols of the Evangelists, two angels and the disciples.

Excursions

Castillo de Javier★

7km/4mi NE on the NA 541. **St Francis Xavier**, the patron saint of Navarra,

Ayuntamiento

born here in 1506, founded the Society of Jesus, with Ignatius Loyola. He died in 1552 and was canonised in 1622.

Open 10.30am-2pm and 3.30-7pm (6pm Nov-Mar). Closed 1 Jan and 24-25 and 31 Dec. 2€. 948 88 40 24.

The fortress, birthplace of the saint, was in part destroyed by Cardinal Cisneros in 1516. The **oratorio**★ (oratory) contains a 13C Christ in walnut and an unusual 15C fresco of the Dance of Death.

Sos del Rey Católico★

13km/8mi SE along the A 127. It was here, in the **Palacio de los Sada** (Sada Palace), that Ferdinand the Catholic, who was to unite Spain, was born in 1452. The town still has a medieval air.

On the **plaza Mayor** stand the imposing 16C Ayuntamiento (town hall), with large carved wood overhangs, and the Lonja (Exchange) with wide arches.

Iglesia de San Esteban★ – *Open 10am-1pm and 3.30-5.30pm (4-6pm Jun-Sep). Sun and public hols, 10am-noon and 4-6pm. 1 €. 948 88 82 03.*

The Church of St Stephen is reached through a vaulted passageway. The 11C **crypt**★ is dedicated to Our Lady of Forgiveness (Virgen del Perdón). Two of the three apses are decorated with fine 14C **frescoes**. The central apse contains outstanding capitals carved with women and birds. The statue columns at the **main door** have the stiff and noble bearing of those at Sangüesa. The church, in transitional style, has a beautiful Renaissance **gallery**★. A chapel contains a 12C Romanesque Christ with eyes open.

Uncastillo

34km/21mi SE. 21km/13mi from Sos del Rey Cátolico. The Romanesque **Iglesia de Santa María** has an unusual 14C tower adorned with machicolations and pinnacle turrets. The delicate carving on the **south portal★** makes it one of the most beautiful doorways of the late Romanesque period. The church gallery with Renaissance **stalls★** and the **cloisters★** are 16C Plateresque.

MONASTERIO DE SANTA MARÍA DE HUERTA★★

MICHELIN MAP 575 I 23 – CASTILLA Y LEÓN (SORIA).

In 1144, a Cistercian community came to the Soria region on the border between Castilla and Aragón. Monks settled in Huerta in 1162. The sober Cistercian style was slightly modified by Renaissance innovations.

- **Orient Yourself:** The monastery stands close to the A 2 highway linking Madrid and Zaragoza (131km/82mi NE).
- **Also See:** Monasterio de PIEDRA (53km/33mi E), SIGÜENZA (67km/42mi SW) and SORIA (85km/53mi NW).

Tour

Approximately 1hr. Open 10am-1pm and 4-6pm; Sun and public hols, 10-11.15am; last admission 15min before closing. 2€. 975 32 70 02.
The monastery is entered through a 16C **triumphal arch**.

Cloisters and Claustro Herreriano (Herreran Cloisters)

16C-17C. The buildings around the cloisters are the monks' living quarters.

Claustro de los Caballeros★ (Knights' Cloisters)

13C-16C. The cloisters owe their name to the many knights buried there. The arches at ground level are elegant, pointed and purely Gothic; above, the 16C gallery has all the exuberance and imagination of the Plateresque *(it is a copy of the gallery in the Palacio de Avellaneda in Peñaranda de Duero)*. The decorative medallions are of Prophets, Apostles and Spanish kings.

Sala de los Conversos (Lay brothers' Hall)

12C. This is divided by stout pillars, crowned with stylised capitals.

Cocina

The kitchen has a monumental central chimney.

Refectorio★★

The refectory, a masterpiece of 13C Gothic, rises 15m/50ft above the 35m/115ft long hall and has a wonderful rose window. A beautiful staircase, its arches on slender columns, leads to the **reader's lectern**.

Iglesia

The church has been restored to its original state although the royal chapel has kept sumptuous Churrigueresque decoration. Between the narthex and the aisles is an intricate 18C wrought-iron screen. The **coro alto** (choir) is beautifully decorated with Renaissance panelling and woodwork. The Talavera *azulejos* on the floor are very old.

SANTANDER★

POPULATION: 196 218.

MICHELIN MAP 572 B18 (ALSO TOWN PLAN) – CANTABRIA.

Santander enjoys a magnificent location★★ on a bay bathed by the azure waters of the Cantabrian Sea. It is best enjoyed on foot, with its long maritime front – one of the finest in Spain – lined by attractive gardens offering incomparable views. Superb beaches draw summer visitors while the university attracts students from around the world.

- **Information:** *Jardines de Pereda, ☎942 20 30 00; Plaza de Velarde 5, ☎ 942 31 07 08.*
- **Orient Yourself:** Santander sprawls to the west of the bay. The A 8 motorway runs SE to Bilbao (116km/72mi).
- Kids See the zoo at Península de la Magdalena.
- **Also See:** SANTILLANA DEL MAR (26km/16mi W) and COSTA DE CANTABRIA.

Worth a Visit

CITY CENTRE

The **paseo de Pereda★**, along the seafront, is lined by the imposing Banco de Santander building and the Palacete del Embarcadero, an exhibition centre.

Museo Regional de Prehistoria y Arqueología★

Open 9am (10am 16 Jun-15 Sep) to 1pm and 4-7pm; Sun and public hols all year, 11am-2pm. Closed Mon, 1 Jan, Good Fri, 1 May and 25 Dec. ☎942 20 71 09.

The archaeological museum in the Diputación shows finds from prehistoric caves in Cantabria, and remains of extinct animals from the Quaternary Era. The richest period is the Upper Palaeolithic from which there are bones engraved with animal silhouettes and **batons★** (from El Pendo) made of horn and finely decorated. Three large circular steles, used for funerary purposes, are representative of the apogee of the Cantabrian culture (Bronze Age). Roman finds are mostly from Julióbriga (*see AGUILAR DE CAMPOO: Tours)* and Castro Urdiales, and include coins, bronzes and pottery figurines. A medieval Mozarabic belt clasp made from bone is dated from the 10C.

A Time of Crisis

At the end of the 19C, the Cabo Machichaco cargo boat disaster, killing more than 500 people, caused widespread shock in Spain.

Half a century later, on 15 February 1941, at a time when the city was attempting to recover from the Civil War, a tornado struck Santander: the sea swept over the quays and a fire broke out, almost completely destroying the centre. Reconstruction was undertaken to a street plan of blocks of no more than four or five storeys, and space was allocated to gardens beside the sea, promenades such as the paseo de Pereda which skirts the pleasure boat harbour known as Puerto Chico, and squares such as plaza Porticada.

Catedral

Entry is through the restored Gothic cloisters. The fortress-like cathedral was badly damaged in a 1941 fire, but has been rebuilt in its original Gothic style. A Baroque altarpiece dominates the presbytery; the **font** to the right of the ambulatory was brought here from Sevilla by soldiers of the Reconquest.

Iglesia del Cristo★ – Access to the fine 13C crypt is through the south portal. Excavations in the Evangelist nave have brought to light the remains of a Roman house with the relics of St Emeterio and St Celedonio, patron saints of the city.

The Baroque Christ at the high altar is from the Castilian School.

Museo de Bellas Artes (Fine Arts Museum)

Open 10.15am-1pm and 5.30-9pm (Sat, mornings only); 15 Jun-15 Sep, 10.45am-1pm and 6-9pm (Sat, mornings only). Closed Sun and public hols. 942 20 31 20.

Works include a portrait of Ferdinand VII by **Goya**; a series of Goya etchings – *Disasters of War, La Tauromaquia* and *Caprichos* – and several 16C-18C paintings by Flemish and Italian artists.

Biblioteca Menéndez y Pelayo

Guided tours (20min), 9.30-11.30am (every half hour). Closed Sat-Sun and public hols. 942 23 45 34.

Marcelino Menéndez y Pelayo (1856-1912), one of Spain's greatest historians, bequeathed this fabulous library of nearly 43 000 books and manuscripts by great Castilian authors.

Península de la Magdalena★★

Kids With its magnificent position and sublime views, this peninsula is one of Santander's major sights. The small zoo (seals, penguins, polar bears etc) on the El Sardinero side, and the replicas of the galleons in which Francisco de Orellana explored the Amazon are popular with children.

A palace, the **Palacio de la Magdalena,** was a summer residence for Alfonso XIII. Today, it is occupied by the Menéndez Pelayo International University.

El Sardinero★★

With its three magnificent **beaches**, the residential and resort area of El Sardinero is one of Santander's main attractions.

Walk to Cabo Mayor★

allow 2hr; 4.5km/3mi round trip from the junction of calle García Lago and calle Gregorio Marañón, at the far end of El Sardinero. By car, 7km/4.5mi N.

This attractive walk, adjoining the Mataleñas golf course, runs along the coast, offering magnificent views all the way.

Excursions

Parque de la Naturaleza de Cabárceno (Cabárceno Nature Reserve)

15km/9.5mi S. Kids *Open 9.30am-6pm (7pm May-Sep). 15 € (12€ low season; children 10€/8€). 942 56 37 36.*

An old iron mine in the Sierra de Cabarga is part of an environmental rehabilitation project which includes a superb **game park**.

J. Malburet/MICHELIN

The beach at El Sardinero

Address Book

For coin ranges, see the Legend at the back of the guide.

WHERE TO STAY

⊜⊜ **Hotel Carlos III** – *Avenida Reina Victoria 135 (El Sardinero) – ☎942 27 16 16 – Open 15 Mar-Oct – 28 rooms – ☕ 4€.* The Carlos III is a small hotel housed in an impressive early-20C mansion opposite the playa del Sardinero. A pleasant mid-range option.

⊜⊜⊜ **Las Brisas** – *La Braña 14 (El Sardinero) – ☎942 27 50 11 – www.hotellasbrisas.net – 13 room.* An attractive building with a tower, in the El Sardinero district next to the beach. Sitting rooms have lovely details, and the service and attention in this small establishement are personalised.

WHERE TO EAT

⊜ **Mesón Rampalay** – *Daoíz y Velarde 9 – ☎942 31 33 67 – Closed Tue.* This bar-restaurant is located in a street running parallel to paseo Pereda, next to the Iglesia de Santa Lucía. A long bar and a number of tables, where you can enjoy traditional specialities such as red peppers with tuna, seafood salad, and mushrooms with cod.

⊜⊜ **Bodega del Riojano** – *Río de la Pila 5 – ☎942 21 67 50 – Closed Sun evening and Mon.* This charming, tavern-style bar-restaurant is decorated with numerous painted barrels both at the entrance to the bar and in the spacious dining room, giving the place a rustic feel. The cuisine here revolves around traditional local dishes.

FIESTAS

In addition to the International Music and Dance Festival held during August in the Palacio de Festivales (designed by Saénz de Oiza, 1991), Santander also hosts the fiesta of St James (Santiago) in July, with its bullfights and range of popular concerts and performances.

BOAT TRIPS

Throughout the year, vessels known as *reginas* provide a shuttle service between Santander and Somo and Pedreña (two districts on the other side of the bay). In summer, excursions around the bay and along the Cubas River are also available for visitors, with departures from the Embarcadero del Palacete dock on paseo de Pereda. *☎942 216 753.*

Castañeda

24km/15mi SW via the N 623 and N 634.
The **antigua Colegiata**, a former collegiate church from the end of the 12C, stands in a pleasant valley. The unusually deep doorway is simple and elegant *(🕓 visits by prior arrangement. ☎942 59 21 57, Señor Luis Carlos Fernández Ruiz).*

Puente Viesgo★

26km/16mi SW along the N 623. The caves were inhabited in prehistoric times.

Cueva del Castillo★ – *Guided tours (45min), Oct-Apr, 9.30am-4pm; May-Sep, 10am-1pm and 4-7.30pm. 🕓 Closed Mon, Tue (Apr-Oct), 1 Jan, 23 May, 29 Sep and 25 and 31 Dec. ⊜ 3 €. ☎942 59 84 25.*
Cave dwellers began engraving and painting the walls towards the end of the Palaeolithic Age.

SANTIAGO DE COMPOSTELA★★★

POPULATION: 105 851.

MICHELIN MAP 571 D 4 (TOWN PLAN) – GALICIA (A CORUÑA/LA CORUÑA).

In the Middle Ages, Santiago de Compostela, attracted pilgrims from all of Europe. It remains one of Spain's most enchanting cities with its old quarters and maze of narrow streets. It is also made lively by its numerous taverns, thousands of university students, and the throng of annual visitors. Contrary to all expectations, the styles of architecture that predominate are Baroque and neo-Classical, rather than Romanesque, lending an air of solemnity to the city.

- **Information:** *Vilar 43, ☎981 58 40 81; Plaza de Galicia, ☎981 57 39 90*
- **Orient Yourself:** This pilgrimage city in NW Spain is connected by the AP 9 to Vigo (84km/52mi S) and A Coruña/La Coruña (72km/45mi N) and by the N 547 with Lugo (107km/67mi E). The AP 53 runs SE to Orense/Ourense (111km/69mi).
- **Don't Miss:** The Cathedral.
- **Also See:** A CORUÑA/La CORUÑA, PONTEVEDRA (57km/35mi S), RÍAS BAJAS, RÍAS ALTAS and The WAY OF ST JAMES.

Background

History, tradition and legends – The Apostle **James the Greater** crossed the seas to convert Spain to Christianity. He returned to Judaea where he fell victim to Herod Agrippa. His disciples fled to Spain with his body. A star is believed to have pointed out the grave to shepherds early in the 9C.

In 844 during an attack against the Moors at **Clavijo**, a knight on a charger, bearing a white standard with a red cross, appeared on the battlefield and brought victory. The Christians recognised St James, naming him *Matamoros* or Moorslayer. The Reconquest and Spain had found a patron saint.

In the 11C devotion spread until a journey to St James' shrine ranked with one to Rome or Jerusalem.

Special Features

PRAÇA DO OBRADOIRO.

The majesty of the square makes it a fitting setting for the cathedral.

Catedral★★★

Open 10.30am-1.30pm and 4-6.30pm (8pm Jun-Sep). ☎981 56 05 27.

The present cathedral dates mostly from the 11C, 12C and 13C, although from the outside it appears Baroque.

Fachada del Obradoiro★★★ (Obradoiro façade) – This Baroque masterpiece by **Fernando Casas y Novoa** was completed in 1750. The central area, given true Baroque movement by the interplay of straight and curved lines, rises to what appears to be a long tongue of flame.

Pórtico de la Gloria★★★ (Doorway of Glory) – Behind the façade stands the narthex and the Portico de la Gloria, a late-12C wonder by **Maestro Mateo**. The statues of the triple doorway are exceptional both as a composition and in detail.

The doorway is slightly more recent than the rest of the cathedral and shows Gothic features. Mateo, who also built bridges, had the crypt reinforced to bear the weight of the portico. The central portal is dedicated to the Christian Church, the one on the left to the Jews, that on the right to the Gentiles. The central portal tympanum shows the Saviour surrounded by the Evangelists while on the archivolt are the 24 Elders of the Apocalypse. The engaged pillars are covered in statues of Apostles and Prophets. Note the figure of Daniel with the hint of a smile, a precursor to the famous Smiling Angel in Reims Cathedral in France. The pillar beneath the seated St James bears finger marks; traditionally, on entering the cathedral, exhausted pilgrims placed their hands here in token of safe arrival. On the other side of the pillar, the statue known as the saint of bumps is believed to impart memory and wisdom.

Interior – The immense Romanesque cathedral displays all the characteristics of medieval pilgrim churches: a Latin cross plan, vast proportions, an ambulatory and a triforium. The side aisles are covered with 13C groin vaults. At major festivals a huge incense burner, the **botafumeiro** *(displayed in the library)*, is swung from the transept dome keystone by eight men.

The **altar mayor** or high altar, surmounted by a sumptuously apparelled 13C statue of St James, is covered by a gigantic baldaquin. Beneath the altar is the **cripta**, a crypt built into the 9C church. It enshrines the relics of the saint and his disciples, St Theodore and St Athanasius.

The Gothic vaulting of the Capilla Mondragón (1521), and the 9C Capilla de la Corticela, formerly separate, are beautiful. The Renaissance doors to the **sacristía** (sacristy) **(1)** and *claustro* (cloisters) **(2)** on the right arm of the transept are noteworthy.

Museo – *Open Oct-May, 10am-1.30pm and 4-6.30pm; Jul-Sep, 10am-2pm and 4-8pm; Sun and public hols, 10am-1.30 (2pm Jul-Sep). Closed 1 and 6 Jan, 25 Jul, 15 Aug and 25 Dec. 5 €. 981 57 23 00.*

Enter the **tesoro** (treasury), in a Gothic chapel to the right of the nave, from inside of the cathedral. Exhibits include a gold and silver monstrance by Antonio de Arfe (1539-66). To visit the 11C **cripta★** (crypt), exit to Plaza del Obradoiro. This is in fact a small Romanesque church with a Latin cross plan. Use the side entry for the rooms devoted to archaeological excavations, the **biblioteca** (library), the **sala capitular** (chapter house) with its granite vault and walls hung with 16C Flemish tapestries, and the rooms with **tapestries★★** by Goya, Bayeu, Rubens and Teniers.

Claustro★ – *Access via the museum.* This Renaissance cloister was designed by

SANTIAGO DE COMPOSTELA

Acibechería	V	2
Algalia de Arriba	V	5
Arco de Palacio	V	9
Caldeirería	X	17
Camiño Porta do	V	20
Castrón Douro	X	22
Cervantes Pr. de	V	25
Faxeiras Porta da	X	37
Ferradura Pas. da	X	40
Galeras	V	42
Galicia Pr. de	X	45
Hórreo	X	53
Immaculada Pr. da	V	58
Nova R.	X	
Orfas	X	70
Patio de Madres	X	72
Pena Porta da	V	75
Praterías Pr. das	VX	77
Preguntoiro	V	80
Rodrigo de Padrón Av. de	X	90
San Francisco	V	99
San Martíño Pr. de	V	101
San Roque	V	104
Senra	X	113
Trinidade	V	116
Troia	V	119
Vilar R. do	X	
Xelmírez	X	122
Xoán Carlos I Av.	V	125
Xoán XXIII Av. de	V	127

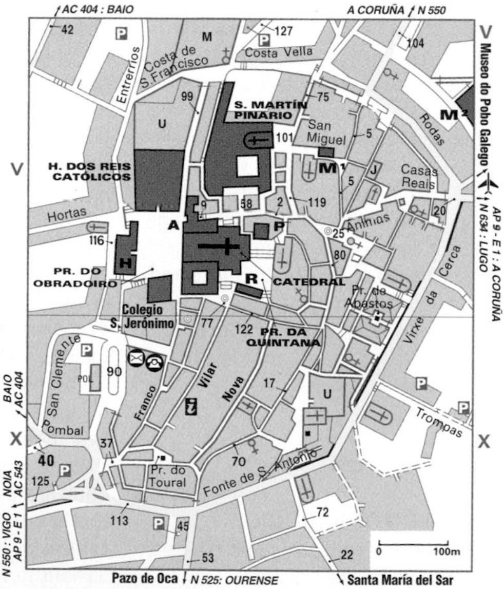

Ayuntamiento	V	H	Museo de las Peregrinaciones	V	M[1]
Casa de la Canónica	V	R	Palacio Gelmírez	V	A
Casa de la Parra	V	P			
Centro Gallego de Arte Contemporáneo	V	M[2]			

Juan de Álava who combined a Gothic structure with Plateresque decoration.

Puerta de las Platerías★★ (Silversmiths' Doorway) – This is the only intact 12C Romanesque doorway. Not all of the entrance is original. The most impressive figure is David playing the viola on the left door. Adam and Eve can be seen being driven out of the Garden of Eden; the Pardoning of the Adulterous Woman is on the right-hand corner of the left tympanum. The **Torre del Reloj** (Clock Tower) was added at the end of the 17C. To the left, stands the **Torre del Tesoro** (Treasury Tower). The 18C Baroque façade of the **Casa del Cabildo**, is opposite the *fuente de los caballos,* or horse trough.

Touring Tip

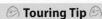

For one of the best views of the cathedral, descend the steps in avenida de Rajoi, to the left of the town hall.

Visit the Cathedral roof

A visit to the roof offers a surprising view of the cathedral and affords unforgettable views of the city. *Enter by Palacio Gelmírez. Guided tours (1hr) 10am-1pm and 4-7pm. 10€. 981 55 29 85 (reservation recommended).*

Palacio Gelmírez

Open Oct-May 10am-1.30pm and 4-6.30pm; Jul-Sep 10am-2pm and 4-8pm.

J. Malburet/MICHELIN

Cathedral

Address Book

For coin ranges, see the Legend on the cover flap.

WHERE TO EAT

Café-Restaurante Casa Manolo – *Plaza de Cervantes 1 – 981 58 29 50 – www.casamanolo.es – Closed in Jan –* . One of the best-known restaurants in town, with a comprehensive menu at unbeatable prices. The two minimalist dining areas are always packed, so go early to avoid a wait.

O Dezaseis – *Rúa de San Pedro 16 – 981 577 633 – www.dezaseis.com – Reservation recommended.* Near the Porta do Camiño and the Museo do Pobo Galego, this restaurant has carved an impressive niche in Santiago gastronomy with delicious tapas and excellent wines, which can be enjoyed beneath the vines on the terrace or in adecor of wood and local stone.

San Clemente – *San Clemente 6 – 981 58 08 82 – www.restaurante-sanclemente.com – Closed Mon –* . Close to the cathedral but in a quiet area off the tourist track, serving what have become legendary fish dishes.

Casa Marcelo – *Rua Hortas 1 – 981 55 85 80 – www.casamarcelo.net – Closed Sun-Tue, 1-15 Feb and 1-15 Oct –* . This charming restaurant just off praça do Obradoiro has a reputation for innovative cuisine. Just one fixed tasting menu, but well-balanced and varied. Pleasant dining environment, splendid wine list and excellent value.

TAPAS

La Bodeguilla de San Roque – *San Roque 13 – 981 564 379.* Despite its simple appearance, this bodega has earned a good reputation for its scrambled egg dishes, chorizos and wines. If you prefer something more substantial, there's also a pleasant restaurant on the first floor.

WHERE TO STAY

Hostal Mapoula – *Entremurallas 10, 3º – 981 58 01 24 – www.mapoula.com – 11 rooms.* A small, family-run hostal in a narrow street in the old quarter, near praça do Toural. Nothing luxurious, but good service and clean rooms with en-suite bathrooms. A recommended choice, both for its location and value for money.

Casa Grande de Cornide – *Cornide – Teo-Casalonga – 11.5km/7mi SW of Santiago on the N 550 towards Padrón – 981 80 55 99 – www.casagrandedecornide.com – Closed Jan – – 10 rooms – 7€.* For those who prefer peace and quiet away from the city, this large, traditional-style Galician house offers the perfect solution. The decor and furnishings are a pleasant fusion of the classic and the modern, creating a comfortable, cosy atmosphere. In summer, guests can take advantage of the pool in the lovely garden surrounding the house.

Hotel San Clemente – *San Clemente 28 – 902 40 58 58 – www.pousadasdecompostela.com – 10 rooms – 5.35€.* The San Clemente enjoys an enviable location a couple of minutes' walk from the praça do Obradoiro. With its ideal size, rooms decorated in brick and wood, and moderate prices, the hotel comes highly recommended.

Parador Hotel Reyes Católicos – *Praça do Obradoiro 1 – 981 58 22 00 – www.parador.es – – 131 rooms from – 12.80 €.* The former Royal Hospital founded by the Catholic Monarchs in 1499 has now been converted into a luxury parador. Particularly worthy of note are its inner patios which trace the typology of hospitals in the 16C. Elegant rooms, some with four-poster beds.

TAKING A BREAK

Café Derby Bar – *Rúa das Orfas 29 – 981 58 59 04.* A timeless bar said to have been popular with the writer Valle Inclán.

Café Literario – *Praça da Quintana.* A stylishly decorated café with a young clientele, located at the top of a flight of steps with a fine view of both the square and the cathedral.

Cafetería Paradiso – *Rúa do Vilar 29 – 981 58 33 94 – Open 8am-2am.* A café with a 19C atmosphere.

Vinatería Don Pinario – *Plazuela de San Martín.* A combination of interesting decor and a good selection of wines in this delightful square.

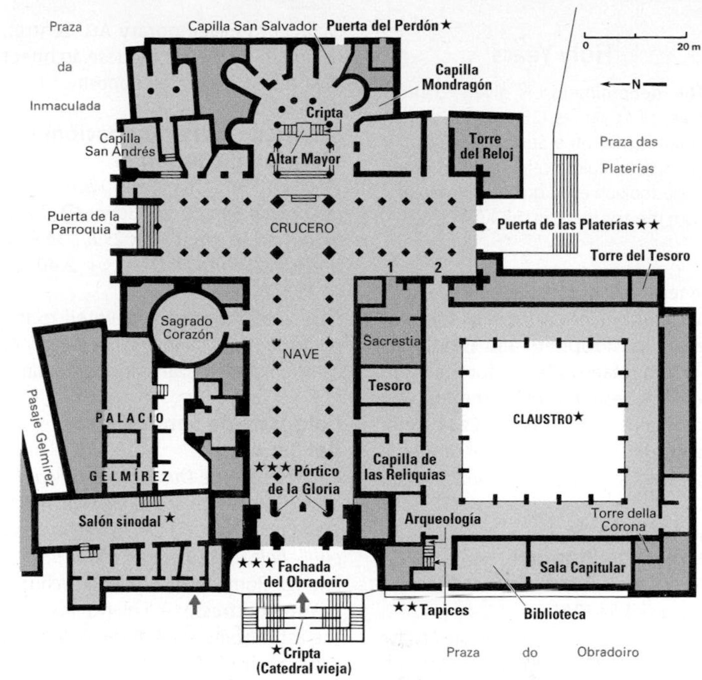

Sun and public hols 10am-1.30pm (2pm Jul-Sep). Closed 1 and 6 Jan, 25 Jul, 15 Aug and 25 Dec. 5 €. 981 57 23 00. This is the bishops' palace (*left of the cathedral*). The **Salón Sinodal**★ (Synod Hall) is more than 30m/98ft long and has sculptured ogive vaulting.

Hostal de los Reyes Católicos★ (Hostelry of the Catholic Monarchs)

This former pilgrim inn and hospital, now a parador, has an impressive **façade**★ with a splendid Plateresque doorway and four elegant *patios*.

Casco Antiguo★★ (Old town)

The old part of the city is a maze of delightful narrow streets which open out onto lively squares.

Rúa do Franco

This street is lined by old colleges, such as Renaissance-style Colegio de Fonseca, and shops and bars. The Porta da Faxeiras leads to paseo de la Herradura, the hill that is the setting for fairs. The excellent **view**★ includes the cathedral and the rooftops of Santiago.

Pazo de Bendaña

Inside this 18C noble building on Plaza do Toural, the Fundación Eugenio Granell (1912-2001) displays surrealist art (*open 11am-2pm and 4-7pm; Jun-Sep 11am-9pm; Sun 10am-2pm; closed Tue and public hols; 2€, no charge Sun; 981 57 63 94*).

Rúa do Vilar

The street leading to the cathedral is bordered by arcaded and ancient houses, as is the parallel **rúa Nova**.

Plaza de la Quintana★★

Along the square at the east end of the cathedral, bustling with students, are the former **Casa de la Canónica** (Canon's Residence) and the 17C Monasterio de San Paio de Antealtares. Inside is the **Museo de Arte Sacro** (Sacred Art Museum (*open Jul-Dec 10.30am-1.30pm and 4-7pm by appointment; closed Sun, public hols and Jan-Jun. 1.50€. 981 58 31 27*).

Opposite, the doorway in the cathedral's east end, known as the **Puerta del Perdón**★ (Door of Pardon), designed by Fernández Lechuga in 1611 and opened only in Holy Years (when

Holy Years

This denomination is given to the feast of St James (25 July) on days when it falls on a Sunday. In recent years, the religious ceremonies in Santiago took on even greater solemnity with the approach of the Jubilee.

the feast day of St James, 25 July, falls on a Sunday), incorporates all the statues of the Prophets and Patriarchs carved by Maestro Mateo for the original Romanesque *coro*. At the top of a large flight of stairs is the **Casa de la Parra,** House of the Bunch of Grapes, a fine late-17C Baroque mansion.

Monasterio de San Martín Pinario★

Open 10am-2pm and 4-6pm. Closed Mon. 981 58 40 81.

The monastery church has an ornate Plateresque front. The interior, with coffered barrel vaulting, is lit by a Byzantine-style lantern without a drum. The Churrigueresque high altar **retable**★ is by the great architect Casa y Novoa (1730). A grand staircase beneath a cupola leads to 16C-18C cloisters.

The façade overlooking plaza de la Inmaculada is colossal with massive Doric columns. Plaza de la Azabachería opposite is named for the jet ornament craftsmen (azabacheros) who had workshops in this square.

Worth a Visit

Museo do Pobo Galego (Museum of the Galician People)

Open 10am-2pm and 4-8pm; Sun and public hols, 11am-2pm. Last admission 30 min before closing. Closed Mon, 1 Jan and 25 Dec. 981 58 36 20.

This regional museum, in the former Convento de Santo Domingo de Bonaval (17C-18C), provides an introduction to Galician culture. Rooms are devoted to the sea, crafts, painting and sculpture. The building has an impressive triple **spiral staircase**★. The **Centro Gallego de Arte Contemporáneo** (Galician Contemporary Art Centre), designed by the Portuguese architect Álvaro Siza, is situated opposite.

Museo de las Peregrinaciones (Pilgrimage Museum)

Open 10am-8pm; Sat, 10am-1.30pm and 5-8pm; Sun, 10.30-1.30pm. Closed Mon, 1 and 6 Jan, 1 May, 25 Jul, 16 Aug, and 24-25 and31 Dec.. 2.40 €. 981 58 15 58.

This small museum is devoted to the pilgrimages to Santiago. Hardly any of its original medieval features remain.

Colegiata de Santa María del Sar★

Calle Castrón de Ouro. Entrance via the apse. Visits by prior arrangement, 10am-1pm and 4-7pm. Closed Sat-Sun and public hols. 0.60 €. 981 56 28 91.

The 12C Romanesque collegiate church has 18C buttresses – a glance inside at the astonishing slant of the pillars will explain why. The only cloister gallery to remain is elegant, with paired **arches**★ decorated with floral and leaf motifs. A museum displays gold and silverwork.

Excursions

Pazo de Oca★

25km/16mi S on the N 525. Open 9am-8pm (9pm in summer); only gardens open to the public. 4 €, no charge Mon (except public hols) until 12.30pm. 986 58 74 35.

This austere Galician **manor**, or *pazo*, with a crenellated tower, lines two sides of a vast square. The romantic **park**★★ behind comes as a complete surprise (*see INTRODUCTION TO SPAIN: Spanish Gardens*). There are shady arbours, terraces covered with rust-coloured lichen, pools, and a silent lake with a stone boat.

Monasterio de Sobrado dos Monxes

56km/35mi W. Open 10.15am-1pm and 4.15-7pm; Sun and public hols, 12.15-1pm and and 4.15-7pm. 0.60 €. 981 78 75 09.

Sobrado is a vast **monastery**, built between the Renaissance and Baroque periods. It is badly weatherworn. Preoccupation with size brought a certain severity in the decoration of the church façade. The interior displays fertile imagination in the design of the **cupolas** in the transept, the sacristy and the Capilla del Rosario (Rosary Chapel). Of the monastery's medieval buildings, there remain a kitchen with a monumental fireplace, a chapter house and the Capilla de la Magdalena (Mary Magdalene Chapel).

SANTILLANA DEL MAR★★

POPULATION: 3 839.
MICHELIN MAP 572 B17 –
COSTA DE CANTABRIA – CANTABRIA.

Santillana del Mar ("of the sea") is in fact located a few kilometres inland. Santillana retains a medieval appearance, its mansions embellished with family coats of arms.

- **Information:** *Plaza Mayor, ☎942 81 82 51.*
- **Orient Yourself:** Santillana is surrounded by verdant hills, between Santander and Comillas (16km/10mi to the W)
- **Especially for Kids:** Visit the zoo on the Puente de San Miguel road.
- **Also See:** SANTANDER (26km/16mi E) and COSTA DE CANTABRIA.

Walking About

The **town**★★ has two main streets, both leading to the collegiate church. Start in **calle de Santo Domingo**, with the 17C Casa del Marqués de Benemejís to the left and the Casa de los Villa, with its semicircular balconies, to the right.

Turn left into calle de Juan Infante.

Plaza de Ramón Pelayo

Along this vast, pleasing triangular square are the **Parador Gil Blas** and the 14C **Torre de Merino** (Merino Tower, *right*); the **Torre de Don Borja**, with its elegant pointed doorway; and (*left*) the 18C Ayuntamiento (town hall), Casa del Águila and Casa de la Parra.
Calle de las Lindas *(end of the square on the right)* runs between massive houses with austere façades to **calle del Cantón** and **calle del Río**, which lead to the collegiate church. On the corner, note the escutcheon of the Casa de Valdivieso (now the Hotel Altamira). Many shops along these streets sell local cheese, chocolates, and crafts.
As you approach the church, you will see several noble residences on the right-hand side: the Casa del **Marqués de Santillana,** with its impressive windows; the **Casa de los Hombrones**, named after the two knights supporting the Villa coat of arm; and the **Casa de Quevedo** and the **Casa de Cossío**, both with magnificent coats of arms. On the left, before the Colegiata, the **house of the Archduchess of Austria** is adorned with three coats of arms.

Colegiata★

Open 10am-1.30pm and 4-7.30pm (6.30pm 15 Jun-15 Sep). Closed Mon (winter), 28 Jun, 16 Aug and 25 Dec.

Historical Notes

Santillana grew up around a monastery which sheltered the relics of St Juliana, who was martyred in Asia Minor – the name Santillana is a contraction of Santa Juliana. Throughout the Middle Ages, the monastery was famous as a place of pilgrimage and was particularly favoured by the Grandees of Castilla. In the 11C it became powerful as a collegiate church; in the 15C, the town, created the seat of a marquisate, was enriched by the fine mansions which still give it so much character.

3 € (includes visit to Museo Diocesano). 942 84 03 17.
The collegiate church dates from the 12C and 13C. The design of the east end is pure Romanesque.

Claustro★
These cloisters are a fine example of 12C Romanesque style. Each pair of capitals is carved by a master craftsman. The **capitals**★★ in the south gallery, which illustrate a scene, often in allegory, are very expressive: look out for Christ and six of the disciples; and the beheading of John the Baptist and Daniel in the Lion's Den, among other themes.

Interior
The vaulting in the aisles was rebuilt at the end of the 13C with intersecting ribs. The aisles and apses are out of line and the cupola, unusually, is almost elliptical. The chancel contains a 17C Mexican beaten **silver altarfront** and Romanesque stone figures of **four Apostles**★. The 16C Hispano-Flemish **altarpiece**★ has the original polychrome wood predella showing the Evangelists in profile.
Skirt around the exterior of the east end to appreciate the Romanesque apses and the restored Renaissance **Palacio de los Velarde**.

Convento de Regina Coeli

Return to your starting point.

The restored 16C Convento de Clarisas (Convent of the Poor Clares) is the **Museo Diocesano** (museum of the diocese), with a collection of paintings, sculptures and religious gold and silver. The Baroque carvings and ivory are noteworthy *(open 10am-2pm and 4-7pm (7.30pm 15 Jun-15 Sep); last admission 30 min before closing; closed Mon (winter), 28 Jun, 16 Aug and 25 Dec; 2.50 € (includes the Colegiata); 942 84 03 17.*
A large coat of arms adorns the 18C **Casa de Los Tagle** *(end of the street)*.
Children will be interested by the **zoo** along the Puente San Miguel road *(Kids open 9.30am-dusk; 12 €, 6 € (child); 942 81 81 25).*

Special Features

MUSEO DE ALTAMIRA★★
2km/1.2mi SW. Kids Guided tours 9.30am-5pm; Jun-Sep, 9.30am-7.30pm (5pm Sun and public hols). Visiting times for the Neocueva are posted. 2.40 €, no charge Sat afternoon and Sun. 942 81 80 05. Purchase tickets in advance at Banco de Santander.

Cueva de Altamira
The original cave is not open.
The Altamira caves consist of galleries with wall paintings and engravings dating back to the Solutrean Age, 20 500 years ago. The most impressive paintings are in the Sala de los Polícromos (Polychrome Chamber). Known as the **Sistine Chapel of Quarternary Art**, it has an outstanding **ceiling**★★★ painted mainly during the Magdalenian Period (15000-12000 BC). Numerous polychrome bison are shown asleep, crouched and galloping with extraordinary realism.

Neocueva
A guided tour (30min) using the latest in technology includes replicas of the cave entrance and the Sala de los Polícromos, with extraordinary wall paintings.

Museo
The museum covers the evolution of man and daily life in the Upper Palaeolithic period. Other caves with wall paintings in Cantabria are also shown.

WHERE TO STAY
Hotel Colegiata – *Carretera Los Hornos 20 – 1km/.6mi N of Santillana on the S 474, towards Suances – 942 84 02 16 – www.hotelcolegiata.com – P – 27 rooms – 3.61 € – Restaurant 30 €.* This rural country house in a hilly setting overlooking Santillana has been converted into a delightful hotel with comfortable rooms and a popular restaurant. An excel-lent alternative for those hoping to escape the hustle and bustle of Santillana.

SEGOVIA★★★

POPULATION: 57 617
MICHELIN MAPS 575 OR 576 J 17 – MAP 121 ALREDEDORES DE MADRID – LOCAL MAP SEE SIERRA DE GUADARRAMA – CASTILLA Y LEÓN (SEGOVIA).

This austere, imposing city, at 1 000m/3 280ft, rises on a triangular rock like an island in the Castilian plain. Its sturdy walls enclose a complicated maze of narrow streets dotted with Roman monuments and mansions.

- **Information:** Plaza Mayor 10, ☎921 46 03 34; Plaza de Azoguejo, 1, ☎921 46 67 20.
- **Orient Yourself:** Segovia is in the Castillian plain NW of Madrid.
- **Parking:** A few spaces are available outside the walled city, near the aqueduct.
- **Don't Miss:** The Alcázar, and a meander along streets lined with palaces.
- **Organizing Your Time:** Enter near the aqueduct, and wander the streets and lanes in the general direction of the Alcázar. Allow time for a scenic drive along cuesta de los Hoyos and paseo de Santo Domingo de Guzmán.
- **Also See:** PEDRAZA (35km/22mi NE), Sierra de GUADARRAMA, ÁVILA (67km/42mi SW) and MADRID (98km/61mi S).

Background

Noble Segovia, residence of King Alfonso X, the Wise, and King Henry IV, played a decisive role in the history of Castilla. The 15C marked its Golden Age, when its population numbered 60 000.

Isabel the Catholic, Queen of Castilla – On the death of Henry IV in 1474 many grandees refused to recognise the legitimacy of his daughter, Doña Juana, known as **La Beltraneja**. In Segovia, the grandees proclaimed Henry's half-sister, Isabel, Queen of Castilla – thus preparing the way for Spain's unification. (Isabel was married to Ferdinand, heir apparent of Aragón.) La Beltraneja, aided by her husband, Alfonso V of Portugal, pressed her claim, but renounced it in 1479 after defeats at Toro and Albuera.

The "Comuneros" – In 1520, just three years after he had landed in Asturias to take possession of his Spanish dominions, the Habsburg Charles I departed in order to be proclaimed Holy Roman Emperor (as Charles V). An uprising started that was to become known as the revolt of the Comunidades. The catalysts included the absence of Charles V, his Flemish court which devalued Castilian nobles, and his attempt to impose new taxes. At the root of the Comuneros movement was the opposition of Castilian towns, the middle classes and merchants to the alliance between Charles V and the landed aristocracy. The comuneros were finally crushed at Villalar in 1521.

Special Features

CIUDAD VIEJA★★ (OLD TOWN)

4hr – Follow the itinerary on the plan

Acueducto romano★★★

This aqueduct is one of the finest examples of Roman engineering standing

Esgrafiados

Geometric designs, or *esgrafiados*, are one of the most characteristic features of Segovian architecture. The word derives from the Italian *graffiare*, meaning "to scratch". The technique consists of scratching – following a pre-existing design – an outer layer, to expose an underlying layer of a different colour tone. The range of motifs could cover simple geometric decoration to biblical and mythological scenes. In Segovia's case, the black stains on some of the city's walls are in fact iron scoria, the purpose of which is purely decorative.

Address Book

For coin ranges, see the Legend on the cover flap.

WHERE TO EAT

Narizotas – *Plaza de Medina del Campo 1 – ☎921 46 26 81 – www.narizotas.net.* Customers in this traditional restaurant can choose between the classic roast suckling pig (cochinillo asado) or a more original tasting menu comprising meat and fish choices. In spring and summer, there's the option of eating on the pleasant street terrace with music.

Mesón de Cándido – *Plaza Azoguejo 5 – ☎921 42 59 11 – www. mesondecandido.es –* . Surely the most famous and traditional restaurant in the entire province, in a 15C house right under the aqueduct. Its rustic Castillian interior is the perfect setting for enjoying roast suckling pig, the indisputable star of the menu.

WHERE TO STAY

Hotel Don Jaime – *Ochoa Ondátegui 8 – ☎921 44 47 90 – www.viasegovia.com/hostaldonjaime – 24 rooms – 3.75€.* The bedrooms in this traditional home, magnificently located at the foot of the Roman aqueduct, are simple, bright and quiet.

Hotel Las Sirenas – *Juan Bravo 30 – ☎921 46 26 63 – www.hotelsirenas.com – – 39 rooms.* This hotel from another age, in the old quarter, has an elegant stone façade and comfortable, adequate rooms. The attractive staircase and old hairdressing salon are reminders of its better days.

today. The simple, elegant structure was built during the reign of Trajan in the 1C to bring water from the River Acebeda in the Sierra de Fuenfría to the upper part of town. It is 728m/2 388ft long, rises to 28m/92ft in plaza del Azoguejo where the ground is lowest, and consists of two tiers of arches.

Casa de los Picos

The house, faced closely with diamond-pointed stones, is the most original of Segovia's 15C mansions.

Casa del Conde de Alpuente

The elegant façade of this 15C Gothic house is adorned with *esgrafiado* designs.

Alhóndiga

This 15C granary is an exhibition room.

Plaza de San Martín★

The square in the heart of the old aristocratic quarter is the most evocative of historic Segovia. It is formed of two small squares joined by a flight of steps. The statue is of Juan Bravo. Around the square stand the **Casa del Siglo XV** (15C House), also known as Juan Bravo's house, with a gallery beneath the eaves, the 16C tower of the **Casa de los Lozoya** as a reminder of the family's power, the Plateresque façade of the **Casa de Solier** (Solier Mansion, also known as Casa de Correas) and the ornate entrances to big houses. In the middle of the square is the 12C **Iglesia de San Martín**★, a church framed on three sides by a covered gallery on pillars with carved strapwork and animal figures on the capitals.

Museo Esteban Vicente

Open Tue-Wed 11am-2pm and 4-7pm; Thu-Sat 11am-8pm; Sun and public hols 11am-3pm. Closed Mon. 2.40 €, no charge Thu. ☎921 46 20 10.

The museum is in the palace of Henry IV in the Hospital de Viejos (Old People's Hospital). The only trace of the original building is the fine chapel with a Mudéjar ceiling, now an auditorium. The museum exhibits the work of artist Esteban Vicente (1903-2001).

The 17C **antigua cárcel** (Old Prison) has a decorative Baroque pediment.

Plaza Mayor

Dominated by the impressive cathedral, the arcaded square with its terrace cafés is a popular meeting-place. Among the buildings surrounding the

SEGOVIA								
			Gobernador F. Jiménez	BY	30	Ruiz de Alda	BY	73
			Independencia	BY	36	Salón Pas. del	BY	76
Azoguejo Pl. de	BY	8	Isabel la Católica	BY	39	San Martín Pl.	BY	78
Cervantes	BY	15	Juan Bravo	BY	47	San Quirze	BX	81
Colón	BY	18	Juderia Vieja	AY	51	Santiago Puerta de	AX	83
Conde de Cheste Pl. del	BY	21	Marqués del Arco	AY	56	Serafín	BY	88
Cronista Lecea	BY	23	Mayor Pl.	ABY	59	Socorro	AY	91
Doctor Laguna	BY	24	Merced Pl. de la	AX	62	Valdeláguila	BX	94
Escuderos	AY	25	Obispo Gandasegui	BY	67	Zuloaga	BY	96
Fernández Ladreda Av.	BY	27	Padre Claret Av.	BY	70			

Alhóndiga	BY	S	Casa del Siglo XV	BY	X	Palacio del Marqués de Lozoya	BY	E
Antigua Cárcel	BY	Y	Museo Esteban Vicente	BY	M^2	Palacio del Marqués de Quintanar	BY	K
Casa de Solier	BY	R	Palacio de los Condes de Cheste	BY	F	San Juan de los Caballeros	BY	M^1
Casa de los Lozoya	BY	V	Palacio de los Marqueses de Moya	BY	B	San Sebastián	BY	L
Casa de los Picos	BY	Z						
Casa del Conde de Alpuente	BY	Q						

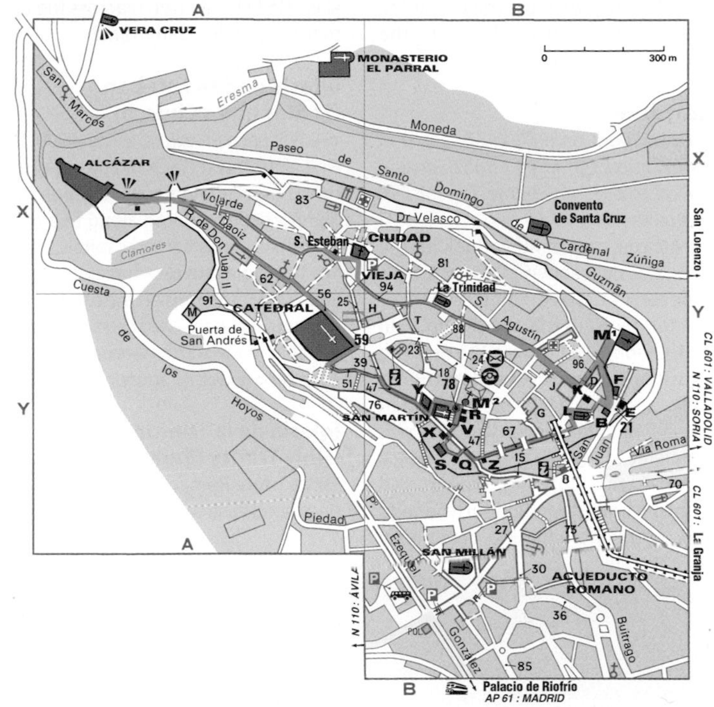

square are the Ayuntamiento (town hall) and the Teatro Juan Bravo.

Catedral★★

Open 9.30am-5.30pm (6.30pm Apr-Oct); Sun and public hols 1.15-5.30pm (6.30pm Apr-Oct). No visits during religious services. 3 € (museum). 921 46 22 05.

This was built during the reign of Emperor Charles V to replace a cathedral destroyed during the Comuneros' Revolt in 1511. It is an example of the survival of the Gothic style in the 16C when Renaissance architecture was at its height. The beautiful golden stone, the stepped east end with pinnacles and delicate balustrades and the tall tower, bring considerable grace to the massive building. The width of the aisles combines with the decorative lines of the pillars and ribs in the vaulting to make the interior both light and elegant. The chapels are closed by fine wrought-iron screens. The first off the south aisle contains as altarpiece an *Entombment* by Juan de Juni. The *coro*

Romanesque Churches

These beautiful churches of golden stone have common architectural features: well-rounded apses, frequently a tall square belfry beside the east end and a covered gallery where weavers' or merchants' guilds used to meet.

stalls, in late-15C Flamboyant Gothic style, are from the earlier cathedral.

Claustro★ – The 15C cloisters from the former cathedral, near the Alcázar, were rebuilt on the new site. In the Sala Capitular (chapter house) beautiful 17C Brussels **tapestries★** illustrate the story of Queen Zenobia.

Alcázar★★

Open 10am-6pm (7pm Apr-Sep and Fri-Sat in Oct). Closed 1 and 6 Jan and 25 Dec. 5 €, no charge Tue for E.U. citizens. 921 46 07 59.

The Alcázar, on a cliff overlooking the valley, was built above a former fortress in the early 13C and modified in the 15C and 16C by Henry IV and Philip II. In 1764, Charles III converted the building into a **Real Colegio de Artillería** (Royal Artillery School), but in 1862 it suffered a devastating fire. Reconstruction was completed at the end of the 19C, hence its neo-Gothic look. The furniture and richly decorated Mudéjar artesonado work, mostly from the 15C, are original and were brought from various Castilian towns. Its keep is flanked by corbelled turrets. The main rooms of note are the Chamber Royal (Cámara Real) and the Sala de los Reyes (Monarchs' Room). The Sala del Cordón and terrace command a fine **panorama** of the fertile Eresma Valley, the Monasterio de El Parral, the Capilla de la Vera Cruz and the meseta. The artillery school houses a museum recalling the chemical laboratory located here in the 18C and the French chemist **Louis Proust**, who formulated his law of constant proportions in Segovia. The **views** from the keep (152 steps) stretch across the city to the Sierra de Guadarrama.

Iglesia de San Esteban (St Stephen's Church)

Not open to visitors. 921 46 00 27.

One of the latest (13C) and most beautiful of Segovia's Romanesque churches. The porticoes running along two of its sides have finely carved capitals.

The five-storey **tower★** has elegant bays and slender columns on the corners. The interior is in Renaissance style. Inside, the altar in the south transept has a 13C polychrome Gothic figure of Christ.

Iglesia de la Trinidad (Holy Trinity Church)

This austere Romanesque church has a decorated apse with blind arcading and

J. Malburet/MICHELIN

Alcázar

capitals carved with imaginary beasts and plant motifs.

Iglesia de San Juan de los Caballerosa

Open 10am-2pm and 4-7pm (8pm in summer); Sun, 10am-2pm. Closed Mon and public hols. 1.20 €, no charge Sat-Sun and public hols. 921 46 33 48.

This is Segovia's oldest Romanesque church (11C). Its portico (taken from the church of San Nicolás) has carvings of portrait heads, plant motifs and animals. The church, which was almost in ruins at the turn of the 20C, was bought by Daniel Zuloaga, who converted it into his home and workshop. Today it houses the **Museo Zuloaga**, exhibiting drawings by the artist and by his nephew, Ignacio Zuloaga.

Plaza del Conde de Cheste

On the square stand the palaces of the **Marqués de Moya**, the **Marqués de Lozoya**, the **Condes de Cheste** and the **Marqués de Quintanar.**

Iglesia de San Sebastián

This small Romanesque church stands on one side of a quiet square.

Worth a Visit

OUTSIDE THE WALLS

Iglesia de San Millán★

Open 10am-2pm and 4.30-7.30pm. Closed Sun, Mon and public hols. 921 46 38 01.

The early-12C church stands in the middle of a large square, which allows a full view of its pure, still primitive Romanesque lines and two porticoes with finely carved modillions and capitals. The three aisles have alternating pillars and columns as in Jaca Cathedral. The apse has blind arcading and a decorative frieze. The transept has Moorish ribbed vaulting.

Monasterio de El Parral★

Open 10am-12.30pm and 4-6.30pm; Sun and public hols, 10-11.30am and 4.30-6.30pm; no visits during religious services. 921 43 12 98.

The monastery was founded by Henry IV in 1445 and later entrusted to the Hieronymites. The **church**, behind its unfinished façade, has a Gothic nave with beautifully carved doors, a 16C altarpiece by Juan Rodríguez and, on either side of the chancel, the Plateresque tombs of the Marquis and Marchioness of Villena.

Capilla de la Vera-Cruz★

Open 10.30am-1.30pm and 3.30-6pm (7pm in spring and summer). Closed Mon and in Nov. 1.75 €, no charge Tue for E.U. citizens. 921 43 14 75.

The unusual polygonal chapel was erected in the 13C, probably by the Templars; it now belongs to the Order of Malta. A circular corridor surrounds two small chambers, one above the other, where secret ceremonies were conducted. The Capilla del Lignum Crucis holds an ornate Flamboyant Gothic altar. There is a good view of Segovia.

Convento de Santa Cruz

The convent pinnacles, the decorated Isabelline **entrance** with a Calvary, a *Pietà*, and the emblems of the Catholic Monarchs, can be seen from the road.

Iglesia de San Lorenzo

The Romanesque church with its unusual brick belfry stands in a picturesque square surrounded by corbelled half-timbered houses.

Excursions

LA GRANJA DE SAN ILDEFONSO★★

(see Sierra de GUADARRAMA)

Riofrío★

11km/7mi S on the N 603. Open 10am-1.30pm and 3-5pm; Sun and public hols, 10am-2pm; Apr-Sep 10am-6pm. Closed Mon, 1, 6 and 23 Jan, 25 Aug, and 25 and 31 Dec. 5 €, no charge Wed for E. U. citizens. 921 47 00 19.

The Palacio Real (Royal Palace) can be seen through holm oaks where deer

J. Malburet/ MICHELIN

Castillo de Coca

roam, below a hill called Mujer Muerta (Dead Woman).

Palacio

Riofrío was planned by Isabel Farnese as the equal of La Granja which she had to vacate on the death of her husband, Philip V. Construction began in 1752 but though it was very big – it measures 84m x 84m (276ft x 276ft) – it was nothing more than a somewhat pretentious hunting lodge. This palatine construction was never completed and Isabel Farnese never lived in it. The furniture belongs to the period of Francisco de Asís de Borbón, the husband of Isabel II, and Alfonso XII, both of whom spent considerable time in the palace.
It is built around a grand Classical-style courtyard. The green and pink façade reflects Isabel's Italian origins. A monumental staircase leads to sumptuously decorated apartments. A **Museo de Caza** (Hunting Museum) illustrates the development of hunting methods since prehistoric times with the aid of paintings and display cases of animals in their natural habitat.

Castillo de Coca★★

52km/32mi NW along the C 605 and SG 341. Guided tours (45min-1hr), 10.30am-1pm and 4.30-6pm (7pm 15 Apr-15 Oct; last admission 30min before closing. Closed two weeks in Jan and first Tue of every month. 2.50 €. 921 57 35 54.
This **castillo** (fortress), on the outskirts of Coca village, is the most outstanding example of Mudéjar military architecture in Spain. It was built in the late 15C by Moorish craftsmen for the archbishop of Sevilla, Fonseca, and consists of three concentric perimeters, flanked by polygonal corner towers and turrets with, at the centre, a massive keep. It is the epitome of all fortresses, but with the sun mellowing the pink brick and the interplay of shadows on battlements and watchtowers, it can be attractive as well as awesome.
The torre del *homenaje* (keep) and *capilla* (chapel), which contains Romanesque wood carvings, are open to the public.

Arévalo

60km/37mi NW along the C 605. Isabel the Catholic spent her childhood in the 14C **castle** with its massive crenellated keep which dominates the town. Of note also are Romanesque-Mudéjar brick churches, and several old mansions.
Plaza de la Villa★, the former Plaza Mayor, is one of the best-preserved town squares in Castilla with its half-timbered brick houses resting on pillared porticoes. They blend in perfectly with the Mudéjar east end of the Iglesia de Santa María and its blind arcading.

SEVILLA★★★

POPULATION: 701 927

MICHELIN MAP 578 T 11-12 (TOWN PLAN) – ANDALUCÍA (SEVILLA).

Sevilla, set in the plain of the Guadalquivir, is capital of Andalucía and Spain's fourth largest city. To appreciate its many moods, take time to stroll the narrow streets of old quarters like Santa Cruz, or ride slowly through peaceful parks and gardens in a horse-drawn carriage. Sevilla is the centre of flamenco, famous for its bullfights, its 18C Maestranza bullring, and for its cafés and tapas bars.

- **Information:** *Avenida Constitución 21 B, ☎95 422 14 04; Paseo de las Delicias 9, ☎95 423 44 65.*
- **Orient Yourself:** Sevilla, in southwestern Spain, is lined by motorways and dual carriageways to Huelva (92km/57mi W), Jerez de la Frontera (90km/56mi SW), Cádiz (123km/77mi SW) and Córdoba (143km/89mi NE).
- **Parking:** Find a space in the centre, leave your car, and stroll the streets.
- **Don't Miss:** The Giralda and the Alcázar.
- **Organizing Your Time:** Take at least a day for the marvels of central Sevilla, then enjoy quarters such as Santa Cruz, María Luisa park and sites nearby.
- **Especially for Kids:** Isla Mágica beckons for at least a day.
- **Also See:** JEREZ DE LA FRONTERA, OSUNA, HUELVA, ARACENA (93km/58mi NW) and COSTA DE LA LUZ.

Background

Historical notes – Sevilla is summed up on the Puerta de Jerez (Jerez Gate): "Hercules built me; Caesar surrounded me with walls and towers; the King Saint took me." Sevilla was chief city of Roman Baetica and capital of the Visigothic kingdom before Toledo. In 712 the Moors arrived; in the 11C, it became capital of a kingdom which prospered under the Almohads. In 1195 **Sultan Yacoub al-Mansur** (1184-99), builder of the Giralda, defeated the Christians at Alarcos. On 19 November 1248, **King Ferdinand III of Castilla**, the Saint, delivered the city from the Moors.

The discoveries brought new prosperity. By 1503, Isabel the Catholic created the *Casa de contratación* or Exchange to control trade with America. This monopoly lasted until 1717.

Art and architecture in Sevilla – The northern ramparts, the Alcázar walls, the **Torre del Oro** *(Golden Tower)* and the Giralda were all built by the Moors. The **Mudéjar style,** a mix of Moorish and Christian, is testimony to the lasting influence of Arab design in the Alcázar

A Tradition of Fiestas

The great festivals, when vast crowds flock to the city from all over Spain and overseas, reveal the provincial capital in many guises. During **Semana Santa**, or **Holy Week**, *pasos* processions are organised nightly in each city quarter by rival brotherhoods. *Pasos* are great litters sumptuously bejewelled and garlanded with flowers on which are mounted religious, polychrome wood statues; these constructions are borne through the crowd on the shoulders of between 25 and 60 men. Accompanying the statues are penitents, hidden beneath tall pointed hoods; from time to time a voice is raised in a *saeta*, an improvised religious lament.

During the **April Fair or Feria,** which began life in the middle of the 19C as an animal fair, the city becomes a fairground with horse and carriage parades. The women in flounced dresses and the men in full Andalucían costume ride up to specially erected canvas pavilions to dance *sevillanas*.

and other monuments after the city's reconquest.

Golden Age painters of the **Seville School** corresponded to three reigns: under Philip III (1598-1621) **Roelas** and **Pacheco**; under Philip IV (1621-65) **Herrera the Elder** and **Zurbarán** (1598-1664) who portrayed figures with spiritual intensity. Finally under Charles II (1665-1700) **Murillo** (1618-82) created radiant Immaculate Conceptions and brilliant everyday scenes. The best work of **Valdés Leal** (1622-90) can be seen in the Hospital de la Caridad. **Velázquez** (1599-1660) was born in Sevilla.

Many statues are the work of 17C sculptor **Martínez Montañés**. Well-known are the **Cristo del Gran Poder** (Christ of Great Power) by **Juan de Mesa** and the **Cachorro** by Francisco Antonio Gijón in the **Capilla del Patrocinio** (calle Castilla). The **Macarena Virgin**, is the most popular figure in Sevilla.

B. Kaufmann/MICHELIN

La Giralda

Special Features

The Giralda and Cathedral★★★

1hr 30min

Open 11am-5pm; Sun, 2.30-6pm. *Closed 1 and 6 Jan, 30 May, Corpus Christi, 15 Aug and 8 and 25 Dec. Restricted opening times on Tue, Maundy Thu and Good Fri during Holy Week.* *7.50€, no charge Sun.* *95 421 49 71.*

La Giralda★★★

When built in the 12C, the 98m/322ft minaret resembled the Koutoubia in Marrakesh. The top storey and Renaissance lantern were added in the 16C. Typically Almohad, it creates grandeur in harmony with the ideal of simplicity. A gently sloping ramp *(accessible from inside the cathedral)* leads to the top (70m/230ft) for excellent **views**★★★.

Cathedral★★★

"Let us build a cathedral so immense that everyone, on beholding it, will take us for madmen", the chapter is said to have declared. Sevilla's cathedral is the third largest in Europe after St Peter's in Rome and St Paul's in London.

The late-Gothic cathedral shows Renaissance influence. The main portals are modern. However, the Puerta de la Natividad (Nativity Doorway) and the Puerta del Bautismo (Baptism Doorway), right and left of the west door, include beautiful sculptures by Mercadente de Bretaña (c 1460). Miguel Perrin (1520) used Renaissance perspective fully in the Renaissance tympana of the Puerta de Los Palos and Puerta de las Campanillas (*east end doorways*).

▸ *Enter by the Puerta de San Cristóbal.*

The **interior** is striking. Massive columns appear slender because they are so tall. Magnificent Flamboyant vaulting rises 56m/184ft above the transept crossing. A **mirror (1)** on the floor affords a striking view.

Capilla Mayor (Chancel)

Splendid Plateresque **grilles**★★ (1518-33) precede an immense Flemish **altarpiece**★★★, profusely carved with

Address Book

TRANSPORT

Airport – Aeropuerto de San Pablo, 8km/5mi toward Madrid on the N IV motorway, ☏95 444 90 00. A bus service operates from the airport to the railway station and city centre.

Trains – Estación de Santa Justa, ☏ 95 441 41 11. The high-speed AVE (Tren de Alta Velocidad) departs from this station, taking just 45min to Córdoba and 2hr 30min to Madrid. For information and bookings, call ☏902 24 02 02 or visit www.renfe.com.

Inter-city buses – Sevilla has two bus stations: **Estación Plaza de Armas**, ☏ 95 490 77 37/ 80 40; and **Estación del Prado de San Sebastián**, ☏ 95 441 71 11.

Taxis – Radio Taxi ☏ 95 458 00 00/95 457 11 11.

SIGHTSEEING

Publications – Two free bilingual publications (Spanish-English) are published for tourists every month. These brochures, **Welcome Olé** and **The Tourist**, can be obtained from major hotels and tourist sites around the city. Sevilla City Hall's Department of Culture (**NODO**) also publishes a monthly brochure listing all the city's cultural events. A monthly publication covering the whole of Andalucía, **El Giraldillo,** contains information on the region's fairs, exhibitions and theatres, as well as details on cinemas, restaurants and shops. www.elgiraldillo.es

Horse-drawn carriages – It is well worth taking a trip in one of the numerous horse-drawn carriages operating in the city. They can normally be hired by the cathedral, in front of the Torre del Oro and in the María Luisa park.

Boat trips on the Guadalquivir – Boat trips lasting 1hr during the day and 1hr 30min at night depart every half-hour from the Torre del Oro. ☏95 456 16 92 *For coin ranges, see the Legend at the back of the guide.*

WHERE TO EAT

◯◯ **Bodegón La Universal** – *Betis 2 (Triana)* – ☏*95 433 47 46 – Closed Wed* – ▤. The terrace, cooled by the fresh air rising from the Guadalquivir, provides a great view of the city and bullring. Traditional cuisine and a pleasant place to eat either before or after exploring the Triana quarter.

◯◯ **Corral del Agua** – *Callejón del Agua 6* – ☏*95 422 48 41 – Closed 15 Jan-1 Mar.* A pleasant, refreshing surprise awaits you in this quiet, atmospheric alley. The terrace, with its abundant vegetation, is delightful in the heat of summer. Classic Andalucían cuisine.

◯◯◯ **Taberna del Alabardero** – *Zaragoza 20* – ☏*95 450 27 21 – www. tabernadelalabardero.com – Closed Aug* – ▤. This 19C mansion houses one of the best restaurants in Sevilla, a high-class hotel with a dozen or so rooms, a very pleasant tea-room and the city's school of hotel management. One of the best tables in Sevilla.

TAPAS

Bar Europa – *Siete Revueltas 35 (Plaza del Pan)* – ☏*95 422 13 54 – www. bareuropa.info* – ▤. The Europa, in a street behind plaza del Salvador, is a traditional bar that has retained its Belle Epoque feel. Popular with a young crowd who head here in the early evening for tapas and people watching. Wines served at cellar temperature.

Bodega San José – *Adriano 10* – ☏ *95 422 41 05* – ▱. Given its location close to the Maestranza bullring, it's not surprising that this typical bodega is popular with aficionados of bullfighting and good fino sherry. The air of authenticity is enhanced by the dirt floor and the aromas emanating from the huge barrels.

R. Mattes/ MICHELIN

A typical tapas bar

Las Teresas – *Santa Teresa 2 (Santa Cruz) – 95 421 30 69.* This small, typically Sevillian tavern, whose doors open onto a picturesque narrow street, is one of the oldest in the Barrio Santa Cruz. Attractive early-19C decor; specialising in Iberian ham. Continue to Casa Plácido opposite for cold tapas.

Sol y Sombra – *Castilla 149-151 – 95 433 39 35 – www.tabernasolysombra.com – Closed Mon-Tue lunchtime and Aug –* . One of the most popular bars in the city. This bustling bar with its characteristic aromas of fine cheeses, cured hams and cigarette smoke, and walls covered with old and modern brightly coloured bullfighting posters is a must for visitors.

El Rinconcillo – *Gerona 40 – 95 422 31 83 – www.elrinconcillo1670.com – Closed 17 Jul-2 Aug –* . One of the oldest and most attractive bars in Sevilla. Although it dates back to 1670, the decor is from the 19C, including the attractive *azulejo* panelling and the wooden ceiling and counter. Complete meals too at a modest price.

Bodeguita Romero – *Harinas 10 – 95 422 95 56 – Closed Mon and 15-31 Aug –* . Held in high esteem by residents, its bar bursts with tapas and larger portions, all made with quality ingredients. The decor has a local flair.

WHERE TO STAY

Sevilla has a huge range of accommodation for visitors, but beware that during Holy Week and the Feria, prices are likely to double or even triple. If you're planning to stay in the city for these events, make sure you check the room rate carefully beforehand.

Hotel Sevilla – *Daóiz 5 – 95 438 41 61 – www.hotel-sevilla.com – 30 rooms.* An excellent location in a pleasant small square near the Palacio de la Condesa de Lebrija. A good option for those looking for basic comfort at budget prices. The faded decor here adds to the hotel's overall charm.

Hotel Londres – *San Pedro Mártir 1 – 954 50 27 45 – www.londreshotel.com – – 25 rooms.* Near the Museo de Bellas Artes. This centrally located hotel has basic but clean rooms, some with balcony. The best rooms have balconies and overlook the street. The hotel is slowly upgrading, while maintaining its traditional charm.

Hotel Doña Blanca – *Plaza Jerónimo de Córdoba 14 – 95 450 13 73 – www.donablanca.com – – 19 rooms.* The rooms in this attractive mansion, with its distinctive red façade, are very reasonably priced given its size, decor and comfort. The other major plus is its central location in a bustling part of the city near the Iglesia de Santa Catalina.

Hotel Simón – *García Vinuesa 19 – 95 422 66 60 – ww.hotelsimonsevilla.com – – 29 rooms – 4.75 €.* This whitewashed mansion, arranged around a cool internal patio, seems to be from a different era, with corridors decorated with antique furniture and large mirrors. All the bedrooms are comfortable, with the best adorned with colourful azulejos. An excellent location close to the cathedral.

Hostal Van Gogh – *Miguel de Mañara 4 – 95 456 37 27 – www.grupo-piramide.com – – 14 rooms.* Despite its name, this *hostal* is typically Sevillian, with a bull's head over the entrance, brightly coloured walls and pots of geraniums on the balconies. Simple, clean rooms and a good location in the Santa Cruz district.

Hotel Amadeus Sevilla – *Farnesio 6 – 954 501 443 – www.hotelamadeussevilla.com – – 19 rooms – 7 €.* A family of musicians converted this typically Sevillian house with courtyard in the heart of the Santa Cruz district into a delightful small hotel, in which the decor enhances the building's original architectural features.

Hotel Las Casas de la Judería – *Callejón Dos Hermanas 7 – 95 441 51 50 – www.casasypalacios.com – – 130 rooms – 16 €.* A pleasant surprise in the city's old Jewish quarter. Elegant, traditional and full of colour, this charming, old hotel is housed in the former mansion of the Duke of Béjar.

Hotel Alfonso XIII – *San Fernando 2 – 95 491 70 00 – www.westin.com – – 127 rooms – 20 €.* Built in 1928 in neo-Mudéjar style, the Alfonso XIII is Sevilla's most luxurious and famous hotel. An excellent location opposite the gardens of the Alcázar.

TAKING A BREAK

Horno San Buenaventura – *Avenida de la Constitución 16 – ☎954 45 87 11 – www.hornosanbuenaventura.com – Open 8am-10pm.* Part of a network of old furnaces over six centuries old. Particularly popular because of its proximity to the cathedral and its spacious lounge on the top floor. Its cakes are justifiably famous.

Confitería La Campana – *Sierpes 1 – ☎ 954 22 35 70 – Open 8am-10pm.* One of Sevilla's classic cafeterias. The Modernist decor creates a pleasant atmosphere in which to enjoy La Campana's pastries, which are famous throughout the city. Varied clientele ranging from the district's senior citizens to tourists passing through the centre.

NIGHTLIFE

Café de la Prensa – *Betis 8 – ☎ 954 33 34 30 – Open 3pm-3am.* This modern café with a young and intellectual ambience is located alongside the riverbank. Its outdoor tables offer a magnificent view of both the Guadalquivir and the monumental heart of the city. Perfect for whiling away the late afternoon or for a few drinks to start the evening.

El Tamboril – *Plaza de Santa Cruz – Open 10pm-5am.* Tucked away in a corner of the Santa Cruz district, this taberna is always heaving with its faithful clientele who occasionally burst into song with an impromptu sevillana or rumba. Always busy until the early hours of the morning. The Salve Rociera, a prayer to Our Lady of El Rocío, is sung at midnight every day.

La Carbonería – *Levíes 18 (Plaza de las Mercaderías) – ☎954 56 37 55 – Open 8pm-4am.* One of Sevilla's institutions and the key to the culture of the city's alter-native crowd. Housed in a former coal warehouse in the Jewish Quarter (Judería), La Carbonería is split up into a number of different areas, where you can listen to a musical recital in intimate surroundings around a chimney or to authentic lively flamenco (live music every night). The venue also hosts art and photography exhibitions. A must!

Paseo de las Delicias – This avenue is home to four venues (Chile, Líbano, Alfonso and Bilindo). Although not open all year round, these venues become lively in summer, when they are perfect for those who prefer to move from bar to bar. On winter afternoons they are ideal for a quiet drink in the middle of the María Luisa park, surrounded by buildings used during the 1929 Ibero-American Exhibition, while in the summer, drinking and dancing outdoors into the early hours is more the scene. The age range is between 25 and 40, but varies from one venue to the next.

ENTERTAINMENT

Teatro de la Maestranza – *Paseo de Cristóbal Colón 22 – ☎954 22 65 73 – www.teatromaestranza.com – box office open 10am-2pm and 6-8.30pm.* This theatre offers a full season of theatre and dance, including performances by leading international stars, particularly in the field of opera.

El Patio Sevillano – *Paseo de Cristóbal Colón 11-A (Arenal) – ☎954 21 41 20 – www.elpatiosevillano.com – closed evening of 24 Dec – show at 7.30 and 10pm, reservation required – 30€ with drink, 55€ with dinner.* A long-running flamenco club catering to aficionados of the art form in its many variations, in a good location by th La Maestranza bullring, with public parking opposite.

Tablao El Arenal – *Rodó 7 (Arenal) – ☎954 21 64 92 – www.tablaoelarenal.com – restaurant open from 7.30pm, shows at 8.30 and 10.30pm, reservation required – 34€ (51€ with tapas, 64€ with dinner).* Rated by those in the know as a place to enjoy flamenco in its pure form.

H. Le Gac/ MICHELIN

Calle Sierpes

SHOPPING

Most of the city's smartest shops and large department stores are located in and around **Sierpes**, O'Donnell and San Pablo streets. A less upmarket shopping area can also be found behind the Iglesia de San Salvador.
Antique-lovers should wander the historic centre of the city, particularly the Santa Cruz district.
The **Jueves** (Thursday) is a weekly small market held along the calle Feria.

Arts and crafts – Sevilla has a rich craft tradition. Potters can still be found in the Santa Cruz and **Triana** districts (in the latter on calle Alfarería, literally Pottery Street). The La Cartuja factory is heir to this tradition which dates back to Roman times and the period of Moorish occupation of the city. Other products from Sevilla include inlaid woodwork, shawls, fans, wrought iron, harnesses, guitars and castanets.

scenes from the life of Christ and gleaming with gold leaf (1482-1525).

Tesoro

The **Sacristía de los Cálices** (Chalice Sacristy) contains canvases by Goya *(Santa Justa and Santa Rufina)*, Valdés Leal, Murillo and Zurburán, and a triptych by Alejo Fernández.
In the 16C **Sacristía Mayor** are a Renaissance **monstrance** by Juan de Arfe, 3.90m/13ft in height and weighing 475kg/1 045lb and paintings by Zurbarán, and Lucas Jordán.

Capilla Real★★ (Chapel Royal)

Closed to visitors. An elegant Renaissance dome is decorated with carved busts. On either side are the tombs of Alfonso X of Castilla (d 1284) and his mother, Beatrice of Swabia. On the high altar is the robed **Virgen de los Reyes**, patron of Sevilla, given by St Louis of

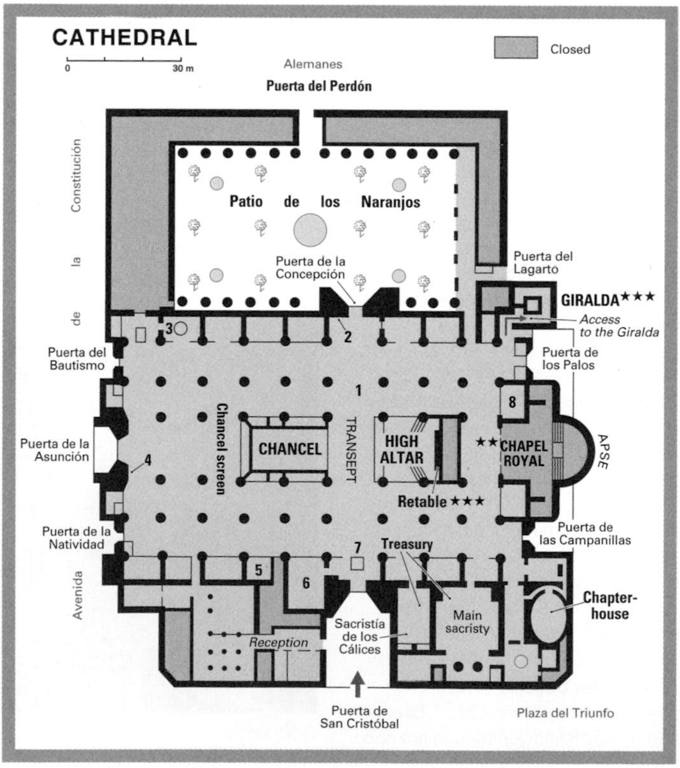

Chapels And Altars

- **Altar de Nuestra Señora de Belén (2)** (Our Lady of Bethlehem): on the north side, to the left of the Puerta de la Concepción. A fine portrayal of the Virgin Mary by Alonso Cano.
- **Capilla de San Antonio (3)**: this chapel contains several interesting canvases dominated by Murillo's *Vision of St Anthony of Padua*, on the right-hand wall. Also worthy of note are *The Baptism of Christ*, also by Murillo, and two paintings of St Peter by Valdés Leal.
- **Altar del Santo Ángel (4)** (at the foot of the cathedral, to the left of the Puerta Mayor): this altar is dominated by a fine *Guardian Angel* by Murillo.
- **Capilla de San Hermenegildo (5)** (next to the Capilla de San José): the 15C alabaster tomb of Cardinal Cervantes sculpted by Lorenzo Mercadante.
- **Capilla de la Vitrgen de la Antigua (6)** (the next chapel): larger than the others and covered with an elevated vault. A fine 14C fresco of the Virgin adorns the altar.
- **19C funerary monument to Christopher Columbus (7)**: the explorer's coffin is borne by four pallbearers, each with the symbol of one of the kingdoms of Castilla, León, Navarra and Aragón on his chest.
- **Capilla de San Pedro (8):** canvases by Zurbarán.

France to St Ferdinand of Spain, who is buried in a silver gilt shrine below.

Patio de los Naranjos (Orange Tree Court) – This patio served as the ablutions area in the mosque.

Exit by the **Puerta del Perdón**, an Almohad arch decorated with stucco and two statues by Miguel Perrin.

REAL ALCÁZAR★★★

Open Oct-Mar, 9.30am-5pm (1.30pm Sun and public hols); Apr-Sep, 9.30am-7pm (5pm Sun and public hols); last admission 1hr before closing time. Closed Mon, 1 and 6 Jan, Good Fri, 25 Dec and for official ceremonies. 7 €; Cuarto Alto: 4 €. 95 450 23 24.

All that remains of the 12C Almohad alcázar are the **Patio de Yeso** and a courtyard wall. In the 13C, Alfonso X, the Wise, built a palace, known today as **Charles V's rooms**. **Peter the Cruel** (1350-69) erected the nucleus of the present building, known as **Peter the Cruel's Palace**, in 1362, using masons from Granada. It is one of the purest examples of the Mudéjar style.

Cuarto del Almirante (Admiral's Apartments)

Right side, the Patio de la Montería. In the Sala de Audiencias (Audience Chamber) the **Virgin of the Navigators**★ altarpiece (1531-36) is by Alejo Fernández.

Palacio de Pedro el Cruel★★★ (Palace of Peter the Cruel)

A passage leads to the **Patio de las Doncellas** (Court of the Maidens), a Moorish arched patio; the upper storey was added in the 16C. An elevated round arch leads to the **Dormitorio de los Reyes Moros** (Bedroom of the Moorish Kings), two rooms decorated with blue-toned stucco and a magnificent *artesonado* ceiling. Through a small room is the **Patio de las Muñecas** (Dolls' Court) with Granada-type decoration. The gallery on the upper floor dates from the 19C. The Catholic Monarchs' bedroom leads to the **Salón de Felipe II** (Philip II Salon), the **Arco de los Pavones** (Peacock Arch), and the **Salón de Embajadores** (Ambassadors

The Cuarto Real Alto

An optional 30min guided tour enables visitors to view the King and Queen of Spain's official residence in Sevilla, The various rooms, with their fine artesonado ceilings, contain an impressive display of 19C furniture and clocks, 18C tapestries and French lamps. Of particular note are the **Capilla de los Reyes Católicos** (Chapel of the Catholic Monarchs) – an exquisite oratory with a ceramic font, by Nicola Pisano – and the Mudéjar **Sala de Audiencias**.

H. Le Gac/MICHELIN

Mercurio pool and Galería del Grutesco

Hall), the most sumptuous room, with a remarkable 15C half-orange cedarwood **cupola**★★★. The **Sala del Techo de Carlos V** (Charles V Room), the former chapel, has a magnificent ceiling.

▸ *Cross the Patio de la Montería and go down a vaulted passage (right).*

Palacio Gótico or Salones de Carlos V (Gothic Palace or Charles V's Rooms)

The palace, built in the reign of Alfonso X, houses magnificent **tapestries**★★ from the Real Fábrica de Tapices illustrating Charles V's conquest of Tunis in 1535.

Jardines★

Continue to the Mercurio pool and 17C **Galería del Grutesco**★ to view the magnificent Moorish gardens. The most enchanting parts are **Charles V's pavilion**, the maze and the English garden. The silhouette of the Giralda rises above the **Patio de Banderas** (Flag Court), bordered by elegant façades.

BARRIO DE SANTA CRUZ★★★ (SANTA CRUZ QUARTER)

The former Jewish quarter is replete with alleys, wrought-iron grilles and flower-filled patios. It is delightful in the evenings when cafés and restaurants overflow into the squares.

Hospital de los Venerables★

Guided tours (15min), 10am-2pm and 4-8pm. Closed 1 Jan, Good Fri and 25 Dec. 4.75 €. 95 422 32 32.
This building, in lively plaza de los Venerables, is one of the best examples of 17C Sevillian Baroque. Its fine **church**★ is covered with frescoes by Valdés Leal and his son Lucas Valdés.

Worth a Visit

NORTH OF THE CATHEDRAL

Museo de Bellas Artes★★★ (Fine Arts Museum)

Open 9am-8.15pm; Tue, 2.30-8.15pm; Sun and public hols, 9am-2.15pm. Closed Mon, 2 and 6 Jan, 28 Feb, 13-14 Apr, 1 and 30 May, 15 Jun, 15 Aug, 12 Oct, 1 Nov and 6, 8 and 25 Dec. 1.50 €, no charge for E.U. citizens. 95 422 07 90.
The Convento de la Merced (Merced Friary) was built in the 17C by Juan de Oviedo around three beautiful patios.
Sala I of the museum inside contains medieval art. **Room II** is dedicated to Renaissance art, in particular a fine sculpture of *St Jerome* by Pietro Torrigiani, a contemporary of Michelangelo. Two magnificent portraits of *A Lady and a Gentleman* by Pedro Pacheco are the highlight in **Room III**.
In **Room V**★★★ walls decorated with paintings by the 18C artist Domingo

Martínez are a stunning backdrop to outstanding work by Murillo and a Zurbarán masterpiece, *The Apotheosis of St Thomas Aquinas* (in the nave), with its skillful play of light and shade. **Murillo**'s monumental *Immaculate Conception,* with its energetic movement, is in the transept. On the right-hand side of the transept is a kindly *Virgen de la Servilleta* (note the effect of the Child approaching).

Upper Floor: Room VI displays a fine collection of saints. **Room VIII** is devoted to Baroque artist Valdés Leal. European Baroque is represented in **Room IX**. **Room X**★★ includes works of **Zurbarán** (1598-1664). In *Christ on the Cross*, the body of Christ appears as if sculpted. His *St Hugh and Carthusian Monks at Table* displays errors in perspective. The ceiling of the inner room should not be missed. In **Room XI** is Goya's *Portrait of Canon José Duato.*

Casa de Pilatos★★ (Pilate's House)

Open 9am-7pm (6pm Oct-Feb). 8 € (5 € ground floor only). ☎95 422 46 77.

The large Mudéjar patio of this 15C-16C palace displays fine stuccowork and magnificent lustre ***azulejos***★★. *Artesonado* ceilings, the chapel with Gothic vaulting and *azulejo* and stucco decoration, and a remarkable wood **dome**★ over the grand **staircase**★★ illustrate the vitality of the Mudéjar style during the Renaissance. The gardens are open to the public.

Iglesia de San Luis de los Franceses★

This church, by Leonardo de Figueroa, is one of the best examples of the Sevillian Baroque. The exuberant **interior**★★ is a mix of outstanding murals, sumptuous retables and fine azulejos.

Convento de Santa Paula★

Open 10am-1pm. Closed Mon and for certain religious ceremonies. 2€. ☎95 453 63 30.

The church's breathtaking **portal**★ (1504) is adorned with ceramics. Despite its mix of styles, the overall effect is harmonious. **Inside**★, the nave is covered by a 17C roof and the chancel by a Gothic vault with attractive frescoes. The **museum**★ (*entrance through nº11 on the plaza*) has works by Ribera, Pedro de Mena, Alonso de Cana and others. The gilded **Capilla de San José**★ **(St Joseph's Chapel)** gleams at night.

Palacio de la Condesa de Lebrija★

Open (including public hols) 10.30am-1.30pm and 4.30-7.30pm (8pm Apr-Sep); Sat, 10am-2pm. Closed Sun. 4 € (8 € both floors). ☎95 422 78 02.

This noble home is decorated with **Roman mosaics**★ from Itálica, Mudé-

Patio, Casa de Pilatos

SEVILLA

Adriano	AX	
Agua Callejón del	CY	4
Águilas	CX	
Alcade Marqués de Contadero Pas.	AXY	
Alemanes	BX	12
Alfarería	AX	
Alfaro Pl. de	CXY	15
Alférez Provisional Glorieta	BZ	18
Alfonso XII	AV	
Alianza Pl.	BX	19
Almirante Apodaca	CV	20
Almirante Lobo	BY	21
Altozano Pl. del	AXY	
Álvarez Quintero	BX	22
Amador de los Ríos	CX	23
Amor de Dios	BV	
Amparo	BV	
Antillano Campos	AX	26
Antonia Díaz	AX	
Aposentadores	BV	29
Arco de la Judería	BY	30
Arcos	AZ	
Ardilla	AY	
Argote de Molina	BX	31
Arjona	AX	
Asunción	AZ	
Bailén	AVX	
Banderas Patio de las	BXY	35
Baños	AV	
Betis	AY	
Borbolla Av. de	CYZ	
Bustos Tavera	CV	
Cádiz Av. de	CY	
Callao Pl.	AX	
Canalejas	AX	
Capitán Vigueras	CY	42
Cardenal Spínola	AV	47
Carlos V Av. de	CY	
Castelar	AX	55
Castellar	BV	
Castilla	AX	
Cervantes	BV	
Chapina Puente	AX	59
Cid Av. del	CY	
Concordia Pl. de la	AV	
Conde de Urbina Av.	CZ	65
Constitución Av. de la	BXY	
Covadonga Glorieta	CZ	67
Cristo de Burgos Pl.	BCV	
Cristóbal Colón Pas. de	AXY	
Cuba Pl. de	AY	
Cuna	BV	
Delicias Pas. de las	BYZ	
Demetrio de los Ríos	CXY	
Diego de Riaño	CY	
Doctor Pedro Castro	CZ	90
Don Juan de Austria Pl.	CY	
Doña Elvira Pl. de	BX	95
Doña Guiomar	AX	97
Doña María Coronel	BCV	
Dos de Mayo	ABXY	
Duque de la Victoria Pl. del	BV	
Ejército Español Pl.	CZ	105
Encarnación Pl. de la	BV	
Enladrillada	CV	
Escuelas Pías	CV	112
España Pl. de	CZ	
Evangelista	AY	

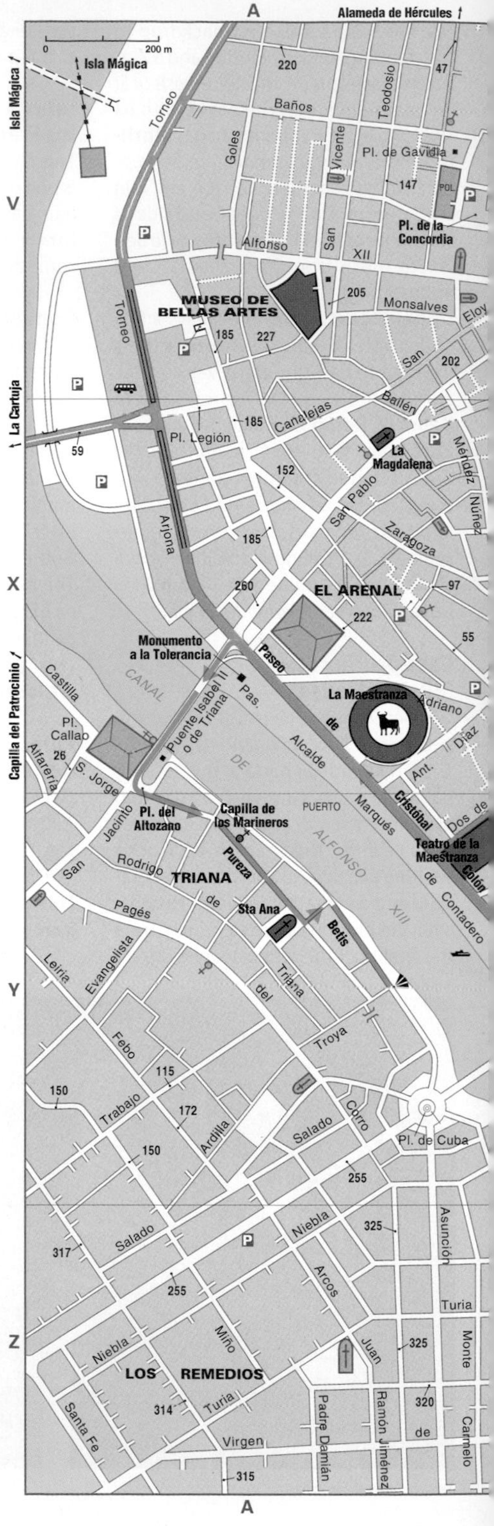

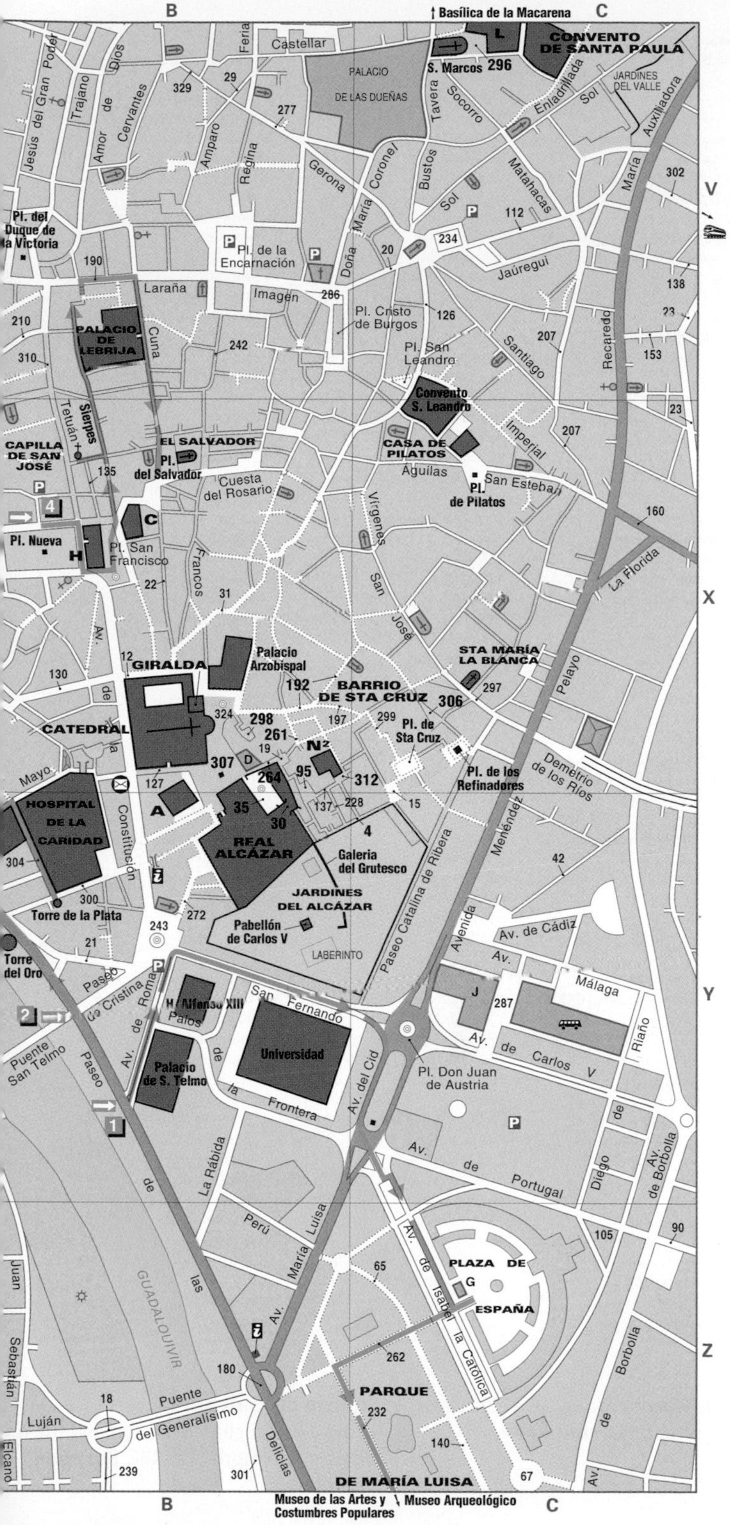
B
↑ Basílica de la Macarena
C
CONVENTO DE SANTA PAULA
L
S. Marcos 296
PALACIO DE LAS DUEÑAS
Castellar
Feria
Jesús del Gran Poder
Trajano
Dios
Amor de
Cervantes
329
29
277
Amparo
Regina
Gerona
Coronel
María
Doña
Tavera
Socorro
Bustos
Sol
Enladrillada
JARDINES DEL VALLE
Auxiliadora
Matahacas
María
302
V
112
234
20
Pl. del Duque de la Victoria
Pl. de la Encarnación
190
Laraña
Imagen
286
Pl. Cristo de Burgos
126
Jáuregui
138
23
210
PALACIO DE LEBRIJA
Cuna
242
Pl. San Leandro
Santiago
207
Recaredo
153
310
Convento S. Leandro
Tetuán
Sierpes
23
Imperial
207
CAPILLA DE SAN JOSÉ
EL SALVADOR
Pl. del Salvador
CASA DE PILATOS
Águilas
Pl. de Pilatos
San Esteban
135
Cuesta del Rosario
Vírgenes
160
4
C
Pl. Nueva
H
Pl. San Francisco
Francos
San José
La Florida
X
22
31
Av.
12
GIRALDA
Palacio Arzobispal
STA MARÍA LA BLANCA
130
de
192
BARRIO DE STA CRUZ
306
297
Pelayo
CATEDRAL
la
324
298
197
299
Pl. de Sta Cruz
261
19
N
307
D
264
95
312
Pl. de los Refinadores
Demetrio de los Ríos
Mayo
127
A
HOSPITAL DE LA CARIDAD
Constitución
35
30
137
228
15
4
REAL ALCÁZAR
Galeria del Grutesco
Menéndez
Paseo Catalina de Ribera
42
304
300
Torre de la Plata
272
JARDINES DEL ALCÁZAR
Pabellón de Carlos V
243
21
LABERINTO
Avenida
Av. de Cádiz
Av.
Torre del Oro
Paseo
Cristina
Roma
H Alfonso XIII
San Fernando
J
287
Málaga
Y
2
Palos
de
Av.
Universidad
Av. del Cid
Pl. Don Juan de Austria
Av. de Carlos V
Riaño
Puente San Telmo
Paseo
Palacio de S. Telmo
la Frontera
1
Av. de Portugal
de
Diego
Av. de Borbolla
La Rábida
Perú
María Luisa
105
90
de
Juan
GUADALQUIVIR
las
65
PLAZA DE ESPAÑA
G
Av. de Isabel la Católica
Av.
Sebastián
262
Borbolla
Z
180
Puente del Generalísimo
PARQUE DE MARÍA LUISA
18
232
Luján
140
de
Delicias
Elcano
239
301
67
Av.
B
Museo de las Artes y Costumbres Populares
Museo Arqueológico
C

Farmacéutico E. Murillo Herrera	AY	115
Febo	AY	
Feria	BV	
La Florida	CX	
Francisco Carrión Mejías	CV	126
Francos	BX	
Fray Ceferino González	BX	127
García de Vinuesa	BX	130
Gavidia Pl. de la	AV	
General Polavieja	BX	135
Generalísimo Puente del	BZ	
Gerona	BCV	
Gloria	BXY	137
Goles	AV	
Gonzalo Bílbao	CV	138
Hernán Cortés Av.	CZ	140
Imagen	BV	
Imperial	CX	
Isabel II o de Triana Puente	AX	
Isabel la Católica Av. de	CZ	
Jaúregui	CV	
Jesús de la Vera Cruz	AV	147
Jesús del Gran Poder	BV	
José Laguillo Av.	CV	302
José María Martínez Sánchez Arjona	AY	150
Juan Ramón Jiménez	AZ	
Juan Sebastián Elcano	BZ	
Julio César	AX	152
Júpiter	CV	153
Laraña	BV	
Leiria	AY	
Luis Montoto	CX	160
Málaga Av.	CY	
Marcelino Champagnat	AY	172
María Auxiliadora	CV	
María Luisa Av.	BZ	
Marineros Voluntarios Glorieta	BZ	180
Marqués de Paradas Av.	AVX	185
Martín Villa	BV	190
Matahacas	CV	
Mateos Gago	BX	192
Méndez Núñez	AX	
Menéndez Pelayo	CXY	
Mesón del Moro	BX	197
Miño	AZ	
Monsalves	AV	
Monte Carmelo	AZ	
Murillo	AV	202
Museo Pl. del	AV	205
Navarros	CVX	207
Niebla	AZ	
Nueva Pl.	BX	
O'Donnell	BV	210
Padre Damián	AZ	
Pagés del Corro	AY	
Palos de la Frontera	BY	
Pascual de Gayangos	AV	220
Pastor Landero	AX	222
Pedro del Toro	AV	227
Perú	BZ	
Pilatos Pl. de	CX	
Pimienta o Susona	BCY	228
Pizarro Av.	CZ	232
Ponce de León Pl.	CV	234
Portugal Av. de	CYZ	
Presidente Carrero Blanco	BZ	239
Puente y Pellón	BV	242
Puerta de Jerez	BY	243
Pureza	AY	
La Rábida	BY	
Recaredo	CV	
Refinadores Pl. de los	CX	
Regina	BV	
República Argentina Av.	AYZ	255
Reyes Católicos	AX	260
Rodrigo Caro Callejón de	BX	261
Rodrigo de Triana	AY	
Rodríguez Caso Av.	CZ	262
Roma Av. de	BY	
Romero Morube	BX	264
Rosario Cuesta del	BX	
Salado	AYZ	
Salvador Pl. del	BX	
San Eloy	AV	
San Esteban	CX	
San Fernando	BY	
San Francisco Pl.	BX	
San Gregorio	BY	272
San Jacinto	AY	
San Jorge	AX	
San José	CX	
San Juan de la Palma	BV	277
San Leandro Pl.	CV	
San Pablo	AX	
San Pedro Pl.	BV	286
San Sebastián Pl.	CY	287
San Telmo Puente	BY	
San Vicente	AV	
Santa Cruz Pl. de	CX	
Santa Fe	AZ	
Santa Isabel Pl. de	CV	296
Santa María La Blanca	CX	297
Santa Marta Pl. de	BX	298
Santa Teresa	CX	299
Santander	BY	300
Santiago	CV	
Santiago Montoto Av.	BZ	301
Sierpes	BVX	
Socorro	CV	
Sol	CV	
Temprado	BY	304
Teodosio	AV	
Tetuán	BX	
Torneo	AV	
Trabajo	AY	
Trajano	BV	
Tres Cruces Pl. de las	CX	306
Triunfo Pl. del	BX	307
Troya	AY	
Turia	AZ	
Velázquez	BV	310
Venerables Pl. de los	BCX	312
Virgen de África	AZ	314
Virgen de Fátima	AZ	317
Virgen de Loreto	AZ	320
Virgen de los Reyes Pl. de la	BX	324
Virgen de Luján	ABZ	
Virgen del Águila	AZ	315
Virgen del Valle	AZ	325
Vírgenes	CX	
Viriato	BV	329
Zaragoza	AX	

Alameda de Hércules	BU	
Archivo General de Indias	BXY	A
Ayuntamiento	BX	H
Barrio de Santa Cruz	BCX	
Basílica de la Macarena	CV	
Caja de Ahorros San Fernando	BX	C
Capilla de San José	BX	
Capilla de los Marineros	AY	
Capilla del Patrocinio	AX	
Casa de Pilatos	CX	
Catedral	BX	
Convento de San Leandro	CVX	
Convento de Santa Isabel	CV	
Convento de Santa Paula	CV	
Hospital de la Caridad	BY	
Hospital de los Venerables	BX	
Iglesia de San Marcos	CV	
Iglesia de Santa Maria la Blanca	CX	
Iglesia de la Magdalena	AX	
Iglesia del Salvador	BX	
Isla Mágica	AV	
Itálica	AVX	
Jardines del Alcázar	BCY	
La Cartuja-Centro Andaluz de Arte Contemporáneo	AVX	
La Giralda	BX	
La Maestranza	AX	
Monumento a la Tolerancia	AX	
Museo Arqueológico de Sevilla	CZ	
Museo de Artes y Costumbres Populares	BCZ	M²
Museo de Bellas Artes	AV	
Palacio Arzobispal	BX	
Palacio de San Telmo	BY	
Palacio de la Condesa de Lebrija	BV	
Parque de María Luisa	CZ	
Parroquia de Santa Ana	AY	
Plaza de España	CZ	
Real Alcázar	BXY	
Teatro de la Maestranza	AY	
Torre de la Plata	BY	
Torre del Oro (Museo de la Marina)	BY	
Triana	AY	
Universidad	BY	

jar artesonado ceilings, 16-17C *azulejos*, and a sumptuous **stairway**★.

Iglesia del Salvador★

It this 17C-18C church are some of the city's most impressive 18C **Baroque retables**★★.

Ayuntamiento (Town Hall)
The attractive **east façade**★ (1527-34) is Renaissance in style and adorned with delicate scrollwork decoration.

AROUND THE CATHEDRAL

Iglesia de Santa María la Blanca★
In the **interior**★ of this former synagogue, exuberant Baroque ceilings are balanced by pink marble columns.

Hospital de la Caridad★ (Hospital of Charity)
Open 9am-1.30pm and 3.30-7.30pm; Sun and public hols, 9am-1pm. Closed some public hols. 5 €. 95 422 32 32.
The hospital was founded in 1625. Great Sevillian artists decorated the **church**★★. Valdés Leal illustrated Death with a striking sense of the macabre. Murillo showed Charity in *The Miracle of the Loaves and Fishes, Moses Smiting Water from the Rock, St John of God* and *St Isabel of Hungary Caring for the Sick*. Pedro Roldan's ***Entombment***★★ adorns the high altar.

Archivo General de Indias (Archives of the Indies)
Open 10am-4pm (2pm Sun and public hols). 95 450 05 28.
The building (1572), designed as an Exchange *(lonja)* by Juan de Herrera, houses priceless documents on America at the time of the conquest, including maps and charts.

South of the Cathedral

Parque de María Luisa★★
The vast **plaza de España**★ of this 19C park remains from the 1929 Ibero-American Exhibition. Each bench represents a province of Spain.

Museo Arqueológico★
Open Tue, 2.30-8.30pm; Wed-Sat, 9am-8.30pm; Sun, 9am-2.30pm. Closed Mon and public hols. 1.50 €, no charge for E.U. citizens. 954 23 24 01.
The archaeological museum is in a palace on plaza de América. The 7C-6C BC **Carambolo Treasure**★ includes a

R. Mattès/MICHELIN
Plaza de España

statue with a Phoenician inscription. In the **Roman section**★ are statues and mosaics from Itálica (*see below*).

Isla de la Cartuja (la Cartuja Island)

Isla Mágica★ (Magic Island)
Kids *Open 1 Apr-1 Nov: all day Jun-Sep (11am-10 pm or midnight); check hours for rest of season and hols. 23.50 €, 15 € (child and over 65); children under 5 no charge; less outside of high season. 902 16 17 16; reservations, 902 16 00 00; www.islamagica.es.*
This amusement park focuses on the Century of Discovery, with such theme areas as **Amazonia** and **The Pirates' Den**, live performances and rides such as **Rapids of the Orinoco**.

La Cartuja–Centro Andaluz de Arte Contemporáneo
Open 10am-8pm (9pm Apr-Sep); Sat, 11am-8pm (9pm Apr-Sep); Sun, 10am-3pm; last admission 30min before closing time. Closed Mon and public hols. 3 €, no charge Tue for E.U. citizens. 95 503 70 96. Buses C-1 and C-2
This modern art museum is in the former La Cartuja monastery; some **convent buildings**★ remain. The collection includes notable 20C artists (Miró and Chillida).
Triana district★; Iglesia de la Magdalena (interior★); Iglesia de San Marcos (Mudéjar tower★).

Excursions

Itálica★

9km/6mi NW on the N 630. Open Oct-Mar, 9am-5.30pm; Sun, 10am-4pm; Apr-Sep, 8.30am-8.30pm; Sun, 9am-3pm. Closed Mon. 1.50 €, no charge for E.U. citizens. 955 99 73 76/ 65 83.

This **Roman town** was the birthplace of emperors Hadrian and Trajan. Mosaics of birds and Neptune are in their original sites.The **Anfiteatro** (amphitheatre), seating 25 000, was one of the largest in the empire.

Carmona★★

40km/25mi W along the A 4. Carmona, with its heritage buildings, overlooks the River Corbones.

Park in the lower part of town.

Old town★

Note the **Baroque tower**★ of the **Iglesia de San Pedro**★, a church with a sumptuous sacrarium chapel (Capilla del Sagrario), and, further along, the **Convento de la Concepción** with its fine cloisters and Mudéjar church.

Through the **Puerta de Sevilla**★ is the 17C-18C **Iglesia de San Bartolomé**. The *capilla mayor* in the Mudéjar church of **San Felipe**★ *(end of calle San Felipe)* is covered with 16C ceramics.

The Baroque **town hall** *(ayuntamiento)*, facing **Plaza de San Fernando** (entrance on calle de El Salvador), has a Roman mosaic. Next door, the 17C-19C **Iglesia del Salvador** is adorned with a magnificent Churrigueresque altarpiece (*open Thu-Mon, 11am-2pm; Mon, Thu and Fri, also open 4-6pm; closed Tue and Wed; 1.20 €. 954 14 12 70.*

The 15C Gothic **Iglesia de Santa María la Mayor**★ is nearby. A monumental **Plateresque altarpiece**★ illustrates the Passion. The **Convento de las Descalzas**★ is a stunning example of 18C Sevillian Baroque. The Mudéjar church of the **Convento de Santa Clara** contains paintings by Valdés Leal.

The **Alcázar de Arriba (Upper Fortress)**, a Roman structure, offers superb **views**★. It is now a parador.

Necrópolis Romana★

Access to the Roman necropolis is indicated along the road to Sevilla.

Open 9am-5pm; 16 Jun-16 Sep, 8.30am-2pm; Sat-Sun in winter, 10am-2pm. Closed Mon and public hols, and Sun in winter. 1.50 €, no charge for E. U. citizens. 95 414 08 11.

Of more than 300 1C tombs, mausoleums and crematoria, the most interesting are the large **Tumba del Elefante** and the huge **Tumba de Servilia**.

SIGÜENZA★

POPULATION: 5 426.

MICHELIN MAP 576 I 22 – CASTILLA-LA MANCHA (GUADALAJARA).

Sigüenza descends in pink and ochre tiers below a cathedral fortress and castle. The old quarter is a maze of narrow streets lined by Romanesque mansions.

- **Information:** *Serrano Sanz 9, 949 34 70 07.*
- **Orient Yourself:** Sigüenza is 128km/75mi NE of Madrid, 22km/14mi from the A 2 road to Zaragoza.
- **Also See:** Monasterio de SANTA MARÍA DE HUERTA (67km/42mi NE), GUADALAJARA (73km/45mi SW) and SORIA (95km/59mi N).

Worth a Visit

Catedral★★

Open 11am-1pm and 4.30-6.30m; Sun, 11am-1pm and 5-6pm; public hols, noon-1pm and 5-6pm. 3 €, no charge Mon. 619 36 27 15.

The nave, begun in the 12C, was completed in 1495. In the **north aisle**, the **doorway**★ into the Capilla de la Anun-

ciación is decorated with Renaissance pilasters, Mudéjar arabesques and Gothic cusping.
In the **north transept** is a fine **sculptured unit**★★: a 16C **porphyry doorway** opens onto cloisters of marble. The **sacristy ceiling**★ by Covarrubias is a profusion of heads and roses between which peer thousands of cherubim.
The **chancel** (*presbiterio*) has a beautiful 17C wrought-iron grille framed by alabaster **pulpits**★. The **Doncel tomb**★★, in the south transept features a realistic figure of a youth which is a major work of sepulchral art.

SITGES★★

POPULATION: 13 096
MICHELIN MAP 574 I 35 – CATALUNYA (BARCELONA).

Sitges is a resort famous for its two lovely beaches. Its 2km/1mi long Passeig Marítim is dotted with hotels and luxury residences. Sitges was an important Modernist centre, which is evident from many of its buildings.

- **Information:** *Sinia Morera 1, ☎93 894 50 04, www.sitgestur.com.*
- **Orient Yourself:** Sitges is a coastal resort between Barcelona and Tarragona.
- **Especially for Kids:** The Museu del Ferrocarril is the place to admire steam engines.
- **Also See:** BARCELONA (45km/28mi NE), TARRAGONA (53km/33mi SW) and MONTBLANC (81km/51mi W).

Worth a Visit

OLD TOWN★★ *1hr 30min*

The parish church dominates the breakwater of La Punta. Balconies of white houses are brilliant with flowers. Museums in neo-Gothic mansions display canvases from the late 19C, when Rusiñol and Miguel Utrillo (father of the French painter) painted here.

Museo del Cau Ferrat★★

Open 10am-1.30pm and 3-6.30pm (15 Jun-15 Oct, 10am-2pm and 5-9pm); Sat, 10am-7pm; Sun and public hols, 10am-3pm. Closed Mon, 1 Jan, 25 Aug and 25-26 Dec. 3.50 € (combined ticket: 6.40 €); no charge first Wed of month. ☎93 894 03 64.

Santiago Rusiñol (1861-1931) added Gothic features to two 16C fishermen's

J. Malburet/MICHELIN

Sitges

Address Book

SIGHTSEEING

A combined ticket provides access to the following museums: Cau Ferrat, Maricel del Mar and the Casa Llopis-Museu Romàntic.

For coin ranges, see the Legend at the back of the guide.

WHERE TO EAT

La Oca – *Parellades 41 – 93 894 79 36 – Closed in Nov –* . This inexpensive, modern restaurant, well located in the centre of Sitges, is known for its grilled meats, roast chicken and fast service. A cheap menu is also available at lunchtime.

Maricel – *Passeig de la Ribera 6 – 93 894 20 54 – www.maricel.es – Closed 15-30 Nov, Tue-Wed for lunch in summer, Tue evenings and Wed rest of year –* . The seafront Maricel specialises in elaborate and innovative Mediterranean cuisine. The specialty is seafood, accompanied by good soups.

WHERE TO STAY

Hotel Romàntic y la Renaixença *– Sant Isidre 33 – 93 894 83 75 – www.hotelromantic.com – Open Apr-Oct – 69 rooms* . This establishment takes up two 19C buildings, each with period decor and a certain decadent charm. Rooms are sombre but cosy, with somewhat antiquated bathrooms. Lovely interior courtyard with trees.

FIESTAS

Sitges is known for its Carnival, its carpets of flowers on the Sunday following Corpus Christi, and for the Catalunya International Cinema Festival *(in October)*. An international theatre festival is also held in the town in June. Its major fiesta, however, is on 24 August, the feast day of San Bartolomé, celebrated with a huge firework display and a traditional parade of giant figures.

houses, which he left to the town, with ceramics, paintings and sculptures. Among the **paintings**, note two remarkable works by El Greco: *Penitent Mary Magdalene* and *The Repentance of St Peter.* The gallery also contains canvases by Picasso, Casas and Rusiñol himself *(Poetry, Music and Painting).*
The museum takes its name from the **wrought iron** collection *(cau ferrat).* Among the objects on display are a set of 16C braziers. There is also a **ceramics** section.

Museo Maricel del Mar★

Open 10am-1.30pm and 3-6.30pm (15 Jun-30 Sep, 10am-2pm and 5-9pm); Sat, 10am-7pm; Sun and public hols, 10am-3pm. Closed Mon, 1 and 6 Jan, 25 Aug and 25-26 Dec. 3 € (combined ticket: 6.40 €), no charge first Wed of month. 93 894 03 64.
This museum in a 14C hospital displays medieval and Baroque art. A footbridge links it to an adjacent mansion.

Casa Llopis-Museu Romàntic★

Open 10am-1.30pm and 3-6.30pm (15 Jun-30 Sep, 10am-2pm and 5-9pm); Sat, 10am-7pm; Sun and public hols, 10am-3pm. 3 € (combined ticket, 6.40€), no charge first Wed of month. 93 894 29 69.
This late-18C bourgeois house gives a good idea of middle- and upper-class life during the Romantic period with frescoes on the walls, English furniture, mechanical devices and musical boxes. Dioramas show scenes of daily life.
The **Lola Anglada collection** is an outstanding display of 17C, 18C and 19C dolls from all over Europe.

Excursions

Vilanova i la Geltrú★

7km/4mi SW. Situated in a small bay, this is an important fishing harbour and a holiday resort.

Museu Romàntic Casa Papiol★

Guided tour (1hr) Wed-Sat 10am-2pm and 6-9pm; Tue, Sun and public hols 10am-2pm. Last entry 1 hr before closing. Closed Mon, 1 Jan, 25 Aug and 25-26 Dec. 3 € (combined ticket, 6.40€), no charge Wed and first Sun of month. 93 893 03 82.

The mansion built by the Papiol family between 1780 and 1801 gives a good idea of the life of the devout, well-to-do industrial middle class. Austerity reigns in the library with its 5 000 or so volumes, in the chapel with its strange relic of St Constance and in the reception rooms with its biblical scenes in grey monochrome. However, the opulence of the house is evident in the furnishings, the ballroom and the Louis XVI apartment where the French General, Suchet, once stayed.

Biblioteca-Museu Balaguer★

Open 10am-2pm and 4-5pm (Jun-Sep, 10am-1.30pm and 4-7.30pm); Thu, 10am-2pm and 6-7pm; Sun and public hols, 10am-2pm. Closed Mon. 2 €, no charge Thu afternoon and first Sun of month. 93 815 42 02.

This library-museum in a curious Egyptian-Greek building was an initiative of poet-historian-politician **Víctor Balaguer** (1824-1901). The **contemporary art collection** includes Catalan works from the 1950s and 1960s (Legado 56). Small works outline the evolution of painting since the end of the 14C. There are also **16C and 17C paintings** (El Greco, Murillo, Carducho, Maino, Carreño etc) and Egyptian and Asian art.

Museu del Ferrocarril★

Kids *Open 10.30am-2.30pm; Sat 5-8pm; Sun and public hols 10.30am-2.30pm. August 11am-2pm and 5-8pm. Closed Mon, 1 and 6 Jan, Easter Mon and 20-26 Dec. 4.50 €, no charge 30 Jan, 18 May 5 Aug, 1-2 Oct and 13 Nov. 93 815 84 91.*

This is one of the most impressive collections of railway engines in Spain.

SOLSONA★★

POPULATION: 6 601

MICHELIN MAP 574 G 34 – CATALUNYA (LLEIDA).

Solsona is a tranquil town with a noble air and attractive squares. Elegant medieval residences line its gently sloping streets.

- **Information:** *Carretera Basella 1, 973 48 23 10, www.elsolsonesinvita.com*
- **Orient Yourself:** The capital of the Solsonès region is on the C 1410 road linking Manresa with the C 1313 heading into the Pyrenees
- **Also See:** PIRINEOS CATALANES, LLEIDA/LÉRIDA (108km/67mi SW) and VIC (97km/60mi E).

Worth a Visit

Museo Diocesano y Comarcal★★ (Diocesan and Regional Museum)

Open 10am-1pm and 4-6pm; May-Sep, 10am-1pm and 4.30-7pm; Sun and public hols, 10am-2pm. Closed Mon (except public hols), 1 Jan and 25 Dec. 2 €. 973 48 21 01.

Romanesque and Gothic **paintings**★★ in the Palacio Episcopal (Episcopal Palace, an 18C Baroque building), are excellent examples of Catalan art.

The frescoes include a painting from the **Sant Quirze de Pedret church**★★, discovered beneath an overpainting.

> **Corpus Christi**
>
> Corpus Christi is the occasion for young men, dressed in ancient costumes, to parade through the streets firing salvoes from blunderbusses. Giant pasteboard figures appear and children dance the local dance, the "Bal de Bastons".

Executed in an archaic style, it shows God, with arms outstretched, in a circle which represents heaven, surmounted by a phoenix symbolising immortality. Totally different are the thinly outlined 13C paintings from **Sant Pau de Caserres**★ – in particular, wonderful **angels**★★ of the Last Judgement.

Known for its **altar fronts**, another highlight of the museum is **La Cena de Santa Constanza**★, a realistic Last Supper, by Jaime Ferrer (15C).

In the **Museo de la Sal** (Salt Museum), everything is carved out of rock salt from Cardona.

Catedral★

Open 9am-1pm and 4-8pm; Jul-Aug, 9am-1pm and 5-9pm; no visits during services (Sun and hols). 973 48 06 19.

Only the belfry and the apse remain of the Romanesque church; the rest is Gothic with Baroque additions such as the portals and the sumptuous 18C Capilla de la Virgen (Lady Chapel) off the south transept. This chapel houses the **Mare de Déu del Claustro**★, a beautifully carved Romanesque figure of the Virgin Mary in black stone.

Museo del Ganivet; Ayuntamiento (town hall – 16C).

Excursions

Cardona★

20km/12mi SE along the C 55. Cardona sits at the foot of an imposing castle.

Castillo de Cardona★

This spectacular hilltop fortress, at 589m/1 933ft, dates back to the 8C. Of the 11C buildings there remain only a truncated tower, the **Torre de la Minyona**, and the collegiate church, surrounded by Vauban-style walls and bulwarks built in the 17C and 18C. The castle is a parador, commanding a marvellous **view**★ of the **montaña de sal**★★, a salt mine worked since Roman times (*guided tours (1hr), 10am-3pm; Sat-Sun and public hols, 10am-2pm and 3-6pm (7pm in Aug); closed Mon exc public hols and in Aug, 12-13 Sep, and19 Dec-15Jan; 9 €; 93 869 24 75).*

Colegiata de Sant Vicenç★★

Open 10am-1.30pm and 3-5.30pm (6.30pm Jun-Sep); last admission 30min before closing. Closed Mon exc public hols, 1 Jan and 25 Dec. 2.40 €, no charge Tue. 93 868 41 69.

The collegiate church built in 1040 has Lombard features. The groined vaulting in the **crypt**★ rests on six graceful columns. The Gothic cloisters date from the 15C.

SORIA★

POPULATION: 35 540

MICHELIN MAP 575 G 22 – CASTILLA Y LEÓN (SORIA).

This tranquil provincial capital stands on the banks of the Duero, the river that relieves the harsh Castilian summer. The desolate scenery and medieval atmosphere have been immortalised by poets such as Antonio Machado.

- **Information:** *Medinaceli 2, 975 21 20 52.*
- **Orient Yourself:** Soria lies in NE Spain at an altitude of 1 050m/3 445ft on a plateau buffeted by the winds of the Meseta.
- **Also See:** El BURGO DE OSMA (56km/35mi SW) and Monasterio de SANTA MARÍA DE HUERTA (85km/53mi SE).

Worth a Visit

Iglesia de Santo Domingo★

The west front of this church has two tiers of blind arcades and a richly carved **portal**★★. The church's founders were Alfonso VIII and his queen, Eleanor Plantagenet (they appear on either side of the portal), hence the French appearance. The figures on the archivolt are shown in great detail. The scenes include the early chapters of Genesis (on the capitals of the jamb shafts), the 24 Elders of the Apocalypse playing stringed instruments, the Massacre of the Innocents, and Christ's childhood,

"Soria Pura, Cabeza de Extremadura"

The motto in the city arms recalls events in the 10C when Soria and its dependent countryside marked the limits of Castile in the face of the Muslim-conquered south. Gradually the Christians built a **fortified line** along the Duero reinforced by bastions such as **Soria, Berlanga, Gormaz, Peñaranda** and **Peñafiel**.

In the Middle Ages, the town grew prosperous partly through its role in the **Mesta**, a powerful association of sheep farmers that organised the seasonal migration of flocks between Extremadura, Castilla and pastures in the north of the country.

Passion and Death (in ascending registers on the archivolt).

Palacio de los Condes de Gómara (Palace of the Counts of Gómara)

The long façade, part Renaissance, part Classical, the bold tower and double patio exemplify late-16C opulence.

Iglesia de San Juan de Rabanera

The Romanesque portal taken from a ruined church dedicated to St Nicholas recalls the events of the saint's life in the capitals on the slender columns on the right and on the tympanum. The decoration at the east end shows Byzantine and Gothic influences. Crucifixes inside are Romanesque over the altar and Baroque in the north transept.

Museo Numantino (Numancia Museum)

Open 10am-2pm and 4-7pm; Jul-Sep 10am-2pm and 5-8pm; Sun and public hols, 10am-2pm. Closed Mon (except Jul-Aug), 1 Jan, local festivals in Jun (Jueves La Saca and Domingo de Calderas), 2 Oct and 25 Dec. 1.20 €, no charge Sat-Sun. ☎975 22 13 97.

The collections in the recently restored museum illustrate the development of Soria from the Palaeolithic Age to today. Note the artefacts from Celt-Iberian necropolises and the coloured pottery from Numancia (*see below*).

Catedral de San Pedro

Open 10am-2pm and 4-7pm (5-8pm Jul-Sep); Sat-Sun and public hols 10am-2pm. Closed Mon in winter. 2 €. ☎975 21 13 34.

The 16C Gothic cathedral is light and spacious; the **cloisters★** are older, with three Romanesque galleries. The capitals have been delicately re sculpted in a pure Romanesque style that recalls Santo Domingo de Silos.

Monasterio de San Juan de Duero

Open 10am-2pm and 4-7pm (5-8pm ;Jul-Sep); Sun and public hols, 10am-2pm. Closed Mon, 1 Jan, 22 Jun, 2 Oct and 24-25 and 31 Dec. 0.60 €, no charge Sat-Sun. ☎975 22 13 97.

The monastery founded by the Hospitallers of St John of Jerusalem is in a rustic setting along the Duero. Only the graceful gallery arcading, with four different orders, remains of the 12C-13C **cloisters★**. The intersecting, overlapping arches owe much to Moorish art. The church contains a small lapidary museum. Two small chambers with beautiful historiated capitals stand at the entrance to the apse; the ciborium effect is unusual, like one might find in an Orthodox church.

Parque del Castillo (Castle Park)

Lines composed about the Soria countryside by Sevillian poet Antonio Machado (1875-1939) come alive here: "violet mountains, poplars beside green waters."

Ermita de San Saturio (San Saturio Hermitage)

1.3km/0.8mi S of the N 122. A shaded path beside the Duero leads to the cave where the holy man sat in meditation. The 18C octagonal chapel is built into the rock.

Excursions

Ruinas de Numancia

7km/4mi NE via ① on the town plan. Open Oct-Mar, 10am-2pm and 3.30-6pm; Apr-Sep, 10am-2pm and 4-8pm;;

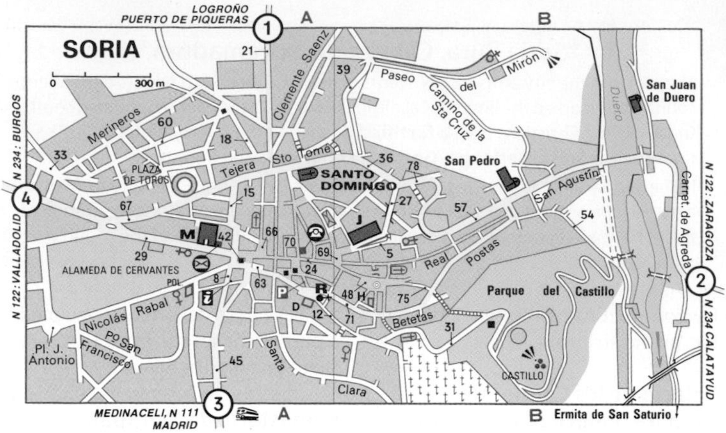

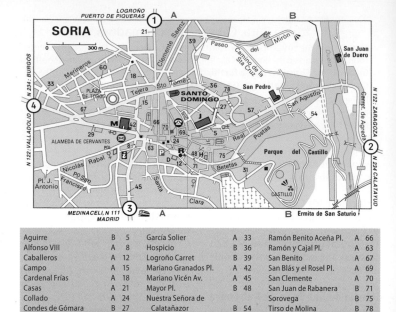

Aguirre	B	5	García Solier	A	33	Ramón Benito Aceña Pl.	A	66
Alfonso VIII	A	8	Hospicio	B	36	Ramón y Cajal Pl.	A	63
Caballeros	A	12	Logroño Carret	B	39	San Benito	A	67
Campo	A	15	Mariano Granados Pl.	A	42	San Blás y el Rosel Pl.	A	69
Cardenal Frías	A	18	Mariano Vicén Av.	A	45	San Clemente	A	70
Casas	A	21	Mayor Pl.	B	48	San Juan de Rabanera	B	71
Collado	A	24	Nuestra Señora de Calatañazor	B	54	Sorovega	B	75
Condes de Gómara	B	27	Obispo Augustín	B	57	Tirso de Molina	B	78
Espolón Pas. del	A	29	Pedrizas	A	60			
Fortún López	B	31						

Iglesia de San Juan de Rabanera	A	R	Museo Numantino	A	M	Palácio de los Condes de Gómara	B	J

Sun and public hols, 10am-2pm. Closed Mon, 1 Jan and 24-25 and 31 Dec. 0.60 €, no charge Sat-Sun. 975 22 13 97.

Scipio Aemilianus, who had destroyed Carthage, directed the Roman siege against Numancia. After eight months the Numantines burned their city and perished. The present ruins are of the town rebuilt by the Romans.

SIERRA DE URBIÓN★★

Roads are liable to be blocked by snow between November and May.

Surprisingly, this part of the Sistema Ibérico mountain range, which rises to 2 228m/7 310ft, is hilly and green. Streams rush through pinewoods and meadows; one is the source of the Duero, one of Spain's longest rivers *(910km/565mi)*.

Laguna Negra de Urbión★★

53km/33mi NW by on the plan and the N 234. About 1hr.

- *At Cidones bear right towards Vinuesa; after 18km/11mi turn*

Address Book

For coin ranges, see the Legend on the cover flap.

WHERE TO EAT

Casa Augusto – *Plaza Mayor 5 – 975 21 30 41 – www.casaaugusto.com* – . This restaurant on the town's main square serves traditional, high-quality regional cuisine in an attractive stone-walled dining room. A daily fixed menu is also available.

WHERE TO STAY

Hostería Solar de Tejada – *Claustrilla 1 – 975 23 00 54 – www.hosteriasolardetejada.com – 18 rooms.* This charming small hotel in the centre of Soria is attractively decorated with a mix of materials, modern design features, bright colours and well-crafted furniture. Excellent value for money.

toward Montenegro de Cameros. After 8km/5mi bear left onto the Laguna road (9km/6mi).

The **road**★★, after skirting the Cuerdo del Pozo reservoir (embalse), continues through pines to **Laguna Negra** (alt 1 700m/5 600ft), a small glacial lake at the foot of a semicircular cliff over which cascade two waterfalls.

Laguna Negra de Neila★★

About 86km/53mi NW by on the plan and the N 234.

▸ *At Abejar turn right towards Molinos de Duero; continue to Quintana de la Sierra then turn right for Neila (12km/7mi), then left for Huerta de Arriba; 2km/1mi on the left is the road to Laguna Negra.*

The **road**★★ through picturesque countryside commands changing views of the valley and Sierra de la Demanda. The lake lies at 2 000m/6 500ft.

TALAVERA DE LA REINA

POPULATION: 69 136

MICHELIN MAP 576 M 15 – CASTILLA-LA MANCHA (TOLEDO).

Talavera is synonymous with the azulejos (ceramic tiles) which brought it fame and prosperity. On the right bank of the Tagus, spanned by a 15C bridge, it retains part of its medieval walls and Mudéjar churches.

- **Information:** *Ronda del Cañillo (Torreón), ☎925 82 63 22.*
- ▸ **Orient Yourself:** Talavera is on the A 5 highway linking Madrid (120km/80mi NE) and Badajoz.
- **Also See:** TOLEDO (80km/50mi E), Monasterio de GUADALUPE (106km/66mi SW) and Sierra de GREDOS (to the N).

Special Features

TALAVERA CERAMICS

Since the 15C, the name Talavera has been associated with **ceramic tiles** with blue and yellow designs used to decorate the lower walls of palaces, mansions and chapels. Today, Talavera manufactures decorative plates, vases and bowls. Green items are made in **El Puente del Arzobispo,** a village *(34km/21mi SW)* which specialises in pottery drinking jars *(cacharros)*.
The **Museo Ruiz de Luna** displays ceramics dating from the 15C to modern times *(open 10am-2pm and 4-6.30pm including public hols; Sun, 10am-2pm; closed Mon, 1 Jan, 1 May and 25 Dec; 0.60 €. ☎925 80 01 49.*

Basílica de la Virgen del Prado (Basilica of the Prado Virgin)

In a park at the entrance to the town coming from Madrid. The church, virtually an *azulejos* museum, gives a good idea of the evolution of the local style.

Excursion

Oropesa

32km/20mi W. The **castle**★ dates from 1366.
Lagartera, 2km/1.2mi west of Oropesa, is known for its embroidery.

B. Brillion/MICHELIN

Talavera de la Reina tiles

TARRAGONA★★

POPULATION: 112 801
MICHELIN MAP 574 I 33 – CATALUNYA (TARRAGONA).

Tarragona, with its ancient and medieval heritage, is also a modern town with wide avenues and a lively commercial centre. Its gardened seafront promenade skirts the cliffside and surrounds the old city and Palace of Augustus, following the city walls in the shadow of the cathedral. Long a major port, Tarragona also has 15km/9.5mi of beaches that attract summer visitors.

- **Information:** *Fortuny 4, ☎977 23 34 15, www.catalunyaturisme.com; Major 39, ☎977 25 07 95, www.tarragonaturisme.es.*
- **Orient Yourself:** Tarragona is in Cataluña in NE Spain, SW along the coast from Barcelona.
- Kids **Especially for Kids:** Visit the Port Aventura theme park, followed by the Costa Caribe water park.
- **Also See:** BARCELONA (109km/68mi to the NE), LLEIDA/LÉRIDA (97km/60mi to the NW) and SITGES (53km/33mi to the NE).

Special Features

ROMAN TARRAGONA★★

Passeig Arqueològic★ (Archaeological Promenade)

Open Oct-Mar, 9am-5pm; Apr-Sep, 9am-9pm; Sun and public hols, 10am-3pm (2pm Apr-Sep, 9pm public hols). Closed Mon, 1 and 6 Jan, 1 May and 25-26 Dec. 2.20€. ☎977 24 22 20.

Scipios built Tarragona's walls in the 3C BC on existing Cyclopean bases. They were so massive that they were long thought to have been barbarian or pre-Roman. Medieval inhabitants rebuilt the ramparts; 18C citizens remodelled them but still left us with walls bearing the marks of 2 000 years of history. A garden walk follows the walls.

Museu Nacional Arqueològic de Tarragona★★ (Archaeological Museum)

Open Jun-Sep, 9.30am-8.30pm; Oct-May, 9.30am-1.30pm and 4-7pm; Sun and public hols, 10am-2pm. 2.40 € (includes visit to Museu y Necrópolis Paleocristianas). ☎977 23 62 09.

The exhibits, mostly from Roman times, are from Tarragona or its environs. The **Roman architecture** *(Room II, ground floor)* section gathers vestiges of the most imposing buildings in Tarraconensis.

Capital of Tarraconensis

The history of Tarragona dates back many centuries. The imposing ramparts built of enormous Cyclopean blocks of stone, indicate that it was founded by peoples from the eastern Mediterranean early in the first millennium BC. In due course it suffered occupation by the Iberians. The Romans, who by 218 BC had control of the larger part of the peninsula, developed Tarraconensis into a major city and overseas capital. Although it could never equal Rome, it enjoyed many of the same privileges as the imperial capital and Augustus, Galba and Hadrian did not disdain to live in it.

Conversion to Christianity, often attributed to the work of St Paul, brought it appointment as a metropolitan seat, and its dignitaries, the primacy of Spain. This honour was retained throughout the barbarian invasions of the 5C and the destruction of the Moors in the 8C but lost finally to the ambition of Toledo in the 11C. The city was then abandoned until the 12C, when it reverted to the Christians.

TARRAGONA								
Àngels Pl.	DZ	2	Enginyer Cabestany	CZ	14	Portalet	DZ	34
Baixada de Misericòrdia	DZ	3	López Peláez	CZ	19	Ramón i Cajal Av.	CZ	40
Baixada de Toro	DZ	5	Mare de Déu del Claustre	DZ	22	Roser Portal del	DZ	43
Baixada Roser	DZ	8	Nova Rambla	CDZ		Sant Agustí	DZ	
Cavallers	DZ	9	Pau Casals Av.	CZ	27	Sant Antoni Portal de	DZ	46
Civadería	DZ	10	Pla de la Seu	DZ	29	Sant Joan Pl.	DZ	52
Coques Les	DZ	12	Pla de Palau	DZ	32	Unió	CZ	
			Ponç d'Icart	CZ	33	William J. Bryant	DZ	55

Antic Hospital	DZ	E	Museo d'Art Modern	DZ	M2	Museu-Casa Castellarnau	DZ	M3
Fòrum Romà	CZ	B	Museu Nacional Arqueològic	DZ	M4	Recinte Monumental del Pretori i Circ Romà	DZ	M1
Fòrum provincial	DZ	D						

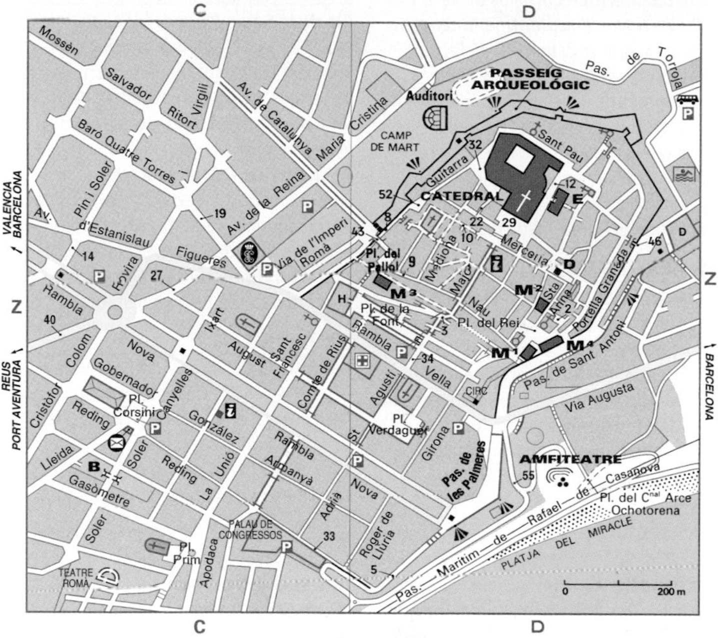

The **Roman mosaics**★★ collection is the finest in Catalunya. Exhibits in Rooms III *(first floor)* and VIII *(second floor)* testify to the high craftsmanship of the Romans. The most extraordinary piece is the **Mosaic of the Medusa**★★ (late 2C), with its penetrating gaze.

Roman sculpture★ *(Rooms VI to X, second floor)* is exemplified by superb **funerary sculptures** *(Room IX)*. Note *(Room VI)* the bust of Lucius Verusa, executed in the 2C, a perfect example of the art, and the small **votive sculpture of Venus**★, with a grace that belies its size.

Recinto Monumental del Pretorio y Circo Romano★ (Praetorium and Roman Circus)

Open Oct-Mar, 9am-7pm; Apr-Sep, 9am-9pm; Sun and public hols, 10am (9am Apr-Sep)-2pm. Closed Mon, 1 and 6 Jan, 1 May and 25-26 Dec. 2.10 €. 977 24 22 20.

Visit the **vaulted underground galleries**★ of a restored 1C BC square tower, or enjoy the sweeping **view**★★ from the top. **Hippolyte's sarcophagus**★★, found virtually intact on the bed of the Mediterranean, bears fine and lively sculptured ornamentation.

The vast **Roman Circus** (325m x 115m/1066ft x 378 ft) was designed for chariot races. Only a few terraces, vaults and sections of the façade remain.

Address Book

SIGHTSEEING

Port Aventura – This theme park, 10km/6mi S of Tarragona, is easily accessible via the A 7 motorway (exit 35) or the N 340.

For coin ranges, see the Legend at the back of the guide.

WHERE TO EAT

Merlot – *Cavallers 6 – 977 22 06 52 – www.restaurantmerlot.com – Closed Sun, Mon at lunch, 1-15 Feb – dinner only in Aug* – . The vaulted ceiling, subtle lighting and high-quality rustic furniture create a refined, intimate ambience. The menu covers a range of Catalan dishes (rice dishes, in particular) as well as an excellent selection of home-made desserts.

WHERE TO STAY

Hotel Urbis Centre – *Plaza Corsini 10* – 977 24 01 16 – www.hotelurbis-centre.com – – *44 rooms – 7.50 € – Restaurant 21 €*. Situated near the convention centre and the old city, this modest family hotel offers functional rooms with updated bathrooms.

Hotel Imperial Tarraco – *Passeig de les Palmeres – 977 23 30 40* – – *170 rooms – 12 €– Restaurant 21 €*. Despite its luxury tag, the rates here are not extortionate. The hotel is housed in a half-moon-shaped modern building near the city's Roman ruins, overlooking the amphitheatre. Many of the international-style rooms enjoy views of the Mediterranean.

TAKING A BREAK

Pla de la Seu – *Plaça de la Seu 5-7 – 977 23 04 07 – www.bettaturst.com.* The best feature of this establishment is its terrace facing the cathedral. Perfect for a refreshment before or after your visit. Live music on weekends.

Rest. Rovira – Vinatería – *Avinguda Prat de la Riba 34 – 977 22 61 58.* The impressive choice at this prestigious wine bar includes a huge selection of sparkling wines from Catalunya. The Sumpta also has its own restaurant.

SHOPPING

Xarcuteria Cuadras – *Rambla Nova 65 – 977 24 28 22.* This is one of the best-known delicatessens in Tarragona, for its own products and local specialties, such as dry fruits, olives, wines, olive oil and Delta rice. A gourmet destination.

Amfiteatre★★

Open Oct-Mar, 9am-5pm; Apr-Sep, 9am-9pm; Sun and public hols 10am-3pm (9am-3pm Apr-Sep). Closed Mon, 1 and 6 Jan, 1 May, and 25-26 Dec. 2.20 €. 977 24 22 00.

The seaside elliptical amphitheatre is in a naturally sloped **site**★. Bishop Fructuosus and his deacons, Augurius and Eulogius, were martyred here in 259. The Iglesia de Santa María del Miracle (church) replaced a Visigothic basilica in the 12C and is itself now in ruins.

Forum Romà

Open Oct-Mar, 9am-5pm; Sun and public hols, 10am-3pm; Jun-Sep, 9am-9pm (3pm, Sun and public hols). Closed Mon, 1 and 6 Jan, 1 May, 11 Sep and 25-26 and 31 Dec. 2.20 €. 977 24 25 01.

The Forum was the core of the Roman city. A few reliefs, pieces of frieze and sections of a street remain.

Museo y Necrópolis Paleocristiana

Open Jun-Sep, 10am-1.30pm and 4-8pm; Oct-May, 9.30am-1.30pm and 3-5.30pm (6pm Mar-May and Oct); Sun and public hols all year, 10am-2pm. Closed Mon, 1 and 6 Jan and 25-26 Dec. 2.40 € (includes visit to Museo Arqueológico), Tue no charge. 977 21 11 75.

During restoration, only a few rooms are open to the public.

Worth a Visit

CIUDAD MEDIEVAL (MEDIEVAL QUARTER)

Catedral★★

Open 16 Mar-May, 10am-1pm and 4-7pm; Jun-15 Oct, 10am-7pm; 16 Oct-15 Nov, 10am-7pm; 16 Oct-15 Mar, 10am-

J. Malburet/MICHELIN

Altarpiece, Capilla de la Virgen de Montserrat

2pm. Closed Sun and public hols. 3.50€. ☎977 23 72 69.

Construction began in 1174 on the site of Jupiter's Temple, in transitional Gothic style, although the side chapels are both Plateresque and Baroque.

Façade★

A Gothic central section with rose window is flanked by Romanesque sections. The **main doorway** displays the Last Judgement, with expressive relief work. The archivolts are carved with Apostles and Prophets. On the pier, the Virgin (13C) receives the Faithful.

Interior★★

Following a Latin cross plan, there are three naves and a transept. The Romanesque apse has semicircular arches. At each end of the transept are 14C rose windows with stained glass. The three naves are mostly Gothic.

The finest work of art is undoubtedly the **altarpiece of Santa Tecla**★★★ (*Capilla Mayor*, 1430), closing off the central apse, which is reached by two Gothic doorways. Santa Tecla (St Thecla) is the city's patron saint. This work by Pere Joan shows a talent for detail, ornamentation and the picturesque. To the right of the altar lies the 14C **Tomb of the Infante Don Juan de Aragón**★★, attributed to an Italian master.

The **Capilla de la Virgen de Montserrat** *(second chapel, left)* houses a **retable**★ by Luis Borrassà (15C). **Reliefs**★ in the Capilla de Santa Tecla (third chapel in the right-hand aisle) recount the saint's life. The **Capilla de los Sastres**★★ *(to the left of the Capilla Major)* features intricate ribbed vaulting, a lovely altarpiece and paintings. Sumptuous tapestries are decorated with allegorical motifs.

Claustro★★

The 12C-13C cloisters are unusually large – each gallery is 45m/148ft long. The arches and geometric decoration are Romanesque, but the vaulting is Gothic, as are the supporting arches . Moorish influence is evident in the *claustra* of geometrically patterned and pierced panels filling the oculi below the arches, the line of multifoil arches at the base of the cathedral roof and the belfry in one corner, rising 70m/230ft. Inlaid in the west gallery is a *mihrab*-like stone niche, dated 960.

A remarkable **Romanesque doorway**★, with a Christ in Majesty, links the cathedral to the cloisters.

Museo Diocesano★★

Open 16 Mar-May, 10am-1pm and 4-7pm; Jun-15 Oct, 10am-7pm; 16 Oct-15 Nov, 10am-5pm; 16 Nov-15 Mar, 10am-2pm. Closed Sun and public hols. 3.50€. ☎977 23 72 69.

The capitular outbuildings contain religious vestments, paintings, altarpieces and reliefs. Tapestries in Room III include the 15C Flemish **La Buena**

Vida★. In the Capilla del Corpus Christi are a richly ornate **monstrance★** (nº105) and a polychrome alabaster relief work depicting St Jerome (16C).

Antiguo Hospital★

This 12C-14C hospital, now used by the local council, is a surprising mix of styles, including the original Romanesque façade and doorway.

Museu-Casa Castellarnau★

Open Oct-Mar 9am-5pm; Apr-Sep 9am-9pm; Sun and public hols, 10am-2pm (9am-2pm Apr-Sep). Closed Mon, 1 and 6 Jan, 1 May and 25-26 Dec. 2.10 €. 977 24 22 20.

The Emperor Charles V is said to have stayed in this wealthy 14C-15C residence. It features a pretty Gothic patio and fine 18C furniture.

El Serrallo★ (19C fishermen's district; fish market)

Excursions

Acueducto de Las Ferreres★★

Leave the city along rambla Nova. 4km/2.5mi from Tarragona you will see the well-preserved two-tier Roman aqueduct on your right, 217m/712ft long. *You can walk (30min)* through the pines to the base.

Mausoleo de Centcelles★★

5km/3mi NW. Exit the city along avenida Ramón i Cajal.

Take the Reus road; bear right after crossing the Francolí. Turn right in Constanti into calle de Centcelles; continue 450m on an unsurfaced road; turn left just before the village.

Open 10am-1.30pm and 3-5.30pm; Jun-Sep, 10am-1.30pm and 4-7.30pm; Sun and public hols, 10am-2pm all year. Closed Mon. 1.80 €. 977 52 33 74.

Two monumental builidings in a vineyard are faced in pink tiles. They were built in the 4C by a wealthy Roman near his vast summer residence. The first chamber is covered by an immense cupola (diameter: 11m/36ft), decorated with **mosaics★★** on themes such as hunting, Daniel in the lion's den etc. The adjoining chamber has an apse on either side.

Torre de los Escipiones★

Leave Tarragona along vía Augusta. After 5km/3mi turn left.

The upper and central parts of this square funerary tower (1C) bear reliefs portraying Atis, a Phrygian divinity associated with death rituals (not the Escipion brothers as once thought).

Villa Romana de Els Munts★

12km/7.5mi E along the N 340. Leave Tarragona along vía Augusta. Open 10am-1.30pm and 3-5.30pm; Jun-Sep, 10am-1.30pm and 4-7.30pm; Sun and public hols, 10am-2pm all year; last admission 20min before closing. Closed Mon, 1 Jan and 25 Dec. 1.80€, no charge Tue. 977 23 62 09.

This Roman villa nestles in Altafulla, in a privileged **site★★** gently sloping towards the sea. The L-shaped arcaded passage was flanked by gardens and **baths★** with a complex plan.

Arco de Berà★

Follow the vía Augusta. The arch is situated in the locality of Roda de Berà, 20km/12mi along the N 340.

The Vía Augusta once passed under this imposing, well-proportioned arch (1C). Its eight grooved pilasters are crowned by Corinthian capitals.

Port Aventura★★

Kids *10km/6mi SW towards Salou. The park is open from 15 Mar to 6 Jan as follows: 15 Mar-22 Jun and 17 Sep-6 Jan, 10am-8pm (10pm Sat-Sun); 23 Jun-16 Sep, 10am-midnight. 902 20 22 20.*

Tickets can be purchased 24hr in advance through the services of Servi-Caixa or at the park ticket offices: adults (12-60 years of age): 28.85 €/day (43.27 € for two consecutive days); children (5-12 years old) and over-60s: 21.64 € (33.06 € for two consecutive days); children under 5: no charge. Parking: cars: 4.21 €; motorbikes: 2.40 €/day; caravans: 4.81 €.

The huge Universal Studios Port Aventura amusement park is divided into five geographical zones, each with its char-

acteristic rides, performances, shops and eateries.
Mediterrània at the park entrance is a coastal town. In **Polynesia**★, a path winds through tropical vegetation.
China★★ is the heart of the park, symbolising the magic and mystery of a millenary civilisation. The star attraction is **Dragon Khan**★★★, the world's most spectacular roller coaster with eight gigantic loops. **Mexico**★★ spans Mayan ruins, colonial Mexico, Mariachi music and traditional Mexican cuisine.
In the **Far West**★★ town of **Penitence**, visitors play the lead in a western or dance in the saloon.

Costa Caribe

Open 10am-7pm (in winter, only Gran Caribe section). Adults 13-59: 18.50 €, children 5-12 and adults over 60: 15 €. 902 20 22 20
Next to Port Aventura, this is a water park with a Caribbean island theme. One covered and heated section remains open through winter.

TERUEL★

POPULATION: 31 068
MICHELIN MAP 574 K 26 – 96KM/60MI FROM DAROCA, ARAGÓN (TERUEL).

Isolated amid rugged hills and deep ravines, Teruel has retained the charm of its narrow streets and splendid buildings which transport visitors back through the centuries. The smallest provincial capital, of Bajo (Lower) Aragón, it is a UNESCO World Heritage Site for its magnificent Mudéjar architecture.

- **Information:** *San Francisco 1, 978 64 14 61.*
- **Orient Yourself:** Teruel is at 916m/3 005ft directly east of Madrid on the Turia river.
- **Also See:** CUENCA (152km/95mi SW) and Costa del AZAHAR.

Worth a Visit

Plaza del Torico, the heart of the town, is lined with Rococo-style houses. It is named for a small statue of a bull calf.

Museo Provincial★

Open 10am-2pm and 4-7pm (including public hols); Sat-Sun, 10am-2pm. Closed Mon, 2 and 6 Jan, 18 Apr, 8-11 Jul and 24-25 and 31 Dec. 978 60 01 50.
The museum, in a mansion with an elegant Renaissance façade crowned by a gallery, displays ethnological and archaeological collections, including tools and everyday objects. Note the reconstitution of a forge and the 15C Gothic door knocker.
The first floor is given over to ceramics, for which Teruel has been renowned since the 13C. The upper floors contain prehistoric (an Iron Age sword from Alcorisa), Iberian, Roman (a catapult) and Arab (an 11C censer) objects.

Catedral

Open 11am-2pm and 4-8pm. 1.80 €. 978 61 99 50.
The cathedral, originating in the 13C (tower), was enlarged in the 16C and

The Legend of the Lovers of Teruel

In the 13C, **Diego de Marcilla** and **Isabel de Segura** were in love and wished to marry but Isabel's father had set his sights on a richer suitor. Diego thereupon went to the wars to win honour and riches. The day of his return, five years later, was Isabel's wedding day to his rival. He died in front of her in despair and the following day Isabel was overcome with grief and died in her turn. This drama inspired many 16C poets and dramatists including Tirso de Molina.

Mudéjar Towers

The great richness of **Mudéjar architecture**★ in Teruel arises because Christians, Jews and Muslims all lived peacefully together in the town until the 15C – the last mosque was closed only in 1502. There are five towers in all, built between the 12C and 16C, in each case to a three-storey plan: at the base, an arch provided access to the street; the centre, pierced only by narrow Romanesque openings, was decorated with Moorish-influenced ornamental brickwork and ceramics, while at the top was a belfry, pierced by bays in pairs below and quadruples above. The two best examples, the **Torre de San Martín** and the **Torre del Salvador**, are both 13C.

B. Brillion/MICHELIN

Torre de San Martín

again in the 17C. The late-13C **artesonado ceiling**★, once hidden beneath star vaulting, is a precious example of Mudéjar art. Its beams and consoles are painted with decorative motifs, people at court and hunting scenes.

In the north transept is a 15C **altarpiece** of the Coronation of the Virgin. Scenes shown in perspective along the second band suggest Flemish influence. The 16C **high altar retable** is by **Gabriel Joli**, known for powerful portraits and skill in illustrating movement by a marked turn of the body.

WHERE TO EAT

⊜⊜ **La Menta** – *Bartolomé Esteban – ☎ 978 60 75 32 – Closed Sun, Mon, 7-24 Jan and 9-24 July –* ▤. A cosy restaurant with a long tradition. Enjoy an original plate or Aragonese specialty, with a selection from the excellent and varied wine list.

Iglesia de San Pedro

Open 10am-2pm and 4-8pm; Aug 10am-8pm. Closed 1 Jan and 25 Dec. 4 €. ☎978 61 83 98.

In spite of 18C alterations, the church retains a Mudéjar tower and east end. The adjoining **Mausoleo de los Amantes de Teruel** (The Mausoleum of the Teruel Lovers) shows the deceased in an alabaster relief by Juan de Ávalos (20C). Glass panes reveal their remains.

Excursions

Albarracín★

38km/24mi W along the N 234 and A 1512. Hidden in the Sierra de Albarracín, this medieval city tinged with pinkish hues stands in an exceptional **site**★, on a cliff above the Guadalaviar river. The ramparts rising behind the town were built by the Moors in the 10C and restored by the Christians in the 14C. Caves in the surrounding sierra contain **rock engravings** from the Upper Palaeolithic era, such as the sites at Callejón del Plou and Cueva del Navaza *(5km/3mi SE towards Bezas and Valdecuenca).*

TOLEDO★★★

POPULATION: 63 561

MICHELIN MAP 576 M 17 (TOWN PLAN) – MAP 121 ALREDEDORES DE MADRID – CASTILLA-LA MANCHA (TOLEDO).

Golden Toledo rises dramatically on a granite eminence encircled by a steep ravine of the Tajo (Tagus). It is as spectacular in setting as it is rich in history, buildings and art. Every corner has a tale to tell, every aspect reflects a brilliant fusion of east and west, of Christian, Jewish and Moorish cultures during the Middle Ages.

- **Information:** *Puerta Bisagra, ☎925 22 08 43; Plaza del Ayuntamiento 1, ☎925 25 40 30.*
- **Orient Yourself:** Toledo is 71km/44mi SW of Madrid.
- **Parking:** Try to park below the centre of the city, and walk or take a taxi up.
- **Don't Miss:** El Greco's masterpiece, *The Burial of the Count of Ordaz.*
- **Organizing Your Time:** Monumental Toledo is compact. Walk around for an overview, then return for a visit to the sites of most interest.
- **Also See:** ARANJUEZ (47km/29mi NE), MADRID (71km/44mi NE) and TALAVERA DE LA REINA (80km/50mi NW).

Background

The city's incomparable **site**★★★ can be appreciated from the *carretera de circunvalación*, a ring-road which parallels the loop of the Tajo from the Puente de Alcántara (Alcántara Bridge) to the Puente de San Martín. For truly memorable views, it is worth going to the **viewpoints** among olive groves on the surrounding hills. The terrace of the parador, above the *carretera de circunvalación*, is a superb vantage point.

Roman town to Holy Roman city – The Romans fortified the strategic settlement into a town they named Toletum. It passed into the hands of the barbarians, and in the 6C to the Visigoths who made it a royal seat until they were defeated by the Moors at Guadelete in 711. After the revolt of the *taifas* in 1012, Toledo was capital of an independent kingdom. In 1085 it was conquered by Alfonso VI, who soon moved his capital from León. Alfonso VII was crowned emperor in Toledo, hence the title of imperial city. The city of Moors, Jews and Christians began to prosper. The Catholic Monarchs gave it the Monastery of St John but lost interest after they reconquered Granada in 1492. Emperor Charles V had the Alcázar rebuilt. In his reign the city took part in the Comuneros' Revolt led by **Juan de Padilla,** a Toledan.
After 1561 when Philip II named Madrid as Spain's capital, Toledo was relegated to the role of spiritual centre.
Toledo and the Visigoths – By 554 the Visigoths had made Toledo their capital. Christianity was adopted in 589. Toledo was abandoned to the Moors amid internal strife in 711.

Toledo and the Jews – In the 12C the Jewish community numbered 12 000. **Ferdinand III** (1217-52) encouraged diversity which brought about a cultural flowering, and the city developed into a great intellectual forum. **Alfonso X, the Wise** (1252-84), gathered a court of learned Jews and established the *School of Translation*. In 1355 a pogrom was instigated by supporters of Henry IV of Trastamara. After repeated attacks, the Jews were expelled in 1492.**Mudéjar art in Toledo** – The Mudéjar style established itself in Toledo after the Reconquest of the city, in palaces (Taller del Moro), synagogues (El Tránsito, Santa María la Blanca) and churches. Brick was widely used. Moorish stuccowork, *artesonado* and *azulejos* became commonplace. In the 13C and 14C, most Toledan churches were given

Romanesque semicircular **east ends**, blind arcades took on variations unknown elsewhere, and **belfries** were built square and decorated until they resembled minarets. The edifices often have a nave and two aisles – a Visigothic influence – Roman tripartite apses and Moorish wood vaulting.

Special Features

CATEDRAL★★★

Open 10.30am-6.30pm; Sun and public hols, 2-6.30pm; last entry 30 min before closing. Closed 1 Jan and 25 Dec. 6 € museum; free Wed afternoon (Spaniards only). 925 22 22 41.

The cathedral dominates the **plaza del Ayuntamiento**. Construction began in the reign of Ferdinand III (St Ferdinand) in 1227. Unusually, the design was French Gothic, but as building continued until the end of the 15C, its architecture came to reflect Spanish Gothic. Despite additions, the church is outstanding for its sculptured decoration and works of religious art.

Exterior

The **Puerta del Reloj** (Clock Doorway), in the north wall, from the 13C, was modified in the 19C.

The **main façade** is pierced by three tall 15C portals; the upper registers were completed in the 16C and 17C. The central **Puerta del Perdón** (Pardon Doorway) is crowded with statues and crowned with a tympanum illustrating the Virgin Mary presenting the 7C bishop of Toledo with a chasuble.

The harmonious tower is 15C; the dome was designed by El Greco's son in the 17C. In the south wall is the 15C **Puerta de los Leones** (Lion Doorway) designed by Master Hanequin of Brussels and decorated by Juan Alemán. The neo-Classical portal is from 1800.

Enter through the Puerta del Mollete, left of the west front.

Interior

The size and sturdy character of the cathedral, with five unequal aisles and great pillars, are striking. Wonderful stained glass (1418-1561) colours the

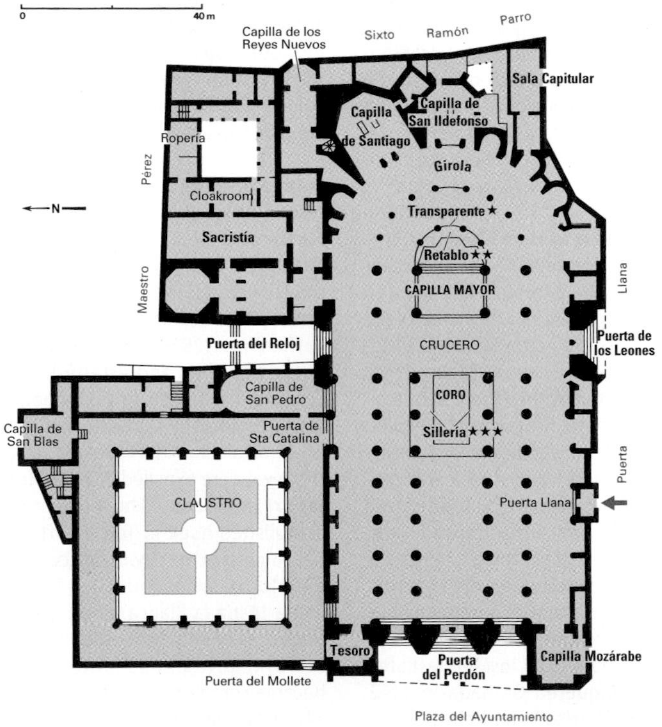

Toledo

windows; magnificent wrought-iron grilles enclose the chancel, *coro* and chapels.

Capilla Mayor

The chancel, the most sumptuous section, was enlarged in the 16C.
The immense polychrome **retable**★★, carved in detail in Flamboyant style with the Life of Christ, is awe-inspiring. The silver statue of the Virgin at the predella dates from 1418. The Plateresque marble tomb of Cardinal Mendoza on the left is by Covarrubias.

Coro

14C high reliefs and wrought-iron enclosed chapels form the perimeter of the choir, itself closed by an elegant iron screen (1547). The lower parts of the 15C and 16C **choir stalls**★★★ were carved by Rodrigo Alemán to recall the conquest of Granada; the alabaster 16C upper parts, by Berruguete *(left)* and Felipe Vigarny *(right)* portray Old Testament figures. The central low relief, the Transfiguration, is also by Berruguete. The style of his work creates the impression of movement. Two organs and a Gothic eagle lectern complete the set. The 14C marble *White Virgin* is French.

Girola

The double ambulatory, surmounted by an elegant triforium with multifoil arches, is bordered by seven apsidal chapels separated by small square chapels. The vaulting is a geometrical wonder.

There is little room to step back for a good look at the **Transparente**★, the contentious but famous work by Narciso Tomé which forms a Baroque island in the Gothic church. Illuminated through an opening in the ambulatory roof (made to allow light to fall on the tabernacle), the *Transparente* appears as an ornamental framework of angels and swirling clouds and rays surrounding the Virgin and the Last Supper. In the **Capilla de San Ildefonso** (Chapel of San Ildefonso), the central tomb of Cardinal Gil de Albornoz (14C) is the most notable.

Sala Capitular (Chapter house)

The antechamber has an impressive Mudéjar ceiling and two Plateresque carved walnut wardrobes. Remarkable Mudéjar stucco doorways and carved Plateresque panels precede the chapter house with its multicoloured **Mudéjar ceiling**★. Below frescoes by Juan de Borgoña are portraits of former archbishops including two by Goya.

Sacristía (Sacristy)

The first gallery, its vaulted ceiling painted by Lucas Jordán, includes **paintings by El Greco**★ of which **El Expolio** (*The Saviour Stripped of His Raiment*) is outstanding. It sets an exalted personality against swirling robes to establish Baroque movement. Other works include a remarkable portrait of *Pope Paul III* by Titian, a *Holy Family* by Van Dyck, a *Mater Dolorosa* by Morales

Address Book

For coin ranges, see the Legend on the cover flap.

GETTING ABOUT

Ave Madrid-Toledo Train – The high-speed train from Madrid reaches Toledo in 30min. Call RENFE, ☎902 24 02 02 or visit www.renfe.es.

WHERE TO EAT

La Abadía – *Nuñez de Arce 3 (Plaza de San Nicolás) – ☎ 925 25 11 40 – www. abadiatoledo.com.* Complex lighting and modern furniture in the basement of a 16C palace create a highly original overall effect and a pleasant backdrop to creative cuisine. Not for the claustrophobic.

Casón de los López de Toledo – *Sillería 3 – ☎925 25 47 74 – www. casontoledo.com – Closed Sun evenings and Mon in Jul-Aug –* . Time has stood still in this stone mansion built around patio. A delightful setting for highly original cuisine. A bar and coffee shop are on the ground floor.

WHERE TO STAY

Hotel La Almazara – *3.5km/2mi SW along the Cuerva road – ☎925 22 38 66 – www.hotelalmazara.com – Closed 11 Dec-25 Feb – P – Reservation recommended – 46 rooms – 4.50 €.* This former cardinal's residence, its walls clad with ivy, is reached via a lane planted with olive trees. Bedrooms are spacious and bright; some terraces have garden or city views.

Hostal del Cardenal – *Paseo Recaredo 24 – ☎925 22 49 00 – www. hostaldelcardenal.com – – 28 rooms – 7.57 € – Restaurant 23.24/36.25 €.* This charming hotel, half-hidden in a delightful garden, stands at the foot of the city walls. Behind the splendid stone façade, the rooms are elegantly decorated with wood furnishings and antiques. The restaurant is superb.

SHOPPING

Toledo is renowned for **damascene ware** (black steel inlaid with gold, silver and copper thread) and such culinary specialities as braised partridge and marzipan.

FIESTAS

Toledo's streets are a splendid setting for the **Corpus Christi** procession, one of the largest in Spain, held on the first Sunday following Corpus Christi.

and the *Taking of Christ* by Goya which displays his skill in composition, use of light and in portraying individuals in a crowd. Pedro de Mena's (17C) famous sculpture, *St Francis of Assisi*, is in a glass case. In the vestry are portraits by Velázquez *(Cardinal Borja)*, Van Dyck *(Pope Innocent XI)* and Ribera.

The old laundry *(ropería)* contains liturgical objects dating back to the 15C. The **Nuevas Salas del Museo Catedralicio** (Cathedral Museum's New Galleries) displays works by Caravaggio, El Greco, Bellini and Morales.

Tesoro (Treasury)

A Plateresque doorway by Covarrubias opens into the chapel under the tower. Beneath a Mudéjar ceiling note the splendid 16C silver-gilt **monstrance**★★ by Enrique de Arfe, weighing 180kg/392lb and 3m/10ft high, paraded at Corpus Christi. The pyx at its centre is fashioned from gold brought by Christopher Columbus.

Capilla Mozárabe (Mozarabic Chapel)

The chapel beneath the dome was built by Cardinal Cisneros (16C) to celebrate Mass according to the Visigothic or Mozarabic ritual which had been threatened with abolition in the 11C.

Claustro (Cloisters)

The simplicity of the 14C lower gallery contrasts with the bold murals by Bayeu of the Lives of Toledan saints (Santa Eugenia and San Ildefonso).

CENTRE OF OLD TOLEDO★★★

Allow 1 day – see town plan

There is something to see and enjoy at every step in Toledo.

Ringing the square before the cathedral are the 18C **Palacio Arzobispal** (Archbishop's Palace), the 17C **Ayuntamiento** (Town Hall) with classical façade and the 14C **Audiencia** (Law Courts).

Iglesia de Santo Tomé

Open 10am-5.45pm (6.45pm Mar-15 Oct); last admission 30 min before closing. Closed 1 Jan and 25 Dec. 1.90 €, no charge non-hol Wed after 2.30pm. 925 25 60 98.

The church, like that of San Román, has a distinctive 14C Mudéjar tower. Inside is El Greco's famous painting **The Burial of the Count of Orgaz**★★★ executed in about 1586. The interment is transformed by the miraculous appearance of St Augustine and St Stephen. Figures in the lower register are portraits of acquaintances of the painter; the sixth from the left is said to be El Greco. Above, Christ prepares to receive the soul of the count.

Museo de El Greco★ (El Greco Museum)

Open 10am-2pm and 4-9pm (6pm Dec-Feb); Sun and public hols, 10am-2pm; last admission 30min before closing. Closed Mon, 1 Jan, 1 May and 24-25 and 31 Dec. 2.40 €. 925 22 40 46.

In 1585, El Greco moved into a house similar to this one. In what would have been the artist's workroom is a signed *St Francis and Brother León*.

On the first floor are an interesting *View and Plan of Toledo* and the complete series of individual portraits of the Apostles and Christ (later and more mature than those in the cathedral).

The **capilla** on the ground floor, with a multicoloured Mudéjar ceiling, has a picture in the altarpiece of *St Bernardino of Siena* by El Greco.

Sinagoga del Tránsito★★

Open 10am-2pm and 4-6pm (9pm Mar-Nov); Sun and public hols, 10am-2pm; last entry 30min before closing. Closed Mon, 1 Jan, 1 May and 24- 25 and 31 Dec. 2.40 €. 925 22 36 65.

Of the 10 synagogues that once stood in the Jewish quarter (Judería), only this and Santa María la Blanca remain. It was financed in the 14C by by Samuel Ha-Levi, treasurer to King Peter the Cruel. In 1492 it was converted into a church.

Unpretentious outside, it is covered inside with amazing **Mudéjar decoration**★★. Above the rectangular hall is an *artesonado* ceiling of cedarwood; just below, are 54 multifoil arches, some blind, others pierced with delicate stone tracery. Below again runs a frieze, decorated at the east end with *mocárabes* and on the walls with inscriptions in Hebrew to the glory of Peter the Cruel, Samuel Ha-Levi and the God of Israel. In the east wall, inscriptions describe the synagogue's foundation. The women's balcony opens from the south wall.

The adjoining rooms, once a Calatrava monastery, are the **Museo Sefardí** (Sephardic Museum) displaying tombs, robes, costumes and books. Several are gifts from descendants of Jews expelled in 1492.

Santa María la Blanca★

Open 10am-3.45pm (6.45pm Mar-Sep). Closed 1 Jan, 24 Dec (afternoon), 25 Dec and 31 Dec (afternoon). 1.90 €, no charge Wed after 3.45pm. 925 22 72 57.

This was the principal synagogue in Toledo in the late 12C. In 1405 it was given to the Knights of Calatrava as a church. Subsequent modifications incredibly left the Almohad-style nave untouched with five tiered aisles separated by octagonal pillars supporting horseshoe-shaped arches. The whitewashed pillars set off intricately carved **capitals**★ adorned with pine cones and strapwork. The polychrome wood altarpiece is 16C.

Monasterio de San Juan de los Reyes★ (St John of the Kings Monastery)

Open 10am-6pm (7pm in summer). Closed 1 Jan and 25 Dec. 1.90 €. 925 22 38 02.

The Franciscan monastery commemmorates the victory over the Portuguese at Toro in 1476. The overall style is Isabelline, which fuses Flamboyant Gothic with Mudéjar and Renaissance art. The exterior is somewhat austere, relieved by pinnacles and a stone balustrade. Covarrubias designed the north portal, including in the decoration the

TOLEDO

Alcántara Puente de	CX	
Alfileritos	BY	
Alfonso VI Pl. de	BX	
Alfonso X el Sabio	BY	2
Alfonso XI	BY	3
América Av. de	AX	
Ángel	AY	
Ave María	BZ	
Ayuntamiento Pl. del	BY	4
Azarquiel Puente de	CX	
Cabestreros Pas. de	CZ	
Cadenas	BY	7
Campana Travesía	BY	8
Cardenal Lorenzana	BY	9
Cardenal Tavera	BX	
Carlos III Av. de	AX	
Carlos V Cuesta de	BY	13
Carmelitas	AY	14
Cava Av. de la	AX	
Cervantes	CY	
Circo Romano Pas. del	AX	
Colegio de Doncellas	AY	17
Comercio	BY	
Conde Pl. del	AY	18
Consistorio Pl. del	BY	19
Cordonerías	BY	20
Cruz Verde Pas. de la	BZ	
Duques de Lerma Av. de los	BX	
Esteban Illán	BY	24
Gerardo Lobo	BX	
Hombre de Palo	BY	27
Honda	BX	28
Juanelo Ronda de	CY	
Mas del Ribero Av. de	AX	
Matías Moreno	AY	
Merced	BY	
Nuncio Viejo	BY	29
Núñez de Arce	BX	32
Padilla Pl. y Calle de	ABY	33
Padre Mariana Pl.	BY	34
Pascuales Cuesta de los	CY	36
Plata	BY	
Pozo Amargo	BZ	
Real del Arrabal	BX	
Recaredo Pas. de	AX	
Reconquista Av. de la	ABX	
Reyes Católicos	AY	
Rosa Pas. de la	CX	
El Salvador	BY	22
San Cristóbal Pas.	BZ	38
San Juan de Dios	AY	40
San Justo Cuesta	CY	
San Justo Pl.	BY	41
San Marcos	BY	42
San Martín Puente	AY	
San Román	BY	44
San Sebastián Carreras de	BZ	
San Torcuato	BZ	
San Vicente Pl. de	BY	45
Santa Leocadia Cuesta de	AY	
Santo Tomé	ABY	
Sillería	BX	
Sixto Ramón Parro	BY	46
Sola	BZ	
Taller del Moro	BY	48
Tendillas	BY	10
Toledo de Ohio	BY	49
Tornerías	BY	50
Tránsito Pas. del	AYZ	52
Trinidad	BY	
Venancio González	CX	53
Zocodover Pl. de	CY	

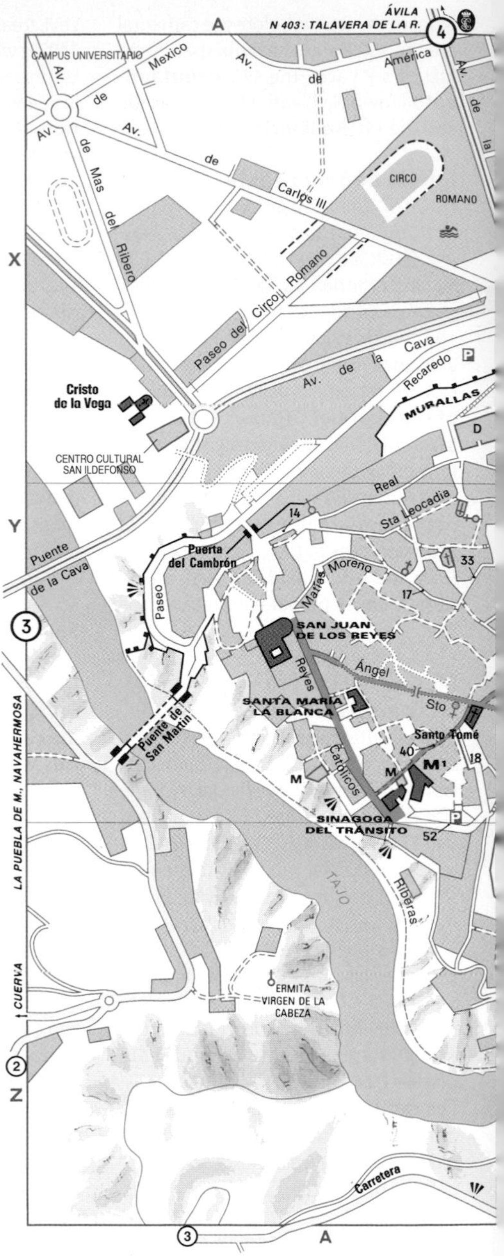

Alcázar	CY		Cristo de la Luz	BX	
Audiencia	BY		Cristo de la Vega	AX	
Ayuntamiento	BY	H	Hospital deTavera	BX	
Casa y Museo de El Greco	AY	M[1]	Iglesia de San Ildefonso	BY	
Castillo de San Servando	CXY		Iglesia de San Pedro	BY	
Catedral	BY		Iglesia de San Román	BY	
Claustro	BY		Iglesia de San Vicente	BY	

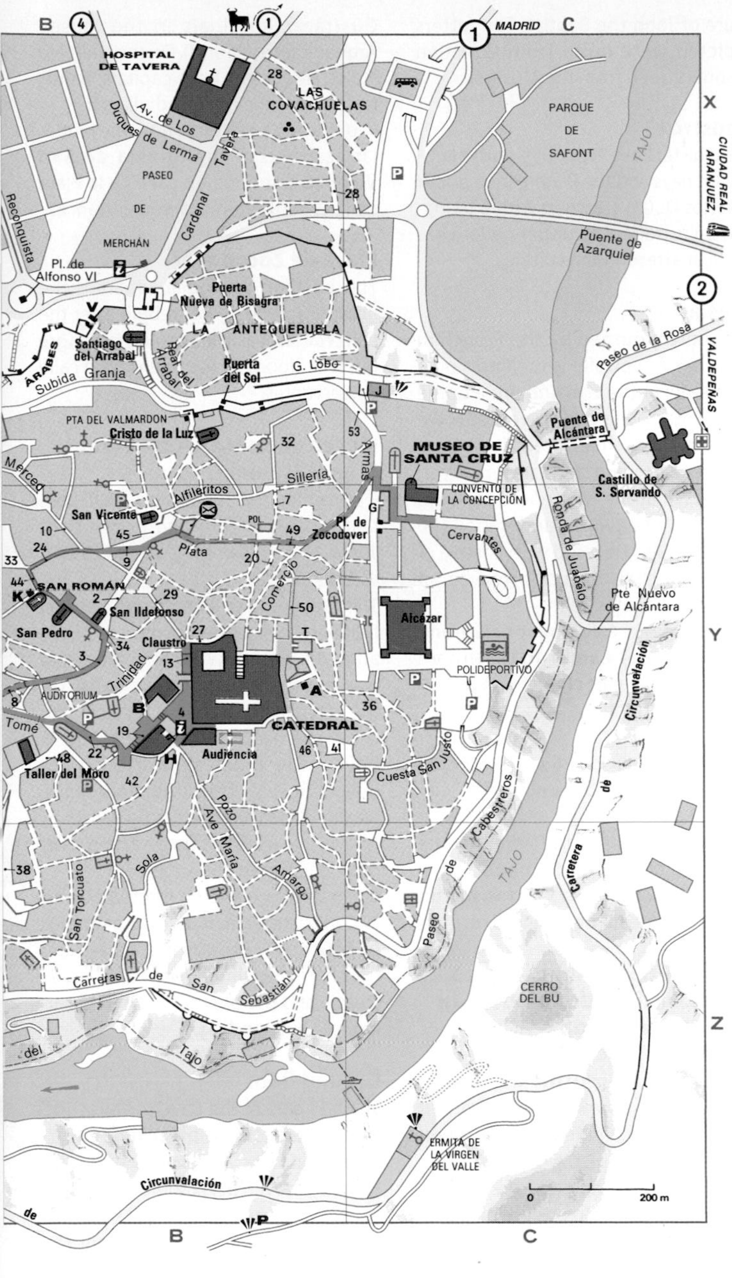

Iglesia de Santiago del Arrabal	BX	Palacio Arzobispal	BY	B	Puerta nueva de Bisagra	BX
Iglesia de Santo Tomé	AY	Parador	BZ	P	Santa María la Blanca	AY
Monasterio de San Juan de los Reyes	AY	Portada de S. Clemente	BY	K	Sinagoga del Tránsito	AYZ
Murallas Árabes	ABX	Posada de la Hermandad	BY	A	Taller del Moro	BY
Museo de Santa Cruz	CXY	Puerta antigua de Bisagra	BX	V		
		Puerta del Cambrón	AY			
		Puerta del Sol	BX			

figure of John the Baptist. The fetters depicted were taken from Christian prisoners freed from the Muslims.

Claustro

The cloisters are attractive with Flamboyant bays and the Plateresque upper galleries (1504) crowned with a pinnacled balustrade. The upper gallery has Mudéjar artesonado vaulting.

Iglesia

The church, burned by the French in 1808, has a typically isabelline single wide aisle; at the crossing are a dome and a lantern. The **sculptured decoration**★ by Flemish architect Juan Guas provides a delicate stone tracery *(crestería)* which at the transept forms twin tribunes for Ferdinand and Isabel. The transept walls are faced with a frieze of royal escutcheons, supported by an eagle, symbol of St John.
Not far away are a Visigothic palace and the **Puerta del Cambrón** (hawthorn gateway), once part of the town perimeter, rebuilt in the 16C.

▸ *Turn left out of calle Santo Tomé onto the Travesía de Campana alley.*

Cross the small plaza del Padre Mariana past the monumental Baroque façade of the **Iglesia de San Ildefonso** and that of the **Iglesia de San Pedro.**

Iglesia de San Román: Museo de los Concilios de Toledo y de la Cultura Visigoda★ (Museum of the Councils of Toledo and Visigothic Culture)

Open 10am-2pm and 4-6.30pm; Sun and public hols, 10am-2pm. Closed Mon, 1 Jan and 25 Dec. ☎925 22 78 72.
The 13C Mudéjar church, at the summit of Toledo, has a tower resembling Santo Tomé's. Aisles are divided by horseshoe arches. The walls are covered in 13C frescoes of the raising of the dead, the Evangelists and, on the far wall, one of the Councils of Toledo. The apse was modified in the 16C with a cupola by Covarrubias. Note the 18C **altarpiece**. The collections include fine bronze jewellery and copies of votive crowns decorated with cabochon stones from Guarrazar (originals in the Museo Arqueológico, Madrid). On the walls are steles, fragments from capitals, balustrades from the choir and pilasters.
In plaza de San Vicente, note the Mudéjar east end of the **Iglesia de San Vicente.** Continue up calle de la Plata with its houses with carved entrances.

Plaza de Zocodover

This bustling triangular square is the heart of Toledo. It was rebuilt after the Civil War as was the Arco de la Sangre (Arch of Blood) which opens onto calle de Cervantes.

Museo de Santa Cruz★★ (Santa Cruz Museum)

Open 10am-6.30pm; Mon, 10am-2pm and 4-6.30pm; Sun and public hols, 10am-2pm. Closed 1 Jan and 25 Dec. ☎925 22 14 02.
This fine group of Plateresque hospital buildings was begun by Enrique Egas and completed by Covarrubias who was responsible for the **façade**★★. On the gateway tympanum Cardinal Mendoza, the hospital's sponsor, kneels before the Cross supported by St Helena, St Peter, St Paul and two pages; on the arches are the cardinal virtues. Above, two windows frame a high relief of St Joachim and St Anne.
The museum is known for its **16C and 17C pictures**★ including 18 paintings by **El Greco**★. The size of the nave and transept – forming a two-tiered Greek cross – and the beautiful coffered ceilings are outstanding.

Ground floor

The first part of the nave contains 16C Flemish tapestries, **primitive paintings**★, and the *Astrolabios* or *Zodiac* tapestry, woven in Flanders in the mid-15C for Toledo cathedral, still strikingly original. Note, in the south transept, the *Ascension* and the *Presentation of Mary in the Temple* by the Maestro de Sijena. In the second part of the nave hangs the immense pennant flown by Don Juan of Austria at the Battle of Lepanto. The north transept contains a *Christ at the Column* by Morales.

El Greco

Domenikos Theotokopoulos, the Greek – El Greco – one of the great figures in Spanish painting, was born in Crete in 1541. After an apprenticeship painting icons, he went to Italy where he worked under Titian and studied Michelangelo before journeying to Spain in 1577 and settling in Toledo where he remained until he died in 1614. Although he did not always succeed in pleasing Philip II he found favour and fortune with Toledans. His work, with its acquired Italian techniques, retained considerable Byzantine influence which appeared as a lengthening of forms – a mannerism which increased as the painter aged. A recurring feature in illustrated scenes was the division of the canvas into two – earth and heaven – demonstrating El Greco's belief that this life was but preparation for an exalted hereafter. The supernatural is a constant preoccupation, figures convey an intense spiritual inner power – all is seen with the eye of the visionary and portrayed sometimes by means of apparent distortion, by brilliant, occasionally crude colours, often by violent, swirling movement so that some pictures have the aspect of hallucinations. But the portraits by contrast are still, the colours deep, expressions meditative in the religious, watchful in the worldly.

First floor

A staircase leads to the upper gallery of the north transept with **paintings by El Greco**★. There are gentle portraits of the Virgin and St Veronica as well as a version of the *Expolio*, later than the original in the cathedral. Most famous is the late **Altarpiece of the Assumption**★, from 1613. The figures are notably elongated, the colours rasping.

The south transept contains a *Holy Family at Nazareth* by Ribera, the specialist in tenebrism who here showed himself a master of light and delicacy.

In the first part of the nave are 16C Brussels tapestries showing the life of Alexander the Great; and 17C statues from the studio of Pascual de Mena.

The **Plateresque patio**★ has bays with elegant lines complemented by the openwork balustrade and enhanced by Mudéjar vaulting and by the magnificent **staircase**★ by Covarrubias. Adjoining rooms house a museum of archaeology and decorative arts.

Worth a Visit

WITHIN THE CITY WALLS

Alcázar

Closed for restoration until 2008. ☎925 22 16 73.

The Alcázar, destroyed and rebuilt so many times, massively dominates all else. Emperor Charles V converted the 13C fortress, of which El Cid had been the first governor, into an imperial residence. The work was entrusted to Covarrubias (1538-51) and then Herrera, who designed the austere south front. The siege and shelling for eight weeks in 1936 left the fortress in ruins. The Falangist commander allowed his son to be shot rather than surrender.

The Alcázar is restored to its appearance at the time of Charles V – an innovation is the *Victory Monument* by Ávalos in the forecourt. Inside are underground galleries where families sheltered in the 1936 siege.

Weapons and uniforms are displayed in museum rooms off the patio.

Posada de la Hermandad (House of the Brotherhood)

This 15C building was once a prison.

Puerta del Sol

The Sun Gate in the second perimeter, rebuilt in the 14C, is a fine Mudéjar construction with two circumscribing horseshoe arches. At the centre a later low relief shows the Virgin presenting San Ildefonso with a chasuble. At the top, the brick decoration of blind arcading incorporates an unusual sculpture of two girls bearing the head of the chief *alguacil* (officer of justice), allegedly a rapist, on a salver.

Puerta Nueva de Bisagra

Cristo de la Luz (Christ of the Light)

This 12C Mudéjar church succeeded a mosque which in turn replaced a Visigothic church. It is named for the miraculous appearance in a mosque of a lamp illuminating a Crucifix when Alfonso VI first entered Toledo. Arches of different periods, intersecting blind arcades, and a line of horizontal brickwork surmounted by Cufic characters make up the façade. Inside, Visigothic pillars support superimposed arches like those in the mosque in Córdoba. Nine domes, each different, rise from square bays. The gardens lead to the Puerta del Sol. Enjoy the panorama from the top.

Iglesia de Santiago del Arrabal (St James on the Outskirts)

San Vicente Ferrer is said to have preached from the Gothic Mudéjar pulpit of this beautifully restored church.

Puerta Nueva de Bisagra (New Bisagra Gate)

The gate was rebuilt by Covarrubias in 1550 and enlarged under Philip II. Massive round crenellated towers, facing the Madrid road, flank a giant imperial crest.

Puerta Antigua de Bisagra (Old Bisagra Gate)

Alfonso VI entered Toledo in triumph through this Moorish gate in 1085.

Taller del Moro

Closed for reconstruction. *925 22 45 00.*

This workshop *(taller)*, a building yard for the cathedral, is an old palace. Mudéjar decoration can still be seen in rooms lit by small openwork windows.

Beyond the Walls

Hospital de Tavera★

Guided tours (30min), 10.30am-1.30pm and 4-5.45pm (6.30pm in summer); Sun and public hols 10.30am-1.30pm and 3.30-5.30pm. Closed Mon, 1 Jan, 25 Dec. 3.60€. 925 22 04 51.

The hospital was begun by Bustamante in 1541 and completed by González de Lara and the Vergaras in the 17C. After the Civil War, the Duchess of Lerma rearranged her **apartments**★ in 17C style. These hold valuable paintings.

In the vast library, the hospital archives contain volumes bound in leather by Moorish craftsmen. El Greco's *Holy Family* is arresting, the portrait of the Virgin perhaps the most beautiful by the artist. Note also the *Birth of the Messiah* by Tintoretto, the *Philosopher* by Ribera and, in an adjoining room, his strange portrait of the *Bearded Woman*.

On the first floor, in the reception hall, is El Greco's sombre portrait of *Cardinal Tavera*, painted from a death mask. Beside it are *Samson and Delilah* (Caravaggio) and two portraits of the *Duke and Duchess of Navas* (Antonio Moro).

A gallery leads to the **church** from the twin patio. The Carrara marble portal is by Alonso Berruguete who also carved the tomb of Cardinal Tavera. The retable at the high altar was designed by El Greco whose last work, a **Baptism of Christ★** is displayed. The artist's use of brilliant colours and elongated figures is at its most magnificent.
The hospital pharmacy, facing the patio, has been restored.

Puente de Alcántara

At the ends of the 13C bridge are a Mudéjar tower and a Baroque arch (*east*). Across the Tajo, behind ramparts, is the restored 14C **Castillo de San Servando** (castle).
A plaque on the town wall by the bridge recalls how **St John of the Cross** (1542-91) escaped through a window from his monastery prison nearby.

Puente de San Martín

The medieval bridge, rebuilt in the 14C, is marked at its south end by an octagonal tower; the north end is 16C.

Cristo de la Vega

The Church of Christ of the Vega, formerly St Leocadia, stands on the site of a 7C Visigothic temple, the venue of early church councils. Although modified in the 18C, it retains a fine Mudéjar apse. A modern Crucifix replaces one which figures in many legends.

Excursions

Guadamur

15km/9mi SW. Leave Toledo by ③ on the map; bear left onto the CM 401. The **castillo** (castle) was built in the 15C. The apartments, occupied for a period by Queen Juana the Mad and her son, the future Emperor Charles V, are furnished in period style. *Currently undergoing restoration. ☎925 29 13 01.*

TORTOSA★

POPULATION: 29 717

MICHELIN MAP 574 J 31 – 65KM/40MI FROM PEÑÍSCOLA – CATALUNYA (TARRAGONA).

Tortosa, for centuries the last town before the sea, once guarded the region's only bridge. From the Castillo de la Suda, a castle (now a parador), enjoy a fine view of the Ebro and the valley. Tortosa's artistic endowment ranges from Gothic monuments to fine examples of Modernism.

- **Information:** *Plaza del Carrilet 1, ☎977 44 25 67, www.tortosa.altanet.org.*
- **Orient Yourself:** Tortosa is 14km/9mi off the coastal motorway in Catalunya.
- **Also See:** TARRAGONA (83km/52mi NE), ALCAÑIZ (94km/59mi NW and COSTA DEL AZAHAR, to the S.

Worth a Visit

Ciudad Antigua★ (Old Town) *3hr*

Catedral★★

Open 9am-1pm and 5-8pm. No visits during religious services. ☎977 44 17 52.
The cathedral was built in pure Gothic style even though construction, begun in 1347, continued for 200 years. The 18C Baroque **façade★** is lavishly decorated: capitals with plant motifs, curved columns and outstanding reliefs.
In Catalan tradition the lines of the **interior★★** are plain, the high arches divided into two tiers only in the nave. The retable at the high altar has a large 14C wood **polyptych★** illustrating the Life of Christ and the Virgin Mary. Another interesting work is the 15C **altarpiece of the Transfiguration★**.
Two stone 15C **pulpits★** in the nave are carved with low reliefs: those on the

left illustrate the Evangelists, those on the right, Saints Gregory, Jerome, Ambrose and Augustine.

Capilla de Nuestra Señora de la Cinta★ (Chapel of Our Lady of the Sash)

Second chapel off the south aisle. Built in Baroque style between 1642 and 1725, it is decorated with paintings and local jasper and marble; at its centre is the sash of Our Lady *(services of special veneration: first week in September).* The stone **font** is said to have stood in the garden of the antipope Benedict XIII, Pedro de Luna, and bears his arms.

Palacio Episcopal★ (Bishop's Palace)

Open 10am-2pm. Closed Sat, Sun and public hols. 977 44 07 00.

The 14C Catalan patio of this palace, built in the 13C-14C, is known for its straight flight of steps which occupies one side, and the arcaded gallery. On the upper floor, the **Gothic chapel**★, has ogive vaulting in which the ribs descend to figured bosses.

Reales Colegios de Tortosa★

Open 10am-1pm and 4-7pm; Jun-15 Sep, 9am-2pm. Closed Sat-Sun and public hols. 977 44 15 25.

In 1564 Emperor Charles V sponsored this lovely Renaissance ensemble.

The **Colegio de Sant Lluís**★ at one time educated newly converted Muslims. The fine oblong **patio**★★ is curiously decorated with characters in a wide range of expressions and attitudes.

The Renaissance façade of the **Colegio de Sant Jordi y de Sant Domingo** bears a Latin inscription *(Domus Sapientiae,* House of Knowledge*).*

Iglesia de Sant Domingo

Built in the 16C, this church was once part of the Reales Colegios.

Llotja de Mar

The maritime exchange is a fine example of Gothic architecture (16C).

Excursions

Parque Natural del Delta del Ebro★★ (Ebro Delta Nature Reserve)

25km/16mi E. Visitors are advised to contact the tourist information office in Deltebre. Centro de Información: Calle Doctor Martín Buera 22, Deltebre. 977 48 96 79. The boat trip from Deltebre to the mouth of the Ebro is highly recommended (45min round trip). Open 10am-2pm and 3-6pm (7pm May-Sep); Sun and public hols, 10am-2pm. Closed 1 Jan and 25 Dec. 1.20 €.

There are boat trips between Deltebre and the river mouth (45min there and back). The reserve, covering 7 736ha/19 116 acres, protects birds. The vast delta, closed by the Isla de Buda (Buda Island), is a swampy stretch of alluvium deposits collected by the Ebro from the Montes Cantábricos range, the Pyrenees and the Aragón plateaux.

TRUJILLO★★

POPULATION: 8 919

MICHELIN MAP 576 N 12 – EXTREMADURA (CÁCERES).

Modern Trujillo conceals the charm of the old town, on a granite ledge above. It was hastily fortified by the Moors in the 13C, and embellished over centuries with mansions built by those who had made their fortunes in the Americas.

- **Information:** *Plaza Mayor, 927 32 26 77.*
- **Orient Yourself:** Trujillo is situated on the A 5 linking Madrid and Badajoz.
- **Don't Miss:** The old town and its mansions.
- **Also See:** CÁCERES (47km/29mi W), PLASENCIA (80km/50mi NE), Monasterio de GUADALUPE (82km/51mi E) and MÉRIDA (89km/55mi SW).

Background

Land of the Conquistadores – "Twenty American nations", it is said, "were conceived in Trujillo". **Francisco de Orellana** left in 1542 to explore the country of the Amazons. Native son **Francisco Pizarro** (1475-1541), plundered the riches of the Emperor Atahualpa and was murdered amid untold riches in his own palace.

Special Features

OLD QUARTER

Trujillo's old quarter is less austere than that of Cáceres. Mansions were built later in the 16C and 17C, decorated with arcades, loggias and corner windows, and whitewashed. They form changing compositions along steep alleys.

Plaza Mayor★★

One of the most beautiful squares in Spain is irregular, lined by mansions, its levels linked by wide flights of steps. By night, it is positively theatrical.

Equestrian statue of Pizarro

This 1927 bronze is by American sculptors Charles Runse and Mary Harriman.

Iglesia de San Martín

16C. The rubble and freestone walls of the church enclose a vast nave chequered with funerary paving stones.

Palacio de los Duques de San Carlos★ (Palace of the Dukes of San Carlos)

17C. Now a convent. The granite façade, decorated in Classical Baroque style, has a corner window topped by a crest with a double-headed eagle. View the **patio** with two tiers of rounded arches and a fine staircase of four flights.

Palacio del Marqués de Piedras Albas (Palace of the Marquis of Piedras Albas)

A Renaissance loggia has been accommodated into the original Gothic wall.

Palacio del Marqués de la Conquista (Palace of the Marquis de la Conquista)

The palace of Hernando Pizarro, the conquistador's brother, has an exceptional number of windows with iron grilles. To the left of a Plateresque corner **window★**, added in the 17C, are busts of Francisco Pizarro and his wife; on the right are Hernando and his niece, whom he married.

Ayuntamiento Viejo (Former town hall)

16C. Three tiers of Renaissance arcades from a palace in ruins form the façade of the Palacio de Justicia (Law Courts).

Casa de las Cadenas (House of Chains)

Christians freed from the Moors left their chains here.

Torre del Alfiler (Alfiler Tower)

The "needle tower", visible from the square, is a Mudéjar belfry and a favourite spot with storks.

Palacio de Orellana-Pizarro

This 16C palace has a beautiful Plateresque upper gallery.

Iglesia de Santiago

This church's 13C Romanesque belfry and the tower of the Palacio de los Chaves frame the Arco de Santiago (St James Arch), one of seven gateways.

Iglesia de Santa María★

Open 10am-2pm and 4.30-7pm (8pm in summer). Closed 1 and 6 Jan and 15 Aug. 1.30€. 927 32 30 05.

This 13C Gothic church is the pantheon of Trujillo's great men. The 24 panels of the Gothic **retable★** are attributed to Fernando Gallego.

From the top of the belfry there is a delightful **view** of brown tile roofs, the Plaza Mayor arcades and the castle.

Castillo

The castle stands out on a granite ledge, its massive crenellated wall reinforced by heavy towers. Above the keep is the patron of Trujillo, Our Lady of Victory. View Trujillo from these walls.

TUDELA★

POPULATION: 26 163

MICHELIN MAP 573 F 25 – NAVARRA.

Tudela was once part of the Córdoba Caliphate, which is evident from its large Moorish quarter, the Morería. interesting churches were built following the 12C Reconquest. Irrigation has made the surrounding Ribera region a market-gardening centre.

- **Information:** *Plaza Mayor, ☎927 32 26 77.*
- **Orient Yourself:** Tudela is on the right bank of the River Ebro in NE Spain.
- **Also See:** ZARAGOZA (81km/51mi SE), PAMPLONA (84km/52mi N), SORIA (90km/56mi SW) and La RIOJA (NW).

Worth a Visit

Catedral★

Open 10am-1pm and 4-7pm. ☎948 40 20 60.

The 12C-13C cathedral examplifies the transitional Romanesque-Gothic style. The **Last Judgement Doorway**★ (Portada del Juicio Final), difficult to see, is incredibly carved with nearly 120 groups of figures.

The **interior** is Romanesque in the elevation of the nave, Gothic in its vaulting and clerestory. Gothic works include early-16C choir stalls, the high altar retable and the Byzantine-looking 13C stone reliquary statue of the White Virgin. In the **Capilla de Nuestra Señora de la Esperanza**★ (Chapel of our Lady of Hope), 15C masterpieces include the tomb of a chancellor of Navarra and the main altarpiece.

The 12C-13C **cloisters**★★ *(claustro)* are harmonious. Romanesque arches rest alternately on columns with historiated capitals with scenes from the New Testament and the lives of the saints in a style inspired by the carvings of Aragón. A door of an earlier mosque remains.

Fiestas

St Anne's feast day (26 July) is celebrated annually, as at Pamplona/Iruña, with several days of great rejoicing including *encierros* and bullfights. During Holy Week, an event known as the Descent of the Angel takes place on the picturesque **plaza de los Fueros**, which served as a bullring in the 18C.

Iglesia de San Nicolás

In the 18C façade of this church in calle Rúa is a 12C Romanesque tympanum showing God the Father holding his Son, amid symbols of the Evangelists.

Excursions

Tarazona

21km/13mi SW on the N 121. Tarazona was once the residence of the kings of Aragón. The royal mansion, now the **Palacio Episcopal** (Episcopal Palace), is in a quarter with narrow streets overlooking the quays of the River Queiles.

Catedral

Closed for restoration.

☎ 948 40 21 61.

The cathedral was largely rebuilt in the 15C and 16C. Its mix of styles includes Aragón Mudéjar in the belfry tower and lantern, Renaissance in the portal and, in the **second chapel**★ as you walk left round the ambulatory, delicately carved Gothic **tombs** of the two Calvillos cardinals from Avignon.

The **Mudéjar cloisters** have bays filled with 16C Moorish plasterwork tracery.

Monasterio de Veruela★★

39km/24mi S from Tudela, From Tarazona (17km/11mi), take the N 122 towards Zaragoza then bear right onto the Z 373.

Open Oct-Mar, 10am-1pm and 3-6pm; Apr-Sep, 10am-2pm and 3-6pm. Apr-Sep 10am-2pm and 4-7pm. Closed Mon, 1

Jan and 25 Dec. 1.80 €. ☎976 64 90 25.

Cistercian monks from France founded a fortified monastery in the mid-12C. The 19C Sevillian poet **Bécquer** stayed here while writing *Letters from My Cell*, in which he described the Aragón countryside much in the manner of later guide books!

Iglesia★★

The church, built in the transitional period between Romanesque and Gothic, has a sober façade with a single oculus, a band of blind arcades lacking a base line, and a doorway decorated with friezes, billets and capitals.

In the large interior, the vault groins are pointed over the nave, and horseshoe-shaped elsewhere. A 16C Plateresque chapel is built onto the north transept. The sacristy door oppsoite is in a surprising Rococo style.

Claustro★

The cloisters are ornate Gothic. At ground level the brackets are carved with the heads of men and beasts; above are three Plateresque galleries. In the **Sala Capitular**★ (chapter house), in pure Cistercian style, are the tombs of the first 15 abbots.

ÚBEDA★★

POPULATION: 32 524

MICHELIN MAP 578 R 19 – ANDALUCÍA (JAÉN).

Úbeda, set amid olive groves, is one of Andalucía's architectural treasures. It flourished in the 16C, when palaces, churches and fine squares were built.

- **Information:** *Plaza Baja del Marqués 4 (Palacio de Contadero), ☎953 75 08 97.*
- **Orient Yourself:** Úbeda is south of Madrid, between the Guadalquivir and Guadalimar rivers.
- **Also See:** BAEZA (9km/5.5mi W), JAÉN (57km/35mi SW) and Parque Natural de las SIERRAS DE CAZORLA, SEGURA Y LAS VILLAS (to the E).

Walking About

Barrio Antiguo★★ (Old Quarter)

allow one day

Plaza Vázquez de Molina★★

The square is lined with historic buildings like the **Palacio del Deán Ortega**, which serves as a parador.

Palacio de las Cadenas★ (House of Chains)

Now the Ayuntamiento (town hall), this mansion is named for the chains round the forecourt. It was designed in 1562 by Vandelvira, also responsible for the Jaén Cathedral. The majestic **façade**★★, relieved by bays and pilasters, is decorated with caryatids and atlantes.

The Renaissance patio is delightful. On the upper floor is the Archivo Histórico Municipal, with pleasant views of the square. In the **Centro Municipal de Interpretación Turística** (tourist centre) downstairs, panels explain Úbeda 's heritage, and craft items are displayed.

Iglesia de Santa María de los Alcázares★

The church was built in the 13C on the site of a mosque and damaged in the civil war. Note the harmonious façade; the main door; the late-16C Puerta de la Consolada (*left side*); and the 16C Renaissance cloisters. Several delightful **chapels**★, are adorned with sculptures and profuse decoration and enclosed by impressive **grilles**★, most the work of Master Bartolomé.

Address Book

For coin ranges, see the Legend on the cover flap.

WHERE TO EAT

Mesón Gabino – *Fuente Seca 2 – 953 75 75 53.* Set in the fortress walls, this traditional restaurant specialises in grilled meats and regional specialties (*andrajos* soup, pork loin, partridge).

WHERE TO STAY

Hotel Victoria – *Alaminos 5 – 953 75 29 52 – – 15 rooms.* This small family-run hotel is clean and reasonably priced with basic but comfortable and well maintained rooms.

Palacio de la Rambla – *Plaza del Marqués 1 – Closed 16 Jul-10 Aug – 953 75 01 96 – www.palaciodelarambla.com – – 8 rooms .* This fine 16C palace treats you like a family guest in a refined yet relaxed atmosphere. It has a magnificent Renaissance patio; on the façade are life-size warriors bearing weapons.

FIESTAS

The nocturnal procession on Good Friday is known for its great solemnity.

Capilla de El Salvador★★

Open Jun-Aug 10am-2pm and 5-7.30pm; Apr-May and Sep Oct 4.30-7pm; Nov-Mar 4-6.30pm. 3 €. 953 75 81 50.

Diego de Siloé designed this sumptuous church in 1536. Its façade is ornamented with Renaissance motifs.

The **interior**★★ is frankly theatrical: the single nave, closed by a monumental grille, has vaulting outlined in blue and gold.The Capilla Mayor (chancel) forms a kind of rotunda. A huge 16C altarpiece includes a baldaquin with a sculpture by Berruguete of the Transfiguration (only the Christ figure remains).

The **sacristy**★★, by Vandelvira, is ornamented with coffered decoration, caryatids and atlantes with all the splendour of the Italian Renaissance style.

Casa de los Salvajes (House of the Savages)

On the façade, two odd savages in animal skins support a bishop's crest.

Iglesia de San Pablo★

The church mixes a Gothic west door and the Isabelline style, in the **south door** (1511). The Capilla de las Calaveras (Skull Chapel) was designed by Vandelvira. The Isabelline Capilla de las Mercedes is enclosed by an extraordinary **grille**★★ – note the highly imaginative depiction of Adam and Eve.

The Palladian-influenced 17C former town hall is on plaza Primero de Mayo.

Convento de San Miguel

The **Museo de San Juan de la Cruz** (St John of the Cross Museum) in this ex-convent traces the final days of this great mystical poet who died in Úbeda. *Open 11am-12.45pm and 5-6.45pm. Closed Mon. 1.20 €. 953 75 06 15.*

Palacio de la Calle Montiel

This early Renaissance palace has a monumental gate flanked by twisted columns.

Casa Mudéjar

In this restored 14C Mudéjar house is the **Museo Arqueológico**, displaying objects discovered in Úbeda and nearby (*open 9am-8.30pm (Tue 2.30-8.30pm); Sun, 9am-2.30pm; closed all day Mon and Tue morning; 1.50 €, no charge for E.U. citizens; 953 75 37 02).*

Palacio del Conde de Guadiana

The early-17C Palace of the Count of Guadiana is crowned by a fine **tower**★ with angular balconies.

Palacio de la Vela de los Cobos

The palace's façade is late-18C. A Renaissance appearance bears witness to the long survival of this style in Úbeda.

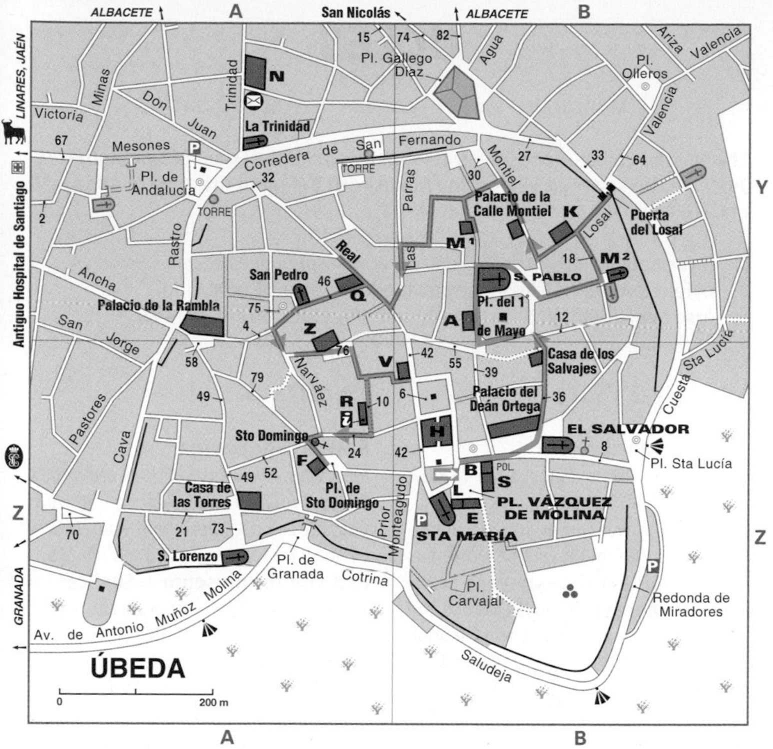

ÚBEDA								
Alaminos	AY	2	Cruz de Hierro	BY	27	Mesones	AY	
Antonio Medina	AY	4	Descalzas Pl.	BY	30	Obispo Cobos	AY	67
Ayuntamiento Pl. del	BZ	6	Doctor Quesada	AY	32	Real	AY	
Baja del Marqués Pl. del	AZ	10	Fuente Seca	BY	33	San Francisco Pl.	AZ	70
Baja del Salvador	BZ	8	Horno Contador	BZ	36	San Lorenzo Pl.	AZ	73
Beltrán de la Cueva	BY	12	Juan González	BZ	39	San Nicólas	BY	74
Campanario	AY	15	Juan Montilla	BZ	42	San Pedro Pl. de	AY	75
Carmen	BY	18	Juan Pasquau	AY	46	Santa Clara Pl. de	AZ	76
Condestable Dávalos	AZ	21	Jurando Gómez	AZ	49	Santo Domingo	AZ	79
Corazón de Jesús	AZ	24	Luna y Sol	AZ	52	Trillo	BY	82
Corredera de San Fernando	ABY		María de Molina	BYZ	55			
			Marqués Pl. del	AZ	58			
			Merced Cuesta de la	BY	64			

Antigo Ayuntamiento	BY	A	Cárcel del Obispo	BZ	E	Palacio del Conde de Guadiana	AY	Q
Antigo Pósito	BZ	B	Museo de San Juan de la Cruz	BY	M²	Palacio del Marqués de Mancera	BZ	S
Casa Mudéjar (Museo Arqueológico)	BY	M¹	Palacio de la Vela de los Cobos	ABZ	V	Palácio del Marqués del Contadero	AZ	R
Casa de los Morales	AZ	F	Palacio de las Cadenas	BZ	H	Real Monasterio de Santa Clara	AY	Z
Casa del Obispo Canastero	BY	K	Palacio de los Bussianos	AY	N			
Casa del Regidor	BZ	L						

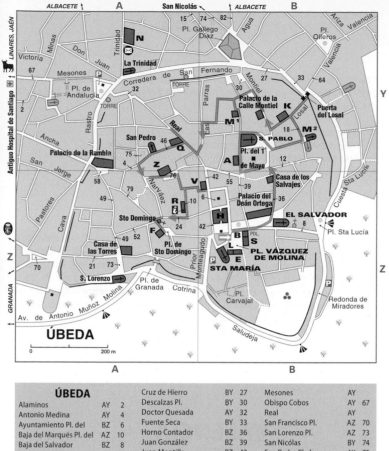

Palacio del Marqués del Contadero (Palace of the Marquis of Contadero)

The late-18C façade, crowned by a gallery, is also Renaissance in style.

Iglesia de Santo Domingo

The church's delicate south door is decorated with Plateresque reliefs.

Antiguo Hospital de Santiago (Museo de la Semana Santa); Palacio de los Bussianos; Iglesia de la Trinidad; Palacio de la Rambla; Casa de las Torres; Iglesia de San Lorenzo.

UCLÉS

POPULATION: 297

MICHELIN MAP 576 M 21 – CASTILLA-LA MANCHA (CUENCA).

The massive castle-monastery was long the seat of the Order of Santiago (1174-1499). At this strategic village, the Almoravids defeated the army of Alfonso VI of Castilla in 1108.

- **Information:** *www.ucles.org and www.monasteriodeucles.com.*
- **Orient Yourself:** Uclés in the province of Cuenca, SE of Madrid.
- **Also See:** CUENCA (70km/44mi E) and ARANJUEZ (77km/48mi W).

Worth a Visit

Castillo-Monasterio

Open 10am-6pm (8pm 15 Apr-15 Sep). 3 €. 969 13 50 58.

The building was begun in 1529 in Plateresque style; most of the work was undertaken by Herrera's disciple, **Francisco de Mora** (1560-1610), hence the building is known as the Little Escorial. Enter by a beautiful Baroque **portal★★**. Note the Baroque well and the magnificent **artesonado★** ceiling in the refectory. The church is Herreran.

The ramparts command a fine view.

Excursion

Roman Segóbriga

In Saelices, 14km/9mi S of Uclés. Leave the A 3 at exit 103/104 and follow signs towards Casas de Luján. Open 9am-9pm (16 Sep-14 Apr 10am-6pm). 4 €. 629 75 22 57.

First visit the **museum** in **Saelices** for an overview. This Celtiberian site, which dates back to the 5C BC, became an important Roman crossroads town. By the 1C AD, it had a theatre and an imposing **amphitheatre★**, with a capacity for 5 000 spectators. Parts of the baths and walls also remain.

VALENCIA★★

POPULATION: 777 427

MICHELIN MAP 577 N28 (TOWN PLAN) OR 574 N 28 – COMUNIDAD VALENCIANA.

Spain's third-largest city is a large Mediterranean town, notable for its mild climate and its light. Wide palm-lined avenues encircle the old quarter with its fortified gateways, quaint shops and Gothic houses. But Valencia is also a city in transition, witnessed in works by Santiago Calatrava and Sir Norman Foster which have propelled this medieval city to the forefront of Spanish design. To top it off, superb beaches are easily reached by tram.

- **Information:** *Plaza del Ayuntamiento 1, 96 351 04 17; Cataluña 5, 96 369 79 32; Paz 48, 96 398 64 22.*
- **Orient Yourself:** Valencia is the main city of the Levante region.
- **Parking:** Don't try to find a space in the old quarter.
- **Don't Miss:** A walk in the old quarter and the Ciutat de les Arts i les Ciències.
- **Organizing Your Time:** Depending on your preferences, you'll start with unmissable modern architecture (Santiago Calatrava's City of Arts and Sciences, and the convention centre) and Sir Norman Foster's Turia bridge; or with the heritage section of the city.
- **Especially for Kids:** L' Oceanogràfic might be the world's greatest aquarium.
- **Also See:** COSTA DEL AZAHAR, COSTA BLANCA and ALACANT/ALICANTE (174km/109mi S)

TRIBUNAL DE LAS AGUAS

Since the Middle Ages disputes in the huerta have been settled by the Water Tribunal: every Thursday at noon, representatives of the areas irrigated by the eight canals, accompanied by an *alguazil* (officer of justice), meet in front of the Portada de los Apóstoles (Apostles' Door) of the cathedral; the offence is read out, judged (the judges all in black) and the sentence pronounced immediately (a fine, deprivation of water) by the most senior judge. The proceedings are oral and there is no appeal.

Background

2 000 years of history – The city founded by the Greeks in 138 BC passed into the hands of Carthaginians, Romans, Visigoths and Arabs, was briefly reconquered in 1094 by **El Cid**, and taken definitively in 1238 by James the Conqueror. Valencia prospered until the discovery of America, and again with a silk renaissance in the 17C.

Valencia sided with Charles of Austria in the War of the Spanish Succession, and lost its privileges. In 1808, it rose against the French. In 1939 it was the last Republican redoubt.

Art in Valencia – Valencia flourished economically in the 15C, and artistically as well, as seen in the Gothic architecture of palaces, the cathedral and the Lonja (Exchange). Among painters were **Luis Dalmau**, who developed a Hispano-Flemish style; **Jaime Baço (Jacomart)**, **Juan Reixach** and the **Osonas**, father and son.

Notable 15C decorative arts were wrought ironwork, gold- and silversmithing, and ceramics (*see the Museo de Cerámica in Worth a Visit*).

The Valencia huerta and Albufera – The Roman irrigation system around Valencia was improved by the Moors. Orchards and market gardens produce fruit and early vegetables for Europe.

South of Valencia lies a vast lagoon, the **Parque Natural de La Albufera** (*see COSTA DEL AZAHAR*).

Special Features

CIUDAD VIEJA★ (OLD TOWN)

Allow 3 hr (see route on town plan)

The best starting point is El Miguelete, the bell tower of the cathedral.

El Miguelete★

Open 10am-1pm and 5pm-dusk. 1.20 €. 96 391 81 27.

"Little Michael" (Micalet in Valencian) is the main bell of this octagonal Gothic tower, consecrated on St Michael's day in 1418. Climb up for a view of the cathedral and the towns glazed roofs.

Catedral★

Open 7.30am-1pm and 5-8.30pm (7pm Jun-Sep). 1.20 € (museum). 96 391 81 27.

Work began in 1262; most of the building is Gothic from the 14C and 15C. The elegant and slender early-18C west face imitates Italian Baroque style. The Assumption on the pediment is by Ignacio Vergara and Esteve.

The south door is Romanesque; the north, the **Portada de los Apóstoles** (Apostles' Door) is Gothic, decorated with time-worn sculptures. A statue of the Virgin and Child on the tympanum is surrounded by angel musicians.

Inside, light filters through the alabaster windows in the beautiful Flamboyant Gothic **lantern**. The **retable** in the capilla mayor (chancel), the work of Fernando de Llanos and Yáñez de la Almedina (early 16C), influenced by Leonardo, illustrates the Lives of Christ and the Virgin.

In the ambulatory, a Renaiassance portico protects an alabaster relief of the Resurrection (1510). Opposite is the 15C late Gothic Virgen del Coro (Chancel Virgin) in polychrome alabaster. In a chapel is a Baroque Cristo de la Buena Muerte (Christ of Good Death).

VALENCIA

Alameda Pas. de la	FXY		Alta	DX		Barón de Cárcer Av.	DY	
Alfonso el Magnánimo Pl.	FY		América Pl.	FY		Blanquerías	DX	
Alicante	EZ		Ángel Guimerá	DY	7	Blasco Ibáñez Av.	FX	
Almirante	EX	3	Aragón Puente de	FYZ		Bolsería	DX	8
Almirante Cadarso	FZ		Ayuntamiento Pl. del	EY		Burriana	FZ	
Almudín	EX	4	Bailén	DZ		Caballeros	DEX	
			Baja	DX		Calatrava Puente	FY	
			Barcas	EY		Carda	DY	

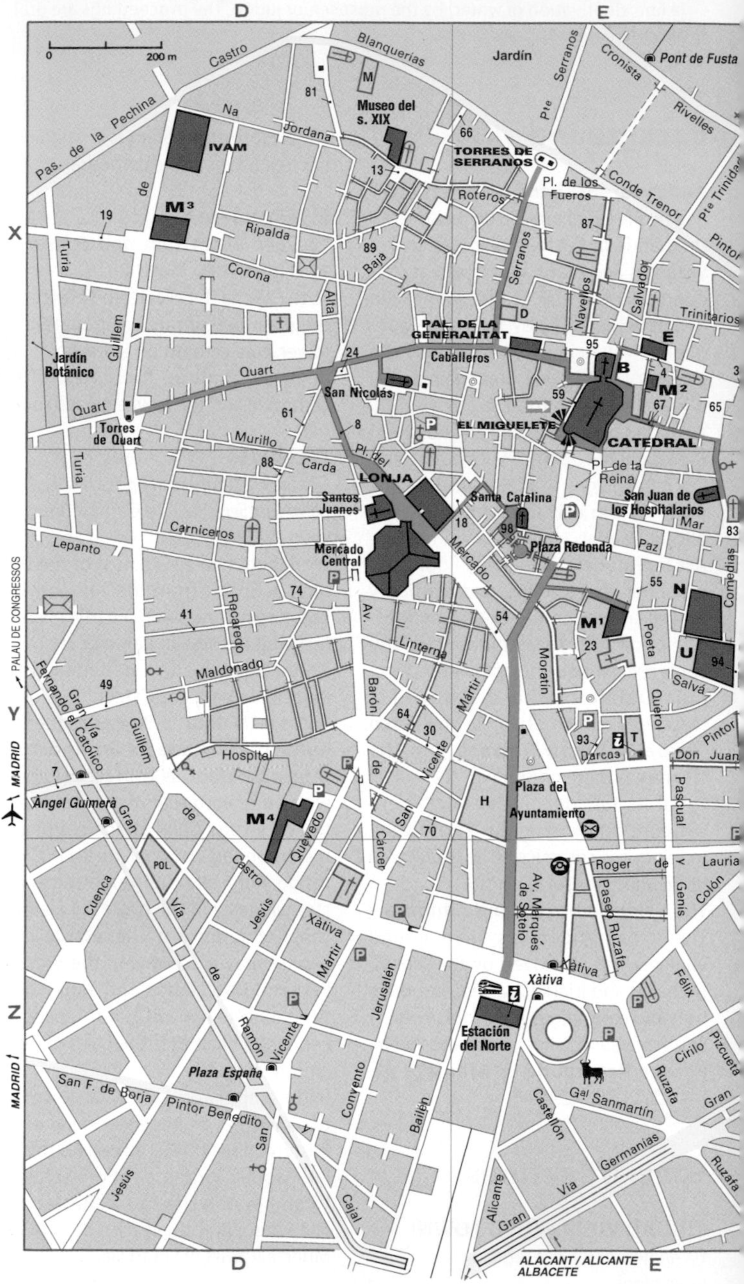

Carmen Pl. del	DX	13
Carniceros	DY	
Castellón	EZ	
Cirilo Amorós	EFZ	
Císcar	FZ	
Ciudadela Pas. de la	FY	
Colón	EFYZ	
Comedias	EY	
Conde de Altea	FZ	
Conde Salvatierra de Alava	FY	
Conde Trenor	EX	
Convento Jerusalén	DZ	
Corona	DX	
Cronista Rivelles	EX	
Cuenca	DZ	
Doctor Collado Pl.	EY	18
Doctor Sanchís Bergón	DX	19
Don Juan de Austria	EFY	
Embajador Vich	EY	23
Esparto Pl. del	DX	24
Félix Pizcueta	EZ	
Fernando el Católico Gran Via	DY	
Fueros Pl. de los	EX	
Garrigues	DY	30
General Elio	FX	
General Palanca	FY	35
General Sanmartín	EZ	
Germanías Gran Via	EZ	
Gobernador Viejo	FXY	
Grabador Esteve	FY	
Guillem de Castro	DXYZ	
Guillem Sorolla	DY	41
Hernán Cortés	FZ	
Hospital	DY	
Isabel la Católica	FYZ	
Jacinto Benavente Av.	FZ	
Jesús	DZ	
Joaquín Costa	FZ	
Jorge Juan	FYZ	
Lepanto	DY	
Linterna	DY	
Llano del Real	FX	
Maestres	FX	48
Maestro Gozalbo	FZ	
Maestro Palau	DY	49
Maldonado	DY	
Mar	EFY	
María Cristina Av.	EY	54
Marqués de Dos Aguas	EY	55
Marqués de Sotelo Av.	EZ	
Marqués del Turia Gran Via	EFZ	
Mercado Pl. del	DEY	
Micalet	EX	59
Micer Mascó	FX	
Moratín	EY	
Moro Zeit	DX	61
Murillo	DX	
Músico Peydró	DY	64
Na Jordana	DX	
Nápoles y Sicilia Pl.	EX	65
Navarro Reverter Av.	FY	
Navellos	EX	
Padre Huérfanos	EX	66
Palau	EX	67
Pascual y Genís	EYZ	
Paz	EFY	
Pechina Pas. de la	DX	
Periodista Azzati	DY	70
Pie de la Cruz	DY	74
Pintor Benedito	DZ	
Pintor López	EFX	
Pintor Sorolla	EFY	
Pizarro	FZ	
Poeta Querol	EY	
Poeta Quintana	FY	77
el Pontó	FY	
Porta de la Mar Pl.	FY	
Quart	DX	
Quevedo	DYZ	
Ramón y Cajal Gran Via de	DZ	
Real Puente del	FX	
Recaredo	DY	
Redonda Pl.	EY	
Regne de València Av.	FZ	

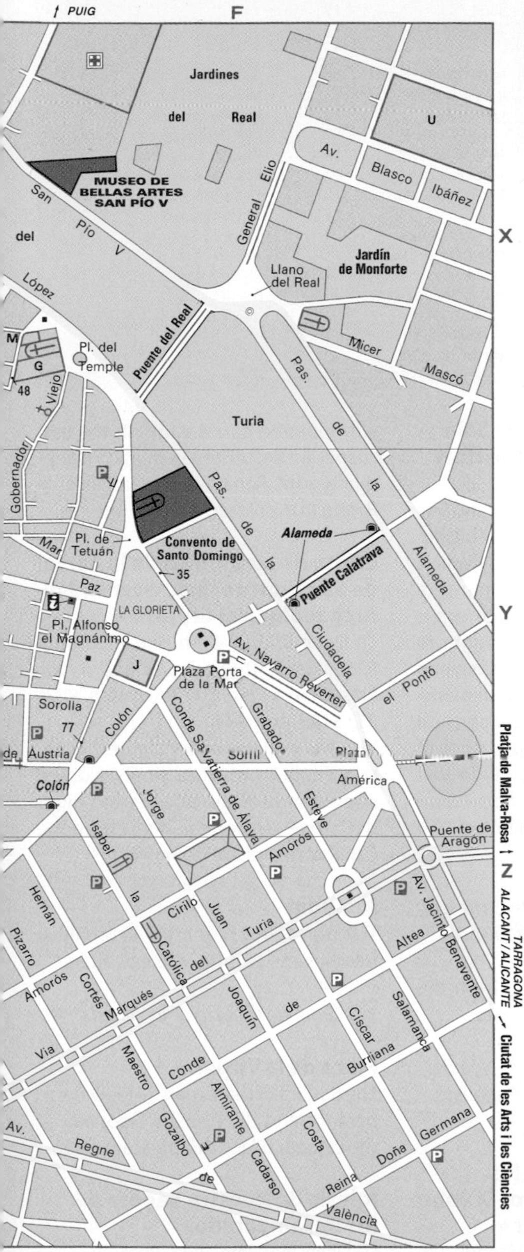

Reina Pl. de la	EY		San Francisco de Borja	DZ		Tetuán Pl. de	FY	
Reina Doña Germana	FZ		San Pío V	FX		Transits	EY	93
Ripalda	DX		San Vicente Ferrer Pl.	EY	83	Trinidad Puente	EX	
Roger de Lauria	EZ		San Vicente Mártír	DEYZ		Trinitarios	EX	
Roteros	EX		Santa Ana Muro	EX	87	Turia	DXY	
Ruzafa	EZ		Santa Teresa	DY	88	Universidad	EY	94
Ruzafa Pas.	EZ		Santo Tomás	DX	89	Virgen Pl. de la	EX	95
Salamanca	FZ		Serranos	EX		Virgen de la Paz Pl.	EY	98
Salvá	EY		Serranos Puente	EX		Xàtiva	DEZ	
Salvador	EX		Sorni	FY				
Salvador Giner	DX	81	Temple Pl. del	FX				

Almudín	EX	E	Iglesia de San Nicolás	DX		Museo de la Ciudad	EX	M^{2}
Catedral	EX		Iglesia de Santa Catalina	EY		Museo del s. XIX	DX	
Centro de la Beneficencia, Museo de Prehistoria y Ethnologia	DX	M^{3}	Iglesia de los Santos Juanes	DY		Nuestra Señora de los Desamparados	EX	B
Ciutat de les Arts i les Ciències	FZ		Jardines del Real	FX		Palau de Congressos	DY	
Colegio del Patriarca o del Corpus Christi	EY	N	Jardín Botánico	DX		Palau de la Generalitat	EX	
Convento de Santo Domingo	FY		Jardín de Montforte	FX		Platja de la Malva-rosa	FYZ	
El Miguelete	EX		Lonja	DY		Torres de Quart	DX	
Estación del Norte	EZ		Mercado Central	DY		Torres de Serranos	EX	
IVAM	DX		Museo Nacional de Cerámica	EY	M^{1}	Universidad	EY	U
Iglesia de San Juan de los Hospitalarios	EY		Museo Valenciano de la Ilustración y la Modernidad	DY	M^{4}			
			Museo de Bellas Artes San Pio V	FX				

Capilla del Santo Cáliz or Sala Capitular★ (Chapel of the Holy Grail or Chapter house)

Last chapel along the north aisle. The chamber has elegant star vaulting. Behind the altar, 12 alabaster low reliefs are by Poggibonsi. In the centre, a magnificent 1C carnelian agate cup is said to be the Holy Grail, brought to Spain in the 3C. The **museum** beyond contains a monumental modern monstrance, works of Juan de Juanes and Vicente Macip and original statues of the Apostles' Door (*open 9am-1pm and 5-7pm; Sun and public hols 10am-1pm; closed afternoons Oct-Mar; ☎96 391 81 27).*

Exit the at the right of the transept; continue to plaza del Arzobispo.

At the left are ruins dating from the Roman era up to Medieval times.

Take calle Palau to plaza de Nápols i Sicilia and turn right ontoTrinquete de los Caballeros

Iglesia de San Juan de los Hospitalarios (Church of St John of the Hospital Brother★

Access through courtyard. This early-13C Gothic church consists of a single nave with pointed barrel vault. In the first chapel are beautiful 13C murals; in another is a 16C Renaissance altarpiece. *Return to the plaza del Arzobispo*

Cripta Arqueológica de la Cárcel de San Vicente (San Vicente Jail Archaeological Crypt)

Open 9.15am-2pm and 4.30-8pm (Oct-Mar, 5.30-9pm); Sun and public hols, 9.15am-2pm. Closed Mon. ☎96 352 54 78, ext. 1184.

Visit the remains of a Visigothic funerary chapel with four finely worked screens and a 6C burial; and two Visigothic stone sarcophagi. Items from the Caliphal period are in showcases.

Almudín

This is a 14C-16C granary with primitive frescoes and two 19C *azulejos* altars.

Continue to plaza de la Virgen.

Plaza de la Virgen★

The Basilica of the Virgen de los Desamparados and the Apostle Doorway of the cathedral face this pleasant plaza.

Iglesia de Nuestra Señora de los Desamparados

Open 7am-2pm and 4-9pm. ☎96 391 92 14.

Plaza de la Virgen

This late-17C church is linked to the apse of the cathedral by a Renaissance arch. The floor plan is oval. Beneath the painted cupola is the venerated statue of the patron of Valencia, the Virgin of the Abandoned *(desamparados)*, which receives a steady flow of devotees.

Palau de la Generalitat★

Open 9am-2pm. Closed Sat-Sun, public hols, 10-20 Mar. ☎96 386 34 61.
A tower was added to this fine 15C Gothic palace in the 17C and an identical one in the 20C. It was until 1707 the meeting place of the Valencia Cortes.
In the Gothic patio is Benlliure's sculpture of Dante's *Inferno* (1900). A golden salon has a wonderful gilt and multicoloured **artesonado ceiling**★ and a large painting of the Tribunal de las Aguas (Water Tribunal, *see above)*. On the first floor are the Sala de los Reyes (Royal Hall) with portraits of the Valencian kings, and the Gran Salón de las Cortes Valencianas (Grand Council Chamber). The *azulejos* frieze and the coffered ceiling are 16C. The rear façade and the Palau de la Batlia (the provincial administration) give onto the pleasant **plaza de Manises**.

Torres de Serranos★

At the end of calle Serranos, which runs from the plaza de Manises. The towers are a good example of late-14C military architecture; they guarded one of the city entrances. Note the flowing lines of the battlements and the delicate tracery above the gateway.

Return to plaza de Manises.

Calle de Caballeros

The most important street of the old city heads from plaza de la Virgen into the traditional Carmen district. Some of the houses preserve their Gothic patios (numbers 22, 26 and 33).

Follow the lane opposite n°26.

Iglesia de San Nicolás

Open 9.30-11am and 6.30-8pm. Sun and public hols 10am-1pm. Closed Mon and Mon-Fri in Aug. ☎96 391 33 17.
In one of the town's oldest churches, in Churrigueresque style, are an altarpiece by Juan de Juanes *(to the left)* and, by the font, a *Calvary* by Osona the Elder.

Continue to plaza del Esparto, then follow calle Quart.

Torres de Quart

These 15C towers were damaged in the 19C by Napoleon's cannons.
From plaza del Esparto, take calle Bolsería.

Las Fallas

The origins of this festival date back to the Middle Ages when on St Joseph's Day, the carpenters' brotherhood, one of the town's traditional crafts, burned their accumulated wood shavings in bonfires known as *Fallas* (from the Latin *fax*: torch). The name became synonymous with a festival for which, in time, objects were made solely for burning – particularly effigies of less popular members of the community! In the 17C single effigies were replaced by pasteboard groups or floats produced by quarters of the town – rivalry is such that the figures today are fantastic in size, artistry and satirical implication. Prizes are awarded during the general festivities, which include fireworks, processions, bullfights etc, before everything goes up in the fires or *cremá* on the evening of 19 March. Figures *(ninots)* dating from 1934 to the present day which have been spared from the bonfires are on display in an interesting museum, the **Museo Fallero.** *Open 9.15am-2pm and 4.30-8pm (5.30-9pm, Apr-Sep); Sun and public hols, 9.15am-2pm. Closed Mon, 1 and 6 Jan, 1 May and 25 Dec. 2 €. 96 352 54 78 (ext. 4625).*

Lonja★ (Silk Exchange)

Open 9.15am-2pm and 4.30-8pm (5.30-9pm Apr-Sep); Sun and public hols, 9.15am-2pm. Closed Mon, 1 Jan, 1 May and 25 Dec. 96 352 54 78, ext. 4153.

This 15C Flamboyant Gothic building replaced an earlier exchange outgrown by prosperous merchants.

The left wing, separated from the entrance by a tower, is crowned by a gallery with a medallion frieze. The old commercial silk **hall**★★ is lofty, with ogival arches supported on slender, elegantly cabled columns; the bays are filled with delicate tracery.

Iglesia de los Santos Juanes

Open 8am (7.30am in summer) to 1pm and 6-8pm. 96 391 63 54.

This is a vast church with a Baroque façade. The single aisle, originally Gothic, was modified in the 17C and 18C with exuberant Baroque stuccowork.

Mercado Central

The enormous metal and glass 1928 Central Market, a fine example of Modernist architecture, is busiest in the mornings with stalls full of fish and local produce.

Iglesia de Santa Catalina

The church is notable for its magnificent 17C **Baroque belfry**★. The interior is soberly Gothic.

▸ *From calle San Vicente Mártir, turn left by the Abadía de San Martín.*

Palacio del Marqués de Dos Aguas★★

This magnificent Baroque building houses the Museo Nacional de Cerámica y de las Artes Suntuarias González Martí (*see Worth a Visit*). The 18C marble portal was once covered by paintings.

▸ *From calle San Vicente Mártir, continue to the plaza del Ayuntamiento*

Plaza del Ayuntamiento

This great square is the meeting point of *Valencianos*, with a showy flower market always in bloom.

Worth a Visit

Ciutat de les Arts i les Ciències★★

This cultural and recreational complex (350 000 m²/420 000 sq yd) is a series of spectacular avant-garde white buildings that reflect onto sheets of water.

L'Oceanogràfic★★

Kids *East end. Open 9.30am-1.30pm. 20.50 € (28 € with L'Hemisfèric and Museu de les Ciències Príncipe Felipe). 902 100 031.*

The facilities of the largest maritime centre of Europe are set around a lake and joined by gardens and tunnels. The exhibit focuses on marine life in the Mediterranean, marshland, temperate and tropical zones (turtles and grey

Address Book

For coin ranges, see the Legend on the cover flap.

WHERE TO EAT

Asador del Carme – *Plaza del Carme 6 – ☎96 392 24 48 – www.asadordelcarme.com – – Closed Mon all year and Sun lunchtime except Oct-Jun.* Customers are attracted by the pleasant covered terrace, extensive menu of grilled meats and copious salads, the quiet of the square and the lovely views of the Iglesia del Carmen.

Casa Chimo – *Avenida Neptuno 40 – ☎ 96 371 20 48 – Closed Wed and 11 Sep-11 Oct – Reservation recommended.* This well-established restaurant is popular with Valencian families who come to enjoy a traditional paella by the sea. The dining room provides a cool retreat from the summer sun.

La Riuá – *Del Mar 27 – ☎96 391 45 71 – closed Holy Week and in Aug – Reservation recommended.* A heavy wooden door provides access to one of the city's best-known restaurants. The split-level dining room, sometimes noisy, is adorned with *azulejos*. A good place to discover Valencian cuisine.

La Rosa – *Neptuno 70 (Playa de Las Arenas) – ☎963 71 20 76 – closed Holy Week and 14 Aug-5 Sep – lunch only in winter –* . Try *arroz abanda*, a variation on *paella*, and a Valencian staple, as well as other seafood in the nautical-style dining room or on the covered terrace with a sea view.

TAPAS

Las Cuevas – *Samaniego 9 – ☎96 391 71 96 – Closed in Aug.* It's just like a cave: tiny windows, narrow doors and beams. Nothing but tapas are served here, prepared in the Valencian way: mussels, stuffed red peppers, sardines etc. At weekends, Las Cuevas fills up with the city's youngsters.

Bar Pilar – *Moro Zeit 13 – ☎96 391 04 97 – Open daily (except Wed) noon-midnight.* Founded in 1917, Pilar is one of the best tapas bars in the city. The house speciality is mussels-based *clochinas*. Another tapas institution, *El Molinón,* is directly opposite, making this a good area in which to discover Valencian nightlife.

Sagardi Euskal Taberna – *San Vicente Mártir 6 – ☎96 391 06 68 – www.sagardi.com –* . Enjoy Basque skewers and cider in the downstairs bar, or go up one flight for a more relaxed meal amid minimalist décor.

WHERE TO STAY

Hostal Antigua Morellana – *En Bou 2 – ☎96 391 57 73 – www.hostalam.com – – 18 rooms (doubles only).* A stone's throw from the Lonja and main market, this family-run hotel offers excellent value for money. The comfortable and bright rooms provide the best views of the picturesque narrow streets in the Carmen district.

Hostal Residencia Venecia – *Plaza Ayuntamiento (enter through Llop 5) – ☎ 96 352 42 67 – www.hotelvenecia.com – – 54 rooms – 4.10 €.* The building is outstanding, with classic façade and balconies facing the plaza del Ayuntamiento, Valencia's social and cultural centre. Rooms are well furnished and the breakfast room enjoys fine views.

Hotel Reina Victoria – *Barcas 4 – ☎96 352 04 87 – www.husa.es – – 95 rooms – 11.50 € – Restaurant 24 €.* It's worth making a journey here if only to admire the immaculate white stone Baroque façade. The interior lives up to expectations, with its charming entry hall set with marble and mirrors, elegant English bar, and classic rooms with modern comforts.

Hotel Ad-Hoc – *Boix 4 – ☎96 391 91 40 – www.adhochoteles.com – – 28 rooms – 10€ – Restaurant 18/50€.* This 19C mansion on a quiet street retains such features as a mosaic floor and exposed beams. Rooms are well-decorated and comfortable. Try for an upstairs room with balcony.

TAKING A BREAK

El Siglo – *Plaza Santa Catalina 11 – ☎ 96 391 84 66 – Closed Sat – Open 8am-9pm.* Founded in 1836, El Siglo (The Century) is a chocolate-maker, ice-cream producer and horchata specialist rolled into one. The extensive building is adorned with *azulejos* from Manises.

Another confectioner, Santa Catalina, less-frequented, is just ten metres away.

NIGHTLIFE

Calle Caballeros – This street is the hub of Valencia's nightlife. Between plaza de la Virgen, with its numerous outdoor cafés, and plaza Tossal, a popular square for tapas, you'll pass by the *Johnny Maracas* salsa bar, the *Babal Hanax* disco, and the fashion *Café Bolsería* with its jet-set clientele.

Café de las Horas – *Conde de Almodóvar 1 – ☎963 91 73 36 – Open 4.30am-1.30am (3am on public hols).* This café with a 19C atmosphere is just steps from the Plaza de la Virgen. The high point is the decor, including trompe-l'œil scenes on the walls, a little fountain, and finely tuned lighting that goes with the music to create an intimate atmosphere.

Café del Negrito – *Plaza Negrito – ☎963 91 42 33 – Open 3pm-3.30am.* This artists' café, situated in a small square in the old town, is a popular meeting-place for friends who come here to enjoy the best "Valencian water" and to enjoy the Negrito's famous orange juice and champagne cocktails. Note the bar opposite, the *Ghecko*, which is completely covered in shells.

La Marxa – *Cocinas 5 – ☎963 917 065 – Open Thu-Sat from 11pm.* At the heart of the famous Carmen district, La Marxa is the emblem of Valencian nightlife, and has been instrumental in developing Valencia's reputation as a city with a vibrant club scene.

SHOPPING

Lladró – *Poeta Querol 9 – ☎ 963 51 16 25 – Open Mon-Sat, 10am-2pm and 4-8pm.* This famous porcelain manufacturer has boutiques around the world selling stunning works of art across a broad price range.

Mercadillo de la Plaza Redonda – *Open 9am-1pm and 4-9pm.* This typical small market in plaza Redonda is the place to buy a whole range of clothes and bric-a-brac, or else simply to watch the world go by over a coffee. On Sundays, animals and pets can also be bought here.

Turrones Ramos – *Sombrerería 11 (next to Plaza Redonda) – Closed Sat-Sun and in Aug – Open 10am-2pm and 5-8pm.* This shop has sold hand-made *turrón* since 1890. The marzipan is worth trying too, especially *casca de batata* and *casca de yema* made with sweet potato or egg yolk."

FIESTAS

During the week of 12-19 March, the city celebrates the festival of St Joseph, with its famous **Las Fallas** (*see below*). Among religious festivals, the solemn **Corpus Christi** procession, dating from 1355 and the festival of the **Virgen de los Desamparados**, patroness of the city (second Sunday in May) are notable.

seals outside and a great 70m/230ft tunnel-aquarium below), the Arctic, the Antarctic (penguins) and Oceans (including a 30m/100ft aquarium-tunnel with sharks and rays). The dolphin centre hosts performances all day.

L'Umbracle★

White parabolic arches shelter this pleasant palm garden on a terrace facing the Museu de les Ciències.

Museu de les Ciències Príncipe Felipe★★

Open 10am-6pm (8pm 14 Jun-14 Sep). 7.50 € (11.20 € combined with L'Hemisfèric, 22.50 € with l'Oceanogràfic). ☎902 10 00 31.

The largest interactive science museum in Europe, designed by Santiago Calatrava, is a hands-on encounter with the human genome, space travel, astronomy and more.

L'Hemisfèric★

Check programmes and prices by calling ☎902 10 00 31.

Also the work of Calatrava, this building symbolizes a human eye open to the world. Set in a huge pool, it houses a planetarium and Omnimax cinema.

Palau de les Arts

The four halls host classical and modern opera, music, theatre and dance.

J. Malburet/MICHELIN

Detail, façade of Palacio del Marqués de Dos Aguas

Museo Nacional de Cerámica y de las Artes Suntuarias González Martí★★ (National Museum of Ceramics and Decorative Art)

Open 10am-2pm and 4-8pm; Sun and public hols, 10am-2pm. Closed Mon, 1 Jan, 1 May and 24-25 and 31 Dec. 2.40 €. No charge Sat afternoon and Sun. 96 351 63 92.

This museum occupies the lovely Baroque **Palacio del Marqués de Dos Aguas**★★. On the **ground floor** is the richly decorated **carriage**★ of the Marquis of Dos Aguas (1753). Rooms on the **first floor** include the Chinese salon, the *fumoir*, and the chapel.

The **ceramic collection** on the **second floor** includes Moorish ceramics (the basis of the craft in Spain), green and black porcelain, and later pieces from Málaga, Murcia and Manises. Christian ceramics of the 13C and 14C evidence continuity from the Moorish. Outstanding are green and manganese ceramics from **Paterna** (*6km/3.8mi N of Valencia*).The golden age of ceramics in **Manises** (*8km/5mi N of Valencia*) is represented by lovely pieces. Also on display are Chinese porcelain and European imitations, and an impressive Toledo urn.

The **Real Fábrica de Alcora**, established in 1727, became the centre of innovation in Spain, spreading the Louis XIV, Classic and Baroque styles. Pieces from 19C **Manises** evidence later styles that spread through southern and eastern Spain. There is also a Valencian kitchen with 18C and 19C tiles.

Colegio del Patriarca o del Corpus Christi★ (Patriarch or Corpus Christi College)

Open 11am-1.30pm. Closed Good Fri. 1.20 €. 96 351 41 76.

This ex-seminary dates back to the 16C. The **church** (*enter by left door*) is one of the few Renaissance churches in Spain with frescoes; on the lower wall sections are Manises tiles. The seminary is built around a harmonious patio decorated with Talavera *azulejo* friezes.

The small **museum** of 15C-17C art includes paintings by Juan de Juanes, a **triptych of the Passion**★ by Dirk Bouts, a 14C Byzantine crucifix from the Monastery of Athos, a 13C Romanesque *Christ* and a portrait of the founder, Ribera, by Ribalta, and paintings by Ribalta, Morales and El Greco.

In the same plaza is the **Universidad** (University).

Museo de Bellas Artes San Pío V★

Open 10am-8pm. Closed Mon, 1 Jan, Good Fri and 25 Dec. 96 360 57 93.

This fine arts museum is in an 18C-19C collegiate church and seminary, and a contemporary extension, near the Jardines del Real (Royal Gardens).

H. Levy/MICHELIN

L'Hemisfèric (Ciutat de les Arts i les Ciències)

The collection is notable for its **Valencian Primitives**★★ with altarpieces by the likes of Jacomart, Reixac, and the Osonas, Elder and Younger.

Representing the Renaissance are Macip, Juan de Juanes and others.

A gallery displays 16C Spanish canvases (among them the works of Ribalta, who introduced tenebrism to Spain) and Valencian artists of the 17C.

On the upper floor are European Baroque works (*St Bartholomew* by Luca Giordano) and Golden Age Spanish painting. Outstanding are *St John the Baptist* by El Greco, an impressive *St Sebastian* by Ribera and a self portrait by Velázquez. The portrait mastery of Goya is shown in his paintings of Francisco Bayeu and Joaquina Candado.

In the lower galleries of the cloister are the Iberian, Roman and Moorish archeaeological collection and a restored 16C Renaissance patio.

Jardines del Real (Royal Gardens)

The city's biggest park is close to the pleasant **Jardín de Monforte**. The **Puente del Real** (Royal Bridge) across the **Jardín del río Turia** is 16C.

Instituto Valenciano de Arte Moderno (IVAM)

Centro Julio González: Open 10-9pm (10pmJun-Sep). Closed Mon, 1 Jan, Good Fri and 25 Dec. 2 €. No charge Sun. ☎96 386 30 00.

This modern building houses more than 7 000 works of contemporary art, on rotating display (*Galleries 3 and 4, upper level*). It also owns the largest collection of the works of **Julio González** (1876-1942), a major 20C sculptor; and a permanent collection of the paintings of **Ignacio Pinazo** (1849-1916) (*Gallery 5, upper level*) , a notable artist of the 19-20C transition to modern styles.

Museo de historia de Valencia★

Calle Valencia 42 (Mislata), BUS 95 or 7. Open 10am-2pm and 4.30-8.30pm; Sun and public hols 10am-3pm. Closed Mon. ☎96 370 11 05.

Located in a 19C water works, this museum tells the story of Valencia from its beginnings to the end of the 20C. Most evocative are the dramatised audiovisual presentations of each era.

Museo Valenciano de la Ilustración y la Modernidad (Museum of Illustration and Modernism); Centro de la Beneficencia; Museo de la Prehistoria; Convento de Santo Domingo; Jardín Botánico (Botanical Garden).

VALLADOLID★

POPULATION: 345 891
MICHELIN MAP 575 H 15 (TOWN PLAN) – CASTILLA Y LEÓN (VALLADOLID).

The former capital of Castilla and of a great empire stands amid a landscape of vineyards and cereal crops. Today, this important provincial capital preserves architectural vestiges that bear witness to its rich and illustrious past.

- **Information:** *Acera de Recoletos (Pabellón de Cristal), ☎983 35 18 01.*
- **Orient Yourself:** The city is at the centre of the northern section of the Spanish Meseta.
- **Especially for Kids:** The interactive Museo de Ciencia (science museum).
- **Also See:**PALENCIA (47km/29mi NE) and ZAMORA (98km/61mi W).

Background

Historical notes – From the 12C, Castilla's kings frequently resided at Valladolid. Peter the Cruel married there, as did Ferdinand and Isabel; it was the birthplace of Philip IV and his sister Anne of Austria, mother of Louis XIV.

Castillo de Simancas *(11km/7mi SW)* – Charles V made this castle a repository for state archives. The collection is a history of Spanish administration from the 15C to the 19C.

Special Features

THE ISABELLINE STYLE

This style emerged in the late 15C as a mixture of Flamboyant Gothic and Mudéjar tradition, the ultimate stage before Plateresque. Rectangular façade panels eventually extended from ground level to cornice and were compartmented like an altarpiece.

The best examples in Valladolid are the Colegio de San Gregorio and the façade of the Iglesia de San Pablo.

Colegio de San Gregorio

This is Valladolid's most impressive Isabelline building. On the sumptuous **entrance**★★★, attributed to Gil de Siloé and Simon of Cologne, fantasies from savages to interwoven thorn branches create a strongly hierarchical composition rising from the doorway.

The college is the seat of the **Museo Nacional de Escultura**★★★ *(sculpture museum, under refurbishment: the collection is at the Palacio de Villena; see under Worth a Visit).*

Iglesia de San Pablo (St Paul's Church)

The **façade**★★★ is outstanding. The lower section, by Simon of Cologne, consists of a portal with an ogee arch all framed in a segmental arch, and above, a large rose window and two coats of arms supported by angels.

Worth a Visit

IN THE CENTRE

The historical centre of Valladolid is a blend of carefully tended plazas, lively pedestrian ways, and a pleasant park, the Campo Grande. The Plaza Mayor, the lovely and spacious focus of the city, dates from the 16C.

Museo Nacional de Escultura★★★ (National Museum of Sculpture)

The temporary home is the Palacio de Villena. Open 10am-2pm and 4-6pm (9pm Apr-Sep); Sun and public hols, 10am-2pm. Closed Mon, 1 and 6 Jan, 1 May, 8 Sep, and 24-25 and 31 Dec. 2.40€, no charge Sat afternoon and Sun. ☎983 25 03 75.

From the 16C to the 17C Valladolid was a major centre for sculpture, reflected in this museum's wonderful collection of religious statues in polychrome wood, a material well suited to the expression of the dramatic.

Address Book

For coin ranges, see the Legend on the cover flap.

WHERE TO EAT

⊖ **Covadonga** – *Zapico 1 – ☎983 33 07 98*. The uninspiring modern appearance of this restaurant is quickly forgotten inside, where the welcome is friendly, the service excellent and the cuisine wholesome and plentiful. Try the house speciality, roast suckling lamb *(lechazo)*.

⊖⊖ **El Figón de Recoletos** – *Acera de Recoletos 3 – ☎983 39 60 43 – Closed Sun evening and 20 Jul-10 Aug –* ▤. This typically Castilian restaurant with its dark wood decor and sturdy chairs is frequented by businessmen and women, families and tourists alike. The roast peppers *(pimientos asados)*, brisket of lamb *(falda de cordero)* and grilled chops *(chuletitas)* tend to be the most popular choices on the menu.

WHERE TO STAY

⊖⊖ **Hotel El Nogal** – *Conde Ansúrez 10 – ☎ 983 34 03 33 – www.hotelelnogal.com –* ▤ *– 26 rooms –* ☕ *7 € – Restaurant 16 €*. This small, recently renovated hotel is located within the triangle of the plaza Mayor, cathedral and Museo de Escultura. The international-style rooms here are bright and airy and are reasonably priced given the quality. The hotel restaurant is pleasant with an often lively ambience.

⊖⊖ **Hotel Imperial** – *Peso 4 – ☎983 33 03 00 – www.himperial.com –* ▤ *– 79 rooms –* ☕ *4 € – Restaurant 16/26 €*. An authentic Valladolid institution of the Renaissance, set in the 16C Gallo mansion, impeccably maintained while meeting mcontemporary requirements. The green marble lobby is popular for afternoon tea.

SHOPPING

Confiterías Cubero – *Pasión 7 – ☎ 983 35 60 77*. This shop has not only delicious patries and authentic local sweets, but also a unique *Museo del Dulce* (museum of sweets) where the sights of Valladolid are re-created in sugar.

Manuel Iborra – *Lencería 2 – ☎ 983 35 11 21 – www.manueliborra.com – closed Feb-Mar – open 10am-2pm and 4-9pm (turrón season)*. The best-known shop for *turrón* and homemade ice cream in Valladolid. Outstanding for *tortas imperiales* (imperial cakes) and all sorts of *turrones* at Christmas.

FIESTAS

The city's Holy Week processions are renowned for their solemnity and impressive statues and floats.

On the ground floor of the Palacio de Villena, aside from paintings (including an attractive *Pieta* by Pedro Berruguete) are the magnificent sculptures of two 16C Mannerist masters: **Alonso Berruguete** (a remarkable altarpiece designed for the San Benito church) and **Juan de Juni** (*The Crucifixion* and the portentous ensemble, **Burial of Christ**). Outstanding works by **Gregorio Fernández**, leading 16C exponent of Castillian Baroque, include *Passage to the Sixth Agony* and **Christ Recumbent**. There are also works of the Andalucian School (Martínez Montañés, Pedro de Mena, Alonso Cano).

On the second floor are works from the Renaissance by **Diego Siloé** (*The Holy Family*) and **Felipe Vigarny** (*Virgin and Child*, a model of grace and elegance). There is also an excellent painting by **Rubens** (*Democritus and Heraclitus*).

On the third floor are Late Baroque (18C) works, such as *St Francis of Assisi* by *Salzillo* and *Head of St Paul* by Juan Alonso de Villabrille y Ron. On the way down, admire a magnificent **Neapolitan nativity** of more than 180 figures.

Capilla del Colegio de San Gregorio★

Designed by Juan Guas, this lovely Gothic chapel with elevated choir contains an altarpiece by Berruguete, a tomb by Felipe Vigarny and carved choir stalls.

Catedral★

▶ *Enter by the Puerta de Santa María in Plaza Universidad.*

VALLADOLID

			Colegio de Santa Cruz Pl.	CY	40	Pasión	BY	30
			Doctrinos	BY	16	Portillo de Balboa	CX	32
Arco de Ladrillo Pas. del	BZ	2	Duque de la Victoria	BY	17	San Ildefonso	BY	36
Arzobispo Gandásegui	CY	3	España Pl. de	BY	18	San Pablo Pl. de	BX	37
Bailarín Vicente Escudero	CY	5	Fuente Dorada Pl. de	BY	20	Santiago	BY	41
Bajada de la Libertad	BCY	6	Gondomar	CX	21	Santuario	CY	42
Cadenas de San Gregorio	CX	8	Industrias	CY	23	Sanz y Forés	CXY	45
Cánovas del Castillo	BCY	9	Jorge Guillén	BXY	24	Teresa Gil	BY	
Cardenal Mendoza	CY	10	Maldonado	CY	25	Zorrilla Pas. de	BZ	47
Chancillería	CX	13	Marqués del Duero	CXY	26			
Claudio Moyano	BY	14	Miguel Iscar	BY	29			

Casa de Cervantes	BY	R	Patio Herreriano-Museo de Arte Contemporáneo Español	BY	M²	Universidad	CY	U
Iglesia de Las Angustias	CY	L						
Museo Oriental	BZ	M¹						

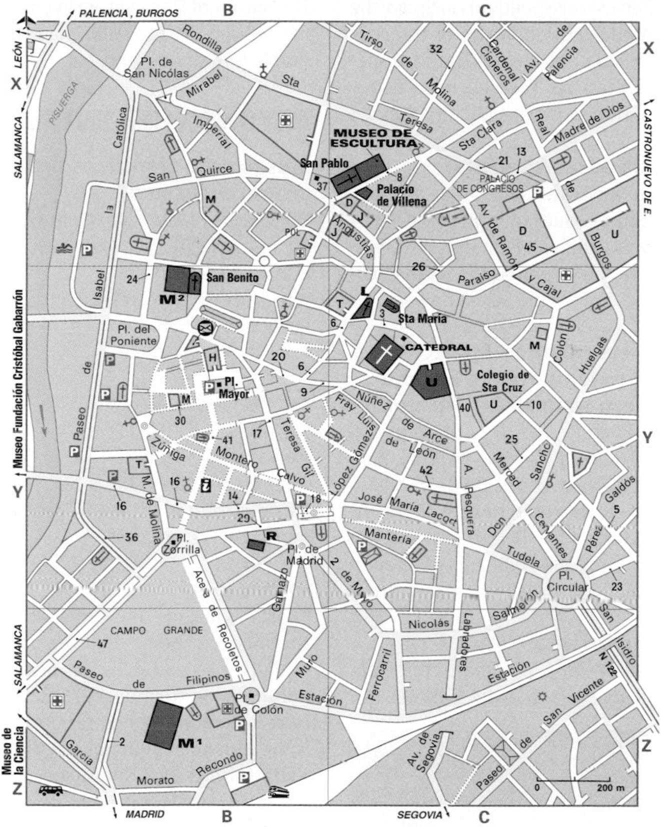

Open 10am-1.30pm and 4.30-7pm; Sat-Sun and public hols, 10am-1.30pm. Closed Mon. ☎*983 30 43 62.*

The cathedral, commissioned in about 1580 by Philip II from Herrera, was distorted by the architect's 17C and 19C successors – in the octagonal tower, and the Baroque upper façade by Alberto Churriguera.

Never completed, the **interior** remains one of Herrera's triumphs. The altarpiece (1551) in the central apsidal chapel, where figures come to life, is by Juan de Juni.

Museo Diocesano y Catedralicio★

In the funerary chapels of the former Gothic cathedral. Note the Mudéjar cupolas in the Capilla de San Llorente. There is a **collection**★ of sculptures, paintings, silverware, and ornaments.

Note two busts by Pedro de Mena (*Ecce Homo* and *Dolorosa*), two 13C tombs, two 13C Christs (one Protogothic with four nails), a dramatic *Ecce Homo* by Gregorio Fernández, the sculpture group *Lament for Christ* (c 1500) and a 16C silver monstrance by Juan de Arfe. Outside, note, on the Baroque university façade, sculptured and heraldic decoration by Narciso and Antonio Tomé.

Colegio de Santa Cruz

This lovely late-15C college is one of the first Renaissance buildings in Spain; the carved decoration at the entrance is Plateresque but the rusticated stonework is Classical. The Neoclassic balconies and windows are 18C additions.

Iglesia de las Angustias

Facing the Teatro Calderón de la Barca. The church, built by one of Herrera's disciples, contains Juan de Juni's masterpiece, the **Virgen de los Siete Cuchillos**★ (Virgin of the Seven Knives).

Patio Herreriano – Museo de Arte Contemporáneo Español (Modern Spanish Art Museum)

Entry by calle Jorge Guillén. Open 11am-8pm. Closed Mon (except public hols) 1 Jan and 25 Dec. 6 €. 983 36 29 08.
The lovely **Herreran patio**★ of the ex-monastery of San Benito and a newer annex house this collection of Spanish art since 1917.

Museo Oriental

Open 4-7pm; Sun and public hols, 10am-2pm. 4 €. 983 30 68 00.

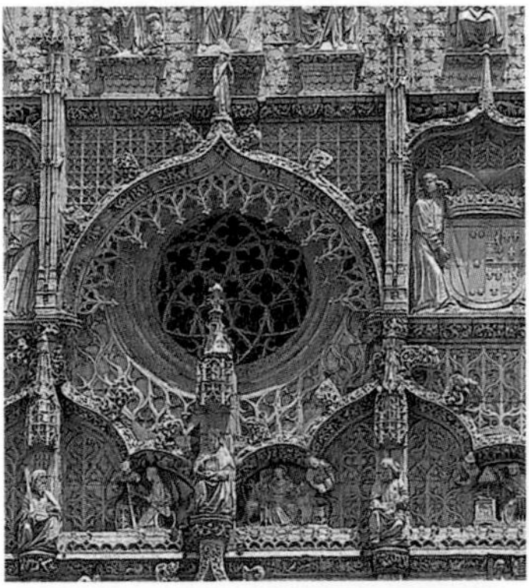

B. Brillion/MICHELIN

Iglesia de San Pablo – detail of the façade

The museum, in a neo-Classical college (18C) designed by Ventura Rodríguez, houses **Chinese art**★ (bronze, porcelain, lacquerware, coins and silk embroidery) and Philippine art with important **ivory pieces**★.

Casa de Cervantes

Enter from calle Rastro. Open 9.30am-3.30pm; Sun and public hols, 10am-3pm. Closed Mon, 1 and 6 Jan, 1 and 13 May, 8 Sep and 24-25 and 31 Dec. 2.40 €, no charge Sun. 983 30 88 10.
The author of *Don Quixote* lived in this house from 1603 to 1606; some of his simple furnishings remain.

BEYOND THE CENTRE

Museo de la Ciencia (Science Museum)

Kids Open 10am-7pm; summer 11am-9pm. 9 €. Closed Mon, 1 Jan and 25 Dec. 983 14 43 00.
This interactive science museum includes a planetarium.

Excursions

Peñafiel★

55km/34mi E along the N 122. Peñafiel was a strong point along the Duero during the Reconquest.

Castillo★

Peñafiel's massive 14C castle is sited at the meeting point of three valleys. Within the second, fairly well preserved perimeter, is an imposing keep, reinforced by machicolated turrets. Inside is the **Museo Provincial del Vino de Valladolid**, a showcase of local wines (*open 11.30am-2.30pm and 4.30-7.30pm (8.30pm in summer); 5 € (castle and museum); 983 88 11 99).*

Iglesia de San Pablo

The church (1324) has a Mudéjar east end, Renaissance vaulting in the 16C Capilla del Infante (Infante Chapel).

Tordesillas

30km/19mi SW along the A 62. The kings of Spain and Portugal signed the famous **Treaty of Tordesillas** here in 1494, dividing up the New World. **Juana the Mad** locked herself away here on the death of her husband Philip the Fair in 1506.

Convento de Santa Clara★

Guided tours (1hr), 10am-1.30pm and 4-5.45pm (to 6.30pm Apr-Sep); Sun and public hols, 10.30am-1.30pm and 3.30-5.30pm. Closed Mon, 1 and 6 Jan, Maundy Thu (afternoon), Good Fri, 1 May, 8 and 16 Sep and 24, 25 and 31 Dec. 3.60 €, no charge Wed for E.U. citizens. 983 77 00 71.

The palace built by Alfonso XI in 1350 was converted to a convent by Peter the Cruel. He installed María de Padilla here, to whom he might have been married. For María, homesick for Sevilla, he commissioned Mudéjar decoration. The **patio**★ has multifoil and horseshoe arches, strapwork decoration and multicoloured ceramic tiles. In the **Capilla Dorada** (Gilded Chapel) are mementoes and works of art.

The choir of the **church** has a particularly intricate **artesonado ceiling**★★.

Medina del Campo

54km/34mi SW along the A 62 and the A 6; 24km/15mi from Tordesillas. In the Middle Ages Medina was famous for its fairs. A large market is held on Sundays. Isabel the Catholic died here in 1504.

Castillo de la Mota★

Juana the Mad often stayed in this large 13C-15C castle. Cesare Borgia was imprisoned in the keep for two years.

Villa de Almenara-Puras: Museo de las Villas Romanas (Museum of Roman Villas)

51 km/31.8mi S by the N 601. Turn at Almenara and continue 3km/1.9mi S. Open 10.30am-2pm and 4-6pm (4.30-8pm in summer). Closed Mon and 24-25 and 31 Dec. 3 €. 983 62 60 36.

This museum brings life in Roman villas into the present. Continue to the remains of a sumptuous villa of the 4C and the underlying 3C structure.

Medina de Rioseco

40km/25mi NW along the N 601. The picturesque narrow main street, or **Rúa,** of this agricultural centre is lined by porticoes on wooden pillars.

Iglesia de Santa María

Open 11am-2pm and 4-7pm (5-8pm in summer). Closed Mon, 1 and 6 Jan and 25 Dec. 3 € (includes Iglesia de Santiago). 983 72 03 19.

The 15C-16C church's central altarpiece was carved by Esteban Jordán. The **Capilla de los Benavente**★ (Benavente Chapel, 16C) contains a 16C retable by Juan de Juni. The treasury holds a 16C monstrance by Antonio Arfe.

Iglesia de Santiago

Open 11am-2pm and 4-7pm. Closed Mon, 1 and 6 Jan and 25 Dec. 3 € (includes Iglesia de Santa María). 983 70 03 27.

The altarpieces in the three apsidal chapels of this 16C-17C church form a spectacular Churrigueresque group.

VIC★★

POPULATION: 29 113

MICHELIN MAP 574 G 36 – CATALUNYA (BARCELONA).

This important commercial centre and thriving industrial town (leather goods, food processing and textiles) was once a Roman centre. Monumental buildings testify to its history. Vic is a good base for exploring Barcelona, Girona and the Pyrenees.

- **Information:** *Ciutat 4, 93 886 20 91, www.ajvic.net.*
- **Orient Yourself:** Vic is in NE Spain, north of Barcelona.
- **Also See:** BARCELONA (66km/41mi S), GIRONA/GERONA (79km/49mi NE) and PIRINEOS CATALANES.

Worth a Visit

OLD QUARTER★

Wide avenues (ramblas) follow the old walls, of which a few remnants remain.

Museu Episcopal★★★

Open 10am-7pm; Oct-Mar 10am-1pm and 4-7pm; Sun and public hols 10am-2pm. Last admission 30 min before closing. Closed Mon, 1 and 6 Jan, Easter Sun and 25-26 Dec. 4 €, no charge first Thu of every month. 93 886 93 60.

This magnificent museum displays Romanesque and Gothic works, along with fabrics and costumes, jewellery, ceramics, and other arts.

Sala del románico★★★ (Romanesque Gallery)

On exhibit are the *Descent of Erill la Vall*, a sculptural ensemble; the painting *Canopy of Ribes de Freser;* and outstanding **altar fronts**. The *Lluça Altar* marks the transition to the Gothic style.

Salas del gótico★★★ (Gothic Galleries)

Among items from the early Gothic period (after 1275) are a magnificent marble altarpiece by **Bernat Saulet** ; a *Virgin of Boixadors*; the altar front of Bellver de Cerdanya and parts of an altarpiece by **Pere Serra**. The impressive collection of international Gothic altarpieces (15C) includes the **Santa Clara** and *Sant Antoni i Santa Margarida* altars, both by Borrasà, the *de Guimerà* altar, the work of Ramón de Mur, and the *Verdú* altarpiece of Jaume Ferrer II.

The paintings of *Jaume Huguet* mark the transition to the Renaissance.

©Museu Episcopal de Vic

Gothic Painting Exhibition in Museu Episcopal de Vic

Tejido e indumentaria★★ – (Textiles and Costumes)

A magnificent display of 13C-18C textiles and liturgical wear (14-19C).

Catedral★

Open 10am-1pm and 4-7pm. No visits during religious services. Closed Mon. 2 €. 93 886 44 49.

An elegant 11C Romanesque belfry and crypt remain from earlier churches.

The neo-Classical cathedral was built between 1781 and 1803. In 1930 the famous Catalan artist **José María Sert** decorated the **interior**★ with wall paintings. These were burned during the Civil War, and repainted by Sert before his death in 1945.

The **paintings**★★ have a power reminiscent of Michelangelo. They evoke the mystery of the Redemption *(chancel)* from the time of Adam's original sin *(transept)* to the Passion (*apse*), the Evangelists and the Martyrs *(nave)*. Scenes on the back of the west door illustrate the triumph of human injustice in the Life of Christ and in the history of Catalunya: Jesus chasing the moneylenders *(right)*; Jesus condemned *(centre)* and the road to Calvary *(left)*. The monochrome golds and browns in the murals lend the effect of a relief.

The former high altar **retable**★★ (*end of the ambulatory*) is a 15C alabaster work in 12 panels. The Gothic tomb is of the canon who commissioned the retable, by the same sculptor.

Claustro★ (Cloister)

Tracery-filled 14C arches surround the small close. In a cloister gallery is the tomb of the painter JM Sert, surmounted by his unfinished *Crucifixion*.

Palau Episcopal

The 12C episcopal palace has been modified significantly. The **Sala dels Sínodes**, decorated in 1845, and the patio are the main features.

Plaça Major★
Note façades with Modernist, Gothic and Baroque details on this busy arcaded square. A popular market is held in the square every Saturday.

Ayuntamiento (Gothic and Baroque town hall); Templo Romano (Roman Temple, 2C); Museo del Arte de la Piel (Museum of Leatherwork).

Excursions

Monasterio de Sant Pere de Casserres★

Open 11am-5.30pm (7pm 15 Jun-15 Sep). Closed Mon, 15-30 Jan and 25 Dec. 3 €. 93 744 71 18.

17/11.6mi NE. Take the C 153 NE from Vic, then turn right toward Tavernoles and Parador. At Parador take a paved lane to the left (3.5km/2.2mi).

Stop just before Parador for a fine **view**★★ (*right*) of the marsh of Sau, between high banks. The small Romaneque montastery enjoys a privileged **location**★★ at the end of a long and narrow peninsula in the marsh.

Monasterio de Santa Maria de L'Estany★

Open 10am-2pm and 4-8pm. Oct-Holy Week 10am-2.30pm, Sat 10am-2pm and 4-6pm. Sun and public hols 10am-2pm. Closed Mon, 1-15 Jan and 25-26 Dec. 2 €. 93 830 30 40.

24km/15mi SW. Leave Vic along the C 25 towards Manresa. Turn right at exit 164 and follow the BP 4313.

The village of **L'Estany**★ grew up around this medieval Augustinian monastery. The bell tower of the 12C Romanesque church was rebuilt in the 15C. The arcades of the beautiful **cloisters**★ are supported by matching columns and decorated with 72 remarkable **capitals**★★. The north gallery is Romanesque and narrative; the west, decorative with palm fronds and gaunt griffons; the south, geometrical and interlaced; the east features wedding scenes and musicians.

Local Specialities

Vic is the centre of the Llonganissa quality label, producing delicious sausages and meat products such as *salchichones* (salami-type sausages), *butifarras* (Catalan sausages) and *fuets*.

EXCURSIONS THROUGH THE SIERRA DE MONTSENY★

The Sierra de Montseny, an extension of the Pyrenees, is a granite massif covered in beeches and cork oaks. To the southeast, the **Parque Natural de Montseny** covers 17 372ha/42 600 acres; its highest peaks are Matagalls (1 695m/5 560ft) and **Turó de l'Home** (1 707m/5 601ft).

From Vic to Sant Celoni via the northern road

60km/37.5mi. Leave Vic to the S; turn left after 6km/3.6mi.

The road goes through pine and beechwoods past delightful **Viladrau**. After **Arbùcies**, it runs beside the river then turns for **Breda**, with the Romanesque tower of the **monasterio de Sant Salvador**★, and Sant Celoni.

From Sant Celoni to la Ermita de Sant Marçal★★

Beyond Campins, the road rises in hairpins, affording coastal **views**, to the lake (*embalse*) of Santa Fè (1 130m/3 707ft). The hermitage is 7km/4mi ahead on Matagalls ridge (1 260m/4 134ft).

From Sant Celoni to Tona via Montseny★

43km/27mi. There are good views of the sierra from the **route**. Beyond Montseny, the road rises to a wild area, then descends to Tona past the Romanesque church in **El Brull** and the tower of **Santa Maria de Seva.**

VITORIA-GASTEIZ★

POPULATION: 209 704

MICHELIN MAP 573 D 21-22 (TOWN PLAN) – PAÍS VASCO (ÁLAVA).

Vitoria-Gasteiz is the capital of the largest Basque province and the seat of the Basque government, sited in a cereal-covered plateau. It was founded in the 12C and was surrounded by walls. The old quarter is in the upper section.

- **Information:** *Plaza del General Loma, ☎945 16 15 98; Dator 11, ☎945 16 15 98; www.vitoria-gasteiz.org/turismo.*
- **Orient Yourself:** The city is at 524m/1 718ft in NE Spain. A 2h30min walking tour of the historic district departs from the Oficina de Turismo (tourist office).
- **Also See:** BILBAO (64km/40mi N), PAMPLONA (93km/58mi E) and La RIOJA.

Walking About

CIUDAD VIEJA★★ (OLD TOWN)

1hr 30min

Concentric streets – each named after a trade – ring the cathedral. The liveliest streets are to the left of the plaza de la Virgen Blanca. The **Iglesia de San Pedro**, with its Gothic façade, can also be found in this part of the old town.

Plaza de la Virgen Blanca

The square, dominated by the Iglesia (church) de San Miguel, is surrounded by house fronts with glassed-in balconies, or *miradores*. The massive monument at the square's centre commemorates Wellington's decisive victory on 21 June 1813, putting to flight King Joseph Bonaparte and his army. It communicates with the nobly ordered 18C **plaza de España** (or plaza Nueva).

Iglesia de San Miguel

In a jasper niche in the church porch is a polychrome Late Gothic statue of the Virgen Blanca, the city's patron. In the late 14C portal, the tympanum shows the Life of St Michael. In the chancel are an altarpiece by Gregorio Fernández and a Plateresque sepulchral arch.

Plaza del Machete

This small, long square lies behind the **Arquillos**, an arcade which links the upper and lower towns. A niche in the east end of San Miguel church contains the *machete* or cutlass, on which the procurator general had to swear to uphold the town's privileges *(fueros)*.

The 16C **Palacio de Villa Suso** on the right side, is now a meeting centre.

Climb the steps adjoining the palace.

A stroll along **calle Fray Zacarías Martínez,** with wood-framed houses and palaces, is pleasant. The Renaissance north doorway of the Palacio de los Escoriaza-Esquivel, built on the old town walls, is worthy of special note; if it is open, enter to view the lovely covered courtyard.

Catedral de Santa María

Closed for restoration. Open for guided tours.

The construction of the Gothic church-fortress, part of the city's first defensive ring, began at the end of the 13C (*see Worth a Visit*).

In the 16C wood and brick **Casa Godeo-Guevara-San Juan** is home to a small archaeological museum (*see Worth a Visit).* The **Casa del Portalón,** opposite, is a typical late 15C-early 16C shop, now a well-known restaurant. The **Torre de los Anda,** part of the medieval defences, forms a triangle with the two houses.

In calle Cuchillería, in the **Palacio de Bendaña,** a building noted for its corner turret and doorway with *alfiz* surround, is a museum devoted to playing cards (*see Worth a Visit).* Part of the delightful **Renaissance patio** has been preserved.

The **Casa del Cordón**, a 16C house at nº24, is used for exhibitions.

CIUDAD NUEVA (MODERN TOWN)

As Vitoria-Gasteiz grew in the 18C, neo-Classical constructions began to appear such as the **Arquillos** arcade**.** In the 19C, the town expanded southwards with the **Parque de la Florida** (Florida Park), the **Catedral Nueva** (New Cathedral, 1907) in neo-Gothic style and two wide avenues: paseo de la Senda and paseo de Fray Francisco, the latter lined by mansions, such as the Palacio de Ajuria Enea, seat of the Lehendakari, or Basque government, and two museums, the Museo de la Armería and the Museo de Bellas Artes.

Near Plaza de España is the modern Plaza de los Fueros, the work of architect José Luis Peña Ganchegui and sculptor Eduardo Chillida.

Worth a Visit

Restoration Work at Catedral de Santa María★★

Guided tour by appointment (60min) 11am-2pm and 5-8pm. 3€. 945 25 51 35.

The diocese has stuggled for centuries to keep this Gothic cathedral from subsiding and tumbling. A program to realign its walls will run at least to 2010. An innovative hard-hat tour along walkways and passages reveals the secrets of this temple fortress.

Museo "Fournier" de Naipes de Álava★

Open 10am-2pm and 4-6.30pm; Sat, 10am (11am Sun and public hols) to 2pm. Last entry 30 min before closing. Closed Mon, 1 Jan, Good Fri and 25 Dec. 945 18 19 20.

In the playing card factory of Heraclio Fournier is a collection of over 15 000 packs from all over the world, dating from the late 14C to the present. Cards illustrate events, geography, politics and traditional dress and pastimes.

Artium★

Open 11am-8pm; Sat-Sun and public hols 10.30am-8pm. Closed Mon exc public hols, 1 Jan and 25 Dec. 4.50 € (5€ with cathedral). 945 20 90 20.

Museo Fournier de Naipes de Álava

A Spanish playing card dating from 1570

This museum and cultural centre focuses on the foundations of modern art. A significant selction from its **magnificent collection**★ is shown on a rotating basis. The museum owns more than 1 800 works of Spanish artists, from the Avant Garde of the twenties and thirties (most of the collection) to the most recent. Names are of the stature of Miró, Gargallo, Tàpies, Canogar, Palazuelo, Oteiza and Chillida.

Museo de Armería★ (Museum of Arms and Armour)

Open 10am-2pm and 4-6.30pm; Sat, 10am (11am Sun and public hols) to 2pm. Closed Mon, Good Fri and 25 Dec. 945 18 19 20.

The well-presented collection housed in a modern building traces the tradition and evolution of weaponry in the Basque country from prehistoric axes to early-20C pistols. Note the 15C-17C **armour**, including suits of 17C **Japanese armour.**

Museo Diocesano de Arte Sacro (Diocesan Sacred Art Museum)

Open 10am-2pm and 4-6pm; Sat, 10am (11am Sun and public hols) to 2pm and 5-8pm. 945 15 06 31

This museum in the ambulatory of the **Catedral Nueva** exhibits Gothic images, Flemish works (*Descent from the Cross* by Van der Goes, *The Crucifixion* by Ambrosius Benson), 16C-18C canvases (*St Francis* by El Greco, several

VITORIA-GASTEIZ								
			España Pl. de	BZ	18	Pascual de Andagoya Pl. de	AY	39
			Gasteiz Av. de	AYZ		Portal del Rey	BZ	42
Angulema	BZ	2	Herrería	AY	24	Postas	BZ	
Becerro de Bengoa	AZ	5	Independencia	BZ	27	Prado	AZ	45
Cadena y Eleta	AZ	8	Machete Pl. del	BZ	30	San Francisco	BZ	48
Dato	BZ		Madre Vedruna	AZ	33	Santa María Cantón de	BY	51
Diputación	AZ	12	Nueva Fuera	BY	34	Virgen Blanca Pl. de la	BZ	55
Escuelas	BY	15	Ortiz de Zárate	BZ	36			

Casa del Portalón	BY	L	Museo "Fournier" de Naipes de Álava	BY	M4	Museo de Arqueología	BY	M1
Catedral Nueva	AZ	N				Museo de Bellas Artes	AZ	M2

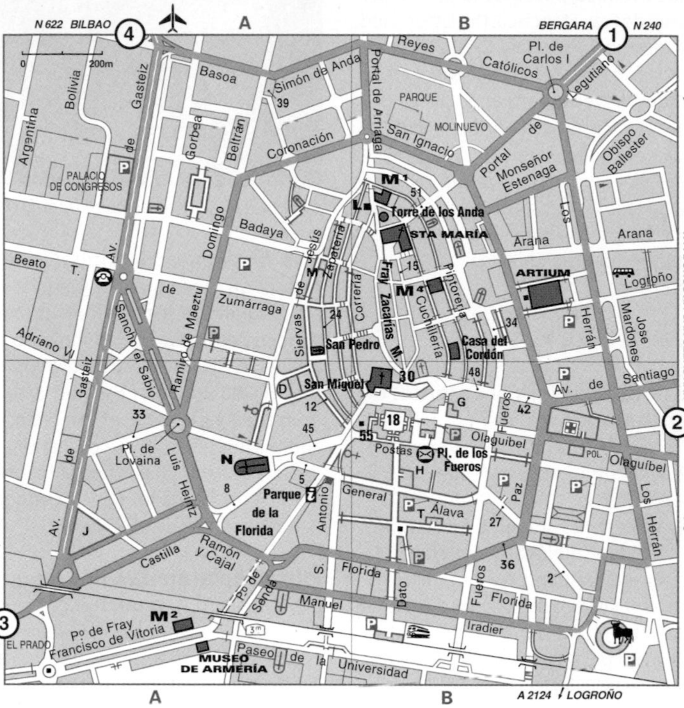

Riberas, *The Immaculate Conception* by Alonso Cano) and silverware.

Museo de Bellas Artes (Fine Arts Museum)

Open 10am-2pm and 4-6.30pm; Sat, 10am (11am Sun and public hols) to 2pm and 5-8pm. Closed Mon, 1 Jan, Good Fri and 25 Dec. 945 18 19 18.

The museum, housed in the early 20C Historicist Palacio de Agustí, displays Spanish art of the 18 and 19C and a comprehensive selection of Basque *costumbrista* painting by such artists as Iturrino, Regoyos and Zuloaga.

Museo de Arqueología (Archaeological Museum)

Open 10am-2pm and 4-6.30pm; Sat, 10am (11am Sun and public hols) to 2pm. Closed Mon, 1 Jan and Good Fri. 945 18 19 22.

This small museum in the half-timbered 16C Godeo-Guevara-San Juan house displays finds from excavations in Álava province. Note the dolmen collections and Roman monuments, including the *Estela del Jinete* (Knight's stele).

Address Book

For coin ranges, see the Legend on the cover flap.

WHERE TO STAY

Hostal Infanta Doña Leonor – *Condes de Toreno 1 – Villalcázar de Sirga – ☎979 88 80 15 – – 9 rooms – 3.50€.* If you're hoping for a good night's sleep in a peaceful setting, this modern hostal in the small town of Villalcázar de Sirga is ideal, with its cosy rooms, parquet floors and wooden furniture.

Hotel San Martín – *Plaza San Martín 7 – Frómista – ☎979 81 00 00 – Closed Jan – – 12 rooms – 3.60 € – Restaurant €7.80.* Despite its simplicity, this hotel on two floors close to the Romanesque church of San Martín has 12 comfortable, well-equipped rooms, all with private bathroom and TV. Much of the cooking in the restaurant is done in the traditional wood-fired oven.

Hotel Madrid – *Avenida de La Puebla 44 – Ponferrada – ☎987 41 15 50 – 45 rooms – 4.21 € – Restaurant 10 €.* A good central location, friendly staff and clean, comfortable rooms are the main features of this well-established hotel, which has been welcoming guests for more than half a century, and whose longevity is reflected in the overall decor.

Hotel Real Monasterio San Zoilo – *Obispo Souto – Carrión de los Condes – ☎ 979 88 00 50 – – 35 rooms – 5.50 €.* This former Benedictine monastery has dispensed with the austerity of former times and is now a delightful hotel where the welcome is both warm and friendly. The architecture – a mix of brick, stone and wood – is soberly elegant, the rooms extremely comfortable and the prices unbeatable.

Pousada de Portomarín – *Avenida de Sarria – Portomarín – ☎ 982 54 52 00 – hpousadalander.es – – 32 rooms – 7.60 €– Restaurant 12.50 €.* A peaceful hotel in a modern stone building with fine views of the River Miño. Spacious, comfortable rooms with wood floors and attractive furniture. Some rooms have the added bonus of a terrace. A good restaurant serving traditional cuisine.

Hotel Achuri – *Rioja 11 – ☎945 25 58 00 – 40 rooms – 3.50 €.* The Achuri has everything you could ask in the budget category: a central position, a friendly welcome and clean, perfectly adequate rooms with bathrooms and TVs. Highly recommended.

Hotel Palacio de Elorriaga – *Elorriaga 15 – Elorriaga – 1.5km/1mi E along avenida de Santiago and the N 104 – ☎945 26 36 16 – www.hotelpalacioelorriaga.com – – 21 rooms – – Restaurant 40 €.* This 16C-17C mansion has been completely restored. Behind the sober walls of stone and brick, the overall effect is delightful with tasteful small touches and an abundance of wood and antique furniture. Guest rooms are cosy with en-suite bathrooms.

WHERE TO EAT

La Peseta – *Plaza San Bartolomé 3 – Astorga – ☎987 61 72 75 – Closed Sun evening and 15-31 Oct – .* This popular, family-run restaurant has a simple, somewhat antiquated dining room, where the cuisine is traditional and reasonably priced. The *cocido maragato* (a stew of assorted animal parts) is popular. There are also 19 modest guest rooms.

Mesón del Peregrino *Irunbidea 10 – Puente la Reina – 1km/0/6mi NE of Puente la Reina on the Pamplona/Iruña road – ☎948 34 00 75 Closed 23 Dec-15 Jan – .* A charming restaurant housed in a magnificent large stone house with dining rooms overlooking the garden and swimming pool. The tasteful decor is rustic in style, creating the perfect atmosphere in which to enjoy the creative cuisine on offer here. The restaurant also has 13 rooms, with prices in the mid- to high price range.

Gurea – *Plaza de la Constitución 10 – ☎945 24 59 33 – .* The attractive wood façade leads to rustic dining areas where traditional foods are served.

Arkupe – *Mateo Moraza 13 – ☎945 23 00 80 – .* This restaurant is behind the town hall in an 18C national monument offers with exposed beams and stone. Meats and fish are prepared according to traditional Basque recipes.

TAPAS

El Rincón de Luis Mari – *Rioja 14 – ☎ 945 25 01 27 – Closed Tue and in Sep –* ▤. A simple bar with a large choice of tapas and raciones, a fine selection of cured hams, and a good location near the old quarter.

LEISURE ACTIVITIES

The inhabitants of Vitoria-Gasteiz have the choice of a river beach in Gamarra, to the north, as well as the Urrúnaga and Ullívarri reservoirs offering fishing and water sports.

For **adventure activites** (mountain biking, hiking, caving, canyoning, parasailing), contact Tura, ☎945 31 25 35

FIESTAS AND FESTIVALS

The August Virgen Blanca festival is colourful and perpetuates a strange tradition: everyone lights a cigar as the angel descends from the Torre de San Miguel (St Michael's Belfry).

Vitoria's noted Festival Internacional de Jazz takes place the third week of July.

Excursions

Santuario de Estíbaliz

10km/6mi E.

▶ *Leave Vitoria-Gasteiz by ② on the town plan and then take the A 132. Bear left after about 4km/2.5mi.* ⏲ *Open 9.30am-1pm and 4-6.30pm.* ⏲ *No visits during religious services.* ☎ *945 29 30 88.*

This Late Romanesque pilgrim shrine has an attractive wall belfry on the south front, and a 12C Romanesque statue of the Virgin.

TOUR EAST OF VITORIA-GASTEIZ: MEDIEVAL PAINTINGS

25km/16mi. ▶*Leave Vitoria-Gasteiz by ② on the town plan and follow the motorway as far as junction 375.*

Gaceo

Ask for the key at house n°10 in Gaceo. ☎945 30 02 37.

Superb 14C **Gothic frescoes**★★ decorate the chancel of the church **(iglesia)**. The south wall shows Hell as a whale's gullet, the north, the Life of the Virgin. On the roof are scenes from the Life of Christ.

Alaiza

▶ *Follow the A 4111 for 3km/2mi, turn right, then left after a few metres.* ⏲ *Visits by prior arrangement. ☎945 30 10 42.*

Obscure **paintings**★ on the walls and roof of the church **(iglesia)** apse probably date from the late 14C. Strange red outlines represent castles, churches, soldiers and many other personages.

THE WAY OF ST JAMES★★

MICHELIN MAPS 571, 573 AND 575 D-E-F 4-26 – NAVARRA, LA RIOJA, CASTILLA Y LEÓN, GALICIA.

The discovery of the body of the Apostle James transformed Santiago de Compostela into the most important pilgrimage centre in Europe in the Middle Ages. From the 11C, the veneration of saintly relics gave rise to a path to this Galician city. Thousands of pilgrims continue to walk the Way of St James. While for some the journey has lost its religious significance, it offers an opportunity to explore the history and culture of a fascinating part of Spain.

- **Information:** *www.xacobeo.es; Astorga: Plaza Eduardo de Castro 5 ☎987 61 82 22; Puente de la Reina: Plaza Mena, ☎948 34 08 45.*
- ▶ **Orient Yourself:** The Way of St James runs east to west from the Pyrenees to Santiago de Compostela across Northern Spain.

Background

The relics of St James (Santiago) discovered early in the 9C soon became a goal of pilgrimage. In the 11C devotion spread until a journey to St James' shrine ranked with one to Rome or Jerusalem. St James had a particular appeal for the French, united with the Spanish against the Moors, but others made the long pilgrimage along routes organised by the Benedictines, Cistercians and the Knights Templars. Hospitals and hospices received the sick, the weary and the stalwart alike who travelled almost all in the uniform of heavy cape, 8ft/2.4m stave with a gourd attached to carry water, stout sandals and broad-brimmed felt hat marked with three or four scallop shells. A Pilgrim Guide of 1130, the first tourist guide ever written, describes the inhabitants, climate, customs and sights on the way. Churches and towns benefited from the passage of from 500 000 to two million pilgrims a year.

In 1175, Pope Alexander III recognised the statutes of the Military Order of Santiago, drawn up to ensure the protection of pilgrims.

Those from England who "took the cockleshell" often sailed from Parson's Quay in the Plymouth estuary to Soulac and followed the French Atlantic coast, or landed at La Coruña or in Portugal. Routes through France from Chartres, St-Denis and Paris joined at Tours.

Villages along the main route (calle Mayor) grew into towns and some were settled by foreigners or minorities (often French or Jewish), who brought a wealth of culture.

With time, the faith that impelled pilgrimages began to diminish; trickery and robbery increased; the Wars of Religion among Christians reduced the faithful. In 1589, Drake attacked La Coruña and the bishop of Compostela removed the relics from the cathedral. They were lost and for 300 years the pilgrimage was virtually abandoned. In 1879 they were recovered, recognised by the pope and the pilgrimage recommenced. In Holy Years, when the feast day of St James (25 July) falls on a Sunday, there are jubilee indulgences and thousands of pilgrims once more visit the shrine.

Special Features

THE WAY IN SPAIN – MAIN HALTS

The ways through France met at Roncesvalles, Behobia and Somport to cross the Pyrenees and continued as the Asturian route from Roncesvalles, and a more secure southerly route from Somport, the **Camino Francés**, marked over the centuries by churches and monasteries in which French architectural influence is obvious. The routes converged at Puente la Reina.

The route from **Roncesvalles** to Puente la Reina was shorter with only one main stop: **Pamplona**; the French Way was via **Jaca, Santa Cruz de la Serós, San Juan de la Peña,** the **Monasterio de Leyre** and **Sangüesa** *(see index)*.

Puente la Reina★

The 11C humpbacked bridge was built for pilgrims. A bronze pilgrim marks where routes converged.

The wide N 111 circles the old town outside whose walls stands the **Iglesia del Crucifijo** (Church of the Crucifix). A second nave was added to the 12C main aisle in the 14C and now contains the famous Y-shaped Cross with a profoundly Expressionist **Christ**★ carved in wood, said to have been brought from Germany in the 14C (*open 9am-8pm; no visits during services; ☎948 34 00 50).*

Walk along the narrow, elegant main street, calle Mayor, fronted by houses of golden brick with carved wood eaves, to the bridge. You will see the **Iglesia de Santiago** (Church of St James), its **doorway**★ crowded with carvings now almost effaced. The nave, remodelled in the 16C, was adorned with altarpieces. Note two statues facing the entrance: St James the Pilgrim in gilded wood, and St Bartholomew (*open 9.45-8pm (8.30pm in summer); ☎948 34 01 32).*

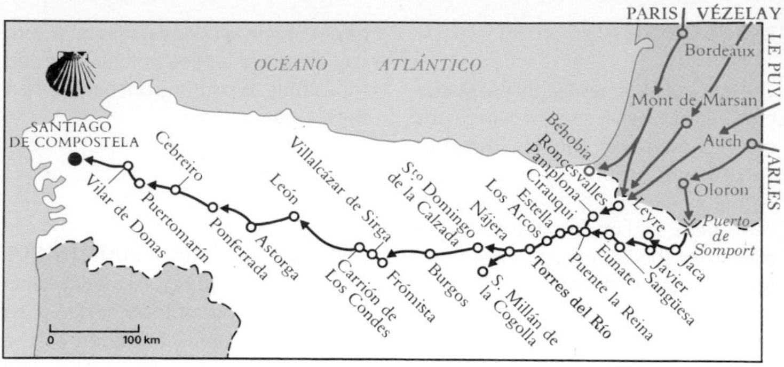

Iglesia de Santa María de Eunate★★

5km/3mi E of Puente la Reina. Human bones indicate that this delightful, isolated 12C **Romanesque** building might have been a funerary chapel like that of Torres del Río (*see below*). The plan is octagonal, with a pentagonal apse outside and a semicircular one inside.

Cirauqui★

Steep, winding alleyways are crowded by houses with rounded doorways, their upper fronts adorned with iron balconies, coats of arms and carved cornices. At the top of the village *(difficult climb)* stands the **Iglesia de San Román** with a multifoil 13C **portal**★ similar to that of San Pedro de la Rúa in Estella/Lizarra.

Estella★ and Monasterio de Irache★ (*See ESTELLA*)

Los Arcos

The **Iglesia de Santa María de los Arcos** (Church of St Mary of the Arches), with its high tower, is Spanish Baroque inside, with overpowering stucco, sculpture and painting covering every available space. The transept, with its imitation Córdoba leather decoration, is noteworthy. Above the high altar rises the 13C polychrome wood statue of the Black Virgin of Santa María de los Arcos. The cloisters illustrate the elegance and lightness of 15C Gothic.

Torres del Río

The **Iglesia del Santo Sepulcro**★ (Church of the Holy Sepulchre) is a tall, octagonal Romanesque building, dating from about 1200. Its resemblance to the chapel in Eunate indicates it might be a funerary chapel. The Mudéjar-inspired, star-shaped **cupola** is geometrical perfection. Decoration is sparse. Note also the fine 13C crucifix.

Nájera and Santo Domingo de la Calzada★ (*See La RIOJA*)

Burgos★★★ (*See BURGOS*)

Iglesia de Frómista★★

(*see PALENCIA*)

Villalcázar de Sirga

The vast Gothic **Iglesia de Santa María la Blanca** has a fine carved **portal**★ and two outstanding Gothic **tombs**★. The recumbent statues of the brother of Alfonso X, who had him murdered in 1271, and his wife Eleanor, are carved with an eye for detail (*open May-Oct 10am-2pm and 4.30-7pm; rest of year Sat-Sun and public hols noon-2pm and 4.30-6.30pm; other days by appointment; closed 22 Dec-31 Jan; 1€; 979 88 80 76*).

Carrión de los Condes

The Poema de Mío Cid narrates the weddings in Valencia of the daughters of El Cid to the counts of Carrión. The daughters were mistreated and abandoned. El Cid executed the counts for their sins.

The 11C **Monasterio de San Zoilo**, rebuilt during the Renaissance, has **cloisters**★ designed by Juan de Badajoz with distinctive vaulting. The keystones and bosses are adorned with figurines and medallions (*open 10.30am-2pm; Sat-Sun and public hols,*

10.30am-2pm and 4-6.30pm; Apr-Oct, 10.30am-2pm and 4.30-8pm; closed Mon exc Jul-15 Sep and 15 Dec-15 Jan; 1.50 €; 979 88 09 02).

The **Iglesia de Santiago** has beautiful 12C carvings on the façade including, on the central coving, an architect with his compass, a barber with his scissors, and other tradesmen. High reliefs above show Gothic influence.

León★★ (*See LEÓN*)

Astorga

Astorga is renowned for its delicious *mantecadas*, a type of light bread roll.

Catedral★

Open 9.30am (9am in summer) to noon and 4.30-6pm (5-6.30pm in summer); Sat-Sun and public hols, 10am-8pm. 987 61 58 20.

Building, begun with the east end in Flamboyant Gothic style in the late 15C, was not completed until the 18C, which explains the rich Renaissance and Baroque façade and towers. The front **porch**★ low reliefs illustrate the Expulsion of the Moneylenders and the Pardoning of the Adulterous Woman, among other events. Above the door is a beautiful Deposition.

The **interior** is surprisingly large, with an upsweeping effect created by innumerable slender columns. Behind the high altar is a 16C **retable**★. Gaspar de Hoyos and Gaspar de Palencia were responsible for the painted, gilt decoration, and **Gaspar Becerra** (1520-70), an Andalucían who after study in Italy developed a style of humanist sensitivity far removed from the Expressionism of his contemporaries.

The **Museo de la Catedral** contains a 13C gold filigree Holy Cross reliquary and a 10C reliquary of Alfonso III, the Great (*open 11am-2pm and 3.30-6.30pm; Mar-Sep, 10am-2pm and 4-8pm; closed 1-15 Jan; 2.50 € (combined entrance with the Museo de los Caminos: 4 €); 987 61 58 20).*

Palacio Episcopal

This fantastic pastiche of a medieval palace was dreamed up by **Gaudí** in 1889. The original, brilliant interior decoration, especially in the neo-Gothic chapel on the first floor, is a profusion of mosaics, stained glass and intersecting ribbed vaults. In the **Museo de los Caminos** (Museum of the Way of St James), medieval art reflects the theme of pilgrimage (*open 11am-2pm and 4-6pm; 21 Mar-18 Sep, 10am-2pm and 4-8pm; Sun and public hols 11am-2pm, 10am-2pm in summer; last entry 45 min before closing; 4 € combined with Museo de la Catedral; 987 61 68 82).*

La Maragatería

Long ago an ethnic group of unknown origin, but possibly of mixed Gothic-Moorish blood, settled in this part of the Astorga region. These Maragatos led an isolated existence in the heart of an inhospitable region where they became muleteers. They may still be seen at religious festivals or weddings in their national costume of voluminous knee breeches, shirt front and wide embroidered belt. Jacks in full Maragato dress can be seen striking the hours on the clock of the **town hall** on the **plaza Mayor** in Astorga.

Ponferrada

The centre of a mining area, Ponferrada owes its name to an 11C iron bridge built across the Sil for pilgrims. Above the town are the ruins of the **Castillo de los Templarios** (Templars' Castle).

Peñalba de Santiago★

21km/13mi SE. Peñalba stands in the heart of the so-called Valle del Silencio (Valley of Silence). Its houses are schist-walled with wooden balconies and slate roofs. The Mozarabic **Iglesia de Santiago**, a church, is all that remains of a 10C monastery. The paired horseshoe portal arch is set off by an *alfiz*.

Las Médulas★

22km/14mi SW. World Heritage Site. Debris from a Roman gold mine has transformed slopes of the Aquilianos mountains into a magical landscape of rocky crags and strangely shaped hillocks of pink and ochre, covered over the ages by gnarled chestnut trees.

Las Médulas Mountains

Cebreiro

Cebreiro, not far from the Puerto de Piedrafita (Piedrafita pass, 1 109m/3 638ft), reflects the hardship of the pilgrim journey. Drystone and thatched houses *(pallozas)* descend from ancient Celtic huts; in one is an **Ethnographic Museum** (Museo Etnográfico). A pilgrim inn remains beside the small 9C mountain church where pilgrims venerated the relics of the miracle of the Holy Eucharist (c1300), when bread was turned to flesh and wine to blood. Relics in silver caskets presented by Isabel may be seen with the miraculous chalice and paten.

Portomarín

Before centuries-old Portomarín was drowned by a dam, the **church**★ of the Knights of St John of Jerusalem was moved stone by stone. It is square, fortified and ornamented with massive arches and Romanesque doors with delicately carved covings. The west door depicts Christ in Majesty with the 24 Old Musicians of the Apocalypse.

Vilar de Donas

6.5km/4mi E of Palas de Rei. Enter the **church**, slightly off the main road, through a Romanesque doorway. Lining the walls are tombs of the Knights of the Order of St James, slain in battle. 15C **frescoes**★ decorate the apse, illustrating Christ in Majesty with St Paul and St Luke on his left and St Peter and St Mark on his right and, on the chancel walls, the faces of the elegant young women who gave the church its name (*donas* in Galician).

Santiago de Compostela★★★

(see SANTIAGO DE COMPOSTELA)

ZAFRA

POPULATION: 14 065

MICHELIN MAP 576 Q 10 – EXTREMADURA (BADAJOZ).

A 15C *alcázar* (now a parador) guards this white-walled town, one of the oldest in Extremadura. It was built by the Dukes of Feria with nine round towers, white marble Renaissance patio and delightful gilded salon.

- **Information:** *Plaza de España , ☎924 55 10 36.*
- **Orient Yourself:** SW of Madrid in Extremadura, 7km/4.5mi W of the N 630.
- **Also See:** MÉRIDA (58km/36mi N), BADAJOZ (76km/47mi NW).

Worth a Visit

Squares★

The large 18C **plaza Grande** and the adjoining smaller 16C **plaza Chica** are line by fine arcaded houses.

Iglesia de la Candelaria

The 16C transitional Gothic-Renaissance church has a massive red-brick belfry. In the south transept is an **altarpiece** by Zurbarán painted in 1644.

Excursions

Llerena

42km/26mi SE along the N 432. The **plaza Mayor** of this country town is one of the most monumental in Extremadura. The composite façade of the **Iglesia de Nuestra Señora de Granada** (Church of Our Lady of Granada) is harmonised by the interplay of white limestone and brick; the delicacy of superimposed arcades contrasts with the mass of a great Baroque belfry.

Fiestas

Zafra's cattle fairs are locally famous, especially the Feria de San Miguel in the week of 5 October.

Jerez de los Caballeros

42km/26mi SW along the EX 101 and EX 112. Jerez de los Caballeros is the birthplace of **Vasco Núñez de Balboa** (1475-1517), who crossed Panama and in 1513 discovered the Pacific Ocean. The town's name, tradition and atmosphere stem from the Knights Templar – Caballeros del Temple – to whom the town was given in 1230 by Alfonso IX of León on its recapture from the Moors. Jerez stands on a hillside and its steep lanes lined by white-walled houses are a foretaste of Andalucía, . On the summit is the ornate San Bartolomé.

ZAMORA★

POPULATION: 68 202

MICHELIN MAP 575 H 12 – CASTILLA Y LEÓN.

Zamora stands in a plain on the banks of the River Duero. The 12C and 13C saw the construction of the cathedral and numerous Romanesque churches.

- **Information:** *Santa Clara 20, ☎980 53 18 45.*
- **Orient Yourself:** Azmora is NW of Madrid.
- **Also See:** SALAMANCA (62km/39mi S) and VALLADOLID (95km/59mi E).

Background

Historical notes – Traces remain of the walls which made Zamora the western bastion along the Duero in the Reconquest. Zamora figured in repeated struggles for the throne of Castilla.

Worth a Visit

Catedral★

Open Oct-Feb, 10am-2pm and 4.30-6.30pm (5-8pm Mar-Sep). Closed Mon, 1 Jan and 25 Dec. 3 € (museum). ☎980 53 06 44.

The cathedral was built between 1151 and 1174 and subsequently altered. The north front is neo-Classical in keeping with the square in front; it contrasts, however, with the Romanesque bell tower and the graceful cupola covered in scallop tiling. The south front, the only original part, has blind arcades and a Romanesque portal with unusual covings featuring openwork festoons. The aisles are transitional Romanesque-Gothic, the vaulting ranging from broken barrel to pointed ogive. Slender painted ribs support the luminous **dome**★ on squinches above the transept. Late Gothic master woodcarvers worked here. Notable are fine **grilles** enclosing the presbytery, the coro and some chapels, two 15C Mudéjar pulpits, and **choir stalls**★★, decorated with biblical figures or with allegorical and burlesque scenes.

Museo Catedralicio (Cathedral Museum)

The museum, off the Herreran cloisters, displays 15C Flemish and 17C **tapestries**★★. Also note the 16C Renaissance monstrance and a Virgin and Child and Little St John sculpted by Bartolomé Ordóñez.

The **Jardín del Castillo** (Castle Garden) to the rear commands fine views.

Romanesque churches★

The 12C saw original Romanesque churches built in Zamora province. Features included portals without tympana, surrounded by multifoil arches and often possessing heavily carved archivolts. Larger churches had domes on squinches over the transept crossing. The best examples in Zamora are the **Magdalena, Santa María la Nueva, San Juan, Santa María de la Orta, Santo Tomé** and **Santiago del Burgo.**

> **Semana Santa**
>
> Zamora's Holy Week solemn celebrations are renowned for the numbers who attend and for the spectacular pasos street processions. On Palm Sunday a children's procession escorts a paso of Christ's entry into Jerusalem; on Maundy Thursday evening a totally silent, torchlight procession follows the poignant *Recumbent Christ,* a sculpture by Gregorio Fernández, borne by white-robed penitents through the streets in imitation of the walk to Golgotha. Most of these *pasos* may be seen in the **Museo de la Semana Santa.** *Open 10am-2pm and 5-8pm; Sun and public hols, 10am-2pm; closed 1 Jan and 25 Dec; 3€. 980 53 22 95.*

Seigniorial mansions

Casa del Cordón and **Casa de los Momos** have elegant Isabelline windows.

Excursions

San Pedro de la Nave★

19km/12mi NW. Leave Zamora by on the town plan. Follow the N 122 for 12km/7mi then turn right.

The late 7C Visigothic **church** *(iglesia)*, endangered by the damming of the Esla, was rebuilt at El Campillo. It is remarkable for the carving on the transept **capitals** with a strong sense of composition: *Daniel in the lion's den, the Sacrifice of Isaac* etc. The frieze, halfway up, presents Christian symbols including grapes and doves (*open Mon-Fri, 4.30-6.30pm; ask for the keys at the nearby bar; 980 55 57 09).*

Arcenillas

7km/4mi SE on the C 605. In the village church *(iglesia)*, 15 **panels**★ depicting the Life, Death and Resurrection of Christ have been reassembled from the late-15C Gothic altarpiece designed for Zamora Cathedral by **Fernando Gallego**, one of the greatest Castilian painters of this age, whose style echoes Van der Weyden with stronger colours and softer facial expressions (*open 9am-2pm and 4-6pm; 980 53 40 05).*

Benavente

66km/41mi N along the N 630. The Renaissance **Castillo de los Condes de Pimentel** (Castle of the Counts of Pimentel), now a parador, retains its 16C Torre del Caracol (snail tower), with fine valley **views**.

The transitional **Iglesia de Santa María del Azogue** is a church with five apses and two Romanesque portals in Zamora style. A beautiful 13C *Annunciation* stands at the transept crossing.

The **Iglesia de San Juan del Mercado** has a 12C carving on the south portal illustrating the journey of the Magi.

ZAMORA								
Alfonso IX	B	2	Feria	B	21	Riego	B	72
Alfonso XII	B	3	Francos Rúa de los	A	22	Sacramento	B	74
Antonio del Aguila Pl.	A	5	Fray Diego de Deza Pl.	A	23	San Torcuato	B	78
Arias Gonzalo Pl. de	A	8	Horta	B	27	San Tortucato Ronda de	B	80
Cabañales	B	12	Ignacio Gazapo	B	36	San Vicente	B	82
Candelaría Pas.	B	13	Leopoldo Alas Clarín	B	40	Santa Clara	B	84
Catedral Pl. de la	A	15	Mayor Pl.	B	42	Santa Lucía Pl.	B	86
Ciento Pl. de los	A	16	Morana Cuesta de la	A	48	Santiago	B	75
Constitución Pl. de	B	18	Notarios Rúa de los	A	60	Tres Cruces Av.	B	88
Corral Pintado	B	19	Príncipe de Asturias Av.	B	66	Víctor Gallego	B	90
Damas	A	20	Puebla de Sanabria	A	70	Viriato Pl.	B	96
			Puentica Pl. de la	A	69	Zorilla Pl. de	B	99
Casa de los Momos	B	J	Casa del Cordón	B	M²	Museo de la Semana Santa	B	M¹

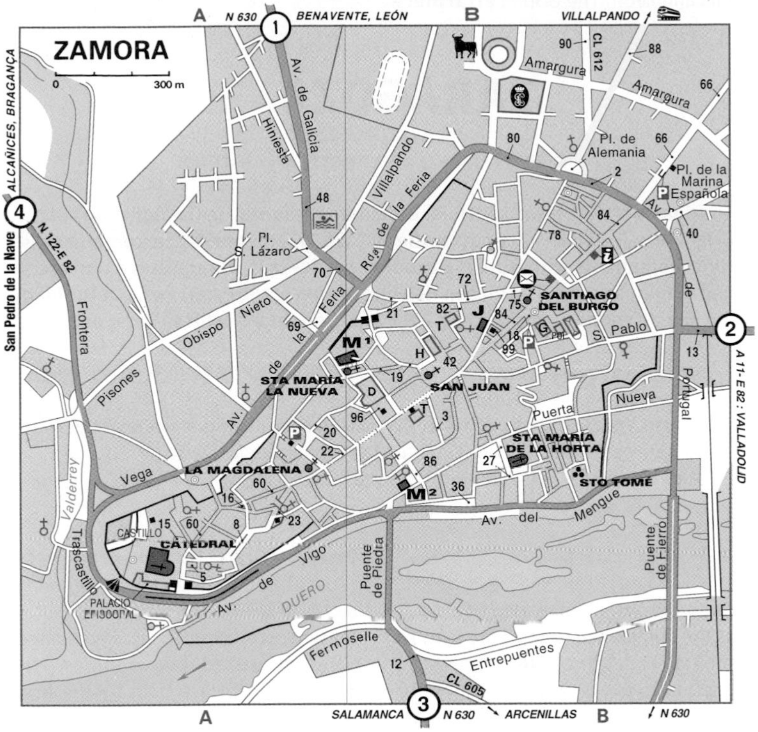

Toro

33km/21mi E along the N 122-E 82. This town on the Duero has a number of Romanesque churches in poor repair. The collegiate church, built of limestone, is in better condition.

Colegiata★

Open 10am-1pm and 5-8pm; Oct-Feb, 10am-2pm and 4-6.30pm. Closed Mon, Fri, 10am-1pm (winter) and Jan. 0.60 €. 980 10 81 07.

Construction of the collegiate church began in 1160 with the elegant transept lantern and ended in 1240 with the west portal. The Romanesque **north portal** illustrates the Old Men of the Apocalypse (above) and angels linked by a rope, symbolising unity of Faith. The Gothic **west portal**★★, repainted in the 18C, is the church treasure. The Celestial Court is shown on the archivolt, an expressive Last Judgement on the coving. Statues on the pier and tympanum jambs have youthful faces. Start beneath the **cupola**★, one of the first of its kind in Spain, with two tiers of windows in the drum. Polychrome wood statues stand against the pillars at the end of the nave on consoles, one carved with an amusing version of the birth of Eve (below the angel). In the sacristy is the **Virgin and the Fly**★, a magnificent Flemish painting by either Gérard David or Hans Memling.

Iglesia de San Lorenzo – *Closed for restoration. ☎980 10 81 07.*

This is the best-preserved of Toro's Romanesque brick churches. With its stone base, blind arcading and dog-tooth decoration on the upper cornice, it has much of the Mudéjar style of Castilla and León. The Gothic **altarpiece** flanked by Plateresque tombs was painted by Fernando Gallego.

San Cebrián de Mazote

57km/35mi NE along the N 122-E 82 or on the C 519 from Toro. The 10C **Iglesia de San Cebrián de Mazote** is a rare Mozarabic church. Capitals and low reliefs bear traces of an earlier, Visigothic style (*open 11am-2pm and 4.30-7pm (by prior arrangement in winter); ☎ 983 78 00 77*).

ZARAGOZA★★

POPULATION: 622 371

MICHELIN MAP 574 H 27 (TOWN PLAN) – ARAGÓN.

The domes of the Basílica del Pilar dominate Zaragoza, on the right bank of the River Ebro. The city, rebuilt after the 19C War of Independence, combines historic monuments with bustling modern boulevards. Zaragoza is a university and religious centre. The Virgen del Pilar (Virgin of the Pillar) makes it the leading Marian shrine in Spain. Expo 2008 has brought a facelift to Zaragoza.

- **Information:** *Glorieta Pio XII (Torreón de la Zuda), ☎976 20 12 91; Plaza Nuestra Señora del Pilar, ☎976 20 12 00.*
- **Orient Yourself:** Zaragoza is in NE Spain in a fertile pocket watered by by the Aragón canal and the Ebro, Gállego, Jalón and Huerva rivers.
- **Also See:** HUESCA (72km/45mi NE) and TUDELA (82km/51mi NW).

Background

Caesaraugusta-Sarakusta – Salduba, at the confluence of the Ebro and its tributaries became Roman Caesaraugusta in 25 BC. On 2 January in AD 40, according to tradition, the Virgin appeared to St James, leaving the pillar around which the **Basílica de Nuestra Señora del Pilar** was later built. The Uncounted Martyrs of the 3C, persecuted by Diocletian, are interred in the crypt of **Santa Engracia.**

To learn more of the Roman city, visit the **Museo del Teatro de Caesaraugusta** (Caesaraugusta Theatre Museum, *San Jorge 12, ☎976 20 50 88*); the **Museo de las Termas Públicas de Caesaraugusta** (Musem of the Public Baths, *calle San Juan y San Pedro 37, ☎976 29 72 79*); the **Museo del Foro de Caesaraugusta** (Forum Museum, *plaza de la Seo 2, ☎ 976 39 97 52*) and the **Museo del Puerto Fluvial de Caesaraugusta** (Port Museum, *plaza de San Bruno 8, ☎976 39 31 57*).

Muslim occupation of the city renamed Sarakusta lasted four centuries. The **Aljafería**, a palace built by the first Benihud monarch of an 11C *taifa* kingdom, is a unique example of Hispano-Muslim art.

Capital of Aragón – The Aragón kings freed Zaragoza from the Moors and proclaimed it capital. The city retained its autonomy and prospered. It protected its Muslim masons, who embellish the apse of **La Seo** (Cathedral), and the **San Pablo** and **Magdalena** church in Mudéjar style. Houses with elegant patios and *artesonado* ceilings reflect prosperity in the 16C.

Two heroic sieges – Zaragoza resisted a siege by Napoleon's army from June to 14 August, 1808. Exultant Zaragozans sang "The Virgin of Pilar will never

ZARAGOZA

			Cinco de Marzo	Z	18	Manifestación	Y	43
			Conde de Aranda	Z		San Pedro Nolasco Pl. de	Z	63
Alfonso I	YZ		Coso	Z		San Vicente de Paul	YZ	
Alfonso V	Z	6	Don Jaime I	YZ		Sancho y Gil	Z	58
Candalija	Z	10	Independencia Pas.	Z		Teniente Coronel Valenzuela	Z	67
Capitán Portolés	Z	13	Magdalena	Z	42			
César Augusto Av.	Z	15						

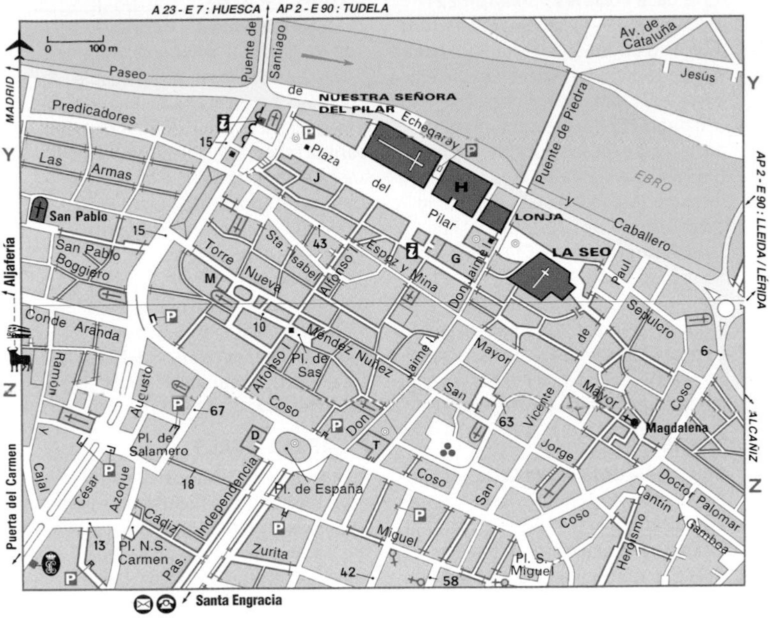

be French." Alas! General Lannes laid siege from 21 December until 20 February, 1809. By its end, 54 000, half of the city, had died. The shrapnel-pitted **Puerta del Carmen** (Carmen Gate) still bears witness.

Worth a Visit

La Seo★★

Open 10am-2pm (1pm Sat, noon Sun and public hols) and 4-6pm ; summer 10am-7pm. Last entry 30 min before closing. Closed Mon. 2 €. 976 29 12 31. The tapestry museum is currently closed.

The Cathedral of Zaragoza, La Seo, of remarkable size, includes all styles from Mudéjar to Churrigueresque, although it is basically Gothic. The tall belfry was added in the 17C, the Baroque façade in the 18C. View the Mudéjar **east end** from calle del Sepulcro.

The interior has five aisles of equal height. Above the high altar is a Gothic **retable**★ with a predella carved by the Catalan, Pere Johan, and three central panels of the Ascension, Epiphany and the Transfiguration sculpted by Hans of Swabia (the stance and modelling of the faces and robes strike a German note).

J. Balanya/ MICHELIN

Basílica de Nuestra Señora del Pilar

Address Book

For coin ranges, see the Legend on the cover flap.

WHERE TO EAT

⊖⊖ **Casa Portolés** – *Santa Cruz 21 – ☎976 39 06 65 – Closed Sun evening and Mon.* This tavern-style restaurant has a bar at the entrance where you can enjoy a range of tapas and *raciones*. The restaurant itself, a pleasant mix of arches and exposed brick, serves fine food and market-based cuisine. A good location close to the plaza del Pilar in a small square by calle Espoz y Mina.

⊖⊖ **Antonio** – *Plaza. San Pedro Nolasco 5 – ☎976 39 74 74 – Closed Sun evenings and Sun all day in Jul-Aug* – ▤. A good restaurant that compensates for its modest size with attentive service. Have a drink at the bar while wating for a table. Often filled up with regulars.

TAPAS

Bodeguilla de la Santa Cruz – *Santa Cruz 3 – ☎976 20 00 18 – Closed Sun* – ▤. The decor in this pleasant, centrally located bar is a throw-back to wine cellars of years gone by. Small, but full of atmosphere, with tapas served at the bar and outside.

Los Victorinos – *José de la Hera 6 – ☎976 39 42 13 – Closed 15-30 Nov* – ▤. This small, lively bar adorned with bullfighting memorabilia is located in a narrow street near the plaza del Pilar and plaza de la Seo. The great selection of delicious, beautifully presented tapas on the bar is not to be missed.

WHERE TO STAY

⊖ **Hotel Las Torres** – *Plaza del Pilar 11 – ☎976 39 42 50 – www.hotellastorres.com* – ▤ – *55 rooms*. An agreeable hotel, lacking great charm, but with a magnficent location in front of the basilica in plaza del Pilar. The rooms are carefully maintained if basic.

⊖⊖**Hotel Sauce** – *Espoz y Mina 33 – ☎976 20 50 50 – www.hotelsauce.com* – P ▤ – *43 rooms* – ☕ *6€*. This friendly, family-run hotel enjoys a good position in the centre of the city, a few metres from Zaragoza's two main squares. The rooms are all different and are perfectly adequate despite being on the small side.

PILAR FESTIVALS

In the week of 12 October, Zaragozans extol their Virgin with incredible pomp and fervour: on the 13th at about 7pm the **Rosario de Cristal** procession moves off by the light of 350 carriage-borne lanterns. Other festivals during the week include the **Gigantes y Cabezudos** procession (cardboard giants and dwarfs with massive heads), *jota* dancing and the famous bullfights.

The **surrounding wall of the chancel** *(trascoro)* and some of the side chapels were adorned in the 16C with carved figures, evidence of the vitality of Renaissance Spanish sculpture. Other chapels, ornamented in the 18C, show Churrigueresque exuberance. One exception is the **Parroquieta**, a Gothic chapel with a Burgundian-influenced 14C tomb and a Moorish **cupola**★ in polychrome wood with stalactites and strapwork (15C).

Museo Capitular★

In the sacristy. Exhibited are paintings, an enamel triptych, and church plate including silver reliquaries, chalices and an enormous processional monstrance made of 24 000 pieces.

Museo de Tapices★★

An outstanding collection of Gothic hangings, woven in Arras and Brussels.

EXPO ZARAGOZA 2008

Zaragoza will host an international exposition on the theme of Water and Sustainable Development from 14 June to 14 September 2008. The exposition, supported by countries, international organizations, NGOs, and water authorities and consumer groups, seeks to promote a culture of water linked to sustainability. Zaragoza is renovating and redeveloping its riverfront in preparation (ℹ*Information: www.expozaragoza2008.es).*

La Lonja★

Currently an exhibition centre. Open 10am-2pm and 5-9pm; Sun and public hols, 10am-2pm. Closed Mon, 1 Jan, 24 (afternoon), 25 and 31 (afternoon) Dec. 976 39 72 39.

Zaragoza, like other trading towns, founded a commercial exchange as early as the 16C. These buildings, in a style between Gothic and Plateresque, include some of the finest civil architecture in Spain. The vast hall is divided in three by tall columns, their shafts ornamented with a band of grotesques. Coats of arms supported by cherubim mark the start of the ribs which open into star **vaulting**.

The **Ayuntamiento** (town hall) has been rebuilt in traditional Aragón style with ornate eaves. Two modern bronzes stand at the entrance.

Basílica de Nuestra Señora del Pilar★

Open 6.45am-8.30pm (9.30pm in summer). 976 29 95 64.

Successive sanctuaries on this site have enshrined the miraculous pillar *(pilar)* above which the Virgin appeared. The present building, Zaragoza's second cathedral, was designed by Francisco Herrera the Younger in about 1677. A buttressed quadrilateral, it is lit by a central dome. The cupolas, with small lantern towers, whose ornamental tiles reflect in the Ebro, were added by Ventura Rodríguez in the 18C.

Inside, some of the frescoes decorating the cupolas were painted by Goya as a young man.

The **Capilla de la Virgen** (Lady Chapel) by Ventura Rodríguez is virtually a miniature church. It contains, in a niche on the right, the pillar and a Gothic wood statue of the Virgin. The Virgin's mantle is changed every day except on the 2nd of the month (the Apparition was on 2 January), and the 12th of the month (for the celebration of the Hispanidad, 12 October). Pilgrims kiss the pillar through an opening at the rear.

The **high altar** is surmounted by a **retable**★ by Damián Forment of which the predella is outstanding. The **coro** is closed by a high grille and adorned with Plateresque stalls.

Museo Pilarista★

Open 9am-2pm and 4-6pm. 1.50 €. 976 29 95 64.

Displayed are sketches made by Goya, González, Velázquez and Bayeu for the cupolas of Our Lady of the Pillar, a model by Ventura Rodríguez, and some of the jewels which adorn the Virgin during the Pilar festivals. Among old ivory pieces are an 11C hunting horn and a Moorish jewellery box.

Aljafería★

Access by calle Conde de Aranda. Open 10am-2pm and 4.30-6.30pm (4.30-8pm Apr-Oct). Last admission 30 min before closing. Closed Sun and afternoons of public hols in winter, 1 Jan and 25 Dec. 3 €, no charge Sun. 976 28 96 84/5.

It is unusual to find such magnificent Moorish architecture in this part of Spain. Built in the 11C by the Benihud family, it was modified by the Aragonese kings (14C) and Catholic Monarchs (15C) before being taken over by the Inquisition and later converted into a barracks. The Moorish palace centres on a rectangular patio bordered by porticoes with delicate tracery and carved capitals. The **musallah**, the mosque of the emirs, is restored with *mihrab* and multifoil arches and floral decoration. The first floor and the staircase are in the Flamboyant Gothic of the Catholic Monarchs. Only the ornate **ceiling**★, its cells divided by geometric interlacing and decorated with fir cones, remains of the throne room.

Excursion

Fuendetodos

45km/28mi SW along the N 330; after 21km/13mi bear left onto the Z 100. It was in a modest house (**Casa-Museo de Goya**) in this village that the great painter Francisco Goya y Lucientes was born in 1746. (*open 11am-2pm and 4-7pm; closed Mon (except public hols); 1.80 €; 976 14 38 30).*

The **Museo de Grabados** next door displays a collection of his engravings (*open 11am-2pm and 4-7pm; closed Mon (except public hols), 1 Jan, and 24-25 and 31 Dec; 1.80 €. 976 14 38 300.*

Mallorca, Playa de Portals Nous

B. Perousse/ MICHELIN

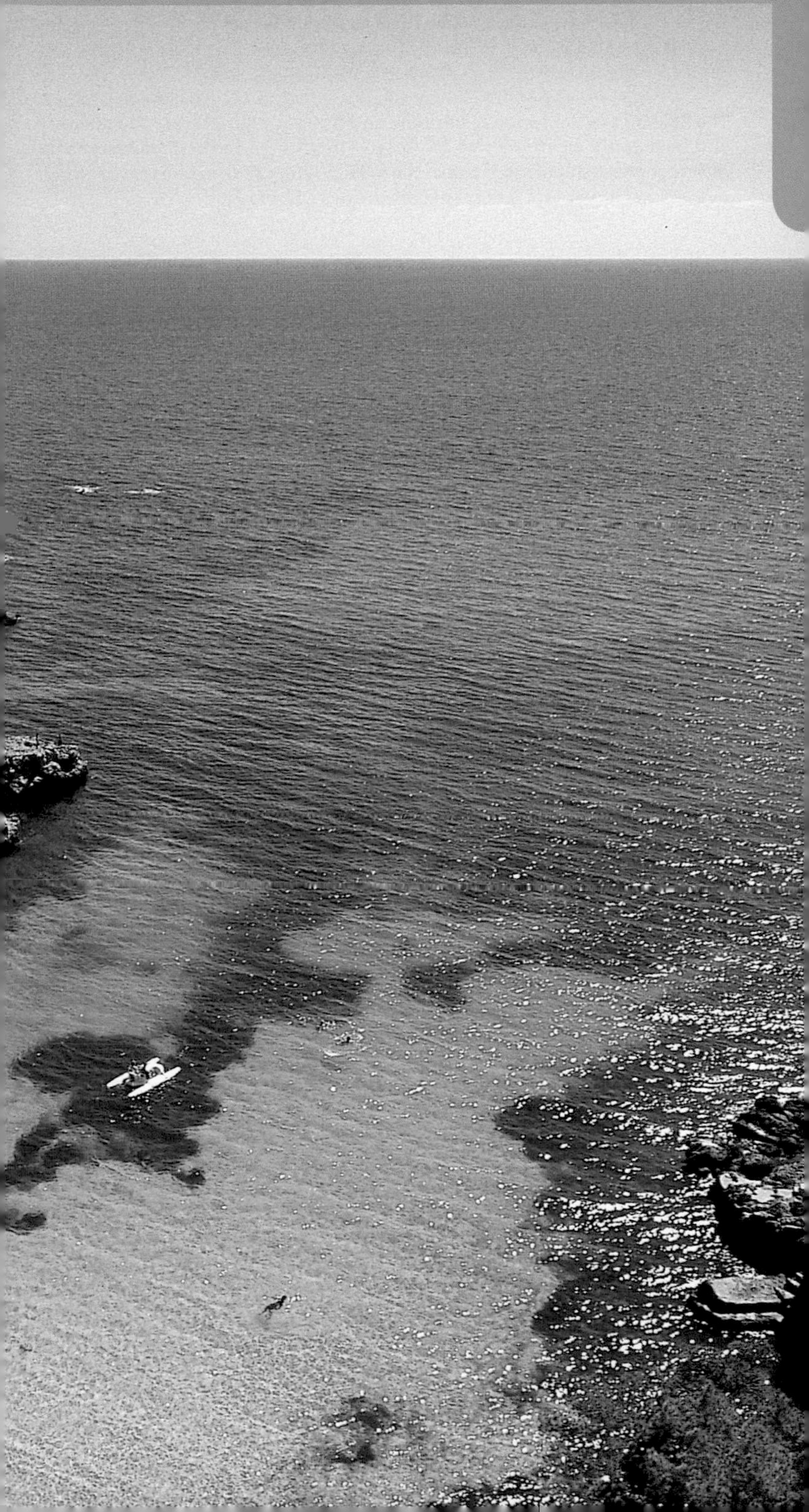

BALEARIC ISLANDS★★★

POPULATION: 825 000

MICHELIN MAP 579.

The Balearics evoke summer sunshine and frenetic nightlife, yet their history and beauty are as impressive as those of any island in the Mediterranean. Although the archipelago is one of the most popular destinations in the world, over 40% of its verdant landscapes are protected by law.

Location

The Balearic Archipelago, in the Mediterranean off Spain's Levante, covers 5 000km²/1 900sq mi. It includes three large islands – Mallorca, Menorca and Ibiza – each with a distinct character, two small ones – Formentera and Cabrera – and many islets. Palma is administrative capital of the Comunidad Autónoma Balear (Balearic Autonomous Community). The language, Balearic, is derived from Catalan but has kept ancient roots. The average annual temperature is 17.6°C/63.6°F.

MALLORCA★★★

POPULATION: 659 000

MICHELIN MAP 579 – BALEARES.

Mallorca is an island paradise where the stunning, steep north shore, indented with coves, contrasts with the beaches of the gentle south coast with their crystalline turquoise waters. Mallorca's picturesque towns and villages speak of history and heritage. Mallorca is the largest of the Balearic Islands, covering 3 640km²/1 405sq mi.

Information: *Palma: Santo Domingo 11, ☎971 72 40 90; Plaza de la Reina 2, ☎971 17 39 39. www.infomallorca.net: Airport: ☎971 26 08 03.*

Kids **Especially for Kids:** Beaches and sand will keep small tourists occupied.

A Bit of History

Landscape – The **Sierra de Tramuntana** in the northwest rises in limestone crests – the highest is **Puig Major** (1 445m/4 740ft) – parallel to the coast. Spectacular cliffs plunging into the sea are high enough to block winds from the mainland.

Pines, junipers and holm oaks cover the slopes, interspersed with Mallorca's famous olive trees. Terraces of vegetables and fruit trees surround hillside villages.

The central plain, **El Pla**, is divided by low walls into fields and fig and almond orchards; market towns, with outlying windmills to pump water, retain the regular medieval fortress plan.

The **Sierras de Levante** to the east are hollowed out into wonderful caves. The rocky coast is indented with sheltered, sand-carpeted coves.

A Short-lived Kingdom (1262-1349) – James (Jaime) I of Aragón recaptured Mallorca from the Muslims in 1229. Thirty years later James united Mallorca-Baleares, Roussillon and Montpellier in a kingdom which he presented to his son, James II. He and his successor, Sancho, founded new Catalan towns. Pedro IV seized the archipelago in 1343 to reunite it with Aragón. A merchant navy was established which brought prosperity, and a school of cartography rapidly became famous.

The Mallorcan Primitives (14C-15C) – Gothic Mallorcan painting, character-

ised by a gentleness of expression, was open to external influences: the so-called **Master of Privileges** (Maestro de los Privilegios) showed a Sienese preference for miniaturisation and warm colours; later, **Joan Daurer** and the **Maestro de Obispo Galiana** were inspired by Catalan painting.
15C artists included **Gabriel Moger**, **Miguel de Alcanyis** and **Martí Torner**, who had studied in Valencia. The **Maestro de Predelas** is distinguishable by his attention to detail, **Rafael Moger** by his realism. **Pedro (Pere) Nisart** and **Alonso de Sedano** introduced the Flemish style *(see Museo de Mallorca).*
Famous Mallorcans and Visitors – **Ramón Llull** (1232-1316) personifies the cosmopolitan 13C outlook of Mallorca. He learned languages and studied philosophy, theology and alchemy, and was beatified. **Fray Junípero Serra** (1713-83) founded missions in California. He was beatified in 1988.
Among the foreign artists to visit in the 19C were **Frédéric Chopin** and **George Sand**. **Robert Graves** (1895-1985), the English poet, lived here from 1929. The Austrian archduke, **Ludwig Salvator** (1847-1915) compiled the most detailed study of the archipelago. He was patron to the French speleologist, E.A. Martel.

Worth a Visit

PALMA★★

Palma spreads along a wide bay. Residential quarters with hotels stretch on either side of the historic centre, in avinguda Gabriel Roca, shaded by palms. The old harbour, bordered by passeig Sagrera, serves passenger and merchant ships. The new harbour at the southern tip of El Terreno accommodates the largest liners.

The Bahía de Palma

The bay, protected from north and west winds by the Puig Major range, has a mild climate all the year. To the west, hotels stand along the indented Bendinat coastline where there is little sand, except at **Palmanova** and **Magaluf**. The coast to the east is less sheltered, but has mile upon mile of fine sand with a series of resorts – **Can Pastilla, ses Meravelles** and **s'Arenal**.

The "Ciutat de Mallorca"

Palma was known by this name after its liberation on 31 December 1229. Trade links were forged with the mainland, Africa and northern Europe; Jews and Genoese established themselves. James II (Jaime II) and his successors endowed the city with beautiful Gothic buildings. Aragonese expansion to Naples and Sicily enabled Palma to extend her commerce.

Palma's old mansions

In the 15C and 16C, the great families of Palma favoured the Italian style. They built elegant residences with stone façades, relieved by windows with Renaissance decoration. In the 18C a characteristic Mallorcan *casa* (house) appeared, with an inner court of massive marble columns, wide shallow arches and a high and graceful loggia.

Modern Palma

Palma is home to a large proportion of the population of the island and is one of the most popular cities in Spain to visit. Tourists congregate in and around **El Terreno** – especially in plaza Gomila – and **Cala Major** quarters in the west of town. The native heart of the city remains the **passeig des Born.** Shops sell pearls, glassware and leather in the old town east of El Born, in pedestrian streets around Plaça Major and in avinguda Jaume III.

Barrio de la Catedral★ (Cathedral Quarter) *3hr*

Catedral★★

Open 10am-3.15pm; Apr-Oct, 10am-5.15 pm (6.15pm Jun-Sep); Sat, 10am-2pm. Closed Sun and public hols. 4 €. 971 72 31 33.
The bold yet elegant cathedral, its buttresses surmounted by pinnacles, rises above the sea. The Santanyi limestone of its walls changes colour according to the time of day: ochre, golden or pink.

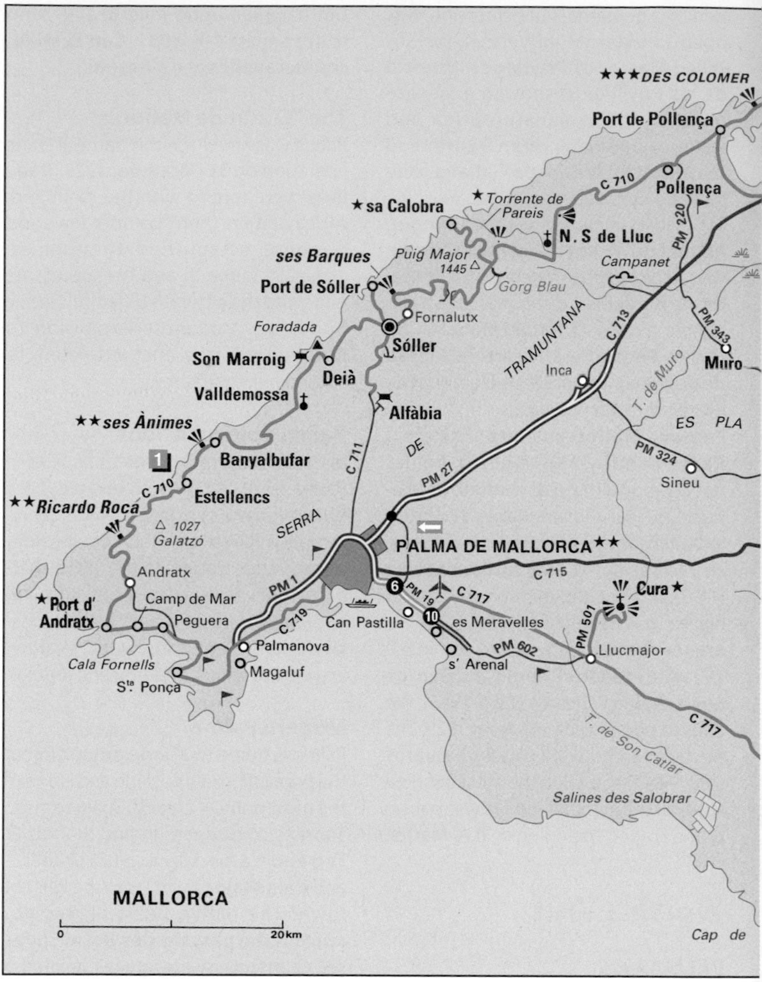

Begun in the early 14C, it is one of the great late-Gothic constructions.

The west face was rebuilt in neo-Gothic style in the 19C after an earthquake; its 16C Renaissance portal remains intact. The south door, the **Portada del Mirador** (Viewpoint Doorway), overlooks the sea, the delicate Gothic decoration dating from the 15C. Statues of St Peter and St Paul on either side prove that Sagrera, architect of the Llotja (Exchange), was a talented sculptor.

The **interior** is large and light, measuring 121m x 55m (397ft x 180ft),and 44m/144ft to the top of the vaulting. Slender octagonal pillars divide the nave from the aisles. The Capilla Mayor or Real (Royal Chapel) contains an enormous wrought-iron baldaquin by Gaudí (1912) with Renaissance choir stalls on either side. Tombs of the kings of Mallorca, James II and Jaime III, lie in the Capilla de la Trinidad (Trinity Chapel).

Museo-Tesoro (Treasury Museum)

In the Gothic chapter house is the Santa Eulàlia altarpiece by the Maestro de los Privilegios (1335). In the oval Baroque chapter house are reliquaries including one of the True Cross.

La Almudaina

Open 10am-1.15pm and 4-5.15pm; Apr-Sep, 10am-5.45pm; Sat and public hols, 10am-1.15pm. Closed Sun, 1, 6

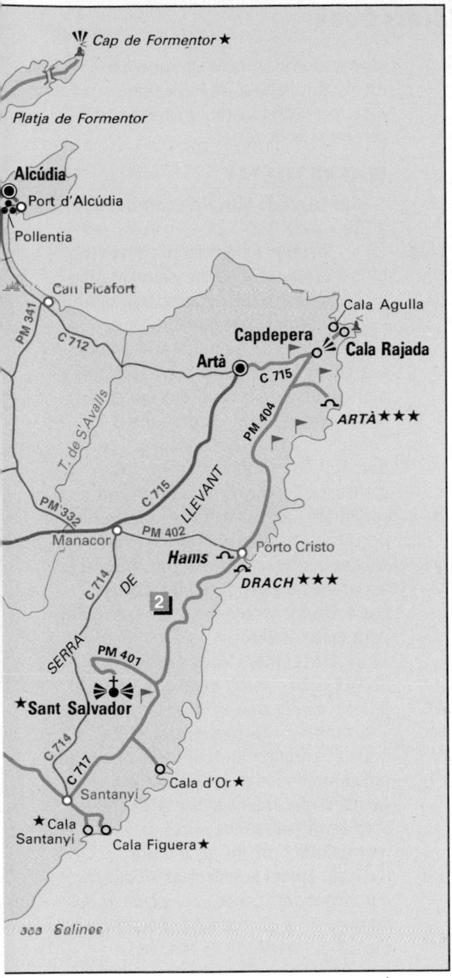

and 20 Jan, 17 Apr, 1 May and 24-25 and 31 Dec. 3.20 €; Wed, no charge for E.U. citizens. ☎971 21 41 34.

This fortress of the Córdoba caliphate, was converted in the 14C and 15C into a royal palace. Today, as a residence of the King of Spain, several rooms have been restored and furnished with Flemish tapestries and paintings. In the courtyard, note the carved eaves and the doorway of the Iglesia de Santa Ana (St Anne's Church), a rare Romanesque structure in the Balearics.

Ayuntamiento

Carved wooden eaves overhang the 17C façade of the town hall.

Iglesia de Santa Eulàlia

13C-15C. The tall nave is unusually bare for a Gothic church. In the first chapel off the south aisle is a 15C altarpiece. Between the churches of Santa Eulàlia and Sant Francesc, at no2 Carrer Savellà, is the 18C **Can Vivot,** its beautiful patio decorated with marble columns.

Iglesia de Sant Francesc

Open 9.30am 12.30pm and 3-6pm; Sun and public hols, 9am-1pm. Closed 1 Jan, Good Fri and 24-25 Dec. 0.60 €. ☎971 71 26 95.

13C-14C. The church façade, rebuilt in the late 17C, has an immense Plateresque rose window and a Baroque portal with a beautifully carved tympanum by Francisco Herrera. The first apsidal chapel on the left contains the tomb of Ramon Llull.

The **cloisters**★ (claustro), begun in 1286, are elegant. Apart from one side of trefoil openings, the architect divided the remaining galleries into multifoil bays on slender columns in varied diameters. The ceiling is painted.

Casa Marqués del Palmer

In Carrer del Sol stands Casa Marqués del Palmer, a mansion built in 1556 in stone now blackened by age. Renaissance decoration around the upper-floor windows mellows the austerity of Gothic walls. The upper gallery, under deep eaves, is a replica of that on the Llotja. The old Jewish quarter, **La Portella,** lies close against the town wall.

Baños Árabes

Open 9.30am-7.30pm (7pm Dec-Mar). 1.20 €. ☎971 72 15 49.

The Moorish baths, the only relic from the caliphate, are beneath small circular windows and a classical dome on 12 columns with rudimentary capitals.

Museo de Mallorca

Open 10am-7pm; Sun and public hols, 10am-2pm. Closed Mon. 2.40 €; Sat-Sun, no charge. ☎971 71 75 40.

Address Book

For coin ranges, see the Legend on the cover flap.

WHERE TO EAT

Ca's Cuiner – *Plaça Cort 5 – Palma – 971 72 12 62 – Closed Sun –* – . This shop selling ready-made meals also has its own restaurant (or vice-versa) and is considered the temple of Mallorcan cuisine. The menus on offer are simple but delicious, ranging from *empanadas de cordero*, (lamb pastries), *tumbet* (a local vegetable stew) to *sobrasada* (a sausage). Mainly popular with locals.

Sa Plaça Petra – *Plaça Ramón Llull 4 – Petra – About 10 km E or Manacor by the PM 332 – – 971 56 16 46 – www.saplacapetra.com – Closed Tue and in Nov –* . This attractive restaurant, a combination of old and new, exemplifies what Mallorcans mean by "isle of calm." It has a pleasant terrace, as well as three guest rooms.

Cás Cosi – *Baronia 1-3 – Banyalbufar – 971 61 82 45 – Closed Tue Nov-Mar –* . A high-quality restaurant in Banyalbufar, an attractive village surrounded by mountains. The pleasant atmosphere is created by the successful combination of the modern and traditional, a mix that is also evident in the copious cuisine.

Stay – *Muelle Nuevo – Port de Pollença – 971 86 40 13 – www.stayrestaurant.com – stay@stayrestaurant.com.* Well-known to locals, this restaurant has a fine location, and modern decor with minimalist details that fit in well.

Es Baluard – *Plaça Porta de Santa Catalina, 9 – Palma – 971 71 96 09 – Closed Sun, second half of Jan, second half of Aug – – Reservation recommended.* With its attentive service, elegant decor, teakwood terrace and refined Mallorcan cuisine, the Es Baluard has become a local favourite. An extensive wine list and a good location close to the port.

Stay – *Estación Marítima – Port de Pollença – 971 86 40 13 – stay@stayrestaurant.com.* Well-known to locals, this restaurant has a fine location, with two dining areas and a serene seaside terrace.

WHERE TO STAY

Santuari de Lluc – *Depatx de cel.les – Lluc – 971 87 15 25 – www.lluc.net – – 110 room.* A number of cells in the oldest monastery on the island (dating to 1286) have been converted into modest but comfortable guest rooms. Monastic silence guaranteed for those searching for complete peace and quiet, along with a daily children's concert.

Hotel Born – *Sant Jaume 3 – Palma – 971 71 29 42 – www.hotelborn.com – 25 rooms.* A good central option if you're planning on staying in Palma itself. The hotel occupies a former 16C palace which was subsequently restored in the 18C and is accessed via a delightful Ibizan-style patio. On the whole the rooms are quiet with tasteful decor.

Hotel Mar i Vent – *Major 49 – Banyalbufar – 971 61 80 00 – www.hotelmarivent.com – Closed Dec-Jan – – 29 rooms – – Restaurant 25 €.* A quite charming hotel converted from an old stone house with views of the wooded mountains to the west and the Mediterranean to the north. Beautifully maintained both inside and out.

Hotel Son Trobat – *Carretera Manacor-Sant Llorenç – Sant Llorenç des Cardassar – 4.8km/3mi NE of Manacor on the C 715. – 971 56 96 74 – www.sontrobat.com – Closed 1 Dec-31 Jan – – 25 rooms – – Restaurant 24 €.* This large property in the heart of the Mallorcan countryside successfully combines the rustic charm of an old building with the facilities of the modern age (two swimming pools, jacuzzi, Turkish bath, sauna etc). Reasonably priced given the standard.

SHOPPING

Mallorca's two gastronomic specialities are **ensaimada**, a light spiral roll dusted with sugar, and **sobrasada**, a hot pork sausage.

Muslim archaeology

The ground floor displays Muslim capitals, *artesonado* ceilings and ceramics.

Fine Arts★

See Background: Mallorcan Primitives.
This section displays Mallorcan Gothic paintings. Works from the early 14C

A View of Palma's Marina and Cathedral

show clear Italian influence. Catalan works begin to appear after 1349 when Mallorca was annexed by Aragón: the *Crucifixion* by Ramón Destorrents, interesting for its composition and expression, was to influence other paintings. Francesch Comes, one of the most prestigious of the early-15C painters, is represented here by his **St George★** (*Room 3*), remarkable for the depth and detail of the landscape.
For the ethnographical section, *see Tours: Muro).*

Museo Diocesano (Diocesan Museum)

On the square behind the cathedral. Open 10am-1pm and 3-6pm (8pm in summer); Sat-Sun and public hols, 10am-1pm. 2 €. 971 71 28 27.
Among the many Gothic works is Pere Nisart's outstanding **St George★** (1568) which shows the saint slaying the dragon against a backdrop of 16C Palma.

To the west of El Born

1hr

La Llotja (La Lonja)★

Open for exhibitions: 11am-2pm and 5-9pm; Sun and public hols, 11am-2pm. Closed Mon. 971 71 17 05.
Guillermo Sagrera designed this 15C commodities exchange. The Llotja's military features are only for appearances, to distract the eye from the buttresses and austerity of the walls. The interior, with pointed arches on spirally fluted columns, is quite elegant.

Antiguo Consulado del Mar (Former Maritime Consulate)

The early-17C building with a Renaissance balcony was the meeting-place of the Tribunal de Comercio Marítimo (Merchant Shipping Tribunal). Today it houses the regional administration.

Walk up the passeig des Born.

Palau Solleric

Open 10.30am-1.30pm and 5.30-8.30pm; Sun and public hols, 10.30am-1.30pm. Closed Mon. 971 72 20 92.
This 18C palace overlooking the Born is completed by an elegant loggia; follow the narrow covered way to the most perfect **patio★** in Palma, along with a double staircase with delicate ironwork.

Outside the Centre

Museu d'Art Espanyol Contemporani – Colecció March★ (Museum of Modern Spanish Art – March Collection)

Open 10am-6.30pm; Sat 10.30am-2pm Closed Sun and public hols. No charge. 971 71 35 15.
In this 18C mansion is a **permanent collection★** of contemporary Spanish artists, from the Avant Garde (Picasso, Miró, Dalí and J. González) to recent figures.

PALMA DE MALLORCA

			Can Serra	HZ	43	Palau Reial	GZ	109
			Conquistador	GZ	50	Portella	GZ	114
			Constitució	GY	51	Ramón Llull	HZ	118
Almoina Pl.	GZ	6	Convent de			Rei Joan Carles I Pl.	GY	119
Antoni Maura Av.	GZ	12	Sant Francesc	HZ	54	Reina Pl.	GZ	120
Antoni Planas i Franch	HZ	13	Corderia	HY	57	Riera	GY	121
Apuntadors	FZ	15	Drassana Pl.	FZ	58	Sant Bartomeu	GY	130
Ballester Travessia	HY	25	Ducs de Palma de			Sant Francesc Pl.	HZ	132
Born Pas. des	GY		Mallorca Rambla dels	GXY	60	Sant Pere Nolasc	GZ	133
Bosseria	HY	34	Forn de la Gloria	FZ	69	Santa Clara	HZ	135
Cadena	GZ	36	Jaume II	GY	85	Sastre Roig	GY	136
Calatrava	HZ	37	Jaume III Av.	FY		Temple	HZ	141
Can Pueyo	GY	40	Josep Maria Quadrado Pl.	HZ	94	Tous i Maroto	GY	144
Can Savellà	HZ	42	Monti-Sion	HZ	108	Weyler Pl.	GY	148

Antiguo Consulado			Casa Berga	GY	J	Museu d'Art Espanyol		
del Mar	FZ	C	Museo Diocesano	GZ	M^2	Contemporani	HY	M^3
Ayuntamiento	GZ	H	Museo del Mallorca	GZ	M^1	Palau Solleric	GY	Z

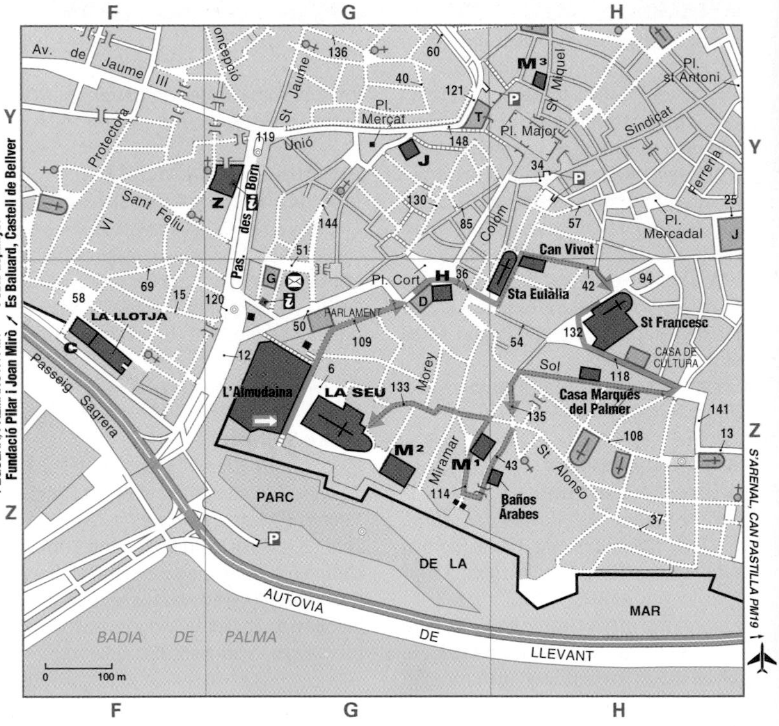

Casa Berga

This 1712 mansion is the Palacio de Justicia (Law Courts). The façade is encumbered with stone balconies but the vast inner courtyard is typically Mallorcan.

Pueblo Español★ (Spanish Village)

Off the town plan, along passeig de Sagrera. Open 9am-6pm (7pm in summer). 5 €. 971 73 70 75.

The buildings are exact reproductions of famous houses or monuments: the Myrtle Court from the Alhambra in Granada, the Casa de El Greco in Toledo, etc. Craftsmen and folk troupes bring the village to life.

Features of all major Roman sites in Spain have been incorporated in the monumental **Palacio de Congresos** (Convention Centre) facing the village.

Castillo de Bellver★

Leave Palma along passeig de Sagrera. *Open 8.15am-7.15pm (8.30pm Apr-Sep); Sun and public hols, 10am-5pm (7pm Apr-Sep); last admission 45min before closing.* *Closed 1 Jan and 25 Dec. 2 €. 971 73 06 57.*

The castle, built by the Mallorcan kings of the 14C as a summer residence, served as a prison until 1915.

The round buildings and circular perimeter and court are highly original; a free-standing keep dominates all. The Roman statues belong to the **Museo Municipal de Historia** (City History Museum). Also displayed are finds from excavations in Pollença. View a **panorama**★★ of the bay from the terrace.

Fundació Pilar i Joan Miró (Pilar and Joan Miró Foundation)

Leave the centre via passeig de Sagrera. Open 10am-6pm (7pm 16 May-15 Sep); Sun and public hols all year, 10am-3pm. Closed Mon, 1 Jan and 25 Dec. 5 €. 971 70 14 20.

The museum is the legacy of Joan Miró (1893-1983) and his wife. In the shadow of Son Abrines, Miró's residence from 1956, works donated by the artist are displayed in a part of the building called the Espacio Estrella.

Es Baluard – Museu d'Art Modern i Contemporani de Palma (Museum of Contemporary Art, in the baluarte de Sant Pere (bastion), facing the port)

Sights

LA COSTA ROCOSA★★★ (THE ROCKY COAST) 1

From Palma to Alcúdia

264km/165mi. Allow 2 days. See map of island on pp 576–577.

Mallorca's west coast is dominated by the limestone Sierra de Tramuntana, rising to 1 436m/4 711ft at Puig Major. In the south, around Estellencs and Banyalbufar, slopes are terraced into *marjades* of olives, almonds and vines.

Leave Palma along passeig Sagrera.

Port d'Andratx★

The small fishing port is now also used by pleasure craft.

The C 710 from Andratx to Sóller is an extremely **scenic road**★★★, mostly along a cliff. It commands outstanding views and is shaded by pine trees.

Mirador Ricardo Roca★★

The **view** from this lookout drops sheer to tiny coves lapped by the limpid sea.

Mirador de Ses Ánimes★★

The **panorama** from the watchtower stretches south from the Isla de Dragonera and north to Port de Sóller.

Cartuja de Valldemossa (Valldemossa Carthusian Monastery)

Open Mar-Oct, 9.30am-5.30pm (6.30pm Jul-Sep); Sun, 10am-1pm. Closed Sun in Dec-Jan, 1 Jan and 25 Dec. 7.50 €. 971 61 21 06.

The monastery was made famous by the visit George Sand and Chopin paid in the winter of 1838-39. Bad weather and local hostility left Sand disenchanted, although she invoked the countryside in *A Winter in Majorca*. From the monks' cells there are pleasant **views** of the surrounding olive groves. An 18C **pharmacy** has a collection of jars and boxes. A small **museum** displays xylographs (wood engravings).

Son Marroig

Open 9.30am-6pm (8pm Apr-Sep). Closed Sun, 1 Jan and 25 Dec. 3 €. 971 63 91 58.

The former residence of Archduke Ludwig Salvator includes an exhibition of archaeological finds and Mallorcan furniture. A belvedere in the garden affords a view of the **Foradada**, a pierced rock rising out of the sea.

Sóller

The delightful 19C houses of Sóller spread in a quiet valley of market gardens, orange trees and olives groves.

Port de Sóller

Port de Sóller, in the curve of an almost circular bay which shelters pleasure boats, is the major seaside resort of the

Port de Sóller

west coast. A train runs between Port de Sóller and Sóller. Coastal boat trips operate from the harbour.

Take the C 711 from Sóller to Alfàbia.

Jardines de Alfàbia (Alfàbia Gardens)

Open 9.30am-5.30pm (6.30pm May-Sep); Sat, 9.30am-1pm (6pm May-Sep). Closed Sun. 4.50 €. 971 61 31 23.

Only the *artesonado* ceiling over the porch remains from a 14C Moorish residence. Follow the path through the gardens to the **library** for a taste of a traditional seigniorial residence.

Return to Sóller. Take the narrow mountain road via the picturesque villages of Biniaraix and Fornalutx., then follow the C 710.

Mirador de Ses Barques

From this viewpoint there is an interesting **panorama** of Port de Sóller. The road heads through a long tunnel before following the upper valley of the Pareís. The land is dominated by **Puig Major** *(military base on the summit).*

After skirting the Gorg Blau reservoir, take the Sa Calobra road.

Sa Calobra road★★★

The magnificently planned road plunges 900m/3 000ft in 14km/9mi through steep, jagged rocks.

Sa Calobra★

Near the village is the mouth of the **Pareís river**★, its clear water pouring over round white shingle. The river bed is accessible along a track through two underground galleries; a 2-3km/1.5-2mi walk along the course gives an idea of how enclosed the stream is.

Return to the C 710.

About 1km/0.6mi north of the Sa Calobra fork, a small **mirador**★ (*lookout*, alt 664m/2 178ft) gives a good view over the cleft hollowed out by the Pareís.

Monasterio de Nuestra Señora de Lluc

Open 8am-10pm. 971 87 15 25.

The monastery dates from the 13C when a young shepherd found a statue of the Virgin. *La Moreneta*, the dark stone statue, is patron of Mallorca. From a pass 5km/3mi north of Lluc, you can see the Bahía de Pollença.

Port de Pollença

This large resort has a perfect **setting**★ in a sheltered bay between the Cabo Formentor headland to the north and Cabo del Pinar to the south, and provides a vast expanse of calm water for water-skiing and sailing.

Cabo de Formentor road★

The road commands spectacular views as it twists upward. The **Mirador des Colomer viewpoint**★★★ *(access along*

a stepped path) overlooks great rock promontories. The **Platja de Formentor** is a sheltered beach. The grand Hotel Formentor was once famous for its casino and millionaire guests.
The road continues through a tunnel and a steep and arid landscape. **Cabo de Formentor★**, with its lighthouse, is the most northerly point of the island.

▶ *Return to Port de Pollença, then skirt the bay until you reach Alcúdia.*

Alcúdia

Alcúdia, encircled by 14C ramparts, guards the promontory which divides the bays of Pollença and Alcúdia. Two gates (**Puerta del Muelle** to the harbour, and the **Puerta de San Sebastián** across town) from early walls were incorporated into 14C ramparts. The streets in the shadow of the walls have a distinctive medieval air.
About 2km south is the site of Roman **Pollentia** founded in the 2C BC. Only the theatre ruins remain.

Museo Monográfico de Pollentia (Pollentia Monographic Museum)

Open 10am-1.30pm and 3.30-5.30pm; Sat-Sun, 10.30am-1pm. Closed Mon and public hols. 2 €. No charge first Sun of month. ☎971 89 71 02.
A chapel in Alcúdia's old quarter houses statues, oil lamps, bronzes and jewellery from the ancient city of Pollentia.

Port d'Alcúdia

2km/1.2mi E. The port of Alcúdia overlooks a vast bay built up with hotels. A beach stretches to the south as far as Can Picafort. The marsh of La Albufera is a nature reserve.

Cuevas de Campanet

17km/11mi SW along the C 713 and a secondary, signposted road. About half of these caves along the 1 300m/1 500yd-long path have ceased formation. In the waterlogged area, the most common features are straight and delicate stalactites *(guided tours, 45min, 10am-6pm (7pm Apr-Oct); closed 1 Jan and 25 Dec; 9.50€; ☎971 51 61 30.*

Muro

▶ *Follow the C 713 SW for 11km/7mi and then bear left for another 7km/4mi via Sa Pobla.*

The road crosses countryside bristling with windmills. The **ethnological section** of the **Museo de Mallorca**, in a large 17C noble residence, displays traditional furniture, dress and farm implements, as well as exhibitions on craftsmen: a blacksmith, cabinetmaker, gilder, engraver, welder, goldsmith and cobbler *(open 10am-7pm; Sun 10am-2pm; closed Mon and public hols; 2.40€; ☎971 71 75 40).*

EAST COAST AND CAVES★★ 2

From Artà to Palma

165km/103mi. Allow one day.
See map.

Artà

The high rock site is crowned by the Iglesia de Sant Salvador (Church of the Saviour) and the ruins of an ancient fortress. The Artà region is rich in **megalithic remains** *(see MENORCA)*, particularly *talayots* which sometimes can be seen over low walls in the fields.

▶ *Continue along the C 715.*

Capdepera

Access to the fortress: by car, along narrow streets; on foot, up steps. The remains of a 14C fortress give Capdepera an angular silhouette of crenellated walls and square towers. The buttressed ramparts enclose only a restored **chapel**. Walk the old sentry path to **view★** the sea and the nearby coves.

Cala Rajada

Cala Rajada is a delightful fishing village and pleasure boat harbour.
Across the pinewood towards the lighthouse are two rocky inlets, relatively wild; 2km/1mi further north, is **Cala Agulla**, with a sandy beach.

▶ *Return to Capdepera and follow the signs to the Coves d'Artà.*

Coves d'Artà★★★

Guided tours (45min), 10am-5.30pm (7pm Jul-Oct); last admission 30min before closing. Closed 1 Jan and 25 Dec. 9 €. 971 84 12 93.

The caves, in the cape closing Canyamel bay to the north, were largely hollowed out by the sea – the giant mouth overlooks the sea from 35m/115ft. The lofty chambers contain massive concretions. The vestibule is blackened by smoke from 19C torches. Inside are the **Reina de las Columnas** (Queen of Columns) 22m/72ft tall, Dantesque surroundings cleverly highlighted in the **Sala del Infierno** (Chamber of Hell) and a fantasy of forms in the **Sala de las Banderas** (Hall of Flags), 45m/148ft high.

Return to the PM 404 and bear left. At Portocristo, take the Manacor road; turn shortly for the Coves dels Hams.

Coves dels Hams

Guided tours (45min), Nov, 11am-5pm; Dec-Feb, 11am-4.30pm, Mar, 10.30am-5pm; Apr, May and Oct, 10.30am-5.30pm; Jun-Sep, 10am-6pm. Closed 25 Dec. 9.80€. 971 82 09 88.

The caves communicate with the sea; the water level in several pools rises and falls with the Mediterranean tide. Some concretions in the **Sala de los Anzuelos**★ (Fish-hook Chamber) are as white as snow.

Return to Portocristo and bear right.

Coves del Drach★★★

Guided tours (1hr) at 10.45am, noon, 2pm and 3.30pm; 15 Mar-Oct at 10am, 11am, noon, 1pm, 2pm, 3pm, 4pm and 5pm. Closed 1 Jan and 25 Dec. 9.50 €. 971 82 07 53.

Four chambers succeed one another over a distance of 2km/1.2mi. The marine origins of the caves seem unquestionable. It is the **roofs**, above all, which are amazing, glittering with countless sharply pointed icicles. **Lago Martel** is vaste and limpid, a lake in a chamber used by musicians as they glide across the water in boats.

Continue along the road towards Santanyí and turn right onto the PM 401.

Monasterio de Sant Salvador★

Open 8am-9pm. No charge. 971 58 00 56.

The monastery on a rise 500m/1 640ft above the plain (tight hairpin bends), commands a wide **panorama**★★.

It was founded in the 14C. In the church, behind the Baroque high altar, is a deeply venerated **Virgin and Child**, while in the south chapels are three **Nativities** set in dioramas and a multi-coloured 14C stone **altarpiece** carved with scenes of the Passion.

Return to the Santanyí road.

Secondary roads lead to resorts built up in the creeks along the coast, namely **Cala d'Or**★, **Cala Figuera**★**,** which is still a delightful little fishing village, and **Cala Santanyí**★.

From Santanyí follow the C 717 towards Palma. In Llucmajor, bear right onto the PM 501.

Santuario de Cura★

Open 10am-1pm and 3.30-6pm. 971 66 09 94.

The road climbs from Randa to the monastery. The buildings have been restored and modernised by the Franciscans. You may visit the 17C **church**, the Sala de Gramática (Grammar Room) and a small **museum**.

From the terrace on the west side there is a **panorama**★★ of Palma, the bay, the Puig Major chain and, in the north-east, Cabo de Formentor headland, the northernmost point on the island.

Return to Llucmajor and continue W along the C 717 to Palma.

MENORCA★★

POPULATION: 70 000

669KM2/258SQ MI – MICHELIN MAP 579.

Menorca has managed to avoid the rampant development that has blighted other Mediterranean islands, preserving picturesque villages and coastline dotted with creeks of crystal-clear water. Other attractions include wildlife, plentiful sunshine, superb cuisine and high standard of hotel accommodation.

- **Information:** *Ciutadella: Plaça de la Catedral 5, 07760, ☎971 38 26 93; Maó: Moll de Llevant 2, 07703, ☎971 35 59 52.*
- **Orient Yourself:** Menorca is the second largest and most populated of the Balearic islands and the farthest from the mainland

A Bit of History

Landscape – Menorca's highest point, Monte Toro, 358m/1 174ft, is in the north of the island, known as the Tramuntana, where there are outcrops of dark slate rock. Along the coast, these ancient, eroded cliffs have been cut into a saw's edge of *rías* (inlets) and deep coves. South of the Maó-Ciutadella line, the Migjorn limestone platform forms cliffs along the coast.

Vegetation is typically Mediterranean: pinewoods, gnarled and twisted wild olives, heather and aromatic herbs such as rosemary, camomile and thyme. Drystone walls divide fields, punctuated by gates of twisted olive branches.

Historical notes – Prehistoric peoples have left monuments throughout the island. Menorca was colonised by the Romans, conquered by Vandals in 427, and came under Muslim control. In the 13C, Alfonso III of Aragón invaded, made Ciutadella capital and encouraged settlers from Catalunya and Aragón. In the 16C, Barbary pirates left Maó and Ciutadella in virtual ruin.

In 1713, Menorca, which had begun to prosper through trade in the late 17C, was ceded to the English crown by the Treaty of Utrecht. Maó became England's stronghold in the Mediterranean. Apart from a short period of French rule from 1756 to 1763, the island remained throughout the 18C under the British,. The first road, between Maó and Ciuta-

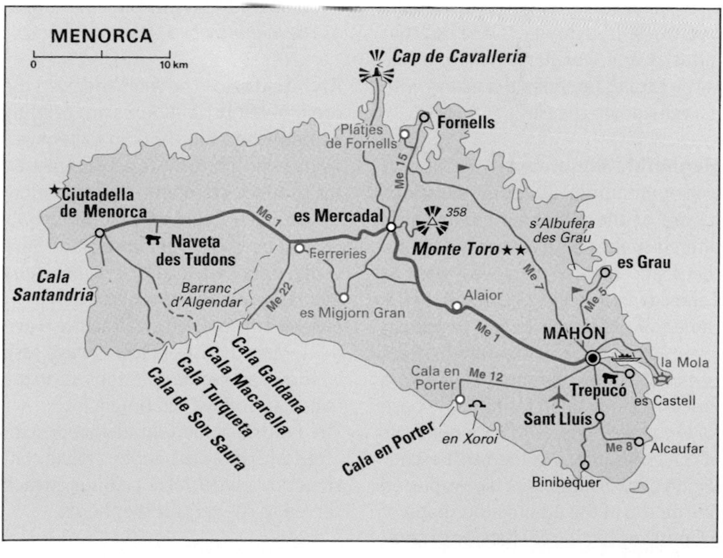

Address Book

For coin ranges, see the Legend on the cover flap.

WHERE TO EAT

Itake – *Moll de Llevant 317 (Puerto) – Mahón – 971 35 45 70 – Closed Sun evening, Mon and 20 Dec-1 Feb – – Reservation recommended.* Understandably, given its location near the port, the colourful decor in this small and inviting restaurant takes its inspiration from the sea and the theme of long ocean voyages. The cuisine here is simple yet original, with signature dishes such as potatoes stuffed with *sobrasada* (sausage), ostrich and kangaroo.

El Horno – *Des Forn, 12 – Ciudadela – 971 38 07 67 – Open Holy Week-Oct –* . A modest family operation in cosy surroundings. The ground floor is rustic, with a French-inspired menu at moderate prices.

S'Engolidor – *Major, 3 – Es Migjorn Gran – 971 37 01 93 – dinner only Apr-Oct –* . This pleasant and simple restaurant assumes the character of a Menorcan house, with its tables set in assorted rooms and on the rear patios in summer. The local cooking is authentic. Modest rooms are also offered (30/54€).

WHERE TO STAY

Hotel Del Almirante – *El Fonduco (Puerto) – es Castell – 971 36 27 00 – www.hoteldelalmirante.com – – 39 rooms –* . The antique furniture, paintings adorning the walls and "very British" clientele confer a special feel to this old mansion. It is also said that the ghost of Admiral Collingwood continues to haunt its walls. Excellent value for money.

Son Triay – *Carretera de Cala Galdana – Ferreries – 3km/2mi from Ferreries towards Cala Galdana – 971 15 50 78 – www.sontriay.com – – 6 rooms (doubles only).* This Italianate mansion with its raspberry-coloured façade stands in a romantic setting surrounded by greenery. The bedrooms are both comfortable and attractive although the bathrooms are on the small side.

della, still exists (north of the C 721), known as camino Kane for a British governor. At the beginning of the 19C, Menorca was restored to Spain.

The island's economy has gradually been oriented towards the leather industry and jewellery-making while cattle raising provides the island with its well-known cheeses.

Megalithic monuments – In the second millennium BC, the cavernous nature of the Minorcan countryside offered shelter both for the living and the dead; some of the caves, such as **Calascoves**, are even decorated. At the same time, **talayots** began to appear (over 200 have been identified), great cones of stones, possibly covering a funeral chamber and forming the base for a wooden house. Other monuments of the civilisation include **taulas**, consisting of two huge stone blocks placed one on top of the other in the shape of a T, possibly serving as altars, and **navetas**, which take the form of upturned boats and contain funeral chambers.

A locally available map shows the monument sites: Mapa Arqueológico de Menorca, by J Mascaró Pasarius.

Architecture – The walls and even the roofs of Minorcan houses are brightly whitewashed; low dividing walls have a white band along the top. Tiles are used for roofing, chimneys and guttering. Houses face south, their fronts characterised by wide, open bays. Northern walls, exposed to fierce *tramontana* winds, have small windows.

English influence on architecture is evident. Many houses in towns have sash windows and some mansions are in the Palladian style of 18C Britain.

The fields around Ciutadella are scattered with *barracas*, curious stone constructions with false ceilings, which served as shelters for shepherds.

Worth a Visit

CIUTADELLA/CIUDADELA★

In the Middle Ages, Ciutadella, citadel and capital of Menorca, was ringed with walls. The fortified aspect of the city becomes evident when viewed from the harbour. Sacked by Turkish pirates in the 16C, Ciutadella was partly rebuilt in the late 17C and 18C.

The **Midsummer's Day Festivities** or **Fiestas de San Juan,** are celebrated in traditional fashion. On the preceding Sunday, a man representing John the Baptist, dressed in skins and carrying a lamb, runs to the sound of *fabiols* (flutes) and *tambourins*. On 24 and 25 June, over 100 horsemen take part in jousting tournaments and processions.

Barrio Antiguo (Old Quarter)

Plaza del Born, the ex-parade ground, is flanked by the eclectic 19C **Ayuntamiento** (town hall) and the early-19C **Palacio de Torre-Saura,** a palace with side loggias. An obelisk commemorates resistance against the Turks in the 16C.

Catedral

Closed for renovation. ☎*971 38 07 39.*

The late-14C fortified church retains a minaret from Islamic days. The single aisle is ogival and the apse pentagonal. View the Baroque doorway from calle del Rosario. At the end of the street, turn left into calle del Santísimo. **Palacio Saura** has a Baroque façade with a cornice. **Palacio Martorell** across the street is more sober.

Take calle del Obispo Vila, passing the Claustro de Socorro (Socorro Cloisters) and the Iglesia de Santo Cristo (Church of the Holy Christ) to the main street which leads to **plaza de España** and the arcaded **carrer de Ses Voltes**.

Puerto (Harbour)

The ramp approach to the harbour, which serves pleasure craft, is along a former counterscarp. Quayside cafés and restaurants bustle with life. The esplanade, pla de Sant Joan, the centre for Midsummer's Day festivities, is bordered by boat shelters hollowed out of rock. The area comes alive at night.

Excursions

Nau or Naveta des Tudons

5km/3mi E of Ciutadella. This funerary monument, shaped like an upturned ship, is notable for the vast stones in the walls and lining the floor.

Cala Santandria

3km/2mi S. This is a small sheltered beach in a creek.

Cala Torre-Saura, Cala Turqueta, Cala Macarella

Ask locally for directions. The three beaches are set in small, beautifully unspoilt creeks fringed by pines.

Mark Fincham/SXC

Naveta des Tudons

MAÓ/MAHÓN

Maó's **site**★ is most striking when approached from the sea, atop a cliff in the curve of a deep, 5km/3mi long natural harbour.

Maó was endowed with Palladian-style mansions during English occupation.

On the north side of the harbour is the Finca de San Antonio – the Golden Farm – where Admiral Nelson put the finishing touches to his book, *Sketches of My Life* (October 1799). Maó gave its name to mayonnaise.

Most of the Maó's shops are between **plaza del Ejército**, a large, lively square lined with cafés and restaurants, and the quieter **plaza de España** with its two churches: **Santa Maria**, with a beautiful Baroque organ, and **Carmen**, the Carmelite church, whose cloisters now hold the municipal market.

Museo de Menorca

Open 9.30am-2pm; Sa-Sun 10am-2pm (Apr-Sep, 10am-2pm and 6-8.30pm; Sun 10am-2pm). Closed Mon and public hols. 2.40 €, no charge Sat (afternoon) and Sun. 971 35 09 55.

The museum is a former Franciscan monastery. Rooms around a sober 18C cloister display prehistoric and other objects relating to Menorcan history. A room is dedicated to *talayot* culture.

Puerto (Harbour)

Walk down the steep ramp from carrer de Ses Voltes, cut by a majestic flight of steps, and follow the quay to the north side. View the town at its most characteristic, with its larger buildings lining the top of the cliff and below, the open-air dance halls, restaurants, shops and fishermen's cottages.

Excursions

La Rada★ (Roadstead)

On the south side are coves and villages, among them Cala Figuera with its fishing harbour and restaurants. **Es Castell** was an English garrison, Georgetown. It has a grid plan, with parade ground at its centre. The islands in the harbour include Lazareto and Cuarentena, which was a quarantine hospital for sailors. A road follows the northern shore to the Faro de la Mola, a lighthouse affording views of Maó.

Talayot de Trepucó

1km/0.6mi S of Maó. This megalithic site is famous for its 4.80m/16ft *taula*.

Sant Lluís

4km/2.5mi S. This town with narrow streets was founded by the French. Small resorts have grown up nearby at **Alcalfar** and **Binibèquer**, a new village made to look like a fishing hamlet.

Es Grau

8km/5mi N. Beside the attractive white village with its long beach is a vast lagoon, **Albufera de es Grau,** 2km/1mi long and 400m/437yd wide. It is an ideal spot to watch migrant birds (rails, ducks and herons).

Cala en Porter

12km/8mi W. Promontories protect a narrow estuary, lined by a sandy beach. Houses perch upon the left cliff. Ancient troglodyte dwellings, the **Coves d'en Xoroi**, overlook the sea.

MERCADAL

Mercadal, a village of brilliantly whitewashed houses halfway between Maó and Ciutadella, is where roads to the coast meet on the north-south axis.

Excursions

Monte Toro

3.5km/2mi along a narrow road. On a clear day, the **view**★★ from the church-crowned summit (358m/1 175ft) is of the entire island: indented Bahía de Fornells (Fornells Bay) to the north, the coastal cliffs and Maó to the south-east.

Fornells

8.5km/5mi N on the C 723. Fornells, a fishing village of whitewashed houses with green shutters, lies at the mouth of a deep inlet, surrounded on all sides by bare moorland. The village lives off crayfish. The local speciality, crayfish soup or caldereta, is a delight.

Cap de Cavalleria

12km/8mi N along the PM 722. The drive to the cape, northernmost point on the island, is through windswept moorland, battered by the *tramontana*, with large, elegant country houses, like that at Finca Santa Teresa. The **view** from the lighthouse is of a rocky, indented coast, more Atlantic than Mediterranean.

Cala Santa Galdana

16km/10mi SW via Ferreries. This cove set in a limpid bay flanked by tall cliffs has been marred by large hotels.

It is also possible to walk to the cove from **the Algendar ravine** *(on leaving Ferreries, take the track left towards Ciutadella)*. The path *(3hr there and back)* winds through a ravine.

IBIZA★

POPULATION: 88 000

572 KM2/221SQ MI – MICHELIN MAP 579 – BALEARES.

Ibiza is renowned for nightlife and visiting hedonists, yet parts of the island remain a natural paradise. There are stunning beaches, hidden coves and delightful villages with narrow streets lined by whitewashed houses all of which forge a personality that is unique in the Balearics.

- **Information:** *Eivissa: Vara de Rey 13, 07800, ☎971 30 19 00.*
- **Orient Yourself:** Ibiza is the closest island to the Spanish mainland (83km/52mi).

A Bit of History

Historical notes – In the 10C BC, Phoenicians made the island a staging-post for ships loaded with Spanish ores; in the 7C BC, Carthage founded a colony; under the Romans the capital grew in size and prosperity.

Landscape – Ibiza, the **Isla Blanca** (White Island), 45 miles southwest of Mallorca, is 41km/25mi in length.

Dazzling whitewashed walls, flat roof terraces, tortuous alleys and an atmosphere similar to that of a Greek island give Ibiza its unique character. It is mountainous, with little space for cultivation. Among pines and junipers on the hillsides stand the cube-shaped houses of many small villages. The shore appears wild and indented; promontories are marked by rocks out to sea, some as high as the limestone needle known as **Vedrá**★ (almost 400m/1 300ft).

Traditional architecture – The typical Ibizan cottage, or **casament**, now largely found inland, is made up of several white cubes with few windows. Arcaded porches provide shade and a sheltered area for storing crops.

Country churches are equally plain with gleaming white exteriors and dark interiors. Façades are square, surmounted by narrow bell gables, pierced by wide porches. Fortified churches once provided shelter from pirates in Sant Carles, Sant Joan, Sant Jordi and Sant Miquel.

Folklore and traditional costume – Ibiza's uncomplicated folklore lives on. Women still wear the traditional long gathered skirt and dark shawl. At festivals the costume is brightened with fine gold filigree necklaces or **emprendades**. Dances are performed to the accompaniment of flute, tambourine and castanets.

Worth a Visit

EIVISSA/IBIZA★

Eivissa's colourful beauty and impressive **site**★★ are best appreciated from the sea; alternatively take the **Talamanca** road and look back *(3km/2mi NE)*. The town, built on a hill, consists of an old quarter ringed by walls, the lively Marina district near the harbour, and, further out, residential and shopping areas. Along the shore are large hotels.

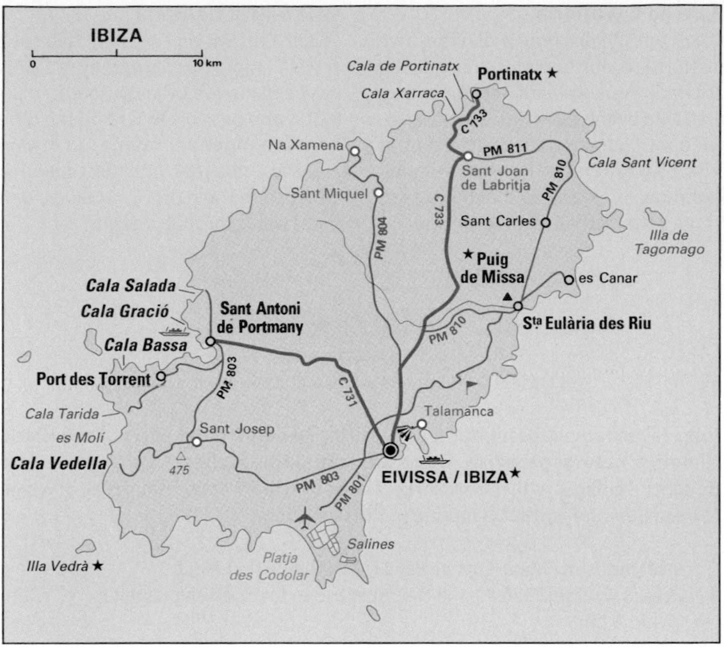

Upper town★ (Dalt Vila)

1hr 30min

The Dalt Vila, enclosed by the 16C walls built under Emperor Charles V, is the heart of the old city and retains even today a rustic, medieval character. There remain many noble houses worth looking at particularly for their vast patios and Gothic windows.

Enter the quarter through the **Porta de Taules**, a gateway surmounted by Philip II's crest. Continue by car up a steep slope to the cathedral square or stroll the quiet meandering streets with their shops and art galleries.

J. Malburet/ MICHELIN

The goddess Tanit

Catedral

10am-1pm and 5-8pm. ☎971 31 27 73

The cathedral's massive 13C belfry, which resembles a keep but for its two storeys of Gothic bays, dominates the town. The nave was rebuilt in the 17C. An ancient bastion behind the east end affords a **panoramic view**★.

Museo Arqueológico de Ibiza y Formentera★

Open 9am-3pm; in summer, 10am-2pm and 6-8pm; Sun 10am-2pm. Closed Mon and public hols. 2.40 €, no charge Sat afternoon and Sun. ☎971 30 12 31.

The most impressive exhibits are its Punic art, which developed around the Mediterranean from the 7C BC to the 3C AD. Particularly impressive are the ex-votos discovered on Ibiza and Formentera, predominantly from excavations at Illa Plana and the Es Cuiram cave. The cave is believed to have been a temple to the goddess **Tanit**, who

Address Book

For coin ranges, see the Legend on the cover flap.

WHERE TO EAT

⊖ **Sa Caleta** – *Playa Es Bol Nou (Sa Caleta) – Sant Josep – ☎971 18 70 95 – Only noon-7pm (Jul-Sep noon-midnight).* The Sa Caleta enjoys a splendid position by the sea in an unspoilt bay surrounded by red earth. Its faithful customers come here in the knowledge that only the freshest fish is served, including seafood produced in the restaurant's own seawater nurseries.

⊖⊖ **Villa Mercedes** – *Passeig del Mar – Sant Antoni de Portmany – ☎ 971 34 85 43 – www.digitalibiza.com/villamercedes* – ▤. The Villa Mercedes is an exclusive restaurant in an attractive Modernist-style house. The views from the dining room windows encompass the ever-changing harbour, which is particularly busy at night. The menu here is on the original side and should satisfy even the most demanding of gourmets.

⊖⊖⊖ **C'an Pujol** – *Carretera Vieja a Port des Torrent (Bahía de San Antonio) – Sant Antoni de Portmany – ☎971 34 14 07 – Closed Wed and in Dec – Reservation recommended.* This restaurant is an island institution. If you're planning on trying the house speciality (*bullit de peix*), a delicious fish stew served with rice made from a broth using the same fish, make sure you call ahead of time.

WHERE TO STAY

⊖ **Sa Pensió** – *Carrrer de Sa Cala 11 – Sant Joan – ☎971 33 30 12 – 12 rooms.* This modest town house to the north of the island has a dozen farily basic but perfectly acceptable rooms, a few with their own terrace. The pleasant dining room offers an attractive setting for a relaxed evening meal.

⊖ **Hostal Parque** – *Plaça del Parque 4 – Ibiza – ☎971 30 13 58 – www.hostal-parque.com* – ▤ – *34 rooms.* Small but pleasing rooms with excellent sound-proofing to block out the noise from the plaza del Parque, a popular meeting-point for local youngsters.

⊖ **Hotel Montesol** – *Passeig Vara de Rei 2 – Ibiza – ☎971 31 01 61 – www.hotelmontesol.com* – ▤ – *55 rooms* – ☕ *5.* Nothing in the town can compare with this large, mustard-coloured building dating from the beginning of the last century, with its comfortable rooms overlooking the streets of the old quarter. Make sure you enjoy a drink on the hotel's terrace café, which continues to be one of Ibiza's famous locations.

⊖⊖ **La Colina** – *5.5km/3.5mi SW of Santa Eulalia del Río – ☎971 33 27 67 – www.lacolina-ibiza.ch – Closed in Nov-Jan* – P – *13 rooms* – ☕. This traditional, Ibizan-style country house stands on the side of a small hill. Now a quiet, family-run hotel, it is increasingly popular with foreign visitors. Pleasant outdoor areas, including a swimming pool.

⊖⊖⊖ **Agroturismo Can Jondal** – *Ibiza – Carretera de San José a Ibiza. – ☎ 971 18 72 70 – www.canjondal.com –* 🚭 🏊 – *6 rooms* – ☕. A pleasant Ibizan house with whitewashed walls, numerous terraces and tastefully decorated rooms, all on an eco-farm using renewable energy, it also a holistic meditation centre. A haven of peace and quiet on the slopes of a hill in the midst of nature. A friendly welcome guaranteed.

⊖⊖⊖ **Hotel Rural Es Cucons** – *Santa Agnès de Corona –1km along Corona – Camí des Plà de Corona – ☎971 80 55 01 – www.escucons.com – Closed Nov-Mar –* 🏊 ▤ – *14 rooms* – ☕ – *Restaurant 10/32 €.* The family who own this hotel have succeeded in converting this former Ibizan farm into an architectural jewel that has been magnificently decorated in keeping with its origins. A superb combination of luxury and simplicity at the heart of an expansive valley carpeted in almond trees.

was venerated from the 5C BC to the 2C BC. Also worthy of note are the polychrome moulded glass and Punic, Roman and Moorish ceramics.

Lower town

Museu Monogràfic de Puig des Molins★ (Puig des Molins Monographic Museum)

🕓 *Open 9am-3pm; Apr-Sep 10am-2pm and*

Portinatx

6-8pm; Sun 10am-2pm. Closed Sun and public hols. 2.40€. 971 30 17 71.
The Puig des Molins hillside necropolis was a burial-ground for the Phoenicians from the 7C BC and for the Romans until the 1C AD. There is a model of the site; some of the hypogea, or funerary chambers, of which over 3 000 have been discovered, may be visited. The objects displayed were found in the tombs and include everyday and ritual articles. The outstanding, partly coloured, 5C BC **bust of the goddess Tanit★**, a Punic version of the Phoenician Astarte, exemplifies Greek beauty. A second bust is more Carthaginian.

La Marina

The Marina district near the market and harbour, with its restaurants, bars and shops, stands in lively contrast to the quieter Dalt Vila.

Sa Penya★

The former fishermen's quarter, now the centre of Ibiza's nightlife, is built on a narrow rock promontory at the harbour mouth. White cubic houses overlap in picturesque chaos, completely blocking streets forcing bypasses via steps cut out of the rock.

SANT ANTONI DE PORTMANY/ SAN ANTONIO ABAD

Sant Antoni with its vast, curved bay has been extensively developed. The old quarter, hidden behind modern apartment blocks, centres on a fortified 14C church rebuilt in the 16C. There is a large pleasure boat harbour. Several coves and creeks are within easy reach.

Excursions

Cala Gració

2km/1.2mi N. A lovely, easily accessible, sheltered creek.

Cala Salada

5km/3mi N. The road descends through pines to a sheltered beach in a cove.

Port des Torrent and Cala Bassa

5km/3mi SW. Port des Torrent is all rocks; Cala Bassa a long, pine-fringed beach. Rocks are smooth and separate and just above or just below the water line, providing perfect underwater swimming conditions.

Cala Vedella

15km/9mi S. A road skirts the shoreline through pine trees between the beaches of Cala Tarida (rather built-up), Es Molí (unspoiled) and Cala Vedella in its enclosed creek. You can return to Sant Antoni along a mountain road cut into the cliffs as far as Sant Josep.

SANTA EULÀRIA DES RIU/SANTA EULALIA DEL RÍO

Santa Eulària des Riu, in a fertile plain watered by Ibiza's only river, is a large seaside resort. Nearby beaches such as **Es Canar** have also been developed.

Puig de Missa★

Bear right off the Eivissa/Ibiza road 50m/55yd after the petrol station (on the left).

This minute, fortified town crowning the hilltop provides a remarkable overview of the island's traditional peasant architecture; in times of danger, the church (16C) served as a refuge.

Portinatx★

27km/17mi N on the PM 810, PM 811 and C 733. The road passes through **Sant Carles** which has a fine church and is a departure point for quiet local beaches. It descends to the vast **Sant Vicent** creek *(cala)* with its sandy beach and opposite, the Isla de Togomago, then crosses a landscape covered in pines. The last section threads between holm oaks and almond trees looking down on **Cala Xarraca.** Creeks sheltered by cliffs and pine-fringed beaches make **Cala de Portinatx** one of the island's most attractive areas.

FORMENTERA

POPULATION: 6 000

84KM2/32SQ MI – MICHELIN MAP 579.

Formentera, the Roman Island of Wheat (from *frumentum*), smallest in the archipelago, is ideal for those in search of peace and quiet, impressive scenery and beautiful beaches lapped by crystal-clear water.

- **Information:** *Port de Sabina (Obras del Puerto bldg), ☎971 32 20 57.*
- **Orient Yourself:** Formentera lies just 7km/4.5mi south of Ibiza.

Background

Formentera is two islets and a sandy isthmus, 14km/9mi long. The "capital", Sant Francesc de Formentera, the passenger port, Cala Savina, the salt pans, Cabo de Barbaria and the dry open expanse where cereals, figs, almonds and a few vines grow, are on the western islet; the island's 192m/630ft "mountain" rises from the **Mola** promontory on the eastern islet. Rock cliffs and sand dunes alternate along the shore. Access to the island is exclusively by sea, and the best way of exploring Formentera is by bicycle.

Special Features

The Beaches (Playas or Platjas)

White sandy beaches with clear water are the main attraction. Long beaches stretch along either side of the isthmus, the rocky Tramuntana to the north and the sheltered, sandy Migjorn to the south. Smaller beaches include Es Pujòls (the most developed), Illetas and Cala Saona.

Cala Savina

Your landing point is in the main harbour: a few white houses stand between two big lagoons, salt-marshes glisten in the distance on the left.

Sant Francesc (San Francisco Javier)

Chief and only town on the island. Its houses are clustered around the 18C church-fortress.

El Pilar de la Mola

The hamlet at the centre of the Mola promontory has this geometrically designed church which is similar to those on Ibiza, only smaller.

Faro de la Mola

The lighthouse overlooks an impressive cliff. There is a monument to Jules Verne who mentioned this spot in one of his books.

Historical Notes

Formentera's inhabitants arrived comparatively recently, the island having been abandoned in the Middle Ages in the face of marauding Barbary pirates and only repopulated at the end of the 17C. Most of the present population consists of fishermen and peasant farmers, shipping figs and fish to Ibiza and salt to Barcelona.

CANARY ISLANDS★★★

POPULATION: 1 600 000

7 273KM²/2 808SQ MI.

These volcanic islands, where nature is at its most generous, provide visitors with myriad contrasts: exuberant vegetation and desert landscapes; steep cliffs and seemingly endless beaches; and picturesque villages and bustling resorts. All this, coupled with a fantastic climate, has turned the "Fortunate Islands" into one of the world's leading destinations, particularly in winter.

Location

The Canary Islands lie slightly north of the Tropic of Cancer in the Atlantic, far nearer to Africa than to Spain. The seven islands together with six smaller islets cover 7 273 km2/2 808sq mi. **Las Palmas** province includes Gran Canaria, Fuerteventura and Lanzarote; **Santa Cruz de Tenerife** province consists of Tenerife, La Palma, La Gomera and El Hierro. The Canary Islands are an autonomous community, in which Santa Cruz de Tenerife and Las Palmas de Gran Canaria share the status of capital.

A Bit of History

Volcanic creation – The islands were thrust up from the Atlantic seabed by volcanic eruptions. La Gomera and Gran Canaria have a conic silhouette and most of the islands, except Fuerteventura and Lanzarote, are hilly and end in steep cliffs. Pico del Teide at 3 718m/12 195ft is the highest point in Spain, exceeding the average depth of the sea round the islands (3 000m/16 640 fathoms). La Palma rises to 2 426m/7 959ft. Lava, slag deserts and fields and cinder cones form what is known as the **malpaís** which is most extensive on Lanzarote.

The Fortunate Islands – The Canary Islands enjoy a mild climate because of trade winds and a cold ocean current. While El Teide is snow-capped for several months in the year, the coastal temperature rarely drops below 18°C/65°F. Rain is practically unknown

Vegetation on the main islands and on the south side of the smaller islands, protected from the wind *(sotavento)*, consists mainly of cactus *(cardón)* and **nopal** *(tunera)*. On the hilly north coasts, exposed to northeast trade winds *(barlovento)*, humidity sustains luxuriant vegetation (laurel and giant ericas) in rich volcanic soil. Water draining from the peaks is stored in huge cisterns. Banana plantations cover the

J. Malburet/ MICHELIN

Mount Teide (Tenerife)

Getting To The Canary Islands

BY PLANE

All the islands have an airport (Tenerife has two), offering easy, rapid access to the Spanish mainland and the rest of Europe, which is where most of the islands tourists come from. A number of inter-island routes also operate throughout the year. The two airports handling the greatest number of flights are Tenerife and Gran Canaria, whereas the airports at El Hierro and La Gomera offer scheduled flights on smaller planes between the different islands.

Iberia ☏902 400 500; www.iberia.com

Binter Canarias: Inter-island flights only. Contact Iberia for information and reservations.

Spanair ☏902 13 14 15; www.spanair.com (flights to Gran Canaria, Tenerife and Lanzarote).

Air Europa ☏902 40 15 01; www.air-europa.com (flights to Gran Canaria, Tenerife and Lanzarote).

By ferry – For those intending to visit the Canary Islands from mainland Spain, there is a two-day boat trip leaving from Cádiz and travelling to Santa Cruz de Tenerife and Las Palmas de Gran Canaria. There are also ferry, jet-foil and hydrofoil services to travel from one island to the other.

Trasmediterránea ☏902 45 46 45; www.trasmediterranea.es

TIME

Clock times on the Canary Islands are the same as Greenwich Mean Time (so one hour behind mainland Spain).

ACCOMMODATION

Refer to the Address Book section under each island.

Visitors must bear in mind that on these islands the **high season** runs from 1 November to 30 April. During this period tourists come here to enjoy the wonderful climate and forget their cold, continental winters and springs. The more touristy areas feature big hotels belonging to well-known hotel chains. It has become difficult for people to book rooms independently, as most of the hotels cater to clients on package tours sent by travel agents. On the two larger islands, the south coast boasts particularly pretty beaches and a very sunny climate. La Palma, El Hierro and La Gomera are perfect resorts for those seeking a quiet, secluded spot.

lowland in the north of Gran Canaria and Tenerife. The only native species to survive is the age-old **dragon tree** *(dracaena)*. Its sap was once used for medicinal purposes.

The Conquest – The first expedition worthy of the name was in 1402. The native population put up fierce resistance. After several years, **Jean de Bethencourt** and **Gadifer de la Salle** subdued only Lanzarote, Fuerteventura and, to a lesser degree, La Gomera and El Hierro. Spanish control was complete only at the end of the century.

The origin of the name "Canaries" remains obscure, although some think it derives from the Latin *canis* (dog), alluding to the large island dogs.

The Guanches – 15C explorers found a Stone Age people. The **Guanches** grew

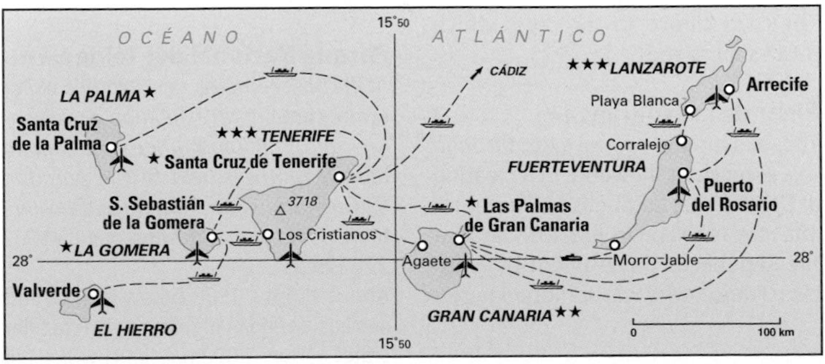

crops and kept cattle. They lived in caves, wore goats' skins and ate meal **(gofio)** made from grilled cereals, and cheese. They mummified their dead and sewed them in goat skins. They appeared somewhat Cro-Magnon, but included fair-skinned individuals. War, plague, famine and eruptions left few survivors.

Local cuisine – Canary Island gastronomy is renowned for *papas arrugadas* (wrinkled potatoes: tiny potatoes cooked in evaporating heavily salted water) and for sauces made with olive oil: *mojos verdes* (flavoured with coriander) or *mojos rojos* (flavoured with paprika). Fish is also popular. Two traditional dishes are *potaje* (vegetable stew) and *sancocho* (stewed grouper with bananas, potatoes and sauce). The islands are renowned for the variety and quality of their fruit.

TENERIFE★★★

POPULATION: 685 583.
2 036KM²/786SQ MI.

The snow-capped silhouette of El Teide, the highest peak in Spain, is the symbol of this beautiful island, literally "snow-covered mountain" in Guanche. The spectacular Las Cañadas crater witnesses Tenerife's volcanic past. A magnificent climate and stunning beauty attract those in search of sea, sand and sunshine as well as visitors who prefer to explore Tenerife's outstanding landscapes.

- **Information:** *Santa Cruz de Tenerife: Plaza de España, ☎922 23 95 92; Puerto de la Cruz: Plaza de Europa, ☎922 38 60 00.*
- **Orient Yourself:** Tenerife is the largest of the Canary Islands.
- Kids **Especially for Kids:** Water and wildlife parks are special attractions for younger visitors.

Special Features

PICO DEL TEIDE★★★

Clouds often enshroud Mount Teide and the superb panoramas from its viewpoints.

Ensure that you have comfortable footwear and a warm jacket. Temperature and weather can change dramatically in a short time.

La Esperanza Approach★

The road climbs to the crest which divides the island.

Pinar de la Esperanza★

The road runs for several miles through this extensive pinewood. In a clearing at **Las Raíces**, an obelisk commemorates the rebellion in July 1936 against the Republican government by Francisco Franco, who was stationed here.

Belvederes★★

When the cloud disperses, admire the stark contrast between the lush north coast and the aridity of the Güimar Valley from roadside belvederes.

After La Crucita, the road enters a high-mountain landscape. The Astronomical Observatory at Izaña is visible *(left)*.

El Portillo

Alt 2 030m/6 660ft. The pass is the gateway to the extraordinary mineral world of Las Cañadas.

Parque Nacional del Teide★★★

At the park entrance, the El Portillo visitor centre contains an exhibition on volcanism, and trail information; the Cañada Blanca centre is next to the parador. Open 9am-4pm. Guided walking tours (2hr) by prior arrangement. ☎922 29 01 29/83.

About 350m/1 150ft below the summit lies Las Cañadas plateau, a spectacular crater at over 2 000m/6 560ft which fell

Address Book

For coin ranges, see the Legend on the cover flap.

WHERE TO EAT

Régulo – *San Felipe 16 – Puerto de la Cruz – ☎922 38 45 06 – www.restauranteregulo.com – Closed Sun, lunchtime Mon and in Jul.* This traditional island house retains all its charm, with a lovely patio and dining areas on two floor. Antiques and plants are prominent in the decor.

Casa del Vino La Baranda – *San Simón 49, La Baranda. El Sauzal – 21km/13mi from Santa Cruz de Tenerife along the Autopista del Norte – ☎ 922 56 38 86 – Closed Mon.* This 17C hacienda is used by the Tenerife council to promote fine island wines. It houses the Wine Museum, a tasting room and shop, as well as the restaurant and tavern where you can try island nouvelle cuisine based on traditional recipes.

El Bacalao de la Cazuela – *General Goded 11 – Santa Cruz de Tenerife – ☎922 29 32 49 – Closed Sat at lunch, Sun and two weeks in Jul and Oct –* . Although its location near the bullring is a little away from the main centre and the menu slightly limited, this cheery restaurant is worth a visit for its high-quality cuisine, excellent daily specials and good wine list. A good balance between traditional meat and fish dishes, enlivened by the occasional modern flourish.

WHERE TO STAY

Hotel Monopol – *Quintana 15 – Puerto de la Cruz – ☎922 38 46 11 – www.monopoltf.com – 92 rooms – – Restaurant 12 €.* This attractive four-storey whitewashed building adorned with wooden balconies stands in a pedestrianised street in a lively shopping district near the seafront. Comfortable rooms, arranged around a Canarian-style patio.

Hotel Aguere – *Obispo Rey Redondo (Calle Carrera) 55 – La Laguna – ☎922 25 94 90 – 21 rooms –* . One of the few hotels on the island to retain its seigniorial charm. The wooden door provides access to a large, patio-style open hall area around which are all the rooms. The wooden floors, antique furniture and somewhat antiquated bathrooms provide further old-world charm. Highly recommended.

EXPENSIVE

Hotel San Roque – *Esteban de Ponte 32 – Garachico – ☎922 13 34 35 – www.hotelsanroque.com – – 20 rooms –* . This luxury hotel is tucked away in a street in the centre of Garachico. The entrance patio, painted in a warm Pompeii red and adorned with a wooden balcony, sets the tonel, a fusion of old and contemporary, and traditional and Avant Garde design. The rooms, some of which are split-level, are both spacious and comfortable.

J. Malburet/ MICHELIN

Parque Nacional del Teide, Mount Teide

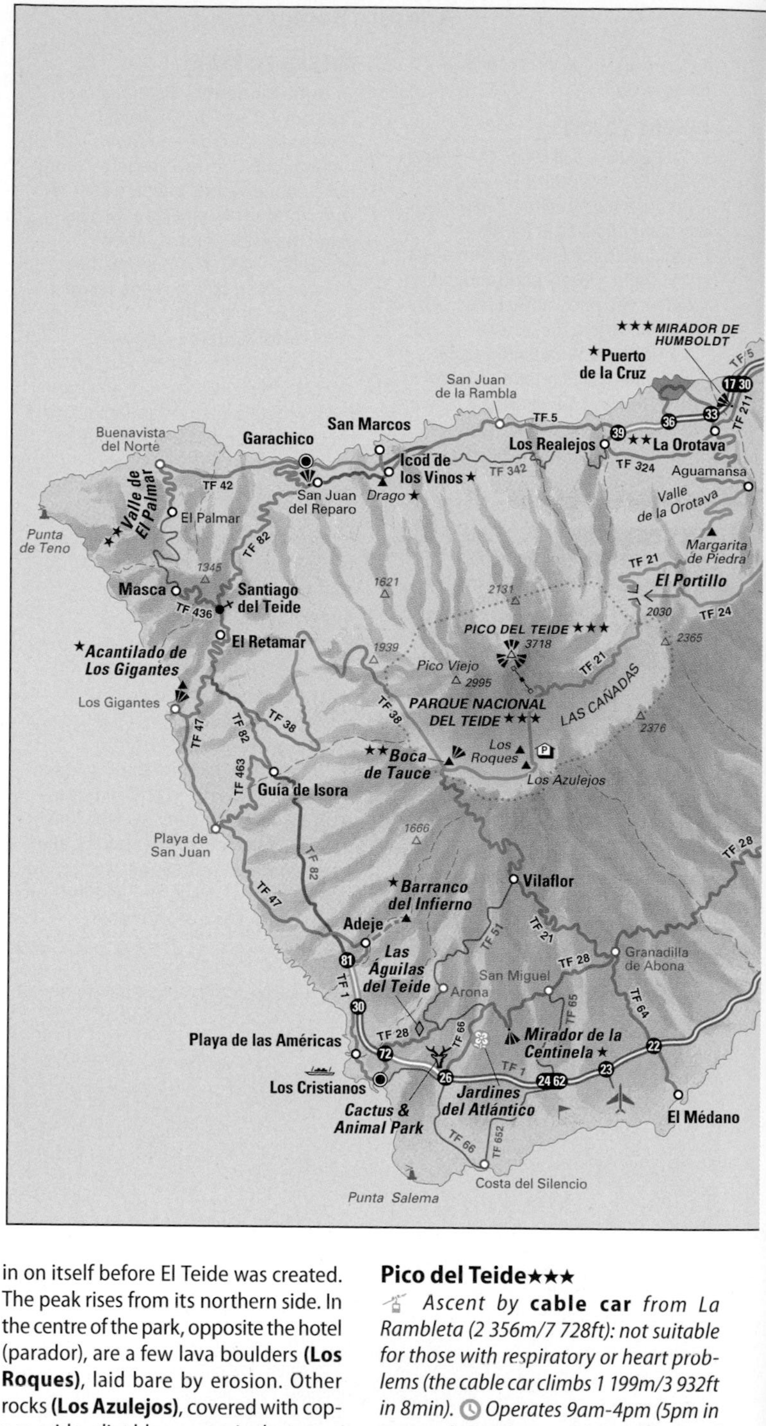

in on itself before El Teide was created. The peak rises from its northern side. In the centre of the park, opposite the hotel (parador), are a few lava boulders **(Los Roques)**, laid bare by erosion. Other rocks **(Los Azulejos)**, covered with copper oxide, glint blue-green in the sun.

Pico del Teide★★★

Ascent by **cable car** *from La Rambleta (2 356m/7 728ft): not suitable for those with respiratory or heart problems (the cable car climbs 1 199m/3 932ft in 8min). Operates 9am-4pm (5pm in summer), weather permitting. Closed*

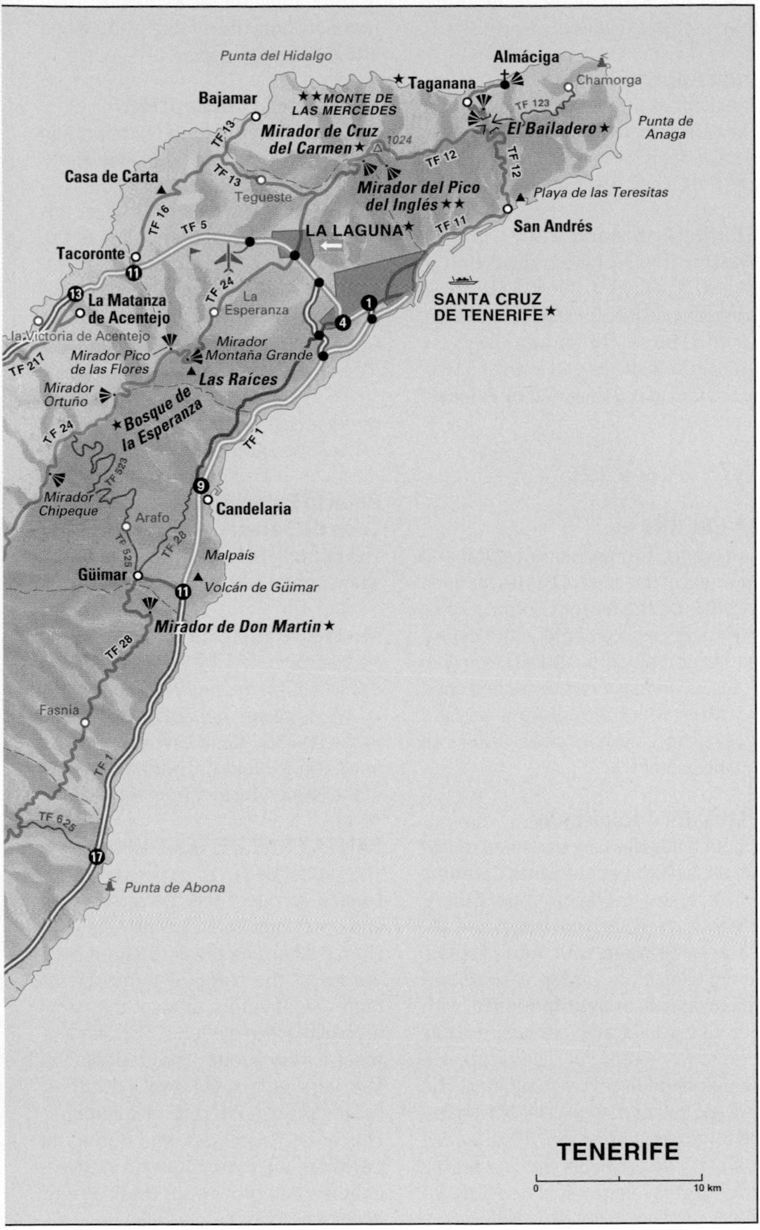

1 Jan and 25 Dec. 20 € round trip. 922 53 37 20.

From the top (3 555m/11 660ft), a steep 30min walk across scree leads to the summit (*the path is currently closed*). The crater at the summit is almost 25m/82ft deep and 50m/164ft across, swathed in wisps of sulphurous smoke. On a clear day, the view covers the whole Canaries archipelago.

La Orotava Approach★

The vegetation on the north coast (bananas, fruit trees and vines) is visible during the climb. Pinewoods begin in **Aguamansa**. Beyond the village at the side of the road, a huge basalt formation resembles a daisy.

Guía Approach

The climb via Guía is more mountainous. The narrow road crosses two defiles, Las Narices del Teide (last eruption in 1798) and the Chinyero volcano (1909).

Vilaflor Approach

Vilaflor is the highest town on the island (1 466m/4 806ft). The road crosses a beautiful pinewood and then, at the **Boca de Tauce pass**★★ (2 055m/6 742ft), reveals a striking view of Las Cañadas dominated by El Teide.

Worth a Visit

LA LAGUNA★

La Laguna, former island capital and now seat of the university, was founded in 1496. On the feast of Corpus Christi the streets are carpeted with flowers; on 14 September the Crucifix from San Francisco monastery is venerated amid festivities which include Canary Island wrestling, which goes back to Guanche times.

Plaza del Adelantado

Fronting this pleasant, tree-lined square are the old **Convent of Santa Catalina**, which retains its original upper gallery, a feature rarely seen nowadays; the 17C **Palacio de Nava** with stone façade, reminiscent of the bishop's palace, and the town hall, or **ayuntamiento**, with neo-Classical façade *(entrance on calle Obispo Rey Redondo)*. The latter is a combination of several buildings. The 16C and 18C portals on calle Obispo Rey Redondo are impressive *(guided tours (45min), 8am-3pm (2pm Jul-Sep) by prior arrangement; closed Sat-Sun and public hols; ☎922 63 11 94)*.

Follow calle Obispo Rey Redondo.

Catedral

Closed for restoration. ☎922 25 89 39.
The elegant neo-Classical façade was erected in 1819; the nave and four aisles were rebuilt in neo-Gothic style in 1905. In the Capilla de los Remedios *(right transept)*, note the retable, a 16C Virgin and 17C Flemish panels.

Iglesia de la Concepción★

Open 8.30am-7.30pm (7pm Sat); Sun 7.30am-8pm. No visits during religious services. 0.60 €. ☎922 25 91 30.
A 17C grey stone tower rises over this 16C church, typical of the time of the conquest. The interior retains several Mudéjar ceilings, a ceiling with Portuguese influence, a Baroque pulpit and choir stalls, and a beaten silver altar *(Capilla del Santísimo)*.

Take calle Belén, then head down calle San Agustín.

Palacio Episcopal or Antigua Casa de Salazar

The bishop's palace has a beautiful 17C stone façade and attractive patio.

Museo de Historia de Tenerife

Open 9am-7pm. Closed Mon, 1 and 6 Jan, Carnival Tue, and 24-25 and 31 Dec. 3 €, no charge Sun. ☎922 82 59 49.
In the late-16C **Casa Lercano**, with its fine patio, exhibits provide an overview of the island's history from the 15C.

SANTA CRUZ DE TENERIFE★

The capital began as a port serving La Laguna. An oil refinery, tobacco factory and other industries operate here.
From the harbour breakwater there is a **view**★ of the stepped semicircle of high-rise buildings against the backdrop of the Pico del Teide. The Guimera theatre, new auditorium (designed by Santiago Calatrava) and exhibition buildings witness a cultural tradition.
This quiet town goes wild during its **Carnival**, the most colourful in Spain. Children and grown-ups dress up and join the mounted procession.

Iglesia de la Concepción

A few houses with balconies around the 16C-18C church (fine Baroque retables) are all that remains of the old city.

SANTA CRUZ DE TENERIFE

Alférez Provisional Pl.	CY	3	Doctor Guigou	CX	12	Imeldo Seris	CY	31
Bethencourt Alfonso	CY	5	Doctor José Naveiras	CX	13	José Murphy	CY	34
Bravo Murillo Av. de	DY	6	Domínguez Alfonso	CY	15	Numancia	BX	39
Candelaria Pl. de la	DY	8	General Galcerán Puente	BY	19	Pérez Galdós	CY	43
Castillo	CY		General Gutiérrez	DY	20	Saludo	DX	46
Costa y Grijalba	BY	10	General O'Donnell	BX	23	San Francisco Pl.	DY	49
			General Serrador Puente	CY	24	San Isidro	DX	50
			General Weyler Pl. del	BY	26	Santo Domingo Pl.	CY	51
			Iglesia Pl. de la	DY	30	Valentín Sanz	CY	53

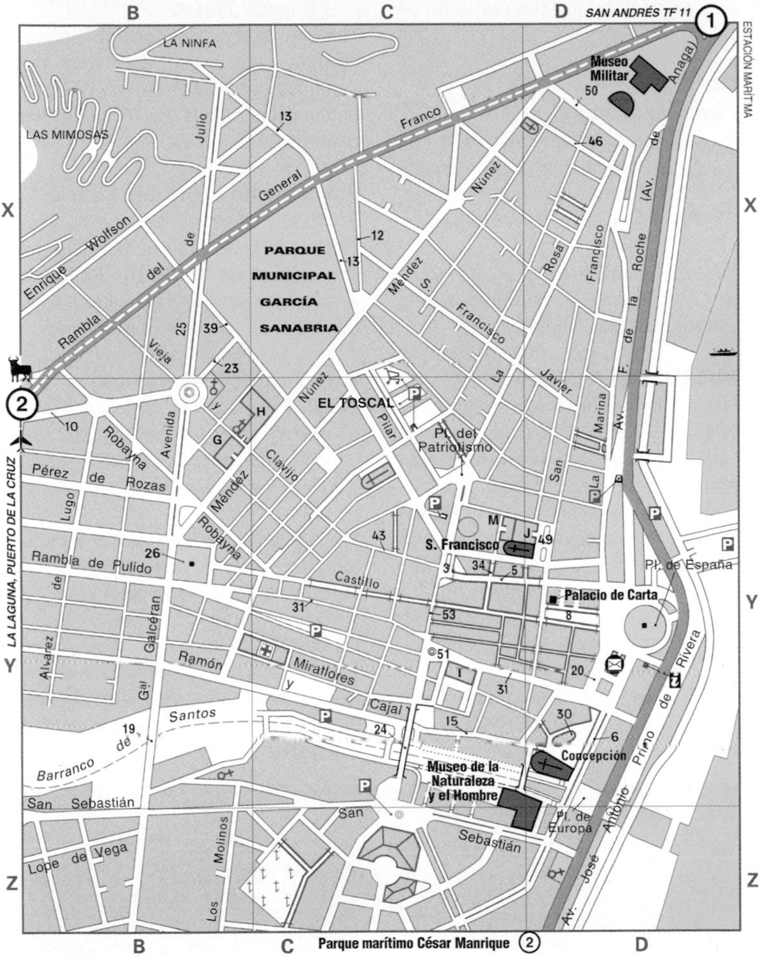

Museo de la Naturaleza y el Hombre★ (Museum of Nature and Man)

Open 9am-7pm. Closed Mon, 1 and 6 Jan, Carnival Tuesday and 24-25 and 31 Dec. 3 €, no charge Sun. 922 53 58 16.

In the ex-Hospital Civil, a large neo-Classical building, are archaeology and natural science collections.

Palacio de Carta

This 18C palace on plaza de la Candelaria, now a bank, retains its delightful wooden arches, galleries and patio.

Iglesia de San Francisco

The 17C-18C church displays the characteristics of Canary Island churches from this period: naves with wooden roofs and cylindrical pillars.

Parque Municipal García Sanabria★

This alluring tropical and Mediterranean garden is close to La Rambia, a landscaped boulevard.

Museo Militar

Nelson lost both the battle and his right arm when attacking the castle on 24 July 1797.

Parque Marítimo César Manrique★

Leave by ② on the town plan. Kids *Open 10am-7pm. Last admission 1 hr before closing. 2.50 € (children 3-10 1.20 €). ☎922 20 29 95.*

This seaside water park, designed by artist César Manrique, combines water, volcanic rock and vegetation.

PUERTO DE LA CRUZ★

Pico del Teide looks down on high-rise buildings proliferating along the rock-strewn coast. A lively **seafront promenade**★ is the main attraction of Tenerife's premier resort. In the old town (between the plazas de la Iglesia and del Charco) are 17C and 18C balconied houses and attractive churches.

Lago Martiánez★ (Martiánez Lake)

Kids *Open 10am-7.30pm. Last entry at 5pm. 3.30 €. ☎922 38 59 55 or 922 37 13 21.*

This seaside pool complex is surrounded by vegetation and volcanic rock.

Jardín de Aclimatación de la Orotava★★

Follow signs to Jardín Botánico. Open 9am-6pm (7pm Apr-Sep). Closed 1 Jan, Good Fri and 25 Dec. 3 €. ☎922 38 35 72.

The botanical garden, on 2ha/5 acres, contain trees and flowers from the Canary Islands and elsewhere. The garden was created in the 18C. A rubber plant is 200 years old,

Playa Jardín★ (Garden Beach)

To the W; follow signposts. This black-sand beach is surrounded by gardens. The **Castillo de San Felipe**, a watchtower now used for cultural functions, can be seen at its eastern end.

Loro Parque (Parrot Park)

W of Playa Jardín; well signposted. Kids *Open 8.30am-6.45pm; last admission at 4pm. 29 €(children 6-11 19 €. ☎922 37 38 41.*

This garden has a collection of animals (gorillas, monkeys, crocodiles etc) and performing parrots and dolphins.

LA OROTAVA★★

This ancient town is arranged in terraces at the foot of the mountain and boasts beautiful balconied mansions and festivals following Corpus Christi.

J. Malburet/ MICHELIN

La Orotava, with a Dragon Tree in the Foreground

Park in plaza de la Constitución and continue on foot.

Plaza de la Constitución
The square is fronted by the 17C Baroque church of San Agustín and the Liceo Taoro cultural centre.

Follow calle Carrera, then descend the street to the right.

Iglesia de la Concepción
Open 9am-1pm and 4-8pm; Sun and public hols, 10am-1pm. Closed Wed afternoon. 922 33 01 87.
The 18C church has a graceful Baroque façade. Visit the treasury.

Return to calle Carrera.

Calle Carrera
Pass the **plaza del Ayuntamiento**, with its neo-Classical Palacio Municipal. The **Hijuela del Jardín Botánico** behind it, a lush park, was a nursery for the botanical gardens in Puerto de la Cruz (*open 9am-2pm; closed Sat-Sun and public hols; 922 38 35 72*).

Calle de San Francisco★
This street is adorned with some of the town's most beautiful balconies.

La Casa de los Balcones
In these two 17C houses (n° 3 and 5), with delightful patios, are a craftwork shop and a small **Museo** which shows the inside of a local bourgeois house (*open 8.30am-7.30pm (1.30pm Sun); 1.50 € (museum); 922 33 06 29*).

La Casa Molina
This 16C-17C Renaissance-style house with craft shop offers a fine view.

Return to calle Carrera, then follow calle Tomás Zerolo to the left.

Museo de Artesanía Iberoamericana
Open 9am-5pm; Sat, 9am-2pm. Closed Sun and public hols. 2 €. 922 32 33 76.
The museum in the ex-Convento de Santo Domingo (17C) displays Spanish and Latin-American handicrafts, including musical instruments and textiles.

Excursions

MONTE DE LAS MERCEDES★★
Round trip of 49km/30mi from La Laguna. Allow 3hr
The Anaga headland traps clouds from the north; tree laurel, giant heather and *fayas*, a local species, flourish.

Mirador de Cruz del Carmen★
See the La Laguna Valley from this viewpoint in Parque Rural de Anaga. Visitor centre (*open 9.30am-3pm (4pm in winter); 922 82 20 56*).

J. Malburet/ MICHELIN

Anaga Mountains

Mirador del Pico del Inglés★★
An impressive panorama spreads from the 1 024m/3 360ft peak of the Anaga headland to distant Pico del Teide.

El Bailadero★
The road crossing this pass commands good views in both directions.

Taganana★
On the way down are magnificent **views**★★. Visit the **Iglesia parroquial de Nuestra Señora de Las Nieves** for its Hispano-Flemish altarpiece (*open 10 am-7pm; no visits during religious services; 922 59 00 75).*

TOUR OF THE ISLAND
310km/194mi – about 3 days

The first section runs along the north coast (La Laguna-Garachico, 100km/62mi); the second along the west coast (Garachico-Los Cristianos, 77km/48mi); the third to the south and west, ending in Santa Cruz de Tenerife (133km/83mi).

Bajamar
Large resort on a picturesque stretch of rocky coast with natural pools.

Casa de Carta
Open 9am-7pm. Closed Mon, 1 and 6 Jan, Carnival Tue, and 24- 25 and 31
Masca
Road in poor repair. Remote hamlet in lovely **countryside**★.

Follow driving tour map for a lovely tour to Acantilado de Los Gigantes.

Acantilado de Los Gigantes★
The Teno mountain range ends in black cliffs called Los Gigantes, "the giants", for their 400m/1 300ft vertical drop.

Adeje
Within walking distance of the village *(2km/1.2mi E)* lies the enormous Hell Canyon, **Barranco del Infierno**★**.**

Playa de las Américas
A large resort with beaches of black sand. Past it is **Los Cristianos**, another busy resort.

Parque Ecológico de Las Águilas del Teide
3km/2mi on the Los Cristianos-Arona road.
Kids Open 10am-6pm. 19 €. 922 72 90 10.
This wildlife park offers bird shows.

Cactus and Animal Park
Motorway exit 26 (Guaza), then take the road to the left. Kids Open 10am-6pm (8pm in summer). 15 € (children 6-14 9€). 922 79 54 24.
The park contains a small animal area and an interesting reptilarium.

Jardines del Atlántico
4km/2.5mi on the Guaza-Valle de San Lorenzo road; the turn-off is indicated to the right. Open 9am-5.30pm. Guided tours (recommended) at 10am, 11.30am, 1pm and 3.30pm. Closed 1 Jan and 25 Dec. 10 €. 922 72 04 03.
The garden provides an introduction to the indigenous flora and traditional agricultural practices of the island.

Follow the TF 82 in the Valle de San Lorenzo.

Mirador de la Centinela★
Like a sentinel, the viewpoint on a rocky projection commands a vast area.

El Médano
One of the best on the island for windsurfing, its beach lies in the shelter of an eroded volcanic cone.

Return to the inland road.

Mirador de Don Martín★
The belvedere provides a view of the Güimar rift valley and its plantations.

Güimar
A major town on the south coast.

Candelaria
This coastal town is a well-known place of pilgrimage. Its **basilica** houses a statue of the Virgin to which islanders make a pilgrimage on 14 and 15 August.

GRAN CANARIA★★

POPULATION: 715 994.
560KM2/602SQ MI.

Diverse landscapes make Gran Canaria a continent in miniature. Almost half of its area is a UNESCO Biosphere Reserve. From the Pozo de las Nieves (1 949m/ 6 393ft) at its centre, ravines fan out in all directions. The mountain barrier divides the wetter landscapes of the north and west from extensive semi-desert-like areas in the south. The north and west coast is steep and rocky; on the accessible south coast are long golden sand beaches and major resorts.

- **Information:** *Las Palmas: León y Castillo 17, ☎928 21 96 00; Maspalomas: Avenida de España 1, ☎928 76 84 09; Plaza de la Constitución 1, ☎928 72 34 44.*
- **Orient Yourself:** Gran Canaria, third largest Canary island, is wedged between Tenerife and Fuerteventura.

Worth a Visit

Las Palmas de Gran Canaria★

Las Palmas de Gran Canaria, founded in a palm grove in 1478, is one of Spain's major ports, extending nearly 10km/6mi between a ravine and the Isleta Peninsula *(N)*, a natural breakwater.
The old city, **Vegueta**, dates from the conquest; **Puerto de la Luz**, and **Las Palmas**, comprise the tourist district, flanked by the harbour and Alcaravaneras beach on the east and Canteras beach on the west; between them lies residential **Ciudad Jardín.**

Vegueta – Triana★

2hr – see plan of old city
These two districts form the historic centre of Las Palmas.

Address Book

WHERE TO EAT

Mesón de la Montaña – *La montaña de Arucas – ☎ 928 60 14 75 – www.mesonarucas.com –* . Despite informal service, this restaurant represents good value. A recommended address for traditional Canarian cuisine served at large round tables in a pleasant location offering good views.

Casa de Galicia – *Salvador Cuyás 8 – Las Palmas de Gran Canaria – ☎ 928 27 98 55 –* . High-quality Galician cuisine where the emphasis is on freshness. A good position between the Playa de las Canteras and the Parque de Santa Catalina. The same owners run restaurant next door.

WHERE TO STAY

Hotel Rural Casa de Los Camellos – *Progreso 12 (on the corner of Retama) – Agüimes – ☎928 78 50 03 – www.hecansa.com – 11 rooms –* . This small hotel, in the old part of Agüimes, has been restored in a welcoming, rustic style, with wooden floors and furniture, and pleasant, attractive bedrooms. The hotel also has two patios and a good restaurant, El Oroval.

Hotel Rural El Refugio – *Cruz de Tejeda – Cruz de Tejeda – ☎928 66 65 13 – www.hotelruralelrefugio.com – P – 10 rooms –* 4.50 €. The somewhat difficult access to this small country hotel is rewarded by its extraordinary setting in an area of lush vegetation near the Roque de Nublo and Roque de Bentayga. An excellent base for excursions through the centre of the island. Cosy bedrooms with wooden floors and attractive furniture.

Tenesoya – *Sagasta, 98 – Las Palmas de Gran Canaria – ☎ 928 46 96 08 – 42 rooms –* *5 €* The best part of this hotel is its value. It's just a step from the beach and offers comfortable rooms with updated, well-equipped bathrooms.

Puerto de la Luz

The port of Las Palmas de Gran Canaria is the engine behind the city's development and is one of the largest in Spain. Its privileged position on the transatlantic routes between Europe, Africa and America has resulted in the development of an international port with a high volume of passenger and goods traffic. It is also one of the largest fishing ports in the region due to its proximity to the fishing grounds off the African coast, and the leading distribution centre for goods in the Canary Islands. The port area also includes a large naval repair centre.

Plaza de Santa Ana

The palm-bordered square is overlooked by the town hall (1842) on one side, and the cathedral on the other. To the side are the Bishop's Palace (Palacio Episcopal, 17C), with an *alfiz*-decorated portal showing clear Mudéjar influence, the Renaissance-style Casa del Regente and the Archivo Histórico Provincial (archives). During the Corpus Christi procession, the square is carpeted with flowers, sawdust and salt.

Catedral – *Open 8-10am; Sat, 6.30-8pm; Sun and public hols, 8am-2pm and 6.30-8pm. 2 €. 928 31 49 89.*

The cathedral, begun in the early 16C was not completed until the 19C. It has three elegant aisles with tierceron vaulting. In the transept are statues by Canarian sculptor **José Luján Pérez** (1756-1815).

Museo Diocesano de Arte Sacro

Entrance in calle Espíritu Santo. Open 10am-4pm; Sat, 10am-1.30pm. Closed Sun and public hols. 2.40 €. 928 31 49 89.

The museum of sacred art, in buildings around the 16C Patio de los Naranjos, contains 16C-19C engravings and gold and silverwork. In the chapter house is a mosaic from Manises (Valencia).

Casa de Colón★

Entrance in calle Colón. Open 9am-7pm; Sat, 9am-3pm. Closed Sun and public hols, 22 May and 24 and 31 Dec. 928 31 23 84.

The palace of the island's first governors, where Columbus stayed in 1502, houses a museum. Maps and instruments evoke Columbus' expeditions. Note the fine *artesonado* ceilings. On the upper floor are 16C-19C paintings.

The **Iglesia de San Antonio Abad,** on the site where Columbus attended Mass, has a fine Baroque interior.

Centro Atlántico de Arte Moderno

Open 10am-9pm; Sun, 10am-2pm. Closed Mon and public hols. 902 31 18 24.

Along **calle de los Balcones** in one of several 18C buildings with fine doorways is this art centre, renovated by the architect Sáenz de Oíza, with works by 20C artists from the Canary Islands, the Spanish mainland and abroad.

Museo Canario★

Open 10am-8pm; Sat-Sun and public hols, 10am-2pm. Closed 1 Jan and 25 Dec. 3 €. 928 33 68 00.

This museum displays a collection of artefacts from pre-Hispanic culture, including mummies, idols and skins. Particularly interesting are the collection of terracotta seals *(pintaderas)* found only on Gran Canaria, whose purpose remains a mystery, Cro-Magnon remains and a re-creation of the cave, Cueva Pintada, in Gáldar.

Two picturesque squares, **plaza del Espíritu Santo** and **plaza de Santo Domingo,** are worth visiting.

Casa-Museo Pérez Galdós

Closed for renovation. 928 37 37 45.

Manuscripts, photographs and objects belonging to Pérez Galdós (1843-1920) are displayed in the house where the writer was born.

Parque de San Telmo

Calle Mayor de Triana, leading from this park, is the main street in the old town. The small **Iglesia de San Bernardo** is full of character with its Baroque altars and paintings. An unusual Modernist kiosk stands in a corner of the park.

LAS PALMAS DE GRAN CANARIA

Alfonso XII	AU	2
Ansite Av.	AT	4
Cornisa Pas.	AT	12
Doctor Marañón	AU	14
Don Benito Pl. de	AU	17
Fernando Guanarteme	AS	20
Ingeniero Léon y Castillo Pl.	AU	28
Juan Rejón	AS	36
Juan XXIII Av.	AT	37
Léon y Castillo	AT	40
Lugo Pas. de	AT	44
Luis Correa Medina	AU	46
M. González Martin	AT	49
Marítima del Sur Av.	AU	52
Mata Carret. de	AU	53
La Naval	AS	
Ortiz de Zàrate	AT	59
Pérez Muñoz	AS	63
Pino Apolinario	AU	65
Pío XII	AT	66
San José Pas.	AU	76
Secretario Padilla	AT	80
Simancas	AT	81
Tecen	AS	83
Tomás Morales Pas.	ATU	85
Zaragoza	AU	90

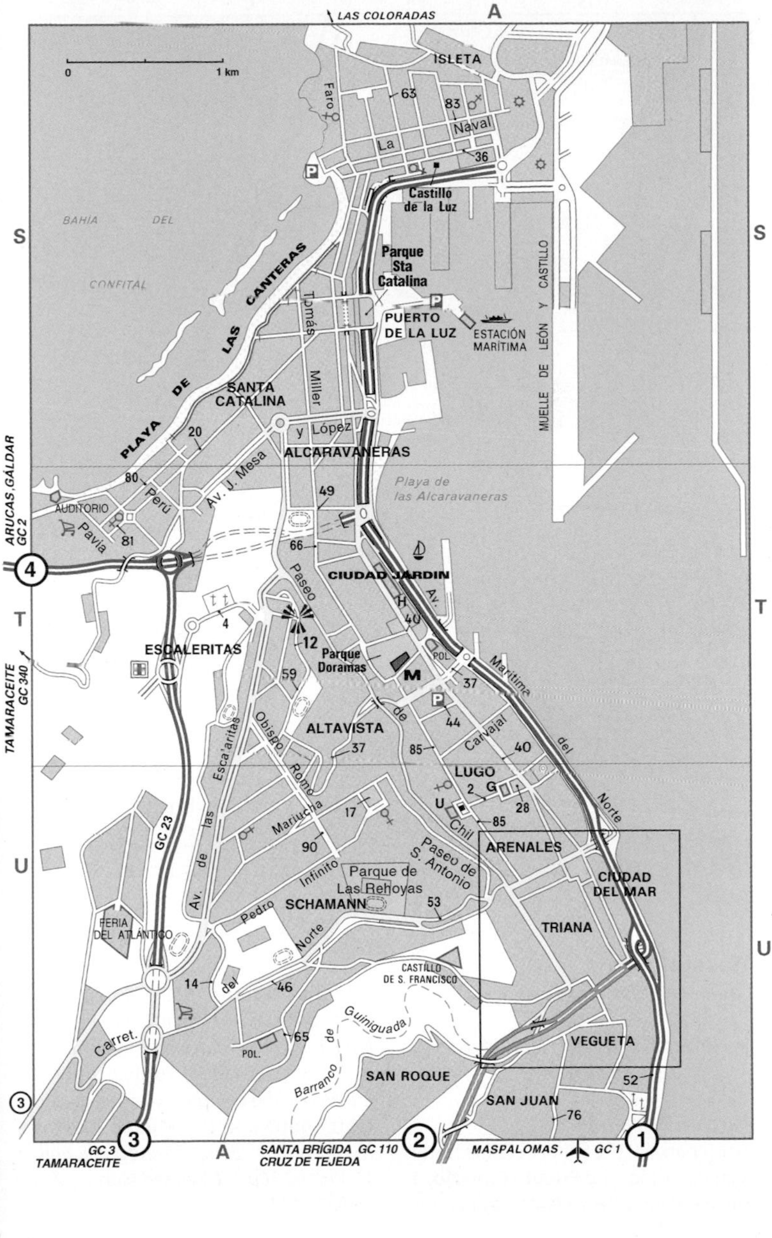

VEGUETA, TRIANA

			Juan E. Doreste	CZ	33	Pérez Galdós	BY	62
			López Botas	CZ	41	Ramón y Cajal	BZ	69
Balcones de los	CZ	5	Luis Millares	CZ	47	San Antonio Pas.	BY	73
Cano	CY	8	Malteses	CZ	50	San Pedro	CZ	78
Doctor Chil	CZ	13	Mayor de Triana	CY		T. Massieu	CZ	84
Domingo J. Navarro	BY	16	Ntra Sra del Pino Pl.	BY	56	Viera Y Clavijo	BY	88
General Bravo	BY	23	Obispo Codina	CZ	57			
General Mola	CZ	24	Las Palmas Muelle de	CY	38			
Juan de Quesada	CZ	31	Pelota	CZ	60			

Centro Atlántico de Arte Moderno (CAAM)	CZ	E	Museo Diocesano de Arte Sacro	CZ	M^1

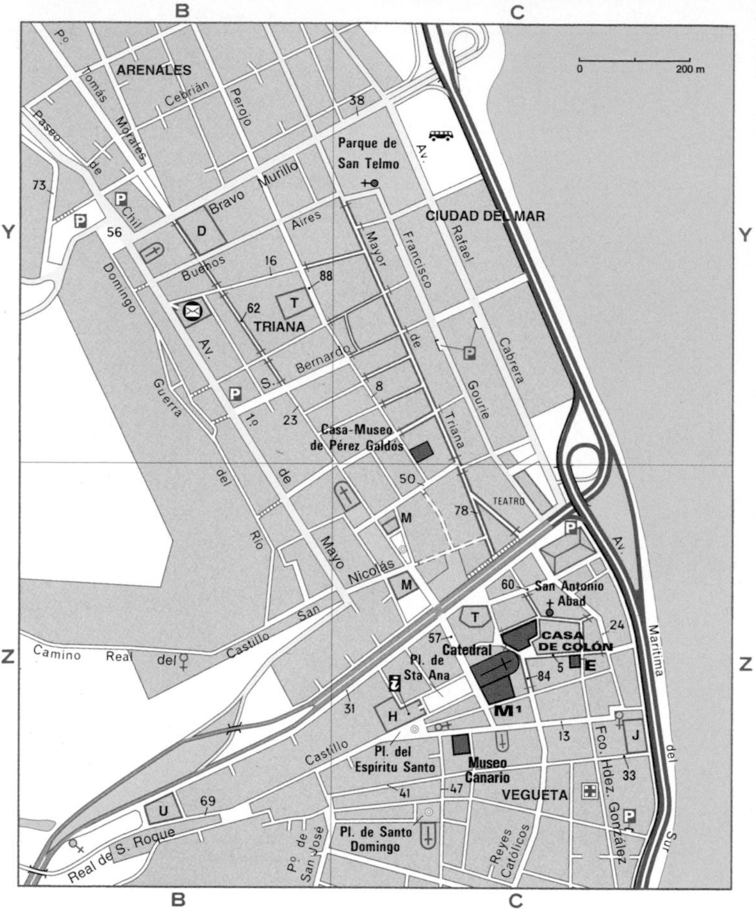

Modern Town

2hr – see plan of city

Drive along avenida Marítima del Norte, skirting the town.

Parque Doramas

In this park are the Santa Catalina Hotel with its casino, and **Pueblo Canario**, a Canary Island village created by painter Néstor de la Torre (1888-1938, *open 10am-8pm; Sun, 10.30am-2.30pm; closed Mon, 1 Jan, Holy Thu, Good Fri and 25 Dec; 2€; 928 24 51 35)*. Folklore festivals are held in the complex, which includes craft shops and the **Museo Néstor** (*open 10am-8pm; Sun and public hols, 11.30am-2.30pm; closed Mon; 2€; 928 24 51 35)*.

Christopher Columbus

It is often maintained that, but for the Canary Islands, Columbus (1451-1506) would never have reached America. His persistence in trying to convince the sovereigns of Portugal, England, France and Castile of the existence of a westerly passage to Asia is well known. Eventually their Catholic Majesties of Castile provided three ships – the *Niña*, the *Pinta* and the *Santa María* – for an expedition to the Indies. He set sail westward from Palos in August 1492 but was forced to put into Las Palmas and La Gomera for repairs to the *Pinta*. On 12 October 1492 he spied land and set foot for the first time on the American continent – on the Caribbean Island of San Salvador. On each of his three subsequent voyages he landed at Las Palmas de Gran Canaria or on La Gomera before going on to discover the other islands of the Antilles (1493), the Orinoco delta (1498) and the shores of Honduras (1502).

Parque Santa Catalina

The park, in **Puerto de la Luz**, includes the Museo de la Ciencia (science museum) and the Miller cultural centre. Nearby streets are lined with restaurants and bars. Bazaars sell electronics at duty-reduced prices.

Playa de las Canteras★

This superb 3.5km/2.2mi beach is sheltered by a line of rocks offshore and backed by a pleasant promenade with restaurants and cafés. At its southeastern end, the **Auditorio Alfredo Kraus**, hosts an opera season. It is the site of the Canaries Music Festival.

Castillo de la Luz

Closed for restoration. ☎928 44 66 23.
The 15C fort is an exhibition locale.

Paseo Cornisa

This avenue in modern Escaleritas provides a fine **panorama**★ of Puerto de la Luz and La Isleta.

Excursions

THE NORTH COAST

From Las Palmas to La Aldea de San Nicolás – *128km/79mi – allow 1 day.*

▸ *Leave Las Palmas on the GC 2, on the plan. Take exit 8.*

Arucas

Arucas is the third largest town on the island. A narrow road leads up **Montaña de Arucas,** shaped like a sugar loaf, offering a **panorama**★ to Las Palmas de Gran Canaria. The black-rock church below stands out against white houses.

▸ *Take the C 813. At Buenlugar, 6km/4mi beyond Arucas, turn left.*

Firgas

This is the source of a popular sparkling mineral water. The paseo de Gran Canaria pays a picturesque homage to the island's communities.

▸ *Return to the main road.*

Los Tilos de Moya

Los Tilos is a protected area with a wood of wild laurel trees.

▸ *At Guía, turn right to join C 810. Head toward Las Palmas for a few metres, then turn off to Cenobio de Valerón.*

Cenobio de Valerón★

Closed for repairs. ☎928 21 94 21.
Tradition has it that native girls were prepared in caves hollowed out of tufa for their role as Sacred Virgins. In fact, these were a granary. Above, chiefs met in council (Tagoror).

▸ *Return to the C 810 and head towards Gáldar.*

Gáldar

At the foot of Mount Gáldar the Guanche king held his court *(guanarteme)*. Outside the heritage centre is the **Cueva Pintada**, a cave with **mural paintings**★.

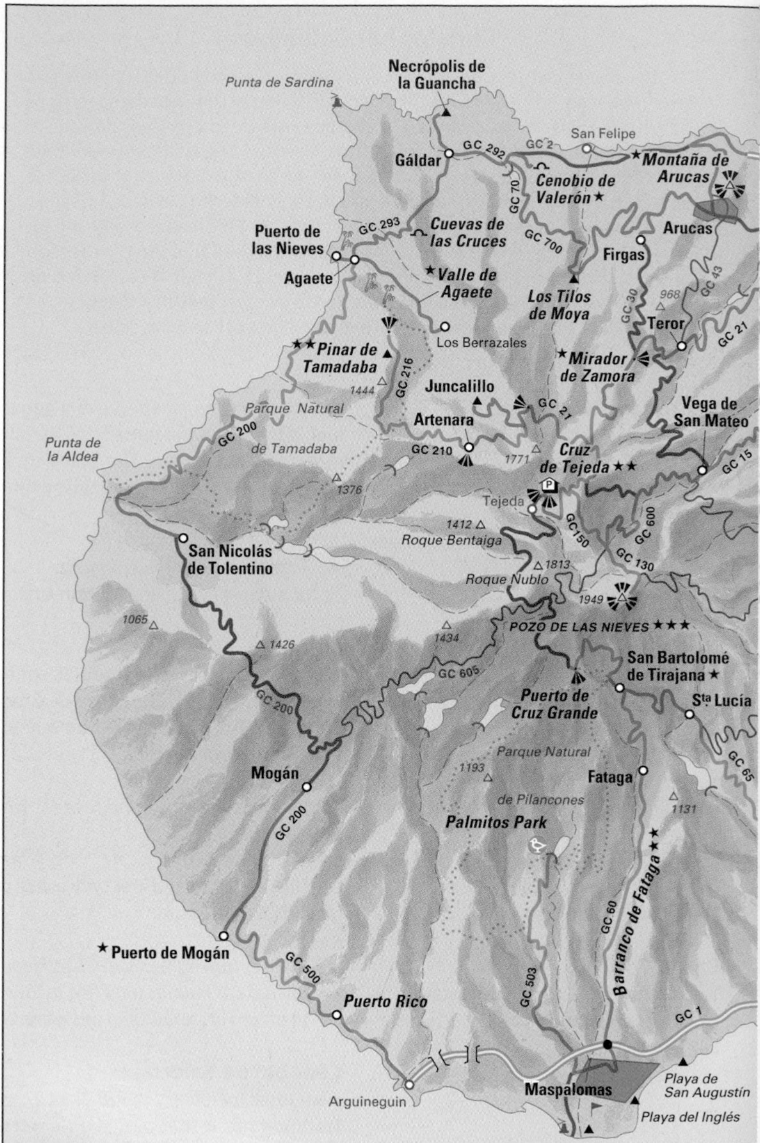

Guanche objects are displayed (*open by appointment, 6€, 928 89 57 46).*

Necrópolis de la Guancha

2km/1.2mi N of Gáldar on coast. *For information, telephone 928 21 94 21.* Excavations have brought to light a Guanche settlement and a necropolis of circular constructions of great blocks of lava and a large burial mound.

Return to Gáldar; take the C 810 S.

Cuevas de las Cruces

Halfway between Gáldar and Agaete. These are attractive caves in the tufa.

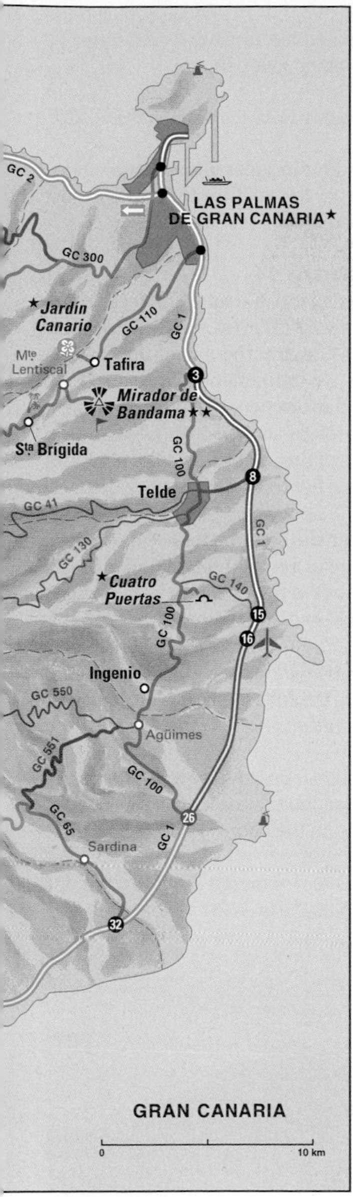

Agaete
In this charming white-walled village is an important burial site, being readied for visitors. On 4 August the village celebrates the **Fiesta de la Rama**, one of the island's most popular festivals.

Los Berrazales road★
SE of Agaete. The road parallels the **Agaete Valley★,** which is sheltered by mountains and covered in vegetation.

Puerto de las Nieves
W of Agaete. This little fishing harbour once shipped bananas. From the quay there is a good view of what remains of the **Finger of God** *(Dedo de Dios)*, a pointed rock mauled by a storm.
The hermitage **(ermita)** contains an interesting 15C Flemish triptych by Joos van Clave *(visits by prior arrangement; 928 55 43 82).*

La Aldea de San Nicolás
A spectacular road follows cliffs and crosses several ravines to La Aldea de San Nicolás, a village in a fertile basin growing sugar cane and tomatoes.

THE CENTRE OF THE ISLAND

156km/97mi – allow 1 day.

▶ *Leave Las Palmas de Gran Canaria on the C 811, ② on the plan*

Tafira
A holiday resort favoured by islanders, the town is the site of a university.

Jardín Canario★
Open 8am-6pm (6.30pm in summer). Closed 1 Jan and 25 Dec. 928 21 95 80.
The largest botanical garden in Spain (27ha/67 acres) is devoted to Canarian flora, with more than 500 species.

▶ *In Monte Lentiscal turn left.*

Mirador de Bandama★★
A road leads to the summit of Bandama (569m/1 867ft) and a superb view of the enormous Caldera de la Bandama, a crater with its eruption formations intact, and a small cultivated area. The **panorama** takes in Tafira, the Montaña de Arucas and Las Palmas to the north, the crater, and the Real Club de Golf (the oldest in Spain) and Telde to the south. In the caldera are old incised drawings.

Return to the C 811.

Santa Brígida

This village sits close to a ravine planted with palms. A plant and flower market is held weekends. The Casa del Vino de Gran Canaria sells wines and offers tastings *(open 10am-6pm, Sat-Sun and public hols 10am-3pm; 928 64 42 45).*

Vega de San Mateo

A large fruit and vegetable market is held Saturdays and Sundays. The **Casa-Museo Cho Zacarías**, in a series of traditional houses, displays pottery, furniture, textiles, traditional implements etc. *(open 10.30am-12.30pm; closed Sun; 3.60 €; 928 66 17 95).*

Continue along the C 811 for 6km/4mi, then bear left.

Pozo de las Nieves★★★

From the summit (1 949m/6 394ft), which is sometimes snow-capped, there is a spectacular **panorama**★★★ of the island. On a clear day, Mount Teide (Tenerife) stands on the horizon.

Cruz de Tejeda★★

NW of Pozo de las Nieves. Near the hotel (parador) at the top of the pass (1 450m/4 757ft) lies the village of **Tejeda** in a huge volcanic basin. From the chaotic landscape, which the Spanish writer Unamuno described as a "petrified tempest", rise Roque Bentaiga and Roque Nublo, formations venerated by the indigenous people.

Bear W to Artenara along the GC 110.

The drive includes **views**★ of the troglodyte village of **Juncalillo** where most people live in lava caves.

Artenara

This village is the highest on the island (1 230m/4 035ft). In the enchanting **Ermita de la Cuevita**, a hermitage dug into the rock, is a statue of the Virgin with Child. The **panorama**★ is impressive. From a cave restaurant (Mesón de la Silla) on the edge of the village, there is a **view**★ of Roque Bentayga.

Pinar de Tamadaba★★

The road passes through Canary pines extending to the edge of a cliff which drops sheer to the sea.

Continue to the end of a tarred road, to the Zona de Acampada, then park and walk 200m/220yd.

On a clear day, the **view**★★ of Agaete, Gáldar and the coast, with the Pico del Teide on the horizon, is superb.

Return by the same road and turn left onto the GC 110 to Valleseco.

J. Malburet/ MICHELIN

Tejeda and the Roque Nublo

Dunes of Maspalomas

Mirador de Zamora★

Just north of Valleseco there is an attractive **view★** of Teror.

Teror

Teror has fine mansions with wooden balconies. The 18C **Basilica de Nuestra Señora del Pino** houses a statue of Our Lady of the Pine Tree, the island's patron, who is said to have appeared in 1481 (*open Mon 1-8.30pm; Tue-Fri 9am-1pm and 3-8.30pm; Sat 9am-8.30pm; Sun and public hols 7.30am-7.30pm. 0.60 € (treasury). 928 63 01 18).*

Thousands gather on 8 September to present their gifts and join in worship. On Sundays a lively market is held.

THE SOUTH COAST

From Las Palmas de Gran Canaria to Maspalomas –

59km/37mi – about 2hr.

Leave Las Palmas de Gran Canaria along the GC 1, ① on the plan, and then take exit 8 (Telde).

Telde

This was an indigenous centre. In the lower town is the 15C **Iglesia de San Juan Bautista**, a church rebuilt in the 17C and 18C, which contains a 16C Flemish retable depicting the Life of the Virgin. The Christ figure was made in Mexico out of reeds and paste.

Take calle Inés Chimida.

The road leads to the quiet **San Francisco district** with narrow streets and whitewashed houses, known for its traditional craftwork.

Follow the C 813 towards Ingenio. Beyond the junction with the C 816 turn left, immediately after some cottages, into a rough track; the last 250m/270yd is on foot.

Yacimiento Arquológico de Cuatro Puertas★

The cave, which has four openings *(cuatro puertas)*, is where the indigenous council *(Tagoror)* used to meet. The east face of the mountain is riddled with caves where the Guanche embalmed their dead. The summit (to the east) is a sacred site, Almogarén.

Maspalomas

The largest resorts with shopping, cafés and recreation are along the sandy coastline to the south: **Maspalomas, Meloneras, Playa del Inglés** and **Playa de San Agustín**. Maspalomas has developed around its spectacular dunes and **beach★**, part of a 400ha/990-acre protected zone. Other attractions are natural pools and a palm grove.

Excursions from Maspalomas

Mogán
38km/24mi NW. **Puerto de Mogán★**, a picturesque resort is built around an attractive marina.

San Bartolomé de Tirajana★
48km/30mi N on the GC 520. The way up passes through the **Barranco de Fataga★★**, a beautiful ravine. San Bartolomé is set in a magnificent green mountain cirque.

Return to San Bartolomé and take the C 815 going SE.

LANZAROTE★★★

POPULATION: 88 849
846KM2/326SQ MI.

Lanzarote, designated a Biosphere Reserve, is the most unusual of the Canary Islands. Its black landscape, dotted with oases of vegetation and crops, is full of contrasting textures and colours. Adaptation to the difficult conditions has shaped the character and activities of its inhabitants over the centuries.

- **Information:** *Arrecife: Parque Municipal, ☎928 81 18 60.*
- **Orient Yourself:** This flat island, just over 100km/62mi from the African coast, is linked by air and ferry to the archipelago, and by ferry to Fuerteventura.

A Bit of History

From the 14C to the present – The island owes its name to Lancelloti Malocello from Genoa, who landed in the 14C. In 1401 the Normans **Gadifer de la Salle** and **Jean de Bethencourt** met captured the island for the King of Castile. Lanzarote was a base for expeditions against the other islands.
Lanzarote became prey to marauding slavers. In 1730, a flaming mountain range, the **Montañas del Fuego,** suddenly arose. The eruption lasted six years and covered one third of the island in lava. In 1824 a new volcano, Tinguatón, engulfed fields and houses.
Lava fields *(malpaís)* and thick black ash and pebbles are pitted with over 100 craters. In **La Geria**, where volcanic pebbles (lapilli) are plentiful, vines are protected by low semicircular walls. The grapes produce an excellent light white wine – Malvasía – with a distinctive bouquet. Throughout the island the fields are covered with a deep layer of the lapilli to retain moisture on an island where it rarely rains. Another feature of this arid land is the dromedary.

Worth a Visit

ARRECIFE
The administrative centre on the coast was defended by the **Castillo de San Gabriel**, built in the 16C on an islet and linked to the town by two bridges; one, the Puente de Bolas, is a drawbridge.
Arrecife has a pleasant beach and a picturesque lagoon, the Charca de San Ginés, where fisherman tie up small boats. To the north is the 18C **Castillo de San José**. Restored by artist César Manrique, it houses the **Museo Internacional de Arte Contemporáneo** *(open 11am-9pm; ☎ 928 81 23 21).*

Excursions
Each tour departs from Arrecife.

THE CENTRE OF THE ISLAND
62km/39mi through the island's centre.

Fundación César Manrique★
In Taro de Tahíche. Open 10am-6pm (7pm Jul-Oct); Sun, 10am-3pm. Last entry 30 min before closing. Closed 1 Jan. 7.50 €. ☎928 84 31 38.

Address Book

WHERE TO EAT

◎◎ **Amura** – *Paseo marítimo – Puerto Calero* – ☎*51 31 81* – *www.puerto-calero.com* – *Closed Mon* – ▤ – . This restaurant in an attractive colonial-style octagonal building has a spectacular terrace. Its location opposite the marina, surrounded by palms, is outstanding.

◎◎ **La Era** – *Barranco 3* – *Yaiza* – ☎ *928 83 00 16* – *www.la-era.com* – *closed Mon.* A family-run restaurant in a lovely 17C country house. Traditional Canarian fare along with a fixed menu.

WHERE TO STAY

◎ **El Hotelito del Golfo** – *Golfo 10* – *Yaiza* – ☎*928 17 32 72* – 🅿 ⛱ – *9 rooms* – ⛱. Although offering limited creature comforts, this hotel has a pool, garden and a spectacular location on a volcanic cliff. The rooms are fairly rudimentary but adequate nonetheless. ◎ **Hotel Miramar** – *Coll 2 – Arrecife* – ☎ *928 80 15 22* – *www.hmiramar.com* – ♿ – *85 rooms* – ⛱ *6 €* – *Restaurant 12 €*. Although this 1980s-style building is lacking in architectural charm, its location, by the sea and opposite the Castillo de San Gabriel in the centre of Arrecife, couldn't be better. Bedroom balconies offer good sea views, although the bedrooms themselves are on the basic side with somewhat antiquated furniture.

The foundation is in a house that sits atop five volcanic bubbles. César Manrique chose this location to demonstrate the bond between architecture and nature.

Monumento al Campesino

This monument near **Mozaga**, in the centre of the island, pays homage to the peasant farmers of Lanzarote. Next to it is the **Casa-Museo del Campesino**, a characteristic country house.

Museo Agrícola El Patio★

In Tiagua. ◷ *Open 10am-5.30pm (including public hols); Sat, 10am-2.30pm. Last admission 30 min before closing.* ◷ *Closed Sun.* ◎ *5 € (including wine tasting and one tapa).* ☎*928 52 91 34.*

The exhibits at this old farm highlight rural life on the island. A tasting of Malvasía wine is also offered.

Museo del Vino El Grifo

◷ *Open 10.30am-6pm (7pm Jul-Sep).* ◷ *Closed 1 Jan and 25 Dec.* ◎ *3 €.* ☎*928 52 49 51.*

The 18C El Grifo wine storehouses are a museum of traditional winemaking.

La Geria★★

La Geria lies between Yaiza and Mozaga in a blackish desert pockmarked with craters. The village is a wine centre.

THE SOUTH OF THE ISLAND

Round trip of 124km/77mi from Arrecife – about 1 day

Parque Nacional de Timanfaya★★★

🚌 *Tours of the park by coach are available from 9am; last tour at 5pm, closing 5.45pm.* ◎ *8 € (including volcano circuit).* ☎*928 84 00 57 or 928 80 15 00.*

The range, which emerged in the 1730-36 eruptions, stands out sometimes red, sometimes black, above cinder and slag. It is the major natural attraction on the island. The **Montañas de Fuego** form the centre of this massif.

Dromedaries wait by the roadside 5km/3mi north of Yaiza to provide a swaying and jolting ride up the mountainside, from where there is a good view of the next crater. Although the volcanoes have not erupted since 1736, their fires burn and bubble still. At **Islote de Hilario**, twigs dropped into a hole 50cm/20in deep catch fire; water poured into a pipe set into the lava steams immediately because of the subsoil temperature (140°C/254°F at 10cm/4in, over 400°C/752°F at 6m/20ft). There are fine views from the El Diablo restaurant, where food is cooked using the heat of the earth.

Buses from Islote follow the 14km/9mi **Ruta de los Volcanes**. A lookout affords

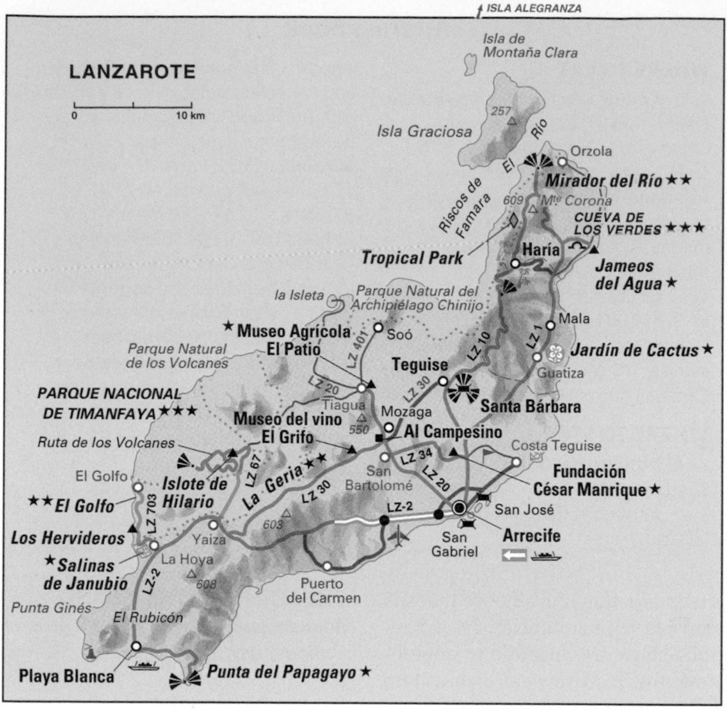

a view over an immense lava field stretching to the sea.

Los Hervideros

In the caverns at the end of the tongue of lava, the sea boils (*hervir*: to boil) in an endlessly fascinating spectacle.

El Golfo★★

A lagoon is filled with vivid emerald-green water; a steep cliff of pitted black rock forms an impressive backdrop.

Salinas de Janubio★

Deep blue seawater entering a crater leaves gleaming white pyramids of salt in square pans.

Playa Blanca

This pleasant resort has a promenade between old fishermen's houses and the white beach.

Punta del Papagayo★

The Rubicón region is where Bethencourt settled. The only trace is the Castillo de las Coloradas, a tower on the cliff edge. From "parrot" point *(by road from the entrance to Playa Blanca to* **Espacio protegido de los Ajaches**, *a protected area)*, with its magnificent rocky creeks, there are **views**★ of Playa Blanca and Fuerteventura (*open 9am-7pm. 3€ vehicle fee), ☎928 17 34 52).*

Take the LZ 2.

Museo de Cetáceos de Canarias (Whale Museum)

In Puerto Calero. Open 10am-6pm (7pm in summer). Closed first Thu of the month, 1 and 6 Jan and 25 Dec. 11 €, children 5 €. ☎928 84 95 60.

One of the best European whale collections uses replicas, skeletons, explanatory panels, sound and images to tell the story of these mammals.

Return to Arrecife via the LZ 2.

THE NORTH OF THE ISLAND

Round trip of 77km/47mi from Arrecife – about half a day

Jardín de Cactus★
In Guatiza. Open 10am-5.45pm. 5 €. 928 52 93 97.
This cactus garden displays many species from the Canary Islands, America and Madagascar, on terraces in an old quarry. In this area are prickly pears, a cactus which attracts cochineal beetles, once crushed to obtain a crimson dye.

Cueva de los Verdes★★★
Guided tours (1hr), 10am-6pm. 8 €. 928 17 32 20 or 928 84 84 84.
At the foot of the Corona volcano are volcanic galleries where the Guanches once took refuge from marauding pirates. There are 2km/1mi of illuminated passages at different levels.

Jameos del Agua★
Open 10am-6.30pm; Tue, Fri and Sat, 7pm-2am, including a folklore show at 11pm. 8€ (day), 9€ (evening). 928 84 80 20.
This leisure complex has a restaurant, bar, dance floor and auditorium. A *jameo* is a cavity formed when the top of a volcanic tube collapses. The lagoon in the cave is the habitat of a minute, blind albino millenary crab. The **Casa de los Volcanes** on the upper level presents information on volcanism.

Mirador del Río★★
Open 10am-5.45pm. 4.70 €. 928 52 65 51.
At the north end of the island stands a steep isolated headland, **Riscos de Famara**. The belvedere commands a superb **panorama★★** across the azure waters of the **El Río** strait to La Graciosa and its neighbouring islands (Montaña Clara, Alegranza, Roque del Oeste and Roque del Este); immediately below are salt pans. A **passenger ferry** operates from Orzola to La Graciosa. *From Orzola to La Graciosa (25min): 10am, noon and 5pm (and 6.30pm in summer); from La Graciosa: 8am, 11am and 4pm (and 6pm in summer). 15 € round trip. 928 84 20 70/55.*

Tropical Park
Kids Open 10am-5pm. 14 €. 928 83 55 00.
These gardens are devoted to exotic birds. Events include parrot shows.

Haría
As on all the islands, the northern end is the least arid. Some 5km/3mi south of the village there is a fine **view★**, from a lookout point, of the lush Haría Valley with its palm trees.

Teguise
Teguise, once the capital, is the home of the *timple*, a miniature guitar which is an element in Canary Island folklore. In the nearby **Castillo de Santa Bárbara,** built in the 16C on the Guanapay volcano, is the **Museo del Emigrante,** which documents the emigration of Canary Islanders to America (*open 10am-5pm, 4pm in summer, 1.80 €; 928 84 50 01).*

FUERTEVENTURA

POPULATION: 49 542
1 731KM2/668SQ MI.

This island calls out with the beauty of its bare landscape, and beaches of white sand with turquoise water all around. Moderate winds and a calm sea on the east coast make this island ideal for sailing, diving, fishing and, in particular, kitesurfing and windsurfing. The world windsurfing championships are held here in July and August.

- **Information:** *Puerto del Rosario: El Almirante Lallermand 1, 928 86 06 04.*
- **Orient Yourself:** Fuerteventura is the largest island after Tenerife and, with the exception of El Hierro, the least densely populated. The coastline is flat with long beaches.

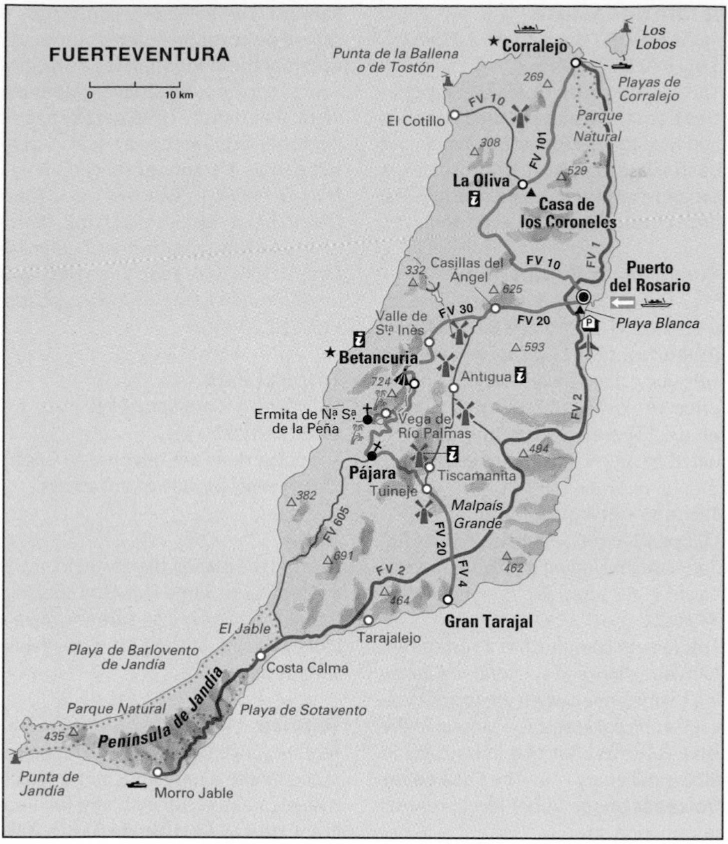

A Bit of History

Landscape – Arid Fuerteventura is dotted with bare crests and extinct volcanoes. It was described as a "skeletal island" by writer **Miguel de Unamuno**, exiled here in 1924. This terrain is only suitable for grazing goats. Villages are marked by palm trees and windmills. Fuerteventura shares the climate of nearby Africa; sand, blown across the sea, formed an isthmus, El Jable, between

Tourism Centres

Open 9.30am-5.30pm. ☎928 86 23 00.

These **leisure and tourist centres** are housed in buildings with typical island architecture and introduce visitors to the traditional ways of life, culture and gastronomy of the island.

La Cilla "Museo del Grano", in La Oliva – This museum in an old granary provides explanations on traditional agriculture.

Mirador de Morro Velosa, in Betancuria – A belvedere with a superb view of the centre of the island. The restaurant serves typical dishes from the Canary Islands.

Centro de Artesanía Molino de Antigua, in Antigua – This arts and crafts centre is in an old mill encircled by a garden of palm and cactus trees. It also contains a craftwork shop and a general information centre providing details on the island.

Centro de Interpretación de los Molinos, in Tiscamanita – A traditional cottage alongside a mill is the setting for this information centre which explains the history of mills (*molinos*) on Fuerteventura.

Address Book

For coin ranges, see the Legend on the cover flap.

WHERE TO EAT

⊜⊜ **Casa Santa María** – *Plaza Santa María – Betancuria – ☎928 87 82 82.* This 16C house with its tiled roof, white-washed walls and at times over-the-top local decoration is set amid lush vegetation with stupendous views. Canarian cuisine at its best.

WHERE TO STAY

⊜⊜ **Hotel Fuerteventura** – *(Playa Blanca) – Puerto del Rosario – 2.5km/1.5mi S of Puerto Rosario – ☎928 85 11 50 – www.hotelfuerteventura.com – P – 50 rooms – 7.21€. Restaurant 21 €.* This hotel occupies the building originally housing the parador. Although slightly old-fashioned, the moderately priced rooms are still pleasant (some have been recently refurbished), with wooden floors and good-quality furniture. Its best feature is undoubtedly its location facing the sea.

the once-separate islets of Maxorata and Jandía. The waters to the east are popular for deep-sea fishing.

Sights

Both in **Puerto del Rosario** and at the airport, taxis and hire cars are available to tour the island. A long beach, Playa Blanca, is located south of the capital.

CORRALEJO★

39km/24mi N of Puerto del Rosario along the FV 10 and FV 101.

La Oliva

Take the path from the church. The **Casa de los Coroneles**, an 18C house, once the residence of the governor of the island, is surmounted by two crenellated towers and ornamented with wooden balconies. Nearby *(right)* stands the **Casa del Capellán**, a minute house enclosed within a drystone wall; the motifs decorating the door and window are very similar to those in Pájara church.

Corralejo★

The fishing village and tourist resort is at the northern end of the island beyond the *malpaís*, or lava fields. Crystal-clear water laps at the immense white dune **beaches** of the Parque Natural Dunas de Corralejo and the Isla de Lobos, a paradise for underwater fishing which can be reached by boat. Lanzarote is visible to the north.

J. Malburet/ MICHELIN

Playa de Sotavento

GRAN TARAJAL

67km/42mi S.

Leave Puerto del Rosario along the FV 20. Beyond Casillas del Angel, turn right onto the FV 30.

Betancuria★

This quiet valley town, once the island capital, was founded in 1404 by Jean de Bethencourt.

Betancuria retains a ruined Franciscan monastery and an ancient **cathedral**, with white walls and a picturesque wooden balcony, now called the **Iglesia de Santa María la Antigua.** The baptistery contains an interesting crucifix; the sacristy has a fine panelled ceiling.

On the south side, a small **Museo Arqueológico** displays Guanche artefacts (*open 10am-6pm; closed Sun-Mon; 1.20 €; 928 87 82 41).*

The road south provides an attractive contrast between the wide horizon of bare rose-tinted peaks and the village of Vega de Río Palmas nestling in its green valley-oasis. Not far away is the hermitage of the Virgen de la Peña, where islanders venerate Fuerteventura's patron saint (third Saturday in September).

Pájara

The carvings on the church doorway betray Aztec inspiration (plumed heads, pumas, snakes and suns).

In Pájara take the FV 20 to the left.

Gran Tarajal

Tamarisk trees surround the port which exports tomatoes and which is the second largest town on the island.

PENÍNSULA DE JANDÍA

Morro del Jable: 54km/34mi SW of Gran Tarajal.

This nature park is famous for fine beaches, half of all those on the island. On the windward side beaches are wild; those on the leeward side are wide and level.

LA PALMA★

POPULATION: 78 198

706KM2/272SQ MI.

With a surface of just 706km²/272sq mi and its highest peak rising to 2 426m/7 949ft, La Palma has the highest average altitude of any island in the world. Rain is more abundant than in the rest of the Canaries, resulting in numerous streams and springs. It is known as the "Beautiful Island" or the "Green Island" because of its woods of laurel and pine and numerous banana plantations. La Palma has distanced itself from major tourist development and will appeal to nature-lovers and those seeking peace and quiet.

Information: *Santa Cruz de la Palma: Plaza de la Constitución, 922 41 21 06.*

Orient Yourself: La Palma is located in the far northwest of the archipelago.

Background

The huge central crater, the Caldera de Taburiente, spreads over 10km/6mi. A chain of peaks, Las Cumbres, extends south; ravines produce an indented coastline. In the mountains, rainwater is collected to irrigate the lower terraces.

Worth a Visit

SANTA CRUZ DE LA PALMA

The administrative centre was founded in 1493 at the foot of an eroded crater. In the 16C, with rising sugar exports and the expansion of the naval yards, Santa Cruz was one of Spain's major ports; now it is a peaceful city where elegant façades line the seafront.

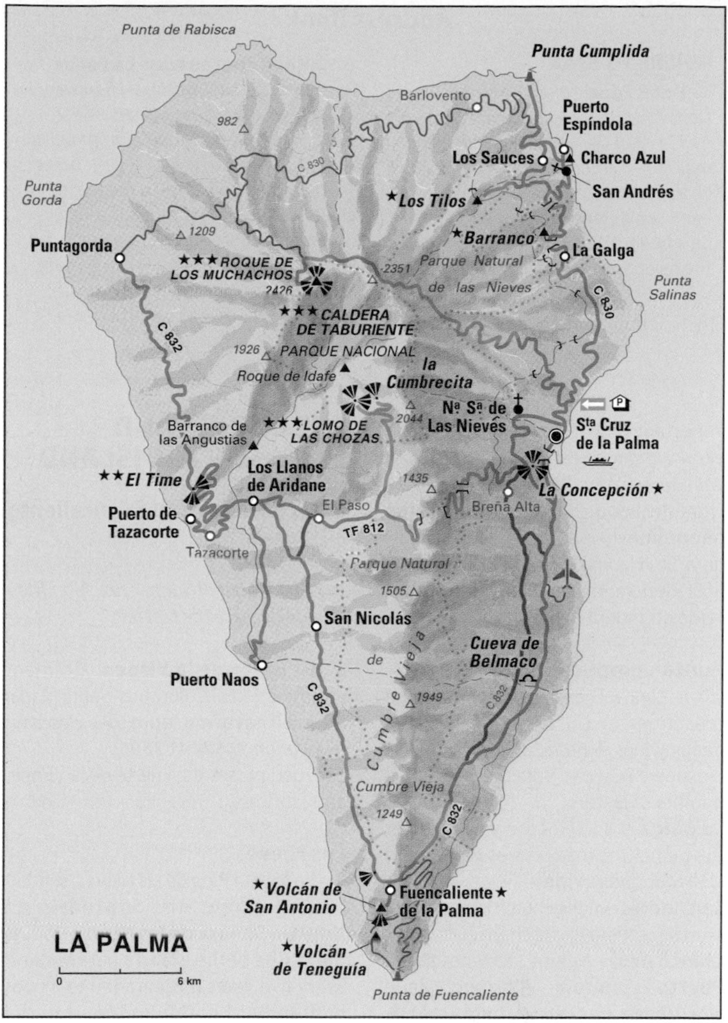

At Playa de Los Cancajos, 5km/3mi S, the beach and rocks are black.

Plaza de España

Several buildings date from the Renaissance. The 16C **Iglesia de El Salvador** has beautiful ceilings with **artesonado ornament★**; the sacristy has Gothic vaulting. Opposite stand the 16C town hall and houses in colonial style.
Walk uphill to the delightful **plaza de Santo Domingo**. Next to a college stands the **chapel** of a former monastery with beautiful Baroque altars. *To visit the chapel, ask for the keys at the Iglesia de El Salvador, ☎ 922 41 32 50.*

Driving Tours

The two tours suggested below both depart from Santa Cruz de la Palma.

THE NORTH OF THE ISLAND

Observatorio Roque de los Muchachos★★★

36km/22mi NW. About 1hr 45min for the ascent.
Laurel bushes and pine trees line the winding road which offers extensive views as it climbs to the **astrophysical observatory**, one of the world's most

Address Book

WHERE TO STAY

⊜ **Hotel Edén** – *Plaza de España – Los Llanos de Aridane – Closed in May – ☎ 922 46 01 04 – www.hoteledenlapalma.com – 19 rooms – ☕ 4 €.* This small hotel in the island's second town, amid banana plantations, is good for those on a budget. Small, comfortable rooms; the reception is upstairs.

⊜⊜ **Hotel-Restaurante La Palma Romántica** – *Las Llanadas – Barlovento – 1km/0.6mi SW of Barlovento – ☎922 18 62 21 – www.hotellapalmaromantica.com – P – 44 rooms – ☕ – Restaurant 14.42 €.* This rural hotel in the north, at 600m/1 950ft, has sweeping views of the coast. Surprisingly large rooms with simple furnishings. Friendly staff and a reasonable restaurant. A good, quiet base for those keen to explore La Palma's wonderful nature.

important, at 2 432m/7 949ft. (*visits by prior arrangement, ☎922 42 57 03 from 9am-3pm or adminorm@iac.es).*
From the Roque de los Muchachos the **panorama**★★★ encompasses the Caldera, Los Llanos de Aridane, the islands of El Hierro and La Gomera, and Mount Teide on Tenerife.

Punta Cumplida

36km/22mi N. There are fine views of the coast from the cliff road which crosses deep ravines *(barrancos)* in the Los Tilos Biosphere Reserve. Note the impressive number of craters.
La Galga – North of the village, after the tunnel, the road crosses a steep and well-wooded **ravine**★.
San Andrés – In the church is a beautiful Mudéjar ceiling in the chancel.
Charco Azul – Natural seawater pools.
Puerto Espíndola – A fishing village where boats are drawn up onto a shingle beach in a breach in the cliff face.
Punta Cumplida – Walk round the lighthouse to see waves breaking on basalt rock piles. The attractive Fajana swimming pools are north of here.
Los Sauces – The main agricultural centre in the north of the island.
Los Tilos★ – Detour up Agua ravine to the lime tree forest. The **Centro de Investigación e Interpretación de la Reserva de la Biosfera de Los Tilos** provides details on flora in the reserve (*open 9am-2pm and 2.30pm-5pm (5.30pm in summer); closed 1 Jan and 24-25 and 31 Dec; ☎922 45 12 46).*

THE CENTRE AND SOUTH OF THE ISLAND

Via Los Llanos and Fuencaliente

– 190km/118mi.

Head N out of Santa Cruz. After the ravine, take the first left.

In the **Barco de la Virgen**, a cement reproduction of Columbus' Santa María, is a small **naval museum** (*closed for renovation. ☎922 41 21 06).*
The road passes the Fuerte de la Virgen, a 16C fortress.

Las Nieves

At the foot of Pico de las Nieves, shaded by laurel trees, the **Santuario de Nuestra Señora de las Nieves** houses the statue of the island's patron saint. Every five years it is paraded to a boat built in her honour and then to the Iglesia de El Salvador in Santa Cruz.

Mirador de la Concepción★

The summit of the Caldereta commands a wonderful **bird's-eye view**★ of Santa Cruz de la Palma, the harbour and the mountains.

Take the TF 812 toward the W.

Parque Nacional de la Caldera de Taburiente★★★

4km/2.5mi W of the tunnel on the right is the **Centro de Visitantes**, *with information on marked footpaths (length, timings, difficulty etc, open 9am-2pm and 4-6.30pm; ☎922 49 72 77).*

J. Malburet/ MICHELIN

La Cumbrecita

▶ *Ahead, turn right for La Cumbrecita.*

The **Cumbrecita Pass** (1 833m/6 014ft) and the **Lomo de las Chozas Pass** *(1km/0.6mi farther on)* provide a splendid **panorama**★★★: the Caldera de Taburiente, dotted with Canary Island pines and crowned by rose-tinted peaks (Roque de los Muchachos).

Los Llanos de Aridane

The island's second largest town is in a plain of bananas and avocado trees.

El Time★★

The top of El Time cliff affords a remarkable **panorama**★★ of the Aridane plain, a sea of banana palms, and of the Barranco de las Angustias, a rock fissure which is the only outlet for the the Caldera de Taburiente.

Puntagorda

The beauty of the landscape makes this drive particularly worthwhile.

▶ *Return to El Time.*

Puerto de Tazacorte

Lugo landed in this small harbour in 1492. The beach is popular on Sundays.

Puerto Naos

Descend through lava fields from the 1949 eruption and then through banana plantations.

San Nicolás

The lava stream from the Nambroque volcano cut the village in two in 1949.

Fuencaliente★

Before reaching Fuencaliente, look back from the Mirador de las Indias for a **glimpse**★ of the coast through the pines. A hot water spring disappeared during the eruption of **San Antonio volcano**★ in 1677. Circle the volcano to see the craters of **Teneguía volcano**★, which appeared in October 1971, and the lava stream which separated the lighthouse from the village.

Cueva de Belmaco

5km/3mi from the airport fork. At the back of the cave are rocks with Guanche inscriptions.

Local Products

Cigars – Tobacco was first introduced to the islands by Cuban Indians. The handmade palm cigars have a deserved reputation and are highly appreciated by cigar connois-seurs the world over.

Silk – La Palma's textile tradition dates back to the 17C. Today, a number of local artisans still work with natural silk.

Cheese – Smoked white goats' cheese is one of La Palma's specialities. The island's goat population numbers some 30 000.

LA GOMERA★

POPULATION: 16 790
378KM²/1 46SQ MI.

La Gomera is ideal for visitors seeking peace, contact with nature and outdoor activities. This round island rises from coastal cliffs, cut by deep ravines, to a *meseta* with a single peak, Mount Garajonay (1 487m/4 879ft). Few traces remain of volcanic activity. Basalt cliffs, Los Órganos, are visible only from the sea. The fertile red soil is carefully husbanded: even the steepest hillsides are terraced.

- **Information:** *Valverde: Dr. Quintero Magdaleno 4, ☎922 55 03 02.*
- **Orient Yourself:** La Gomera is the second smallest island in the Canaries. Until 1999, the island was only accessible by sea.

Worth a Visit

San Sebastián de la Gomera

Christopher Columbus stopped in what is now the administrative centre of the island. His route can be traced down the main street from the corner house where he took on water *(ask to see the well, el pozo, in the patio)*, past the **Iglesia de la Asunción** where he heard Mass, to the two-storey white house, a little before the post office, where he is said to have slept.

The Whistling Language

In former times, the steep terrain in the interior of the island posed huge communication problems for the inhabitants of La Gomera. As a result, an unusual whistling language was created by the Guanches to provide contact from valley to valley. Despite its ancient roots, this language continues to be used today.

Driving Tour

- *15km/9mi. Leave San Sebastián de la Gomera on the TF 711.*

The road emerges from the first tunnel in the **Hermigua valley**★★ amid white houses, palms and banana plantations.

Agulo★

Very picturesque seaside site; Tenerife is visible on the horizon.

Parque Nacional de Garajonay★★

Stop at the Juego de Bolas visitor centre. Open 9.30am-4.30pm; guided walking tours on Wed and Sat by prior arrangement. Closed Mon, 1 Jan and 25 Dec. ☎922 80 09 93.
The national park is covered by laurels, traces of the Tertiary Era, and giant heathers, punctuated by rocks. Mist caused by trade winds lends an air of mystery.

Valle Gran Rey★★

55km/34mi from San Sebastián de la Gomera on the TF 713. The road ascends the slopes to the south; the climb to the central *meseta* in the park is less steep.
Chipude – Attractive potters' village.
Arure – After the bridge there is a good **panorama**★ of Taguluche.
Barranco del Valle Gran Rey★★ – The most spectacular ravine on the island.

EL HIERRO

POPULATION: 6 995
278KM2/107SQ MI.

This small island combines fertile farmland, spectacular cliffs plunging into the sea, volcanic cones, fields of lava carpeted in laurel, and an underwater world popular with divers.

- **Information:** *Valverde: Dr. Quintero Magdaleno 4, 38900 Valverde, ☎ 922 55 03 02.*
- **Orient Yourself:** El Hierro is in the far southwest of the archipelago. Ferries run to neighbouring islands.

Driving Tours

The excursions below depart from **Valverde**, the capital of the island, at an altitude of 571m/1 873ft.

Tamaduste

8km/5mi NE. A large sandbank by the small seaside resort forms a lagoon.

El Golfo★★

8km/5mi W. There is a fine **view**★★ of El Golfo from the **Mirador de La Peña.** The rim of a crater is covered with laurels and giant heather; the level floor is cultivated. La Fuga de Gorreta, near the Salmor rocks *(NE)*, is the habitat of a primeval lizard.

Tour through La Dehesa

- *105km/65mi. Head S from Valverde along the TF 912.*

Tiñor – Until 1610, when it was blown down, a Garoé tree was venerated by natives. Its leaves condensed water.
Sabinosa – A spa-hotel treats skin and digestive diseases.
La Dehesa – A track from 3km/2mi on crosses the arid La Dehesa region and provides extensive **views**★ of the south coast where the fiery red earth, pitted with craters, slopes to the sea.
Punta de Orchilla – Orchilla Point was the zero meridian before Greenwich. Beyond the lighthouse are sabine trees, conifers with twisted trunks found only on El Hierro.
Ermita de Nuestra Señora de los Reyes – In this hermitage are statues of the three Wise Men (los Reyes), and one of the Virgin Mary carried in procession every four years to Valverde.
El Pinar – A pleasant **pine forest**★ extends all over this region.

A

B

N

O

P

T

U

V

W

X

Y

Z

WHERE TO EAT

WHERE TO STAY

MAPS AND PLANS

LIST OF MAPS AND PLANS

THEMATIC MAPS

TOWN PLANS

PLANS OF MONUMENTS AND SITES

TOURING MAPS

Abbreviations

D	Provincial Council (Diputación)
G	Central government representation (Delegación del Gobierno)
H	Town hall (Ayuntamiento)
J	Law courts/Courthouse (Palacio de Justicia)
M	Museum (Museo)
POL.	Police station (Policía)
T	Theatre (Teatro)
U	University (Universidad)

Sports and recreation

- Racecourse
- Skating rink
- Outdoor, indoor swimming pool
- Multiplex Cinema
- Marina, sailing centre
- Trail refuge hut
- Cable cars, gondolas
- Funicular, rack railway
- Tourist train
- Recreation area, park
- Theme, amusement park
- Wildlife park, zoo
- Gardens, park, arboretum
- Bird sanctuary, aviary
- Walking tour, footpath
- Of special interest to children

LEGEN

Highly recommended	★★★
Recommended	★★
Interesting	★

Additional symbols

	Tourist information
	Motorway or other primary route
❶ ❶	Junction: complete, limited
	Pedestrian street
	Unsuitable for traffic, street subject to restrictions
	Steps – Footpath
	Train station – Auto-train station
S.N.C.F.	Coach (bus) station
	Tram
	Metro, underground
	Park-and-Ride
♿	Access for the disabled
	Post office
	Telephone
	Covered market
	Barracks
	Drawbridge
	Quarry
⚒	Mine
B F	Car ferry (river or lake)
	Ferry service: cars and passengers
	Foot passengers only
③	Access route number common to Michelin maps and town plans
Bert (R.)...	Main shopping street
AZ B	Map co-ordinates

Selected monuments and sights

◉	Tour - Departure point
	Catholic church
	Protestant church, other temple
	Synagogue - Mosque
	Building
■	Statue, small building
	Calvary, wayside cross
◎	Fountain
	Rampart - Tower - Gate
	Château, castle, historic house
	Ruins
	Dam
☼	Factory, power plant
	Fort
	Cave
	Troglodyte dwelling
	Prehistoric site
	Viewing table
	Viewpoint
▲	Other place of interest

Special symbols

	Civil Guard (Guardia Civil)
P	Parador (hotel run by the State)
	Bullring
	Olive grove
	Orange grove

Principal Sights

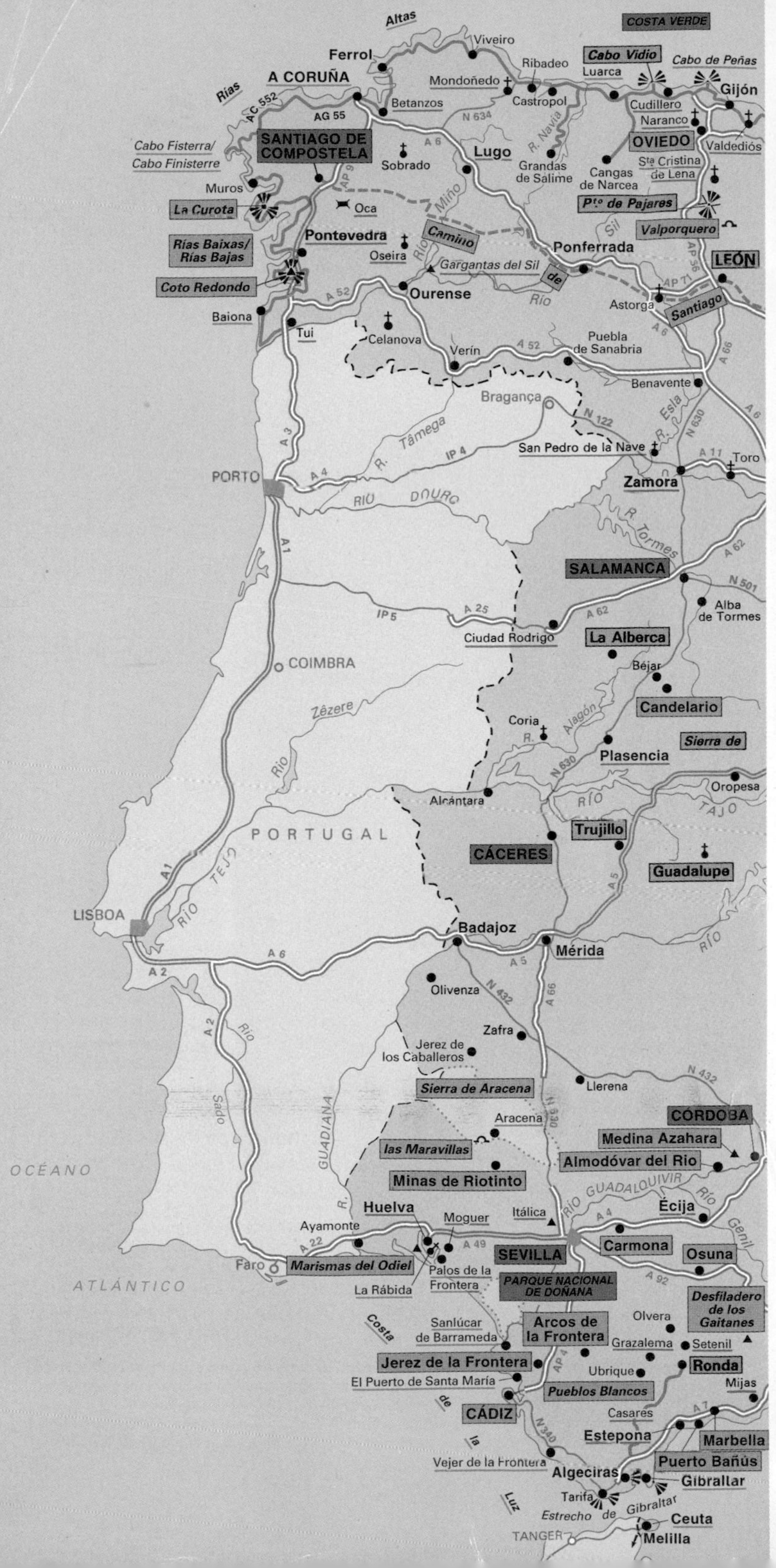

Michelin Apa Publications Ltd

A joint venture between Michelin and Langenscheidt

Suite 6, Tulip House, 70 Borough High Street, London SE1 1XF, United Kingdom

ISBN 978-1-906261-22-1
Printed: October 2007
Printed and bound in Germany